PEARSON EDEXCEL INTERNATIONAL GCSE (9–1)

SCIENCE DOUBLE AWARD

Student Book

BIOLOGY
Phil Bradfield
Steve Potter

CHEMISTRY
Jim Clark
Steve Owen
Rachel Yu

PHYSICS
Brian Arnold
Penny Johnson
Steve Woolley

Published by Pearson Education Limited, 80 Strand, London, WC2R 0RL.

www.pearsonglobalschools.com

Copies of official specifications for all Edexcel qualifications may be found on the website: https://qualifications.pearson.com

Edited by Stephen Cunningham
Designed by Cobalt id
Typeset by Tech-Set Ltd, Gateshead, UK

Illustrated by Tech-Set Ltd, Gateshead, UK
Cover design by Pearson Education Limited
Cover photo/illustration © Getty Images: Jeffrey Rotman
Picture research by: Frances Topp, Andreas Schindler and Penny Bowden.

First published 2017

21
10

British Library Cataloguing in Publication Data
A catalogue record for this book is available from the British Library

ISBN 9780435185282

Printed in Slovakia by Neografia

Endorsement Statement
In order to ensure that this resource offers high-quality support for the associated Pearson qualification, it has been through a review process by the awarding body. This process confirms that this resource fully covers the teaching and learning content of the specification or part of a specification at which it is aimed. It also confirms that it demonstrates an appropriate balance between the development of subject skills, knowledge and understanding, in addition to preparation for assessment.

Endorsement does not cover any guidance on assessment activities or processes (e.g. practice questions or advice on how to answer assessment questions), included in the resource nor does it prescribe any particular approach to the teaching or delivery of a related course.

While the publishers have made every attempt to ensure that advice on the qualification and its assessment is accurate, the official specification and associated assessment guidance materials are the only authoritative source of information and should always be referred to for definitive guidance.
Pearson examiners have not contributed to any sections in this resource relevant to examination papers for which they have responsibility.

Examiners will not use endorsed resources as a source of material for any assessment set by Pearson. Endorsement of a resource does not mean that the resource is required to achieve this Pearson qualification, nor does it mean that it is the only suitable material available to support the qualification, and any resource lists produced by the awarding body shall include this and other appropriate resources.

Picture Credits
The authors and publisher would like to thank the following individuals and organisations for permission to reproduce photographs:

(Key: b-bottom; c-centre; l-left; r-right; t-top)

123RF.com: 163bl, 378t, 381r, 326, choneschones 533, cristimatei 698tl, Feliks Gurevich 550bl, homestudio 543, Eric Isselee 230bl, Jozsef Szasz-Fabian 495tr, leungchopan 528, Melinda Nagy 504tc, Scandal 468; **Alamy Stock Photo:** age fotostock 514r, 666, Ageev Rostislav 600, Alison Eckett 650, Nathan Allred 22b, Ange 679r, Archive Pics 669l, Art Directors & TRIP 695, Aurora 456, Authentic Creations 582tl, Blend-Memento 196, blickwinkel 3cl, 3cr, 3bl, 3br, 25l, 230c, Bon Appetit 476, Nigel Cattlin 27l, 229, Charles Stirling 504tl, Chris Cooper-Smith 509tl, Chris Rose 572tr, Trevor Chriss 322, 529, David Colbran 218, Ashley Cooper 481r, Cultura Creative 381l, Cultura Creative (RF) 652, Design Pics Inc 621r, Digital Image Library 613c, Dorling Kindersley ltd 239tl, Emmanuel Lacoste 624l, Hayley Evans 22tr, FineArt 223, Flake 530, frans lemmens 602tr, GL Archive 669r, Granger Historical Picture Archive 520, Henry Westheim Photography 591tl, Horizon International Images Limited 601, 697, Rachel Husband 22tl, IanDagnall Computing 23tc, Image Source 545, ImagineThat 573, INTERFOTO 625, Jeff Rotman 621c, JLImages 24tl, John Joannides 597, Juniors Bildarchiv GmbH 230tr, LGPL / Ian Cartwright 378b, Linda Richards 508tr, Andrew Michael 559t, Michele Burgess 489tr, NASA 701, NASA / S.Dupuis 412, NASA Archive 523t, NASA Photo 488, National Geographic Creative 71, The Natural History Museum 629, Naturfoto-Online 225, Nick Greening 489tl, Sergey Nivens 236, paul ridsdale pictures 639, Nikos Pavlakis 366r, philipus 552, Pictorial Press Ltd 211, 608, 630t, 656, pixel shepherd 533, PjrStudio 572bl, Pulsar Images 684l, Radoslav Radev 582bl, Richard Wainscoat 698b, Rodney_X 145cr, samart boonyang 646, sciencephotos 549c, 550c, 565, Scott Ramsey 504tr, Sean Pavone 591, Trevor Smith 95, Studioshots 533b, David Taylor 401l, Trevor Chriss 322, 529, Genevieve Vallee 145cl, Jan Wlodarczyk 163br, World History Archive 282, Zoonar GmbH 162, 482b, Zoonar GmbH 162, 482b, Владимир Галкин 495tc; **Fotolia.com:** annavaczi 602tl, artush 518, bit24 48, Grinchh 269, izzzy71 602bl, Jess8 230br, Dr_Kateryna 51, Kateryna_Kon 198, ktsdesign 568, Arpad Nagy-Bagoly 478c, nengredeye 131, schankz 624r, troninphoto 509bl, Pavla Zakova 230tl; **Getty Images:** Aleksandrs Podskocijs / EyeEm 598, Thomas Barwick 120, BlackJack3D 34, Carlos Herrera / Icon Sportswire / Corbis 591c, Graiki 522, In Pictures / Corbis / Gideon Mendel 425, Muditha Madushan / EyeEm 2, Miguel Malo 366l, Maxim Grigoryev 344, mevans 507bl, NASA / National Geographic 258, PaulFleet 414, Peter Turnley 514tl, qbanczyk 93r, ROBERT SULLIVAN / AFP 572c, Science & Society Picture Library 613b, Scott Eells / Bloomberg 575b, ViewStock 507tl, YinYang 508tl; **Maritime & Coastguard Agency:** 571r; **Nature Picture Library:** Nature Production 436t; **Pearson Education Ltd:** Studio 8 541, Gareth Boden 549tl, Coleman Yuen. Pearson Education Asia Ltd 530bl, Oxford Designers & Illustrators Ltd 481l, Jules Selmes 538, 602br, Jules Selmes 538, 602br, Tsz-shan Kwok 531; **Science Photo Library Ltd:** 73, 123, 352b, 393t, 401c, 401r, 436b, AJ PHOTO 42, Andrew Lambert Photography 152, 272, 306, 309, 352t, 354r, 362t, 363, 403t, 403b, 498, 511, 630b, Animated Healthcare Ltd 104l, STEPHEN AUSMUS / US DEPARTMENT OF AGRICULTURE 23tl, Biomedical Imaging Unit, Southampton General Hospital 19, BIOPHOTO ASSOCIATES 43, 52, 53, 72, 124, Robert Brook 188, Carol and Mike Werner 446, Martyn F Chillmaid 54b, 165, 296, 345, 346, 348, 362b, 376, 384, 388, 390, 393l, 400, 401b, 401br, 402, 413, 420, 438b, 475, 478l, 565r, CNRI 226, 677, Crown Copyright / Health and Safety Laboratory 398, David Parker 179, 611b, Phil Degginger 415, Alan L. Detrick 180, Dorling Kindersley / UIG 24bl, 599, Dr Brad Mogan / Visuals Unlimited 250, DR GOPAL MURTI 6t, 25r, John Durham 6b, ESA - A. Le Floc'h 523c, MAURO FERMARIELLO 50b, Fundamental Photos 370, Gastrolab 60, GIPhotoStock 54t, 382, 383, 395, 401cr, 428cl, Dr Gopal Murti 6t, 25r, Steve Gschmeissner 139cr, 142, 203, Gusto Images 262, Adam Hart-Davis 146, RALPH HUTCHINGS, VISUALS UNLIMITED 36, Mikkel Juul Jensen 316, Keith R. Porter 5, Leonard Lessin 78t, 78b, DR P. MARAZZI 678, Microscope 111, CORDELIA MOLLOY 506tl, 540tl, 540tc, National Library of Medicine 222, NATURAL HISTORY MUSEUM, LONDON 224t, 224b, NIBSC 37, Susumu Nishinaga 139cl, Omikron 104r, David Parker 179, 611b, Alfred Pasieka 455, Lea Paterson 447l, PATRICK LANDMANN 684r, POWER AND SYRED 23b, R. MEGNA / FUNDAMENTAL PHOTOS 537, JC Revy, ISM 139tl, Saturn Stills 94, Science Pictures Ltd 204, Martin Shields 145b, Lee D. Simon 27c, Sinclair Stammers 25c, Volker Steger 478r, Steve Gschmeissner 139cr, 142, 203, David Taylor 401cl, TONY & DAPHNE HALLAS 611t, Trevor Clifford Photography 136, UIG / Dorking Kindersley 433, Charles D Winters 330, 353, 354l, 482t; **Shutterstock.com:** 279, photo Studio 178, 805084 590, 463c, 573r, 463c, 573r, Africa Studio 50t, Aivolie 298, Anastasios71 358, Vartanov Anatoly 572tl, Galyna Andrushko 386, arka38 239br, H E Benson 259l, best images. 462b, bikeriderlondon 571l, Bitt24 473, Sinisa Botas 462t, Brian Kinney 613t, Sherri R. Camp 428tl, Cardens Design 694, Norman Chan 542, Checubus 438t, Marcel Clemens 288b, Dashu 459, Demarcomedia 287, Dencg 266l, devy 495tl, Digieva 239tr, Dr.OGA 447c, EpicStockMedia 558, Peter Hermes Furian 323, Mauricio Graiki 93l, Jiri Hera 335bl, IANG HONGYAN 251, imagedb.com 532, Joanne Harris and Daniel Bubnich 583, Anan Kaewkhammul 460, karrapavan 638, KDEdesign 335tl, Jatuporn Khuansuwan 308, Kateryna Kon 26t, Ktsdesign 26b, 290, Robyn Mackenzie 121, Ilya Malov 428cr, MidoSemsem 582c, MIGUEL GARCIA SAAVEDRA 530br, Minerva Studio 627b, morchella 584, Resul Muslu 239bl, Mylisa 266r, Romanova Natali 276r, Oleg1969 276l, Olga Selyutina 559b, Palmaria 483, Pavel L Photo and Video 575t, Werayuth Piriyapornprapa 463t, Przemyslaw Skibinski 577, ra3rn 644, Vadim Ratnikov 463b, Remedios55 335br, Sander van Sinttruye 702l, Aygul Sarvarova 481, Scanrail1 336, Jeff Schultes 428tr, sciencepics 79, SFC 564, Smileus 562, Sozaijiten 23tr, Sam Strickler 447r, STUDIOMAX 603c, Mary Terriberry 464b, Tiago Ladeira 605, Reinhard Tiburzy 241, topseller 621l, Dave Turner 347, Valeriy Lebedev 702bl, VanHart. 259r, Ventin 288t, Volodymyr Goinyk 620, Voyagerix 506bl, Wolfgang Kloehr 702r, XXLPhoto 464t, YanLev 491, Ron Zmiri 377.

Inside front cover: **Shutterstock.com**: Dmitry Lobanov

All other images © Pearson Education

Disclaimer: **neither Pearson, Edexcel nor the authors take responsibility for the safety of any activity.** Before doing any practical activity you are legally required to carry out your own risk assessment. In particular, any local rules issued by your employer must be obeyed, regardless of what is recommended in this resource. Where students are required to write their own risk assessments they must always be checked by the teacher and revised, as necessary, to cover any issues the students may have overlooked. The teacher should always have the final control as to how the practical is conducted.

BIOLOGY

UNIT 1: ORGANISMS AND LIFE PROCESSES

UNIT 2: ANIMAL PHYSIOLOGY

UNIT 3: PLANT PHYSIOLOGY

UNIT 4: ECOLOGY AND THE ENVIRONMENT

UNIT 5: VARIATION AND SELECTION

UNIT 6: MICROORGANISMS AND GENETIC MODIFICATION

CHEMISTRY

UNIT 1: PRINCIPLES OF CHEMISTRY

UNIT 2: INORGANIC CHEMISTRY

UNIT 3: PHYSICAL CHEMISTRY

UNIT 4: ORGANIC CHEMISTRY

PHYSICS

UNIT 1: FORCES AND MOTION

UNIT 2: ELECTRICITY

UNIT 3: WAVES

UNIT 4: ENERGY RESOURCES AND ENERGY TRANSFER

UNIT 5: SOLIDS, LIQUIDS AND GASES

UNIT 6: MAGNETISM AND ELECTROMAGNETISM

UNIT 7: RADIOACTIVITY AND PARTICLES

UNIT 8: ASTROPHYSICS

ABOUT THIS BOOK

This book is written for students following the Pearson Edexcel International GCSE (9–1) Science Double Award specification. You will need to study all of the content in this book for your examinations, except anything in Extension boxes.

In each unit of this book, there are concise explanations and worked examples, plus numerous exercises that will help you build up confidence. The book also describes the methods for carrying out all of the required practicals.

The language throughout this textbook is graded for speakers of English as an additional language (EAL), with advanced Science-specific terminology highlighted and defined in the glossaries on the eBook. A list of command words at the back of the book will help you to learn the language you will need in your examinations.

You will also find that questions in this book have Progression icons and Skills tags. The Progression icons refer to Pearson's Progression scale. This scale – from 1 to 12 – tells you what level you have reached in your learning and will help you to see what you need to do to progress to the next level. Furthermore, Edexcel have developed a Skills grid showing the skills you will practise throughout your time on the course. The skills in the grid have been matched to questions in this book to help you see which skills you are developing. You can find Pearson's Progression scale at www.pearsonglobalschools.com/igscienceprogression along with guidelines on how to use it. Edexcel's skills grid can be found on their website.

Learning Objectives show what you will learn in each chapter.

Unit boxes tell you which units – for example, metres, grams and seconds – you will need to know and use for the study of a topic.

Looking Ahead tells you what you would learn if you continued your study of Science to a higher level, such as International A Level.

WAVES PROPERTIES OF WAVES 559

7 PROPERTIES OF WAVES

Talking to someone using a mobile phone is something most of us do several times a day. The technology that had to be developed for this to happen was based on a thorough understanding of the properties of waves.

In this chapter you will learn about different types of waves and their properties (characteristics).

▲ Figure 7.1 Using microwaves to communicate

LEARNING OBJECTIVES

- Explain the difference between longitudinal and transverse waves
- Know the definitions of amplitude, wavefront, frequency, wavelength and period of a wave
- Know that waves transfer energy and information without transferring matter
- Know and use the relationship between the speed, frequency and wavelength of a wave:
  wave speed = frequency × wavelength
  $v = f \times \lambda$
- Use the relationship between frequency and time period:
  $\text{frequency} = \frac{1}{\text{time period}}$
  $f = \frac{1}{T}$
- Use the above relationships in different contexts including sound waves and electromagnetic waves
- Explain that all waves can be reflected and refracted
- Explain why there is a change in the observed frequency and wavelength of a wave when its source is moving relative to an observer, and that this is known as the Doppler effect

UNITS

In this unit, you will need to use degrees (°) as the unit of angle, hertz (Hz) as the unit of frequency, metre (m) as the unit of length, metre per second (m/s) as the unit of speed and second (s) as the unit of time.

WHAT ARE WAVES?

Waves are a way of transferring energy from place to place. As we can see in Figure 7.1 we often use them to transfer information. All these transfers take place with no matter being transferred.

▲ Figure 7.2 Waves are produced if we drop a stone into a pond. The circular wavefronts spread out from the point of impact, carrying energy in all directions, but the water in the pond does not move from the centre to the edges.

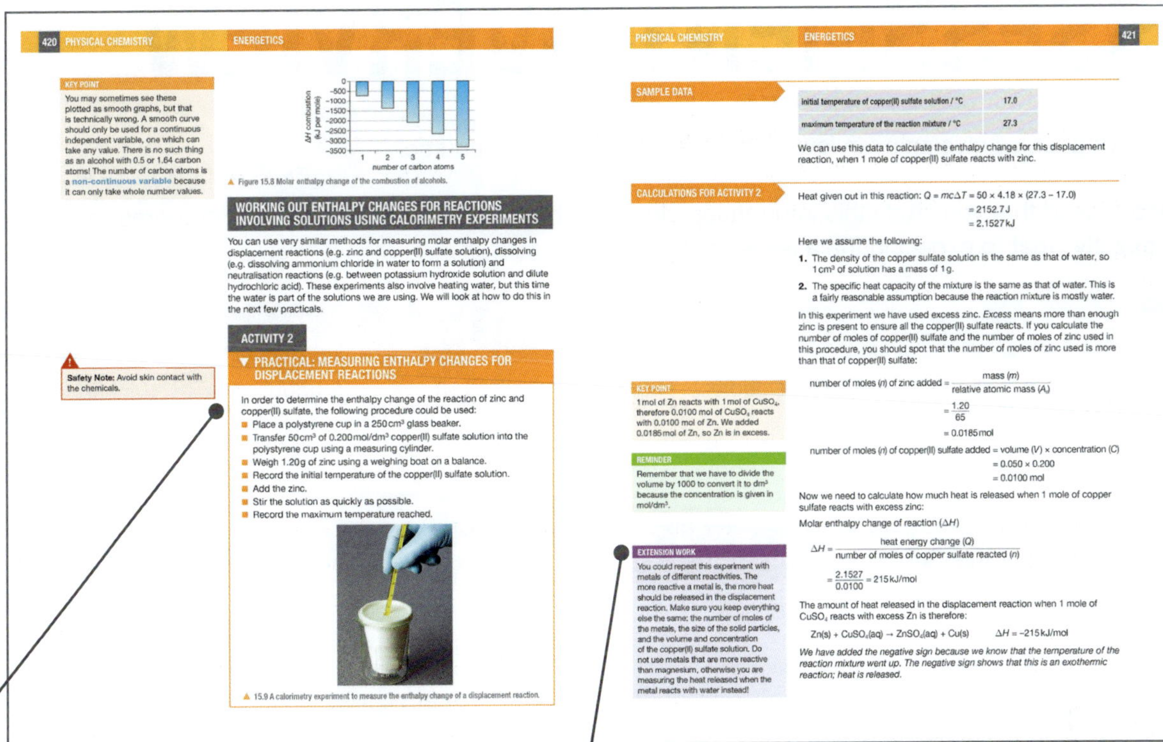

Practicals describe the methods for carrying out all of the practicals you will need to know for your examination.

Extension work boxes include content that is not on the specification and which you do not have to learn for your examination. However, it will help to extend your understanding of the topic.

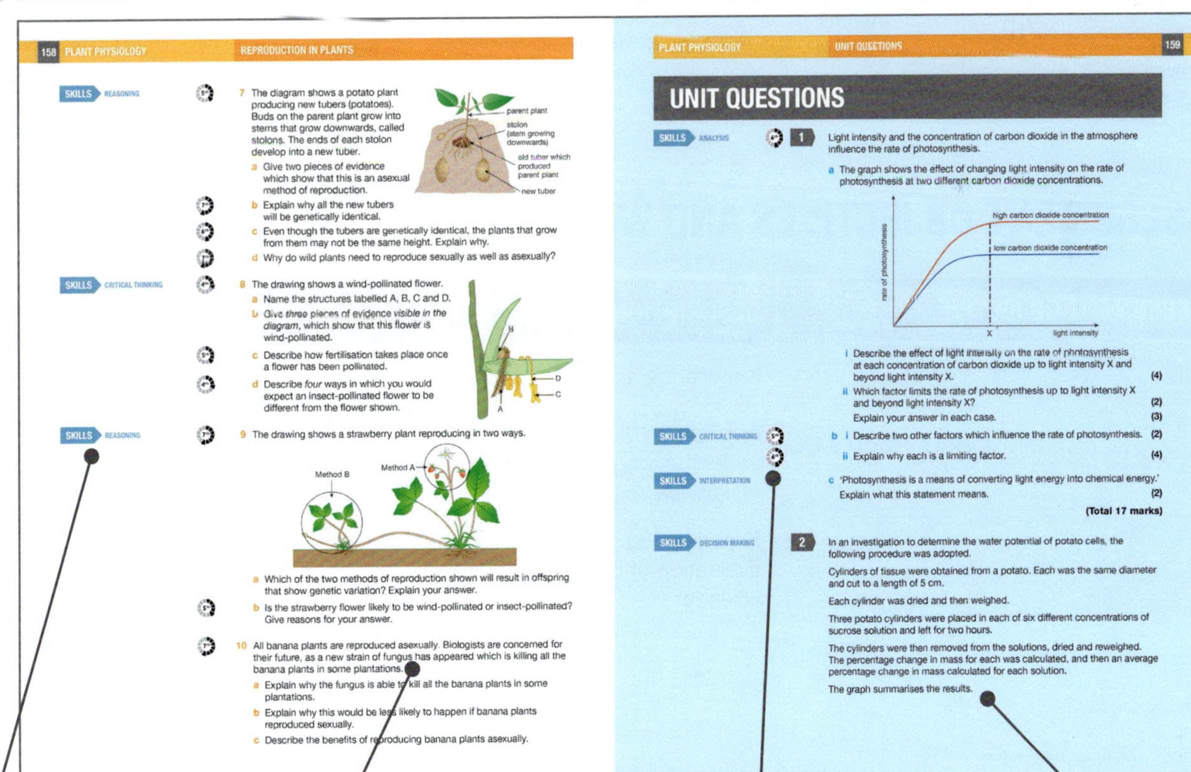

Skills tags tell you which skills you are practising in each question.

Chapter Questions test your knowledge of the topic in that chapter.

Progression icons show the level of difficulty according to the Pearson International GCSE Science Progression Scale.

Unit Questions test your knowledge of the whole unit and provide quick, effective feedback on your progress.

ASSESSMENT OVERVIEW

The following tables give an overview of the assessment for this course.

We recommend that you study this information closely to help ensure that you are fully prepared for this course and know exactly what to expect in the assessment.

BIOLOGY PAPER 1	SPECIFICATION	PERCENTAGE	MARK	TIME	AVAILABILITY
Written examination paper Paper code 4SD0/1B Externally set and assessed by Edexcel	Science Double Award	33.3%	110	2 hours	January and June examination series First assessment June 2019
CHEMISTRY PAPER 1	**SPECIFICATION**	**PERCENTAGE**	**MARK**	**TIME**	**AVAILABILITY**
Written examination paper Paper code 4SD0/1C Externally set and assessed by Edexcel	Science Double Award	33.3%	110	2 hours	January and June examination series First assessment June 2019
PHYSICS PAPER 1	**SPECIFICATION**	**PERCENTAGE**	**MARK**	**TIME**	**AVAILABILITY**
Written examination paper Paper code 4SD0/1P Externally set and assessed by Edexcel	Science Double Award	33.3%	110	2 hours	January and June examination series First assessment June 2019

ASSESSMENT OBJECTIVES AND WEIGHTINGS

ASSESSMENT OBJECTIVE	DESCRIPTION	% IN INTERNATIONAL GCSE
AO1	Knowledge and understanding of science	38%–42%
AO2	Application of knowledge and understanding, analysis and evaluation of science	38%–42%
AO3	Experimental skills, analysis and evaluation of data and methods in science	19%–21%

EXPERIMENTAL SKILLS

In the assessment of experimental skills, students may be tested on their ability to:

- solve problems set in a practical context
- apply scientific knowledge and understanding in questions with a practical context
- devise and plan investigations, using scientific knowledge and understanding when selecting appropriate techniques
- demonstrate or describe appropriate experimental and investigative methods, including safe and skilful practical techniques
- make observations and measurements with appropriate precision, record these methodically and present them in appropriate ways
- identify independent, dependent and control variables
- use scientific knowledge and understanding to analyse and interpret data to draw conclusions from experimental activities that are consistent with the evidence
- communicate the findings from experimental activities, using appropriate technical language, relevant calculations and graphs
- assess the reliability of an experimental activity
- evaluate data and methods taking into account factors that affect accuracy and validity.

CALCULATORS

Students are permitted to take a suitable calculator into the examinations. Calculators with QWERTY keyboards or that can retrieve text or formulae will not be permitted.

BIOLOGY UNIT 1 ORGANISMS AND LIFE PROCESSES

All living organisms are composed of microscopic units known as cells. These building blocks of life have a number of features in common, which allow them to grow, reproduce, and generate more organisms. In Chapter 1 we start by looking at the structure and function of cells, and the essential life processes that go on within them. Despite the fact that cells are similar in structure, there are many millions of different species of organisms. Chapter 2 looks at the diversity of living things and how we can classify them into groups on the basis of the features that they show.

1 LIFE PROCESSES

There are structural features that are common to the cells of all living organisms. In this chapter you will find out about these features and look at some of the processes that keep cells alive.

LEARNING OBJECTIVES

- Understand the characteristics shared by living organisms
- Describe cell structures and their functions, including the nucleus, cytoplasm, cell membrane, cell wall, mitochondria, chloroplasts, ribosomes and vacuole
- Know the similarities and differences in the structures of plant and animal cells
- Understand the role of enzymes as biological catalysts in metabolic reactions
- Understand how temperature changes can affect enzyme function, including changes to the shape of the active site
- Understand how enzyme function can be affected by changes in pH altering the active site
- Investigate how enzyme activity can be affected by changes in temperature
- Describe the differences between aerobic and anaerobic respiration
- Understand how the process of respiration produces ATP in living organisms
- Know that ATP provides energy for cells
- Know the word equation and balanced chemical symbol equation for aerobic respiration
- Know the word equations for anaerobic respiration
- Investigate the evolution of carbon dioxide and heat from respiring seeds or other suitable living organisms
- Understand the processes of diffusion, osmosis and active transport by which substances move into and out of cells
- Understand how factors affect the rate of movement of substances into and out of cells
- Investigate diffusion in a non-living system (agar jelly)
- Describe the levels of organisation within organisms – organelles, cells, tissues, organ systems

All living organisms are composed of units called **cells**. The simplest organisms are made from single cells (Figure 1.1) but more complex plants and animals are composed of millions of cells. In many-celled (**multicellular**) organisms, there may be hundreds of different types of cells with different structures. They are specialised so that they can carry out particular functions in the animal or plant. Despite all the differences, there are basic features that are the same in all cells.

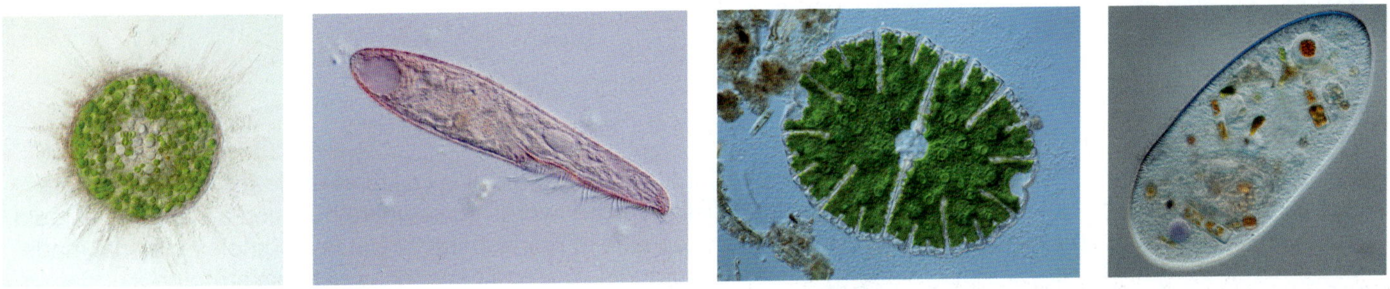

▲ Figure 1.1 Many simple organisms have 'bodies' made from single cells. Here are four examples.

There are eight life processes which take place in most living things. Organisms:

- require nutrition – plants make their own food, animals eat other organisms
- respire – release energy from their food
- excrete – get rid of waste products
- respond to stimuli – are sensitive to changes in their surroundings
- move – by the action of muscles in animals, and slow growth movements in plants
- control their internal conditions – maintain a steady state inside the body
- reproduce – produce offspring
- grow and develop – increase in size and complexity, using materials from their food.

CELL STRUCTURE

This part of the book describes the cell structure of 'higher' organisms such as animals, plants and fungi. The cells of bacteria are simpler in structure and will be described in Chapter 2.

Most cells contain certain parts such as the nucleus, cytoplasm and cell membrane. Some cells have structures missing, for instance red blood cells are unusual in that they have no nucleus. The first chapter in a biology textbook will usually present diagrams of 'typical' plant and animal cells. In fact, there is really no such thing as a 'typical' cell. Humans, for example, are composed of hundreds of different kinds of cells – from nerve cells to blood cells, skin cells to liver cells. What we really mean by a 'typical' cell is a general diagram that shows all the features that you will find in most cells (Figure 1.2). However, not all these are present in *all* cells – for example the cells in the parts of a plant that are not green do not contain chloroplasts.

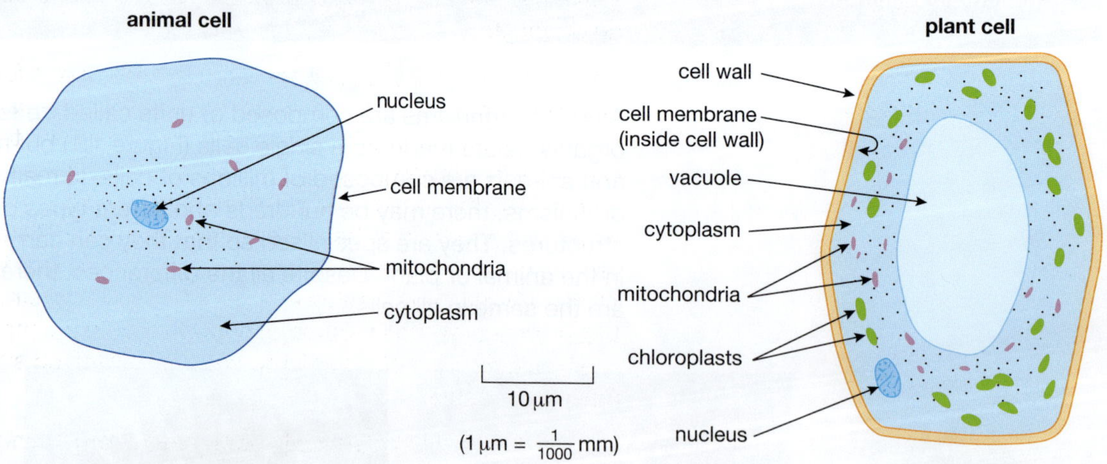

▲ Figure 1.2 The structure of a 'typical' animal and plant cell.

The living material that makes up a cell is called **cytoplasm**. It has a texture rather like sloppy jelly, in other words somewhere between a solid and a liquid. Unlike a jelly, it is not made of one substance but is a complex material made of many different structures. You can't see many of these structures under an ordinary light microscope. An electron microscope has a much higher magnification and can show the details of these structures, which are called **organelles** (Figure 1.3).

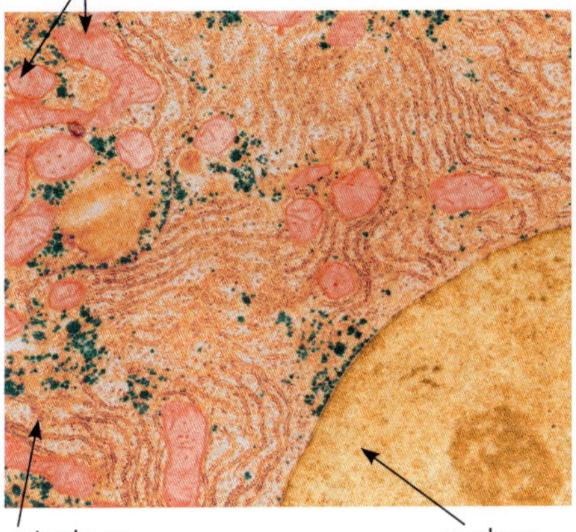

▲ Figure 1.3 The organelles in a cell can be seen using an electron micropscope.

The largest organelle in the cell is the **nucleus**. Nearly all cells have a nucleus. The few types that don't are usually dead (e.g. the xylem vessels in a stem, Chapter 11) or don't live for very long (e.g. red blood cells, Chapter 5). The nucleus controls the activities of the cell. It contains **chromosomes** (46 in human cells) which carry the genetic material, or **genes**. Genes control the activities in the cell by determining which proteins the cell can make. The DNA remains in the nucleus, but the instructions for making proteins are carried out of the nucleus to the cytoplasm, where the proteins are assembled on tiny structures called **ribosomes**. A cell contains thousands of ribosomes, but they are too small to be seen through a light microscope.

One very important group of proteins found in cells are **enzymes.** Enzymes control the chemical reactions that take place in the cytoplasm.

All cells are surrounded by a **cell membrane**, sometimes called the cell *surface* membrane to distinguish it from other membranes inside the cell. This is a thin layer like a 'skin' on the surface of the cell. It forms a boundary between the cytoplasm of the cell and the outside. However, it is not a complete barrier. Some chemicals can pass into the cell and others can pass out. We say that the membrane is **partially permeable**. The membrane can go further than this and actually *control* the movement of some substances – it is **selectively permeable**.

One organelle that is found in the cytoplasm of all living cells is the **mitochondrion** (plural mitochondria). In cells that need a lot of energy such as muscle or nerve cells, there are many mitochondria. This gives us a clue to their function. They carry out some of the reactions of **respiration** (see page 11) releasing energy that the cell can use. Most of the energy from respiration is released in the mitochondria.

PLANT CELLS

All of the structures you have seen so far are found in both animal and plant cells. However, some structures are only ever found in plant cells. There are three in particular – the cell wall, a permanent vacuole and chloroplasts.

The **cell wall** is a layer of non-living material that is found outside the cell membrane of plant cells. It is made mainly of a carbohydrate called **cellulose**, although other chemicals may be added to the wall in some cells. Cellulose is a tough material that helps the cell keep its shape and is one reason why the 'body' of a plant has a fixed shape. Animal cells do not have a cell wall and tend to be more variable in shape. Plant cells absorb water, producing an internal pressure that pushes against adjacent cells, giving the plant support (see Chapter 11). Without a cell wall strong enough to resist these pressures, this method of support would be impossible. The cell wall is porous, so it is not a barrier to water or dissolved substances. We call it *freely permeable*.

Mature (fully grown) plant cells often have a large central space surrounded by a membrane, called a **vacuole**. This vacuole is a permanent feature of the cell. It is filled with a watery liquid called cell sap, which is a store of dissolved sugars, mineral ions and other solutes. Animal cells do contain vacuoles, but they are only small, temporary structures.

Cells of the green parts of plants, especially the leaves, contain another very important organelle, the **chloroplast**. Chloroplasts absorb light energy to make food in the process of photosynthesis (see Chapter 10). They contain a green pigment called **chlorophyll**. Cells from the parts of a plant that are not green, such as the flowers, roots and woody stems, have no chloroplasts.

KEY POINT

Nearly all cells contain cytoplasm, a nucleus, a cell membrane and mitochondria. As well as these structures, plant cells have a cell wall and a permanent vacuole, and plant cells that photosynthesise contain chloroplasts.

Figure 1.4 shows some animal and plant cells seen through the light microscope.

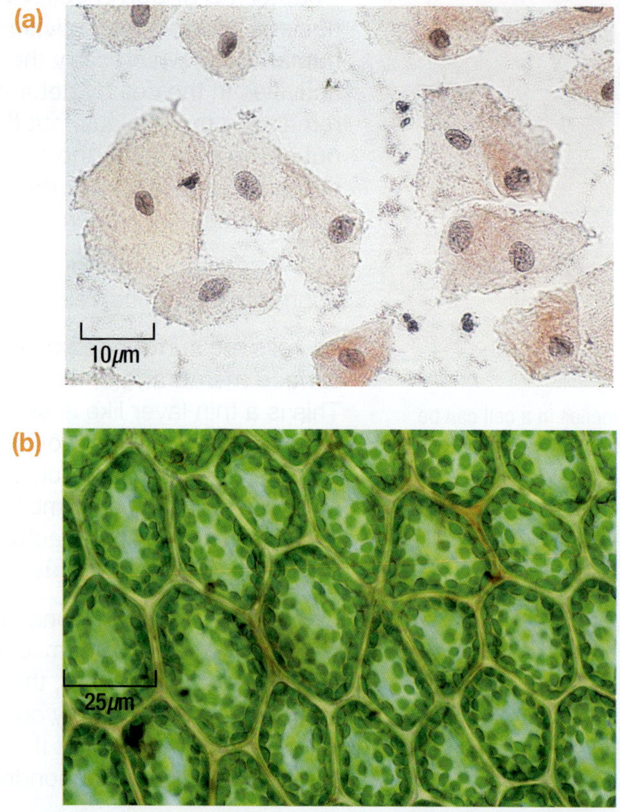

▲ Figure 1.4 (a) Cells from the lining of a human cheek. (b) Cells from the photosynthetic tissue of a leaf.

ENZYMES: CONTROLLING REACTIONS IN THE CELL

The chemical reactions that take place in a cell are controlled by a group of proteins called enzymes. Enzymes are biological **catalysts**. A catalyst is a chemical which speeds up a reaction without being used up itself. It takes part in the reaction, but afterwards is unchanged and free to catalyse more reactions. Cells contain hundreds of different enzymes, each catalysing a different reaction. This is how the activities of a cell are controlled – the nucleus contains the genes, which control the production of enzymes, which then catalyse reactions in the cytoplasm:

genes → proteins (enzymes) → catalyse reactions

Everything a cell does depends on which enzymes it can make, which in turn depends on which genes in its nucleus are working.

What hasn't been mentioned is why enzymes are needed at all. They are necessary because the temperatures inside organisms are low (e.g. the human body temperature is about 37 °C) and without catalysts, most of the reactions that happen in cells would be far too slow to allow life to go on. The reactions can only take place quickly enough when enzymes are present to speed them up.

It is possible for there to be thousands of different sorts of enzymes because they are proteins, and protein molecules have an enormous range of structures and shapes (see Chapter 4).

KEY POINT

The chemical reactions taking place in a cell are known as metabolic reactions. The sum of all the metabolic reactions is known as the **metabolism** of the cell. The function of enzymes is to catalyse metabolic reactions.

KEY POINT

You have probably heard of enzymes being involved in digestion of food. In the intestine enzymes are secreted onto the food to break it down. These are called *extracellular* enzymes, which means they function 'outside cells'. However, most enzymes stay inside cells and carry out their function there; they are *intracellular*. You will find out about digestive enzymes in Chapter 4.

KEY POINT

Secretion is the release of a fluid or substances from a cell or tissue.

The molecule that an enzyme acts on is called its **substrate**. Each enzyme has a small area on its surface called the **active site**. The substrate attaches to the active site of the enzyme. The reaction then takes place and products are formed. When the substrate joins up with the active site it lowers the energy needed for the reaction to start, allowing the products to be formed more easily.

Enzymes also catalyse reactions where large molecules are built up from smaller ones. In this case, several substrate molecules attach to the active site, the reaction takes place and the larger product molecule is formed. The product then leaves the active site.

The substrate fits into the active site of the enzyme like a key fitting into a lock. Just as a key will only fit one lock, a substrate will only fit into the active site of a particular enzyme. This is known as the **lock and key model** of enzyme action. It is the reason why enzymes are *specific*, i.e. an enzyme will only catalyse one reaction.

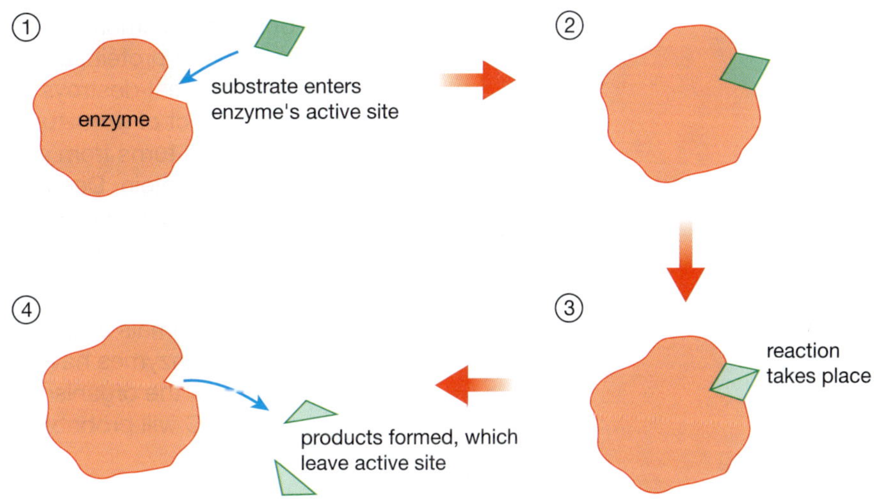

▲ Figure 1.5 Enzymes catalyse reactions at their active site. This acts like a 'lock' to the substrate 'key'. The substrate fits into the active site, and products are formed. This happens more easily than without the enzyme – so enzymes act as catalysts.

After an enzyme molecule has catalysed a reaction, the product is released from the active site, and the enzyme is free to act on more substrate molecules.

FACTORS AFFECTING ENZYMES

KEY POINT

'Optimum' temperature means the 'best' temperature, in other words the temperature at which the reaction takes place most rapidly.

DID YOU KNOW?

Kinetic energy is the energy an object has because of its movement. The molecules of enzyme and substrate are moving faster, so they have more kinetic energy.

A number of factors affect the activity of enzymes. The rate of reaction may be increased by raising the concentration of the enzyme or the substrate. Two other factors that affect enzymes are temperature and pH.

TEMPERATURE

The effect of temperature on the action of an enzyme is easiest to see as a graph, where we plot the rate of the reaction against temperature (Figure 1.6).

Enzymes in the human body have evolved to work best at body temperature (37 °C). The graph in Figure 1.6 shows a peak on the curve at this temperature, which is called the *optimum temperature* for the enzyme.

As the enzyme is heated up to the optimum temperature, the rise in temperature increases the rate of reaction. This is because higher temperatures give the molecules of the enzyme and the substrate more kinetic energy, so they collide more often. More collisions means that the reaction will take place more frequently.

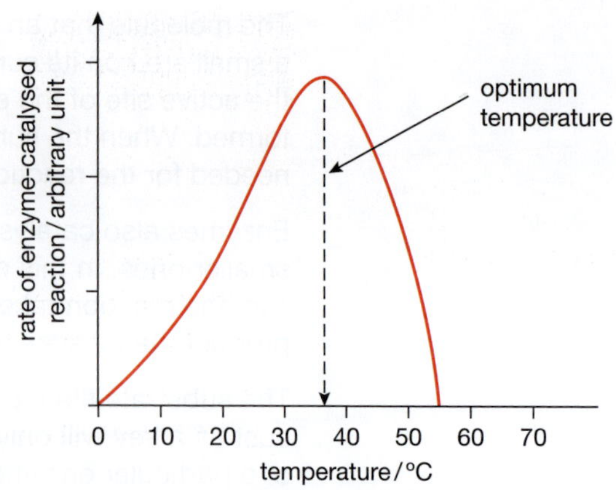

▲ Figure 1.6 Effect of temperature on the action of an enzyme.

However, above the optimum, temperature starts to have another effect. Enzymes are made of protein, and proteins are broken down by heat. From 40 °C upwards, the heat destroys the enzyme. We say that it is denatured. You can see the effect of **denaturing** when you boil an egg. The egg white is made of protein, and turns from a clear runny liquid into a white solid as the heat denatures the protein. Denaturing changes the shape of the active site so that the substrate will no longer fit into it. Denaturing is permanent – the enzyme molecules will no longer catalyse the reaction.

Not all enzymes have an optimum temperature near 37 °C, only those of animals such as mammals and birds, which all have body temperatures close to this value. Enzymes have evolved to work best at the normal body temperature of the organism. Bacteria that always live at an average temperature of 10 °C will probably have enzymes with an optimum temperature near 10 °C.

pH

The pH around the enzyme is also important. The pH inside cells is neutral (pH 7) and most enzymes have evolved to work best at this pH. At extremes of pH either side of neutral, the enzyme activity decreases, as shown in Figure 1.7. The pH at which the enzyme works best is called its *optimum pH*. Either side of the optimum, the pH affects the structure of the enzyme molecule and changes the shape of its active site, so that the substrate will not fit into it so well.

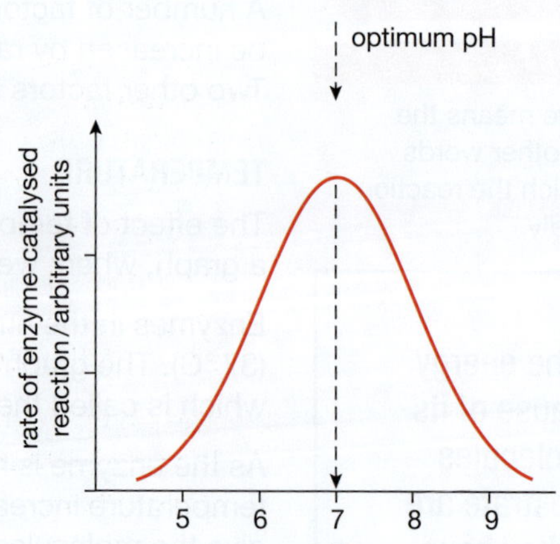

▲ Figure 1.7 Most enzymes work best at a neutral pH.

KEY POINT

Although most enzymes work best at a neutral pH, a few have an optimum below or above pH 7. The stomach produces hydrochloric acid, which makes its contents very acidic (see Chapter 4). Most enzymes stop working at a low pH, but the stomach makes an enzyme called pepsin which has an optimum pH of about 2, so that it is adapted to work well in these unusually acidic surroundings.

Safety note: Wear eye protection and avoid skin contact with the liquids. Amylase is hazardous to the eyes.

ACTIVITY 1

▼ PRACTICAL: AN INVESTIGATION INTO THE EFFECT OF TEMPERATURE ON THE ACTIVITY OF AMYLASE

The digestive enzyme amylase breaks down starch into the sugar maltose. If the speed at which the starch disappears is recorded, this is a measure of the activity of the amylase.

Figure 1.8 shows apparatus which can be used to record how quickly the starch is used up.

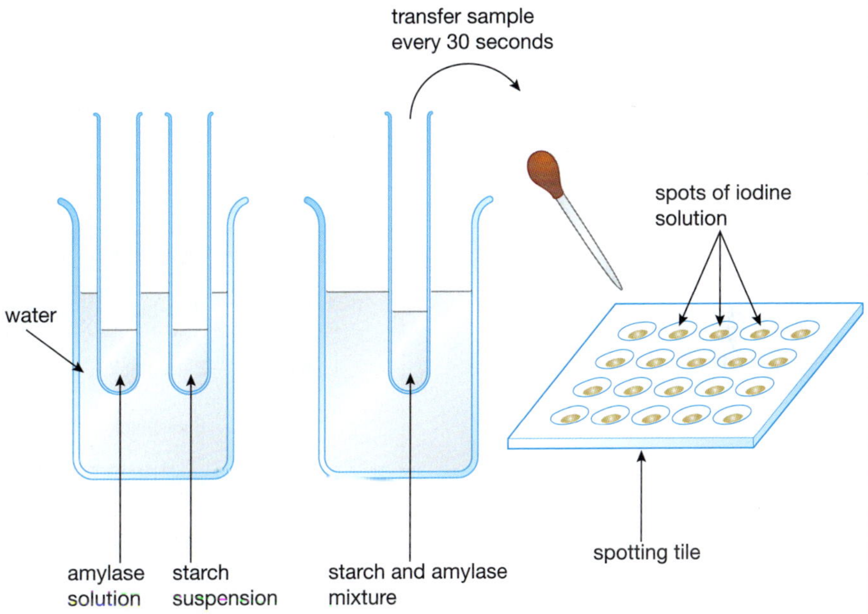

▲ Figure 1.8 Investigating the breakdown of starch by amylase at different temperatures.

Spots of iodine solution are placed into the dips on the spotting tile. Using a syringe, 5 cm^3 of starch suspension is placed in one boiling tube, and 5 cm^3 of amylase solution in another tube, using a different syringe. The beaker is filled with water at 20 °C. Both boiling tubes are placed in the beaker of water for 5 minutes, and the temperature recorded.

The amylase solution is then poured into the starch suspension, leaving the tube containing the mixture in the water bath. Immediately, a small sample of the mixture is removed from the tube with a pipette and added to the first drop of iodine solution on the spotting tile. The colour of the iodine solution is recorded.

A sample of the mixture is taken every 30 seconds for 10 minutes and tested for starch as above, until the iodine solution remains yellow, showing that all the starch is used up.

The experiment is repeated, maintaining the water bath at different temperatures between 20 °C and 60 °C. A set of results is shown in the table below.

	Colour of mixture at different temperatures / (°C)				
Time / min	20	30	40	50	60
0.0	Blue-black	Blue-black	Blue-black	Blue-black	Blue-black
0.5	Blue-black	Blue-black	Brown	Blue-black	Blue-black
1.0	Blue-black	Blue-black	Yellow	Blue-black	Blue-black
1.5	Blue-black	Blue-black	Yellow	Blue-black	Blue-black
2.0	Blue-black	Blue-black	Yellow	Brown	Blue-black
2.5	Blue-black	Blue-black	Yellow	Brown	Blue-black
3.0	Blue-black	Blue-black	Yellow	Brown	Blue-black
3.5	Blue-black	Blue-black	Yellow	Yellow	Blue-black
4.0	Blue-black	Blue-black	Yellow	Yellow	Blue-black
5.5	Blue-black	Blue-black	Yellow	Yellow	Blue-black
6.0	Blue-black	Brown	Yellow	Yellow	Blue-black
6.5	Blue-black	Brown	Yellow	Yellow	Blue-black
7.0	Blue-black	Yellow	Yellow	Yellow	Blue-black
7.5	Blue-black	Yellow	Yellow	Yellow	Brown
8.0	Blue-black	Yellow	Yellow	Yellow	Brown
8.5	Brown	Yellow	Yellow	Yellow	Yellow
9.0	Brown	Yellow	Yellow	Yellow	Yellow
9.5	Yellow	Yellow	Yellow	Yellow	Yellow
10.0	Yellow	Yellow	Yellow	Yellow	Yellow

The rate of reaction can be calculated from the time taken for the starch to be fully broken down, as shown by the colour change from blue-black to yellow. For example, at 50 °C the starch had all been digested after 3.5 minutes. The rate is found by dividing the volume of the starch (5 cm^3) by the time:

$$\text{Rate} = \frac{5.0\,\text{cm}^3}{3.5\,\text{min}} = 1.4\,\text{cm}^3 \text{ per min}$$

Plotting a graph of rate against temperature should produce a curve similar to the one shown in Figure 1.6. Try this, using the results in the table. Better still, you may be able to do this experiment and provide your own results.

If the curve doesn't turn out quite like the one in Figure 1.6, can you suggest why this is? How could you improve the experiment to get more reliable results?

HOW THE CELL GETS ITS ENERGY

A cell needs a source of energy in order to be able to carry out all the processes needed for life. It gets this energy by breaking down food molecules to release the stored chemical energy that they contain. This process is called respiration. Many people think that respiration means the same as 'breathing', but although there are links between the two processes, the biological meaning of respiration is very different.

KEY POINT

Respiration is called an *oxidation* reaction, because oxygen is used to break down food molecules.

Respiration happens in all the cells of our body. Oxygen is used to oxidise food, and carbon dioxide (and water) are released as waste products. The main food oxidised is a sugar called **glucose**. Glucose contains stored chemical energy that can be converted into other forms of energy that the cell can use. It is rather like burning a fuel to get the energy out of it, except that burning releases most of the energy as heat. Respiration releases some heat energy, but most is used to make a substance called ATP (see below). The energy stored in the ATP molecules can then be used for a variety of purposes, such as:

- contraction of muscle cells, producing movement
- active transport of molecules and ions (see page 17)
- building large molecules, such as proteins
- cell division.

The energy released as heat is also used to maintain a constant body temperature in mammals and birds (see Chapter 8).

The overall reaction for respiration is:

$$\text{glucose} + \text{oxygen} \rightarrow \text{carbon dioxide} + \text{water} \quad (+\text{ energy})$$
$$C_6H_{12}O_6 + 6O_2 \rightarrow 6CO_2 + 6H_2O \quad (+\text{ energy})$$

DID YOU KNOW?

Carbon from the respired glucose passes out into the atmosphere as carbon dioxide. The carbon can be traced through this pathway using a radioactive form of carbon called carbon-14.

This is called **aerobic respiration**, because it uses oxygen. Aerobic respiration happens in the cells of humans and those of animals, plants and many other organisms. It is important to realise that the equation above is only a *summary* of the process. It actually takes place gradually, as a sequence of small steps, which release the energy of the glucose in small amounts. Each step in the process is catalysed by a different enzyme. The later steps in the process are the aerobic ones, and these release the most energy. They happen in the mitochondria of the cell.

ATP – THE ENERGEY 'CURRENCY' OF THE CELL

Respiration releases energy while other cell processes use it up. Cells have a way of passing the energy from respiration to the other processes that need it. They do this using a chemical called **adenosine triphosphate** or **ATP**. ATP is present in all living cells.

ATP is composed of an organic molecule called adenosine attached to three phosphate groups. In a cell, ATP can be broken down losing one phosphate group and forming adenosine diphosphate or ADP (Figure 1.9 (a)).

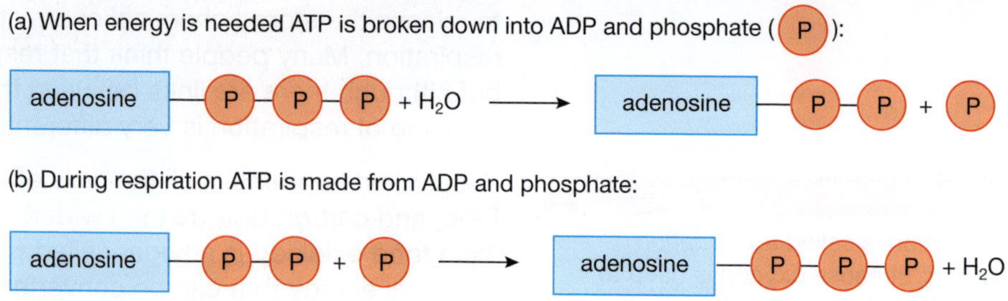

▲ Figure 1.9 ATP is the energy 'currency' of the cell.

When this reaction takes place, chemical energy is released and can be used to drive metabolic processes that need it.

During respiration the opposite happens – energy from the oxidation of glucose is used to drive the reverse reaction and a phosphate is added onto ADP (Figure 1.9 (b)).

ATP is often described as the energy 'currency' of the cell. It transfers energy between the process that releases it (respiration) and the processes in a cell that use it up.

ANAEROBIC RESPIRATION

There are some situations where cells can respire *without* using oxygen. This is called **anaerobic respiration**. In anaerobic respiration, glucose is not completely broken down, so less energy is released. The advantage of anaerobic respiration is that it can occur in situations where oxygen is in short supply. Two important examples of this are in yeast cells and muscle cells.

Yeasts are single-celled fungi. They are used in processes such as baking bread. When yeast cells are prevented from getting enough oxygen, they stop respiring aerobically and start to respire anaerobically instead. The glucose is partly broken down into ethanol (alcohol) and carbon dioxide:

glucose → ethanol + carbon dioxide (+ some energy)

This process is described in more detail in Chapter 21.

Think about the properties of ethanol – it makes a good fuel and will burn to produce a lot of heat, so it still has a lot of chemical energy 'stored' in it.

Muscle cells can also respire anaerobically when they are short of oxygen. If muscles are overworked, the blood cannot reach them fast enough to deliver enough oxygen for aerobic respiration. This happens when a person does a 'burst' of activity, such as a sprint, or quickly lifting a heavy weight. This time the glucose is broken down into a substance called **lactate**:

glucose → lactate (+ some energy)

Anaerobic respiration provides enough energy to keep the overworked muscles going for a short period. During the exercise, the level of lactate rises in the muscle cells and bloodstream.

DID YOU KNOW?

It was once thought that lactate was toxic and caused muscle fatigue. We now know that this is *not* true. In fact physiologists have shown that lactate actually *delays* muscle fatigue. Fatigue is caused by other changes that happen in the muscles during exercise.

DID YOU KNOW?

Lactate is sometims called lactic acid.

After the exercise the lactate is respired aerobically in the mitochondria. The volume of oxygen needed to completely oxidise the lactate that builds up in the body during anaerobic respiration is called the **oxygen debt**.

ACTIVITY 2

▼ PRACTICAL: DEMONSTRATION OF THE PRODUCTION OF CARBON DIOXIDE BY SMALL LIVING ORGANISMS

Safety note: Wear eye protection, treat all living organisms with care and avoid skin contact.

Hydrogen carbonate indicator solution is normally orange, but turns yellow if carbon dioxide is added to it. The indicator is sensitive to small changes in carbon dioxide concentration, and can be used to show production of carbon dioxide by small organisms such as woodlice, maggots (fly larvae) or germinating seeds.

The organisms are placed in a stoppered boiling tube with the indicator, as shown in Figure 1.10. The gauze platform supports the organisms above the hydrogen carbonate indicator solution and stops them from coming into contact with the chemical.

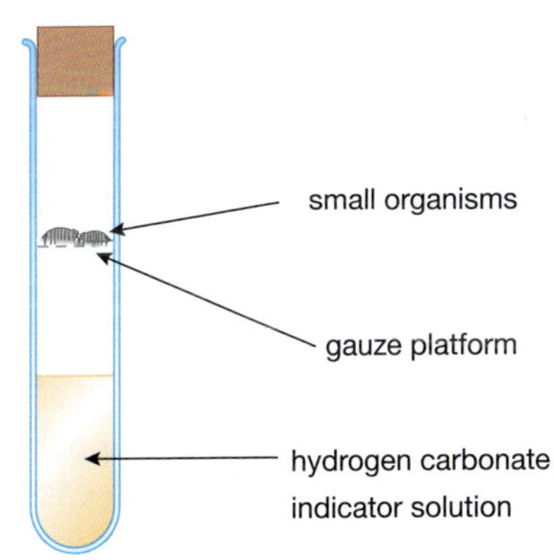

▲ Figure 1.10 Testing for carbon dioxide production by small organisms.

Of the three species of organisms mentioned above, which do you think would change the colour of the indicator most quickly? If you are able to observe each of the organisms, this might help with your prediction.

When you have made your prediction (called a 'hypothesis'), plan an investigation to test it. Take care to consider the variables that need to be **controlled variable**, and don't forget to include a description of a fourth tube that you would need to set up as the experimental Control (see Appendix A for an explanation of these terms).

It may be possible for you to carry out the investigation using similar apparatus and organisms.

Safety note: Eye protection should be worn when using bleach to wash the peas and skin contact avoided.

ACTIVITY 3

▼ PRACTICAL: DEMONSTRATION THAT HEAT IS PRODUCED BY RESPIRATION

Some peas are soaked in water for 24 hours, so that they start to germinate. A second batch of peas is boiled, to kill them. Each set of peas is washed in a 1% bleach solution, which acts as a disinfectant, killing any bacteria present on the surface of the peas. The peas are then rinsed twice in distilled water to remove any traces of bleach.

Each batch of peas is placed in an inverted vacuum flask as shown in Figure 1.11, leaving some air in each flask. A vacuum flask insulates its contents, so that any small temperature change inside the flask can be measured.

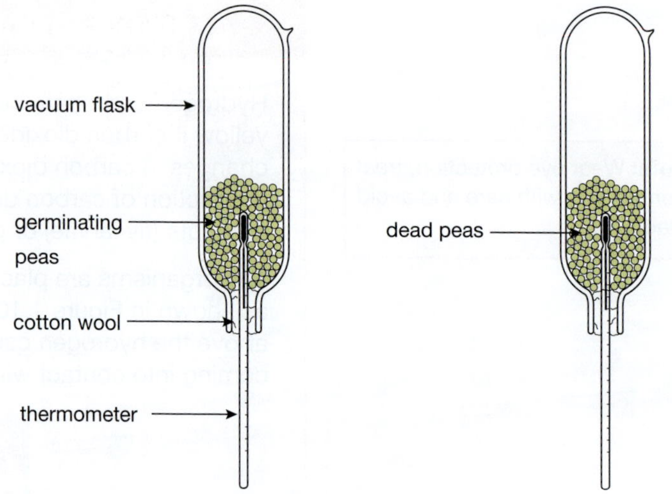

▲ Figure 1.11 Experiment to show that heat is produced during respiration in germinating peas.

The seeds produce carbon dioxide gas, which is denser than air. The inverted flasks and cotton wool allow this to escape. It might otherwise kill the peas.

The apparatus is left set up for a couple of days, and the temperature inside each flask measured at the start and end of the experiment.

The following results were obtained from this experiment:

Temperature in both flasks at the start = 21 °C

Temperature in flask with dead peas at the end = 21 °C

Temperature in flask with living peas at the end = 24 °C

Can you explain these results? Why is it necessary to kill any microorganisms on the surface of the peas? Explain the importance of the flask containing dead peas.

MOVEMENT OF MATERIALS IN AND OUT OF CELLS

Cell respiration shows the need for cells to be able to take in certain substances from their surroundings, such as glucose and oxygen, and get rid of others, such as carbon dioxide and water. As you have seen, the cell surface membrane can control which chemicals can pass in and out – it is described as selectively permeable.

There are three main ways that molecules and ions can move through the membrane. They are diffusion, active transport and osmosis.

DIFFUSION

Many substances can pass through the membrane by **diffusion**. Diffusion happens when a substance is more concentrated in one place than another. For example, if the cell is making carbon dioxide by respiration, the concentration of carbon dioxide inside the cell will be higher than outside. This difference in concentration is called a concentration gradient. The molecules of carbon dioxide are constantly moving about because of their kinetic energy. The cell membrane is permeable to carbon dioxide, so the molecules can move in either direction through it. Since there is a higher concentration of carbon dioxide molecules inside the cell than outside, over time, more molecules will move from inside to outside than move in the other direction. We say that there is a *net* movement of the molecules out of the cell (Figure 1.12).

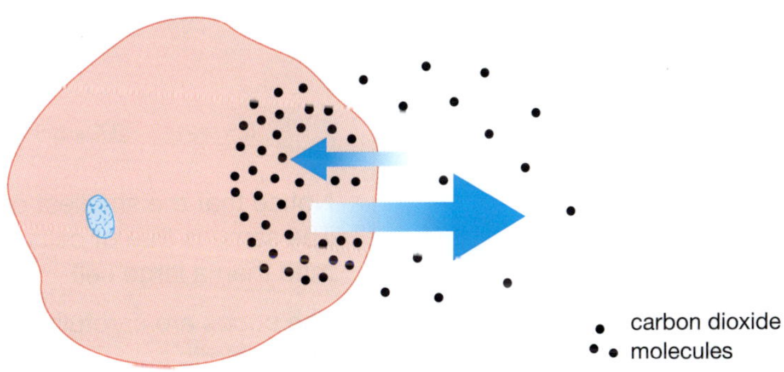

▲ Figure 1.12 Carbon dioxide is produced by respiration, so its concentration builds up inside the cell. Although the carbon dioxide molecules diffuse in both directions across the cell membrane, the overall (net) movement is out of the cell, down the concentration gradient.

KEY POINT

Diffusion is the net movement of particles (molecules or ions) from a region of high concentration to a region of low concentration, i.e. down a concentration gradient.

The opposite happens with oxygen. Respiration uses up oxygen, so there is a concentration gradient of oxygen from outside to inside the cell. There is therefore a net movement of oxygen *into* the cell by diffusion.

The rate of diffusion is affected by various factors.

- The concentration gradient. Diffusion happens more quickly when there is a steep concentration gradient (i.e. a big difference in concentrations between two areas).
- The surface area to volume ratio. A larger surface area in proportion to the volume will increase the rate.
- The distance. The rate is decreased if the distance over which diffusion has to take place is greater.
- The temperature. The rate is greater at higher temperatures. This is because a high temperature provides the particles with more kinetic energy.

Safety note: Wear eye protection and avoid all skin contact with the acid and the dyed agar blocks.

ACTIVITY 4

▼ PRACTICAL: DEMONSTRATION OF DIFFUSION IN A JELLY

Agar is a jelly that is used for growing cultures of bacteria. It has a consistency similar to the cytoplasm of a cell. Like cytoplasm, it has a high water content. Agar can be used to show how substances diffuse through a cell.

This demonstration uses the reaction between hydrochloric acid and potassium permanganate solution. When hydrochloric acid comes into contact with potassium permanganate, the purple colour of the permanganate disappears.

A Petri dish is prepared which contains a 2 cm deep layer of agar jelly, dyed purple with potassium permanganate. Three cubes of different sizes are cut out of the jelly, with side lengths 2 cm, 1 cm and 0.5 cm. The cubes have different volumes and total surface areas. They also have a different surface area to volume ratio, as shown in the table below.

Length of side of cube / cm	Volume of cube / cm^3 (length × width × height)	Surface area of cube / cm^2 (length × width of one side) × 6	Ratio of surface area to volume of cube (surface area divided by volume)
2	(2 × 2 × 2) = 8	(2 × 2) × 6 = 24	24/8 = 3
1	(1 × 1 × 1) = 1	(1 × 1) × 6 = 6	6/1 = 6
0.5	(0.5 × 0.5 × 0.5) = 0.125	(0.5 × 0.5) × 6 = 1.5	1.5/0.125 = 12

Notice that the smallest cube has the largest surface area to volume ratio. The same is true of cells – a small cell has a larger surface area to volume ratio than a large cell.

The cubes are carefully dropped, at the same time, into a beaker of dilute hydrochloric acid (Figure 1.13).

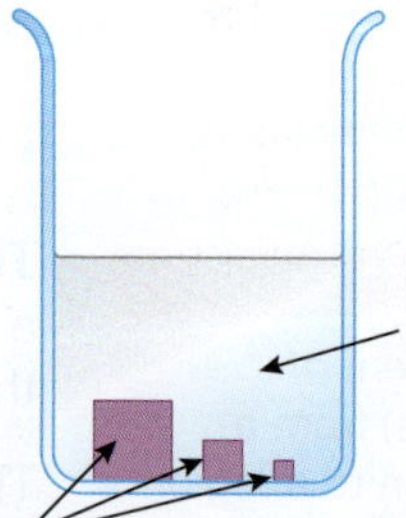

▶ Figure 1.13 Investigating diffusion in a jelly.

The time taken for each cube to turn colourless is noted.

Which cube would be the first to turn colourless and which the last? Explain the reasoning behind your prediction.

If the three cubes represented cells of different sizes, which cell would have the most difficulty in obtaining substances by diffusion?

It may be possible for you to try this experiment, using similar apparatus.

ACTIVE TRANSPORT

Diffusion happens because of the kinetic energy of the particles. It does not need an 'extra' source of energy from respiration. However, sometimes a cell needs to take in a substance when there is very little of that substance outside the cell, in other words *against* a concentration gradient. It can do this by another process, called **active transport**.

During active transport a cell uses energy from respiration to take up substances, rather like a pump uses energy to move a liquid from one place to another. In fact, biologists speak of the cell 'pumping' ions or molecules in or out. The pumps are large protein molecules located in the cell membrane, and they are driven by the breakdown of ATP. An example of a place where this happens is in the human small intestine, where some glucose in the gut is absorbed into the cells lining the intestine by active transport. The roots of plants also take up certain mineral ions in this way. Cells use active transport to control the uptake of many substances.

KEY POINT

Active transport is the movement of substances against a concentration gradient, using energy from respiration.

OSMOSIS

Water moves across cell membranes by a special sort of diffusion, called **osmosis**. Osmosis happens when the total concentrations of all dissolved substances inside and outside the cell are different. Water will move across the membrane from the more dilute solution to the more concentrated one. Notice that this is still obeying the rules of diffusion – the water moves from where there is a higher concentration of *water* molecules to a lower concentration of *water* molecules. Osmosis can only happen if the membrane is permeable to water but not to some other solutes. We say that it is partially permeable.

Osmosis is important for moving water from cell to cell, for example in plant roots. You will find out more about osmosis in Chapter 11.

KEY POINT

Osmosis in cells is the net movement of water from a dilute solution to a more concentrated solution across the partially permeable cell membrane.

SPECIALISED EXCHANGE SURFACES

KEY POINT

'Adapted' or 'an **adaptation**' means that the structure of a cell or an organism is suited to its function. It is a word that is very commonly used in biology, and will appear again in many of the chapters of this book. We also use it when we say that organisms are adapted to their environment.

All cells exchange substances with their surroundings, but some parts of animals or plants are specially adapted for the exchange of materials because they have a very large surface area in proportion to their volume. In animals, two examples are the alveoli (air sacs) of the lungs (Chapter 3) and the villi of the small intestine (Chapter 4). Diffusion is a slow process, and organs that rely on diffusion need a large surface over which it can take place. The alveoli allow the exchange of oxygen and carbon dioxide to take place between the air and the blood during breathing. The villi of the small intestine provide a large surface area for the absorption of digested food. In plants, exchange surfaces are also adapted by having a large surface area, such as the spongy mesophyll of the leaf (Chapter 10) and the **root hairs**.

CELLS, TISSUES AND ORGANS

Cells with a similar function are grouped together as **tissues**. For example, the muscle of your arm contains millions of similar muscle cells, all specialised for one function – contraction to move the arm bones. This is muscle tissue. However, a muscle also contains other tissues, such as blood, nervous tissue and epithelium (lining tissue). A collection of several tissues carrying out a particular function is called an **organ**. The main organs of the human body are shown in Figure 1.14. Plants also have tissues and organs. Leaves, roots, stems and flowers are all plant organs.

In animals, jobs are usually carried out by several different organs working together. This is called an **organ system**. For example, the digestive system consists of the gut, along with glands such as the pancreas and gall bladder.

The function of the whole system is to digest food and absorb the digested products into the blood. There are seven main systems in the human body. These are the:

- digestive system
- gas exchange system – including the lungs, which exchange oxygen and carbon dioxide
- circulatory system – including the heart and blood vessels, which transport materials around the body
- excretory system – including the kidneys, which filter toxic waste materials from the blood
- nervous system – consisting of the brain, spinal cord and nerves, which coordinate the body's actions
- endocrine system – glands secreting hormones, which act as chemical messengers
- reproductive system – producing sperm in males and eggs in females, and allowing the development of the embryo.

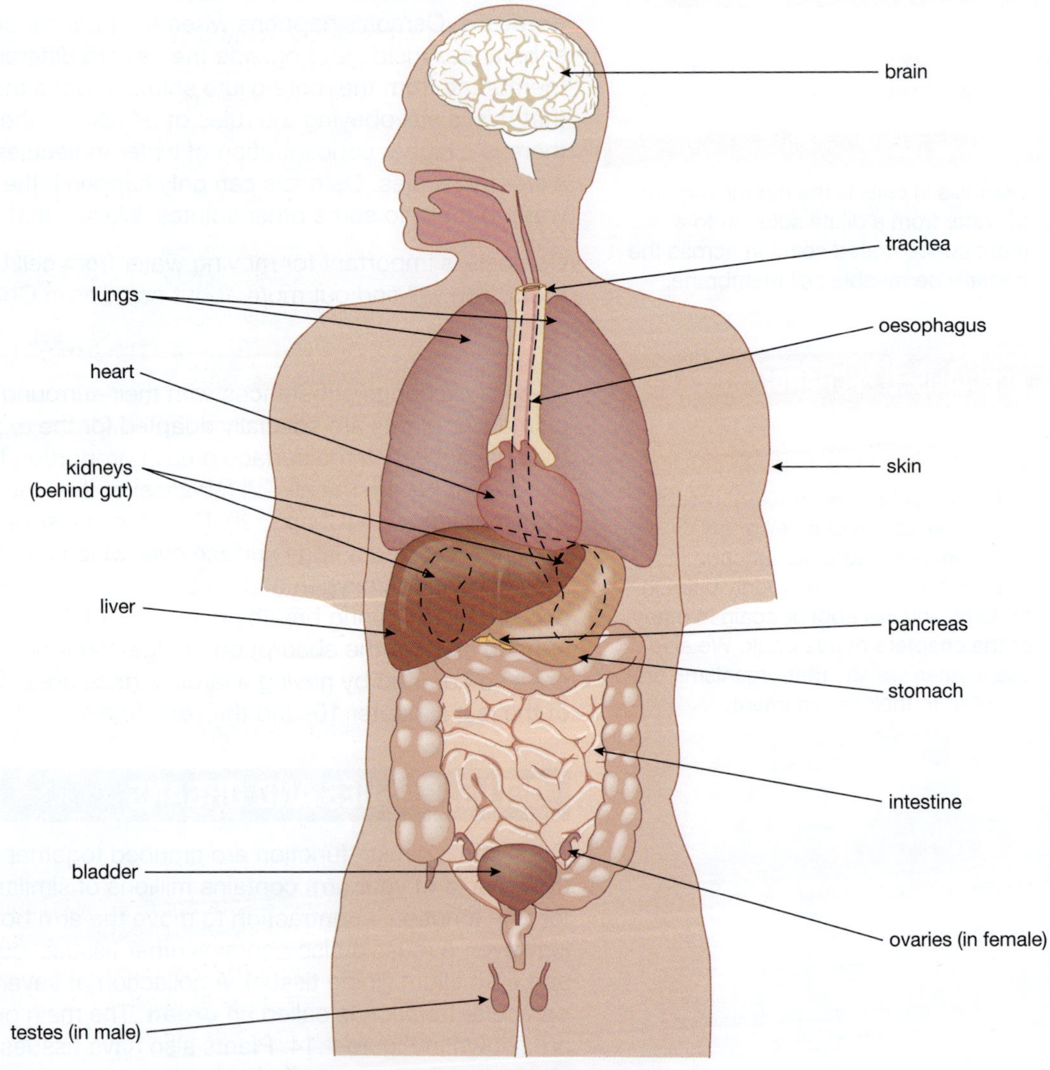

▲ Figure 1.14 Some of the main organs of the human body.

LOOKING AHEAD – MEMBRANES IN CELLS

If you continue to study biology beyond International GCSE, you will learn more about the structure and function of cells. You might like to look on the Internet for some electron micrographs and carry out some further research into cells.

Electron micrographs allow us to see cells at a much greater magnification than by using a light microscope. They also reveal more detail. The image produced by a light microscope can only distinguish features about the size of a mitochondrion. The electron microscope has a much greater *resolution*. Resolution is the ability to distinguish two points in an image as being separate. The maximum resolution of a light microscope is about 200 nanometres (nm), while with an electron microscope we can distinguish structures less than 1 nm in size. That is why ribosomes are only visible using an electron microscope – they are about 25 nm in diameter. A nanometre (nm) is 10^{-9} m, or one millionth of a milimetre.

Electron microscopy reveals that much of the cytoplasm is made up of membranes. As well as the cell surface membrane, there are membranes around organelles such as the nucleus, mitochondria and chloroplasts. In addition, there is an extensive system of membranes running throughout the cytoplasm, called the endoplasmic reticulum (ER). Some ER is covered in ribosomes, and is called rough ER (Figure 1.15).

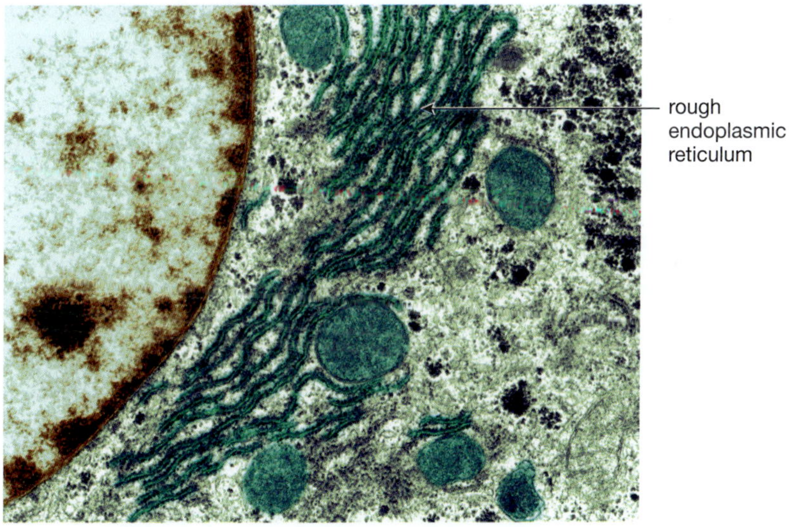

▲ Figure 1.15 Rough endoplasmic reticulum is a system of membranes extending throughout the cytoplasm of a cell. It is covered with ribosomes the (tiny dots). Ribosomes are the site of protein synthesis.

There are thousands of different chemical reactions that take place inside cells. A key function of a cell membrane is to separate cell functions into different compartments so they don't take place together. For example, the reactions and enzymes of aerobic respiration are kept inside the mitochondria, separate from the rest of the cytoplasm.

CHAPTER QUESTIONS

More questions on life processes can be found at the end of Unit 1 on page 29.

SKILLS CRITICAL THINKING 5th

1 Which of the following comparisons of animal and plant cells is *not* true?

	Animal cells	Plant cells
A	do not have chloroplasts	have chloroplasts
B	have mitochondria	do not have mitochondria
C	have temporary vacuoles	have permanent vacuoles
D	do not have cellulose cell walls	have cellulose cell walls

2 Which of the following descriptions is correct?

A The cell wall is freely permeable and the cell membrane is partially permeable

B The cell wall is partially permeable and the cell membrane is freely permeable

C Both the cell wall and the cell membrane are freely permeable

D Both the cell wall and the cell membrane are partially permeable

6th

3 What are the products of anaerobic respiration in yeast?

A ethanol and carbon dioxide

B lactate and carbon dioxide

C carbon dioxide and water

D ethanol and water

SKILLS INTERPRETATION

4 **a** Draw a diagram of a plant cell. Label all of the parts. Alongside each label write the function of that part.

SKILLS CRITICAL THINKING 5th

b Write down three differences between the cell you have drawn and a 'typical' animal cell.

5 Write a short description of the nature and function of enzymes. Include in your description:

- a definition of an enzyme
- a description of the 'lock and key' model of enzyme action
- an explanation of the difference between intracellular and extracellular enzymes.

Your description should be about a page in length, including a labelled diagram.

SKILLS ANALYSIS 6th

6 The graph shows the effect of temperature on an enzyme. The enzyme was extracted from microorganism that lives in hot mineral springs near a volcano.

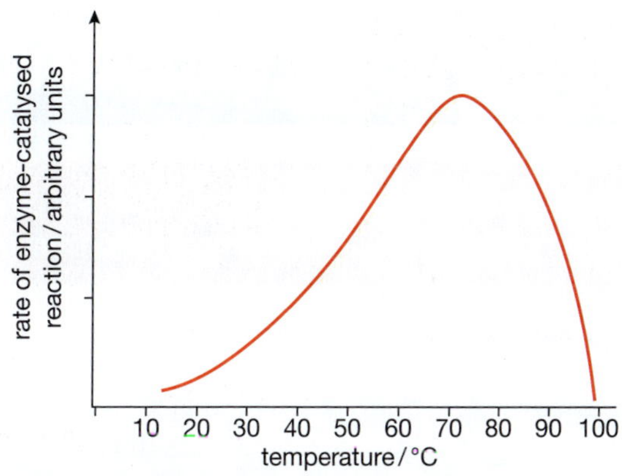

a What is the optimum temperature of this enzyme?

8th b Explain why the activity of the enzyme is greater at 60 °C than at 30 °C.

9th c The optimum temperature of enzymes in the human body is about 37 °C. Explain why this enzyme is different.

8th d What happens to the enzyme at 90 °C?

SKILLS INTERPRETATION

7th 7 Explain the differences between diffusion and active transport.

SKILLS CRITICAL THINKING, INTERPRETATION

6th 8 The diagram shows a cell from the lining of a human kidney tubule. A major role of the cell is to absorb glucose from the fluid passing along the tubule and pass it into the blood, as shown by the arrow on the diagram.

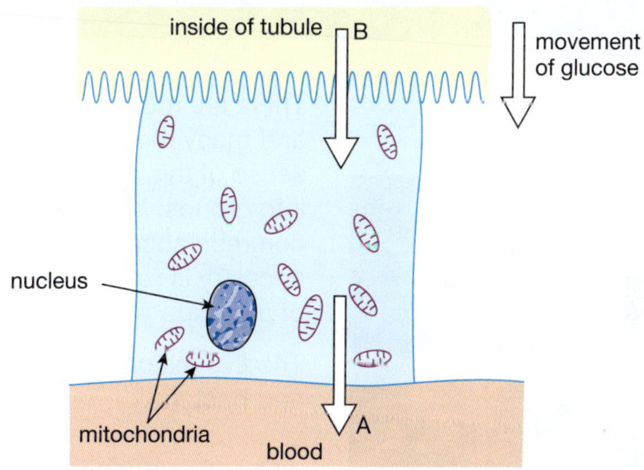

SKILLS ANALYSIS, INTERPRETATION

5th a What is the function of the mitochondria?

7th b The tubule cell contains a large number of mitochondria. They are needed for the cell to transport glucose across the cell membrane into the blood at 'A'. Suggest the method that the cell uses to do this and explain your answer.

6th c The mitochondria are *not* needed to transport the glucose into the cell from the tubule at 'B'. Name the process by which the ions move across the membrane at 'B' and explain your answer.

7th d The surface membrane of the tubule cell at 'B' is greatly folded. Suggest how this adaptation helps the cell to carry out its function.

2 THE VARIETY OF LIVING ORGANISMS

There is an enormous variety of living organisms. Biologists put them into groups according to their structure and function. The members of each group have certain features in common.

LEARNING OBJECTIVES

- Understand the difference between eukaryotic and prokaryotic organisms
- Describe the features common to plants and recognise examples of flowering plants such as maize, peas and beans
- Describe the features common to animals and recognise examples such as mammals and insects
- Describe the features common to fungi and recognise examples such as *Mucor* and yeast
- Describe the features common to protoctists and recognise examples such as *Amoeba*, *Chlorella* and *Plasmodium*
- Describe the features common to bacteria and recognise examples such as *Lactobacillus bulgaricus* and *Pneumococcus*
- Describe the features common to viruses and recognise examples such as the influenza virus, the HIV virus and the tobacco mosaic virus
- Understand the term 'pathogen' and know that pathogens may include fungi, bacteria, protoctists or viruses.

There are more than ten million species of organisms alive on Earth today, and many more that once lived on Earth but are now extinct. In order to make sense of this enormous variety biologists classify organisms, putting them into groups. Members of each group are related – they are descended from a common ancestor by the process of evolution (see Chapter 19). This common ancestry is reflected in the similarities of structure and function of the members of a group.

The five major groups of living organisms are plants, animals, fungi, protoctists and bacteria.

▲ Figure 2.1 (a) A pea plant. Its leaves and **stem cells** contain chloroplasts, giving them their green colour. The white flowers are pollinated by insects. (b) Maize plants are pollinated by wind. These are the male flowers, which make the pollen. (c) The female maize flowers produce seeds after pollination.

PLANTS

You will be familiar with flowering plants, such as those shown in Figure 2.1. This group, or **kingdom**, also contains simpler plants, such as mosses and ferns. All plants are multicellular, which means that their 'bodies' are made up of many cells. Their main distinguishing feature is that their cells contain chloroplasts and they carry out photosynthesis – the process that uses light energy to convert simple inorganic molecules such as water and carbon dioxide into complex organic compounds (see Chapter 10). One of these organic compounds is the carbohydrate cellulose, and all plants have cell walls made of this material.

Plants can make many other organic compounds as a result of photosynthesis. One of the first to be made is the storage carbohydrate **starch**, which is often found inside plant cells. Another is the sugar **sucrose**, which is transported around the plant and is sometimes stored in fruits and other plant organs. The structure and function of flowering plants is dealt with in Unit 3 of this book.

ANIMALS

You will be even more familiar with this kingdom, since it contains the species *Homo sapiens*, i.e. humans! The variety of the animal kingdom is also enormous, including organisms such as sponges, molluscs, worms, starfish, insects and crustaceans, through to larger animals such as fish, amphibians, reptiles, birds and mammals (Figure 2.2). The last five groups are all **vertebrates**, which means that they have a vertebral column, or backbone. All other animals lack this feature, and are called **invertebrates**.

(a)  (b) 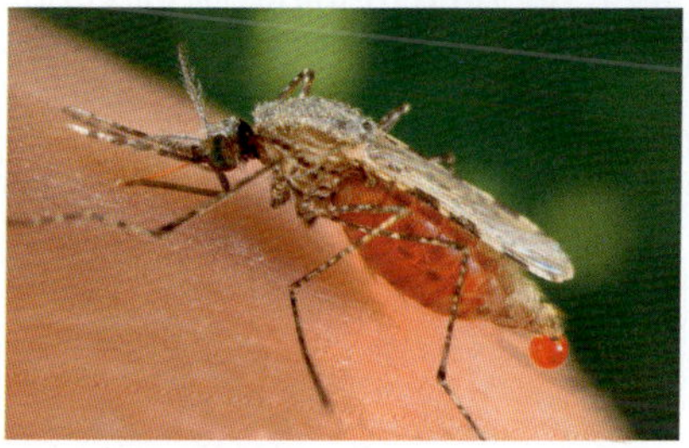 (c) 

▲ Figure 2.2 (a) A housefly. (b) A mosquito, feeding on human blood. Houseflies and mosquitoes are both insects, which make up the largest sub-group of all the animals. About 60% of all animal species are insects. (c) This high jumper's movement is coordinated by a complex nervous system.

Animals are also multicellular organisms. Their cells never contain chloroplasts, so they are unable to carry out photosynthesis. Instead, they gain their nutrition by feeding on other animals or plants. Animal cells also lack cell walls, which allows their cells to change shape, an important feature for organisms that need to move from place to place. Movement in animals is achieved in various ways, but often involves coordination by a nervous system (see Chapter 6). Another feature common to most animals is that they store carbohydrate in their cells as a compound called **glycogen** (see Chapter 4). The structure and function of animals is dealt with in Unit 2 of this book.

FUNGI

Fungi include mushrooms and toadstools, as well as moulds. These groups of fungi are multicellular. Another group of fungi is the yeasts, which are **unicellular** (made of single cells). Different species of yeasts live everywhere – on the surface of fruits, in soil, water, and even on dust in the air. The yeast powder used for baking contains millions of yeast cells (Figure 2.3). The cells of fungi never contain chloroplasts, so they cannot photosynthesise. Their cells have cell walls, but they are not composed of cellulose (Figure 2.4).

EXTENSION WORK

Because fungi have cell walls, they were once thought to be plants that had lost their chlorophyll. We now know that their cell wall is not made of cellulose as in plants, but of a different chemical called **chitin** (the same material that makes up the outside skeleton of insects). There are many ways that fungi are very different from plants (the most obvious is that fungi do not photosynthesise) and they are not closely related to plants at all.

▲ Figure 2.3 Yeast cells, highly magnified

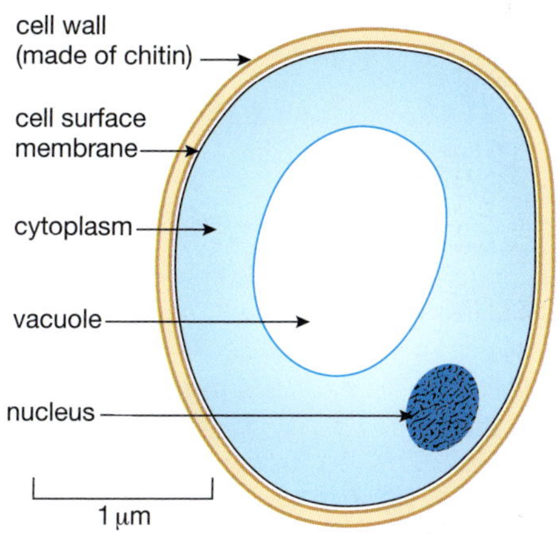

▲ Figure 2.4 Structure of a yeast cell

KEY POINT

The singular of hyphae is hypha.

A mushroom or toadstool is the reproductive structure of the organism, called a fruiting body (Figure 2.5). Under the soil, the mushroom has many fine thread-like filaments called **hyphae** (pronounced high-fee). A mould is rather like a mushroom without the fruiting body. It just consists of the network of hyphae (Figure 2.6). The whole network is called a **mycelium** (pronounced my-sea-lee-um). Moulds feed by absorbing nutrients from dead (or sometimes living) material, so they are found wherever this is present, for example, in soil, rotting leaves or decaying fruit.

▲ Figure 2.5 Toadstools growing on a rotting tree trunk

If you leave a piece of bread or fruit exposed to the air for a few days, it will soon become mouldy. Mould spores carried in the air have landed on the food and grown into a mycelium of hyphae (Figure 2.7).

▲ Figure 2.6 The 'pin mould' *Mucor* growing on a piece of bread. The dark spots are structures that produce spores for reproduction.

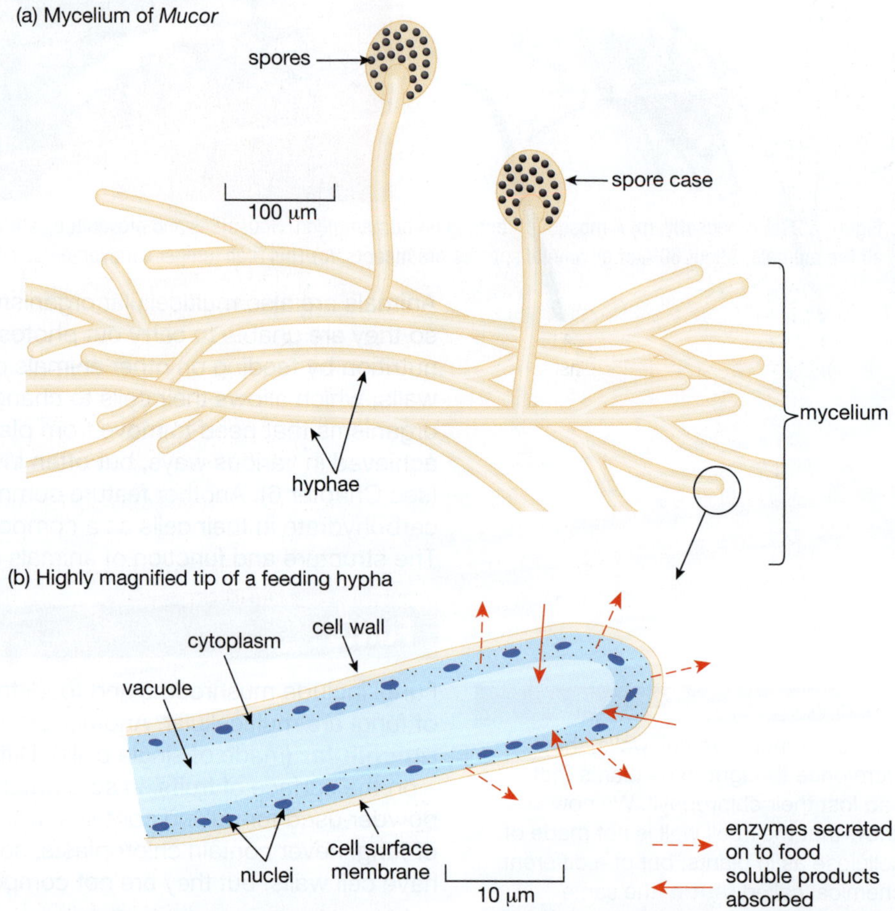

▲ Figure 2.7 The structure of a typical mould fungus, the 'pin mould' *Mucor*.

The thread-like hyphae of *Mucor* have cell walls surrounding their cytoplasm. The cytoplasm contains many nuclei. In other words the hyphae are not divided up into separate cells.

When a spore from *Mucor* lands on the food, a hypha grows out from it. The hypha grows and branches again and again, until the mycelium covers the surface of the food. The hyphae secrete digestive enzymes on to the food, breaking it down into soluble substances such as sugars, which are then absorbed by the mould. Eventually, the food is used up and the mould must infect another source of food by producing more spores.

When an organism feeds on dead organic material in this way, and digestion takes place outside of the organism, this is called **saprotrophic** nutrition. Enzymes that are secreted out of cells for this purpose are called *extracellular* enzymes (see Chapter 1).

PROTOCTISTS

Protoctists are sometimes called the 'dustbin kingdom', because they are a mixed group of organisms that don't fit into the plants, animals or fungi. Most protoctists are microscopic single-celled organisms (Figure 2.8). Some look like animal cells, such as *Amoeba*, which lives in pond water. These are known as **protozoa**. Other protoctists have chloroplasts and carry out photosynthesis, so are more like plants. These are called **algae**. Most algae are unicellular, but some species such as seaweeds are multicellular and can grow to a great size. Some protoctists are the agents of disease, such as *Plasmodium*, the organism that causes malaria.

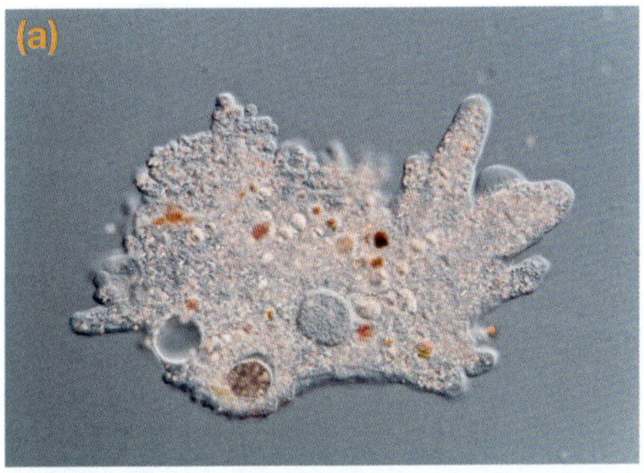

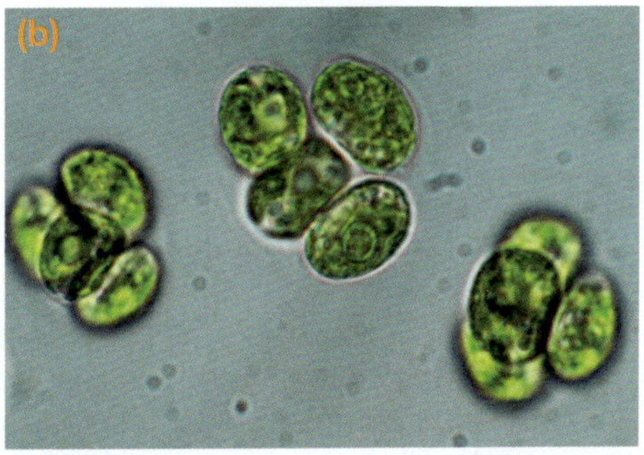

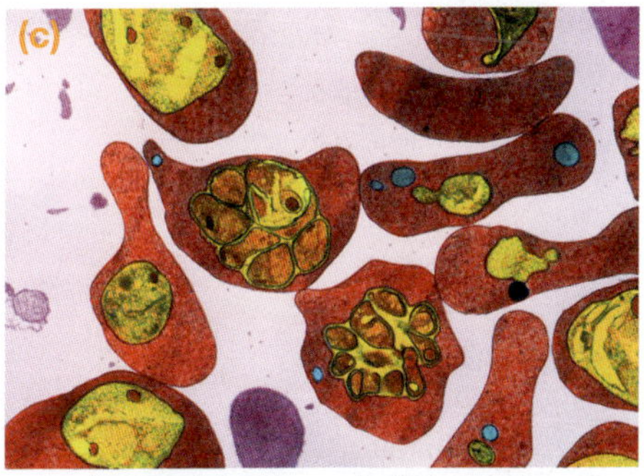

▲ Figure 2.8 (a) *Amoeba*, a protozoan that lives in ponds (b) *Chlorella*, a unicellular freshwater alga (c) Blood cells containing the protoctist parasite *Plasmodium*, the organism responsible for causing malaria

EUKARYOTIC AND PROKARYOTIC ORGANISMS

All the organisms described so far are composed of **eukaryotic** cells and are known as eukaryotic organisms. 'Eukaryotic' means 'having a nucleus' – their cells contain a nucleus surrounded by a membrane, along with other membrane bound organelles, such as mitochondria and chloroplasts.

There are also organisms made of simpler cells, which have no nucleus, mitochondria or chloroplasts. These are called **prokaryotic** cells. 'Prokaryotic' means 'before nucleus'. The main forms of prokaryotic organisms are the bacteria.

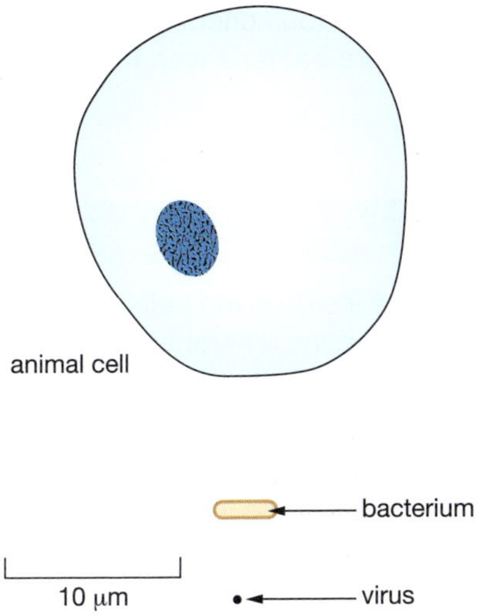

▲ Figure 2.9 A bacterium is much smaller than an animal cell. The relative size of a virus is also shown.

BACTERIA

Bacteria are small single-celled organisms. Their cells are much smaller than those of eukaryotic organisms and have a much simpler structure. To give you some idea of their size, a typical animal cell might be 10 to 50 μm in diameter (1 μm, or one micrometre, is a millionth of a metre). Compared with this, a typical bacterium is only 1 to 5 μm in length (Figure 2.9) and its volume is thousands of times smaller than that of the animal cell.

There are three basic shapes of bacteria: spheres, rods and spirals, but they all have a similar internal structure (Figure 2.10).

All bacteria are surrounded by a cell wall, which protects the bacterium and keeps the shape of the cell. Bacterial cell walls are not made of cellulose but a complex compound of sugars and proteins called peptidoglycan. Some species have another layer outside this wall, called a **capsule** or slime layer. Both give the bacterium extra protection. Underneath the cell wall is the cell membrane, as in other cells. The middle of the cell is made of cytoplasm. Since it is a prokaryotic cell, the bacterium has no nucleus. Instead, its genetic material (DNA) is in a single chromosome, loose in the cytoplasm, forming a circular loop.

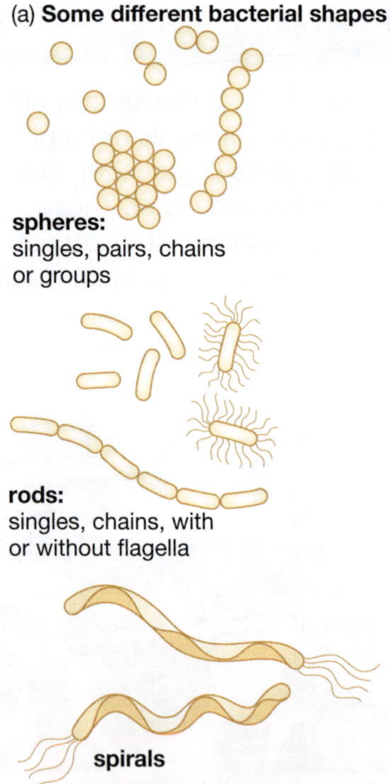

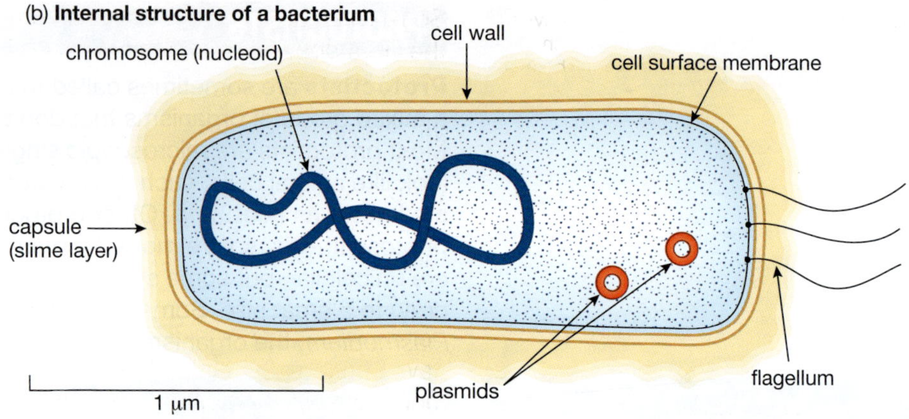

Figure 2.10 Structure of bacteria

Some bacteria can swim, and are propelled through water by corkscrew-like movements of structures called flagella (a single one of these is called a **flagellum**). However, many bacteria do not have flagella and cannot move by themselves. Other structures present in the cytoplasm include the **plasmids**. These are small circular rings of DNA, carrying some of the bacterium's genes. Not all bacteria contain plasmids, although about three-quarters of all known species do. Plasmids have very important uses in genetic engineering (see Chapter 21).

Some bacteria contain a form of chlorophyll in their cytoplasm, and can carry out photosynthesis. However, most bacteria feed off other living or dead organisms. Along with the fungi, many bacteria are important **decomposers** (see Chapter 14), recycling dead organisms and waste products in the soil and elsewhere. Some bacteria are used by humans to make food, such as *Lactobacillus bulgaricus*, a rod-shaped species used in the production of yoghurt from milk (Figure 2.11). Other species are **pathogens**, which means that they cause disease (Figure 2.12).

Despite the relatively simple structure of the bacterial cell, it is still a living cell that carries out the normal processes of life, such as respiration, feeding, excretion, growth and reproduction. As you have seen, some bacteria can move, and they can also respond to a range of stimuli. For example, they may move towards a source of food, or away from a poisonous chemical. You should think about these features when you compare bacteria with the next group, the much simpler viruses.

KEY POINT

'Pathogens are organisms that cause disease. Many common animal and plant diseases are caused by bacteria or viruses. Most protoctists are free-living, but a few species are pathogens, such as *Plasmodium* (Figure 2.8). Even some species of fungi can cause disease, e.g. the skin infection called 'athlete's foot' is caused by a mould.

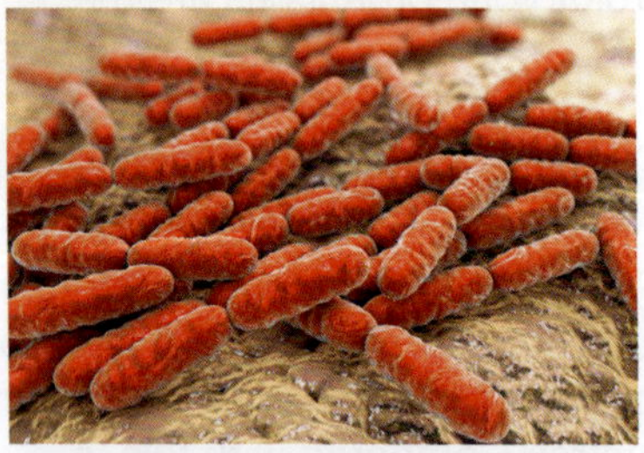

Figure 2.11 The bacterium *Lactobacillus bulgaricus*, used in the production of yoghurt.

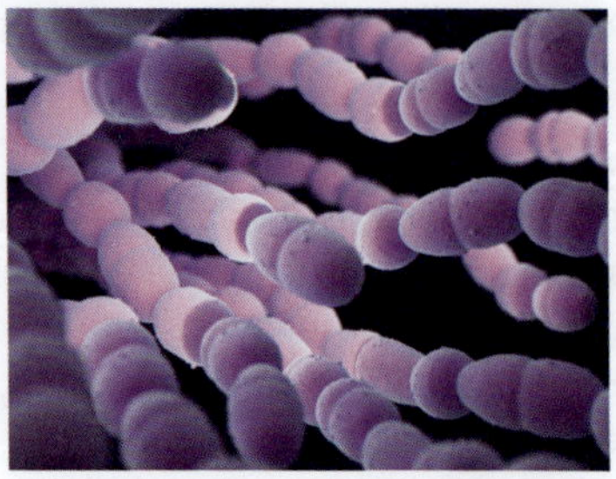

Figure 2.12 Rounded cells of the bacterium *Pneumococcus*, one cause of pneumonia.

VIRUSES

All **viruses** are **parasites**, and can only reproduce inside living cells. The cell in which the virus lives is called the host. There are many different types of viruses. Some live in the cells of animals or plants, and there are even viruses which infect bacteria. Viruses are much smaller than bacterial cells: most are between 0.01 and 0.1 μm in diameter (Figure 2.9).

Viruses are not made of cells. A virus particle is very simple. It has no nucleus or cytoplasm, and is composed of a core of genetic material surrounded by a protein coat (Figure 2.13). The genetic material can be either **DNA**, or a similar chemical called **ribonucleic acid (RNA)**. In either case, the genetic material makes up just a few genes – all that is needed for the virus to reproduce inside its host cell.

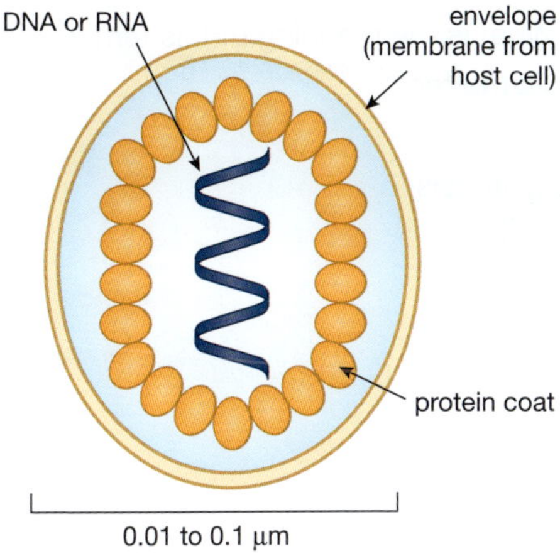

▲ Figure 2.13 The structure of a typical virus, such as the type causing influenza (flu).

Sometimes a membrane called an envelope may surround a virus particle, but the virus does not make this. Instead it is 'stolen' from the surface membrane of the host cell.

Viruses do not feed, respire, excrete, move, grow or respond to their surroundings. They do not carry out any of the normal 'characteristics' of living things except reproduction, and they can only do this parasitically. This is why biologists do not consider viruses to be living organisms. You can think of them as being on the border between an organism and a non-living chemical.

A virus reproduces by entering the host cell and taking over the host's genetic machinery to make more virus particles. After many virus particles have been made, the host cell dies and the particles are released to infect more cells. Many human diseases are caused in this way, such as influenza ('flu'). Other examples include colds, measles, mumps, polio and rubella ('German measles'). Of course, the reproduction process does not continue forever. Usually, the body's immune system destroys the virus and the person recovers. Sometimes, however, a virus cannot be destroyed by the immune system quickly enough, and it may cause permanent damage or death. With other infections, the virus may attack cells of the immune system itself. This is the case with HIV (the Human Immunodeficiency Virus), which causes the illness called AIDS (Acquired Immune Deficiency Syndrome).

EXTENSION WORK

AIDS is not actually a disease but a 'syndrome'. A syndrome is a set of symptoms caused by a medical condition. In the case of HIV, the virus severely damages the person's immune system, so they are more likely to get other diseases, such as tuberculosis. They may also develop some unusual types of cancer. This collection of different symptoms is referred to as AIDS.

Viruses don't just parasitise animal cells. Some infect plant cells, such as the tobacco mosaic virus (Figure 2.14), which interferes with the ability of the tobacco plant to make chloroplasts, causing mottled patches to develop on the leaves (Figure 2.15).

▲ Figure 2.15 Discolouration of the leaves of a tobacco plant, caused by infection with tobacco mosaic virus.

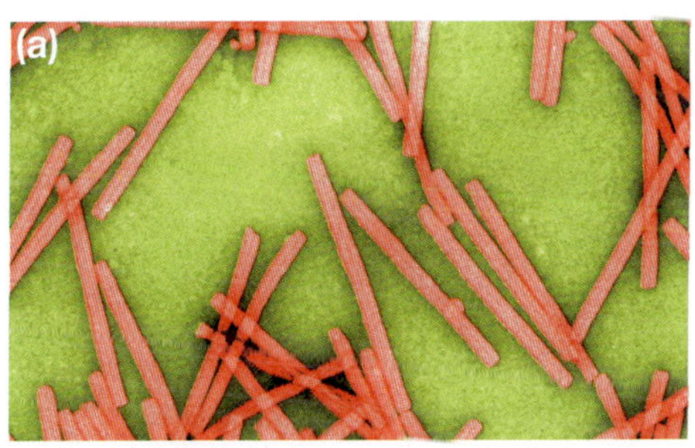

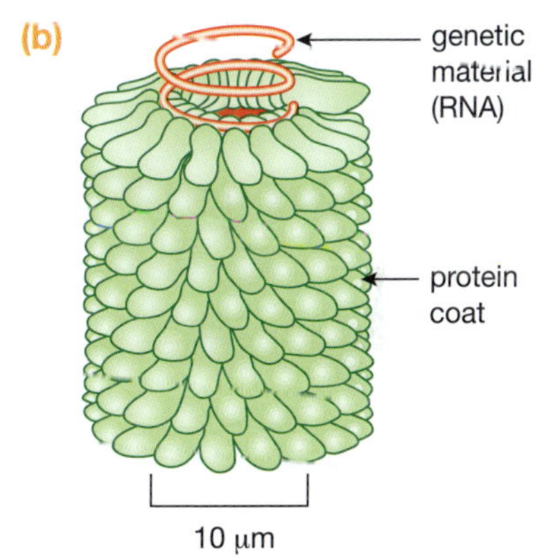

▲ Figure 2.14 (a) Tobacco mosaic virus (TMV), seen through an electron microscope. (b) Structure of part of a TMV particle, magnified 1.25 million times.

CHAPTER QUESTIONS

More questions on the variety of living organisms can be found at the end of Unit 1 on page 29.

SKILLS CRITICAL THINKING 4th

1 Which of the following is *not* a characteristic of plants?

A cells contain chloroplasts

B cell wall made of cellulose

C bodies are multicellular

D store carbohydrate as glycogen

SKILLS CRITICAL THINKING

2 Fungi carry out *saprotrophic nutrition*. What is the meaning of this term?

A extracellular digestion of dead organic matter

B feeding on other living organisms

C making organic molecules by photosynthesis

D secreting digestive enzymes

3 Below are three groups of organisms.

1. viruses
2. bacteria
3. yeasts

Which of these organisms are prokaryotic?

A 1 only

B 2 only

C 1 and 2

D 1, 2 and 3

4 Which of the following diseases is *not* caused by a virus?

A influenza

B measles

C malaria

D AIDS

5 a Name the kingdom to which each of the following organisms belongs:

i mushroom

ii *Chlorella*

iii moss

iv *Lactobacillus*

SKILLS ANALYSIS, REASONING

b The diagram shows a species of protoctist called *Euglena*. Use the diagram to explain why *Euglena* is classified as a protoctist and not as an animal or plant.

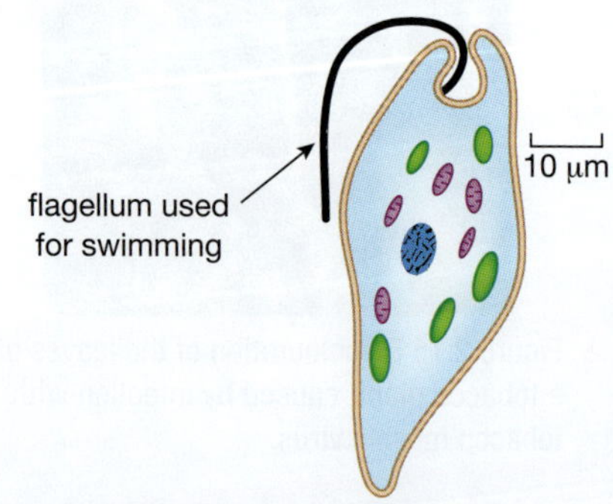

SKILLS INTERPRETATION

SKILLS CRITICAL THINKING

6 a Draw a diagram to show the structure of a typical virus particle.

b Is a virus a living organism? Explain your answer.

c Explain the statement ‘viruses are all parasites’.

7 Explain the meanings of the following terms:

a invertebrate

b hyphae

c saprotrophic

UNIT QUESTIONS

SKILLS CRITICAL THINKING 5th

1 These three organelles are found in cells: nucleus, chloroplast and mitochondrion.

a Which of the above organelles would be found in:

i a cell from a human muscle? **(1)**

ii a palisade cell from a leaf? **(1)**

iii a cell from the root of a plant? **(1)**

SKILLS REASONING

b Explain fully why the answers to ii) and iii) above are different. **(1)**

SKILLS INTERPRETATION

c What is the function of each organelle? **(3)**

(Total 7 marks)

SKILLS INTERPRETATION, REASONING

2 In multicellular organisms, cells are organised into tissues, organs and organ systems.

a The diagram shows a section through an artery and a capillary.

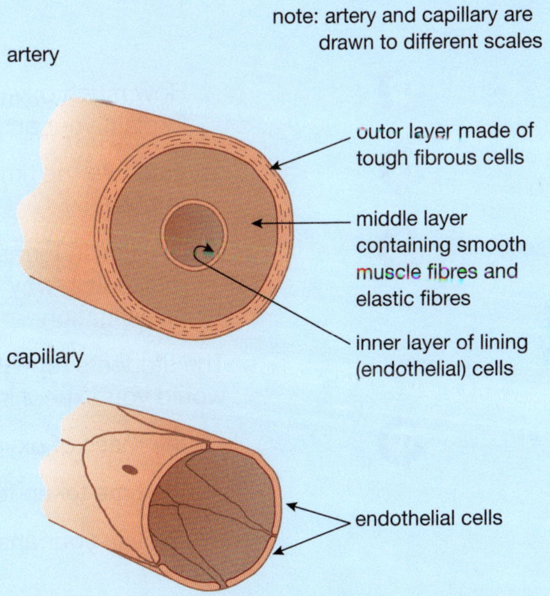

Explain why an artery can be considered to be an organ whereas a capillary cannot. **(2)**

b Organ systems contain two or more organs whose functions are linked. The digestive system is one human organ system. (See Chapter 4.)

SKILLS CRITICAL THINKING 4th

i What does the digestive system do? **(2)**

5th

ii Name three organs in the human digestive system. Explain what each organ does as part of the digestive system. **(6)**

4th

iii Name two other human organ systems and, for each system, name two organs that are part of the system. **(6)**

(Total 16 marks)

SKILLS ANALYSIS 4th

3 Catalase is an enzyme found in many plant and animal cells. It catalyses the breakdown of hydrogen peroxide into water and oxygen.

$$\text{hydrogen peroxide} \xrightarrow{\textit{catalase}} \text{water + oxygen}$$

a In an investigation into the action of catalase in potato, 20 g of potato tissue was put into a small beaker containing hydrogen peroxide weighing 80 g in total. The temperature was maintained at 20 °C throughout the investigation. As soon as the potato was added, the mass of the beaker and its contents was recorded until there was no further change in mass. The results are shown in the graph.

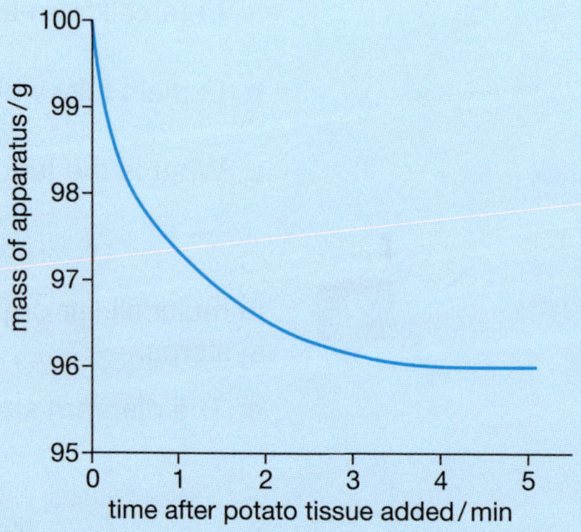

5th **i** How much oxygen was formed in this investigation? Explain your answer. **(2)**

6th **ii** Estimate the time by which half this mass of oxygen had been formed. **(2)**

SKILLS REASONING 8th **iii** Explain, in terms of collisions between enzyme and substrate molecules, why the rate of reaction changes during the course of the investigation. **(2)**

b The students repeated the investigation at 30 °C. What difference, if any, would you expect in:

SKILLS DECISION MAKING 9th **i** the mass of oxygen formed?

ii the time taken to form this mass of oxygen?

Explain your answers. **(4)**

(Total 10 marks)

CRITICAL THINKING 7th

4 Different particles move across cell membranes using different processes.

a The table below shows some ways in which active transport, osmosis and diffusion are similar and some ways in which they are different. Copy and complete the table with ticks and crosses. **(3)**

Feature	Active transport	Osmosis	Diffusion
particles must have kinetic energy			
requires energy from respiration			
particles move down a concentration gradient			

SKILLS CRITICAL THINKING 7th

b The graph shows the results of an investigation into the rate of diffusion of sodium ions across the membranes of potato cells.

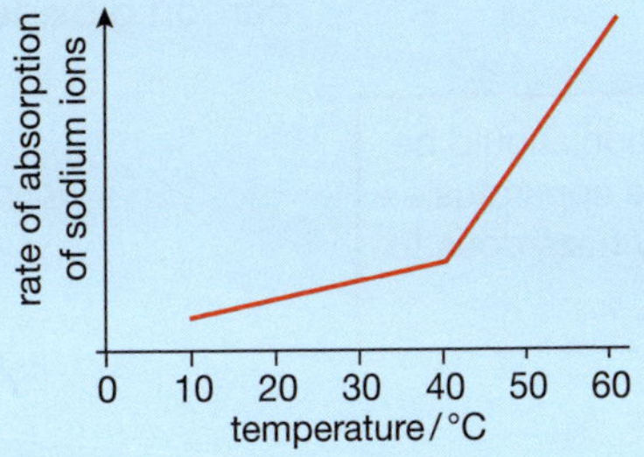

SKILLS ANALYSIS, REASONING 6th

i Explain the increase in the rate of diffusion up to 40 °C. **(2)**

ii Suggest why the rate of increase is much steeper at temperatures above 40 °C. **(2)**

(Total 7 marks)

SKILLS REASONING 8th

5 Cells in the wall of the small intestine divide by mitosis to replace cells lost as food passes through.

a Chromosomes contain DNA. The graph shows the changes in the DNA content of a cell in the wall of the small intestine as it divides by mitosis.

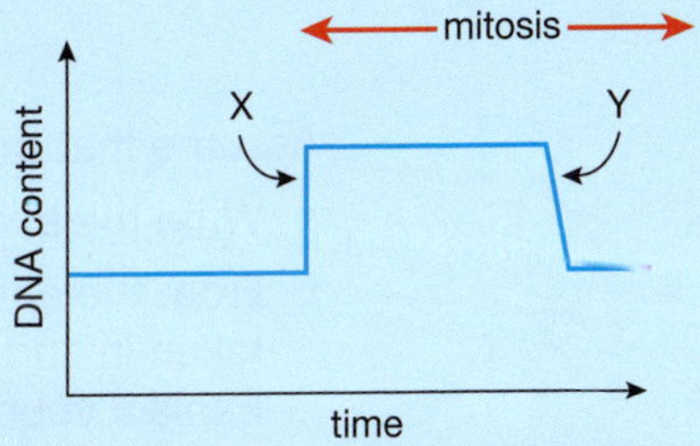

i Why is it essential that the DNA content is doubled (X) before mitosis begins? **(2)**

SKILLS ANALYSIS

ii What do you think happens to the cell at point Y? **(1)**

b The diagram shows a cell in the wall of a villus in the small intestine. Some of the processes involved in the absorption of glucose are also shown.

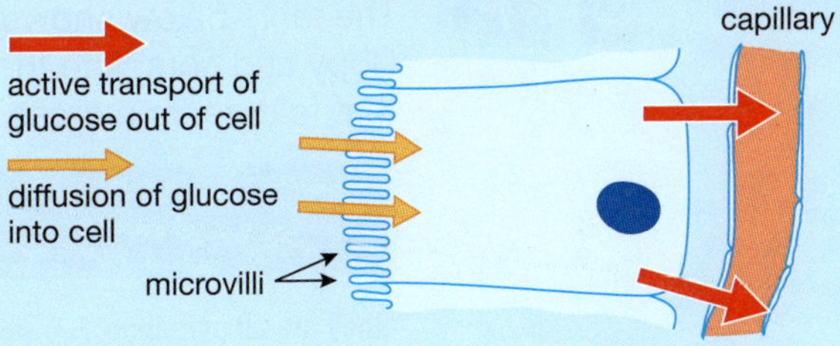

SKILLS INTERPRETATION 6th 7th 8th

i What is the importance of the small intestine having villi? **(1)**

ii Suggest how the microvilli adapt this cell to its function of absorbing glucose. **(1)**

iii Suggest how the active transport of glucose out of the cell and into the blood stream helps with the absorption of glucose from the small intestine. **(2)**

(Total 7 marks)

SKILLS REASONING 8th

6 A respirometer is used to measure the rate of respiration. The diagram shows a simple respirometer. The sodium hydroxide solution in the apparatus absorbs carbon dioxide. Some results from the investigation are also shown.

Safety note: Eye protection should be worn when setting up the apparatus as sodium hydroxide is very hazardous to the eyes.

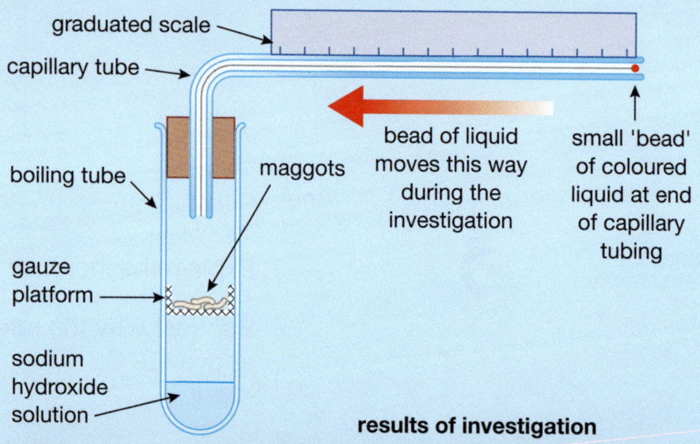

results of investigation

Experiment	Distance moved by bead / mm
1	20
2	3
3	18

Assume that the maggots in the apparatus respire aerobically.

a Write the symbol equation for aerobic respiration. (4)

b From the equation, what can you assume about the amount of oxygen taken in and carbon dioxide given off by the maggots? Explain your answer. (3)

c Result 2 is significantly different from the other two results. Suggest a reason for this. (2)

9th **d** How would the results be different if the organisms under investigation respired anaerobically? **(2)**

(Total 11 marks)

SKILLS INTERPRETATION 5th

7 The table below shows some features of different groups of organisms. Copy and complete the table by putting a tick in the box if the organism has that feature, or a cross if it lacks the feature.

Feature	Type of organism		
	Plant	Fungus	Virus
they are all parasites			
they are made up of a mycelium of hyphae			
they can only reproduce inside living cells			
they feed by extracellular digestion by enzymes			
they store carbohydrate as starch			

(Total 5 marks)

SKILLS CRITICAL THINKING 6th

8 Copy and complete the following account.

Plants have cell walls made of ________________ . They store carbohydrate as the insoluble compound called ________________ or sometimes as the sugar ________________ . Plants make these substances as a result of the process called ________________ . Animals, on the other hand, store carbohydrate as the compound ________________ . Both animals' and plants' cells have nuclei, but the cells of bacteria lack a true nucleus, having their DNA in a circular chromosome. They sometimes also contain small rings of DNA called ________________ , which are used in genetic engineering. Bacteria and fungi break down organic matter in the soil. They are known as ________________ . Some bacteria are pathogens, which means that they ________________ .

(Total 8 marks)

SKILLS DECISION MAKING

9 The diagram shows the apparatus used to investigate germination of pea seeds. At the start of the experiment the temperature in both flasks was 19 °C

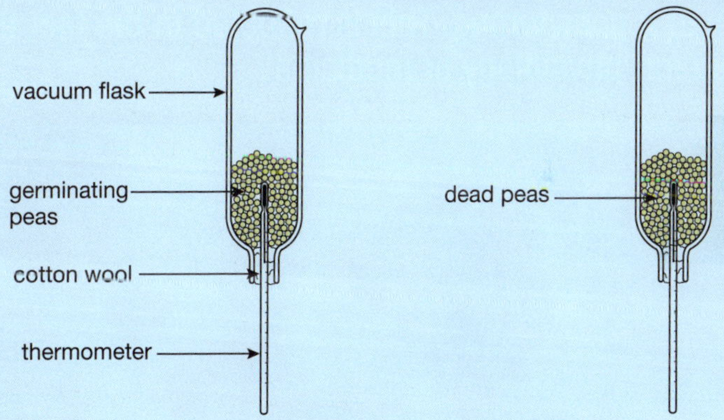

The apparatus was left for 24 hours. At the end of this time the temperature in the flask with germinating peas was 22 °C, while the temperature in the flask with dead peas was 19 °C.

a Explain the biological reason for this difference in temperature. **(2)**

b The seeds in both flasks were washed in disinfectant before the experiment. Explain why this was done. **(1)**

c Cotton wool was used to hold the seeds in the flasks. Suggest why cotton wool was used instead of a rubber bung. **(1)**

SKILLS EXECUTIVE FUNCTION 5th

d Pea seeds were used in both flasks. State another variable that should have been controlled in the experiment. **(1)**

(Total 5 marks)

7th **10** A piece of meat is a tissue composed of muscle fibres. Muscle fibres use ATP when they contract. Describe an investigation to find out if a solution of ATP will cause the contraction of muscle fibres.

(Total 6 marks)

BIOLOGY UNIT 2 ANIMAL PHYSIOLOGY

Physiology is the branch of biology that looks at how living things function. It studies the workings of an organism at different levels from cells, tissues and organs through to the whole organism. In this unit we look at animal physiology and in particular how the human body works. It is important to study physiology, not least because knowledge of the body is essential in understanding how to treat it when it goes wrong. This is reflected in the fact that one of the six categories of Nobel Prize is awarded for 'physiology or medicine'.

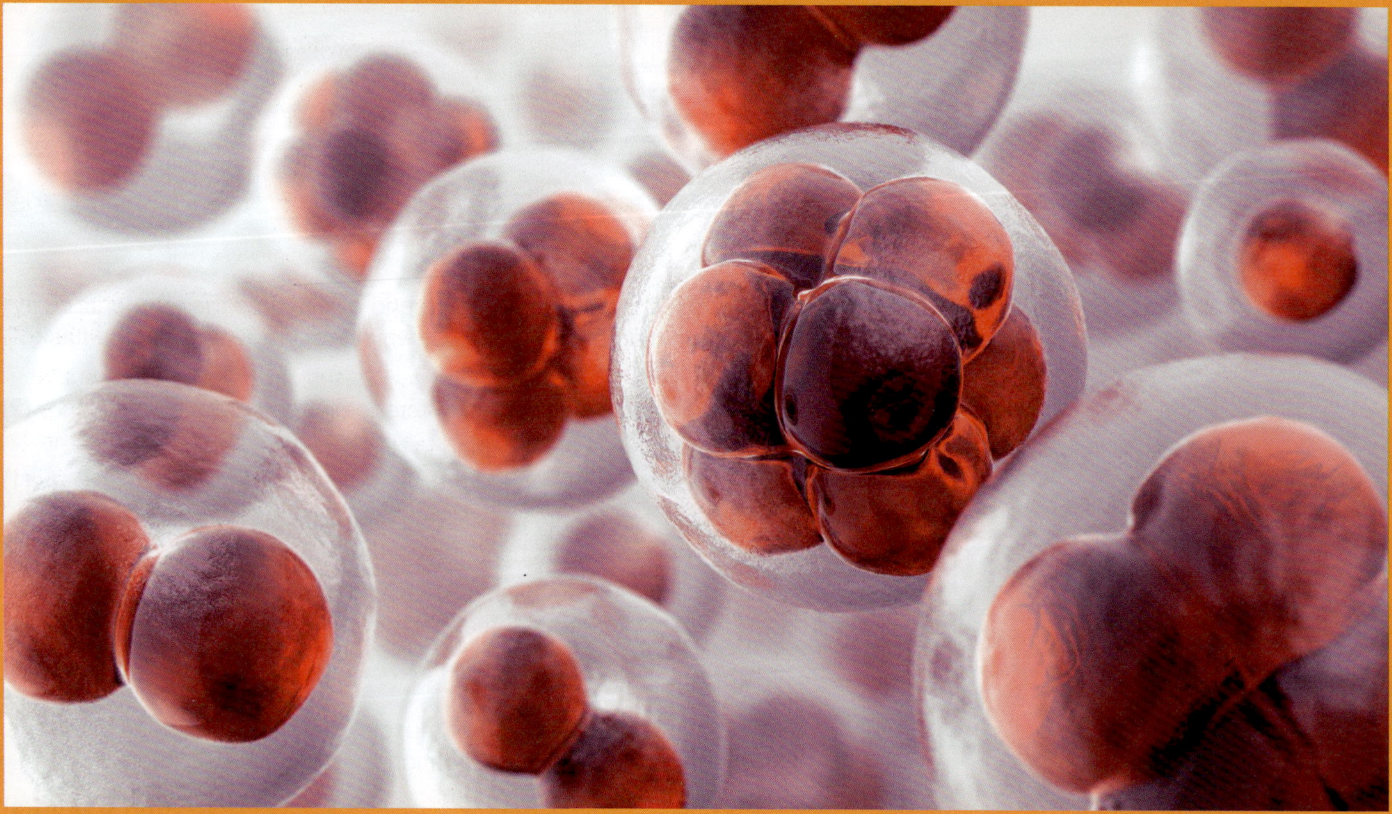

3 BREATHING AND GAS EXCHANGE

When we breathe, air is moved in and out of the lungs so that gas exchange can take place between the air and the blood. This chapter looks at these processes, and also deals with some ways that smoking can damage the lungs and stop these vital organs from working properly.

LEARNING OBJECTIVES

- Describe the structure of the thorax, including the ribs, intercostal muscles, diaphragm, trachea, bronchi, bronchioles, alveoli and pleural membranes
- Understand the role of the intercostal muscles and the diaphragm in ventilation
- Explain how alveoli are adapted for gas exchange by diffusion between air in the lungs and blood in capillaries
- Investigate breathing in humans, including the release of carbon dioxide and the effect of exercise
- Understand the biological consequences of smoking in relation to the lungs and circulatory system, including coronary heart disease.

Cells get their energy by oxidising foods such as glucose, during the process called **respiration**. If cells are to respire aerobically, they need a continuous supply of oxygen from the blood. In addition, carbon dioxide from respiration needs to be removed from the body. In humans, these gases are exchanged between the blood and the air in the lungs.

RESPIRATION AND BREATHING

You need to understand the difference between respiration and breathing. Respiration is the oxidation reaction that releases energy from foods such as glucose (Chapter 1). Breathing is the mechanism that moves air into and out of the lungs, allowing gas exchange to take place. The lungs and associated structures are often called the 'respiratory system' but this can be confusing. It is better to call them the gas exchange system and this is the term we use in this book.

THE STRUCTURE OF THE GAS EXCHANGE SYSTEM

The lungs are enclosed in the chest or **thorax** by the ribcage and a muscular sheet of tissue called the **diaphragm** (Figure 3.1). As you will see, the actions of these two structures bring about the movements of air into and out of the lungs. Joining each rib to the next are two sets of muscles called **intercostal muscles** ('costals' are rib bones). The diaphragm separates the contents of the thorax from the abdomen. It is not flat, but a shallow dome shape, with a fibrous middle part forming the 'roof' of the dome, and muscular edges forming the walls.

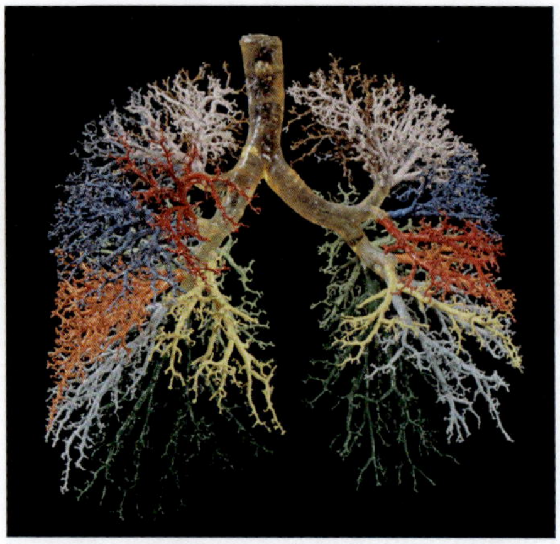

▲ Figure 3.2 This cast of the human lungs was made by injecting a pair of lungs with a liquid plastic. The plastic was allowed to set, then the lung tissue was dissolved away with acid.

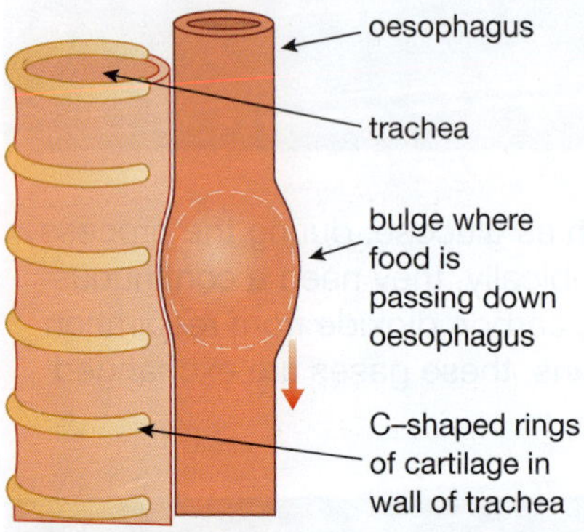

▲ Figure 3.3 C-shaped cartilage rings in the trachea.

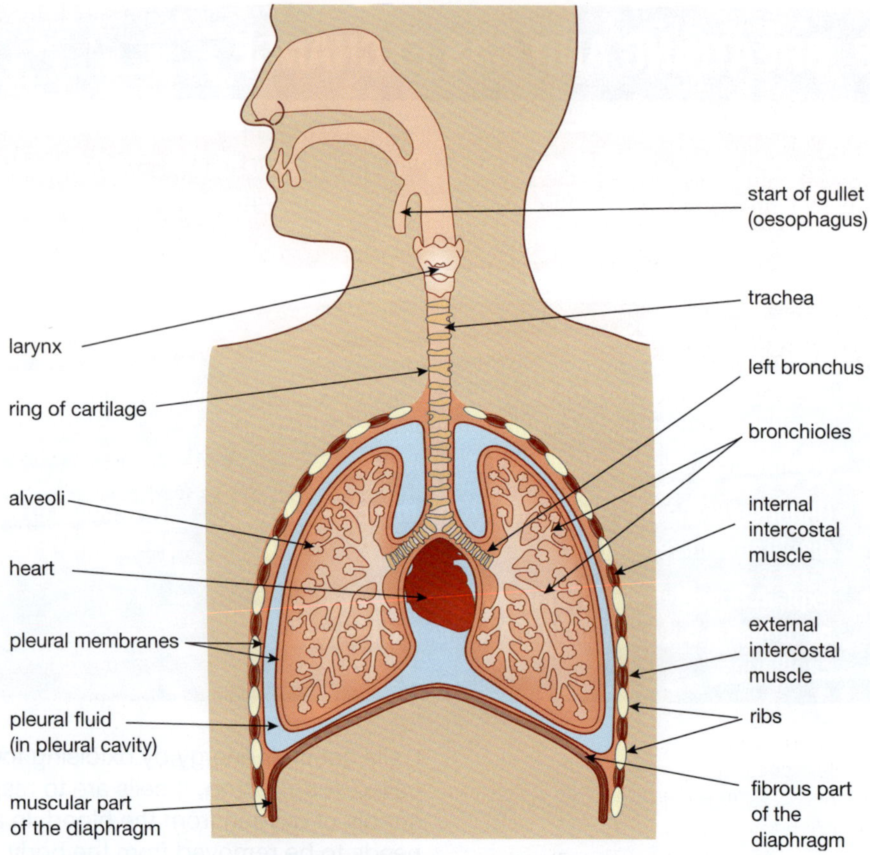

▲ Figure 3.1 The human gas exchange system

The air passages of the lungs form a highly branching network (Figure 3.2). This is why it is sometimes called the **bronchial tree**.

When we breathe in, air enters our nose or mouth and passes down the windpipe or **trachea**. The trachea splits into two tubes called the **bronchi** (singular **bronchus**), one leading to each lung. Each bronchus divides into smaller and smaller tubes called **bronchioles**, eventually ending at microscopic air sacs, called **alveoli** (singular **alveolus**). It is here that gas exchange with the blood takes place.

The walls of trachea and bronchi contain rings of gristle or **cartilage**. These support the airways and keep them open when we breathe in. They are rather like the rings in a vacuum cleaner hose – without them the hose would squash flat when the cleaner sucks air in.

The inside of the thorax is separated from the lungs by two thin, moist membranes called the **pleural membranes**. They make up a continuous envelope around the lungs, forming an airtight seal. Between the two membranes is a space called the **pleural cavity**, filled with a thin layer of liquid called **pleural fluid**. This acts as lubrication, so that the surfaces of the lungs don't stick to the inside of the chest wall when we breathe.

EXTENSION WORK

In the bronchi, the cartilage forms complete, circular rings. In the trachea, the rings are incomplete, and shaped like a letter 'C'. The open part of the ring is at the back of the trachea, next to where the oesophagus (gullet) lies as it passes through the thorax. When food passes along the oesophagus by peristalsis (see Chapter 4) the gaps in the rings allow the lumps of food to pass through more easily, without the peristaltic wave 'catching' on the rings (Figure 3.3).

KEEPING THE AIRWAYS CLEAN

The trachea and larger airways are lined with a layer of cells that have an important role in keeping the airways clean. Some cells in this lining secrete a sticky liquid called **mucus**, which traps particles of dirt or bacteria that are breathed in. Other cells are covered with tiny hair-like structures called **cilia** (Figure 3.4). The cilia beat backward and forward, sweeping the mucus and trapped particles out towards the mouth. In this way, dirt and bacteria are

▲ Figure 3.4 This electron microscope picture shows cilia from the lining of the trachea.

prevented from entering the lungs, where they might cause an infection. As you will see, one of the effects of smoking is that it destroys the cilia and stops this protection mechanism from working properly.

VENTILATION OF THE LUNGS

Ventilation means moving air in and out of the lungs. This requires a difference in air pressure – the air moves from a place where the pressure is high to one where it is low. Ventilation depends on the fact that the thorax is an airtight cavity. When we breathe, we change the volume of our thorax, which alters the pressure inside it. This causes air to move in or out of the lungs.

There are two movements that bring about ventilation: those of the ribs and the diaphragm. If you put your hands on your chest and breathe in deeply, you can feel your ribs move upwards and outwards. They are moved by the intercostal muscles (Figure 3.5). The outer (external) intercostals contract, pulling the ribs up. At the same time, the muscles of the diaphragm contract, pulling the diaphragm down into a more flattened shape (Figure 3.6a). Both these movements increase the volume of the chest and cause a slight drop in pressure inside the thorax compared with the air outside. Air then enters the lungs (inhalation).

The opposite happens when you breathe out deeply. The external intercostals relax, and the internal intercostals contract, pulling the ribs down and in. At the same time, the diaphragm muscles relax and the diaphragm goes back to its normal dome shape. The volume of the thorax decreases, and the pressure in the thorax is raised slightly above atmospheric pressure. This time the difference in pressure forces air out of the lungs (Figure 3.6b). Exhalation is helped by the fact that the lungs are elastic, so that they have a tendency to collapse and empty like a balloon.

EXTENSION WORK

During normal (shallow) breathing, the elasticity of the lungs and the weight of the ribs acting downwards is enough to cause exhalation. The internal intercostals are only really used for deep (forced) breathing out, for instance when we are exercising.

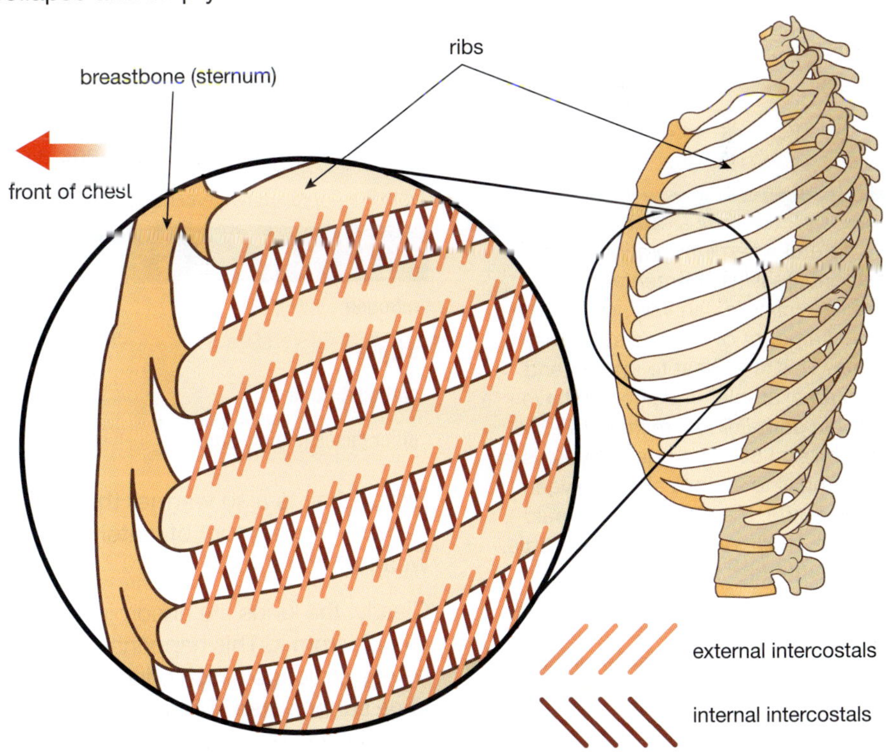

▲ Figure 3.5 Side view of the chest wall, showing the ribs. The diagram shows how the two sets of intercostal muscles run between the ribs. When the external intercostals contract, they move the ribs upwards. When the internal intercostals contract, the ribs are moved downwards.

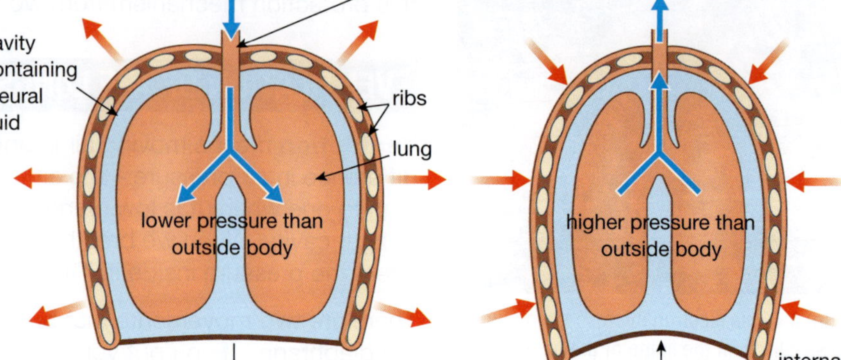

▲ Figure 3.6 Changes in the position of the ribs and diaphragm during breathing. (a) Breathing in (inhalation). (b) Breathing out (exhalation).

KEY POINT

It is important that you remember the changes in volume and pressure during ventilation. If you have trouble understanding these, think of what happens when you use a bicycle pump. If you push the pump handle, the air in the pump is squashed, its pressure rises and it is forced out of the pump. If you pull on the handle, the air pressure inside the pump falls a little, and air is drawn in from outside. This is similar to what happens in the lungs. In exams, students sometimes talk about the lungs *forcing* the air in and out – they don't!

GAS EXCHANGE IN THE ALVEOLI

You can tell what is happening during gas exchange if you compare the amounts of different gases in atmospheric air with the air breathed out (Table 3.1).

Table 3.1 Approximate percentage volume of gases in atmospheric (inhaled) and exhaled air.

Gas	Atmospheric air / %	Exhaled air / %
nitrogen	78	79
oxygen	21	16
carbon dioxide	0.04	4
other gases (mainly argon)	1	1

HINT

Be careful when interpreting percentages! The *percentage* of a gas in a mixture can vary, even if the actual *amount* of the gas stays the same. This is easiest to understand from an example. Imagine you have a bottle containing a mixture of 20% oxygen and 80% nitrogen. If you used a chemical to absorb all the oxygen in the bottle, the nitrogen left would now be 100% of the gas in the bottle, despite the fact that the *amount* of nitrogen would still be the same. That is why the percentage of nitrogen in inhaled and exhaled air is slightly different.

Exhaled air is also warmer than atmospheric air, and is saturated with water vapour. The amount of water vapour in the atmosphere varies depending on weather conditions.

Clearly, the lungs are absorbing oxygen into the blood and removing carbon dioxide from it. This happens in the alveoli. To do this efficiently, the alveoli must have a structure which brings the air and blood very close together, over a very large surface area. There are enormous numbers of alveoli. It has been calculated that the two lungs contain about 700 000 000 of these tiny air sacs, giving a total surface area of 60 m^2. That's bigger than the floor area of an average classroom! Viewed through a high-powered microscope, the alveoli look rather like bunches of grapes, and are covered with tiny blood capillaries (Figure 3.7).

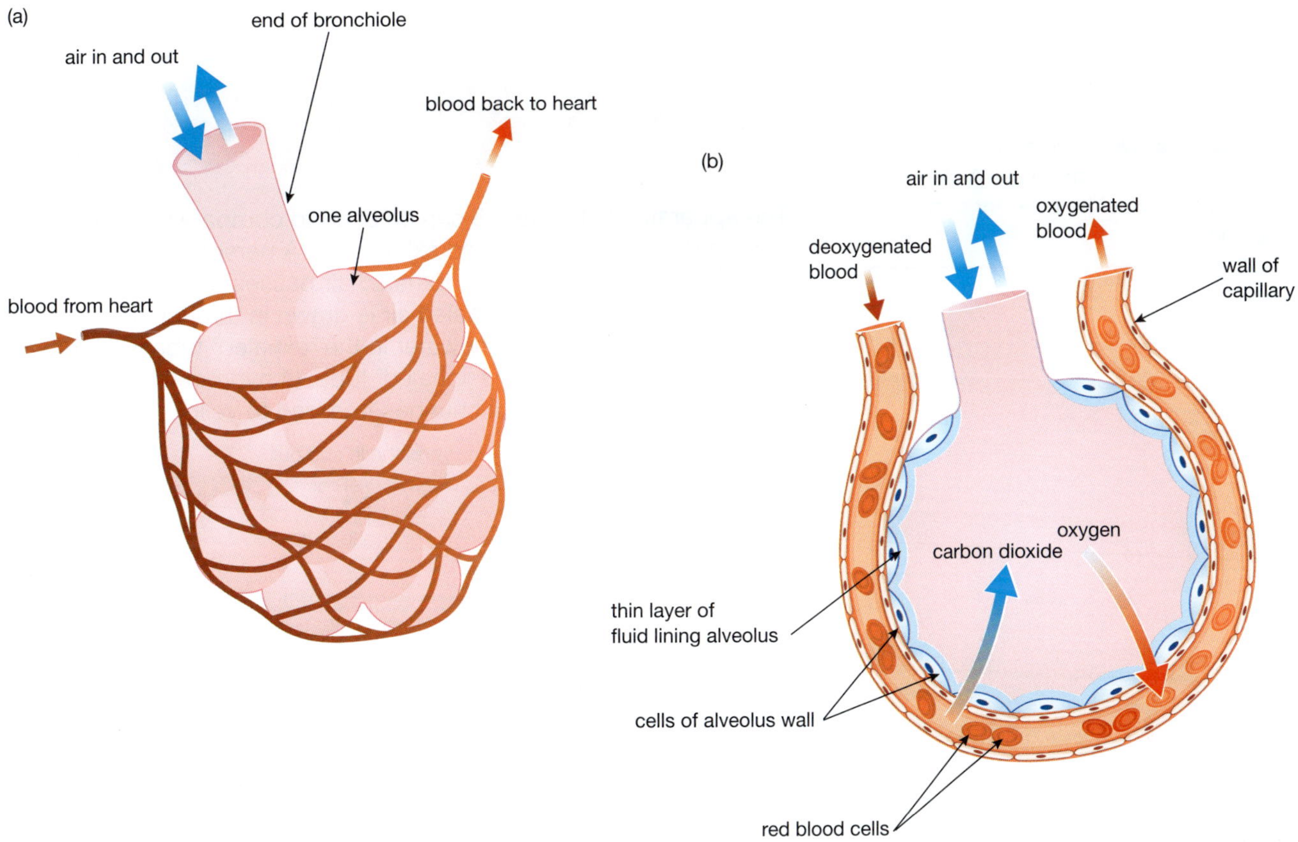

▲ Figure 3.7 (a) Alveoli and the surrounding capillary network. (b) Diffusion of oxygen and carbon dioxide takes place between the air in the alveolus and the blood in the capillaries.

HINT

Be careful – students sometimes write 'The alveolus has *cell walls*'. This statement is not correct – a cell wall is part of a plant cell! The correct way to describe the structure is: 'The alveolus has *a wall made of cells*'.

Deoxygenated blood is pumped from the heart to the lungs and passes through the capillaries surrounding the alveoli. The blood has come from the respiring tissues of the body, where it has given up some of its oxygen to the cells, and gained carbon dioxide. Around the lungs, the blood is separated from the air inside each alveolus by only two cell layers; the cells making up the wall of the alveolus, and the capillary wall itself. This is a distance of less than a thousandth of a millimetre.

EXTENSION WORK

The thin layer of fluid lining the inside of the alveoli comes from the blood. The capillaries and cells of the alveolar wall are 'leaky' and the blood pressure pushes fluid out from the blood plasma into the alveolus. Oxygen dissolves in this moist surface before it passes through the alveolar wall into the blood.

Because the air in the alveolus has a higher concentration of oxygen than the blood entering the **capillary** network, oxygen diffuses from the air, across the wall of the alveolus and into the blood. At the same time there is more carbon dioxide in the blood than there is in the air in the lungs. This means that there is a diffusion gradient for carbon dioxide in the other direction, so carbon dioxide diffuses the other way, out of the blood and into the alveolus. The result is that the blood which leaves the capillaries and flows back to the heart has gained oxygen and lost carbon dioxide. The heart then pumps the oxygenated blood around the body again, to supply the respiring cells (see Chapter 5).

Safety note: Wear eye protection and breathe gently; do not blow. A clean mouthpiece must be used for each person.

ACTIVITY 1

▼ PRACTICAL: COMPARING THE CARBON DIOXIDE CONTENT OF INHALED AND EXHALED AIR

The apparatus in Figure 3.8 can be used to compare the amount of carbon dioxide in inhaled and exhaled air. A person breathes gently in and out through the middle tube. Exhaled air passes out through one tube of indicator solution and inhaled air is drawn in through the other tube. If limewater is used, the limewater in the 'exhaled' tube will turn cloudy before the limewater in the 'inhaled' tube. (If hydrogen carbonate indicator solution is used instead, it changes from red to yellow.)

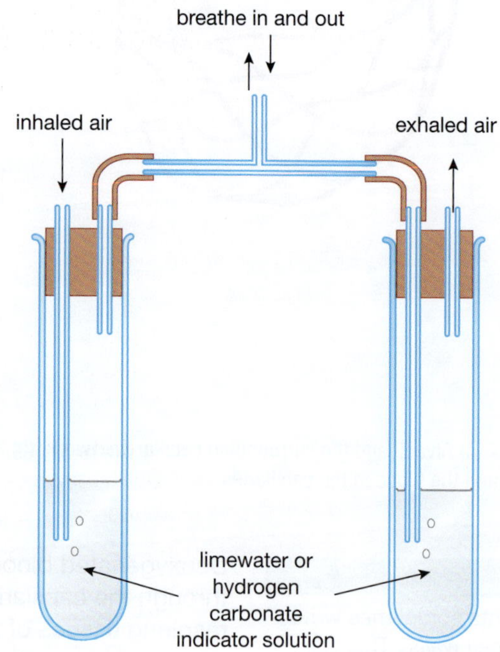

▲ Figure 3.8 Apparatus for Experiment 6.

Safety note: Wear suitable footwear for exercising and if doing step-ups use a sturdy secure low box or a PE bench.

ACTIVITY 2

▼ PRACTICAL: AN INVESTIGATION INTO THE EFFECT OF EXERCISE ON BREATHING RATE

It is easy to show the effect of exercise on a person's breathing rate. They sit quietly for five minutes, making sure that they are completely relaxed. They then count the number of breaths they take in one minute, recording their results in a table. They wait a minute, and then count their breaths again, recording the result, and repeating if necessary until they get a steady value for the 'resting rate'.

The person then carries out some vigorous exercise, such as running on the spot for three minutes. Immediately after they finish the exercise, they sit down and record the breathing rate as before. They then continue to record their breaths per minute, every minute, until they return to their normal resting rate.

The table shows the results from an investigation into the breathing rate of two girls, A and B, before and after exercise.

Time from start of experiment (min)	Breathing rate / breaths per min	
	A	B
1	13	13
2	14	12
3	14	12
Rate after 3 min vigorous exercise:		
7	28	17
8	24	13
9	17	12
10	14	12

Plot a line graph of these results, using the same axes for both subjects. Join the data points using straight lines, and leave a gap during the period of exercise, when no readings were taken.

Why does breathing rate need to rise during exercise? Explain as fully as possible. Why does the rate not return to normal as soon as a subject finishes the exercise? (see Chapter 1).

Describe the difference in the breathing rates of the two girls (A and B) after exercise. Which girl is more fit? Explain your reasoning.

THE EFFECTS OF SMOKING

In order for the lungs to exchange gases properly, the air passages need to be clear, the alveoli need to be free from dirt particles and bacteria, and they must have as big a surface area as possible in contact with the blood. There is one habit that can upset all of these conditions – smoking.

Links between smoking and diseases of the lungs are now a proven fact. Smoking is associated with lung cancer, bronchitis and emphysema. It is also a major contributing factor to other conditions, such as coronary heart disease and ulcers of the stomach and intestine. Pregnant women who smoke are more likely to give birth to underweight babies.

Coronary heart disease will be described in Chapter 5 after you have studied the structure of the heart. Here we will look at a number of other medical conditions that are caused by smoking.

EFFECTS OF SMOKE ON THE LINING OF THE AIR PASSAGES

You saw above how the lungs are kept free of particles of dirt and bacteria by the action of mucus and cilia. In the trachea and bronchi of a smoker, the cilia are destroyed by the chemicals in cigarette smoke.

The reduced numbers of cilia mean that the mucus is not swept away from the lungs, but remains to block the air passages. This is made worse by the fact that the smoke irritates the lining of the airways, stimulating the cells to secrete more mucus. The sticky mucus blocking the airways is the source of 'smoker's cough'. Irritation of the bronchial tree, along with infections from bacteria in the mucus, can cause the lung disease **bronchitis**. Bronchitis blocks normal air flow, so the sufferer has difficulty breathing properly.

EMPHYSEMA

Emphysema is another lung disease that kills about 20 000 people in Britain every year. Smoking is the cause of one type of emphysema. Smoke damages the walls of the alveoli, which break down and fuse together again, forming enlarged, irregular air spaces (Figure 3.9).

This greatly reduces the surface area for gas exchange, which becomes very inefficient. The blood of a person with emphysema carries less oxygen. In serious cases, this leads to the sufferer being unable to carry out even mild exercise, such as walking. Emphysema patients often have to have a supply of oxygen nearby at all times (Figure 3.10). There is no cure for emphysema, and usually the sufferer dies after a long and distressing illness.

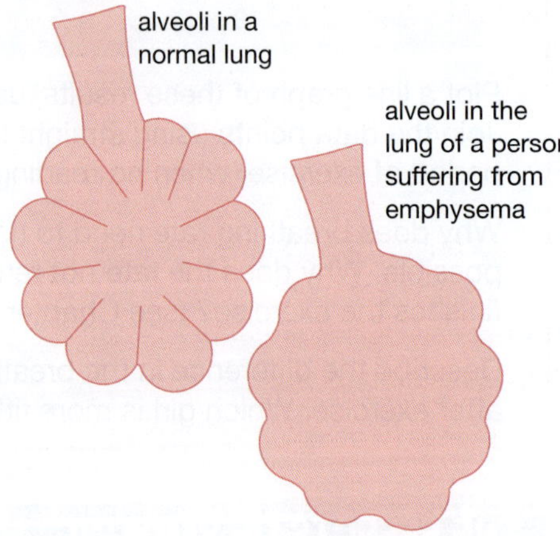

▲ Figure 3.9 The alveoli of a person suffering from emphysema have a greatly reduced surface area and inefficient gas exchange.

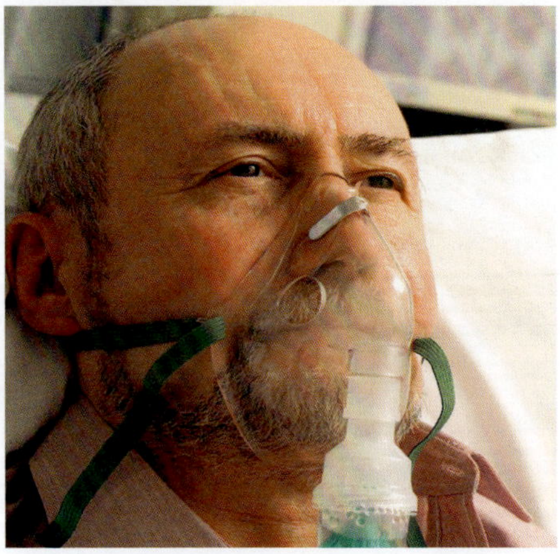

▲ Figure 3.10 Patients with emphysema often need to breathe air enriched with oxygen in order to stay alive.

EXTENSION WORK

A person who has chronic (long-term) bronchitis and emphysema is said to be suffering from chronic obstructive pulmonary disease, or COPD. COPD is a progressive disease for which there is no cure.

LUNG CANCER

Evidence of the link between smoking and lung cancer first appeared in the 1950s. In one study, a number of patients in hospital were given a series of questions about their lifestyles. They were asked about their work, hobbies, housing and so on, including a question about how many cigarettes they smoked. The same questionnaire was given to two groups of patients. The first group were all suffering from lung cancer. The second (**Control**) group were in hospital with various other illnesses, but not lung cancer. To make it a fair comparison, the Control patients were matched with the lung cancer patients for sex, age and so on.

When the results were compared, one difference stood out (Table 3.2). A greater proportion of the lung cancer patients were smokers than in the Control patients. There seemed to be a connection between smoking and getting lung cancer.

Table 3.2 Comparison of the smoking habits of lung cancer patients and other patients.

	Percentage of patients who were non-smokers	Percentage of patients who smoked more than 15 cigarettes a day
lung cancer patients	0.5	25
Control patients (with illnesses other than lung cancer)	4.5	13

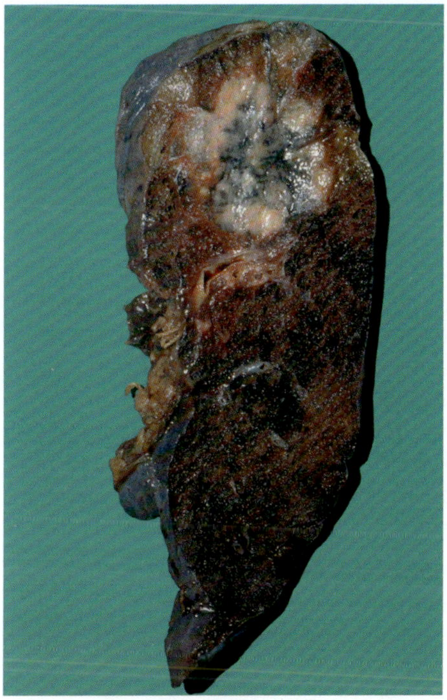

▲ Figure 3.11 This lung is from a patient with lung cancer.

Although the results didn't prove that smoking caused lung cancer, there was a statistically significant link between smoking and the disease: this is called a 'correlation'.

Over 20 similar investigations in nine countries have revealed the same findings. In 1962 a report called 'Smoking and health' was published by the Royal College of Physicians of London, which warned the public about the dangers of smoking. Not surprisingly, the first people to take the findings seriously were doctors, many of whom stopped smoking. This was reflected in their death rates from lung cancer. In ten years, while deaths among the general male population had risen by 7%, the deaths of male doctors from the disease had *fallen* by 38%.

Cigarette smoke contains a strongly addictive drug – **nicotine**. Smoke contains over 7000 chemicals, including; carbon monoxide, arsenic, ammonia, formaldehyde, cyanide, benzene, and toluene. More than 60 of the chemicals are known to cause cancer. These chemicals are called **carcinogens**, and are contained in the tar that collects in a smoker's lungs. Cancer happens when cells mutate and start to divide uncontrollably, forming a **tumour** (Figure 3.11). If a lung cancer patient is lucky, they may have the tumour removed by an operation before the cancer cells spread to other tissues of the body. Unfortunately tumours in the lungs usually cause no pain, so they are not discovered until it is too late – it may be inoperable, or tumours may have developed elsewhere.

If you smoke you are not *bound* to get lung cancer, but the risk that you will get it is much greater. In fact, the more cigarettes you smoke, the more the risk increases (Figure 3.12).

DID YOU KNOW?

People often talk about 'yellow nicotine stains'. In fact it is the *tar* that stains a smoker's fingers and teeth. Nicotine is a colourless, odourless chemical.

DID YOU KNOW?

Studies have shown that the type of cigarette smoked makes very little difference to the smoker's risk of getting lung cancer. Filtered and 'low tar' cigarettes only reduce the risk slightly.

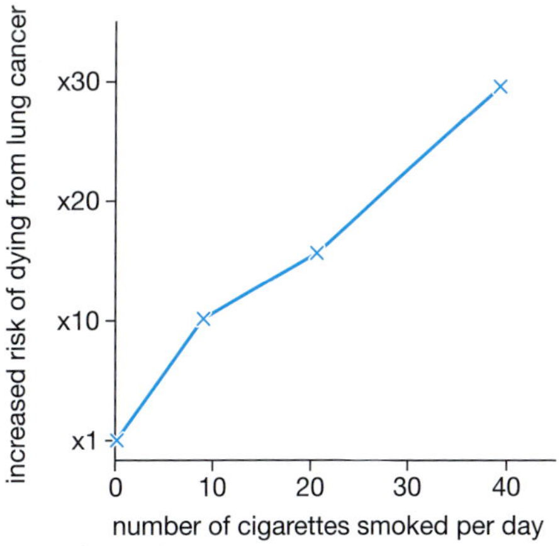

▲ Figure 3.12 The more cigarettes a person smokes, the more likely it is they will die of lung cancer. For example, smoking 20 cigarettes a day increases the risk by about 15 times.

The obvious thing to do is not to start smoking. However, if you are a smoker, giving up the habit soon improves your chance of survival (Figure 3.13). After a few years, the likelihood of your dying from a smoking-related disease is almost back to the level of a non-smoker.

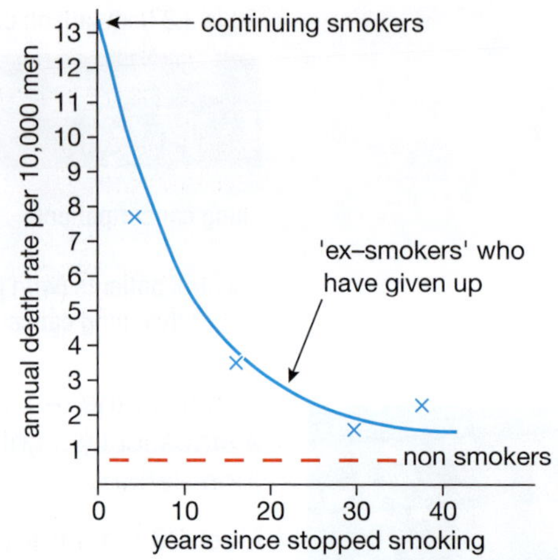

▲ Figure 3.13 Death rates from lung cancer for smokers, non-smokers and ex-smokers.

CARBON MONOXIDE IN SMOKE

One of the harmful chemicals in cigarette smoke is the poisonous gas **carbon monoxide**. When this gas is breathed in with the smoke, it enters the bloodstream and interferes with the ability of the blood to carry oxygen. Oxygen is carried around in the blood in the red blood cells, attached to a chemical called **haemoglobin** (see Chapter 5). Carbon monoxide can combine with the haemoglobin much more tightly than oxygen can, forming a compound called **carboxyhaemoglobin**. The haemoglobin will combine with carbon monoxide in preference to oxygen. When this happens, the blood carries much less oxygen around the body. Carbon monoxide from smoking is also a major cause of heart disease (Chapter 5).

If a pregnant woman smokes, she will be depriving her unborn **fetus** of oxygen (Figure 3.14). This has an effect on its growth and development, and leads to the mass of the baby at birth being lower, on average, than the mass of babies born to non-smokers.

SOME SMOKING STATISTICS

- It is estimated that there are over 1 billion smokers worldwide. In 2014 they consumed 5.8 *trillion* cigarettes.
- Every year nearly 6 million people are killed by tobacco-related illnesses. If the current trend continues, by 2030 this will rise to 8 million deaths per year and 80% of these premature deaths will be in developing countries.
- Smoking causes almost 80% of deaths from lung cancer, 80% of deaths from bronchitis and emphysema, and 14% of deaths from heart disease.
- More than a quarter of all cancer deaths are attributable to smoking. These include cancer of the lung, mouth, lip, throat, **bladder**, kidney, pancreas, stomach, liver and cervix.
- While demand for tobacco has steadily fallen in developed countries like the UK, cigarette consumption is being increasingly concentrated in the developing world.
- 9.6 million adults in the UK smoke cigarettes, 20% of men and 17% of women. However, 22% of women and 30% of men in the UK are now ex-smokers. Surveys show that about two-thirds of current smokers would like to stop smoking.
- It is estimated that worldwide, 31% of men and 8% of women are smokers. Consumption varies widely between different countries, but generally the areas of the world where there has been no change in consumption, or an increase, are southern and central Asia, Eastern Europe and Africa.

- In China alone there are about 350 million smokers, who consume about one-third of all cigarettes smoked worldwide. Large multinational tobacco companies have long been keen to enter the Chinese market.
- In China there are over a million deaths a year from smoking-related diseases. This figure is expected to double by 2025.
- In developing countries, smoking has a greater economic impact. Poorer smokers spend significant amounts of their income on cigarettes rather than necessities like food, healthcare and education.
- Tobacco farming uses up land that could be used for growing food crops. In 2012, 7.5 million tonnes of tobacco leaf were grown on almost 4.3 million hectares of land (an area larger than Switzerland).

Sources: Action on Smoking and Health (ASH) fact sheets (2015- 2016); ASH research reports (2014-2016)]

GIVING UP SMOKING

Most smokers admit that they would like to find a way to give up the habit. The trouble is that the nicotine in tobacco is a very addictive drug, and causes withdrawal symptoms when people stop smoking. These include cravings for a cigarette, restlessness and a tendency to put on weight (nicotine depresses the appetite).

There are various ways that smokers can be helped to give up their habit. One method is 'vaping', which involves inhaling a vapour containing nicotine from an electronic cigarette or e-cigarette (Figure 3.15). Other methods use nicotine patches (Figure 3.16) or nicotine chewing gum. They all work in a similar way, providing the smoker with a source of nicotine without the harmful tar from cigarettes. The nicotine is absorbed by the body and reduces the craving for a cigarette. Gradually, the patient reduces the nicotine dose until they are weaned off the habit.

EXTENSION WORK

You could carry out an Internet search to find out about the different methods people use to help them give up smoking. Which methods have the highest success rate? Is there any evidence that suggests e-cigarettes are not safe?

There are several other ways that people use to help them give up smoking, including the use of drugs that reduce withdrawal symptoms, acupuncture and even hypnotism.

CHAPTER QUESTIONS

More questions on breathing can be found at the end of Unit 2 on page 116.

SKILLS CRITICAL THINKING

4th

1 The structures below are found in the human bronchial tree

1. alveoli	3. bronchioles
2. trachea	4. bronchi

Which of the following shows the route taken by air after it is breathed in through the mouth?

A 2 → 3 → 4 → 1 **C** 2 → 4 → 3 → 1
B 1 → 4 → 3 → 2 **D** 4 → 1 → 2 → 3

5th

2 Which of the following is *not* a feature of an efficient gas exchange surface?

A thick walls **C** close proximity to blood capillaries
B moist lining **D** large surface area

SKILLS CRITICAL THINKING

3rd

3 Which row in the table shows the correct percentage of oxygen in atmospheric and exhaled air?

	Atmospheric air / %	Exhaled air / %
A	78	21
B	21	16
C	16	4
D	4	0.04

4 Chemicals in cigarette smoke lead to the breakdown of the walls of the alveoli. What is the name given to this disease?

A bronchitis

B emphysema

C coronary heart disease

D lung cancer

4th

5 Copy and complete the table, which shows what happens in the thorax during ventilation of the lungs. Two boxes have been completed for you.

	Action during inhalation	Action during exhalation
external intercostal muscles	contract	
internal intercostal muscles		
ribs		move down and in
diaphragm		
volume of thorax		
pressure in thorax		
volume of air in lungs		

5th

6 A student wrote the following about the lungs.

When we breathe in, our lungs inflate, sucking air in and pushing the ribs up and out, and forcing the diaphragm down. This is called respiration. In the air sacs of the lungs, the air enters the blood. The blood then takes the air around the body, where it is used by the cells. The blood returns to the lungs to be cleaned. When we breathe out, our lungs deflate, pulling the diaphragm up and the ribs down. The stale air is pushed out of the lungs.

The student did not have a good understanding of the workings of the lungs. Re-write their description, using correct biological words and ideas.

SKILLS REASONING

7 Sometimes, people injured in an accident such as a car crash suffer from a *pneumothorax*. This is an injury where the chest wall is punctured, allowing air to enter the pleural cavity (see Figure 3.1). A patient was brought to the casualty department of a hospital, suffering from a pneumothorax on the left side of his chest. His left lung had collapsed, but he was able to breathe normally with his right lung.

6th

a Explain why a pneumothorax caused the left lung to collapse.

b Explain why the right lung was not affected.

c If a patient's lung is injured or infected, a surgeon can sometimes 'rest' it by performing an operation called an *artificial pneumothorax*. What do you think might be involved in this operation?

SKILLS CRITICAL THINKING

5th

8 Briefly explain the importance of the following.

a The trachea wall contains C-shaped rings of cartilage.

6th

b The distance between the air in an alveolus and the blood in an alveolar capillary is less than 1/1000th of a millimetre.

c The lining of the trachea contains mucus-secreting cells and cells with cilia.

5th

d Smokers have a lower concentration of oxygen in their blood than non-smokers.

e Nicotine patches and nicotine chewing gum can help someone give up smoking.

7th

f The lungs have a surface area of about 60 m^2 and a good blood supply.

6th

9 Explain the differences between the lung diseases bronchitis and emphysema.

SKILLS ANALYSIS

10 A long-term investigation was carried out into the link between smoking and lung cancer. The smoking habits of male doctors aged 35 or over were determined while they were still alive, then the number and causes of deaths among them were monitored over a number of years. (Note that this survey was carried out in the 1950s – very few doctors smoke these days!) The results are shown in the graph.

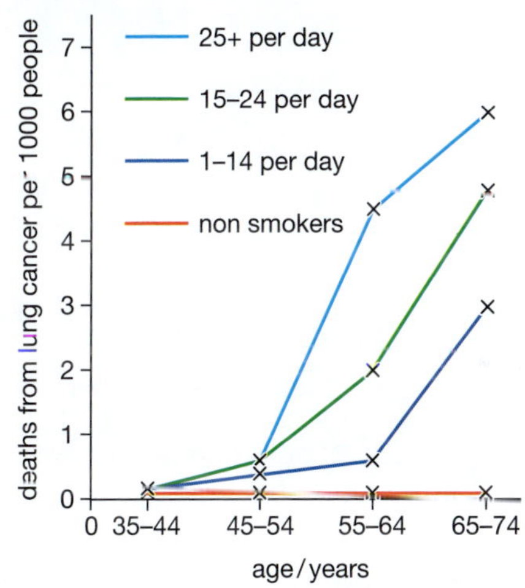

5th

a Write a paragraph to explain what the researchers found out from the investigation.

SKILLS ANALYSIS, PROBLEM SOLVING

6th

b How many deaths from lung cancer would be expected for men aged 55 who smoked 25 cigarettes a day up until their death? How many deaths from lung cancer would be expected for men in the same age group smoking 10 a day?

SKILLS ANALYSIS, REASONING

c Table 3.2 (page 43) shows the findings of another study linking lung cancer with smoking. Which do you think is the more convincing evidence of the link, this investigation or the findings illustrated in Table 3.2?

SKILLS CREATIVITY

7th

11 Design and make a hard-hitting leaflet explaining the link between smoking and lung cancer. It should be aimed at encouraging an adult smoker to give up the habit. You could use suitable computer software to produce your design. Include some smoking statistics, perhaps from an Internet search. However don't use too many, or they may put the person off reading the leaflet!

4 FOOD AND DIGESTION

Food is essential for life. The nutrients obtained from it are used in many different ways by the body. This chapter looks at the different kinds of food, and how the food is broken down by the digestive system and absorbed into the blood, so that it can be carried to all the tissues of the body.

LEARNING OBJECTIVES

- Identify the chemical elements present in carbohydrates, proteins and lipids (fats and oils)
- Describe the structure of carbohydrates, proteins and lipids as large molecules made up from smaller basic units – starch and glycogen from simple sugars, protein from amino acids, and lipids from fatty acids and glycerol
- Investigate food samples for the presence of glucose, starch, protein and fat
- Understand that a balanced diet should include appropriate proportions of carbohydrate, protein, lipid, vitamins, minerals, water and dietary fibre
- Identify the sources and describe the functions of carbohydrate, lipid, protein, vitamins A, C and D, the mineral ions calcium and iron, water, and dietary fibre as components of the diet
- Understand how energy requirements vary with activity levels, age and pregnancy
- Describe the structure and function of the human alimentary canal, including the mouth, oesophagus, stomach, small intestine (duodenum and ileum), large intestine (colon and rectum) and pancreas
- Understand how food is moved through the gut by peristalsis
- Understand the role of digestive enzymes, including the digestion of starch to glucose by amylase and maltase, the digestion of proteins to amino acids by proteases and the digestion of lipids to fatty acids and glycerol by lipases
- Understand that bile is produced by the liver and stored in the gall bladder, and understand the role of bile in neutralising stomach acid and emulsifying lipids
- Understand how the small intestine is adapted for absorption, including the structure of a villus

Figure 4.1 A balanced diet contains all the types of food the body needs, in just the right amounts.

We need food for three main reasons:

- to supply us with a 'fuel' for energy
- to provide materials for growth and repair of tissues
- to help fight disease and keep our bodies healthy.

A BALANCED DIET

The food that we eat is called our diet. No matter what you like to eat, your diet must include the following five groups of food substances if your body is to work properly and stay healthy – **carbohydrates**, **lipids**, **proteins**, **minerals** and **vitamins** – along with **dietary fibre** and water. Food should provide you with all of these substances, but they must also be present in the *right* amounts. A diet that provides enough of these substances and in the correct proportions to keep you healthy is called a **balanced diet** (Figure 4.1). We will look at each type of food in turn, to find out about its chemistry and the role that it plays in the body.

CARBOHYDRATES

DID YOU KNOW?

The chemical formula for glucose is $C_6H_{12}O_6$. Like all carbohydrates, glucose contains only the elements carbon, hydrogen and oxygen. The 'carbo' part of the name refers to carbon, and the 'hydrate' part refers to the fact that the hydrogen and oxygen atoms are in the ratio two to one, as in water (H_2O).

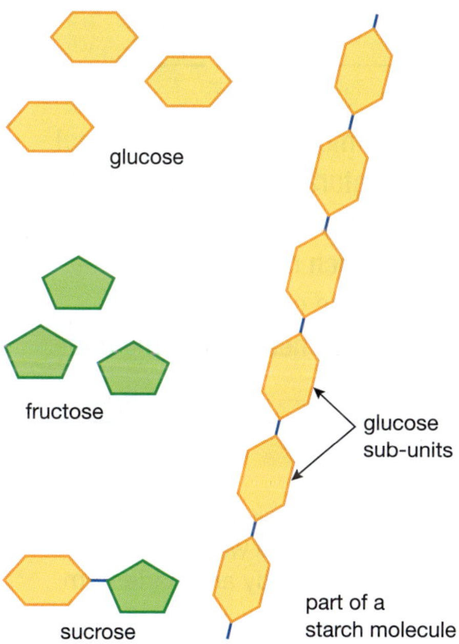

▲ Figure 4.2 Glucose and fructose are 'single sugar' molecules. A molecule of glucose joined to a molecule of fructose forms the 'double sugar' called sucrose. Starch is a polymer of many glucose sub-units.

Carbohydrates only make up about 1% of the mass of the human body, but they have a very important role. They are the body's main 'fuel' for supplying cells with energy. Cells release this energy by oxidising a sugar called **glucose**, in the process called cell respiration (see Chapter 1). Glucose and other sugars belong to one group of carbohydrates.

Glucose is found naturally in many sweet-tasting foods, such as fruits and vegetables. Other foods contain different sugars, such as the fruit sugar called **fructose**, and the milk sugar, **lactose**. Ordinary table sugar, the sort some people put in their tea or coffee, is called **sucrose**. Sucrose is the main sugar that is transported through plant stems. This is why we can extract it from sugar cane, which is the stem of a large grass-like plant. Sugars have two physical properties that you will probably know: they all taste sweet, and they are all soluble in water.

We can get all the sugar we need from natural foods such as fruits and vegetables, and from the **digestion** of starch. Many processed foods contain large amounts of *added* sugar. For example, a typical can of cola can contain up to seven teaspoons (27 g) of sugar! There is hidden sugar in many other foods. A tin of baked beans contains about 10 g of added sugar. This is on top of all the food that we eat with a more obvious sugar content, such as cakes, biscuits and sweets.

In fact, we get most of the carbohydrate in our diet not from sugars, but from **starch**. Starch is a large, *insoluble* molecule. Because it does not dissolve, it is found as a storage carbohydrate in many plants, such as potato, rice, wheat and millet. The 'staple diets' of people from around the world are starchy foods like rice, potatoes, bread and pasta. Starch is a polymer of glucose – it is made of long chains of hundreds of glucose molecules joined together (Figure 4.2).

Starch is only found in plant tissues, but animal cells sometimes contain a very similar carbohydrate called **glycogen**. This is also a polymer of glucose, and is found in tissues such as liver and muscle, where it acts as a store of energy for these organs.

As you will see, large carbohydrates such as starch and glycogen have to be broken down into simple sugars during digestion, so that they can be absorbed into the blood.

Another carbohydrate that is a polymer of glucose is **cellulose**, the material that makes up plant cell walls. Humans are *not* able to digest cellulose, because our gut doesn't make the enzyme needed to break down the cellulose molecule. This means that we are not able to use cellulose as a source of energy. However, it still has a vitally important function in our diet. It forms **dietary fibre** or 'roughage', which gives the muscles of the gut something to push against as the food is moved through the intestine. This keeps the gut contents moving, avoiding constipation and helping to prevent serious diseases of the intestine, such as colitis and bowel cancer.

EXTENSION WORK

'Single' sugars such as glucose and fructose are called **monosaccharides**. Sucrose molecules are made of two monosaccharides (glucose and fructose) joined together, so sucrose is called a **disaccharide**. Lactose is also a disaccharide, made of glucose joined to another monosaccharide called galactose. Polymers of sugars, such as starch, glycogen and cellulose, are called polysaccharides.

LIPIDS (FATS AND OILS)

Lipids contain the same three elements as carbohydrates – carbon, hydrogen and oxygen – but the proportion of oxygen in a lipid is much lower than in a carbohydrate. For example, beef and lamb both contain a fat called tristearin, which has the formula $C_{51}H_{98}O_6$. This fat, like other animal fats, is a solid at room

▲ Figure 4.3 These foods are all rich in lipids.

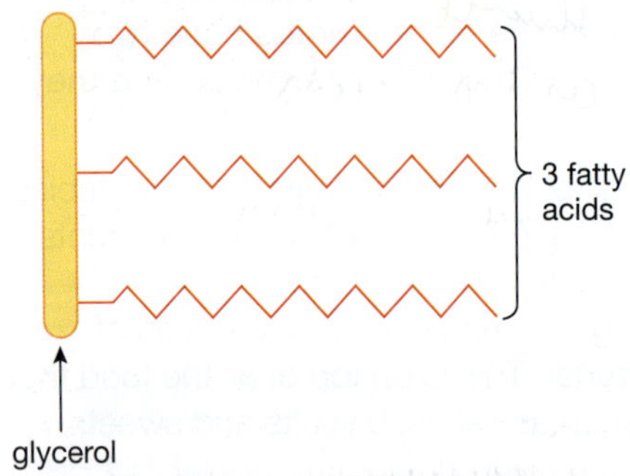

▲ Figure 4.4 Lipids are made up of a molecule of glycerol joined to three fatty acids. The many different fatty acids form the variable part of the molecule.

KEY POINT

Cholesterol is a substance that the body gets from food such as eggs and meat, but we also make cholesterol in our liver. It is an essential part of all cells, but too much cholesterol causes heart disease.

temperature, but melts if you warm it up. On the other hand, plant lipids are usually liquid at room temperature, and are called oils. Meat, butter, cheese, milk, eggs and oily fish are all rich in animal fats, as well as foods fried in animal fat. Vegetable oils include many types used for cooking, such as olive oil, corn oil and rapeseed oil, as well as products made from oils, such as margarine (Figure 4.3).

Lipids make up about 10% of our body's mass. They form an essential part of the structure of all cells, and fat is deposited in certain parts of the body as a long-term store of energy, for example under the skin and around the heart and kidneys. The fat layer under the skin acts as insulation, reducing heat loss through the surface of the body. Fat around organs such as the kidneys also helps to protect them from mechanical damage.

The chemical 'building blocks' of lipids are two types of molecule called **glycerol** and **fatty acids**. Glycerol is an oily liquid. It is also known as glycerine, and is used in many types of cosmetics. In lipids, a molecule of glycerol is joined to three fatty acid molecules. There are many different fatty acid molecules, which give us the many different kinds of lipid found in food (Figure 4.4).

Although lipids are an essential part of our diet, too much lipid is unhealthy, especially a type called *saturated* fat, and a lipid compound called **cholesterol**. These substances have been linked to heart disease (see Chapter 5).

DID YOU KNOW?

Saturated lipids (saturated fats) are more common in food from animal sources, such as meat and dairy products. 'Saturated' is a word used in chemistry, which means that the fatty acids of the lipids contain no double bonds. Other lipids are *unsaturated*, which means that their fatty acids contain double bonds. These are more common in plant oils. There is evidence that unsaturated lipids are healthier for us than saturated ones.

PROTEINS

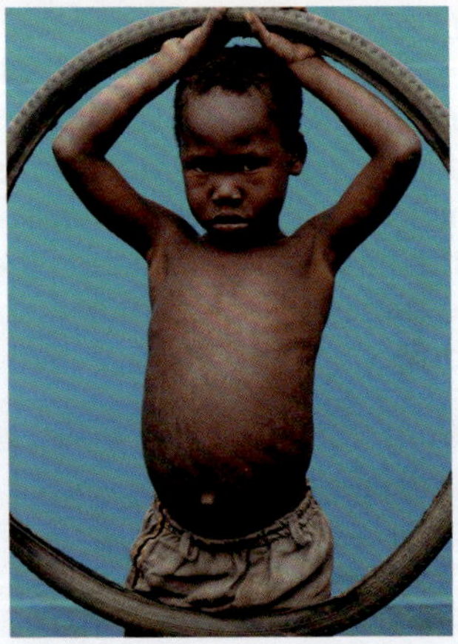

▲ Figure 4.5 This child is suffering from a lack of protein in his diet, a disease called kwashiorkor. His swollen belly is not due to a full stomach, but is caused by fluid collecting in the tissues. Other symptoms include loss of weight, poor muscle growth, general weakness and flaky skin.

Proteins make up about 18% of the mass of the body. This is the second largest percentage after water. All cells contain protein, so we need it for growth and repair of tissues. Many compounds in the body are made from protein, including enzymes.

Most foods contain some protein, but certain foods such as meat, fish, cheese and eggs are particularly rich in it. You will notice that these foods are animal products. Plant material generally contains less protein, but some foods, especially beans, peas and nuts, are richer in protein than others.

However, we don't need much protein in our diet to stay healthy. Doctors recommend a maximum daily intake of about 70 g. In more economically developed countries, people often eat far more protein than they need, whereas in many poorer countries a protein-deficiency disease called **kwashiorkor** is common (Figure 4.5).

Like starch, proteins are also polymers, but whereas starch is made from a single molecular building block (glucose), proteins are made from 20 different sub-units called **amino acids**. All amino acids contain four chemical elements: carbon, hydrogen and oxygen (as in carbohydrates and fats) along with nitrogen. Two amino acids also contain sulfur. The amino acids are linked together in long chains, which are usually folded up or twisted into spirals, with cross-links holding the chains together (Figure 4.6).

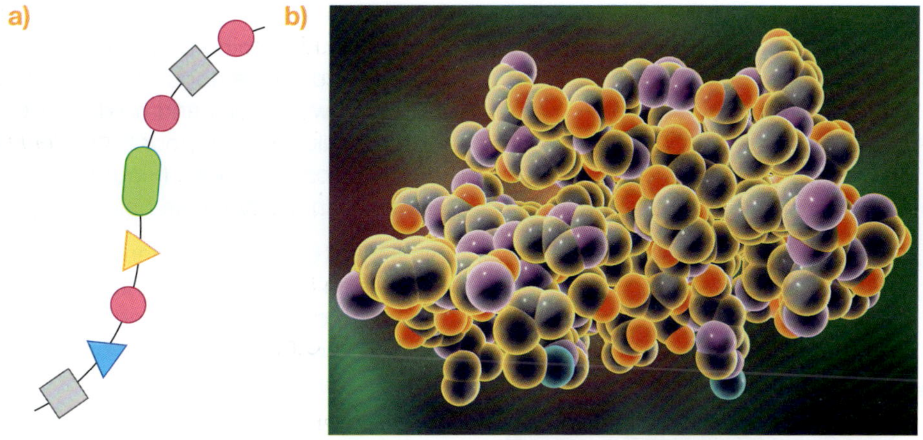

▲ Figure 4.6 (a) A chain of amino acids forming part of a protein molecule. Each shape represents a different amino acid. (b) A computer model of the protein insulin. This substance, like all proteins, is made of a long chain of amino acids arranged in a particular order and folded into a specific shape.

EXTENSION WORK

Humans can make about half of the 20 amino acids that they need, but the other 10 have to be taken in as part of the diet. These 10 are called essential amino acids. There are higher amounts of essential amino acids in meat, fish, eggs and dairy products. If you are a vegetarian, you can still get all the essential amino acids you need, as long as you eat a varied diet that includes a range of different plant materials.

The *shape* of a protein is very important in allowing it to carry out its function, and the *order* of amino acids in the protein decides its shape. Because there are 20 different amino acids, and they can be arranged in any order, the number of different protein structures that can be made is enormous. As a result, there are thousands of different kinds of proteins in organisms, from structural proteins such as collagen and keratin in skin and nails, to proteins with more specific functions, such as enzymes and haemoglobin.

MINERALS

All the foods you have read about so far are made from just five chemical elements: carbon, hydrogen, oxygen, nitrogen and sulfur. Our bodies contain many other elements that we get from our food as 'minerals' or 'mineral ions'. Some are present in large amounts in the body, for example calcium, which is used for making teeth and bones. Others are present in much smaller amounts, but still have essential jobs to do. For instance our bodies contain about 3 g of iron, but without it our blood would not be able to carry oxygen. Table 4.1 shows just a few of these minerals and the reasons they are needed.

Table 4.1 Some examples of minerals needed by the body.

Mineral	Approximate mass in an adult body / g	Location or role in body	Examples of foods rich in minerals
calcium	1000	making teeth and bones	dairy products, fish, bread, vegetables
phosphorus	650	making teeth and bones; part of many chemicals, e.g. DNA and ATP	most foods
sodium	100	in body fluids, e.g. blood	common salt, most foods
chlorine	100	in body fluids, e.g. blood	common salt, most foods
magnesium	30	making bones; found inside cells	green vegetables
iron	3	part of haemoglobin in red blood cells, helps carry oxygen	red meat, liver, eggs, some vegetables, e.g. spinach

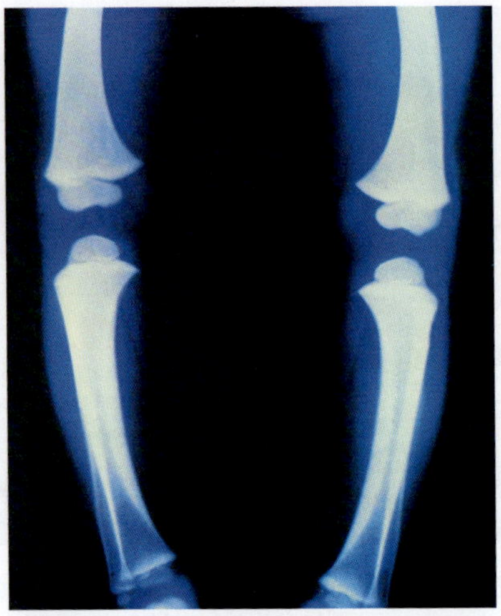

▲ Figure 4.7 An x-ray of the legs of a child showing the symptoms of rickets.

If a person doesn't get enough of a mineral from their diet, they will show the symptoms of a 'mineral deficiency disease'. For example, a one-year-old child needs to consume about 0.6 g (600 mg) of calcium every day, to make the bones grow properly and harden. Anything less than this over a prolonged period could result in poor bone development. The bones become deformed, a disease called rickets (Figure 4.7). Rickets can also be caused by lack of vitamin D in the diet (see below).

Similarly, 16-year-olds need about 12 mg of iron in their daily food intake. If they don't get this amount, they can't make enough haemoglobin for their red blood cells (see Chapter 5). This causes a condition called anaemia. People who are anaemic become tired and lack energy, because their blood doesn't carry enough oxygen.

VITAMINS

During the early part of the twentieth century, experiments were carried out that identified another class of food substances. When young laboratory rats were fed a diet of pure carbohydrate, lipid and protein, they all became ill and died. If they were fed on the same pure foods with a little added milk, they grew normally. The milk contained chemicals that the rats needed in small amounts to stay healthy. These chemicals are called vitamins. The results of one of these experiments are shown in Figure 4.8.

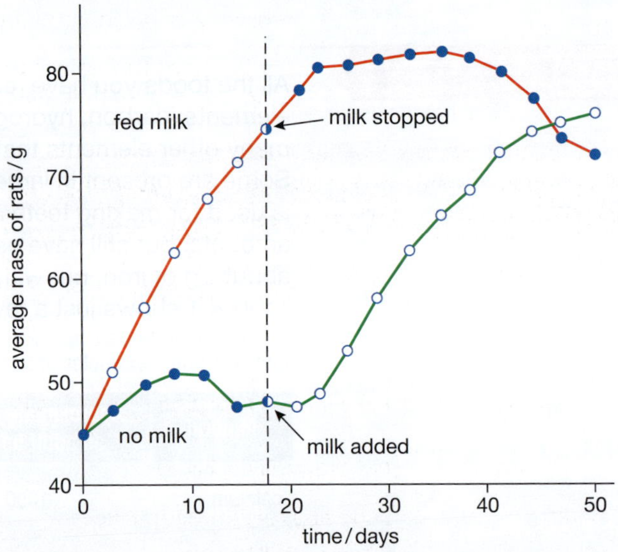

▲ Figure 4.8 Rats were fed a diet of pure carbohydrate, lipid and protein, with and without added milk. Vitamins in the milk had a dramatic effect on their growth.

At first, the chemical nature of vitamins was not known, and they were given letters to distinguish between them, such as vitamin A, vitamin B and so on. Each was identified by the effect a lack of the vitamin (vitamin deficiency) had on the body. For example, vitamin D is needed for growing bones to take up calcium salts. A deficiency of this vitamin can result in rickets (Figure 4.7), just as a lack of calcium can.

We now know the chemical structure of the vitamins and the exact ways in which they work in the body. As with vitamin D, each has a particular function. Vitamin A is needed to make a light-sensitive chemical in the retina of the eye (see Chapter 6). A lack of this vitamin causes night blindness, where the

DID YOU KNOW?

The cure for scurvy was discovered as long ago as 1753. Sailors on long voyages often got scurvy because they ate very little fresh fruit and vegetables (the main source of vitamin C). A ship's doctor called James Lind wrote an account of how the disease could quickly be cured by eating fresh oranges and lemons. The famous explorer Captain Cook, on his world voyages in 1772 and 1775, kept his sailors healthy by making sure that they ate fresh fruit. By 1804, all British sailors were made to drink lime juice to prevent scurvy. This is how they came to be called 'limeys', a word that was later used by Americans for all British people.

person finds it difficult to see in dim light. Vitamin C is needed to make fibres of a material called connective tissue. This acts as a 'glue', bonding cells together in a tissue. It is found in the walls of blood vessels and in the skin and lining surfaces of the body. Vitamin C deficiency leads to a disease called **scurvy**, where wounds fail to heal, and bleeding occurs in various places in the body. This is especially noticeable in the gums (Figure 4.9).

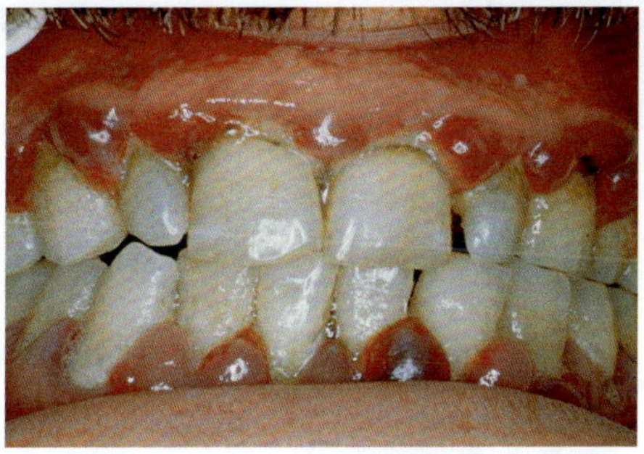

▲ Figure 4.9 Vitamin C helps lining cells such as those in the mouth and gums stick to each other. Lack of vitamin C causes scurvy, where the mouth and gums become damaged and bleed.

Vitamin B is not a single substance, but a collection of many different substances called the vitamin B group. It includes vitamins B1 (thiamine), B2 (riboflavin) and B3 (niacin). These compounds are involved in the process of cell respiration. Different deficiency diseases result if any of them are missing from the diet. For example, lack of vitamin B1 results in the weakening of the muscles and paralysis, a disease called **beri-beri**.

The main vitamins, their role in the body and some foods which are good sources of each, are summarised in Table 4.2.

Notice that the amounts of vitamins that we need are very small, but we cannot stay healthy without them.

Table 4.2 Summary of the main vitamins. Note that you only need remember the sources and functions of vitamins A, C and D.

Vitamin	Recommended daily amount in diet[1]	Use in the body	Effect of deficiency	Some foods that are a good source of the vitamin
A	0.8 mg	making a chemical in the retina; also protects the surface of the eye	night blindness, damaged cornea of eye	fish liver oils, liver, butter, margarine, carrots
B1	1.1 mg	helps with cell respiration	beri-beri	yeast extract, cereals
B2	1.4 mg	helps with cell respiration	poor growth, dry skin	green vegetables, eggs, fish
B3	16 mg	helps with cell respiration	pellagra (dry red skin, poor growth, and digestive disorders)	liver, meat, fish.
C	80 mg	sticks together cells lining surfaces such as the mouth	scurvy	fresh fruit and vegetables
D	5 μg	helps bones absorb calcium and phosphate	rickets, poor teeth	fish liver oils; also made in skin in sunlight

[1]Figures are the European Union's recommended daily intake for an adult (2012). 'mg' stands for milligram (a thousandth of a gram) and 'μg' for microgram (a millionth of a gram).

FOOD TESTS

It is possible to carry out simple chemical tests to find out if a food contains starch, glucose, protein or lipid. Practical 8 uses pure substances for the tests, but it is possible to do them on normal foods too. Unless the food is a liquid like milk, it needs to be cut up into small pieces and ground with a pestle and mortar, then shaken with some water in a test tube. This is done to extract the components of the food and dissolve any soluble substances such as sugars.

▲ Figure 4.10a Testing for starch using iodine

▲ Figure 4.10b Glucose with Benedict's solution, before and after heating

ACTIVITY 3

▼ PRACTICAL: TEST FOR STARCH

A little starch is placed on a spotting tile. A drop of yellow-brown iodine solution is added to the starch. The iodine reacts with the starch, forming a very dark blue, or 'blue-black' colour (Figure 4.10 (a)). Starch is insoluble, but this test will work on a solid sample of food, such as potato, or a suspension of starch in water.

▼ PRACTICAL: TEST FOR GLUCOSE

Glucose is called a reducing sugar. This is because the test for glucose involves reducing an alkaline solution of copper (II) sulfate to copper (I) oxide.

A small spatula measure of glucose is placed in a test tube and a little water added (about 2 cm deep). The tube is shaken to dissolve the glucose. Several drops of Benedict's solution are added to the tube, enough to colour the mixture blue (Figure 4.10 (b)).

A water bath is prepared by half-filling a beaker with water and heating it on a tripod and gauze. The test tube is placed in the beaker and the water allowed to boil (using a water bath is safer than heating the tube directly in the Bunsen burner). After a few seconds the clear blue solution gradually changes colour, forming a cloudy orange or 'brick red' precipitate of copper (I) oxide (Figure 4.10 (b)).

All other 'single' sugars (monosaccharides), such as fructose, are reducing sugars, as well as some 'double' sugars (disaccharides), such as the milk sugar, lactose. However, ordinary table sugar (sucrose) is not. If sucrose is boiled with Benedict's solution it will stay a clear blue colour.

▼ PRACTICAL: TEST FOR PROTEIN

The test for protein is sometimes called the 'biuret' test, after the coloured compound that is formed.

A little protein, such as powdered egg white (albumen), is placed in a test tube and about 2 cm depth of water added. The tube is shaken to mix the powder with the water. An equal volume of dilute (5%) potassium hydroxide solution is added and the tube shaken again. Finally two drops of 1% copper sulfate solution are added. A purple colour develops. (Sometimes these two solutions are supplied already mixed together as 'biuret solution'.)

▼ PRACTICAL: TEST FOR LIPID

Fats and oils are insoluble in water, but will dissolve in ethanol (alcohol). The test for lipid uses this fact.

A pipette is used to place one drop of olive oil in the bottom of a test tube. About 2 cm depth of ethanol is added, and the tube is shaken to dissolve the oil. The solution is poured into a test tube that is about three-quarters full with cold water. A white cloudy layer forms on the top of the water. The white layer is caused by the ethanol dissolving in the water and leaving the lipid behind as a suspension of tiny droplets, called an emulsion.

▲ Figure 4.11 Food packaging is labelled with the proportions of different food types that it contains, along with its energy content. The energy in units called kilocalories (kcal) is also shown, but scientists no longer use this old-fashioned unit.

ENERGY FROM FOOD

Some foods contain more energy than others. It depends on the proportions of carbohydrate, lipid and protein that they contain. Their energy content is measured in kilojoules (kJ). If a gram of carbohydrate is fully oxidised, it produces about 17 kJ, whereas a gram of lipid yields over twice as much as this (39 kJ). Protein can produce about 18 kJ per gram. If you look on a food label, it usually shows the energy content of the food, along with the amounts of different nutrients that it contains (Figure 4.11).

Foods with a high percentage of lipid, such as butter or nuts, contain a large amount of energy. Others, like fruits and vegetables, which are mainly composed of water, have a much lower energy content (Table 4.3).

Table 4.3 Energy content of some common foods

Food	kJ per 100g	Food	kJ per 100g
margarine	3200	white bread	1060
butter	3120	chips	990
peanuts	2400	grilled beef steak	930
samosa	2400	fried cod	850
chocolate	2300	roast chicken	770
Cheddar cheese	1700	boiled potatoes	340
table sugar	1650	milk	270
cornflakes	1530	baked beans	270
rice	1500	yoghurt	200
spaghetti	1450	boiled cabbage	60
fried beefburger	1100	lettuce	40

EXTENSION WORK

Food scientists measure the amount of energy in a sample of food by burning it in a calorimeter (Figure 4.12). The calorimeter is filled with oxygen, to make sure that the food will burn easily. A heating filament carrying an electrical current ignites the food. The energy given out by the burning food is measured by using it to heat up water flowing through a coil in the calorimeter.

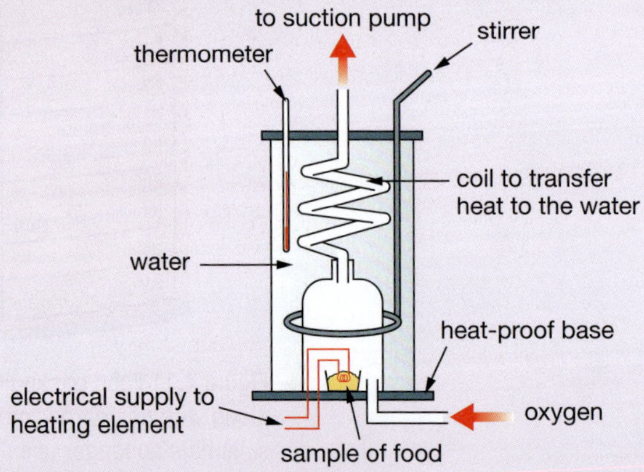

▶ Figure 4.12 A food calorimeter

If you have samples of food that will easily burn in air, you can measure the energy in them by a similar method, using the heat from the burning food to warm up water in a test tube.

Table 4.4 The daily energy needs of different types of people.

Age/sex/occupation of person	Energy needed per day / kJ
newborn baby	2000
child aged 2	5000
child aged 6	7500
girl aged 12–14	9000
boy aged 12–14	11000
girl aged 15–17	9000
boy aged 15–17	12000
female office worker	9500
male office worker	10500
heavy manual worker	15000
pregnant woman	10000
breast-feeding woman	11300

Even while you are asleep you need a supply of energy – in order to keep warm, for your heart to keep beating, to allow messages to be sent through your nerves, and for other body functions. However, the energy you need at other times depends on the physical work you do. The total amount of energy that a person needs to keep healthy depends on their age and body size, and also on the amount of activity they do. Table 4.4 shows some examples of how much energy is needed each day by people of different age, sex and occupation.

Remember that these are approximate figures, and they are averages. Generally, the greater a person's weight, the more energy that person needs. This is why men, with a greater average body mass, need more energy than women. The energy needs of a pregnant woman are increased, mainly because of the extra weight that she has to carry. A heavy manual worker, such as a labourer, needs extra energy for increased muscle activity.

It is not only the recommended energy requirements that vary with age, sex and pregnancy, but also the *content* of the diet. For instance, during pregnancy a woman may need extra iron or calcium in her diet, for the growth of the fetus. In younger women, the blood loss during menstruation (periods) can result in anaemia, producing a need for extra iron in the diet.

DIGESTION

Food, such as a piece of bread, contains carbohydrates, lipids and proteins, but they are not the same carbohydrates, lipids and proteins as in our tissues. The components of the bread must first be broken down into their 'building blocks' before they can be absorbed through the wall of the gut. This process is called **digestion**. The digested molecules – sugars, fatty acids, glycerol and amino acids – along with minerals, vitamins and water, can then be carried around the body in the blood. When they reach the tissues they are reassembled into the molecules that make up our cells.

HINT

A good definition of digestion is: 'Digestion is the chemical and mechanical breakdown of food. It converts large insoluble molecules into small soluble molecules, which can be absorbed into the blood.'

Digestion is speeded up by **enzymes**, which are biological catalysts (see Chapter 1). Although most enzymes stay inside cells, the digestive enzymes are made by the tissues and glands in the gut and pass out of cells – on to the gut contents where they act on the food. This *chemical* digestion is helped by *mechanical* digestion. Mechanical digestion is the physical breakdown of food. The most obvious place where this happens is in the mouth, where the teeth bite and chew the food, cutting it into smaller pieces that have a larger surface area. This means that enzymes can act on the food more quickly. Other parts of the gut also help with mechanical digestion. For example, muscles in the wall of the stomach contract to churn up the food while it is being chemically digested.

PERISTALSIS

Muscles are also responsible for moving the food along the gut. The walls of the intestine contain two layers of muscles. One layer has fibres arranged in rings around the gut. This is the circular muscle layer. The other has fibres running along the length of the gut, and is called the longitudinal muscle layer. Together these two layers act to push the food along. When the circular muscles contract and the longitudinal muscles relax, the gut is made narrower. When the opposite happens, i.e. the longitudinal muscles contract and the circular muscles relax, the gut becomes wider. Waves of muscle contraction like this pass along the gut, pushing the food along, rather like squeezing toothpaste from a tube. This is called **peristalsis** (Figure 4.13). It means that movement of food in the gut doesn't depend on gravity – we can still eat standing on our heads!

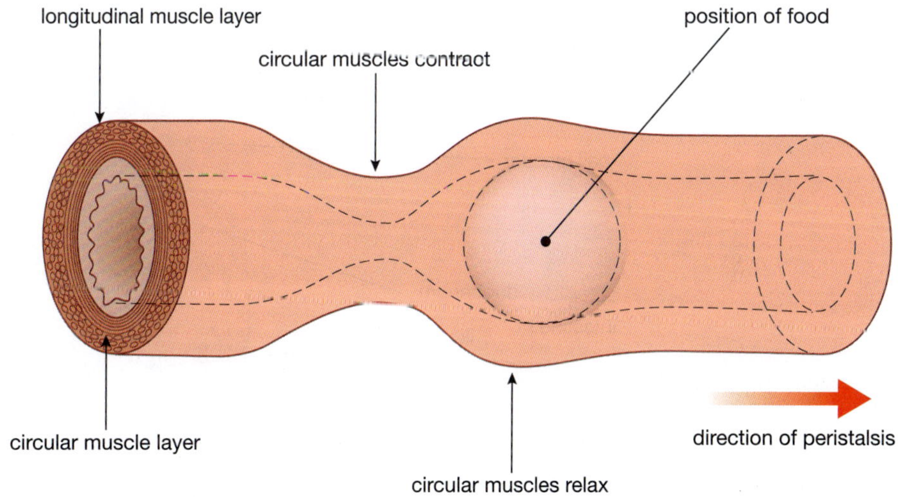

▲ Figure 4.13 Peristalsis: contraction of circular muscles behind the food narrows the gut, pushing the food along. When the circular muscles are contracted, the longitudinal ones are relaxed, and vice versa.

THE DIGESTIVE SYSTEM

Figure 4.14 shows a simplified diagram of the human digestive system. It is simplified so that you can see the order of the organs along the gut. The real gut is much longer than this, and coiled up so that it fills the whole space of the abdomen. Overall, its length in an adult is about 8 m. This gives plenty of time for the food to be broken down and absorbed as it passes through the gut.

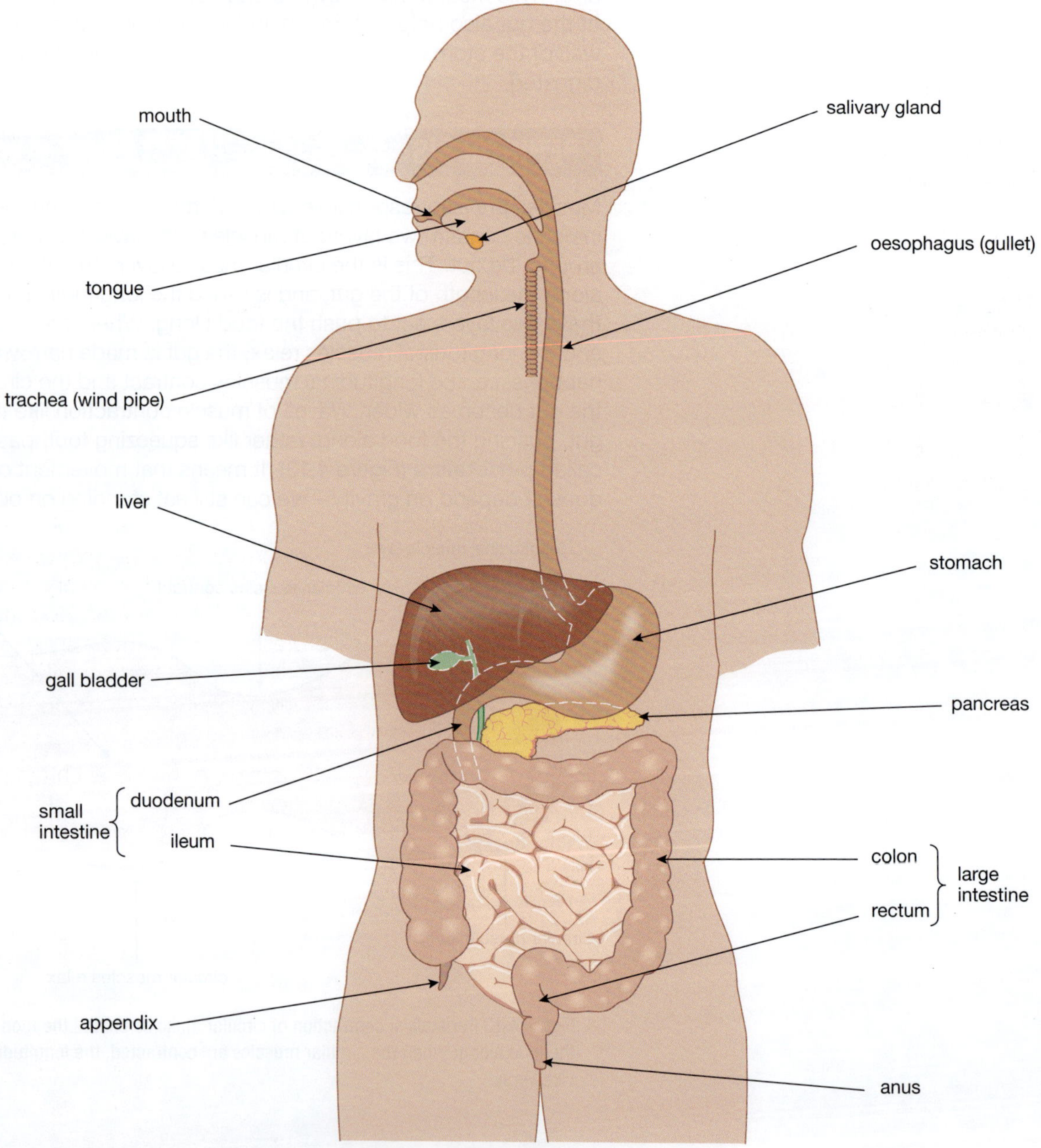

▲ Figure 4.14 The human digestive system

The mouth, stomach and the first part of the small intestine (called the **duodenum**) all break down the food using enzymes, either made in the gut wall itself, or by glands such as the **pancreas**. Digestion continues in the last part of the small intestine (the **ileum**) and it is here that the digested food is absorbed. The last part of the gut, the large intestine, is mainly concerned with absorbing water out of the remains, and storing the waste products (**faeces**) before they are removed from the body.

The three main classes of food are broken down by three classes of enzymes. Carbohydrates are digested by enzymes called **carbohydrases**. Proteins are acted upon by **proteases**, and enzymes called **lipases** break down lipids. Some of the places in the gut where these enzymes are made are shown in Table 4.5.

KEY POINT

Amylase digests starch into maltose. Amylase is the enzyme, starch is the substrate and maltose is the product.

Digestion begins in the mouth. **Saliva** helps moisten the food and contains the enzyme **amylase**, which starts the breakdown of starch. The chewed lump of food, mixed with saliva, then passes along the **oesophagus** (gullet) to the stomach.

Table 4.5 Some of the enzymes that digest food in the human gut. The substances shown in bold are the end products of digestion that can be absorbed from the gut into the blood.

Class of enzyme	Examples	Digestive action	Source of enzyme	Where it acts in the gut
carbohydrases	amylase amylase maltase	starch → maltose[1] starch → maltose maltose → **glucose**	salivary glands pancreas wall of small intestine	mouth small intestine small intestine
proteases	pepsin trypsin peptidases	proteins → peptides[2] proteins → peptides peptides → **amino acids**	stomach wall pancreas wall of small intestine	stomach small intestine small intestine
lipases	lipase	lipids → **glycerol** and **fatty acids**	pancreas	small intestine

[1]Maltose is a disaccharide made of two glucose molecules joined together.

[2]Peptides are short chains of amino acids.

The food is held in the stomach for several hours, while initial digestion of protein takes place. The stomach wall secretes hydrochloric acid, so the stomach contents are strongly acidic. This has a very important function. It kills bacteria that are taken into the gut along with the food, helping to protect us from food poisoning. The protease enzyme that is made in the stomach, called **pepsin**, has to be able to work in these acidic conditions, and has an optimum pH value of about 2. This is unusually low – most enzymes work best at near neutral conditions (see Chapter 1).

The semi-digested food is held back in the stomach by a ring of muscle at the outlet of the stomach, called a **sphincter muscle**. When this relaxes, it releases the food into the first part of the small intestine, called the duodenum (Figure 4.15).

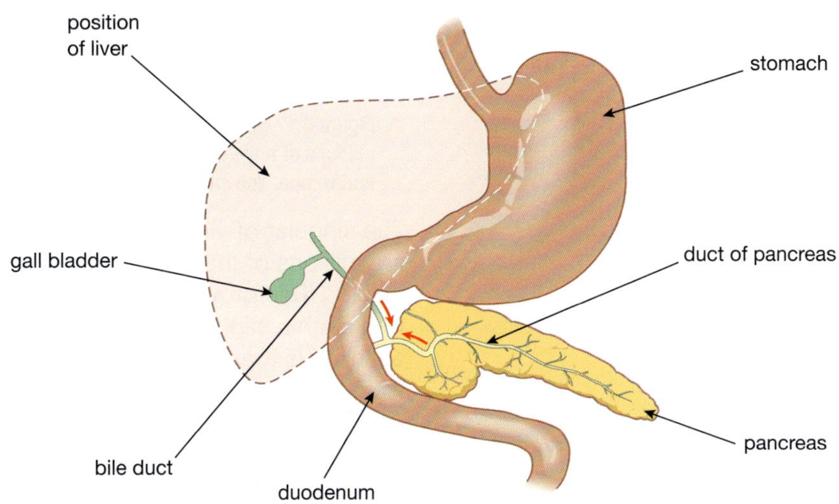

▲ Figure 4.15 The first part of the small intestine, the duodenum, receives digestive juices from the liver and pancreas through tubes called ducts.

▲ Figure 4.16 Bile turns fats into an emulsion of tiny droplets for easier digestion.

Several digestive enzymes are added to the food in the duodenum. These are made by the pancreas, and digest starch, proteins and lipids (Table 4.5). As well as this, the **liver** makes a digestive juice called **bile**. Bile is a green liquid that is stored in the **gall bladder** and passes down the **bile duct** on to the food. Bile does not contain enzymes, but has another important function. It turns any large lipid globules in the food into an emulsion of tiny droplets (Figure 4.16). This increases the surface area of the lipid, so that lipase enzymes can break it down more easily.

Bile and pancreatic juice have another function. They are both alkaline. The mixture of semi-digested food and enzymes coming from the stomach is acidic, and needs to be neutralised by the addition of alkali before it continues on its way through the gut.

As the food continues along the intestine, more enzymes are added, until the parts of the food that can be digested have been fully broken down into soluble end products, which can be absorbed. This is the role of the last part of the small intestine, the ileum.

ABSORPTION IN THE ILEUM

The ileum is highly adapted to absorb the digested food. The lining of the ileum has a very large surface area, which means that it can quickly and efficiently absorb the soluble products of digestion into the blood. The length of the intestine helps to provide a large surface area, and this is aided by folds in its lining, but the greatest increase in area is due to tiny projections from the lining, called **villi** (Figure 4.17).

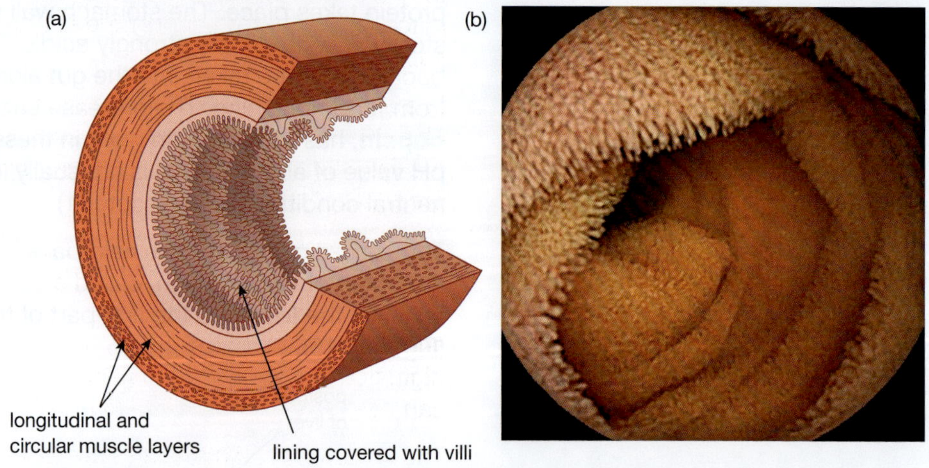

▲ Figure 4.17 (a) The inside lining of the ileum is adapted to absorb digested food by the presence of millions of tiny villi. (b) Photo of the inside a patient's ileum, taken using a camera attached to an endoscope. You can see thousands of tiny villi covering the lining.

The singular of villi is 'villus'. Each villus is only about 1–2 mm long, but there are millions of them, so that the total area of the lining is thought to be about 300 m^2. This provides a massive area in contact with the digested food. As well as this, high-powered microscopy has revealed that the surface cells of each villus themselves have hundreds of minute projections, called **microvilli**, which increase the surface area for absorption even more (Figure 4.18).

Each villus contains a network of blood capillaries. Most of the digested food enters these blood vessels, but the products of fat digestion, as well as tiny fat droplets, enter a tube in the middle of the villus, called a **lacteal**. The lacteals form part of the body's lymphatic system, which transports a liquid called lymph. This lymph eventually drains into the blood system too.

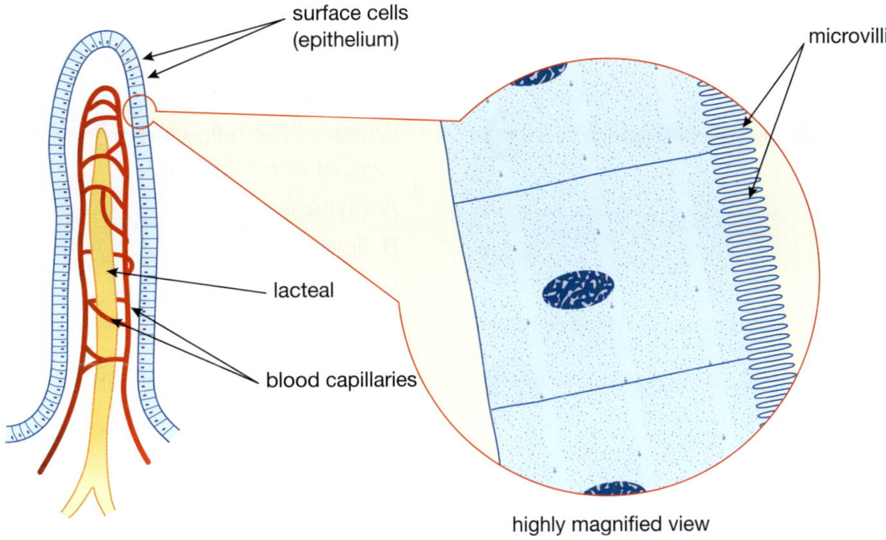

▲ Figure 4.18 Each villus contains blood vessels and a lacteal, which absorb the products of digestion. The surface cells of the villus are covered with microvilli, which further increase the surface area for absorption.

The surface of a villus is made of a single layer of cells called an epithelium. This means that there is only a short distance between the digested food in the ileum and the blood capillaries making it easier for the products of digestion to diffuse through and enter the blood. The epithelium cells contain many mitochondria, which supply the energy needed for active transport of some substances.

In addition each villus contains muscle fibres which contract to move the villus. The villi are in constant motion, keeping them in contact with the contents of the ileum and maintaining a steep concentration gradient for diffusion of the products of digestion.

The blood vessels from the ileum join up to form a large blood vessel called the **hepatic portal vein**, which leads to the liver (see Chapter 5). The liver acts rather like a food processing factory, breaking some molecules down, and building up and storing others. For example, glucose from carbohydrate digestion is converted into glycogen and stored in the liver. Later, the glycogen can be converted back into glucose when the body needs it (see Chapter 7).

The digested food molecules are distributed around the body by the blood system (see Chapter 5). The soluble food molecules are absorbed from the blood into cells of tissues, and are used to build new parts of cells. This is called assimilation.

KEY POINT

Removal of faeces by the body is sometimes incorrectly called excretion. Excretion is a word that only applies to materials that are the waste products of cells of the body, such as carbon dioxide. Faeces are not products of cell metabolism – they consist of waste that has passed through the gut and left the body via the anus, without entering the cells. The correct name for this process is egestion.

THE LARGE INTESTINE – ELIMINATION OF WASTE

By the time that the contents of the gut have reached the end of the small intestine, most of the digested food, as well as most of the water, has been absorbed. The waste material consists mainly of cellulose (fibre) and other indigestible remains, water, dead and living bacteria and cells lost from the lining of the gut. The function of the first part of the large intestine, called the **colon**, is to absorb most of the remaining water from the contents, leaving a semi-solid waste material called faeces. This is stored in the **rectum**, until expelled out of the body through the **anus**.

CHAPTER QUESTIONS

More questions on food and digestion can be found at the end of Unit 2 on page 116.

SKILLS CRITICAL THINKING

6th

1 Which of the following organic molecules contains carbon, hydrogen, oxygen and nitrogen?

A glycogen

B lipid

C cellulose

D protein

5th

2 Which of the following substances would give a positive test when boiled with Benedict's solution?

A fructose

B lipid

C starch

D protein

6th

3 Which of the following statements about digestion is *not* correct?

A Digestion produces fatty acids and glycerol

B Digestion converts insoluble molecules into soluble molecules

C Digestion changes proteins into amino acids

D Digestion releases energy from food

4th

4 Which of the following organs does *not* produce digestive enzymes?

A salivary gland

B gall bladder

C stomach

D pancreas

SKILLS EXECUTIVE FUNCTION

5 The diagram shows an experiment that was set up as a model to show why food needs to be digested.

The Visking tubing acts as a model of the small intestine because it has tiny holes in it that some molecules can pass through. The tubing was left in the boiling tube for an hour, then the water in the tube was tested for starch and glucose.

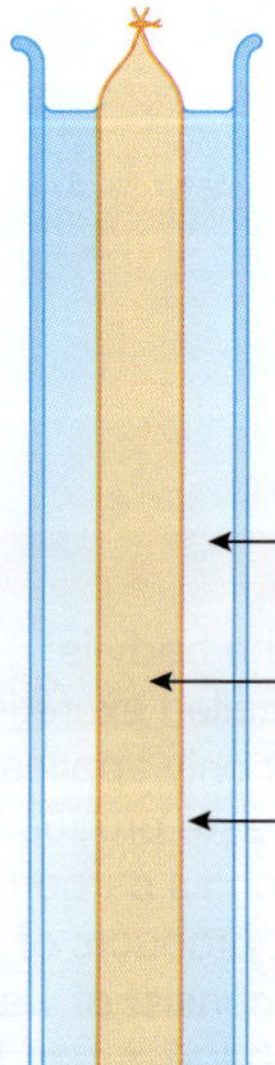

5th

a Describe how you would test the water for starch, and for glucose. What would the results be for a 'positive' test in each case?

SKILLS REASONING

6th

b The tests showed that glucose was present in the water, but starch was not. Explain why.

5th

c If the tubing takes the place of the intestine, what part of the body does the water in the boiling tube represent?

SKILLS CRITICAL THINKING

6th

d What does 'digested' mean?

SKILLS DECISION MAKING

4th

6 A student carried out an experiment to find out the best conditions for the enzyme pepsin to digest protein. For the protein, she used egg white powder, which forms a cloudy white suspension in water. The table below shows how the four tubes were set up.

Tube	Contents
A	5 cm^3 egg white suspension, 2 cm^3 pepsin, 3 drops of dilute acid. Tube kept at 37 °C
B	5 cm^3 egg white suspension, 2 cm^3 distilled water, 3 drops of dilute acid. Tube kept at 37 °C
C	5 cm^3 egg white suspension, 2 cm^3 pepsin, 3 drops of dilute acid. Tube kept at 20 °C
D	5 cm^3 egg white suspension, 2 cm^3 pepsin, 3 drops of dilute alkali. Tube kept at 37 °C

The tubes were left for 2 hours and the results were then observed. Tubes B, C and D were still cloudy. Tube A had gone clear.

a Three tubes were kept at 37 °C. Why was this temperature chosen?

SKILLS REASONING

6th

b Explain what had happened to the protein in tube A.

7th

c Why did tube D stay cloudy?

SKILLS CRITICAL THINKING

5th

d Tube B is called a **Control**. Explain what this means.

SKILLS REASONING

8th

e Tube C was left for another 3 hours. Gradually it started to clear. Explain why digestion of the protein happened more slowly in this tube.

SKILLS CRITICAL THINKING

5th

f The lining of the stomach secretes hydrochloric acid. Explain the function of this.

4th

g When the stomach contents pass into the duodenum, they are still acidic. How are they neutralised?

6th

7 Copy and complete the following table of digestive enzymes.

Enzyme	Food on which it acts	Products
amylase		
trypsin		
		fatty acids and glycerol

7th

8 Describe four adaptations of the small intestine (ileum) that allow it to absorb digested food efficiently.

SKILLS CRITICAL THINKING, CREATIVITY

9th

9 Bread is made mainly of starch, protein and lipid. Imagine a piece of bread about to start its journey through the human gut. Describe what happens to the bread as it passes through the mouth, stomach, duodenum, ileum and colon. Explain how the bread is moved along the gut. Your description should be illustrated by two or three simplified diagrams.

5 BLOOD AND CIRCULATION

Large, multicellular animals need a circulatory system to transport substances to and from the cells of the body. This chapter looks at the structure and function of the circulatory systems of humans and other animals, the composition of mammalian blood, and disorders associated with the heart and circulation.

LEARNING OBJECTIVES

- Understand why simple unicellular organisms can rely on diffusion for movement of substances in and out of the cell
- Understand the need for a transport system in multicellular organisms
- Understand the general structure of the circulation system, including the blood vessels to and from the heart and lungs, liver and kidneys
- Describe the structure of the heart and how it functions
- Understand how factors may increase the risk of developing coronary heart disease
- Explain how the heart rate changes during exercise and under the influence of adrenaline
- Understand how the structures of arteries, veins and capillaries relate to their functions
- Describe the composition of blood: red blood cells, white blood cells, platelets and plasma
- Understand the role of plasma in the transport of carbon dioxide, digested food, urea, hormones and heat energy
- Understand how the adaptations of red blood cells make them suitable for the transport of oxygen, including shape, the absence of a nucleus and the presence of haemoglobin
- Understand how the immune system responds to infection using white blood cells, illustrated by phagocytes ingesting pathogens and lymphocytes releasing antibodies specific to the pathogen

THE NEED FOR CIRCULATORY SYSTEMS

Figure 5.1 shows the circulatory system of a mammal.

Blood is pumped around a closed circuit made up of the heart and blood vessels. As it travels around the body, it collects materials from some places and unloads them in others. In mammals, blood transports:

- oxygen from the lungs to all other parts of the body
- carbon dioxide from all parts of the body to the lungs
- nutrients from the gut to all parts of the body
- urea from the liver to the kidneys.

Hormones, antibodies and many other substances are also transported by the blood. It also distributes heat around the body.

Single-celled organisms, like the ones shown in Figure 5.2, do not have circulatory systems.

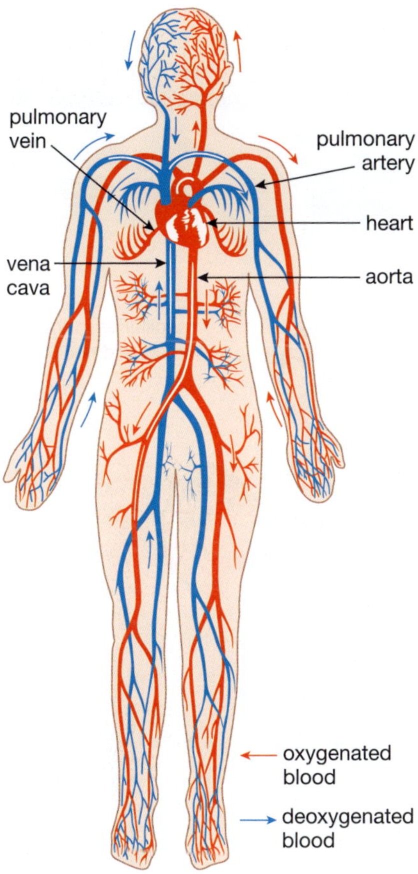

▲ Figure 5.1 The human circulatory system.

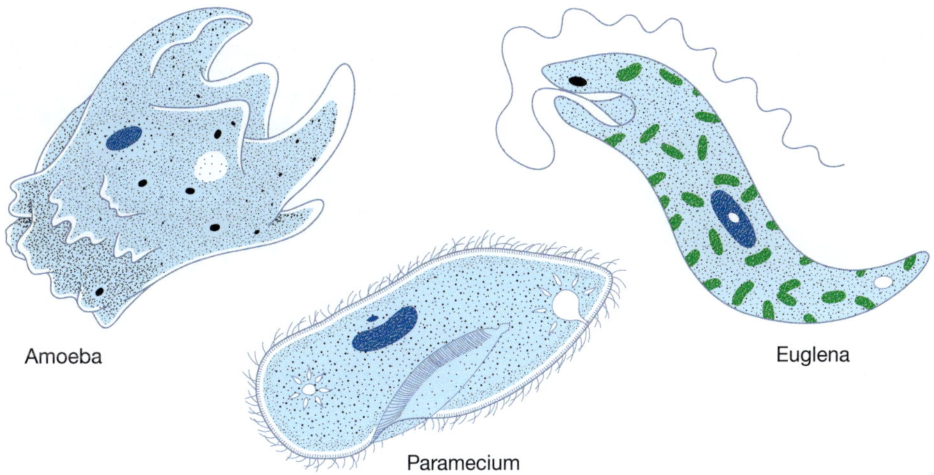

▲ Figure 5.2 Unicellular organisms do not have circulatory systems.

There is no circulatory system to carry materials around the very small 'bodies' of these single-celled organisms. Materials can easily move around the cell without a special system. There is no need for lungs or gills to obtain oxygen from the environment either. Single-celled organisms obtain oxygen by diffusion through the surface membrane of the cell. The rest of the cell then uses the oxygen. The area of the cell's surface determines how much oxygen the organism can get (the supply rate), and the volume of the cell determines how much oxygen the organism uses (the demand rate).

The ratio of supply to demand can be written as: $\frac{\text{surface area}}{\text{volume}}$

This is called the 'surface area to volume ratio' and it is affected by the size of an organism (see Chapter 1, Activity 4). Single-celled organisms have a high surface area to volume ratio. Their cell surface membrane has a large enough area to supply all the oxygen that their volume demands. In larger animals, the surface area to volume ratio is lower.

Large animals cannot get all the oxygen they need through their surface (even if the body surface would allow it to pass through) – there just isn't enough surface to supply all that volume. To overcome this problem, large organisms have evolved special gas exchange organs and circulatory systems. The gills of fish and the lungs of mammals are linked to a circulatory system that carries oxygen to all parts of the body. The same idea applies to obtaining nutrients – the gut obtains nutrients from food and the circulatory system distributes the nutrients around the body.

THE CIRCULATORY SYSTEMS OF DIFFERENT ANIMALS

One of the main functions of a circulatory system in animals is to transport oxygen. Blood is pumped to a gas exchange organ to load oxygen. It is then pumped to other parts of the body where it unloads the oxygen. There are two main types of circulatory systems in animals.

- In a **single circulatory** system the blood is pumped from the heart to the gas exchange organ and then directly to the rest of the body.
- In a **double circulatory** system the blood is pumped from the heart to the gas exchange organ, back to the heart and then to the rest of the body.

Figure 5.3 shows the difference between these systems.

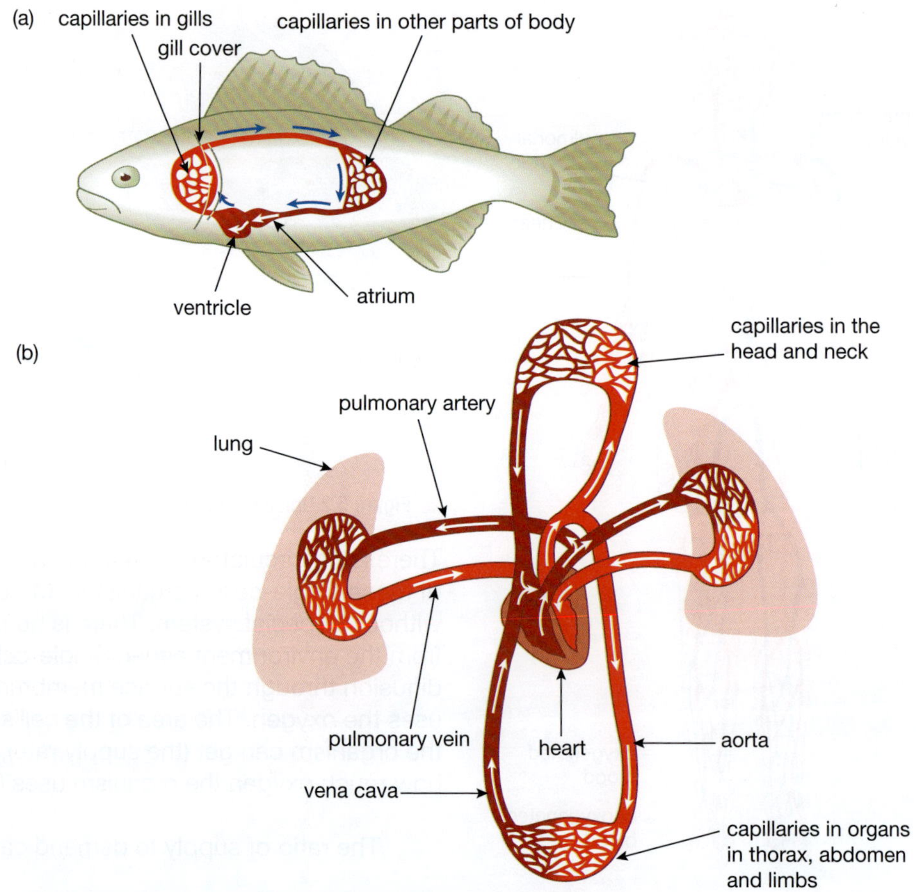

▲ Figure 5.3 (a) The single circulatory system of a fish. The blood passes through the heart only once in a complete circuit of the body. (b) The double circulatory system of a human (and other mammals). The blood passes through the heart twice in one complete circuit of the body.

There are two parts to a double circulatory system:

- The **pulmonary circulation**. Deoxygenated blood leaves the heart through the pulmonary arteries, and is circulated through the lungs, where it becomes oxygenated. The oxygenated blood returns to the heart through the pulmonary veins.
- The **systemic circulation**. Oxygenated blood leaves the heart through the aorta and is circulated through all other parts of the body, where it unloads its oxygen. Deoxygenated blood returns to the heart through the vena cava.

A double circulatory system is more efficient than a single circulatory system. The heart pumps the blood twice, so higher pressures can be maintained. The blood travels more quickly to organs. In the single circulatory system of a fish, blood loses pressure as it passes through the gills. It then travels more slowly to the other organs.

The human circulatory system comprises:

- the heart – this is a pump
- blood vessels – these carry the blood around the body; **arteries** carry blood away from the heart and towards other organs, **veins** carry blood towards the heart and away from other organs and **capillaries** carry blood through organs, linking the arteries and veins
- blood – the transport medium.

Figure 5.4 shows the main blood vessels in the human circulatory system.

KEY POINT

'Pulmonary' means 'relating to the lungs'.

DID YOU KNOW?

There are actually two vena cavae (the plural of vena cava). One brings blood back from the head and arms and the other returns blood from the rest of the body (see Figure 5.4).

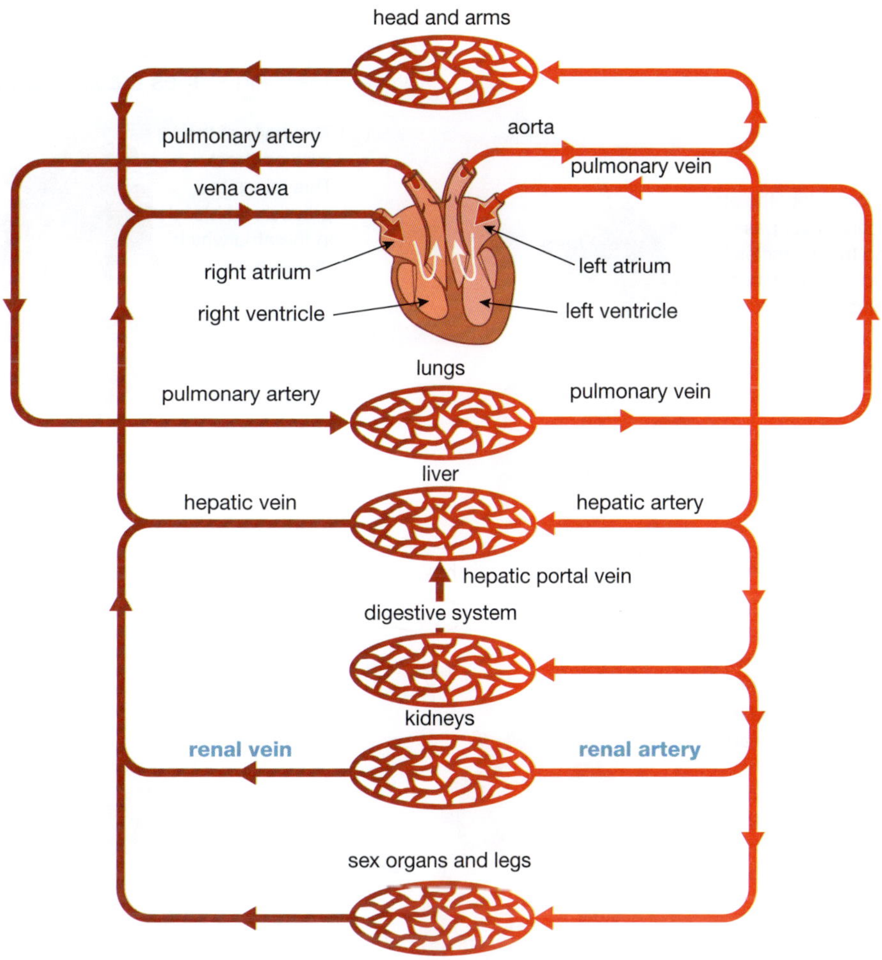

Figure 5.4 The main components of the human circulatory system

THE STRUCTURE AND FUNCTION OF THE HUMAN HEART

> **DID YOU KNOW?**
> 'Cardiac' means 'related to the heart'.

> **DID YOU KNOW?**
> The **bicuspid** (mitral) and **tricuspid valves** are both sometimes called atrioventricular valves, as each controls the passage of blood from an atrium to a ventricle.

The human heart is a pump (Figure 5.5). It pumps blood around the body at different speeds and at different pressures according to the body's needs.

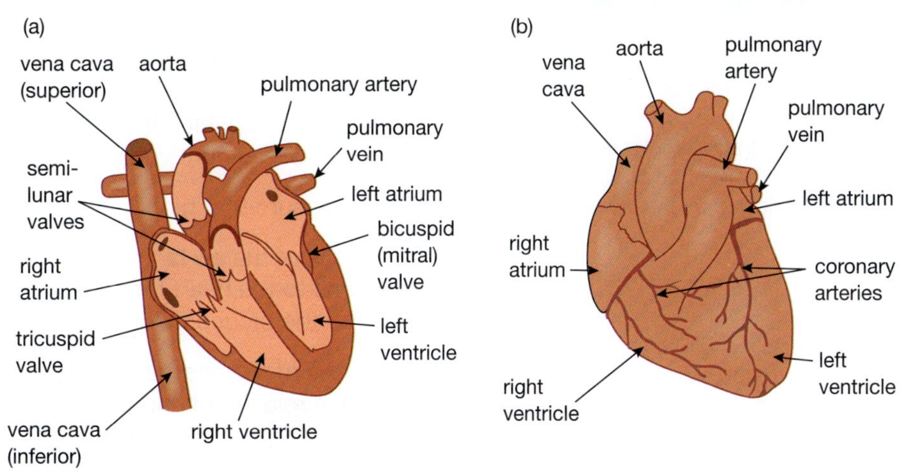

Figure 5.5 The human heart: (a) vertical section; (b) external view

Blood is moved through the heart by a series of contractions and relaxations of the muscle in the walls of the four chambers. These events form the **cardiac cycle**. The main stages are illustrated in Figure 5.6.

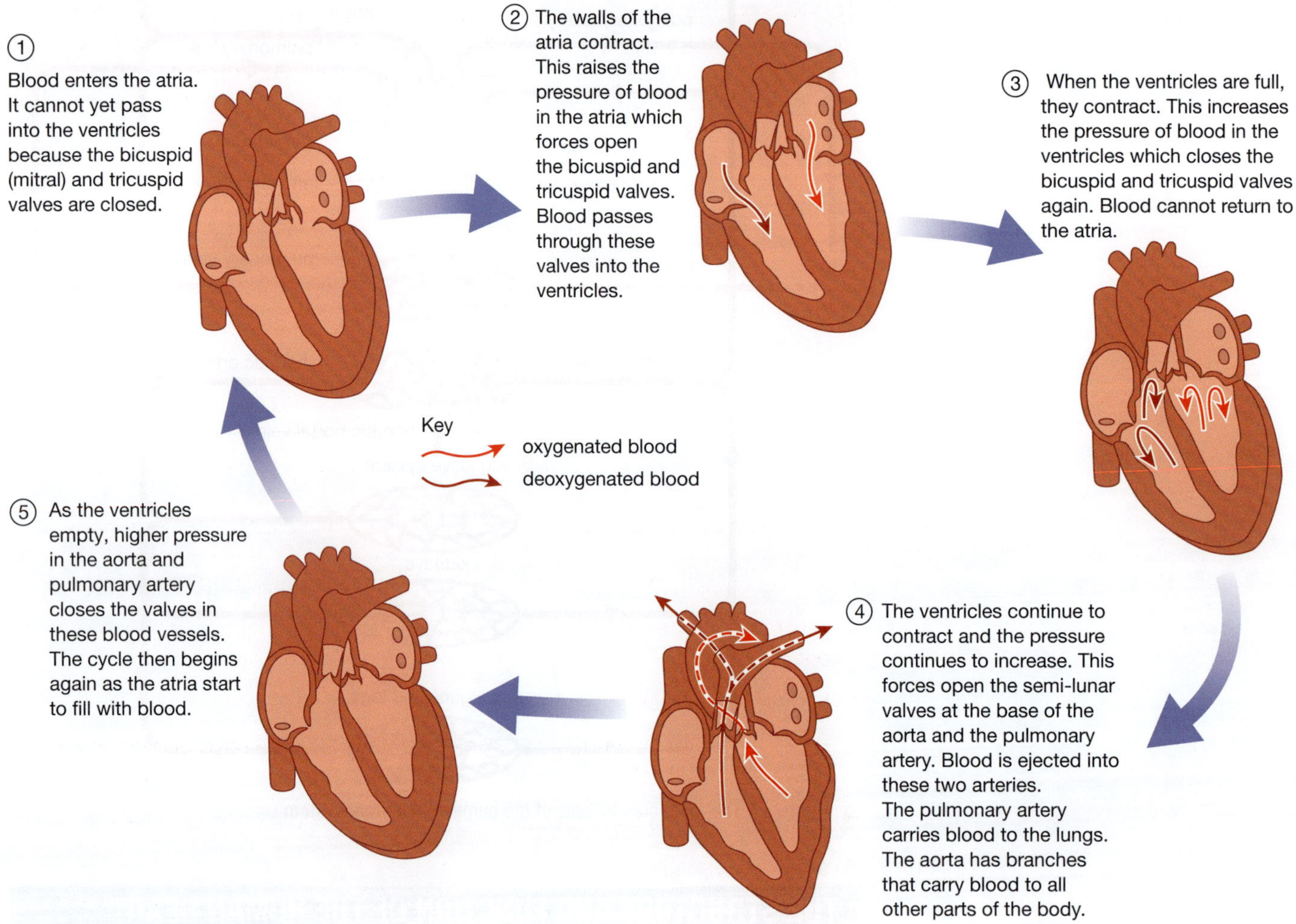

▲ Figure 5.6 The cardiac cycle.

HINT

Note that during the cardiac cycle both atria contract at the same time (and then relax). After this both ventricles contract at the same time (and then relax). Students are sometimes confused about this, and think that one ventricle contracts, followed by the other.

KEY POINT

Cardiac muscle is unlike any other muscle in our bodies. It never gets fatigued ('tired') like skeletal muscle. On average, cardiac muscle fibres contract and then relax again about 70 times a minute. In a lifetime of 70 years, this special muscle will contract over two billion times – without taking a rest!

The structure of the heart is adapted to its function in several ways:

- It is divided into a left side and a right side by a wall of muscle called the septum. The right **ventricle** pumps blood only to the lungs while the left ventricle pumps blood to all other parts of the body. This requires much more pressure, which is why the wall of the left ventricle is much thicker than that of the right ventricle.
- Valves ensure that blood can flow only in one direction through the heart.
- The walls of the **atria** are thin. They can be stretched to receive blood as it returns to the heart but can contract with enough force to push blood through the bicuspid and tricuspid valves into the ventricles.
- The walls of the heart are made of **cardiac muscle**, which can contract and then relax continuously without becoming fatigued.
- The cardiac muscle has its own blood supply – the coronary circulation. Blood reaches the muscle via **coronary arteries**. These carry blood to capillaries that supply the heart muscle with oxygen and nutrients. Blood is returned to the right atrium via **coronary veins**.

CORONARY HEART DISEASE

The coronary arteries are among the narrowest in the body. They are easily blocked by a build-up of fatty substances (including **cholesterol**) in their walls. This can cut off the blood supply to an area of cardiac muscle. The affected muscle can no longer receive oxygen and glucose, so it cannot respire and release energy. This means it is unable to contract, resulting in a heart attack. This is called **coronary heart disease (CHD)**. It can lead to severe health problems and is often fatal.

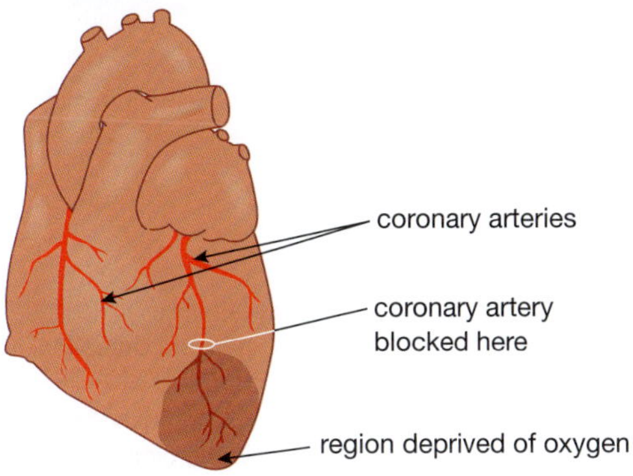

▲ Figure 5.7 A blockage of a coronary artery cuts off the blood supply to part of the heart muscle.

A number of factors make coronary heart disease more likely:

- heredity – some people inherit a tendency to develop coronary heart disease
- high blood pressure – puts more strain on the heart
- diet – eating large amounts of saturated fat is likely to raise cholesterol levels
- smoking – raises blood pressure and makes blood clots more likely to form
- stress – raises blood pressure
- lack of exercise – regular exercise helps to reduce blood pressure and strengthens the heart.

HEART RATE

Normally the heart beats about 70 times a minute, but this can change according to the needs of the body. When we exercise, muscles must release more energy. They need an increased supply of oxygen for aerobic respiration (see Chapter 1). To deliver the extra oxygen, both the number of beats per minute (heart rate) and the volume of blood pumped with each beat (called stroke volume) increase.

When we are angry or afraid our heart rate again increases. The increased output supplies extra blood to the muscles, enabling them to release extra energy through aerobic respiration. This allows us to fight or run away and is called the 'fight or flight' response. It is triggered by **secretion** of the hormone **adrenaline** from the adrenal glands (see Chapter 7).

When we sleep, our heart rate decreases as all our organs are working more slowly. They need to release less energy and so need less oxygen.

These changes in the heart rate are controlled by nerve impulses from a part of the brain called the **medulla** (Figure 5.8). When we start to

DID YOU KNOW?

Have you noticed a 'hollow' or 'fluttering' feeling in your stomach when you are anxious? It happens because blood that would normally flow to your stomach and intestines has been diverted to the muscles to allow the 'fight or flight' response.

exercise, our muscles produce more carbon dioxide in aerobic respiration. Receptors in the aorta and the carotid **artery** (the artery leading to the head) detect this increase. They send electrical signals called nerve impulses through the sensory nerve to the medulla. The medulla responds by sending nerve impulses along the accelerator nerve. When carbon dioxide production returns to normal, the medulla receives fewer impulses. It responds by sending nerve impulses along a decelerator nerve.

KEY POINT

The precise region of the medulla that controls heart functions is called the **cardiac centre**.

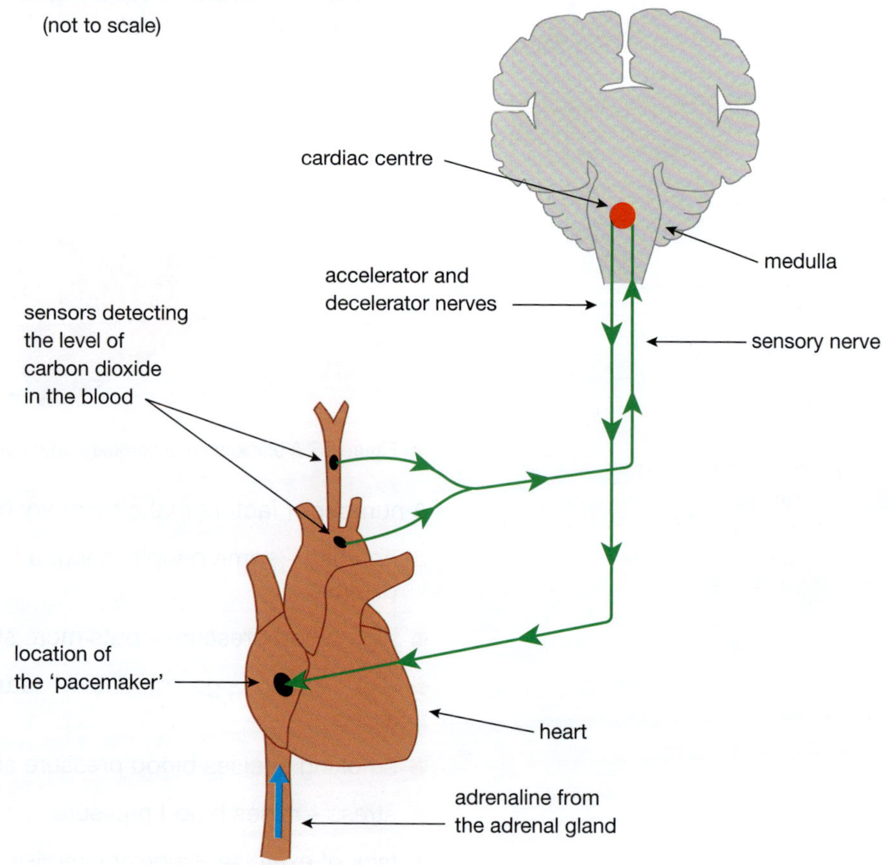

▲ Figure 5.8 How the heart rate is controlled.

The accelerator nerve increases the heart rate. It also causes the heart to beat with more force and so increases blood pressure. The decelerator nerve decreases the heart rate. It also reduces the force of the contractions. Blood pressure then returns to normal.

These controls are both examples of **reflex actions** (see Chapter 6).

ARTERIES, VEINS AND CAPILLARIES

Arteries carry blood from the heart to the organs of the body. This arterial blood is pumped out by the ventricles at a high pressure. Elastic tissue in the walls of the arteries allows them to stretch and recoil (spring back into shape), maintaining the high blood pressure. A thick muscular wall helps control the flow of blood by dilating (widening) or constricting (narrowing) the vessels.

Veins carry blood from organs back towards the heart. The pressure of this venous blood is much lower than that in the arteries. It puts very little pressure on the walls of the veins, so they can be thinner than those of arteries, and contain less elastic tissue and muscle. Figure 5.9 shows the structure of a typical artery and a typical vein with the same diameter.

EXTENSION WORK

Arterioles are small arteries. They carry blood into organs from arteries. Their structure is similar to the larger arteries, but they have a larger proportion of muscle fibres in their walls. They are also supplied with nerve endings in their walls and so can be made to dilate (become wider) or constrict (become narrower) to allow more or less blood into the organ.

If *all* the arterioles constrict, it is harder for blood to pass through them – there is more resistance. This increases blood pressure. Prolonged stress can cause arterioles to constrict and so increase blood pressure.

KEY POINT

All arteries carry oxygenated blood (blood containing a lot of oxygen) except the pulmonary artery and the umbilical artery of an unborn baby. All veins carry deoxygenated blood (blood containing less oxygen) except the pulmonary vein and umbilical vein.

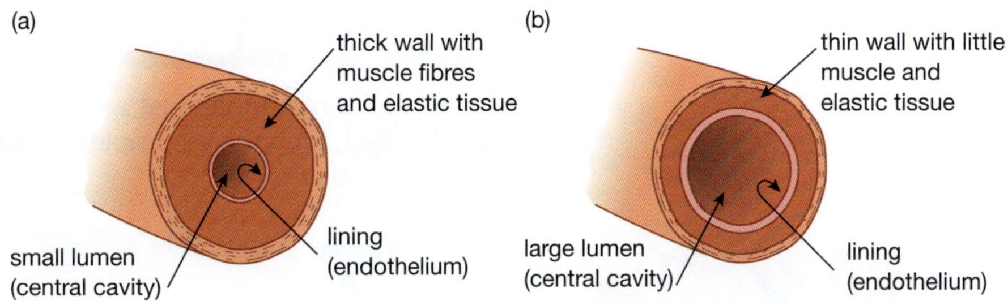

▲ Figure 5.9 The structure of (a) an artery and (b) a vein as seen in cross section.

Veins also have **semilunar** (half-moon shaped) **valves**, which prevent the backflow of blood. The action of these valves is explained in Figure 5.10.

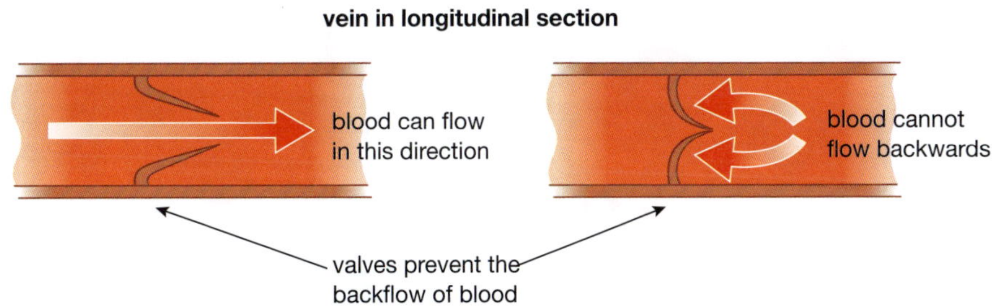

▲ Figure 5.10 The action of semilunar valves in veins

Capillaries carry blood through organs, bringing the blood close to every cell in the organ. Substances are transferred between the blood in the capillary and the cells. To do this, capillaries must be small enough to 'fit' between cells, and allow materials to pass through their walls easily. Figure 5.11 shows the structure of a capillary and how exchange of substances takes place between the capillary and nearby cells. The walls of capillaries are one cell thick, providing a short distance for diffusion of materials into and out of the blood. Red blood cells just fit through the tiny diameter of capillaries, so they are close to the capillary wall. This means that there is a short distance for oxygen to diffuse. Figure 5.12 shows a photograph of a cross-section through an artery and a vein.

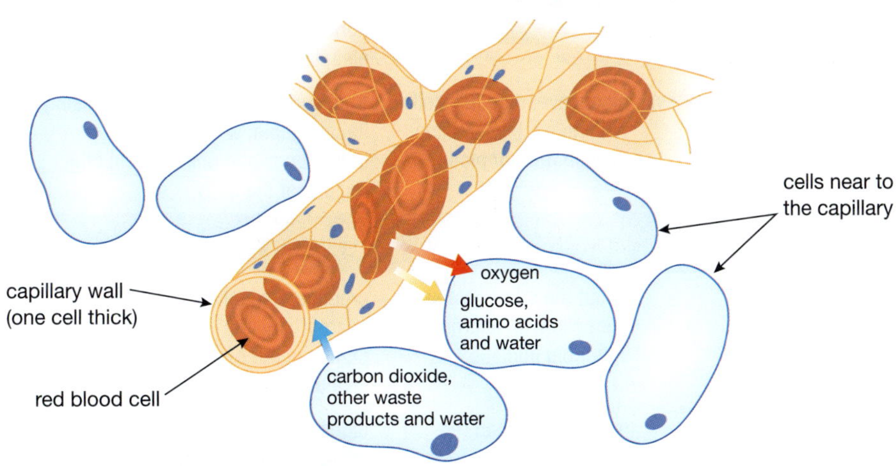

▲ Figure 5.11 How capillaries exchange materials with cells

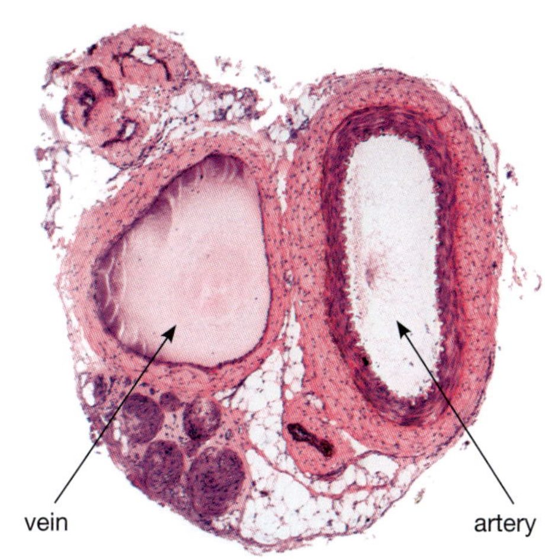

▲ Figure 5.12 The lumen of the artery is the same size as the lumen of the vein – but note the difference in the thickness of the walls of these two vessels.

THE COMPOSITION OF BLOOD

Blood is a lot more than just a red liquid flowing through your arteries and veins! In fact, blood is a complex tissue. Figure 5.13 illustrates the main types of cells found in blood.

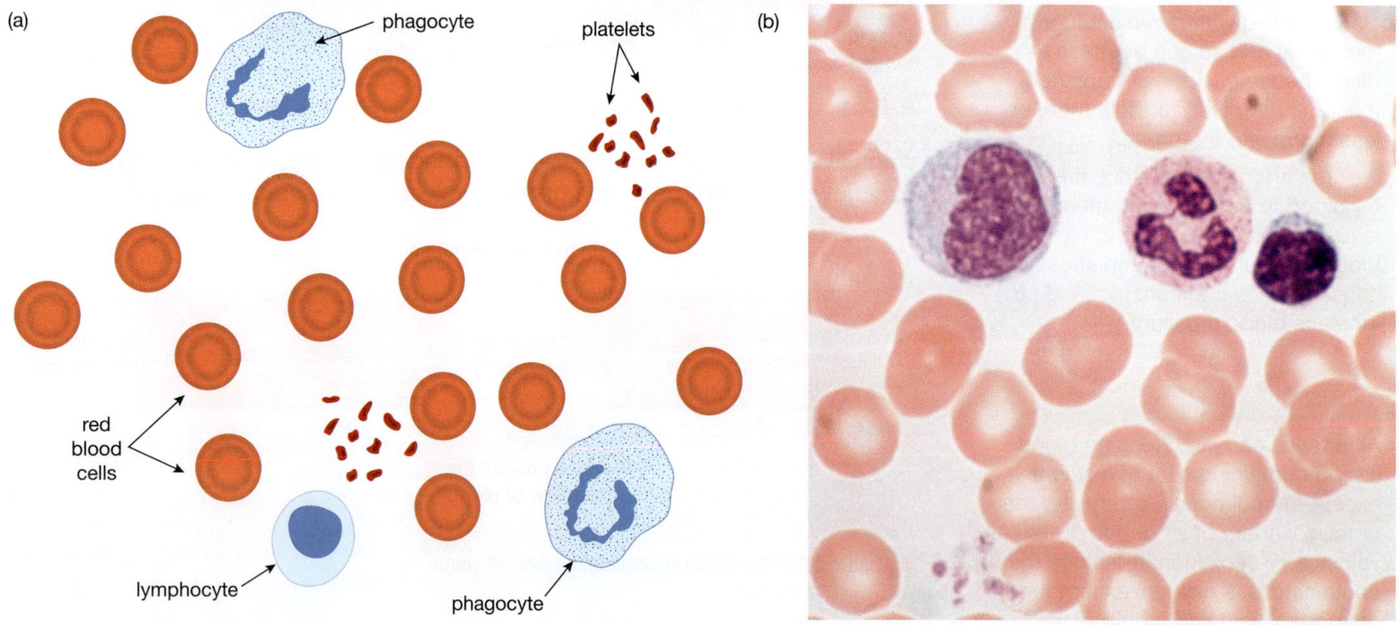

▲ Figure 5.13 The different types of blood cells. (a) Diagram of the different cells. (b) A blood smear seen through a light microscope. The smear shows many red blood cells and three different kinds of white blood cell.

The different parts of blood have different functions. These are described in Table 5.1.

Table 5.1 Functions of the different components of blood.

COMPONENT OF BLOOD	DESCRIPTION OF COMPONENT	FUNCTION OF COMPONENT
plasma	liquid part of blood: mainly water	carries the blood cells around the body; carries dissolved nutrients, hormones, carbon dioxide and urea; also distributes heat around the body
red blood cells (erythrocytes)	biconcave, disc-like cells with no nucleus; millions in each mm^3 of blood	transport of oxygen – contain mainly haemoglobin, which loads oxygen in the lungs and unloads it in other regions of the body
WHITE BLOOD CELLS:		
lymphocytes	about the same size as red cells with a large spherical nucleus	produce antibodies to destroy microorganisms – some lymphocytes persist in our blood after infection and give us immunity to specific diseases
phagocytes	much larger than red cells, with a large spherical or lobed nucleus	digest and destroy bacteria and other microorganisms that have infected our bodies
platelets	the smallest cells – are really fragments of other cells	release chemicals to make blood clot when we cut ourselves

RED BLOOD CELLS

The red blood cells or **erythrocytes** are highly specialised cells made in the bone marrow. They have a limited life span of about 100 days after which time they are destroyed in the spleen. They have only one function – to transport oxygen. Several features enable them to carry out this function very efficiently.

Red blood cells contain **haemoglobin**. This is an iron-containing protein that associates (combines) with oxygen to form **oxyhaemoglobin** when there is a high concentration of oxygen in the surroundings. We say that the red blood cell is loading oxygen. When the concentration of oxygen is low, oxyhaemoglobin turns back into haemoglobin and the red blood cell unloads its oxygen.

As red blood cells pass through the lungs, they load oxygen. As they pass through active tissues they unload oxygen.

$$\text{haemoglobin} + \text{oxygen} \underset{\text{in the tissues}}{\overset{\text{in the lungs}}{\rightleftharpoons}} \text{oxyhaemoglobin}$$

Red blood cells do not contain a nucleus. It is lost during their development in the bone marrow. This means that more haemoglobin can be packed into each red blood cell so more oxygen can be transported. Their biconcave shape allows efficient exchange of oxygen in and out of the cell. Each red blood cell has a high surface area to volume ratio, giving a large area for diffusion. The thin shape of the cell results in a short diffusion distance to the centre of the cell.

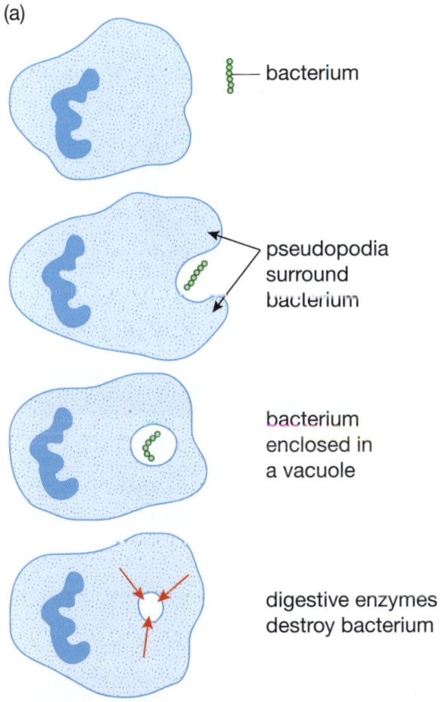

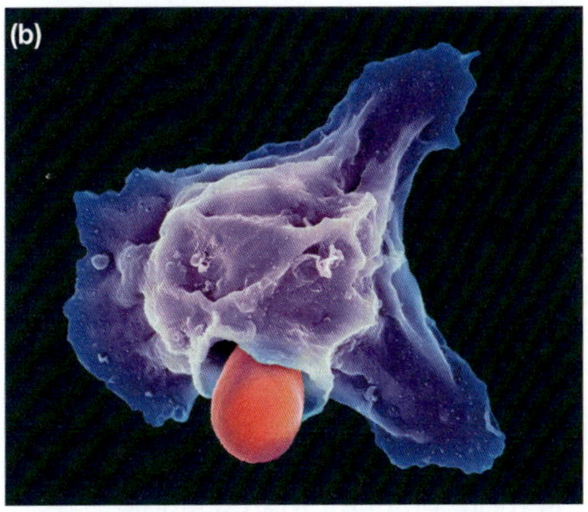

▲ Figure 5.14 (a) Phagocytosis by a white blood cell. (b) A phagocyte engulfing a pathogenic microorganism (a species of yeast).

WHITE BLOOD CELLS

There are several types of white blood cell. Their main role is to protect the body against invasion by disease-causing microorganisms (pathogens), such as bacteria and viruses. They do this in two main ways: **phagocytosis** and production of **antibodies**.

About 70% of white blood cells can ingest (take in) microorganisms such as bacteria. This is called phagocytosis, and the cells are **phagocytes**. They do this by changing their shape, producing extensions of their cytoplasm, called pseudopodia. The pseudopodia surround and enclose the microorganism in a vacuole. Once it is inside, the phagocyte secretes enzymes into the vacuole to break the microorganism down (Figure 5.14). Phagocytosis means 'cell eating' – you can see why it is called this.

Approximately 25% of white blood cells are **lymphocytes**. Their function is to make chemicals called antibodies. Antibodies are soluble proteins that pass into the plasma. Pathogens such as bacteria and viruses have chemical 'markers' on their surfaces, which the antibodies recognise. These markers are called **antigens**. The antibodies stick to the surface antigens and destroy the pathogen. They do this in a number of ways, for example by:

- causing bacteria to stick together, so that phagocytes can ingest them more easily
- acting as a 'label' on the pathogen, so that it is more easily recognised by a phagocyte
- causing bacterial cells to burst open
- neutralising poisons (toxins) produced by pathogens.

The production of antibodies following the first exposure to a foreign antigen is called the primary **immune response**.

CHAPTER QUESTIONS

More questions on blood and circulation can be found at the end of Unit 2 on page 116.

SKILLS CRITICAL THINKING

6th

1 After a period of exercise, which blood vessel will contain the highest concentration of carbon dioxide?

A aorta
B vena cava
C hepatic artery
D pulmonary vein

2 When the right ventricle contracts, to which of the following structures does the blood flow next?

A aorta
B left atrium
C pulmonary artery
D left ventricle

3 The diagram below shows sections through three blood vessels (not drawn to scale).

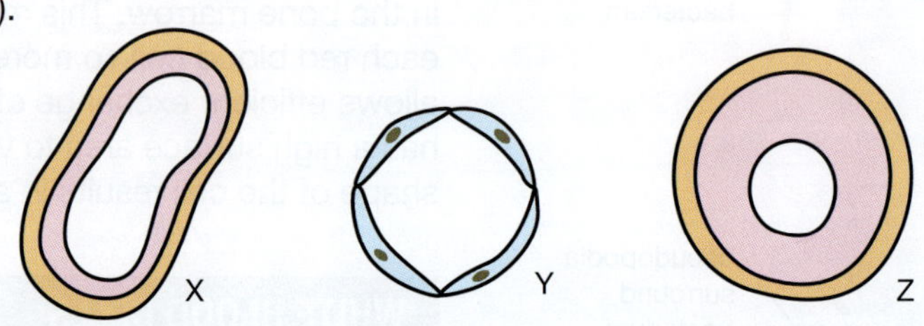

Which row in the table shows the correct names of vessels X, Y and Z?

	X	Y	Z
A	vein	capillary	artery
B	artery	capillary	vein
C	vein	artery	capillary
D	capillary	vein	artery

5th

4 Which component of the blood makes antibodies?

A red blood cells
B white blood cells
C plasma
D platelets

6th

5 Some animals have a single circulatory system, some have a double circulatory system and some organisms have no circulatory system at all.

a Name one type of animal with a single circulatory system and one type of animal with a double circulatory system.

b Explain:

SKILLS REASONING

i the difference between single and double circulatory systems

7th

ii why a double circulatory system is more efficient than a single circulatory system.

6th

c Explain why single-celled organisms do not need a circulatory system.

SKILLS CRITICAL THINKING

6th

6 Blood transports oxygen and carbon dioxide around the body. Oxygen is transported by the red blood cells.

a Give three ways in which a red blood cell is adapted to its function of transporting oxygen.

b Describe how oxygen:

5th

i enters a red blood cell from the alveoli in the lungs

ii passes from a red blood cell to an actively respiring muscle cell.

6th

c Describe how carbon dioxide is transported around the body.

SKILLS REASONING

7 Blood is carried around the body in arteries, veins and capillaries.

a Describe two ways in which the structure of an artery is adapted to its function.

b Describe three differences between arteries and veins.

c Describe two ways in which the structure of a capillary is adapted to its function.

SKILLS ANALYSIS

8 The diagram shows a section through a human heart.

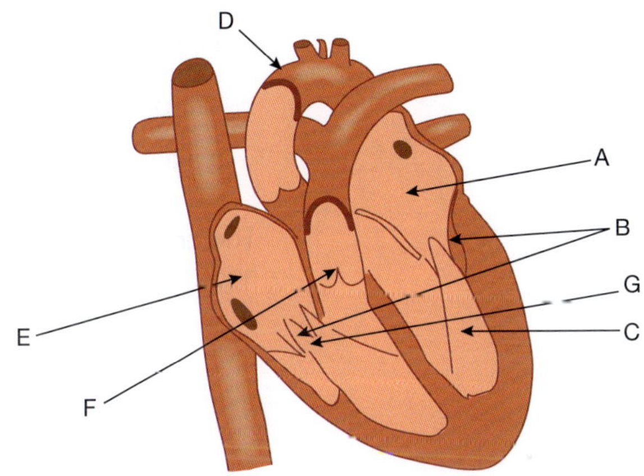

4th

a Name the structures labelled A, B, C, D and E.

SKILLS CRITICAL THINKING

6th

b What is the importance of the structures labelled B and F?

SKILLS ANALYSIS

5th

c Which letters represent the chambers of the heart to which blood returns:

i from the lungs

ii from all the other organs of the body?

9 The diagram shows three types of cells found in human blood.

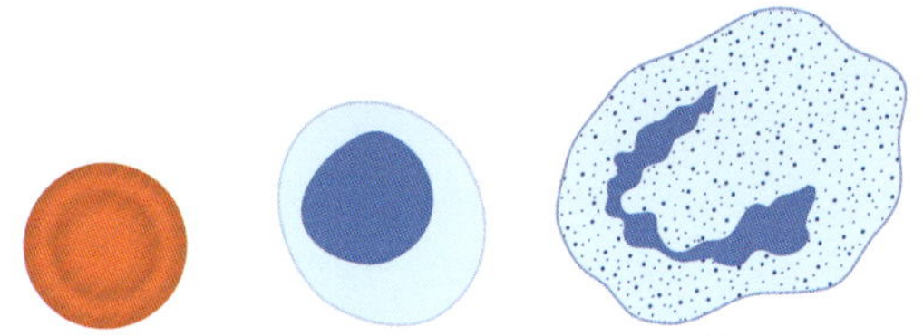

a Giving a reason for each answer, identify the blood cell which:

i transports oxygen around the body

ii produces antibodies to destroy bacteria

iii engulfs and digests bacteria.

SKILLS CRITICAL THINKING

b Name one other component of blood found in the plasma and state its function.

SKILLS ANALYSIS 6th

10 The graph shows changes in a person's heart rate over a period of time.

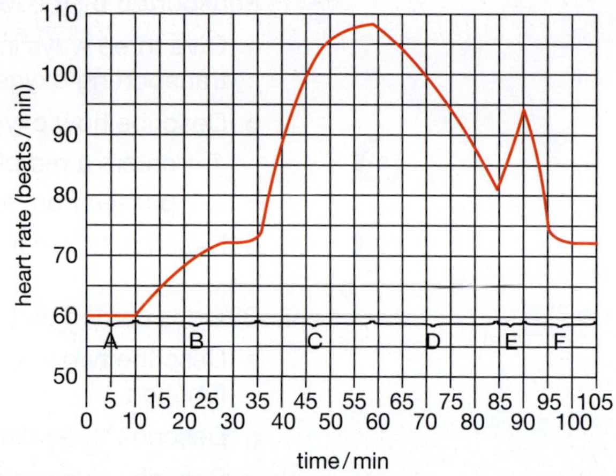

Giving reasons for your answers, give the letter of the time period when the person was:

a running

b frightened by a sudden loud noise

c sleeping

d waking.

11 The graph shows the changes that take place in heart rate before, during and after a period of exercise.

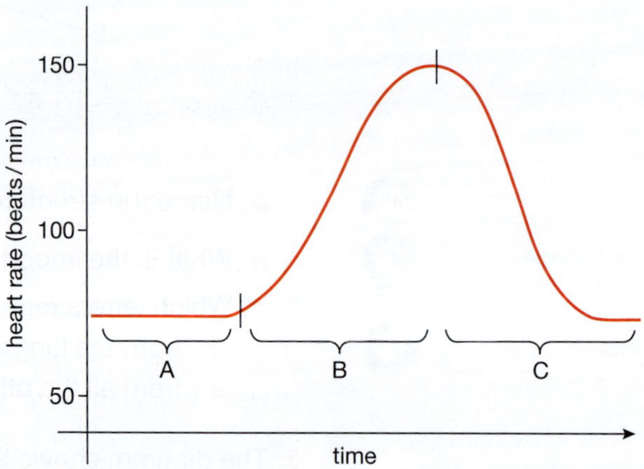

a Describe and explain the heart rates found:

- **i** at rest, before exercise (period A)
- **ii** as the person commences the exercise (period B)
- **iii** as the person recovers from the exercise (period C).

SKILLS REASONING 7th

b How can the recovery period (period C) be used to assess a person's fitness?

6 COORDINATION

In the body 'coordination' means making things happen at the right time by linking up different body activities. Humans and other animals have two organ systems which do this. The first is the nervous system, which is the subject of this chapter. The second is the hormone or endocrine system, which is dealt with in Chapter 7.

LEARNING OBJECTIVES

- Understand how organisms are able to respond to changes in their environment
- Understand that a coordinated response requires a stimulus, a receptor and an effector
- Understand that the central nervous system consists of the brain and spinal cord and is linked to sense organs by nerves
- Describe how the nervous system controls responses
- Understand how stimulation of receptors in the sense organs sends electrical impulses along nerves into and out of the central nervous system, resulting in rapid responses
- Describe the structure and function of the eye as a receptor
- Understand the function of the eye in focusing on near and distant objects, and in responding to changes in light intensity
- Describe the structure and functioning of a simple reflex arc, illustrated by the withdrawal of a finger from a hot object
- Understand the role of neurotransmitters at synapses

STIMULUS AND RESPONSE

Suppose you are walking along when you see a football coming at high speed towards your head. If your nerves are working properly, you will probably move or duck quickly to avoid contact. Imagine another situation where you are very hungry, and you smell food cooking. Your mouth might begin to 'water', in other words secrete saliva.

KEY POINT

The surroundings outside the body are called the *external* environment. The inside of the body is known as the *internal* environment. The body also responds to changes in its internal environment, such as temperature and blood glucose levels. You will read about these responses in Chapters 7 and 8.

Each of these situations is an example of a **stimulus** and a **response**. A *stimulus* is a change in an animal's surroundings, and a *response* is a reaction to that change. In the first example, the approaching ball was the stimulus, and your movement to avoid it hitting you was the response. The change in your environment was detected by your eyes, which are an example of a **receptor** organ. The response was brought about by contraction of muscles, which are a type of **effector** organ (they produce an effect). The nervous system links the two, and is an example of a coordination system. A summary of the sequence of events is:

stimulus → receptor → coordination → effector → response

In the second example, the receptor for the smell of food was the nose, and the response was the secretion of saliva from glands. Glands secrete (release) chemical substances, and they are the second type of effector organ. Again, the link between the stimulus and the response is the nervous system. The information in the nerve cells is transmitted in the form of tiny electrical signals called **nerve impulses**.

DID YOU KNOW?

Some animals can detect changes in their environment that are not sensed by humans. Insects such as bees can see ultraviolet (UV) light. The wavelengths of UV are invisible to humans (Figure 6.1).

▲ Figure 6.1 This yellow flower (a) looks very different to a bee, which sees patterns on the petals reflecting UV light (b).

Some organisms can even detect the direction of magnetic fields. Many birds, such as pigeons, have a built-in compass in their brain, which they use for navigation. A species of bacterium can also do this, but as yet no one can explain why this might be an advantage to it!

RECEPTORS

The role of any receptor is to detect the stimulus by changing its energy into the electrical energy of the nerve impulses. For example, the eye converts light energy into nerve impulses, and the ear converts sound energy into nerve impulses (Table 6.1).

Table 6.1 Human receptors and the energy they receive.

Receptor	Type of energy received
eye (retina)	light
ear (organ of hearing)	sound
ear (organ of balance)	mechanical (kinetic)
tongue (taste buds)	chemical
nose (organ of smell)	chemical
skin (touch/pressure/pain receptors)	mechanical (kinetic)
skin (temperature receptors)	heat
muscle (stretch receptors)	mechanical (kinetic)

Notice how a 'sense' like touch is made up of several components. When we touch a warm surface we will be stimulating several types of receptor, including touch and temperature receptors, as well as stretch receptors in the muscles (see the section on skin in Chapter 8). As well as this, each sense detects different aspects of the energy it receives. For example, the ears don't just detect sounds, but different loudness and frequencies of sound, while the eye not only forms an image, but also detects brightness of light and in humans can tell the difference between different light wavelengths (colours). Senses tell us a great deal about changes in our environment.

THE CENTRAL NERVOUS SYSTEM

The biological name for a nerve cell is a **neurone**. The impulses that travel along a neurone are not an electric current, as in a wire. They are caused by movements of charged particles (ions) in and out of the neurone. Impulses travel at speeds between about 10 and 100 metres per second, which is much slower than an electric current, but fast enough to produce a rapid response (see the 'Looking ahead' feature at the end of this chapter).

Impulses from receptors pass along nerves containing **sensory neurones**, until they reach the brain and spinal cord. These two organs are together known as the **central nervous system**, or **CNS** (Figure 6.2).

Other nerves contain **motor neurones**, transmitting impulses to the muscles and glands. Some nerves contain only sensory or motor cells, while other nerves contain both – they are 'mixed'. A typical nerve contains thousands of individual neurones.

DID YOU KNOW?

The CNS is well protected by the skeleton. The brain is inside the skull or cranium (nerves connected to the brain are *cranial* nerves) and the spinal cord runs down the middle of the spinal column, passing through a hole in each vertebra. Nerves connected to the spinal cord are called *spinal* nerves.

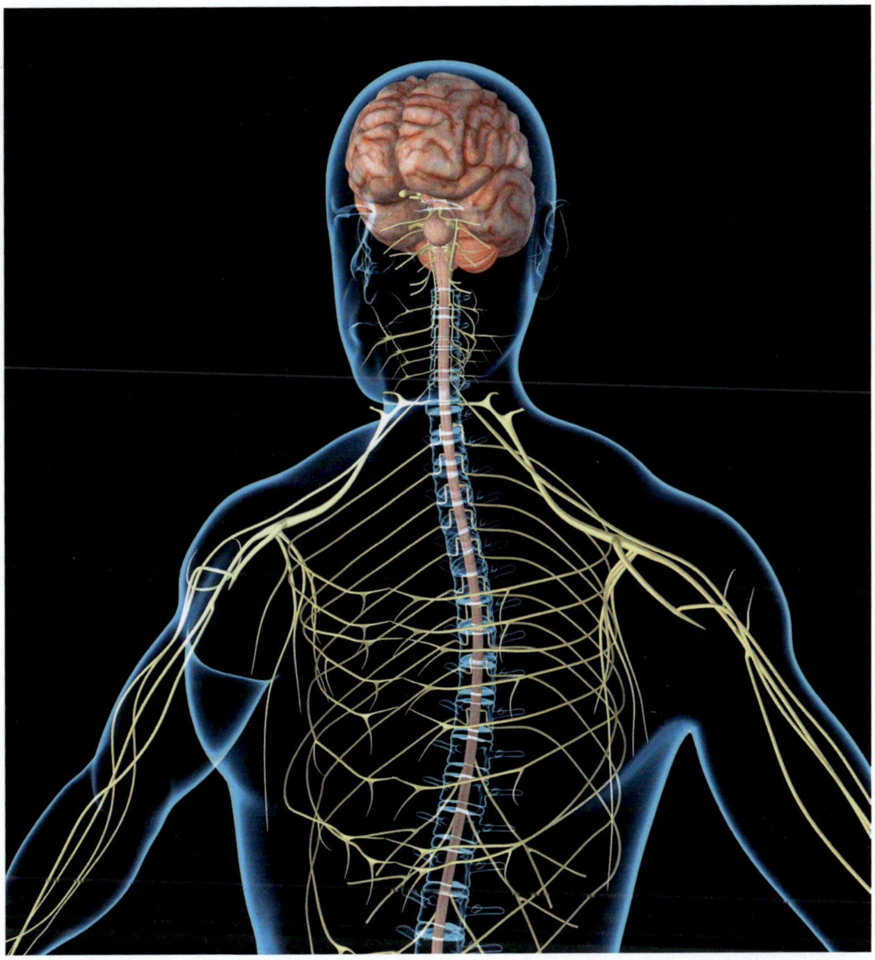

▲ Figure 6.2 The brain and spinal cord form the central nervous system. Cranial and spinal nerves lead to and from the CNS. The CNS sorts out information from the senses and sends messages to muscles.

THE STRUCTURE OF NEURONES

Both sensory and motor neurones can be very long. For example, a motor neurone leading from the CNS to the muscles in the finger has a fibre about a metre in length, which is 100 000 times the length of the cell body (Figure 6.3).

The cell body of a motor neurone is at one end of the fibre, in the CNS. The cell body has fine cytoplasmic extensions, called **dendrons**. These in turn form finer extensions, called **dendrites**. There can be junctions with other neurones on any part of the cell body, dendrons or dendrites. These junctions are called **synapses**. Later in this chapter we will deal with the importance of synapses in nerve pathways. One of the extensions from the motor neurone cell body is much longer than the other dendrons. This is the fibre that carries impulses to the effector organ, and is called the **axon**. At the end of the axon furthest from the cell body, it divides into many nerve endings. These fine branches of the axon connect with a muscle at a special sort of synapse called a **neuromuscular junction**. In this way impulses are carried from the CNS out to the muscle. The signals from nerve impulses are transmitted across the neuromuscular junction, causing the muscle fibres to contract. The axon is covered by a sheath made of a fatty material called myelin. The **myelin sheath** insulates the axon, preventing 'short circuits' with other axons, and also speeds up the conduction of the impulses. The sheath is formed by the membranes of special cells that wrap themselves around the axon as it develops.

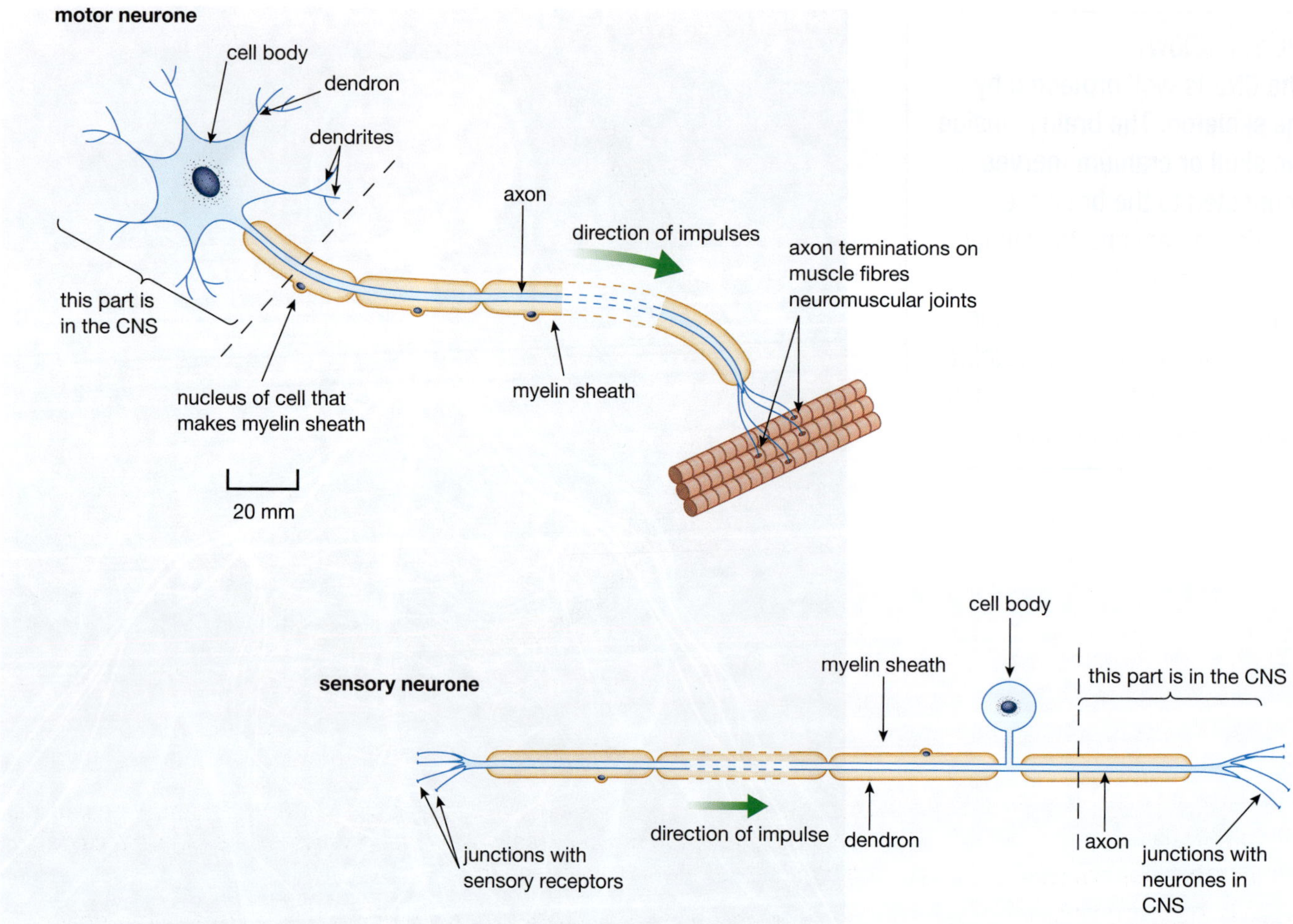

▲ Figure 6.3 The structure of motor and sensory neurones. The cell fibres (axon/dendron) are very long, which is indicated by the dashed sections.

A **sensory neurone** has a similar structure to the motor neurone, but the cell body is located on a side branch of the fibre, just outside the CNS. The fibre from the sensory receptor to the cell body is actually a dendron, while the fibre from the cell body to the CNS is a short axon. As with motor neurones, fibres of sensory neurones are often myelinated.

THE EYE

Many animals have eyes, but few show the complexity of the human eye. Simpler animals, such as snails, use their eyes to detect light but cannot form a proper image. Other animals, such as dogs, can form images but cannot distinguish colours. The human eye does all three. Of course it is not really the eye that 'sees' anything at all, but the brain that interprets the impulses from the eye. To find out how light from an object is converted into impulses representing an image, we need to look at the structure of this complex organ (Figure 6.4).

The tough outer coat of the eye is called the **sclera**, which is the visible, white part of the eye. At the front of the eye the sclera becomes a transparent 'window' called the **cornea**, which lets light into the eye. Behind the cornea is the coloured ring of tissue called the **iris**. In the middle of the iris is a hole called the **pupil**, which lets the light through. It is black because there is no light escaping from the inside of the eye.

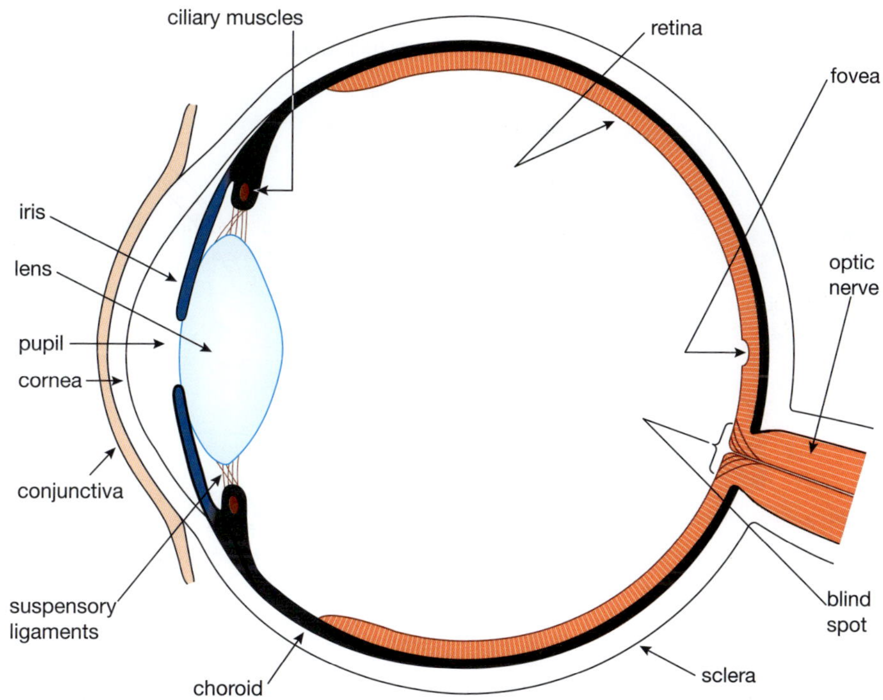

▲ Figure 6.4 A horizontal section through the human eye

Underneath the sclera is a dark layer called the **choroid**. It is dark because it contains many pigment cells, as well as blood vessels. The pigment stops light being reflected around inside the eye.

The innermost layer of the back of the eye is the **retina**. This is the light-sensitive layer, the place where light energy is converted into the electrical energy of nerve impulses. The retina contains receptor cells called **rods** and **cones**. These cells react to light, producing impulses in sensory neurones. The sensory neurones then pass the impulses to the brain through the **optic nerve**. Rod cells work well in dim light, but they cannot distinguish between different colours, so the brain 'sees' an image produced by the rods in black and white. This is why we can't see colours very well in dim light: only our rods are working properly. The cones, on the other hand, will only work in bright light, and there are three types which respond to different wavelengths or colours of light – red, green and blue. We can see all the colours of visible light as a result of these three types of cones being stimulated to different degrees. For example, if red, green and blue are stimulated equally, we see white. Both rods and cones are found throughout the retina, but cones are particularly concentrated at the centre of the retina, in an area called the **fovea**. Cones give a sharper image than rods, which is why we can only see objects clearly if we are looking directly at them, so that the image falls on the fovea.

DID YOU KNOW?

The fact that the inverted image is seen the right way up by the brain makes the point that it is the brain which 'sees' things, not the eye. An interesting experiment was carried out to test this. Volunteers were made to wear special inverting goggles for long periods. These turned the view of their surroundings upside down. At first this completely disorientated them, and they found it difficult to make even simple coordinated movements. However, after a while their brains adapted, until the view through the goggles looked normal. In fact, when the volunteers removed the goggles, the world then looked upside down!

FORMING AN IMAGE

To form an image on the retina, light needs to be bent or *refracted.* Refraction takes place when light passes from one medium to another of a different density. In the eye, this happens first at the air/cornea boundary, and again at the lens (Figure 6.5). In fact the cornea acts as the first lens of the eye.

As a result of refraction at the cornea and lens, the image on the retina is inverted (upside down). The brain interprets the image the right way up.

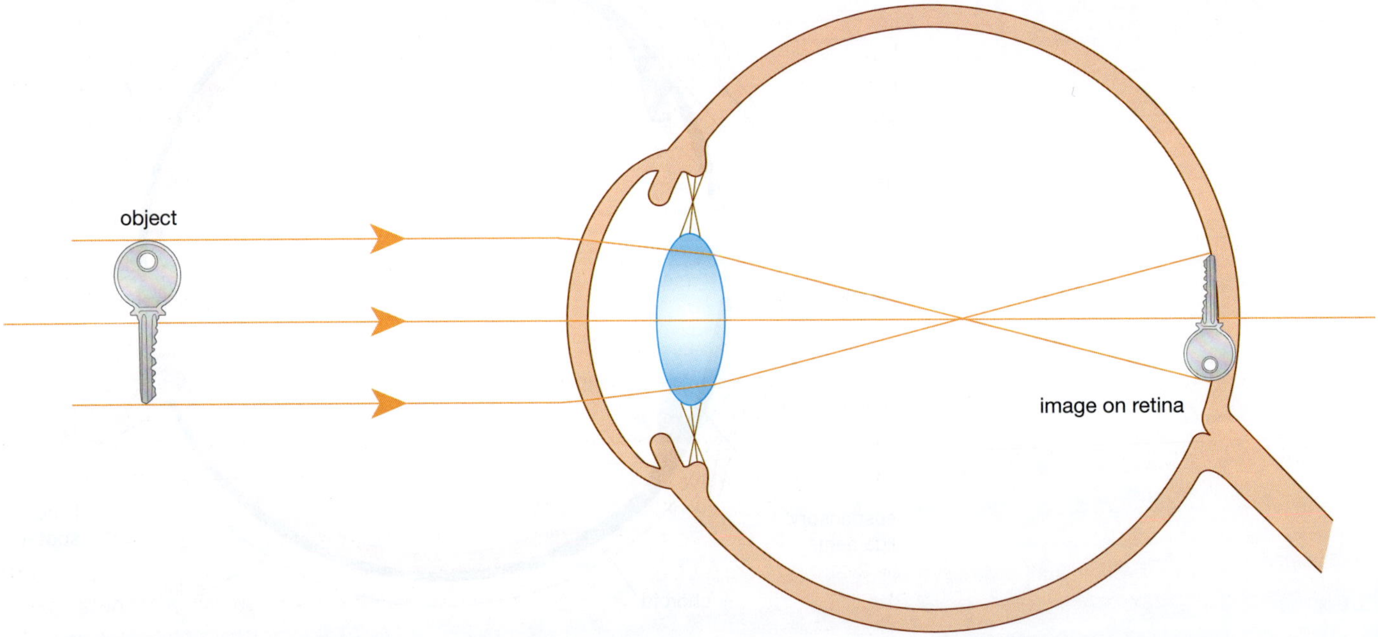

▲ Figure 6.5 How the eye forms an image. Refraction of light occurs at the cornea and lens, producing an inverted image on the retina.

THE IRIS REFLEX

The role of the iris is to control the amount of light entering the eye, by changing the size of the pupil. The iris contains two types of muscles. Circular muscles form a ring shape in the iris, and radial muscles lie like the spokes of a wheel. In bright light, the pupil is constricted (made smaller).

This happens because the circular muscles contract and the radial muscles relax. In dim light, the opposite happens. The radial muscles contract and the circular muscles relax, dilating (widening) the pupil (Figure 6.6).

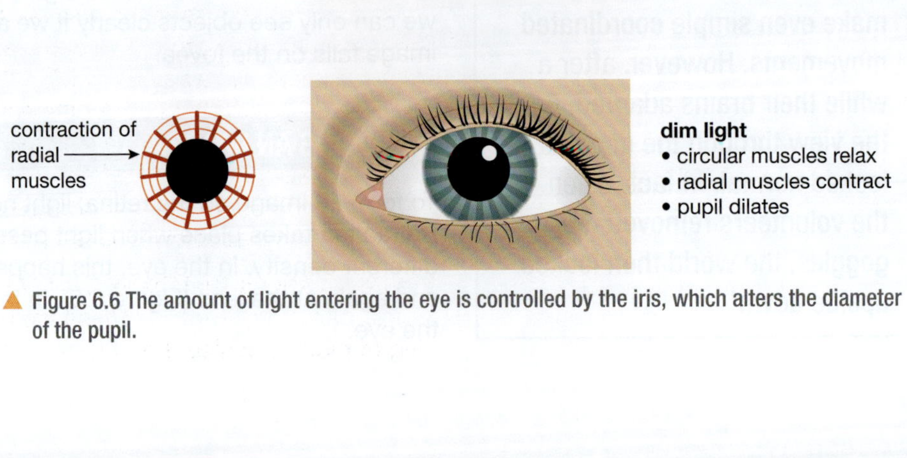

▲ Figure 6.6 The amount of light entering the eye is controlled by the iris, which alters the diameter of the pupil.

KEY POINT

In the iris reflex, the route from stimulus to response is this:

stimulus (light intensity)
↓
retina (receptor)
↓
sensory neurones in optic nerve
↓
unconscious part of brain
↓
motor neurones in nerve to iris
↓
iris muscles (effector)
↓
response (change in size of pupil)

Whenever our eyes look from a dim light to a bright one, the iris rapidly and automatically adjusts the pupil size. This is an example of a **reflex action**. You will find out more about reflexes later in this chapter. The purpose of the iris reflex is to allow the right intensity (brightness) of light to fall on the retina. Light that is too bright could damage the rods and cones, and light that is too dim would not form an image. The intensity of light hitting the retina is the stimulus for this reflex. Impulses pass to the brain through the optic nerve, and straight back to the iris muscles, adjusting the diameter of the pupil. It all happens without the need for conscious thought – in fact we are not even aware of it happening.

THE BLIND SPOT

There is one area of the retina where an image cannot be formed; this is where the optic nerve leaves the eye. At this position there are no rods or cones, so it is called the **blind spot**. The retina of each eye has a blind spot, but they are not a problem, because the brain puts the images from each eye together, cancelling out the blind spots of both eyes. As well as this, the optic nerve leaves the eye towards the edge of the retina, where vision is not very sharp anyway. To 'see' your own blind spot you can do a simple experiment. Cover or close your right eye. Hold this page about 30 cm from your eyes and look at the black dot below. Now, without moving the book or turning your head, read the numbers from left to right by moving your left eye slowly towards the right.

• 1 2 3 4 5 6 7 8 9 10 11 12 13 14 15

You should find that when the image of the dot falls on the blind spot it disappears. If you try doing this with both eyes open, the image of the dot will not disappear.

DID YOU KNOW?

A way to prove to yourself that the eyes form two overlapping images is to try the 'sausage test'. Focus your eyes on a distant object. Place your two index fingers tip to tip, and bring them up in front of your eyes, about 30 cm from your face, while still focusing at a distance. You should see a finger 'sausage' between the two fingers. Now try this with one eye closed. What is the difference?

ACCOMMODATION

The changes that take place in the eye which allow us to see objects at different distances are called **accommodation**.

You have probably seen the results of a camera or projector not being in focus – a blurred picture. In a camera, we can focus light from objects that are different distances away by moving the lens backward or forward, until the picture is sharp. In the eye, a different method is used. Rather than altering its position, the shape of the lens can be changed. A lens that is fatter in the middle (more convex) will refract light rays more than a thinner (less convex) lens. The lens in the eye can change shape because it is made of cells containing an elastic crystalline protein.

Figure 6.4 shows that the lens is held in place by a series of fibres called the **suspensory ligaments**. These are attached like the spokes of a wheel to a ring of muscle, called the **ciliary muscle**. The inside of the eye is filled with a transparent watery fluid which pushes outwards on the eye. In other words, there is a slight positive pressure within the eye. The changes to the eye that take place during accommodation are shown in Figure 6.7.

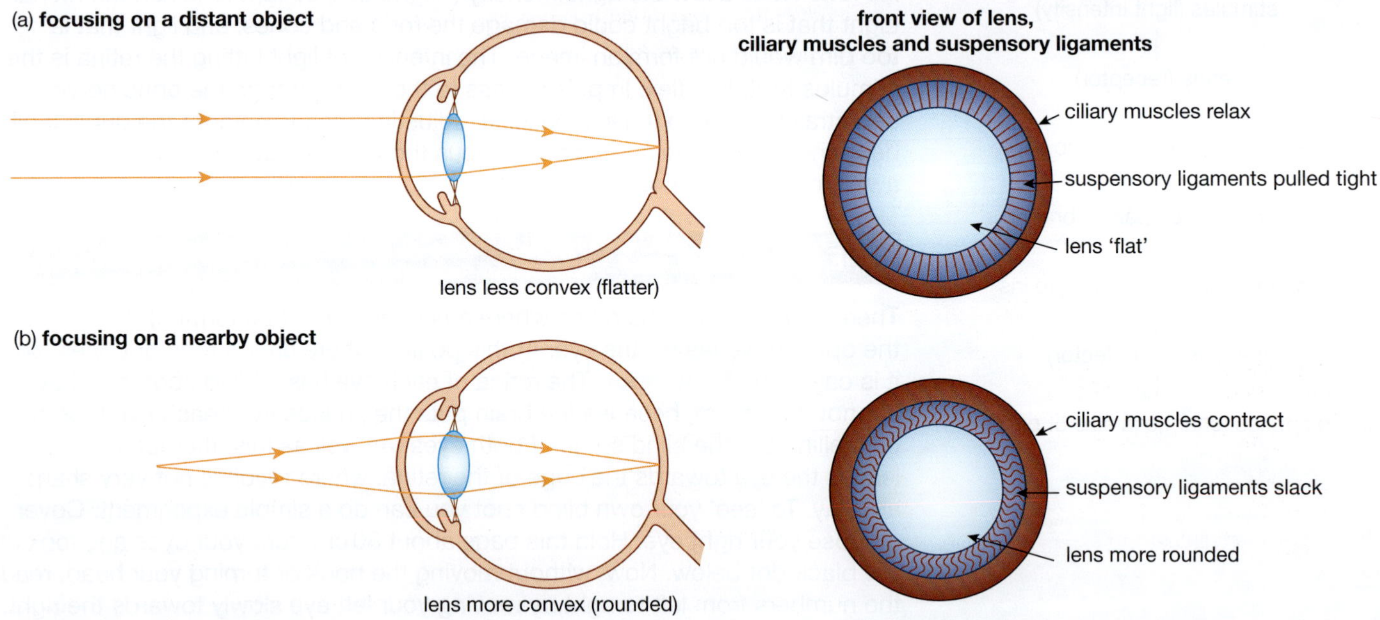

▲ Figure 6.7 Accommodation: how the eye focuses on objects at different distances

When the eye is focused on a distant object, the rays of light from the object are almost parallel when they reach the cornea (Figure 6.7(a)). The cornea refracts the rays, but the lens does not need to refract them much more to focus the light on the retina, so it does not need to be very convex. The ciliary muscles relax and the pressure in the eye pushes outwards on the lens, flattening it and stretching the suspensory ligaments. This is the condition when the eye is at rest – our eyes are focused for long distances.

When we focus on a nearby object, for example when reading a book, the light rays from the object are spreading out (diverging) when they enter the eye (Figure 6.7(b)). In this situation, the lens has to be more convex in order to refract the rays enough to focus them on the retina. The ciliary muscles now contract, the suspensory ligaments become slack and the elastic lens bulges outwards into a more convex shape.

REFLEX ACTIONS

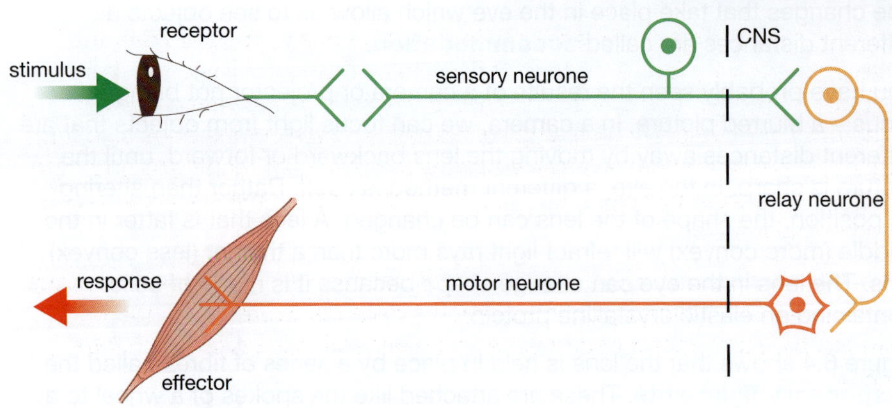

▲ Figure 6.8 Simplified diagram of a reflex arc

You saw on page 82 that the dilation and constriction of the pupil by the iris is an example of a reflex action. You now need to understand a little more about the nerves involved in a reflex. The nerve pathway of a reflex is called the **reflex arc**. The 'arc' part means that the pathway goes into the CNS and then straight back out again, in a sort of curve or arc (Figure 6.8).

The iris–pupil reflex protects the eye against damage by bright light. Other reflexes are protective too, preventing serious harm to the body. Take, for example, the reflex response to a painful stimulus. This happens when part of your body, such as your hand, touches a sharp or hot object. The reflex results in your hand being quickly withdrawn. Figure 6.9 shows the nerve pathway of this reflex in more detail.

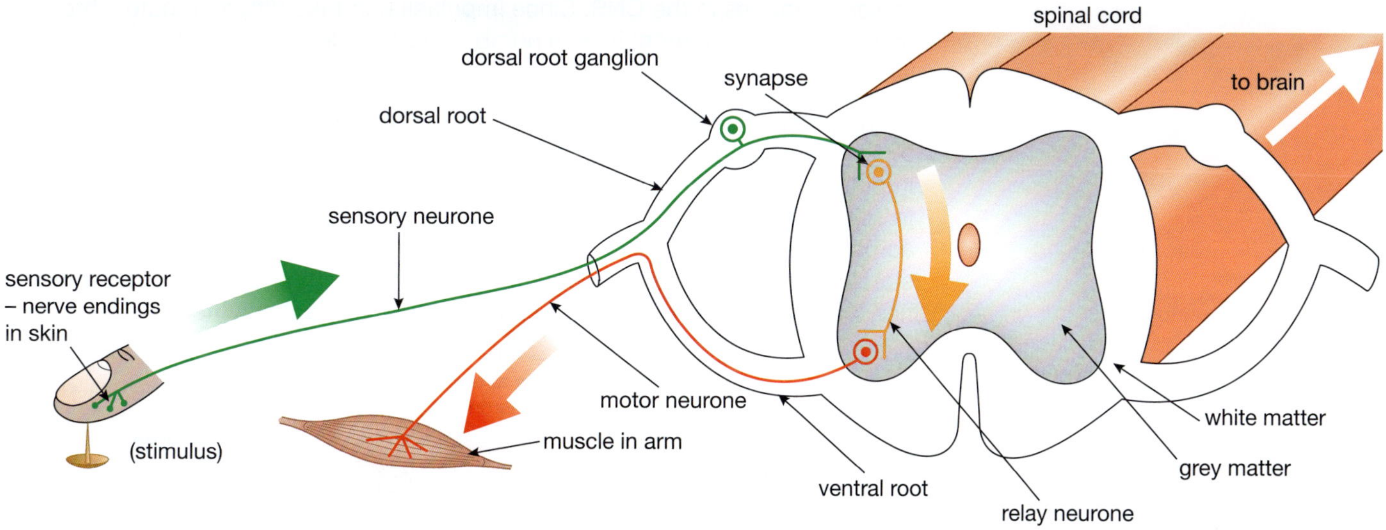

▲ Figure 6.9 A reflex arc in more detail

KEY POINT

A reflex action is a *rapid*, *automatic* (or *involuntary*) response to a stimulus. The action often (but not always) protects the body. 'Involuntary' means that it is not started by impulses from the brain.

The stimulus is detected by temperature or pain receptors in the skin. These generate impulses in sensory neurones. The impulses enter the CNS through a part of the spinal nerve called the **dorsal root**. In the spinal cord the sensory neurones connect by synapses with short **relay neurones**, which in turn connect with motor neurones. The motor neurones emerge from the spinal cord through the **ventral root**, and send impulses back out to the muscles of the arm. These muscles then contract, pulling the arm (and thus finger) away from the harmful stimulus.

The middle part of the spinal cord consists mainly of nerve cell bodies, which gives it a grey colour. This is why it is known as **grey matter**. The outer part of the spinal cord is called **white matter**, and has a whiter appearance because it contains many axons with their fatty myelin sheaths. (In the brain this is reversed – the grey matter is on the outside and the white matter in the middle of the brain.)

Impulses travel through the reflex arc in a fraction of a second, so that the reflex action is very fast, and doesn't need to be started by impulses from the brain. However, this doesn't mean that the brain is unaware of what is going on. This is because in the spinal cord, the reflex arc neurones also form connections called synapses (see below) with nerve cells leading to and from the brain. The brain therefore receives information about the stimulus. This is how we feel the pain.

Movements are sometimes a result of reflex actions, but we can also contract our muscles as a voluntary action, using nerve cell pathways from the brain linked to the same motor neurones. A voluntary action is under *conscious control*.

DID YOU KNOW?

'Dorsal' and 'ventral' are words describing the back and front of the body. The dorsal roots of spinal nerves emerge from the spinal cord towards the back of the person, while the ventral roots emerge towards the front. Notice that the cell bodies of the sensory neurones are all located in a swelling in the dorsal root, called the **dorsal root ganglion**.

SYNAPSES

Synapses are critical to the working of the nervous system. The CNS is made of many billions of nerve cells, and these have links with many others, through synapses. In the brain, each neurone may form synapses with thousands of other neurones. It is estimated that there are between 100 and 1000 million *million* synapses in the CNS. Since impulses can take different routes through these, there is an almost infinite number of possible pathways through the system.

A synapse is actually a *gap* between two nerve cells. The gap is not crossed by the electrical impulses passing through the neurones, but by chemicals. Impulses arriving at a synapse cause the ends of the fine branches of the axon to secrete a chemical, called a **neurotransmitter**. This chemical diffuses across the gap and attaches to the membrane of the second neurone. It then starts off impulses in the second cell (Figure 6.10). After the neurotransmitter has 'passed on the message', it is broken down by an enzyme.

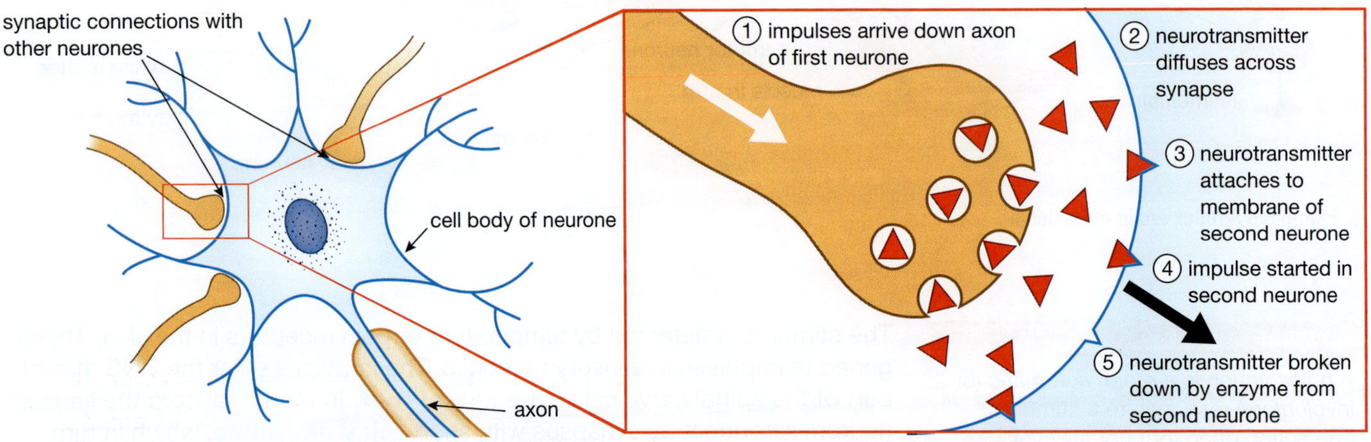

▲ Figure 6.10 The sequence of events happening at a synapse

Remember that many nerve cells, particularly those in the brain, have thousands of synapses with other neurones. The output of one cell may depend on the inputs from many cells adding together. In this way, synapses are important for integrating information in the CNS (Figure 6.11).

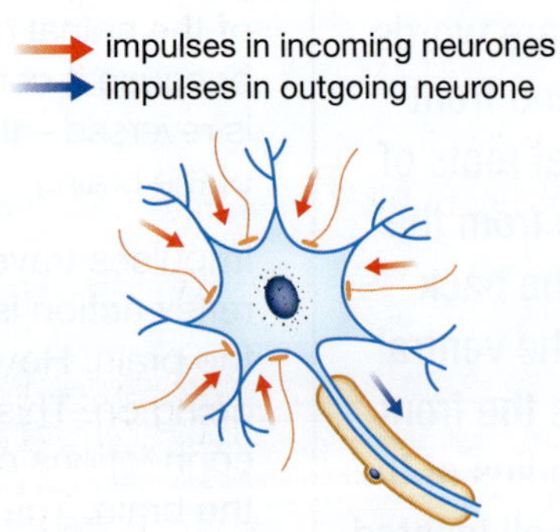

▲ Figure 6.11 Synapses allow the output of one nerve cell to be a result of integration of information from many other cells.

Because synapses are crossed by chemicals, it is easy for other chemicals to interfere with the working of the synapse. They may imitate the neurotransmitter, or block its action. This is the way that many drugs work.

LOOKING AHEAD – WHAT IS A NERVE IMPULSE?

A nerve impulse is an electrical signal that travels along the axon of a nerve cell. When the cell is not transmitting an impulse, there is small potential difference (voltage) across the nerve cell membrane. The potential inside the axon is about –70 mV lower than outside. This 'resting potential' is caused by differences in concentrations of various ions inside and outside the cell.

When the cell is stimulated, sodium ions (Na^+) rush into the axon through the membrane. The inflow of positively charged ions causes the potential to become positive – we say that it is *depolarised*. This sudden switch in voltage is called an 'action potential'. It only lasts for a few milliseconds (Figure 6.12). After a brief 'overshoot' below –70 mV it returns to normal (*repolarised*), as other positive ions (potassium, K^+) pass out through the membrane.

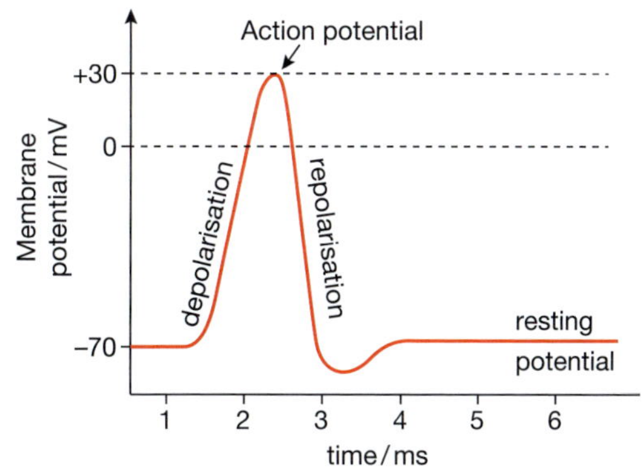

▲ Figure 6.12 Nerve cell action potential.

A nerve impulse is a *propagated* action potential. The action potential stimulates the next part of the cell membrane, so that the depolarisation spreads along the axon. After the action potential has passed, ion exchange pumps in the membrane sort out the imbalance of Na^+ and K^+ ions. The pumps use ATP for active transport – this is one reason why nerve cells need a lot of metabolic energy from respiration.

Nerve cells are called 'excitable cells' because they can change their membrane potential in this way. Other excitable cells include muscle and receptor cells. If you continue to study biology beyond International GCSE you will probably learn more about this interesting topic.

CHAPTER QUESTIONS

More questions on coordination can be found at the end of Unit 2 on page 116.

SKILLS CRITICAL THINKING 5th

1 Which row in the table correctly describes the three types of neurone?

	Sensory neurone	Relay neurone	Motor neurone
A	connects neurones within the CNS	connects impulses to the effector from the CNS	connects impulses from the receptor to the CNS
B	connects impulses from the effector to the CNS	connects neurones within the CNS	connects impulses from the CNS to the receptor
C	connects neurones within the CNS	connects impulses from the receptor to the CNS	connects impulses to the effector from the CNS
D	connects impulses from the receptor to the CNS	connects neurones within the CNS	connects impulses to the effector from the CNS

SKILLS CRITICAL THINKING

4th

2 The diagram below shows a section through the eye.

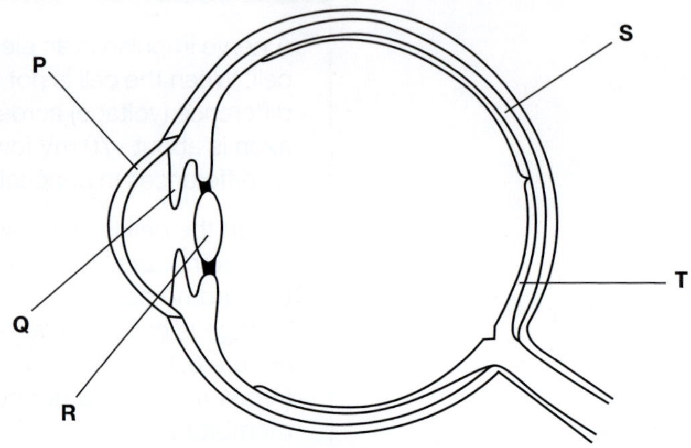

Which row in the table shows the cornea and the choroid?

	Cornea	Choroid
A	R	T
B	P	S
C	R	P
D	Q	T

5th

3 A boy sits in the shade under a tree, reading a book. He looks up into the sunny sky at an aeroplane. Which of the following changes will take place in his eyes?

A The pupils dilate and the lens becomes less convex

B The pupils dilate and the lens becomes more convex

C The pupils constrict and the lens becomes less convex

D The pupils constrict and the lens becomes more convex

6th

4 Below are two statements about how nerve cells work.

1. Neurotransmitters carry a nerve impulse along a neurone
2. An electrical charge carries a nerve impulse across a synapse

Which of these statements is/are true?

A 1 **B** 2

C 1 and 2 **D** neither

5th

5 A cataract is an eye problem suffered by some people, especially the elderly. The lens of the eye becomes opaque (cloudy) which blocks the passage of light. It can lead to blindness. Cataracts can be treated by a simple eye operation, where a surgeon removes the lens and replaces it with an artificial lens. After the operation, the patient is able to see again, but the eye is unable to carry out accommodation, and the patient will probably need to wear glasses for close-up work, such as reading.

a What is meant by 'accommodation'?

SKILLS REASONING

6th

b Why is accommodation not possible after a cataract operation?

7th

c Explain how a normal eye accommodates to focus on a nearby object.

SKILLS ANALYSIS

4th

6 The diagram shows a section through a human eye.

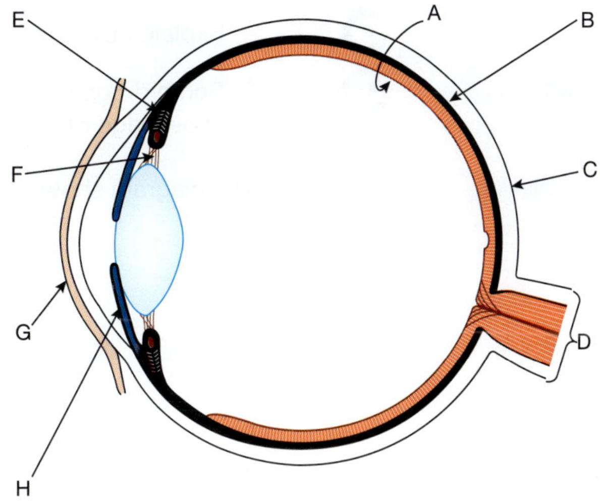

a The table below lists the functions of some of parts A to H. Copy the table and write the letters of the correct parts in the boxes.

Function	Letter
refracts light rays	
converts light into nerve impulses	
contains pigment to stop internal reflection	
contracts to change the shape of the lens	
takes nerve impulses to the brain	

b i Which label shows the iris?

5th

ii Explain how the iris controls the amount of light entering the eye.

iii Why is this important?

7th

7 The diagram shows some parts of the nervous system involved in a simple reflex action that happens when a finger touches a hot object.

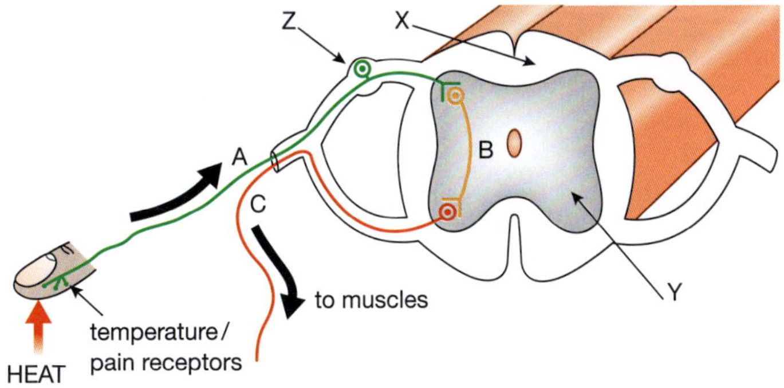

a What type of neurone is:

i neurone A

ii neurone B

iii neurone C?

b Describe the function of each of these types of neurone.

c Which parts of the nervous system are shown by the labels X, Y and Z?

SKILLS CRITICAL THINKING

6th

d In what form is information passed along neurones?

7th

e Explain how information passes from one neurone to another.

SKILLS REASONING

8th

f Some drugs act at a synapse to prevent a person feeling pain. From your knowledge of synapses, suggest how they might work.

SKILLS PROBLEM SOLVING

8 The diagram shows a motor neurone.

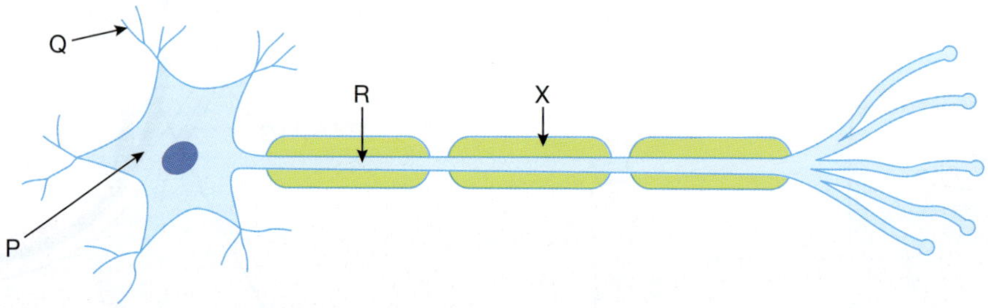

Name the parts of the neurone labelled P, Q and R.

a This motor neurone is 1.2 metres in length. It takes 0.016 seconds for an impulse to pass along the neurone. Calculate the speed of conduction of the impulse.

SKILLS CRITICAL THINKING

5th

b Neurones need energy from ATP to conduct impulses. Name the organelle in the cell that provides most of this ATP.

6th

c Structure R is surrounded by a sheath, labelled X in the diagram. What is the function of this sheath?

SKILLS REASONING

7th

d Some diseases can cause damage to this sheath. Suggest what would happen to a person's nervous responses if this sheath were to be damaged.

SKILLS CRITICAL THINKING

5th

9 **a** List five examples of stimuli that affect the body and state the response produced by each stimulus.

b For one of your five examples, explain:

i the nature and role of the receptor

ii the nature and role of the effector organ.

c For the same example, describe the chain of events from stimulus to response.

7 CHEMICAL COORDINATION

The nervous system (Chapter 6) is a coordination system forming a link between stimulus and response. The body has a second coordination system, which does not involve nerves. This is the endocrine system. It consists of organs called endocrine glands, which make chemical messenger substances called hormones. Hormones are carried in the bloodstream.

LEARNING OBJECTIVES

- Describe how responses can be controlled by hormonal communication
- Understand the differences between nervous and hormonal control
- Understand the sources, roles and effects of the following hormones:
  - adrenaline
  - insulin
  - testosterone*
  - progesterone*
  - oestrogen*

*These hormones will be dealt with in more detail in later chapters.

GLANDS AND HORMONES

A gland is an organ that releases or *secretes* a substance. This means that cells in the gland make a chemical which leaves the cells through the cell membrane. The chemical then travels somewhere else in the body, where it carries out its function. There are two types of glands – exocrine and endocrine glands. **Exocrine glands** secrete their products through a tube called a duct. For example, salivary glands in your mouth secrete saliva down salivary ducts, and tear glands secrete tears through ducts that lead to the surface of the eye. **Endocrine glands** have no duct, and so are called ductless glands. Instead, their products, the **hormones**, are secreted into the blood vessels that pass through the gland (Figure 7.1).

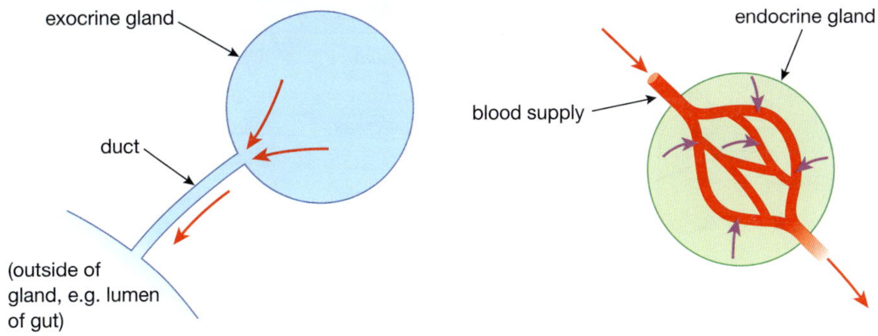

▲ Figure 7.1 Exocrine glands secrete their products though a duct, while endocrine glands secrete hormones into the blood.

This chapter looks at some of the main endocrine glands and the functions of the hormones they produce. Because hormones are carried in the blood, they can travel to all areas of the body. They usually only affect certain tissues or organs, called 'target organs', which can be a long distance from the gland

KEY POINT

The receptors for some hormones are located in the cell membrane of the target cell. Other hormones have receptors in the cytoplasm, and some in the nucleus. Without specific receptors, a cell will not respond to a hormone at all.

that made the hormone. Hormones only affect particular tissues or organs if the cells of that tissue or organ have special chemical receptors for the particular hormone. For example, the hormone **insulin** affects the cells of the liver, which have insulin receptors.

THE DIFFERENCES BETWEEN NERVOUS AND ENDOCRINE CONTROL

Although the nervous and endocrine systems both act to coordinate body functions, there are differences in the way that they do this. These are summarised in Table 7.1.

Table 7.1 The nervous and endocrine systems compared.

Nervous system	Endocrine system
works by nerve impulses transmitted through nerve cells (although chemicals are used at synapses)	works by hormones transmitted through the bloodstream
nerve impulses travel fast and usually have an 'instant' effect	hormones travel more slowly and generally take longer to act
response is usually short-lived	response is usually longer-lasting
impulses act on individual cells such as muscle fibres, so have a very localised effect	hormones can have widespread effects on different organs (although they only act on particular tissues or organs if the cells have the correct receptors)

THE ENDOCRINE GLANDS

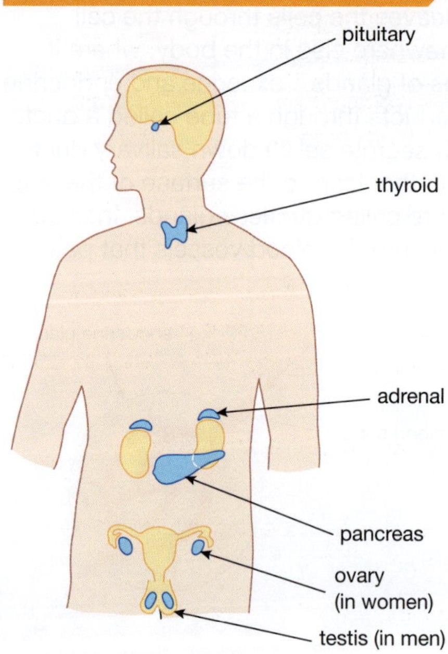

▲ Figure 7.2 The main endocrine glands of the body.

The positions of the main endocrine glands are shown in Figure 7.2. A summary of some of the hormones that they make and their functions is given in Table 7.2.

The **pituitary gland** (often just called 'the pituitary') is found at the base of the brain. It produces a number of hormones controlling various processes in the body. It also controls the release of certain hormones from other endocrine glands.

Table 7.2: Some of the main endocrine glands, the hormones they produce and their functions.

Gland	Hormone	Some functions of the hormones
thyroid	thyroxine	controls the body's metabolic rate (how fast chemical reactions take place in cells)
pancreas	insulin glucagon	lowers blood glucose raises blood glucose
adrenals	adrenaline	prepares the body for physical activity
testes	testosterone	controls the development of male secondary sexual characteristics
ovaries	oestrogen progesterone	controls the development of female secondary sexual characteristics regulates the menstrual cycle

The **pancreas** is both an endocrine *and* an exocrine gland. It secretes two hormones involved in the regulation of blood glucose, and is also a gland of the digestive system, secreting enzymes through the pancreatic duct into the small intestine (see Chapter 4). The sex organs of males (**testes**) and females (**ovaries**) are also endocrine organs. In addition to their role in producing sex cells, the testes and ovaries make hormones that are involved in controlling reproduction. This topic is covered more fully in Chapter 9. We will now look at the functions of two hormones in more detail.

ADRENALINE – THE 'FIGHT OR FLIGHT' HORMONE

DID YOU KNOW?
'Adrenal' means 'next to the kidneys', which describes where the adrenal glands are located – on top of these organs (see Figure 7.2).

When you are frightened, excited or angry, your **adrenal glands** secrete the hormone adrenaline.

Adrenaline acts at a number of target organs and tissues, preparing the body for action. In animals other than humans this action usually means dealing with an attack by an enemy, where the animal can stay and fight or run away – hence 'fight or flight'. This is not often a problem with humans, but there are plenty of other times when adrenaline is released (Figure 7.3).

▲ Figure 7.3 Many human activities cause adrenaline to be produced, not just a 'fight or flight' situation!

▲ Figure 7.4 Adrenaline affects the body of an animal in many ways.

If an animal's body is going to be prepared for action, the muscles need a good supply of oxygen and glucose for respiration. Adrenaline produces several changes in the body that make this happen (Figure 7.4) as well as other changes to prepare for fight or flight.

- The breathing rate increases and breaths become deeper, taking more oxygen into the body.
- The heart beats faster, sending more blood to the muscles, so that they receive more glucose and oxygen for respiration.
- Blood is diverted away from the intestine and into the muscles.
- In the liver, stored carbohydrate (glycogen) is changed into glucose and released into the blood. The muscle cells absorb more glucose and use it for respiration.
- The pupils dilate, increasing visual sensitivity to movement.
- Body hair stands upright, making the animal look larger to an enemy.
- Mental awareness is increased, so reactions are faster.

In humans, adrenaline is not just released in a 'fight or flight' situation, but in many other stressful activities too, such as preparing for a race, going for a job interview or taking an exam.

INSULIN – CONTROL OF BLOOD GLUCOSE

You saw earlier that adrenaline can raise blood glucose from stores in the liver. The liver cells contain carbohydrate in the form of **glycogen**. Glycogen is made from long chains of glucose sub-units joined together, forming a large insoluble molecule (see Chapter 4). Being insoluble makes glycogen a good storage product. When the body is short of glucose, the glycogen can be broken down into glucose, which then passes into the bloodstream.

Adrenaline raises blood glucose concentration in an emergency, but other hormones act all the time to control the level, keeping it fairly constant at a little less than 1 g of glucose in every dm^3 (cubic decimetre) of blood. The main hormone controlling glucose is insulin. Insulin is made by special cells in the pancreas. It stimulates the liver cells to take up glucose and convert it into glycogen, lowering the level of glucose in the blood.

The concentration of glucose in your blood will start to rise after you have had a meal. Sugars from digested carbohydrate pass into the blood and are carried to the liver in the hepatic portal vein (Chapter 5). In the liver the glucose is converted to glycogen, so the blood leaving the liver in the hepatic vein has a lower concentration of glucose than when it enters the liver.

DID YOU KNOW?

The pancreas also makes a hormone called **glucagon**, which has the opposite effect to insulin – it raises blood glucose.

DIABETES

Some people have a disease where their pancreas cannot make enough insulin to keep their blood glucose level constant – it rises to very high concentrations. The disease is called **diabetes**. One symptom of diabetes can be detected by a chemical test on urine. Normally, people have no glucose at all in their urine. Someone suffering from diabetes may have such a high concentration of glucose in the blood that it is excreted in their urine. This can be shown up by using coloured test strips (Figure 7.5).

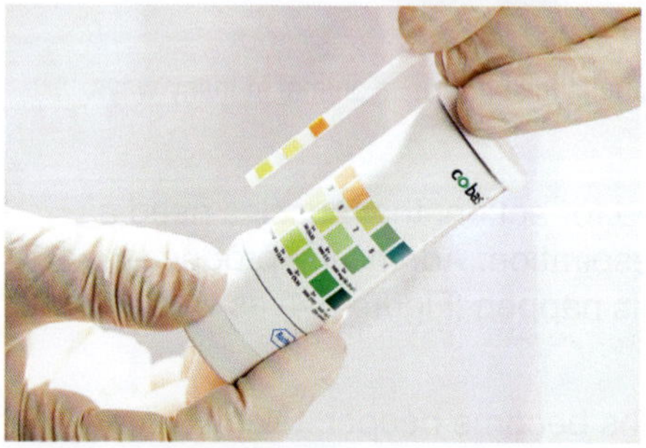

▲ Figure 7.5 Coloured test strips are used to detect glucose in urine.

KEY POINT

We should really refer to this disease by its full name, which is 'type 1' diabetes. There is also a 'type 2' diabetes, where the pancreas produces insulin but the body shows *insulin resistance*, where insulin has less effect than it should do. At first the pancreas makes extra insulin, but eventually it can't continue to make enough to maintain blood glucose at a normal level. Type 2 diabetes is common in people who are overweight and eat a poor diet that is high in sugar and other carbohydrates. It can be prevented and controlled by eating a good diet and doing regular exercise. Type 2 diabetes also tends to happen in middle-aged or older people, whereas type 1 can happen at any age, and is common in childhood.

Another symptom of diabetes is a constant thirst. This is because the high blood glucose concentration stimulates receptors in the **hypothalamus** of the brain. These 'thirst centres' are stimulated, so that by drinking, the person will dilute their blood.

Severe diabetes is very serious. If it is untreated, the sufferer loses weight and becomes weak and eventually falls into a coma and dies.

Carbohydrates in the diet, such as starch and sugars, are the source of glucose in the blood, so a person with diabetes can help to control their blood sugar if they limit the amount of carbohydrate that they eat. However a person

KEY POINT

Insulin is a protein, and if it were to be taken by mouth in tablet form, it would be broken down by protease enzymes in the gut. Instead it is injected into muscle tissue, where it is slowly absorbed into the bloodstream.

DID YOU KNOW?

Insulin for the treatment of diabetes has been available since 1921, and has kept millions of people alive. It was originally extracted from the pancreases of animals and much insulin is still obtained in this way. However, since the 1970s, human insulin has been produced commercially, from genetically modified (GM) bacteria. The bacteria have their DNA 'engineered' to contain the gene for human insulin (see Chapter 21).

with diabetes (type 1) also needs to receive daily injections of insulin to keep the glucose in their blood at the right level.

People with diabetes can check their blood glucose using a special sensor. They prick their finger and place a drop of blood on a test strip. The strip is then put into the sensor, which gives them an accurate reading of how much glucose is in their blood (Figure 7.6). They can then tell when to inject insulin and how much to inject.

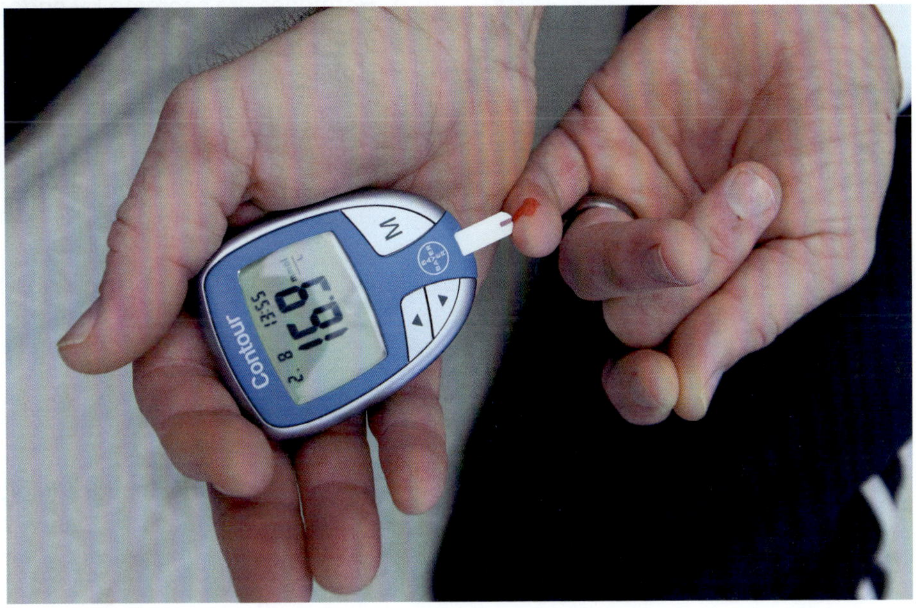

▲ Figure 7.6 Sensor for measuring blood glucose

CHAPTER QUESTIONS

More questions on chemical coordination can be found at the end of Unit 2 on page 116.

SKILLS CRITICAL THINKING 6th

1 Which of the following statement(s) is/are true?

1. Insulin converts glucose to glycogen
2. Insulin causes blood glucose levels to fall
3. Glucose is stored as glucagon in the liver
4. Glycogen can be broken down to release glucose into the blood

A 2 only

B 2 and 4

C 3 and 4

D 1 and 2

2 Which of the following will *not* happen when the hormone adrenaline is released?

A an increase in heart rate

B an increase in blood flow to the gut

C dilation of the pupils

D an increase in breathing rate

SKILLS CRITICAL THINKING

6th

3 Which of the following is a symptom of type 1 diabetes?

A high insulin level in the blood

B low glucose level in the blood

C glucose present in the urine

D insulin present in the urine

7th

4 a *Hormones* are *secreted* by *endocrine glands*. Explain the meaning of the four words in italics

SKILLS ANALYSIS

6th

b Identify the hormones A to D in the table.

Hormone	One function of this hormone
A	stimulates the liver to convert glucose to glycogen
B	controls the 'fight or flight' responses
C	controls the breaking of the voice at puberty in boys
D	completes the development of the uterus lining during the menstrual cycle

8th

5 The graph shows the changes in blood glucose in a healthy woman over a 12-hour period.

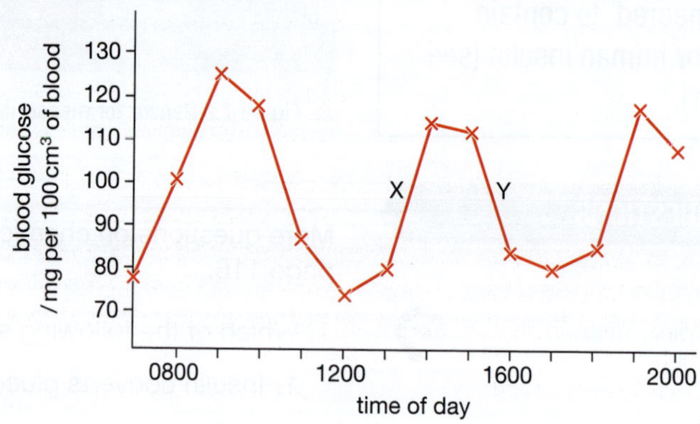

a Explain why there was a rise in blood glucose at X.

b How does the body bring about a decrease in blood glucose at Y? Your answer should include the words insulin, liver and pancreas.

c Diabetes is a disease where the body cannot control the concentration of glucose in the blood.

SKILLS CRITICAL THINKING

i Why is this dangerous?

7th

ii Describe two ways a person with diabetes can monitor their blood glucose level.

8th

iii Explain two ways that a person with diabetes can help to control their blood glucose level.

8 HOMEOSTASIS AND EXCRETION

The kidneys have major roles to play in both homeostasis and excretion. This chapter is mainly concerned with the structure and function of the kidneys. It also deals with another important aspect of homeostasis – maintaining a steady body temperature.

LEARNING OBJECTIVES

- Understand that homeostasis is the maintenance of a constant internal environment
- Understand that control of body water content and body temperature are examples of homeostasis
- Know the excretory products of the lungs, kidneys and skin
- Understand the origin of carbon dioxide and oxygen as waste products of metabolism and their loss from the stomata of a leaf
- Describe the role of the skin in temperature regulation, with reference to sweating, vasoconstriction and vasodilation

Inside our bodies, conditions are kept relatively constant. This is called **homeostasis**. The kidneys are organs which have a major role to play in both homeostasis and in the removal of waste products, or **excretion**. They filter the blood, removing substances and controlling the concentration of water and solutes (dissolved substances) in the blood and other body fluids.

HOMEOSTASIS

KEY POINT

The meaning of 'homeostasis' is 'keeping the conditions in the internal environment of the body relatively constant'. One aspect of homeostasis is the maintenance of the water and salt content of the internal environment. This is called **osmoregulation**.

If you were to drink a litre of water and wait for half an hour, your body would soon respond to this change by producing about the same volume of urine. In other words, it would automatically balance your water input and water loss. Drinking is the main way that our bodies gain water, but there are other sources (Figure 8.1). Some water is present in the food that we eat, and a small amount is formed by cell respiration. The body also loses water, mostly in urine, but also smaller volumes in sweat, faeces and exhaled air. Every day, we gain and lose about the same volume of water, so that the total content of our bodies stays more or less the same. This is an example of homeostasis. The word 'homeostasis' means 'steady state', and refers to keeping conditions inside the body relatively constant.

The inside of the body is known as the **internal environment.** You have probably heard of the 'environment', which means the 'surroundings' of an organism. The *internal* environment is the surroundings of the cells inside the body. It particularly means the blood, together with another liquid called **tissue fluid**.

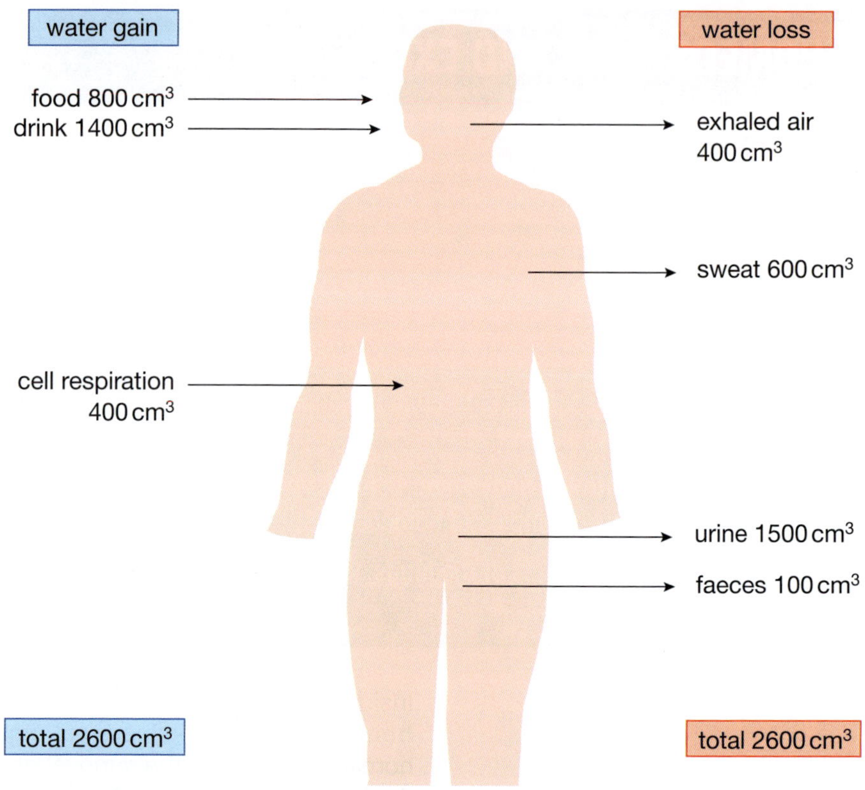

▲ Figure 8.1 The daily water balance of an adult

Tissue fluid is a watery solution of salts, glucose and other solutes. It surrounds all the cells of the body, forming a pathway for the transfer of nutrients between the blood and the cells. Tissue fluid is formed by leakage from blood capillaries. It is similar in composition to blood plasma, but lacks the plasma proteins.

It is not just water and salts that are kept constant in the body. Many other components of the internal environment are maintained. For example, the level of carbon dioxide in the blood is regulated, along with the blood pH, the concentration of dissolved glucose (see Chapter 7) and the body temperature.

Homeostasis is important because cells will only function properly if they are bathed in a tissue fluid which provides them with their optimum conditions. For instance, if the tissue fluid contains too many solutes, the cells will lose water by osmosis, and become dehydrated. If the tissue fluid is too dilute, the cells will swell up with water. Both conditions will prevent them working efficiently and might cause permanent damage. If the pH of the tissue fluid is not correct, it will affect the activity of the cell's enzymes, as will a body temperature much different from 37 °C. It is also important that excretory products are removed. Substances such as urea must be prevented from building up in the blood and tissue fluid, where they would be toxic to cells.

DID YOU KNOW?

'Salts' in urine or in the blood are present as ions. For example, the sodium chloride in Table 8.1 will be in solution as sodium ions (Na^+) and chloride ions (Cl^-). Urine contains many other ions, such as potassium (K^+), phosphate (HPO_4^{2-}) and ammonium (NH_4^+), and removes excess ions from the blood.

URINE

An adult human produces about 1.5 dm^3 of urine every day, although this volume depends very much on the amount of water drunk and the volume lost in other forms, such as sweat. Every litre of urine contains about 40 g of waste products and salts (Table 8.1).

KEY POINT

If you are studying for the Double Award, you only need to be aware that urea is an excretory product of the kidneys.

Table 8.1 Some of the main solutes in urine.

Substance	Amount / g per dm^3
urea	23.3
ammonia	0.4
other nitrogenous waste	1.6
sodium chloride (salt)	10.0
potassium	1.3
phosphate	2.3

Notice the words *nitrogenous waste*. Urea and ammonia are two examples of nitrogenous waste. It means that they contain the element nitrogen. All animals have to excrete a nitrogenous waste product.

The reason behind this is quite complicated. Carbohydrates and fats only contain the elements carbon, hydrogen and oxygen. However, proteins also contain nitrogen. If the body has too much carbohydrate or fat, these substances can be stored, for example as glycogen in the liver, or as fat under the skin and around other organs. Excess proteins, or their building blocks (called amino acids) *cannot* be stored. The amino acids are first broken down in the liver. They are converted into carbohydrate (which is stored as glycogen) and the main nitrogen-containing waste product, urea. The urea passes into the blood, to be filtered out by the kidneys during the formation of urine. Notice that the urea is made by chemical reactions in the cells of the body (the body's metabolism). 'Excretion' means getting rid of waste of this kind. When the body gets rid of solid waste from the digestive system (faeces), this is not excretion, since it contains few products of *metabolism*, just the 'remains' of undigested food, along with bacteria and dead cells.

So the kidney is in fact carrying out two functions. It is a *homeostatic* organ, controlling the water and salt (ion) concentration in the body as well as an *excretory* organ, concentrating nitrogenous waste in a form that can be eliminated.

KEY POINT

Excretion is the process by which waste products of metabolism are removed from the body. In humans, the main nitrogenous excretory substance is **urea**. Another excretory product is carbon dioxide, produced by cell respiration and excreted by the lungs (Chapter 3). The human skin is also an excretory organ, since the sweat that it secretes contains small amounts of urea.

Plants also excrete waste products of metabolism. In light, their leaves produce oxygen from photosynthesis. In the dark they excrete carbon dioxide from respiration. Plants exchange these gases through pores in the leaf called stomata (see Chapter 11).

CONTROL OF BODY TEMPERATURE

You may have heard mammals and birds described as 'warm blooded'. A better word for this is homeothermic. It means that they keep their body temperature constant, despite changes in the temperature of their surroundings. For example, the body temperature of humans is kept steady at about 37 °C, give or take a few tenths of a degree. This is another example of homeostasis. All other animals are 'cold blooded'. For example, if a lizard is kept in an aquarium at 20 °C, its body temperature will be 20 °C too. If the temperature of the aquarium is raised to 25 °C, the lizard's body temperature will rise to 25 °C as well. We can show this difference between **homeotherms** and other animals as a graph (Figure 8.2).

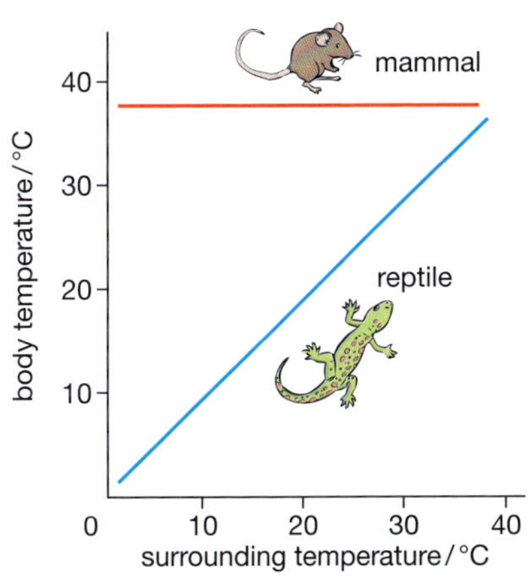

▲ Figure 8.2 The temperature of a homeotherm, such as a mammal, is kept constant at different external temperatures, whereas the lizard's body temperature changes.

In the wild, lizards keep their temperature more constant than in Figure 8.2, by adapting their behaviour. For example, in the morning they may stay in the sun to warm their bodies, or at midday, if the sun is too hot, retreat to holes in the ground to cool down.

DID YOU KNOW?
Physiology is the branch of biology that deals with how the bodies of animals or plants work, for example how muscles contract, how nerves send impulses, or how xylem carries water through plants. In this chapter you have read about kidney physiology.

The real difference between homeotherms and all other animals is that homeotherms can keep their temperatures constant by using *physiological* changes for generating or losing heat. For this reason, mammals and birds are also called 'endotherms', meaning 'heat from inside'.

An endotherm uses heat from the chemical reactions in its cells to warm its body. It then controls its heat loss by regulating processes like sweating and blood flow through the skin. Endotherms use behavioural ways to control their temperature too. For example, penguins 'huddle' together in groups to keep warm, and humans put on extra clothes in winter.

What is the advantage of a human maintaining a body temperature of 37 °C? It means that all the chemical reactions taking place in the cells of the body can go on at a steady, predictable rate. The metabolism doesn't slow down in cold environments. If you watch goldfish in a garden pond, you will notice that in summer, when the pond water is warm, they are very active, swimming about quickly. In winter, when the temperature drops, the fish slow down and become very sluggish in their actions. This would happen to a mammal too, if its body temperature varied.

It is also important that the body does not become *too* hot. The cells' enzymes work best at 37 °C. At higher temperatures enzymes, like all proteins, are destroyed by **denaturing** (see Chapter 1). Endotherms have all evolved a body temperature of around 40 °C (Table 8.2) and enzymes that work best at this temperature.

Table 8.2 The body temperatures of a range of mammals and birds

Species	Average and normal range of body temperature / °C	Species	Average and normal range of body temperature / °C
brown bear	38.0 ± 1.0	shrew	35.7 ± 1.2
camel	37.5 ± 0.5	whale	35.7 ± 0.1
elephant	36.2 ± 0.5	duck	43.1 ± 0.3
fox	38.8 ± 1.3	ostrich	39.2 ± 0.7
human	36.9 ± 0.7	penguin	39.0 ± 0.2
mouse	39.3 ± 1.3	thrush	40.0 ± 1.7
polar bear	37.5 ± 0.4	wren	41.0 ± 1.0

MONITORING BODY TEMPERATURE

In humans and other mammals the core body temperature is monitored by a part of the brain called the **thermoregulatory centre**. This is located in the hypothalamus of the brain. It acts as the body's 'thermostat'.

If a person goes into a warm or cold environment, the first thing that happens is that temperature receptors in the skin send electrical impulses to the hypothalamus, which stimulates the brain to alter our behaviour. We start to feel hot or cold, and usually do something about it, such as finding shade, having a cold drink, or putting on more clothes.

If changes to our behaviour are not enough to keep our body temperature constant, the thermoregulatory centre in the hypothalamus detects a change in the temperature of the blood flowing through it. It then sends signals via nerves to other organs of the body, which regulate the temperature by physiological means.

DID YOU KNOW?
A thermostat is a switch that is turned on or off by a change in temperature. It is used in electrical appliances to keep their temperature steady. For example, a thermostat in an iron can be set to 'hot' or 'cool' to keep the temperature of the iron set for ironing different materials.

THE SKIN AND TEMPERATURE CONTROL

The human skin has a number of functions related to the fact that it forms the outer surface of the body. These include:

- forming a tough outer layer able to resist mechanical damage
- acting as a barrier to the entry of pathogens
- forming an impermeable surface, preventing loss of water
- acting as a sense organ for touch and temperature changes
- controlling the loss of heat through the body surface.

Figure 8.3 shows the structure of human skin. It is made up of three layers: the epidermis, dermis and hypodermis.

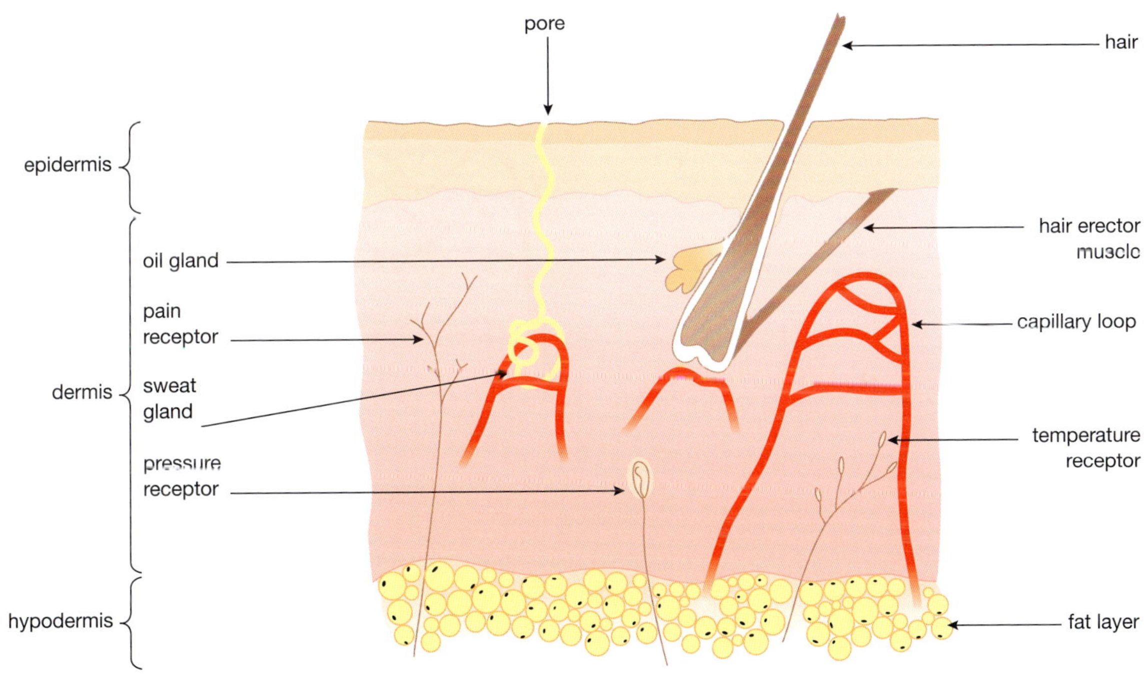

▲ Figure 8.3 A section through human skin

The outer **epidermis** consists of dead cells that stop water loss and protect the body against invasion by microorganisms such as bacteria. The **hypodermis** contains fatty tissue, which insulates the body against heat loss and is a store of energy. The middle layer, the **dermis**, contains many sensory receptors. It is also the location of sweat glands and many small blood vessels, as well as hair follicles. These last three structures are involved in temperature control.

Imagine that the hypothalamus detects a rise in the central (core) body temperature. Immediately it sends nerve impulses to the skin. These bring about changes to correct the rise in temperature.

First of all, the **sweat glands** produce greater amounts of sweat. This liquid is secreted onto the surface of the skin. When a liquid evaporates, it turns into a gas. This change needs energy, called the latent heat of vaporisation. When sweat evaporates, the energy is supplied by the body's heat, cooling the body down. It is not that the sweat is cool – it is secreted at body temperature. It only has a cooling action when it evaporates. In very humid atmospheres (e.g. a tropical rainforest) the sweat stays on the skin and doesn't evaporate. It then has very little cooling effect.

Secondly, hairs on the surface of the skin lie flat against the skin's surface. This happens because of the relaxation of tiny muscles called **hair erector muscles** attached to the base of each hair. In cold conditions, these contract and the hairs are pulled upright. The hairs trap a layer of air next to the skin, and since air is a poor conductor of heat, this acts as insulation. In warm conditions, the thinner layer of trapped air means that more heat will be lost. This is not very effective in humans, because the hairs over most of our body do not grow very large. It is very effective in hairy mammals like cats or dogs. The same principle is used by birds, which 'fluff out' their feathers in cold weather.

HINT

Students often describe vasodilation incorrectly. They talk about the blood vessels 'moving nearer the surface of the skin'. They don't *move* at all, it's just that more blood flows through the surface vessels.

Lastly, there are tiny blood vessels called capillary loops in the dermis. Blood flows through these loops, radiating heat to the outside, and cooling the body down. If the body is too hot, **arterioles** (small arteries) leading to the capillary loops dilate (widen). This increases the blood flow to the skin's surface (Figure 8.4) and is called **vasodilation**.

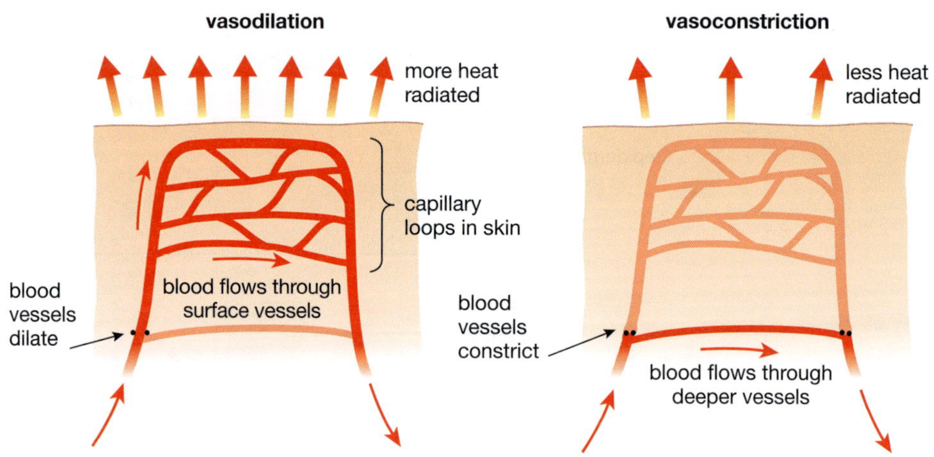

▲ Figure 8.4 Blood flow through the surface of the skin is controlled by vasodilation or vasoconstriction.

In cold conditions, the opposite happens. The arterioles leading to the surface capillary loops constrict (become narrower) and blood flow to the surface of the skin is reduced, so that less heat is lost. This is called **vasoconstriction**. Vasoconstriction and vasodilation are brought about by tiny rings of muscles in the walls of the arterioles, called sphincter muscles, like the sphincters you read about earlier in this chapter, at the outlet of the bladder.

There are other ways that the body can control heat loss and heat gain. In cold conditions, the body's metabolism speeds up, generating more heat. The liver, a large organ, can produce a lot of metabolic heat in this way. The hormone adrenaline stimulates the increase in metabolism (see Chapter 7). **Shivering** also takes place, where the muscles contract and relax rapidly. This also generates a large amount of heat.

Sweating, vasodilation and vasoconstriction, hair erection, shivering and changes to the metabolism, along with behavioural actions, work together to keep the body temperature to within a few tenths of a degree of the 'normal' 37 °C. If the difference is any bigger than this it shows that something is wrong. For instance, a temperature of 39 °C might be due to an illness.

CHAPTER QUESTIONS

More questions on homeostasis and excretion can be found at the end of Unit 2 on page 116.

SKILLS CRITICAL THINKING

4th

1 Which of the following is *not* an example of excretion?

A loss of carbon dioxide by a plant in the dark
B removal of carbon dioxide from the lungs
C removal of urea in urine
D elimination of faeces from the alimentary canal

7th

2 If the human body temperature starts to rise, which of the following happens?

A vasoconstriction of arterioles in the skin
B contraction of hair erector muscles
C decrease in the rate of metabolism
D decrease in production of sweat by glands in the skin

SKILLS INTERPRETATION

3 Construct a table like the one below to show the changes that take place when a person is put in a hot or cold environment. Your table should have three columns.

Changes taking place	Hot environment	Cold environment
sweating		
blood flow through capillary loops		vasoconstriction decreases blood flow through surface capillaries so that less heat is radiated from the skin
hairs in skin		
shivering		
metabolism		

SKILLS ANALYSIS, REASONING

5th

4 Look at the body temperatures of mammals and birds shown in Table 8.2 on page 100. Use the information in the table to answer these questions:

a How does the average temperature of birds differ from the average temperature of mammals? Can you suggest why this is an advantage for birds?

b Is there a relationship between the body temperature of a mammal and the temperature of its habitat? Give an example to support your answer.

6th

c Polar bears have thick white fur covering their bodies. Explain two ways in which this is an adaptation to their habitat (the place where the animal lives).

9 REPRODUCTION IN HUMANS

One of the characteristics of living organisms that makes them different from non-living things is their ability to produce offspring, or **reproduce**. Reproduction is all about an organism passing on its genes. This can be through special sex cells, or gametes. It can also be asexually, without the production of gametes. In this chapter we look at the differences between sexual and asexual reproduction, and study in detail the process of human reproduction.

LEARNING OBJECTIVES

- Understand the differences between sexual and asexual reproduction
- Understand that fertilisation involves the fusion of a male and female gamete to produce a zygote
- Understand that a zygote undergoes cell division and develops into an embryo
- Understand how the structure and function of the human male and female reproductive systems are adapted for their functions
- Describe the role of the placenta in the nutrition of the developing embryo
- Understand how the developing embryo is protected by amniotic fluid
- Understand the roles of oestrogen and testosterone in the development of secondary sexual characteristics
- Understand the roles of oestrogen and progesterone in the menstrual cycle

SEXUAL AND ASEXUAL REPRODUCTION COMPARED

In any method of reproduction, the end result is the production of more organisms of the same species. Humans produce more humans, pea plants produce more pea plants and salmonella bacteria produce more salmonella bacteria. However, the way in which they reproduce differs. There are two types of reproduction: **sexual reproduction** and **asexual reproduction**.

In sexual reproduction, specialised sex cells called **gametes** are produced. There are usually two types, a mobile male gamete called a **sperm** and a stationary female gamete called an egg cell or **ovum** (plural **ova**).

The sperm must move to the egg and fuse (join) with it. This is called **fertilisation** (Figure 9.1). The single cell formed by fertilisation is called a **zygote**. This cell will divide many times by mitosis to form all the cells of the new animal.

In asexual reproduction, there are no specialised gametes and there is no fertilisation. Instead, cells in one part of the body divide by mitosis to form a structure that breaks away from the parent body and grows into a new organism. Not many animals reproduce in this way. Figure 9.2 shows *Hydra* (a small animal similar to jellyfish) reproducing by budding. Cells in the body wall divide to form a small version of the adult. This eventually breaks off and becomes a free-living *Hydra*. One animal may produce several 'buds' in a short space of time.

▲ Figure 9.1 A sperm fertilising an egg

▲ Figure 9.2 *Hydra* reproducing asexually by budding

KEY POINT

Individuals produced asexually from the same adult organism are called **clones**.

KEY POINT

A **gene** is a section of DNA that determines a particular characteristic or feature. Genes are found in the nucleus of a cell on the chromosomes (see Chapter 18).

All the offspring produced from *Hydra* buds are genetically identical – they have exactly the same genes. This is because all the cells of the new individual are produced by **mitosis** from just one cell in the body of the adult. When cells divide by mitosis, the new cells that are produced are exact copies of the original cell (see Chapter 17 for a description of mitosis). As a result, all the cells of an organism that are produced asexually have the same genes as the cell that produced them – the original adult cell. So *all* asexually produced offspring from one adult will have the same genes as the cells of the adult. They will *all* be genetic copies of that adult and so will be identical to each other.

Asexual reproduction is useful to a species when the environment in which it lives is relatively stable. If an organism is well adapted to this stable environment, asexual reproduction will produce offspring that are also well adapted. However, if the environment changes significantly, then *all* the individuals will be affected equally by the change. It may be such a dramatic change that none of the individuals are adapted well enough to survive. The species will die out in that area.

SEXUAL REPRODUCTION

There are four stages in any method of sexual reproduction.

- Gametes (sperm and egg cells) are produced.
- The male gamete (sperm) is transferred to the female gamete (egg cell).
- Fertilisation must occur – the sperm fuses with the egg.
- The zygote formed develops into a new individual.

The offspring produced by sexual reproduction show a great deal of genetic variation as a result of both gamete production and fertilisation.

PRODUCTION OF GAMETES

Sperm are produced in the male sex organs – the testes. Eggs are produced in the female sex organs – the ovaries. Both are produced when cells inside these organs divide. These cells do not divide by mitosis but by **meiosis** (see Chapter 17). Meiosis produces cells that are not genetically identical and have only half the number of chromosomes as the original cell.

KEY POINT

Cells that have the full number of chromosomes are called **diploid** cells. Cells that only have half the normal number of chromosomes are called **haploid** cells.

TRANSFER OF THE SPERM TO THE EGG

Sperm are specialised for swimming. They have a tail-like **flagellum** that moves them through a fluid. Figure 9.3 shows the structure of a sperm.

Some male animals, such as those of most fish, release their sperm into the water in which they live. The female animals release their eggs into the water and the sperm then swim through the water to fertilise the eggs. This is called *external* fertilisation as it takes place *outside* the body. Before the release takes place, there is usually some mating behaviour to ensure that male and female are in the same place at the same time. This gives the best chance of fertilisation occurring before water currents sweep the sex cells away.

▲ Figure 9.3 The structure of a sperm

Other male animals, such as those of birds and mammals, ejaculate their sperm in a special fluid into the bodies of the females. *Internal* fertilisation then takes place *inside* the female's body. Fertilisation is much more likely as there are no external factors to prevent the sperm from reaching the eggs. Some form of **sexual intercourse** precedes **ejaculation**.

FERTILISATION

Once the sperm has reached the egg, its nucleus must enter the egg and fuse with the egg nucleus. As each gamete has only half the normal number of chromosomes, the zygote formed by fertilisation will have the full number of chromosomes. In humans, the sperm and egg each have only 23 chromosomes. The zygote has 46 chromosomes, like all other cells in the body. Figure 9.4 shows the main stages in fertilisation.

REMINDER

Red blood cells are exceptions. They have no nucleus, so have no chromosomes.

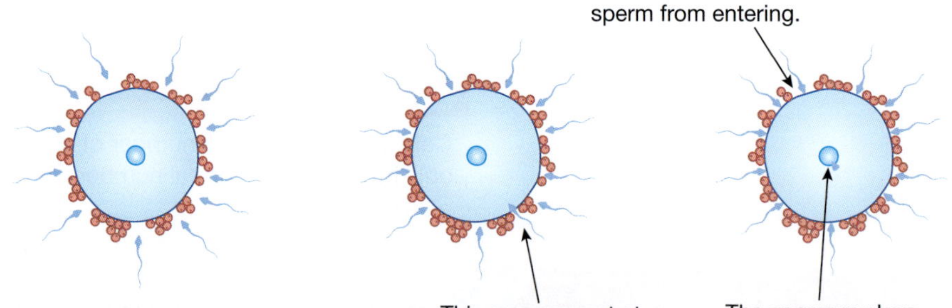

▲ Figure 9.4 The main stages in fertilisation

Fertilisation does more than just restore the diploid chromosome number; it provides an additional source of genetic variation. The sperm and eggs are all genetically different because they are formed by meiosis. Therefore, each time fertilisation takes place, it brings together a different combination of genes.

SUMMARY OF THE HUMAN LIFE CYCLE

Each zygote that is formed must divide to produce all the cells that will make up the adult. All these cells must have the full number of chromosomes, so the zygote divides repeatedly by mitosis. Figure 9.5 shows the importance of meiosis, mitosis and fertilisation in the human life cycle.

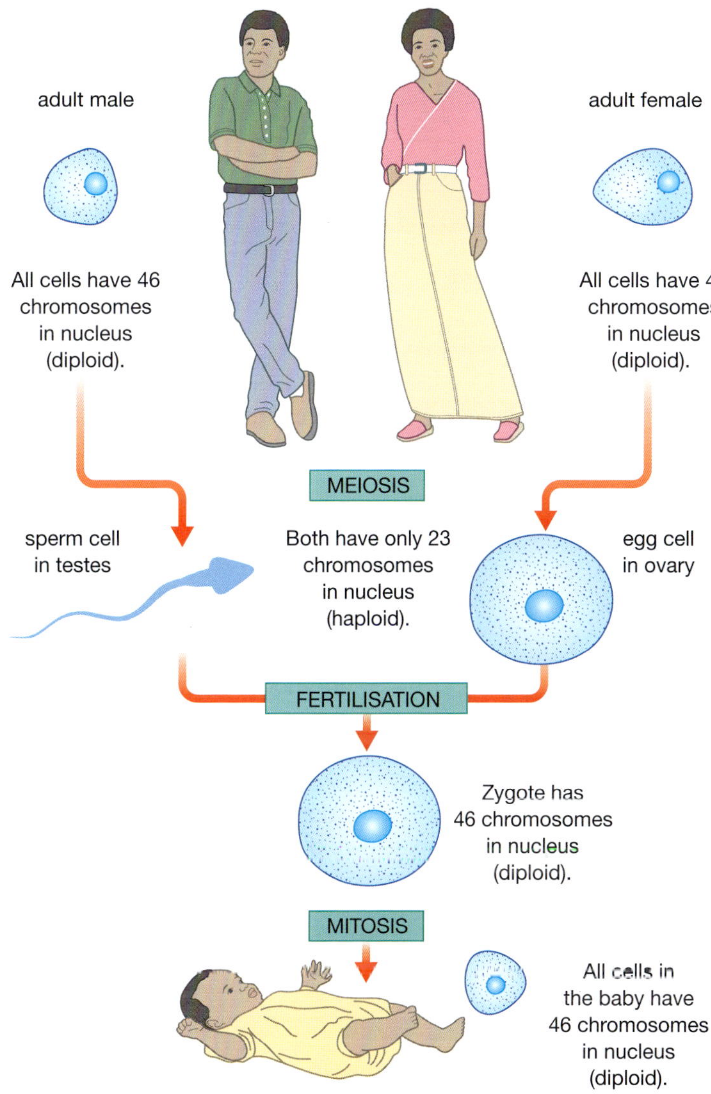

▲ Figure 9.5 The importance of meiosis, mitosis and fertilisation in the human life cycle.

Mitosis is not the only process involved in development, otherwise all that would be produced would be a ball of cells. During the process, cells move around and different shaped structures are formed. Also, different cells specialise to become bone cells, nerve cells, muscle cells, and so on (the process called **differentiation**).

REPRODUCTION IN HUMANS

Humans reproduce sexually and fertilisation is internal. Figures 9.6 and 9.7 show the structure of the human female and male reproductive systems.

The sperm are produced in the testes by meiosis. During sexual intercourse, they pass along the sperm duct and are mixed with a fluid from the seminal vesicles. This mixture, called **semen**, is ejaculated through the **urethra** into the vagina of the female. The sperm then begin to swim towards the oviducts.

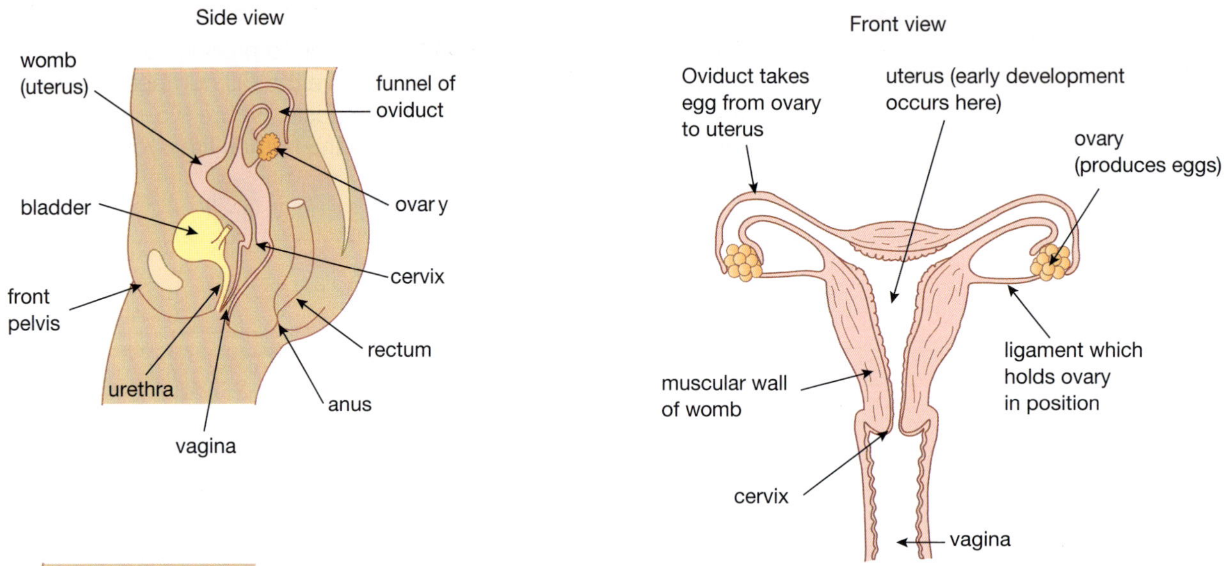

▲ Figure 9.6 The human female reproductive system

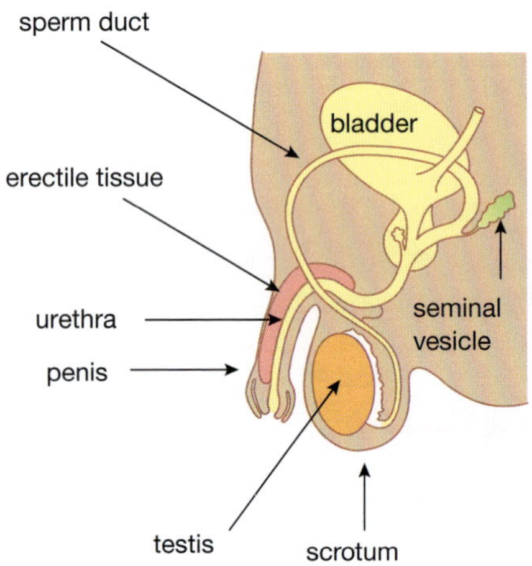

▲ Figure 9.7 The human male reproductive system.

Each month, an egg is released into an **oviduct** from one of the ovaries. (The oviduct is also known as the Fallopian tube.) This is called **ovulation**. If an egg is present in the oviduct, then it may be fertilised by sperm introduced during intercourse. The zygote formed will begin to develop into an **embryo**, which will implant in the lining of the uterus. Here, the embryo will develop a **placenta**, which will allow the embryo to obtain materials such as oxygen and nutrients from the mother's blood. It also allows the embryo to get rid of waste products such as urea and carbon dioxide, as well as anchoring the embryo in the uterus. The placenta secretes female hormones, in particular **progesterone**, which maintain the pregnancy and prevent the embryo from aborting (being rejected by the mother's body). Figure 9.8 shows the structure and position of the placenta.

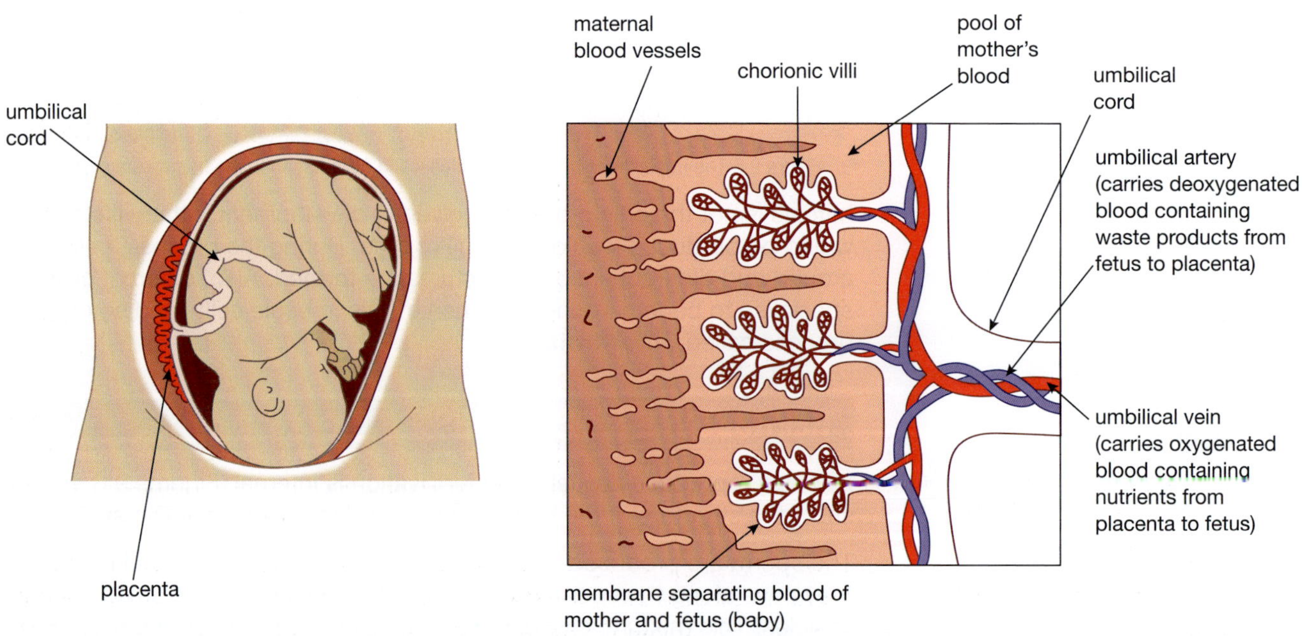

▲ Figure 9.8 The position of the fetus just before birth, and the structure of the placenta.

DID YOU KNOW?
Just before birth, the fetus takes up so much room that many of the mother's organs are moved out of position. The heart is pushed upwards and rotates so that the base points towards the left breast.

During pregnancy, a membrane called the **amnion** encloses the developing embryo. The amnion secretes a fluid called **amniotic fluid**, which protects the developing embryo against sudden movements and bumps. As the embryo develops, it becomes more and more complex. When it becomes recognisably human, we no longer call it an embryo but a **fetus**. At the end of nine months of development, there just isn't any room left for the fetus to grow and it sends a hormonal 'signal' to the mother to begin the birth process. Figure 9.8 also shows the position of a human fetus just before birth.

There are three stages to the birth of a child.

1. **Dilation of the cervix**. The **cervix** is the 'neck' of the uterus. It gets wider to allow the baby to pass through. The muscles of the uterus contract quite strongly and tears the amnion, allowing the amniotic fluid to escape. (In some countries the woman describes this as 'her waters have broken'.)
2. **Delivery of the baby**. Strong contractions of the muscles of the uterus push the baby's head through the cervix and then through the vagina to the outside world.
3. **Delivery of the afterbirth**. After the baby has been born, the uterus continues to contract and pushes the placenta out, together with the membranes that surrounded the baby. These are known as the afterbirth.

Figure 9.9 shows the stages of birth.

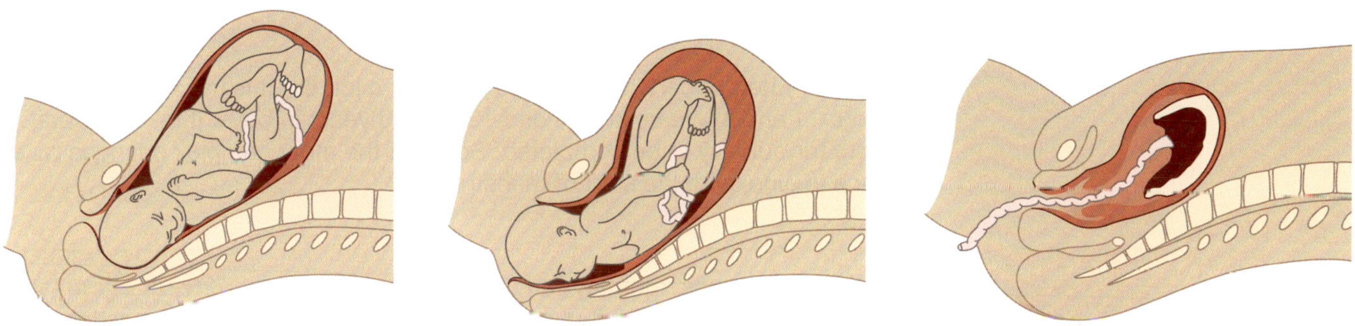

1 Baby's head pushes cervix; mucous pluq dislodges and waters break.

2 Uterus contracts to push baby out through the vagina.

3 The placenta becomes detached from the wall of the uterus and is expelled through the vagina as the afterbirth.

▲ Figure 9.9 The stages of birth

HORMONES CONTROLLING REPRODUCTION

Most animals are unable to reproduce when they are young. We say that they are sexually immature. When a baby is born, it is recognisable as a boy or girl by its sex organs.

The presence of male or female sex organs is known as the primary sex characteristics. During their teens, changes happen to boys and girls that lead to sexual maturity. These changes are controlled by hormones, and the time when they happen is called **puberty**. Puberty involves two developments. The first is that the gametes (eggs and sperm) start to mature and be released. The second is that the bodies of both sexes adapt to allow reproduction to take place. These events are started by hormones released by the pituitary gland.

DID YOU KNOW?
Sperm production is most efficient at a temperature of about 34 °C, just below the core body temperature (37 °C). This is why the testes are outside the body in the scrotum, where the temperature is a little lower.

In boys, these pituitary hormones stimulate sperm production and instruct the testes to secrete the male sex hormone, **testosterone**. Testosterone controls the development of the male **secondary sexual characteristics**. These include growth of the penis and testes, growth of facial and body hair, muscle development and breaking of the voice (Table 9.1).

In girls, the pituitary hormones control the release of a female sex hormone called **oestrogen**, from the ovaries. Oestrogen produces the female secondary sexual characteristics, such as breast development and the beginning of menstruation ('periods').

Table 9.1 Changes at puberty.

In boys	In girls
sperm production starts	the menstrual cycle begins, and eggs are released by the ovaries every month
growth and development of male sexual organs	growth and development of female sexual organs
growth of armpit and pubic hair, and chest and facial hair (beard)	growth of armpit and pubic hair
increase in body mass; growth of muscles, e.g. chest	increase in body mass; development of 'rounded' shape to hips
voice breaks	voice deepens without sudden 'breaking'
sexual 'drive' develops	sexual 'drive' develops
	breasts develop

The age when puberty takes place can vary a lot, but it is usually between about 11 and 14 years in girls and 13 and 16 years in boys. It takes several years for puberty to be completed. Some of the most complex changes take place in girls, with the start of menstruation.

HORMONES AND THE MENSTRUAL CYCLE

'Menstrual' means 'monthly', and in most women the **menstrual cycle** takes about a month, although it can vary from as little as two weeks to as long as six weeks (Figures 9.10 and 9.11). In the middle of the cycle is an event called **ovulation**, which is the release of a mature egg cell, or egg.

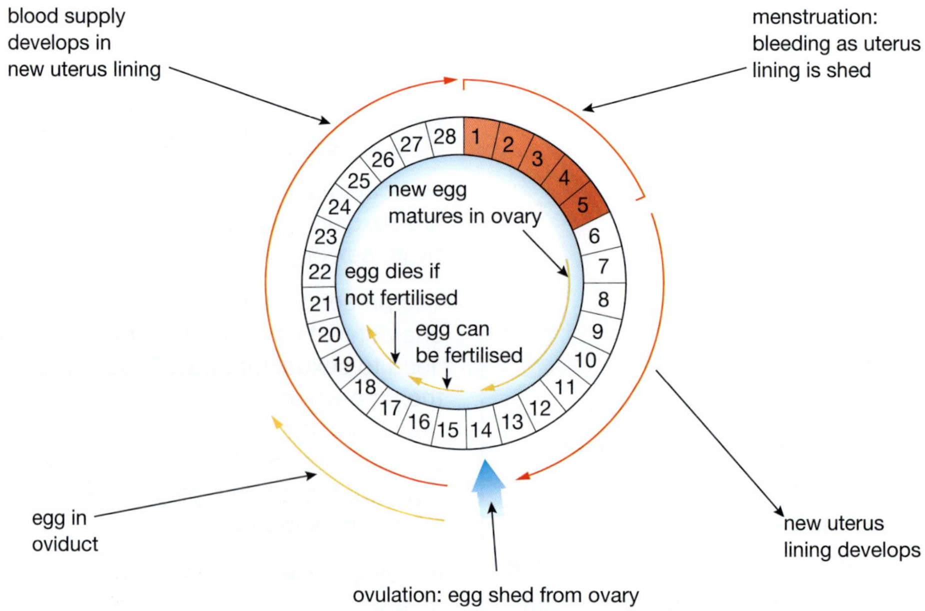

▲ Figure 9.10 The menstrual cycle

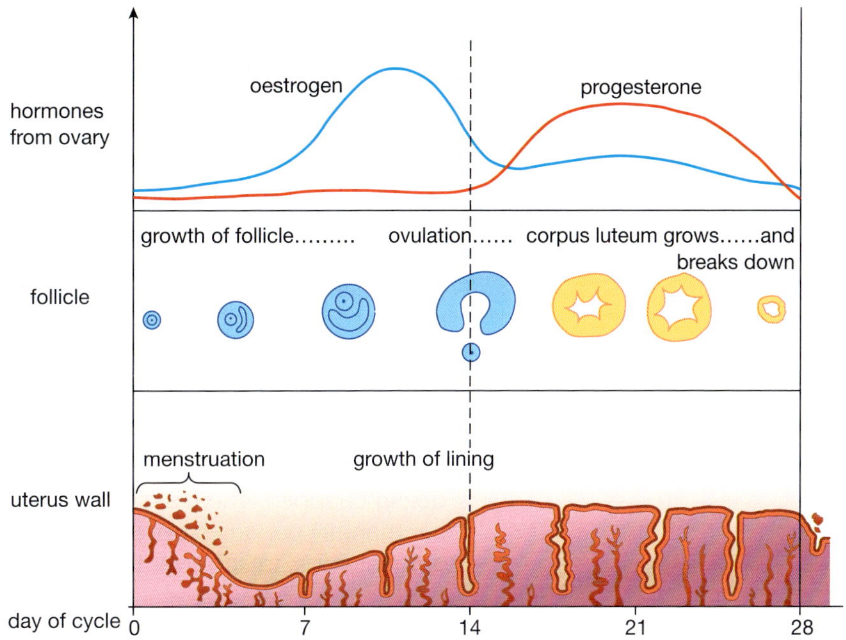

▲ Figure 9.11 Changes taking place during the menstrual cycle

One function of the cycle is to control the development of the lining of the uterus (womb), so that if the egg is fertilised, the lining will be ready to receive the fertilised egg. If the egg is not fertilised, the lining of the uterus is lost from the woman's body as the flow of menstrual blood and cells of the lining, called a **period**.

A cycle is a continuous process, so it doesn't really have a beginning, but the first day of menstruation is usually called day 1.

Inside a woman's ovaries are hundreds of thousands of cells that could develop into mature eggs. Every month, one of these grows inside a ball of cells called a **follicle** (Figure 9.12). At the middle of the cycle (about day 14) the follicle moves towards the edge of the **ovary** and the egg is released as the follicle bursts open. This is the moment of ovulation.

DID YOU KNOW?

A small percentage of women are able to sense the exact moment that ovulation happens, as the egg bursts out of an ovary.

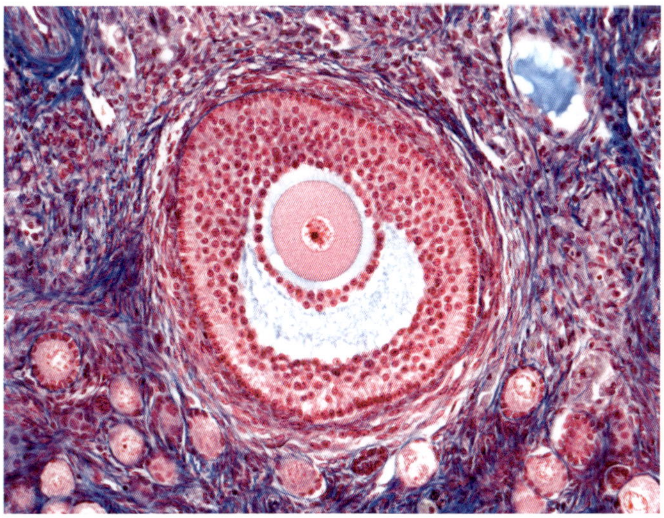

▲ Figure 9.12 Eggs developing inside the follicles of an ovary. The large follicle contains a fully developed egg ready for ovulation.

While this is going on, the lining of the uterus has been repaired after menstruation, and has thickened. This change is brought about by the hormone oestrogen, which is secreted by the ovaries.

EXTENSION WORK

'Corpus luteum' is Latin for 'yellow body'. A corpus luteum appears as a large yellow swelling in an ovary after the egg has been released.

After the egg has been released, it travels down the oviduct to the uterus. It is here in the oviduct that fertilisation may happen, if sexual intercourse has taken place. What's left of the follicle now forms a structure in the ovary called the **corpus luteum**. The corpus luteum makes another hormone called **progesterone**. Progesterone completes the development of the uterus lining, by thickening and maintaining it, ready for the fertilised egg to sink into it and develop into an embryo.

If the egg is not fertilised, the corpus luteum breaks down and stops making progesterone. The lining of the uterus then passes out through the woman's vagina during menstruation. If, however, the egg is fertilised, the corpus luteum carries on making progesterone, the lining is not shed, and menstruation doesn't happen. The first sign that tells a woman she is pregnant is when her monthly periods stop. Later on in pregnancy, the **placenta** secretes progesterone, taking over the role of the corpus luteum.

CHAPTER QUESTIONS

More questions on human reproduction can be found at the end of Unit 2 on page 116.

SKILLS CRITICAL THINKING

7th

1 Which of the following describes sex cells (gametes)?

A diploid cells produced by meiosis

B diploid cells produced by mitosis

C haploid cells produced by meiosis

D haploid cells produced by mitosis

6th

2 Which of the following is *not* a function of the ovaries?

A the secretion of progesterone

B the production of eggs

C the secretion of oestrogen

D the site of fertilisation

3 Which of the following organs produce(s) the hormone progesterone?

1. pituitary gland
2. ovary
3. uterus
4. placenta

A 1 and 2

B 2 and 3

C 3 and 4

D 2 and 4

SKILLS CRITICAL THINKING

5th

4 A woman's first day of menstruation was on 1st June. Assuming she has a 28-day menstrual cycle, when was she most likely to ovulate?

A 7 June

B 10 June

C 14 June

D 21 June

SKILLS ANALYSIS

4th

5 The diagram shows a baby about to be born.

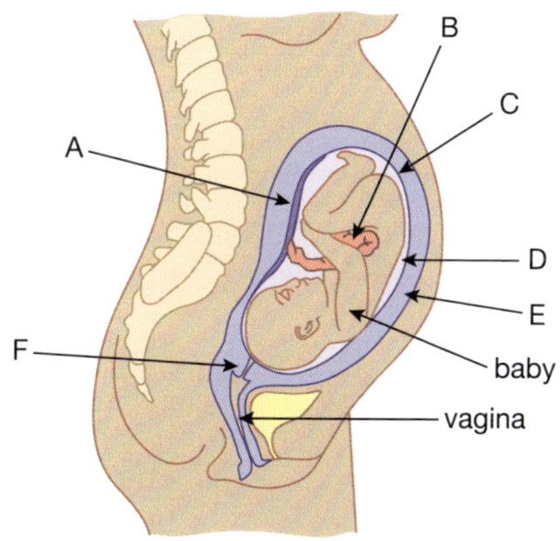

a Name parts A to F on the diagram.

5th

b What is the function of A during pregnancy?

c What must happen to D and E just before birth?

d What must E and F do during birth?

SKILLS CRITICAL THINKING

6th

6 The diagram shows *Hydra* (a small water animal) reproducing in two ways.

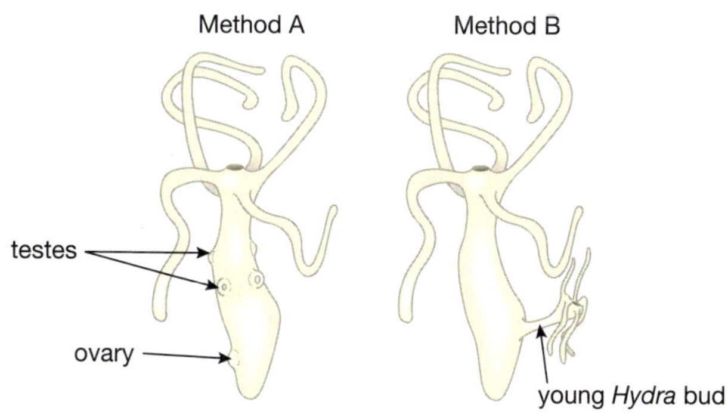

a Which of the two methods shows asexual reproduction? Give a reason for your answer.

7th

b Explain why organisms produced asexually are genetically identical to each other and to the organism that produced them.

c When the surroundings do not change for long periods, *Hydra* reproduces mainly asexually. When the conditions change, *Hydra* begins to reproduce sexually. How does this pattern of sexual and asexual reproduction help *Hydra* to survive?

SKILLS ANALYSIS

5th

7 a The diagram shows the female reproductive system.

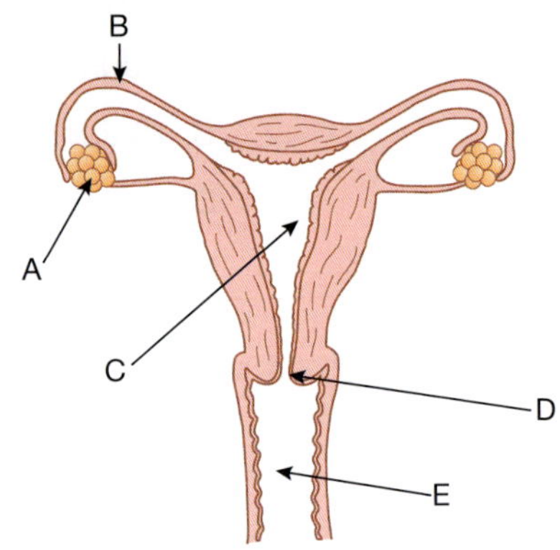

Which letter represents:

i the site of production of oestrogen and progesterone

4th

ii the structure where fertilisation usually occurs

iii the structure that must dilate when birth commences

iv the structure that releases ova?

b The graph shows the changes in the thickness of the lining of a woman's uterus over 100 days.

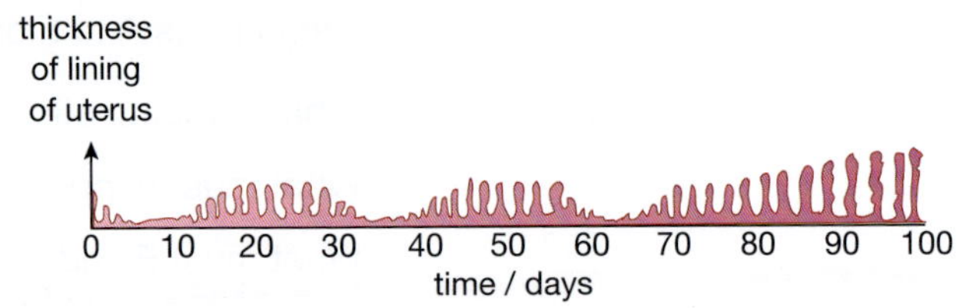

SKILLS CRITICAL THINKING

SKILLS INTERPRETATION

6th

i Name the hormone that causes the thickening of the uterine lining.

ii Use the graph to determine the duration of *this* woman's menstrual cycle. Explain how you arrived at your answer.

iii From the graph, deduce the approximate day on which fertilisation leading to pregnancy took place. Explain how you arrived at your answer.

SKILLS CRITICAL THINKING

5th

iv Why must the uterus lining remain thickened throughout pregnancy?

SKILLS INTERPERSONAL SKILLS

9th

8 The number of sperm cells per cm^3 of semen (the fluid containing sperm) is called the 'sperm count'. Some scientists believe that over the last 50 years, the sperm counts of adult male humans have decreased. They think that this is caused by a number of factors, including drinking water polluted with oestrogens and other chemicals. Carry out an Internet search to find out the evidence for this. Summarise your findings in about two sides of A4 paper.

SKILLS ANALYSIS

6th

9 The graph shows some of the changes taking place during the menstrual cycle.

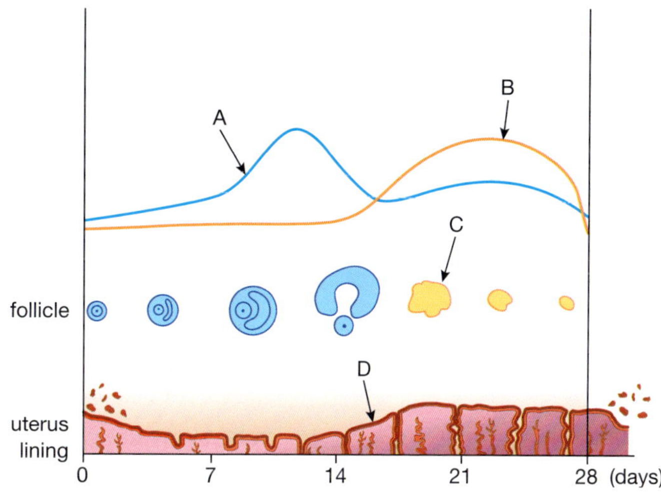

a Identify the two hormones produced by the ovary, which are shown by the lines A and B on the graph.

5th

b Name the structure C.

c What is the purpose of the thickening of the uterus lining at D?

d When is sexual intercourse most likely to result in pregnancy: at day 6, 10, 13, 20 or 23?

SKILLS REASONING

6th

e Why is it important that the level of progesterone remains high in the blood of a woman during pregnancy? How does her body achieve this:

  i just after she becomes pregnant

  ii later on in pregnancy?

UNIT QUESTIONS

SKILLS CRITICAL THINKING 3rd

1 The table shows the percentage of gases in inhaled and exhaled air.

Gas	Inhaled air / %	Exhaled air / %
nitrogen	78	79
oxygen		
carbon dioxide		
other gases (mainly argon)	1	1

a Copy the table and fill in the gaps by choosing from the following numbers:

21 4 0.04 16 **(2)**

SKILLS REASONING 6th

b Explain why the percentage of carbon dioxide is different in inhaled and exhaled air. **(2)**

c Explain why exhaling is a form of excretion. **(2)**

d The following features can be seen in the lungs:

7th

i thin membranes between the alveoli and the blood supply

ii a good blood supply

iii a large surface area.

In each case explain how the feature helps gas exchange to happen quickly. **(6)**

(Total 12 marks)

SKILLS ANALYSIS

2 Digestion is brought about by enzymes converting large insoluble molecules into smaller soluble molecules that can be more easily absorbed.

a The activity of enzymes is influenced by pH and temperature. The graph shows the activity of two human enzymes from different regions of the gut at different pH values.

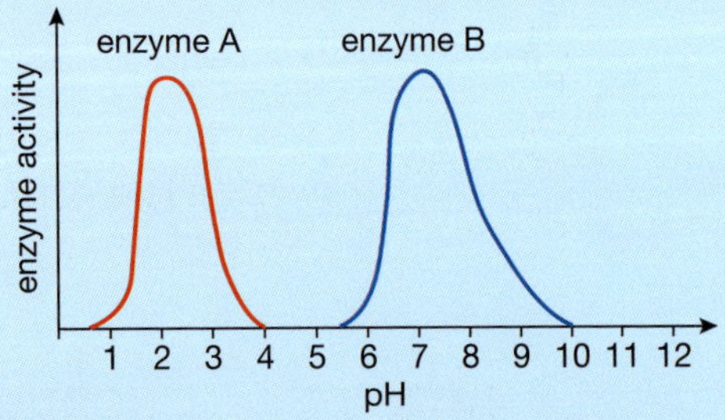

i Suggest which regions of the gut the two enzymes come from. Explain your answer. **(4)**

6th

ii Which nutrient does enzyme A digest? **(1)**

b Farmers sometimes include urea in cattle food. The microorganisms in the rumen can use urea to make protein.

SKILLS CRITICAL THINKING 4th

i In mammals, where in the body is urea made? **(1)**

5th

ii What is urea made from? **(1)**

8th

iii Suggest how feeding urea to cattle can result in an increased growth rate. **(1)**

(Total 8 marks)

SKILLS ANALYSIS 6th

3 The diagram shows the human circulatory system. The system carries nutrients, oxygen and carbon dioxide around the body.

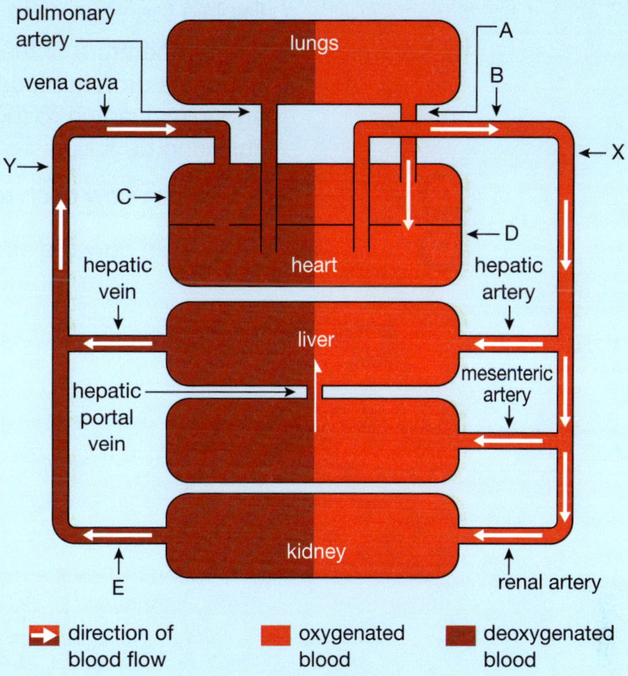

a Write down the names of the structures labelled A to E. **(5)**

7th **b** Give two differences between the blood vessels at point X and point Y. **(2)**

c During exercise, the adrenal gland releases the hormone adrenaline. Reflexes involving the medulla of the brain influence the heartbeat and breathing.

SKILLS CRITICAL THINKING 6th

i Describe two effects of adrenaline on the heartbeat. **(2)**

ii Describe two other effects of adrenaline on the body. **(2)**

SKILLS REASONING 7th

d How is a reflex action different from a voluntary action? **(2)**

6th **e** Following exercise there is a recovery period in which breathing rate and heart rate gradually return to pre-exercise levels. Explain why they do not return immediately to these levels. **(3)**

(Total 16 marks)

SKILLS INTERPRETATION

4 The immune system responds to infections using white blood cells. A phagocyte is one type of white blood cell.

a Draw and label a phagocyte. **(3)**

SKILLS CRITICAL THINKING 5th

b State one way that the structure of a phagocyte differs from that of a red blood cell. **(1)**

c Phagocytes carry out phagocytosis. Describe this process. **(2)**

6th **d** Describe how other white blood cells are involved in the immune response. **(3)**

(Total 9 marks)

SKILLS REASONING 7th

5 Humans and other mammals are able to maintain a constant body temperature which is usually higher than that of their surroundings.

a Explain the advantage in maintaining a constant, high body temperature. **(1)**

b The temperature of the blood is constantly monitored by the brain. If it detects a drop in blood temperature, the following things happen: the arterioles leading to the skin capillaries constrict, less sweat is formed and shivering begins.

8th **i** Explain how each response helps the body to keep warm. **(3)**

7th **ii** Explain how the structure of arterioles allows them to constrict. **(2)**

(Total 6 marks)

SKILLS ANALYSIS

6 The diagram represents a typical menstrual cycle.

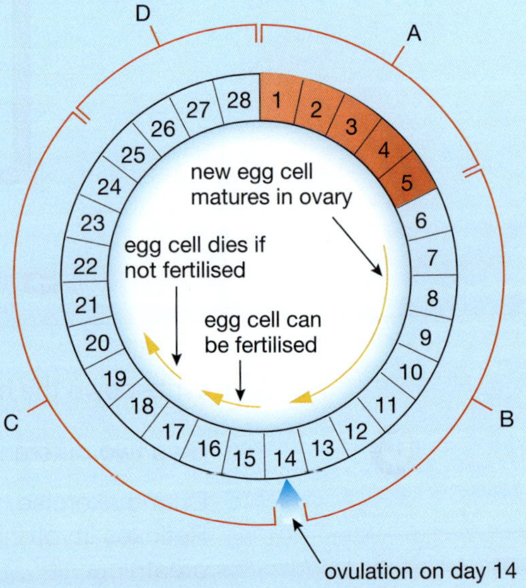

a Using evidence from the diagram, answer the following questions.

During which of the stages A, B, C or D does:

5th **i** the level of the hormone oestrogen increase in the blood

ii the level of the hormone progesterone increase in the blood

4th **iii** the uterine lining become more vascular

5th **iv** the levels of oestrogen and progesterone in the blood fall

4th **v** the uterine lining begin to break down? **(5)**

SKILLS REASONING 5th

b Explain how knowledge of the menstrual cycle can be used to avoid pregnancy. **(3)**

(Total 8 marks)

SKILLS CRITICAL THINKING 8th

7 Cells can divide by mitosis or by meiosis. Human cells contain 46 chromosomes. The graphs show the changes in the number of chromosomes per cell as two different human cells undergo cell division.

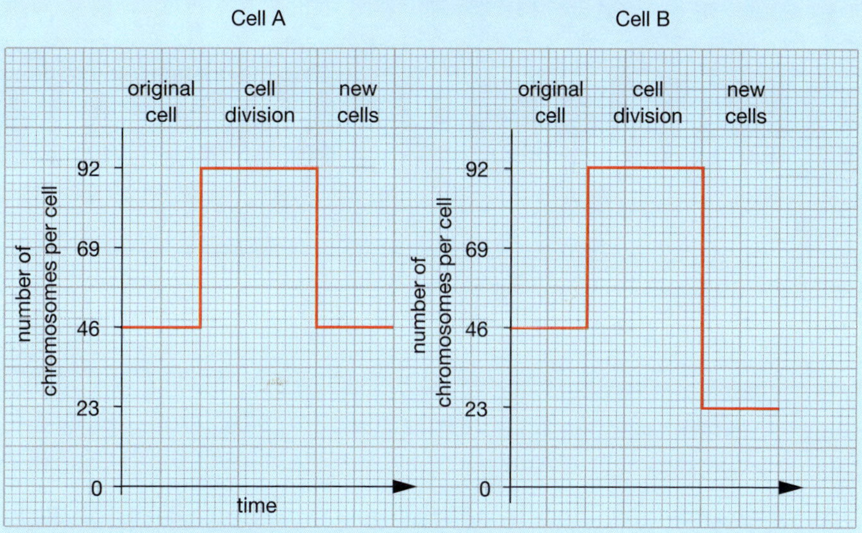

a Which of the two cells, A or B, is dividing by meiosis? Explain how you arrived at your answer. **(3)**

b Explain the importance of meiosis, mitosis and fertilisation in maintaining the human chromosome number constant at 46 chromosomes per cell, generation after generation. **(6)**

7th

c Give *three* differences between mitosis and meiosis. **(3)**

(Total 12 marks)

SKILLS EXECUTIVE FUNCTION 6th

8 Protein supplements are foods that some body-builders use to increase the growth of their muscles. Describe an investigation to find out if adding a protein supplement to the diet of rats will increase their growth.

Your answer should include experimental details and be written in full sentences. **(6)**

(Total 6 marks)

BIOLOGY UNIT 3 PLANT PHYSIOLOGY

Plant physiology is the branch of biology that deals with the internal activities of plants. It covers many aspects of plant life, including nutrition (photosynthesis), movement of materials around the plant, and reproduction. There are many reasons why we need to study how plants work, not least because they provide the world's food supply and oxygen. Animals, including humans, could not exist without plants. Modern agriculture depends on the scientific study of plant physiology, as does our understanding of eccosystems.

10 PLANTS AND FOOD

This chapter looks at photosynthesis, the process by which plants make starch, and the structure of leaves in relation to photosynthesis. It also deals with how plants obtain other nutrients, and their uses in the plant.

LEARNING OBJECTIVES

- Investigate photosynthesis by testing for the production of starch in a leaf
- Investigate the need for light, carbon dioxide and chlorophyll for photosynthesis
- Understand the process of photosynthesis and its importance in the conversion of light energy to chemical energy
- Know the word equation and the balanced symbol equation for photosynthesis
- Describe the structure of the leaf and explain how it is adapted for photosynthesis
- Understand how light intensity, carbon dioxide concentration and temperature affect the rate of photosynthesis
- Investigate photosynthesis using the evolution of oxygen from a water plant
- Understand that plants require mineral ions for growth, and that magnesium ions are needed to make chlorophyll and nitrate ions are needed to make amino acids

PLANTS MAKE STARCH

All the foods shown in Figure 10.1 are products of plants. Some, such as potatoes, rice and bread (made from cereals such as wheat or rye), form the staple diet of humans. They all contain starch, which is the main storage carbohydrate made by plants. Starch is a good way of storing carbohydrate because it insoluble, compact and can be broken down easily.

▲ Figure 10.1 All these foods are made by plants or made from products of plants. They all contain starch.

ACTIVITY 1

▼ PRACTICAL: TESTING LEAVES FOR STARCH

You can test for starch in food by adding a few drops of yellow-brown iodine solution (see Chapter 4). If the food contains starch, a blue-black colour is produced.

Leaves that have been in sunlight also contain starch, but you can't test for it by adding iodine solution to a fresh leaf. The outer waxy surface of the leaf will not absorb the solution, and besides, the green colour of the leaf would hide the colour change. To test for starch in a leaf, the outer waxy layer needs to be removed and the leaf decolourised. This is done by placing the leaf in boiling ethanol (see Figure 10.2).

A beaker of water is set up on a tripod and gauze and the water heated until it boils. A leaf is removed from a plant and killed by placing it in boiling water for 30 seconds (this stops all chemical reactions in the leaf).

The Bunsen burner is turned off (this is important because ethanol is highly flammable), the leaf is placed in a boiling tube containing ethanol, and the tube is placed in the beaker of hot water. The boiling point of ethanol (about 78 °C) is lower than that of water (100 °C) so the ethanol will boil for a few minutes, until the water cools down. This is long enough to remove most of the chlorophyll from the leaf.

When the leaf has turned colourless or pale yellow, it is removed and washed in cold water to soften it, then spread out on a tile and covered with a few drops of iodine solution. After a few minutes, any parts of the leaf that contain starch will turn a dark blue-black colour. This only works if the plant has had plenty of light for some hours before the test.

Safety note: Wash your hands after handling the leaves. Take care not to splash boiling water. Do not heat the ethanol directly with any flame: instead use a beaker of hot water. Iodine solution will badly stain everything – including skin.

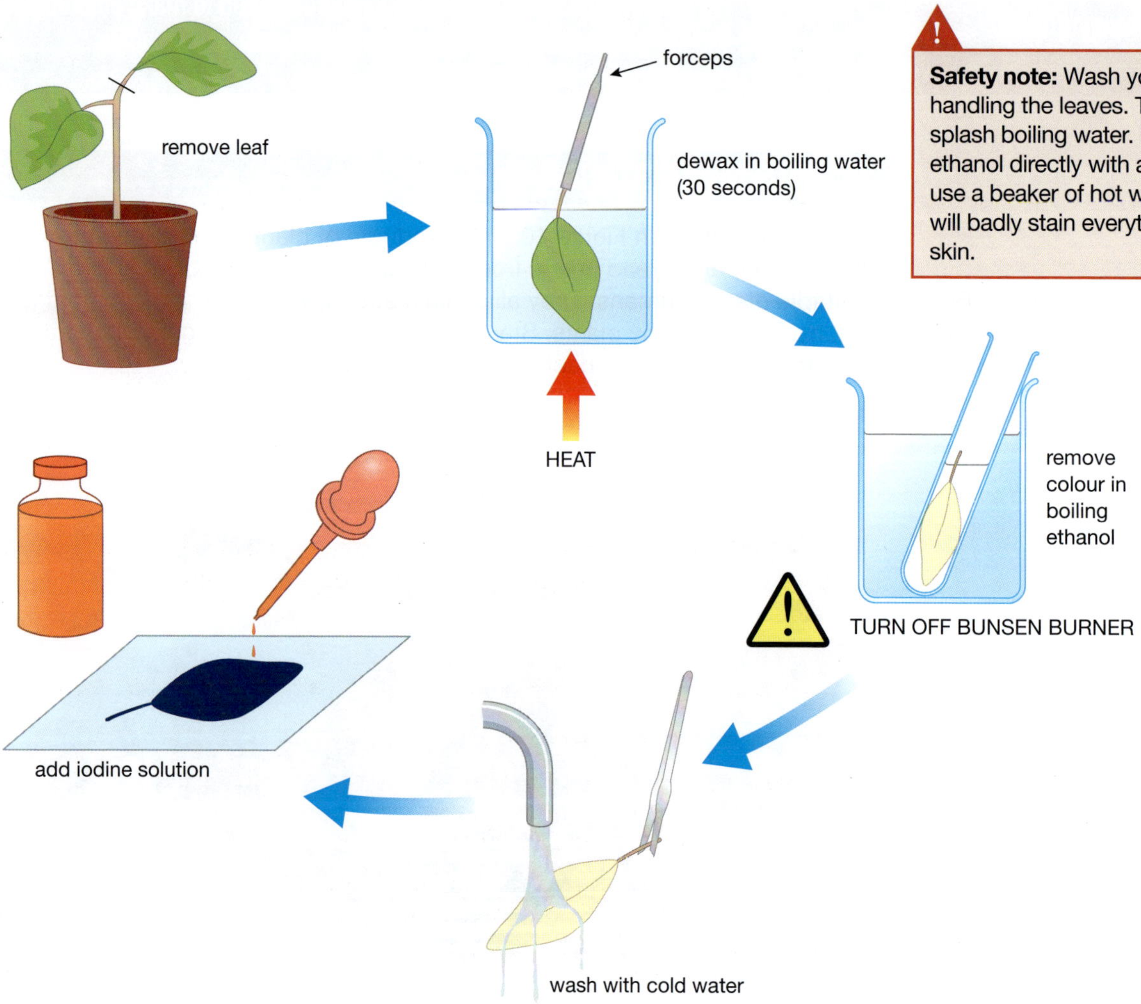

▲ Figure 10.2 How to test a leaf for starch

KEY POINT

You can 'de-starch' a plant by placing it in the dark for 2 or 3 days. The plant uses up the starch stores in its leaves. De-starched plants are used to find out the conditions needed for the plant to make more starch by photosynthesis.

Starch is only made in the parts of plants that contain chlorophyll. You can show this by testing a leaf from a variegated plant, which has green and white areas to its leaves. The white parts of the leaf will give a negative starch test, staining yellow-brown with iodine solution. Only the green areas will stain blue-black. Figure 10.3 shows the results of a starch test on a leaf. The leaf was taken from a plant that had been under a bright light for 24 hours.

▲ Figure 10.3 Testing a leaf for starch. (a) Leaf before test (b) Decolourised leaf (c) Leaf after test, stained blue-black with iodine solution.

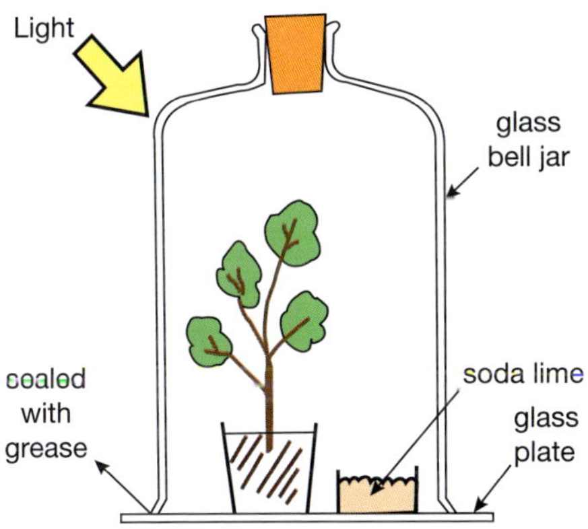

▲ Figure 10.4 Demonstration that carbon dioxide is needed for photosynthesis. The soda lime absorbs carbon dioxide from the air in the bell jar. A Control experiment should be set up, using exactly the same apparatus but without the soda lime.

HINT

You might think that the results of the test on the variegated leaf prove that chlorophyll is needed for photosynthesis. But is this conclusion fully justified? The leaf could have photosynthesised in the white areas and the sugars been transported elsewhere in the plant. Similarly, the green areas may not be photosynthesising at all, but simply laying down starch from glucose made somewhere else. All it really shows is that starch is present in the green areas and not in the white areas of the leaf. We *assume* this is because chlorophyll is needed for photosynthesis.

Taking away the source of light is not the only way you can prevent a plant making starch in its leaves. You can also place it in a closed container containing a chemical called soda lime (Figure 10.4). This substance absorbs carbon dioxide from the air around the plant. If the plant is kept under a bright light but with no carbon dioxide, it again won't be able to make starch.

WHERE DOES THE STARCH COME FROM?

You have now found out three important facts about starch production by leaves:

- it uses carbon dioxide from the air
- it needs light
- it needs chlorophyll in the leaves.

As well as starch, there is another product of this process which is essential to the existence of most living things on the Earth – oxygen. When a plant is in the light, it makes oxygen gas. You can show this using an aquatic plant such as *Elodea* (Canadian pondweed). When a piece of this plant is placed in a test tube of water under a bright light, it produces a stream of small bubbles. If the bubbles are collected and their contents analysed, they are found to contain a high concentration of oxygen (Figure 10.5).

▲ Figure 10.5 The bubbles of gas released from this pondweed contain a higher concentration of oxygen than in atmospheric air.

Starch is composed of long chains of glucose (see Chapter 4). A plant does not make starch directly, but first produces glucose, which is then joined together in chains to form starch molecules. A carbohydrate made of many sugar sub-units is called a **polysaccharide**. Glucose has the formula $C_6H_{12}O_6$. The carbon and oxygen atoms of the glucose molecule come from the carbon dioxide gas in the air around the plant. The hydrogen atoms come from another molecule essential to the living plant – water.

It would be very difficult in a school laboratory to show that a plant uses water to make starch. If you deprived a plant of water in the same way as you deprived it of carbon dioxide, it would soon wilt and eventually die. However, scientists have proved that water is used in photosynthesis. They have done this by supplying the plant with water with 'labelled' atoms, for example using the 'heavy' isotope of oxygen (^{18}O). This isotope ends up in the oxygen gas produced by the plant. A summary of the sources of the atoms in the glucose and oxygen looks like this:

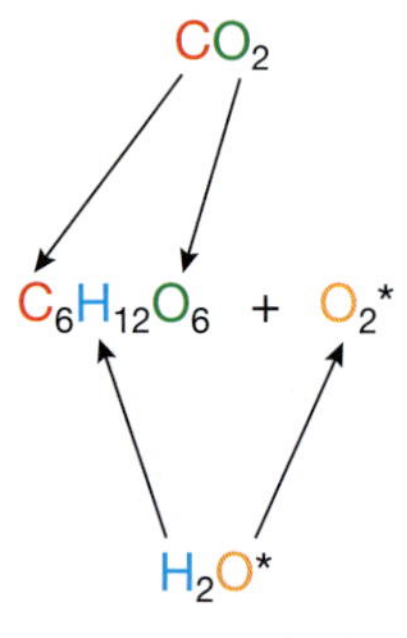

(*oxygen labelled with ^{18}O)

EXTENSION WORK

Isotopes are forms of the same element with the same atomic number but different mass numbers (due to extra neutrons in the nucleus). Isotopes of some elements are radioactive and can be used as 'labels' to follow chemical pathways. Others like ^{18}O are identified by their mass.

PHOTOSYNTHESIS

Plants use the simple inorganic molecules carbon dioxide and water, in the presence of chlorophyll and light, to make glucose and oxygen. This process is called **photosynthesis**.

It is summarised by the equation:

$$\text{carbon dioxide + water} \xrightarrow[\text{chlorophyll}]{\text{light}} \text{glucose + oxygen}$$

or: $$6CO_2 + 6H_2O \xrightarrow[\text{chlorophyll}]{\text{light}} C_6H_{12}O_6 + 6O_2$$

DID YOU KNOW?

The 'photo' in photosynthesis comes from the Greek word *photos*, meaning light, and a 'synthesis' reaction is one where small molecules are built up into larger ones.

The role of the green pigment, chlorophyll, is to absorb the light energy needed for the reaction to take place. The products of the reaction (glucose and oxygen) contain more energy than the carbon dioxide and water. In other words, photosynthesis converts light energy into chemical energy.

You will probably have noticed that the overall equation for photosynthesis is the reverse of the one for aerobic respiration (see Chapter 1):

$$C_6H_{12}O_6 + 6O_2 \rightarrow 6CO_2 + 6H_2O \text{ (plus energy)}$$

Respiration, which is carried out by both animals and plants, *releases* energy (but not as light) from the breakdown of glucose. The chemical energy in the glucose came originally from light 'trapped' by the process of photosynthesis.

THE STRUCTURE OF LEAVES

Most green parts of a plant can photosynthesise, but the leaves are the plant organs which are best adapted for this function. To be able to photosynthesise efficiently, leaves need to have a large surface area to absorb light, many chloroplasts containing the chlorophyll, a supply of water and carbon dioxide, and a system for carrying away the products of photosynthesis to other parts of the plant. They also need to release oxygen (and water vapour) from the leaf cells. Most leaves are thin, flat structures supported by a leaf stalk which can grow to allow the blade of the leaf to be angled to receive the maximum amount of sunlight (Figure 10.6).

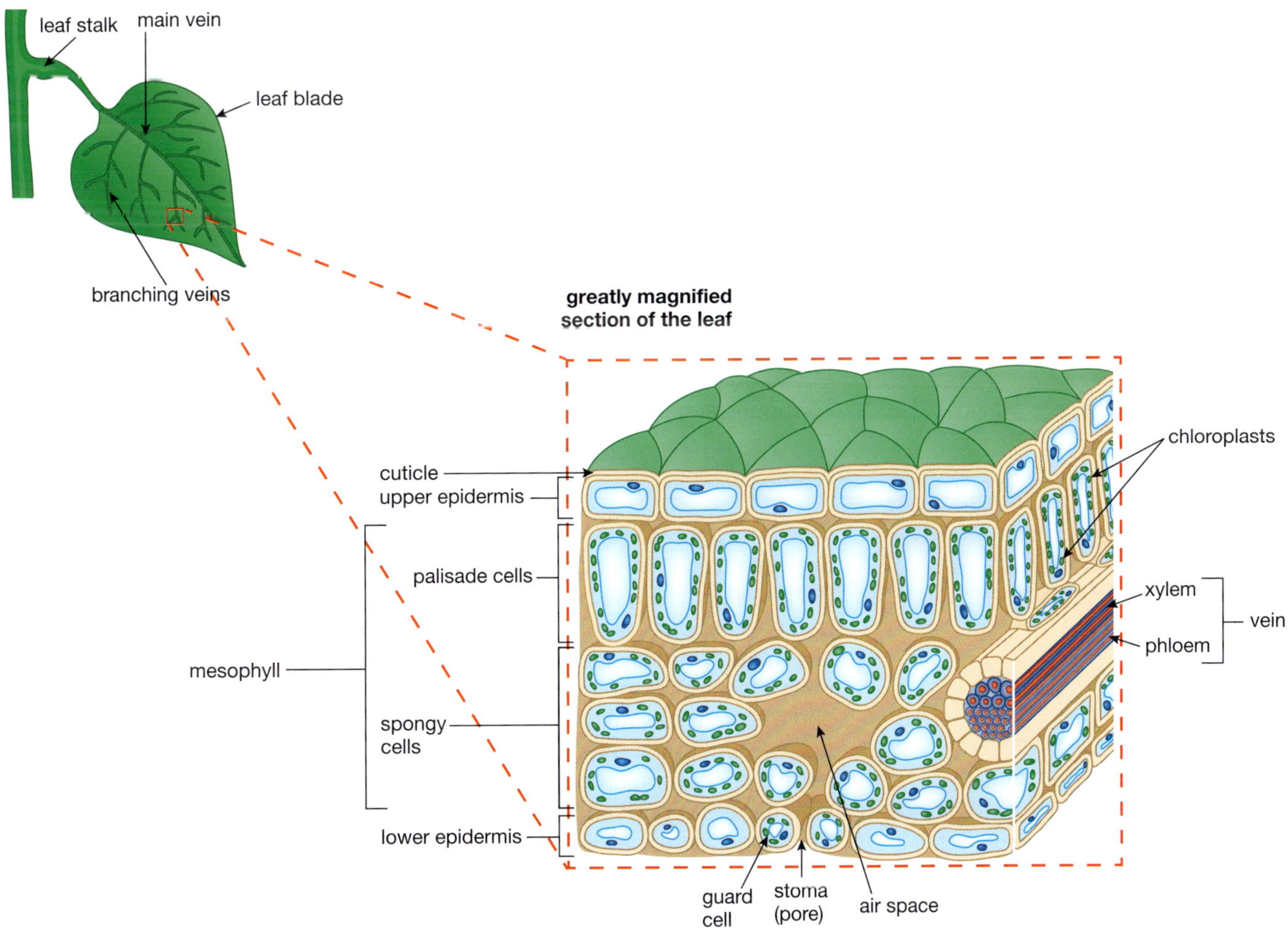

▲ Figure 10.6 External and internal features of a leaf

Inside the leaf are layers of cells with different functions.

- The two outer layers of cells (the upper and lower **epidermis**) have few chloroplasts and are covered by a thin layer of a waxy material called the **cuticle**. This reduces water loss by evaporation, and acts as a barrier to the entry of disease-causing microorganisms such as bacteria and fungi.
- The lower epidermis has many holes or pores called **stomata** (a single pore is a **stoma**). Usually the upper epidermis contains fewer or no stomata. The stomata allow carbon dioxide to diffuse into the leaf, to reach the photosynthetic tissues. They also allow oxygen and water vapour to diffuse out. Each stoma is formed as a gap between two highly specialised cells called **guard cells**, which can change their shape to open or close the stoma.
- In the middle of the leaf are two layers of photosynthetic cells called the mesophyll ('mesophyll' just means 'middle of the leaf'). Just below the upper epidermis is the **palisade mesophyll** layer. This is a tissue made of long, narrow cells, each containing hundreds of chloroplasts, and is the main site of photosynthesis. The palisade cells are close to the source of light, and the upper epidermis is relatively transparent, allowing light to pass through to the enormous numbers of chloroplasts which lie below.
- Below the palisade layer is a tissue made of more rounded, loosely packed cells, with air spaces between them, called the **spongy mesophyll** layer. These cells also photosynthesise, but have fewer chloroplasts than the palisade cells. They form the main gas exchange surface of the leaf, absorbing carbon dioxide and releasing oxygen and water vapour. The air spaces allow these gases to diffuse in and out of the mesophyll.
- Water and mineral ions are supplied to the leaf by vessels in a tissue called the **xylem**. This forms a continuous transport system throughout the plant. Water is absorbed by the roots and passes up through the stem and through veins in the leaves in the **transpiration stream**. In the leaves, the water leaves the xylem and supplies the mesophyll cells.
- The products of photosynthesis, such as sugars, are carried away from the mesophyll cells by another transport system, the **phloem**. The phloem supplies all other parts of the plant, so that tissues and organs that can't make their own food receive products of photosynthesis. The veins in the leaf contain both xylem and phloem tissue, and branch again and again to supply all parts of the leaf.

You will find out more about both plant transport systems in Chapter 11.

KEY POINT

Starch is insoluble and so cannot be transported around the plant. The phloem carries only soluble substances such as sugars (mainly sucrose) and amino acids. These are converted into other compounds when they reach their destination.

FACTORS AFFECTING THE RATE OF PHOTOSYNTHESIS

When the light intensity rises, the rate of photosynthesis begins by rising too, but eventually it reaches a maximum rate. What makes the rate 'level off' (flatten) like this? It is because some other factor needed for photosynthesis is in short supply, so that increasing the light intensity does not affect the rate any more. Normally, the factor which 'holds back' the rate of photosynthesis is the concentration of carbon dioxide in the air. This is only about 0.03 to 0.04%, and the plant can only take up the carbon dioxide and fix it into carbohydrate at a certain rate. If the plant is put in a closed container with a higher than normal concentration of carbon dioxide, it will photosynthesise at a faster rate. If there is both a high light intensity and a high level of carbon dioxide, the temperature may limit the rate of photosynthesis, by limiting the rate of the chemical reactions in the leaf. A rise in temperature will then increase the rate. With normal levels of carbon dioxide, very low temperatures (close to 0 °C) slow the reactions, but high temperatures (above about 35 °C) also reduce photosynthesis by denaturing enzymes in the plant cells (see Chapter 1).

KEY POINT

A limiting factor is the component of a reaction that is in 'shortest supply' so that it prevents the rate of the reaction increasing, in other words sets a 'limit' to it.

KEY POINT

Knowledge of limiting factors is used in some glasshouses (greenhouses) to speed up the growth of crop plants such as tomatoes and lettuces (see Chapter 15). Extra carbon dioxide is added to the air around the plants, by using gas burners. The higher concentration of carbon dioxide, along with the high temperature in the glasshouse, increases the rate of photosynthesis and the growth of the leaves and fruits.

Light intensity, carbon dioxide concentration and temperature can all act as what are called **limiting factors** in this way. This is easier to see as a graph (Figure 10.7).

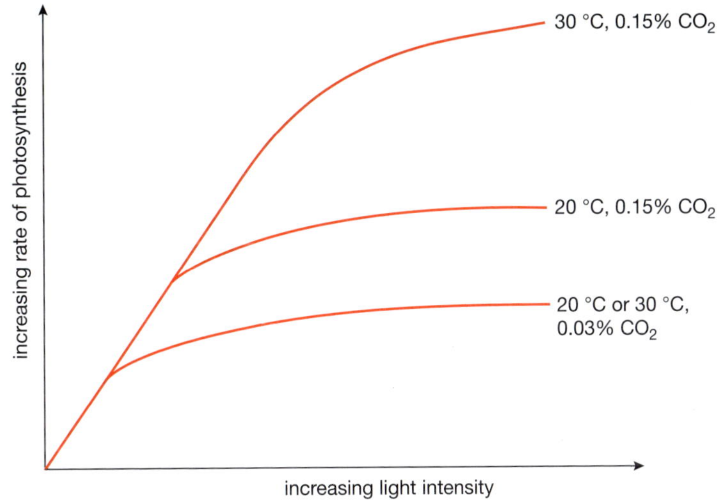

▲ Figure 10.7 Light intensity, carbon dioxide concentration and temperature can all act as limiting factors on the rate of photosynthesis.

Safety note: Wash hands after collecting and preparing pondweed. Do not handle the lamp, plug or switch with wet hands.

ACTIVITY 2

▼ PRACTICAL: MEASURING THE RATE OF PHOTOSYNTHESIS USING PONDWEED

You can measure the rate of photosynthesis of a plant by measuring how quickly it produces oxygen. With a land plant this is difficult, because the oxygen is released into the air, but with an aquatic plant such as the pondweed *Elodea*, bubbles of oxygen are released into the water around the plant (Figure 10.5).

If the bubbles formed per minute are counted, this is a measure of the rate of photosynthesis of the plant. It is easiest to count the bubbles if the cut piece of weed is placed upside down in a test tube, as shown in Figure 10.8. A small paperclip attached to the bottom of the piece of weed makes it sink.

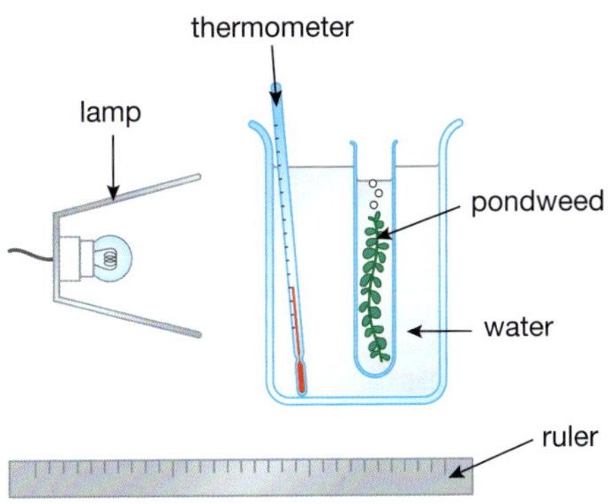

▲ Figure 10.8 Measuring the rate of photosynthesis in an aquatic plant.

The light intensity is changed by moving the lamp, altering the distance between the lamp and the pondweed. The beaker of water keeps the temperature of the plant constant.

Design an experiment using this apparatus to find out if the rate of photosynthesis is affected by the light intensity. In your plan you should include:

- a hypothesis – state what you think will happen when you change the light intensity, and why
- a systematic way of changing the light intensity
- how the experiment will be controlled so that nothing else is changed apart from the light intensity (e.g. what will you do about the background light in the laboratory?)
- a Control that you could use, to show that it is the effect of light on the pondweed that is producing the bubbles
- how you will ensure that your results are reliable.

When you have completed your plan, you may be allowed to use similar apparatus to carry out the experiment. How could you modify your plan to find the effect of changing the *temperature* on the rate of photosynthesis? What factors would you need to keep constant this time? What would be a suitable range of temperatures to use?

THE PLANT'S USES FOR GLUCOSE

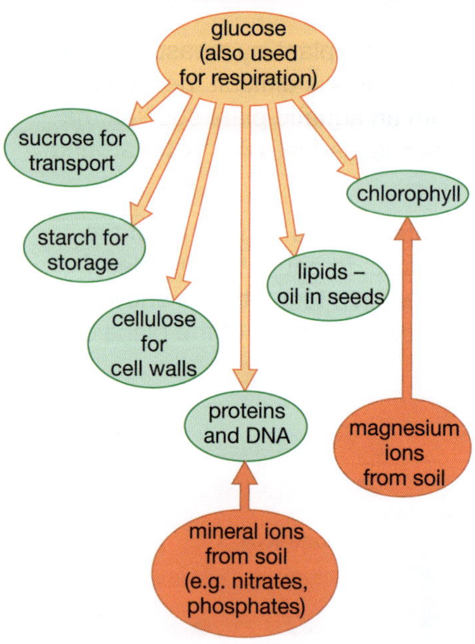

▲ Figure 10.9 Compounds that plant cells can make from glucose.

As you have seen, some glucose that the plant makes is used in respiration to provide the plant's cells with energy. Some glucose is quickly converted into starch for storage. However, a plant is not made up of just glucose and starch, and must make all of its organic molecules, starting from glucose.

Glucose is a single sugar unit (a **monosaccharide**). Plant cells can convert it into other sugars, such as a monosaccharide called **fructose** (found in fruits) and the disaccharide sucrose, which is the main sugar carried in the phloem. It can also be changed into another polymer, the polysaccharide called **cellulose**, which forms plant cell walls.

All these compounds are carbohydrates. Plant cells can also convert glucose into lipids (fats and oils). Lipids are needed for the membranes of all cells, and are also an energy store in many seeds and fruits, such as peanuts, sunflower seeds and olives.

Carbohydrates and lipids both contain only three elements – carbon, hydrogen and oxygen – and so they can be inter-converted without the need for a supply of other elements. Proteins contain these elements too, but all amino acids (the building blocks of proteins) also contain nitrogen. This is obtained as nitrate ions from the soil, through the plant's roots. Other compounds in plants contain other elements. For example, chlorophyll contains magnesium ions, which are also absorbed from water in the soil. Some of the products that a plant makes from glucose are summarised in Figure 10.9.

KEY POINT

Glucose from photosynthesis is not just used as the *raw material* for the production of molecules such as starch, cellulose, lipids and proteins. Reactions like these, which synthesise large molecules from smaller ones, also need a source of energy. This energy is provided by the plant's *respiration* of glucose.

MINERAL NUTRITION

Nitrate ions are absorbed from the soil water, along with other minerals such as phosphate, potassium and magnesium ions. The element phosphorus is needed for the plant cells to make many important compounds, including DNA. Potassium ions are required for enzymes in respiration and photosynthesis to work, and magnesium forms a part of the chlorophyll molecule.

WATER CULTURE EXPERIMENTS

A plant takes only water and mineral ions from the soil for growth. Plants can be grown in soil-free cultures (water cultures) if the correct balance of minerals is added to the water. In the nineteenth century, the German biologist Wilhelm Knop invented one example of a culture solution. Knop's solution contains the following chemicals (per dm^3 of water):

0.8 g	calcium nitrate
0.2 g	magnesium sulfate
0.2 g	potassium nitrate
0.2 g	potassium dihydrogenphosphate
(trace)	iron(III) phosphate

Notice that these chemicals provide all of the main elements that the plant needs to make proteins, DNA and chlorophyll, as well as other compounds, from glucose. It is called a *complete* culture solution. If you were to make a similar solution, but to replace, for example, magnesium sulfate with more calcium sulfate, this would produce a culture solution which was *deficient* (lacking) in magnesium. You could then grow plants in the complete and deficient solutions, and compare the results. There are several ways to grow the plants, such as using the apparatus shown in Figure 10.10, which is useful for plant cuttings. Seedlings can be grown by packing cotton wool around the seed, instead of using a rubber bung.

DID YOU KNOW?

In fact, in addition to the ions listed in Knop's solution, plants need very small amounts of other mineral ions for healthy growth. Knop's culture solution only worked because the chemicals he used to make his solutions weren't very pure, and supplied enough of these additional ions by mistake!

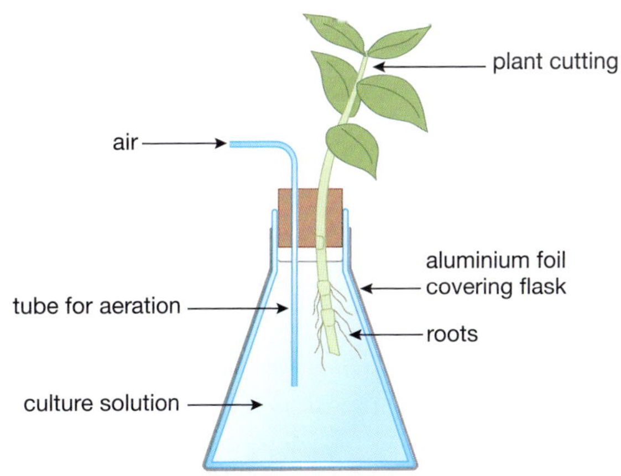

▲ Figure 10.10 A simple water culture method

The plant is kept in bright light, so that it can photosynthesise. The covering around the flask prevents algae from growing in the culture solution. The aeration tube is used for short periods to supply the roots with oxygen for respiration of the root cells, since some ions are taken up by active transport. Using methods like this, it soon becomes clear that mineral deficiencies result in poor plant growth. A shortage of a particular mineral results in particular symptoms in the plant, called a *mineral deficiency disease*. For example, lack of magnesium means that the plant won't be able to make chlorophyll, and the leaves will turn yellow. Lack of nitrate limits a plant's growth, because it is unable to make enough protein. Some of the mineral ions that a plant needs, their uses, and the deficiency symptoms are shown in Table 10.1. Compare the photographs of the mineral deficient plants to those of the control plant in Figure 10.11(a).

▲ Figure 10.11 (a) A healthy bean plant

Table 10.1: Mineral ions needed by plants

Mineral ion	Use	Deficiency symptoms
nitrate	making amino acids, proteins, chlorophyll, DNA and many other compounds	limited growth of plant; older leaves turn yellow  ▲ Figure 10.11 (b) A plant showing symptoms of nitrate deficiency.
phosphate	making DNA and many other compounds; part of cell membranes	poor root growth; younger leaves turn purple  ▲ Figure 10.11 (c) A plant showing symptoms of phosphate deficiency.
potassium	needed for enzymes of respiration and photosynthesis to work	leaves turn yellow with dead spots  ▲ Figure 10.11 (d) A plant showing symptoms of potassium deficiency.
magnesium	part of chlorophyll molecule	leaves turn yellow  ▲ Figure 10.11 (e) A plant showing symptoms of magnesium deficiency.

DID YOU KNOW?

Some commercial crops such as lettuces can be grown without soil in culture solutions. This is called **hydroponics**. The plants' roots grow in a long plastic tube that has culture solution passing through it (Figure 10.12). The composition of the solution can be carefully adjusted to ensure the plants grow well. Pests such as insects, which might live in soil, are also less of a problem.

▲ Figure 10.12 Lettuce plants grown by hydroponics

LOOKING AHEAD – MORE ABOUT PHOTOSYNTHESIS

The role of chlorophyll is to absorb the light energy needed to drive photosynthesis. The products of the reaction (glucose and oxygen) contain more chemical energy than the reactants (carbon dioxide and water). The simple equation for photosynthesis that you saw earlier in this chapter is actually a summary of a series of reactions. They take place in two stages (Figure 10.13).

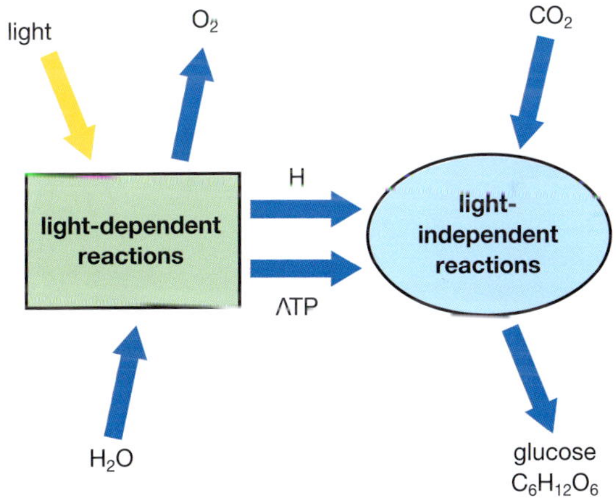

▲ Figure 10.13 Photosynthesis takes place in two stages called light-dependent and light-independent reactions.

The light energy absorbed by the chlorophyll is used to split water molecules into hydrogen and oxygen. The waste product, oxygen, is given off as a gas. At the same time, the light energy is used to convert ADP and phosphate into ATP. Because this stage needs light, the steps in the process are known as the *light-dependent reactions*.

Next, the hydrogen atoms from the water and energy from the ATP are used to reduce carbon dioxide to glucose. This takes place in another series of reactions in the chloroplast. Because these do not need light, they are called the *light-independent reactions*.

If you continue with biology beyond International GCSE, you will find out more about the biochemistry of photosynthesis.

CHAPTER QUESTIONS

More questions on plants and food can be found at the end of Unit 3 on page 159.

SKILLS REASONING

1 A variegated leaf attached to a plant was placed in a test tube as shown below. The test tube contained soda lime to absorb carbon dioxide.

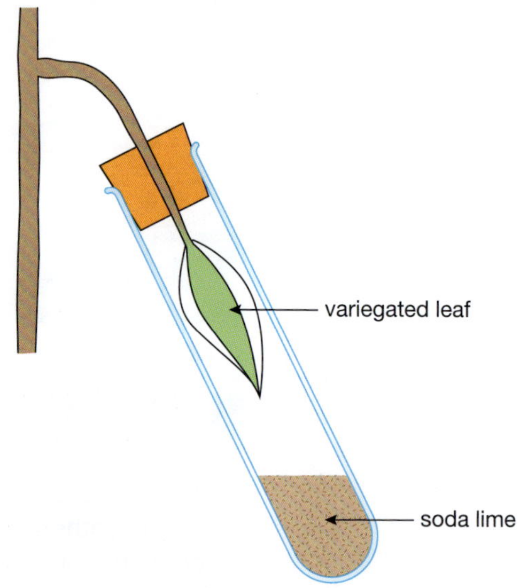

The plant was left in bright light for 24 hours and tested for starch using iodine solution. Which of the following diagrams shows the expected results?

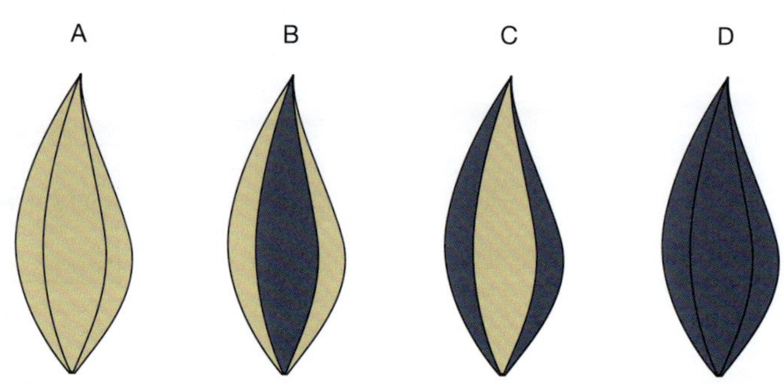

SKILLS CRITICAL THINKING

2 Which of the following is not normally a factor that limits the rate of photosynthesis?

A temperature

B oxygen concentration

C carbon dioxide concentration

D light intensity

3 Which of the following compounds can only be made by a plant if it has access to magnesium ions?

A chlorophyll

B cellulose

C starch

D protein

SKILLS CRITICAL THINKING

5th

4 A plant with variegated leaves had a piece of black paper attached to one leaf as shown in the diagram.

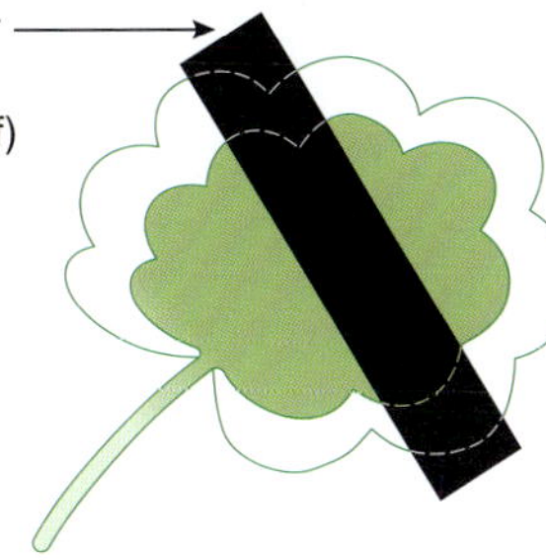

The plant was kept under a bright light for 24 hours. The leaf was then removed, the paper taken off and the leaf was tested for starch.

a Name the chemical used to test for starch, and describe the colour change if the test is positive.

6th

b Copy the leaf outline and shade in the areas which would contain starch.

c Explain how you arrived at your answer to (b).

SKILLS REASONING

5th

d What is starch used for in a plant? How do the properties of starch make it suitable for this function?

SKILLS INTERPRETATION

5 Copy and complete the following table to show the functions of different parts of a leaf, and how that part is adapted for its function. One row has been done for you.

Part of leaf	Function	How the part is adapted for its function
palisade mesophyll layer	main site of photosynthesis	cells contain many chloroplasts for photosynthesis
spongy mesophyll layer		
stomata		
xylem		
phloem		

6 The table below shows some of the substances that can be made by plants. Give one use in the plant for each. The first has been done for you.

Substance	Use
glucose	oxidised in respiration to give energy
sucrose	
starch	
cellulose	
protein	
lipid	

SKILLS REASONING

6th

7 The apparatus shown in the diagram was used to grow a pea seedling in a water culture experiment.

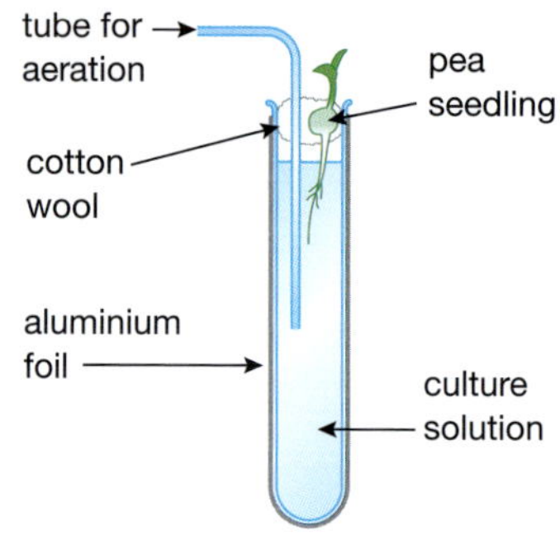

a Explain the purpose of the aeration tube and the aluminium foil around the test tube.

5th

b After two weeks, the roots of the pea seedling had grown less than normal, although the leaves were well developed. What mineral ion is likely to be deficient in the culture solution?

SKILLS INTERPRETATION

7th

8 A piece of Canadian pondweed was placed upside down in a test tube of water, as shown in the diagram.

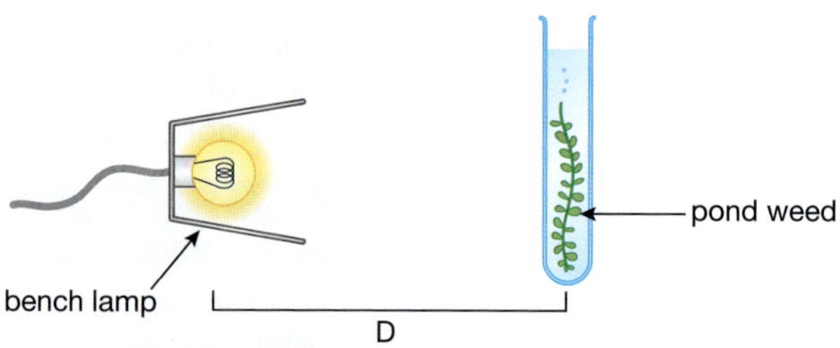

Light from a bench lamp was shone onto the weed, and bubbles of gas appeared at the cut end of the stem. The distance of the lamp from the weed was changed, and the number of bubbles produced per minute was recorded. The results are shown in the table below.

Distance of lamp (D) / cm	Number of bubbles per minute
5	126
10	89
15	64
20	42
25	31
30	17
35	14
40	10

a Plot a graph of the number of bubbles per minute against the distance of the weed from the lamp.

SKILLS REASONING

6th

b Using your graph, predict the number of bubbles per minute that would be produced if the lamp was placed 17 cm from the weed.

c The student who carried out this experiment arrived at the following conclusion:

'The gas made by the weed is oxygen from photosynthesis, so the faster production of bubbles shows that the rate of photosynthesis is greater at higher light intensities.'

Write down three reasons why his conclusion could be criticised. (Hint: is counting the bubbles a reliable method of measuring the rate of photosynthesis?)

SKILLS INTERPRETATION

9th

9 Write a summary account of photosynthesis. You should include a description of the process, a summary equation, an account of how a leaf is adapted for photosynthesis and a note of how photosynthesis is important to other organisms, such as animals. You must keep your summary to less than two sides (about 500 words).

11 TRANSPORT IN PLANTS

Chapter 10 described how plants make food by photosynthesis. Photosynthesis requires water from the roots to be transported to the leaves, and sugars and other products of photosynthesis to be transported away from the leaves to the rest of the plant. This chapter explains how these materials are moved through the plant.

LEARNING OBJECTIVES

- Understand how water can move in or out of plant cells by osmosis
- Investigate osmosis in living and non-living systems (plant cells and Visking tubing)
- Describe the role of the xylem in the transport of water and mineral ions from the roots to other parts of a plant
- Describe the role of phloem in the transport of sucrose and amino acids from the leaves to other parts of a plant
- Understand the origin of carbon dioxide and oxygen as waste products of metabolism and their loss from the stomata of a leaf

OSMOSIS

Osmosis is the name of a process by which water moves into and out of cells. In order to understand how water moves through a plant, you need to understand the mechanism of osmosis. Osmosis happens when a material called a **partially permeable membrane** separates two solutions. One artificial partially permeable membrane is called Visking tubing. This is used in kidney dialysis machines. Visking tubing has microscopic holes in it, which let small molecules like water pass through (it is *permeable* to them) but is not permeable to some larger molecules, such as the sugar sucrose. This is why it is called 'partially' permeable. You can show the effects of osmosis by filling a Visking tubing 'sausage' with concentrated sucrose solution, attaching it to a capillary tube and placing the Visking tubing in a beaker of water (Figure 11.1).

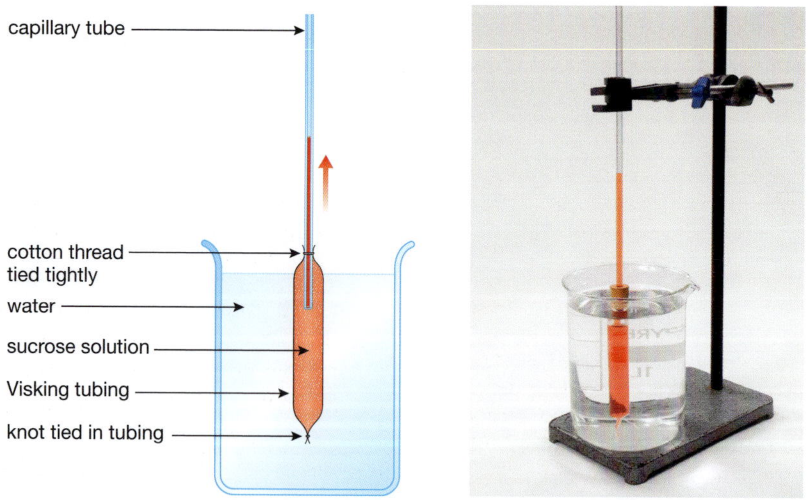

▲ Figure 11.1 Water enters the Visking tubing 'sausage' by osmosis. This causes the level of liquid in the capillary tube to rise. In the photograph, the contents of the Visking tubing have had a red dye added to make it easier to see the movement of the liquid.

The level in the capillary tube rises as water moves from the beaker to the inside of the Visking tubing. This movement is due to osmosis. You can understand what's happening if you imagine a highly magnified view of the Visking tubing separating the two liquids (Figure 11.2).

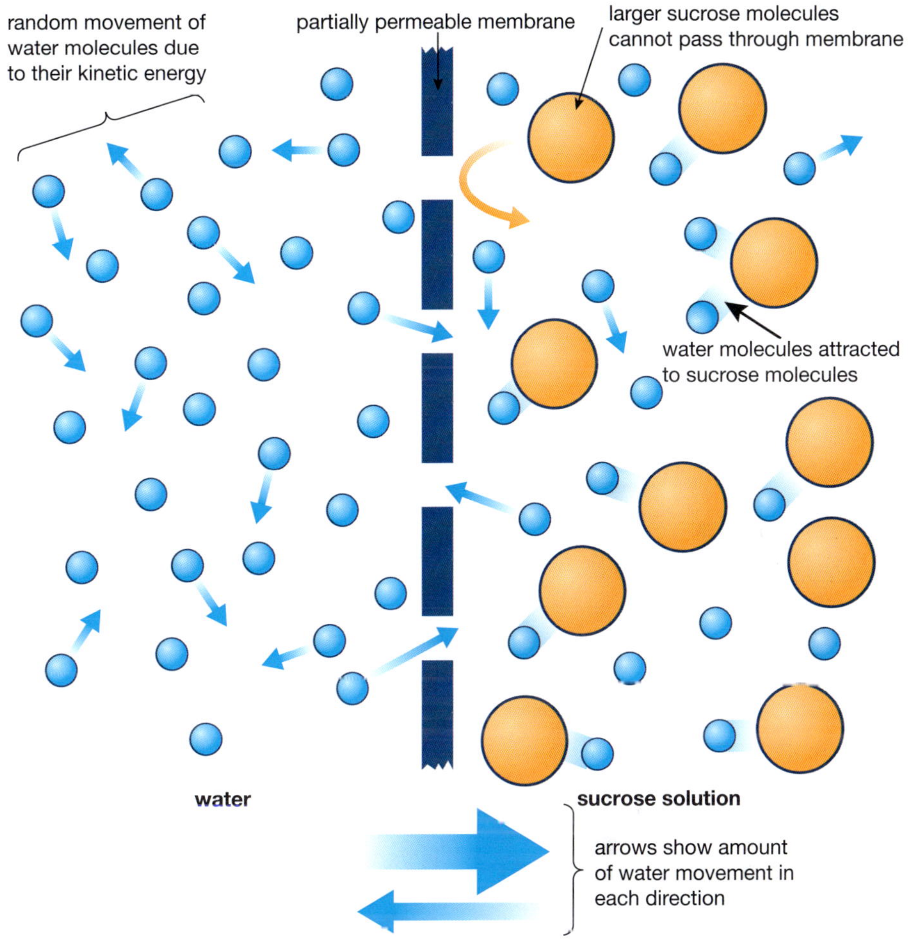

▲ Figure 11.2 In this model of osmosis, more water molecules diffuse from left to right than from right to left.

KEY POINT

Diffusion is the net movement of particles (molecules or ions) due to their kinetic energy, down a concentration gradient (see Chapter 1).

The sucrose molecules are too big to pass through the holes in the partially permeable membrane. The water molecules can pass through the membrane in either direction, but those on the right are attracted to the sugar molecules. This slows them down and means that they are less free to move – they have less kinetic energy. As a result of this, more water molecules diffuse from left to right than from right to left. In other words, there is a greater diffusion of water molecules from the more dilute solution (in this case pure water) to the more concentrated solution.

KEY POINT

It is important to realise that neither of the two solutions has to be pure water. As long as there is a difference in their concentrations (and their water potentials), and they are separated by a partially permeable membrane, osmosis can still take place.

How 'free' the water molecules are to move is called the **water potential**. The molecules in pure water can move most freely, so pure water has the highest water potential. The more concentrated a solution is, the lower is its water potential. In the model in Figure 11.2, water moves from a high to a low water potential. This is a law which applies whenever water moves by osmosis. We can bring these ideas together in a definition of osmosis.

KEY POINT

Osmosis is the net diffusion of water across a partially permeable membrane, from a solution with a higher water potential to one with lower water potential.

OSMOSIS IN PLANT CELLS

So far we have only been dealing with osmosis through Visking tubing. However, there are partially permeable membranes in cells too. The cell surface membranes of both animal and plant cells are partially permeable, and so is the inner membrane around the plant cell's sap vacuole (Figure 11.3).

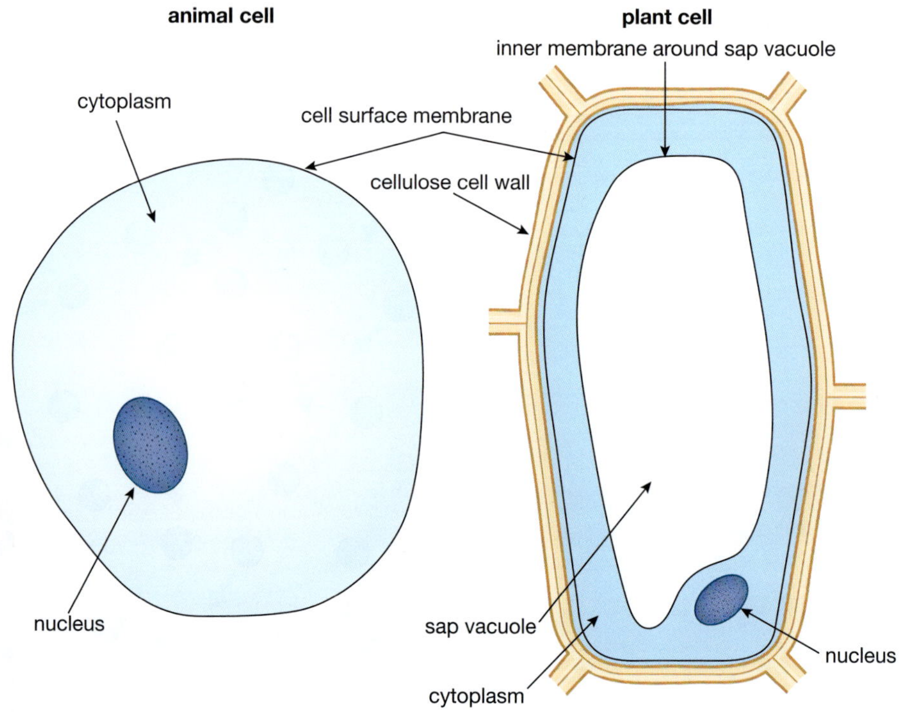

▲ Figure 11.3 Membranes in animal and plant cells

KEY POINT

The cell *wall* has large holes in it, making it fully permeable to water and solutes. Only the cell *membranes* are partially permeable barriers that allow osmosis to take place.

Around the plant cell is the tough cellulose cell wall. This outer structure keeps the shape of the cell, and can resist changes in pressure inside the cell. This is very important, and critical in explaining the way that plants are supported. The cell contents, including the sap vacuole, contain many dissolved solutes, such as sugars and ions.

If a plant cell is put into pure water or a dilute solution, the contents of the cell have a lower water potential than the external solution, so the cell will absorb water by osmosis (Figure 11.4). The cell then swells up and the cytoplasm pushes against the cell wall. A plant cell that has developed an internal pressure like this is called **turgid**.

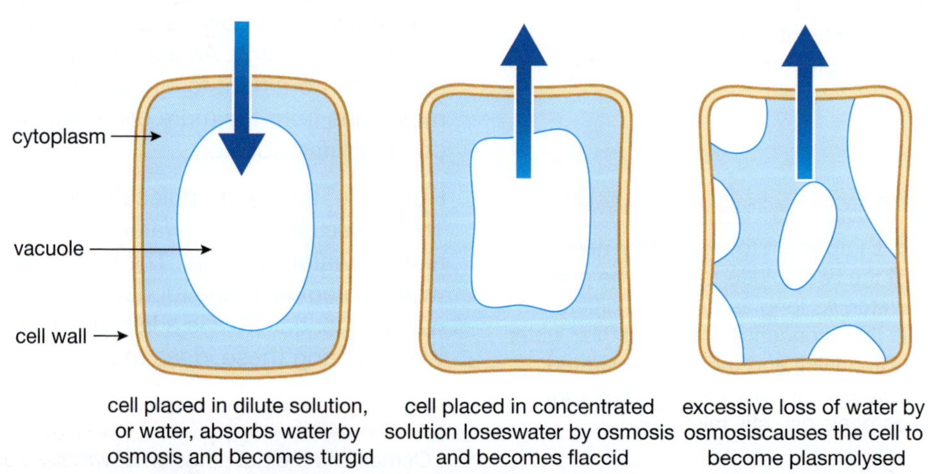

▲ Figure 11.4 The effects of osmosis on plant cells

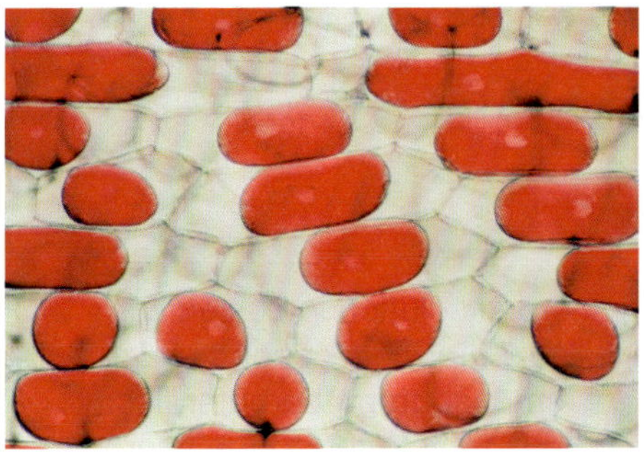

Figure 11.5 Cells of onion epidermis, showing plasmolysis. The cell membranes and cytoplasm can be seen to have pulled away from the cell wall.

On the other hand, if the cell is placed in a concentrated sucrose solution that has a lower water potential than the cell contents, it will *lose* water by osmosis. The cell decreases in volume and the cytoplasm no longer pushes against the cell wall. In this state, the cell is called **flaccid**. Eventually the cell contents shrink so much that the membrane and cytoplasm split away from the cell wall and gaps appear between the wall and the membrane. A cell like this is called **plasmolysed**. You can see plasmolysis happening in the plant cells shown in Figure 11.5. The space between the cell wall and the cell surface membrane will now be filled with the sucrose solution.

KEY POINT

This chapter only covers plant cells. Osmosis also happens in animal cells, but there is much less water movement. This is because animal cells do not have a strong cell wall around them, and can't resist the changes in internal pressure resulting from large movements of water. For example, if red blood cells are put into water, they will swell up and burst. If the same cells are put into a concentrated salt solution, they lose water by osmosis and shrink, producing cells with crinkly edges (Figure 11.6).

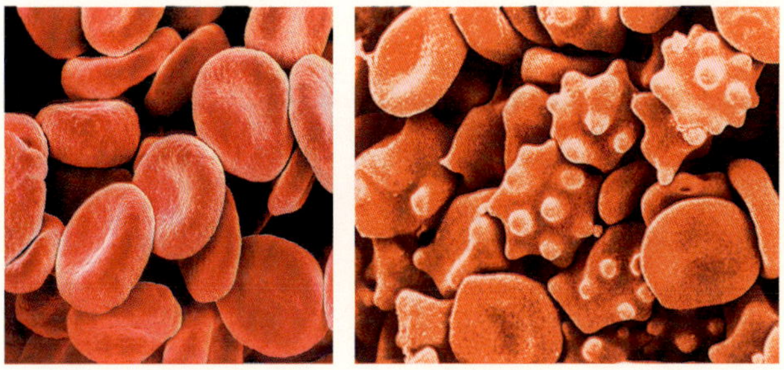

Figure 11.6 Compare the red blood cells on the right, which were placed in a 3% salt solution, with the normal cells on the left. Blood plasma has a concentration equal to a 0.85% salt solution.

Turgor (the state a plant is in when its cells are turgid) is very important to plants. The pressure inside the cells pushes neighbouring cells against each other, like a box full of inflated balloons. This supports the non-woody parts of the plant, such as young stems and leaves, and holds stems upright, so the leaves can carry out photosynthesis properly. Turgor is also important in the functioning of stomata. If a plant loses too much water from its cells so that they become flaccid, this makes the plant **wilt**. You can see wilting in a pot plant which has been left for too long without water. The leaves droop and collapse. In fact this is a protective action. It cuts down water loss by reducing the exposed surface area of the leaves and closing the stomata.

Inside the plant, water moves from cell to cell by osmosis. If a cell has a higher water potential than the cell next to it, water will move from the first cell to the second. In turn, this will dilute the contents of the second cell, so that it has a higher water potential than the next cell. In this way, water can move across a plant tissue, down a gradient of water potential (Figure 11.7).

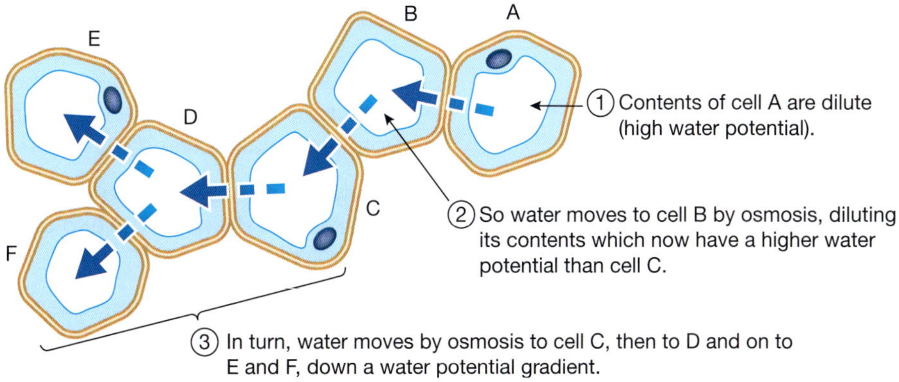

Figure 11.7 Water moves from cell to cell down a water potential gradient.

Safety note: Wash hands after handling and preparing the onion. Microscopes using a mirror for daylight illumination must never be placed where direct sunlight might strike the mirror otherwise permanent retinal damage may occur.

ACTIVITY 3

▼ PRACTICAL: INVESTIGATING THE EFFECTS OF OSMOSIS IN ONION EPIDERMIS CELLS

A drop of concentrated (1 mol per dm^3) sucrose solution is placed on one microscope slide, and a drop of distilled water on a second slide. Two small squares of inner epidermis are removed from the outer fleshy layers of an onion (Figure 11.8). One square is transferred to the sucrose solution, and the second to the water. This is done as quickly as possible, so that the cells do not dry out.

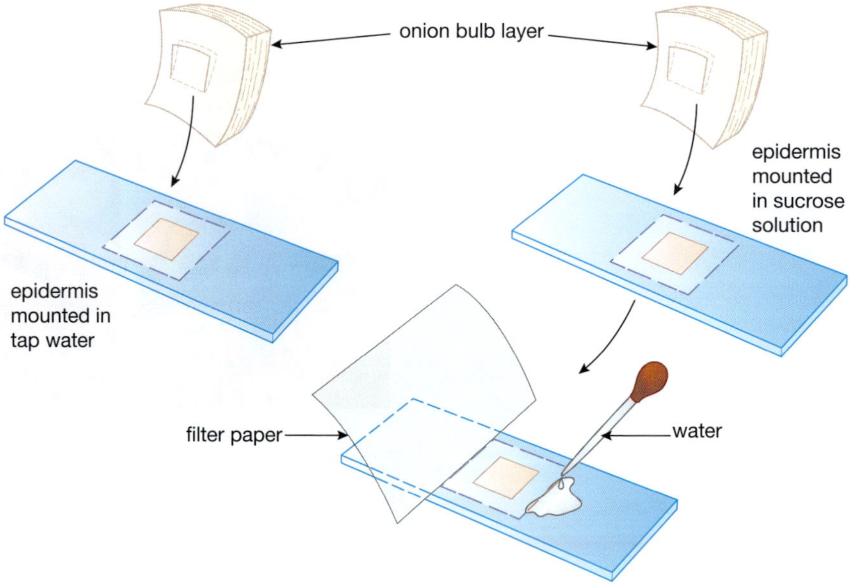

▲ Figure 11.8 Investigating osmosis in onion epidermis cells

A drop of the correct solution is added to the top of each specimen, followed by a cover slip. Any excess liquid is blotted (cleaned) up with filter paper.

Each slide is examined through the microscope for several minutes. The specimen in water will show turgid cells, similar to the first cell in Figure 11.4. The cells in sucrose solution will gradually plasmolyse, as shown in the last diagram of Figure 11.4, and Figure 11.5.

It is interesting to replace the sugar solution on the first slide with distilled water, to see the effect on the plasmolysed cells. This can be done quite easily without removing the cover slip. Some water is placed on one side of the cover slip and drawn across the slide using filter paper, as shown in Figure 11.8. After a while all the sucrose solution is replaced by water. If the cells are now observed for a few minutes, they will gradually recover from their plasmolysed condition until they are fully turgid again.

It may be possible for you to carry out these procedures. If you can, observe and draw one or two turgid cells, and one or two that are plasmolysed.

Can you explain all these observations in terms of osmosis?

If you use a red onion, the contents of the cells are coloured and easier to see.

Safety note: Take great care when cutting the potato into 'chips' and wash hands afterwards.

ACTIVITY 4

▼ PRACTICAL: INVESTIGATING THE EFFECTS OF OSMOSIS ON POTATO TUBER TISSUE

A potato tuber is a plant storage organ. It is a convenient tissue to use to investigate the effects of osmosis on the mass of the tissue.

A boiling tube is half filled with distilled water and a second with concentrated (1 mol per dm^3) sucrose solution. A third tube is left empty.

A potato is cut into chips 5 cm × 1 cm × 1 cm, making these measurements as accurate as possible so that the three chips are the same size. No skin is left on the potato tissue.

Each chip is gently blotted to remove excess moisture, and the mass of each is found by weighing on a balance. One chip is placed in each of the three boiling tubes (Figure 11.9).

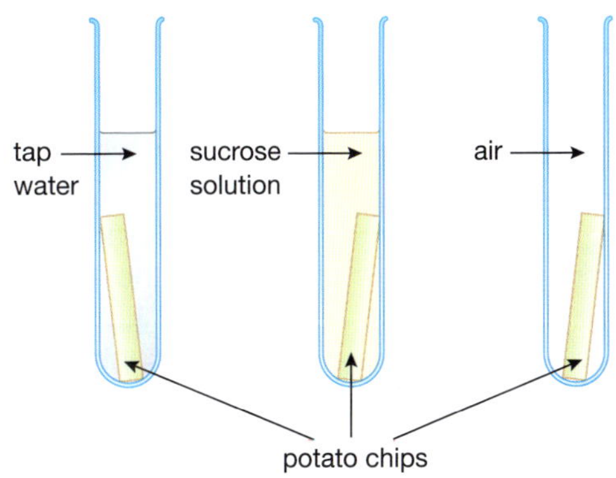

▲ Figure 11.9 Investigating osmosis in potato tissue

After 30 minutes, the chips are removed from the tubes and gently blotted to remove excess liquid, then re-weighed. Each is felt in turn, to compare how flexible or stiff they are.

The change in mass (+ or –) of each chip is calculated, and the percentage change found from the equation:

$$\% \text{ change} = \frac{\text{change in mass}}{\text{starting mass}} \times 100$$

The table below shows a set of results from this experiment.

Tube contents	Starting mass / g	Final mass / g	Change in mass / g	Change in mass / %	Condition (flexible / stiff)
water	6.25	6.76	+0.51	+8.16	stiff
sucrose solution	7.10	6.31	–0.79	–11.1	flexible
air	6.66	6.57	–0.09	–1.35	stiff

What conclusions can you make from these results? Explain them in terms of osmosis.

How large are the percentage changes in mass of the chips in the two liquids, compared with the chip in air?

Can you explain the final 'condition' of the chips, using terms such as 'flaccid' and 'turgid'?

Can you think of any criticisms of this experiment? For example, does using one chip per tube yield reliable evidence?

You may be able to perform an experiment similar to the one above. You don't have to use potato; other tissues such as carrot or sweet potato should work. An alternative to weighing is to measure the length of the chips at the end of the experiment, and compare these measurements with the starting lengths. However, weighing is much more accurate and gives a bigger percentage change.

You could try extending the experiment into a more complete investigation. For example you could make predictions about what would happen to chips placed in solutions that are intermediate in concentration between water and molar sucrose solution.

Plan a method to test your hypothesis. You should include a list of the apparatus and materials to be used, a description of the procedure, and a statement of the expected results.

TRANSPORT IN THE XYLEM

▲ Figure 11.10 Xylem vessels in a stem. The spirals and rings (stained red) are made of lignin.

Xylem transports water and minerals throughout the plant. Xylem contains dead cells arranged end-to-end, forming continuous vessels. When they are mature, the vessels contain no cytoplasm. Instead, they have a hollow central space or **lumen** through which the water passes. The walls of the xylem vessels contain a woody material called **lignin** (Figure 11.10).

The xylem vessels begin life as living cells with normal cytoplasm and cellulose cell walls. As they develop they become elongated, and gradually their original cellulose cell walls become impregnated with lignin, made by the cytoplasm. As this happens, the cells die, forming hollow tubes. Lignification makes them very strong, and enables them to carry water up tall plants without collapsing. Lignin is also impermeable to water.

TRANSPORT IN THE PHLOEM

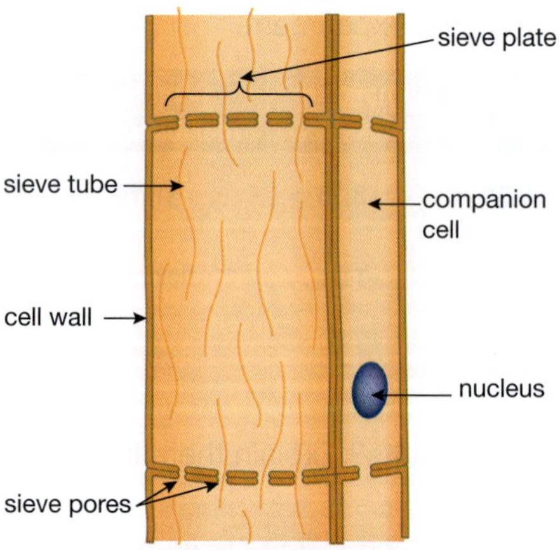

▲ Figure 11.11 Xylem vessels in a stem

The other plant transport tissue, the phloem, consists of living cells at all stages in its development. Tubes in the phloem are also formed by cells arranged end-to-end, but they have cell walls made of cellulose, and retain their cytoplasm. The end of each cell is formed by a cross-wall of cellulose with holes, called a **sieve plate**. The living cytoplasm extends through the holes in the sieve plates, linking each cell with the next, forming a long **sieve tube** (Figure 11.11). The sieve tubes transport the products of photosynthesis from the leaves to other parts of the plant. Sugars for energy, or amino acids for building proteins, are carried to young leaves and other growing points in the plant. Sugar may also be taken to the roots and converted into starch for storage. Despite being living cells, the phloem sieve tubes have no nucleus. They seem to be controlled by other cells that lie alongside the sieve tubes, called **companion cells** (Figure 11.11).

REMINDER

Remember: xylem carries water and minerals up from the roots. Phloem carries products of photosynthesis away from the leaves. The contents of the phloem can travel up or down the plant.

STRUCTURE OF A STEM

In a young stem, xylem and phloem are grouped together in areas called **vascular bundles**. Unlike in the root, where the vascular tissue is in the central core, the vascular bundles are arranged in a circle around the outer part of the stem (Figure 11.12).

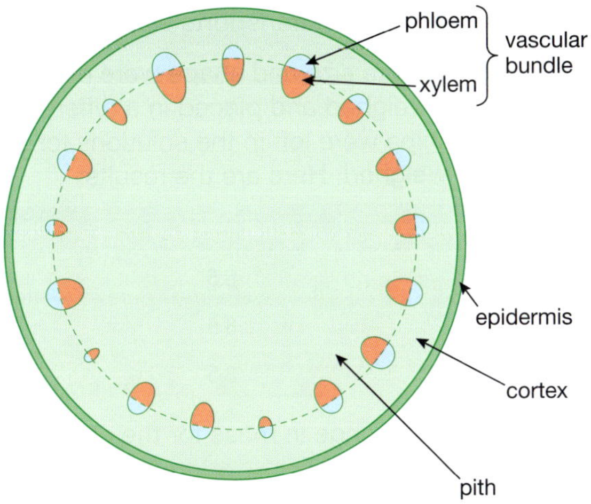

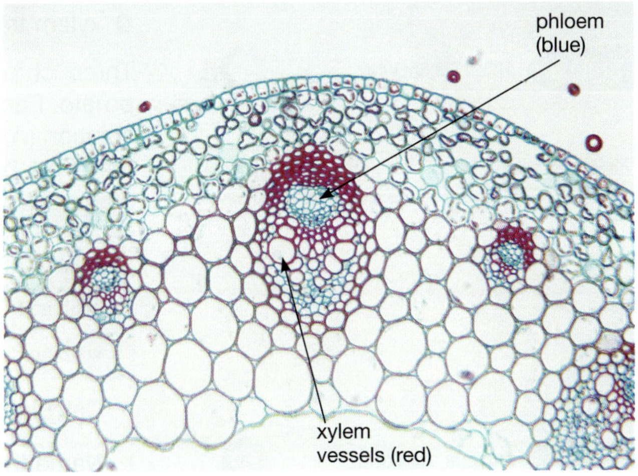

▲ Figure 11.12 (a) This cross-section of a stem shows the arrangement of xylem and phloem tissue in vascular bundles. (b) Three vascular bundles in part of a stem section. The outer red cells are lignified fibres for extra support.

KEY POINT

'Vascular' means 'made of vessels'. A vascular bundle is a group of vessels or tubes (xylem and phloem).

In older stems, the vascular tissue grows to form complete rings around the stem. The inner xylem forms the woody central core of a stem, with the living layer of phloem outside this.

CHAPTER QUESTIONS

More questions on transport in plants can be found at the end of Unit 3 on page 159.

SKILLS CRITICAL THINKING 8th

1 A plant cell was placed in a concentrated sucrose solution. The diagram below shows the appearance of the cell after an hour in the solution.

What is the best description of this cell?

A turgid

B flaccid

C plasmolysed

D wilted

SKILLS CRITICAL THINKING 4th

2 What are the functions of xylem and phloem?

A xylem transports water and sugars, phloem transports mineral ions

B xylem transports water and mineral ions, phloem transports sugars

C xylem transports sugars and mineral ions, phloem transports water

D xylem transports sugars, phloem transports water and mineral ions

SKILLS PROBLEM SOLVING 6th

3 Three 'chips' of about the same size and shape were cut from the same potato. Each was blotted, weighed and placed in a different sucrose solution (A, B or C). The chips were left in the solutions for an hour, then removed, blotted and re-weighed. Here are the results:

	Starting mass / g	Final mass / g	Change in mass / %
solution A	7.4	6.5	−12.2
solution B	8.2	8.0	
solution C	7.7	8.5	+10.4

a Calculate the percentage change in mass for the chip in solution B.

SKILLS CRITICAL THINKING 7th

b Name the process that caused the chips to lose or gain mass.

SKILLS ANALYSIS 8th

c Which solution was likely to have been the most concentrated?

d Which solution had the highest water potential?

e Which solution had a water potential most similar to the water potential of the potato cells?

SKILLS CRITICAL THINKING 7th

f The cell membrane is described as 'partially permeable'. Explain the meaning of this.

SKILLS ANALYSIS 5th

4 The diagram shows a cross-section through the stem of a plant.

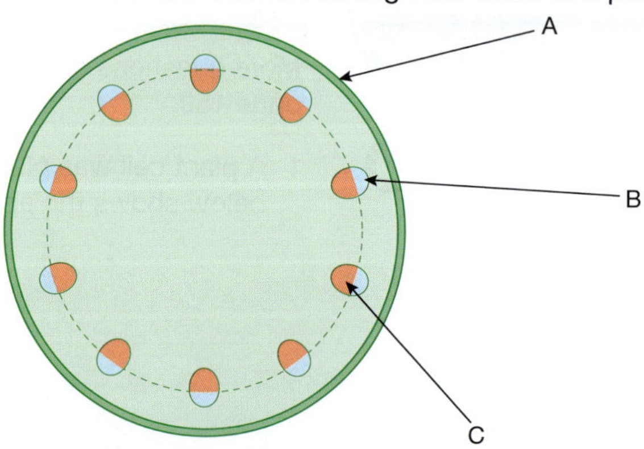

a Identify the tissues labelled A, B and C.

SKILLS REASONING 6th

b A young stem was placed in a solution of a red dye for an hour. Which tissue in the diagram would be most likely to contain the dye? Explain your answer.

12 CHEMICAL COORDINATION IN PLANTS

Plants can detect changes in their environment and respond to them, but the responses are much slower than those in animals. This is because movements in a plant are brought about by changes in the plant's growth. This chapter is about these growth responses, and the chemicals that coordinate them.

LEARNING OBJECTIVES

- Understand that plants respond to stimuli
- Describe the phototropic response of roots and stems
- Describe the geotropic responses of roots and stems
- Understand the role of auxin in the phototropic response of stems

Chapter 6 explains how animals detect and respond to changes in their environment. Animals usually respond very quickly – for example the reflex action resulting from a painful stimulus (page 83) is over in a fraction of a second.

As in animals, some species of plant can respond rapidly to a stimulus, for example the Venus flytrap (Figure 12.1). This plant has modified leaves, which close quickly around their 'prey', trapping it. The plant then secretes enzymes to digest the insect. The movement is brought about by rapid changes in turgor of specialised cells at the base of the leaves.

▲ Figure 12.1 The Venus flytrap catches and digests insects to gain extra nutrients. The plant responds very quickly to a fly landing on one of its leaves.

▲ Figure 12.2 This bean has responded to being placed horizontally. The growing shoot has started to bend upwards.

TROPISMS

Most plants do not respond to stimuli as quickly as the Venus flytrap, because their response normally involves a change in their rate of growth. Different parts of plants may grow at different rates, and a plant may respond to a stimulus by increasing growth near the tip of its shoot or roots.

Imagine a plant growing normally in a pot. Usually, most light will be falling on the plant from above. If you turn the plant on its side and leave it for a day or so, you will see that its shoot starts to grow upwards (Figure 12.2).

▲ Figure 12.3 The shoots of these tomato seedlings are showing a positive phototropism.

KEY POINT

Phototropisms are growth responses to light from one direction. Geotropisms are growth responses to the direction of gravity ('geo' refers to the Earth).

KEY POINT

Light from one direction is called 'unidirectional'. If light shines on the plant evenly from all directions, this is called 'uniform' light.

There are two stimuli acting on the plant in Figure 12.2. One is the direction of the light that falls on the plant. The other stimulus is gravity. Both light and gravity are *directional* stimuli (they act in a particular direction). The growth response of a plant to a directional stimulus is called a **tropism**. If the growth response is *towards* the direction of the stimulus, it is a *positive* tropism, and if it is *away* from the direction of the stimulus, it is a *negative* tropism. The stem of the plant in Figure 12.2 is showing a positive **phototropism** and a negative **geotropism**, which both make the stem grow upwards.

The aerial part of a plant (the 'shoot') needs light to carry out photosynthesis. This means that in most species, a positive phototropism is the strongest tropic response of the shoot. If a shoot grows towards the light, it ensures that the leaves, held out at an angle to the stem, will receive the maximum amount of sunlight. This response is easily seen in any plant placed near a window, or another source of 'one-way' or *unidirectional* light (Figure 12.3).

In darkness or uniform light, the shoot shows a negative geotropism. As you might expect, the roots of plants are strongly positively geotropic. This response makes sure that the roots grow down into the soil, where they can reach water and mineral ions. Roots also fix a plant firmly in place – they provide 'anchorage'.

The roots of some species that have been studied are also negatively phototropic, but most roots don't respond to directional light at all. Table 12.1 summarises the main tropisms.

Table 12.1: The main responses of plants to directional stimuli (tropisms).

Stimulus	Name of response	Response of shoots	Response of roots
light	phototropism	grow towards light source (positive phototropism)	most species show no response; some grow away from light (negative phototropism)
gravity	geotropism	grow away from direction of gravity (negative geotropism)	grow towards direction of gravity (positive geotropism)

DETECTING THE LIGHT STIMULUS – PLANT HORMONES

Plants do not have the obvious sense organs and nervous system of animals. However, since they respond to stimuli such as light and gravity, they must have some way of detecting them and coordinating the response. The detection system of phototropism was first investigated by the great English biologist Charles Darwin (see Chapter 19) in the late nineteenth century. Instead of using stems, Darwin (and later scientists) used cereal coleoptiles, which are easier to grow and use in experiments.

A **coleoptile** is a protective sheath that covers the first leaves of a cereal seedling. It protects the delicate leaves as the shoot emerges through the soil (Figure 12.4). Coleoptiles have a simple structure and are easy to grow, so they are often used to investigate tropisms.

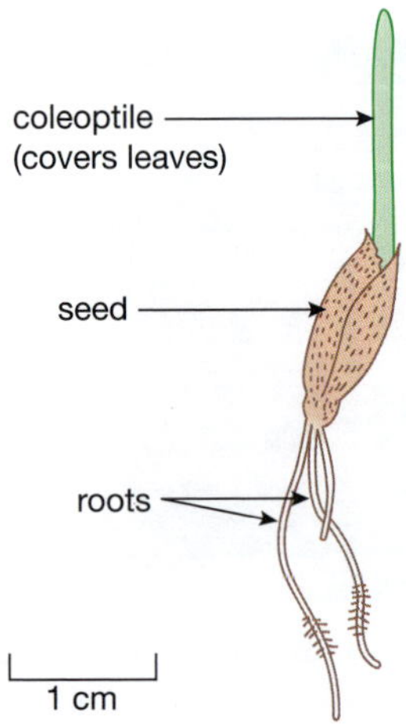

▲ Figure 12.4 Germinating oat seedling

EXTENSION WORK

Charles Darwin is best known for his theory of evolution by natural selection (Chapter 19). However, he carried out research in other areas of biology, including studying plant hormones. You could do some research to find out more about his life and work. Make a list of his achievements.

Darwin showed that the stimulus of unidirectional light was detected by the tip of the coleoptile, and transmitted to a growth zone, just behind the tip (Figure 12.5).

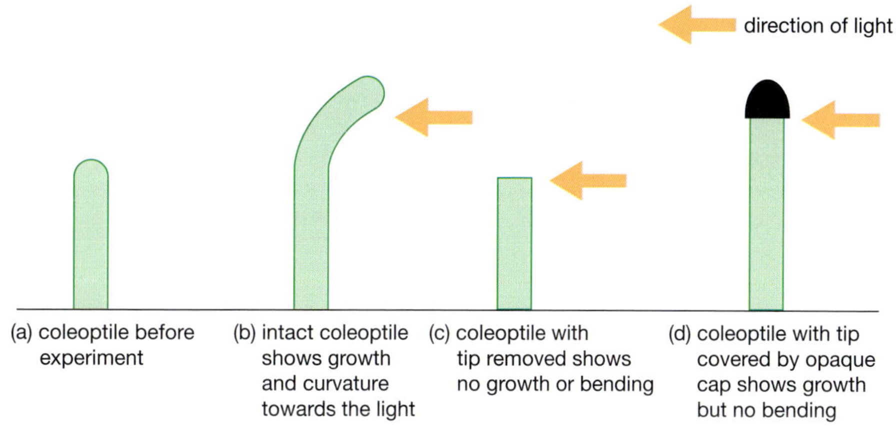

▲ Figure 12.5 Darwin's experiments with phototropism (1880)

Since plants don't have a nervous system, biologists began to look for a chemical messenger (or plant **hormone)** that might be the cause of phototropism in coleoptiles. Between 1910 and 1926 several scientists investigated this problem. Some of their results are summarised in Figure 12.6.

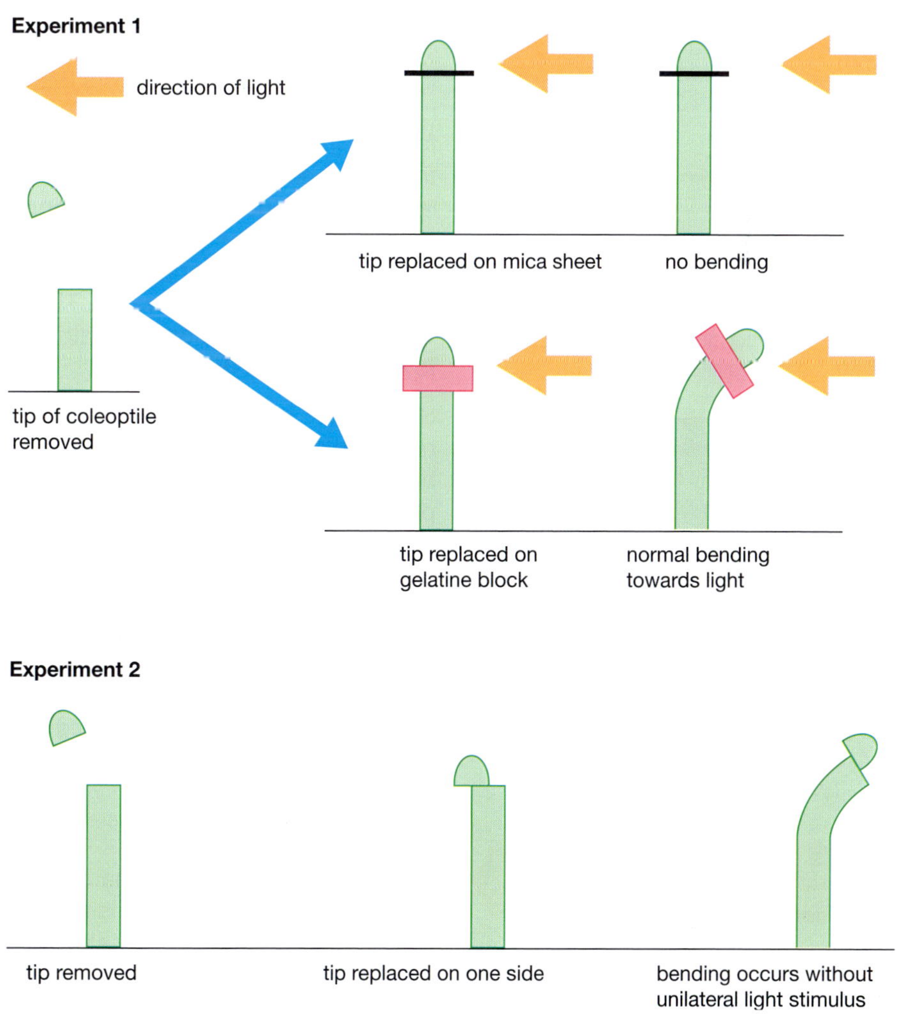

Experiment 3

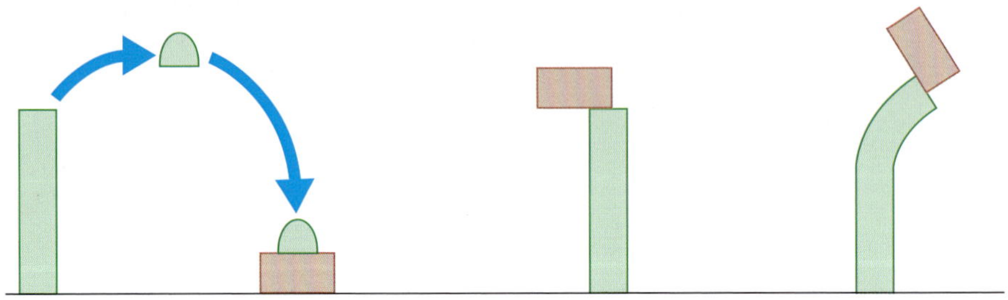

▲ Figure 12.6 Experiments on coleoptiles that helped to explain the mechanism of phototropism.

In experiment 1, the stimulus for growth was found to pass through materials such as gelatine, which absorbs water-soluble chemicals, but not through materials such as mica (a mineral), which is impermeable to water. This made biologists think that the stimulus was a chemical that was soluble in water.

In experiment 2, it was shown that the phototropic response could be brought about, even *without* unidirectional light, by removing a coleoptile tip ('decapitating' the coleoptile) and placing the tip on one side of the decapitated stalk.

In experiment 3, it was found that the hormone could be collected in another water-absorbing material (a block of agar jelly). Placing the agar block on one side of the decapitated coleoptile stalk caused it to bend.

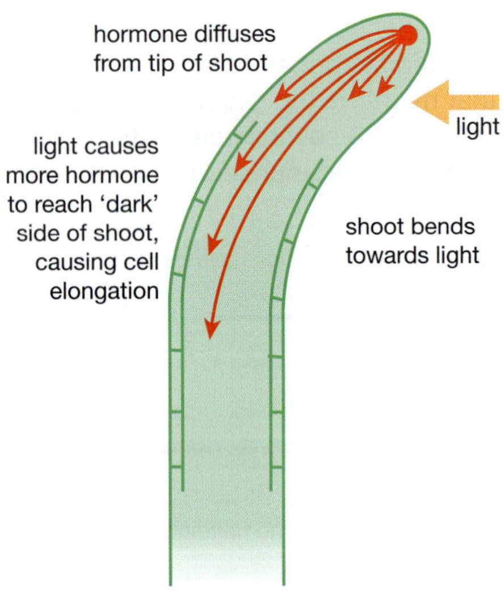

▲ Figure 12.7 How movement of a plant hormone causes phototropism.

Investigations like experiments 2 and 3 led scientists to believe that the hormone caused bending by stimulating growth on the side of the coleoptile furthest from the light. The theory is that the hormone is produced in the tip of the shoot, and diffuses back down the shoot. If the shoot is in the dark, or if light is all around the shoot, the hormone diffuses at equal rates on each side of the shoot, so it stimulates the shoot equally on all sides. However, if the shoot is receiving light from one direction, the hormone moves away from the light as it diffuses downwards. The higher concentration of hormone on the 'dark' side of the shoot stimulates cells there to grow, making the shoot bend towards the light (Figure 12.7).

Since these experiments were carried out, scientists have identified the hormone responsible. It is called **auxin**. Several other types of plant hormone have been found. Like auxin, they all influence growth and development of plants in one way or another, so that many scientists prefer to call them **plant growth substances** rather than plant hormones.

EXTENSION WORK

'Auxin' should really be 'auxins', since there are a number of chemicals with very similar structures making up a group of closely related plant hormones.

EXTENSION WORK

As well as auxins, there are four other main groups of plant hormones, called gibberellins, cytokinins, abscisic acid and ethene. They control many aspects of plant growth and development, apart from tropisms. These include growth of buds, leaves and fruit, fruit ripening, seed germination, leaf fall and opening of stomata, to name just a few.

USING A CLINOSTAT TO SHOW TROPISMS

A clinostat is a piece of apparatus consisting of an electric motor turning a cork disc. Germinating seeds are attached to the disc. The motor turns the disc and seeds around very slowly, so that the movement eliminates the effect of any directional stimulus that may be acting on the seeds. The clinostat can be turned through 90°, so that the disc rotates either horizontally or vertically.

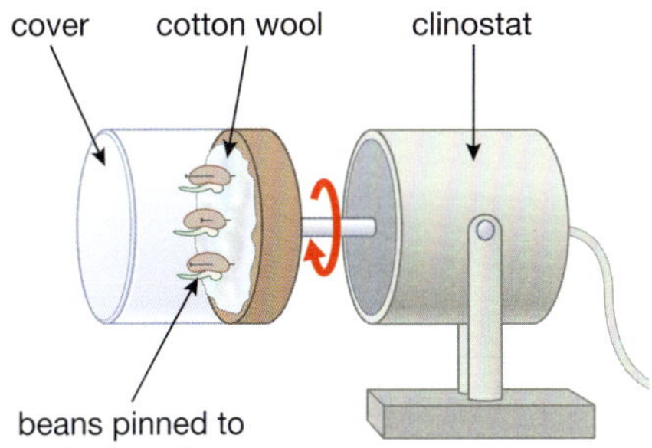

▲ Figure 12.8 A clinostat

The clinostat can be used to demonstrate tropisms, for example geotropism in roots. A few beans are soaked in water overnight and then placed on wet cotton wool for a day or two, until the first root of each seed (called the radicle) grows to a length of about 2 cm.

Wet cotton wool is attached to the cork disc of two clinostats. Three or four of the germinating bean seeds are pinned on to each of the discs, with their radicles pointing outwards. Covers are placed over them to keep the air around the beans moist.

The clinostats are turned on their sides, as shown in Figure 12.8. One clinostat is switched on, with the other left switched off, as a control. Both clinostats are left set up for a few days. The cotton wool is watered regularly to keep it damp.

After this time, the radicles of the beans on the control clinostat will have grown downwards, under the influence of gravity. Those on the moving clinostat will have grown straight out horizontally. The continuously changing direction of the gravitational stimulus acting on the seeds of the moving clinostat cancels out the geotropic response.

CHAPTER QUESTIONS

More questions on chemical coordination in plants can be found at the end of Unit 3 on page 159.

SKILLS CRITICAL THINKING

1 Which of the following statements about tropisms is correct?

A Roots show positive phototropism and negative geotropism

B Roots show negative phototropism and positive geotropism

C Stems show negative phototropism and negative geotropism

D Stems show positive phototropism and positive geotropism

2 Below are three statements about phototropism in a coleoptile.

1. Auxin is made in the tip of the coleoptile
2. Auxin diffuses towards the light
3. A high concentration of auxin stimulates growth of the coleoptile towards the light.

Which of these statements are true?

A 1 and 2

B 1 and 3

C 2 and 3

D 1, 2 and 3

3 The diagram below shows a bean seedling that has been growing in the dark.

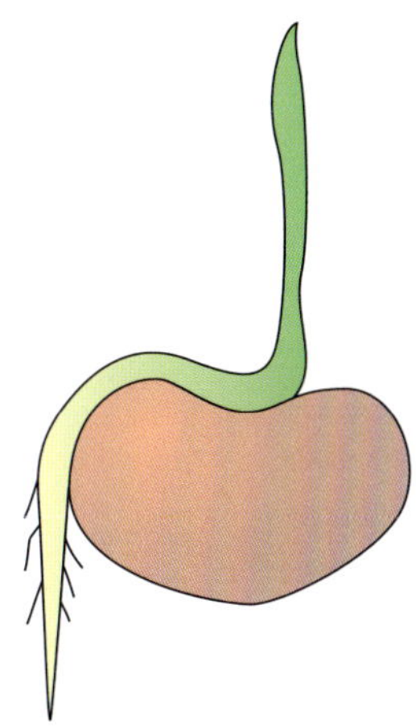

What is the name given to the response of the shoot?

A positive phototropism

B negative phototropism

C positive geotropism

D negative geotropism

SKILLS CRITICAL THINKING

5th

4 Movement of auxin is thought to take place by which of the following methods?

A diffusion

B active transport

C osmosis

D mass flow in the phloem

5 a What are the main stimuli affecting the growth of

i the shoot? ii the root?

6th

b How does a plant benefit from a positive phototropism in its stem?

SKILLS INTERPRETATION

7th

6 Draw a labelled diagram to show how auxin brings about phototropism in a coleoptile that has light shining on it from one direction.

SKILLS REASONING

8th

7 An experiment was carried out to investigate phototropism in a coleoptile. The diagram shows what was done. Predict the results you would expect to get in each of the experiments a) to c). Explain your answers.

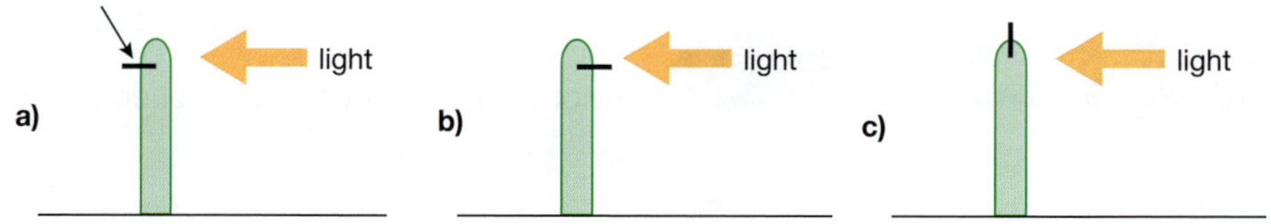

SKILLS EXECUTIVE FUNCTION

8 An experiment was carried out to investigate which part of a coleoptile is sensitive to a light stimulus. Three dishes containing wheat seedlings were subjected to different treatments:

- Dish 1 – 2 mm was removed from the growing coleoptiles ('decapitated' coleoptiles)
- Dish 2 – the tips of the coleoptiles were covered with caps of aluminium foil
- Dish 3 – the seedlings were left untreated as a control.

The coleoptiles were measured and the mean length of each treatment group was calculated. Each batch of seedlings was then placed in a box with a hole cut in one side to provide a unidirectional source of light.

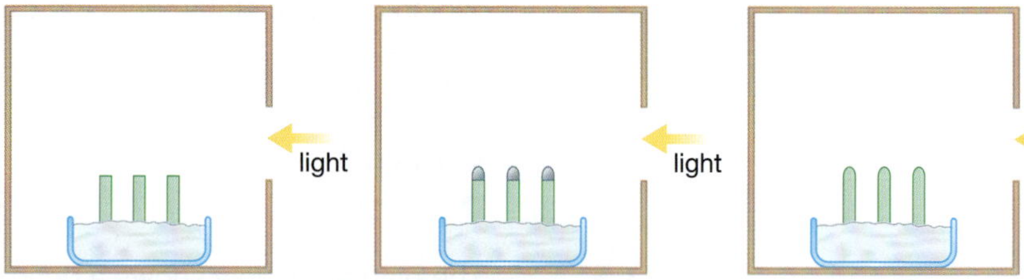

After 48 hours the new mean length of the coleoptiles was found for each treatment group, and the percentage increase in length calculated. Any change in direction of growth of the coleoptiles was noted.

a Suggest which treatment would produce the greatest percentage increase in length and which the least. Explain your answer.

SKILLS REASONING

b What differences in direction of growth would you expect to see as a result of the three treatments? Explain your answer.

5th

c Explain why it is necessary to calculate the *percentage* increase in the length of the coleoptiles, rather than simply the increase in length.

13 REPRODUCTION IN PLANTS

Plants, like animals, can reproduce sexually and asexually. The sexual organs of a flowering plant are its flowers, which produce pollen and ovules containing the flower's gametes. This chapter looks at both types of reproduction in flowering plants.

LEARNING OBJECTIVES

- Describe the differences between sexual and asexual reproduction in plants
- Understand that plants can reproduce asexually by natural methods (illustrated by runners) and by artificial methods (illustrated by cuttings)
- Describe the structures of an insect-pollinated and a wind-pollinated flower and explain how each is adapted for pollination
- Understand that the growth of the pollen tube followed by fertilisation leads to seed and fruit formation
- Understand how germinating seeds utilise food reserves until the seedling can carry out photosynthesis
- Investigate the conditions needed for seed germination

SEXUAL AND ASEXUAL REPRODUCTION

You have seen how animals can reproduce sexually and asexually (Chapter 9). Plants can also carry out both types of reproduction. Table 13.1 summarises some of the differences between the two methods of reproduction.

Table 13.1 Sexual and asexual reproduction compared.

Feature of the process	Sexual reproduction	Asexual reproduction
gametes produced	yes	no
fertilisation takes place	yes	no
genetic variation in offspring	yes	no
has survival value in:	changing environment	stable environment

KEY POINT

As each method of asexual reproduction involves some part of the plant growing, new cells must be produced. These cells are produced by **mitosis** and so are all genetically identical. This means that all the offspring formed by asexual reproduction will also be genetically identical.

ASEXUAL REPRODUCTION IN PLANTS

There are many different methods of asexual reproduction in plants. Most involve some part of the plant growing, and then breaking away from the parent plant before developing into a new plant (Figure 13.1).

Gardeners often take advantage of the ways that plants can reproduce asexually. They use runners, bulbs and tubers to produce more plants.

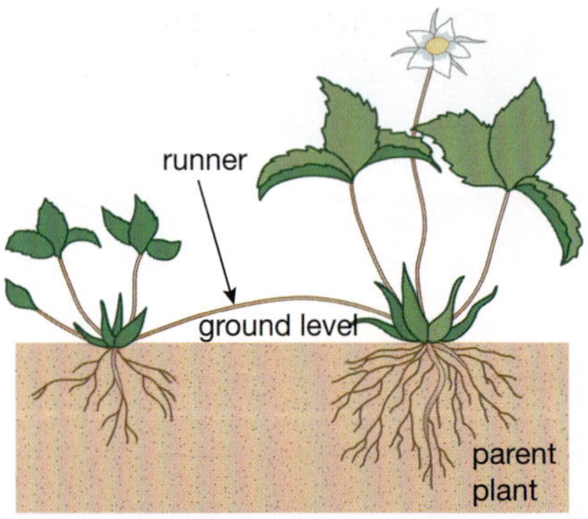

A new plant is produced where the runner touches the ground.

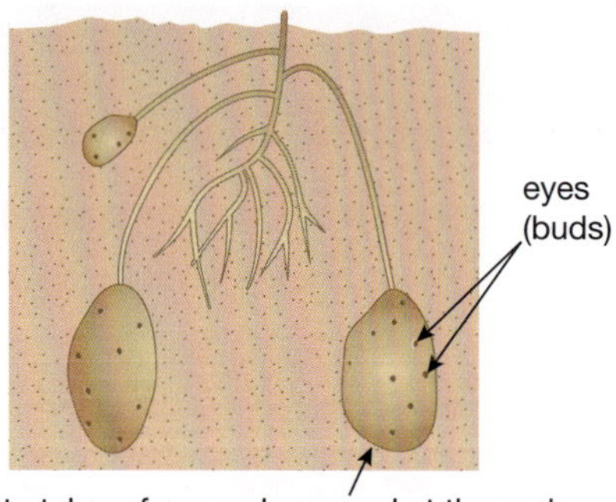

Potato tubers form underground at the ends of branches from the main stem. Each potato can produce several new plants from the 'eyes' which are buds.

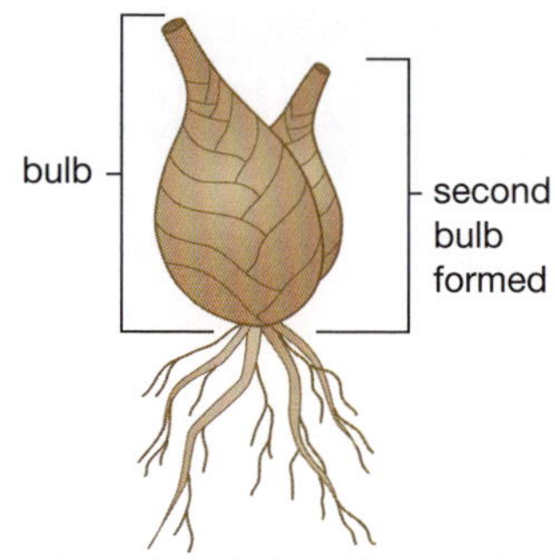

Some plants form bulbs. They are the bases of leaves which have become swollen with food. Buds in them can develop into new plants. Plants can form more than one bulb.

▲ Figure 13.1 Some methods of asexual reproduction in plants

Another type of asexual reproduction is to grow plants from **cuttings**. A piece of a plant's stem, with a few leaves attached, is cut from a healthy plant. This is planted in damp soil or compost, where it will grow roots and develop into a new plant (Figure 13.2).

▲ Figure 13.2 These geranium cuttings have started to grow roots

SEXUAL REPRODUCTION IN PLANTS

REMINDER

Haploid cells have only half the number of chromosomes of other body cells of that species.

Plants produce specialised, haploid gametes in their flowers. The male gametes are contained within the **pollen grains** and the female gametes are egg cells or **ova**. Just as in animals, the male gametes must be transferred to the female gametes. This takes place through **pollination,** which is normally carried out either by wind or insects. Following pollination, fertilisation takes place and the zygote formed develops into a **seed**, which, in turn, becomes enclosed in a **fruit**.

PRODUCTION OF GAMETES AND POLLINATION

The gametes are produced by meiosis in structures in the flowers. Pollen grains are produced in the **anthers** of the **stamens**. The ova are produced in **ovules** in the **ovaries**.

In pollination, pollen grains are transferred from the anthers of a flower to the **stigma**. If this occurs within the same flower it is called **self-pollination**. If the pollen grains are transferred to a different flower, it is called **cross-pollination**. Pollination can occur by wind or by insect in either case.

Plants that are wind-pollinated produce flowers with a different structure to those of insect-pollinated flowers. These differences are related to the different methods of pollination of the flowers. Figure 13.3 shows the structure of a typical insect-pollinated flower and Figure 13.4 shows the structure of a typical wind-pollinated flower. Table 13.2 summarises the main differences between insect-pollinated flowers and wind-pollinated flowers.

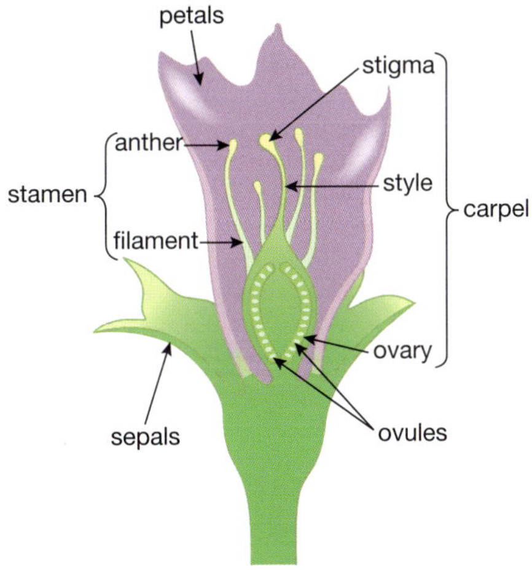

▲ Figure 13.3 The main structures in an insect-pollinated flower.

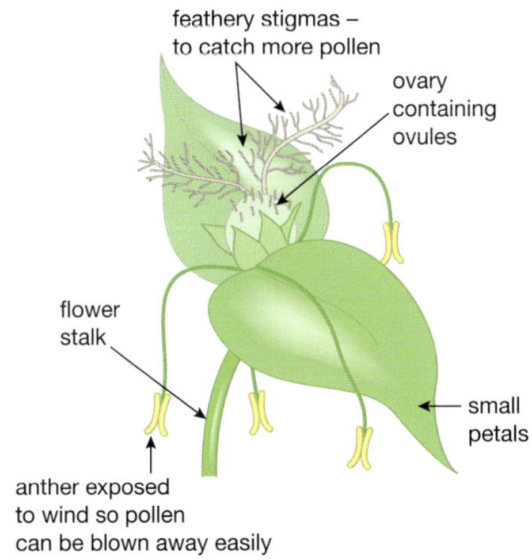

▲ Figure 13.4 The main structures in an wind-pollinated flower.

Table 13.2 Differences between insect-pollinated and wind-pollinated flowers.

Feature of flower	Type of flower	
	Insect-pollinated	Wind-pollinated
position of stamens	enclosed within flower so that insect must make contact	exposed so that wind can easily blow pollen away
position of stigma	enclosed within flower so that insect must make contact	exposed to catch pollen blowing in the wind
type of stigma	sticky so pollen grains attach from insects	feathery, to catch pollen grains blowing in the wind
size of petals	large to attract insects	small
colour of petals	brightly coloured to attract insects	not brightly coloured, usually green
nectaries	present – they produce nectar, a sweet liquid containing sugars as a 'reward' for insects	absent
pollen grains	larger, sticky grains or grains with hooks, to stick to insects' bodies	smaller, smooth, inflated grains to carry in the wind

FERTILISATION

Pollination transfers the pollen grain to the stigma. However, for fertilisation to take place, the nucleus of the pollen grain (the male gamete) must fuse with the nucleus of the ovum, which is inside an ovule in the ovary. To transfer the nucleus to the ovum, the pollen grain forms a **pollen tube**, which grows down through the tissue of the **style** and into the ovary. Here it curves around to enter the opening in an ovule. The tip of the tube dissolves and allows the pollen grain nucleus to move out of the tube and into the ovule. Here it fertilises the ovum nucleus. These events are summarised in Figure 13.5.

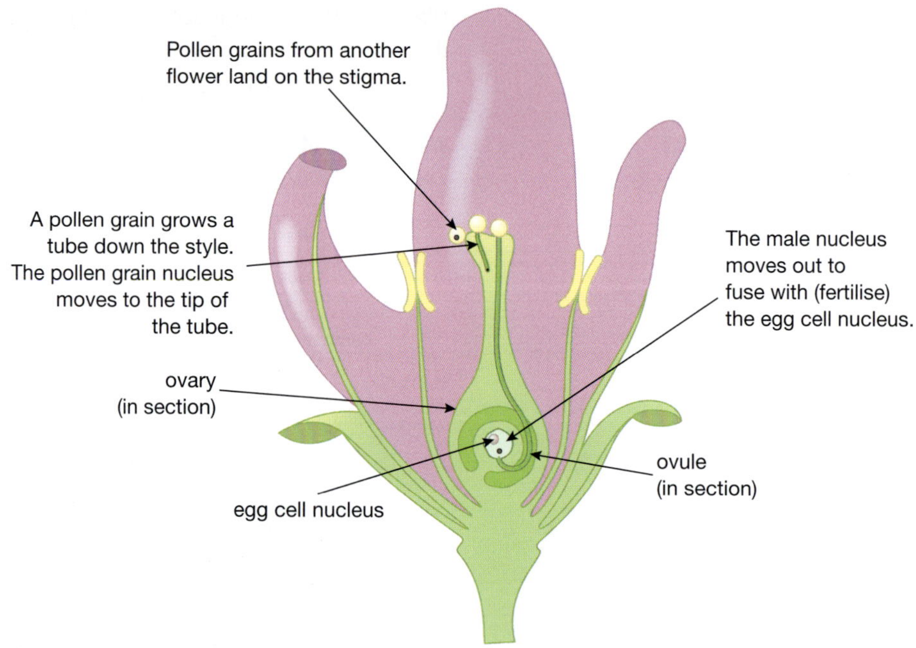

▲ Figure 13.5 Pollination and fertilisation

SEED AND FRUIT FORMATION

Once fertilisation has occurred, a number of changes take place in the ovule and ovary that will lead to the fertilised ovule becoming a seed and the ovary in which it is found becoming a fruit. Different flowers produce different types of fruits, but in all cases the following four changes take place.

1 The zygote develops into an embryonic plant with small root (**radicle**) and shoot (**plumule**).

2 Other contents of the ovule develop into a food store for the young plant when the seed germinates.

3 The ovule wall becomes the seed coat or **testa**.

4 The ovary wall becomes the fruit coat; this can take many forms depending on the type of fruit.

Figure 13.6 summarises these changes as they occur in the plum flower, which forms a fleshy fruit.

DID YOU KNOW?

Any structure that contains seeds is a fruit. A pea pod is a fruit. The 'pod' is the fruit wall, formed from the ovary wall, and the peas are individual seeds. Each forms from a fertilised ovule.

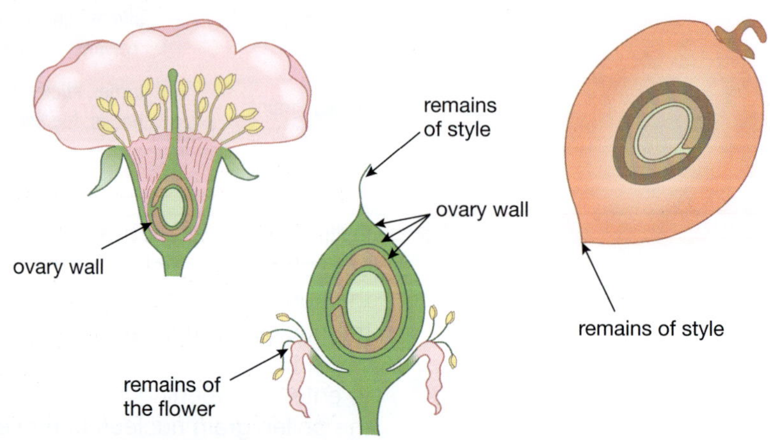

▲ Figure 13.6 How a plum fruit forms

GERMINATION

A seed contains a plant embryo, consisting of a root (radicle), shoot (plumule) and one or two seed leaves, called **cotyledons**. It also contains a food store, either in the cotyledons or another part of the seed. During germination, the food store is used up, providing the nutrients to allow the radicle and plumule to grow. The radicle grows down into the soil, where it will absorb water and mineral ions. The plumule grows upwards towards the light, where it can start the process of photosynthesis (Figure 13.7). Once the small plant (seedling) is able to photosynthesise, germination is over.

The seeds of plants such as peas or beans have two cotyledons. They are called dicotyledonous plants, or **dicots**. Seeds of grasses and other narrow-leaved plants, such as irises and orchids have only one cotyledon. They are monocotyledonous plants, or **monocots**.

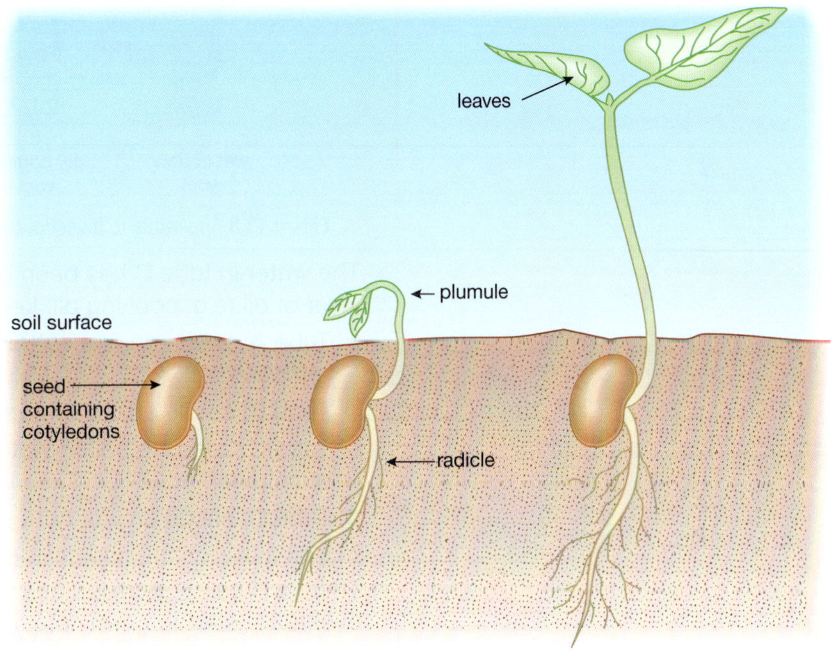

▲ Figure 13.7 Germination in the broad bean. In this species, the cotyledons contain a food store. They remain below the ground when the seed germinates. In other species (e.g. the French bean), they are carried above the ground during germination.

The food store of peas or beans is present in the cotyledons. It consists mainly of starch and protein. In monocots such as maize, there is a separate food store of starch.

THE CONDITIONS NEEDED FOR GERMINATION

The growth of a new plant from a seed is called **germination**. When seeds are dispersed from the parent plant they are usually very dry, containing only about 10% water. This low water content restricts a seed's metabolism, so that it can remain alive but dormant (inactive) for a long time, sometimes for many years.

When a seed germinates, dormancy comes to an end. The seed's food store is broken down by enzymes and respired aerobically. This means that germination needs the following conditions:

- warm temperatures, so that enzymes can act efficiently (see Chapter 1)
- water, for chemical reactions to take place in solution
- oxygen, for respiration.

Safety note: Wash hands after handling seeds.

ACTIVITY 5

▼ PRACTICAL: INVESTIGATING THE CONDITIONS NEEDED FOR GERMINATION

Small seeds such as peas or mustard will grow on wet cotton wool in a test tube. Figure 13.8 shows four tubes set up to investigate the conditions needed for the seeds to germinate.

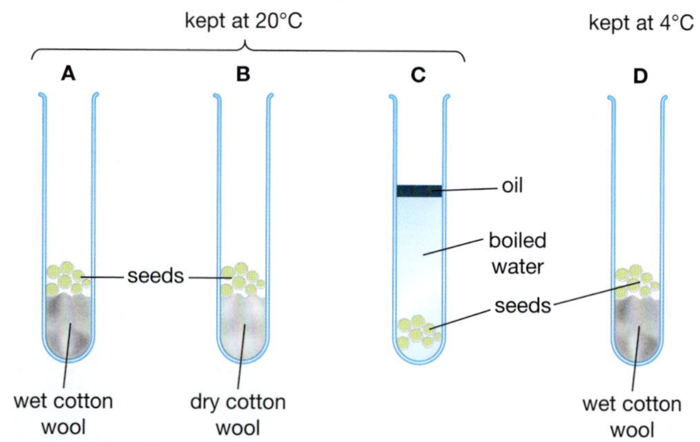

▲ Figure 13.8 Apparatus to investigate the conditions needed for germination

The water in tube C has been boiled to remove dissolved oxygen. The layer of oil (e.g. cooking oil) keeps out oxygen from the air.

- Tube A: seeds on wet cotton wool, maintained at 20 °C (room temperature)
- Tube B: seeds on dry cotton wool, maintained at 20 °C
- Tube C: seeds in boiled water, with a thin surface layer of oil; maintained at 20 °C
- Tube D: seeds on wet cotton wool, placed in a refrigerator at 4 °C

After a few days the seeds in the control tube (A) will start to germinate. There will be no germination in tubes B or C. The seeds in tube D may eventually start to germinate, but much more slowly than in tube A.

What do the results tell you about the conditions needed for germination? Do you have any criticisms of this method? (Hint – are all the variables fully controlled?)

CHAPTER QUESTIONS

More questions on reproduction in plants can be found at the end of Unit 3 on page 159.

SKILLS CRITICAL THINKING 4th

1 Which of the following features are shown by wind-pollinated flowers?

A large petals, a scent and sticky pollen grains
B small petals, no scent and light pollen grains
C large petals, no scent and light pollen grains
D small petals, a scent and sticky pollen grains

2 During pollination, between which of the following structures are pollen grains transferred?

A from anther to stigma
B from anther to ovary
C from stigma to style
D from stigma to ovary

SKILLS CRITICAL THINKING

4th

3 Following fertilisation, which of the following takes place?

A The ovule becomes the fruit and the ovary becomes the seed

B The carpel becomes the fruit and the anther becomes the seed

C The anther becomes the fruit and the carpel becomes the seed

D The ovary becomes the fruit and the ovule becomes the seed

5th

4 Read the three statements below.

1. Uptake of water 2. Uptake of oxygen 3. Increase in metabolism

Which of these events are associated with seed germination?

A 1 and 2 **B** 1 and 3 **C** 2 and 3 **D** 1, 2 and 3

SKILLS ANALYSIS

4th

5 The diagram below shows a section through an insect-pollinated flower. Pollination happens when pollen grains land on part X.

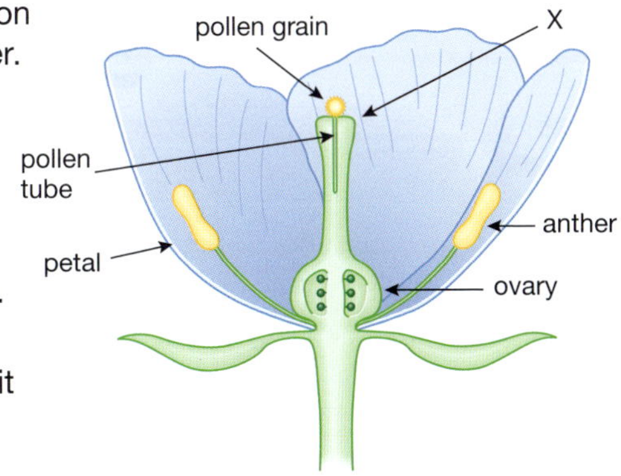

a Name part X.

SKILLS REASONING

b How are insects attracted to a flower like this? Give two ways.

SKILLS INTERPRETATION

5th

c Copy the diagram and extend the pollen tube to show where it would go when fully grown.

SKILLS CRITICAL THINKING

6th

6 A student investigated whether temperature affected the germination of seeds. He set up three boiling tubes, each containing 10 seeds placed on wet cotton wool.

- Tube A was kept at room temperature (20 °C) in the light.
- Tube B was placed in a fridge at 4 °C.
- Tube C was placed in an incubator at 30 °C.

The student monitored the seeds for 3 days, making sure that the cotton wool remained damp. At the end of this time he observed the results and measured the height of any seedlings that had germinated. His results are shown in the table.

Tube	Height of any seedlings that germinated / cm	% seeds germinated	Average height of seeds that germinated / cm
A	2.3, 2.7, 1.9, 2.5, 2.6, 3.1, 1.9, 2.2, 2.6, 3.2	100	2.5
B	0.3, 0.5 (the other seeds did not germinate)	20	0.4
C	3.4, 4.5, 2.5, 3.7, 2.8, 4.4, 4.3, 2.9, 2.1, 3.7	100	

a State the independent variable and the dependent variable in the student's experiment.

SKILLS PROBLEM SOLVING

5th

b Calculate the average height of the seedlings that germinated in tube C.

SKILLS DECISION MAKING

c Summarise the conclusions that can be drawn from this experiment.

SKILLS REASONING

6th

d Why does temperature affect the germination of seeds?

SKILLS EXECUTIVE FUNCTION

5th

e Another student suggested that the experiment was not properly controlled. Explain what she meant, and suggest how the experiment could be modified.

SKILLS REASONING

7 The diagram shows a potato plant producing new tubers (potatoes). Buds on the parent plant grow into stems that grow downwards, called stolons. The ends of each stolon develop into a new tuber.

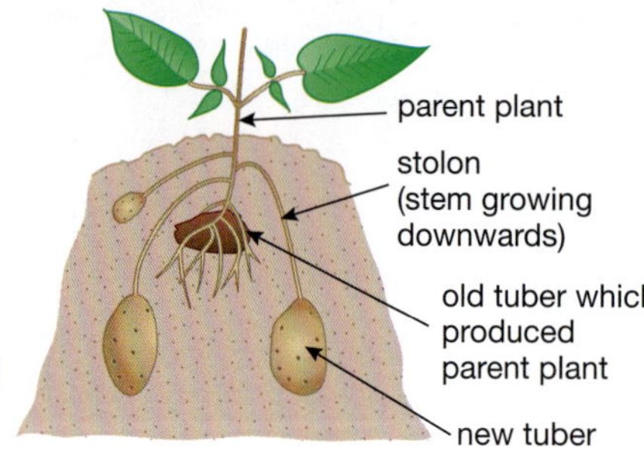

a Give two pieces of evidence which show that this is an asexual method of reproduction.

b Explain why all the new tubers will be genetically identical.

c Even though the tubers are genetically identical, the plants that grow from them may not be the same height. Explain why.

d Why do wild plants need to reproduce sexually as well as asexually?

SKILLS CRITICAL THINKING

8 The drawing shows a wind-pollinated flower.

a Name the structures labelled A, B, C and D.

b Give *three* pieces of evidence *visible in the diagram*, which show that this flower is wind-pollinated.

c Describe how fertilisation takes place once a flower has been pollinated.

d Describe *four* ways in which you would expect an insect-pollinated flower to be different from the flower shown.

SKILLS REASONING

9 The drawing shows a strawberry plant reproducing in two ways.

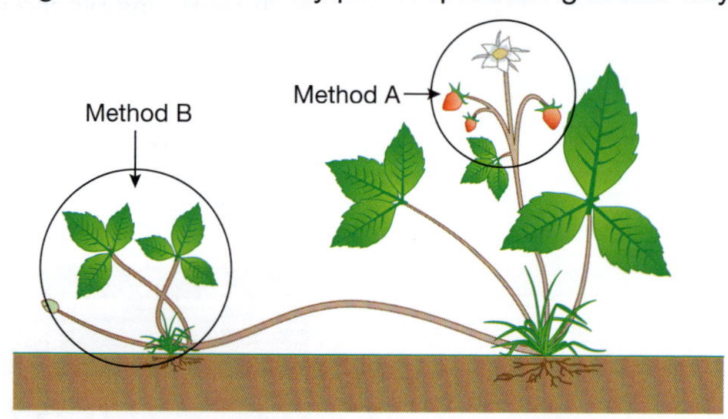

a Which of the two methods of reproduction shown will result in offspring that show genetic variation? Explain your answer.

b Is the strawberry flower likely to be wind-pollinated or insect-pollinated? Give reasons for your answer.

10 All banana plants are reproduced asexually. Biologists are concerned for their future, as a new strain of fungus has appeared which is killing all the banana plants in some plantations.

a Explain why the fungus is able to kill all the banana plants in some plantations.

b Explain why this would be less likely to happen if banana plants reproduced sexually.

c Describe the benefits of reproducing banana plants asexually.

UNIT QUESTIONS

SKILLS ANALYSIS 6th

1 Light intensity and the concentration of carbon dioxide in the atmosphere influence the rate of photosynthesis.

a The graph shows the effect of changing light intensity on the rate of photosynthesis at two different carbon dioxide concentrations.

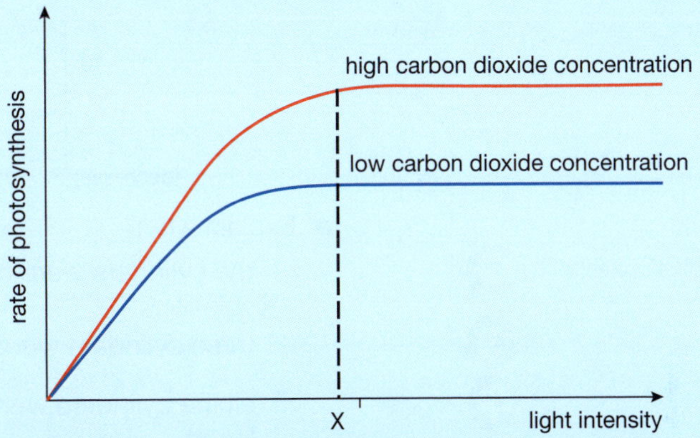

i Describe the effect of light intensity on the rate of photosynthesis at each concentration of carbon dioxide up to light intensity X and beyond light intensity X. **(4)**

ii Which factor limits the rate of photosynthesis up to light intensity X and beyond light intensity X? **(2)**

Explain your answer in each case. **(3)**

SKILLS CRITICAL THINKING 5th 6th

b **i** Describe two other factors which influence the rate of photosynthesis. **(2)**

ii Explain why each is a limiting factor. **(4)**

SKILLS INTERPRETATION

c 'Photosynthesis is a means of converting light energy into chemical energy.'

Explain what this statement means. **(2)**

(Total 17 marks)

SKILLS DECISION MAKING

2 In an investigation to determine the water potential of potato cells, the following procedure was adopted.

Cylinders of tissue were obtained from a potato. Each was the same diameter and cut to a length of 5 cm.

Each cylinder was dried and then weighed.

Three potato cylinders were placed in each of six different concentrations of sucrose solution and left for two hours.

The cylinders were then removed from the solutions, dried and reweighed. The percentage change in mass for each was calculated, and then an average percentage change in mass calculated for each solution.

The graph summarises the results.

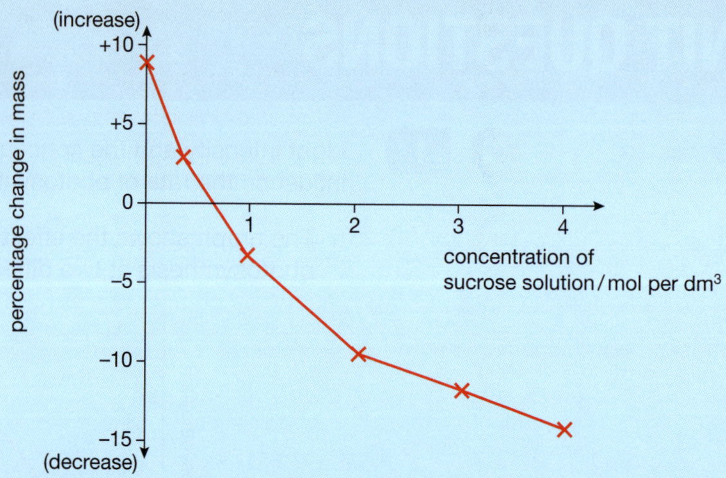

SKILLS DECISION MAKING

a Explain why:

- **i** the cylinders were dried before and after being placed in the sucrose solutions **(1)**
- **ii** three cylinders were used for each solution **(1)**
- **iii** all the cylinders were the same diameter and were cut to the same length. **(1)**

SKILLS PROBLEM SOLVING

b **i** In terms of water potential, explain the result obtained with a 3 mol per dm^3 sucrose solution. **(3)**

- **ii** What concentration of sucrose has a water potential equivalent to that of the potato cells? Explain your answer. **(3)**

SKILLS EXECUTIVE FUNCTION

c How could the water potential of the potato tissue be determined more accurately? **(2)**

(Total 11 marks)

SKILLS CRITICAL THINKING

3 Plants can respond to a range of stimuli.

a Plant shoots detect and grow towards light.

- **i** What is this process called? **(1)**
- **ii** Explain how a plant bends towards the light. **(3)**
- **iii** Explain the advantage to the plant of this response. **(1)**

b In an investigation, young plant shoots were exposed to light from one side. The wavelength of the light was varied. The graph summarises the results of the investigation.

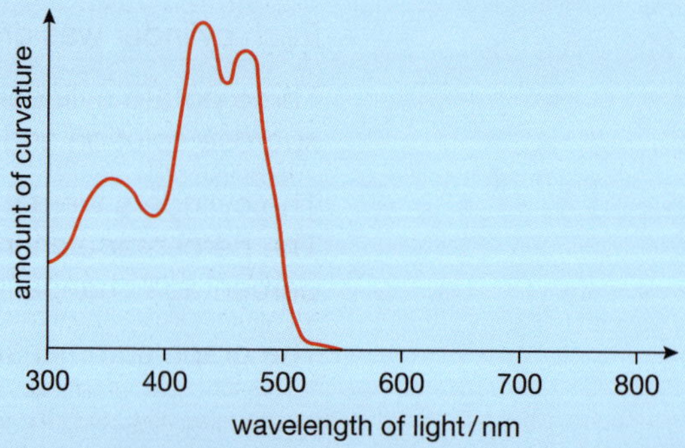

SKILLS ANALYSIS

- **i** Describe the results shown in the graph. **(2)**

SKILLS ANALYSIS 7th

ii Suggest why the results show this pattern. (2)

SKILLS CRITICAL THINKING 5th

c i Name another stimulus that produces a growth response in plants. (1)

ii Describe the ways roots and shoots respond to this stimulus (2)

6th

iii What is the benefit to the plant of these responses? (2)

(Total 14 marks)

SKILLS ANALYSIS 4th

4 The diagram below shows a flower.

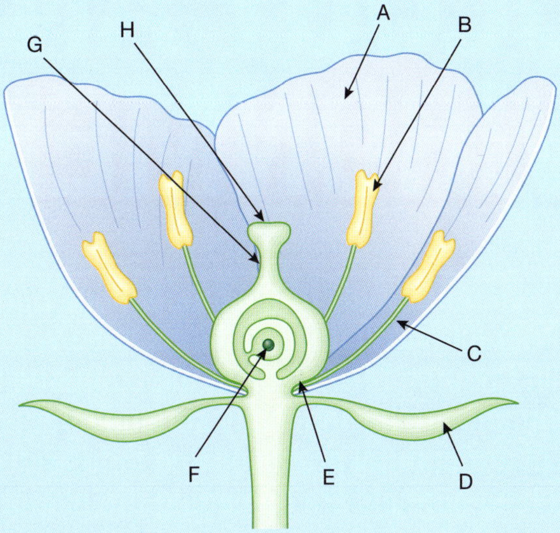

a Give the letter of the structure which:

i produces pollen grains ii becomes the seed

iii becomes the fruit wall. (3)

b Write down two ways that you can see in the diagram that this flower is adapted for insect pollination. (2)

c Give the letter of the structure which is:

i the stigma ii the style iii the filament. (3)

SKILLS INTERPRETATION 5th

d Explain the difference between:

i pollination and fertilisation

ii self-pollination and **cross-pollination**. (4)

(Total 12 marks)

SKILLS EXECUTIVE FUNCTION 8th

5 When pollen grains land on the stigma of a plant they germinate (grow a pollen tube). Growth of the pollen tube is thought to be stimulated by sugars produced by the stigma.

If pollen grains are placed in certain solutions they will germinate. The drawing shows some grains seen through a microscope after 2 hours in a solution.

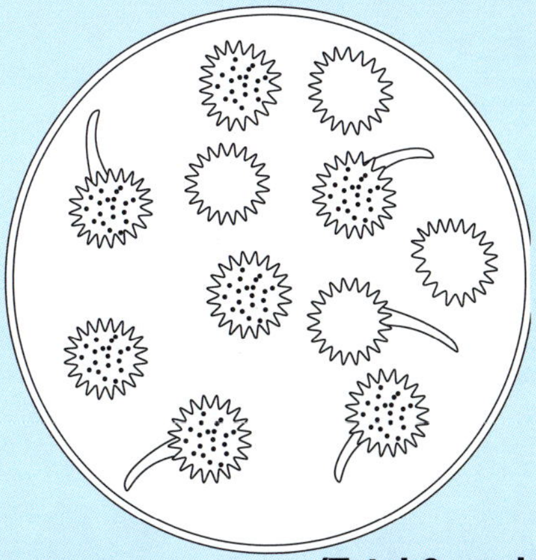

Design an investigation to find out if germination of pollen grains is stimulated by sucrose.

Your answer should include experimental details and be written in full sentences.

(Total 6 marks)

BIOLOGY UNIT 4 ECOLOGY AND THE ENVIRONMENT

Ecology is the scientific study of the interactions between organisms and their surroundings. It analyses the interactions that living things have with each other and with their non-living, physical environment. In Chapter 14 we look at the components of ecosystems and these interactions. The activities of humans are having many serious effects on the world ecosystems, in particular as a consequence of agricultural practices and industrial pollution. Chapter 15 looks at these activities and considers how humans are damaging the planet.

14 ECOSYSTEMS

An ecosystem is a distinct, self-supporting system of organisms interacting with each other and with a physical environment. An ecosystem can be small, such as a pond, or large, such as a mangrove swamp or a large forest. This chapter looks at a variety of ecosystems and the interactions that happen within them.

LEARNING OBJECTIVES

- Understand the terms ecosystem, habitat, population and community
- Investigate the population size of an organism in two different areas using quadrats
- Understand how biotic and abiotic factors affect the population size and distribution of organisms
- Understand the names given to different trophic levels, including producers, primary, secondary and tertiary consumers, and decomposers
- Understand the concepts of food chains, food webs, pyramids of number, pyramids of biomass and pyramids of energy transfe
- Understand the transfer of substances and energy along a food chain
- Understand why only about 10% of energy is transferred from one trophic level to the next
- Describe the stages in the carbon cycle, including respiration, photosynthesis, decomposition and combustion

Figure 14.1 A pond is a small ecosystem.

Figure 14.2 A mangrove swamp is a larger ecosystem.

THE COMPONENTS OF ECOSYSTEMS

Whatever their size, **ecosystems** usually have the same components:

- **producers** – plants which photosynthesise to produce food
- **consumers** – animals that eat plants or other animals
- **decomposers** – organisms that break down dead material and help to recycle nutrients
- the physical environment – all the non-biological components of the ecosystem; for example, the water and soil in a pond or the soil and air in a forest.

KEY POINT

Decomposers are fungi and some species of bacteria. They feed by saprotrophic nutrition (see Chapter 2)

The living components of an ecosystem are called the *biotic* components. The non-living (physical) components are the *abiotic* components (compare these with **biotic** and **abiotic factors**, below).

An ecosystem contains a variety of habitats. A **habitat** is the place where an organism lives. For example, habitats in a pond ecosystem include the open water, the mud at the bottom of the pond, and the surface water.

All the organisms of a particular species found in an ecosystem at a certain time form the **population** of that species. All the immature frogs (tadpoles) swimming in a pond are a population of tadpoles; all the water lily plants growing in the pond make up a population of water lilies.

The populations of *all* species (animals, plants and other organisms) found in an ecosystem at a particular time form the **community**. Figure 14.3 illustrates the main components of a pond ecosystem.

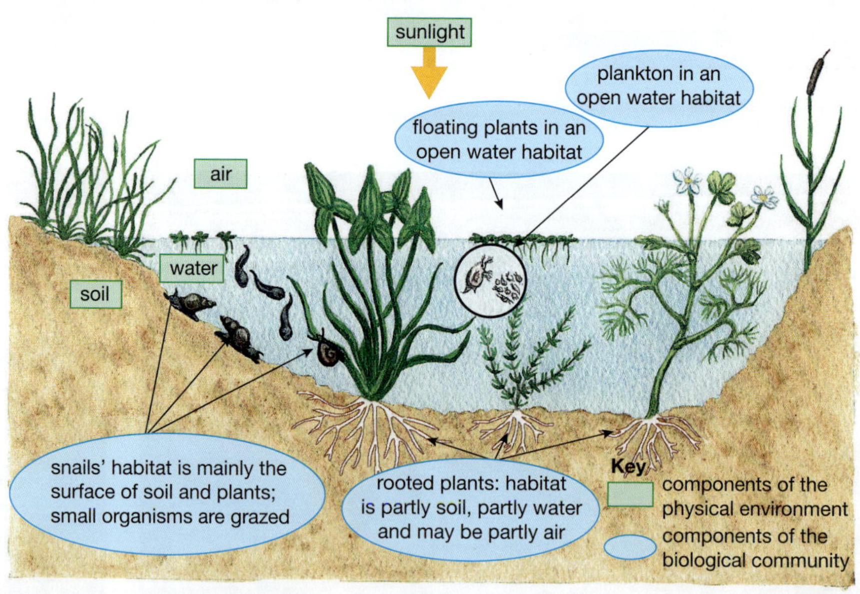

▲ Figure 14.3 A pond ecosystem

USING QUADRATS TO SAMPLE FROM A HABITAT

When an ecologist wants to know how many organisms there are in a particular habitat, it would not be possible for him to count them all. Instead, he is forced to count a smaller representative part of the population, called a *sample*. Sampling of plants, or animals that do not move much (such as snails), can be done using a sampling square called a **quadrat**. A quadrat is usually made from metal, wood or plastic. The size of quadrat you use depends on the size of the organisms being sampled. For example, to count plants growing on a school field, you could use a quadrat with sides 0.5 or 1 metre in length (Figure 14.4).

HINT

People often mistakenly call quadrats 'quadrants'. A *quadrant* is quite different – it is a quarter of a circle.

▲ Figure 14.4 A student sampling with a quadrat

KEY POINT

Some books (and teachers!) talk about 'throwing' quadrats. The idea is that you stand in the middle of a field and throw the quadrat over your shoulder. This is supposed to be random, but it isn't! The place where the quadrat falls will depend on where you stand, how hard you throw it, etc. It is wrong to use this method.

It is important that sampling in an area is carried out *at random*, to avoid bias. For example, if you were sampling from a school field, but for convenience only placed your quadrats next to a path, this probably wouldn't give you a sample that was representative of the whole field! It would be a *biased* sample.

Safety note: Wash hands after handling the quadrat, plants and soil. Take care if working near a pond or stream or in any areas which may contain animal faeces.

ACTIVITY 1

▼ PRACTICAL: USING QUADRATS TO COMPARE THE SIZE OF A PLANT POPULATION IN TWO AREAS OF A FIELD

One way that you can sample randomly is to place quadrats at coordinates on a numbered grid.

Imagine that there are two areas of a school field (A and B) that seem to contain different numbers of dandelion plants. Area A is more trampled than area B and looks like it contains fewer dandelions. This might lead you to propose the hypothesis: 'The dandelion population in area A is smaller than the dandelion population in area B'.

In area A, two 10-metre tape measures are arranged to form the sides of a square (Figure 14.5).

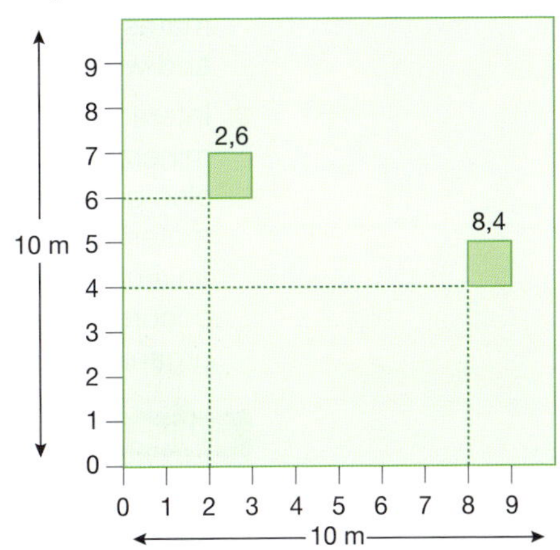

▲ Figure 14.5 A 10-m^2 grid with 1-m^2 quadrats positioned at coordinates 2,6 and 8,4.

A pair of random numbers is generated, using the random number function on a calculator. These numbers are used as coordinates to position the quadrat in the large square.

The numbers of dandelions in the quadrat are counted. The process is then repeated for nine more quadrats.

The tape measures are then moved to area B and the process repeated to sample from ten more quadrats in that part of the field.

The table below shows a set of results for a study like this.

Table 14.1

Quadrat number	Number of dandelions in each quadrat in area A	Number of dandelions in each quadrat in area B
1	4	10
2	7	7
3	1	9
4	0	14
5	3	12
6	8	7
7	3	16
8	12	9
9	1	11
10	6	15

Calculate the mean number of dandelions per m^2 in each area. Do the results support the hypothesis that the population numbers are different? How could you improve the **reliability** of the results?

INTERACTIONS IN ECOSYSTEMS

The organisms in an ecosystem are continually interacting with each other and with their physical environment. Interactions include the following.

- Feeding among the organisms – the plants, animals and decomposers are continually recycling the same nutrients through the ecosystem.
- Competition among the organisms – animals compete for food, shelter, mates, nesting sites; plants compete for carbon dioxide, mineral ions, light and water.
- Interactions between organisms and the environment – plants absorb mineral ions, carbon dioxide and water from the environment; plants also give off water vapour and oxygen into the environment; animals use materials from the environment to build shelters; the temperature of the environment can affect processes occurring in the organisms; processes occurring in organisms can affect the temperature of the environment (all organisms produce some heat).

REMINDER

Don't forget that plants take in carbon dioxide and give out oxygen only when there is sufficient light for photosynthesis to occur efficiently. When there is little light, plants take in oxygen and give out carbon dioxide. You should be able to explain the reasons for this (see Chapter 10).

BIOTIC AND ABIOTIC FACTORS

There are many factors that influence the numbers and distribution of organisms in an ecosystem. There are two types of factor – *biotic* and *abiotic*.

Biotic factors are biological. Many (but not all) involve feeding relationships. They include:

- availability of food and competition for food resources
- predation
- parasitism
- disease
- presence of pollinating insects
- availability of nest sites.

KEY POINT

A **predator** is an animal that kills and eats another animal. A **parasite** is an organism (animal or plant) that lives in or on another organism (called its host) and gets its nutrition from the host. e.g. mosquitoes are parasites of humans (and other animals), and the human is the host of the mosquito.

Abiotic factors are physical or chemical factors. They include:

- climate, such as light intensity, temperature and water availability
- hours of daylight
- soil conditions, such as clay content, nitrate level, particle size, water content and pH
- other factors specific to a particular habitat, such as salinity (salt content) in an estuary, flow rate in a river, or oxygen concentration in a lake
- pollution.

Clearly *which* factors affect population sizes and distribution of organisms will depend on the *type* of ecosystem. If you take the example of a river, some of the main abiotic factors could be:

- depth of water
- flow rate
- type of material at the bottom of the stream (stones, sand, mud etc.)
- concentration of minerals in the water
- pH
- oxygen concentration
- cloudiness of the water
- presence of any pollution.

The main biotic factors affecting animals in the river will be food supply, either from plants or other animals. But other factors are important too – large fish could not live in a shallow stream!

It is impossible to generalise about which factors are the most important. In a heavily polluted river all the organisms could be killed by the pollution, while in a clean river depth and flow rate might have a greater effect on the animals that could live there. The different factors may also affect one another. For example, a faster flow rate could mix the water with air, increasing the amount of dissolved oxygen.

KEY POINT

Large areas of the Earth dominated by a specific type of vegetation are called *biomes*. Temperate grassland and tropical rain forest are two examples of biomes. You could carry out some research to find out about these and other biomes.

The main factor affecting large ecosystems is climate, particularly temperature and rainfall. Climate is the reason why **tropical rainforests** are restricted to a strip near the equator of the Earth, while pine forests grow in the higher latitudes of the northern hemisphere.

FEEDING RELATIONSHIPS

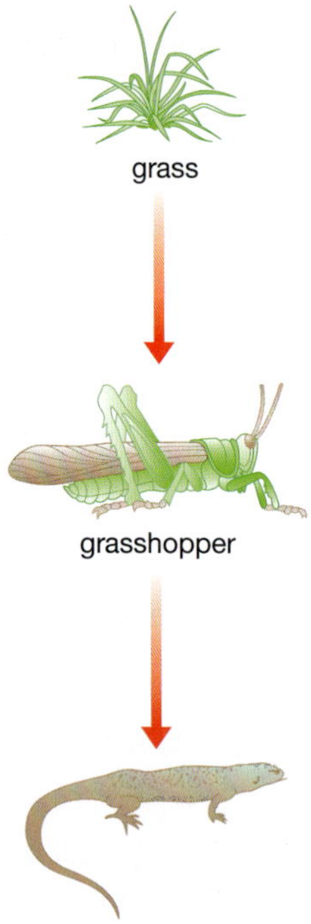

▲ Figure 14.6 A simple food chain.

The simplest way of showing feeding relationships within an ecosystem is a **food chain** (Figure 14.6).

In any food chain, the arrow (→) means 'is eaten by'. In the food chain illustrated, the grass is the **producer**. It is a plant so it can photosynthesise and produce food materials. The grasshopper is the **primary consumer**. It is an animal which eats the producer and is also a **herbivore**. The lizard is the **secondary consumer**. It eats the primary consumer and is also a **carnivore**. The different stages in a food chain (producer, primary consumer and secondary consumer) are called **trophic levels**.

Many food chains have more than three links in them. Here are two examples of longer food chains:

filamentous algae → mayfly nymph → caddis fly larvae → salmon

In this freshwater food chain, the extra link in the chain makes the salmon a **tertiary consumer**.

plankton → crustacean → fish → ringed seal → polar bear

In this marine (sea) food chain, the fifth link makes the polar bear a **quaternary consumer**. Because nothing eats the polar bear, it is also called the *top carnivore*.

Food chains are a convenient way of showing the feeding relationships between a few organisms in an ecosystem, but they oversimplify the situation. The marine food chain above implies that only crustaceans feed on plankton, which is not true. Some whales and other mammals also feed on plankton. For a fuller understanding, you need to consider how the different food chains in an ecosystem relate to each other. Figure 14.7 gives a clearer picture of the feeding relationships involved in a freshwater ecosystem in which salmon are the top carnivores. This is the **food web** of the salmon.

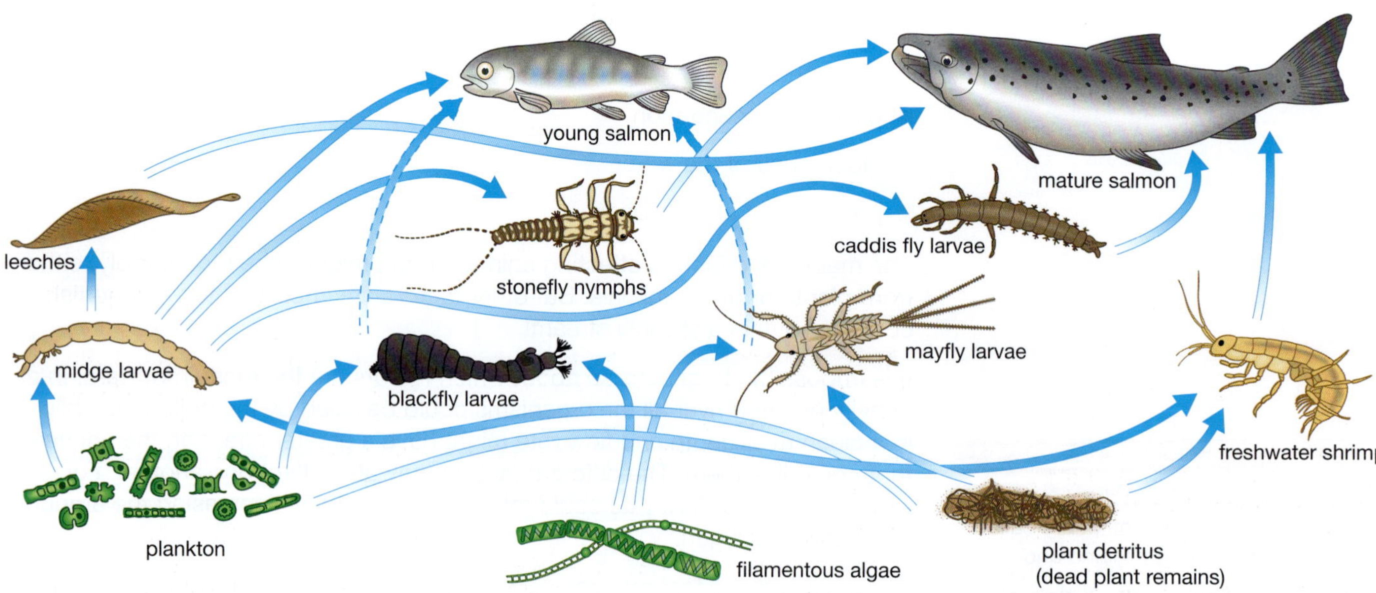

▲ Figure 14.7 The food web of the salmon. As you can see, young salmon have a slightly different diet to mature salmon.

This is still an oversimplification of the true situation, as some feeding relationships are still not shown. It does, however, give some indication of the interrelationships that exist between food chains in an ecosystem. With a little thought, you can predict how changes in the numbers of an organism in one food chain in the food web might affect those in another food chain. For example, if the leech population were to decline through disease, there could be several possible consequences:

- the stonefly nymph population could increase as there would be more midge larvae to feed on
- the stonefly nymph population could decrease as the mature salmon might eat more of them as there would be fewer leeches
- the numbers could remain the same due to a combination of the above.

Although food webs give us more information than food chains, they don't give any information about how many, or what mass of organisms is involved. Neither do they show the role of the decomposers. To see this, we must look at other ways of presenting information about feeding relationships in an ecosystem.

ECOLOGICAL PYRAMIDS

Ecological pyramids are diagrams that represent the relative amounts of organisms at each trophic level in a food chain. There are two main types:

- **pyramids of numbers**, which represent the numbers of organisms in each trophic level in a food chain, irrespective of their mass
- **pyramids of biomass**, which show the total mass of the organisms in each trophic level, irrespective of their numbers.

Consider these two food chains:

a grass → grasshopper → frog → bird

b oak tree → aphid → ladybird → bird

Figures 14.8 and 14.9 show the pyramids of numbers and biomass for these two food chains.

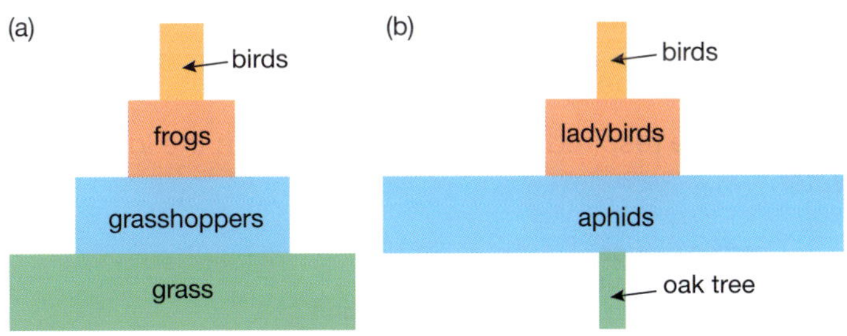

▲ Figure 14.8 Pyramids of numbers for two food chains

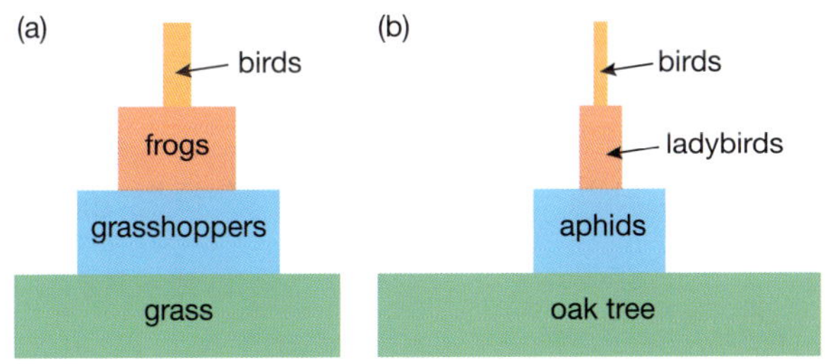

▲ Figure 14.9 Pyramids of biomass for the two food chains

KEY POINT

Biomass is the total mass of organisms. If it refers to living organisms, this is called the *fresh biomass*. More commonly the *dry biomass* is used. This is the mass of plant or animal material after water has been removed, by drying in an oven. Dry biomass is a more reliable measure, since the water content of organisms (especially plants) varies with environmental conditions.

The two pyramids for the 'grass' food chain look the same – the numbers at each trophic level decrease. The *total* biomass also decreases along the food chain – the mass of *all* the grass plants in a large field would be more than that of *all* the grasshoppers which would be more than that of *all* the frogs, and so on.

The two pyramids for the 'oak tree' food chain look different because of the size of the oak trees. Each oak tree can support many thousands of aphids, so the numbers *increase* from first to second trophic levels. But each ladybird will need to eat many aphids and each bird will need to eat many ladybirds, so the numbers *decrease* at the third and fourth trophic levels. However, the total biomass *decreases* at each trophic level – the biomass of one oak tree is much greater than that of the thousands of aphids it supports. The total biomass of all these aphids is greater than that of the ladybirds, which is greater than that of the birds.

Suppose the birds in the second food chain are parasitised by nematode worms (small worms living in the bird's gut). The food chain now becomes:

oak tree → aphid → ladybird → bird → nematode worm

The pyramid of numbers now takes on a very strange appearance (Figure 14.10a) because of the large numbers of parasites on each bird. The pyramid of biomass, however, has a true pyramid shape because the total biomass (Figure 14.10b) of the nematode worms must be less than that of the birds they parasitise.

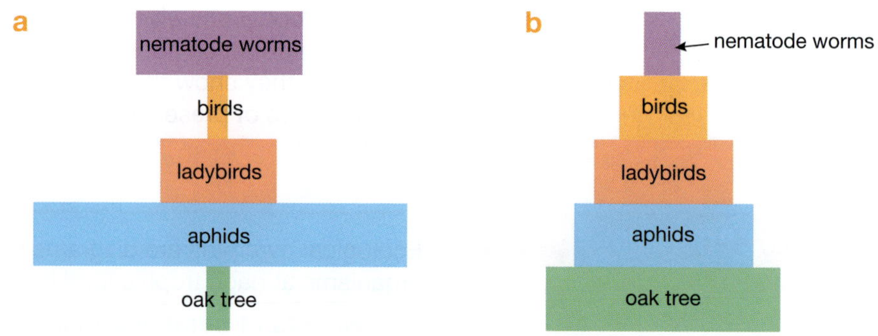

Figure 14.10 (a) A pyramid of numbers and (b) a pyramid of biomass for the parasitised food chain.

KEY POINT

Another way of describing the food chain is that it shows how energy is moved from one organism to another as a result of feeding. The arrows show the direction of energy flow.

The explanation is relatively straightforward (Figure 14.11). When a rabbit eats grass, not all of the materials in the grass plant end up as rabbit! There are losses:

- some parts of the grass are not eaten (the roots for example)
- some parts are not digested and so are not absorbed – even though rabbits have a very efficient digestive system
- some of the materials absorbed form excretory products
- many of the materials are respired to release energy, with the loss of carbon dioxide and water.

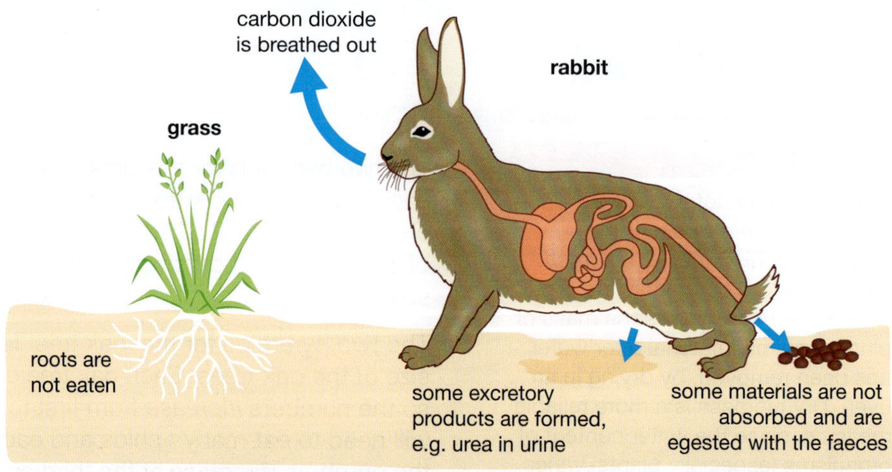

Figure 14.11 Not all the grass eaten by a rabbit ends up as rabbit tissue.

In fact, only a small fraction of the materials in the grass ends up in new cells in the rabbit. Similar losses are repeated at each stage in the food chain, so smaller and smaller amounts of biomass are available for growth at successive trophic levels. The shape of pyramids of biomass reflects this.

Feeding is a way of transferring energy between organisms. Another way of modelling ecosystems looks at the energy flow between the various trophic levels.

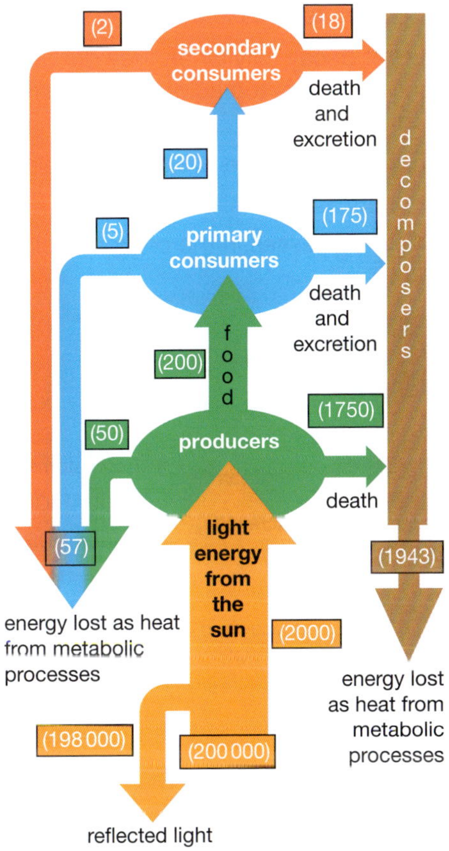

▲ Figure 14.12 The main ways in which energy is transferred in an ecosystem. The amounts of energy transferred through 1 m^2 of a grassland ecosystem per year are shown in brackets.

THE FLOW OF ENERGY THROUGH ECOSYSTEMS

This approach focuses less on individual organisms and food chains and rather more on energy transfer between trophic levels (producers, consumers and decomposers) in the whole ecosystem. There are a number of key ideas involved:

- Photosynthesis 'fixes' sunlight energy into chemicals such as glucose and starch.
- Respiration releases energy from organic compounds such as glucose.
- Almost all other biological processes (e.g. muscle contraction, growth, reproduction, excretion, active transport) use the energy released in respiration.
- If the energy released in respiration is used to produce new cells, then the energy remains 'fixed' in molecules in that organism. It can be passed on to the next trophic level through feeding.
- If the energy released in respiration is used for other processes then it will, once used, eventually escape as heat from the organism. Energy is therefore lost from food chains and webs at each trophic level.

Figure 14.12 is an energy flow diagram. It shows the main ways in which energy is transferred in an ecosystem. It also gives the amounts of energy transferred between the trophic levels of this particular (grassland) ecosystem.

As you can see, only about 10% of the energy entering a trophic level is passed on to the next trophic level. This explains why not many food chains have more than five trophic levels. Think of the food chain:

$$A \rightarrow B \rightarrow C \rightarrow D \rightarrow E$$

If we use the idea that only about 10% of the energy entering a trophic level is passed on to the next level, then, of the original 100% reaching A (a producer), 10% passes to B, 1% (10% of 10%) passes to C, 0.1% passes to D and only 0.001% passes to E. There just isn't enough energy left for another trophic level. In certain parts of the world, some marine food chains have six trophic levels because of the huge amount of light energy reaching the surface waters.

CYCLING NUTRIENTS THROUGH ECOSYSTEMS

The chemicals that make up our bodies have all been around before – probably many times! You may have in your body some carbon atoms that were part of the body of Mahatma Gandhi or were in carbon dioxide molecules breathed out by Winston Churchill. This constant recycling of substances is all part of the cycle of life, death and decay.

Microorganisms play a key role in recycling. They break down complex organic molecules in the bodies of dead animals and plants into simpler substances, which they release into the environment.

THE CARBON CYCLE

Carbon is a component of all major biological molecules. Carbohydrates, lipids, proteins, DNA, vitamins and many other molecules all contain carbon. The following processes are important in cycling carbon through ecosystems.

- Photosynthesis 'fixes' carbon atoms from carbon dioxide into organic compounds
- Feeding and **assimilation** pass carbon atoms already in organic compounds along food chains
- Respiration produces inorganic carbon dioxide from organic compounds (mainly carbohydrates) as they are broken down to release energy
- Fossilisation – sometimes living things do not decay fully when they die due to the conditions in the soil (decay is prevented if it is too acidic) and fossil fuels (coal, oil, natural gas and peat) are formed
- Combustion releases carbon dioxide into the atmosphere when fossil fuels are burned.

DID YOU KNOW?

What exactly is an organic compound? There is no precise definition! All organic compounds contain carbon, and *most* contain hydrogen. Starch and glucose are organic molecules, but carbon dioxide (CO_2) isn't (it is inorganic).

Figures 14.13 and 14.14 show the role of these processes in the carbon cycle in different ways.

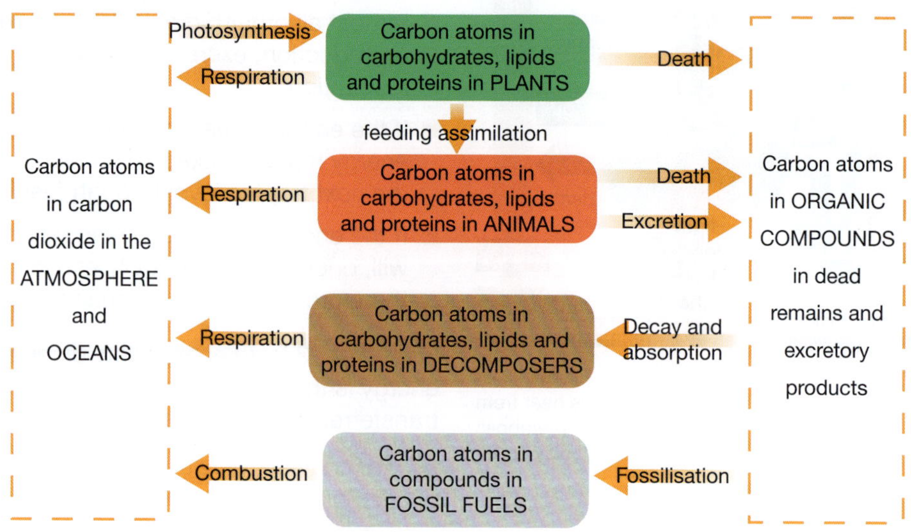

▲ Figure 14.13 The main stages in the carbon cycle

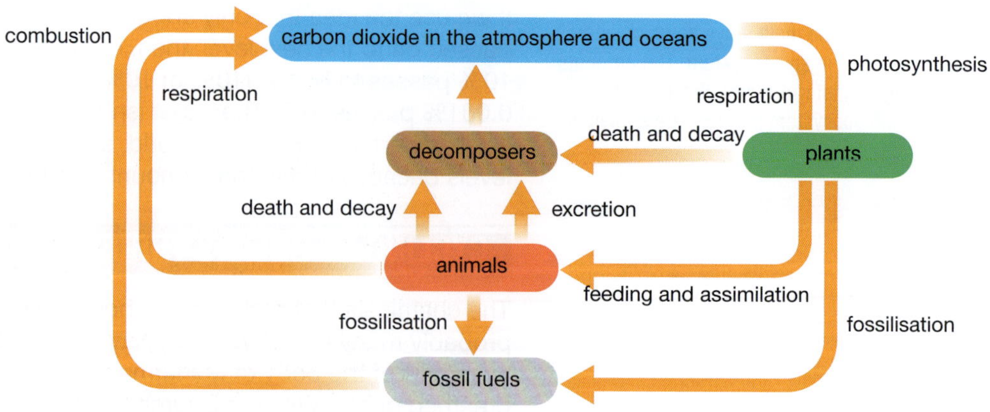

▲ Figure 14.14 A typical illustration of the carbon cycle

LOOKING AHEAD – MEASURING BIODIVERSITY

Ecology is a very mathematical branch of biology. An example of this is that **biodiversity** can be measured by calculating a *diversity index*. One example is called Simpson's Index. One formula for Simpson's Index (D) is:

$$D = 1 - \sum\left(\frac{n}{N}\right)^2$$

In this formula:

N = the total number of individuals of all species

n = the total number of individuals of a particular species.

You calculate $\frac{n}{N}$ for each species, square each of these numbers, and then sum (Σ) all the squares. Subtracting this value from 1 gives you D. Values of D range from 0 to 1, where 0 represents a low diversity and 1 a high diversity.

Take the data you saw in Table 14.1:

Species	Number of individuals of each species in community 1	Number of individuals of each species in community 2
A	10	1
B	10	1
C	10	1
D	10	1
E	10	46

For community 1:

The total number of individuals of all species (N) = 50

For each species the total number of individuals (n) = 10.

So $\frac{n}{N} = \frac{10}{50} = 0.2$ for each species

$$\sum\left(\frac{n}{N}\right)^2 = \left(\frac{10}{50}\right)^2 + \left(\frac{10}{50}\right)^2 + \left(\frac{10}{50}\right)^2 + \left(\frac{10}{50}\right)^2 + \left(\frac{10}{50}\right)^2$$

$$= 0.2^2 + 0.2^2 + 0.2^2 + 0.2^2 + 0.2^2$$

$$= 0.04 + 0.04 + 0.04 + 0.04 + 0.04$$

$$= 0.20$$

To find Simpson's Index you subtract this value from 1:

$D = (1 - 0.20) = 0.80$

This value is close to 1.0, showing that community 1 has a high biodiversity.

Can you calculate Simpson's Index for community 2? If you do it carefully you should get the answer $D = 0.152$, showing that community 2 has a lower biodiversity.

EXTENSION WORK

If you are interested, you can do some background research about Simpson's Index. You will find that there are different formulae used for the Index. It doesn't matter which one you use, as long as you are consistent.

CHAPTER QUESTIONS

More questions on ecosystems can be found at the end of Unit 4 on page 191.

SKILLS CRITICAL THINKING

4th

1 Which of the following terms is defined as 'all the organisms living in a particular place and their interactions with each other and with their environment'?

A habitat

B population

C community

D ecosystem

2 Which of the following is a biotic factor?

A light intensity

B food supply

C pollution

D temperature

5th

3 The diagram below shows a food web containing four food chains.

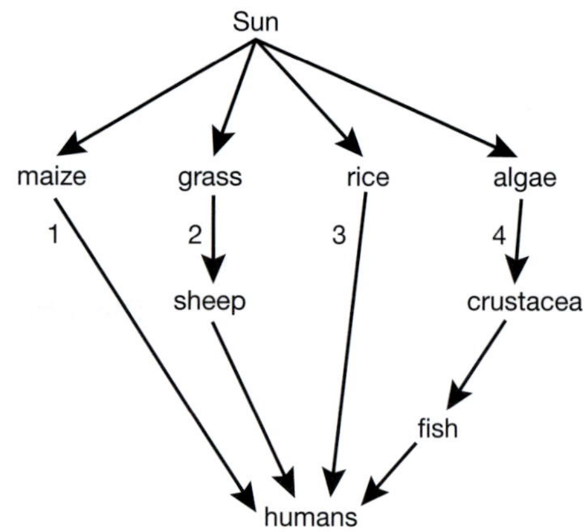

Which food chains are most efficient at using energy from the Sun?

A 1 and 3

B 2 and 4

C 2 and 3

D 3 and 4

4th

4 a Explain what is meant by the terms habitat, community, environment and population.

5th

b What are the roles of plants, animals and decomposers in an ecosystem?

5 A marine food chain is shown below.

plankton → small crustacean → krill → seal → killer whale

4th

a Which organism is i the producer, ii the secondary consumer?

b What term best describes the killer whale?

SKILLS REASONING

5th

c Suggest why five trophic levels are possible in this case, when many food chains only have three or four.

SKILLS INTERPRETATION

6 Part *(a)* of the diagram shows a woodland food web. Part *(b)* shows a pyramid of numbers and a pyramid of biomass for a small part of this wood.

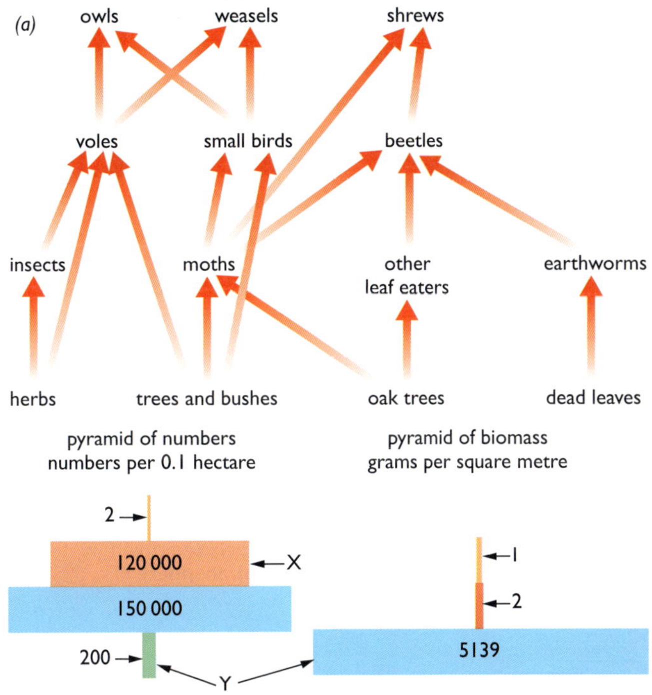

a Write out *two* food chains (from the food web) containing four organisms, both involving moths.

b Name *one* organism in the food web which is both a primary consumer and a secondary consumer.

SKILLS REASONING

c Suggest how a reduction in the dead leaves may lead to a reduction in the numbers of shrews.

SKILLS ANALYSIS, REASONING

d In part *(b)* of the diagram, explain why level Y is such a different width in the two pyramids.

SKILLS PROBLEM SOLVING

7 In a year, 1 m^2 of grass produces 21 500 kJ of energy. The diagram below shows the fate of the energy transferred to a cow feeding on the grass.

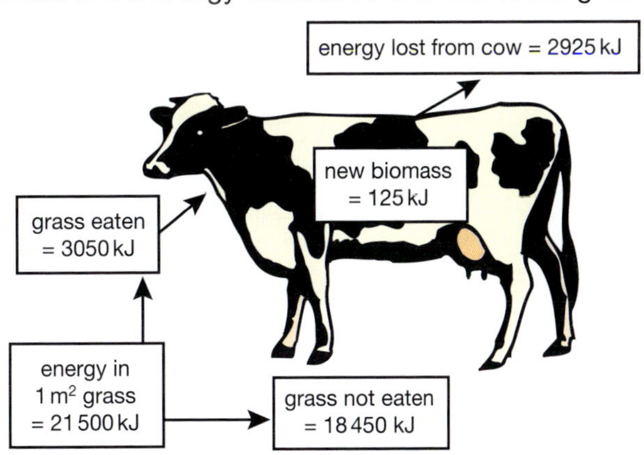

a Calculate the energy efficiency of the cow from the following equation.

$$\text{Energy efficiency} = \frac{\text{energy that ends up as part of cow's biomas}}{\text{energy available}} \times 100$$

SKILLS CRITICAL THINKING

b State two ways that energy is lost from the cow.

SKILLS REASONING

c Suggest what may happen to the 18 450 kJ of energy in the grass that was not eaten by the cow.

15 HUMAN INFLUENCES ON THE ENVIRONMENT

Humans have intelligence far beyond that of any other animal on Earth. This chapter looks at the ways in which we have used our intelligence to influence natural environments, and some of the problems we have caused.

▲ Figure 15.1 How the actions of humans influence the environment.

LEARNING OBJECTIVES

- Describe how glasshouses and polythene tunnels can be used to increase the yield of certain crops
- Understand the effects on crop yield of increased carbon dioxide and increased temperature in glasshouses
- Understand how the use of fertiliser can increase crop yield
- Understand the reasons for pest control and the advantages and disadvantages of using pesticides and biological control with crop plants
- Understand that water vapour, carbon dioxide, nitrous oxide, methane and CFCs are greenhouse gases
- Understand how human activities contribute to greenhouse gases
- Understand how an increase in greenhouse gases results in an enhanced greenhouse effect and that this may lead to global warming and its consequences
- Understand the biological consequences of pollution of air by sulfur dioxide and carbon monoxide
- Understand the biological consequences of pollution of water by sewage
- Understand the biological consequences of eutrophication caused by leached minerals from fertiliser

Since humans first appeared on Earth, our numbers have grown dramatically (Figure 15.2). The secret of our success has been our intelligence. Unlike other species, we have not adapted to one specific environment, we have changed many environments to suit our needs.

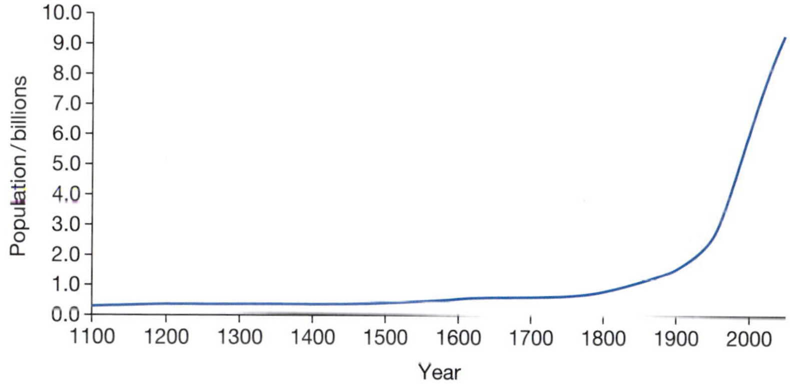

▲ Figure 15.2 The rate of increase of the human population has been particularly steep over the last 200 years. The curve has been extended to 2050, showing that the population is expected to reach 10 billion by that date..

As our numbers have grown, so has the sophistication of our technology. Early humans made tools from materials readily to hand. Today's technology involves much more complex processes. As a result, we produce ever-increasing amounts of materials that pollute our air, soil and waterways.

Early humans influenced their environment, but the enormous size of the population today and the extent of our industries mean that we affect the environment much more significantly. We make increasing demands on the environment for:

- food to sustain an ever-increasing population
- materials to build homes, schools and industries
- fuel to heat homes and power vehicles
- space in which to build homes, schools and factories, as well as for leisure facilities
- space in which to dump our waste materials.

MODERN AGRICULTURE – PRODUCING THE FOOD WE NEED

A modern farm is a sort of managed ecosystem. Many of the interactions are the same as in natural ecosystems. Crop plants depend on light and mineral ions from the soil as well as other factors in the environment. Stock animals (sheep, cattle, etc.) depend on crop plants for food (see Figure 15.3).

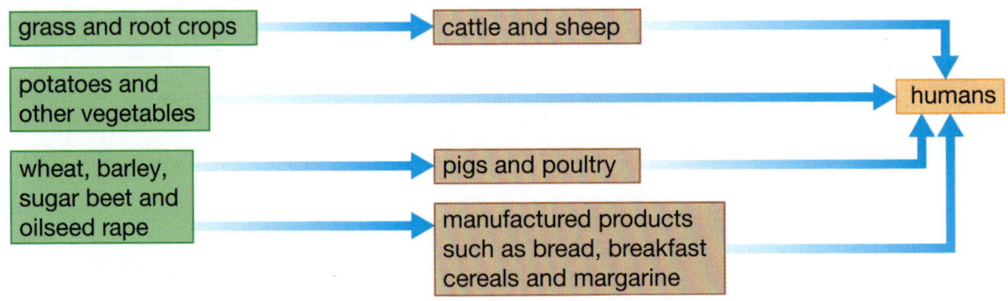

▲ Figure 15.3 A food web on a farm

Farmers must make a profit from their farms. To do this, they try to control the environment in such a way as to maximise the yield from crop plants and livestock.

IMPROVING YIELDS FROM CROP PLANTS

Table 15.1 summaries some factors that can be controlled by the farmer in order to maximise crop yield.

> **DID YOU KNOW?**
> Soil pH can vary between about pH 3 to 8. Soil pH is tested using indicator kits or pH meters. Some soils are too acidic – they can be made more alkaline by adding lime.

Table 15.1 Some ways the yield from crops can be improved.

Factor controlled	How it is controlled	Reason for controlling the factor
soil ions (e.g. nitrates)	adding fertilisers to the soil or growing in a hydroponic culture (Figure 15.4a)	extra mineral ions can be taken up and used to make proteins and other compounds for growth
soil structure	ploughing fields to break up compacted soil; adding manure to improve drainage and aeration of heavy, clay soils	good aeration and drainage allow better uptake of mineral ions (by active transport) and water
soil pH	adding lime (calcium salts) to acidic soils; few soils are too alkaline to need treatment	soil pH can affect crop growth as an unsuitable pH reduces uptake of mineral ions
carbon dioxide, light and heat	these cannot be controlled for field crops but in a glasshouse or polytunnel all can be altered to maximise yield of crops (Figure 15.4b); burning fuels produces heat and carbon dioxide	all may limit the rate of photosynthesis and the production of the organic substances needed for growth

a

▲ Figure 15.4 (a) A glasshouse maintains a favourable environment for plants. Crops grown by hydroponics in a glasshouse.

Glasshouses (otherwise known as 'greenhouses') and polytunnels can provide very controlled conditions for plants to grow (Figure 15.4). There are several reasons for this.

- The transparent walls of the glasshouse allow enough natural light for photosynthesis during the summer months, while additional lighting gives a 'longer day' during the winter.

▲ Figure 15.4 (b) Many crops are grown in large tunnels made of transparent polythene, called polytunnels.

- The 'greenhouse effect' doesn't just happen to the Earth, but also in greenhouses! Short wavelength infrared radiation entering the glasshouse is absorbed and re-radiated as longer wavelength infrared radiation. This radiation cannot escape through the glass, so the glasshouse heats up (see the section on the Earth's greenhouse effect later in this chapter). The glasshouse also reduces convection currents that would cause cooling.
- The glasshouse can be heated to raise the temperature if the outside temperature is too low.
- If heaters use fossil fuels such as gas, this produces carbon dioxide and water vapour. The carbon dioxide is a raw material of photosynthesis. The water vapour maintains a moist atmosphere and reduces water loss by transpiration.
- If the plants are grown in a hydroponic culture this provides *exactly* the right balance of mineral ions for the particular crop.

KEY POINT

By heating glasshouses to the optimum temperature for photosynthesis, a farmer can maximise his yield. Heating above this temperature is a waste of money as there is no further increase in yield.

CYCLING NUTRIENTS ON A FARM

In Chapter 14 you saw how carbon is cycled in nature. On a farm, the situation is quite different, particularly with regard to the circulation of nitrogen.

Nitrates from the soil supply nitrogen that is needed to make proteins in plants. Some of these plants are crops that will be sold; others are used as food for the stock animals (fodder). When the crops are sold, the nitrogen in the proteins goes with them and is lost from the farm ecosystem. Similarly, when livestock is sold, the nitrogen in their proteins (gained from the fodder) goes with them and is lost from the farm ecosystem. To replace the lost nitrogen, a farmer usually adds some kind of fertiliser. The amount of fertiliser added must be carefully monitored to ensure the maximum growth and yield of the crop – using excess fertiliser wastes money.

Figure 15.5 summarises the circulation of nitrogen on a farm.

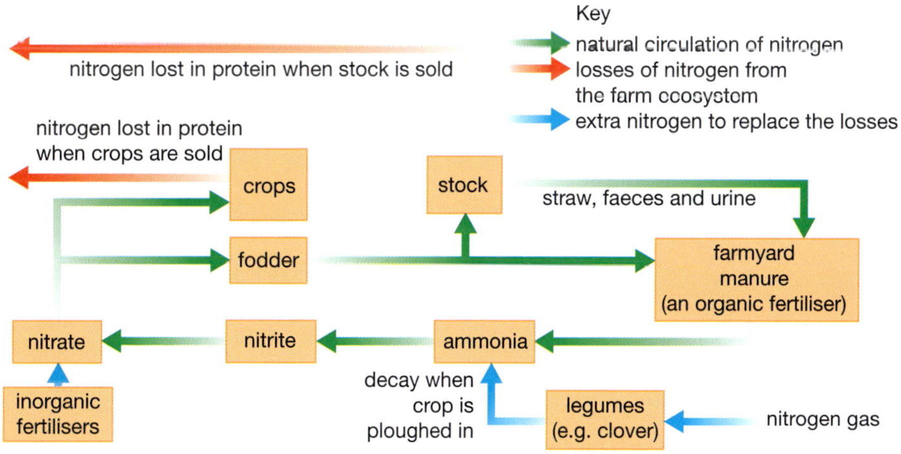

▲ Figure 15.5 The nitrogen cycle on a farm.

FERTILISERS INCREASE CROP YIELD

There are two main types of fertilisers – *organic* and *inorganic*. Many organic fertilisers (such as farmyard manure) are made from the faeces of farm animals mixed with straw. Inorganic fertilisers are simply inorganic compounds such as potassium nitrate or ammonium nitrate, carefully formulated to provide a specific amount of nitrate (or some other ion) when applied according to the manufacturer's instructions.

Adding farmyard manure returns some nitrogen to the soil. But, as farmyard manure is made from livestock faeces and indigestible fodder, it can only replace a portion of the lost nitrogen. Most farmers apply inorganic fertilisers to replace the nitrates and other mineral ions lost. While this can replace *all* the lost ions, it can also lead to pollution problems, which we will discuss later. Inorganic fertilisers do not improve soil structure in the way that organic fertilisers can, because they do not contain any decaying matter that is an essential part of the soil.

Another way to replace lost nitrates is to grow a legume crop (e.g. clover) in a field one year in four. Legumes have **nitrogen-fixing bacteria** in nodules on their roots. These bacteria convert nitrogen gas in the soil air to ammonium ions. Some of this is passed to the plants, which use it to make proteins. At the end of the season, the crop is ploughed back into the soil, and decomposers convert the nitrogen in the proteins to ammonia. This is then oxidised to nitrate by **nitrifying bacteria** and made available for next year's crop.

PEST CONTROL

Pests are organisms that reduce the yield of crop plants or stock animals. The 'yield' of a crop is the amount produced for sale. A pest can harm this in two ways:

- lowering the amount by reducing growth, e.g. by damaging leaves and reducing photosynthesis
- affecting the appearance or quality of a crop, making it unsuitable for sale (Figure 15.6).

▲ Figure 15.6 Damage to a maize (corn) cob caused by the corn earworm caterpillar.

DID YOU KNOW?

In Britain, about 30% of the potential maize crop is lost to weeds, insects and fungal diseases (Figure 15.6).

Any type of organism – plants, animals, bacteria, fungi or protoctists, as well as viruses – can be a pest. Pests can be controlled in a number of ways. Chemicals called **pesticides** can be used to kill them, or their numbers can be reduced by using **biological control** methods.

DID YOU KNOW?

A weed is a plant that is growing where it is not wanted. Weeds can be controlled mechanically or chemically. Mechanical control involves physically removing the weeds. Chemical control uses herbicides.

Pesticides are named according to the type of organism they kill:

- herbicides kill plant pests (they are weedkillers)
- insecticides kill insects
- fungicides kill fungi
- molluscicides kill snails and slugs.

A farmer uses pesticides to kill particular pests and improve the yield from the crops or livestock. Pests are only a problem when they are present in big enough numbers to cause economic damage – a few whiteflies in a tomato crop are not a problem; the real damage arises when there are millions of them. Whether or not a farmer uses pesticides is largely a decision based on cost. The increase in income due to higher yields must be set against the cost of the pesticides.

PROBLEMS WITH PESTICIDES

One problem with using pesticides is that a pest may develop *resistance* to the chemical. This happens through **natural selection** (see Chapter 19). It makes the existing pesticide useless, so that another must be found. Other problems are to do with the fact that pesticides can cause environmental damage. There are several reasons for this:

- they may be slow to decompose – they are *persistent* in the environment
- they build up in the tissues of organisms – *bioaccumulation*
- they build up and become more concentrated along food chains – *biomagnification*
- they kill other insects that are harmless, as well as helpful species, such as bees.

An ideal pesticide should:

- control the pest effectively
- be biodegradable, so that no toxic products are left in the soil or on crops
- be specific, so that only the pest is killed
- not accumulate in organisms
- be safe to transport, store and apply
- be easy to apply.

We can explain these problems by looking at one well-documented example – the insecticide DDT (dichlorodiphenyltrichloroethane).

DDT was invented in 1874, and first discovered to be an insecticide in 1939. In World War II it was used with great success to kill malaria carrying mosquitoes and the lice that carried typhus. Its use increased up until the 1960s, when we began to understand its harmful effects. It was banned from general use in the USA in 1972, and worldwide in 2004. Limited use of DDT is still allowed for control of insects that transmit disease, although this is still regarded as controversial.

DDT is a very effective insecticide, so why has it been banned?

- DDT is very persistent, remaining active in the environment for many years. If DDT is sprayed onto a field, around half will still be there ten years later. To make things worse, the missing half won't have degraded to harmless products – some will have broken down to form a similar compound called DDE, which is also a potent insecticide, and some will have spread to other habitats. DDT is carried all around the world by wind, and has been identified in polar ice caps and deserts, thousands of kilometres away from where it was applied.
- By the 1950s, many types of insect began to appear that were resistant to DDT. These insects had developed a genetic **mutation** that prevented them from being killed by the insecticide. While DDT continued to be used, the resistant insects had an advantage over the non-resistant ones. Their numbers increased with every generation since they were able to survive exposure to the pesticide. They reproduced, passing on their resistance genes to their offspring. This is an example of natural selection (see Chapter 19). There are now hundreds of examples of pest species that have

DID YOU KNOW?

Cultivating large areas of land with a single crop (a *monoculture*) encourages pests. Monocultures make harvesting the crop easier. But if a pest arrives, it can easily spread through the crop. During the winter the pest can lie dormant in the soil ready to attack next year's crop.

Crop rotation breaks the pest cycle. This is where a different crop is grown each year (Figure 15.7). When over-wintering pests emerge, their preferred crop is no longer there.

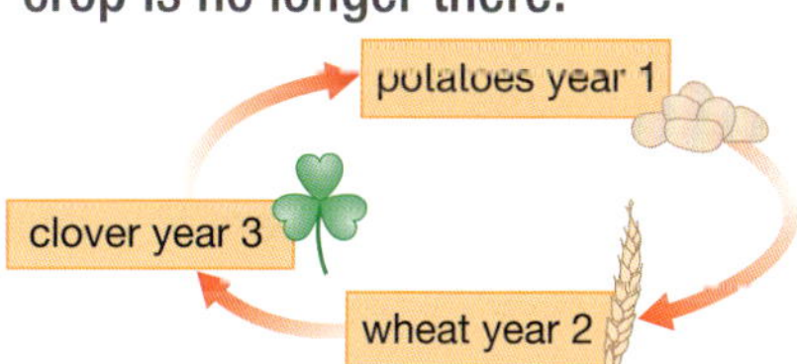

▲ Figure 15.7 A three-year crop rotation.

DID YOU KNOW?

DDT is a historical case, but there are problems with many modern pesticides. One recent example involves a class of insecticides called *neonicotinoids* (chemicals similar to nicotine). They have been linked to several serious ecological problems, including honey bee colony collapse disorder (CCD) and loss of birds due to a reduction in insect populations.

developed resistance to different insecticides.

- DDT doesn't just kill pests. It will kill any type of insect, including harmless ones such as butterflies and useful species such as bees, as well as natural predators such as wasps, which might themselves kill the pest insects. Insecticides damage ecosystems by disrupting food chains.
- DDT is very soluble in fats. When a herbivore feeds on plants that are contaminated with DDT, the insecticide is not broken down or excreted. Instead it becomes concentrated in the fatty tissues of the animal. This is called **bioaccumulation**. When a carnivore eats the herbivore this process is repeated, so that the insecticide builds up in concentration along the food chain. This is known as **biomagnification** (Figure 15.8). The levels at the top of the food chain may be toxic, leading to the death of the top carnivores in the chain. This can disrupt the food web of an ecosystem.

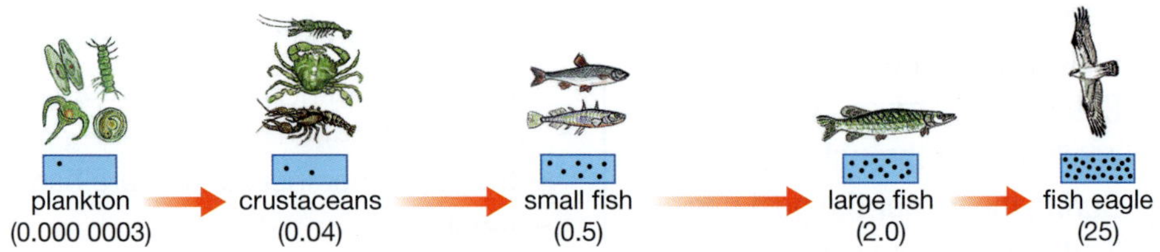

▲ Figure 15.8 Biomagnification of DDT in a food chain

BIOLOGICAL CONTROL

Another option that may be used to control pests is biological control. Instead of using a toxic chemical, biological control uses another organism to reduce the numbers of a pest. We have already mentioned whiteflies as pests of tomatoes. One way of controlling them in large glasshouses is to introduce a parasite that will kill the whiteflies. A tiny wasp called *Encarsia* parasitises and kills their larvae, reducing the numbers of adult whitefly.

A problem with biological control is that it never fully gets rid of a pest. If the control organism killed *all* the pests, then it too would die out, as it would have no food supply. Biological control aims to reduce pest numbers to a level where they no longer cause significant economic damage (Figure 15.9).

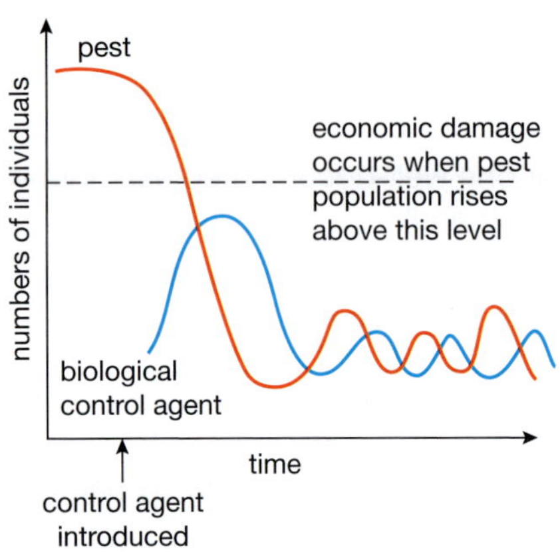

▲ Figure 15.9 Biological control.

There are several methods of biological control. Some examples include:

- introducing a natural predator – ladybirds can be used to control the populations of aphids in orange groves
- introducing a herbivore – a moth was introduced from South America to control the prickly pear cactus that was becoming a serious weed in grazing land in Australia
- introducing a parasite – the wasp *Encarsia* is used to control whitefly populations in glasshouse tomato crops
- introducing a pathogenic (disease-causing) microorganism – the myxomatosis virus was deliberately released in Australia to control the rabbit population
- introducing sterile males – these mate with the females but no offspring are produced from these matings, so numbers fall
- using pheromones – these are natural chemicals produced by insects to attract a mate. They are used to attract pests (either males or females) to traps. The pests are then destroyed, reducing the reproductive potential of the population. Male-attracting pheromones are used to control aphids (greenfly) in plum crops.

AIR POLLUTION

One definition of **pollution** is:

> 'Pollution is the contamination of the environment by harmful substances that are produced by the activities of humans'.

Human activities pollute the air with many gases. Some major examples that we will look at in this chapter are carbon dioxide, methane, carbon monoxide and sulfur dioxide.

CARBON DIOXIDE AND GLOBAL WARMING

KEY POINT

In any one year, there is a peak and a trough in the levels of carbon dioxide in the atmosphere

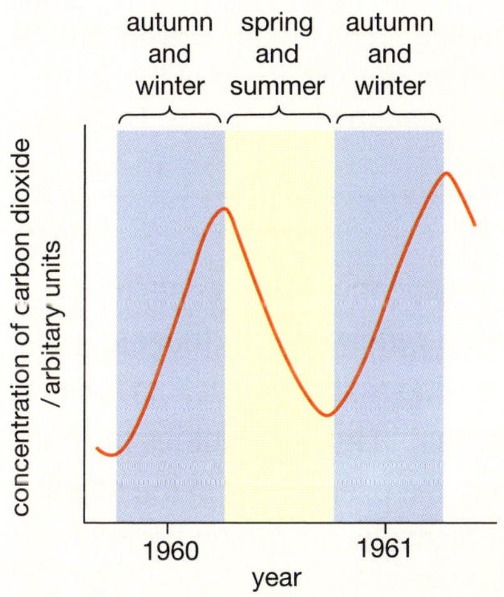

Figure 15.11 Seasonal fluctuations in carbon dioxide levels.

In the autumn and winter, trees lose their leaves. Without leaves they cannot photosynthesise and so do not absorb carbon dioxide. They still respire, which produces carbon dioxide, so in the winter months, they give out carbon dioxide and the level in the atmosphere rises. In the spring and summer, with new leaves and brighter sunlight, the trees photosynthesise faster than they respire. As a result, they absorb more carbon dioxide from the atmosphere than they produce, so the level decreases. However, because there are fewer trees overall, it doesn't quite return to the low level of the previous summer.

The levels of carbon dioxide have been rising for several hundred years. Over the last 100 years alone, the level of carbon dioxide in the atmosphere has increased by nearly 30%. This rise is mainly due to the increased burning of fossil fuels, such as coal, oil and natural gas, as well as petrol and diesel in vehicle engines. It has been made worse by cutting down large areas of tropical rainforest (see later in this chapter). These extensive forests have been called 'the lungs of the Earth' because they absorb such vast quantities of carbon dioxide and produce equally large amounts of oxygen. Extensive deforestation (see below) means that less carbon dioxide is being absorbed. Figure 15.10 shows changes in the level of carbon dioxide in the atmosphere (in parts per million) from 1960 to 2010.

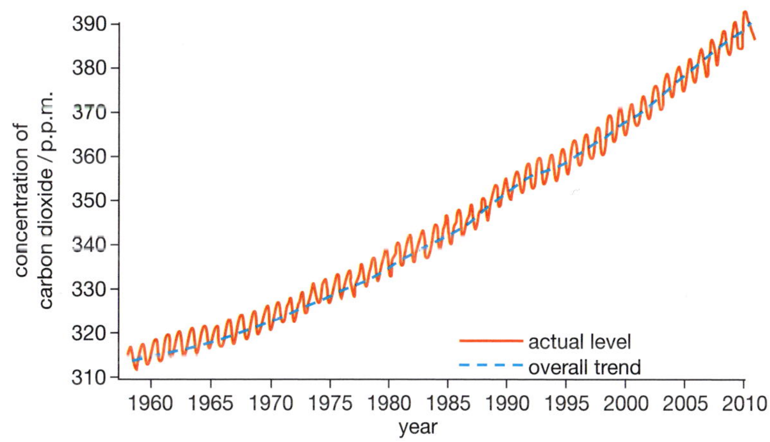

▲ Figure 15.10 Changes in the level of carbon dioxide in the atmosphere.

The increased levels of carbon dioxide and other gases contribute to global warming, or the enhanced greenhouse effect. It is important to understand that the 'normal' greenhouse effect occurs naturally – without it, more heat would be lost into space and the surface temperature of the Earth would be about 30 °C lower than it is today, and life as we know it would be impossible.

Carbon dioxide is one of the 'greenhouse gases' that are present in the Earth's upper atmosphere. Other greenhouse gases include water vapour (H_2O), methane (CH_4), nitrous oxide (N_2O) and chlorofluorocarbons (CFCs). Most greenhouse gases occur naturally, while some (like CFCs) are only produced by human activities.

The 'normal' greenhouse effect is shown in Figure 15.12.

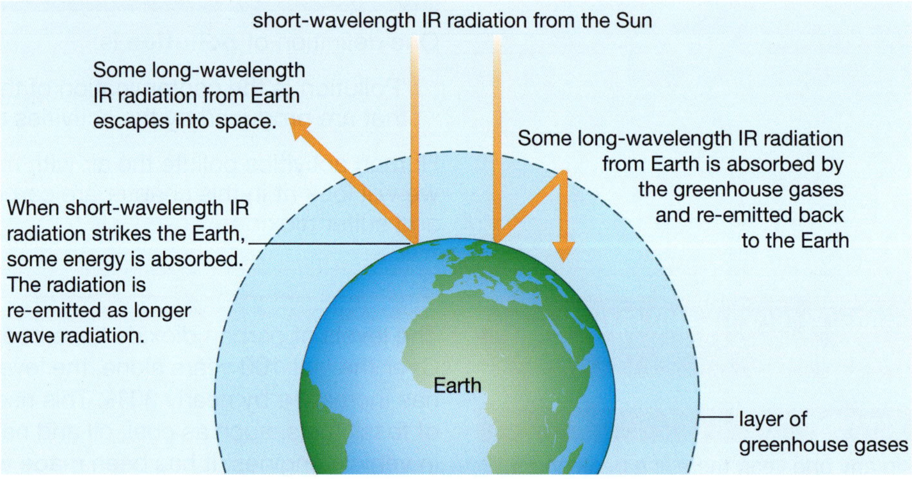

Figure 15.12 The Greenhouse effect

Short-wavelength infrared (IR) radiation from the Sun reaches the Earth. Some is absorbed by the Earth's surface and emitted again as longer-wavelength IR radiation. The greenhouse gases absorb and then re-emit some of this long-wavelength IR radiation, which would otherwise escape into space. This then heats up the surface of the Earth.

DID YOU KNOW?

Chlorofluorocarbons or CFCs are complex organic molecules containing carbon, chlorine and fluorine. They were once widely used in fridges, spray cans and as solvents, as well as in making materials such as foam packaging. Their use was banned or phased out in many countries in 1987, when they were found to be damaging the ozone layer in the upper atmosphere. (This layer protects living organisms by absorbing harmful ultraviolet radiation from the Sun.)

The problem is that human activities are polluting the atmosphere with *extra* greenhouse gases such as carbon dioxide. This is thought to be causing a rise in the Earth's surface temperature – the enhanced greenhouse effect, or global warming.

A rise in the Earth's temperature of only a few degrees would have many effects.

- Polar ice caps would melt and sea levels would rise.
- A change in the major ocean currents would result in warm water flowing into previously cooler areas.
- A change in global rainfall patterns could result. With a rise in temperature, there will be more evaporation from the surface of the sea, leading to more water vapour in the atmosphere and more rainfall in some areas. Other areas could experience a decrease in rainfall. Long-term climate change could occur.
- It could change the nature of many ecosystems. If species could not migrate quickly enough to a new, appropriate habitat, or adapt quickly enough to the changed conditions in their original habitat, they could become extinct.
- Changes in farming practices would be necessary as some pests became more abundant. Higher temperatures might allow some pests to complete their life cycles more quickly.

DID YOU KNOW?

Infrared radiation is radiated heat. The heat you can feel from an electric fire is IR radiation.

METHANE

Methane (CH_4) is an organic gas. It is produced when microorganisms ferment larger organic molecules to release energy. The most significant sources of methane are:

- **decomposition** of waste buried in the ground ('landfill sites'), by microorganisms
- fermentation by microorganisms in the rumen (stomach) of cattle and other ruminants
- fermentation by bacteria in rice fields.

Methane is a greenhouse gas, with effects similar to carbon dioxide. Although there is less methane in the atmosphere than carbon dioxide, each molecule has a much bigger greenhouse effect.

DID YOU KNOW?
Cattle can produce up to 40 dm^3 of methane per animal per hour.

CARBON MONOXIDE

When substances containing carbon are burned in a limited supply of oxygen, carbon monoxide (CO) is formed. This happens when petrol and diesel are burned in vehicle engines. Exhaust gases contain significant amounts of carbon monoxide. It is a dangerous pollutant as it is colourless, odourless and tasteless and can be fatal. Haemoglobin binds more strongly with carbon monoxide than with oxygen. If a person inhales carbon monoxide for a period of time, more and more haemoglobin becomes bound to carbon monoxide and so cannot bind with oxygen. The person may lose consciousness and eventually die, as a result of a lack of oxygen reaching the cells, so that organs such as the heart and brain stop working.

KEY POINT
In many countries there are now strict laws controlling the permitted levels of carbon monoxide in the exhaust gases produced by newly designed engines.

SULFUR DIOXIDE

Sulfur dioxide (SO_2) is an important air pollutant. It is formed when fossil fuels are burned, and combines with water droplets in the air. It can be carried hundreds of miles in the atmosphere before falling as **acid rain**. Rain normally has a pH of about 5.5 – it is slightly acidic due to the carbon dioxide dissolved in it. Both sulfur dioxide and nitrogen oxides dissolve in rainwater to form a mixture of acids, including sulfuric acid and nitric acid. As a result, the rainwater is more acidic with a much lower pH than normal rain (Figure 15.13).

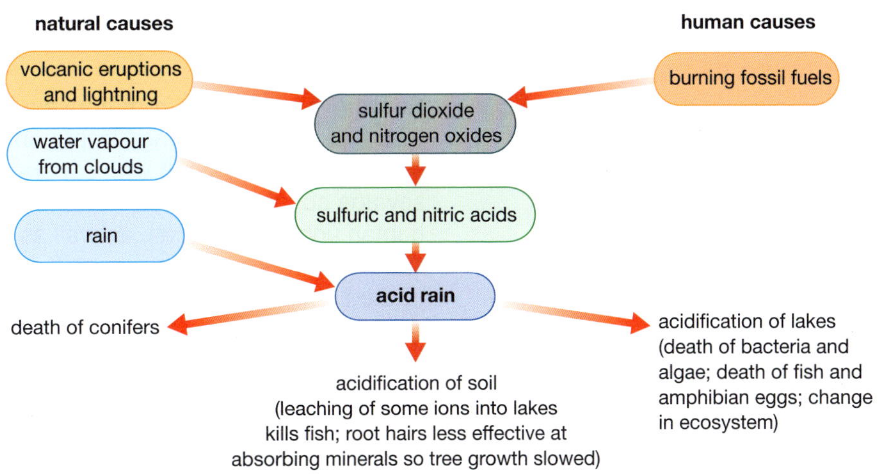

▲ Figure 15.13 The formation of acid rain and its effects on living organisms.

Lichens are small moss-like organisms. Some lichens are more tolerant of sulfur dioxide than others. In some countries, patterns of lichen growth can be used to monitor the level of pollution by sulfur dioxide. The different lichens are called *indicator species* as they 'indicate' different levels of sulfur dioxide pollution.

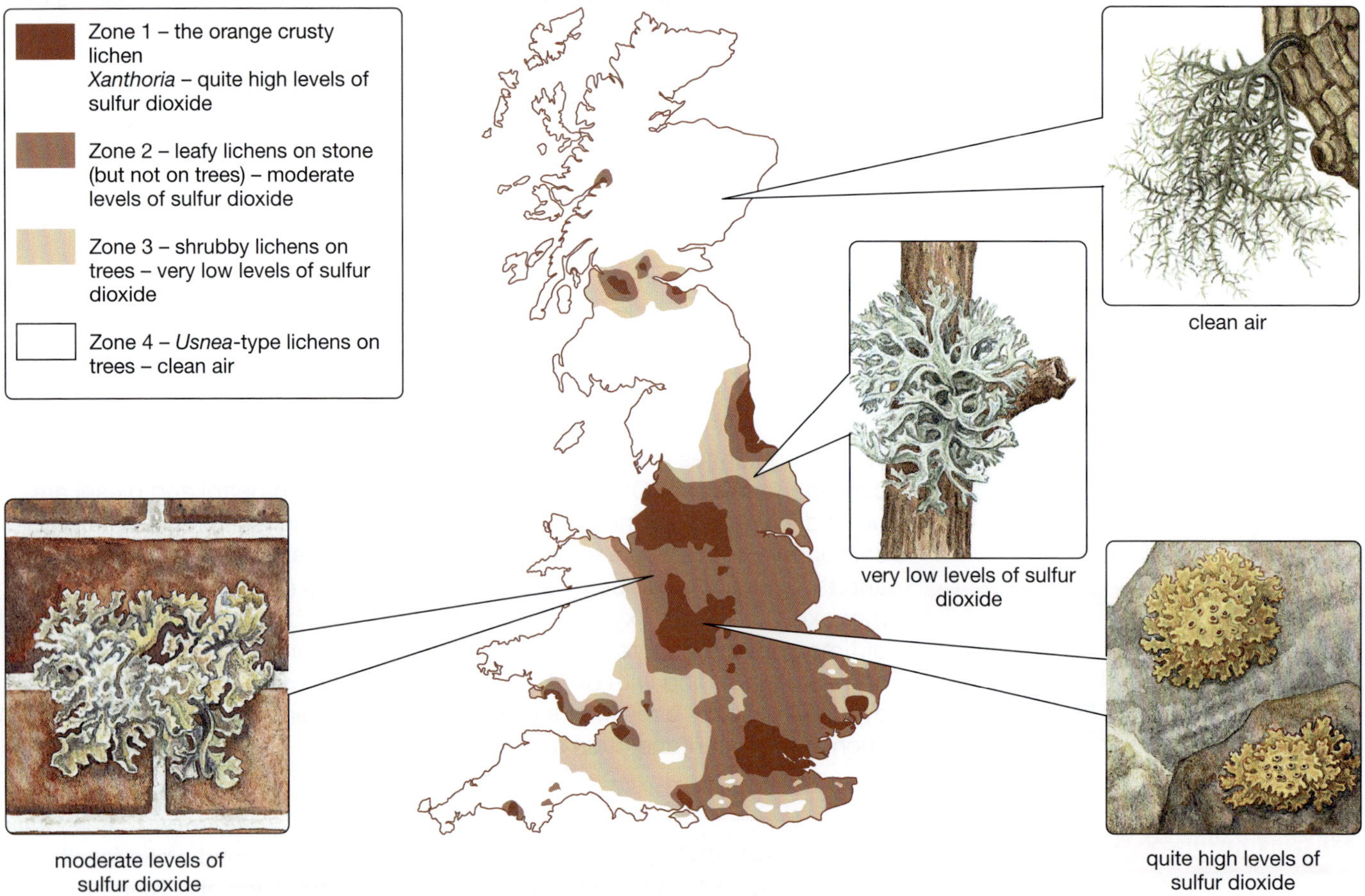

▲ Figure 15.14 Lichens are sensitive to pollution levels.

The map in Figure 15.14 shows zones in Britain where different types of lichen are found.

WATER POLLUTION

Two major pollutants of freshwater are sewage and minerals from fertiliser.

POLLUTION OF WATER BY SEWAGE

Sewage is wet waste from houses, factories and farms. In developed countries where large-scale sewage treatment takes place, industrial and agricultural sewage is usually dealt with separately from household sewage. Household sewage consists of wastewater from kitchens and bathrooms and contains human urine and faeces, as well as dissolved organic and inorganic chemicals such as soaps and detergents. It is carried away in pipes called sewers, to be treated before it enters waterways such as rivers or the sea.

If sewage is discharged untreated into waterways, it produces two major problems:

- Aerobic bacteria in the water polluted by the sewage use up the dissolved oxygen in the water as they break down the organic materials. This reduction in the level of oxygen kills larger animals such as freshwater insects and fish.
- Untreated sewage contains pathogenic bacteria, which are a danger to human health.

Where untreated or 'raw' sewage enters a river, the level of oxygen in the water becomes very low as the aerobic bacteria and other microorganisms from the sewage decompose the organic matter. Only species that are adapted to live in low-oxygen conditions, such as anaerobic bacteria, can survive. As the water moves away from the outlet, it becomes oxygenated again as it mixes with clean water and absorbs oxygen from the air. The increase in dissolved oxygen levels allows more clean-water species to survive. Figure 15.15 shows the changes in oxygen content, numbers of clean-water animals, and numbers of polluted-water animals downstream from a sewage outlet.

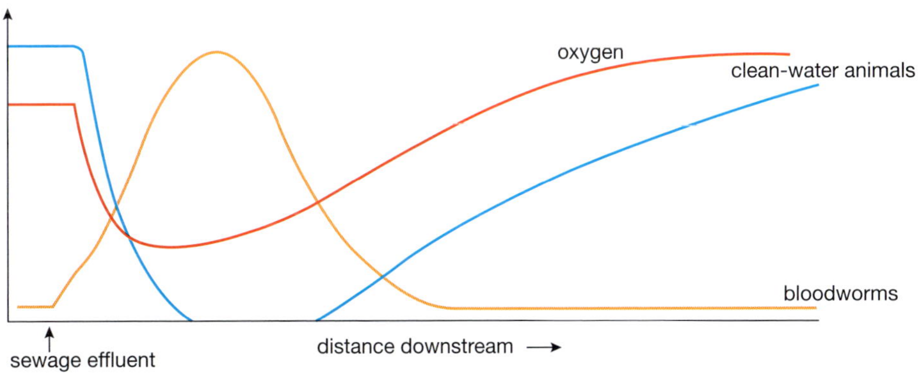

▲ Figure 15.15 Changes in oxygen levels and types of organism living downstream from a sewage outlet into a river.

The aim of sewage treatment is to remove solid and suspended organic matter and pathogenic microorganisms, so that cleaner waste can be discharged into waterways.

As with air pollution by sulfur dioxide, the level of pollution by organic material can be monitored by the presence or absence of indicator species. Figure 15.16 shows some of these.

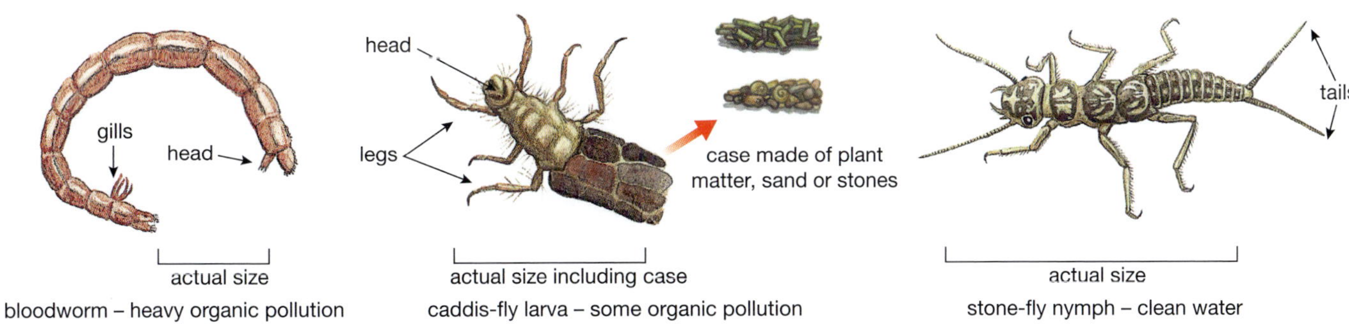

▲ Figure 15.16 Some freshwater animals will only live in very clean water, while others can survive in very polluted areas.

EUTROPHICATION

Eutrophication comes from a Greek word, meaning 'well-fed'. It refers to a situation where large amounts of nutrients enter a body of water, such as a river, lake or even the sea. The nutrients in question are inorganic mineral ions, usually nitrates or phosphates. Pollution by these minerals can have very harmful effects on an aquatic ecosystem.

There are two main sources of excess minerals:

- from untreated or treated sewage
- from artificial nitrate or phosphate fertilisers.

Eutrophication is often caused by the use of artificial fertiliser. Streams and rivers that run through agricultural land that have been treated with fertiliser can contain high concentrations of nitrate and phosphate. This is because nitrate is very soluble in water, and is easily washed out of the soil by rain, a process known as **leaching**. This is less of a problem with phosphate fertiliser, but phosphate is also washed into waterways by surface run-off of water.

The excess mineral ions stimulate the growth of all plants in the river or lake, but this is usually seen first as a rapid growth of algae, called an **algal bloom**. The algae can increase in numbers so rapidly that they form a thick scum on the surface of the water (Figure 15.17).

Figure 15.17 An algal bloom caused by fertiliser

The algae soon start to die, and are decomposed by aerobic bacteria in the water. Because the bacteria respire aerobically, they use up the oxygen in the water. In addition, the algae block the light from reaching other rooted plants, further decreasing the oxygen produced by photosynthesis. The low oxygen levels can result in fish and other aerobic animals dying. In severe cases, the water becomes *anoxic* (containing very little oxygen) and smelly from gases like hydrogen sulfide and methane from the bacteria. By this stage only anaerobic bacteria can survive.

Rapid eutrophication is less likely when farmers use organic fertiliser (manure). The organic nitrogen-containing compounds in manure are less soluble and so are leached less quickly from the soil.

REMINDER

The sequence of events following eutrophication is:

increase in mineral ions
↓
algal bloom
↓
death of algae
↓
decomposition by aerobic bacteria
↓
bacteria use up oxygen
↓
fish and other animals die

CHAPTER QUESTIONS

More questions on human influences on the environment can be found at the end of Unit 4 on page 191.

SKILLS CRITICAL THINKING 5th

1 Which of the following is a desirable property for a pesticide?

A It kills all insects

B It does not show bioaccumulation

C It is persistent in the environment

D It is not biodegradable

2 The following gases are found in atmospheric air:

1. nitrogen
2. methane
3. carbon dioxide
4. water vapour

Which of these is/are *not* a greenhouse gas?

A 1 only

B 1 and 4

C 2 and 3

D 2 and 4

3 In a lake affected by eutrophication, which of the following causes the death of aquatic plants?

A Poisoning by excess minerals

B Lack of oxygen in the water

C Lack of light reaching the plants

D Lack of carbon dioxide in the water

SKILLS REASONING 6th

4 Why are humans having much more of an impact on their environment now than they did 500 years ago?

SKILLS ANALYSIS 4th

5 The graph shows the changing concentrations of carbon dioxide at Mauna Loa, Hawaii over a number of years.

a Describe the overall trend shown by the graph.

SKILLS REASONING 5th

b Explain the trend described in a).

6th

c In any one year, the level of atmospheric carbon dioxide shows a peak and a trough. Explain why.

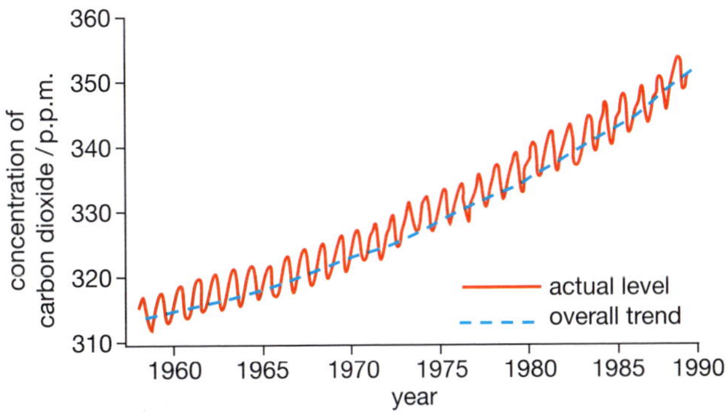

SKILLS REASONING

4th

6 The diagram shows how the greenhouse effect is thought to operate.

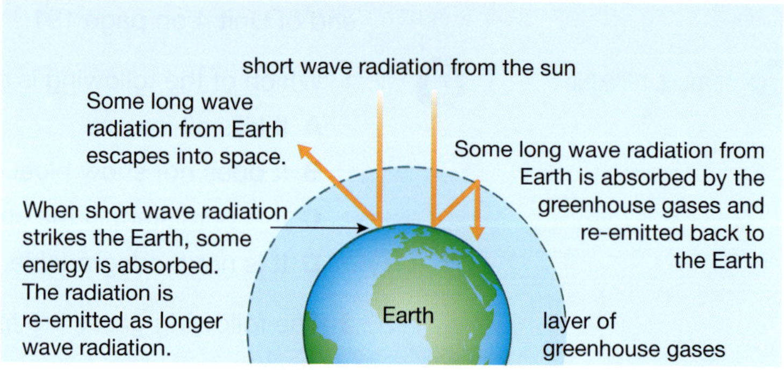

a Name two greenhouse gases.

6th

b Explain one benefit to the Earth of the greenhouse effect.

c Suggest why global warming may lead to malaria becoming more common in Europe.

7 The diagram shows the profile of the ground on a farm either side of a pond.

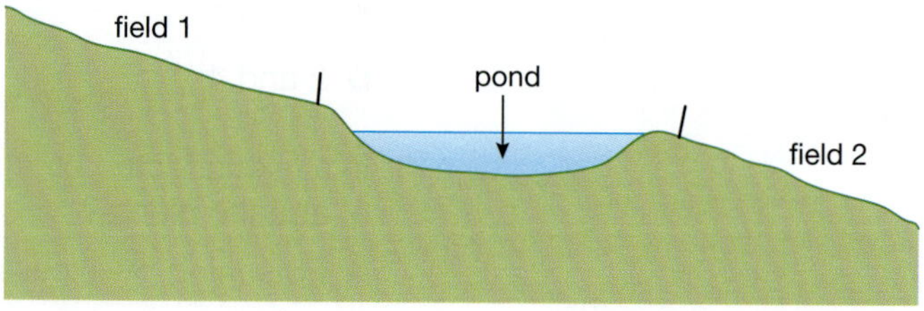

The farmer applied nitrate fertiliser to the two fields in alternate years. When he applied the fertiliser to Field 1, the pond often developed an algal bloom. This did not happen when fertiliser was applied to Field 2.

a Explain why an algal bloom developed when he applied the fertiliser to Field 1.

b Explain why no algal bloom developed when he applies the fertiliser to Field 2.

c Suggest why the algal bloom is greater in hot weather.

8th

8 Some untreated sewage was accidentally discharged into a small river. A short time afterwards, a number of dead fish are seen downstream of the point of discharge. Explain, as fully as you can, how the discharge might have led to the death of the fish.

6th

9 Some farmers use pesticides and fertilisers to improve crop yields. Those practising 'organic' farming techniques do not use any artificial products.

a Describe how the use of pesticides and fertilisers can improve crop yields.

SKILLS CRITICAL THINKING

b Explain how organic farmers can maintain fertile soil and keep their crops free of pests.

UNIT QUESTIONS

SKILLS INTERPRETATION 5th

1 The diagram shows a simplified food web of a fish, the herring.

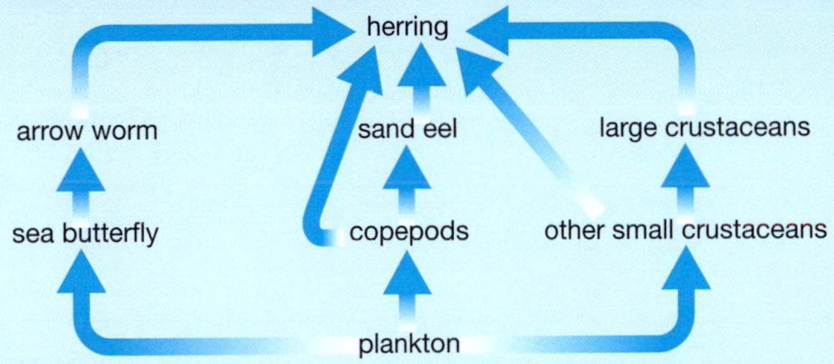

a **i** Write out a food chain from the above food web containing four organisms. **(1)**

SKILLS ANALYSIS 4th

ii From your food chain, name the primary consumer and secondary consumer. **(2)**

iii Name one organism in the web that is both a secondary consumer and a tertiary consumer. Explain your answer. **(2)**

b The amount of energy in each trophic level has been provided for the following food chain. The units are kJ per m^2 per year

plankton (8869) → copepod (892) → herring (91)

SKILLS INTERPRETATION 6th

i Sketch a pyramid of energy for this food chain. **(1)**

SKILLS PROBLEM SOLVING 7th

ii Calculate the percentage of energy entering the plankton that passes to the copepod. **(2)**

iii Calculate the percentage of energy entering the copepod that passes to the herring. **(2)**

8th

iv Calculate the amount of energy that enters the food chain per year if the plankton use 0.1% of the available energy. **(2)**

SKILLS REASONING 6th

v Explain two ways in which energy is lost in the transfer from the copepod to the herring. **(2)**

(Total 14 marks)

SKILLS INTERPRETATION 7th

2 A farmer added nitrate fertiliser to his wheat crop to try to increase yield. The table below shows the wheat yield when he added different amounts of nitrate fertiliser.

Fertiliser added / kg per hectare	Wheat yield / tonnes per hectare
0	15
50	18
100	22
150	31
200	30
250	31

a Use the information in the table to draw a line graph showing the effects of fertiliser on wheat yield. **(4)**

SKILLS PROBLEM SOLVING 6th

b What amount of fertiliser would you advise the farmer to use on his wheat crop? Explain your answer. **(3)**

SKILLS REASONING 5th

c Why is nitrate needed to help plants grow? **(1)**

7th

d Excess nitrate can be washed into rivers. Explain the effects that this could have on the river ecosystem. **(5)**

(Total 13 marks)

SKILLS ANALYSIS, REASONING

3 Insecticides are used by farmers to control the populations of insect pests. New insecticides are continually being developed.

a A new insecticide was trialled over three years to test its effectiveness in controlling an insect pest of potato plants. Three different concentrations of the insecticide were tested. Some results are shown in the table.

Concentration	Percentage of insect pest killed each year of insecticide		
	Year 1	Year 2	Year 3
1 (weakest)	95	72	18
2 (intermediate)	98	90	43
3 (strongest)	99	91	47

i Describe, and suggest an explanation for, the change in the effectiveness of the insecticide over the three years. **(3)**

6th

ii Which concentration would a farmer be most likely to choose to apply to potato crops? Explain your answer. **(3)**

b The trials also showed that there was no significant bioaccumulation of the insecticide.

SKILLS CRITICAL THINKING 5th

i What is bioaccumulation? **(1)**

6th

ii Give an example of bioaccumulation of an insecticide and describe its consequences. **(2)**

iii Explain why it is particularly important that there is no bioaccumulation of this insecticide. **(1)**

(Total 10 marks)

8th **4** Carbon is passed through ecosystems by the actions of plants, animals and decomposers, in the carbon cycle. Humans influence the carbon cycle more than other animals.

a Explain the importance of plants in the carbon cycle. **(2)**

7th

b Describe two human activities that have significant effects on the world carbon cycle. **(2)**

SKILLS ANALYSIS, REASONING

c The graph shows the activity of decomposers acting on the bodies of dead animals under different conditions.

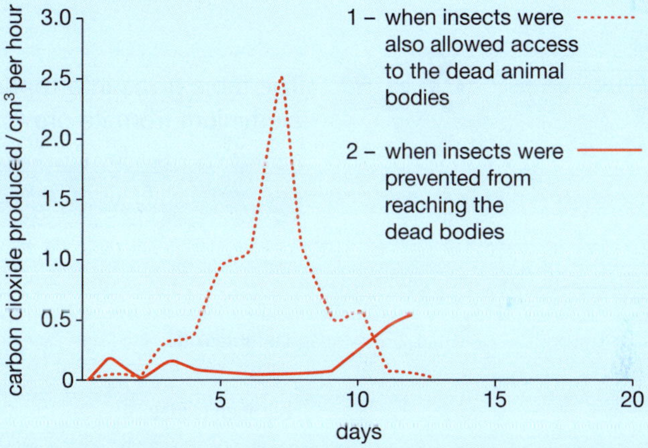

i Explain why carbon dioxide production was used as a measure of the activity of the decomposers. **(2)**

ii Describe and explain the changes in decomposer activity when insects were also allowed access to the dead bodies (curve 1) **(3)**

iii Describe two differences between curves (1) and (2). Suggest an explanation for the differences you describe. **(4)**

(Total 13 marks)

SKILLS REASONING 6th **5** In natural ecosystems, there is competition between members of the same species as well as between different species.

a Explain how competition between members of the same species helps to control population growth. **(3)**

b Crop plants must often compete with weeds for resources. Farmers often control weeds by spraying herbicides (weedkillers).

SKILLS CRITICAL THINKING

i Name two factors that the crop plants and weeds may compete for and explain the importance of each. **(4)**

SKILLS REASONING 7th

ii Farmers usually prefer to spray herbicides on weeds early in the growing season. Suggest why. **(2)**

SKILLS ANALYSIS 8th

c Two species of the flour beetle, *Tribolium*, compete with each other for flour. Both are parasitised by a protozoan. The graphs show the changes in numbers of the two species over 900 days when the parasite is absent and when it is present.

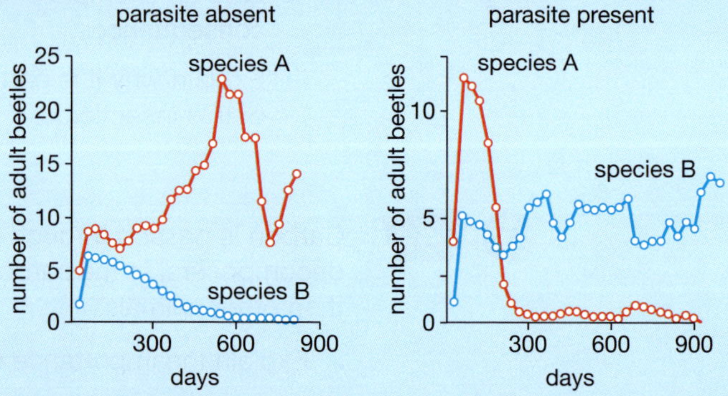

i Which species is the most successful when the parasite is absent? Justify your answer. **(2)**

ii What is the effect of the parasite on the relative success of the two beetles? Suggest an explanation for your answer. **(4)**

(Total 15 marks)

SKILLS PROBLEM SOLVING 6th

6 The table gives information about the pollutants produced in extracting aluminium from its ore (bauxite) and in recycling aluminium.

Pollutants	Amount / g per kg aluminium produced	
air	extraction from bauxite	recycling aluminium
sulfur dioxide	88 600	886
nitrogen oxides	139 000	6760
carbon monoxide	34 600	2440
Water		
dissolved solids	18 600	575
suspended solids	1600	175

a Calculate the percentage reduction in sulfur dioxide pollution by recycling aluminium. **(2)**

SKILLS REASONING 7th

b Explain how extraction of aluminium from bauxite may contribute to the acidification of water hundreds of miles from the factory where the aluminium is extracted. **(3)**

c Suggest two reasons why there may be little plant life in water near an extraction. **(4)**

(Total 9 marks)

SKILLS INTERPRETATION 7th

7 Rust fungi infect the leaves of many crop plants.

a Explain two ways in which an infection by rust fungi can reduce crop yield. **(2)**

b Infections of rust fungi can be controlled by spraying the crops with a fungicide. In an investigation into the effectiveness of this method of control, a field of wheat was divided into two plots. As soon as the first signs of infection appeared, one plot was sprayed with fungicide. The other plot was left unsprayed.

The relative amount of infection in the two plots was monitored over 50 days. The table shows the results of the investigation.

Day	Relative amount of infection / arbitrary units	
	Unsprayed (control)	Sprayed plants
0	0	3
10	17	8
20	32	10
30	48	15
40	62	17
50	65	18

i Plot a line graph of these data. **(5)**

SKILLS ANALYSIS 6th

ii From your graph, find the relative infection of sprayed and unsprayed plants on day 24. **(2)**

SKILLS EXECUTIVE FUNCTION

iii Explain why it is necessary to have a control group. **(2)**

SKILLS ANALYSIS

iv The investigation was repeated every year for five years. Each year seeds were kept for planting the following year. On day 30 in Year 5, the relative amounts of infection were 46 (unsprayed) and 38 (sprayed). Compare these results with Year 1 and suggest an explanation for the difference. **(3)**

(Total 14 marks)

BIOLOGY UNIT 5 VARIATION AND SELECTION

The genetic code is contained within a chemical in the nucleus of the cell, called DNA. DNA is organised into units called genes. The discovery of the structure of DNA in 1953 was the beginning of a new discipline called molecular biology. Molecular biology looks at how the genetic code in the DNA affects the function of the cell. Molecular biology is closely linked with genetics, which concerns the visible effects of the genes on living organisms . This Unit starts with a look at how DNA forms the genetic code, and how it is passed from cell to cell when a cell divides. Chapter 18 deals with genetics – how the DNA shows itself in organisms. Chapter 19 describes the theory that underpins all of biology – Darwin's theory of evolution by natural selection and the principles of selective breeding.

16 CHROMOSOMES, GENES AND DNA

This chapter looks at the structure and organisation of genetic material, namely chromosomes, genes and DNA.

LEARNING OBJECTIVES

- Understand that the nucleus of a cell contains chromosomes on which genes are located
- Understand that a gene is a section of a molecule of DNA that codes for a specific protein
- Understand that mutation is a rare, random change in genetic material that can be inherited
- Know that in human cells the diploid number of chromosomes is 46 and the haploid number is 23
- Understand that the genome is the entire DNA of an organism
- Understand how genes exist in alternative forms called alleles, which give rise to different inherited characteristics

DID YOU KNOW?

DNA is short for **deoxyribonucleic acid**. It gets the 'deoxyribo' part of its name from the sugar in the DNA molecule – deoxyribose, a sugar containing five carbon atoms.

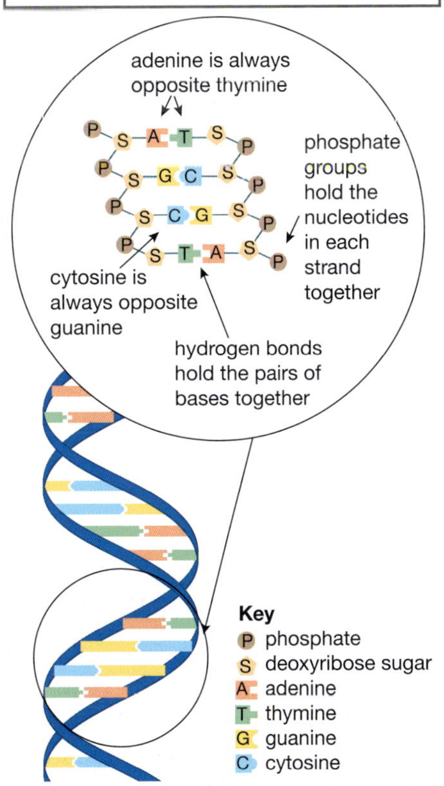

▲ Figure 16.2 Part of a molecule of DNA.

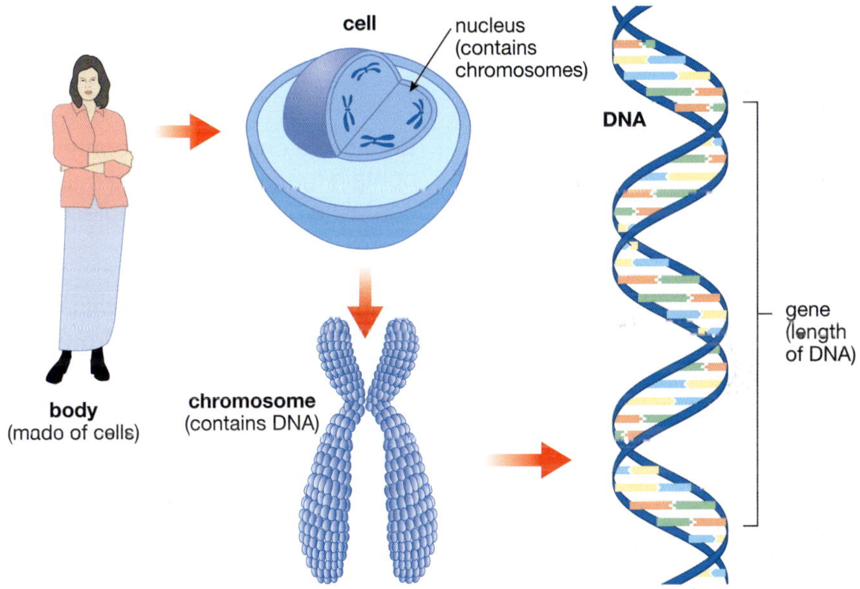

▲ Figure 16.1 Our genetic make-up

The chemical that is the basis of inheritance in nearly all organisms is **DNA**. DNA consists of two strands looking like a twisted ladder - the famous 'double helix'. The 'sides' of the ladder are made of alternating sugar and phosphate groups. The 'rungs' of the ladder are made of pairs of nitrogen-containing groups called bases (Figure 16.2). There are four bases called adenine, thymine, cytosine and guanine. The base adenine always pairs with thymine, and cytosine with guanine. These are called complementary base pairs. DNA is usually found in the nucleus of a cell, in the **chromosomes** (Figure 16.1). A small section of DNA that determines a particular feature is called a **gene**. Genes determine features by instructing cells to produce particular proteins which then lead to the development of the feature. So a gene can also be described as a section of DNA that codes for a particular protein.

DNA can replicate (make an exact copy of) itself. When a cell divides by mitosis (see Chapter 17), each new cell receives exactly the same type and amount of DNA. The cells formed are *genetically identical*.

THE STRUCTURE OF CHROMOSOMES

Each chromosome contains one double-stranded DNA molecule. The DNA is folded and coiled so that it can be packed into a small space. The DNA is coiled around proteins called **histones** (Figure 16.3).

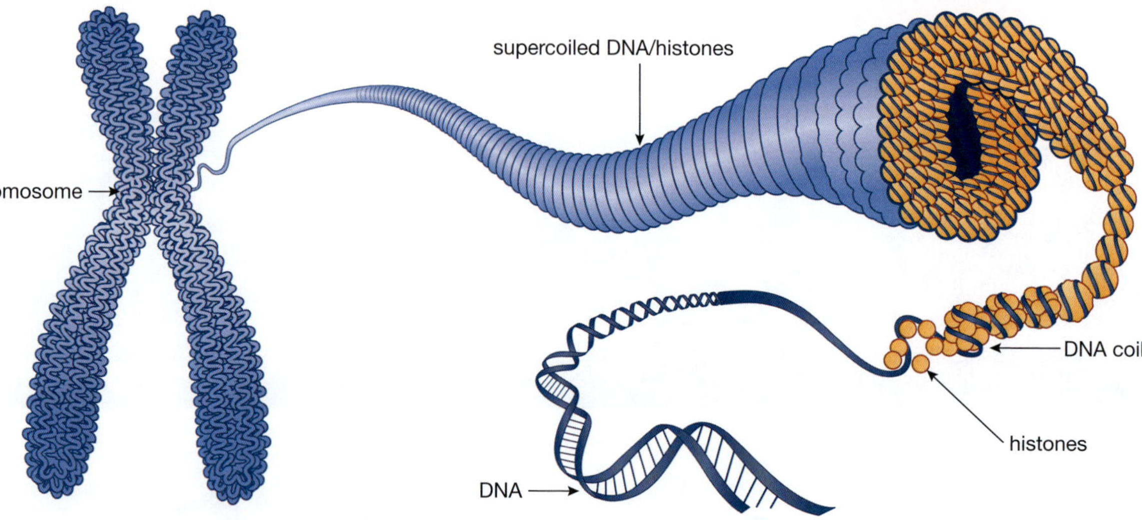

▲ Figure 16.3 The structure of a chromosome

Because a chromosome contains a particular DNA molecule, it will also contain the genes that make up that DNA molecule. Another chromosome will contain a different DNA molecule, and so will contain different genes.

HOW MANY CHROMOSOMES?

Nearly all human cells contain 46 chromosomes. The photographs in Figure 16.4 show the 46 chromosomes from the body cells of a human male.

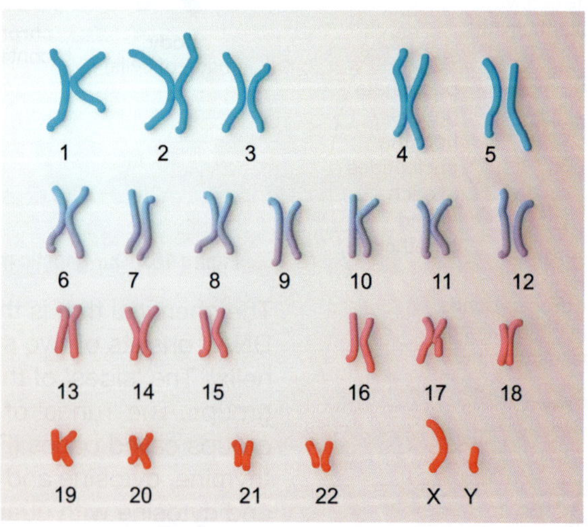

▲ Figure 16.4 A man's chromosomes. One of each of the 22 homologous pairs are shown, along with the X and Y sex chromosomes. A woman's chromosomes are the same, except that she has two X chromosomes. A picture of all the chromosomes in a cell is called a karyotype.

The chromosomes are not arranged like this in the cell. The original photograph has been cut up and chromosomes of the same size and shape 'paired up'. The cell from the male has 22 pairs of chromosomes and two that do not form a pair – the X and Y chromosomes. A body cell from a female has 23 matching pairs including a pair of X chromosomes.

REMINDER

Red blood cells have no nucleus and therefore no chromosomes. (The lack of a nucleus means there is more room for carrying oxygen.)

KEY POINT

The X and the Y chromosomes are the **sex chromosomes**. They determine whether a person is male or female (see Chapter 18).

Pairs of matching chromosomes are called **homologous pairs**. They carry genes for the same features, and these genes are arranged at the same positions and sequence along the chromosome (Figure 16.5). Cells with chromosomes in pairs like this are **diploid** cells.

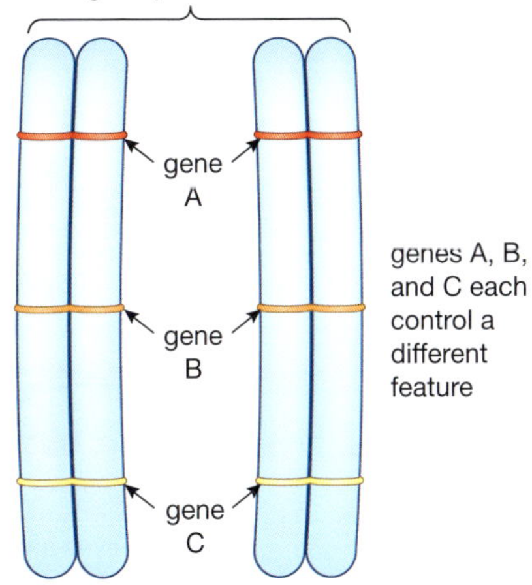

▲ Figure 16.5 Both chromosomes in a homologous pair have the same sequence of genes.

Not all human cells have 46 chromosomes. Red blood cells have no nucleus and so have none. Sex cells have only 23 – just half the number of other cells. They are formed by a cell division called **meiosis** (see Chapter 17). Each cell formed has one chromosome from each homologous pair, and one of the sex chromosomes. Cells with only half the normal diploid number of chromosomes, and therefore only half the DNA content of other cells, are **haploid** cells.

When two gametes fuse in **fertilisation**, the two nuclei join to form a single diploid cell (a **zygote**). This cell has, once again, all its chromosomes in homologous pairs and two copies of every gene. It has the normal DNA content.

HOW MANY GENES?

The entire DNA of an organism (the amount present in a diploid cell) is known as its **genome**. The human genome is made up of about 3.2 billion **base** pairs. One of the surprise discoveries of modern molecular biology is that only a small fraction of the genome consists of protein-coding genes. For example, the human genome contains about 20 000-25 000 genes coding for proteins, which is only about 1.5% of the total DNA. The rest have other functions, or functions yet to be discovered! (See the 'Looking ahead' feature at the end of this chapter.)

GENES AND ALLELES

Genes are sections of DNA that control the production of proteins in a cell. Each protein contributes towards a particular body feature. Sometimes the feature is visible, such as eye colour or skin pigmentation. Sometimes the feature is not visible, such as the type of haemoglobin in red blood cells or the type of blood group antigen on the red blood cells.

Some genes have more than one form. For example, the genes controlling several facial features have alternative forms, which result in alternative forms of the feature (Figure 16.6).

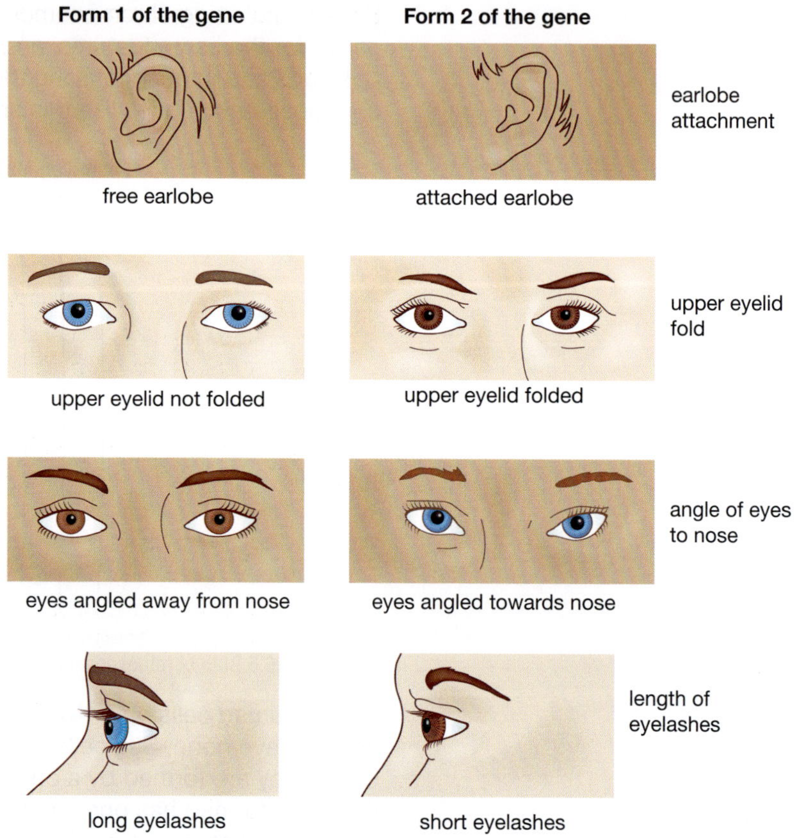

▲ Figure 16.6 The alternate forms of four facial features

The gene for earlobe attachment has the forms 'attached earlobe' and 'free earlobe'. These different forms of the gene are called **alleles**. Homologous chromosomes carry genes for the same features in the same sequence, but the alleles of the genes may not be the same (Figure 16.7). The DNA in the two chromosomes is not quite identical.

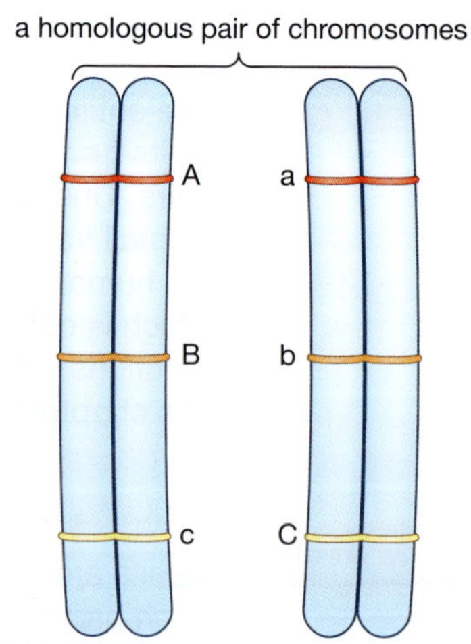

▲ Figure 16.7 A and a, B and b, and C and c are different alleles of the same gene. They control the same feature but code for different expressions of that feature.

Each cell with two copies of a chromosome also has two copies of the genes on those chromosomes. Suppose that, for the gene controlling earlobe attachment, a person has one allele for attached earlobes and one for free earlobes. What happens? Is one ear free and the other attached? Are they both partly attached? Neither. In this case, both earlobes are free. The 'free' allele is **dominant.** This means that it will show its effect, whether or not the allele for 'attached' is present. The allele for 'attached' is called **recessive**. The recessive allele will only show up in the appearance of the person if there is no dominant allele present. You will find out more about how genes work in Chapter 18.

LOOKING AHEAD – REGULATING GENES

You have seen how 'normal' gene coding for proteins (known as structural genes) make up only 1.5% of the genome. Some of the rest of the genome is DNA that regulates the action of the structural genes, switching them on and off. One way this happens is in regions of the DNA called operons.

An operon is a group of structural genes headed by a non-coding length of DNA called an operator, along with another sequence of DNA called a promoter. The promoter starts **transcription** by binding to an enzyme called RNA polymerase. Close to the promoter is a regulatory gene, which codes for a protein called a repressor. The repressor can bind with the operator, preventing the promoter from binding with RNA polymerase, and stopping transcription (Figure 16.8).

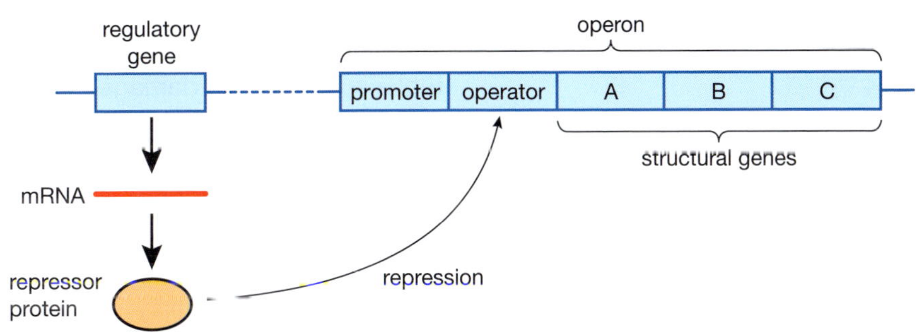

Figure 16.8 An operon is a group of structural genes linked to an operator and a promoter. It is under the control of a regulatory gene.

The structural genes are in groups because they are related – e.g. they code for different enzymes in a metabolic pathway. Operons were first discovered in bacteria. At first we thought they only existed in prokaryotes, but molecular biologists have now found them in eukaryotic cells too.

CHAPTER QUESTIONS

More questions on DNA can be found at the end of Unit 5 on page 234.

SKILLS CRITICAL THINKING

6th

1 How many chromosomes are there in the body cells of a man?

A 23 pairs + XX
B 23 pairs + XY
C 22 pairs + XX
D 22 pairs + XY

2 a What is:
  i a gene
  ii an allele?

7th

b Describe the structure of a chromosome.

c How are the chromosomes in a woman's skin cells:
  i similar to
  ii different from those in a man's skin cells?

17 CELL DIVISION

Growth and reproduction are two characteristics of living things. Both involve cell division, which is the subject of this chapter.

LEARNING OBJECTIVES

- Understand how division of a diploid cell by mitosis produces two cells that contain identical sets of chromosomes
- Understand that mitosis occurs during growth, repair, cloning and asexual reproduction
- Understand how division of a cell by meiosis produces four cells, each with half the number of chromosomes, and that this results in the formation of genetically different haploid gametes
- Understand how random fertilisation produces genetic variation of offspring
- Understand that variation within a species can be genetic, environmental or a combination of both

In most parts of the body, cells need to divide so that organisms can grow and replace worn out or damaged cells. The cells that are produced in this type of cell division should be exactly the same as the cells they are replacing. This is the most common form of cell division.

Only in the sex organs is cell division different. Here, some cells divide to produce gametes (sex cells), which contain only half the original number of chromosomes. This is so that when male and female gametes fuse together (fertilisation) the resulting cell (called a **zygote**) will contain the full set of chromosomes and can then divide and grow into a new individual.

Human body cells are **diploid** – they have 46 chromosomes in 23 homologous pairs. The gametes, with 23 chromosomes (one copy of each homologous chromosome), are **haploid** cells.

There are two kind of cell division: **mitosis** and **meiosis**. When cells divide by mitosis, two cells are formed. These have the same number and type of chromosomes as the original cell. Mitosis forms all the cells in our bodies except the gametes.

When cells divide by meiosis, four cells are formed. These have only half the number of chromosomes of the original cell. Meiosis forms gametes

KEY POINT

Meiosis is sometimes called a *reduction division*. This is because it produces cells with only half the number of chromosomes of the original cell.

MITOSIS

When a 'parent' cell divides it produces 'daughter' cells. Mitosis produces two daughter cells that are genetically identical to the parent cell – both daughter cells have the same number and type of chromosomes as the parent cell.

To achieve this, the dividing cell must do two things.

- It must copy each chromosome before it divides. This involves the DNA replicating and more proteins being added to the structure. Each daughter cell will then be able to receive a copy of each chromosome (and each molecule of DNA) when the cell divides.

- It must divide in such a way that each daughter cell receives one copy of every chromosome. If it does not do this, both daughter cells will not contain all the genes.

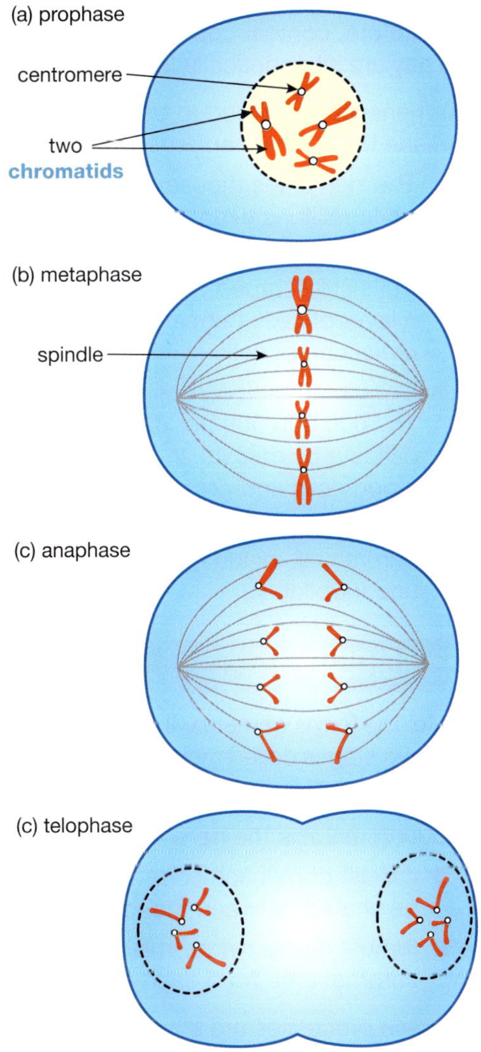

Before mitosis the DNA replicates and the chromosomes form two exact copies called chromatids. During the first stage of mitosis (prophase) the chromatids become visible, joined at a centromere. The nuclear membrane breaks down.

During metaphase a structure called the spindle forms. The chromosomes line up at the 'equator' of the spindle, attached to it by their centromeres.

During anaphase, the spindle fibres shorten and pull the chromatids to the opposite ends ('poles') of the cell. The chromatids separate to become the chromosomes of the two daughter cells.

In the last stage (telophase) two new nuclei form at the poles of the cell. The cytoplasm starts to divide to produce two daughter cells. Both daughter cells have a copy of each chromosome from the parent cell.

▲ Figure 17.1 The stages of mitosis. For simplicity the cell shown contains two homologous pairs of chromosomes (one long pair, one short). (You do not need to remember the names of the stages.)

A number of distinct stages occur when a cell divides by mitosis. These are shown in Figure 17.1. Figure 17.2 is a photograph of some cells from the root tip of an onion. Cells in this region of the root divide by mitosis to allow growth of the root.

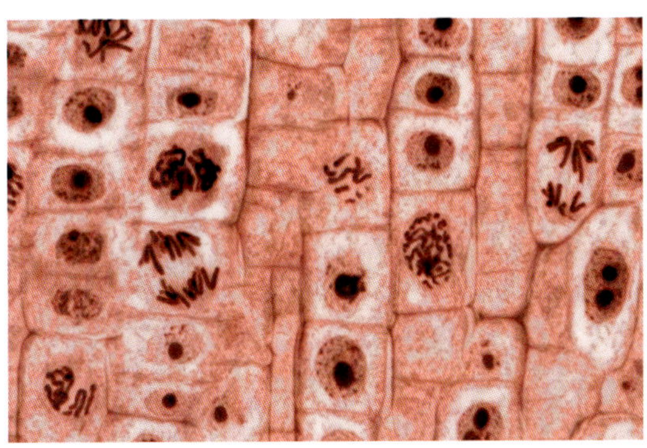

▲ Figure 17.2 Cells in the root tip of an onion dividing by mitosis. Can you identify any of the stages shown in Figure 17.1?

Each daughter cell formed by mitosis receives a copy of every chromosome, and therefore every gene, from the parent cell. Each daughter cell is genetically identical to the others. All the cells in our body (except the gametes) are formed by mitosis from the zygote (single cell formed at fertilisation). They all, therefore, contain copies of all the chromosomes and genes of that zygote. They are all genetically identical.

Whenever cells need to be replaced in our bodies, cells divide by mitosis to make them. This happens more frequently in some regions than in others.

- The skin loses thousands of cells every time we touch something. This adds up to millions every day that need replacing. A layer of cells beneath the surface is constantly dividing to produce replacements.
- Cells are scraped off the lining of the gut as food passes along. Again, a layer of cells beneath the gut lining is constantly dividing to produce replacement cells.
- Cells in our spleen destroy worn out red blood cells at the rate of 100 000 000 000 per day! These are replaced by cells in the bone marrow dividing by mitosis. In addition, the bone marrow forms all our new white blood cells and **platelets**.
- Cancer cells also divide by mitosis. The cells formed are exact copies of the parent cell, including the mutation in the genes that makes the cells divide uncontrollably.

MEIOSIS

Meiosis forms gametes. It is a more complex process than mitosis and takes place in two stages called meiosis I and meiosis II, resulting in four haploid cells. Each daughter cell is genetically different from the other three and from the parent cell.

During meiosis the parent cell must do two things:

- It must copy each chromosome so that there is enough genetic material to be shared between the four daughter cells
- It must divide twice, in such a way that each daughter cell receives just one chromosome from each homologous pair.

These processes are summarised in Figure 17.4. Figure 17.3 shows cells in the anther of a flower dividing by meiosis.

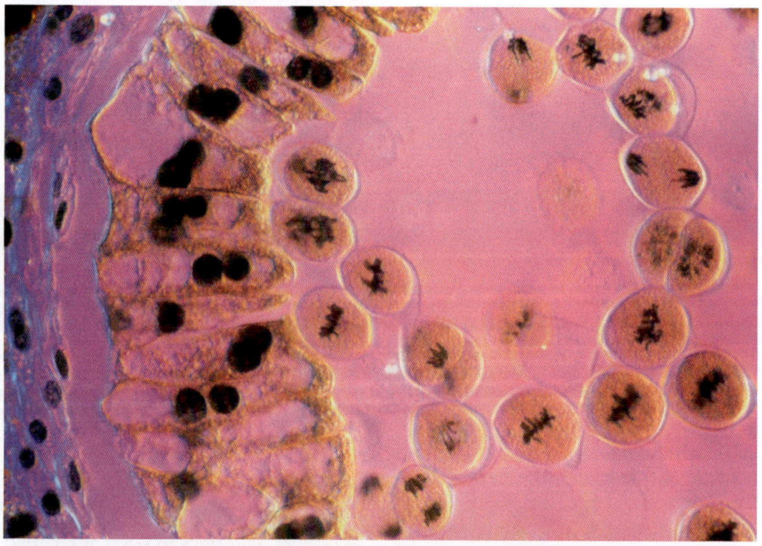

▲ Figure 17.3 Photomicrograph of an anther showing cells dividing by meiosis.

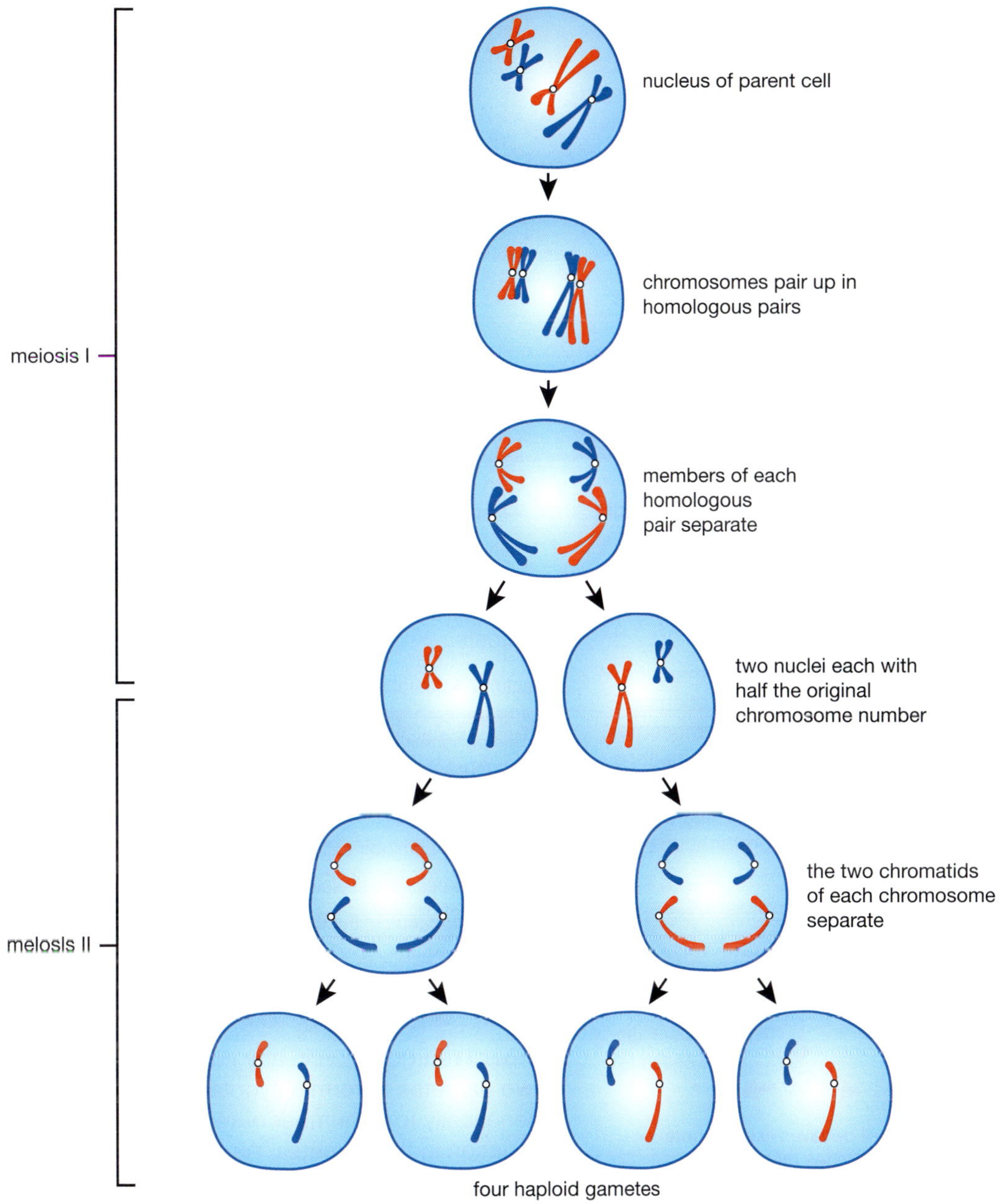

▲ Figure 17.4: The stages of meiosis. For simplicity the parent cell contains only two homologous pairs of chromosomes (one long pair, one short). To help you to see what happens, one member of each pair is coloured red and one blue. The cell membrane is shown, but the nuclear membrane has been omitted. A spindle forms during each division, but these have also been omitted for clarity.

There are two main events during meiosis:

- during the first division, one chromosome from each homologous pair goes into each daughter cell
- during the second division, the chromosome separates into two parts. One part goes into each daughter cell.

The gametes formed by meiosis don't all have the same combinations of alleles – there is *genetic variation* in the cells. During the two cell divisions of meiosis, the chromosomes of each homologous pair are shared between the two daughter cells independently of each of the other homologous pairs. This allows for much possible genetic variation in the daughter cells (Figure 17.5).

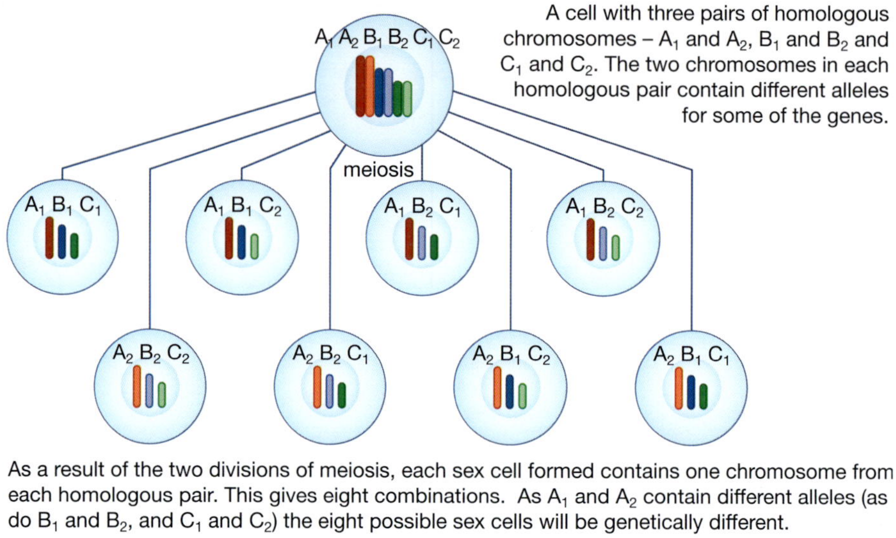

▲ Figure 17.5 How meiosis produces variation

EXTENSION WORK

There is a mathematical rule for predicting how many combinations of chromosomes there can be. The rule is:

number of possible combinations = 2^n

where n = number of pairs of chromosomes.

With two pairs of chromosomes, the number of possible combinations = 2^2 = 4. With three pairs of chromosomes, the number of possible combinations = 2^3 = 8. With the 23 pairs of chromosomes in human cells, the number of possible combinations = 2^{23} = 8 388 608!

Table 17.1 summarises the similarities and differences between mitosis and meiosis.

Table 17.1 Comparison of meiosis and mitosis.

Feature of the process	Mitosis	Meiosis
Chromosomes are copied before division begins	Yes	Yes
Number of cell divisions	One	Two
Number of daughter cells produced	Two	Four
Daughter cells are haploid or diploid	Diploid	Haploid
Genetic variation in the daughter cells	No	Yes

SEXUAL REPRODUCTION AND VARIATION

Sexual reproduction in any multicellular organism involves the fusion of two gametes to form a zygote. The offspring from sexual reproduction vary genetically for a number of reasons. One reason is because of the huge variation in the gametes. Another reason is because of the random way in which fertilisation takes place. In humans, any one of the billions of sperm formed by a male during his life could, potentially, fertilise any one of the thousands of ova formed by a female.

This variation applies to both male and female gametes. So, just using our 'low' estimate of about 8.5 million different types of human gametes means that there can be 8.5 million different types of sperm and 8.5 million different types of ova. When fertilisation takes place, any sperm could fertilise any ovum. The number of possible combinations of chromosomes (and genes) in the zygote is 8.5 million × 8.5 million = 7.2×10^{13}, or 72 trillion! And remember, this is using our 'low' number!

This means that every individual is likely to be genetically unique. The only exceptions are identical twins. Identical twins are formed from the *same* zygote – they are sometimes called *monozygotic* twins. When the zygote divides by mitosis, the two *genetically identical* cells formed do not 'stay together'. Instead, they separate and each cell behaves as though it were an individual zygote, dividing and developing into an embryo (Figure 17.6). Because they have developed from genetically identical cells (and, originally, from the same

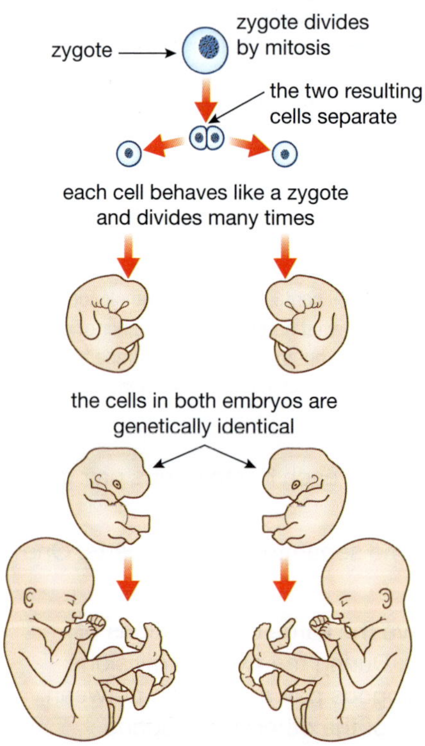

▲ Figure 17.6 How identical twins are formed

zygote), the embryos (and, later, the children and the adults they become) will be genetically identical.

Non-identical twins develop from different zygotes and so are not genetically identical.

Seeds are made by sexual reproduction in plants. Each seed contains an embryo, which results from a pollen grain nucleus fusing with an egg cell nucleus. Embryos from the same plant will vary genetically because they are formed by different pollen grains fertilising different egg cells and so contain different combinations of genes.

ASEXUAL REPRODUCTION AND CLONING

KEY POINT

Cloning is a process that produces a group of genetically identical offspring (a **clone**) from part of the parent organism. Gametes are not involved.

Plant breeders have known for a long time that sexual reproduction produces variation. They realised that if a plant had some desirable feature, the best way to get more of that plant was not to collect and plant its seeds, but to **clone** it in some way. Modern plant-breeding techniques allow the production of many thousands of identical plants from just a few cells of the original (see Chapter 19).

When organisms reproduce asexually, there is no fusion of gametes. A part of the organism grows and somehow breaks away from the parent organism. The cells it contains were formed by mitosis, so contain exactly the same genes as the parent. Asexual reproduction produces offspring that are genetically identical to the parent, and genetically identical to each other.

Asexual reproduction is common in plants (see Chapter 13). For example, flower bulbs grow and divide asexually each season to produce more bulbs. Asexual reproduction also occurs in some animals (see Chapter 9).

GENES AND ENVIRONMENT BOTH PRODUCE VARIATION

DID YOU KNOW?

Short pea plants are called 'dwarf' varieties. The genetics controlling the height of pea plants is described in Chapter 18.

There are two varieties of pea plants that are either tall or short. This difference in height is due to the genes they inherit. There are no 'intermediate height' pea plants. However, all the tall pea plants are not *exactly* the same height and neither are all the short pea plants *exactly* the same height. Figure 17.7 illustrates the variation in height of pea plants.

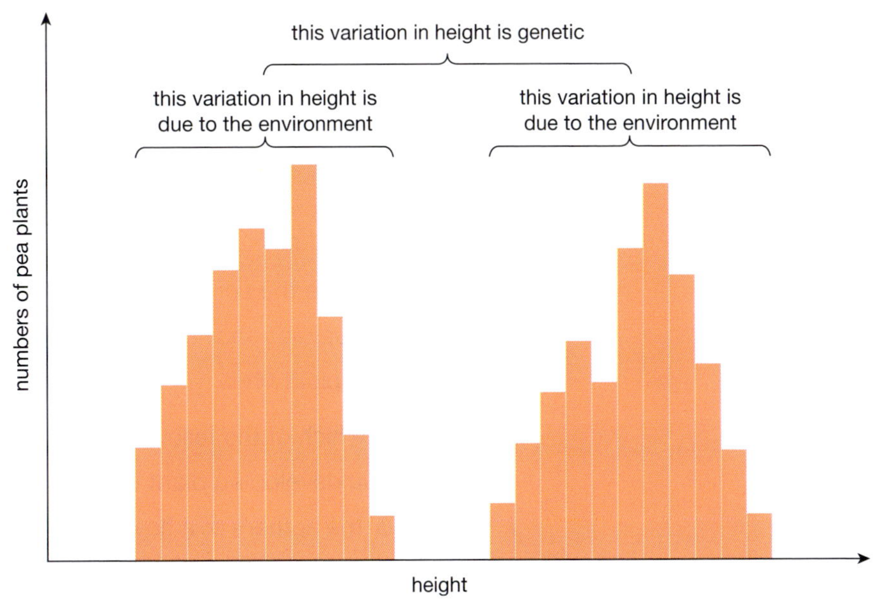

Figure 17.7 Bar chart showing variation in height of pea plants.

Several environmental factors can influence the height of the plants.

- They may not all receive the same amount of light and so some will not photosynthesise as well as others.
- They may not all receive the same amount of water and mineral ions from the soil – this could affect the manufacture of a range of substances in the plant.
- They may not all receive the same amount of carbon dioxide. Again, some plants will not photosynthesise as well as others.

Similar principles apply in humans. Identical twins have the same genes, and often grow up to look very alike (although not quite identical). Also, they often develop similar talents. However, identical twins never look *exactly* the same. This is especially true if, for some reason, they grow up apart. The different environments affect their physical, social and intellectual development in different ways.

CHAPTER QUESTIONS

SKILLS CRITICAL THINKING 6th

More questions on cell division can be found at the end of Unit 5 on page 234.

1 A species of mammal has 32 chromosomes in its muscle cells. Which row in the table below shows the number of chromosomes in the mammal's skin cells and sperm cells?

	Skin cells	Sperm cells
A	32	32
B	16	16
C	16	32
D	32	16

2 Consider the following statements about reproduction in plants:

1. Large numbers of offspring are quickly produced

2. There is little genetic variation in the offspring.

3. A mechanism such as wind or insects is not needed for pollination.

Which of the above are advantages of *asexual* reproduction in plants?

A 1 and 2 **C** 2 and 3

B 1 and 3 **D** 1, 2 and 3

7th

3 Mitosis results in two _______ cells, while meiosis results in _______ haploid cells

Choose the correct pair of answers to fill the gaps in the sentence:

A haploid / four **C** diploid / four

B diploid / two **D** haploid / two

4 In which of the following does meiosis occur?

A a developing plant embryo

B the anthers of a flower

C the skin of a mammal.

D the tip of a shoot of a plant

SKILLS CRITICAL THINKING 7th

5 Cells can divide by mitosis or by meiosis.

a Give one similarity and two differences between the two processes.

8th

b Do cancer cells divide by mitosis or meiosis? Explain your answer.

c Why is meiosis sometimes called a reduction division?

SKILLS REASONING 7th

6 Daffodils reproduce sexually by forming seeds and asexually by forming bulbs. Explain why:

a the bulbs formed from a single daffodil plant produce plants very similar to each other and to the parent plant

b the seeds formed by a single daffodil plant produce plants that vary considerably.

SKILLS CRITICAL THINKING 4th

7 The diagram shows two cuttings. They were both taken from the same clover plant and planted in identical soil. Both were left for several days to become established in their new pots. Some nitrogen-fixing bacteria were then added to the pot labelled 'inoculated'. The other pot was left untreated and labelled 'not inoculated'. The diagram shows the plants three weeks after the treatment to the 'inoculated' pot.

a What is the name given to the part of the experiment represented by the untreated pot of seeds?

SKILLS EXECUTIVE FUNCTION, REASONING 7th

b Why were cuttings from the same plant used rather than seeds from the same plant?

SKILLS REASONING 6th

c What does this experiment suggest about the influence of genes and the environment on variation in the height of clover plants?

SKILLS CRITICAL THINKING 7th

8 Some cells divide by mitosis, others divide by meiosis. For each of the following examples, say whether mitosis or meiosis is involved. In each case, give a reason for your answers.

a Cells in the testes dividing to form sperm.

b Cells in the lining of the small intestine dividing to replace cells that have been lost.

c Cells in the bone marrow dividing to form white blood cells.

d Cells in an anther of a flower dividing to form pollen grains.

e A zygote dividing to form an embryo.

SKILLS CRITICAL THINKING, REASONING 4th

9 Variation in organisms can be caused by the environment as well as by the genes they inherit. For each of the following examples, state whether the variation described is likely to be genetic, environmental or both. In each case, give a reason for your answers.

a Humans have brown, blue or green eyes.

b Half the human population is male, half is female.

c Cuttings of hydrangea plants grown in soils with different pH values develop flowers with slightly different colours.

SKILLS CRITICAL THINKING, REASONING

5th

d Some pea plants are tall; others are dwarf. However, the tall plants are not exactly the same height and neither are all the dwarf plants the same height.

e People in some families are more at risk of heart disease than people in other families. However, not every member of the 'high risk' families have a heart attack and some members of the 'low risk' families do.

SKILLS ANALYSIS, NTERPRETATION

9th

10 In an investigation into mitosis, the distance between a chromosome and the pole (end) of a cell was measured.

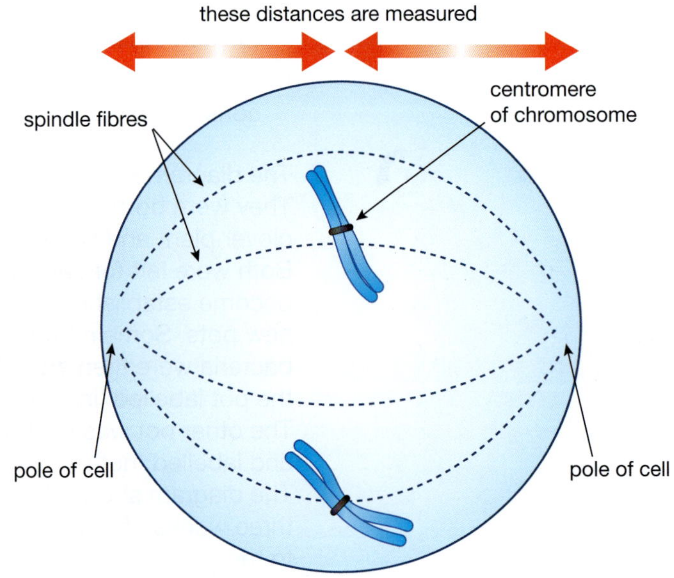

The graph shows how these distances changed during mitosis.

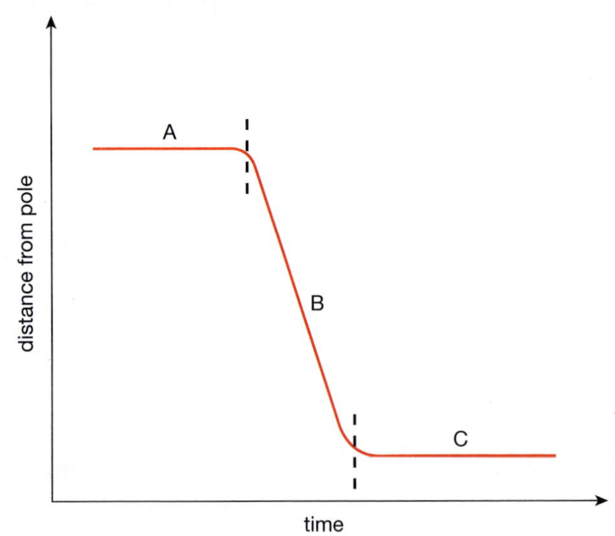

a Describe two events that occur during stage A.

b Explain what is happening during stage B.

c Describe two events that occur during stage C.

18 GENES AND INHERITANCE

How and why do we inherit features from our parents? This chapter answers these questions by looking at the work of Gregor Mendel and how he has helped us to understand the mysteries of inheritance.

LEARNING OBJECTIVES

- Understand that genes exist in alternative forms called alleles which give rise to differences in inherited characteristics
- Understand the meaning of the terms dominant, recessive, homozygous, heterozygous, phenotype and genotype
- Describe patterns of monohybrid inheritance using genetic diagrams
- Predict probabilities of outcomes from monohybrid crosses
- Understand how to interpret family pedigrees
- Understand how the sex of a person is controlled by one pair of chromosomes, XX in a female and XY in a male
- Describe the determination of the sex of offspring at fertilisation, using a genetic diagram
- Understand that most phenotypic features are the result of polygenic inheritance rather than single genes

The groundbreaking research that uncovered the rules of how genes are inherited was carried out by Gregor Mendel and published in 1865. The rules of inheritance are now known as 'Mendelian genetics' in his honour.

GREGOR MENDEL

▲ Figure 18.1 Gregor Mendel.

Gregor Mendel was a monk who lived in a monastery in Brno in what is now the Czech Republic (Figure 18.1). He became interested in the science of heredity, and carried out hundreds of breeding experiments using pea plants. From his research Mendel was able to explain the laws governing inheritance.

Mendel found that for every feature or 'character' he investigated:

- a 'heritable unit' (what we now call a **gene**) is passed from one generation to the next
- the heritable unit (gene) can have alternative forms (we now call these different forms **alleles**)
- each individual must have two alternative forms (alleles) per feature
- the gametes only have one of the alternative forms (allele) per feature
- one allele can be dominant over the other.

Mendel used these ideas to predict outcomes of cross-breeding or 'crosses' between plants, which he tested in his breeding experiments. He published his results and ideas in 1865 but few people took any notice, and his work went unrecognised for many years. It wasn't until 1900 that other biologists working on inheritance rediscovered Mendel's work and realised its importance. In 1903, the connection between the behaviour of genes in Mendelian genetics and the behaviour of chromosomes in meiosis was noticed and the science of genetics was established.

MENDEL'S EXPERIMENTS ON INHERITANCE

Mendel noticed that many of the features of pea plants had two alternative forms. For example, plants were either tall or very short (called a 'dwarf' variety); they either had purple or white flowers; they produced yellow seeds or green seeds. There were no intermediate forms, no pale purple flowers or green/yellow seeds or intermediate height plants. Figure 18.2 shows some of the contrasting features of pea plants that Mendel used in his breeding experiments.

▲ Figure 18.2 Some features of pea plants used by Mendel in his breeding experiments.

KEY POINT

In his breeding experiments, Mendel initially used only plants that had 'bred true' for several generations. For example, any tall pea plants he used came from generations of pea plants that had all been tall.

Mendel decided to investigate, systematically, the results of cross breeding plants that had contrasting features. These were the 'parent plants', referred to as 'P' in genetic diagrams. He transferred pollen from one experimental plant to another. He also made sure that the plants could not be self-fertilised.

He collected all the seeds formed, grew them and noted the features that each plant developed. These plants were the first generation of offspring, called the **F_1 generation**. He did not cross-pollinate these plants, but allowed them to self-fertilise. Again, he collected the seeds, grew them and noted the features that each plant developed. These plants formed the second generation of offspring or **F_2 generation**. When Mendel used pure-breeding tall and pure-breeding dwarf plants as his parents, he obtained the results shown in Figure 18.3.

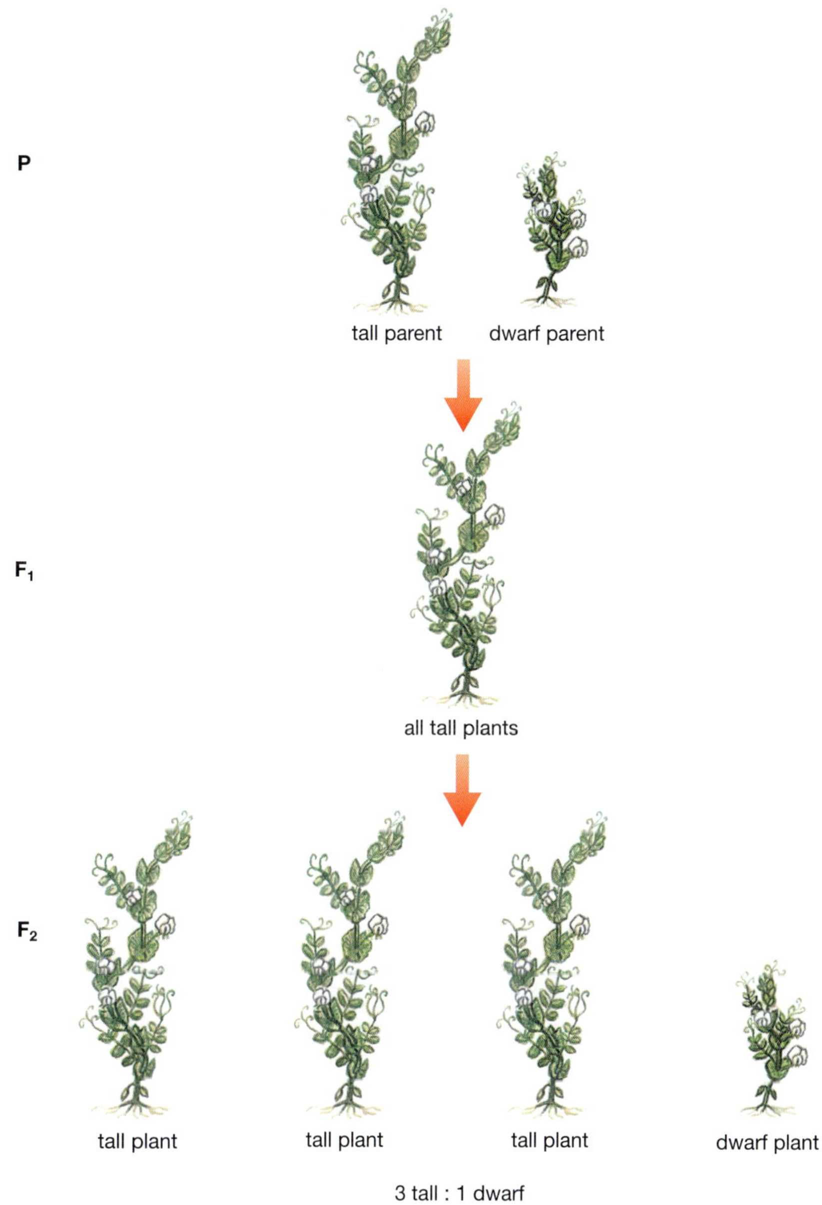

▲ Figure 18.3 A summary of Mendel's results from breeding tall pea plants with dwarf pea plants.

Mendel obtained similar results when he carried out breeding experiments using plants with other pairs of contrasting characters (Figure 18.4). He noticed two things in particular.

- All the plants of the F_1 generation were of one type. This type was not a blend of the two parental features, but one or the other. For example, when tall and dwarf parents were crossed, all the F_1 plants were tall.
- There was always a 3:1 ratio of types in the F_2 generation. Three-quarters of the plants in the F_2 generation were of the type that appeared in the F_1 generation. One-quarter showed the other parental feature. For example, when tall F_1 plants were crossed, three-quarters of the F_2 plants were tall and one-quarter were dwarf.

Mendel was able to use his findings to work out how features were inherited, despite having no knowledge of chromosomes, genes or meiosis. Nowadays we can use our understanding of these ideas to explain Mendel's results.

EXPLAINING MENDEL'S RESULTS

- Each feature is controlled by a gene, which is found on a chromosome.
- There are two copies of each chromosome and each gene in all body cells, except the gametes.
- The gametes have only one copy of each chromosome and each gene (i.e. one allele).
- There are two alleles of each gene.
- One allele is **dominant** over the other allele, which is **recessive**.
- When two different alleles (one dominant and one recessive) are in the same cell, only the dominant allele is expressed (shown in the appearance of the organism).
- An individual can have two dominant alleles, two recessive alleles or a dominant allele and a recessive allele in each cell.

KEY POINT

Normally, we use the first letter of the dominant feature to represent the gene, with a capital letter indicating the dominant allele and a lower case letter the recessive allele. Tall is dominant to dwarf in pea plants, so we use T for the allele for tall and t for dwarf.

We can use the cross between tall and dwarf pea plants as an example (Figure 18.4). In pea plants, there are tall and dwarf alleles of the gene for height. We will use the symbol T for the tall allele and t for the dwarf allele. The term **genotype** describes the alleles each cell has for a certain feature (e.g. TT). The **phenotype** is the feature that results from the genotype (e.g. a tall plant).

KEY POINT

It is the accepted practice in genetics diagrams to show the gene present in a gamete as a letter in a circle.

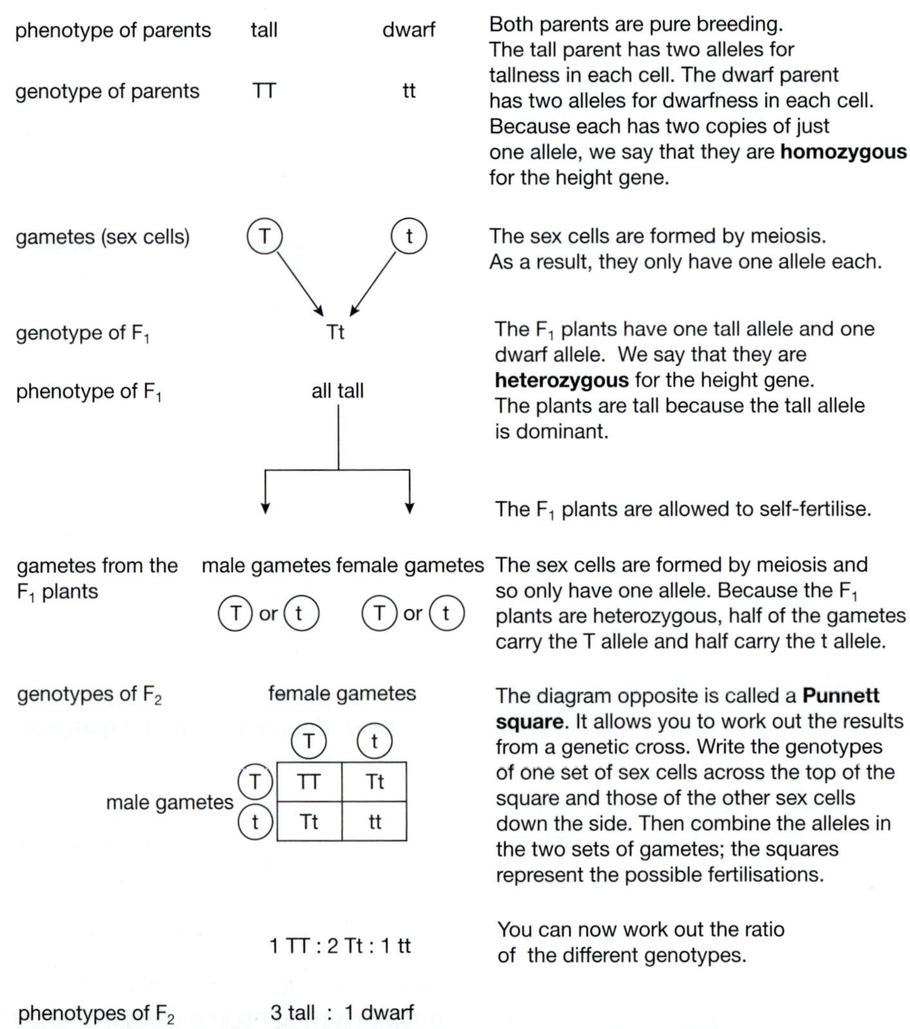

▲ Figure 18.4 Results of crosses using true-breeding tall and dwarf pea plants.

KEY POINT

Mendel's experiments described above, all involve single genes (e.g. the gene for height, or the gene for flower colour). The name given for inheritance involving one gene is **monohybrid** inheritance. It is possible to draw genetic diagrams involving two or more genes (e.g height and flower colour together), but for International GCSE you only need to interpret monohybrid crosses.

It is important to remember that in genetic crosses, ratios such as 3:1 are *predicted* ratios. In breeding experiments the *actual* numbers of offspring are unlikely to *exactly* fit a 3:1 ratio.

Imagine you flip a coin 20 times. The most likely outcome is that you will get 10 heads and 10 tails. However, you wouldn't be surprised to get, by chance, 11 heads and 9 tails, or 8 heads and 12 tails. The same principle applies to the outcome of a breeding experiment.

For example, one of Mendel's experiments produced 787 tall plants and 277 dwarf plants. This is a ratio of 2.84:1, not quite the expected 3:1. The reason for this is that there are a number of factors that affect survival of the plants – some pollen may not fertilise some ova, some seedlings may die before they mature, and so on. These are unpredictable or 'chance' events. The numbers that Mendel found were statistically close enough to the expected 3:1 ratio, and he found the same thing when he repeated his experiments with other characteristics.

WORKING OUT GENOTYPES – THE TEST CROSS

You cannot tell just by looking at a tall pea plant whether it is **homozygous** (TT) or **heterozygous** (Tt). Both these genotypes would appear equally tall because the tall allele is dominant.

It would help if you knew the genotypes of its parents. You could then write out a genetic cross and perhaps work out the genotype of your tall plant. If you don't know the genotypes of the parents, the only way you can find out is by carrying out a breeding experiment called a **test cross**.

In a test cross, the factor under investigation is the unknown genotype of an organism showing the dominant phenotype. A tall pea plant could have the genotype TT or Tt. You must control every other possible variable *including the genotype of the plant you breed it with*. The only genotype you can be *certain* of is the genotype of plants showing the *recessive* phenotype (in this case dwarf plants). They *must* have the genotype tt.

KEY POINT

In a test cross, you breed an organism showing the dominant feature with one showing the recessive feature.

In this example, you must breed the 'unknown' tall pea plant (TT or Tt) with a dwarf pea plant (tt). You can write out a genetic cross for both possibilities (TT ´ tt and Tt ´ tt) and *predict* the outcome for each (Figure 18.5). You can then compare the result of the breeding experiment with the predicted outcome, to see which result matches the prediction most closely.

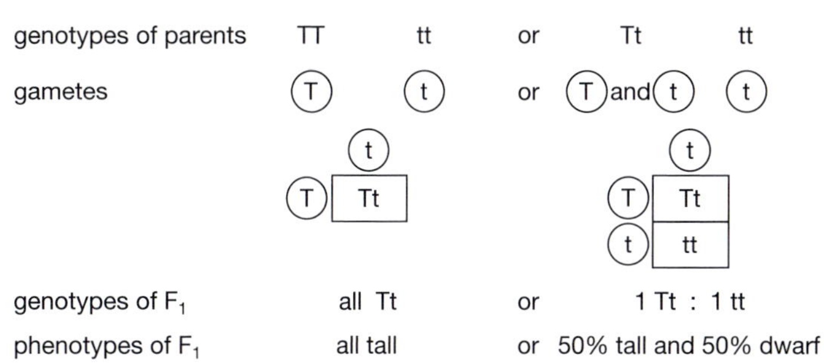

▲ Figure 18.5 A test cross

From our crosses we would expect:

- *all* the offspring to be tall if the tall parent was homozygous (TT)
- *half* the offspring to be tall and *half* to be dwarf if the tall parent was heterozygous (Tt).

WAYS OF PRESENTING GENETIC INFORMATION

Writing out a genetic cross is a useful way of showing how genes are passed through one or two generations, starting from the parents. To show a family history of a genetic condition requires more than this. We can use a diagram called a **pedigree**.

Polydactyly is an inherited condition in which a person develops an extra digit (finger or toe) on the hands and feet. It is determined by a dominant allele. The recessive allele causes the normal number of digits to develop.

If we use the symbol D for the polydactyly allele and d for the normal-number allele, the possible genotypes and phenotypes are:

- DD – person has polydactyly (has two dominant polydactyly alleles)
- Dd – person has polydactyly (has a dominant polydactyly allele and a recessive normal allele)
- dd – person has the normal number of digits (has two recessive, normal-number alleles).

We don't use P and p to represent the alleles as you would expect, because the letters P and p look very similar and could easily be confused. The pedigree for polydactyly is shown in Figure 18.6.

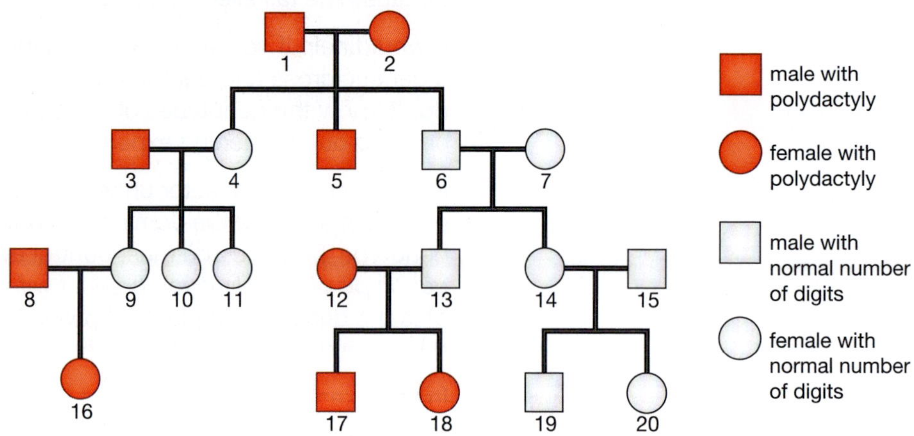

▲ Figure 18.6 A pedigree showing the inheritance of polydactyly in a family.

We can extract a lot of information from a pedigree. In this case:

- there are four generations shown (individuals are arranged in four horizontal lines)
- individuals 4, 5 and 6 are children of individuals 1 and 2 (a family line connects each one directly to 1 and 2)
- individual 4 is the first-born child of 1 and 2 (the first-born child is shown to the left, then second born to the right of this, then the third born and so on)
- individuals 3 and 7 are not children of 1 and 2 (no family line connects them directly to 1 and 2)
- individuals 3 and 4 are father and mother of the same children – as are 1 and 2, 6 and 7, 8 and 9, 12 and 13, 14 and 15 (a horizontal line joins them).

It is usually possible to work out which allele is dominant from a pedigree. You look for a situation where two parents show the same feature and at least one child shows the contrasting feature. In Figure 18.6, individuals 1 and 2 both have polydactyly, but children 4 and 6 do not. There is only one way to explain this:

- the normal alleles in 4 and 6 can only have come from their parents (1 and 2), so 1 and 2 must both carry normal alleles
- 1 and 2 show polydactyly, so they must have polydactyly alleles as well
- if they have both polydactyly alleles *and* normal alleles but show polydactyly, the polydactyly allele must be the dominant allele.

Now that we know which allele is dominant, we can work out most of the genotypes in the pedigree. All the people with the normal number of digits *must* have the genotype dd (if they had even one D allele, they would show polydactyly). All the people with polydactyly must have at least one polydactyly allele (they must be either DD or Dd).

From here, we can begin to work out the genotypes of the people with polydactyly. To do this we need to remember that people with the normal number of digits must inherit one 'normal-number' allele from each parent, and also that people with the normal number of digits will pass on one 'normal-number' allele to each of their children.

From this we can say that any person with polydactyly who has children with the normal number of digits must be heterozygous (the child must have inherited one of their two 'normal-number' alleles from this parent), and also that any person with polydactyly who has one parent with the normal number of digits must also be heterozygous (the 'normal-number' parent can only have passed on a 'normal-number' allele). Individuals 1, 2, 3, 16, 17 and 18 fall into one or other of these categories and must be heterozygous.

We can now add this genetic information to the pedigree. This is shown in Figure 18.7.

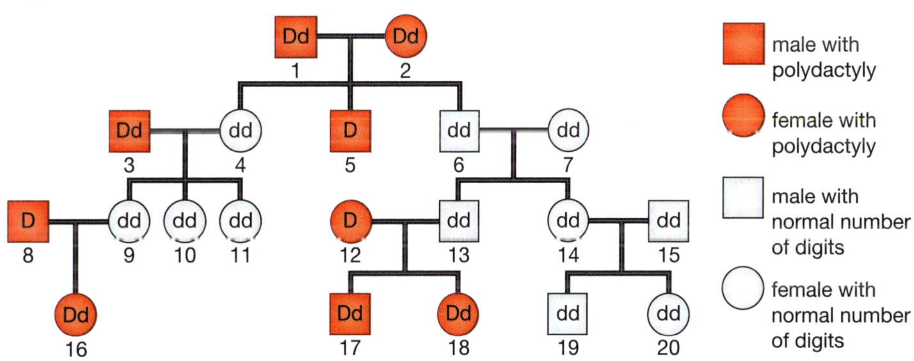

▲ Figure 18.7 A pedigree showing the inheritance of polydactyly in a family, with details of genotypes added.

We are still uncertain about individuals 5, 8 and 12. They could be homozygous or heterozygous. For example, individuals 1 and 2 are both heterozygous. Figure 18.8 shows the possible outcomes from a genetic cross between them. Individual 5 could be any of the outcomes indicated by the shading. It is impossible to distinguish between DD and Dd.

genotypes of parents: Dd Dd

gametes: (D) and (d) (D) and (d)

genotypes of children:

	female gametes (D)	female gametes (d)
male gametes (D)	DD	Dd
male gametes (d)	Dd	dd

▲ Figure 18.8 Possible outcomes from a genetic cross between two parents, both heterozygous for polydactyly.

SEX DETERMINATION

Our sex – whether we are male or female – is not under the control of a single gene. It is determined by the X and Y chromosomes – the **sex chromosomes**. As well as the 44 non-sex chromosomes, there are two X chromosomes in all cells of females (except the egg cells) and one X and one Y chromosome in all cells of males (except the sperm). Our sex is effectively determined by the presence or absence of the Y chromosome. The full chromosome complement of male and female is shown in Figure 16.4 on page 198.

DID YOU KNOW?
Because the Y chromosome, when present, causes a zygote to develop into a male, some people describe it it as 'dominant'. This is incorrect: dominant and recessive are terms that are only applied to individual alleles.

The inheritance of sex follows the pattern shown in Figure 18.9. In any one family, however, this ratio may well not be met. Predicted genetic ratios are usually only met when large numbers are involved. The overall ratio of male and female births in all countries is 1 : 1.

phenotypes of parents	male	female
genotypes of parents	XY	XX
gametes	(X) and (Y)	(X)

	female gametes: (X)
male gametes (X)	XX
male gametes (Y)	XY

ratio of genotypes: 50% XX : 50% XY

ratio of phenotypes: 50% female : 50% male

▲ Figure 18.9 Determination of sex in humans

POLYGENIC INHERITANCE

All of the genetic crosses that you have seen in this chapter have been examples of inheritance involving single genes. The reason for this is that it is easier to draw genetics diagrams and explain what is happening if we start by considering alleles of a single gene. However, many characteristics are controlled by two or more genes working together. This is called **polygenic inheritance**.

DID YOU KNOW?
Melanin protects the skin against the harmful effects of ultraviolet radiation, which is a mutagen that can cause skin cancer.

A good example is human skin colour. Darker skins contain greater amounts of a black pigment called melanin. This is controlled by several genes, which act together to determine the amount of melanin in the skin. Each gene has alleles that promote melanin production and alleles which do not. This produces a wide range of phenotypes (Figure 18.10).

◀ Figure 18.10 Skin colour depends on the amount of melanin in the skin. It is a result of polygenic inheritance.

Other human characteristics determined by several genes (**polygenes**) are human height and body mass (weight).

CHAPTER QUESTIONS

More questions on chromosomes, genes and inheritance can be found at the end of Unit 5 on page 234.

SKILLS CRITICAL THINKING

1 Which of the following is true of dominant alleles?

A they are only expressed if present as a pair

B they determine the most favourable of a pair of alternative features

C they are inherited in preference to recessive alleles

D a dominant allele is expressed if present with a recessive allele

SKILLS PROBLEM SOLVING

2 In pea plants, the allele for purple petals is dominant to the allele for white petals. A plant heterozygous for petal colour was crossed with a plant with white petals. What would be the ratio of genotypes in the offspring?

A 1 : 1 **B** 2 : 1 **C** 1 : 0 **D** 3 : 1

3 The allele for yellow coat colour in mice (Y) is dominant to the allele for non-yellow coat colour (y).

Mice with the genotype yy have non-yellow coats.

Mice with the genotype Yy have yellow coats.

Mice with the genotype YY die as embryos.

Two heterozygous mice were crossed. What is the probability that a surviving mouse in the F1 generation will be yellow?

A 0.00 **B** 0.25 **C** 0.50 **D** 0.67

4 Predict the *ratios* of offspring from the following crosses between tall/dwarf pea plants.

a TT × TT

b TT × Tt

c TT × tt

d Tt × Tt

e Tt × tt

f tt × tt.

SKILLS CRITICAL THINKING

5 In cattle, a pair of alleles controls coat colour. The allele for black coat colour is dominant over the allele for red coat colour. The genetic diagram represents a cross between a pure-breeding black bull and a pure-breeding red cow. B = dominant allele for black coat colour; b = recessive allele for red coat colour.

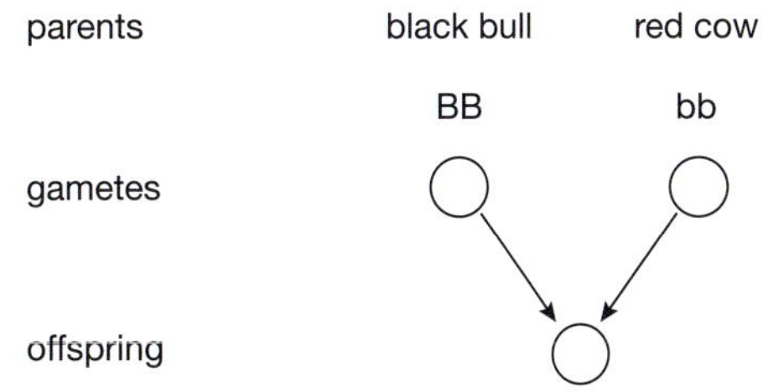

a i What term describes the genotypes of the pure-breeding parents?

ii Explain the terms dominant and recessive.

SKILLS CRITICAL THINKING 7th

b i What are the genotypes of the gametes of each parent?

ii What is the genotype of the offspring?

c Cows with the same genotype as the offspring were bred with bulls with the same genotype.

6th

i What genetic term describes this genotype?

SKILLS INTERPRETATION, PROBLEM SOLVING 9th

ii Draw a genetic diagram to work out the ratios of:

the genotypes of the offspring

the phenotypes of the offspring.

SKILLS INTERPRETATION

6 In nasturtiums, a single pair of alleles controls flower colour.

The allele for red flower colour is dominant over the allele for yellow flower colour. The diagram represents the results of a cross between a pure-breeding red-flowered nasturtium and a pure-breeding yellow-flowered nasturtium. R = dominant allele for red flower colour; r = recessive allele for yellow flower colour.

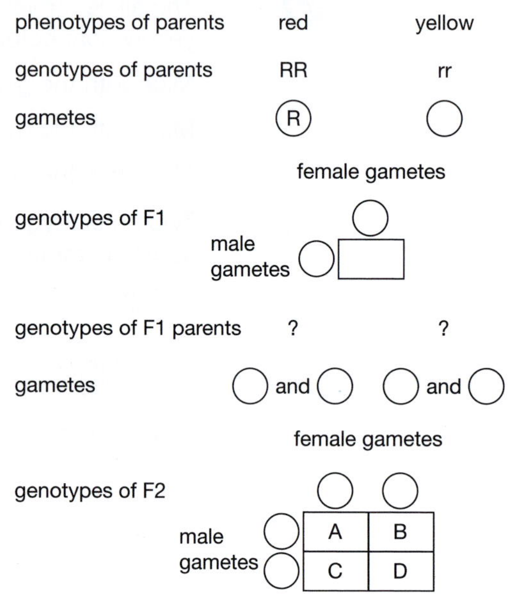

a Copy and complete the genetic diagram.

SKILLS ANALYSIS

b What are the colours of the flowers of A, B, C and D?

SKILLS ANALYSIS

7 Cystic fibrosis is an inherited condition. The diagram shows the incidence of cystic fibrosis in a family over four generations.

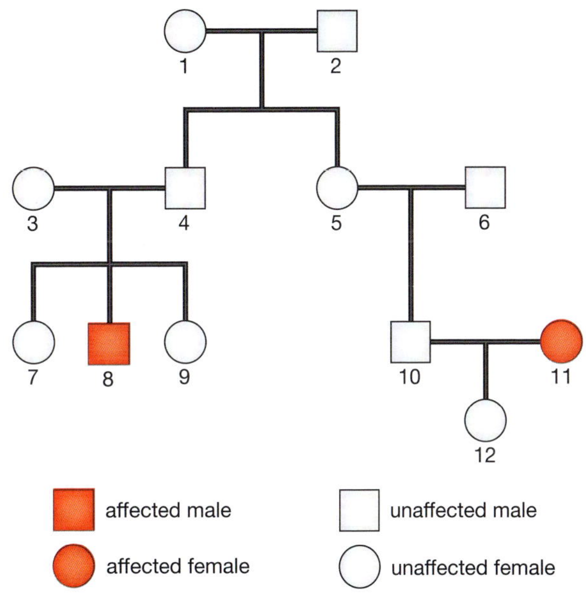

a What evidence in the pedigree suggests that cystic fibrosis is determined by a recessive allele?

b What are the genotypes of individuals 3, 4 and 11? Explain your answers.

c Draw genetic diagrams to work out the probability that the next child born to individuals 10 and 11 will

i be male,

ii suffer from cystic fibrosis.

SKILLS INTERPRETATION

SKILLS REASONING

8 In guinea pigs, the allele for short hair is dominant to that for long hair.

a Two short-haired guinea pigs were bred and their offspring included some long-haired guinea pigs. Explain these results.

b How could you find out if a short-haired guinea pig was homozygous or heterozygous for hair length?

19 NATURAL SELECTION, EVOLUTION AND SELECTIVE BREEDING

Over millions of years, life on this planet has evolved from its simple beginnings into the vast range of organisms present today. This has happened by a process called natural selection. This chapter looks at natural selection, as well as traditional methods of selective breeding and modern developments involving cloned organisms.

LEARNING OBJECTIVES

- Explain Darwin's theory of evolution by natural selection
- Understand how resistance to antibiotics can increase in bacterial populations
- Understand how selective breeding can be used to produce plants with desired characteristics
- Understand how selective breeding can be used to produce animals with desirable characteristics

▲ Figure 19.1 Charles Darwin (1809–1882).

The meaning of '**evolution**' is that species of animals and plants are not fixed in their form, but change over time. It is not a new idea. For thousands of years philosophers have discussed this theory. By the beginning of the nineteenth century there was overwhelming evidence for evolution, and many scientists had accepted that it had taken place. What was missing was an understanding of the *mechanism* by which evolution could have occurred.

The person who proposed the mechanism for evolution that is widely accepted today was the English biologist Charles Darwin (Figure 19.1). He called the mechanism **natural selection**.

THE WORK OF CHARLES DARWIN

Charles Darwin was the son of a country doctor. He did not do particularly well at school or university and was unable to decide on a profession. His father is supposed to have said: 'you're good for nothing but shooting guns and rat-catching … you'll be a disgrace to yourself and all of your family'. He was wrong – Darwin went on to become one of the most famous scientists of all time!

At the age of 22, Charles Darwin became the unpaid biologist aboard the survey ship HMS *Beagle*, which left England for a five-year voyage in 1831 (Figure 19.2).

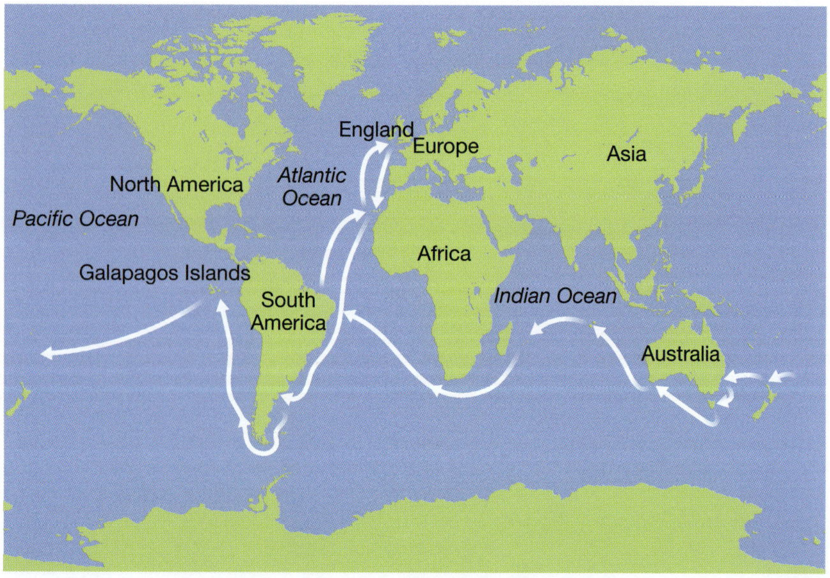

Figure 19.2 The five-year journey of HMS *Beagle* ▶

DID YOU KNOW?

A fossil is the remains of an animal or plant that lived thousands or millions of years ago, preserved in sedimentary rocks. Fossils are formed when minerals replace the materials in bone and tissue, creating a replica of the original organism in the rock.

During the voyage, Darwin collected hundreds of specimens and made many observations about the variety of organisms and the ways in which they were adapted to their environments. He gained much information, in particular, from the variety of life forms in South America and the Galapagos Islands. Darwin was influenced by the work of Charles Lyell who was, at the time, laying the foundations of modern geology. Lyell was using the evidence of rock layers to suggest that the surface of the Earth was constantly changing. The layers of sediments in rocks represented different time periods. Darwin noticed that the fossils found in successive layers of rocks often changed slightly through the layers. He suggested that life forms were continually changing – evolving.

On his return to England, Darwin began to evaluate his data and wrote several essays, introducing the ideas of natural selection. He arrived at his theory of natural selection from observations made during his voyage on HMS *Beagle* and from deductions made from those observations. Darwin's observations were that:

- organisms generally produce more offspring than are needed to replace them – a single female salmon can release 5 million eggs per year; a giant puffball fungus produces 40 million spores
- despite this over-reproduction, stable, established populations of organisms generally remain the same size – the seas are not overflowing with salmon, and we are not surrounded by lots of giant puffball fungi!
- members of the same species are not identical – they show variation.

He made two important deductions from these observations.

- From the first two observations he deduced that there is a 'struggle for existence'. Many offspring are produced, yet the population stays the same size. There must be competition for resources and many individuals must die.
- From the third observation he deduced that, if some offspring survive while others die, those organisms best suited to their environment would survive to reproduce. Those less suited will die. This gave rise to the phrase 'survival of the fittest'.

KEY POINT

The phrase 'survival of the fittest' does not mean *physical* fitness, but *biological* fitness. This depends on how well adapted an organism is to its environment so that it is successful in *reproducing*. A good way of putting it is; 'survival of the individuals that will leave most offspring in later generations'.

Notice a key phrase in the second deduction – the best-suited organisms survive *to reproduce*. This means that those characteristics that give the organism a better chance of surviving will be passed on to the next generation. Fewer of the individuals that are less suited to the environment survive to reproduce. The next generation will have more of the type that is better adapted and fewer of the less well adapted type. This will be repeated in each generation.

Another naturalist, Alfred Russell Wallace, had also studied life forms in South America and Indonesia and had reached the same conclusions as Darwin. Darwin and Wallace published a scientific paper on natural selection jointly, although it was Darwin who went on to develop the ideas further. In 1859, he published his now famous book *On the Origin of Species by Means of Natural Selection* (usually shortened to *The Origin of Species*).

▲ Figure 19.3 Darwin's ideas were unpopular and many newspapers of the time made fun of them.

This book changed forever the way in which biologists think about how species originate. Darwin went on to suggest that humans could have evolved from ape-like ancestors. For this he was ridiculed, largely by people who had misunderstood his ideas (Figure 19.3). He also carried out considerable research in other areas of biology, such as plant tropisms (see Chapter 12).

KEY POINT

When Darwin proposed his theory of natural selection, he did not know about genes and how they control characteristics. Gregor Mendel had yet to publish his work on inheritance, and as you have seen, the significance of Mendel's work was not recognised until 1903.

The theory of natural selection proposes that some factor in the environment 'selects' which forms of a species will survive to reproduce. Forms that are not well adapted will not survive.

The following is a summary of how we think natural selection works:

1. there is variation within the species
2. changing conditions in the environment (called a selection pressure) favours one particular form of the species (which has a selective advantage)
3. the frequency of the favoured form increases (it is selected for) under these conditions (survival of the fittest)
4. the frequency of the less well adapted form decreases under these conditions (it is selected against).

As you have seen, many gene mutations are harmful, and cells that carry them will not usually survive. Some mutations are 'neutral' and if they arise in the gametes, may be passed on without affecting the survival of the offspring. However, a few mutations can actually be beneficial to an organism. Beneficial mutations are the 'raw material' that are ultimately the source of new inherited variation.

SOME EXAMPLES OF HOW NATURAL SELECTION MIGHT HAVE WORKED

THE HOVERFLY

(a)

(b)

▲ Figure 19.4 Two insects showing 'warning colouration'. (a) A wasp, which has a sting. (b) A harmless hoverfly.

Figure 19.4 shows two species of insect: a wasp and a hoverfly. Wasps can defend themselves against predators using a sting. They also have a body with yellow and black stripes. This is called a 'warning colouration'. Predators such as birds soon learn that these colours mean that wasps have the sting, and they avoid attacking them.

Hoverflies do not have a sting. However, they have an appearance that is very like a wasp, with similar yellow and black stripes – they are 'mimics' of wasps. Predators treat hoverflies as if they do have a sting.

Clearly, mimicking a wasp is an advantage to the hoverfly. How could they have evolved this appearance? We can explain how it could have happened by natural selection.

The selection pressure was predation by birds and other animals. Among the ancestors of present-day hoverflies there would have been variation in colours. As a result of mutations, some hoverflies gained genes that produced stripes on their bodies. These insects were less likely to be eaten by predators than hoverflies without the stripes – they had a *selective advantage*.

Since the hoverflies with stripes were more likely to survive being eaten, they were more likely to reproduce, and would pass on the genes for stripes to their offspring. This process continued over many generations. Gradually more mutations and selection for 'better' stripes took place, until the hoverflies evolved the excellent warning colouration that they have today.

KEY POINT

Note that perfect stripes didn't have to appear straight away. Even a slight stripy appearance could give a small selective advantage over hoverflies without stripes. This would be enough to result in an increase in stripy hoverflies in the next generation.

THE POLAR BEAR

▲ Figure 19.5 A polar bear hunting on the Arctic sea ice.

The polar bear lives in the Arctic, inhabiting landmasses and sea ice covering the waters within the Arctic Circle (Figure 19.5). It is a large predatory carnivore, mainly hunting seals. One way the bear hunts is to wait near holes in the ice where seals come up to breathe. It also silently approaches and attacks seals that are resting on the ice.

Polar bears have many **adaptations** that suit them to their habitat. These include:

- a thick layer of white fur, which reduces heat loss and acts as camouflage in the snow
- wide, large paws. These help with walking in the snow, and are used for swimming
- strong, muscular legs – a bear can swim continuously in the cold Arctic waters for days
- nostrils that close when the bear is swimming under water
- a large body mass. Polar bears are the largest bears on Earth. An adult male averages 350 to 550 kilograms, and the record is over 1000 kilograms. This large size results in the animal having a small surface area to volume ratio, which reduces heat loss
- a 10 centimetre thick layer of insulating fat under the skin
- a well developed sense of smell – used to detect the bear's prey
- bumps on the pads of the paws to provide grip on the ice
- short, powerful claws, which also provide grip, and are needed for holding the heavy prey.

DID YOU KNOW?

Polar bear fur appears to be white, but in fact the individual hairs are actually transparent. The white colour results from light being refracted through the clear hair strands.

The polar bear is thought to have evolved from a smaller species, the brown bear, about 150,000 years ago. How did it evolve its adaptations for life in the Arctic? Let's consider just one of the adaptations, the thick white fur.

There are two main selection pressures in favour of thick white fur. The first is the need for insulation to reduce heat loss. The polar bear often has to survive temperatures of –30°C, and temperatures in the Arctic can fall as low as –70°C. The second is camouflage; white fur camouflages the animal against the snow so that it can approach its prey unseen and then attack it.

Among the brown bears that were the ancestors of the polar bear there would have been variations in fur length and colour. When some of these bears came to live in colder, more northerly habitats, those individuals with longer and paler fur would have had a selective advantage over others with shorter, darker fur. Any gene mutations that produced long, pale fur increased this advantage. Bears with these genes were less likely to die from the cold, or from lack of food. As a result, well-adapted bears were more likely to reproduce and pass on their genes. Over many thousands of years more mutations and selection for long, white fur produced the adaptation we see in the polar bear today. The same process of natural selection is thought to have happened to bring about the other adaptations shown by the polar bear.

CAN WE OBSERVE NATURAL SELECTION IN ACTION?

Most animals and plants reproduce slowly, so it takes a long time for natural selection to have an observable effect. To observe natural selection happening we can study organisms that reproduce quickly, such as bacteria or insects.

ANTIBIOTIC RESISTANCE IN BACTERIA

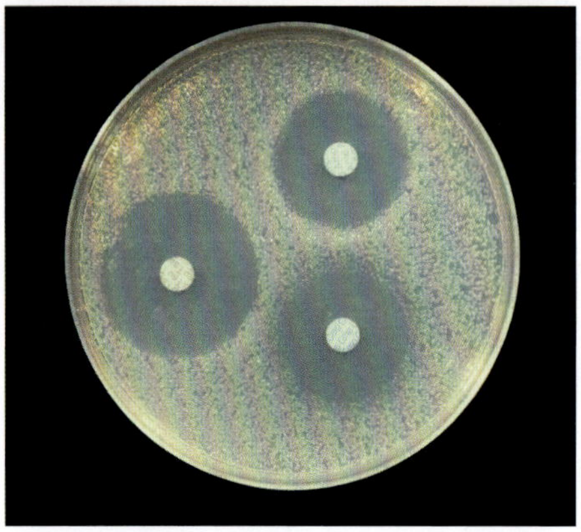

▲ Figure 19.6 This photo shows a colony of bacteria growing on a petri dish of nutrient agar. The circular discs contain different antibiotics. The discs have clear areas around them, where the bacteria have been killed by the antibiotic diffusing out from the discs.

Antibiotics are chemicals that kill or reduce the growth of microorganisms (Figure 19.6). They are used in medicine mainly to treat bacterial infections, although a few antibiotics are effective against fungal pathogens. Antibiotics do not work on viruses, so they are no use in treating any disease caused by a virus.

Natural antibiotics are produced by bacteria and fungi. They give a microorganism an advantage over other microorganisms when competing for nutrients and other resources, since the antibiotic kills the competing organisms.

Alexander Fleming discovered the first antibiotic in 1929. It is made by the mould *Penicillium*, and is called **penicillin**. Penicillin kills bacteria, and was first used to treat bacterial infections in the 1940s. Since then other natural antibiotics have been discovered, and many more have been chemically synthesised in laboratories. The use of antibiotics has increased dramatically, particularly over the last 20 years. We now almost expect to be given an antibiotic for even the most minor of ailments. This can be dangerous, as it leads to the development of bacterial resistance to antibiotics, so that the antibiotics are no longer effective in preventing bacterial infection.

DID YOU KNOW?

A particularly worrying example of a resistant bacterium is MRSA. MRSA stands for methicillin-resistant *Staphylococcus aureus*. It is sometimes called a 'super bug' because it is resistant to many antibiotics including methicillin (a type of penicillin). It is a particular problem in hospitals where it is responsible for many difficult-to-treat infections.

Resistance starts when a random mutation gives a bacterium resistance to a particular antibiotic. In a situation where the antibiotic is widely used, the new resistant bacterium has an advantage over non-resistant bacteria of the same type. The resistant strain of bacterium will survive and multiply in greater numbers than the non-resistant type. Bacteria reproduce very quickly – the generation time of a bacterium (the time it takes to divide into two daughter cells) can be as short as 20 minutes. This means that there could be 72 generations in a single day, producing a population of millions of resistant bacteria.

Resistant bacteria will not be killed by the antibiotic, meaning the antibiotic is no longer effective in controlling the disease.

Bacterial resistance to antibiotics was first noticed in hospitals in the 1950s, and has grown to be a major problem today. The resistant bacteria have a selective advantage over non-resistant bacteria – they are 'fitter'. In effect, the bacteria have evolved as a result of natural selection.

Doctors are now more reluctant to prescribe antibiotics. They know that by using them less, the bacteria with resistance have less of an advantage and will not become as widespread.

HINT

Some people talk about bacteria becoming *immune* to antibiotics. This is a misunderstanding. Immunity happens in people – we become immune to microorganisms that infect us, as a result of the immune response.

Bacteria become *resistant* to antibiotics.

PESTICIDE RESISTANCE IN INSECTS

Just as pathogenic bacteria can become resistant to antibiotics, insect pests can develop resistance to insecticides. The powerful insecticide DDT was first used in the 1940s (see Chapter 15). By the 1950s many species of insect (e.g. mosquitoes) appeared to be resistant to DDT. The resistant insects had developed a gene mutation that stopped them being killed by the insecticide.

While DDT continued to be used, the resistant insects had a selective advantage over the non-resistant ones. They survived to breed, so that with each generation the numbers of resistant insects in the population increased.

The same thing has happened with modern insecticides. There are now hundreds of examples of insect pests that have developed resistance to different insecticides.

SELECTIVE BREEDING

About 12 000 years ago, the human way of life changed significantly. Humans began to grow plants and keep animals for milk and meat. They became farmers rather than hunters. This change first took place in the Middle East. Similar changes took place a little later in the Americas (where potatoes and maize were being grown) and in the Far East (where rice was first cultivated).

In the Middle East, humans first grew the cereal plants wheat and barley, and kept sheep and goats. Later, their livestock included cattle and pigs. Cultivating crops and keeping stock animals made it possible for permanent settlements to appear – life in villages began. Because of the more certain food supply, there was spare time, for the first time ever, for some people to do things other than hunt for food.

Ever since the cultivation of the first wheat and barley and the domestication of the first stock animals, humans have tried to obtain bigger yields from them. They cross-bred different maize plants (and barley plants) to obtain strains that produced more grain. They bred sheep and goats to give more milk and meat – selective breeding had begun. Today, animals and plants are bred for more than just food. For example, animals are used to produce a range of medicines and for research into the action of drugs.

Selective breeding is best described as the breeding of only those individuals with desirable features. It is sometimes called '**artificial selection**', as human choice, rather than environmental factors, is providing the selection pressure (compare this with natural selection, described above).

The methods used today for selective breeding are very different from those used only 50 years ago. Modern gene technology makes it possible to create a new strain of plant within weeks, rather than years.

TRADITIONAL SELECTIVE BREEDING

PLANTS

Traditionally, farmers have bred crop plants of all kinds to obtain increased yields. Probably the earliest example of selective breeding was the cross-breeding of strains of wild wheat. The aim was to produce wheat with a much increased yield of grain and with shorter, stronger stems (Figure 19.7). This wheat was used to make bread.

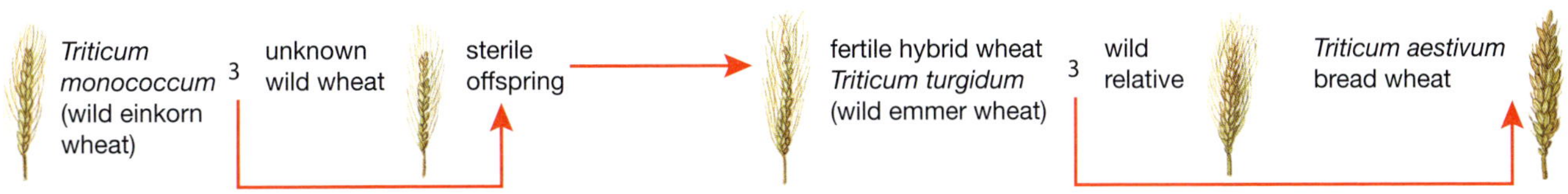

1 About 11 000 years ago, two strains of wild wheat were cultivated by farmers. Initially, all attempts at cross-breeding to produce wheats with a better yield gave only sterile offspring.

2 About 8000 years ago, a fertile hybrid wheat appeared from these two wild wheats. This was called emmer wheat and had a much higher yield than either of the original wheats.

3 The emmer wheat was cross-bred with another wild wheat to produce wheat very similar to the wheats used today to make bread. This new wheat had an even bigger yield and was much easier to 'process' to make flour.

▲ Figure 19.7 Modern wheat is the result of selective breeding by early farmers.

DID YOU KNOW?

The production of modern bread wheats by selective breeding is probably one of the earliest examples of producing genetically modified food. Each original wild wheat species had 14 chromosomes per cell. The wild emmer hybrid had 28 chromosomes per cell. Modern bread wheat has 42 chromosomes per cell. Selective breeding has modified the genetic make-up of wheat.

Other plants have been selectively bred for certain characteristics. *Brassica* is a genus of cabbage-like plants. One species of wild brassica (*Brassica olera*) was selectively bred to give several strains, each with specific features (see Figure 19.8). Some of the strains had large leaves, others had large flower heads, and others produced large buds.

▲ Figure 19.8 Selectively breeding the original wild brassica plants to enhance certain features has produced several familiar vegetables.

Selective breeding has produced many familiar vegetables. Besides the ones produced from *Brassica*, selective breeding of wild *Solanum* plants has produced the many strains of potatoes that are eaten today. Carrots and parsnips are also the result of selective breeding programmes. Crop plants are bred to produce strains that:

- give higher yields
- are resistant to certain diseases (the diseases would reduce the yields)
- are resistant to certain insect pest damage (the damage would reduce the yield)
- are hardier (so that they survive in harsher climates or are productive for longer periods of the year)
- have a better balance of nutrients in the crop (for example, plants that contain more of the types of amino acids needed by humans).

DID YOU KNOW?
Plant breeders do not just breed plants for food. Nearly all garden flowers are the result of selective breeding. Breeders have selected flowers to have a particular size, shape, colour and fragrance. Roses and orchids are among the most selectively bred of our garden plants.

Figure 19.9 shows a field of potato plants. Some have been bred to be resistant to insect pests, while others were not selectively bred in this way.

▲ Figure 19.9 Selective breeding can reduce damage by pests. The plants on the right have been bred to be resistant to a fungal pest. Plants on the left are not resistant to the pest.

ANIMALS

Farmers have bred stock animals for similar reasons to the breeding of crops. They have selected for animals that:

- produce more meat, milk or eggs
- produce more fur or better quality fur
- produce more offspring
- show increased resistance to diseases and parasites.

Again, like crop breeding, breeding animals for increased productivity has been practised for thousands of years. A stone tablet found in Iran appears to record the results of breeding domesticated donkeys. It was dated at over 5000 years old.

For many thousands of years, the only way to improve livestock was to mate a male and a female with the features that were desired in the offspring. In cattle, milk yield is an important factor and so high-yielding cows would be bred with bulls from other high-yielding cows.

Since about 1950, the technique of **artificial insemination** (**AI**) has become widely available. Bulls with many desirable features are kept and semen is obtained from them. The semen is diluted, frozen and stored. Farmers can buy quantities of this semen to inseminate their cows. the semen is transferred into the cow's uterus using a syringe. AI makes it possible for the semen from one prize bull to be used to fertilise many thousands of cows.

Modern sheep are domesticated wild sheep, and cows have been derived from wild aurochs. Just think of all the varieties of dogs that now exist. All these have been derived from one ancestral type. This original 'dog' was a domesticated wolf (Figure 19.10). In domesticating the wolf, humans gained an animal that was capable of herding stock animals. The sheepdog has all the same instincts as the wolf except the instinct to kill. This has been selectively 'bred out'.

▲ Figure 19.10 The many different breeds of dog all originate from a common ancestor – the wolf.

CHAPTER QUESTIONS

More questions on natural selection, evolution and selective breeding can be found at the end of Unit 5 on page 234.

SKILLS CRITICAL THINKING

1 Which of the following statements is/are correct?

1. Antibiotics are made by bacteria
2. Antibiotics kill bacteria
3. Antibiotics do not work on viruses

A 1 and 2 **B** 2 only
C 2 and 3 **D** 1, 2 and 3

2 Which of the following best describes the meaning of biological 'fitness'

A a measure of an organism's ability to survive in different habitats
B a measure of the reproductive success of an organism
C a measure of the relative health of an organism
D a measure of the strength of an organism

3 What is the source of genetic variation?

A mutations
B mitosis
C selection pressures
D changes in the environment

4 Why is natural selection easy to observe in bacteria?

A they are very small
B they can be killed by antibiotics
C they are composed of simple cells
D they reproduce very quickly

5 Which of the following is another term for selective breeding?

A cloning **B** natural selection
C artificial insemination **D** artificial selection

SKILLS CRITICAL THINKING

7th

6 Which of the following best describes artificial insemination?

A transplanting an embryo in the uterus

B taking sperm and placing it directly in the uterus

C selectively breeding healthy animals

D fertilisation of an egg in a test tube

7 a What does the term 'survival of the fittest' mean?

4th

b Which two biologists arrived at the same idea concerning the 'survival of the fittest' at the same time?

5th

8 Antibiotics are chemicals that are used to kill pathogens.

a What is a pathogen?

b Name two types of organism that make natural antibiotics.

SKILLS REASONING

9th

c Some antibiotics are no longer effective in killing pathogens. Use your understanding of natural selection to explain why.

9 Warfarin is a pesticide that was developed to kill rats. When it was first used in 1950, it was very effective. Some rats, however, had a mutant allele that made them resistant to warfarin. Nowadays the pesticide is much less effective.

a Use the ideas of natural selection to explain why warfarin is much less effective than it used to be.

10th

b Suggest what might happen to the number of rats carrying the allele for warfarin resistance, if warfarin were no longer used. Explain your answer.

SKILLS ANALYSIS

7th

10 In the Galapagos Islands, Charles Darwin identified a number of species of birds, now known as Darwin's finches. He found evidence to suggest that they had all evolved from one ancestral type, which had colonised the islands from South America. The main differences between the finches were their beaks. The diagram shows some of the beak types and that of the likely ancestral finch.

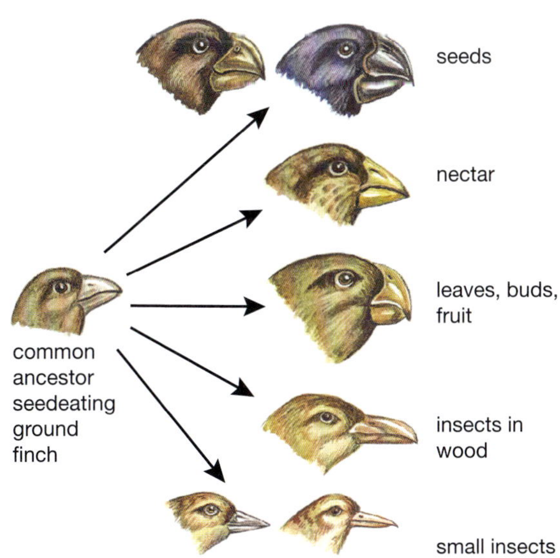

a Explain how the seed-eating finches are adapted to their environment.

b Explain how the finches that eat insects and live in woodland are adapted to their environment.

SKILLS REASONING

9th

c Use the information in the diagram to help you explain how the common ancestor could have evolved into the different type of finches.

SKILLS CRITICAL THINKING 8th

11 Read the description below and answer the questions that follow.

Natural selection happens when a selection pressure favours individuals with particular characteristics, so that they have a selective advantage.

Some plants growing in areas contaminated by waste from mines have developed a tolerance to toxic metals such as lead and copper. They are able to grow on polluted soil, while non-tolerant plants are killed by the metals in the soil.

a How did the new tolerant varieties of plants arise?

9th

b With reference to this example, explain the terms

i selection pressure

ii selective advantage

iii natural selection

SKILLS REASONING 10th

c When metal-tolerant plants are grown on uncontaminated soil, they are out-competed by non-tolerant plants. Suggest a reason for this.

SKILLS CRITICAL THINKING 8th

12 a How is selective breeding similar to natural selection?

b How is selective breeding different from natural selection?

SKILLS ANALYSIS 7th

13 The diagram shows some of the features of a cow that might be used as a basis for a breeding programme.

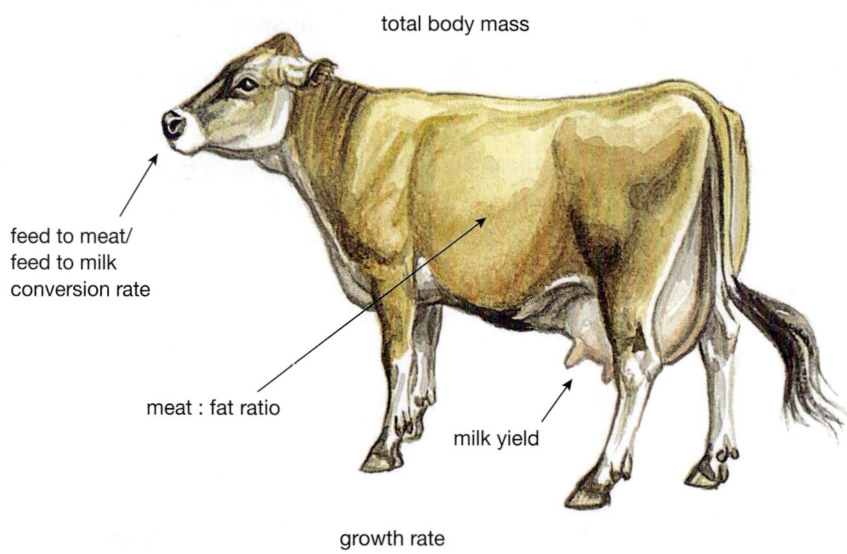

a Which features would you consider important in a breeding programme for dairy cattle?

SKILLS REASONING 8th

b Assume that you had all the techniques of modern selective breeding available to you. Describe how you would set about producing a herd of high-yielding beef cattle.

SKILLS ANALYSIS

9th

14 The diagram shows the results of a breeding programme to improve the yield of maize (sweetcorn).

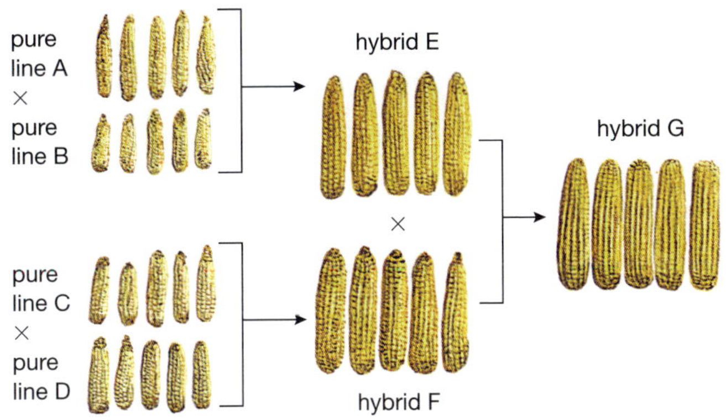

a Describe the breeding procedure used to produce hybrid G.

6th

b Describe three differences between the corn cobs of hybrid G and those of C.

SKILLS REASONING

9th

c How could you show that the differences between hybrid G and hybrid C are genetic?

SKILLS INTRAPERSONAL

15 Carry out some research and write an essay about the benefits and concerns of selective breeding of animals. You should write about one side of A4.

UNIT QUESTIONS

SKILLS REASONING 9th

1 For natural selection to operate, some factor has to exert a 'selection pressure'. In each of the following situations, identify both the selection pressure and the likely result of this selection pressure.

a Near old copper mines, the soil becomes polluted with copper ions that are toxic to most plants. **(2)**

b In the Serengeti of Africa, wildebeest are hunted by lions. **(2)**

c A farmer uses a pesticide to try to eliminate pests of a potato crop. **(2)**

(Total 6 marks)

SKILLS ANALYSIS

2 PTC (phenylthiocarbamide) is a chemical that to some people has a very bitter taste, while other people cannot taste it at all. The diagram shows the inheritance of PTC tasting in a family.

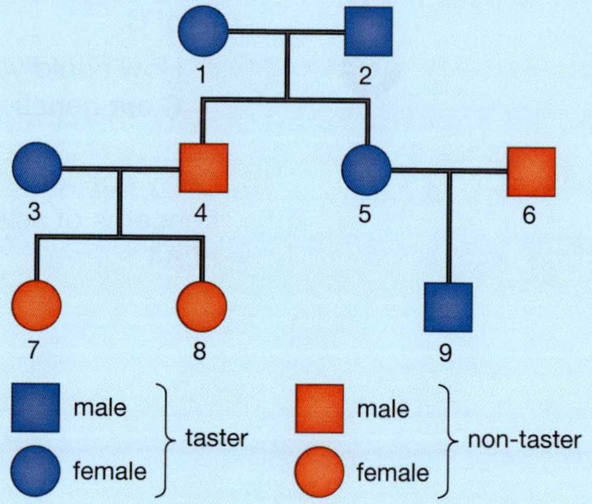

a What evidence in the diagram suggests that the allele for PTC tasting is dominant? **(2)**

SKILLS REASONING

b Using T to represent the tasting allele and t to represent the non-tasting allele, give the genotypes of individuals 3 and 7. Explain how you arrived at your answers. **(4)**

SKILLS ANALYSIS

c Why can we not be sure of the genotype of individual 5? **(2)**

SKILLS INTRPRETATION 10th

d If individuals 3 and 4 had another child, what is the chance that the child would be able to taste PTC? Construct a genetic diagram to show how you arrived at your answer. **(4)**

(Total 12 marks)

SKILLS ANALYSIS

7th

3 The diagrams A to F show an animal cell during cell division. The diploid number of this cell is eight.

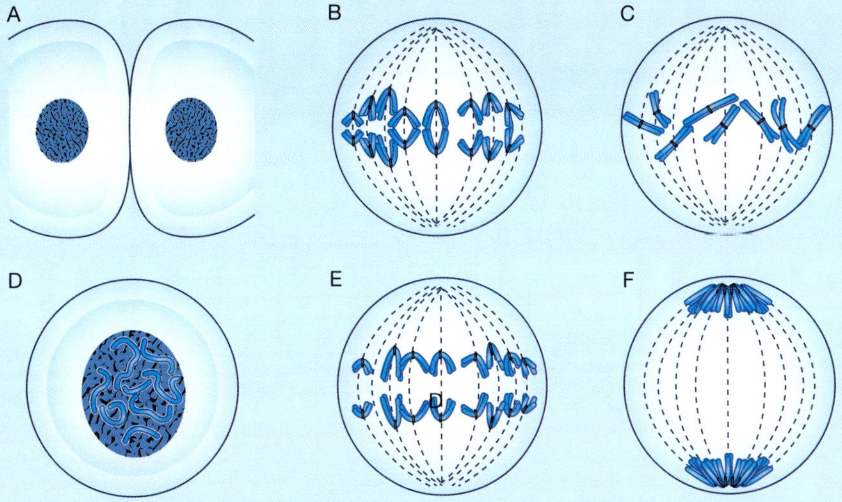

a Put the pictures in the correct order. **(2)**

8th

b Is the cell going through mitosis or meiosis? Explain your answer. **(2)**

SKILLS CRITIACL THINKING

6th

c What is the diploid number of a human cell? **(1)**

7th

d Describe two differences between mitosis and meiosis. **(2)**

(Total 7 marks)

BIOLOGY UNIT 6 MICROORGANISMS AND GENETIC MODIFICATION

You have seen how some microorganisms are essential decomposers in ecosystems and recycle nutrients, while others are pathogens, causing diseases of animals and plants. There are a few species of microorganisms that are grown by humans in order to make useful products. In this unit we look at this last group, and consider traditional and modern biotechnology. In addition, microorganisms are sometimes genetically engineered to produce new products. This is described in the final chapter, along with some examples of genetically modified plants and animals.

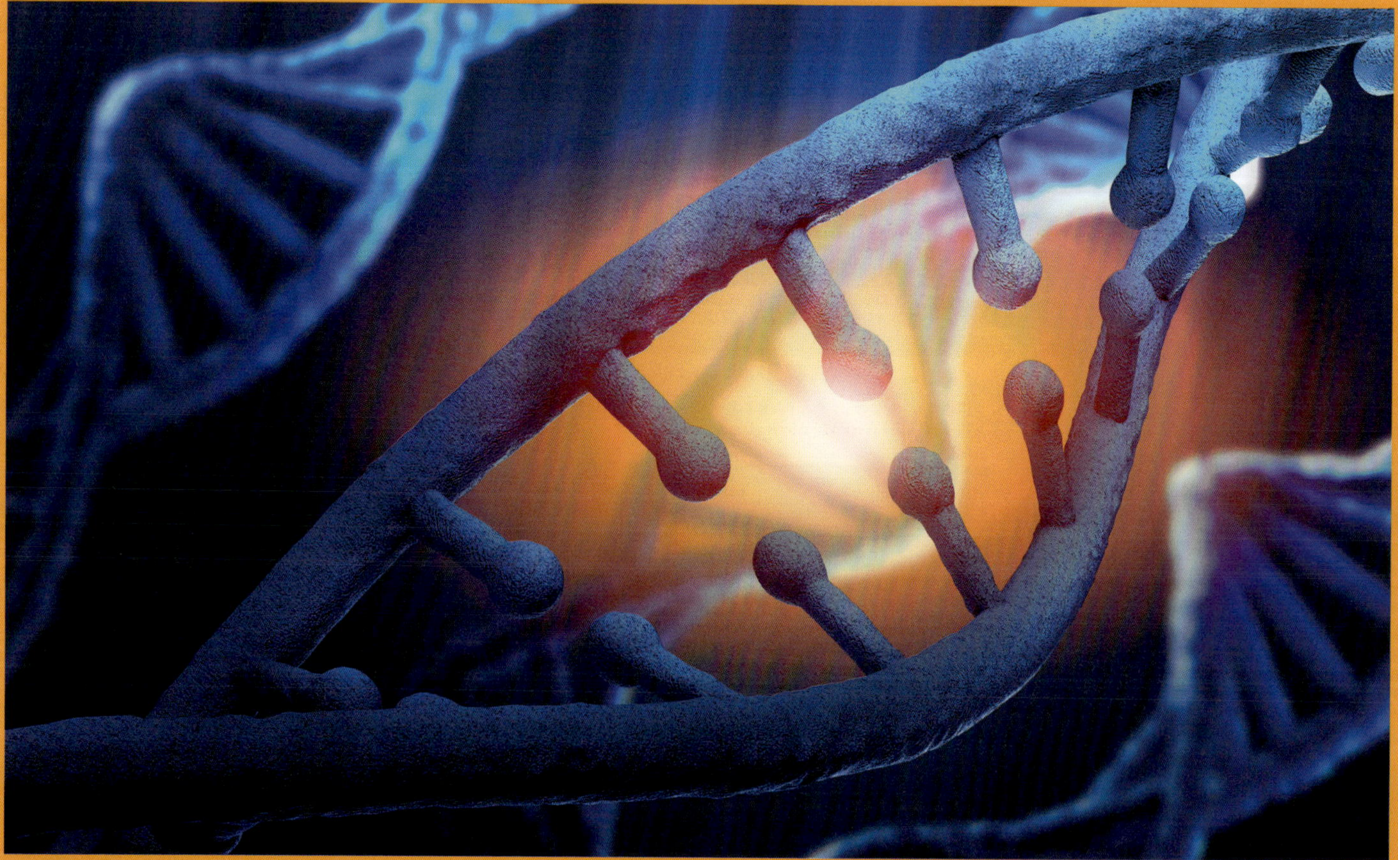

20 USING MICROORGANISMS

In this chapter we look at microorganisms that are grown in order to make products that are of use to humans.

LEARNING OBJECTIVES

- Understand the role of yeast in the production of food, including bread
- Investigate the rate of anaerobic respiration by yeast in different conditions
- Understand the role of bacteria (*Lactobacillus*) in the production of yoghurt
- Understand the use of an industrial fermenter and explain the need to provide suitable conditions for the growth of microorganisms in the fermenter, including aseptic precautions, nutrients, optimum temperature and pH, oxygenation, and agitation

WHAT ARE MICROORGANISMS?

Microorganisms are living things that you can only see with the help of a microscope. The 'bodies' of most microorganisms are made of a single cell, although sometimes millions of cells are gathered together to form a colony. The colony of cells may then be visible to the human eye.

Microorganisms have critical roles to play in recycling the waste products of organisms, as well as recycling the organisms themselves when they die. Many types of microorganisms are studied because they cause disease in animals and plants. On the other hand, humans have made use of the great reproductive capacity of microorganisms to make useful products, such as food, drink and medicines.

There are several groups that we call microorganisms, including protoctists, bacteria, viruses and some fungi (see Chapter 2).

Figure 20.1 shows a few examples of the many types of microorganisms.

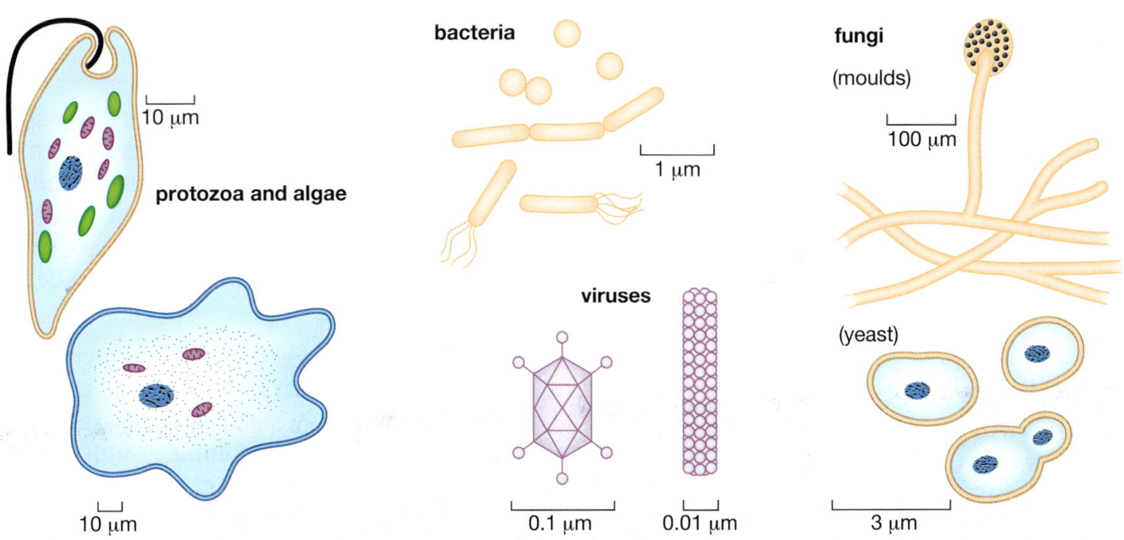

▲ Figure 20.1 Some examples of microorganisms. They are not drawn to the same scale. Notice the range of size, as shown by the scale bar alongside each organism. One micrometre (1 µm) is a millionth of a metre, or a thousandth of a millimetre.

FERMENTATION AND BIOTECHNOLOGY

Fermentation and **fermenters** are terms that you will encounter if you are involved in the growth of microorganisms. What do these words mean? Many microorganisms respire anaerobically (see Chapter 1), and originally, fermentation meant any anaerobic respiration process involving microorganisms, such as the fermentation of sugars by yeast. Nowadays, the word is used more generally to define other metabolic processes carried out by microorganisms, many of which are aerobic. Fermentation is normally used to make a useful product.

This overlaps with the definition of **biotechnology**, which means using any organisms (but mainly microbes) to make products that are useful to humans. Although the word itself is relatively new, humans have been using biotechnology processes for thousands of years without knowing it. Since ancient times, fermentation by yeast has been used to produce bread. Yoghurt is made by the action of bacteria on milk, and other bacteria and moulds are used in cheese manufacture.

Our ancestors used biotechnology to make products like these, but they did not understand *how* they were made and had no idea of the existence of microorganisms. Nowadays we understand what is happening when fermentation takes place, and can use biotechnology to produce not just foods but also a huge range of products, from medicines like penicillin to chemicals such as enzymes and fuels.

Modern biotechnology also allows us to alter the genes of microorganisms so that they code for new products. This is called **genetic engineering**. It is a topic that you will read about in Chapter 21.

TRADITIONAL BIOTECHNOLOGY – MAKING FOOD AND DRINKS

When yeast cells are deprived of oxygen, they respire anaerobically, breaking sugar down into ethanol and carbon dioxide:

glucose → ethanol + carbon dioxide

This process has been used for thousands of years to make bread using a species of yeast called *Saccharomyces cerevisiae.*

MAKING ALCOHOLIC DRINKS

Wine is made by using yeast to ferment sugars in grape juice. Commercial wine production takes place in large containers called vats which prevent air reaching the wine and ensure conditions remain anaerobic. Homemade wine is produced in small-scale fermenters fitted with an 'airlock', which allows carbon dioxide to escape but prevents the entry of oxygen (Figure 20.2). The alcohol increases in concentration until it kills the yeast cells, at which point fermentation stops.

Beer is made from barley. Barley contains starch rather than sugars so the starch needs to be broken down first. This happens by allowing the barley seeds to germinate. When they start to germinate they produce the enzyme amylase, which breaks down starch into the sugar maltose. Amylase breaks down starch into the sugar maltose. Later, the maltose from the seeds is fermented by yeast in a large open vat (Figure 20.3).

▲ Figure 20.2 A small fermenter for producing homemade wine. The U-shaped tube at the top is a water-filled airlock that prevents oxygen entering the fermenter but allows carbon dioxide to escape.

▲ Figure 20.3 A froth forming on the surface of the beer as yeast ferments the sugar to alcohol and carbon dioxide. The carbon dioxide in the froth prevents oxygen entering the mixture from the air – keeping conditions anaerobic.

MAKING BREAD

Yeast is also used to make bread. Wheat flour and water are mixed together and yeast added, forming the bread dough. Enzymes from the original cereal grains break down starch to sugars, which are respired by the yeast. Extra sugar may be added at this stage. In bread-making, the yeast begins by respiring aerobically, producing water and carbon dioxide. The carbon dioxide makes the dough rise. When the air runs out, conditions become anaerobic, so the yeast begins to respire anaerobically making ethanol and more carbon dioxide.

Later, when the dough is baked in the oven, the gas bubbles expand. This gives the bread a light, cellular texture (Figure 20.4). Baking also kills the yeast cells and evaporates any ethanol from the fermentation.

a **b**

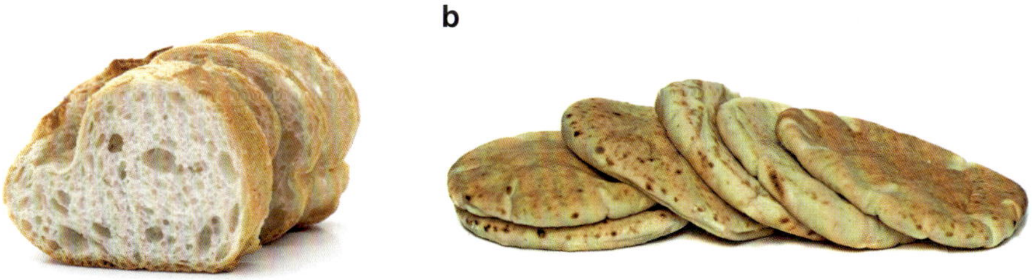

▲ Figure 20.4 (a) The 'holes' in this bread were produced by bubbles of carbon dioxide released from the respiration of the yeast. (b) Bread that is made without yeast is called unleavened bread. What is the difference in texture and appearance between leavened and unleavened bread?

Safety note: Wear eye protection and avoid skin contact with the indicator.

ACTIVITY 1

▼ PRACTICAL: INVESTIGATING THE RATE OF ANAEROBIC RESPIRATION IN YEAST

Some simple apparatus and materials can be used to investigate the rate of anaerobic respiration in yeast.

A small amount of water is gently boiled in a boiling tube to remove any air that is dissolved in the water. The water is allowed to cool, and a small amount of sugar (glucose or sucrose) is dissolved in the water. Finally, a little yeast is added and the mixture is stirred.

The apparatus is set up as shown in Figure 20.5.

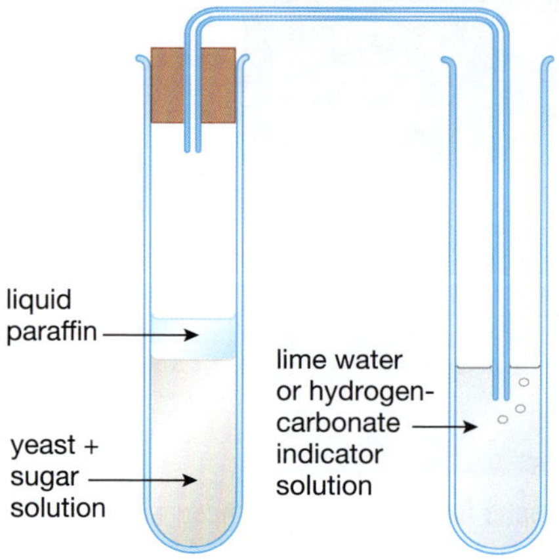

▲ Figure 20.5 Apparatus to test for carbon dioxide produced by anaerobic respiration in yeast.

A thin layer of liquid paraffin is added to the surface of the mixture, using a pipette. The boiled water ensures that there is no oxygen in the mixture, and the layer of paraffin stops any oxygen diffusing in from the air. A control apparatus is set up. This is exactly the same as that shown in Figure 20.5, except that boiled (killed) yeast is used instead of living yeast.

Both sets of apparatus are left in a warm place for an hour or two. The mixture with living yeast will be seen to produce gas bubbles. The gas passes through the delivery tube and into the indicator in the second boiling tube.

If this tube contains limewater, it will turn cloudy (milky). If it contains hydrogen carbonate indicator, the indicator will change from orange to yellow. This shows that the gas is carbon dioxide. The time taken for the indicator to change colour is recorded and compared with the control (which will not change).

(If the bung is taken out of the first boiling tube and the liquid paraffin removed using a pipette, the tube will smell of alcohol.)

This method can be used to test predictions, such as:

- the type of sugar (glucose, sucrose, maltose etc.) affects the rate of respiration of the yeast
- the concentration of sugar affects the rate of respiration of the yeast
- how temperature affects the rate of respiration of the yeast.

The rate can be found by timing how quickly the indicator changes colour, or from the rate of production of bubbles of carbon dioxide. You could plan experiments to test these hypotheses.

MAKING YOGHURT

Yoghurt is milk that has been fermented by certain species of bacteria, called **lactic acid bacteria**. The effect of the fermentation is to turn the liquid milk into a semi-solid food with a sour taste.

To make yoghurt, milk is first pasteurised at 85–95 °C for 15–30 minutes, to kill any natural bacteria that it contains, then homogenised to disperse the fat globules. The milk is then cooled to 40–45 °C and inoculated with a starter culture of two species of bacteria, called *Lactobacillus* and *Streptococcus*.

DID YOU KNOW?
Different species of *Lactobacillus* and *Streptococcus* bacteria are also used in the production of cheese.

DID YOU KNOW?
The process called pasteurisation is named after the famous French microbiologist, Louis Pasteur. He was trying to find a way to kill the bacteria in beverages that caused them to go sour. In 1864 Pasteur discovered that short periods of heating killed most of the bacteria responsible for this 'spoilage', without affecting the quality. Today, pasteurisation is used to treat many products, such as milk, fruit juices and canned food.

These bacteria produce lactic acid, as well as starting to digest the milk proteins. The culture is kept at this temperature for several hours while the pH falls to about 4.4 (these are the optimum conditions for the bacteria). The mixture coagulates (thickens) as the drop in pH causes the milk proteins to denature and turn into semi-solids.

When fermentation is finished, the yoghurt is stirred and cooled to 5 °C. Flavourings, colourants and fruit may then be added before it is packaged for sale.

The drop in pH (as the yoghurt forms) gradually reduces the reproduction of the lactic acid bacteria (although it doesn't kill them). It also helps to prevent the growth of other microorganisms, and so preserves the nutrients in the milk. The steps in yoghurt production are summarised in the flow chart (Figure 20.6).

Milk is pasteurised at 85–95 °C for 15–30 minutes.

↓

Milk is homogenised.

↓

Milk is cooled to 40–45 °C and inoculated with a starter culture of lactic acid bacteria.

↓

Mixture is incubated at this temperature for several hours, while bacteria digest milk proteins and ferment lactose to lactic acid.

↓

Thickened yoghurt is stirred and cooled to 5 °C.

↓

Flavourings, colorants and fruit may be added before packaging.

▲ Figure 20.6 Flow chart showing the stages in yoghurt production.

INDUSTRIAL FERMENTERS

A **fermenter** is any vessel that is used to grow microorganisms used for fermentation. Even a baking tray containing a ball of dough could be defined as a fermenter!

Industrial fermenters are large tanks that can hold up to 200 000 dm^3 of a liquid culture (Figure 20.7). They enable the environmental conditions such as temperature, oxygen and carbon dioxide concentrations, pH and nutrient supply to be carefully controlled so that the microorganisms will yield their product most efficiently. A simplified diagram of the inside of a fermenter is shown in Figure 20.8.

◀ Figure 20.7 An industrial fermenter holds hundreds of thousands of dm^3 of a liquid culture.

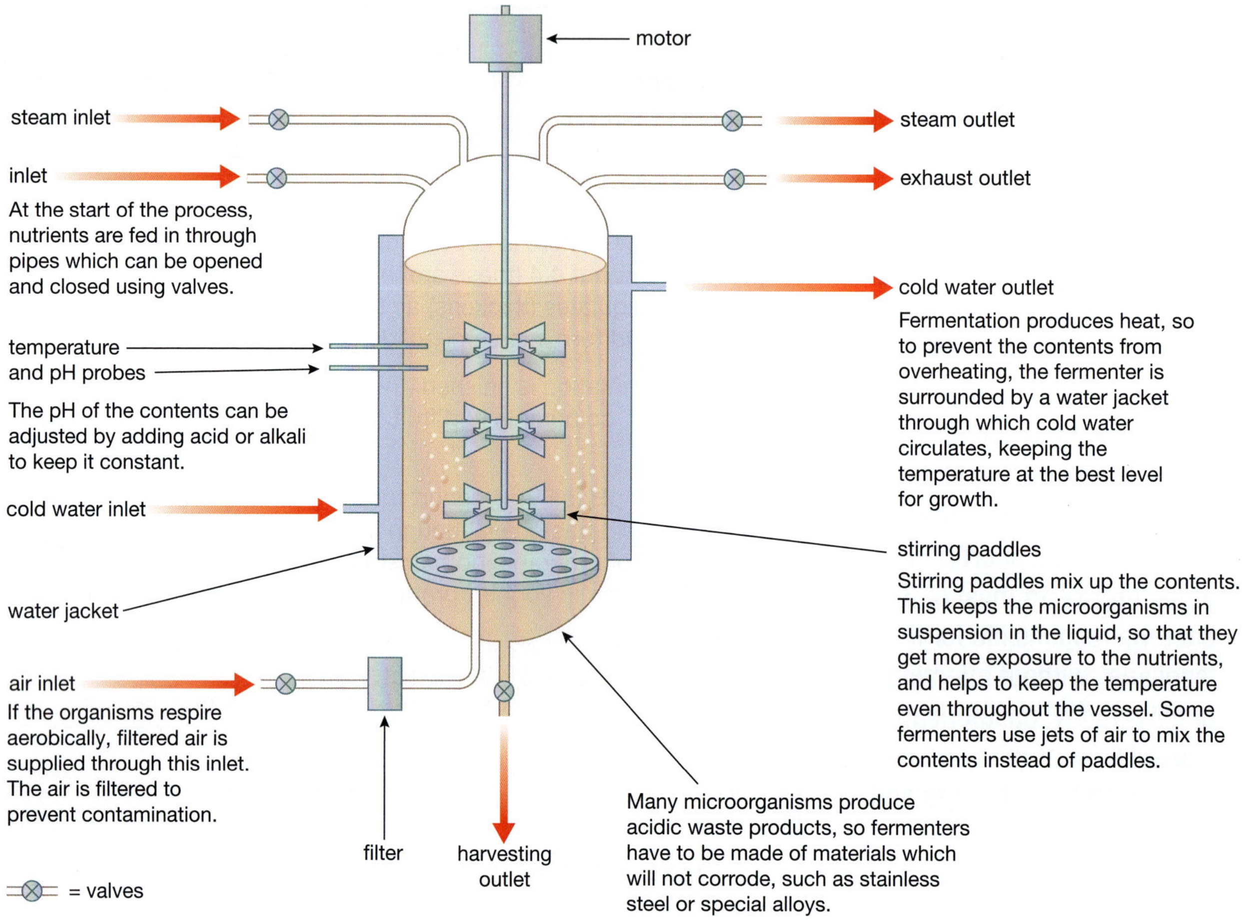

▲ Figure 20.8 An industrial fermenter. Fermenters like this are used to make many products, such as the antibiotic penicillin.

KEY POINT

Many microorganisms use an external food source from their growth medium to obtain energy. In doing this, they change substances in the medium. This is the modern meaning of fermentation. It is used by humans to make many important products. The use of microorganisms to make products useful to humans is called biotechnology.

When fermentation is completed, the products are collected through an outlet pipe. Before the fermenter is filled with new nutrients and culture, the inside of the tank and all the pipes must be cleaned and sterilised. This is usually done with very hot steam under high pressure.

If the inside of the fermenter and the new nutrients are not sterile, two problems are likely to develop. Firstly, any bacteria or fungi that manage to get in would compete with the organism in the culture, reducing the yield of product. Secondly, the product would become contaminated with waste products or cells of the 'foreign' organism. The methods used to prevent contamination by unwanted microorganisms such as filtering the air and sterilising the fermenter using steam, are known as 'aseptic precautions'.

CHAPTER QUESTIONS

More questions on growing useful organisms can be found at the end of Unit 6 on page 256.

SKILLS CRITICAL THINKING 6th

1 Which of the following is *not* normally controlled in an industrial fermenter?

A Temperature **B** Light intensity **C** pH **D** Oxygen

2 During the manufacture of yoghurt, the pH of the milk changes. What causes this change in pH?

A denaturing of the milk proteins

B pasteurisation of the milk

C the conversion of lactose into lactic acid

D yhe action of an enzyme in the milk

3 Yoghurt can be made at home by adding a small amount of old yoghurt to some fresh milk. What is present in the old yoghurt to cause this to happen?

A fat **B** sugar **C** protein **D** bacteria

4 The diagram shows an industrial fermenter which is used to grow the mould *Penicillium* to make the antibiotic penicillin.

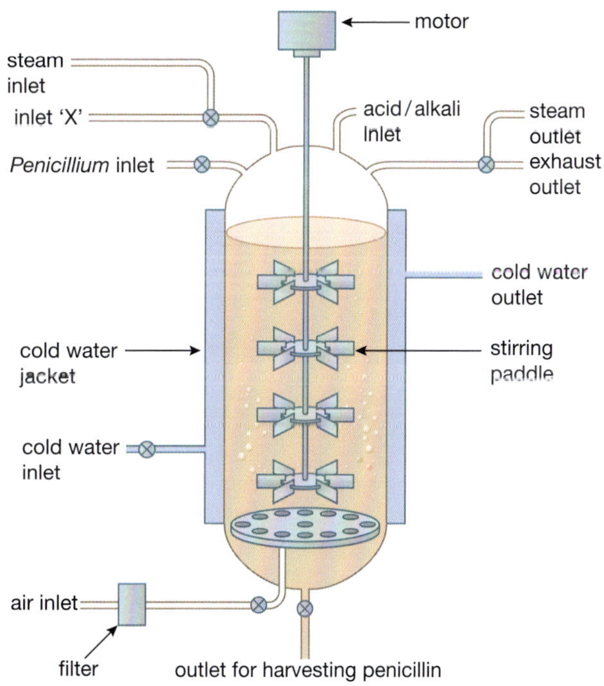

a Explain how the fermenter is sterilised before use.

SKILLS REASONING

b Why does air need to be pumped through the fermenter? Why is the air filtered?

SKILLS REASONING 6th

c Explain how a steady temperature is maintained in the fermenter.

d What is supplied through the inlet marked 'X'?

7th

e Suggest what would happen to the growth of *Penicillium* in the fermenter if the paddles stopped working.

SKILLS CRITICAL THINKING

5th

5 Answer these questions about making yoghurt. Try at first to answer them without looking back to the section on page 241.

a Why is the milk pasteurised at the start of the process?

b Why is the mixture of milk and bacteria incubated at 45 °C?

c What causes the milk to thicken?

d Why does fermentation eventually stop?

e Explain how making yoghurt is a way of preserving the nutrients from milk.

21 GENETIC MODIFICATION

In this chapter we will look at ways in which it is now possible to manipulate genes and produce genetically modified organisms – the science of 'genetic engineering'.

LEARNING OBJECTIVES

- Understand that the term 'transgenic' means the transfer of genetic material from one species to a different species
- Understand how restriction enzymes are used to cut DNA at specific sites and ligase enzymes are used to join pieces of DNA together
- Understand how plasmids and viruses can act as vectors, which take up pieces of DNA, and then insert this recombinant DNA into other cells
- Understand how large amounts of human insulin can be manufactured from genetically modified bacteria that are grown in a fermenter
- Understand how genetically modified plants can be used to improve food production

In Chapter 16 you saw that a gene is a section of a molecule of DNA that codes for the production of a protein. One strand of the DNA (called the coding strand) contains triplets of bases, each triplet coding for one amino acid. Different genes produce different proteins because each has a unique sequence of bases that codes for a unique sequence of amino acids (Figure 21.1).

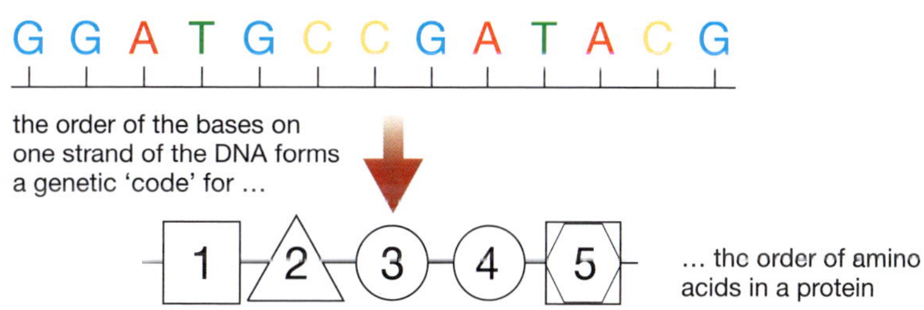

Figure 21.1 The role of DNA in protein synthesis

The protein that is produced could be:

- an enzyme that controls a particular reaction inside a cell or in the digestive system
- a structural protein like keratin in hair, collagen in skin or one of the many proteins found in the membranes of cells
- a protein hormone such as insulin
- a protein with a specific function such as haemoglobin or an **antibody**.

KEY POINT

A transgenic organism is one that contains a gene that has been introduced from another species. For example, some bacteria have had human genes transferred to them that allow them to make human insulin. Some sheep secrete the protein alpha-1-antitrypsin (AAT) in their milk because they have the human gene that directs the manufacture of this substance. Because they contain 'foreign' genes, they are no longer quite the same organisms. They are transgenic.

RECOMBINANT DNA

The production of **recombinant DNA** is the basis of genetic engineering. A section of DNA – a gene – is cut out of the DNA of one species and inserted into the DNA of another. This new DNA is called 'recombinant' DNA because the DNA from two different organisms has been 'recombined'. The organism that receives the gene from a different species is a **transgenic** organism.

The organism receiving the new gene now has an added capability. It will manufacture the protein that the new gene codes for. For example, a bacterium receiving the human gene that codes for insulin production will make human insulin. If these transgenic bacteria are cultured by the billion in a fermenter, they become a factory for making human insulin.

PRODUCING GENETICALLY MODIFIED (TRANSGENIC) BACTERIA

The breakthrough in being able to transfer DNA from cell to cell came when it was found that bacteria have two sorts of DNA – the DNA found in their bacterial 'chromosome' and much smaller circular pieces of DNA called **plasmids** (see Unit 1, Figure 2.10).

Bacteria naturally 'swap' plasmids, and biologists found ways of transferring plasmids from one bacterium to another. The next stage was to find molecular 'scissors' and a molecular 'glue' that could cut out genes from one molecule of DNA and stick them back into another. Further research found the following enzymes that were able to do this.

- **Restriction endonucleases** (usually shortened to **restriction enzymes**) are enzymes that cut DNA molecules at specific points. Different restriction enzymes cut DNA at different places. They can be used to cut out specific genes from a molecule of DNA.
- **Ligases** (or DNA ligases) are enzymes that join the cut ends of DNA molecules.

Each restriction enzyme recognises a certain base sequence in a DNA strand. Wherever it encounters that sequence, it will cut the DNA molecule. Suppose a restriction enzyme recognises the base sequence G-A-A-T-T-C. It will only cut the DNA molecule if it can 'see' the base sequence on both strands. Figure 21.3 illustrates this.

Some restriction enzymes make a straight cut and the fragments of DNA they produce are said to have 'blunt ends' (Figure 21.3(a)). Other restriction enzymes make a staggered cut. These produce fragments of DNA with overlapping ends with complementary bases. These overlapping ends are called 'sticky ends' because fragments of DNA with exposed bases are more easily joined by ligase enzymes (Figure 21.3(b)).

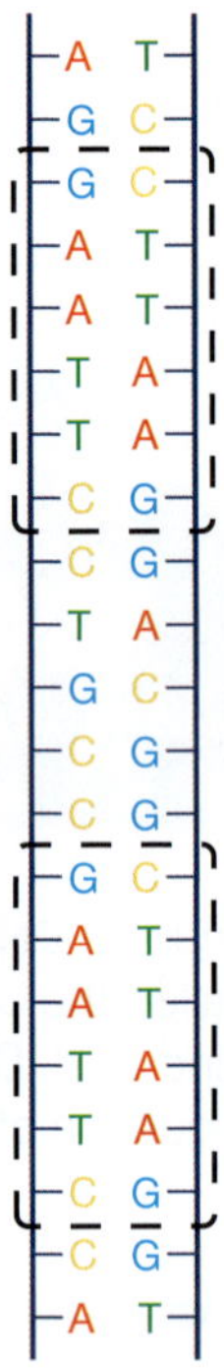

▲ Figure 21.2 Part of a DNA molecule containing the base sequence G-A-A-T-T-C. Notice that the sequence is present on both strands, but running in opposite directions.

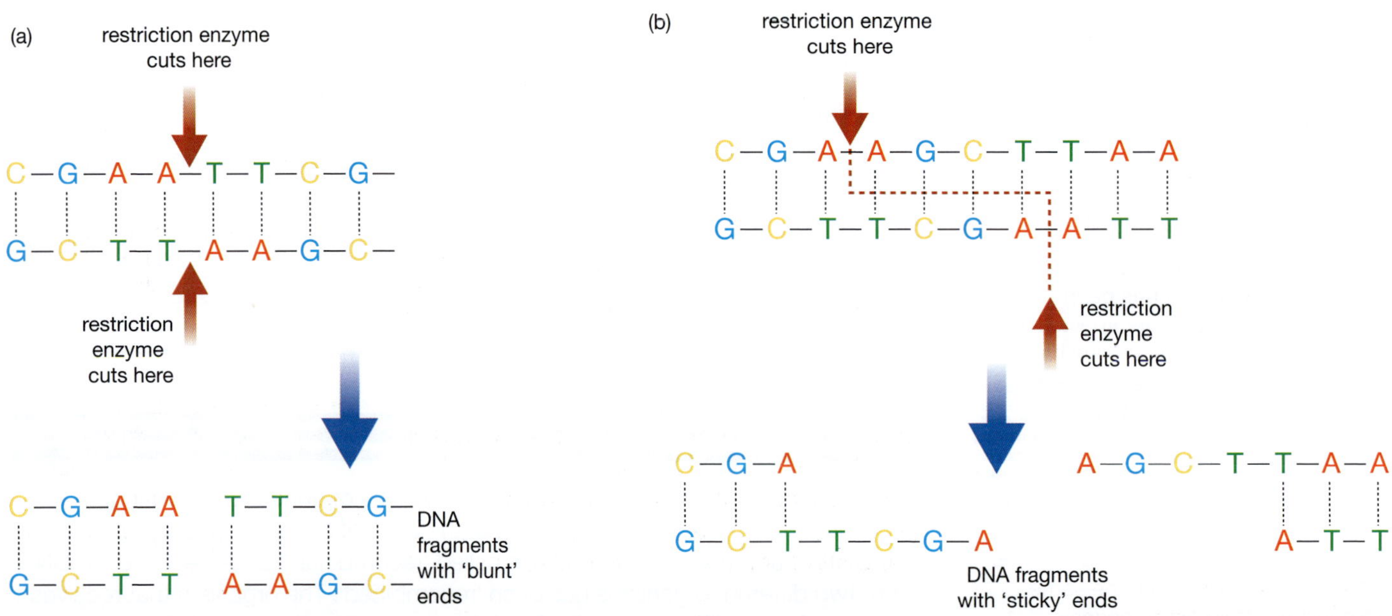

▲ Figure 21.3 How restriction enzymes cut DNA. (a) Forming blunt ends. (b) Forming sticky ends.

EXTENSION WORK

There is a lot more to producing recombinant DNA and transgenic bacteria than is shown here. You could carry out an some research to find out more about this topic.

Biologists now had a method of transferring a gene from any cell into a bacterium. They could insert the gene into a plasmid and then transfer the plasmid into a bacterium. The plasmid is called a **vector** because it is the means of transferring the gene. The main processes involved in producing a transgenic bacterium are shown in Figure 21.4.

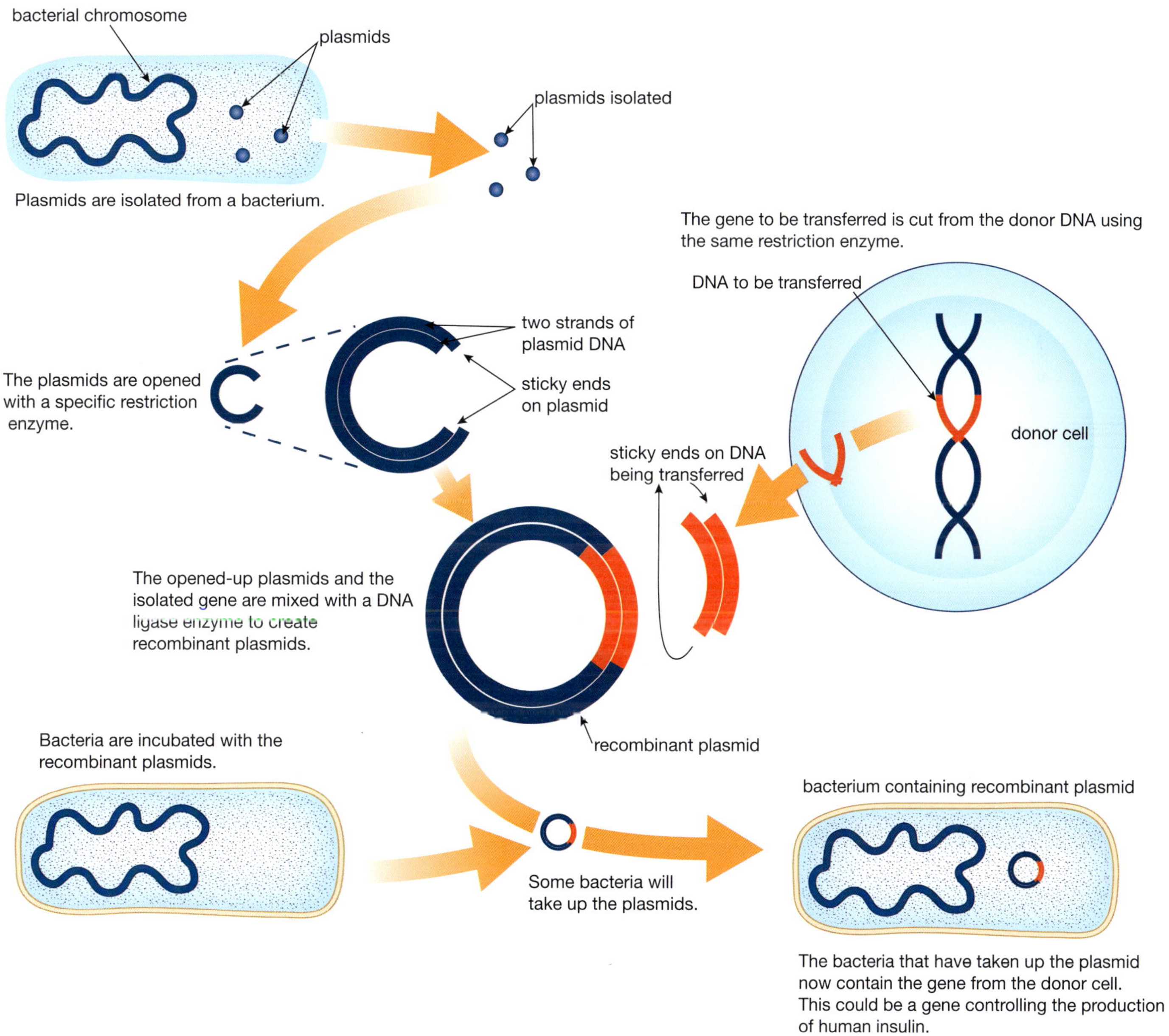

▲ Figure 21.4 Stages in producing a transgenic bacterium.

Another vector that has been used to introduce foreign DNA into bacterial cells is the **bacteriophage**. A bacteriophage, or 'phage', is a virus that attacks a bacterium. It does this by attaching to the cell wall of the bacterium and injecting its own DNA into the bacterial cell (Figure 21.5). This DNA becomes incorporated into the DNA of the host cell, and eventually causes the production of many virus particles.

If a foreign gene can be inserted into the DNA of the virus, the virus will inject it into the bacterium along with its own genes. Viruses were used as vectors in the early days of genetic modification, but most gene transfer is now carried out using plasmids.

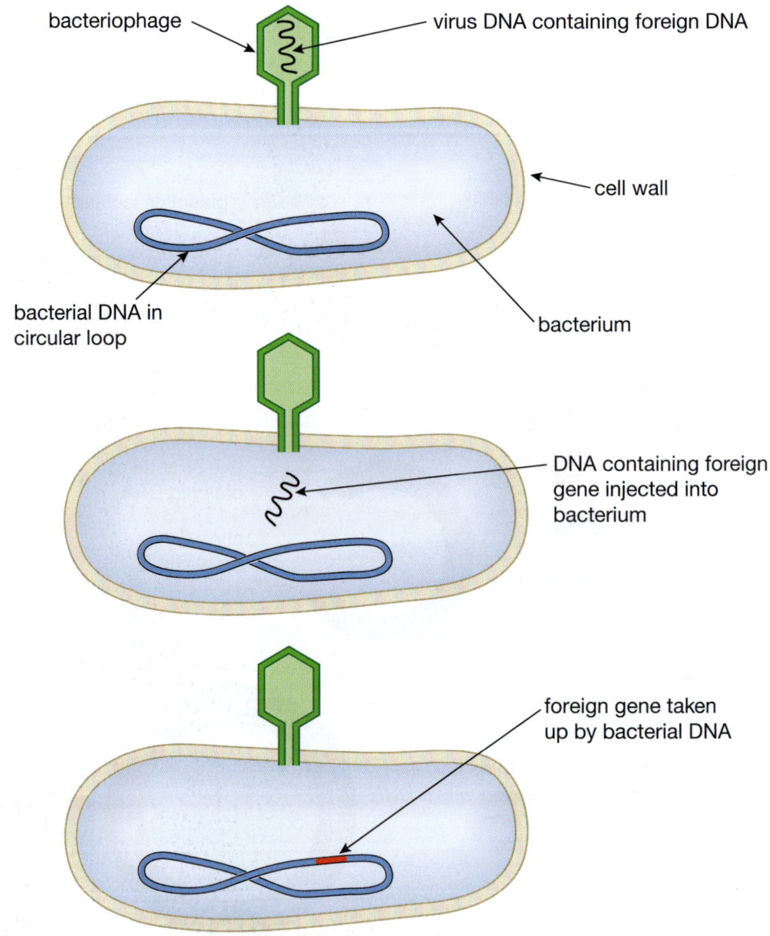

▲ Figure 21.5 A bacteriophage attacking a bacterial cell.

MAKING USE OF GENETICALLY MODIFIED BACTERIA

Different bacteria have been genetically modified to manufacture a range of products. Once they have been genetically modified, they are cultured in fermenters to produce large amounts of the product (see Chapter 20). Some examples are described below.

DID YOU KNOW?
More insulin is required every year because the number of diabetics increases worldwide each year and diabetics now have longer life spans.

1. **Human insulin** People suffering from diabetes need a reliable source of insulin. Before the use of genetic engineering to make human insulin, the only insulin available was extracted from the pancreases of other animals such as cattle or pigs. This is not quite the same as human insulin and does not give the same level of control of blood glucose levels.
2. **Enzymes for washing powders** Many stains on clothing are biological. Blood stains are largely proteins, grease marks are largely lipids. Enzymes can digest these large, insoluble molecules into smaller, soluble ones. These then dissolve in the water. Amylases digest starch, proteases digest proteins and lipases digest lipids. Bacteria have been genetically engineered to produce enzymes that work at higher temperatures, allowing even faster and more effective action.

3. **Enzymes in the food industry** One bacterial enzyme used in the food industry is glucose isomerase. This enzyme catalyses a reaction which converts glucose into a similar sugar called fructose. Fructose is much sweeter than glucose and so less is needed to sweeten foods. This has two advantages – it saves money (since less is used) and it means that the food contains less sugar and is healthier.

4. **Human growth hormone** The pituitary gland of some children does not produce enough of this hormone and they show a slow rate of growth. Injections of growth hormone from genetically modified bacteria restore normal growth patterns.

5. **Bovine somatotrophin** *(BST)* (a growth hormone in cattle) This hormone increases the milk yield of cows and increases the muscle (meat) production of bulls. Giving injections of BST to dairy cattle can increase the milk yield by up to 10 kg per day. To do this they need more food, but this increased cost is more than offset by the increased income from the increased milk yield (Table 21.1).

6. **Human vaccines** Bacteria have been genetically modified to produce the antigens of the hepatitis B virus. This is used in the vaccine against hepatitis B. The body makes antibodies against the antigens but there is no risk of contracting the actual disease from the **vaccination**.

DID YOU KNOW?
Before human growth hormone from genetically modified bacteria was available, the only source of the hormone was from human corpses. This was a rather gruesome procedure and had health risks. A number of children treated in this way developed Creutzfeld–Jacob disease (the human form of 'mad cow' disease). When this became apparent, the treatment was withdrawn.

Table 21.1 Effects of BST on milk yield.

	Feed / kg per day	Milk output / kg per day	Milk to feed ratio
without BST	34.1	27.9	0.82
with BST	37.8	37.3	0.99

Since the basic techniques of transferring genes were developed, many unicellular organisms have been genetically modified to produce useful products. Techniques for transferring genes into plants and animals have also been developed.

PRODUCING GENETICALLY MODIFIED PLANTS

The gene technology described so far can transfer DNA from one cell to another cell. In the case of bacteria, this is fine – a bacterium only has one cell. But plants have billions of cells and to genetically modify a plant, each cell must receive the new gene. So, any procedure for genetically modifying plants has two main stages:

- introducing the new gene or genes into plant cells
- producing whole plants from just a few cells.

Biologists initially had problems in inserting genes into plant cells. They then discovered a soil bacterium called *Agrobacterium*, which regularly inserts plasmids into plant cells. Now that a vector had been found, the rest became possible. Figure 21.6 outlines one procedure that uses *Agrobacterium* as a vector.

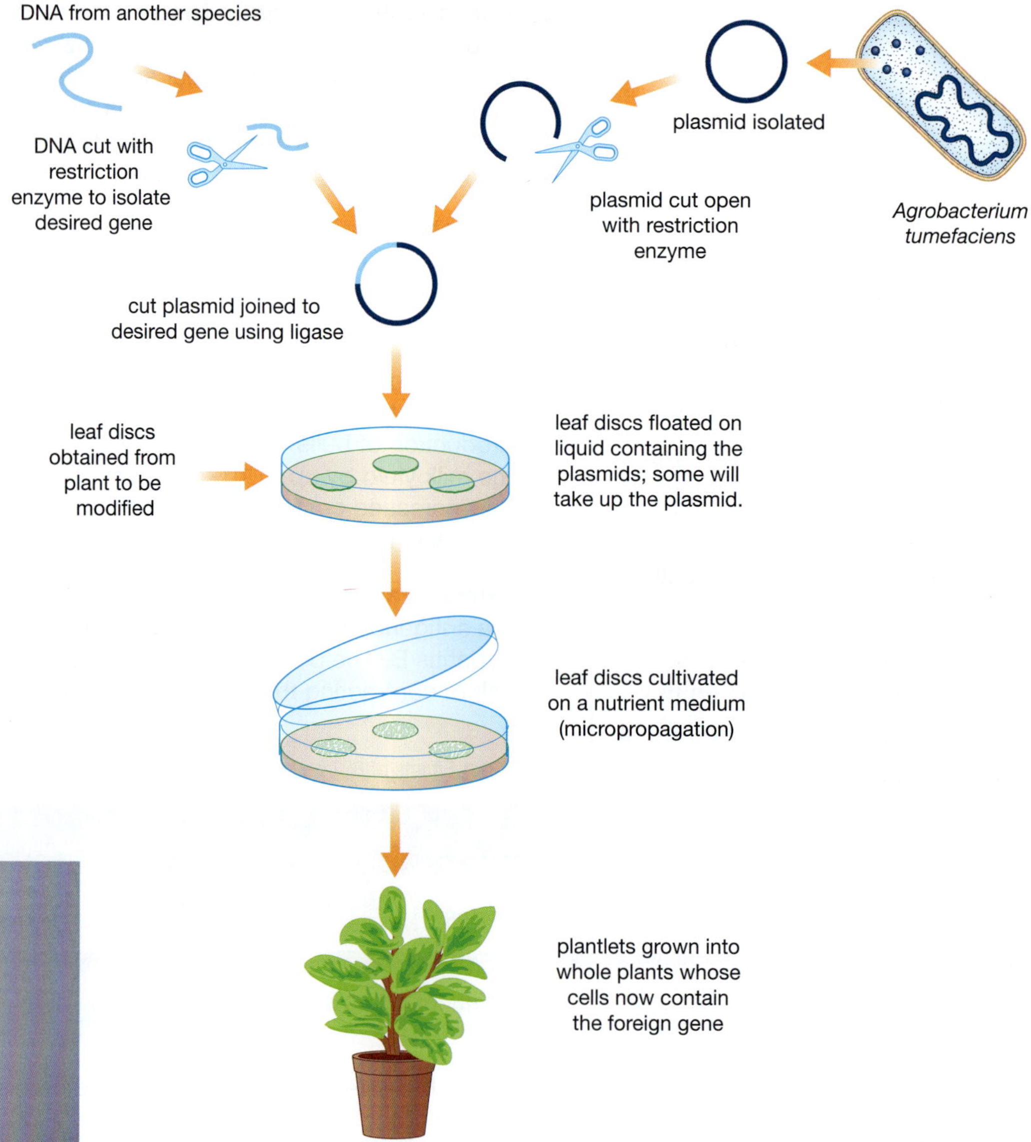

▲ Figure 21.6 Genetically modifying plants using *Agrobacterium*.

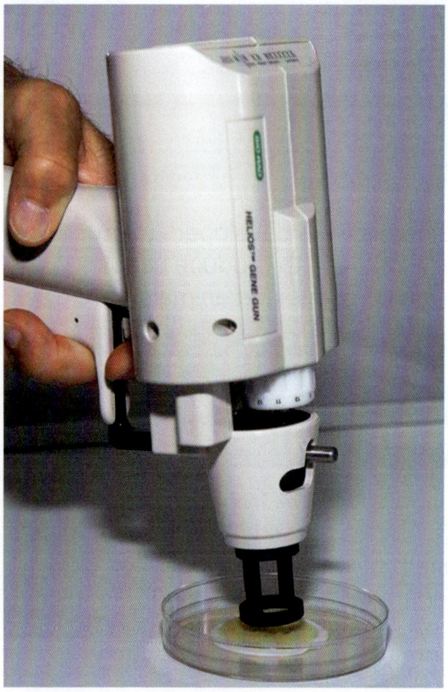

▲ Figure 21.7 A gene gun

This technique cannot be used on all plants. *Agrobacterium* will not infect cereals and so another technique was needed for these. The 'gene gun' was invented. This is, quite literally, a gun that fires a golden bullet (Figure 21.7). Tiny pellets of gold are coated with DNA that contains the desired gene. These are then 'fired' directly into plant tissue. Research has shown that if young, delicate tissue is used, there is a good uptake of the DNA. The genetically modified tissue can then be grown into new plants using the same **micropropagation** techniques as those used in the *Agrobacterium* procedure. The gene gun has made it possible to genetically modify many cereal plants as well as tobacco, carrot, soybean, apple, oilseed rape, cotton and many others. There is, however, much debate about the rights and wrongs of GM crops. You may like to carry out some further research on this topic.

MAKING USE OF GENETICALLY MODIFIED PLANTS

Large numbers of genetically modified plants are already available to plant growers and farmers.

Some fruit and vegetables have been engineered to have extended 'shelf lives' – they last longer before they start to go bad. Other crop plants have been modified to be resistant to herbicides (weedkillers). This allows farmers to spray herbicides at times when they will have maximum effect on the weeds, without affecting the crop plant.. There are concerns that this will encourage farmers to be less careful in their use of herbicides. In another example, genes from Arctic fish that code for an 'anti-freeze' in their blood have been transferred to some plants to make them frost resistant.

▲ Figure 21.8 Golden rice

The gene gun allowed biologists to produce genetically modified rice called 'golden rice' (Figure 21.8). This rice has three genes added to its normal DNA content. Two of these come from daffodils and one from a bacterium. Together, these genes allow the rice to make beta-carotene – the chemical that gives carrots their colour. It also colours the rice, hence the name 'golden rice'. More importantly, the beta-carotene is converted to vitamin A when eaten. This could save the eyesight of millions of children in less economically developed countries, who go blind because they do not have enough vitamin A in their diet.

EXTENSION WORK

Golden rice sounds like a good idea, but there have been several problems with it. Some people believe that there are ethical and environmental reasons why golden rice should not be grown and that it is better to provide other, natural crops containing enough beta-carotene. You could carry out some research into the advantages and disadvantages of golden rice.

Genetically modified plants are also helping humans to resist infection. Biologists have succeeded in modifying tobacco plants and soybeans to produce antibodies against a range of infectious diseases. If these can be produced on a large scale, they could be given to people who are failing to produce their own antibodies. Other modified tobacco plants produce the hepatitis B antigens that could be used as the basis for a vaccine. There is always a risk with a vaccine containing viruses that they may somehow become infectious again. This could not happen with a vaccine containing only plant-produced antigens.

KEY POINT

What if you could receive a 'vaccination' every time you ate a banana? Scientists are researching the possibility of transferring the genes that produce the antigens for certain diseases to bananas. If they succeed, then when you eat the banana, the antigens will stimulate an immune response. There will be no risk of you catching the disease – and no need to have needles stuck in you!

Besides the specific examples given, research into the genetic modification of plants provides, or hopes to provide, plants with:

- increased resistance to a range of pests and pathogens
- increased heat and drought tolerance
- increased salt tolerance
- a better balance of proteins, carbohydrates, lipids, vitamins and minerals.

In addition, some genetically modified oilseed rape plants will be used in large-scale production of biodegradable plastics and anti-coagulants.

One of the biggest achievements would be to modify crop plants like cereals and potatoes to allow nodules of nitrogen-fixing bacteria to form on their roots. At the moment only legumes (peas, beans and other plants with seeds in 'pods') can do this. Biologists know that the ability is genetically controlled. So far, they have not been able to transfer these genes to other plants. If they could, vast areas of infertile soil would be able to yield good crops of cereals without the need to use large quantities of fertilisers.

The bacteria in the **root nodules** would obtain nitrogen from the air in the soil and 'fix' it in a more usable form (usually ammonia). By doing this, they would make a supply of usable nitrogen available to the plants. The plants would convert this into plant protein and use the protein for growth. The cost of producing these crops would decrease dramatically.

PRODUCING GENETICALLY MODIFIED ANIMALS

Producing genetically modified animals presents some of the same problems as those connected with modifying plants. Animals, like plants, are multicellular. It is not enough simply to transfer a gene to a cell. That cell must then grow into a whole organism. The plasmid technology used to create

DID YOU KNOW?

'Xenotransplantation' means transplanting organs from other animals into humans. Transgenic pigs have been produced with genes that code for the main human 'marker antigens'. The cells of the pig's organs therefore have these human antigens on their surface and the organs would be less likely to be rejected by a recipient. If this became possible on a large scale, it could help to overcome the shortage of donor organs for transplantation. However, many people have ethical concerns about using animal organs for transplanting into humans.

genetically modified plants depends on the modified cells being grown into whole plants using micropropagation. No such micropropagation techniques exist for animals.

Scientists researching the production of genetically modified animals had to find other techniques. The most successful involves injecting DNA directly into a newly fertilised egg cell. This develops into an embryo, then an adult (Figure 21.9).

Research of this kind can produce beneficial results similar to those achieved by genetically modifying plants, such as:

- manufacture of human proteins, such as antibodies, blood clotting factors or alpha-1-antitrypsin (AAT) – see below
- increased production of a particular product, e.g. higher milk yield in cows, greater muscle mass in animals used for meat
- increased resistance to disease
- production of organs for transplantation (xenotransplantation).

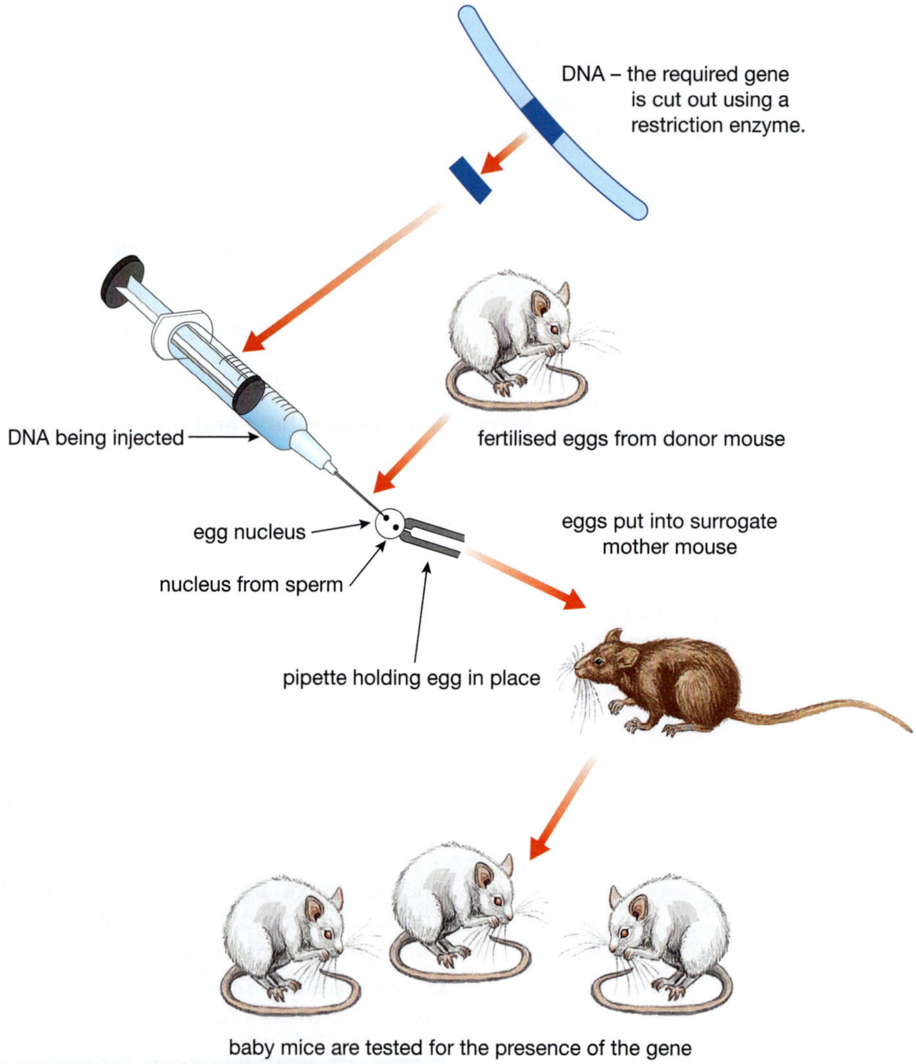

▲ Figure 21.9 The procedures used in producing genetically modified animals.

LOOKING AHEAD – THE POLYMERASE CHAIN REACTION

The polymerase chain reaction (PCR) is a laboratory process that amplifies DNA. This means that it rapidly produces a large number of copies of a piece of DNA, starting from as little as one molecule. The invention of PCR revolutionised gene technology and is used in virtually every application of the science.

Each cycle of PCR doubles the amount of DNA, producing an exponential increase in the numbers of copies (Figure 21.10). Thirty cycles produces over a billion copies of the original DNA.

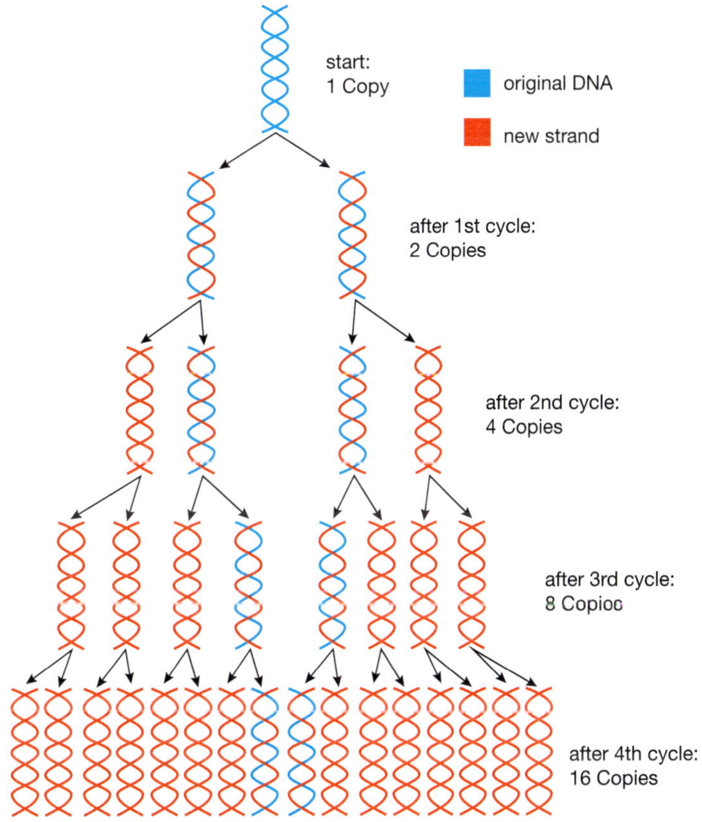

▲ Figure 21.10 PCR produces an exponential increase in the number of copies of a piece of DNA.

The procedure uses short lengths of single-stranded DNA called primers, which are precisely complementary to one end of each strand of the DNA you wish to amplify. The DNA is heated to separate the strands and the primers added to the ends of each strand. An enzyme called DNA polymerase builds up two new complimentary strands by adding nucleotides - one at a time - along each strand.

Nowadays, PCR is an automated process and can be performed in as little as 2–3 hours in a PCR machine. You just place small tubes containing the DNA sample, primers, free nucleotides, DNA polymerase and a buffer solution in the machine, switch on, and wait for the results.

CHAPTER QUESTIONS

More questions on gene technology can be found at the end of Unit 6 on page 256.

SKILLS CRITICAL THINKING

8th

1 Why is it relatively easy to genetically modify bacteria?

A they reproduce slowly and accurately

B they are able to take up plasmids

C they only contain a single chromosome

D they make restriction enzymes

9th

2 The statements below show some stages in the production of human insulin from genetically modified bacteria.

1. DNA for insulin inserted into plasmids
2. bacteria cloned
3. plasmids inserted into bacteria
4. DNA for insulin cut out using restriction enzyme

Which of the following shows the correct sequence of steps in the process?

A 2 → 1 → 4 → 3

B 4 → 2 → 3 → 1

C 4 → 1 → 3 → 2

D 2 → 3 → 4 → 1

8th

3 Which of the following genetically modified plants have not been produced yet?

A rice that is rich in beta-carotene to make vitamin A

B plants resistant to weedkiller

C plants containing an anti-freeze

D cereals with nitrogen-fixing bacteria in root nodules

4 Which of the following enzymes is used to join together pieces of DNA?

A ligase

B DNA polymerase

C protease

D restriction enzyme

SKILLS ANALYSIS 8th

5 The diagram shows the main stages in transferring the human insulin gene to a bacterium.

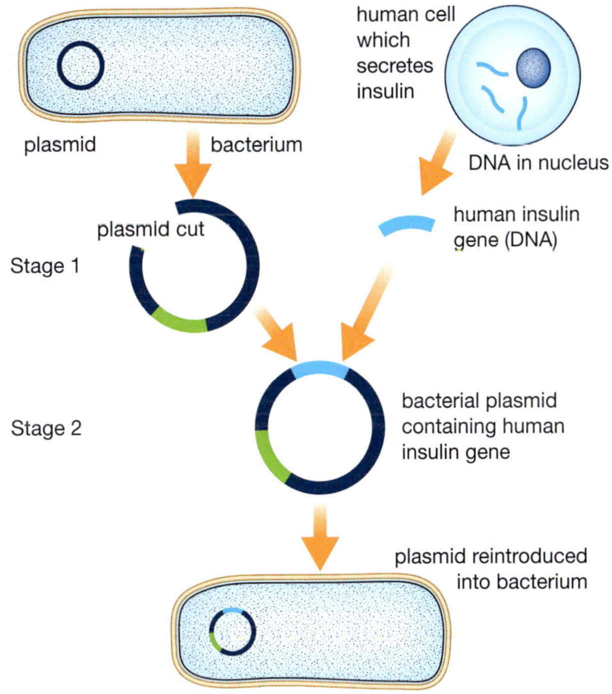

a Name the enzymes used at stages 1 and 2.

SKILLS CRITICAL THINKING

b What is the role of the plasmid in this procedure?

c How would the insulin-producing bacteria be used to produce significant amounts of insulin?

SKILLS REASONING 9th

d Why is the insulin produced this way preferred to insulin extracted from other animals?

SKILLS INTRAPERSONAL 12th

6 Carry out some research to find out more about the use of transgenic animals for organ transplantation. What are the arguments for and against its use? What are the ethical objections?

SKILLS CRITICAL THINKING 8th

7 Producing genetically modified plants and animals is more complex than producing genetically modified bacteria.

a Describe two ways in which genes can be introduced into plant cells.

b How are these genetically modified cells used to produce whole organisms?

c What sort of animal cell is genetically modified and then used to produce the whole organism?

SKILLS INTRAPERSONAL 12th

8 Write an essay about the importance of genetic engineering. In your essay you should make reference to:

a important potential benefits resulting from genetic engineering in animals and plants

b concerns about the risks resulting from genetic engineering in animals and plants.

UNIT QUESTIONS

SKILLS CRITICAL THINKING

8th **1** Some experimental sheep were genetically modified, using a human gene. The gene codes for a protein involved in blood clotting, called factor IX.

The gene for factor IX was cut from human DNA and injected into a sheep body cell. The nucleus of this body cell was transferred to an enucleated sheep ovum. The ovum was cultured in a dish and then implanted in the uterus of a surrogate sheep to complete its development.

Two lambs produced by this method grew to maturity. They produced milk from which Factor IX could be extracted.

a Name an enzyme that can be used to cut DNA. **(1)**

7th b What is an *enucleated ovum*? **(2)**

8th c The sheep produced by this method are called *transgenic*. What is meant by this term? **(1)**

SKILLS REASONING

7th d The transgenic sheep were reproduced by *cloning*. What are the advantages of producing the sheep in this way? **(3)**

6th e Factor IX can be used to treat people with a blood clotting disorder called haemophilia. Why is important to have blood that clots? **(2)**

SKILLS CRITICAL THINKING

5th f Blood contains plasma, white blood cells, red blood cells and platelets. Which *two* components of the blood are involved with blood clotting? **(2)**

(Total 11 marks)

9th **2** Some genes are transferred from one plant species to another. These genes are called 'jumping genes'. Environmentalists are concerned that genetically modified plants may transfer some of their genes to wild species. Explain their concern about genetically modified plants that:

a have genes that make them resistant to herbicides (weedkillers) **(2)**

b have genes that make them resistant to pests **(2)**

c have genes that increase the yield of the crop they can produce. **(2)**

(Total 6 marks)

SKILLS REASONING

6th **3** The diagram shows a fermenter of the type used to grow microorganisms used to produce human insulin. Insulin is used to treat people with diabetes.

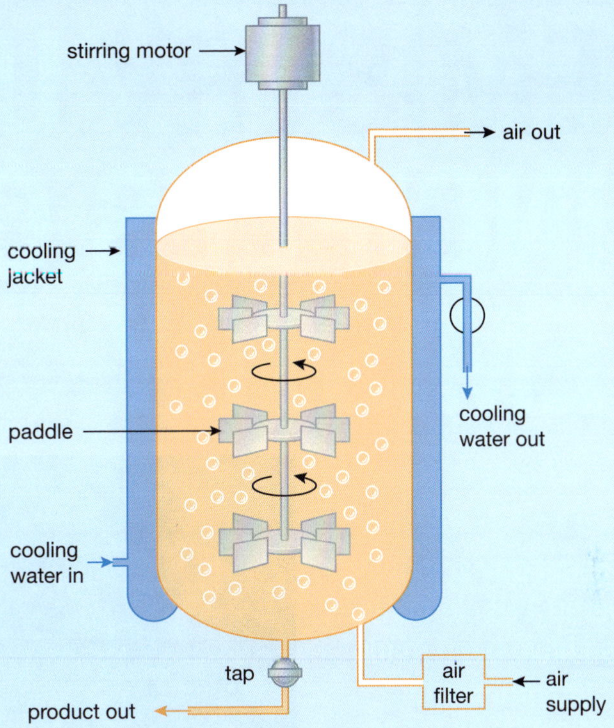

a Explain why air is pumped through the fermenter. **(2)**

b Why is it necessary to keep the temperature in the fermenter constant? **(2)**

7th **c** Suggest one other condition that must be kept constant inside the fermenter. **(1)**

d The fermenter is sterilised by steam. Suggest why this is better than using disinfectants. **(2)**

9th **e** Insulin can also be obtained from animal pancreases. Suggest two advantages of using microorganisms to produce the insulin needed by diabetics. **(2)**

(Total 9 marks)

SKILLS CRITICAL THINKING

8th **4** **a** Explain the meaning of the following terms:

i a plasmid

ii a bacteriophage. **(6)**

9th **b** Explain the importance of the following enzymes in genetic engineering:

i restriction enzymes

ii ligase enzymes. **(6)**

(Total 12 marks)

CHEMISTRY UNIT 1 PRINCIPLES OF CHEMISTRY

The universe is made of three things!

Up to the present day scientists have discovered 118 elements. Most of these have been made naturally in stars but some are made artificially. As far as we know these are the only elements in the universe, so we basically have a model kit containing 118 different atoms. Chemistry can be described as the study of how these different atoms are joined together in various ways to make everything around us, from a tree, to a person, to the tallest skyscraper. Many of these elements are not very common so most of the things we see around us are made up of different combinations of only about a quarter of these elements. What makes this even more amazing is that each atom is made up of just three subatomic particles, which are called protons, neutrons and electrons. So, the world around us is made of only three things arranged in different ways.

1 STATES OF MATTER

Everything around us is made of particles that we can't see because they are so small. This chapter looks at the arrangement of particles in solids, liquids and gases, and the ways in which the particles can move around. The nature of the different sorts of particles will be explored in Chapter 3.

▲ Figure 1.1 Everything you look at is a solid, a liquid or a gas . . .

▲ Figure 1.2 . . . metals, concrete, water, air, clouds – everything!

LEARNING OBJECTIVES

- Understand the three states of matter in terms of the arrangement, movement and energy of the particles
- Understand the interconversions between the three states of matter in terms of:
  - the names of the interconversions
  - how they are achieved
  - the changes in arrangement, movement and energy of the particles
- Understand how the results of experiments involving the dilution of coloured solutions and diffusion of gases can be explained
- Know what is meant by the terms:
  - solvent
  - solute
  - solution
  - saturated solution

STATES OF MATTER

Solids, liquids and gases are known as the three states of matter.

THE ARRANGEMENT OF THE PARTICLES

Think about these facts:

- You can't walk through a brick wall, but you can move (with some resistance – it pushes against you) through water. Moving through air is easy.
- When you melt most solids their volume increases slightly. Most liquids are less dense than the solid they come from.
- If you boil about 5 cm^3 of water, the steam will fill an average bucket.

HINT

The packing in the solid might be completely different. What is important is that the particles are close together and, usually, regularly packed. When you draw a liquid, make sure the particles are mostly touching the particles next to them.

KEY POINTS

- You can't walk through a brick wall because of the strong forces of attraction between the particles – the particles can't move out of your way.
- You can swim through water because you can push the particles out of the way.
- It is easy to move through a gas because there are no forces between the particles.

The arrangement of the **particles** in solids, liquids and gases explains these facts.

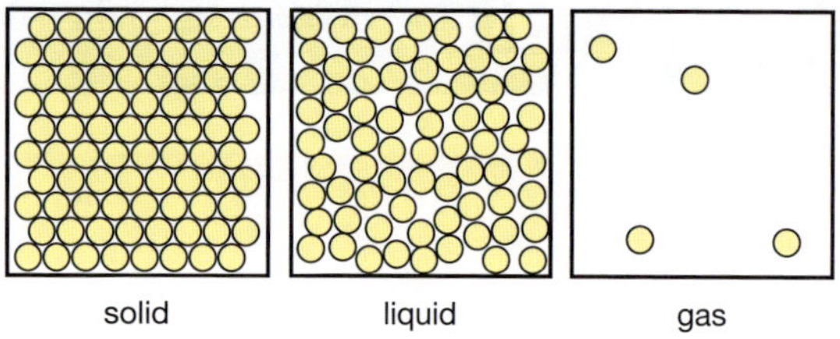

▲ Figure 1.3 The arrangement of particles in different states of matter

In a solid, the particles are usually arranged regularly and packed closely together. The particles are only able to vibrate about fixed positions; they can't move around. The particles have strong forces of attraction between them, which keep them together.

In a liquid, the particles are still mostly touching, but some gaps have appeared. This is why liquids are usually less dense than solids. The forces between the particles are less effective, and the particles can move around each other. The particles in a liquid are arranged randomly.

The particles in a gas are moving randomly at high speed in all directions. In a gas, the particles are much further apart and there are (almost) no forces of attraction between them.

The particles in a solid have less kinetic (movement) energy than the particles in a liquid, which have less **kinetic energy** than the particles in a gas.

INTERCONVERSIONS BETWEEN THE THREE STATES OF MATTER

CHANGING STATE BETWEEN SOLID AND LIQUID

If you heat a solid, the energy provided by the heat source makes the particles in the solid vibrate faster and faster. Eventually, they vibrate so fast that the forces of attraction between the particles are no longer strong enough to hold them together; the particles are then able to move around each other – the solid melts to form a liquid. The temperature at which the solid **melts** is called its **melting point**. The particles in the liquid have more kinetic energy than the particles in the solid so energy has to be supplied to convert a solid to a liquid.

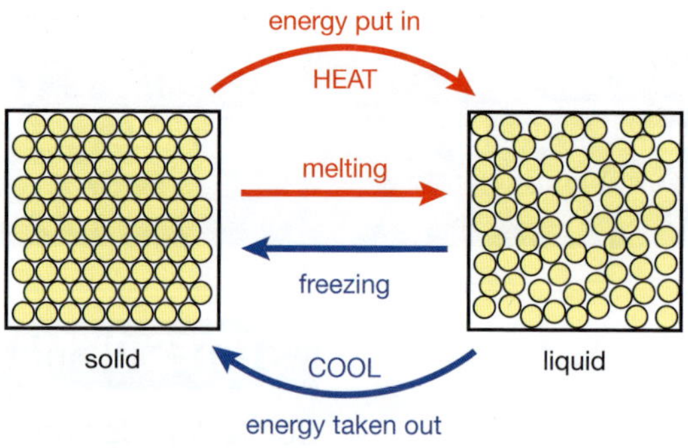

▲ Figure 1.4 Melting to become a liquid – and **freezing** to become a solid.

If the liquid is cooled again, the liquid particles will move around more and more slowly. Eventually, they are moving so slowly that the forces of attraction between them will hold them in a fixed position and the particles pack more closely together into a solid. The liquid freezes, forming a solid. The temperature at which this occurs is called the **freezing point**.

Although they are called different things depending which way you are going, the temperature of the melting point and that of the freezing point of a substance are exactly the same.

CHANGING STATE BETWEEN LIQUID AND GAS

There are two different ways this can happen, called **boiling** and **evaporation**.

BOILING

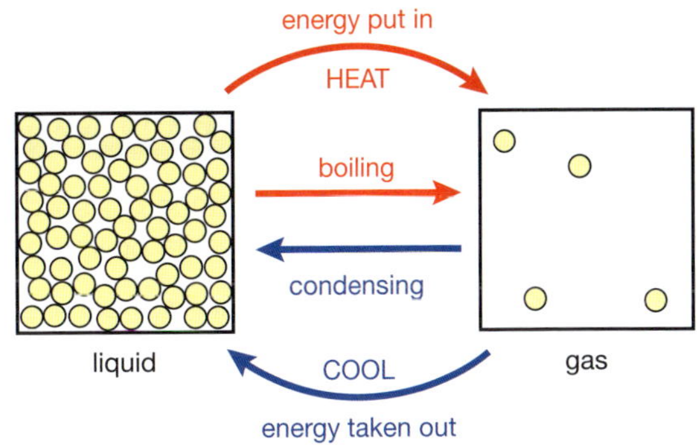

▲ Figure 1.5 Boiling to become a gas – and condensing to become a liquid.

KEY POINT

Evaporation occurs at any temperature, but boiling only occurs at one temperature – the boiling point of the liquid. Puddles of water disappear quite quickly despite the outside temperature often being below 5 °C in the winter in the UK. The water in the puddles certainly does not boil at this temperature; the water evaporates. So water will evaporate at, for example, 5 °C but only boil at 100 °C.

Boiling occurs when a liquid is heated so strongly that the particles are moving fast enough to overcome all the forces of attraction between them. The stronger the forces of attraction between particles, the higher the boiling point of the liquid. This is because more energy is needed to overcome these forces of attraction.

If a gas is cooled, the particles eventually move slowly enough that forces of attraction between them start to form and hold them together as a liquid. The gas condenses.

EVAPORATION

Evaporation is different. In any liquid or gas, the average speed of the particles varies with the temperature. But at each temperature, some particles will be moving faster than the average and others more slowly.

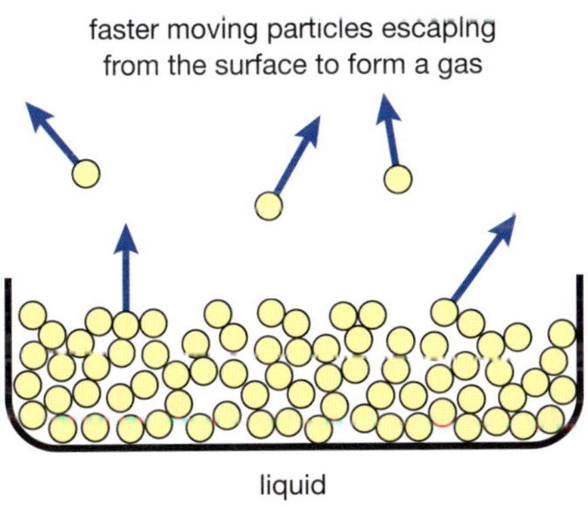

▲ Figure 1.6 Evaporation.

Some very fast particles at the surface of the liquid will have enough energy to overcome the forces of attraction between the particles – they will break away to form a gas. This is evaporation. You don't see any **bubbling**; the liquid just slowly disappears if it is open to the air. If the liquid is in a closed container, particles in the gas will also be colliding with particles at the surface of the liquid. If they are moving slowly enough they will be held by the attractive forces and become part of the liquid. In a closed container evaporation and **condensation** will both be occurring at the same time.

CHANGING STATE BETWEEN SOLID AND GAS: SUBLIMATION

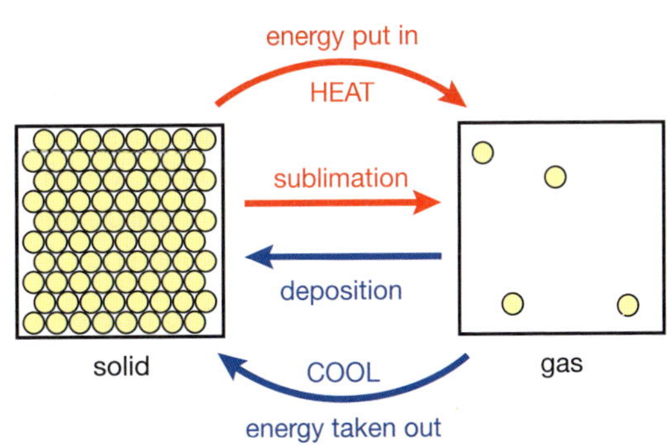

▲ Figure 1.7 This change of state goes directly from a solid to a gas and from a gas to a solid.

KEY POINT

The process of a gas changing into a solid is given various names. Some people call it 'de-sublimation' or 'deposition' and others just use the word 'sublimation' again.

A small number of substances can change directly from a solid to a gas, or from a gas to a solid, at normal **pressure** without involving any liquid in the process. The conversion of a solid into a gas is known as **sublimation** and the reverse process is usually called **deposition**.

▲ Figure 1.8 Dry ice subliming. Notice the white solid carbon dioxide in the beaker. The white cloud is because the carbon dioxide gas produced is so cold that it causes water vapour in the air to condense. Carbon dioxide gas itself is invisible.

An example of a substance that sublimes is carbon dioxide. At ordinary pressures, there is no such thing as liquid carbon dioxide – it turns directly from a solid to a gas at –78.5 °C. Solid carbon dioxide is known as **dry ice**.

WORKING OUT THE PHYSICAL STATE OF A SUBSTANCE AT A PARTICULAR TEMPERATURE

A substance is a solid at temperatures below its melting point, between its melting point and its boiling point it is a liquid, and above its boiling point it is a gas.

In science we can decide whether a substance is a solid, a liquid or a gas at room temperature by looking at where its melting and boiling points are in relation to room temperature.

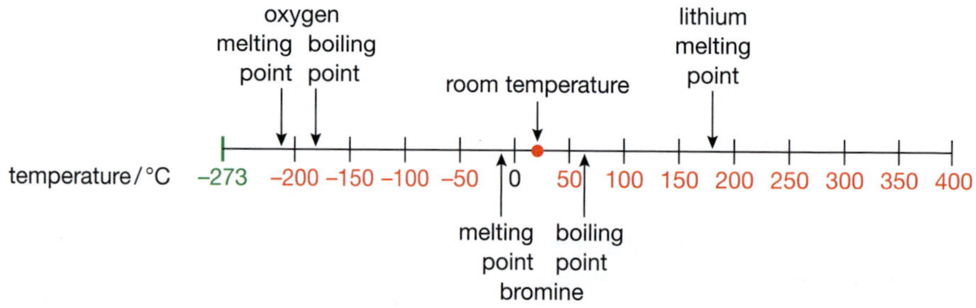

▲ Figure 1.9 A temperature line can be used to work out whether substances are solids, liquids or gases.

KEY POINT

Room temperature is different in different places but in science it is usually taken to mean a temperature between 20 and 25 °C. Because there is not just one fixed value, for changes of state that occur near room temperature we must be careful when making comparisons and make clear what value is being used as room temperature.

If we look at the temperature line in Figure 1.9 we can see that room temperature is above the boiling point of oxygen; this means that oxygen is a gas at room temperature.

Let's look at what happens when we heat bromine from –100 °C to 100 °C. As –100 °C is below bromine's melting point, bromine is a solid at –100 °C. As it is heated to –7 °C (its melting point) it becomes a liquid and it remains as a liquid until its temperature reaches the boiling point at 59 °C. Room temperature is between the melting point and the boiling point, which means that bromine is a liquid at room temperature. Above 59 °C bromine is a gas.

Lithium's melting point is above room temperature and so it is a solid at room temperature.

DIFFUSION

DIFFUSION IN GASES

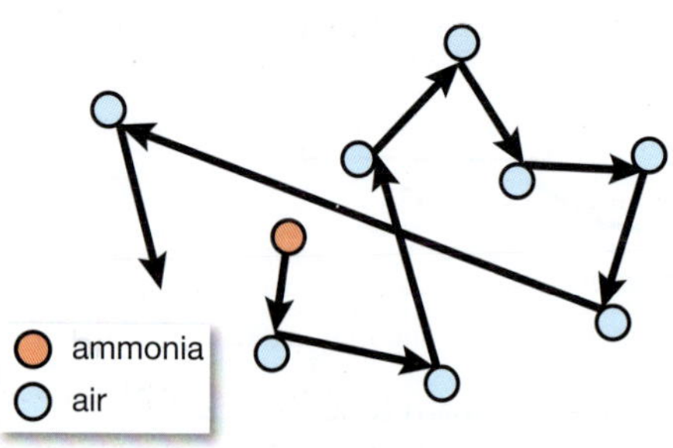

▲ Figure 1.10 An ammonia particle bouncing off air particles.

Suppose someone accidentally releases some smelly gas in the lab, ammonia for example. Within a minute or so, everybody in the lab will be able to smell it. That isn't surprising – particles in the gas are free to move around. What does need explaining, though, is why it takes so long.

At room temperature, ammonia particles travel at speeds of about 600 metres per second so they should be able to travel from one end of a lab to the other in less than 1/100 s (0.01 s). This would be the case if they travelled in a straight line without bumping into anything else. However, each particle is bouncing off air particles on its way. In the time that it takes for the smell to reach all corners of the lab, each ammonia particle may have travelled 30 or more kilometres!

The spreading out of particles in a gas or liquid is known as **diffusion**. We say that ammonia particles *diffuse* through the air. A formal definition of diffusion is:

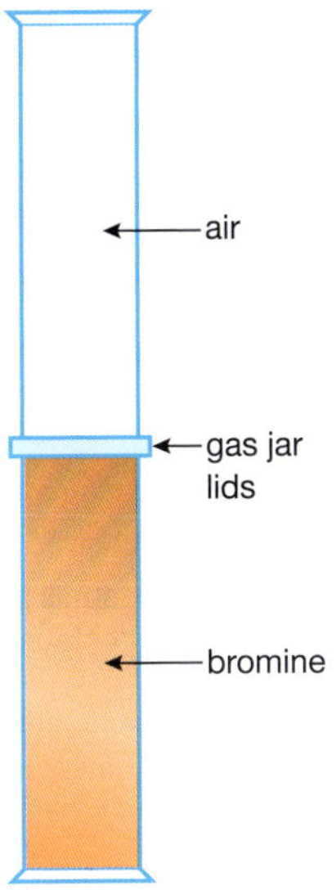

▲ Figure 1.12 Demonstrating diffusion in gases

Safety note: The teacher demonstration must be prepared in a working fume cupboard wearing eye protection and chemical-resistant gloves. Inhalation of bromine by anyone with breathing difficulties may produce a reaction, possibly delayed, requiring urgent medical attention.

Diffusion is the spreading out of particles from where they are at a high concentration (there are lots of them in a certain volume) to where they are at a low concentration (there are fewer of them in a certain volume).

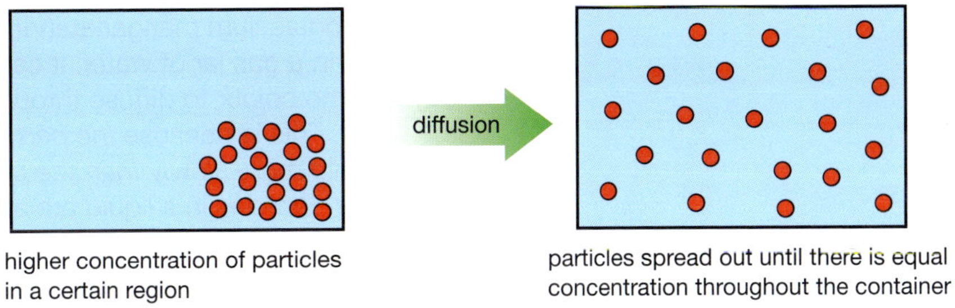

▲ Figure 1.11 Diffusion involves the spreading out of particles.

You can show diffusion in gases very easily by using the apparatus in Figure 1.12. The lower gas jar contains bromine gas; the top one contains air. If the lids are removed, the brown colour of the bromine diffuses upwards until both gas jars are uniformly brown (the air particles also diffuse downwards). The bromine particles and air particles move around at random to give an even mixture – both gas jars contain air and bromine particles.

You can carry out the same experiment with hydrogen and air, but in this example you have to put a lighted splint in at the end to find out where the gases have gone. People often expect that the much less dense hydrogen will all go to the top gas jar. In fact, you will get identical explosions from both jars.

SHOWING THAT PARTICLES OF DIFFERENT GASES TRAVEL AT DIFFERENT SPEEDS

HINT

Don't worry if you don't know how to write symbol equations. This one is included here so that you can refer to it again in later revision.

Safety note: The teacher demonstration requires eye protection and the avoidance of skin contact and inhalation of any fumes. The apparatus has to be cleaned up in a working fume cupboard.

KEY POINT

You will learn about relative molecular mass in Chapter 5. The relative molecular mass of ammonia is 17 and that of hydrogen chloride is 36.5.

This experiment relies on the reaction between ammonia (NH_3) and hydrogen chloride (HCl) gases to give white solid ammonium chloride (NH_4Cl):

$$NH_3(g) + HCl(g) \rightarrow NH_4Cl(s)$$

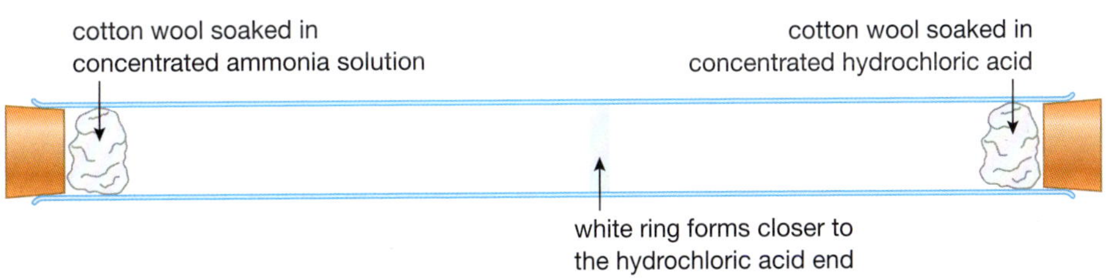

▲ Figure 1.13 Demonstrating that particles in ammonia and hydrogen chloride travel at different speeds.

Pieces of cotton wool are **soaked** in concentrated ammonia solution (as a source of ammonia gas) and concentrated hydrochloric acid (as a source of hydrogen chloride gas). These are placed in the ends of a long glass tube with rubber bungs to stop the poisonous gases escaping.

Ammonia particles and hydrogen chloride particles diffuse along the tube. A white ring of solid ammonium chloride forms where they meet. The white ring of ammonium chloride takes time to form (as it takes some time for the particles of ammonia and hydrogen chloride to diffuse along the tube), and appears *closer to the hydrochloric acid end*. Ammonia particles are lighter than hydrogen chloride particles and therefore move faster. The ammonia particles travel further in the same amount of time, which means that the ring forms further away from the ammonia end.

DIFFUSION IN LIQUIDS

Diffusion through a liquid is very slow if the liquid is completely still. For example, if a small jar of strongly coloured solution (such as potassium manganate(VII) solution) is placed in a gas jar of water, it can take days for the colour to diffuse throughout all the water. This is because *the particles in a liquid move more slowly than the particles in a gas*.The particles in a liquid are also much closer together than those in a gas and so there is less space for particles to move into without colliding with another one.

▲ Figure 1.14 Demonstrating diffusion in liquids

THE DILUTION OF COLOURED SOLUTIONS

Imagine you dissolve 0.01 g of potassium manganate(VII) in 1 cm^3 of water to make a deep purple solution. If we take the volume of 1 drop as 0.05 cm^3 we can work out that there are 20 drops in 1 cm^3 and each drop will contain 0.0005 g of potassium manganate(VII).

If you dilute this solution by adding water until the total volume is 10 000 cm^3, you should still just be able to see the purple colour.

There are now 200 000 drops in the solution. In order to see the colour each drop must contain at least one 'particle' of potassium manganate(VII), so there must be at least 200 000 'particles' in 0.01 g of potassium manganate(VII). This means that each 'particle' can't weigh more than 50 billionths of a gram (0.00000005 g).

This answer is not even close to the real answer. A potassium manganate(VII) 'particle' actually weighs about 0.00000000000000000000026 g and there are about 38 000 000 000 000 000 000 particles in 0.01 g! In reality, you need very large numbers of particles in each drop in order to see the colour.

REMINDER

Why the inverted commas around 'particle'? Potassium manganate(VII) is an *ionic compound* and contains more than one sort of particle. You will find out more about ionic compounds in Chapter 6.

THE SOLUBILITY OF SOLIDS

SOLUTES, SOLVENTS AND SOLUTIONS

When a solid dissolves in a liquid:

- the substance that dissolves is called the **solute**
- the liquid it dissolves in is called the **solvent**
- the liquid formed is a **solution**.

When you make a solution, the attractive forces between the particles in the solute (the solid) are being broken. At the same time, new attractive forces are being formed between the solvent particles and the solute particles. Whether a particular solid is soluble in any solvent depends on whether the new attractive forces are strong enough to overcome the old ones.

Only a certain amount of solute will dissolve in a fixed amount of solute at a particular temperature. When the maximum amount is dissolved a saturated solution is obtained.

A **saturated solution** is a solution which contains as much dissolved solid as possible at a particular temperature. There must be some undissolved solute present.

CHAPTER QUESTIONS

SKILLS CRITICAL THINKING 2nd

1 What name is given to each of the following changes of state?

a Solid to liquid b Liquid to solid c Solid to gas d Gas to solid

SKILLS INTERPRETATION 5th

2 a Draw diagrams to show the arrangement of the particles in a solid, a liquid and a gas.

b Describe the difference between the movement of particles in a solid and a liquid.

c The change of state from a liquid to a gas can be either evaporation or boiling. Explain the difference between evaporation and boiling.

SKILLS ANALYSIS

3 The questions refer to the substances in the table.

	Melting point / °C	Boiling point / °C
A	–259	–253
B	0	100
C	3700 (sublimes)	
D	–116	34.5
E	801	1413

a Write down the physical states of each compound at

i 30 °C.

ii –100 °C

iii 80 °C

SKILLS PROBLEM SOLVING 6th

b Which substance has the greatest distance between its particles at 25 °C? Explain your answer.

SKILLS REASONING 5th

c Why is no boiling point given for substance **C**?

6th

d Which liquid substance would evaporate most quickly in the open air at 25 °C? Explain your answer.

4 Refer to Figure 1.13 on page 263 showing the diffusion experiment.

a Explain why the ring takes a few minutes to form.

5th

b i If you heat a gas, what effect will this have on the movement of the particles?

6th

ii In the light of your answer to i, what difference would you find if you did this experiment outside on a day when the temperature was 2 °C instead of in a warm lab at 25 °C? Explain your answer.

c Explain why the ring was formed nearer the hydrochloric acid end of the tube.

d Suppose you replaced the concentrated hydrochloric acid with concentrated hydrobromic acid. This releases the gas hydrogen bromide (HBr). Hydrogen bromide also reacts with ammonia to form a white ring.

i Suggest a name for the white ring in this case.

7th

ii Hydrogen bromide particles are about twice as heavy as hydrogen chloride particles. What effects do you think this would have on the experiment?

2 ELEMENTS, COMPOUNDS AND MIXTURES

Most of the substances that we are familiar with from everyday life are mixtures. For example, the air that we breathe is a mixture containing elements such as nitrogen and oxygen, and compounds such as carbon dioxide and nitrogen oxides. The food that we eat and the drinks that we drink are mixtures. This chapter looks at the properties of elements, compounds and mixtures, and also how to separate the components of a mixture. Separation of mixtures is very important in the analysis of substances, such as in forensics.

▲ Figure 2.1 Gold is an element, but a gold ring made from 18-carat gold only contains 75% gold. The metal is a mixture of gold and, usually, copper.

▲ Figure 2.2 Pure water is a compound, but the water we drink is a mixture of water and other dissolved substances.

LEARNING OBJECTIVES

- Understand how to classify a substance as an element, compound or mixture
- Understand that a pure substance has a fixed melting and boiling point, but that a mixture may melt or boil over a range of temperatures
- Describe these experimental techniques for the separation of mixtures:
  - simple distillation
  - filtration
  - paper chromatography
  - fractional distillation
  - crystallisation
- Understand how a chromatogram provides information about the composition of a mixture
- Understand how to use the calculation of R_f values to identify the components of a mixture
- Practical: Investigate paper chromatography using inks/food colourings

REMINDER

You might want to look at Chapter 3 if you do not already know the term 'atom'.

KEY POINT

It isn't completely true to say that elements consist of only one type of atom. A better way of saying it would be that *all the atoms in an element have the same atomic number*. Most elements consist of mixtures of isotopes, which have the same atomic number, but different mass numbers (due to different numbers of neutrons). When we draw diagrams or make models, we aren't usually interested in the differences between the isotopes. Isotopes will be discussed in Chapter 3.

ELEMENTS

Elements are *substances that can't be split into anything simpler by* **chemical means**. An element contains only one type of atom (but see the key point in the margin). In models or diagrams they are shown as atoms of a single colour or size.

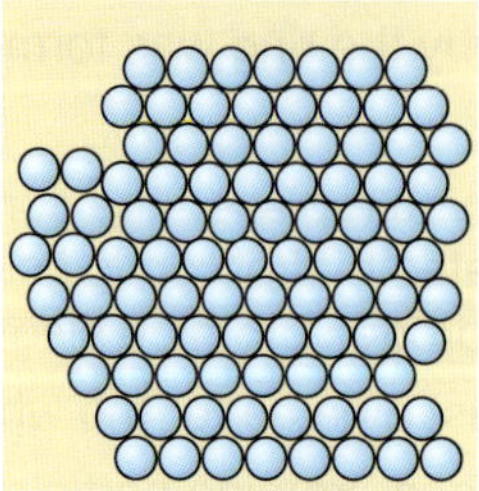

a pure metal such as magnesium

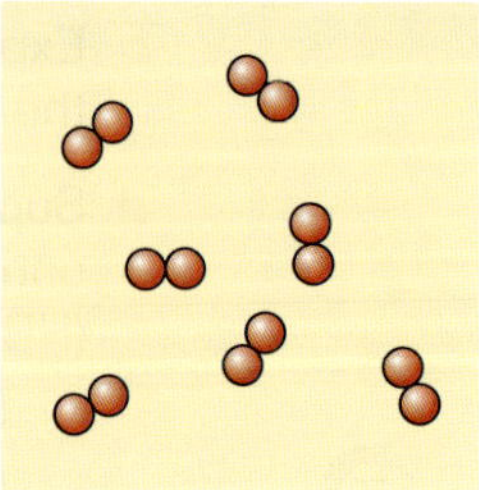

oxygen gas

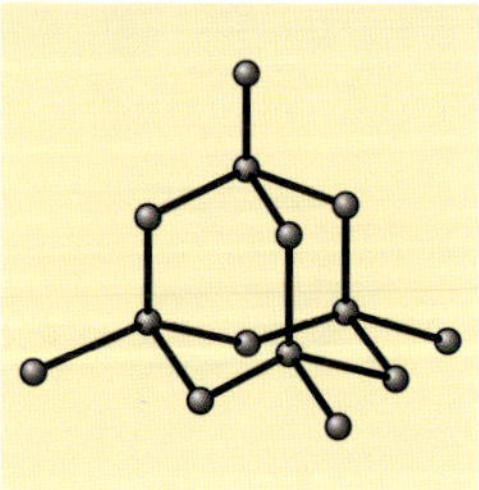

diamond (a form of carbon)

▲ Figure 2.3 Elements contain only one type of atom.

There are 118 elements and these are shown in the **Periodic Table**. Most of the elements occur naturally, such as hydrogen, helium and sulfur. Some others have to be made artificially, such as einsteinium.

COMPOUNDS

Compounds are formed when *two or more elements chemically combine*. The elements always combine in fixed proportions. For example, hydrogen and fluorine always combine to form hydrogen fluoride, with formula HF, whereas magnesium and fluorine always combine to form magnesium fluoride, with formula MgF_2 – the elements must combine in these ratios. Examples of other compounds are carbon dioxide (CO_2) and methane (CH_4). Diagrams of compounds show more than one type of atom bonded together.

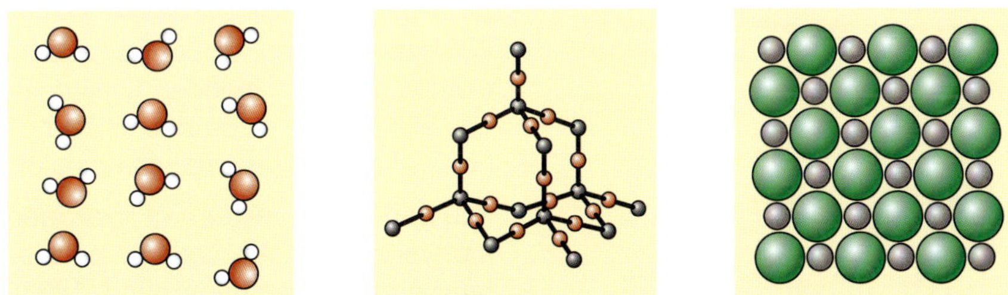

water silicon dioxide sodium chloride

▲ Figure 2.4 Some compounds

MIXTURES

In a **mixture**, the various substances are mixed together and no chemical reaction occurs. Mixtures can be made from elements and/or compounds. The various components can be in any proportion, for example you can put any amount of sugar into your cup of tea or coffee (until it becomes saturated).

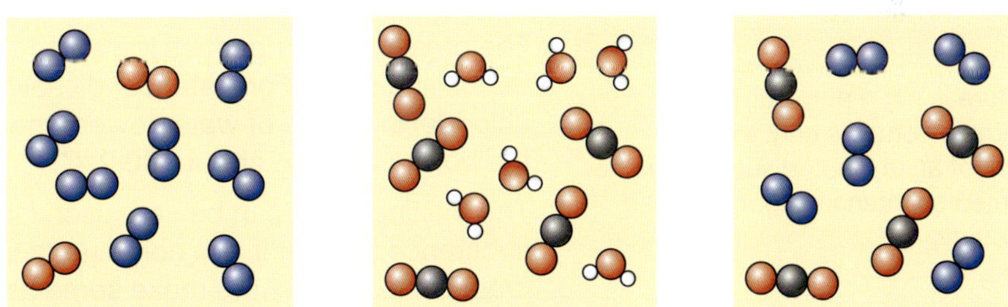

mixture of elements – nitrogen and oxygen

mixture of compounds – carbon dioxide and water (vapour)

mixture of an element with a compound – carbon dioxide and nitrogen

▲ Figure 2.5 Some mixtures

SIMPLE DIFFERENCES BETWEEN MIXTURES AND COMPOUNDS

PROPORTIONS

In water (a compound), every single water molecule has two hydrogen atoms combined with one oxygen atom. It never varies. In a mixture of hydrogen and oxygen gases, the two could be mixed together in any proportion.

If you had some iron metal and some sulfur, you could mix them in any proportion you wanted to. In iron sulfide (FeS), a compound, the proportion of iron to sulfur is always exactly the same.

PROPERTIES

REMINDER

You can find out about the reactions of metals with dilute acids on pages 387–388. The reaction between iron sulfide and acids isn't needed for exam purposes at International GCSE.

In a mixture of elements, each element keeps its own properties, but the properties of the compound are quite different. For example, in a mixture of iron and sulfur, the iron is grey and the sulfur is yellow. The iron reacts with dilute acids such as hydrochloric acid to produce hydrogen; the sulfur doesn't react with the acid. However, the compound iron sulfide (FeS) reacts quite differently with acids to produce poisonous hydrogen sulfide gas, which smells of bad eggs.

A mixture of hydrogen and oxygen is a colourless gas which explodes when you put a flame to it. The compound, water, is a colourless liquid which just puts out a flame.

EASE OF SEPARATION

Mixtures can be separated by **physical means**. Physical means are things like changing the temperature or dissolving part of the mixture in a solvent such as water; in other words, methods that don't involve any chemical reactions.

For example, a mixture of iron and sulfur is quite easy to separate into the two elements using a magnet. The iron sticks to the magnet and the sulfur doesn't. The elements in a compound cannot be separated by physical means. To convert iron sulfide into separate samples of iron and sulfur requires chemical reactions.

You can cool a mixture of hydrogen and oxygen gases to separate it by a physical process. Oxygen condenses into a liquid at a much higher temperature than hydrogen (–183 °C as opposed to –253 °C). This would leave you with liquid oxygen and hydrogen gas, which are easy to separate. But to separate water into hydrogen and oxygen, you have to change it chemically using **electrolysis**.

MELTING POINT AND BOILING POINT

Pure substances, such as elements and pure compounds, melt and boil at fixed temperatures. For example, the melting point of water is 0 °C and the boiling point 100 °C. However, mixtures usually melt or boil over a ***range*** *of temperatures*.

KEY POINT

A mixture is not a pure substance. If a sample contains only a small amount of an unwanted substance, the unwanted substance might be called an *impurity*.

The presence of impurities lowers the melting point of a substance and raises the boiling point. For instance, dissolving 10 g of common (table) salt (sodium chloride) in 1 **litre** of water lowers the melting point to about –0.6 °C and raises the boiling point to about 100.2 °C.

The melting point can be very useful in determining whether or not a substance is pure. If you continue to study chemistry you might carry out a practical experiment to make some aspirin. In order to determine whether your sample is pure or not you can measure the melting point. You would record the temperature at which your sample starts to melt, and then you would record the temperature at which it has fully melted to completely form a liquid. Aspirin is a white powder that melts at 138 °C. If the melting point of the sample you made is 128–134 °C you can see that it is quite impure because it melts over a wide range of temperature (below the melting point of pure aspirin).

SEPARATION OF MIXTURES

Separating mixtures is extremely important in chemistry. For example, we can see this in the processing of crude oil, in producing fresh water from salt water and in the enrichment of uranium. In forensic science, the components of a mixture usually have to be separated before they can be analysed.

FILTRATION

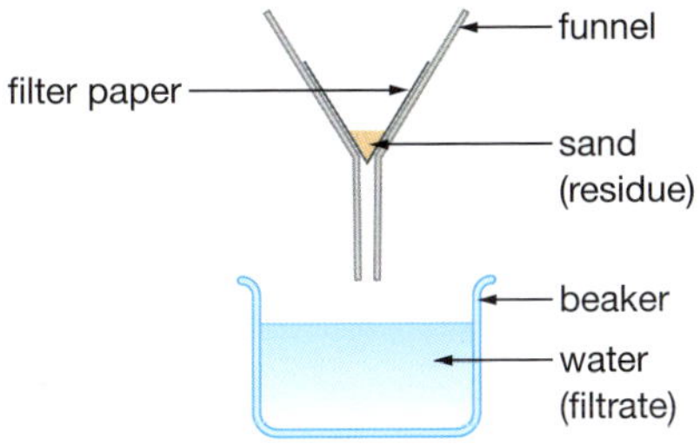

Figure 2.6 Filtration can be used to separate a mixture of sand and water.

Filtration can be used to separate a solid from a liquid.

For example, sand can be separated from water by filtration. The apparatus for filtration is shown in Figure 2.6.

The substance left in the filter paper is called the **residue** and the liquid that comes through is called the **filtrate**.

Filtration can also be used to separate two solids from each other if only one of them is soluble in water (see below – rock salt).

CRYSTALLISATION

Crystallisation can be used to separate a solute from a solution. For example, it could be used to separate sodium chloride from a sodium chloride solution. The solution is heated in an evaporating basin to boil off some of the water until an almost saturated solution is formed. This can be tested by dipping a glass rod into the solution and seeing if crystals form quickly on its surface when it is removed. The Bunsen burner is then turned off and the crystals allowed to form as more water evaporates and the solution cools. The crystals can now be removed from the mixture by filtration.

The apparatus for crystallisation is shown in Figure 2.7.

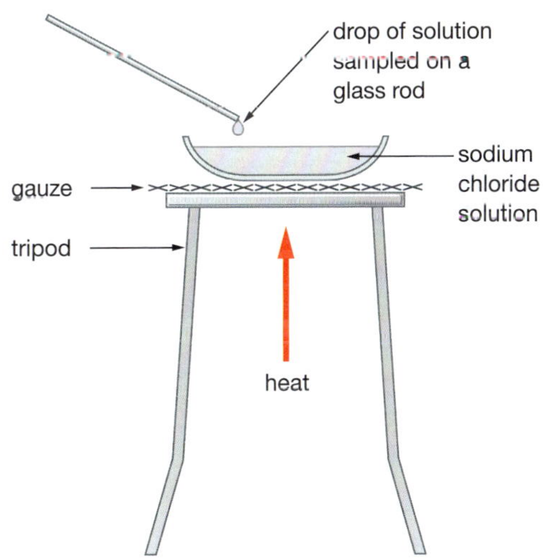

Figure 2.7 Crystallisation can be used to separate a solute from a solution.

MAKING PURE SALT FROM ROCK SALT

Figure 2.8 Rock salt

We can use filtration and crystallisation to obtain pure salt from rock salt.

Rock salt consists of salt contaminated by various earthy or rocky impurities. These impurities aren't soluble in water.

If you crush the rock salt and mix it with hot water, the salt dissolves, but the impurities don't. The impurities can be filtered off, and remain on the filter paper. The filtrate is then a salt solution. The solid salt can be obtained from the solution by crystallisation.

This is typical of the way you can separate any mixture of two solids, one of which is soluble in water and one of which isn't.

SIMPLE DISTILLATION

Simple distillation can be used to separate the components of a solution. Although we can use crystallisation to separate sodium chloride from a sodium chloride solution, we can also collect the water if we use simple distillation.

The water boils and is condensed back to a liquid by the condenser. The salt remains in the flask.

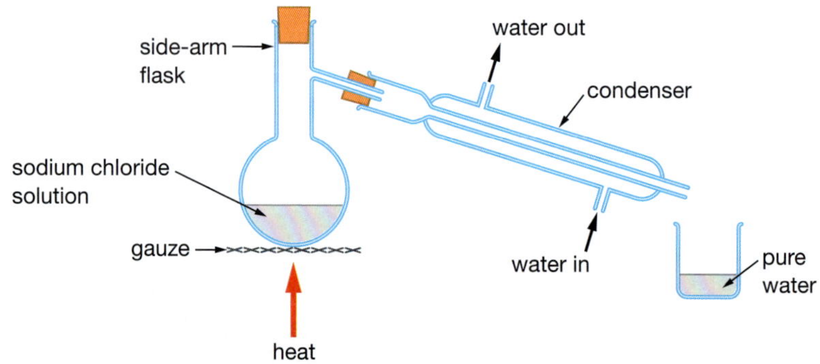

▲ Figure 2.9 Distilling pure water from sodium chloride solution.

You could, of course, collect the salt from the solution as well as collecting pure water. The sodium chloride solution eventually becomes so concentrated that the salt will crystallise out.

KEY POINT

Notice that water is always fed into the condenser at the lower end. That way it fills the condenser jacket better and if the flow of water stops for any reason the condenser jacket remains full of water.

FRACTIONAL DISTILLATION

Fractional distillation is used to separate a mixture of liquids such as ethanol (alcohol) and water. Ethanol and water are completely **miscible** with each other. That means you can mix them together in any proportion and they will form a single liquid layer. You can separate them by taking advantage of their different boiling points: water boils at 100 °C, ethanol at 78 °C.

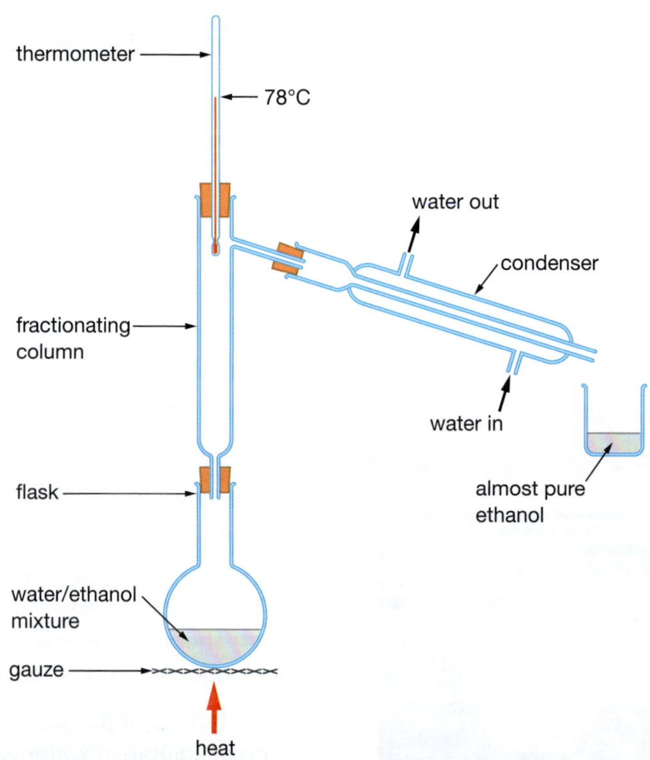

▲ Figure 2.10 Fractional distillation

EXTENSION WORK

The fractionating column is often packed with glass beads or something similar, although the separation of ethanol and water in the lab works perfectly well just with an empty column. For reasons that are beyond International GCSE, a high surface area in the column helps separation of the two vapours. The ethanol produced by this experiment is about 96% pure. For complicated reasons, again beyond International GCSE, it is impossible to remove the last 4% of water by distillation.

Both liquids boil, but by careful heating you can control the temperature of the column so that all the water condenses in the column and **trickles** back into the flask. Only the ethanol remains as a vapour all the way to the top of the **fractionating column** and out into the condenser.

PAPER CHROMATOGRAPHY

Paper chromatography can be used to separate a variety of mixtures. However, at International GCSE level we will usually use it to separate mixtures of coloured inks or food colourings. Most inks and food colourings are not just made up of one colour but contain a mixture of dyes.

Paper chromatography can also be used to separate a mixture of colourless substances such as sugars, but then some method must be used to make the spots visible on the paper.

Safety note: Avoid skin contact with the solvents and dyes, especially if you have sensitive skin.

ACTIVITY 1

PRACTICAL: INVESTIGATING THE COMPOSITION OF DYE WITH PAPER CHROMATOGRAPHY

We can investigate the composition of a mixture of coloured dyes using paper chromatography. To do this we carry out the following steps.

1. Draw a line with a pencil across a piece of chromatography paper; this line should be about 1 cm from the bottom of the paper. Do not use a pen as the colours in the ink may move up the chromatography paper with the solvent.
2. Put a spot (use a teat pipette or a capillary tube) of the mixture of dyes on the pencil line and allow it to dry.
3. Suspend the chromatography paper in a beaker that contains a small amount of solvent so that the bottom of the paper goes into the solvent. It is important that the solvent is below the pencil line so that the inks/colourings don't just dissolve in the solvent.
4. Put a lid (such as a watch glass) on the beaker so that the atmosphere becomes saturated with the solvent. This is to stop evaporation of the solvent from the surface of the paper.
5. When the solvent has moved up the paper to about 1 cm from the top, remove the paper from the beaker and draw a pencil line to show where the solvent got to. The highest level of the solvent on the paper at any time is called the *solvent front*.
6. Leave the paper to dry so that all the solvent evaporates.

For the solvent you can use water or a non-aqueous solvent (a solvent other than water). Which solvent you use depends on what substances are present in the mixture. A suitable solvent is usually found by experimenting with different ones.

The dyes that make up the mixture will be different in two important ways:

- the affinity they have for the paper (how well they 'stick' to the paper)
- how soluble they are in the solvent which moves up the paper.

In Figure 2.11 spot C has hardly moved. Either it was not very soluble in the solvent or it has a very high affinity for the paper (or both). On the other hand, spot A has moved almost as far as the solvent. It must be very soluble in the solvent and not have much affinity for the paper. The pattern you get is called a **chromatogram**.

KEY POINT

If the dye does not move from the pencil line during an experiment, then the dye is not at all soluble in the solvent you are using. In this case, you need to find a different solvent. If the dye moves up the paper with the solvent front, the dye is too soluble in that solvent and, again, you have to try a different solvent.

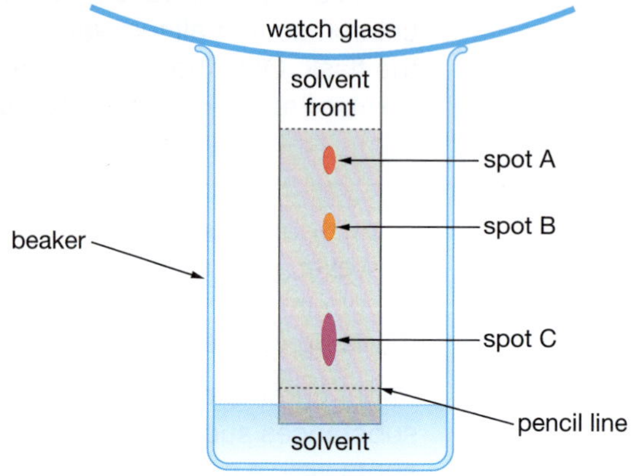

Figure 2.11 Paper chromatography

In this example, the mixture must have contained a minimum of three different dyes. We say a *minimum* of three dyes because there could be more – it is possible that one of the spots is made up of two coloured dyes that by concidence moved the same distance. You could only confirm this by doing the experiment again with a different solvent.

Figure 2.12 A paper chromatography experiment

USING PAPER CHROMATOGRAPHY IN ANALYSIS

You can use paper chromatography to identify the particular dyes in a mixture. If you think that your mixture (m) could contain dyes d1, d2, d3 and d4, you can carry out an experiment to determine this.

A pencil line is drawn on a larger sheet of paper and pencil marks are drawn along the line to show the original positions of the various dyes placed on the line (see Figure 2.13). One spot is your unknown mixture; the others are single, known dyes. The chromatogram is then allowed to develop as before.

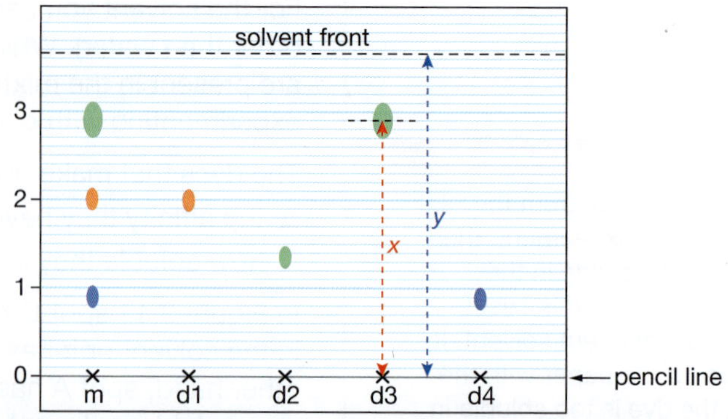

Figure 2.13 Paper chromatography can be used to analyse a mixture. Lines will not be present on your paper, but they have been added here to help you measure the distances.

The mixture (m) has spots corresponding to dyes d1, d3 and d4. They have the same colour as spots in the mixture, and have travelled the same distance on the paper. Although dye d2 is the same colour as one of the spots in the mixture, it has travelled a different distance and so must be a different compound.

Instead of just saying the spots move different distances we can use the **R_f value** to describe how far the spots move. R_f stands for **retardation factor**. Each time we do a chromatography experiment the solvent (and therefore the spots) will move different distances along the paper. This means we can't just report the distance moved by a particular spot so we have to work out a ratio instead.

$$R_f = \frac{\text{distance moved by a spot (from the pencil line)}}{\text{distance moved by the solvent front (from the pencil line)}}$$

In Figure 2.13 $R_f = \frac{x}{y}$.

So in Figure 2.13 the R_f value for dye d3 is:

$$R_f = \frac{2.9}{3.6} = 0.81$$

HINT

Measure to the centre of the spot.

The R_f values of the dyes in mixture m are:

blue spot: $R_f = \frac{0.9}{3.6} = 0.25$

orange spot: $R_f = \frac{2.0}{3.6} = 0.56$

green spot: $R_f = \frac{2.9}{3.6} = 0.81$

The R_f values of dyes d1 to d4 are:

d1: $R_f = 0.56$

d2: $R_f = 0.36$

d3: $R_f - 0.81$

d4: $R_f = 0.25$

Because the spots in mixture m have the same R_f values as d1, d3 and d4, we can conclude that the mixture contains these dyes.

An R_f value must be between 0 and 1. If you get a number bigger than 1 you have probably divided the numbers the wrong way round. An R_f value has no units.

You have to be careful when using R_f values as they depend on the solvent used and on the type of paper. There was no problem in the experiment described above because the mixture and the individual dyes were all put on the same piece of paper. However, if the mixture was put on one piece of chromatography paper and the individual dyes on a separate piece, you can still compare R_f values as long as you use the same type of paper and the same solvent.

CHAPTER QUESTIONS

SKILLS CRITICAL THINKING 6th

1 Classify each of the following substances as an element, compound or mixture:

sea water	hydrogen	honey
magnesium oxide	copper(II) sulfate	blood
calcium	mud	potassium iodide solution

SKILLS ANALYSIS

2 Look at the diagrams below and classify each one as an element, compound or mixture.

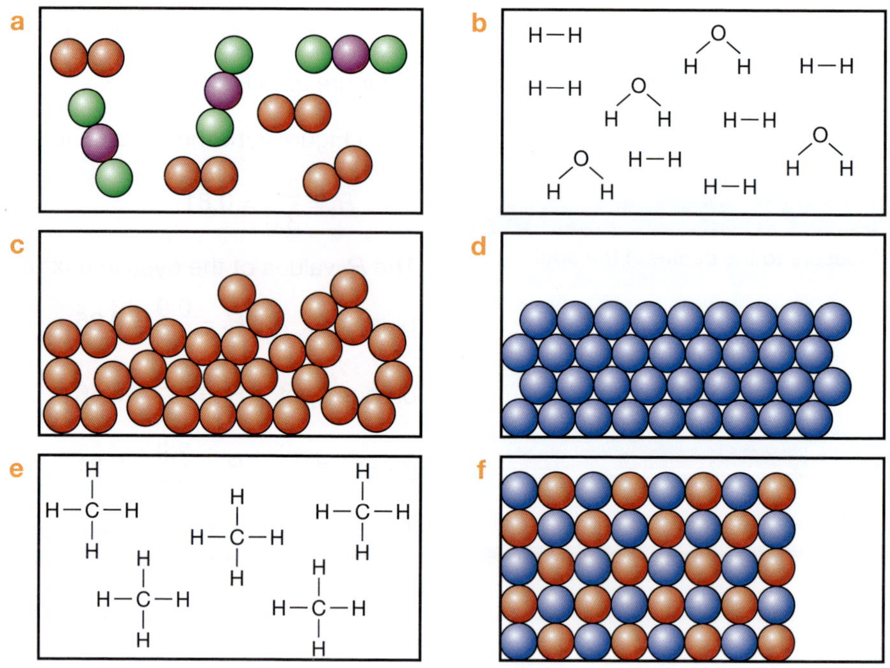

SKILLS REASONING, PROBLEM SOLVING 5th

3 A teacher has found two white powders on a desk in the chemistry laboratory. She wants to test to see if they are pure substances, so she measures the melting points. Substance X melts at 122 °C and substance Y melts between 87 and 93 °C. Explain which one is the pure substance.

SKILLS DECISION MAKING 6th

4 State which separation method you would use to carry out the following separations:

a Potassium iodide from a potassium iodide solution.

b Water from a potassium iodide solution.

c Ethanol from a mixture of ethanol and water.

d Red dye from a mixture of red and blue dyes.

e Calcium carbonate (insoluble in water) from a mixture of calcium carbonate and water.

SKILLS CREATIVITY, DECISION MAKING 5th

5 Suppose you had a valuable collection of small diamonds, which you kept safe from thieves by mixing them with white sugar crystals. You store the mixture in a jar labelled 'sugar'. Now you want to sell the diamonds. Describe how you would separate all the diamonds from the sugar.

SKILLS ANALYSIS 5th

6 In order to identify the writer of an anonymous letter, a sample of ink from the letter was dissolved in a solvent and then placed on some chromatography paper. Spots of ink from the pens of five possible writers, **G**, **M**, **P**, **R** and **T**, were placed next to the sample on the chromatography paper. The final chromatogram looked like this:

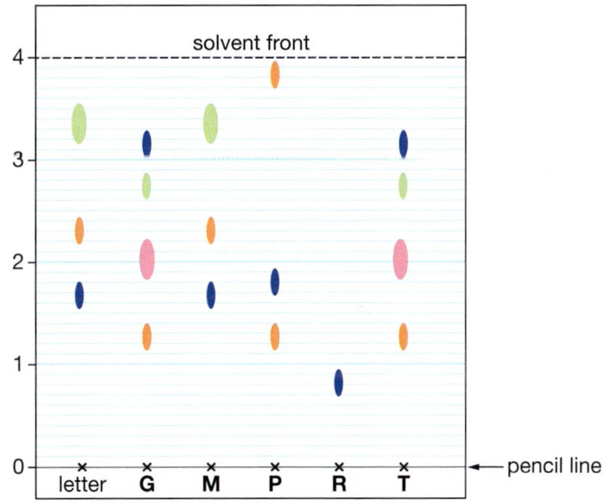

a Which of the five writers is using ink that matches the sample from the letter?

b Which of the writers is using a pen that contains ink made from a single dye?

SKILLS PROBLEM SOLVING 6th

c What is the R_f value of the blue dye in suspect **P**'s pen?

SKILLS ANALYSIS 5th

d Which two of the five writers are using pens containing the same ink?

6th

e Whose pen contained the dye that was most soluble in the solvent?

3 ATOMIC STRUCTURE

This chapter explores the nature of atoms and how they differ from element to element. The 118 elements are the building blocks from which everything is made, from a simple substance, such as carbon, to a more complex one, such as DNA.

LEARNING OBJECTIVES

- Know what is meant by the terms atom and molecule
- Know the structure of an atom in terms of the positions, relative masses and relative charges of sub-atomic particles
- Know what is meant by the terms atomic number, mass number, isotopes and relative atomic mass (A_r)
- Be able to calculate the relative atomic mass of an element (A_r) from isotopic abundances

Copper is an element. If you tried to cut it up into smaller and smaller pieces, the final result would be the smallest possible piece of copper. At that stage, you would have an individual copper atom. You can, of course, split that atom into smaller pieces (**protons**, **neutrons** and **electrons**), but you would no longer have copper. Therefore, an **atom** is the smallest piece of an element that can still be recognised as that element.

Figure 3.1 New atoms are produced in stars . . .

Figure 3.2 . . . or in nuclear processes such as nuclear bombs, nuclear reactors or radioactive decay.

ATOMS AND MOLECULES

Atoms can be joined together to make molecules. A **molecule** consists of two or more atoms chemically bonded (by covalent bonds). The atoms that make up a molecule can be from the same elements or different elements. A hydrogen (H_2) molecule (Figure 3.3a) consists of 2 hydrogen atoms chemically bonded together. A water (H_2O) molecule (Figure 3.3b) consists of 2 hydrogen atoms and an oxygen atom chemically bonded.

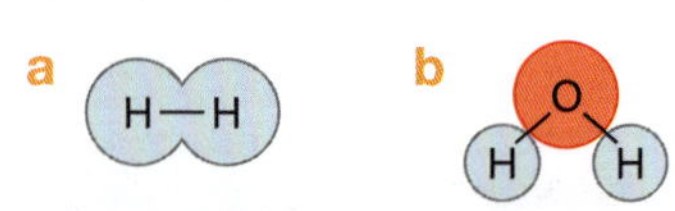

Figure 3.3 (a) A H_2 molecule and (b) a H_2O molecule. The lines between the atoms represent chemical bonds.

THE STRUCTURE OF THE ATOM

Atoms are made of protons, neutrons and electrons. These particles are sometimes called *sub-atomic particles* because they are smaller than an atom.

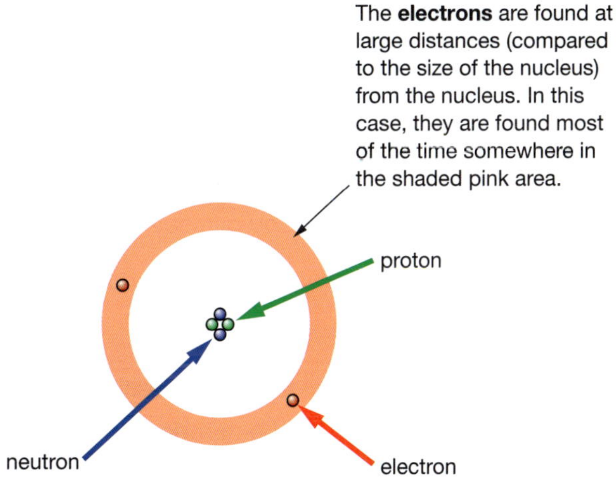

▲ Figure 3.4 The structure of a helium atom

The **nucleus** of the atom contains protons and neutrons, and is shown highly magnified in Figure 3.4. In reality, if you **scale up** a helium atom to the size of a sports hall the nucleus would be no more than the size of a grain of sand.

The relative masses and charges of protons, neutrons and electrons are shown in Table 3.1.

Table 3.1 The properties of protons, neutrons and electrons

Particle	Relative mass	Relative charge
proton	1	+1
neutron	1	0
electron	1/1836	−1

Virtually all the mass of the atom is concentrated in the nucleus because electrons have a much smaller mass than protons and neutrons.

The masses and charges are measured relative to each other because the actual values are incredibly small. For example, it would take about 600 000 000 000 000 000 000 000 (6×10^{23}) protons to weigh 1 g.

ATOMIC NUMBER AND MASS NUMBER

The number of protons in an atom's nucleus is called its **atomic number** or **proton number**. Each of the 118 different elements has a different number of protons. For example, if an atom has 8 protons it must be an oxygen atom:

atomic number = number of protons

The **mass number** (sometimes known as the **nucleon number**) counts the total number of protons and neutrons in the nucleus of the atom:

mass number = number of protons + number of neutrons

KEY POINT

You may have come across diagrams of the atom in which the electrons are drawn orbiting the nucleus rather like planets around the sun. This can be misleading.
Electrons are constantly moving in the atom and it is impossible to know exactly where they are at any moment in time. You can only identify that they have a particular energy and that they are likely to be found in a certain region of space at some particular distance from the nucleus. Electrons with different energies are found at different distances from the nucleus.

HINT

$\frac{1}{1836}$ is approximately 0.0005.

KEY POINT

The atomic number defines an element and is unique to that element. We can identify an element by its atomic number instead of its name. We could talk about a wristwatch made from the element with atomic number 79 instead of talking about 'a gold wristwatch', or say that the element with atomic number 17 is poisonous instead of saying 'chlorine is poisonous'. However, these are more complicated ways of describing things!

HINT

Be careful! When you are writing symbols with two letters, the first is a capital letter and the second must be lower case. If you write CO you are talking about carbon monoxide, not cobalt.

For any particular atom, this information can be shown as, for example:

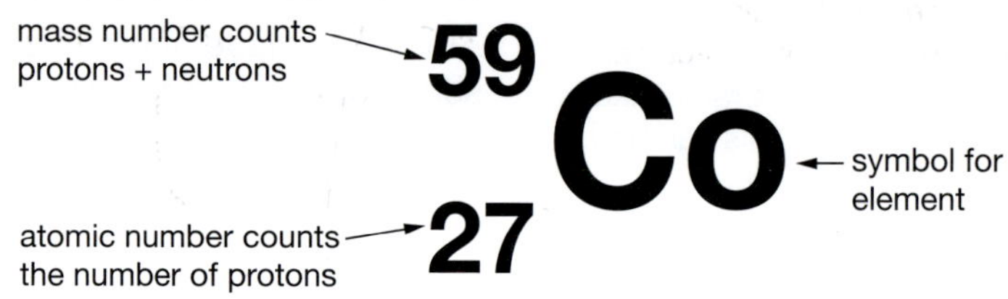

This particular atom of cobalt contains 27 protons. To make the total number of protons and neutrons up to 59, there must also be 32 neutrons.

You can see from this that:

number of neutrons = mass number – atomic number

ISOTOPES

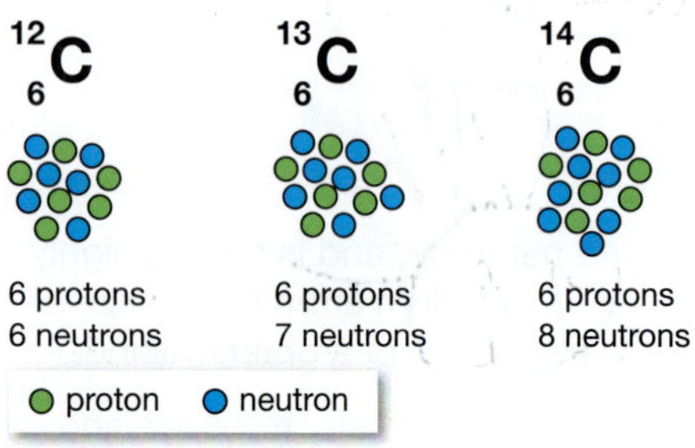

▲ Figure 3.5 The nuclei of the three isotopes of carbon

The number of neutrons in an atom can vary slightly. For example, there are three kinds of carbon atom called carbon-12, carbon-13 and carbon-14. They all have the same number of protons (because all carbon atoms have 6 protons, its atomic number), but the number of neutrons varies. These different atoms of carbon are called **isotopes**.

Isotopes are atoms (of the same element) which have the same atomic number but different mass numbers. They have the same number of protons but different numbers of neutrons.

The fact that they have varying numbers of neutrons makes no difference to their chemical reactions. The chemical properties (how something reacts) are controlled by the number and arrangement of the electrons, and that is identical for all three isotopes.

RELATIVE ATOMIC MASS

You might have seen the following in a Periodic Table:

35.5 **Cl** chlorine 17

Chlorine appears to have a mass number of 35.5. If you calculate the number of neutrons for chlorine you obtain:

number of neutrons = 35.5 – 17 = 18.5

It is not possible to have half a neutron and so there must be something wrong with this. The number 35.5 is not actually the mass number for chlorine but rather the **relative atomic mass** (A_r). Chlorine consists of two isotopes, ^{35}Cl and ^{37}Cl, and a naturally occurring sample contains a mixture of these.

KEY POINT

The number above each symbol in the International GCSE Periodic Table papers is a relative atomic mass and not a mass number. However, in most cases the relative atomic mass stated is the same as the mass number of the most common isotope. The only exceptions to this are chlorine (35.5) and copper (63.5).

KEY POINT

This type of average is called a **weighted average** or weighted mean.

Relative atomic mass is the average mass of an atom, taking into account the amount of each isotope present in a naturally occurring sample of an element. It is explained in more detail in Chapter 5.

You can probably see that a naturally occurring sample of chlorine must contain more of the ^{35}Cl isotope than the ^{37}Cl isotope. This is because the relative atomic mass is closer to 35 than to 37.

We can calculate the relative atomic mass of an element by knowing how much of each isotope is present in a sample (the isotopic abundances) of that element, and then working out the average mass of an atom. This is done in exactly the same way as you would calculate a weighted average in maths. It can be understood more easily by looking at a worked example.

EXAMPLE 1

A naturally occurring sample of the element boron contains 20% ^{10}B and 80% ^{11}B. Calculate the relative atomic mass.

If we imagine there are 100 atoms we can work out that 20% of them, that is 20, will have mass 10 and 80 will have mass 11.

The total mass of the 20 atoms with mass 10 is 20 × 10.

The total mass of the 80 atoms with mass 11 is 80 × 11.

The total mass of all the atoms in the sample is 20 × 10 + 80 × 11.

There are 100 atoms so we can work out the average by dividing the total mass by the total number of atoms (100):

$$\text{relative atomic mass} = \frac{20 \times 10 + 80 \times 11}{100} = 10.8$$

Therefore, the relative atomic mass of boron is 10.8.

Even if there are three or four different isotopes, you still do the calculation in the same way: calculate the total mass of 100 atoms, then divide the answer by 100.

THE ELECTRONS

COUNTING THE NUMBER OF ELECTRONS IN AN ATOM

Atoms are electrically neutral (they have no overall charge). The charge on a proton (+1) is equal but opposite to the charge on an electron (–1), and therefore in an atom:

number of electrons = number of protons

HINT

Remember that the number of protons is the same as the atomic number of the element.

So, if an oxygen atom (atomic number = 8) has 8 protons, it must also have 8 electrons; if a chlorine atom (atomic number = 17) has 17 protons, it must also have 17 electrons.

You will see that the key feature in this is knowing the atomic number. You can find the atomic number from the Periodic Table.

The number of protons in an atom is equal to the number of electrons. However, the atomic number is defined in terms of the number of protons because the number of electrons can change in chemical reactions, for example when atoms form **ions** (see Chapter 6).

THE PERIODIC TABLE

Chapter 4 deals in detail with what you need to know about the Periodic Table for International GCSE purposes.

Atoms are arranged in the Periodic Table in order of increasing atomic number. You will find a full version of the Periodic Table in Appendix A on page 708. Most Periodic Tables have two numbers against each symbol; be careful to choose the right one. The atomic number will always be the smaller number. The other number will either be the mass number of the most common isotope of the element or the relative atomic mass of the element. The Periodic Table will clarify this.

You can use a Periodic Table to find out the number of protons, neutrons and electrons in an atom. Remember:

- the number of protons in an atom is equal to the atomic number
- the number of electrons in an atom is equal to the number of protons
- the number of neutrons in an atom = mass number – atomic number.

EXAMPLE 2

The symbol for uranium is given in a Periodic Table as:

238 **U** Uranium 92

Calculate the number of protons, neutrons and electrons in an atom of uranium.

The atomic number is the smaller number, so the atomic number of uranium is 92. The atomic number tells us the number of protons, therefore a uranium atom contains 92 protons.

The number of protons is equal to the number of electrons, therefore a uranium atom contains 92 electrons.

The number of neutrons = mass number – atomic number.

The number of neutrons = 238 – 92 = 146.

CHAPTER QUESTIONS

You will need to use the Periodic Table in Appendix A on page 708.

SKILLS CRITICAL THINKING 7th

1 Atoms contain three types of particle: proton, neutron and electron.

  a State where the protons and neutrons are in an atom.

  b State which type of particle in the atom orbits the nucleus.

  c State which one of the particles has a positive charge.

  d State which two particles have approximately the same mass.

SKILLS CRITICAL THINKING

7th

2 Fluorine atoms have a mass number of 19.

a Use the Periodic Table to find the atomic number of fluorine.

b Explain what *mass number* means.

c State the number of protons, neutrons and electrons in a fluorine atom.

SKILLS REASONING

8th

d Explain why the number of protons in an atom must always equal the number of electrons.

SKILLS PROBLEM SOLVING

9th

3 Work out the numbers of protons, neutrons and electrons in each of the following atoms:

a $^{56}_{26}Fe$ b $^{93}_{41}Nb$ c $^{235}_{92}U$

SKILLS CRITICAL THINKING

7th

4 Chlorine has two isotopes, chlorine-35 and chlorine-37.

a Explain what *isotopes* are.

SKILLS PROBLEM SOLVING

b State the numbers of protons, neutrons and electrons in the two isotopes.

10th

5 Lithium has two naturally occurring isotopes, ^{6}Li (abundance 7%) and ^{7}Li (abundance 93%). Calculate the relative atomic mass of lithium, giving your answer to 2 decimal places.

6 Magnesium has three naturally occurring stable isotopes, ^{24}Mg (abundance 78.99%), ^{25}Mg (abundance 10.00%) and ^{26}Mg (abundance 11.01%). Calculate the relative atomic mass of magnesium, giving your answer to 2 decimal places.

7 Lead has four naturally occurring stable isotopes. Calculate the relative atomic mass of lead given the data in the table.

Mass number	Natural abundance / %
204	1.4
206	24.1
207	22.1
208	52.4

7th

8 Iridium has two naturally occurring isotopes, ^{191}Ir and ^{193}Ir.

a State the number of protons, neutrons and electrons in an ^{191}Ir atom.

SKILLS REASONING

8th

b Explain the difference between the two isotopes.

9th

c The relative atomic mass of iridium is 192.22. Explain whether a naturally occurring sample of iridium contains more ^{191}Ir or ^{193}Ir.

10th

9 Use the Periodic Table to explain whether the following statement is true or false.

Considering only the most common isotope of each element, there is only one element that has more protons than neutrons.

4 THE PERIODIC TABLE

The Periodic Table shows all the elements in the universe and is one of the most important tools that a chemist has. The arrangement of the elements allows us to understand trends in properties and make predictions. The modern Periodic Table was first presented in 1869 by a famous Russian chemist, Dmitri Mendeleev (left). This chapter explores some of the features of the Periodic Table.

LEARNING OBJECTIVES

- Understand how elements are arranged in the Periodic Table:
  - in order of atomic number
  - in groups and periods
- Understand how to deduce the electronic configurations of the first 20 elements from their positions in the Periodic Table
- Understand how to use electrical conductivity and the acid–base character of oxides to classify elements as metals or non-metals
- Identify an element as a metal or a non-metal according to its position in the Periodic Table
- Understand how the electronic configuration of a main group element is related to its position in the Periodic Table
- Understand why elements in the same group of the Periodic Table have similar chemical properties
- Understand why the noble gases (Group 0) do not readily react

THE PERIODIC TABLE

The search for patterns in chemistry during the 19th century resulted in the modern Periodic Table. *The elements are arranged in order of atomic number* – the number of protons in the nuclei of the atoms.

The vertical columns are called **groups**

The horizontal rows are called **periods**

Period	1	2											3	4	5	6	7	0
1	H																	He
2	Li	Be											B	C	N	O	F	Ne
3	Na	Mg					transition metals						Al	Si	P	S	Cl	Ar
4	K	Ca	Sc	Ti	V	Cr	Mn	Fe	Co	Ni	Cu	Zn	Ga	Ge	As	Se	Br	Kr
5	Rb	Sr	Y	Zr	Nb	Mo	Tc	Ru	Rh	Pd	Ag	Cd	In	Sn	Sb	Te	I	Xe
6	Cs	Ba	•	Hf	Ta	W	Re	Os	Ir	Pt	Au	Hg	Tl	Pb	Bi	Po	At	Rn
7	Fr	Ra	:	Rf	Db	Sg	Bh	Hs	Mt	Ds	Rg	Cn	Nh	Fl	Mc	Lv	Ts	Og

lanthanoids

•	La	Ce	Pr	Nd	Pm	Sm	Eu	Gd	Tb	Dy	Ho	Er	Tm	Yb	Lu
:	Ac	Th	Pa	U	Np	Pu	Am	Cm	Bk	Cf	Es	Fm	Md	No	Lr

actinoids

▲ Figure 4.1 The Periodic Table

DID YOU KNOW?

You will sometimes see Group 0 labelled as Group 8. In more advanced Periodic Tables the groups are numbered from 1 to 18, including the transition metals.

REMINDER

For a larger version of the Periodic Table, including atomic numbers and other information, see Appendix A.

DID YOU KNOW?

Most International GCSE Periodic Tables stop at the end of the actinoid series, even though more elements continue to be discovered. Some tables completely omit the lanthanoids and actinoids because the emphasis in International GCSE is placed on a general understanding, which can easily be achieved with the main group and transition elements. Although sometimes called the rare earth metals, the lanthanoids are actually not that rare and are quite important in modern technology. Most of the actinoids are unstable and **undergo** radioactive decay.

EXTENSION WORK

The third shell can actually hold up to 18 electrons. To explain why 2 electrons go into the fourth shell before the third shell is completely filled requires a more advanced understanding of electronic configurations. Each shell is actually made up of a series of subshells and some of these subshells overlap from one shell to another. The 4s subshell (which can hold 2 electrons) is lower in energy than the 3d subshell (which can hold 10 electrons) and so 2 electrons go into the fourth shell before the next 10 go into the third shell.

The vertical columns in the Periodic Table are called **groups**. The first seven groups are numbered from 1 to 7 and the final group is numbered 0. The elements in orange in Figure 4.1 are called the transition metals or transition elements. At this level, they are not usually included in the numbering of the groups. Some of the groups have names, e.g. Group 1 is the *alkali metals*, Group 7 is the ***halogens*** and Group 0 is the *noble gases*.

The horizontal rows in the Periodic Table are called **periods**. It is important to remember that hydrogen and helium make up Period 1.

The lanthanoids and actinoids are usually dropped out of their proper places and written separately at the bottom of the Periodic Table. There is a good reason for this. If you put them where they should be (as in Figure 4.2), everything has to be drawn slightly smaller to fit on the page. That makes it more difficult to read.

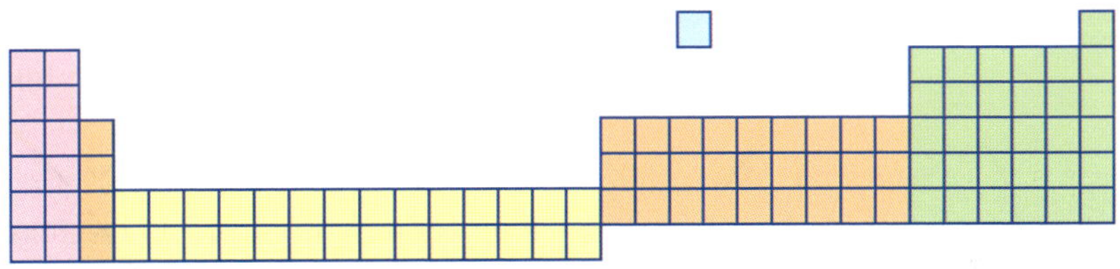

▲ Figure 4.2 The real shape of the Periodic Table

THE PERIODIC TABLE AND THE NUMBER OF PROTONS, NEUTRONS AND ELECTRONS

Most Periodic Tables have two numbers against each symbol. The atomic number will always be the smaller number. The other number will either be the mass number of the most common isotope of the element or the relative atomic mass of the element. The Periodic Table will tell you which.

You can use a Periodic Table to work out the number of protons, neutrons and electrons there are in atoms. Remember:

- the number of protons in an atom is equal to the atomic number
- the number of electrons in an atom is equal to the number of protons
- the number of neutrons in an atom = mass number – atomic number.

THE ARRANGEMENT OF THE ELECTRONS IN AN ATOM

The electrons move around the nucleus in a series of levels called **energy levels** or **shells**. Each energy level (shell) can only hold a certain number of electrons. Lower energy levels are always filled before higher ones. The lowest energy level is the closest one to the nucleus.

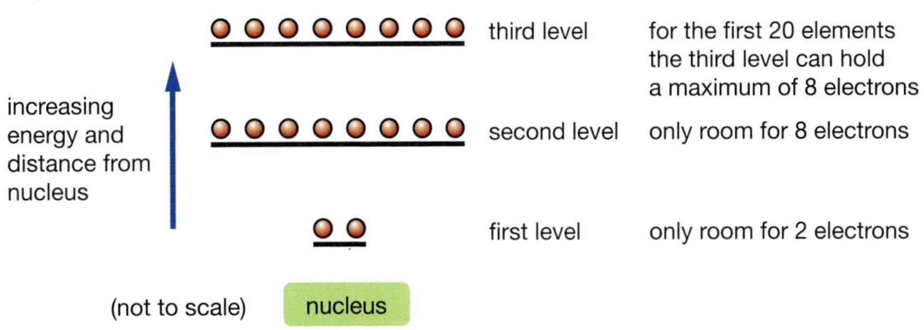

▲ Figure 4.3 The different energy levels for electrons in an atom showing the maximum number of electrons that each energy level (shell) can hold.

HOW TO WORK OUT THE ARRANGEMENT OF ELECTRONS IN AN ATOM

The arrangement of electrons in an atom is called its **electronic configuration**.

We will use chlorine as an example.

Look up the atomic number in the Periodic Table. (Make sure that you don't use the wrong number if you have a choice. The atomic number will always be the smaller one.)

The Periodic Table tells you that chlorine's atomic number is 17.

This tells you the number of protons. The number of electrons is equal to the number of protons.

There are 17 protons and so 17 electrons in a neutral chlorine atom.

Arrange the electrons in shells (energy levels), always completing an inner shell (lower energy level) before you go to an outer one. Remember that the first shell (lowest energy level) can take up to 2 electrons, the second one can take up to 8, and the third one also takes up to 8.

For chlorine the electrons will be arranged as follows: 2 in the first shell, 8 in the second shell and 7 in the third shell. This is written as 2, 8, 7. When you have finished, always check to make sure that the electrons add up to the right number, in this case 17.

DRAWING DIAGRAMS OF ELECTRONIC CONFIGURATIONS

When we draw a diagram of an atom we usually draw circles to represent the shells (energy levels); dots or crosses are then drawn on the circles to represent the electrons. You can choose to draw dots or crosses.

Hydrogen has 1 electron and helium has 2 in the first shell (lowest energy level).

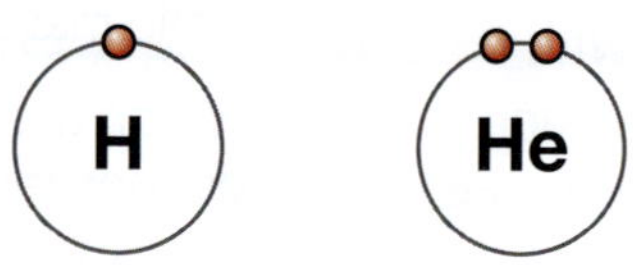

▲ Figure 4.4 Electronic arrangements of hydrogen and helium

KEY POINT

Drawing circles like this does not imply that the electrons are orbiting the nucleus along the circles.
The circles represent energy levels. The further away the level is from the nucleus, the higher its energy.
It is impossible to work out exactly how an electron is moving in that energy level.

The helium electrons are sometimes shown as a pair (as here), and sometimes as two separate electrons on opposite sides of the circle. Either form is acceptable.

The next 8 atoms are drawn like this:

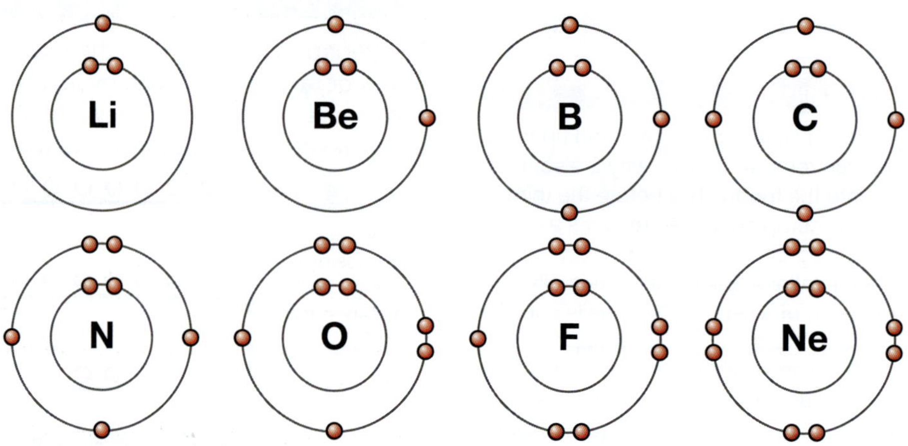

▲ Figure 4.5 The electronic arrangements of the elements in Period 2

HINT

The terms 'shell' and 'energy level' are used quite interchangeably by chemists. To make things easier, we will just use one term, shell, from now on. If, however, you prefer the term energy level, that is absolutely fine and both terms will be accepted in the examination.

It does not matter at this level whether you draw the electrons singly or in pairs.

The atoms in the Periodic Table from sodium to argon fill the third shell in exactly the same way, and potassium and calcium start to fill the fourth shell.

Potassium and calcium will look like this:

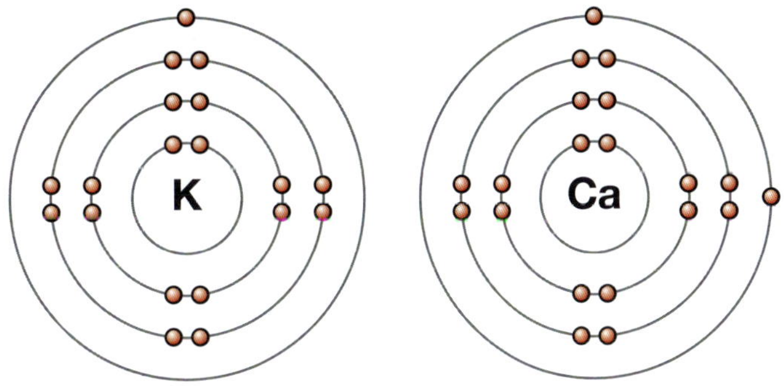

▲ Figure 4.6 Electronic arrangements of potassium and calcium

ELECTRONIC CONFIGURATIONS AND THE PERIODIC TABLE

The electronic configurations of the first 20 elements in the Periodic Table are shown in Figure 4.7.

Group 1	Group 2		Group 3	Group 4	Group 5	Group 6	Group 7	Group 0
		H 1						He 2
Li 2,1	Be 2,2		B 2,3	C 2,4	N 2,5	O 2,6	F 2,7	Ne 2,8
Na 2,8,1	Mg 2,8,2		Al 2,8,3	Si 2,8,4	P 2,8,5	S 2,8,6	Cl 2,8,7	Ar 2,8,8
K 2,8,8,1	Ca 2,8,8,2	10 more elements						

▲ Figure 4.7 The electronic configurations of the first 20 elements in the Periodic Table

Two important facts:

- ***Elements in the same group in the Periodic Table have the same number of electrons in their outer shell.***
- ***The number of electrons in the outer shell is the same as the group number for Groups 1 to 7.***

So if you know that barium is in Group 2, you know it has 2 electrons in its outer shell, the same as all the other elements in Group 2. Iodine (Group 7) has 7 electrons in its outer shell. Lead (Group 4) has 4 electrons in its outer shell. Working out what is in their inner shells is much more difficult – the simple patterns we have described don't work beyond calcium.

The period number gives the number of occupied shells or the highest occupied shell.

So, calcium (electronic configuration = 2, 8, 8, 2) is in Period 4 and has four shells occupied; the outermost electron is in the fourth shell. Iodine is in Period 5 and has five occupied shells, and because it is also in Group 7 we can deduce that it has 7 electrons in the fifth shell.

ELEMENTS IN THE SAME GROUP IN THE PERIODIC TABLE HAVE SIMILAR CHEMICAL PROPERTIES

Groups in the Periodic Table contain elements with similar chemical properties – they react in the same way.

For example:

- all the elements in Group 1 react vigorously with water to form hydrogen and hydroxides with similar formulae: LiOH (lithium hydroxide), NaOH (sodium hydroxide), KOH (potassium hydroxide)
- all the elements in Group 7 react with hydrogen to form compounds with similar formulae: HF (hydrogen fluoride), HCl (hydrogen chloride), HBr (hydrogen bromide)
- all the elements in Group 2 form chlorides with similar formulae: $MgCl_2$, $CaCl_2$.

The reactions of atoms depend on how many electrons there are in their outer shell. These are the electrons which normally get involved when elements bond to other elements. Elements in the same group (apart from helium in Group 0) have the same number of electrons in their outer shell, therefore they react in similar ways.

THE NOBLE GASES

The Group 0 elements are known as the **noble gases** because they are almost completely unreactive, in fact the two at the top of the group, helium and neon, don't react with anything. The elements in Group 0 have 8 electrons in their outer shell (apart from helium, which has 2).

The lack of reactivity of the elements in Group 0 is associated with their electronic configurations. The noble gases are unreactive because *the outer shell is full, and so there is no tendency to lose, gain or share electrons in a chemical reaction*. You will learn more about how elements form compounds in Chapters 6 and 7.

He
Ne
Ar
Kr
Xe
Rn

▲ Figure 4.8 The noble gases

KEY POINT

The reason the noble gas group is usually called Group 0 and not Group 8 (which would seem more sensible because most of the elements have 8 electrons in their outer shell) is because when they were first discovered it was believed that noble gases did not combine with anything, they had zero combining power (valency). This is the only group where the group number does not tell you the number of electrons in the outer shell! The key point is that the noble gases (except helium) have 8 electrons in their outer shell. You will see in Chapters 6 and 7 that atoms tend to form compounds by losing/gaining or sharing electrons so that they have 8 electrons in their outer shell. The noble gases already have 8 electrons in their outer shell so they do not do that.

EXTENSION WORK

In reality, the outer shells of argon, krypton, xenon and radon are not full; in fact only helium and neon have full outer shells. The third shell can actually hold up to 18 electrons and the fourth up to 32 electrons.

METALS AND NON-METALS IN THE PERIODIC TABLE

The metals are on the left-hand side of the Periodic Table and the non-metals are on the right-hand side. Although the division into metals and non-metals is shown clearly in Figure 4.9, in practice there is a lot of uncertainty on the dividing line. For example, arsenic (As) has properties of both metals and non-metals.

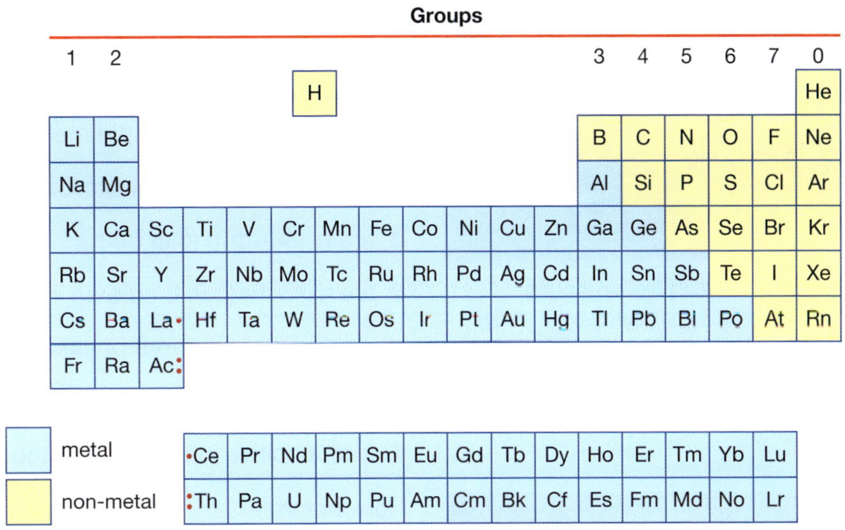

▲ Figure 4.9 Metals and non-metals

KEY POINT

You may have noticed by now that hydrogen does not really fit into the Periodic Table properly. Although it has 1 electron in its outer shell, it is not in Group 1 because it does not have similar properties to the other elements in Group 1: it is not a metal and does not have similar chemical properties to the alkali metals.

EXTENSION WORK

If you are interested you could try an internet search for 'metallic hydrogen'.

DIFFERENCES BETWEEN THE PROPERTIES OF METALS AND NON-METALS

There are many differences between the properties of metals and non-metals. Here, we will use two main ones to classify them: electrical conductivity and the acid–base character of their oxides.

Metals conduct electricity and non-metals do not generally conduct electricity. You may be familiar with the use of metals such as copper in electrical wires.

Non-metals do not conduct electricity (because there are no electrons that are free to move or mobile ions) but there are a few exceptions, such as graphite (a form of carbon) and silicon.

Metals generally form basic oxides. A basic oxide is one which reacts with acids to form salts. For example, copper forms copper(II) oxide (CuO). This reacts, for example, with sulfuric acid to form the salt copper(II) sulfate:

$$CuO + H_2SO_4 \rightarrow CuSO_4 + H_2O$$

copper(II) oxide + sulfuric acid → copper(II) sulfate + water

The reactions between **bases** and acids will be discussed in more detail in Chapter 13.

Non-metals generally form acidic oxides. You may be familiar, for example, with sulfur(IV) oxide (SO_2) being one of the gases responsible for acid rain. Acidic oxides react with bases/alkalis to form salts. For example, carbon dioxide, an acidic oxide, reacts with sodium hydroxide, an alkali:

$$CO_2 + 2NaOH \rightarrow Na_2CO_3 + H_2O$$

carbon dioxide + sodium hydroxide → sodium carbonate + water

Some other properties you might also associate with metals and non-metals are included in the list on the next page.

▲ Figure 4.10 Copper, like all other metals, conducts electricity.

EXTENSION WORK

The reason that metals conduct electricity is due to the presence of delocalised electrons that are free to move.

KEY POINT

If a basic oxide is soluble in water it will dissolve to form an alkali. For example, sodium oxide reacts with water to form sodium hydroxide solution, an alkali. If an acidic oxide is soluble in water it will dissolve to form an acidic solution. For example, sulfur(IV) oxide reacts with water to form sulfurous acid.

KEY POINT

There are some exceptions to the rules. For example, some metals form **amphoteric** oxides (e.g. Al_2O_3), which react with acids and bases, and some non-metal oxides (e.g. CO) are neutral.

▲ Figure 4.11 Mercury has most of the properties of a metal (high density, shiny, conducts electricity, forms positive ions); the exception is that it is a liquid at room temperature.

▲ Figure 4.12 Sulfur crystals are shiny, but you wouldn't mistake them for a metal.

Metals:

- tend to be solids with high melting and boiling points, and with relatively high densities (but as with several of the properties in this list, there are exceptions, for example mercury is a liquid)
- are shiny (have a metallic lustre) when they are polished or freshly cut
- are **malleable** (can be **hammered** into shape)
- are **ductile** (can be drawn into wires)
- are good conductors of electricity and heat
- form ionic compounds (see Chapter 6)
- form positive ions in their compounds (see Chapter 6).

Non-metals:

- tend to have low melting and boiling points (there are some exceptions, e.g. carbon and silicon)
- tend to be brittle when they are solids
- don't have the same type of shine as metals
- don't usually conduct electricity; carbon (in the form of graphite) and silicon are again exceptions
- are poor conductors of heat (diamond is an exception; it is the best conductor of heat of all the elements)
- form both ionic and covalent compounds (see Chapters 6 and 7)
- tend to form negative ions in ionic compounds (see Chapter 6).

CHAPTER QUESTIONS

You will need to use the Periodic Table in Appendix A on page 708.

SKILLS CRITICAL THINKING 6th

1 Answer the questions that follow using only the elements in this list:

caesium, chlorine, molybdenum, neon, nickel, nitrogen, strontium, tin.

a State the name of an element which is:

i in Group 2

ii in the same period as silicon

iii in the same group as phosphorus

iv in Period 6

v a noble gas

b Divide the list of elements at the beginning of the question into two groups, metals and non-metals.

SKILLS INTERPRETATION 8th

2 Draw diagrams to show the arrangement of the electrons in:

a sodium

b silicon

c sulfur

SKILLS CRITICAL THINKING

8th

3 State the electronic configurations of the following atoms:

a fluorine

b aluminium

c calcium

SKILLS PROBLEM SOLVING

9th

4 Find each of the following elements in the Periodic Table and state the number of electrons in its outer shell:

a arsenic, As

b bromine, Br

c tin, Sn

d xenon, Xe

SKILLS REASONING

8th

5 The questions refer to the electronic configurations below. Don't worry if some of these are unfamiliar to you. All of these are the electronic configurations of neutral atoms.

A 2, 4

B 2, 8, 8

C 2, 8, 18, 18, 7

D 2, 8, 18, 18, 8

E 2, 8, 8, 2

F 2, 8, 18, 32, 18, 4

a Explain which of these atoms are in Group 4 of the Periodic Table.

b State which of these electronic configurations represents carbon.

c Explain which atoms are in Period 5 of the Periodic Table.

d Explain which of these electronic configurations represents an element in Group 7 of the Periodic Table.

e State which of these electronic configurations represent noble gases.

SKILLS PROBLEM SOLVING

f State the name of element **E** and explain how you arrived at your answer.

g State how many protons are present in an atom of element **F**. State the name of the element.

SKILLS INTERPRETATION

h Element **G** has one more electron than element **B**. Draw a diagram to show how the electrons are arranged in an atom of **G**.

SKILLS REASONING

6 Predict two properties of the element palladium, Pd (atomic number 46), or its compounds. The properties can be either physical or chemical.

7 Helium and neon do not form any compounds. Explain why the noble gases are unreactive.

9th

8 The elements in the Periodic Table are arranged in order of atomic number. If they were arranged in order of mass number give the names of two elements that would be in different positions. Explain why this would cause a problem.

5 CHEMICAL FORMULAE, EQUATIONS AND CALCULATIONS

It is often important in chemistry to know how much of one substance reacts with a certain amount of another. To do this, we will learn about moles in this chapter.

▲ Figure 5.1 Each gold bar contains almost 4×10^{25} gold atoms. That's 4 followed by 25 noughts! Learning about the mole allows us to work out how many atoms are in something.

LEARNING OBJECTIVES

- Write word equations and balanced chemical equations (including state symbols):
  - for reactions studied in this course
  - for unfamiliar reactions where suitable information is provided
- Calculate relative formula masses (including relative molecular masses) (M_r) from relative atomic masses (A_r)
- Know that the mole (mol) is the unit for the amount of a substance
- Understand how to carry out calculations involving amount of substance, relative atomic mass (A_r) and relative formula mass (M_r)
- Calculate reacting masses using experimental data and chemical equations
- Calculate percentage yield
- Understand how the formulae of simple compounds can be obtained experimentally, including metal oxides, water and salts containing water of crystallisation
- Know what is meant by the terms empirical formula and molecular formula
- Calculate empirical and molecular formulae from experimental data
- Practical: Know how to determine the formula of a metal oxide by combustion (e.g. magnesium oxide) or by reduction (e.g. copper(II) oxide)

WRITING EQUATIONS

There are two types of chemical equation that you could be asked to write: **word equations** and symbol equations. Symbol equations are usually called *chemical equations* and you should only write a word equation if you are specifically asked to. All chemical equations must be balanced.

WHAT ALL THE NUMBERS MEAN

An example of a balanced chemical equation is:

$$CaCO_3 + 2HCl \rightarrow CaCl_2 + CO_2 + H_2O$$

When you write equations, it is important to be able to count how many of each type of atom you have. In particular, you must understand the difference between big numbers written in front of formulae (sometimes called **coefficients**), such as the **2** in **2**HCl, and the smaller, **subscript** (slightly lower on the line) numbers, such as the **3** in $CaCO_3$.

Another chemical equation is $2Cl \rightarrow Cl_2$. Here, **2Cl** represents 2 separate Cl atoms and $\mathbf{Cl_2}$ means that the atoms are joined together in a molecule.

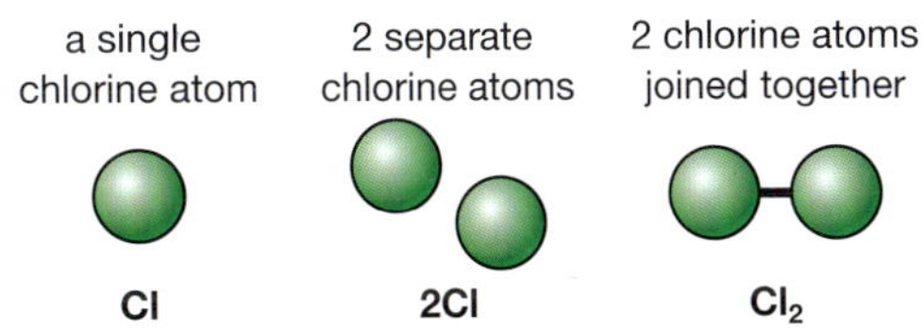

▲ Figure 5.2 The difference between 2Cl and Cl_2

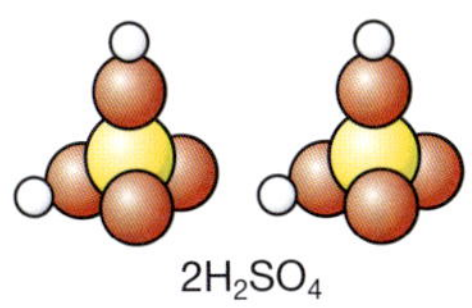

▲ Figure 5.3 $2H_2SO_4$. The sulfur atoms are shown in yellow, the oxygens in red and the hydrogens in white.

Another balanced chemical equation is $H_2S_2O_7 + H_2O \rightarrow 2H_2SO_4$.

Look at the way the numbers work in $2H_2SO_4$. The big number in front tells you that you have 2 sulfuric acid (H_2SO_4) molecules. The subscript 4 tells you that you have 4 oxygen atoms in each molecule. A small, subscript number in a **formula** applies only to the atom immediately before it in the formula. If you count the atoms in $2H_2SO_4$ you will find 4 hydrogens, 2 sulfurs and 8 oxygens.

If you have brackets in a formula, the small number refers to everything inside the brackets. For example, in the formula $Ca(OH)_2$, the 2 applies to both the oxygen and the hydrogen. The formula shows 1 calcium, 2 oxygens and 2 hydrogens. You will learn more about how to work out the formulae of compounds in Chapter 6.

BALANCING EQUATIONS

Chemical reactions involve taking elements or compounds and moving their atoms around into new combinations. It follows that you must always end up with the same number of atoms that you started with.

Imagine you had to write an equation for the reaction between methane, CH_4, and oxygen, O_2. Methane burns in oxygen to form carbon dioxide and water. Think of this in terms of rearranging the atoms in some models.

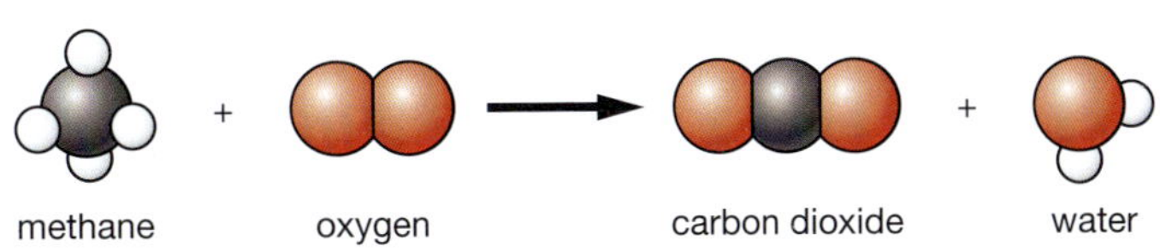

▲ Figure 5.4 Rearranging the atoms in methane and oxygen

If you count the atoms you had at the beginning (on the left-hand side of the arrow) and the atoms you have at the end (on the right-hand side of the arrow), you can see that this can't be right! During the rearrangement, we seem to have gained an oxygen atom and lost two hydrogens. The reaction must be more complicated than this. Since the substances are all correct, the proportions must be wrong.

Try again:

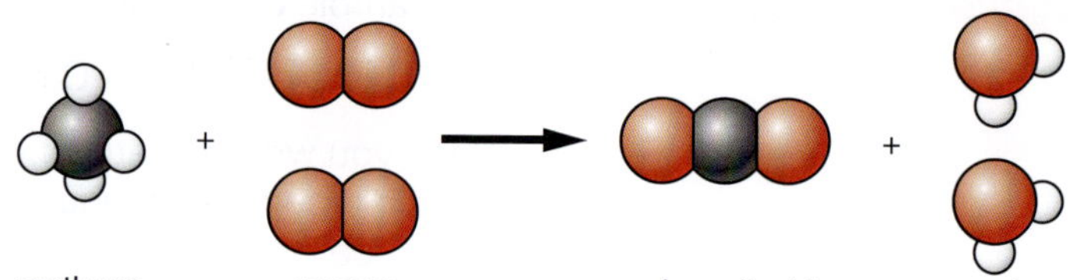

▲ Figure 5.5 A balanced equation for the reaction between methane and oxygen.

There are now the same number of each type of atom before and after. This is called **balancing the equation**.

In symbols, this equation would be:

$$CH_4 + 2O_2 \rightarrow CO_2 + 2H_2O$$

Think of each symbol (C or H or O) as representing one atom of that element. Count them up in the equation, and check that there is the same number of atoms on both sides.

HOW TO BALANCE EQUATIONS

In order to balance equations you should adopt a systematic approach.

- Work across the equation from left to right, checking one element after another, except if an element appears in several places in the equation. In that case, leave the element until the end and you will often find that it has sorted itself out.
- If you have a group of atoms (like a sulfate group (SO_4), for example), which is unchanged from one side of the equation to the other, there is no reason why you can't just count that up as a whole group, rather than counting individual sulfurs and oxygens. It saves time.
- Check everything at the end to make sure you haven't changed something that you have already counted.

HINT

This is really important! You must never, never change a formula when balancing an equation. All you are allowed to do is to write big numbers in front of the formula.

EXAMPLE 1

Balance the equation for the reaction between zinc and hydrochloric acid:

$$Zn + HCl \rightarrow ZnCl_2 + H_2$$

Work from left to right. Count the zinc atoms: 1 on each side; no problem!

Count the hydrogen atoms: 1 on the left, 2 on the right. If you have 2 at the end, you must have started with 2. The only way of achieving this is to have 2HCl. (You must not change the formula to H_2Cl because this substance does not exist.)

$$Zn + 2HCl \rightarrow ZnCl_2 + H_2$$

Now count the chlorines: there are 2 on each side. Good! Finally check everything again to make sure and you've finished.

	Zn + 2HCl		→	$ZnCl_2 + H_2$	
numbers of atoms	Zn	1		Zn	1
	H	2		H	2
	Cl	2		Cl	2

EXAMPLE 2

Balance the equation for the **combustion** of ethane:

$$C_2H_6 + O_2 \rightarrow CO_2 + H_2O$$

Starting from the left, balance the carbons:

$$C_2H_6 + O_2 \rightarrow 2CO_2 + H_2O$$

Now the hydrogens:

$$C_2H_6 + O_2 \rightarrow 2CO_2 + 3H_2O$$

Finally the oxygens: there are 7 oxygens ((2 × 2) + 3) on the right-hand side, but only 2 on the left. The problem is that the oxygens have to go around in pairs. So how can you obtain an odd number (7) of oxygens on the left-hand side?

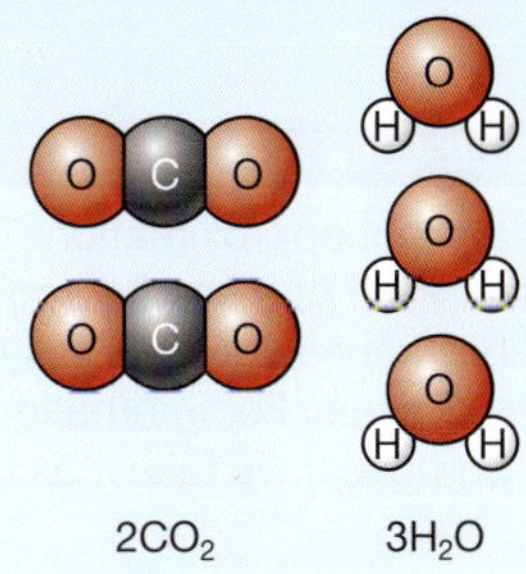

Figure 5.6 There are 7 O atoms in $2CO_2 + 3H_2O$

The trick with this is to allow yourself to have halves in your equation. 7 oxygen atoms, O, is the same as $3\frac{1}{2}$ oxygen molecules, O_2.

$$C_2H_6 + 3\tfrac{1}{2}O_2 \rightarrow 2CO_2 + 3H_2O$$

Now double everything to get rid of the half:

$$2C_2H_6 + 7O_2 \rightarrow 4CO_2 + 6H_2O$$

KEY POINT

In fact, it is acceptable to have halves in equations, but you don't usually come across them at Internaional GCSE.
You might reasonably argue that you can't have half an oxygen molecule, but to remove that problem all you have to do is double everything.

STATE SYMBOLS

State symbols are often, but not always, written after the formulae of the various substances in an equation to show what physical state everything is in. You need to know four different state symbols:

(s) solid (l) liquid (g) gas (aq) in **aqueous** solution (dissolved in water)

So an equation might look like this:

$$2K(s) + 2H_2O(l) \rightarrow 2KOH(aq) + H_2(g)$$

This shows that *solid* potassium reacts with *liquid* water to make a *solution* of potassium hydroxide in water and hydrogen *gas*.

HINT

Don't worry if this chemistry is new to you, or if at this stage you don't know what the state symbols should be. That is not important at the moment.

HINT

Remember that water is a liquid (l), not an aqueous solution (aq). An aqueous solution is formed when something is *dissolved in water*.

HOW MUCH OF EACH SUBSTANCE REACTS IN A CHEMICAL REACTION?

You can make iron(II) sulfide by heating a mixture of iron and sulfur:

$$Fe + S \rightarrow FeS$$

How do you know what proportions to mix them in? You can't just mix equal masses of them because iron and sulfur atoms don't weigh the same. Iron atoms contain more protons and neutrons than sulfur atoms, so an iron atom is one and three-quarter times heavier than a sulfur atom. In this or any other reaction, you can get the right proportions only if you know about the masses of the individual atoms that take part in the reaction.

RELATIVE ATOMIC MASS (A_r)

We have already looked at how to calculate relative atomic masses from the isotopic abundances in Chapter 3. Here we will look a little more closely at what exactly the relative atomic mass is.

REMINDER

Remember that isotopes are atoms of the same element, but with different masses. Isotopes are explained in Chapter 3 (page 276).

EXTENSION WORK

This is a slight approximation. To be accurate, each of these hydrogen atoms has a mass of 1.008 on the carbon-12 scale. For International GCSE purposes, we take it as being exactly 1.

Atoms are amazingly small. The mass of a hydrogen atom is about 1.67×10^{-24} g (0.00000000000000000000000167 g). It is really difficult to use numbers such as this and so we use a scale of *relative* masses instead. The masses of atoms (and molecules) are compared with the mass of an atom of the carbon-12 isotope. We call this the carbon-12 scale. On this scale, one atom of the carbon-12 isotope weighs *exactly* 12 units and the mass of the most common hydrogen isotope is 1, which is a much simpler number to use!

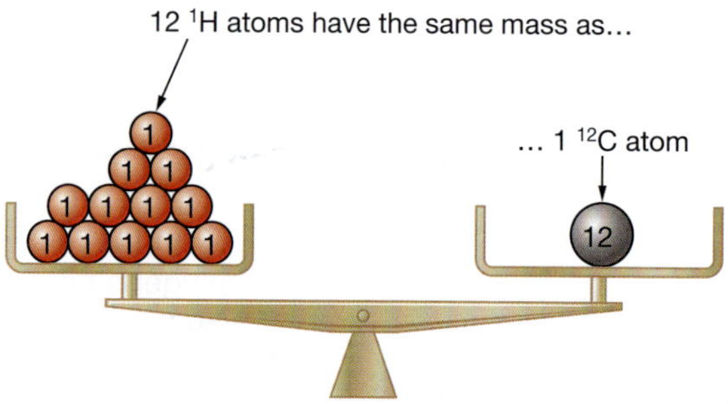

▲ Figure 5.7 The most common hydrogen atom weighs one-twelfth as much as a ^{12}C atom.

The basic unit on the carbon-12 scale is $\frac{1}{12}$ of the mass of a ^{12}C atom, which is approximately the mass of the most common hydrogen atom. A fluorine-19 atom has a relative mass of 19 because its atoms have a mass 19 times that of $\frac{1}{12}$ of a ^{12}C atom. An atom of the most common isotope of magnesium weighs 24 times as much as $\frac{1}{12}$ of a ^{12}C atom, and is therefore said to have a relative mass of 24.

The masses we are talking about here are the masses of individual *isotopes*, but samples of an actual element contain different isotopes and so we need a measure of the average mass of an *atom* taking into account the different isotopes. This is the relative atomic mass.

The relative atomic mass of an element (as opposed to one of its isotopes) is given the symbol $\boldsymbol{A_r}$ and it is defined like this:

KEY POINT

Remember, to work out a weighted average we have to know how much of each isotope is present in a sample.

The relative atomic mass of an element is the weighted average mass of the isotopes of the element. It is measured on a scale on which a carbon-12 (^{12}C) atom has a mass of exactly 12.

Because we are talking here about *relative* masses they have no units.

On this scale, the relative atomic mass of chlorine is 35.45, that of lithium is 6.94 and that of sodium is 22.99 because we are taking into account the different isotopes, and are quoting an average mass for an atom. Although all elements consist of a mixture of isotopes, at International GCSE we only use relative atomic masses, including decimal places for Cl (35.5) and Cu (63.5), therefore we will take the relative atomic mass of lithium as 7 and that of sodium as 23.

HINT

Avoid the term 'relative molecular mass' because it can only properly be applied to substances which are actually molecules, that is, to covalent substances. You shouldn't use it for things like magnesium oxide or sodium chloride, which are ionic. Relative formula mass covers everything.

RELATIVE FORMULA MASS (M_r)

You can measure the masses of compounds on the same carbon-12 scale. For example, a water molecule, H_2O, has a mass of 18 on the carbon-12 scale. This means that a water molecule has 18 times the mass of $\frac{1}{12}$ of a ^{12}C atom.

If you are talking about compounds, you use the term **relative formula mass**. Relative formula mass is sometimes called relative molecular mass.

Relative formula mass is given the symbol $\boldsymbol{M_r}$.

CALCULATING SOME RELATIVE FORMULA MASSES

To find the relative formula mass (M_r) of magnesium carbonate, $MgCO_3$

Relative atomic masses: C = 12, O = 16, Mg = 24.

Add up the relative atomic masses to give the relative formula mass of the whole compound. In this case, you need to add up the masses of 1 × Mg, 1 × C and 3 × O.

$$M_r = \underset{Mg}{24} + \underset{C}{12} + \underset{(3 \times O)}{(3 \times 16)}$$

$$M_r = 84$$

To find the relative formula mass of calcium hydroxide, $Ca(OH)_2$

Relative atomic masses: H = 1, O = 16, Ca = 40.

$$M_r = \underset{Ca}{40} + (\underset{O}{16} + \underset{H}{1}) \times 2$$

$$M_r = 74$$

HINT

Remember, you do not have to calculate the relative atomic masses, they will always be given to you in an exam, either in the question or on the Periodic Table. **If you use a Periodic Table, be sure to use the right number!** It will always be the larger of the two numbers given.

To find the M_r of copper(II) sulfate crystals, $CuSO_4{\cdot}5H_2O$

This formula looks very different and a lot more complicated than the ones we have looked at above. When some substances crystallise from solution, water becomes chemically bound up with the salt. This is called **water of crystallisation**. The $5H_2O$ is water of crystallisation. The water is necessary to form crystals of copper(II) sulfate (and some other substances). There are always 5 water molecules associated with 1 $CuSO_4$ unit and they are part of the formula. Salts containing water of crystallisation are said to be **hydrated**. Other examples include $Na_2CO_3{\cdot}10H_2O$ and $MgCl_2{\cdot}6H_2O$.

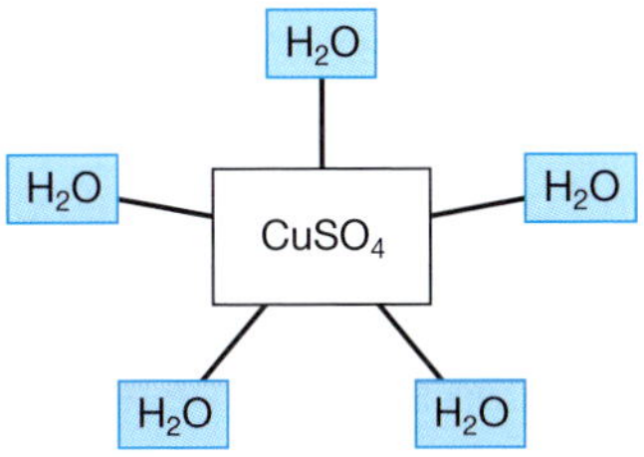

▲ Figure 5.8 A schematic diagram showing the formula of copper(II) sulfate crystals: there are five water molecules bonded to each copper(II) sulfate unit.

Relative atomic masses: H = 1, O = 16, S = 32, Cu = 63.5.

It is easiest to work out the relative formula mass of water first:

$$H_2O: \quad M_r = 2 \times 1 + 16 = 18$$

Now add the correct number of waters on to the rest of the formula:

$$CuSO_4{\cdot}5H_2O: \quad M_r = \underset{Cu}{63.5} + \underset{S}{32} + \underset{(4 \times O)}{(4 \times 16)} + \underset{(5 \times H_2O)}{(5 \times 18)} = 249.5$$

HINT

It is dangerous to calculate the number of hydrogens and oxygens separately. The common mistake is to work out 10 hydrogens (quite correctly!), but then only count 1 oxygen rather than 5.

USING RELATIVE FORMULA MASS TO FIND PERCENTAGE COMPOSITION

Having found the relative formula mass of a compound, we can work out the percentage by mass of any part of it. Examples make this clear.

To find the percentage by mass of copper in copper(II) oxide, CuO

Relative atomic masses: O = 16, Cu = 63.5.

$$M_r \text{ of CuO} = 63.5 + 16 = 79.5$$

Of this, 63.5 is copper.

$$\text{Percentage of copper} = \frac{63.5}{79.5} \times 100$$

$$= 79.9\%$$

To find the percentage by mass of oxygen in sodium carbonate, Na_2CO_3

Relative atomic masses: Na = 23, C = 12, O = 16.

$$M_r = (2 \times 23) + 12 + (3 \times 16)$$

$$= 106$$

48 of this 106 is due to the oxygen (remember that there are 3 oxygens in the formula, so the total mass of oxygen is 3 × 16 = 48).

$$\text{Percentage of oxygen} = \frac{3 \times 16}{106} \times 100 = 45.3\%$$

▲ Figure 5.9 1-mole quantities (clockwise from upper left) of carbon (12 g), sulfur (32 g), iron (56 g), copper (63.5 g) and magnesium (24 g).

THE MOLE

In chemistry, the **mole** is a unit of the amount of substance. We can talk about an amount of substance in grams or an amount of substance in moles. The difference between expressing the amount of substance in moles or in grams is that 1 mole of any substance has its own particular mass. For example, 1 mole of water has a mass of 18 g, 1 mole of sulfur has a mass of 32 g and 1 mole of magnesium oxide has a mass of 40 g. The abbreviation for mole is **mol**.

We can therefore talk, for example, about an amount of water as 36 g or 2 mol, since 1 mol of water has a mass of 18 g. 36 g of sulfur, however, would only be 1.125 mol and 36 g of magnesium would be 1.5 mol because the mass of 1 mol of sulfur is 32 g and that of 1 mol of magnesium is 24 g.

Some people talk about the *amount in moles* and others talk about the *number of moles*. This is like talking about the *mass of a substance* or the *number of grams*. For example, we could say that the amount in grams of water is 36 g or the number of grams of water is 36 g. Similarly, we can say that the amount in moles of water is 2 mol or the number of moles of water is 2 mol.

CALCULATING THE MASSES OF A MOLE OF SUBSTANCE

You find the mass of 1 mole of a substance by calculating the relative formula mass (M_r) and attaching the units, grams.

1 mole of oxygen gas, O_2

Relative atomic mass: O = 16.

$$M_r \text{ of } O_2 = 2 \times 16 = 32$$

1 mole of oxygen, O_2, has a mass of 32 g.

1 mole of calcium chloride, $CaCl_2$

Relative atomic masses: Cl = 35.5, Ca = 40.

$$M_r \text{ of } CaCl_2 = 40 + (2 \times 35.5) = 111$$

1 mole of calcium chloride has a mass of 111 g.

1 mole of iron(II) sulfate crystals, $FeSO_4{\cdot}7H_2O$

Relative atomic masses: H = 1, O = 16, S = 32, Fe = 56.

$$M_r \text{ of crystals} = 56 + 32 + (4 \times 16) + \{7 \times [(2 \times 1) + 16]\}$$

1 mole of iron(II) sulfate crystals has a mass of 278 g.

THE IMPORTANCE OF QUOTING THE FORMULA

Whenever you talk about a mole of something, you *must* quote its formula, otherwise there is a risk of confusion.

For example, if you talk about 1 mole of oxygen, this could mean:

1 mole of oxygen atoms, O, with a mass of 16 g

1 mole of oxygen molecules, O_2, with a mass of 32 g.

HINT

We often use the term '**molar mass**' instead of 'mass of 1 mole'.

EXTENSION WORK

To be 100% correct 'molar mass' and 'mass of 1 mole' are not exactly the same thing and have different units: molar mass has units of g/mol and the mass of 1 mole has units of g. You are unlikely to come across the distinction between these at International GCSE.

SIMPLE CALCULATIONS WITH MOLES

You need to be able to interconvert between a mass in grams and an amount in moles for a given substance. There is a simple formula that you can learn:

$$\text{number of moles} = \frac{\text{mass (g)}}{\text{mass of 1 mole (g)}}$$

You can rearrange this formula to find whatever you want. If rearranging this expression causes you problems, you can learn a simple triangular arrangement to help you.

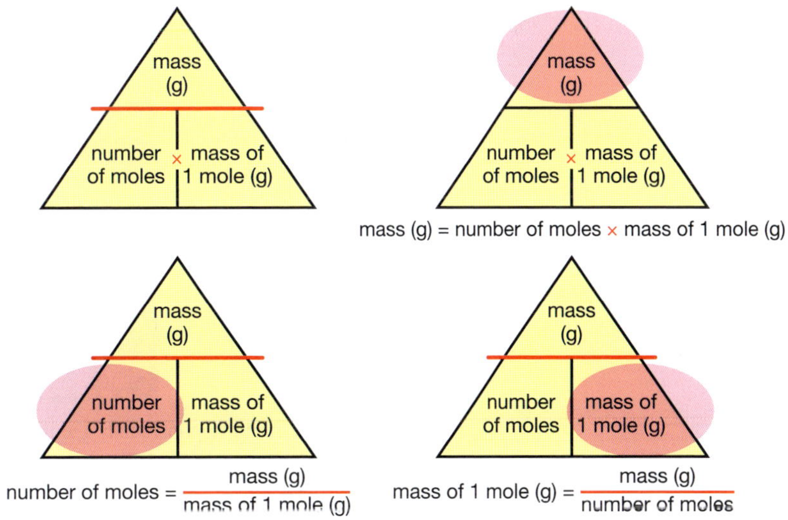

Figure 5.10 Converting between mass in grams and number of moles.

Look at this carefully and make sure that you understand how you can use it to deduce the three equations that you might need.

Finding the mass of 0.2 mol of calcium carbonate, $CaCO_3$

Relative atomic masses: C = 12, O = 16, Ca = 40.

First find the relative formula mass of calcium carbonate.

$$M_r \text{ of } CaCO_3 = 40 + 12 + (3 \times 16)$$
$$= 100$$

1 mol of $CaCO_3$ has a mass of 100 g.

$$\text{Mass (g)} = \text{number of moles} \times \text{mass of 1 mole (g)}$$
$$= 0.2 \times 100$$
$$= 20\,\text{g}$$

0.2 mol of $CaCO_3$ has a mass of 20 g.

HINT

Don't get too reliant on learning formulae for doing simple calculations. If 1 mole weighs 100 g, it should be fairly obvious to you that 2 moles will weigh twice as much, 10 moles will weigh 10 times as much and 0.2 moles will weigh 0.2 times as much.

Finding the number of moles in 54 g of water, H_2O

Relative atomic masses: H = 1, O = 16.

1 mol of H_2O has a mass of 18 g.

$$\text{Number of moles} = \frac{\text{mass (g)}}{\text{mass of 1 mole (g)}}$$
$$= \frac{54}{18}$$
$$= 3\,\text{mol}$$

54 g of water is 3 mol.

HINT

If 1 mol weighs 18 g, then you need to find out how many times 18 goes into 54 to find out how many moles you have. On the other hand, if you feel safer using a formula, use it.

EXTENSION WORK

Moles and the Avogadro constant

Imagine you had 1 mole of ^{12}C. It would have a mass of 12 g and contain a very large number of carbon atoms, in fact about 6×10^{23} carbon atoms, which is 6 followed by 23 noughts. This number of atoms in 12 g of ^{12}C is called the **Avogadro constant**.

1 mole of anything else contains this same number of particles. For example:

1 mole of magnesium contains 6×10^{23} magnesium atoms, Mg, and has a mass of 24 g.

1 mole of water contains 6×10^{23} water molecules, H_2O, and has a mass of 18 g.

This is the reason that we use moles: if we know the number of moles we also know how many particles are present. If we know how many particles are present, we can work out how much of one substance reacts with a certain amount of another.

▲ Figure 5.11 Approximately 1×10^{32} water molecules go over Niagara Falls every second during the summer. That's 100 million million million million million water molecules per second.

FORMULAE

The formula of sulfur dioxide is SO_2. We can see that there are 2 O atoms for each S atom. If we had 1 mol SO_2 we would still have twice as many O atoms as S atoms; there would be 1 mol S atoms and 2 mol O atoms. If we know that in a certain sample of sulfur dioxide we have 0.1 mol of S atoms we also know that we must have 0.2 mol O atoms. 0.2 mol contains twice as many atoms as 0.1 mol.

If we did an experiment and found that a compound contained 0.2 mol Ca and 0.2 mol O, then we could work out that the formula must be CaO because there are the same number of Ca atoms as O atoms.

If a compound contains 0.4 mol Mn and 0.8 mol O then the formula must be MnO_2 because there are twice as many O atoms as Mn atoms.

The formulae that we have found here are called *empirical formulae*.

The* empirical formula *shows the simplest whole number ratio of the atoms present in a compound.

There is another type of formula that we will come across, called the *molecular formula*.

The* molecular formula *shows the actual number of atoms of each element present in a molecule (covalent compound) or formula unit (ionic compound) of a compound.

The molecular formula can be the same as the empirical formula or a multiple of the empirical formula. The empirical formula of calcium oxide is CaO and the molecular formula is also CaO. The empirical formula of hydrogen peroxide is HO and the molecular formula is H_2O_2.

In order to work out the molecular formula from the empirical formula we need more information – the M_r of the compound. We will look at this again below.

WORKING OUT EMPIRICAL FORMULAE

In order to find out the empirical formula of a compound such as copper oxide, we need to know how many atoms of copper combine with how many atoms of oxygen. We can work out the number of atoms from the number of moles. If we know the ratio between the number of copper atoms and oxygen atoms in the compound we know the formula.

KEY POINT

0.02 mol of atoms is twice as many atoms as 0.01 mol of atoms.

HINT

More significant figures should have been used for the number of moles in the examples on this page but these have been omitted for simplicity.

EXAMPLE 3

A sample of a compound contains 1.27 g of Cu and 0.16 g of O. Calculate the empirical formula. (A_r of Cu – 63.5, A_r of O – 16)

It is easiest to do this in columns using a table:

	Cu	O
masses / g	1.27	0.16
find the number of moles of atoms by dividing the mass by the mass of 1 mole of atoms	1.27/63.5	0.16/16
number of moles of atoms	0.02	0.01
divide by the smaller number to find the ratio	0.02/0.01	0.01/0.01
ratio of moles	2	1
empirical formula	Cu_2O	

From calculating the number of moles of Cu and O we can see that there are twice as many moles of Cu and therefore there must be twice as many Cu atoms as O atoms in the compound.

It is important to remember in this calculation that we are working out how many *atoms* of copper combine with how many *atoms* of oxygen so we divide the mass of oxygen by 16 (the mass of 1 mole of oxygen atoms) rather than by 32 (the mass of 1 mole of oxygen molecules).

EXAMPLE 4

A sample of a compound contains 0.78 g of K, 1.10 g of Mn and 1.28 g of O. (A_r of K = 39, A_r of Mn = 55, A_r of O = 16)

Again, we use a table:

	K	Mn	O
masses / g	0.78	1.10	1.28
find the number of moles of atoms by dividing the mass by the mass of 1 mole of atoms	0.78/39	1.10/55	1.28/16
number of moles of atoms	0.02	0.02	0.08
divide by the smallest number to find the ratio	0.02/0.02	0.02/0.02	0.08/0.02
ratio of moles	1	1	4
empirical formula		$KMnO_4$	

The empirical formula of this compound is $KMnO_4$.

Safety note: Wear eye protection and take care not to get burned when raising the crucible lid with tongs. The crucible will stay very hot for some time.

KEY POINT

How do we know when the reaction has finished? We can generally see when there is no more reaction because nothing is happening in the crucible. We can also check by weighing the crucible and contents, then heating it and weighing again. If the mass is higher when we weigh it again then this indicates that a reaction has occurred. We keep heating and weighing until the mass stays constant.

ACTIVITY 2

▼ PRACTICAL: INVESTIGATING THE FORMULA OF A METAL OXIDE BY COMBUSTION

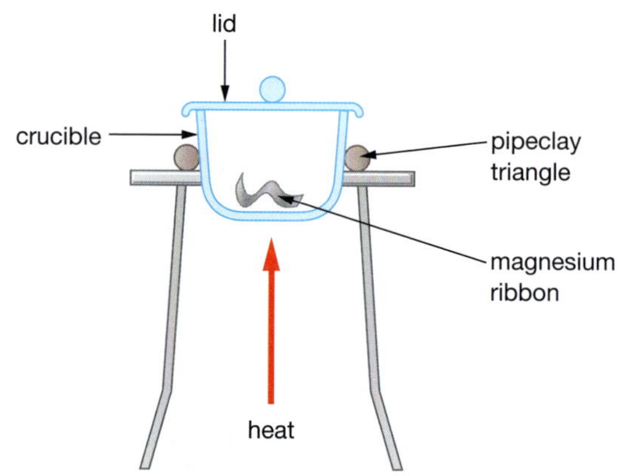

▲ Figure 5.12 Apparatus for determining the formula of magnesium oxide

We can find the formula of magnesium oxide by burning magnesium in oxygen and looking at how the mass changes. The following procedure is usually used:

- Weigh a crucible with a lid.
- Place a piece of magnesium ribbon about 10 cm long in the crucible and weigh the crucible and contents.
- Set up the apparatus as shown in Figure 5.12.
- Heat the crucible strongly (a roaring flame).
- Lift the lid every few seconds.
- When the reaction is finished, allow the crucible and contents to cool.
- Weigh the crucible and contents.

When the magnesium burns it does so with a bright white flame. Magnesium oxide, a white powder, is produced in the reaction.

A lid is placed on the crucible to prevent the white powder (magnesium oxide) escaping but the lid must be lifted every few seconds to allow oxygen into the crucible to react with the magnesium.

A set of results for this practical could be:

mass of empty crucible / g	32.46
mass of crucible + magnesium / g	32.70
mass of crucible + contents at end of experiment / g	32.86

We can work out the mass of magnesium by subtracting the mass of the crucible from the mass of the crucible + magnesium:

mass of magnesium = 32.70 − 32.46 = 0.24 g

The reason that the mass increases is because the magnesium combines with the oxygen in the air. The mass of magnesium oxide is greater than the mass of just magnesium due to the extra oxygen.

KEY POINT

Remember: Number of moles is mass in grams divided by the mass of 1 mole in grams.

The overall reaction that occurred was:

$2Mg + O_2 \rightarrow 2MgO$

magnesium + oxygen → magnesium oxide

The type of reaction that occurred was combustion.

When we do this experiment in practice, it is not very often that the ratio comes out as 1:1. There are things that may go wrong with this experiment which could affect the results, such as:

- some of the magnesium oxide powder might escape when the lid is lifted
- not all the magnesium might have reacted
- the magnesium can also react with nitrogen in the air.

HINT

The original masses were measured to 2 significant figures so the number of moles should also be given to 2 significant figures (0.010). If you write 0.01 for the number of moles of atoms in the exam, this will be fine and still give you the correct answer.

Safety note: The teacher demonstrating needs to wear a face shield and use safety screens. The pupils require eye protection and should be no closer than 2 metres. If a drying agent is needed anhydrous calcium chloride should be used NOT concentrated sulfuric acid.

KEY POINT

We must always make sure that the tube is filled with hydrogen before lighting the stream of hydrogen because a mixture of hydrogen and oxygen is explosive! It is therefore important to let the stream of hydrogen gas flow through the tube for a little while (to **flush out** all the oxygen) before lighting it or lighting the Bunsen burner.

We can work out the mass of oxygen that combines with the magnesium:

mass of oxygen = 32.86 − 32.70 = 0.16 g

In order to find the formula of magnesium oxide we need to work out how many moles of magnesium atoms combine with how many moles of oxygen atoms.

	Mg	O
masses / g	0.24	0.16
find the number of moles of atoms by dividing the mass by the mass of 1 mole	0.24/24	0.16/16
number of moles of atoms	0.010	0.010
divide by the smaller number to find the ratio	0.010/0.010	0.010/0.010
ratio of moles	1	1
empirical formula	MgO	

The empirical formula of magnesium oxide is MgO.

THE FORMULA FOR COPPER OXIDE

ACTIVITY 3

▼ PRACTICAL: INVESTIGATING THE FORMULA OF A METAL OXIDE BY REDUCTION

We can also find the formula of an oxide by removing the oxygen from it and looking at how the mass changes.

The following procedure can be used to find the formula of copper oxide:

- Weigh a ceramic dish.
- Put about 3 g of copper oxide in the ceramic dish and weigh the dish again.
- Place the ceramic dish in a tube as shown in Figure 5.13.
- Pass hydrogen gas over the copper oxide.
- Ignite the excess hydrogen, which comes out of the small hole in the boiling tube.
- Heat the copper oxide strongly until the reaction is finished (pink-brown copper metal will be seen).

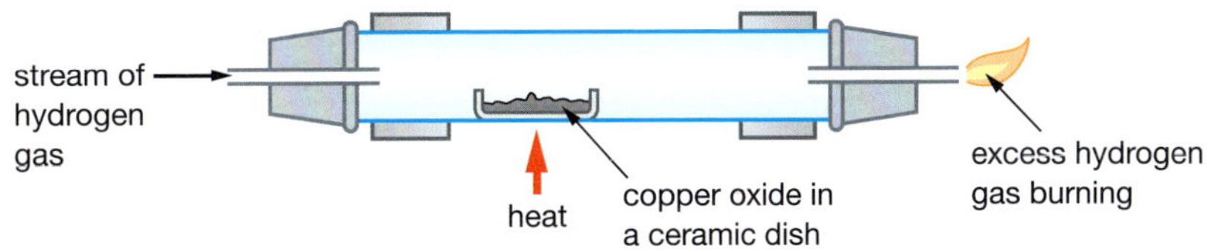

▲ Figure 5.13 The experimental set-up for finding the formula of copper oxide.

A set of results for this practical could be:

mass of empty dish / g	23.78
mass of dish + copper oxide / g	26.96
mass of dish + contents at end of experiment / g	26.32

KEY POINT

This is a displacement (or competition) reaction. Hydrogen is more reactive than copper and displaces it from copper oxide. Displacement reactions are discussed in Chapter 11.

The reason that the mass decreases is because the hydrogen combines with the oxygen from the copper oxide to form water. The oxygen is removed from the copper oxide and we are left with only copper in the dish at the end of the experiment. Because oxygen is removed from the copper oxide we say that the copper oxide has been reduced. Reduction is explained in Chapter 11.

From this data we can calculate the mass of copper oxide at the beginning by subtracting the mass of the dish from the mass of the dish + copper oxide:

mass of copper oxide = 26.96 – 23.78 = 3.18 g

We can work out the mass of copper remaining at the end by subtracting the mass of the dish from the mass of the dish + copper at the end.

mass of copper = 26.32 – 23.78 = 2.54 g

The mass has decreased because the oxygen has been removed from the copper oxide and we can calculate the mass of oxygen by subtracting the mass of copper at the end from the mass of copper oxide:

mass of oxygen = 3.18 – 2.54 = 0.64 g

We now know that 2.54 g of copper combines with 0.64 g of oxygen in copper oxide and can deduce the empirical formula:

KEY POINT

The equation for the reaction that occurs in this experiment is:

$$CuO + H_2 \rightarrow Cu + H_2O$$

copper(II) oxide + hydrogen → copper + water

As well as a displacement reaction, this type of reaction can also be called a redox reaction. Redox reactions are discussed in Chapter 11.

	Cu	O
masses / g	2.54	0.64
find the number of moles of atoms by dividing the mass by the mass of 1 mole	2.54/63.5	0.64/16
number of moles of atoms	0.0400	0.040
divide by the smaller number to find the ratio	0.0400/0.040	0.040/0.040
ratio of moles	1	1
empirical formula	CuO	

Safety note: The teacher demonstrating needs to wear a face shield and use safety screens. The pupils require eye protection and should be no closer than 2 metres. If a drying agent is needed anhydrous calcium chloride should be used NOT concentrated sulfuric acid.

DETERMINING THE FORMULA OF WATER

We can modify the apparatus in Figure 5.13 to allow us to determine the formula of water.

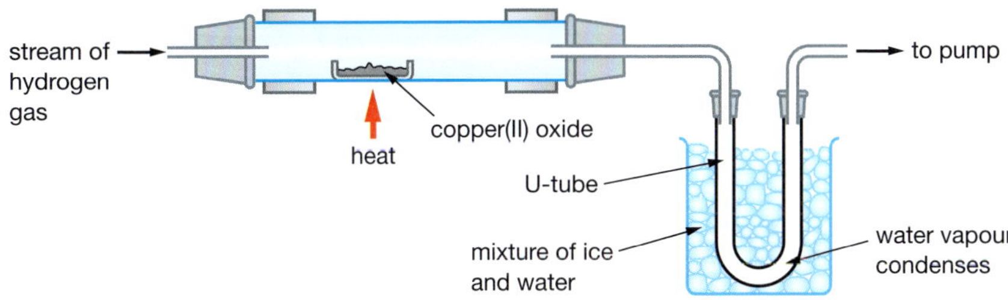

▲ Figure 5.14 Apparatus that can be used to determine the formula of water.

The experiment is conducted in the same way except that this time the water vapour that is produced from the reaction between copper(II) oxide and hydrogen is condensed. The contents of the dish at the beginning and the end of the experiment are again weighed but this time the mass of water that collects in the U-tube must also be measured.

mass of empty dish / g	23.78
mass of dish + copper oxide / g	26.96
mass of dish + contents at end of experiment / g	26.32
mass of water / g	0.72

Here we are using the same results as above. The mass of oxygen lost from the copper(II) oxide is 0.64g.

All the oxygen lost from the copper(II) oxide combines with hydrogen to form water. This means that the water contains 0.64g of oxygen. 0.72g of water was collected so the mass of hydrogen in the water must be 0.72 – 0.64 = 0.08g. We can now determine the empirical formula of water:

	H	O
masses / g	0.08	0.64
number of moles of atoms	0.08/1	0.64/16
number of moles of atoms	0.08	0.040
divide by the smaller number to find the ratio	0.08/0.040	0.040/0.040
ratio of moles	2	1
empirical formula	H_2O	

WORKING OUT FORMULAE USING PERCENTAGE COMPOSITION FIGURES

In the worked examples and practical examples above, we have determined the empirical formulae of compounds using masses. However, we are often given percentages by mass instead of just masses.

EXAMPLE 5

Find the empirical formula of a compound containing 82.7% C and 17.3% H by mass (A_r of H = 1, A_r of C = 12).

The percentage figures apply to any amount of substance you choose, so let's choose 100 g. In this case the percentages convert simply into masses: 82.7% of 100 g is 82.7 g (Table 5.1).

Table 5.1 Finding the ratio from percentage by mass

	C	H
percentages / %	82.7	17.3
masses in 100 g / g	82.7	17.3
number of moles of atoms	82.7/12	17.3/1
number of moles	6.89	17.3
divide by smallest to get ratio	6.89/6.89	17.3/6.89
ratio of moles	1	2.5

From this we can see that there are 2.5 mol of H atoms for every mole of C atoms. The empirical formula, however, is the *whole number ratio* of the elements present in a compound. To obtain a whole number here we multiply both numbers by 2 to get C_2H_5, which is the empirical formula.

HINT

When you calculate 17.3/6.89 you actually obtain 2.51. When doing these calculations it is fine to round 2.51 to 2.5 or 1.01 to 1 but what you must not do is round 2.51 to 3!
If you got a ratio of C:H of 1:1.33 you would not round this down to 1:1 but rather multiply by 3 to obtain C_3H_4.

CONVERTING EMPIRICAL FORMULAE INTO MOLECULAR FORMULAE

When you have learned a bit more **organic chemistry** in Unit 4 you will realise that, in the example we have just looked at, C_2H_5 can't possibly be the real formula of the compound. The molecular formula (the actual number of each atom present in a molecule) has to be a multiple of C_2H_5, like C_4H_{10}.

We can find the molecular formula if we know the relative formula mass of the compound (or the mass of 1 mole, which is just the M_r in grams).

In the previous example, suppose you were told that the relative formula mass of the compound was 58.

C_2H_5 has a relative formula mass of 29 (A_r of H = 1, A_r of C = 12).

All you need to find out is how many times 29 goes into 58.

$$58/29 = 2$$

So you need 2 lots of C_2H_5, in other words, C_4H_{10}.

The molecular formula is C_4H_{10}.

EXAMPLE 6

A compound has the empirical formula CH_2. If the relative formula mass is 56, work out the molecular formula.

The relative formula mass of CH_2 is $12 + (2 \times 1) = 14$.

$$56/14 = 4$$

Therefore there must be 4 lots of CH_2 in the actual molecule and the molecular formula is C_4H_8.

Remember, the ratio of elements in the molecular formula must be the same as in the empirical formula: C_4H_8 cancels down to CH_2.

EMPIRICAL FORMULA CALCULATIONS INVOLVING WATER OF CRYSTALLISATION

FINDING THE *n* IN $BaCl_2 \cdot nH_2O$

REMINDER

Remember that when some substances crystallise from solution, water becomes chemically bound up with the salt. This is called **water of crystallisation**. The salt is said to be **hydrated**.

REMINDER

Anhydrous means without water.

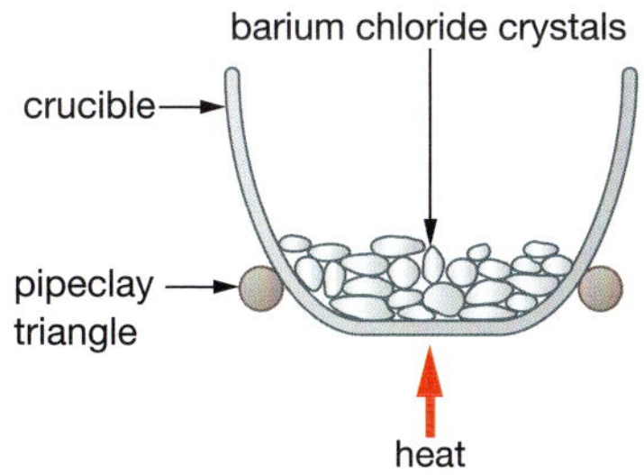

Figure 5.15 Heating barium chloride crystals in a crucible

Safety note: Barium chloride is toxic but a Bunsen flame is not hot enough to release it into the atmosphere.

HINT

If you are doing this experiment, how can you be sure that all the water has been driven off? The best way to do this is to heat it to constant mass. You heat the crucible and weigh it. Keep doing this until the mass remains constant. If the mass has gone down after heating there may still be water present, but when the mass remains constant after heating you know that all the water has been driven off.

Usually, when you heat a salt that contains water of crystallisation, the water is driven off, leaving the **anhydrous** salt behind. Hydrated barium chloride is a commonly used example because the barium chloride itself doesn't decompose even on quite strong heating.

If you heated barium chloride crystals in a crucible you might obtain these results:

Mass of crucible = 30.00 g

Mass of crucible + barium chloride crystals, $BaCl_2 \cdot nH_2O$ = 32.44 g

Mass of crucible + anhydrous barium chloride, $BaCl_2$ = 32.08 g

To find *n*, you need to find the ratio of the number of moles of $BaCl_2$ to the number of moles of water. It's just another empirical formula calculation (A_r of H = 1, A_r of O = 16, A_r of Cl = 35.5, A_r of Ba = 137).

Mass of $BaCl_2$ = 32.08 – 30.00 = 2.08 g

Mass of water = 32.44 – 32.08 = 0.36 g

Table 5.2 Finding the *n* in $BaCl_2 \cdot nH_2O$

	$BaCl_2$	H_2O
masses / g	2.08	0.36
divide by M_r to find the number of moles	2.08/208	0.36/18
number of moles	0.0100	0.020
ratio of moles	1	2
empirical formula	$BaCl_2 \cdot 2H_2O$	

CALCULATIONS USING MOLES, CHEMICAL EQUATIONS AND MASSES OF SUBSTANCES

INTERPRETING SYMBOLS IN EQUATIONS IN TERMS OF MOLES

KEY POINT

The big numbers in front of the formulae tell us the number of moles of each substance that react. Although there does not appear to be a big number in front of the CH_4 and CO_2, there should actually be a '1' in front of each but we just don't write it.

If we write a chemical equation:

$$CH_4 + 2O_2 \rightarrow CO_2 + 2H_2O$$

we can say that 1 molecule of CH_4 combines with 2 molecules of O_2 to form 1 molecule of CO_2 and 2 molecules of water. When doing calculations, however, it is often more useful to think about this in terms of moles and take symbols as meaning moles of each substance. So here we can say:

1 mol CH_4 reacts with 2 mol O_2 to form 1 mol CO_2 and 2 mol H_2O

We have not changed the meaning of the equation as the ratios are still the same.

KEY POINT

Remember that 2 mol of O_2 contains twice as many molecules as 1 mol of CH_4.

We can therefore tell from this equation that 16 g of CH_4 (1 mol) reacts exactly with 64 g of O_2 (2 mol) to form 44 g of CO_2 (1 mol) and 36 g of H_2O (2 mol).

CALCULATIONS INVOLVING ONLY MASSES

Typical calculations will give you a mass of starting material and ask you to calculate how much product you are likely to obtain. You will also find examples done in reverse, where you are told the mass of the product and are asked to find out how much of the starting material you would need. In almost all the cases you will see at International GCSE you will be given the equation for the reaction.

▲ Figure 5.16 A glowing piece of limestone. Limestone is impure calcium carbonate – it decomposes when heated to form calcium oxide (quicklime) and carbon dioxide. This is a thermal **decomposition reaction**.

A PROBLEM INVOLVING HEATING CALCIUM CARBONATE

When calcium carbonate, $CaCO_3$, is heated, calcium oxide is formed. Imagine you wanted to calculate the mass of calcium oxide produced by heating 25 g of calcium carbonate (A_r: C = 12, O = 16, Ca = 40).

$$CaCO_3 \rightarrow CaO + CO_2$$

THE CALCULATION

The method we will use has three steps:

Step 1: Calculate the number of moles using the mass that you have been given.

Step 2: Use the chemical equation to work out the number of moles of the substance you are interested in.

Step 3: Convert the number of moles to a mass.

KEY POINT

The M_r of $CaCO_3$ is 100 and the M_r of CaO is 56.

In this reaction we have 25 g of $CaCO_3$ and the number of moles can be calculated as:

$$\text{number of moles} = \frac{\text{mass}}{\text{mass of 1 mole}} = \frac{25}{100} = 0.25\,\text{mol}$$

The chemical equation for this reaction is

$$CaCO_3 \rightarrow CaO + CO_2$$

We can see from the equation that 1 mole of $CaCO_3$ will decompose to produce 1 mole of CaO. In other words, the equation is telling us that if we start with a certain number of moles of $CaCO_3$ we will obtain the same number of moles of CaO at the end.

Therefore, we can deduce that 0.25 mol $CaCO_3$ will decompose to produce 0.25 mol CaO. Now that we know the number of moles of CaO (M_r = 56) we can convert this to a mass:

$$\text{mass} = \text{number of moles} \times \text{mass of 1 mole}$$

$$\text{mass} = 0.25 \times 56 = 14\,\text{g}$$

Therefore, the reaction will produce 14 g of calcium oxide.

ALTERNATIVE METHOD

The calculation can also be done in a different way using ratios:

$CaCO_3(s) \rightarrow CaO(s) + CO_2(g)$

Interpret the equation in terms of moles:

1 mol $CaCO_3$ produces 1 mol CaO (and 1 mol CO_2)

Substitute masses where relevant:

100 g (1 mol) $CaCO_3$ produces 56 g (1 mol) CaO

Do a proportion calculation:

If 100 g of calcium carbonate gives 56 g of calcium oxide

1 g of calcium carbonate gives $\frac{56}{100}$ g of calcium oxide = 0.56 g

25 g of calcium carbonate gives 25 × 0.56 g of calcium oxide = 14 g of calcium oxide

HINT

You do not have to learn both methods, just learn whichever method you are happier with.
Your maths may be so good that you don't need to take all these steps to find the answer. If you can do it more quickly, that's fine. However, you must still show all your calculations.
When you have finished a chemistry calculation, the impression should nearly always be that there are a lot of words with a few numbers between them, not vice versa.

A PROBLEM ABOUT EXTRACTING IRON

The equation below is for a reaction that occurs in the extraction of iron:

$Fe_2O_3 + 3C \rightarrow 2Fe + 3CO$

Calculate the mass of iron which can be formed from 1000 g of iron oxide.

We are given the mass of Fe_2O_3 in the question and so we can calculate the number of moles of Fe_2O_3:

$$\text{number of moles} = \frac{\text{mass}}{\text{mass of 1 mole}}$$

$$\text{number of moles} = \frac{1000}{160} = 6.25\,\text{mol}$$

From the chemical equation we can see that 1 mol Fe_2O_3 produces 2 mol Fe. We know this because of the big numbers in front of the formulae.

So we know that, if we start with a certain number of moles of Fe_2O_3, we will obtain twice as many moles of Fe.

So 6.25 mol Fe_2O_3 produces 2 × 6.25 = 12.5 mol Fe:

mass = number of moles × mass of 1 mole

The mass of 12.5 mol Fe is 12.5 × 56 = 700 g.

KEY POINT

The A_r of Fe is 56.
The M_r of $Fe_2O_3 = 2 \times 56 + 3 \times 18 = 160$.

HINT

To find the mass of Fe we multiply the number of moles of Fe by the mass of 1 mole of Fe (56 g). A common mistake is to multiply the number of moles by the mass of 2Fe (112 g), but we have already used the '2' when we worked out the number of moles of Fe.

ALTERNATIVE METHOD IN TERMS OF RATIOS

First interpret the equation in terms of moles:

1 mol Fe_2O_3 reacts with C to form 2 mol Fe (and CO_2).

We are only looking at how much iron is produced, so let's introduce just these masses.

160 g (1 mol) of Fe_2O_3 produces 2 × 56 g (2 mol) of Fe.

That is, 160 g of Fe_2O_3 produces 112 g of Fe.

From this we can calculate that 1 g of Fe_2O_3 will produce 112/160 g of Fe, and therefore 1000 g of Fe will produce 1000 × 112/160 = 700 g.

A PROBLEM INVOLVING THE EXTRACTION OF LEAD

Lead is extracted from galena, PbS. The **ore** is roasted in air to produce lead(II) oxide, PbO:

$$2PbS(s) + 3O_2(g) \rightarrow 2PbO(s) + 2SO_2(g)$$

The lead(II) oxide is then converted to lead by heating it with carbon in a blast furnace:

$$PbO(s) + C(s) \rightarrow Pb(l) + CO(g)$$

The molten lead is tapped from the bottom of the furnace.

Calculate the mass of lead that would be produced from 1 tonne of galena.

(A_r: O = 16, S = 32, Pb = 207)

▲ Figure 5.17 Molten lead tapped from the bottom of a furnace.

HINT

You should be told how many grams there are in a tonne if you need this information in the exam.

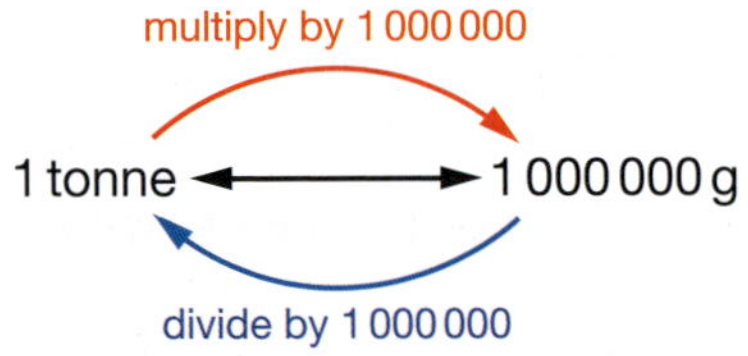

▲ Figure 5.18 How to convert between grams and tonnes

HINT

1 000 000 might be given to you as 10^6 or 1×10^6. These are both the same.

We have been given the mass of PbS so we can calculate the number of moles. However, we have to be careful because the mass is in tonnes but to calculate a number of moles we need to know the mass in grams, so we must convert tonnes to grams. The conversion for this is shown in Figure 5.18. Just write down this relationship: *1* tonne is equivalent to *1 000 000* g so, to change from tonnes to grams, the number has to *increase* (from 1 to 1 000 000), so we *multiply* by 1 000 000.

Therefore we have 1 000 000 g PbS.

$$\text{Number of moles} = \frac{\text{mass}}{\text{mass of 1 mole}}$$

$$\text{The number of moles of PbS} = \frac{1\,000\,000}{239} = 4184\,\text{mol.}$$

From the first equation:

$$2PbS(s) + 3O_2(g) \rightarrow 2PbO(s) + 2SO_2(g)$$

we can see that 2 mol PbS produce 2 mol PbO, therefore we can work out that 4184 mol PbS will produce 4184 mol PbO.

From the second equation:

$$PbO(s) + C(s) \rightarrow Pb(l) + CO(g)$$

we can see that 1 mol PbO produces 1 mol Pb. But we are starting this reaction with 4184 mol PbO and so we can work out that we will produce 4184 mol Pb.

The mass of 4184 mol Pb is $4184 \times 207 = 866\,000$ g.

We can convert this to tonnes by dividing by 1 000 000:

$$866\,000/1\,000\,000 = 0.866\ \text{tonne}$$

ALTERNATIVE METHOD

KEY POINT

We've doubled the second equation so that we can trace what happens to all the 2PbO from the first one.
This could also be simplified to 1 mol PbS produces 1 mol Pb. This would save you doing some arithmetic as you would not have to multiply everything by 2. However, in the end it does not make any difference to the answer, so you do not have to simplify it if you don't want to.

$$2PbS(s) + 3O_2(g) \rightarrow 2PbO(s) + 2SO_2(g)$$

$$PbO(s) + C(s) \rightarrow Pb(l) + CO(g)$$

Interpret the equation in terms of moles and trace the lead through the equations:

2 mol PbS produces 2 mol PbO

If we double the second equation:

$$2PbO(s) + 2C(s) \rightarrow 2Pb(l) + 2CO(g)$$

we can see that 2 mol PbO produces 2 mol Pb.

In other words, every 2 mol of PbS produces 2 mol of Pb.

Substitute masses where relevant. In this case, the relevant masses are only the PbS and the Pb:

2 × 239 g PbS produces 2 × 207 g Pb

478 g PbS produces 414 g Pb

HINT

There are advantages and disadvantages of both methods.
For the first method, we can use the same three steps in more advanced work that you might meet at the next level. However, a bit more maths will be involved: converting tonnes to grams and back again. The alternative method has fewer steps but we cannot use it in the same way when doing some of the calculations you will meet if you continue with Chemistry.

Now there seems to be a problem. The question is asking about tonnes and not grams. You could calculate how many grams there are in a tonne. However, it's much easier to think a bit, and realise that the ratio is always going to be the same, whatever the units, which means that:

478 tonnes PbS produces 414 tonnes Pb

Do the proportion calculation:

If 478 tonnes PbS produces 414 tonnes Pb

then 1 tonne PbS gives $\frac{417}{478}$ tonne Pb = 0.866 tonne

0.866 tonne of lead is produced from 1 tonne of galena.

CALCULATING PERCENTAGE YIELDS

WHAT IS A PERCENTAGE YIELD?

If you calculate how much product a reaction might produce, in real life you rarely obtain as much as you expected. If you expect to get 100 g, but only get 80 g, your percentage **yield** is 80%. The rest of it has been lost in some way. This could be due to spillages, or losses when you transfer a liquid from one container to another. Or it may be that there are all sorts of side reactions going on, so that some of your starting materials are changed into unwanted products. That happens a lot during reactions in organic chemistry.

Figure 5.19 Experiments done by students to make and purify organic compounds rarely give a high percentage yield.

CALCULATING THE PERCENTAGE YIELD

HINT

The percentage yield should always come out as less than 100%. If it comes out as more than 100% either you have made a mistake in the calculation or the question will continue by asking about what might have gone wrong in the experiment to give a value greater than 100%. If you are making a salt (see Chapter 13), for instance, a possible reason you could get a percentage yield greater than 100% is that it was not completely dry.

Suppose you do a calculation and work out that you should get 12.5 g of copper sulfate crystals, but you only get 11.2 g when you actually do the experiment. 12.5 g is the *theoretical yield* and can be obtained by carrying out a moles calculation. 11.2 g is the *actual yield* – this is what is obtained in the actual experiment and will be given to you in the question.

$$\text{Percentage yield} = \frac{\text{actual yield}}{\text{theoretical yield}} \times 100$$

The percentage yield is $\frac{11.2}{12.5} \times 100 = 89.6\%$.

EXAMPLE 7

A student reacted 2.40 g of copper(II) oxide (CuO) with hot sulfuric acid. She made 5.21 g of copper(II) sulfate crystals ($CuSO_4 \cdot 5H_2O$).

The equations for the reactions are:

$$CuO(s) + H_2SO_4(aq) \rightarrow CuSO_4(aq) + H_2O(l)$$

$$CuSO_4(aq) + 5H_2O(l) \rightarrow CuSO_4 \cdot 5H_2O(l)$$

First we need to calculate the theoretical yield. This is done by carrying out a moles calculation. We have enough information to calculate the number of moles of copper(II) oxide:

$$\text{number of moles of CuO} = \frac{2.40}{79.5} = 0.0302\,\text{mol}$$

From the first equation we can deduce that 0.0302 mol CuO will produce 0.0302 mol $CuSO_4$.

From the second equation we can deduce that 0.0302 mol $CuSO_4$ will produce 0.0302 mol $CuSO_4 \cdot 5H_2O$.

Now we need to calculate the mass of $CuSO_4 \cdot 5H_2O$ by multiplying the number of moles by the mass of 1 mole:

$$\text{mass} = 0.0302 \times 249.5 = 7.53\,\text{g}$$

This is the theoretical yield of copper(II) sulfate crystals.

The actual yield is what was obtained in the experiment. This was 5.21 g.

The percentage yield = (actual yield/theoretical yield) × 100

The percentage yield is 5.21/7.53 × 100 = 69.2%.

CALCULATIONS IN WHICH YOU HAVE TO CALCULATE WHICH SUBSTANCE IS IN EXCESS

When you make something in the lab, you rarely mix things together in exactly the right proportions. Usually, something is in **excess**, and you remove the excess (by filtering, for example) when the reaction is complete. If something is in excess there is more than enough of it to react with the other substance and so we don't need to worry about it.

In all the examples we have done above, we have only ever been given enough information to calculate the number of moles of one thing at the beginning of the problem. We have used this number of moles throughout the calculations. But what would happen if we were given the following question?

Magnesium reacts with hydrochloric acid according to the following equation:

$$Mg(s) + 2HCl(aq) \rightarrow MgCl_2(aq) + H_2(g)$$

0.2 mol Mg is reacted with 0.2 mol HCl. Calculate the mass of hydrogen gas produced.

We might be tempted to say that 0.2 mol Mg produces 0.2 mol $H_2(g)$ and the mass of $H_2 = 0.2 \times 2 = 0.4$ g. Unfortunately this is not the correct answer!

We can understand why it is not correct by looking at the chemical equation. 1 mol Mg reacts with 2 mol HCl and therefore 0.2 mol Mg would react with $2 \times 0.2 = 0.4$ mol HCl.

But we only used 0.2 mol HCl and so we did not have enough to react with all the Mg. Because all the Mg did not react we cannot use the number of moles of Mg to work out how much hydrogen is produced.

If we try starting with the number of moles of HCl, we can deduce from the chemical equation that 2 mol HCl reacts with 1 mol Mg, therefore 0.2 mol HCl reacts with 0.1 mol Mg. We added 0.2 mol Mg and so there is more than enough to react with all the HCl – the Mg is in excess.

KEY POINT

You always have to use the chemical equation to determine which substance is in excess. If we had been given 0.2 mol Mg and 0.3 mol HCl in this reaction it would look like the HCl is in excess because there is more of it. But if you look at the chemical equation you can see that 0.3 mol HCl only reacts with 0.15 mol Mg so there is still not enough HCl to react with all the Mg, so the Mg is still in excess.

Because we know that all the HCl reacts we can use the number of moles of HCl to work out how much H_2 is produced.

2 mol HCl produce 1 mol H_2: the number of moles of H_2 is half the number of moles of HCl.

Therefore 0.2 mol HCl produce 0.1 mol H_2.

The mass of $H_2 = 0.1 \times 2 = 0.2$ g.

This is the correct answer!

To deduce which substance is in excess we try both numbers of moles in the chemical equation and compare the numbers.

KEY POINT

A reagent is just something that reacts.

EXAMPLE 8

Copper reacts with concentrated nitric acid according to the equation:

$$Cu(s) + 4HNO_3(aq) \rightarrow Cu(NO_3)_2(aq) + 2H_2O(l) + 2NO_2(g)$$

3.2 g of copper is reacted with 0.40 mol concentrated nitric acid. Work out which reagent is in excess.

We need to convert the mass of Cu to a number of moles:

$$\text{number of moles of Cu} = \frac{3.2}{63.5} = 0.050\text{ mol}$$

Looking at the chemical equation we can see that 1 mol Cu reacts with 4 mol HNO_3, so we can calculate that:

$$0.050\text{ mol Cu reacts with } 4 \times 0.050 = 0.20\text{ mol } HNO_3$$

We have more than 0.20 mol HNO_3 therefore HNO_3 is in excess.

If the question went further and asked us to calculate the amount in moles of NO_2 produced using these quantities we would have to use the number of moles of Cu because not all the HNO_3 is used up. We would obtain $2 \times 0.050 = 0.10$ mol NO_2.

CHAPTER QUESTIONS

SKILLS PROBLEM SOLVING

8th

1 Balance the following equations:

a $Fe + HCl \rightarrow FeCl_2 + H_2$

b $Zn + H_2SO_4 \rightarrow ZnSO_4 + H_2$

c $Ca + H_2O \rightarrow Ca(OH)_2 + H_2$

d $Al + Cr_2O_3 \rightarrow Al_2O_3 + Cr$

e $Fe_2O_3 + CO \rightarrow Fe + CO_2$

f $NaHCO_3 + H_2SO_4 \rightarrow Na_2SO_4 + CO_2 + H_2O$

g $C_8H_{18} + O_2 \rightarrow CO_2 + H_2O$

h $Fe_3O_4 + H_2 \rightarrow Fe + H_2O$

i $Pb + AgNO_3 \rightarrow Pb(NO_3)_2 + Ag$

j $AgNO_3 + MgCl_2 \rightarrow Mg(NO_3)_2 + AgCl$

k $C_3H_8 + O_2 \rightarrow CO_2 + H_2O$

2 Calculate the relative formula masses of the following compounds:

a CO_2

b CH_3CO_2H

c Na_2SO_4

d $(NH_4)_2SO_4$

e $Na_2CO_3{\cdot}10H_2O$

f $Cr_2(SO_4)_3$

(A_r: H = 1, C = 12, N = 14, O = 16, Na = 23, S = 32, Ca = 40, Cr = 52, Fe = 56)

9th

3 Calculate the percentage of nitrogen in each of the following substances (all used as nitrogen fertilisers):

a potassium nitrate, KNO_3

b ammonium nitrate, NH_4NO_3

c ammonium sulfate, $(NH_4)_2SO_4$

(A_r: H = 1, N = 14, O = 16, S = 32, K = 39)

4 Calculate the mass of the following:

a 1 mol of HCN

b 1 mol of lead(II) nitrate, $Pb(NO_3)_2$

c 4.30 mol of methane, CH_4

d 0.70 mol of Na_2O

e 0.015 mol of $NaNO_3$

f 0.24 mol of sodium carbonate crystals, $Na_2CO_3{\cdot}10H_2O$

(A_r: H = 1, C = 12, N = 14, O = 16, Na = 23, Pb = 207)

SKILLS PROBLEM SOLVING 9th

5 Calculate the number of moles represented by each of the following:

a 20 g of magnesium oxide, MgO

b 3.20 g of iron(III) oxide, Fe_2O_3

c 2 kg of copper(II) oxide, CuO

d 50 g of copper(II) sulfate crystals, $CuSO_4{\cdot}5H_2O$

e 1 tonne of iron, Fe (1 tonne is 1 000 000 g)

f 0.032 g of sulfur dioxide, SO_2

(A_r: H = 1, O = 16, S = 32, Mg = 24, Fe = 56, Cu = 63.5)

6 The following calculations use A_r: H = 1, O = 16, Na = 23, Cl = 35.5, Ca = 40, Cu = 63.5.

a Calculate the mass of 4 mol of sodium chloride, NaCl.

b Calculate how many moles is 37 g of calcium hydroxide, $Ca(OH)_2$.

c Calculate how many moles is 1 kg (1000 g) of calcium, Ca.

d Calculate the mass of 0.125 mol of copper(II) oxide, CuO.

e 0.1 mol of a substance has a mass of 4 g. Calculate the mass of 1 mole.

f 0.004 mol of a substance has a mass of 1 g. Calculate the relative formula mass of the compound.

7 Determine the empirical formulae of the compounds which contain:

a 9.39 g P, 0.61 g H

b 5.85 g K, 2.10 g N, 4.80 g O

c 3.22 g Na, 4.48 g S, 3.36 g O

d 22.0% C, 4.6% H, 73.4% Br (by mass)

(A_r: H = 1, C = 12, N = 14, O = 16, Na = 23, S = 32, K = 39, Br = 80)

8 1.24 g of phosphorus was burned completely in oxygen to give 2.84 g of phosphorus oxide. Find:

a the empirical formula of the oxide

b the molecular formula of the oxide given that 1 mole of the oxide has a mass of 284 g.

(A_r: O = 16, P = 31)

9 An organic compound contained C 66.7%, H 11.1%, O 22.2% by mass. Its relative formula mass was 72. Find:

a the empirical formula of the compound

b the molecular formula of the compound.

(A_r: H = 1, C = 12, O = 16)

10 In an experiment to find the number of molecules of water of crystallisation in sodium sulfate crystals, $Na_2SO_4{\cdot}nH_2O$, 3.22 g of sodium sulfate crystals were heated gently. When all the water of crystallisation had been driven off, 1.42 g of anhydrous sodium sulfate was left. Find the value of n in the formula. (A_r: H = 1, O = 16, Na = 23, S = 32)

SKILLS PROBLEM SOLVING

9th

11 Gypsum is hydrated calcium sulfate, $CaSO_4{\cdot}nH_2O$. A sample of gypsum was heated in a crucible until all the water of crystallisation had been driven off. The following results were obtained:

Mass of crucible = 37.34 g

Mass of crucible + gypsum, $CaSO_4{\cdot}nH_2O$ = 45.94 g

Mass of crucible + anhydrous calcium sulfate, $CaSO_4$ = 44.14 g

Calculate the value of n in the formula $CaSO_4{\cdot}nH_2O$.

(A_r: H = 1, O = 16, S = 32, Ca = 40)

12 a Calculate the amount in moles of SO_3 formed when 0.36 mol SO_2 reacts with excess O_2.

$2SO_2 + O_2 \rightarrow 2SO_3$

b Calculate the amount in moles of HCl that reacts with 0.4 mol $CaCO_3$.

$CaCO_3(s) + 2HCl(aq) \rightarrow CaCl_2(aq) + H_2O(l) + CO_2(g)$

c Calculate the amount in moles of H_2S formed when 0.4 mol of HCl reacts with excess Sb_2S_3.

$Sb_2S_3 + 6HCl \rightarrow 2SbCl_3 + 3H_2S$

d Calculate the amount in moles of iron formed when 0.9 mol carbon monoxide reacts with excess iron(III) oxide.

$Fe_2O_3 + 3CO \rightarrow 2Fe + 3CO_2$

e Calculate the amount in moles of hydrogen that would be required to make 0.8 mol NH_3.

$N_2 + 3H_2 \rightarrow 2NH_3$

13 The reaction between iron and bromine is

$2Fe + 3Br_2 \rightarrow 2FeBr_3$

10 g of iron is reacted with bromine.

a Calculate the amount in moles of iron that reacted.

b Calculate the amount in moles of bromine that the iron reacted with.

c Calculate the amount in moles of $FeBr_3$ that will be formed.

d Calculate the mass of $FeBr_3$ formed.

(A_r: Fe = 56, Br = 80)

14 Titanium is manufactured by heating titanium(IV) chloride with sodium.

$TiCl_4(g) + 4Na(l) \rightarrow Ti(s) + 4NaCl(s)$

1.0 g of $TiCl_4$ is reacted with excess sodium

(A_r: Na = 23, Ti = 48, Cl = 35.5)

a Calculate the amount in moles of $TiCl_4$ reacted.

b Calculate the amount in moles of Ti formed.

c Calculate the mass of Ti formed.

d Calculate the mass of NaCl formed.

e Calculate the mass of Ti formed when 1 tonne of $TiCl_4$ reacts with excess sodium (1 tonne is 1 000 000 g).

SKILLS PROBLEM SOLVING

9th

15 2.67 g of aluminium chloride was dissolved in water and an excess of silver nitrate solution was added to give a precipitate of silver chloride (AgCl).

$AlCl_3(aq) + 3AgNO_3(aq) \rightarrow Al(NO_3)_3(aq) + 3AgCl(s)$

Calculate the mass of silver chloride that would be formed.

(A_r: Al = 27, Cl = 35.5, Ag = 108)

16 Chromium is manufactured by heating a mixture of chromium(III) oxide with aluminium powder.

$Cr_2O_3(s) + 2Al(s) \rightarrow 2Cr(s) + Al_2O_3(s)$

a Calculate the mass of aluminium needed to react with 50 g of Cr_2O_3.

b Calculate the mass of chromium produced from 50 g of Cr_2O_3.

c Calculate the mass of chromium produced from 5 kg of Cr_2O_3.

d Calculate the mass of chromium produced from 5 tonnes of Cr_2O_3.

(1 tonne is 1 000 000 g)

(A_r: Cr = 52, O = 16, Al = 27)

17 Copper(II) sulfate crystals, $CuSO_4{\cdot}5H_2O$, can be made by heating copper(II) oxide with dilute sulfuric acid and then crystallising the solution formed.

a Calculate the maximum mass of crystals that could be made from 4.00 g of copper(II) oxide using an excess of sulfuric acid.

$CuO(s) + H_2SO_4(aq) \rightarrow CuSO_4(aq) + H_2O(l)$

$CuSO_4(aq) + 5H_2O(l) \rightarrow CuSO_4{\cdot}5H_2O(s)$

b If the actual mass of copper(II) sulfate collected at the end of the experiment was 11.25 g, calculate the percentage yield.

(A_r: H = 1, O = 16, S = 32, Cu = 63.5)

18 Ethanol reacts with ethanoic acid to form ethyl ethanoate and water:

$C_2H_5OH(l) + CH_3COOH(l) \rightarrow CH_3COOC_2H_5(l) + H_2O(l)$

ethanol ethanoic acid ethyl ethanoate water

a Calculate the mass of ethyl ethanoate produced when 20.0 g of ethanol reacts with excess ethanoic acid.

7th

b The actual yield in this experiment is 30.0 g of ethyl ethanoate. Calculate the percentage yield.

(A_r: C = 12, H = 1, O = 16)

SKILLS REASONING

8th

19 Determine which reactant is in excess in each case.

a 0.5 mol of Na_2CO_3 is reacted with 0.5 mol hydrochloric acid:

$Na_2CO_3(s) + 2HCl(aq) \rightarrow 2NaCl(aq) + H_2O(l) + CO_2(g)$

b 0.01 mol C_3H_8 is reacted with 0.02 mol O_2:

$C_3H_8 + 5O_2 \rightarrow 3CO_2 + 4H_2O$

c 28 g CO is reacted with 0.6 mol Fe_2O_3:

$Fe_2O_3 + 3CO \rightarrow 2Fe + 3CO_2$

d 16 g O_2 is reacted with 16 g SO_2:

$2SO_2 + O_2 \rightarrow 2SO_3$

(A_r : C = 12, O = 16, S = 32)

20 1.0 g of $CaCO_3$ is reacted with 0.015 mol of HCl:

$CaCO_3(s) + 2HCl(aq) \rightarrow CaCl_2(aq) + H_2O(l) + CO_2(g)$

a Determine which reagent is present in excess.

SKILLS PROBLEM SOLVING

9th

b Calculate the mass of CO_2 produced.

(A_r: Ca = 40, C = 12, O = 16)

6 IONIC BONDING

We have already looked at the definition of a compound. A compound is formed when two or more elements chemically combine. In this chapter we are going to look at one way in which elements can chemically combine: by the transfer of electrons to form ionic compounds.

▲ Figure 6.1 The properties of a compound are very different from those of the elements. Sodium (an element) is a dangerously reactive metal. It is stored under oil to prevent it reacting with air or water. Chlorine (an element) is a very poisonous, reactive gas. But salt, sodium chloride (an ionic compound), is safe to eat in small quantities.

LEARNING OBJECTIVES

- Understand how ions are formed by electron loss or gain
- Know the charges of these ions:
  - metals in Groups 1, 2 and 3
  - non-metals in Groups 5, 6 and 7
  - Ag^+, Cu^{2+}, Fe^{2+}, Fe^{3+}, Pb^{2+}, Zn^{2+}
  - hydrogen (H^+), hydroxide (OH^-), ammonium (NH_4^+), carbonate (CO_3^{2-}), nitrate (NO_3^-), sulfate (SO_4^{2-})
- Write formulae for compounds formed between the ions listed above
- Draw dot-and-cross diagrams to show the formation of ionic compounds by electron transfer, limited to combinations of elements from Groups 1, 2, 3, 5, 6 and 7 *(only outer electrons need be shown)*
- Understand ionic bonding in terms of electrostatic attractions
- Understand why compounds with giant ionic lattices have high melting and boiling points
- Know that ionic compounds do not conduct electricity when solid, but do conduct electricity when molten and in aqueous solution

IONIC BONDING

Sodium chloride is probably the best-known example of an ionic compound – one that is held together by **ionic bonding**. There are lots of other ionic compounds, such as magnesium oxide, calcium fluoride and zinc bromide. What you will realise about all these compounds is that they all contain a metal combined with a non-metal.

You can recognise ionic compounds because they (usually) contain a metal.

HINT

There are one or two exceptions to this: there are ionic compounds that do not contain a metal, for example those containing the ammonium ion (such as NH_4Cl, $(NH_4)_2SO_4$. We will look at these later.

KEY POINT

This is a simplification! In reality, you don't react sodium with chlorine atoms, but with chlorine molecules, Cl_2.

KEY POINT

You can check that sodium does have a positive charge. If you look at the Periodic Table you will see that sodium has an atomic number of 11, so it has 11 protons in its nucleus. Protons have a positive charge so the charge on the nucleus is 11+. In the sodium **atom** there are 11 electrons, each with a negative charge. These cancel out the 11+ on the nucleus and there is no overall charge. However, in the sodium ion there are only 10 electrons, so with 11+ and 10– there is an overall charge of 1+.

KEY POINT

Electrostatic attraction simply means that positively charged particles attract negatively charged particles.

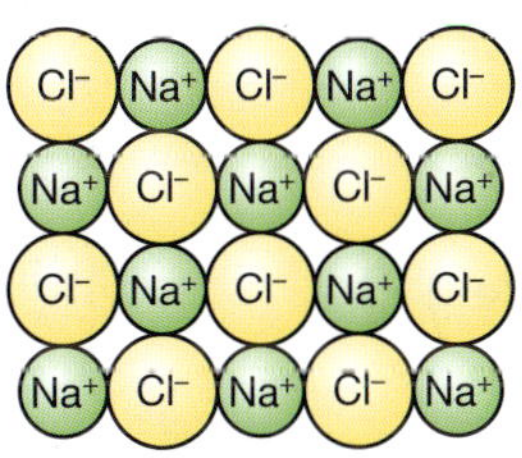

▲ Figure 6.3 Part of the structure of a sodium chloride crystal. The structure is held together by the attraction between positive and negative ions.

When a non-metal such as chlorine combines with a metal such as sodium, the chlorine atom has a stronger attraction for electrons than the sodium atom and *an electron is transferred from the outer shell of the sodium atom to the outer shell of the chlorine atom*. Because an electron has a negative charge, when something gains an electron it becomes negatively charged, and when something loses an electron it becomes positively charged.

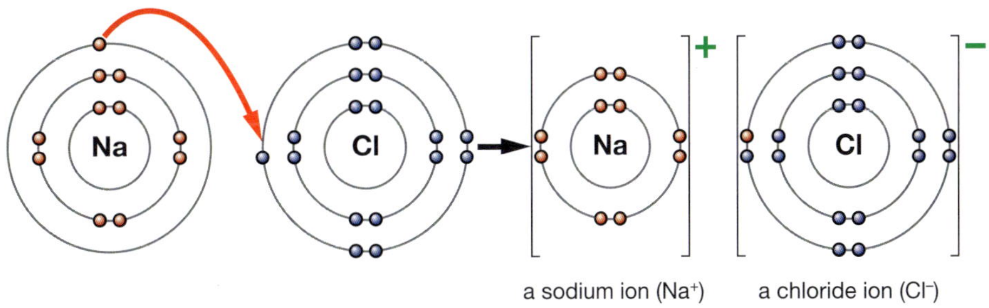

▲ Figure 6.2 Ionic bonding in sodium chloride. Ionic bonding involves the transfer of electron(s).

The charged particles that are formed are called **ions**.

Ions are charged particles formed when atoms (or groups of atoms) lose or gain electrons. Ions can have either a positive or a negative charge.

- A positive ion is called a **cation**, for example Na^+.
- A negative ion is called an **anion**, for example Cl^-.

When an ionic compound is formed, electron(s) are transferred from a metal atom to a non-metal atom to form positive and negative ions. Ionic compounds have ionic bonding. *Ionic bonding is the strong* ***electrostatic attraction*** *between positive and negative ions.*

Ionic bonding is often shown using **dot-and-cross diagrams**. Figure 6.4 is an example of a dot-and-cross diagram. Although the electrons are drawn as dots or as crosses, there is absolutely no difference between them in reality. The dots and the crosses simply show that the electrons have come from two different atoms. You could equally well use two different coloured dots (as in Figure 6.2), or two different coloured crosses.

IONIC BONDING IN MAGNESIUM OXIDE

A dot-and-cross diagram for MgO is shown in Figure 6.4.

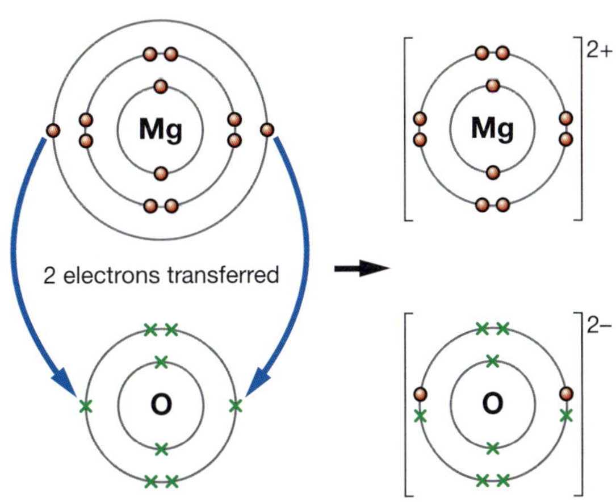

▲ Figure 6.4 A dot-and-cross diagram for magnesium oxide. When drawing these diagrams, don't forget the charges on the ions.

Two electrons are transferred from a magnesium atom to an oxygen atom to form Mg^{2+} and O^{2-} ions.

THE SIGNIFICANCE OF NOBLE GAS ELECTRONIC CONFIGURATIONS IN IONIC BONDING

If you look at the electronic arrangements of the ions formed in Figures 6.2, 6.4, 6.5 and 6.6, each of them has a noble gas electronic configuration: [2, 8] (the same as neon) or [2, 8, 8] (the same as argon). For the first 20 elements, atoms lose or gain electrons so that they achieve a noble gas electronic configuration. The elements in Groups 1, 2 and 3 of the Periodic Table will lose their outer shell electrons to form 1+, 2+ and 3+ ions, and the elements in Groups 5, 6 and 7 will gain electrons to form 3–, 2– and 1– ions.

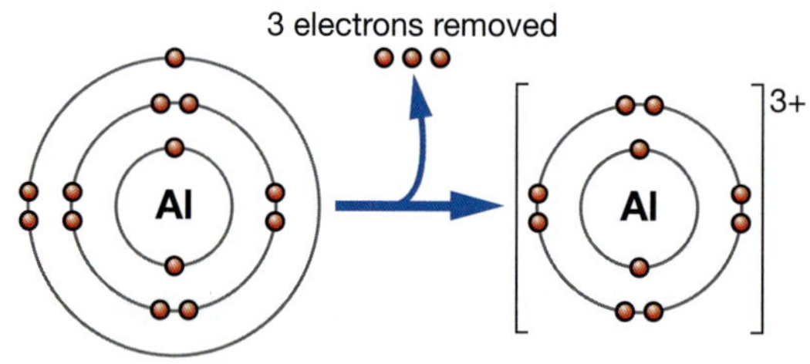

▲ Figure 6.5 An aluminium atom loses its 3 outer shell electrons to form an Al^{3+} ion.

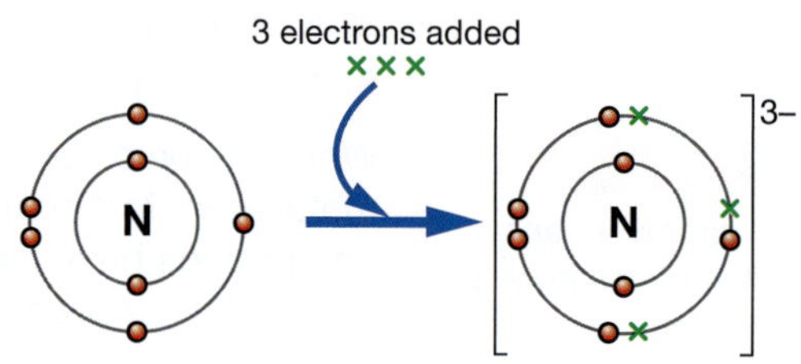

▲ Figure 6.6 A nitrogen atom gains 3 electrons to form the nitride ion (N^{3-}).

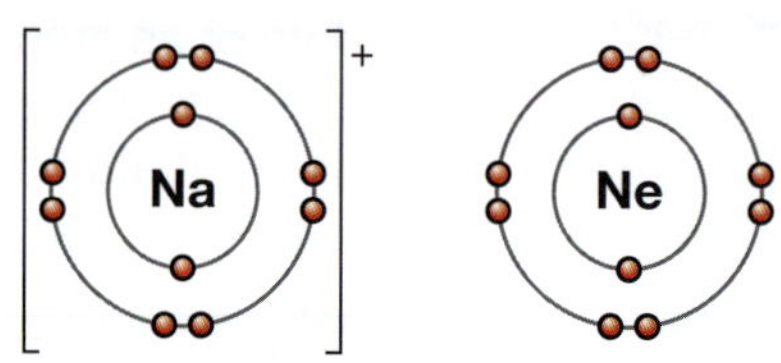

▲ Figure 6.7 Na^+ and Ne are isoelectronic – they have the same number of electrons.

KEY POINT

We sometimes use the word **isoelectronic**, which means 'have the same number of electrons'. So, when sodium forms an ion (electronic configuration [2, 8]) it becomes isoelectronic with neon [2, 8].

Elements in Groups 1, 2, 6 and 7 always form ions that are **isoelectronic** with the nearest noble gas atom. For example, rubidium (Rb), which is in Group 1, has 1 electron in its outer shell and will lose this outer shell electron to form a 1+ ion, which has the same number of electrons as a krypton (Kr) atom. Iodine is in Group 7, so it has 7 electrons in its outer shell; it will gain 1 electron when it forms an ion to form a 1– ion. This 1– ion has the same number of electrons as a xenon (Xe) atom.

However, there are a lot of common ions that don't have noble gas structures. Fe^{2+}, Fe^{3+}, Cu^{2+}, Zn^{2+}, Ag^+ and Pb^{2+} are all ions that you will come across during the International GSCE course, although you won't have to write their electronic structures. Not one of them has a noble gas structure.

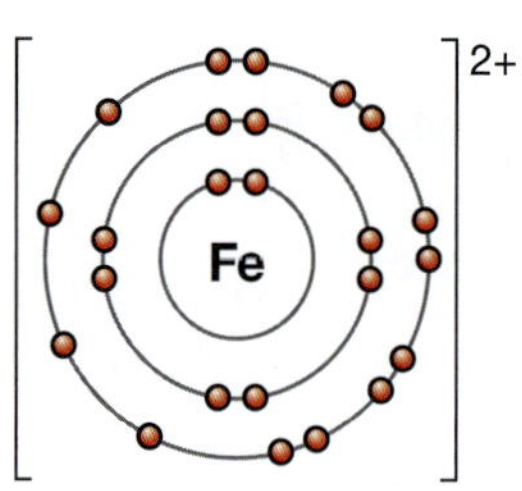

▲ Figure 6.8 An Fe^{2+} ion – definitely not a noble gas structure!

OTHER EXAMPLES OF IONIC BONDING

Ionic bonds are usually formed only if small numbers of electrons need to be transferred, typically 1 or 2, but occasionally 3.

LITHIUM FLUORIDE

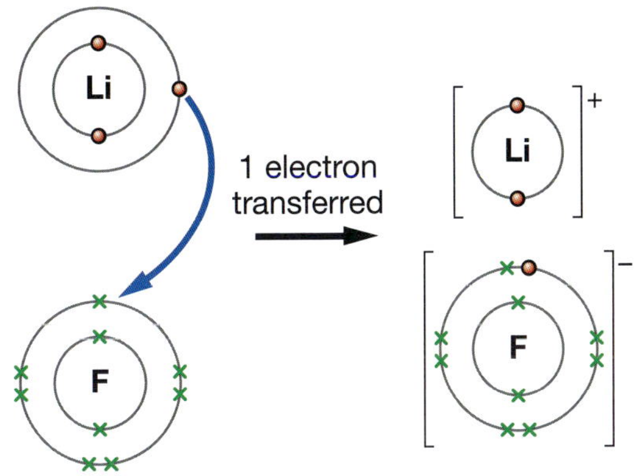

▲ Figure 6.9 A dot-and-cross diagram for lithium fluoride

The lithium atom has 1 electron in its outer shell that is easily lost, and the fluorine has space to receive one. One electron is transferred from the lithium atom to the fluorine atom. Lithium fluoride is held together by the strong electrostatic attractions between positive lithium (Li^+) ions and the negative fluoride (F^-) ions.

CALCIUM CHLORIDE

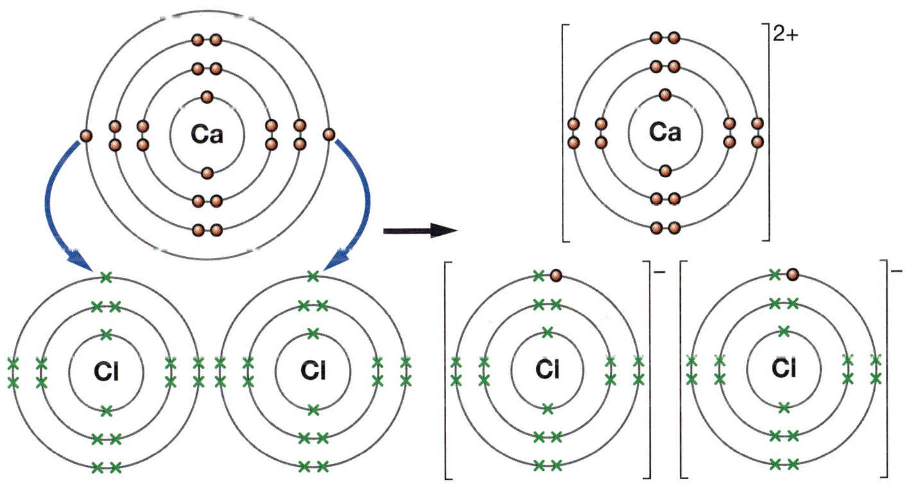

▲ Figure 6.10 A dot-and-cross diagram to show the formation of calcium chloride.

The calcium atom [2, 8, 8, 2] has 2 electrons in its outer shell but each chlorine atom [2, 8, 7] only has room in its outer shell to take one of them. You need two chlorines for every calcium. The 2 electrons are transferred from the outer shell of a calcium atom to two chlorine atoms, one to each. The formula for calcium chloride is therefore $CaCl_2$. There will be very strong electrostatic attractions holding the ions together because of the 2+ charge on the calcium ions.

FORMULAE FOR IONIC COMPOUNDS

There are so many different ionic compounds that you might encounter at International GSCE that it would be impossible to learn all their formulae. You need a simple way to work them out. You could work out a few from first principles, using their electronic structures, but that would take ages. Others would be too difficult. You need a simple, shortcut method.

THE NEED FOR EQUAL NUMBERS OF PLUSES AND MINUSES

Ions are formed when atoms, or groups of atoms, lose or gain electrons. They carry an electrical charge, either positive or negative. Compounds are electrically neutral. Therefore in an ionic compound there must be the right number of each sort of ion, so that the total positive charge exactly cancels out the total negative charge. Obviously, then, if you are going to work out a formula, you need to know the charges on the ions.

CASES WHERE YOU CAN WORK OUT THE CHARGE ON AN ION

Any element in Group 2 has 2 outer electrons, which it will lose to form a 2+ ion. Any element in Group 6 has 6 outer electrons, and it has room to gain 2 more; this leads to a 2– ion. Similar arguments apply in the other groups shown in Table 6.1.

HINT

You will always have a copy of the Periodic Table, even in an exam. That means that you can always find out which group an element is in. Elements in Group 4 only form a few ionic compounds and the situation is a bit more complicated. You will need to learn that lead forms a 2+ ion (Pb^{2+}).

REMINDER

Remember that all metals form positive ions.

Table 6.1 The charges on an ion in Groups 1–7

Group in Periodic Table	Charge on ion	Example
1	1+	Na^{+}
2	2+	Mg^{2+}
3	3+	Al^{3+}
5	3–	N^{3-}
6	2–	O^{2-}
7	1–	Br^{-}

CASES WHERE THE NAME TELLS YOU THE CHARGE

All metals form positive ions. Names such as lead(II) oxide, iron(III) chloride or copper(II) sulfate tell you directly about the charge on the metal ion. The number after the metal tells you the number of charges, so:

- lead(II) oxide contains a Pb^{2+} ion
- iron(III) chloride contains an Fe^{3+} ion
- copper(II) sulfate contains a Cu^{2+} ion.

You cannot work out the charges for some ions, you have to learn them. Ions that need to be learned are shown in Table 6.2.

Table 6.2 Ions that you should learn.

Charge	Substance	Ion
positive	zinc	Zn^{2+}
	silver	Ag^{+}
	hydrogen	H^{+}
	ammonium	NH_4^{+}

Charge	Substance	Ion
negative	nitrate	NO_3^{-}
	hydroxide	OH^{-}
	carbonate	CO_3^{2-}
	sulfate	SO_4^{2-}

You will encounter other ions during the course, but these are the important ones for now. The ions in this list are the difficult ones – be sure to learn both the formula and the charge for each ion.

KEY POINT

Ammonium chloride (NH_4Cl) is an example of an ionic compound that does not contain a metal. There is ionic bonding between the NH_4^{+} and Cl^{-} ions. There is, however, also covalent bonding (see Chapter 7) in this compound: the NH_4^{+} ion is held together by covalent bonding.

CONFUSING ENDINGS!

Don't confuse ions such as sulf**ate** and sulf**ide**. A name like copper(II) sulf**ide** means that it contains copper and sulfur **only**. Any '**ide**' ending means that there isn't anything complicated there. Sodium chloride, for example, is just sodium and chlorine combined together. So copper(II) sulfide contains Cu^{2+} and S^{2-} ions.

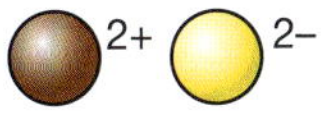

▲ Figure 6.11 Copper(II) sulfide is CuS.

Once you have an '**ate**' ending, it means that there is oxygen (and possibly other things) there as well. So, for example, copper(II) sulfate contains copper, sulfur and oxygen.

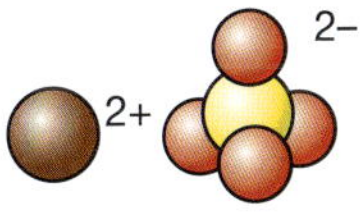

▲ Figure 6.12 Copper(II) sulfate is $CuSO_4$.

HINT

Not looking carefully at word endings is one of the most common mistakes students make when they start to write formulae. Be careful!

DEDUCING THE FORMULA FOR AN IONIC COMPOUND

EXAMPLE 1

To find the formula for sodium oxide

Sodium is in Group 1, so the ion is Na^+.

Oxygen is in Group 6, so the ion is O^{2-}.

To have equal numbers of positive and negative charges, you would need two sodium ions to provide the two positive charges to cancel the two negative charges on one oxide ion. In other words, you need:

Na^+ Na^+ O^{2-}

The formula is therefore $\mathbf{Na_2O}$.

EXAMPLE 2

To find the formula for barium nitrate

Barium is in Group 2, so the ion is Ba^{2+}.

Nitrate ions are NO_3^-. You will have to remember this.

To have equal numbers of positive and negative charges, you would need two nitrate ions for each barium ion.

The formula is $\mathbf{Ba(NO_3)_2}$.

Notice the brackets around the nitrate group. *Brackets must be written if you have more than one of these complex ions* (ions containing more than one atom). In any other situation, they are completely unnecessary.

KEY POINT

If you didn't write the brackets, the formula would look like this: $BaNO_{32}$. That would read as 1 barium, 1 nitrogen and 32 oxygens!

EXAMPLE 3

To find the formula for iron(III) sulfate

Iron(III) tells you that the metal ion is Fe^{3+}.

Sulfate ions are SO_4^{2-}.

To have equal numbers of positive and negative charges, you would need two iron(III) ions for every three sulfate ions, giving 6+ and 6– in total.

The formula is $\mathbf{Fe_2(SO_4)_3}$.

A shortcut to working out complicated formulae such as these is to just swap over the numbers in the charges. This is shown in Figure 6.13.

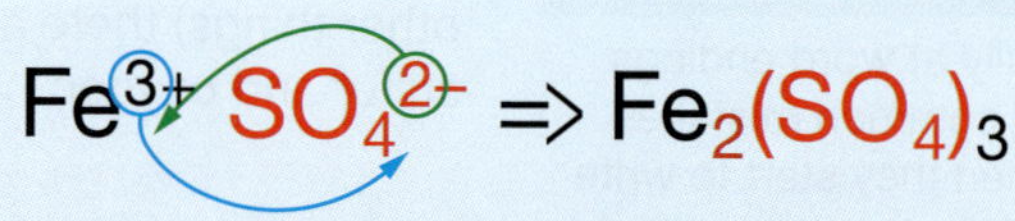

▲ Figure 6.13 If you cross over the numbers in the charges you will get the formula.

CALCIUM CHLORIDE PROVIDES ANOTHER EXAMPLE

▲ Figure 6.14 To work out the formula of calcium chloride we cross over the numbers in the charges. There is no extra number in front of the charge in Cl^- because we do not tend to write in a 1.

KEY POINT

Why aren't ion charges shown in formulae? Actually, they can be shown. For example, the formula for sodium chloride is NaCl. It is sometimes written Na^+Cl^- if you are trying to make a particular point, but for most purposes the charges are left out. In an ionic compound, the charges are there, whether you write them or not.

You have to be careful using this method because you can get the wrong answer when the charges on the ions are the same. For example, the formula of calcium oxide is CaO and not Ca_2O_2. When the charges on the positive and negative ions are the same you can deduce that there will be 1 of each ion in the formula, so there is no need to swap anything over.

▲ Figure 6.15 The formula of calcium oxide is CaO and not Ca_2O_2.

GIANT IONIC STRUCTURES

All ionic compounds form crystals that consist of lattices of positive and negative ions packed together in a regular way. A **lattice** is a regular **array** of particles. The lattice is held together by the strong electrostatic attractions between the positively and negatively charged ions.

▲ Figure 6.16 A lattice fence. A lattice is a regular, repeating structure.

THE STRUCTURE OF SODIUM CHLORIDE

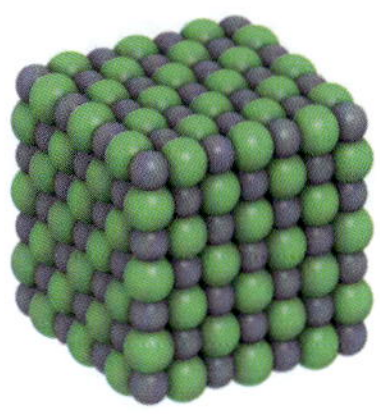

▲ Figure 6.17 A model of a small part of a sodium chloride crystal

Figure 6.17 shows how the ions in a crystal of sodium chloride are arranged.

In diagrams, the ions are usually drawn in an 'exploded' view (Figure 6.18). Each sodium ion is surrounded by 6 chloride ions. In turn, each chloride ion is surrounded by 6 sodium ions. You have to remember that this pattern repeats itself throughout the structure over vast numbers of ions.

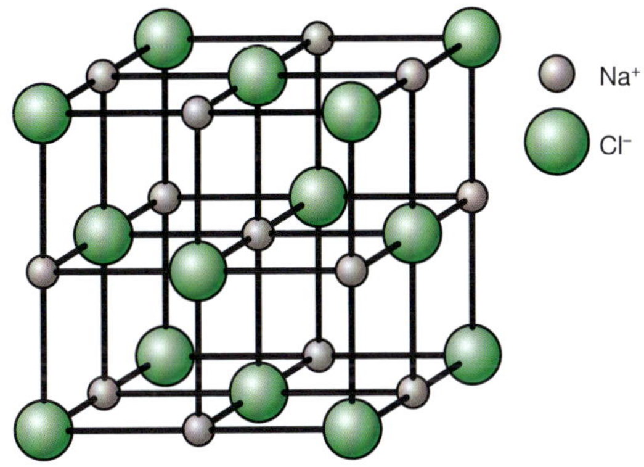

▲ Figure 6.18 An 'exploded' view of sodium chloride. The lines in this diagram are not bonds, they are just there to help show the arrangement of the ions. Those ions joined by lines are touching each other.

The structure of sodium chloride is described as a **giant ionic lattice**. We are using the word '**giant**' here not in the sense of big but rather to describe a structure where there are no individual molecules. All the sodium ions in the structure attract all the chloride ions, we cannot pick out sodium chloride molecules; there are no individual molecules. The bonding in a giant ionic lattice extends throughout the structure in all directions. There is no limit to the number of particles present, all we know is that there must be the same number of sodium and chloride ions.

HINT

This is really important: you must not talk about *molecules* of an ionic compound. This will be marked wrong in the exam and you could lose all the marks for a question!

THE STRUCTURE OF MAGNESIUM OXIDE

Magnesium oxide, MgO, contains magnesium ions, Mg^{2+}, and oxide ions, O^{2-}. It has exactly the same structure as sodium chloride. The only difference is that the magnesium oxide lattice is held together by stronger forces of attraction. This is because in magnesium oxide, 2+ ions are attracting 2– ions. In sodium chloride, the electrostatic attractions are weaker because they are only between 1+ and 1– ions.

EXTENSION WORK

The Mg^{2+} ion is also smaller than the Na^+ ion, and the O^{2-} ion is smaller than the Cl^- ion. This causes stronger attractions but the effect of the charge on the ions is more important.

▲ Figure 6.19 Sodium chloride is crystalline

THE PHYSICAL PROPERTIES OF IONIC SUBSTANCES

Ionic compounds have high melting points and boiling points because of the strong electrostatic forces of attraction holding the lattice together. A lot of energy has to be supplied to break the strong electrostatic forces of attraction between oppositely charged ions in the giant lattice structure.

Ionic compounds tend to be crystalline. This reflects the regular arrangement of ions in the lattice. Sometimes the crystals are too small to be seen except under powerful microscopes. Magnesium oxide, for example, is always seen as a white powder because the individual crystals are too small to be seen with the naked eye.

Ionic crystals tend to be brittle. This is because any small distortion of a crystal will bring ions with the same charge alongside each other. Like charges repel and so the crystal splits itself apart.

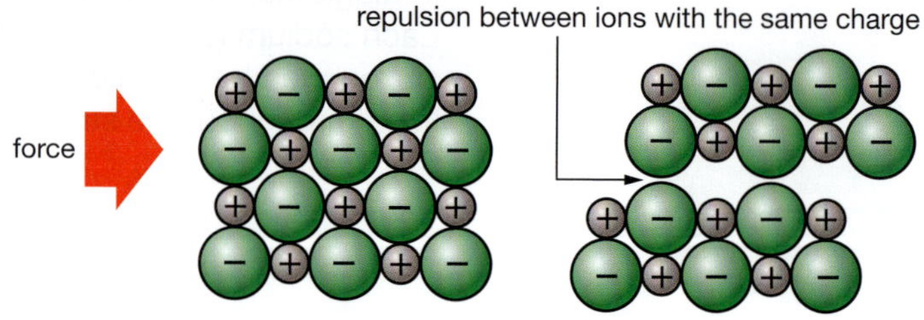

▲ Figure 6.20 Ionic crystals tend to be brittle

KEY POINT

Organic solvents include ethanol (alcohol) and **hydrocarbons**, such as hexane and those found in petrol. If you are interested in these, you could explore the organic chemistry section of this book (Unit 4).

Ionic substances tend to be soluble in water.

Ionic compounds tend to be insoluble in organic solvents.

EXTENSION WORK

The reasons that ionic compounds tend to be soluble in water are quite complicated. Water is a covalent molecule (Chapter 7) but the electrons in the bonds are more attracted towards the oxygen end of the bond. This makes the oxygen slightly negative and the hydrogen slightly positive – the molecule is called **polar**. This means that reasonably strong forces can be formed between water molecules and ions, which provide the energy to break the lattice apart.

Not all ionic substances are soluble in water: magnesium oxide isn't soluble in water because the attractions between the water molecules and the ions aren't strong enough to overcome the very strong electrostatic forces of attraction between magnesium and oxide ions.

Hexane is non-polar and does not form strong enough attractions to the ions to break apart the ionic lattice.

THE ELECTRICAL CONDUCTIVITY OF IONIC SUBSTANCES

HINT

Molten just means that the salt has been melted – it is a liquid.

Ionic compounds don't conduct electricity when they are solid because the *ions* are fixed in position and are not free to move around. They do, however, conduct electricity when they are **molten** (have melted) or if they are dissolved in water (in aqueous solution). This happens because the *ions* then become free to move around. It is really important that you use the correct words when explaining this. Do not use the word 'electrons'. You must talk about the **ions** being free to move.

CHAPTER QUESTIONS

SKILLS INTERPRETATION

1 a Explain what is meant by i an ion and ii ionic bonding.

SKILLS CRITICAL THINKING

b In each of the following cases, write down the electronic configurations of the original atoms and then explain (in words or diagrams) what happens when:

i sodium bonds with chlorine to make sodium chloride

ii lithium bonds with oxygen to make lithium oxide

iii magnesium bonds with fluorine to make magnesium fluoride.

SKILLS INTERPRETATION

2 Draw dot-and-cross diagrams to show the ions formed (outer electrons only) when:

a potassium combines with fluorine

b calcium combines with bromine

c magnesium combines with iodine.

SKILLS CRITICAL THINKING

6th

3 a State the formula of the ion formed by:

i magnesium
ii strontium
iii potassium
iv oxygen
v sulfur
vi caesium
vii chlorine
viii iodine
ix aluminium
x calcium
xi nitrogen

b State the name of each negative ion in a.

8th

4 Work out the formulae of the following compounds:

lead(II) oxide
magnesium sulfate
potassium carbonate
calcium nitrate
iron(II) sulfate
aluminium sulfate
cobalt(II) chloride
silver nitrate
ammonium nitrate
sodium sulfate
sodium bromide
zinc chloride
ammonium sulfide
iron(III) hydroxide
copper(II) carbonate
calcium hydroxide
calcium oxide
iron(III) fluoride
rubidium iodide
chromium(III) oxide

SKILLS REASONING

6th

5 Explain why sodium chloride:

a has a high melting point
b does not conduct electricity when solid
c conducts electricity when molten.

7th

6 Predict, giving reasons, whether you would expect potassium chloride to have a higher or lower melting point than calcium oxide.

7 COVALENT BONDING

We met ionic compounds in Chapter 6 and in this chapter we will understand what covalent bonding is. There are a lot more covalent compounds than ionic compounds so it is important that you understand how the bonding works.

▲ Figure 7.1 Water is a covalent compound but the salt dissolved in sea water is an ionic compound.

LEARNING OBJECTIVES

- Know that a covalent bond is formed between atoms by the sharing of a pair of electrons
- Understand covalent bonds in terms of electrostatic attractions
- Understand how to use dot-and-cross diagrams to represent covalent bonds in:
  - diatomic molecules, including hydrogen, oxygen, nitrogen, halogens and hydrogen halides
  - inorganic molecules, including water, ammonia and carbon dioxide
  - organic molecules containing up to two carbon atoms, including methane, ethane, ethene and those containing halogen atoms
- Explain why substances with a simple molecular structure are gases or liquids, or solids with low melting and boiling points
- Understand that the term intermolecular forces of attraction can be used to represent all forces between molecules
- Explain why the melting and boiling points of substances with simple molecular structures increase, in general, with increasing relative molecular mass
- Explain why substances with giant covalent structures are solids with high melting and boiling points
- Explain how the structures of diamond, graphite and C_{60} fullerene influence their physical properties, including electrical conductivity and hardness
- Know that covalent compounds do not usually conduct electricity

COVALENT BONDING

WHAT IS A COVALENT BOND?

In any bond, particles are held together by electrostatic attractions between something positively charged and something negatively charged. In a **covalent bond**, *a pair of electrons is shared between two atoms*. What holds the atoms together is *the strong electrostatic attraction between the nuclei (positively charged) of the atoms that make up the bond, and the shared pair of electrons (negatively charged).*

EXTENSION WORK

In most of the simple examples you will meet at International GCSE, each atom in a covalent bond supplies one electron to the shared pair of electrons. That doesn't have to be the case. Both electrons may come from the same atom.

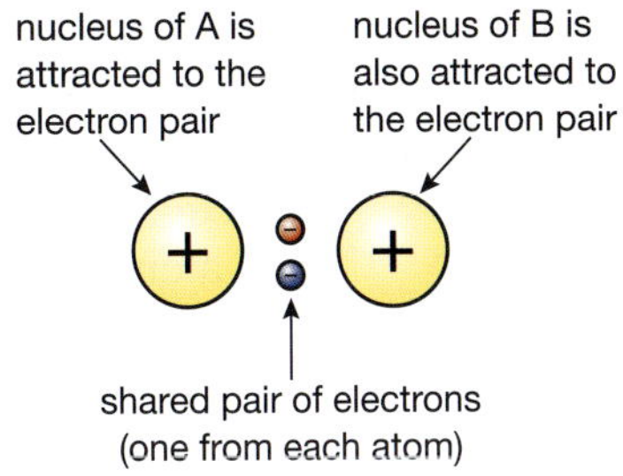

▲ Figure 7.2 The shared pair of electrons is attracted to the nuclei of both atoms.

COVALENT BONDING IN A HYDROGEN MOLECULE

HINT

Remember that, although the electrons are drawn as dots or as crosses, there is absolutely no difference between them in reality; the dots and the crosses simply show that the electrons have come from two different atoms.

Covalent bonds are often shown using dot-and-cross diagrams.

Both hydrogen nuclei in Figure 7.3 are strongly attracted to the shared pair of electrons.

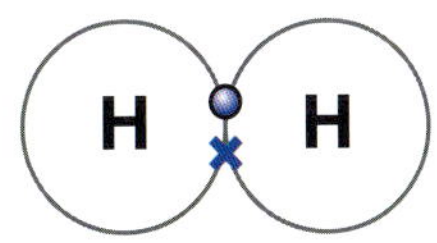

▲ Figure 7.3 A dot-and-cross diagram for H_2

Hydrogen atoms form diatomic molecules with the formula H_2. The atoms in an H_2 molecule are joined together by a covalent bond. The covalent bond between two hydrogen atoms is very strong.

Molecules contain a certain fixed number of atoms, which are joined together by covalent bonds. Hydrogen molecules are said to be **diatomic** because they contain two atoms. Other sorts of molecule may have as many as thousands of atoms joined together, for example proteins and DNA.

THE SIGNIFICANCE OF NOBLE GAS STRUCTURES IN COVALENT BONDING

In H_2, each hydrogen atom has only one electron to share, so it can only form one covalent bond. The shared pair of electrons is in the outer shell of both, therefore each atom has the same number of electrons as a noble gas atom (helium in this case).

Does that mean that the hydrogen has turned into helium? No. The number of protons in the nucleus hasn't changed, it is the number of protons that defines what an atom is.

REMINDER

If atoms have 8 electrons in their outer shell they have the same number of electrons as a noble gas atom – they are isoelectronic with a noble gas atom.

In virtually all of the molecules you will meet at this level, electrons will be shared so that H atoms have a total of 2 electrons in their outer shell and all other atoms will have 8 electrons in their outer shell. Some people talk about the '**octet** rule', referring to this 8. Remember, we are counting shared electrons as belonging to the outer shells of both atoms.

When there is one atom in the middle and other atoms are joined to it (as in CH_4 or PCl_3) the *outer* atoms will virtually always have 8 electrons in their outer shell (or 2 if they are H). In fact, it is very difficult to think of an example where the outer atoms do not have 8 electrons. There are some molecules where the *central* atom does not have 8 electrons in the outer shell, and we will look at a couple of examples of those later on.

KEY POINT

In chemistry, we talk about things being more stable or less stable. When we do this we are usually talking about how much energy something has. Generally, the lower the energy something has, the more stable it is. Chemical reactions usually occur so that something becomes more stable. Think about holding a book: if you let go of the book, it will fall to the floor, where it has less (potential) energy, therefore it becomes more stable. When bonds form energy is given out and so the substance formed has less energy, therefore it is more stable.

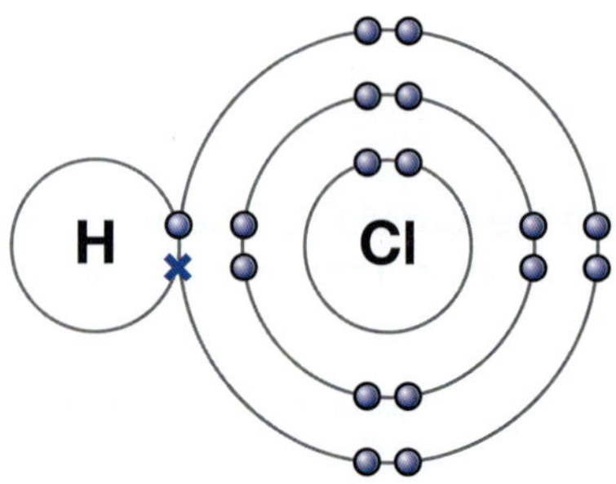

Figure 7.4 A dot-and-cross diagram for HCl.

Figure 7.5 The covalent bonding in HCl showing outer shell electrons only.

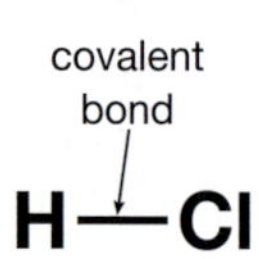

Figure 7.6 The line between the atoms represents a covalent bond.

WHY DOES HYDROGEN FORM MOLECULES?

Whenever a bond is formed (of whatever kind), energy is released, and that makes the things involved more stable than they were before. The more bonds an atom can form, the more energy is released and the more stable the system becomes. The H_2 molecule is much more stable than two separate hydrogen atoms.

COVALENT BONDING IN A HYDROGEN CHLORIDE MOLECULE

A chlorine atom has 7 electrons in its outer shell. By sharing 1 electron with a hydrogen atom, both atoms will have the same number of electrons as the nearest noble gas atom. If you look at the arrangement of electrons around the chlorine atom in the covalently bonded molecule of HCl (Figure 7.4), you will see that its electronic configuration is now [2, 8, 8]. That is the same as an argon atom. Similarly, the hydrogen now has 2 electrons in its outer shell – the same as helium.

Notice in Figure 7.4 that only the electrons in the outer shell of the chlorine are used in bonding. In the examples you will meet at International GCSE, the inner electrons never get used. In fact, the inner electrons are often left out of bonding diagrams. But be careful! In an exam, only leave out the inner electrons if the question tells you to. Another way of representing the covalent bonding in HCl is shown in Figure 7.5.

We also use lines to represent the covalent bonds between atoms, but be careful, the diagram shown in Figure 7.6 is not a dot-and-cross diagram.

COVALENT BONDING IN A CHLORINE MOLECULE (Cl_2)

A chlorine atom has 7 electrons in its outer shell. Each Cl shares 1 electron so that both Cl atoms will have 8 electrons in their outer shell.

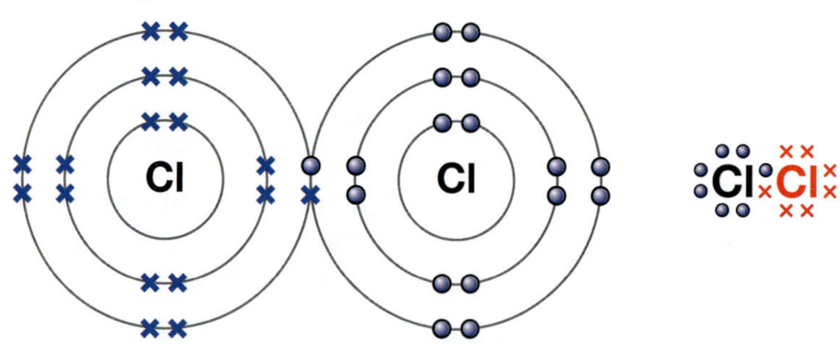

Figure 7.7 Two ways of showing the covalent bonding in Cl_2

COVALENT BONDING IN METHANE, AMMONIA AND WATER

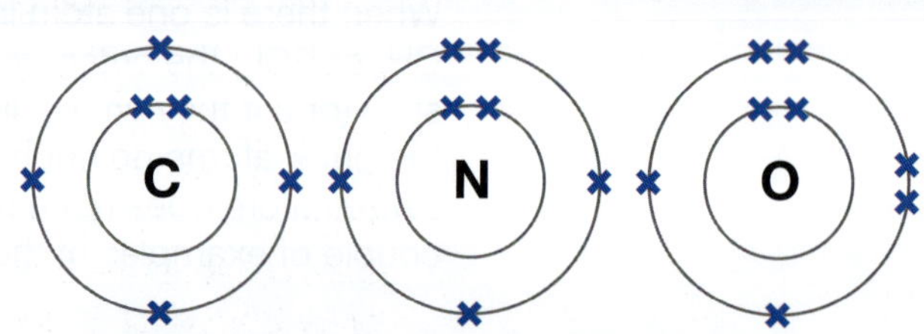

Figure 7.8 The electronic configurations of C, N and O atoms

COVALENT BONDING IN METHANE

A carbon atom has 4 electrons in its outer shell. By sharing 1 electron with each of 4 hydrogen atoms the C will have 8 electrons in its outer shell and each H will have 2 electrons in its outer shell. Therefore C forms 4 covalent bonds, 1 with each H atom. Methane has the formula CH_4.

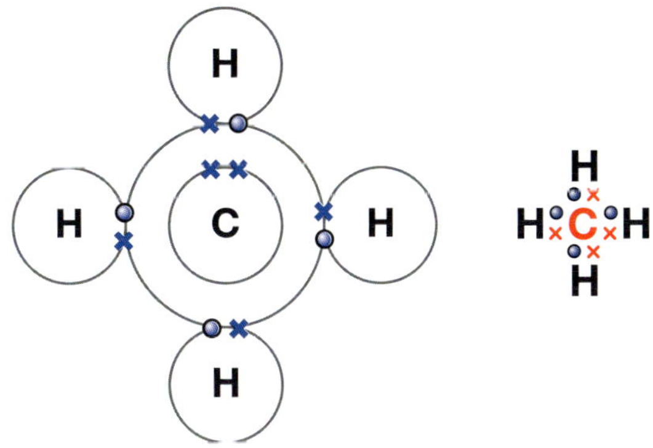

▲ Figure 7.9 Dot-and-cross diagrams for methane

COVALENT BONDING IN AMMONIA

A nitrogen atom has 5 electrons in its outer shell. It will therefore share 3 other electrons to have 8 electrons in its outer shell. In ammonia, a nitrogen atom forms 3 covalent bonds, 1 with each H atom.

The formula of ammonia is NH_3.

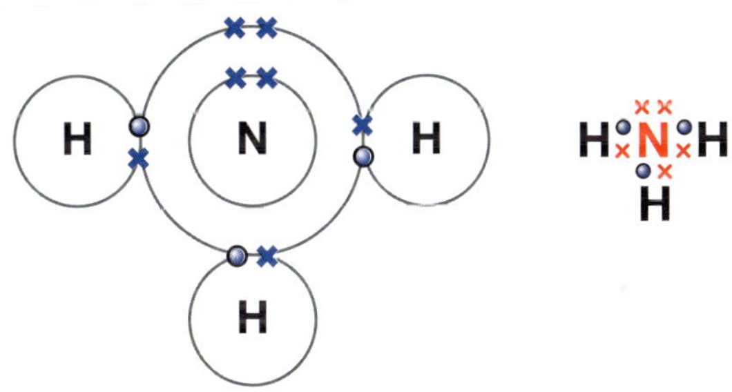

▲ Figure 7.10 Dot-and-cross diagrams for ammonia

COVALENT BONDING IN WATER

An oxygen atom has 6 electrons in its outer shell. It will therefore share 2 other electrons to have 8 electrons in its outer shell. In water, an oxygen atom forms 2 covalent bonds – 1 with each H atom. The formula of water is H_2O.

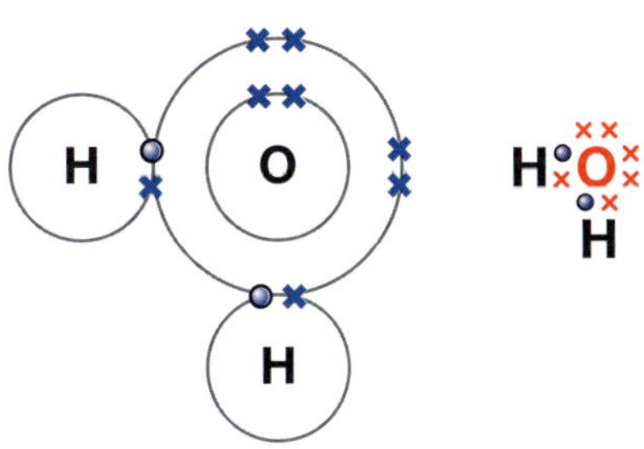

▲ Figure 7.11 Dot-and-cross diagrams for water

LOOKING AHEAD

Shapes of molecules

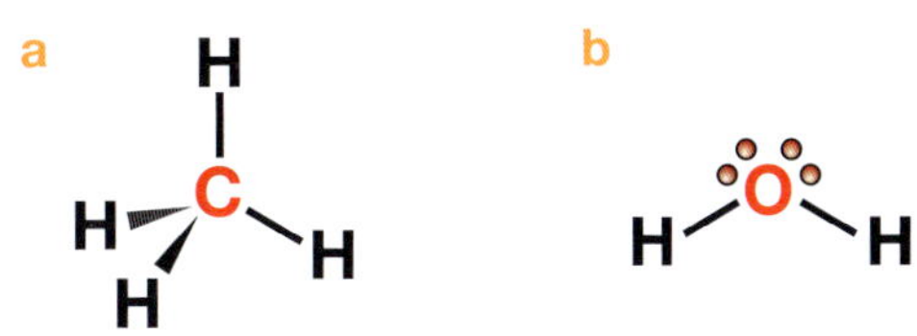

▲ Figure 7.12 (a) A methane molecule is tetrahedral and (b) a water molecule is bent.

By understanding the bonding in a covalent molecule it is possible to work out the shape of the molecule. Pairs of electrons in the outer shell of the central atom repel each other and will therefore tend to get as far apart as possible. For example, in a methane molecule there are four pairs of electrons around the central C atom and for these to be as far away from each other as possible, they must be arranged in a tetrahedral shape. A tetrahedron (adjective: tetrahedral) is a triangular pyramid.

There are also four pairs of electrons around the central atom in water: two of these are pairs of electrons involved in covalent bonds and two are pairs of electrons in the outer shell of the oxygen which are not involved in bonding (these are often called *lone pairs of electrons* or just *lone pairs*). These four pairs of electrons are also arranged in a tetrahedral arrangement so the actual shape of a water molecule (how the atoms are arranged) is described as 'bent' or 'V-shaped'. The fact that a water molecule is bent and the electrons are attracted to a different extent by the oxygen and hydrogen atoms means that a water molecule is polar (has a slightly negative and a slightly positive end) and that a stream of water can be bent by an electrically charged object.

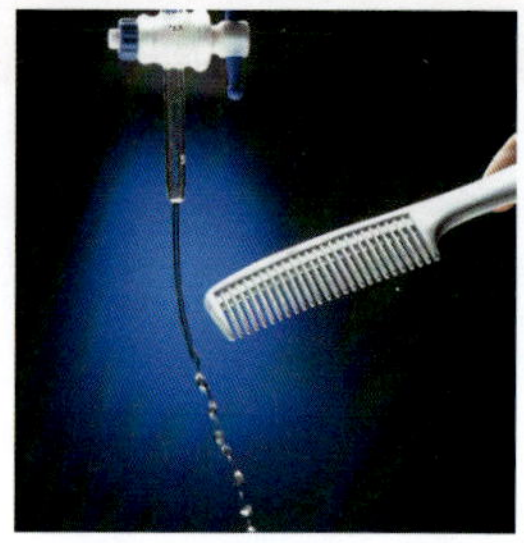

▲ Figure 7.13 Water being bent by an electrically charged comb.

COVALENT BONDING IN A SLIGHTLY MORE COMPLICATED MOLECULE: ETHANE

Ethane has the formula C_2H_6. The bonding is similar to methane (Figure 7.9), except that there is a carbon–carbon covalent bond as well as the carbon–hydrogen bonds.

This is called an organic compound. You will learn more about molecules such as this in Unit 4.

HINT

When drawing molecules containing carbon and hydrogen it is useful to remember that carbon always forms 4 bonds by sharing 4 electrons, and hydrogen always forms 1 bond by sharing 1 electron. The hydrogen atoms always go on the outside, never in the middle.

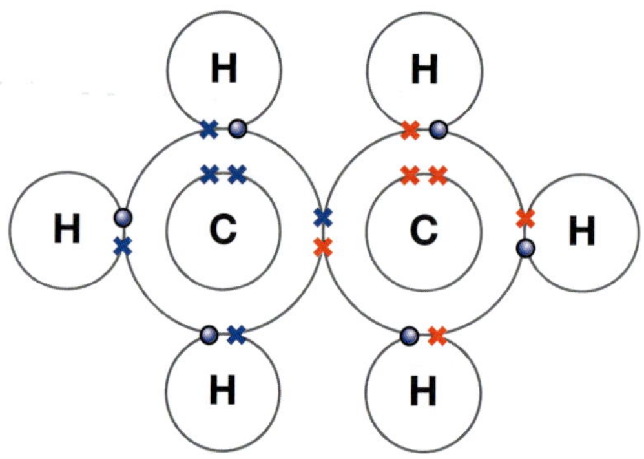

▲ Figure 7.14 A dot-and-cross diagram for ethane

MULTIPLE COVALENT BONDING

COVALENT BONDING IN AN OXYGEN MOLECULE: DOUBLE BONDING

An oxygen atom has 6 electrons in its outer shell and so if two oxygen atoms combine, they will both share 2 electrons each; this means that each atom will have 8 electrons in its outer shell. There are therefore two shared pairs of electrons between the oxygen atoms; this is called a double covalent bond or, usually, just a **double bond**.

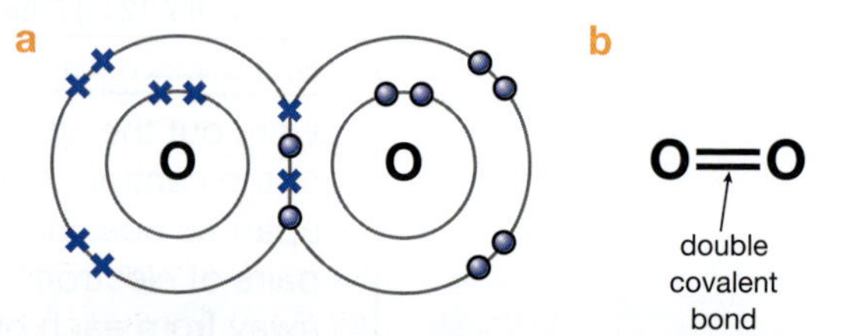

▲ Figure 7.15 (a) A dot-and-cross diagram for O_2 and (b) the double covalent bond.

THE TRIPLE BOND IN A NITROGEN MOLECULE

A nitrogen atom has 5 electrons in its outer shell and so if two nitrogen atoms combine they will both share 3 electrons each; this means that each atom will have 8 electrons in its outer shell. There are, therefore, three shared pairs of electrons between the nitrogen atoms; this is called a triple covalent bond or, usually, just a **triple bond**.

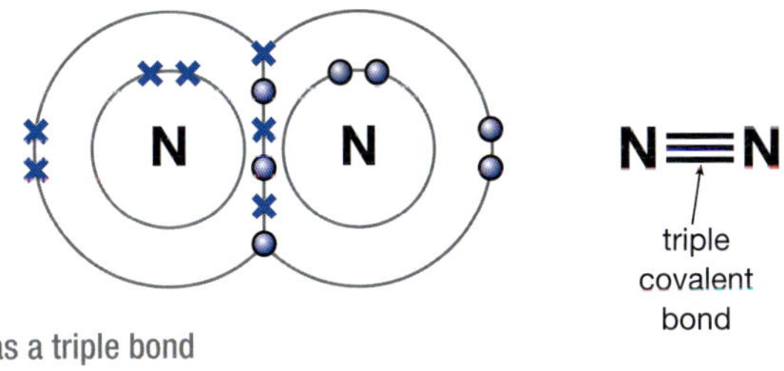

▲ Figure 7.16 N_2 has a triple bond

Nitrogen gas consists of nitrogen molecules bonded like this. The triple bond from the sharing of three pairs of electrons between the two nitrogen atoms is very strong and needs a lot of energy to break. That is why nitrogen is relatively unreactive.

COVALENT DOUBLE BONDING IN CARBON DIOXIDE, CO_2

An oxygen atom has 6 electrons in its outer shell and a carbon atom has 4. Each oxygen atom will share 2 electrons with the carbon atom. Two double bonds are formed between the carbon and the two oxygens (Figure 7.17). All atoms have 8 electrons in their outer shells.

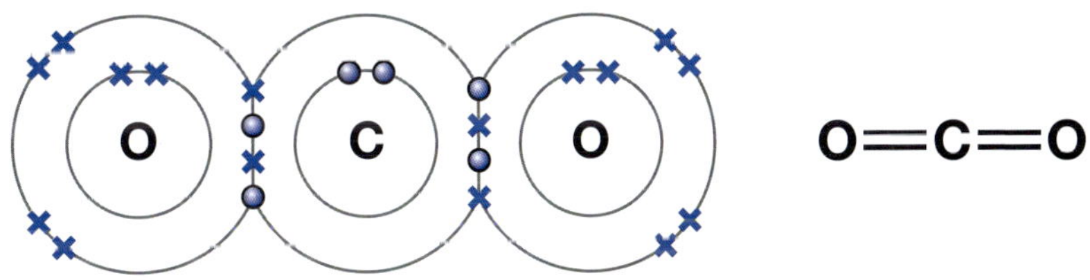

▲ Figure 7.17 CO_2 has two double bonds between atoms.

THE DOUBLE BOND IN ETHENE, C_2H_4

HINT

With organic compounds such as ethane and ethene you have to look at their names very carefully, even one different letter in the name can matter. Here, for example, ethane and ethene are completely different compounds. You will find out more about this in Unit 4.

Ethene is rather like ethane in Figure 7.14, except that it only has two hydrogen atoms attached to each carbon atom and a double bond between the carbon atoms.

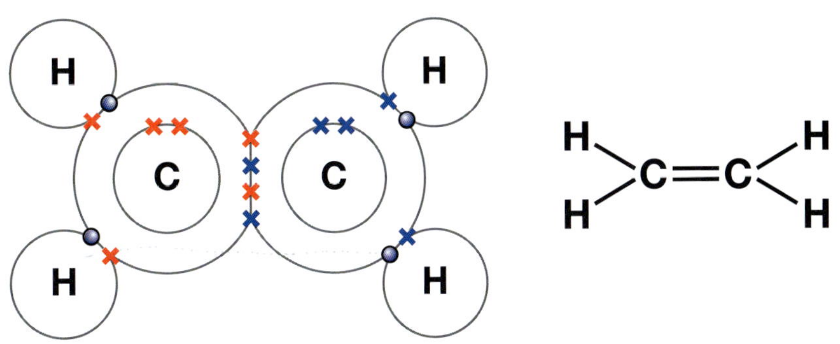

▲ Figure 7.18 Ethene has a double bond between the C atoms.

ORGANIC MOLECULES CONTAINING HALOGEN ATOMS

Bromomethane has the formula CH_3Br: the 3 H atoms and the Br atom are joined to the central C atom. Br has 35 electrons and we have not learned how to work out the electronic configuration of an atom with 35 electrons, but if you look at the Periodic Table you will see that Br is in Group 7. Because it is in Group 7 we know that it has 7 electrons in its outer shell, and will share 1 electron so that it has 8 in its outer shell. Therefore, we know that Br will form just 1 covalent bond. When you draw a dot-and-cross diagram for CH_3Br you will only be asked to show the outer electrons (Figure 7.19).

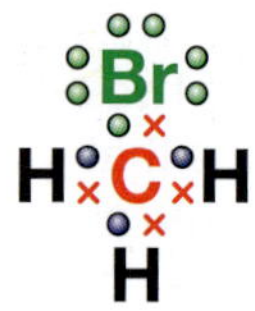

▲ Figure 7.19 A dot-and-cross diagram for CH_3Br showing outer shells only. Although we have used different colours here for clarity, you do not need to use different colours in the exam.

Probably the most complicated molecule for which you could be asked to draw a dot-and-cross diagram would be something like chloroethene (CH_2CHCl). When drawing chloroethene, remember that C will form 4 covalent bonds, H will form 1 and Cl will form 1. The dot-and-cross diagram (outer shells only) is shown in Figure 7.20.

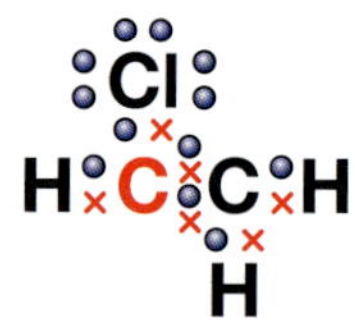

▲ Figure 7.20 There is a double bond between the 2 C atoms. It does not matter where you put the H and Cl atoms relative to the C, and you do not have to use different colours.

The structure of chloroethene can also be shown as illustrated in Figure 7.21.

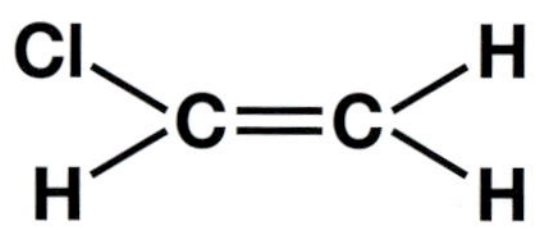

▲ Figure 7.21 The structure of chloroethene showing the covalent bonds. This is not, however, a dot-and-cross diagram and you must not draw this if you are asked to draw a dot-and-cross diagram.

SOME MORE DIFFICULT MOLECULES WHERE THE CENTRAL ATOM DOES NOT HAVE 8 ELECTRONS IN ITS OUTER SHELL

Although the *outer* atoms in a molecule will always have 8 (or 2 in the case of hydrogen) electrons in their outer shell, there are a few examples you may encounter where the *central* atom has more or fewer than 8 electrons in the outer shell.

BF_3

Boron is the central atom and the Fs are the outer atoms. Each F will share 1 other electron to have 8 electrons in its outer shell. This means that B only has a total of 6 electrons in its outer shell. Another way of thinking about this is that a B atom only has 3 electrons in its outer shell, and so this is the maximum number that it can share.

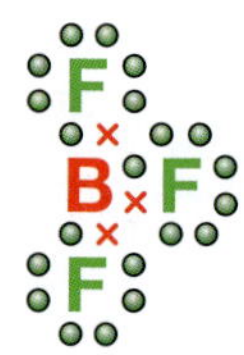

▲ Figure 7.22 A dot-and-cross diagram for BF_3

SO_2

EXTENSION WORK

Atoms in Periods 3 and below (4, 5, 6, 7) can have more than 8 electrons in their outer shells. The maximum number of electrons that the central atom in a molecule can share is equal to the number of electrons in its outer shell. So, sulfur can form up to 6 bonds (in SF_6) and chlorine 7 (in $HClO_4$).

This is called sulfur dioxide or sulfur(IV) oxide. The central atom is S and the outer atoms are O. Each O atom has 6 electrons in its outer shell and so will need to share 2 other electrons to have 8 electrons in the outer shell. So the S atom shares 2 electrons with each of the O atoms to form two double bonds. A sulfur atom originally had 6 electrons in its outer shell and so now, if it shares 4 electrons, it has 10 electrons in its outer shell.

▲ Figure 7.23 There are two double bonds in SO_2.

SIMPLE MOLECULAR STRUCTURES

Molecules contain fixed numbers of atoms joined by strong covalent bonds. If we look closely at liquid water, there are individual water molecules, where the H and O atoms are joined together with strong covalent bonds. But there must also be some forces between water molecules which keep them in the liquid state. These forces are **intermolecular forces**.

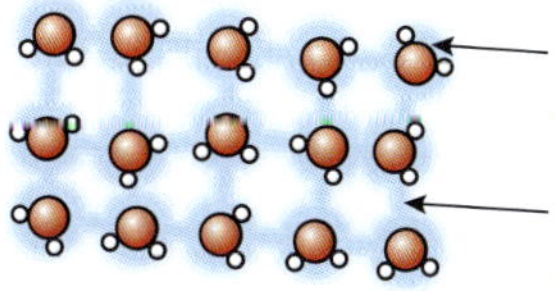

▲ Figure 7.24 Water is a simple molecular compound.

DID YOU KNOW?
Intermolecular literally means between molecules.

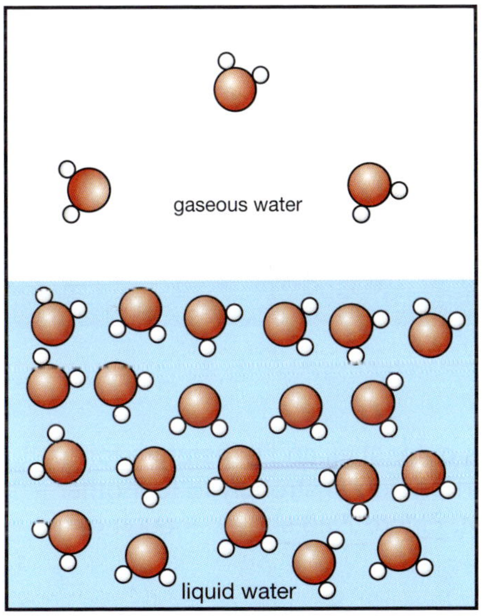

▲ Figure 7.25 Only intermolecular forces are broken when water evaporates/boils.

These intermolecular forces between molecules are much weaker than covalent bonds. When we boil water it is only these weak intermolecular forces of attraction that are broken; covalent bonds are not broken. Looking at Figure 7.25 you can see that there are H_2O molecules in liquid water and in gaseous water. The covalent bonds between the H and O atoms in the molecules have not changed in any way. All that has changed in gaseous water is that there are no intermolecular forces, they have been broken.

When a substance consists of molecules with intermolecular forces of attraction between them, we say that it has a *simple molecular structure*. Examples of things that have simple molecular structures are H_2O, CO_2, CH_4, NH_3 and C_2H_4. These are all the things that we have drawn dot-and-cross diagrams for above. Virtually all the compounds you will encounter that have covalent bonding will have simple molecular structures.

Substances with simple molecular structures tend to be gases or liquids or solids with low melting points and boiling points. The reason for this is that not much energy is required to break the weak intermolecular forces of attractions between molecules. Remember, no covalent bonds are broken, covalent bonds are strong.

EXTENSION WORK

If you continue with chemistry you will learn that there are different types of intermolecular forces. You will come across terms like van der Waals' forces, London dispersion forces and hydrogen bonds. There is a special type of intermolecular force between water molecules called **hydrogen bonds**. Hydrogen bonding gives water some of its very special properties, for example the solid form (ice) is less dense than the liquid form.

MELTING AND BOILING POINTS INCREASE AS RELATIVE MOLECULAR MASS INCREASES

The halogens (Group 7 in the Periodic Table) all have a simple molecular structure consisting of diatomic molecules with intermolecular forces between them.

You can see from Table 7.1 that the melting points and boiling points increase as the relative molecular mass increases.

Table 7.1 The melting points and boiling points of the halogens.

Halogen	Formula	Relative molecular mass / M_r	Melting point / °C	Boiling point / °C
fluorine	F_2	38	−220	−188
chlorine	Cl_2	71	−101	−34
bromine	Br_2	160	−7	59
iodine	I_2	254	114	184

EXTENSION WORK

It is not always the case that melting and boiling points increase as the M_r increases and really the rule only applies to sets of very similar substances, such as the halogens or the alkanes (see Chapter 18). Some examples where the rule does not work are water ($M_r = 18$, boiling point = 100 °C), ethane ($M_r = 30$, boiling point = −89 °C), NH_3 ($M_r = 17$, boiling point = −33 °C) and PH_3 ($M_r = 34$, boiling point = −88 °C).

Remember, as we melt or boil these substances we are only breaking the intermolecular forces of attraction between molecules. The boiling points increase down this group, which means we have to put in more energy to break the intermolecular forces as the relative molecular mass increases. This means that the *intermolecular forces of attraction must become stronger as relative molecular mass increases*.

This is something that we see quite often in chemistry, for example boiling points increase along the series CH_4, C_2H_6, C_3H_8 as relative molecular mass increases. This is discussed further in Chapter 18.

SOME OTHER PHYSICAL PROPERTIES OF COVALENT COMPOUNDS

KEY POINT

We are using the term covalent molecular compounds to mean covalent compounds with a simple molecular structure.

Covalent molecular compounds do not conduct electricity. This is because the molecules don't have any overall electrical charge (there are no ions) and all the electrons are held tightly in the atoms or in covalent bonds and so are not able to move from molecule to molecule.

Covalent molecular substances tend to be insoluble in water. There are some exceptions to this, for example ethanol (C_2H_5OH) and substances such as NH_3 and HCl that react with water as they dissolve.

Covalent molecular substances are often soluble in organic solvents.

GIANT COVALENT STRUCTURES

DIAMOND

KEY POINT

A tetrahedron is a triangular-based pyramid. In a tetrahedral arrangement, one atom is at the centre of the tetrahedron, and the atoms it is attached to are at the four corners. Look carefully at the top five atoms in Figure 7.26 to see what this looks like. You will find other similar arrangements in this diagram.
In Figure 7.26 some carbon atoms seem to be forming only two bonds (or even one bond), but that's not really the case. We are only showing a small part of the whole structure. The structure continues in three dimensions, and each of the atoms drawn here is attached to four others. Each of the lines in this diagram represents a covalent bond.

Diamond is a form of pure carbon.

Each carbon atom has four electrons in its outer shell and it therefore forms four covalent bonds. In diamond, each carbon bonds strongly to four other carbon atoms in a *tetrahedral* arrangement. Figure 7.26 shows enough of the structure to see what is happening.

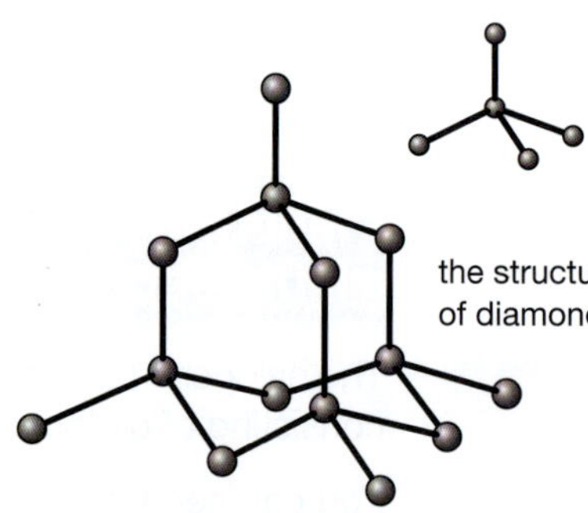

▲ Figure 7.26 Part of the structure of diamond

This is a giant covalent structure; it continues on and on in three dimensions. It is *not* a molecule because the number of atoms joined up in a real diamond is completely variable and depends on the size of the crystal. Molecules always contain *fixed numbers* of atoms joined by covalent bonds.

Diamond has a very high melting and boiling point. This is because of the very strong carbon–carbon covalent bonds, which extend throughout the whole crystal in three dimensions. A lot of energy has to be supplied to break these strong covalent bonds, therefore diamond has very high melting and boiling points. It is important to realise how this is different from the simple molecular structures that we saw above. In order to melt or boil a substance with a simple molecular structure, such as CH_4, we only had to supply enough

▲ Figure 7.27 Diamond (a form of carbon) is crystalline, and is the hardest naturally occurring substance.

energy to break the relatively weak intermolecular forces of attraction. In diamond there are no intermolecular forces (it has a giant structure, there are no molecules). Covalent bonds, which are very strong, must be broken in order to melt or boil it.

In general, *all substances with giant covalent structures are solids with high melting and boiling points* because a lot of energy has to be supplied to break all the strong covalent bonds throughout the giant structure. Other substances with giant covalent structures include graphite (discussed below) and silicon dioxide (SiO_2).

Diamond is very hard. Again, a lot of energy has to be supplied to break the strong covalent bonds in the giant structure. Drill bits can be tipped with diamonds for drills used on stone and rock.

Diamond doesn't conduct electricity. All the electrons in the outer shells of the carbon atoms are tightly held in covalent bonds between the atoms. None are free to move around.

EXTENSION WORK

Diamond doesn't dissolve in water or in any other solvent. This is again because of the strong covalent bonds between the carbon atoms. If the diamond dissolved, these bonds would have to be broken.
Diamond conducts heat very well (better than any other element). As one end of the crystal is heated the atoms vibrate more. The strong bonds throughout the giant structure mean that these vibrations are quickly transmitted from one end of the crystal to the other.

GRAPHITE

Graphite is also a form of carbon, but the atoms are arranged differently, although it still has a giant structure. Graphite has a *layer structure*, rather like a pack of playing cards. In a pack of cards, each card is strong but the individual cards are easily separated. The same is true in graphite.

▲ Figure 7.28 Graphite has a structure rather like a pack of playing cards.

▲ Figure 7.29 Graphite is soft with a layer structure.

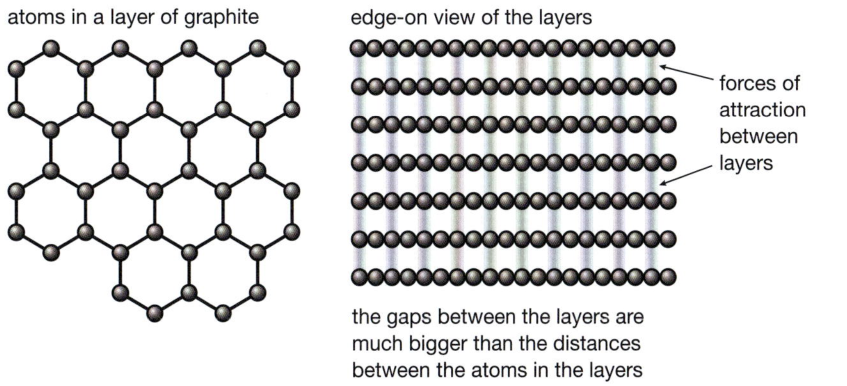

▲ Figure 7.30 The structure of graphite. Some forces of attraction between layers have been shown. These are not bonds and could have been drawn anywhere between the layers.

EXTENSION WORK

Actually, the reason that the layers slide over each other fairly easily is more complicated than this and graphite is not a lubricant in a vacuum. Graphite being a lubricant relies on water molecules sticking to the surface; this does not happen in a vacuum.

Graphite is a soft material. Although the forces holding the atoms together in each layer are very strong, the attractions between the layers are much weaker and not much energy is needed to overcome them. Layers slide over each other and can easily be flaked off.

Graphite (mixed with clay to make it harder) is used in pencils. When you write with a pencil, you are leaving a trail of graphite layers behind on the paper. Pure graphite is so slippery that it is used as a dry lubricant, for example powdered graphite is used to lubricate locks.

Graphite has high melting and boiling points. To melt/boil graphite, you don't just have to separate the layers, you have to break up the whole structure, including the covalent bonds. That needs very large amounts of energy because the covalent bonds are so strong.

▲ Figure 7.31 Three graphite **electrodes** glow red hot after their removal from an electric arc furnace used to produce steel.

Graphite conducts electricity. If you look back at Figure 7.30, you will see that each carbon atom is joined to only three others. Each carbon atom uses three of its outer shell electrons to form three single covalent bonds. The fourth electron in the outer shell of each atom is free to move around throughout the whole of the layer. The electrons that are free to move throughout the layers are called **delocalised electrons**. The movement of these delocalised electrons allows graphite to conduct electricity.

EXTENSION WORK

Some other properties of graphite are:

- *Graphite is insoluble in all solvents* because it would take too much energy to break all the strong covalent bonds.
- *Graphite is less dense than diamond* because the layers in graphite are relatively far apart. The distance between the graphite layers is more than twice the distance between atoms in each layer. In a sense, a graphite crystal contains a lot of wasted space, which isn't there in a diamond crystal.

C_{60} FULLERENE

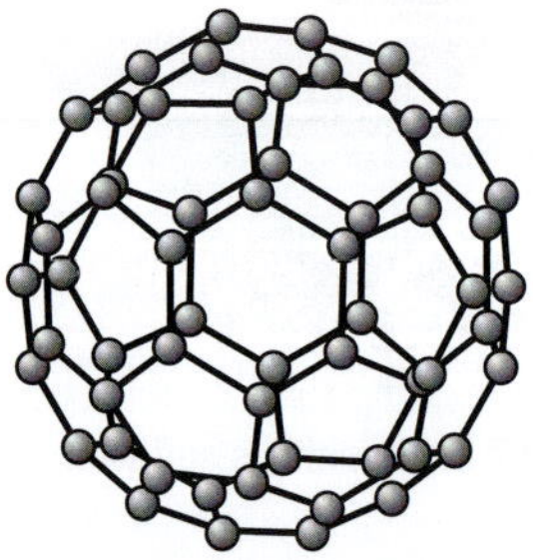

▲ Figure 7.32 A C_{60} fullerene molecule. Remember that molecules consist of fixed number of atoms; each C_{60} fullerene molecule contains 60 carbon atoms joined by covalent bonds.

Diamond and graphite are two **allotropes** of carbon. Allotropes are different forms of the same element. Another allotrope of carbon is C_{60} fullerene. Diamond and graphite both have giant structures but C_{60} fullerene has a simple molecular structure.

In solid or liquid C_{60} fullerene there are C_{60} molecules with weak intermolecular forces between them. The fact that C_{60} has a simple molecular structure has a big influence on its physical properties.

C_{60} fullerene has lower melting and boiling points than diamond and graphite. When fullerene is melted, only the relatively weak intermolecular forces of attraction must be broken. This does not require as much energy as breaking all the strong covalent bonds when diamond and graphite are melted.

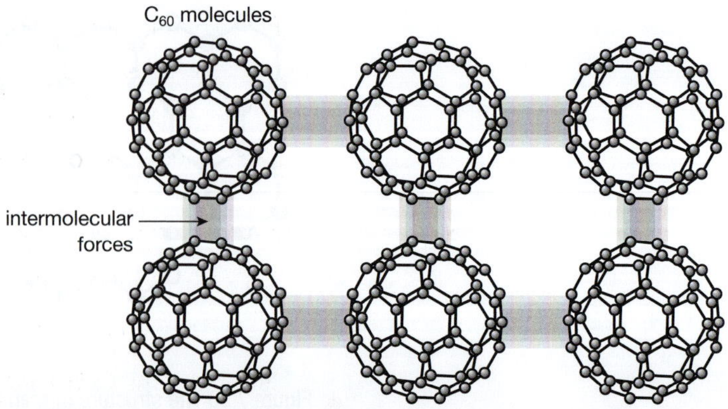

▲ Figure 7.33 C_{60} fullerene has a simple molecular structure.

KEY POINT

There are different fullerenes, where the molecules contain different numbers of carbon atoms. This is why we include the C_{60} in the name.

EXTENSION WORK

Unlike diamond and graphite C_{60} fullerene does dissolve in some solvents; only relatively weak intermolecular forces of attraction have to be broken for it to dissolve.

C_{60} fullerene is not as hard as diamond. It does not take as much energy to break the intermolecular forces of attraction in C_{60} fullerene compared to breaking the strong covalent bonds in diamond.

C_{60} fullerene does not conduct electricity. Although all the carbon atoms in C_{60} only form three bonds, the fourth electron on each atom can only move around *within* each C_{60} molecule; the electrons cannot jump from molecule to molecule.

CHAPTER QUESTIONS

You will need to use the Periodic Table in Appendix A on page 708.

SKILLS CRITICAL THINKING 6th

1 State whether each of the following compounds is ionic or covalent:

a MgO b CH_3Br c H_2O_2

d $FeCl_2$ e NaF f HCN

SKILLS INTERPRETATION 8th

2 a What is meant by a covalent bond? How does this bond hold two atoms together?

b Draw dot-and-cross diagrams (showing outer shell electrons only) to show the covalent bonding in

i methane (CH_4)

ii hydrogen sulfide (H_2S)

iii phosphine (PH_3)

iv silicon tetrachloride ($SiCl_4$)

c Draw dot-and-cross diagrams (showing outer shell electrons only) to show the covalent bonding in

i O_2

ii N_2

3 Draw dot-and-cross diagrams (showing outer shell electrons only) to show the covalent bonding in

a ethane (C_2H_6) b ethene (C_2H_4) c chloroethane (CH_3CH_2Cl)

SKILLS REASONING

4 Explain why carbon dioxide sublimes at −78.5 °C but diamond sublimes at around 4000 °C.

5 Hexane has the formula C_6H_{14}. It is a liquid at room temperature.

a Explain whether hexane has a simple molecular or giant structure.

b Explain whether you would expect pentane (C_5H_{12}) to have a higher or lower boiling point than hexane.

c Explain whether or not you would expect hexane to conduct electricity.

9th

6 Explain the following in terms of structure and bonding:

a diamond is harder than graphite

b C_{60} fullerene has a lower melting point than graphite

c graphite conducts electricity

d diamond does not conduct electricity.

SKILLS ANALYSIS

8th

7 The table below gives details of the boiling temperatures of some substances made of covalent molecules. Arrange these substances in increasing order of the strength of their intermolecular forces and explain your order.

Substance	Boiling point / °C
ammonia	–33
ethanamide	221
ethanol	78.5
hydrogen	–253
phosphorus trifluoride	–101
water	100

(Don't panic if you don't recognise some of the names. The substances could also have been labelled A, B, C, D, E and F.)

SKILLS REASONING

8 The compound N_2F_2 has the structure:

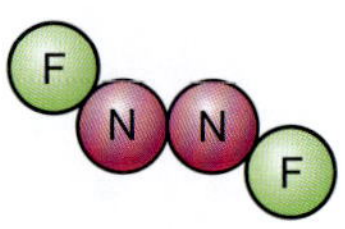

a Explain whether you would expect the bond between the nitrogen atoms to be a single, double or triple bond.

SKILLS INTERPRETATION

b Draw a dot-and-cross diagram for N_2F_2 showing outer electrons only.

SKILLS REASONING

9 a Draw a dot-and-cross diagram (showing outer electrons only) to show the covalent bonding in BCl_3.

9th

b BCl_3 is sometimes described as an *electron-deficient* compound. Explain what you think that means.

UNIT QUESTIONS

You may need to refer to the Periodic Table on page 708.

SKILLS CRITICAL THINKING 4th

1 Hydrogen is the most common element in the universe.

The melting point and boiling point of hydrogen are shown in the table:

Melting point / °C	**–259**
Boiling point / °C	**–253**

a Put a cross in the box to show a temperature at which hydrogen is a liquid. **(1)**

–265 °C ☐   –260 °C ☐   –255 °C ☐   –250 °C ☐

SKILLS INTERPRETATION 6th

b The circle in the diagram represents 1 molecule of hydrogen. Complete the diagram to show the arrangement of particles in liquid hydrogen. You should add at least 10 more circles to the diagram. **(2)**

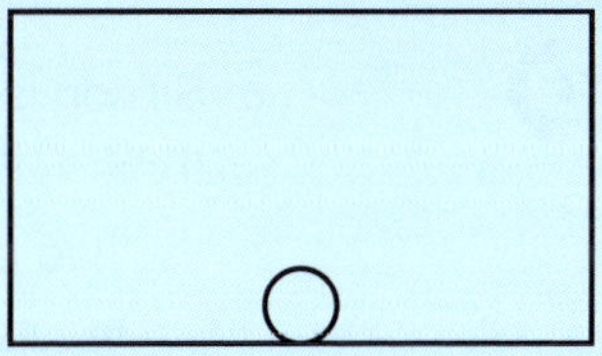

SKILLS PROBLEM SOLVING 8th

c Hydrogen has three isotopes, the least common of which is tritium, ^3H. Use the Periodic Table to work out the number of protons, neutrons and electrons in an atom of tritium. **(3)**

Number of protons:

Number of neutrons:

Number of electrons:

d Hydrogen reacts with nitrogen to form ammonia (NH_3).

7th

i The electronic configuration of a nitrogen atom is (put a cross in one box): **(1)**

2, 2, 3 ☐   2, 5 ☐   2, 8, 4 ☐   2, 2, 8, 2 ☐

SKILLS CRITICAL THINKING 8th

ii Draw a dot-and-cross diagram, showing outer electrons only, to show the bonding in an ammonia molecule. **(2)**

6th

e Ammonia forms salts that contain the ammonium ion. Put a cross in the box to show which of the following formulae for ammonium compounds is incorrect.

NH_4SO_4 ☐ NH_4NO_3 ☐ NH_4Cl ☐ $(NH_4)_2CO_3$ ☐

SKILLS CRITICAL THINKING 5th

f Two more compounds that contain hydrogen are water and ethanol. Put a cross in the box to show a method that can be used to separate a mixture of ethanol and water. **(1)**

crystallisation ☐ simple distillation ☐

filtration ☐ fractional distillation ☐

(Total 10 marks)

6th **2**

a Complete the following passage by using the words below. You may use the words once, more than once, or not at all. **(4)**

mass number	atomic number	groups	periods
protons	electrons	outer shell	nucleus

The elements in the Periodic Table are arranged in order of ______________.

The vertical columns are called ______________ and contain elements

which have the same number of ______________ in their ______________.

5th

b Put a cross next to the symbol(s) of elements that are non-metals. **(2)**

H ☐ V ☐ Pb ☐ Ar ☐ W ☐

SKILLS REASONING 6th

c Silicon is an element that shows some of the properties of metals and non-metals. It is sometimes called a *metalloid*.

i Two properties of silicon are:

- silicon conducts electricity
- silicon forms an oxide (SiO_2) that reacts with hot concentrated sodium hydroxide.

Explain which of these is not a property of metals. **(2)**

SKILLS ANALYSIS, REASONING 8th

ii The structure of silicon dioxide (SiO_2) is shown in the diagram. This structure continues in all directions.

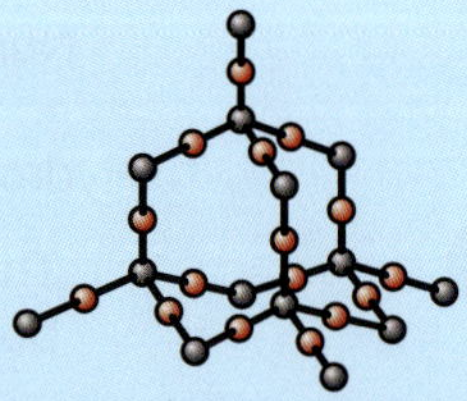

Explain in terms of electronic configurations and bonding whether the grey or red circles in this diagram represent silicon atoms. **(3)**

iii By referring to the diagram in part **ii** explain whether you would expect SiO_2 to be a solid, liquid or gas at room temperature. **(2)**

(Total 13 marks)

SKILLS INTERPRETATION, REASONING 7th

3 Strontium is an element in Group 2 of the Periodic Table and bromine is an element in Group 7.

a Explain what happens in terms of electrons when an atom of strontium combines with an atom of bromine to form strontium bromide. You may draw a diagram to illustrate your answer. **(3)**

b Explain in terms of structure and bonding whether you would expect strontium bromide to have a high or a low melting point. **(3)**

c Explain what you understand by the term 'relative atomic mass' of an element. **(2)**

SKILLS PROBLEM SOLVING 10th

d The natural abundances of the two isotopes of bromine are:

^{79}Br 50.69%

^{81}Br 49.31%

Calculate the relative atomic mass of bromine. Give your answer to 2 decimal places. **(2)**

SKILLS CRITICAL THINKING 6th

e The formula of strontium nitrate is (put a cross in one box): **(1)**

$SrNO_3$ ☐ $Sr(NO_3)_2$ ☐ $SrNO_{32}$ ☐ Sr_3N_2 ☐

(Total 11 marks)

SKILLS REASONING 9th

4 The diagram represents the structure of diamond, a form of carbon.

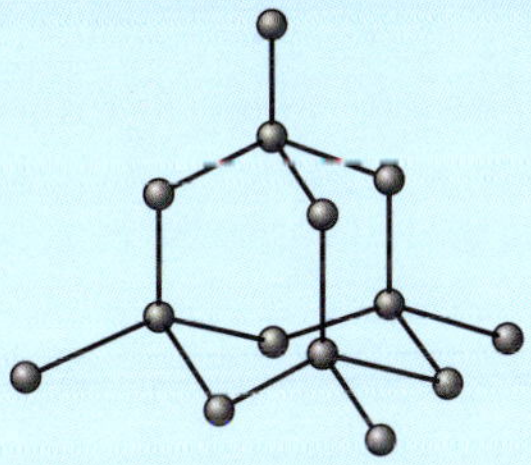

a Explain in terms of structure and bonding why diamond is very hard. **(2)**

b Two more forms of carbon are graphite and C_{60} fullerene. Part of the structure of graphite and a molecule of C_{60} fullerene are shown in the diagram.

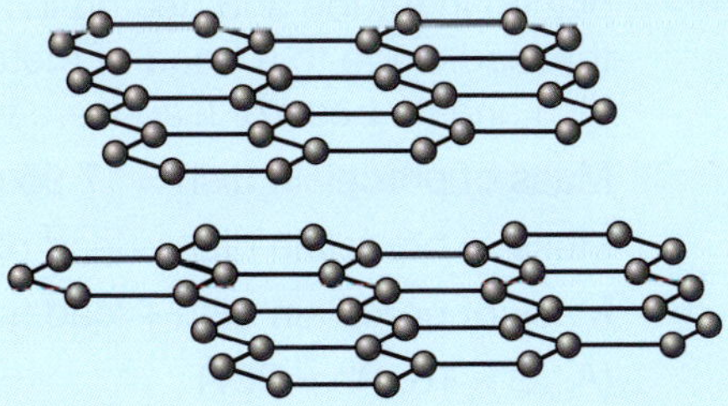

graphite

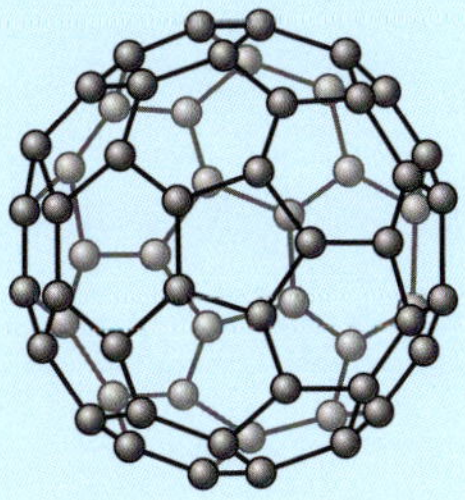

C_{60} fullerene

i Explain whether graphite or C_{60} fullerene has the higher boiling point. **(4)**

ii Explain why graphite conducts electricity. **(2)**

iii Explain why C_{60} fullerene does not conduct electricity. **(2)**

(Total 10 marks)

SKILLS ANALYSIS

5 a Oxygen gas has the formula O_2. Which of the following is a correct dot-and-cross diagram showing the bonding in O_2 (outer shells of electrons only are shown). Circle one of the diagrams. **(1)**

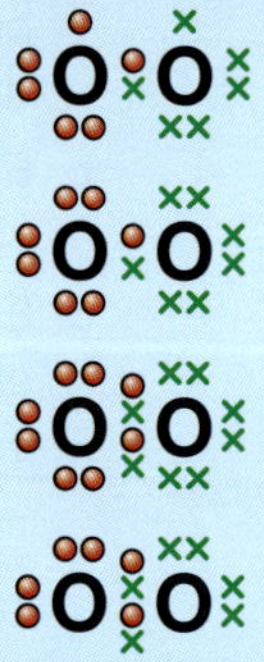

SKILLS CRITICAL THINKING

b Oxygen reacts with potassium to form potassium oxide. Put a cross in one box to indicate what the formula of potassium oxide is. **(1)**

PO ☐ KO ☐ K_2O ☐ KO_2 ☐

SKILLS ANALYSIS

c Oxygen reacts with carbon to form carbon dioxide. Which diagram shows the covalent bonds in carbon dioxide? Circle one diagram. **(1)**

O=C—O

O=C=O

O=C≡O

O—C—O

(Total 3 marks)

SKILLS PROBLEM SOLVING

6 In an experiment to find the empirical formula of lead oxide, a small porcelain dish was weighed, filled with lead oxide and weighed again. The dish was placed in a tube and heated in a stream of hydrogen. The hydrogen reduced the lead oxide to a bead of metallic lead. When the apparatus was cool, the dish and its bead of lead were weighed together.

Mass of porcelain dish = 17.95 g

Mass of porcelain dish + lead oxide = 24.80 g

Mass of porcelain dish + lead = 24.16 g

(A_r: O = 16, Pb = 207)

a Calculate the mass of lead in the lead oxide. **(1)**

b Calculate the mass of oxygen in the lead oxide. **(1)**

c There are three different oxides of lead: PbO, PbO_2 and Pb_3O_4. Use your results from **a** and **b** to find the empirical formula of the oxide used in the experiment. **(3)**

(Total 5 marks)

SKILLS PROBLEM SOLVING 7th

7 Copper reacts with concentrated nitric acid to produce copper(II) nitrate solution and nitrogen dioxide gas.

$$Cu(s) + 4HNO_3(aq) \rightarrow Cu(NO_3)_2(aq) + 2NO_2(g) + 2H_2O(l)$$

A student carried out an experiment to make some copper(II) nitrate crystals.

a The student started with 2.00 g of copper and added excess nitric acid. Calculate the maximum mass of copper(II) nitrate, $Cu(NO_3)_2$, which could be obtained. (A_r: N = 14, O = 16, Cu = 63.5) **(3)**

SKILLS EXECUTIVE FUNCTION 5th

b Explain the method the student could use to obtain crystals of copper(II) nitrate from the copper nitrate solution. **(3)**

SKILLS PROBLEM SOLVING 7th

c The copper nitrate crystallises out of the solution as $Cu(NO_3)_2{\cdot}3H_2O$. The student did some calculations and worked out that he should make 7.61 g of crystals. He actually only made 5.23 g. Calculate the percentage yield of the student's experiment. **(2)**

(Total 8 marks)

CHEMISTRY UNIT 2 INORGANIC CHEMISTRY

Inorganic chemistry is the study of all the elements in the Periodic Table and the compounds they form, except organic compounds formed by carbon. The properties of these elements are very different and they form a huge variety of compounds. The Periodic Table is the great unifying principle used by inorganic chemists as a guide to understanding the behaviour of the elements and their compounds. Most of the elements in the Periodic Table are metals and these are some of the most important materials that we use in everyday life. However, scientists are always searching for new materials with exciting properties. Inorganic chemists are involved in the development of these new materials, for instance high-temperature superconductors that are used in trains that levitate above the tracks.

8 THE ALKALI METALS

We have already looked at the Periodic Table in Chapter 4. Here we will look at the properties of the elements in Group 1 of the Periodic Table: the alkali metals.

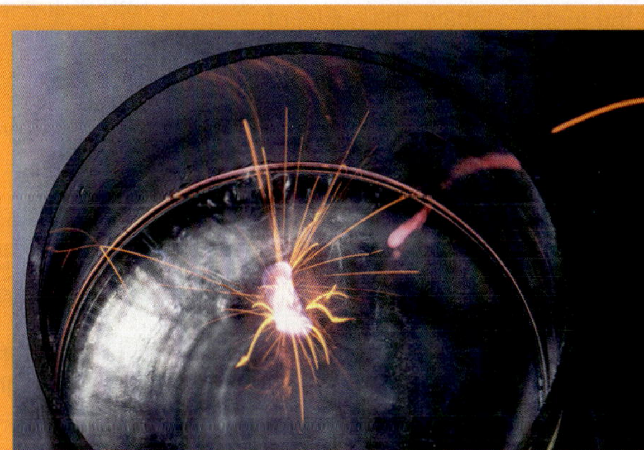

▶ Figure 8.1 Potassium reacting with water. The alkali metals are all reactive metals that react vigorously with water.

LEARNING OBJECTIVES

- Understand how the similarities in the reactions of these elements with water provide evidence for their recognition as a family of elements
- Understand how the differences between the reactions of these elements with air and water provide evidence for the trend in reactivity in Group 1
- Use knowledge of trends in Group 1 to predict the properties of other alkali metals

Li	lithium
Na	sodium
K	potassium
Rb	rubidium
Cs	caesium
Fr	francium

▲ Figure 8.2 The alkali metals

The elements in Group 1 of the Periodic Table are called the **alkali metals**. The group contains the elements shown in Figure 8.2.

Francium (pronounced france-ee-um), at the bottom of the group, is **radioactive**. One of its isotopes is produced during the radioactive decay of uranium-235, but is extremely short-lived. At any one time scientists estimate that there is only about 20–30 g of francium present in the whole of the Earth's crust and no one has ever seen a piece of francium. When you know about the rest of Group 1 you can predict what francium would be like. We will make those predictions later.

PHYSICAL PROPERTIES

	Melting point / °C	Boiling point / °C	Density / g / cm^3
Li	181	1342	0.53
Na	98	883	0.97
K	63	760	0.86
Rb	39	686	1.53
Cs	29	669	1.88

EXTENSION WORK

The reason that the melting points decrease is that the atoms get bigger as we go down the group. In the metallic lattice, the nuclei of the positive ions are further from the delocalised electrons in caesium than in sodium and therefore there is weaker electrostatic attraction.

The melting and boiling points of the elements are very low for metals, and get lower as you move down the group.

Their densities tend to increase down the group, although not regularly. Lithium, sodium and potassium are all less dense than water, and so will float on it.

The metals are also very soft and are easily cut with a knife, becoming softer as you move down the group. They are shiny and silver when freshly cut, but **tarnish** very quickly on exposure to air.

STORAGE AND HANDLING

▲ Figure 8.3 Lithium, sodium and potassium have to be kept in oil to stop them reacting with oxygen in the air.

All these metals are extremely reactive and get more reactive as you go down the group. They all react quickly with oxygen in the air to form oxides, and react rapidly with water to form strongly alkaline solutions of the metal hydroxides. This is why the Group 1 metals are commonly known as the alkali metals.

To stop them reacting with oxygen or water vapour in the air, lithium, sodium and potassium are stored under oil. Rubidium and caesium are so reactive that they have to be stored in sealed glass tubes to stop any possibility of oxygen getting at them.

Great care must be taken not to touch any of these metals with bare fingers. There could be enough sweat on your skin to give a reaction, producing lots of heat and a very **corrosive** metal hydroxide.

A FAMILY OF ELEMENTS

DID YOU KNOW?

Historically alkali metals were put in the same group because of similarities in properties, before anyone knew anything about electrons!

There are two reasons that we put these elements in Group 1:

1 They all have *one* electron in their outer shell. The electronic configurations are:

lithium	2, 1
sodium	2, 8, 1
potassium	2, 8, 8, 1

2 They have similar chemical properties, for example:

- they all react with water (this will be discussed below) in the same way to form a hydroxide with the formula MOH (e.g. LiOH, NaOH) and hydrogen
- they react with oxygen to form an oxide with the formula M_2O (Na_2O, K_2O)
- they react with halogens to form compounds with the formula MX (e.g. LiCl, KBr)
- they form ionic compounds which contain an M^+ ion (e.g. Na^+, K^+).

KEY POINT

'M' simply represents any one of the alkali metals. 'X' represents any one of the halogens.

The chemical properties depend on the number of electrons in the outer shell. The Group 1 elements react in very similar ways because they all have the same number of electrons in the outer shell (one), so reason 2 is really just a consequence of reason 1.

We will discuss the chemical properties in more detail below.

REACTIONS WITH WATER

All these metals react in the same way with water to produce a metal hydroxide and hydrogen:

alkali metal + water → alkali metal hydroxide + hydrogen

$$2M + 2H_2O \rightarrow 2MOH + H_2$$

The main difference between the reactions is how quickly they happen.

As you go down the group, the metals become more reactive and the reactions occur more rapidly.

The reaction between sodium and water is typical.

WITH SODIUM

$$2Na(s) + 2H_2O(l) \rightarrow 2NaOH(aq) + H_2(g)$$

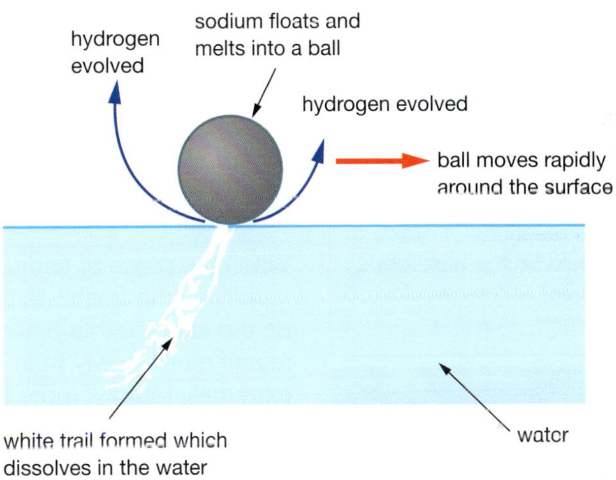

▲ Figure 8.4 Sodium reacting with water. The white trail is the sodium hydroxide, which dissolves in water to form a strongly alkaline solution.

The main observations you can make when this reaction occurs are:

- The sodium floats because it is less dense than water.
- The sodium melts into a ball because its melting point is low and a lot of heat is produced by the reaction.
- There is **fizzing** because hydrogen gas is produced.
- The sodium moves around on the surface of the water. Because the hydrogen isn't given off symmetrically around the ball, the sodium is pushed around the surface of the water, like a hovercraft.
- The piece of sodium gets smaller and eventually disappears. The sodium is used up in the reaction.
- If you test the solution that is formed with universal indicator solution, you will see that the universal indicator goes blue, indicating an alkaline solution has been formed. The metal hydroxide is alkaline (the solution contains the OH^- ion).

REMINDER

You might need to remind yourself why the formula is MOH by looking at Chapter 6. The charge on the hydroxide ion is 1–.

HINT

Strictly speaking, most of the time the sodium is reacting it is present as molten sodium, not solid sodium. Writing (l) for the state symbol has the potential to confuse an examiner and is probably best avoided!

HINT

When asked to write *observations* in the exam it is better to write 'fizzing/bubbling/effervescing' rather than 'a gas is given off' because the fizzing/bubbling/effervescing is what you actually see.

▲ Figure 8.5 A hovercraft

LITHIUM

$$2Li(s) + 2H_2O(l) \rightarrow 2LiOH(aq) + H_2(g)$$

The reaction is very similar to sodium's reaction, except that it is slower. Lithium's melting point is higher and the heat isn't produced so quickly, so the lithium doesn't melt.

HINT

When you are asked about this in the exam, you are often asked to compare the reactions of sodium and lithium so you should explain how you can see that the reaction of lithium is slower. So, for example, you can say that it fizzes more slowly, or the lithium moves around more slowly, or takes longer to disappear.

POTASSIUM

$$2K(s) + 2H_2O(l) \rightarrow 2KOH(aq) + H_2(g)$$

Potassium's reaction is faster than sodium's. Enough heat is produced to ignite the hydrogen, which burns with a lilac flame. The reaction often ends with the potassium **spitting** around and exploding.

HINT

Again, if you are asked to compare potassium with sodium use phrases such as:
'fizzes *more* vigorously'
'moves around *more* quickly'
'disappears *more* quickly'
The key difference though is that with potassium the hydrogen bursts into flames but with sodium it usually does not.

RUBIDIUM AND CAESIUM

These react even more violently than potassium, and the reaction can be explosive. Rubidium hydroxide and caesium hydroxide are formed.

Safety note: The reactions of rubidium and caesium would be too hazardous to attempt in school as they would explode.

REACTIONS OF THE ALKALI METALS WITH THE AIR

Lithium, sodium and potassium are all stored in oil because they react with the air. If we look at a piece of sodium which has been taken out of the oil, it usually has a crust on the outside. It is not shiny unless it has been freshly cut.

Figure 8.6 A piece of sodium. The left-hand edge has been freshly cut, so it is shiny.

When the piece of sodium is cut, the fresh surface is shiny but it tarnishes rapidly as the freshly exposed sodium reacts with oxygen in the air. If we do the same with a piece of lithium it tarnishes more slowly because lithium reacts more slowly than sodium. A freshly cut piece of potassium tarnishes extremely rapidly, more quickly than sodium. In this way we can see again that potassium is more reactive than sodium, which is more reactive than lithium. In each case the metal reacts with oxygen in the air to form an oxide with the formula M_2O.

If we heat each of the metals in the air using a Bunsen burner, we get a much more vigorous reaction and it is more difficult to see which metal is most reactive because all the reactions are so rapid.

Lithium burns with a red flame to form lithium oxide.

Sodium burns with a yellow flame to form sodium oxide.

Potassium burns with a lilac flame to form potassium oxide.

REMINDER

Remember the charge on the oxide ion is O^{2-} and the charge on an alkali metal ion is M^+.

The equation for all these reactions is:

$$4M(s) + O_2(g) \rightarrow 2M_2O(s)$$

In each case the product formed is a white powder – the alkali metal oxide.

EXTENSION WORK

When the alkali metals react with air, other types of oxide can also be formed, called peroxides (M_2O_2) and superoxides (MO_2). These all still contain the M^+ ion, it is the oxygen bit which is different. Lithium can also form a nitride (Li_3N).

COMPOUNDS OF THE ALKALI METALS

All Group 1 metal ions are colourless. That means that their compounds will be colourless or white unless they are combined with a coloured negative ion. Potassium dichromate(VI) is orange, for example, because the dichromate(VI) ion is orange, and potassium manganate(VII) is purple because the manganate(VII) ion is purple. Group 1 compounds are typical ionic solids and are mostly soluble in water.

SUMMARISING THE MAIN FEATURES OF THE GROUP 1 ELEMENTS

Group 1 elements:

- are metals
- are soft with melting points and densities which are very low for metals
- have to be stored out of contact with air or water
- react rapidly with air to form coatings of the metal oxide
- react with water to produce an alkaline solution of the metal hydroxide and hydrogen gas
- increase in reactivity as you go down the group
- form compounds in which the metal has a 1+ ion
- have mainly white/colourless compounds which dissolve to produce colourless solutions.

PREDICTING THE PROPERTIES OF FRANCIUM

As we move down a group in the Periodic Table the properties of the elements change gradually. So, if we know the properties of most of the elements in a group, we should be able to predict the properties of elements we don't know. Francium is extremely radioactive and at any time, anywhere in the world, there is only a tiny amount present; nobody has actually seen a piece of francium. We can, however, predict the properties of francium using the properties of the other alkali metals.

We can predict that francium:

- is very soft
- will have a melting point around room temperature
- has density which is probably just over 2 g/cm^3
- will be a silvery metal, but will tarnish almost instantly in air
- will react violently with water to give francium hydroxide and hydrogen
- will be more reactive than caesium
- will have a hydroxide, francium hydroxide, with the formula FrOH, which will be soluble in water and form a strongly alkaline solution
- will form compounds that are white/colourless and dissolve in water to give colourless solutions.

REMINDER

Remember, you can't actually observe any of these things.

We could use a graphical method to predict the melting point of francium. If we **plot** the melting point of the alkali metals against atomic number then draw a line of best fit we get:

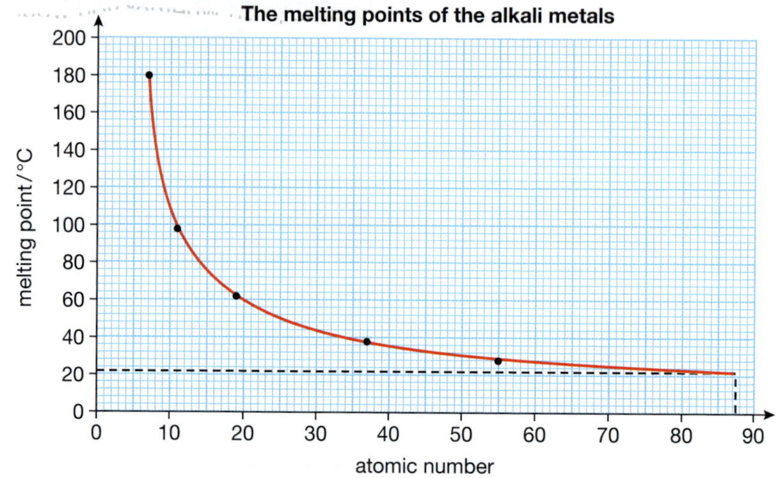

▲ Figure 8.7 This graph allows us to predict the melting point of francium.

If we carry on the line to atomic number 87 we can predict a melting point of about 22 °C.

KEY POINT

Various other predictions give a melting point for francium between 21 °C and 27 °C.

CHAPTER QUESTIONS

SKILLS REASONING

1 Explain why lithium, sodium and potassium are put in the same group in the Periodic Table.

SKILLS CRITICAL THINKING

2 This question concerns the chemistry of the elements Li, Na, K, Rb and Cs. In a and b, you should name the substances represented by letters.

a **A** is the least dense of all the metals.

b When metal **B** is dropped onto water it melts into a small ball and moves rapidly around the surface. A gas, **C**, is given off and this burns with a lilac flame. A solution of **D** is formed.

c Write an equation for the reaction of **B** with water.

SKILLS REASONING

d What would you expect to see if solution **D** was tested with universal indicator paper?

e Explain why **B** melts into a small ball when it is dropped onto water.

SKILLS CRITICAL THINKING

f **E** burns in air with a yellow flame to form compound **F**. Write a word equation and balanced symbol equation for the reaction that occurs.

3 Explain whether each of the following statements is true or false.

a Sodium forms mostly covalent compounds.

b A rubidium atom is larger than a potassium atom.

c All the alkali metals react with air to form oxides.

d Lithium reacts with chlorine to form lithium chloride, which has the formula Li_2Cl.

SKILLS REASONING 8th

4 Imagine that a new alkali metal has recently been discovered and that it fits into the Periodic Table below francium. We will call this new element edexcelium.

a Explain whether you would expect edexcelium to be more or less dense than francium.

SKILLS PROBLEM SOLVING 9th

b State how many electrons edexcelium will have in its outer shell.

SKILLS CRITICAL THINKING 8th

c State the names of the products that will be formed when edexcelium reacts with water.

d Explain whether edexcelium will be more or less reactive than francium.

SKILLS PROBLEM SOLVING 9th

e If the symbol for edexcelium is Ed, write a balanced chemical equation for the reaction of edexcelium with water.

SKILLS CRITICAL THINKING 6th

f When edexcelium reacts with water, will the solution formed be acidic, alkaline or neutral?

SKILLS PROBLEM SOLVING 7th

g Write the formula for the compound formed when edexcelium reacts with air.

9 THE HALOGENS

The elements in Group 7 of the Periodic Table are called the halogens. In this chapter we will look at some of the properties of these elements. When we first look at them, it is hard to see that they form a family of elements because they look so different, but they react in very similar ways.

▶ Figure 9.1 Chlorine, bromine and iodine are three of the halogens.

LEARNING OBJECTIVES

- Know the colours, physical states (at room temperature) and trends in physical properties of the halogens
- Use knowledge of trends in Group 7 to predict the properties of other halogens
- Understand how displacement reactions involving halogens and halides provide evidence for the trend in reactivity in Group 7

F	fluorine
Cl	chlorine
Br	bromine
I	iodine
At	astatine

▲ Figure 9.2 The halogens

▲ Figure 9.3 Iodine is a grey solid but has a purple vapour.

THE HALOGENS

The atoms of fluorine, chlorine, bromine, iodine and astatine all have 7 electrons in their outer shell, therefore these elements are put in Group 7 in the Periodic Table. The number of electrons in the outer shell of an atom determines how something reacts, so all the elements in Group 7 react in a similar way.

The name '**halogen**' means 'salt-producing'. When they react with metals, these elements produce a wide range of salts, including calcium fluoride, sodium chloride, silver bromide and potassium iodide. All the salts contain the X^- ion (where X stands for any halogen atom).

The halogens are non-metallic elements with diatomic molecules: F_2, Cl_2, etc.

Table 9.1 The melting and boiling points of the halogens increase and the colour becomes darker down the group

	Physical state at room temperature	Colour
F_2	gas	yellow
Cl_2	gas	green
Br_2	liquid	red-brown liquid, orange/brown vapour
I_2	solid	grey solid, purple vapour

REMINDER

Remember that intermolecular forces are the forces of attraction between molecules.

The melting and boiling points increase down the group. The halogens are all covalent molecular substances and the melting and boiling points increase as the relative molecular mass increases. As the relative molecular mass increases, the intermolecular forces of attraction become stronger and therefore more energy must be put in to overcome these stronger forces of attraction. Remember, no covalent bonds are broken when these melt/boil.

Because the halogens are non-metals, they are poor conductors of heat and electricity.

Astatine is radioactive and is formed during the radioactive decay of other elements, such as uranium and thorium. Most of its isotopes are so unstable that their lives can be measured in seconds or fractions of a second.

SAFETY

Fluorine is so dangerously reactive that you would never expect to find it in a school lab. Apart from any safety problems, due to the reactivity of the elements (especially fluorine and chlorine), all the halogens have extremely poisonous **vapours** and have to be handled in a **fume** cupboard. Liquid bromine is also very corrosive, and great care has to be taken to keep it off the skin.

REACTIONS OF THE HALOGENS

The halogens react with hydrogen to form **hydrogen halides**: hydrogen fluoride, hydrogen chloride, hydrogen bromide and hydrogen iodide. For example:

$$H_2(g) + Br_2(g) \rightarrow 2HBr(g)$$

The hydrogen halides are all acidic, poisonous gases. In common with all the compounds formed between the halogens and non-metals, the gases are covalently bonded. They are very soluble in water, reacting with it to produce solutions of acids. For example, hydrochloric acid is a solution of hydrogen chloride in water:

$$\underset{\text{hydrogen chloride}}{HCl(g)} \xrightarrow{\text{dissolve in water}} \underset{\text{hydrochloric acid}}{HCl(aq)}$$

KEY POINT

This is something that can be confusing. Hydrogen chloride is a gas and when it dissolves in water it becomes hydrochloric acid. Hydrogen chloride is a gas consisting of HCl molecules and hydrochloric acid is a solution containing H^+ and Cl^- ions. The acids formed by other hydrogen halides are:

HF(aq)	hydrofluoric acid
HBr(aq)	hydrobromic acid
HI(aq)	hydroiodic acid

The halogens react with alkali metals to form salts. For instance, sodium burns in chlorine with its typical yellow flame to produce white, solid sodium chloride:

$$2Na(s) + Cl_2(g) \rightarrow 2NaCl(s)$$

Sodium chloride is an ionic solid. Typically, when the halogens react with metals from Groups 1 and 2, they form ions.

▲ Figure 9.4 Sodium burning in chlorine to produce sodium chloride.

DISPLACEMENT REACTIONS INVOLVING THE HALOGENS

In this section we will look at what happens when we react a solution of a halogen with a solution containing halide ions. These are called **displacement reactions** – you will see why below. We can use these displacement reactions to show that chlorine is more reactive than bromine, which is more reactive than iodine.

KEY POINT

We will concentrate on the three commonly used halogens, but the trend continues for the rest of the group.

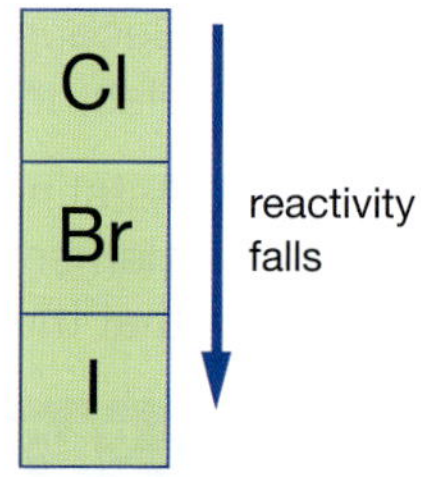

▲ Figure 9.5 Reactivity decreases down the group.

REACTING CHLORINE WITH POTASSIUM BROMIDE OR POTASSIUM IODIDE SOLUTIONS

KEY POINT

Although pure liquid bromine is red-brown, in solution it is orange. If the solution is very dilute it may even look yellow.

HINT

You have to be careful with the words you use here. In the exam you must write 'chlorine displaces bromine' not 'chlorine displaces bromide'.

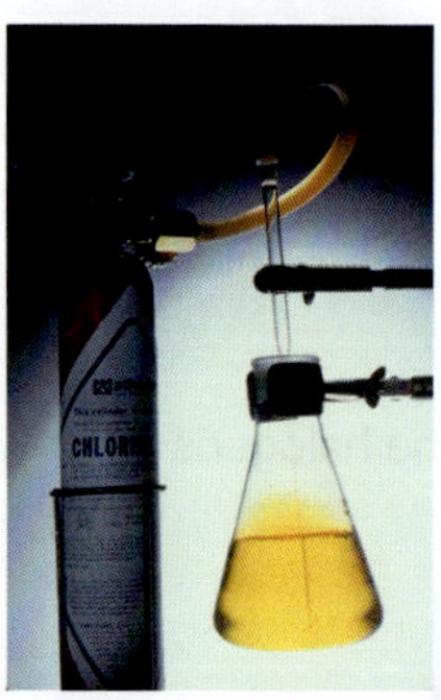

▲ Figure 9.6 Chlorine displaces bromine from potassium bromide solution.

If you add chlorine solution ('chlorine water') to colourless potassium bromide solution, the solution becomes orange as bromine is formed:

$$2KBr(aq) + Cl_2(aq) \rightarrow 2KCl(aq) + Br_2(aq)$$

potassium bromide + chlorine → potassium chloride + bromine

Chlorine is more reactive than bromine and has displaced the bromine from solution. You can think about this in the following way: if something is more reactive, it has a greater tendency to *react* to form a compound. Something that is less reactive is more likely to go back to being the element (the unreacted form).

Similarly, adding chlorine solution to potassium iodide solution gives a brown (orange if it is very dilute) solution of iodine.

$$2KI(aq) + Cl_2(aq) \rightarrow 2KCl(aq) + I_2(aq)$$

In exactly the same way, the more reactive bromine displaces the less reactive iodine from potassium iodide solution. Adding bromine solution ('bromine water') to colourless potassium iodide solution gives a brown solution of iodine:

$$2KI(aq) + Br_2(aq) \rightarrow 2KBr(aq) + I_2(aq)$$

▲ Figure 9.7 Chlorine displaces iodine from potassium iodide solution.

All of the following experiments show no reaction:

- bromine + potassium chloride solution: the less reactive bromine cannot displace the more reactive chlorine
- iodine + potassium chloride solution: the less reactive iodine cannot displace the more reactive chlorine
- iodine + potassium bromide solution: the less reactive iodine cannot displace the more reactive bromine.

IONIC EQUATIONS FOR DISPLACEMENT REACTIONS

REMINDER

Remember when an ionic compound dissolves in water, it splits into its ions.

In all of the above reactions it would not have mattered if we had reacted chlorine with *sodium* bromide or *magnesium* bromide, for example. The reaction occurs between the chlorine molecule and the bromide ion; the metal ion does not do anything, we call it a **spectator ion**. If we write the reaction between chlorine and potassium iodide showing all the charges, we can see this more clearly:

$$2K^+(aq) + 2Br^-(aq) + Cl_2(aq) \rightarrow 2K^+(aq) + 2Cl^-(aq) + Br_2(aq)$$

You can see that the potassium ions are the same on each side. They have not changed and so we can write a new equation simply concentrating on the things that have changed:

$$2Br^-(aq) + Cl_2(aq) \rightarrow 2Cl^-(aq) + Br_2(aq)$$

This is called an *ionic equation* and does not include the spectator ions.

DISPLACEMENT REACTIONS AS REDOX REACTIONS

REMINDER

Some reminders about oxidation and reduction:

oxidation is loss of electrons
reduction is gain of electrons

An oxidising agent is something that oxidises something else by taking electrons away from it. Oxidising agents accept electrons and therefore are the things that are reduced in a reaction.

A reducing agent is something that reduces something else by giving electrons to it. Reducing agents give away electrons and therefore are the things that are oxidised in a reaction.

The reactions above that do show a colour change are often discussed in terms of oxidation and reduction, they are *redox reactions*. If you have not already covered redox reactions, you should look at Chapter 11 before reading the next section.

If we look at the reaction between chlorine and either bromide ions or iodide ions, we can see why they are described as redox reactions.

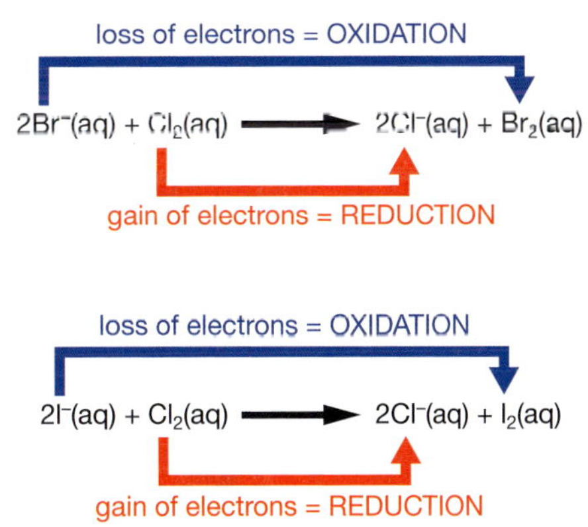

▲ Figure 9.8 The reaction of chlorine with potassium bromide (top) or potassium iodide (below).

In each case, the chlorine is acting as an oxidising agent. In the first equation it oxidises the Br^- ions by taking electrons away from them. Because the oxidising agent takes electrons away from something else, it is reduced itself: the Cl_2 is reduced to $2Cl^-$ ions.

In the reaction between bromine and iodide ions, the bromine is the oxidising agent:

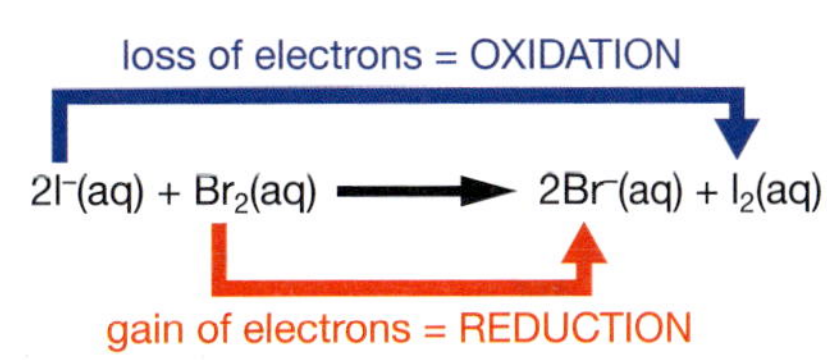

▲ Figure 9.9 The reaction between bromine solution and potassium iodide solution.

EXTENSION WORK

This only works for non-metals. For metals, the most reactive one is the best reducing agent. The difference comes because non-metals react to form negative ions but metals react to form positive ions.

EXTENSION WORK

We can now say a bit more than just 'chlorine is more reactive than bromine, which is more reactive than iodine'. We can describe the reactivity in terms of how good an oxidising agent something is: chlorine is a stronger oxidising agent than bromine, which is a stronger oxidising agent than iodine. Chlorine can oxidise (take electrons away from) bromide ions and iodide ions; bromine can oxidise (take electrons away from) iodide ions, but not chloride ions; iodine cannot oxidise bromide ions or chloride ions.

SUMMARISING THE MAIN FEATURES OF THE GROUP 7 ELEMENTS

Group 7 elements:

- have diatomic molecules, X_2 (e.g. F_2, Cl_2, Br_2)
- go from gases to liquid to solid as you move down the group: the melting points and boiling points increase down the group
- have coloured poisonous vapours: the colours of the elements get darker down the group
- form compounds with the formula HX (e.g. HF, HCl, HBr) when reacted with hydrogen and these dissolve in water to form acids
- form ionic salts with metals and covalent compounds with non-metals
- form X^- (e.g. F^-, Cl^-, Br^-) ions in ionic compounds
- become less reactive towards the bottom of the group
- will displace elements lower down the group from their salts.

We can use these properties and trends to predict the properties of astatine, the element below iodine in Group 7. Astatine is an extremely rare radioactive element and no one has ever seen a sample of it, but we can predict that it:

- will be a darker colour than iodine, very dark grey or black
- will be a solid at room temperature and have a higher melting point than iodine
- will be diatomic and contain At_2 molecules
- will react with hydrogen to form HAt, which will dissolve in water to form an acid
- will form the salt NaAt with sodium or KAt with potassium
- will contain the astatide ion (At^-) in its ionic salts
- will be less reactive than iodine
- will be displaced from solution by iodine

CHAPTER QUESTIONS

SKILLS INTERPRETATION 8th

1 a Draw a diagram to show the arrangement of electrons in a fluorine atom.

SKILLS REASONING 7th

b Explain why fluorine is placed in Group 7 in the Periodic Table.

SKILLS INTERPRETATION 8th

c Draw a dot-and-cross diagram (showing outer electrons only) of the molecule formed when fluorine reacts with hydrogen.

SKILLS REASONING 7th

d Explain why fluorine has a lower melting point than chlorine.

e Explain what you would observe when a chlorine solution is added to a solution of potassium fluoride.

SKILLS INTERPRETATION 8th

2 This question is about astatine, At, at the bottom of Group 7 of the Periodic Table. You are asked to make some predictions about astatine and its chemistry.

a Showing only the outer electrons, draw diagrams to show the arrangement of electrons in an astatine *atom*, an astatide *ion* and an astatine *molecule*.

SKILLS REASONING 7th

b Explain what physical state you would expect astatine to be in at room temperature.

c Explain whether you would expect astatine to be more or less reactive than iodine.

6th

d Suggest a likely pH for a reasonably concentrated solution of hydrogen astatide in water.

8th

e Explain what you would expect caesium astatide to look like. Will it be soluble in water? Explain your reasoning.

SKILLS PROBLEM SOLVING, REASONING 10th

f Write an ionic equation for the reaction that will occur if you add chlorine water to a solution of sodium astatide. Assume that astatine is insoluble in water. Explain clearly why this reaction would be counted as a redox reaction.

SKILLS PROBLEM SOLVING 9th

3 Chlorine reacts with fluorine to form chlorine monofluoride (ClF).

a Write an equation for this reaction, including state symbols. All the substances are gases at room temperature.

SKILLS INTERPRETATION 8th

b Draw a dot-and-cross diagram for ClF.

SKILLS REASONING

c Arrange the substances Cl_2, F_2 and ClF in order of increasing boiling point and explain your order.

SKILLS PROBLEM SOLVING

d Chlorine and fluorine can also react together to form chlorine trifluoride, which is a gas at room temperature and pressure.

i State the formula of chlorine trifluoride.

9th

ii Chlorine trifluoride is an extremely reactive substance and, for instance, reacts explosively with water. The products of the reaction are hydrofluoric acid, hydrochloric acid and oxygen gas. Write an equation, including state symbols, for the reaction of chlorine trifluoride with water.

10 GASES IN THE ATMOSPHERE

This chapter looks at the most common gases in the atmosphere, concentrating on oxygen. We will also look at carbon dioxide, which is a greenhouse gas and may contribute to climate change.

▶ Figure 10.1 Despite the gases added by industry, the air around us is mostly nitrogen and oxygen.

LEARNING OBJECTIVES

- Know the approximate percentages by volume of the four most abundant gases in dry air
- Understand how to determine the percentage by volume of oxygen in air using experiments involving the reactions of metals (e.g. iron) and non-metals (e.g. phosphorus) with air
- Describe the combustion of elements in oxygen, including magnesium, hydrogen and sulfur
- Describe the formation of carbon dioxide from the thermal decomposition of metal carbonates, including copper(II) carbonate
- Know that carbon dioxide is a greenhouse gas and that increasing amounts in the atmosphere may contribute to climate change
- Practical: Determine the approximate percentage by volume of oxygen in air using a metal or a non-metal

THE COMPOSITION OF THE AIR

The approximate percentages (by volume) of the four most abundant gases present in *unpolluted, dry* air are shown in Table 10.1.

Table 10.1 Approximate percentages (by volume) of the main gases in unpolluted, dry air

Gas	Amount in air (%)	Amount in air (fraction)
nitrogen	78.1	about 4/5
oxygen	21.0	about 1/5
argon	0.9	
carbon dioxide	0.04	

KEY POINT

It is important to realise that these figures apply only to dry, unpolluted air. Air can have anywhere between 0 and 4% water vapour. The percentage of carbon dioxide in the air, although very small, is rising steadily because of human activity.

There are also very small amounts of the other noble gases in the air.

SHOWING THAT AIR CONTAINS ABOUT ONE-FIFTH OXYGEN

We will look at a few different methods for measuring the percentage of oxygen in the air. All the methods rely on the same basic principle: we react something with the oxygen in the air and look at how much the volume decreases as the oxygen is removed.

Safety note: Wear eye protection and heat carefully to avoid cracking the glass syringe with the flame. Take care not to push the opposite plunger completely out!.

ACTIVITY 1

▼ PRACTICAL: USING COPPER

The apparatus shown in Figure 10.2 can be used to find the percentage of oxygen in the air.

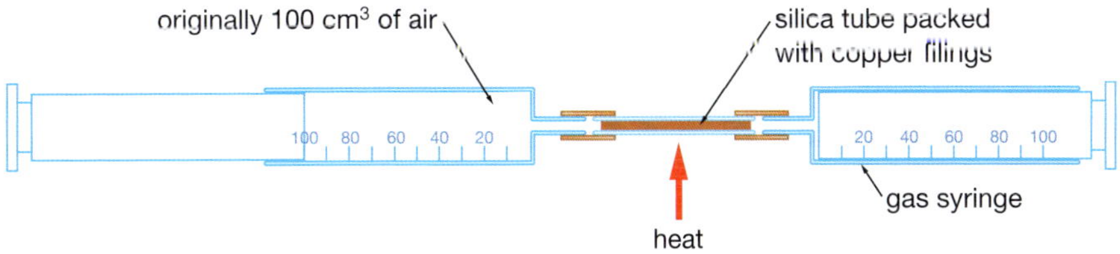

▲ Figure 10.2 Using copper to measure the percentage of oxygen in air.

- The **plunger** on one of the gas syringes is pushed all the way in and the other moved out to 100 cm^3. We now know that the apparatus contains 100 cm^3 air.
- The silica tube is heated strongly (roaring Bunsen flame).
- The plunger in the left-hand gas syringe is pushed in. This causes the air to pass over the heated copper. This pushes out the plunger on the right-hand gas syringe.
- The plungers are pushed in sequence so that the air in the system keeps passing over the heated copper. The pink-brown copper turns black as copper(II) oxide is formed.
- As the copper reacts, the Bunsen burner is moved along the tube so that it is always heating fresh copper.
- The volume of gas in the syringes falls as the oxygen is consumed.
- We keep pushing the plungers in and out until there is no change in volume.
- The apparatus is then allowed to cool to room temperature again before taking the final volume of gas (because gases expand as they are heated).

RESULTS

initial volume of air In the system / cm^3	100
final volume of 'air' in the system / cm^3	79

The volume of the air has decreased because the oxygen has been removed as it reacts with the copper. The reaction that occurs is

$$2Cu(s) + O_2(g) \rightarrow 2CuO(s)$$

copper + oxygen → copper(II) oxide

We can work out from these data that the volume of oxygen that reacted was 100 − 79 = 21 cm^3.

The original volume of air was 100 cm^3 so we can work out the percentage of oxygen in the air:

percentage oxygen = 21/100 × 100 = 21%

KEY POINT

When doing this experiment we need to make sure that we use enough copper to react with *all* the oxygen in the air - the copper must be in excess. There will be some unreacted copper metal at the end. If we do not use enough copper then the value we will get for the percentage of oxygen will be too low because not all of the oxygen will have been removed.

KEY POINT

We have put inverted commas around 'air' because we are now talking about air from which the oxygen has been removed, so it is mostly nitrogen. Nitrogen is very unreactive and so if you put a lighted splint into this 'air' it would be extinguished. Oxygen is needed for things to burn.

KEY POINT

Iron needs oxygen and water to rust. The rusting of iron is discussed in Chapter 11.

Safety note: Iron filings can irritate the skin and are a particular hazard if they get in the eyes.

ACTIVITY 2

▼ PRACTICAL: USING THE RUSTING OF IRON

Iron rusts in **damp** air, using up oxygen as it does so. We can use this reaction to determine how much oxygen there is in the air.

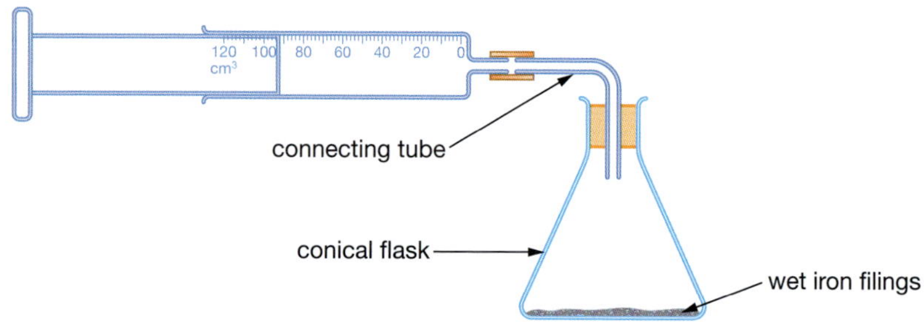

▲ Figure 10.3 This apparatus can be used to find the percentage of oxygen in the air.

We will use the apparatus from Figure 10.3, but before we start we need to know the volume of air present in the apparatus. We can find this by filling up the conical flask and connecting tube with water and then transferring the water to a measuring cylinder. On the conical flask we mark the position of the bung and only fill with water to that point. We will assume that the small volume occupied by the **iron filings** is negligible (very small compared to the overall volume).

The procedure for the experiment is as follows:

- Set up the apparatus as shown in Figure 10.3.
- Put wet iron filings into the conical flask.
- Record the initial reading on the gas syringe.
- Leave the apparatus in place for about a week, until the reading on the gas syringe stops changing.
- Record the final reading on the gas syringe.

volume of air in conical flask / cm^3	130
volume of air in connecting tube / cm^3	12
initial reading on gas syringe / cm^3	92
final reading on gas syringe / cm^3	43

So, the total volume of air inside the apparatus at the beginning of the experiment is $130 + 12 + 92 = 234\,cm^3$.

The total volume of 'air' in the apparatus at the end $= 130 + 12 + 43$
$= 185\,cm^3$

Volume of oxygen used up $= 234 - 185 = 49\,cm^3$

The percentage of oxygen in the air is $49/234 \times 100 = 21\%$.

Sometimes when you do this experiment, the answer comes out as less than 21%. Possible reasons for this could be:

- The experiment was not left set up for long enough. The iron has not had enough chance to react with all the oxygen in the apparatus.
- Not enough iron was added at the beginning. The iron must be in excess, that is, there must be enough iron to react with all the oxygen present.

KEY POINT

Phosphorus does not react with water.

Safety note: The teacher demonstrating needs to wear goggles or a face shield, and have the room well ventilated. After igniting the phosphorous the bell-jar needs to be held down as pressure rises initially. After all the fumes have gone the evaporating basin needs to be sunk using a glass rod to prevent any unreacted phosphorous re-igniting.

ACTIVITY 3

▼ PRACTICAL: USING PHOSPHORUS

Phosphorus is a very reactive element that reacts with the oxygen in the air to form a phosphorus oxide. This oxide is very soluble in water.

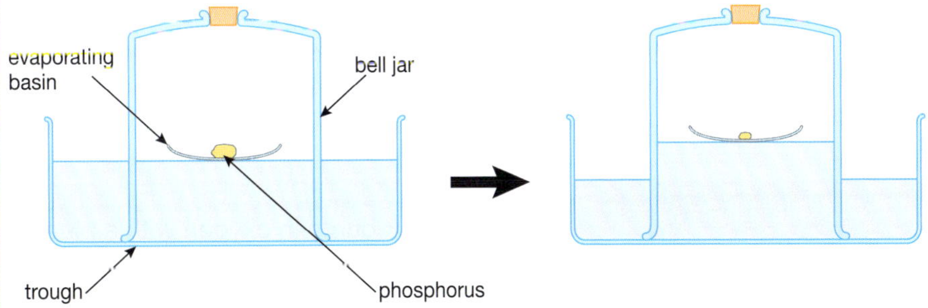

▲ Figure 10.4 Finding the percentage of oxygen in air using phosphorus.

- The apparatus shown in Figure 10.4 is set up with the piece of phosphorus on an evaporating basin, which is floating in the water.
- The initial level of water is marked on the side of the bell jar with a waterproof pen or a sticker.
- The bung is removed from the bell jar and the phosphorus is touched with a hot metal wire in order to ignite it.
- The bung is quickly put back into the bell jar.
- The phosphorus burns, the bell jar becomes filled with a white smoke (phosphorus oxide) and the level of water rises inside the bell jar. The smoke eventually clears as the phosphorus oxide dissolves in the water.
- When the level of water inside the bell jar stops rising, the final level is marked.
- To find how much the water level has changed, the bell jar is turned upside down, filled with water to each mark in turn and the water is poured into a large measuring cylinder.

It is important that there is still some phosphorus left on the evaporating basin at the end of the experiment. We have used an excess of phosphorus so that there is more than enough to react with all the oxygen. If there was no phosphorus left, then we would probably get a lower value for the percentage of oxygen in the air because not all the oxygen might have been used up.

THE COMBUSTION OF ELEMENTS IN OXYGEN

Some elements burn in oxygen, these reactions are called *combustion reactions*. Elements burn more brightly and rapidly in pure oxygen than in air because air only contains 21% oxygen.

BURNING MAGNESIUM

Magnesium burns in oxygen with an extremely bright white flame to give a white, powdery **ash** of magnesium oxide:

$$2Mg(s) + O_2(g) \rightarrow 2MgO(s)$$

The white powder formed is not very soluble in water but a very small amount does dissolve to form an alkaline solution:

$$MgO(s) + H_2O(l) \rightarrow Mg(OH)_2(aq)$$

▲ Figure 10.5 Magnesium ribbon burning in air

BURNING SULFUR

KEY POINT

Sulfur dioxide is also called sulfur(IV) oxide.

Sulfur burns in oxygen with a blue flame. Poisonous, colourless sulfur dioxide gas is produced.

$$S(s) + O_2(g) \rightarrow SO_2(g)$$

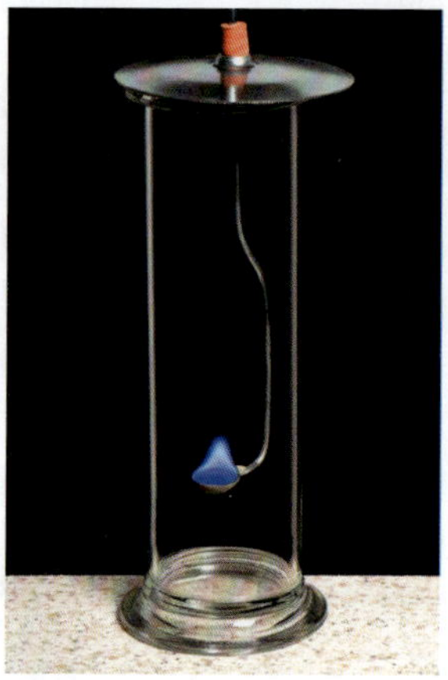

▲ Figure 10.6 Sulfur burning in oxygen

KEY POINT

Sulfurous acid (H_2SO_3), not sulfuric acid (H_2SO_4), is formed.

The sulfur dioxide dissolves in water to form an acidic solution of *sulfurous acid*:

$$SO_2(g) + H_2O(l) \rightarrow H_2SO_3(aq)$$

BURNING HYDROGEN

Hydrogen burns in oxygen with a pale blue flame. The product is water:

$$2H_2(g) + O_2(g) \rightarrow 2H_2O(l)$$

If you ignite a mixture of hydrogen and oxygen it will explode. This is the basis of the 'squeaky **pop**' test for hydrogen (see Chapter 14).

THE PROPERTIES OF OXIDES

We can make some generalisations about the properties of oxides formed when elements burn in oxygen.

METAL OXIDES

- Metal oxides are ionic compounds containing O^{2-} ions.
- Metal oxides are usually basic oxides, which means that they react with acids to form salts.
- Metal oxides are usually insoluble in water. Those metal oxides that are soluble in water react with it to form alkaline solutions containing hydroxide (OH^-) ions.

NON-METAL OXIDES

- Non-metal oxides are covalent compounds.
- Non-metal oxides are usually acidic oxides, which react with alkalis/bases to form salts.
- Non-metal oxides are often soluble in water and react with it to form acidic solutions containing hydrogen (H^+) ions.

CARBON DIOXIDE

▲ Figure 10.7 Copper(II) carbonate decomposes to form carbon dioxide when heated.

HINT

You should remember the colours of copper(II) carbonate and copper(II) oxide.

Carbon dioxide is a colourless gas that is most easily made in the laboratory by the reaction between dilute hydrochloric acid and calcium carbonate in the form of marble chips:

$$CaCO_3(s) + 2HCl(aq) \rightarrow CaCl_2(aq) + CO_2(g) + H_2O(l)$$

Carbon dioxide can also be obtained when metal carbonates are heated strongly.

Most carbonates split to give the metal oxide and carbon dioxide when you heat them. This is an example of **thermal decomposition**, breaking up something by heating it.

For example, copper(II) carbonate is a *green* powder which decomposes on heating to produce *black* copper(II) oxide:

$$CuCO_3(s) \rightarrow CuO(s) + CO_2(g)$$

Calcium carbonate doesn't decompose unless it is heated at quite high temperatures. This is a commercially important reaction because it is used to convert limestone (calcium carbonate) into **quicklime** (calcium oxide):

$$CaCO_3(s) \rightarrow CaO(s) + CO_2(g)$$

CARBON DIOXIDE AND GLOBAL WARMING: THE GREENHOUSE EFFECT

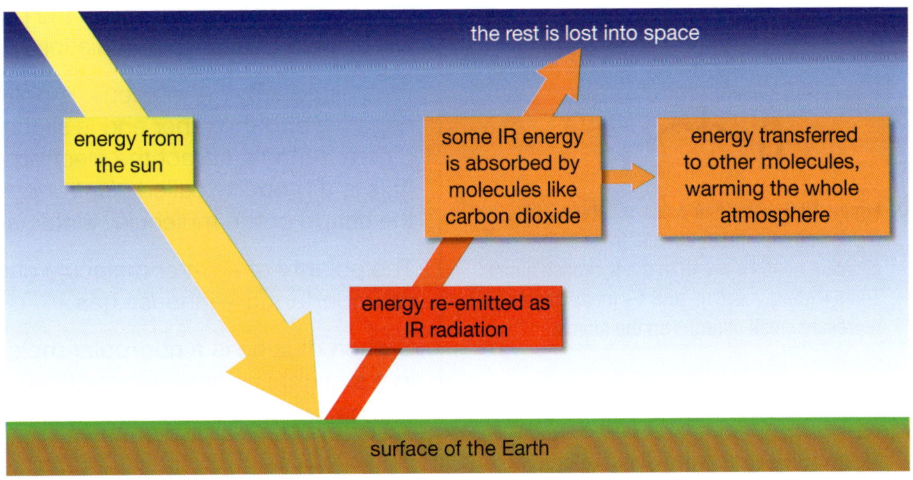

▲ Figure 10.8 The greenhouse effect

REMINDER

A hydrocarbon is a molecule containing carbon and hydrogen only. These are discussed more fully in Unit 4.

Carbon dioxide is produced when fossil fuels (coal, oil and gas) burn. For instance, when coal, which is mostly carbon, burns in excess oxygen:

$$C(s) + O_2(g) \rightarrow CO_2(g)$$

Petrol is a mixture containing many different hydrocarbons. An example of a reaction that occurs when petrol burns is:

$$2C_8H_{18}(l) + 25O_2(g) \rightarrow 16CO_2(g) + 18H_2O(l)$$

DID YOU KNOW?

Although most scientists believe that increases in carbon dioxide will cause devastating climate change, there are others who reject this. They claim that the increases in average world temperatures during the 20th century were part of natural heating and cooling cycles caused by the sun and changes to ocean currents. They believe the effect of carbon dioxide is small compared with these.

Carbon dioxide is a **greenhouse gas**. The greenhouse effect occurs when high-energy **UV** and visible light from the sun pass through the atmosphere and warm up the surface of the Earth. The surface of the Earth (like any other warm surface) radiates infrared (IR) radiation. This IR radiation is absorbed by molecules such as CO_2 in the atmosphere. These then give out this energy again in all directions, heating the atmosphere.

For approximately the last 200 years the level of CO_2 in the atmosphere has been increasing. This has occurred since the industrial revolution and is due to the burning of fossil fuels and deforestation (cutting down trees to create more land for agriculture). Many people believe that the increase in the level of carbon dioxide in the atmosphere may contribute to climate change. The exact nature of this climate change is difficult to know, but some of the things that scientists believe could happen are:

- polar ice caps could melt
- sea levels could rise
- there could be more extreme weather (such as floods, droughts and heat waves).

LOOKING AHEAD

Why is CO_2 a greenhouse gas and oxygen and nitrogen are not?

The presence of greenhouse gases in the atmosphere is essential to the maintenance of life on Earth as they keep the planet at a temperature at which water is mostly a liquid. However, it is very important that we do not have too much of these greenhouse gases. If nitrogen and oxygen, the main constituents of the atmosphere, were greenhouse gases the temperature of the Earth would be too high to support life as we know it. So, what makes something a greenhouse gas? A greenhouse gas must be able to **absorb** IR radiation emitted by the surface of the Earth and then emit it again in all directions, warming the atmosphere. All molecules vibrate and if these vibrations involve a change in the polarity of the molecule then the molecule will be able to absorb IR radiation and be a greenhouse gas.

What is polarity? A molecule is polar if one end of the molecule is slightly negative and the other end is slightly positive. Polarity arises because different atoms attract the electrons in a covalent bond to different extents (this is a property called *electronegativity*). The polarity also depends on the shape of the molecule. Water is a good example of a polar molecule.

The polarity of a water molecule changes as it vibrates and water vapour is an important greenhouse gas.

Carbon dioxide is a non-polar molecule because it is linear (the atoms are in a straight line) and symmetrical, and therefore there is no positive end and no negative end of the molecule.

However, as a CO_2 molecule vibrates it becomes non-symmetrical and polar. Because the polarity changes as a CO_2 molecule vibrates it can absorb IR radiation and is a greenhouse gas.

O_2 and N_2 are non-polar because both the atoms are the same and therefore attract the electrons in the covalent bonds equally, so there are no small charges. The molecules can only vibrate in one way and the molecules remain non-polar as they vibrate. This means that there is no change in polarity as they vibrate, therefore N_2 and O_2 cannot absorb IR radiation and are not greenhouse gases.

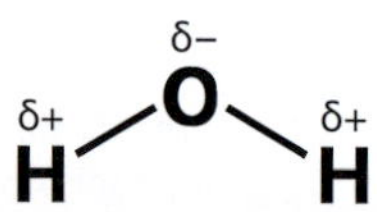

▲ Figure 10.9 Water is a polar molecule. The oxygen atoms attract the electrons in the covalent bonds more than the hydrogen atoms. The δ+ (delta positive) and δ– (delta negative) represent small charges on the atoms.

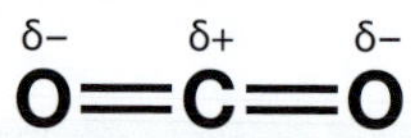

▲ Figure 10.10 The oxygen atoms attract the electrons in the covalent bonds more than the carbon atoms do (oxygen is more electronegative than carbon) but the charges cancel due to the shape (a better way of saying this is that the dipoles cancel).

CHAPTER QUESTIONS

SKILLS CRITICAL THINKING 5th

1 State the approximate percentage of each of the following gases in dry air:

a nitrogen b oxygen c carbon dioxide d argon

SKILLS PROBLEM SOLVING 7th

2 A student carried out an experiment to measure the percentage oxygen in the air by using the rusting of iron. The experimental set-up is shown below. The initial reading on the measuring cylinder was 95 cm^3. They left the apparatus for 2 days and the new reading on the measuring cylinder was 80 cm^3.

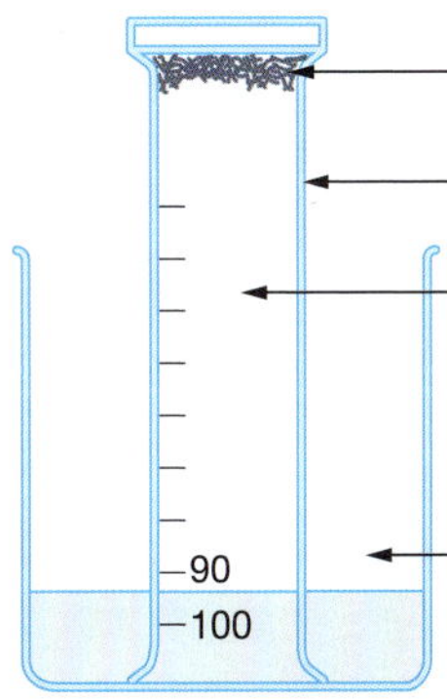

SKILLS REASONING, DECISION MAKING

a Calculate the percentage oxygen in the air using this data.

b Explain why the answer is not the same as you had expected and how the experiment could be improved.

SKILLS DECISION MAKING 6th

3 A student carries out an experiment to investigate how much gas is produced when various metal carbonates are heated. Their data are shown in the table.

Metal carbonate	Mass of carbonate used / g	Volume of gas collected at rtp / cm^3	Mass of solid left at the end / g
lead(II) carbonate	1.00	89	0.84
copper(II) carbonate	1.00	194	0.64
sodium carbonate	1.00	0	1.00

a Describe an experiment that would allow the student to collect these data.

SKILLS CRITICAL THINKING 5th

b Name the gas collected.

SKILLS PROBLEM SOLVING 9th

c Write an equation for the reaction occurring with lead(II) carbonate.

SKILLS CRITICAL THINKING 5th

d Name the type of reaction occurring with lead(II) carbonate and copper(II) carbonate.

SKILLS REASONING 6th

e Explain what these results indicate about the thermal **stability** of sodium carbonate compared to the other two substances.

7th

f Explain why much more gas is given off in the copper(II) carbonate experiment than in the lead(II) carbonate experiment.

SKILLS PROBLEM SOLVING

g Use the data from the lead(II) carbonate experiment to calculate the mass of 100 cm^3 of the gas.

SKILLS EXECUTIVE FUNCTION

h The student repeated the experiment for copper(II) carbonate and only obtained 152 cm^3 of gas this time. Explain two things that could have gone wrong with the second experiment to give this result.

SKILLS CRITICAL THINKING 6th

4 Carbon dioxide is described as a *greenhouse gas*. Explain what this means.

11 REACTIVITY SERIES

The reactivity series lists elements (mainly metals) in order of decreasing reactivity. It is likely that you will have come across some of this chemistry already in earlier years. This chapter looks at some of the reactions of metals and introduces the idea of redox reactions.

▲ Figure 11.1 Rails are welded together using molten iron, produced by a reaction between aluminium and iron(III) oxide.

▲ Figure 11.2 Gold is so unreactive that it will remain chemically unchanged in contact with air or water basically forever.

LEARNING OBJECTIVES

- Understand how metals can be arranged in a reactivity series based on their reactions with:
  - water
  - dilute hydrochloric or sulfuric acid
- Understand how metals can be arranged in a reactivity series based on their displacement reactions between:
  - metals and metal oxides
  - metals and aqueous solutions of metal salts
- Know the order of reactivity of these metals: potassium, sodium, lithium, calcium, magnesium, aluminium, zinc, iron, copper, silver, gold
- Know the conditions under which iron rusts
- Understand how the rusting of iron may be prevented by:
  - barrier methods
  - galvanising
  - sacrificial protection
- Understand the terms:
  - oxidation
  - reduction
  - redox
  - oxidising agent
  - reducing agent

  in terms of gain or loss of oxygen and loss or gain of electrons
- Practical: Investigate reactions between dilute hydrochloric and sulfuric acids and metals (e.g. magnesium, zinc and iron)

DISPLACEMENT REACTIONS INVOLVING METAL OXIDES

THE REACTION BETWEEN MAGNESIUM AND COPPER(II) OXIDE

potassium
sodium
lithium
calcium
magnesium
aluminium
(carbon)
zinc
iron
(hydrogen)
copper
silver
gold

↓ decreasing reactivity

▲ Figure 11.4 The reactivity series. Although carbon and hydrogen are not metals they are usually included in the series. You will learn why in this chapter.

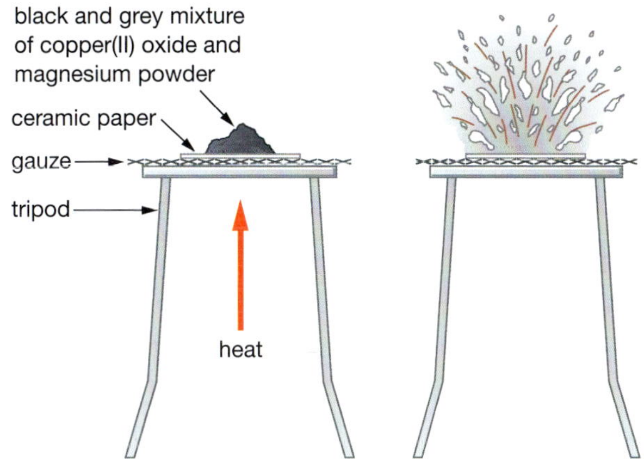

▲ Figure 11.3 Magnesium reacts with copper(II) oxide.

Safety note: For this demonstration goggles or a face shield are needed, together with safety screens in a well-ventilated room. The bench should be protected by a large sheet of hardboard. The pupils should be at the back of the room. One gram of the mixture is strongly heated in a metal crown bottle cap before retiring to the back of the room to await a violent reaction. If nothing happens after a minute or so turn off the gas and do not touch the mixture but leave it to cool and dispose of it in water.

Magnesium powder and copper(II) oxide are mixed together and heated very strongly. At the end, **traces** of white magnesium oxide are left on the ceramic paper.

magnesium + copper(II) oxide → magnesium oxide + copper

$$Mg(s) + CuO(s) \rightarrow MgO(s) + Cu(s)$$

This is an example of a displacement reaction. The less reactive metal, copper, has been displaced from its compound by the more reactive magnesium. Any metal higher in the **reactivity series** will displace one lower down from a compound.

If you heated copper with magnesium oxide, nothing would happen because copper is less reactive than magnesium. Copper isn't capable of displacing magnesium from magnesium oxide.

KEY POINT

These reactions involving metals and metal oxides are often called **competition reactions**.

THE REACTION BETWEEN MAGNESIUM AND ZINC OXIDE

Heating magnesium with zinc oxide produces zinc metal:

magnesium + zinc oxide → magnesium oxide + zinc

$$Mg(s) + ZnO(s) \rightarrow MgO(s) + Zn(s)$$

THE REACTION BETWEEN CARBON AND COPPER(II) OXIDE

Safety note: Wear eye protection. The tube will get very hot and remain so for some time.

A black mixture of carbon and copper(II) oxide is heated in a test-tube. The mixture **glows** red hot because of the heat given out during the reaction, and you are left with pink-brown copper in the tube.

$$C(s) + 2CuO(s) \rightarrow CO_2(g) + 2Cu(s)$$

Carbon is above copper in the reactivity series and displaces the copper from copper(II) oxide.

OXIDATION AND REDUCTION

OXYGEN TRANSFER

DID YOU KNOW?

Many metals are found as metal oxides in nature. If they are found as other compounds these are often converted to metal oxides before the metal is extracted.

A substance has been oxidised if it gains oxygen. **Oxidation** is gain of oxygen.

A substance has been reduced if it loses oxygen. **Reduction** is loss of oxygen.

Consider the reaction between magnesium and copper(II) oxide again. Figure 11.5 shows what happens in terms of oxidation and reduction.

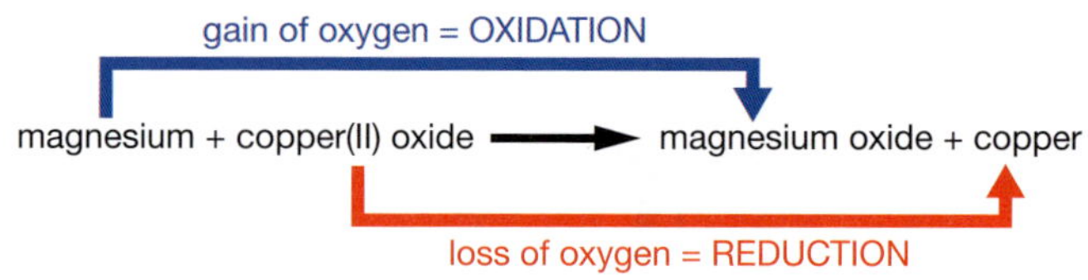

▲ Figure 11.5 Magnesium reacting with copper(II) oxide

A **redox** reaction is one in which both **red**uction and **ox**idation are occurring. Oxidation and reduction always occur together because if something loses oxygen, something else must gain it.

- A **reducing agent** is a substance that reduces something else. In this case, the magnesium is the reducing agent because it takes the oxygen away from the copper oxide, reducing it.
- An **oxidising agent** is a substance that oxidises something else. The copper(II) oxide is the oxidising agent in this reaction because it gives oxygen to the magnesium, oxidising it.

An oxidising agent always gets reduced in a chemical reaction because it oxidises something else by giving away its oxygen.

A reducing agent always gets oxidised in a chemical reaction because it takes the oxygen away from something else and therefore gains oxygen itself.

In the reaction between magnesium and zinc oxide on page 367, the magnesium is the reducing agent and the zinc oxide is the oxidising agent. In the reaction between copper(II) oxide and carbon, the carbon is the reducing agent and the copper(II) oxide is the oxidising agent.

ELECTRON TRANSFER

We are now going to look very closely at what happens in the reaction between magnesium and copper(II) oxide in terms of the various particles involved. Here is the equation again:

$$Mg(s) + CuO(s) \rightarrow MgO(s) + Cu(s)$$

The magnesium and the copper are metals, and are made of metal atoms, but the copper(II) oxide and the magnesium oxide are both ionic compounds.

The copper(II) oxide contains Cu^{2+} and O^{2-} ions, and the magnesium oxide contains Mg^{2+} and O^{2-} ions. Writing these into the equation gives:

$$Mg(s) + Cu^{2+}O^{2-}(s) \rightarrow Mg^{2+}O^{2-}(s) + Cu(s)$$

The oxide ion (O^{2-}) does not change in this reaction. It ends up with a different partner, but is totally unchanged itself.

What is happening in this reaction is that magnesium *atoms* are turning into magnesium *ions*. The magnesium atoms lose electrons to form magnesium ions. These electrons are gained by the copper ions to form copper atoms. We have described this as a redox reaction above in terms of loss/gain of oxygen, but now we can see that it was not the oxygen that was actually the important part, it has not changed! To understand what is happening better, we need a more fundamental definition of oxidation and reduction:

- *oxidation is loss of electrons*
- *reduction is gain of electrons.*

The mnemonic OILRIG can be helpful in remembering this:

Oxidation

Is

Loss of electrons

Reduction

Is

Gain of electrons

DISPLACEMENT REACTIONS INVOLVING SOLUTIONS OF SALTS

Salts are compounds such as copper(II) sulfate, silver nitrate or sodium chloride. You will find a definition of what a salt is on page 386. This section explores some reactions between metals and solutions of salts in water.

THE REACTION BETWEEN ZINC AND COPPER(II) SULFATE SOLUTION

The copper is displaced by the more reactive zinc. The blue colour of the copper(II) sulfate solution **fades** as colourless zinc sulfate solution is formed:

$$Zn(s) + CuSO_4(aq) \rightarrow ZnSO_4(aq) + Cu(s)$$

The zinc and the copper are metals consisting simply of atoms, but the copper(II) sulfate and the zinc sulfate are metal compounds and so are ionic.

The equation can be rewritten showing the ions:

$$Zn(s) + Cu^{2+}(aq) + SO_4^{2-}(aq) \rightarrow Zn^{2+}(aq) + SO_4^{2-}(aq) + Cu(s)$$

We can see that the sulfate ions are exactly the same on both sides of the equation – they have not changed at all in the reaction. We call the sulfate ions here *spectator ions*. Removing the spectator ions (because they aren't changed during the reaction) leaves:

$$Zn(s) + Cu^{2+}(aq) \rightarrow Zn^{2+}(aq) + Cu(s)$$

This is called an ionic equation and just shows the things that change in the reaction.

This is another redox reaction.

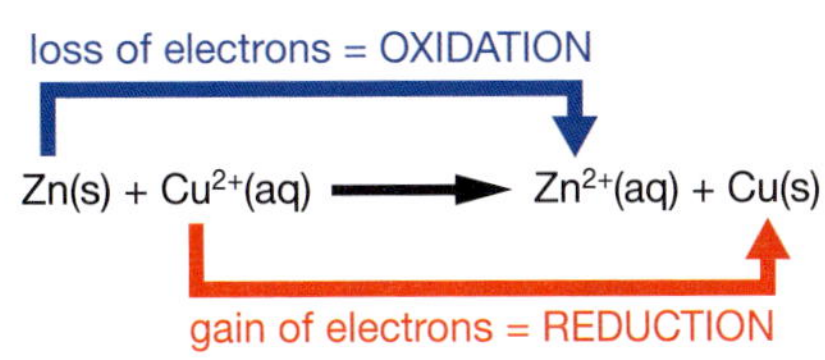

▲ Figure 11.6 The reaction between zinc and copper(II) sulfate solution

The Zn atoms are oxidised to Zn^{2+} ions because they lose electrons. The Cu^{2+} ions gain electrons and are reduced to Cu atoms. We can split up the ionic equation to show the individual oxidation and reduction processes:

$$Zn(s) \rightarrow Zn^{2+}(aq) + 2e^- \quad \text{oxidation}$$

$$Cu^{2+}(aq) + 2e^- \rightarrow Cu(s) \quad \text{reduction}$$

These are called *ionic* ***half-equations*** as they each only show one of the processes (either oxidation or reduction) occurring in the reaction. In reality, these processes cannot occur one without the other: if something gains electrons, it has to get them from somewhere, so something else must lose electrons.

KEY POINT

When we looked at the reaction between Mg and CuO above, we also wrote ions in the equation but we did not separate them completely because the ions are in a solid. We only separate everything like this when things are in solution. In a solution the ions are free to move around separately, in a solid they are not.

KEY POINT

Which copper(II) salt you started with would not matter, as long as it was soluble in water. Copper(II) chloride or copper(II) nitrate would react in exactly the same way with zinc because the chloride ions or the nitrate ions would again be spectator ions, not participating in the reaction.

OXIDISING AND REDUCING AGENTS IN TERMS OF ELECTRONS

A couple more definitions (this time in terms of electrons):

- *An oxidising agent is something that oxidises something else by taking electrons away from it. Oxidising agents accept electrons and therefore are reduced in a reaction.*
- *A reducing agent is something that reduces something else by giving electrons to it. Reducing agents give away electrons and therefore are oxidised in a reaction.*

Let us look again at the overall ionic equation for the displacement reaction between zinc and copper ions:

$$Zn(s) + Cu^{2+}(aq) \rightarrow Zn^{2+}(aq) + Cu(s)$$

The Zn reduces the Cu^{2+} by giving electrons to it and therefore the Zn is the reducing agent. In the process of the reaction the Zn is oxidised because it has given electrons away (lost them).

The Cu^{2+} oxidises the Zn by taking electrons away from it, therefore the Cu^{2+} is the oxidising agent. In the process the Cu^{2+} is reduced because it has taken electrons (gained them).

HINT

You now have two definitions of oxidation (and its reverse, reduction). Which one should you use? Use whichever is simpler in the case you are asked about! Both definitions are true. Don't worry too much about this at the moment. With a little experience, you will find it is obvious which one you need to use in various cases.

▲ Figure 11.7 Displacing silver from silver nitrate solution

THE REACTION BETWEEN COPPER AND SILVER NITRATE SOLUTION

Silver is below copper in the reactivity series, so a **coil** of copper wire in silver nitrate solution will produce metallic silver. Figure 11.7 shows the silver being produced as a mixture of grey 'fur' and delicate crystals. Notice the solution becoming blue, as copper(II) nitrate is produced:

$$Cu(s) + 2AgNO_3(aq) \rightarrow Cu(NO_3)_2(aq) + 2Ag(s)$$

This time the nitrate ions are spectator ions, and the final version of the ionic equation looks like this:

$$Cu(s) + 2Ag^+(aq) \rightarrow Cu^{2+}(aq) + 2Ag(s)$$

This is another redox reaction.

The Cu is the reducing agent (it is oxidised) because it gives electrons to the Ag^+ ions to reduce them to Ag. The Ag^+ ion is the oxidising agent (it is reduced) because it takes electrons away from the Cu atoms.

The ionic half-equations are:

$$Cu(s) \rightarrow Cu^{2+}(aq) + 2e^- \quad \text{oxidation}$$

$$Ag^+(aq) + e^- \rightarrow Ag(s) \quad \text{reduction}$$

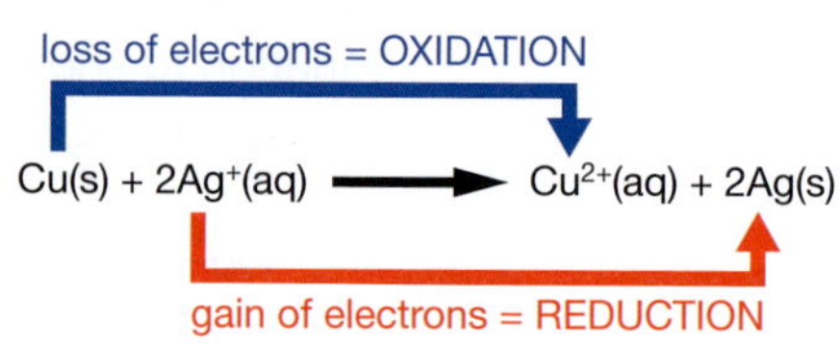

▲ Figure 11.8 Copper reacting with silver nitrate solution

REACTIONS OF METALS WITH WATER

A GENERAL SUMMARY

METALS ABOVE HYDROGEN IN THE REACTIVITY SERIES

Metals above hydrogen in the reactivity series react with water (or steam) to produce hydrogen.

If the metal reacts with *cold water*, the metal *hydroxide* and hydrogen are formed.

metal + cold water → metal hydroxide + hydrogen

If the metal reacts with *steam*, the metal *oxide* and hydrogen are formed.

metal + steam → metal oxide + hydrogen

As you move down the reactivity series, the reactions become less and less vigorous.

METALS BELOW HYDROGEN IN THE REACTIVITY SERIES

Metals below hydrogen in the reactivity series (such as copper) don't react with water or steam. This is why copper can be used for both hot and cold water pipes.

REACTIONS OF POTASSIUM, SODIUM OR LITHIUM WITH COLD WATER

These reactions are described in detail on pages 347–348. They are very vigorous reactions, but become less violent in the following order: potassium > sodium > lithium. The equations all look like this:

$$2M(s) + 2H_2O(l) \rightarrow 2MOH(aq) + H_2(g)$$

Replace M by K, Na or Li, depending on which metal you want.

REACTION OF CALCIUM WITH COLD WATER

Calcium reacts gently with cold water. The grey granules sink, but are carried back to the surface again as bubbles of hydrogen are formed around them. The mixture becomes warm as heat is produced.

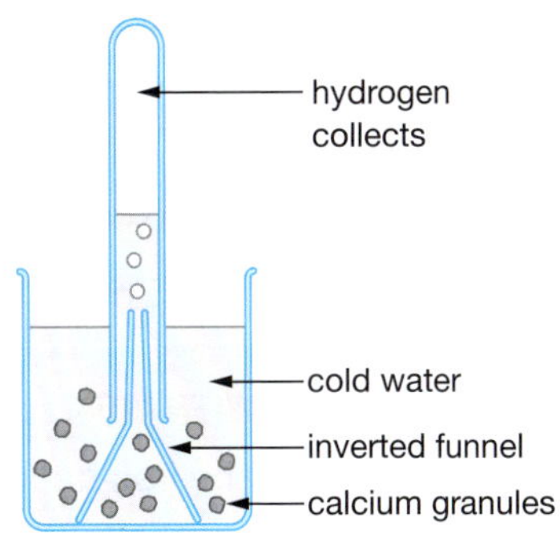

▲ Figure 11.9 Calcium reacting with cold water

Calcium hydroxide is formed. This isn't very soluble in water. Some of it dissolves to give a colourless solution, but most of it is left as a white, insoluble solid.

$$Ca(s) + 2H_2O(l) \rightarrow Ca(OH)_2(aq \text{ or } s) + H_2(g)$$

REACTION OF MAGNESIUM WITH COLD WATER

There is almost no reaction. If the magnesium is very clean, a few bubbles of hydrogen form on it, but the reaction soon stops again. This is because the magnesium becomes coated with insoluble magnesium hydroxide, which prevents any more water coming into contact with the magnesium.

REACTION OF MAGNESIUM WITH STEAM

KEY POINT

You might wonder why there is no description for aluminium and steam. The reactivity of aluminium is supposed to be between that of magnesium and that of zinc. However, aluminium has only a very slow reaction with steam because it is covered in a very thin, but very strong, layer of aluminium oxide. It only really shows its true reactivity if that layer can be penetrated in some way. Water or steam don't do that very well. We will talk about this again when we look at reactions between metals and acids.

Magnesium ribbon can be heated in steam using the apparatus shown in Figure 11.10.

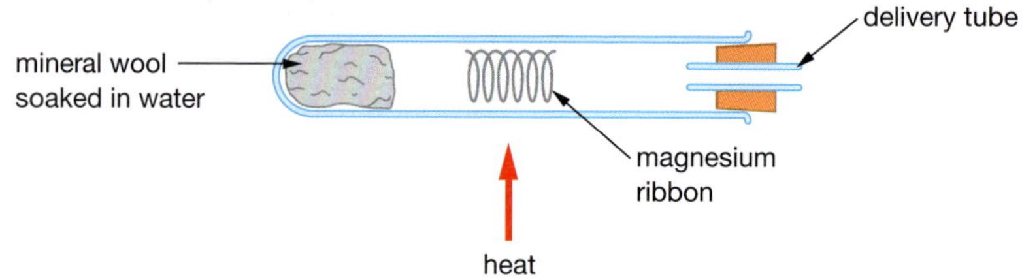

▲ Figure 11.10 Magnesium reacting with steam

The mineral wool isn't heated directly. Enough heat moves back along the test-tube to turn the water to steam.

The magnesium burns with a bright white flame in the steam, producing hydrogen, which can be ignited at the end of the delivery tube. White magnesium oxide is formed:

$$Mg(s) + H_2O(g) \rightarrow MgO(s) + H_2(g)$$

REACTIONS OF ZINC OR IRON WITH STEAM

Safety note: For both reactions wear eye protection. The tube will get very hot and remain so for some time.

KEY POINT

Care has to be taken during this experiment to avoid 'suck-back'. If you stop heating while the delivery tube is still under the surface of the water, water is sucked back into the hot tube, which often results in it cracking.

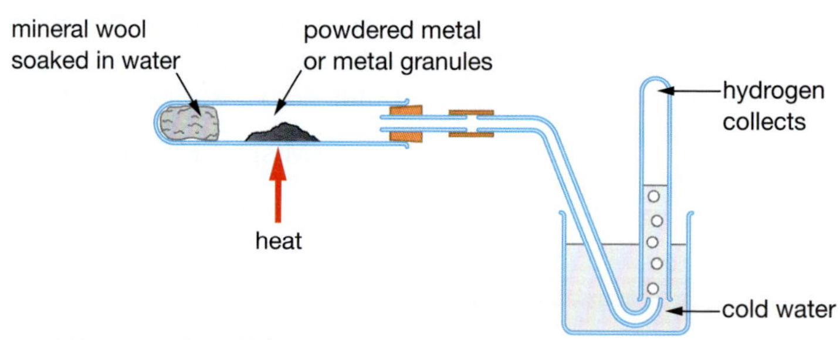

▲ Figure 11.11 Zinc or iron reacting with steam

With both zinc and iron, the hydrogen comes off slowly enough to be collected. Neither metal burns.

WITH ZINC

Zinc oxide is formed. This is yellow when it is hot, but white on cooling.

$$Zn(s) + H_2O(g) \rightarrow ZnO(s) + H_2(g)$$

WITH IRON

The iron becomes slightly darker grey. A complicated oxide is formed, called tri-iron tetroxide, Fe_3O_4:

$$3Fe(s) + 4H_2O(g) \rightarrow Fe_3O_4(s) + 4H_2(g)$$

KEY POINT

Notice that in these equations, water now has a state symbol (g) because we are talking about it as steam.

REMINDER

Remember that *metals below hydrogen* in the reactivity series, such as copper, *don't react* with water or steam.

REACTIONS OF METALS WITH DILUTE ACIDS

Safety note: Wear eye protection. Keep hands and face away from the mouths of the tubes as some acid aerosol (tiny droplets) may be carried out by the gas.

ACTIVITY 4

▼ PRACTICAL: INVESTIGATION INTO THE REACTIONS BETWEEN METALS AND DILUTE ACIDS

- Set up four test-tubes and put about 2 cm^3 of dilute hydrochloric acid into each one.
- Put a small piece of magnesium, zinc, iron or copper into each test-tube and observe any reaction that occurs.
- If there is fizzing, collect or trap the gas and test with a lighted splint – a squeaky pop indicates the presence of hydrogen gas.
- Repeat the experiments with dilute sulfuric acid.

The results that we could obtain from the experiments with dilute hydrochloric acid are shown in Figure 11.12 and Table 11.1.

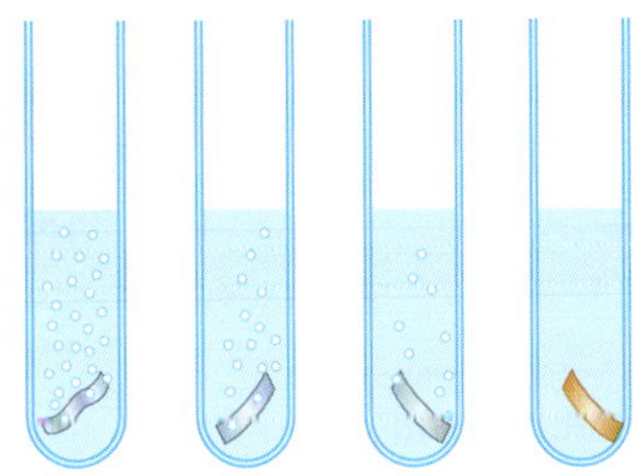

▲ Figure 11.12 The reactions between metals and hydrochloric acid

Table 11.1 The results of experiments on the reaction between hydrochloric acid and some metals

Metal	Reaction with dilute hydrochloric acid
Magnesium	Reacts vigorously with lots of fizzing. The gas produced gave a squeaky pop with a lighted splint. A colourless solution is formed. The test-tube gets hot.
Zinc	Steady reaction. Fizzing. Enough gas eventually collected to produce a squeaky pop with a lighted splint. A colourless solution formed. The test-tube gets warmer.
Iron	Slow fizzing. Very little gas was collected in the time available. A very pale green solution formed. The test-tube got slightly warmer.
Copper	No change.

These reactions are all **exothermic** (they give out heat). See Chapter 15 for more about exothermic reactions.

Now that we have noticed that there is a temperature change in the reaction we could measure this temperature change to compare the reactivity of the metals. However, in order to do this we will have to think more carefully about the things that we have to keep the same in order to make this a valid (fair) test.

The volume and concentration of the hydrochloric acid are perhaps the most obvious things that we have to keep the same, but what about the mass of the metal? This is a more difficult question. If we use 0.24 g of metal in each experiment, we can work out that this is 0.24/24 = 0.010 mol magnesium but 0.24/56 = 0.0040 mol iron.

KEY POINT

If the reaction occurs very slowly, the heat will be given out over a long period of time. As the heat is being given out it will also be lost to the surroundings and the temperature change will be quite low. If the reaction occurs more quickly, the heat is given out more quickly to the solution, and there is less time for heat to be lost to the surroundings – we obtain a larger temperature change. A large surface area causes a faster rate of reaction, so we should use metal powders in these reactions. These things are discussed more in Chapters 15 and 16.

Safety note: Wear eye protection and avoid splashing the acid when stirring.

Now, chemical reactions depend on how many particles are present: more moles and therefore more particles are present in the Mg experiment and more heat would be given out because of this. It is therefore important that we use the same number of moles in each experiment rather than the same number of grams.

The other variable that we should control is the surface area of the metal. Although this does not affect the overall amount of heat given out in the reaction, it will affect the speed at which the heat is given out, which can affect the temperature change.

We will use the following procedure to investigate this reaction quantitatively (involving numbers):

- Measure out 50 cm³ of 1 mol/dm³ hydrochloric acid using a 50 cm³ measuring cylinder (this amount was chosen so that the hydrochloric acid is in excess – there is more than enough to react with all the metal in each case).
- **Pour** the hydrochloric acid into a polystyrene cup (this is an insulator).
- Measure the initial temperature of the hydrochloric acid.
- Weigh out 0.010 mol of magnesium ($0.010 \times 24 = 0.24$ g) powder.
- Add the magnesium powder to the polystyrene cup, stirring rapidly, and measure the maximum temperature reached.
- Repeat with the other metals using 0.010 mol in each case.

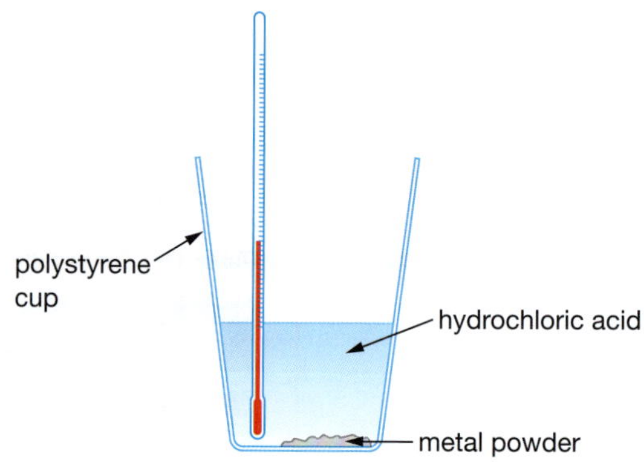

Figure 11.13 Measuring the temperature change when a metal reacts with dilute hydrochloric acid.

The data for this experiment could be:

Metal	Mass / g	Initial temperature / °C	Maximum temperature / °C
magnesium	0.24	18	40
zinc	0.65	19	26
iron	0.56	18	22
copper	0.64	18	18

We can work out the temperature change for each experiment and plot this as a bar chart. We use a bar chart because the type of metal is not continuous data: the metal can be either magnesium or zinc, it cannot be anything in between.

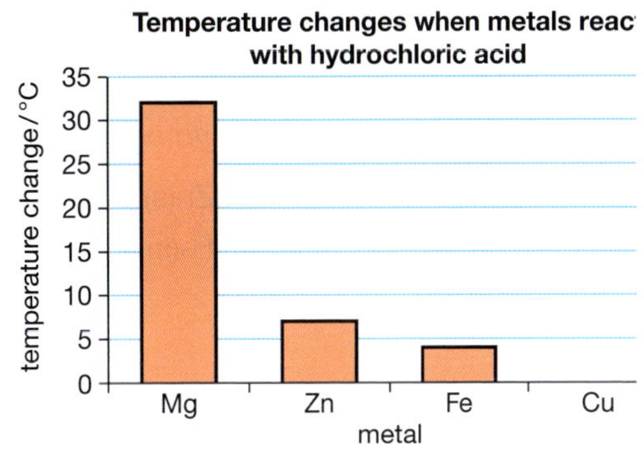

▲ Figure 11.14 Magnesium gives out the most heat when reacted with hydrochloric acid.

We can see from this data that magnesium caused the greatest temperature change and so is the most reactive metal of the four; copper caused no change and is the least reactive.

KEY POINT

We could also calculate the molar enthalpy change for each reaction – see Chapter 15 to learn how to do this.

A GENERAL SUMMARY

The pattern for the reaction of metals with acids is the same as for the reaction between the metals and water, but in each case the reaction is much more vigorous.

KEY POINT

The general trends on this page apply to simple acids such as dilute sulfuric acid or dilute hydrochloric acid. Nitric acid and concentrated sulfuric acid behave completely differently with most metals. These are problems beyond International GCSE.

METALS ABOVE HYDROGEN IN THE REACTIVITY SERIES

Metals above hydrogen react with acids to form a salt (e.g. magnesium sulfate or zinc chloride) and hydrogen. The higher the metal in the series, the more violent the reaction.

metal + acid → salt + hydrogen

metal + dilute sulfuric acid → metal sulfate + hydrogen

metal + dilute hydrochloric acid → metal chloride + hydrogen

HINT

You can remember this using the mnemonic MASH.

METALS BELOW HYDROGEN IN THE REACTIVITY SERIES

Metals such as copper, silver and gold do not react with simple dilute acids such as sulfuric or hydrochloric acid.

POTASSIUM, SODIUM, LITHIUM AND CALCIUM WITH DILUTE ACIDS

These are too reactive to add safely to acids, the reaction is too violent. Calcium can be used if the acid is very dilute.

METALS FROM MAGNESIUM TO IRON IN THE REACTIVITY SERIES

Magnesium reacts vigorously with cold dilute acids, and the mixture becomes hot. A colourless solution of magnesium sulfate or chloride is formed. With dilute sulfuric acid:

$$Mg(s) + H_2SO_4(aq) \rightarrow MgSO_4(aq) + H_2(g)$$

Safety note: Wear eye protection and avoid splashing the acid when stirring.

Aluminium is slow to start reacting, but after warming it reacts very vigorously. There is a very thin, but very strong, layer of aluminium oxide on the surface of the aluminium, which stops the acid from getting to it. On heating, the acid removes this layer, and the aluminium can show its true reactivity. With dilute hydrochloric acid:

$$2Al(s) + 6HCl(aq) \rightarrow 2AlCl_3(aq) + 3H_2(g)$$

Zinc and ***iron*** react slowly in the cold, but more rapidly on heating. The vigour of the reactions is less than that of aluminium. The zinc forms zinc sulfate or zinc chloride and hydrogen. The iron forms iron(II) sulfate or iron(II) chloride and hydrogen. For example:

$$Zn(s) + H_2SO_4(aq) \rightarrow ZnSO_4(aq) + H_2(g)$$

$$Fe(s) + 2HCl(aq) \rightarrow FeCl_2(aq) + H_2(g)$$

▲ Figure 11.15 Iron reacting with dilute hydrochloric acid

KEY POINT

There are two ranges of iron salts containing either Fe^{2+} or Fe^{3+} ions. These reactions produce iron(II) salts, containing Fe^{2+} ions.

FINDING THE APPROXIMATE POSITION OF A METAL IN THE REACTIVITY SERIES USING WATER AND DILUTE ACIDS

Add a very small piece of metal to some cold water. If there is any rapid reaction, then the metal must be above magnesium in the reactivity series.

If there isn't any reaction, add a small amount of metal to some dilute hydrochloric acid (or dilute sulfuric acid). If there isn't any reaction in the cold acid, warm it carefully.

If there is still no reaction, the metal is probably below hydrogen in the reactivity series. If there is a reaction, then it is somewhere between magnesium and hydrogen.

KEY POINT

It would be impossible to place a metal exactly in the reactivity series using this sequence. How vigorously a metal reacts with a dilute acid depends on its position in the series, but it also depends on its surface area, and whether the surface is free from dirt or an oxide coating.

MAKING PREDICTIONS USING THE REACTIVITY SERIES

You can make predictions about the reactions of unfamiliar metals if you know their position in the reactivity series.

A PROBLEM INVOLVING MANGANESE

Suppose you have a question as follows.

Manganese (Mn) lies between aluminium and zinc in the reactivity series, and forms a 2+ ion. Solutions of manganese(II) salts are very pale pink (almost colourless).

a Use the reactivity series to predict whether manganese will react with copper(II) sulfate solution. If it will react, describe what you would see, name the products and write an equation for the reaction.

b Explain why you would expect manganese to react with steam. Name the products of the reaction and write the equation.

KEY POINT

You need to know the charge on the ion so that you can deduce the formulae of the manganese compounds. If you aren't sure about working out the formula of an ionic compound, look again at Chapter 6.

potassium
sodium
lithium
calcium
magnesium
aluminium
manganese
zinc
iron
(hydrogen)
copper

▲ Figure 11.16 Where is manganese in the reactivity series?

a The reaction between manganese and copper(II) sulfate solution

Manganese is above copper in the reactivity series and so will displace it from the copper(II) sulfate:

A pink-brown deposit of copper will be formed. The colour of the solution will fade from blue and leave a very pale pink (virtually colourless) solution of manganese(II) sulfate.

$$Mn(s) + CuSO_4(aq) \rightarrow MnSO_4(aq) + Cu(s)$$

b The reaction between manganese and steam

Manganese is above hydrogen in the reactivity series and so reacts with steam to give hydrogen and the metal oxide, in this case manganese(II) oxide.

You couldn't predict the colour of the manganese(II) oxide, and the question doesn't ask you to do this.

$$Mn(s) + H_2O(g) \rightarrow MnO(s) + H_2(g)$$

RUSTING OF IRON

Iron **rusts** in the presence of *oxygen* and *water*. Rusting occurs with iron and the most common **alloy** of iron, mild steel (see below).

The formula of rust is $Fe_2O_3{\cdot}xH_2O$, where *x* is a variable number. It can be called 'hydrated iron(III) oxide'. Rusting can be described as a redox reaction – the iron is oxidised.

HINT

Warning! Many metals corrode, but it is only the corrosion of iron that is referred to as *rusting*.

▲ Figure 11.17 Rusting is accelerated by salty water.

KEY POINT

Forming rust from iron is a surprisingly complicated process. The iron loses electrons to form iron(II) ions, Fe^{2+}, which are then oxidised by the air to iron(III) ions, Fe^{3+}. Reactions involving the water produce the actual rust.

PREVENTING RUSTING BY USING BARRIERS

The most obvious way of preventing rusting is to keep water and oxygen away from the iron. You can do this by painting it, coating it in oil or grease, or covering it in plastic. Coating the iron with a metal *below* it in the reactivity series (e.g. coating steel with tin for tin cans) is also a **barrier method**.

Barrier methods are usually quite cheap ways of preventing rusting. A problem with barrier methods is that once the coating is broken, the iron underneath is exposed to oxygen and water and the iron will rust (even the bits that are not directly exposed to the air/water).

PREVENTING RUSTING BY GALVANISING

Galvanised iron is iron that is coated with a layer of zinc. As long as the zinc layer is unscratched, it serves as a barrier to air and water. However, the iron still doesn't rust, even when some of the zinc on the surface is scratched away

EXTENSION WORK

During the process, the zinc loses electrons (is oxidised) to form zinc ions.

$$Zn(s) \rightarrow Zn^{2+}(aq) + 2e^-$$

These electrons flow into the iron. Any iron atom which has lost electrons to form an ion immediately regains them. If the iron can't form ions, it can't rust.

to expose the iron. This is because the zinc is more reactive than iron, and so reacts with oxygen/water more readily than the iron does. The zinc corrodes instead of the iron.

▲ Figure 11.18 Galvanised iron doesn't rust even in constant contact with air and water.

PREVENTING RUSTING BY USING SACRIFICIAL PROTECTION

▲ Figure 11.19 A sacrificial anode on a ship

Zinc, magnesium or aluminium blocks are attached to metal hulls or keels of ships to prevent the iron/steel from rusting. For this to work, you have to use a metal that is *more reactive than iron;* the more reactive metal reacts (is oxidised) more readily in the presence of oxygen/water than the iron. The corrosion of the more reactive metal prevents the iron from rusting. Such blocks are called sacrificial **anodes**.

These sacrificial anodes have to be replaced occasionally when all the more reactive metal has been oxidised. This type of protection is used on large structures where it would be very difficult to use a barrier method effectively.

Galvanising is a combination of a barrier method and **sacrificial protection**.

Underground pipelines are also protected using sacrificial anodes. In this case, **lumps** of magnesium are attached at intervals along the pipe. The very reactive magnesium corrodes in preference to the iron. The electrons produced as the magnesium forms its ions prevent the ionisation of the iron.

CHAPTER QUESTIONS

SKILLS CRITICAL THINKING — 6th

1 a List the following metals in order of decreasing reactivity: aluminium, copper, iron, sodium.

b Some magnesium powder was mixed with some copper(II) oxide and heated strongly. There was a vigorous reaction, producing a lot of sparks and a bright **flash** of light.

5th

i State the names of the products of the reaction.

SKILLS PROBLEM SOLVING — 9th

ii Write a balanced symbol equation for the reaction.

SKILLS REASONING

iii Explain which substance in the reaction has been reduced.

iv Explain which substance is the oxidising agent.

c If a mixture of zinc powder and cobalt(II) oxide is heated, the following reaction occurs:

$$Zn(s) + CoO(s) \rightarrow ZnO(s) + Co(s)$$

7th

i Explain which metal is higher in the reactivity series.

SKILLS CRITICAL THINKING — 9th

ii The zinc can be described as a reducing agent. Using this example, explain what is meant by the term 'reducing agent'.

iii Explain which substance in this reaction has been oxidised.

SKILLS REASONING

8th

d Aluminium, chromium and manganese are all moderately reactive metals. Use the following information to arrange them in the correct reactivity series order. Start with the most reactive one.

- Chromium is manufactured by heating chromium(III) oxide with aluminium.
- If manganese is heated with aluminium oxide there is no reaction.
- If manganese is heated with chromium(III) oxide, chromium is produced.

10th

2 Study the following equations and in each case decide whether the substance in bold type is oxidised or reduced. Explain your choice in terms of either oxygen transfer or electron transfer as appropriate.

a $\mathbf{Zn(s)} + CuO(s) \rightarrow ZnO(s) + Cu(s)$

b $\mathbf{Fe_2O_3(s)} + 3C(s) \rightarrow 2Fe(s) + 3CO(g)$

c $\mathbf{Mg(s)} + Zn^{2+}(aq) \rightarrow Mg^{2+}(aq) + Zn(s)$

d $Zn(s) + \mathbf{Cu^{2+}(aq)} \rightarrow Zn^{2+}(aq) + Cu(s)$

8th

3 The equation for the reaction when solid magnesium and solid lead(II) oxide are heated together is:

$$Mg(s) + PbO(s) \rightarrow MgO(s) + Pb(s)$$

Explain what this tells you about the position of lead in the reactivity series.

6th

4 Some iron filings were shaken with some copper(II) sulfate solution. The ionic equation for the reaction is:

$$Fe(s) + Cu^{2+}(aq) \rightarrow Fe^{2+}(aq) + Cu(s)$$

a Explain any one change that you would observe during this reaction.

9th

b Explain which substance has been oxidised in this reaction.

SKILLS CRITICAL THINKING

c Write down the full (not ionic) equation for this reaction.

SKILLS REASONING

8th

5 Some experiments were carried out to place the metals copper, nickel and silver in reactivity series order.

Experiment 1: A piece of copper was placed in some green nickel(II) sulfate solution. There was no change to either the copper or the solution.

Experiment 2: A coil of copper wire was suspended in some silver nitrate solution. A furry grey growth appeared on the copper wire, out of which grew spiky silvery crystals. The solution gradually turned from colourless to blue.

a Use this information to place copper, nickel and silver in reactivity series order, starting with the most reactive one.

b In another experiment, a piece of nickel was placed in some copper(II) sulfate solution.

6th

i State one change that you would observe during this reaction.

SKILLS PROBLEM SOLVING

9th

ii Write the full balanced equation for this reaction.

iii Write the ionic equation for this reaction and use it to explain which substance has been oxidised during the reaction.

SKILLS REASONING

8th

6 a Look carefully at the following equations and then explain what you can say about the position of the metal X in the reactivity series.

$$X(s) + 2HCl(aq) \rightarrow XCl_2(aq) + H_2(g)$$

$$X(s) + CuSO_4(aq) \rightarrow XSO_4(aq) + Cu(s)$$

$$X(s) + FeSO_4(aq) \rightarrow \text{no reaction}$$

SKILLS REASONING — 8th

b Decide whether X will react with the following substances. If it will react, state the names of the products, if not state 'no reaction'.

- **i** Silver nitrate solution
- **ii** Zinc oxide
- **iii** Cold water
- **iv** Copper(II) chloride solution
- **v** Dilute sulfuric acid

SKILLS CRITICAL THINKING — 5th

7 If you add some powdered aluminium to a small amount of cold dilute hydrochloric acid in a boiling tube, very little happens. If you warm this gently, it starts to fizz very rapidly.

a State the name of the gas given off to produce the fizzing.

b If you used an excess of hydrochloric acid, the result would be a colourless solution. State the name of the solution.

SKILLS PROBLEM SOLVING — 9th

c Write the full balanced equation for the reaction.

SKILLS REASONING — 6th

d Explain why the aluminium hardly reacts at all with the dilute acid in the cold, but reacts vigorously after even gentle heating.

SKILLS EXECUTIVE FUNCTION — 8th

8 If you have some small pieces of the metal titanium and any simple apparatus that you might need, describe how you would find out the approximate position of titanium in the reactivity series, using only water and dilute hydrochloric acid. You only need to find out that the reactivity is 'similar to iron' or 'similar to magnesium', for example. Your experiments should be done in an order that guarantees maximum safety. For example, if titanium's reactivity turned out to be similar to potassium, dropping it into dilute hydrochloric acid wouldn't be a good idea!

SKILLS CRITICAL THINKING — 5th

9 In the past, cars were made from mild steel, which was then painted. In more modern cars, the mild steel is galvanised before it is painted.

a State the conditions under which iron/steel rusts.

6th

b Explain how painting prevents iron/steel from rusting.

c What is meant by *galvanised steel*?

7th

d Describe and explain the effect that galvanised steel has on the life of the car.

SKILLS INTERPRETATION — 8th

10 A student tested four unknown metals (the names are all imaginary) with different metal salt solutions. She put a tick (✔) if there was a reaction and a cross (✖) if there was no change. Some of her results are shown in the table.

	Pearsonium chloride solution	Mollium chloride solution	Rosium chloride solution	Amelium chloride solution
pearsonium	✖		✖	
mollium	✔	✖	✔	✔
rosium			✖	✖
amelium				✖

a Copy and complete the table.

SKILLS CRITICAL THINKING

b Arrange the metals in an order of reactivity (most reactive first).

SKILLS PROBLEM SOLVING — 6th

c Copy and complete the equation:

mollium + pearsonium chloride →

12 ACIDS AND ALKALIS

This chapter explores what indicators, acids and alkalis are. The reactions of acids are also discussed in Chapter 13.

▲ Figure 12.1 Acids range from the extremely dangerous, needing protective clothing to clean up spills . . .

▲ Figure 12.2 . . . to a natural part of our diet: oranges contain citric acid.

LEARNING OBJECTIVES

- Describe the use of litmus, phenolphthalein and methyl orange to distinguish between acidic and alkaline solutions
- Understand how the pH scale, from 0–14, can be used to classify solutions as strongly acidic (0–3), weakly acidic (4–6), neutral (7), weakly alkaline (8–10) and strongly alkaline (11–14)
- Describe the use of universal indicator to measure the approximate pH value of an aqueous solution
- Know that acids in aqueous solution are a source of hydrogen ions, and alkalis in an aqueous solution are a source of hydroxide ions
- Know that alkalis can neutralise acids

pH AND INDICATORS

THE pH SCALE

The **pH scale** ranges from about 0 to about 14, and tells you how acidic or how alkaline a solution is.

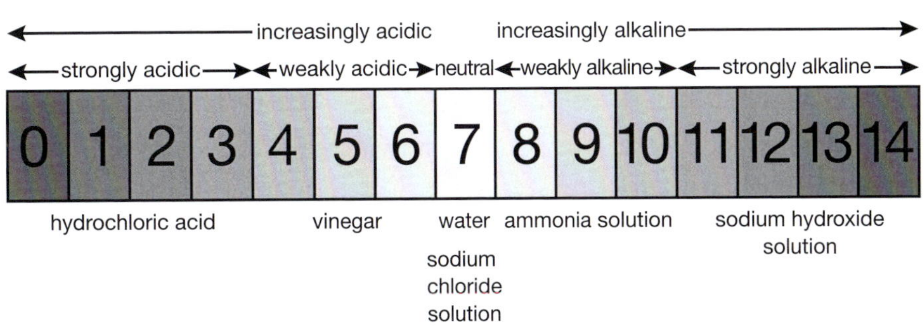

▲ Figure 12.3 The pH scale. **Vinegar** is a solution of ethanoic acid.

We can classify substances as strongly acidic/alkaline or weakly acidic/alkaline based on their pH. Remember, when writing pH, it is a small p and a big H (the symbol for hydrogen).

EXTENSION WORK

These are actually only approximate ranges and depend on the concentration of the acid/alkali solution. A 0.10 mol/dm^3 solution of ethanoic acid actually has a pH of 2.88.

Table 12.1 We can classify solutions according to their pH

	pH	Solution
strongly acidic	0–3	hydrochloric acid
weakly acidic	4–6	ethanoic acid (vinegar)
neutral	7	sodium chloride
weakly alkaline	8–10	ammonia
strongly alkaline	11–14	sodium hydroxide

MEASURING pH

USING UNIVERSAL INDICATOR

HINT

You can measure pH much more accurately using a pH meter.

Universal indicator is made from a mixture of **indicators**, which change colour in a gradual way over a range of pH values. It can be used as a solution or as paper. The most common form is known as *full-range* universal indicator. It changes through a variety of colours from pH 1 right up to pH 14, but it isn't very accurate.

▲ Figure 12.4 Using universal indicator solution to measure the pH of various solutions.

The colour of the paper or solution is checked against a chart to find the pH.

ACID–ALKALI INDICATORS

Any substance that has different colours depending on the pH can be used as an indicator. Some common indicators and their colours in acidic and alkaline solutions are shown in Table 12.2.

Table 12.2 The colours of various indicators in acidic and alkaline solutions

	Acid	Alkali
litmus	red	blue
methyl orange	red	yellow
phenolphthalein	colourless	pink
universal indicator	red	blue

KEY POINT

Litmus can be used as a solution or as litmus paper.

Litmus is red in acidic solutions and blue in alkaline ones. In neutral solutions, the colour is purple, which is an equal mixture of the red and blue forms. Universal indicator is green in neutral solutions.

ACIDS

Table 12.3 Some acids showing the replaceable hydrogen

Acid	Formula
hydrochloric acid	HCl
nitric acid	HNO_3
sulfuric acid	H_2SO_4
ethanoic acid	CH_3COOH
phosphoric acid	H_3PO_4

The formulae of some acids are given in Table 12.3.

All acids contain hydrogen and when acids react the hydrogen shown in red in Table 12.3 is replaced by something else; all acids have replaceable H. For example, when hydrochloric acid reacts with sodium hydroxide we obtain:

$$HCl(aq) + NaOH(aq) \rightarrow NaCl(aq) + H_2O(l)$$

The H of the HCl has been replaced by an Na.

Not all of the hydrogens in acids are replaceable, for example in ethanoic acid only the H attached to the O is replaceable, not the ones joined to the C.

When acids are in water they dissociate (break apart) to form hydrogen ions (H^+), for example:

$$HCl(aq) \rightarrow H^+(aq) + Cl^-(aq)$$
$$HNO_3(aq) \rightarrow H^+(aq) + NO_3^-(aq)$$
$$H_2SO_4(aq) \rightarrow 2H^+(aq) + SO_4^{2-}(aq)$$

When we are measuring pH we are actually measuring the concentration of these H^+ ions in the solution. This is why the H in pH is written with a capital letter.

We can define acids as *substances that act as a source of hydrogen ions (H^+) in solution*.

EXTENSION WORK

At the next level, you will discover that pH is defined by a mathematical equation: $pH = -\log_{10}[H^+(aq)]$.

BASES

Bases are substances that neutralise acids by combining with the hydrogen ions in them. When we are referring to a base at this level we usually mean a metal oxide, a metal hydroxide or ammonia (NH_3).

ALKALIS

Some bases dissolve in water to form solutions containing hydroxide ions. These are alkalis.

Alkalis are a source of hydroxide (OH^-) ions in solution.

Examples of alkalis are sodium hydroxide and potassium hydroxide (all the Group 1 hydroxides). When sodium hydroxide is in water it breaks apart to form sodium and hydroxide ions:

$$NaOH(aq) \rightarrow Na^+(aq) + OH^-(aq)$$

The other alkali you will meet is a solution of ammonia (NH_3). The ammonia reacts with the water to form ammonium ions and hydroxide ions:

$$NH_3(aq) + H_2O(l) \rightleftharpoons NH_4^+(aq) + OH^-(aq)$$

These alkalis all have a pH greater than 7.

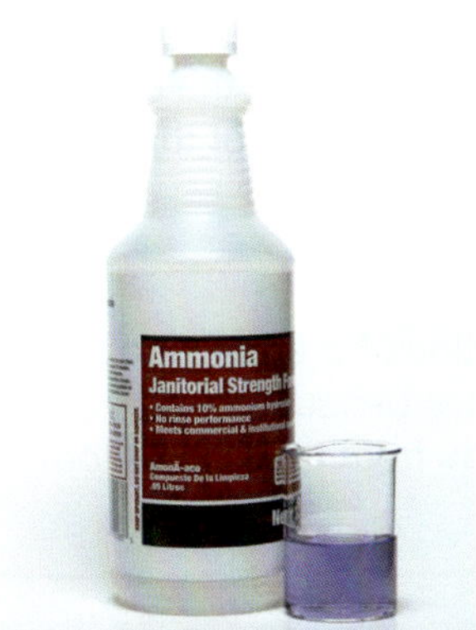

▲ Figure 12.5 Ammonia solution is sometimes called ammonium hydroxide. It is an alkali and is used in some cleaning products. Some universal indicator solution has been added to it in the beaker.

OTHER ALKALINE SOLUTIONS

There are some other substances, such as soluble metal carbonates, that react with water to form hydroxide ions:

$$Na_2CO_3(aq) + H_2O(l) \rightleftharpoons NaOH(aq) + NaHCO_3(aq)$$

EXTENSION WORK

The ionic equation for a carbonate reacting with water is:

$CO_3^{2-}(aq) + H_2O(l) \rightleftharpoons OH^-(aq) + HCO_3^-(aq)$

There are not many soluble carbonates, but sodium carbonate and potassium carbonate are both alkalis with a pH greater than 7. This is due to the OH^- ions in the solution. Only some of the carbonate ions react with water, so these solutions are only weakly alkaline.

REACTING ACIDS WITH BASES AND ALKALIS

Acids react with bases or alkalis in a ***neutralisation reaction***.

REACTING ACIDS WITH BASES

Metal oxides, such as copper(II) oxide and magnesium oxide, are bases.

Copper(II) oxide reacts with hot dilute sulfuric acid, in a neutralisation reaction, to produce a solution of copper(II) sulfate and water:

$$CuO(s) + H_2SO_4(aq) \rightarrow CuSO_4(aq) + H_2O(l)$$

Copper(II) oxide is an ionic compound containing the O^{2-} ion and what has happened in this reaction is that the H^+ ions from the acid have combined with the O^{2-} ions from the base to form water (H_2O).

▲ Figure 12.6 Copper(II) oxide reacts with hot dilute sulfuric acid to form blue copper(II) sulfate solution.

REACTING ACIDS WITH ALKALIS

Sodium hydroxide solution (an alkali) reacts with dilute hydrochloric acid to form sodium chloride and water:

$$NaOH(aq) + HCl(aq) \rightarrow NaCl(aq) + H_2O(l)$$

This is a neutralisation reaction. Sodium hydroxide and sodium chloride are both ionic compounds and so will be present as ions in solution. HCl(aq) is an acid and so will dissociate into $H^+(aq)$ and $Cl^-(aq)$. We can therefore re-write this equation showing all the ions.

$$Na^+(aq) + OH^-(aq) + H^+(aq) + Cl^-(aq) \rightarrow Na^+(aq) + Cl^-(aq) + H_2O(l)$$

The $Na^+(aq)$ and $Cl^-(aq)$ ions are the same on both sides of the equation and so are spectator ions. We can leave the spectator ions out of this equation to just show the things that have changed:

$$OH^-(aq) + H^+(aq) \rightarrow H_2O(l)$$

This is an ionic equation. All neutralisation reactions for an acid reacting with an alkali will have the same ionic equation. This is because they all involve the OH^- ions from the alkali reacting with the H^+ ions from the acid to form water.

CHAPTER QUESTIONS

SKILLS CRITICAL THINKING 4th

1 State the colours of methyl orange, phenolphthalein and litmus in each of the following solutions:

a sodium hydroxide solution

b hydrochloric acid solution.

SKILLS ANALYSIS 4th

2 Table 12.4 gives the pH of some solutions. Classify each as strongly acidic, strongly alkaline, weakly acidic, weakly alkaline or neutral by copying the table and putting ticks in the appropriate boxes.

Table 12.4

Solution	pH	Strongly acidic	Weakly acidic	Neutral	Weakly alkaline	Strongly alkaline
potassium iodide	7					
propanoic acid	4.2					
sodium carbonate	9.5					
potassium hydroxide	13					
iron(III) chloride	2.4					
nitric acid	1.3					

SKILLS PROBLEM SOLVING 9th

3 Write equations for the reactions between:

a sodium oxide and nitric acid

b potassium hydroxide and sulfuric acid.

SKILLS CRITICAL THINKING 6th

4 Explain what type of reaction is occurring in 3.

13 ACIDS, BASES AND SALT PREPARATIONS

Acids were introduced in Chapter 12. In this chapter we will look more closely at some of the reactions of acids and how to make salts.

▲ Figure 13.1 Sodium chloride is common salt. You don't normally make it. It occurs naturally.

LEARNING OBJECTIVES

- Know the general rules for predicting the solubility of ionic compounds in water:
  - common sodium, potassium and ammonium compounds are soluble
  - all nitrates are soluble
  - common chlorides are soluble, except those of silver and lead(II)
  - common hydroxides are insoluble except for those of sodium, potassium and calcium (calcium hydroxide is slightly soluble)
- Understand acids and bases in terms of proton transfer
- Understand that an acid is a proton donor and a base is a proton acceptor
- Describe the reactions of hydrochloric acid, sulfuric acid and nitric acid with metals, bases and metal carbonates (excluding the reactions between nitric acid and metals) to form salts
- Know that metal oxides, metal hydroxides and ammonia can act as bases, and that alkalis are bases that are soluble in water
- Describe an experiment to prepare a pure, dry sample of a soluble salt, starting from an insoluble reactant
- Practical: Prepare a sample of pure, dry hydrated copper(II) sulfate crystals, starting from copper(II) oxide

SALTS

All acids contain hydrogen. When that hydrogen is replaced by a metal, the compound formed is called a **salt**. Magnesium sulfate is a salt, and so is zinc chloride, and so is potassium nitrate.

The formulae of some acids and salts are given in Table 13.1.

Table 13.1 Some acids and salts

Acid	Formula	Example of salt	Name of salts
hydrochloric acid	HCl	$NaCl$	chlorides
nitric acid	HNO_3	KNO_3	nitrates
sulfuric acid	H_2SO_4	$CuSO_4$	sulfates
ethanoic acid	CH_3COOH	CH_3COONa	ethanoates
phosphoric acid	H_3PO_4	K_3PO_4	phosphates

Sulfuric acid can be thought of as the **parent acid** of all the sulfates (the salts formed trom sulfuric acid are all called sulfates). It doesn't matter if the replacement of the hydrogen can't be done directly. For example, you can't make copper(II) sulfate from copper and dilute sulfuric acid because they don't react. There are, however, other ways of making it from sulfuric acid – copper(II) sulfate is still a salt.

REMINDER

These salts contain the NH_4^+ ion.

Salts are also formed when the hydrogen in an acid is replaced with NH_4. These are ammonium salts, for example NH_4Cl (ammonium chloride) and $(NH_4)_2SO_4$ (ammonium sulfate).

REACTIONS OF ACIDS

Before we look at some practical methods to make salts, we need to study the reactions of acids.

REACTING ACIDS WITH METALS

KEY POINT

Of the common acids in the lab, nitric acid has much more complex reactions with metals. You won't be asked about this at International GCSE.

Simple dilute acids react with metals depending on their positions in the reactivity series.

- Metals below hydrogen in the series don't react with dilute acids.
- Metals above hydrogen in the series react to produce hydrogen gas.
- The higher the metal is in the reactivity series, the more vigorous the reaction. You would never mix metals such as sodium or potassium with acids because their reactions are too violent.

REMINDER

Remember: MASH

A summary equation for metals above hydrogen in the reactivity series:

metal + acid → salt + hydrogen

REACTIONS INVOLVING MAGNESIUM AND ACIDS

WITH DILUTE SULFURIC ACID

There is rapid fizzing and a colourless gas is evolved, which pops with a lighted splint (the test for hydrogen). The reaction mixture becomes very warm as heat is produced. The magnesium gradually disappears to leave a colourless solution of magnesium sulfate.

$$Mg(s) + H_2SO_4(aq) \rightarrow MgSO_4(aq) + H_2(g)$$

This is a displacement reaction. The more reactive magnesium has displaced the less reactive hydrogen.

▲ Figure 13.2 Magnesium reacting with dilute sulfuric acid

WITH DILUTE HYDROCHLORIC ACID

The reaction looks exactly the same. The only difference is that this time a solution of magnesium chloride is formed.

$$Mg(s) + 2HCl(aq) \rightarrow MgCl_2(aq) + H_2(g)$$

EXTENSION WORK

Acids in solution form ions. Dilute sulfuric acid contains hydrogen ions and sulfate ions. Dilute hydrochloric acid contains hydrogen ions and chloride ions.

You can rewrite the equations above as ionic equations. In the case of sulfuric acid:

$$Mg(s) + 2H^+(aq) + SO_4^{2-}(aq) \rightarrow Mg^{2+}(aq) + SO_4^{2-}(aq) + H_2(g)$$

The sulfate ion hasn't been changed by the reaction. It is a spectator ion, and so we don't include it in the ionic equation:

$$Mg(s) + 2H^+(aq) \rightarrow Mg^{2+}(aq) + H_2(g)$$

Repeating this with hydrochloric acid, we find that the chloride ions are also spectator ions:

$$Mg(s) + 2H^+(aq) + 2Cl^-(aq) \rightarrow Mg^{2+}(aq) + 2Cl^-(aq) + H_2(g)$$

Not including the spectator ions produces the ionic equation:

$$Mg(s) + 2H^+(aq) \rightarrow Mg^{2+}(aq) + H_2(g)$$

The reactions look the same because they are the same. All solutions of acids contain hydrogen ions. That means that magnesium will react with any simple dilute acid in the same way.

REMINDER

Ionic compounds are present as separate ions in solution, so in $MgSO_4(aq)$ the $Mg^{2+}(aq)$ and $SO_4^{2-}(aq)$ ions are separated from each other.

REACTIONS INVOLVING ZINC AND ACIDS

Again, the reactions between zinc and the two acids look exactly the same. The reactions are slower because zinc is lower down the reactivity series than magnesium.

The equations are:

$$Zn(s) + H_2SO_4(aq) \rightarrow ZnSO_4(aq) + H_2(g)$$
$$Zn(s) + 2HCl(aq) \rightarrow ZnCl_2(aq) + H_2(g)$$

EXTENSION WORK

The ionic equations are both the same:

$$Zn(s) + 2H^+(aq) \rightarrow Zn^{2+}(aq) + H_2(g)$$

BASES

We saw in Chapter 12 that bases are substances that neutralise acids by combining with the hydrogen ions in them to produce water. When we are referring to a base at this level, we usually mean a metal oxide, a metal hydroxide or ammonia.

REACTING ACIDS WITH BASES

Metal oxides, such as copper(II) oxide and magnesium oxide, are bases.

REACTING DILUTE SULFURIC ACID WITH COPPER(II) OXIDE

The copper(II) oxide (black powder) reacts with hot dilute sulfuric acid to produce a blue solution of copper(II) sulfate.

$$CuO(s) + H_2SO_4(aq) \rightarrow CuSO_4(aq) + H_2O(l)$$

All the metal oxide and acid combinations that you will meet at International GCSE behave in exactly the same way as the reaction between copper(II) oxide and dilute sulfuric acid, that is, they produce a salt and water. Most need to be heated for the reaction to start.

Copper(II) oxide is an ionic compound containing the O^{2-} ion. What has happened in this reaction is that the H^+ ions from the acid have combined with the O^{2-} ions to form water (H_2O).

The general equation for the reaction of a metal oxide (base) with an acid is

metal oxide + acid → salt + water

This is a neutralisation reaction – the base neutralises the acid (water is formed).

BASES AND ALKALIS

Some metal oxides are soluble in water and react with it to form solutions of metal hydroxides, for example:

$$Na_2O(s) + H_2O(l) \rightarrow 2NaOH(aq)$$

All the Group 1 oxides do this reaction, so for potassium oxide we would get:

$$K_2O(s) + H_2O(l) \rightarrow 2KOH(aq)$$

Most other metal oxides are not soluble in water.

Calcium oxide dissolves slightly to form calcium hydroxide:

$$CaO(s) + H_2O(l) \rightarrow Ca(OH)_2(aq)$$

Another alkali you will meet is a solution of ammonia (NH_3). The ammonia reacts with the water to form ammonium ions and hydroxide ions:

$$NH_3(aq) + H_2O(l) \rightleftharpoons NH_4^+(aq) + OH^-(aq)$$

All these solutions contain hydroxide ions. We learned in the last chapter that we can define alkalis as solutions that are a source of hydroxide (OH^-) ions, so all of these solutions are alkalis.

REACTING ACIDS WITH METAL HYDROXIDES

All metal hydroxides react with acids in a neutralisation reaction:

metal hydroxide + acid → salt + water

REACTING DILUTE HYDROCHLORIC ACID WITH SODIUM HYDROXIDE SOLUTION

Mixing sodium hydroxide solution and dilute hydrochloric acid produces a colourless solution so not much seems to have happened. But if you repeat the reaction with a thermometer in the beaker, the temperature rises several degrees, showing that there has been a chemical change. Sodium chloride solution has been formed:

$$NaOH(aq) + HCl(aq) \rightarrow NaCl(aq) + H_2O(l)$$

We saw in Chapter 12 that the ionic equation for this reaction is:

$$OH^-(aq) + H^+(aq) \rightarrow H_2O(l)$$

All neutralisation reactions for an acid reacting with an alkali have the same ionic equation: they all involve the hydroxide ions from the alkali reacting with the H^+ ions from the acid to form water.

REACTING ACIDS WITH CARBONATES

Carbonates react with cold dilute acids to produce carbon dioxide gas.

A summary equation for acids and carbonates:

carbonate + acid → salt + carbon dioxide + water

THE REACTION BETWEEN COPPER(II) CARBONATE AND DILUTE ACIDS

Green copper(II) carbonate reacts with the common dilute acids to give a blue or blue-green solution of copper(II) sulfate, copper(II) nitrate or copper(II) chloride. Carbon dioxide gas is given off. You can recognise this because it turns limewater milky.

All the equations have the same form:

$$CuCO_3(s) + H_2SO_4(aq) \rightarrow CuSO_4(aq) + CO_2(g) + H_2O(l)$$

$$CuCO_3(s) + 2HNO_3(aq) \rightarrow Cu(NO_3)_2(aq) + CO_2(g) + H_2O(l)$$

$$CuCO_3(s) + 2HCl(aq) \rightarrow CuCl_2(aq) + CO_2(g) + H_2O(l)$$

▲ Figure 13.3 The reaction between copper(II) carbonate and dilute sulfuric acid.

THE REACTION BETWEEN SODIUM CARBONATE AND DILUTE ACIDS

Sodium carbonate is soluble in water. The equation for the reaction of sodium carbonate with hydrochloric acid is:

$$Na_2CO_3(aq) + 2HCl(aq) \rightarrow 2NaCl(aq) + CO_2(g) + H_2O(l)$$

HINT

Carbonates are not mentioned as bases on the syllabus; only metal oxides, metal hydroxides and ammonia.

EXTENSION WORK

If we show the ions (remembering that HCl splits apart into its ions in solution):

$$2Na^+(aq) + CO_3^{2-}(aq) + 2H^+(aq) + 2Cl^-(aq) \rightarrow 2Na^+(aq) + 2Cl^-(aq) + CO_2(g) + H_2O(l)$$

By not including the spectator ions we obtain the ionic equation:

$$CO_3^{2-}(aq) + 2H^+(aq) \rightarrow CO_2(g) + H_2O(l)$$

Because carbonate ions react by accepting hydrogen ions, we can classify carbonate ions as bases.

SALT PREPARATIONS

In the next section we will learn about a method to make soluble salts. Before we can do this, we need to know which substances are soluble and which are insoluble in water.

THE SOLUBILITY OF IONIC COMPOUNDS IN WATER

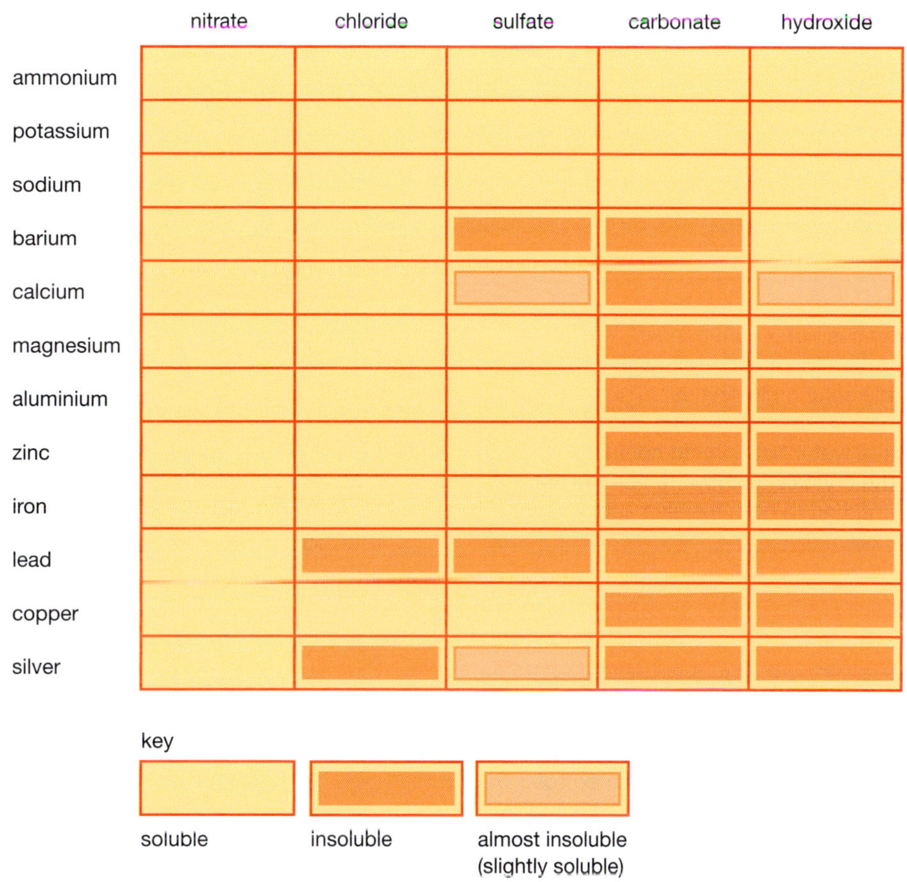

▲ Figure 13.4 Solubility patterns

NOTES ON THE TABLE

To keep the table simple, it includes one or two compounds (aluminium carbonate, for example) which don't actually exist. Don't worry about these. The problem won't arise at International GCSE.

There is no clear line between 'insoluble' and 'almost insoluble' compounds. The ones picked out as 'almost insoluble' include the more common ones that you might need to know about elsewhere in the course.

Note that:

- all sodium, potassium and ammonium compounds are *soluble*
- all nitrates are *soluble*
- most common chlorides are *soluble*, except lead(II) chloride and silver chloride
- most common sulfates are *soluble*, except lead(II) sulfate, barium sulfate, silver sulfate and calcium sulfate
- most common carbonates are *insoluble*, except sodium, potassium and ammonium carbonates
- most metal hydroxides are *insoluble* (or *almost insoluble*), except sodium, potassium and ammonium hydroxides. Calcium hydroxide is slightly soluble in water.

HINT

It can seem a bit frightening to have to remember all this, but it isn't as difficult as it looks at first sight.

Except for the carbonates and hydroxides, most of these compounds are soluble. Learn the exceptions in the sulfates and chlorides.

The reason for the exceptions in the carbonates and hydroxides is that all sodium, potassium and ammonium compounds are soluble.

MAKING SOLUBLE SALTS (EXCEPT SODIUM, POTASSIUM AND AMMONIUM SALTS)

These all involve reacting a solid with an acid. You can use any of the following mixtures:

- acid + metal (but only for the moderately reactive metals from magnesium to iron in the reactivity series)
- acid + metal oxide or hydroxide
- acid + carbonate.

Whatever mixture you use, the method is basically the same.

Safety note: Direct heating of the acid is not recommended. Wear eye protection and do not evaporate the solution to dryness. The acid is best heated in a boiling tube placed in a water bath. Avoid contact with the crystals as they are harmful and irritating to both the skin and eyes.

ACTIVITY 5

▼ PRACTICAL: MAKING COPPER(II) SULFATE CRYSTALS

The practical procedure for this is as follows:

- Measure 50 cm^3 of dilute sulfuric acid into a beaker and heat it on a tripod and gauze using a Bunsen burner.
- Add a spatula full of black copper(II) oxide and continue heating. If all the copper(II) oxide disappears add more copper(II) oxide until there is some left in the beaker. Stir the mixture well to make sure that no more will react. At this stage, we have added *excess* copper(II) oxide – there is more than enough to react with all the acid present. When there is copper(II) oxide left, we know that all the acid has been neutralised.
- Filter off the excess copper(II) oxide and transfer the filtrate (solution), which is blue, to an evaporating basin. The solution we have now is copper(II) sulfate.

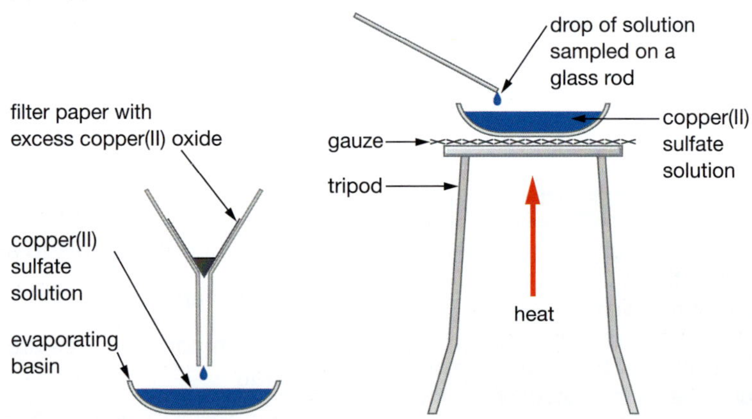

▲ Figure 13.5 Making copper(II) sulfate crystals

The equation for the formation of the solution is:

$$CuO(s) + H_2SO_4(aq) \rightarrow CuSO_4(aq) + H_2O(l)$$

- Heat the solution of copper(II) sulfate over a Bunsen burner to boil off some of the water and concentrate the solution.
- Keep heating until a saturated solution is formed. We can test this by dipping a glass rod into the solution. If crystals form on the glass rod when we remove it we know that the solution is very close to saturated and crystals will also begin to form in the solution.

EXTENSION WORK

In the method described here, you add an excess of a solid to an acid, and then filter off the unreacted solid. You do this to make sure all the acid is used up. This method does not work for making sodium, potassium and ammonium salts. The problem is that all sodium, potassium and ammonium compounds are soluble in water. The solid you added to the acid would not only react with the acid, but any excess would just dissolve in the water present. You wouldn't have any visible excess to filter off. There's no simple way of seeing when you have added just enough of the solid to neutralise the acid. A different method therefore has to be used for making sodium, potassium and ammonium salts.

- Stop heating the reaction mixture and allow it to cool slowly at room temperature so that larger crystals can form.
- Remove the blue crystals from the reaction mixture by filtration, or by just pouring off the remaining solution.
- The crystals can be dried by blotting them with a paper towel, or they can be left to dry in a warm place.

WHY NOT SIMPLY EVAPORATE THE SOLUTION TO DRYNESS?

It would seem much easier to just evaporate off all the water by boiling rather than crystallising the solution slowly, but evaporating to dryness wouldn't give you blue copper(II) sulfate crystals. Instead, you would produce a white powder of anhydrous copper(II) sulfate.

KEY POINT

'Anhydrous' means 'without water'.

When many salts form their crystals water from the solution becomes chemically bound up with the salt. This is called *water of crystallisation*. A salt which contains water of crystallisation is said to be *hydrated*. We can show the crystallisation part of the reaction as:

$$CuSO_4(aq) + 5H_2O(l) \rightarrow CuSO_4{\cdot}5H_2O(s)$$

Safety note: Wear eye protection. Heating must be very gentle to avoid 'spitting' of hot particles.

▲ Figure 13.6 Copper(II) sulfate crystals

MAKING MAGNESIUM SULFATE CRYSTALS

We can add excess magnesium to sulfuric acid. This time the acid does not have to be heated.

When we add the magnesium the reaction mixture will fizz (hydrogen is given off). We keep adding magnesium until the fizzing stops and there is magnesium left in the beaker. This means that all the acid has reacted. The equation for the formation of the solution of magnesium sulfate is:

$$Mg(s) + H_2SO_4(aq) \rightarrow MgSO_4(aq) + H_2(g)$$

▲ Figure 13.7 Dilute sulfuric acid with magnesium

Again the solution is concentrated by heating it and allowed to crystallise. The crystallisation reaction is:

$$MgSO_4(aq) + 7H_2O(l) \rightarrow MgSO_4{\cdot}7H_2O(s)$$

HOW DO YOU KNOW WHETHER YOU NEED TO HEAT THE MIXTURE?

Carbonates react with dilute acids in the cold, and so does magnesium. Most other things that you are likely to come across need to be heated.

cold	hot
carbonates magnesium	most other substances

▲ Figure 13.8 Do you need to heat the mixture?

THEORIES OF ACIDS AND BASES

In Chapter 12, we met the idea that an acid is something that produces $H^+(aq)$ ions in solution and an alkali is something that produces $OH^-(aq)$ ions in solution. This is called the Arrhenius theory of acids and bases. For example, when hydrogen chloride gas is dissolved in water to form hydrochloric acid the molecules dissociate to form H^+ ions:

$$HCl(aq) \rightarrow H^+(aq) + Cl^-(aq)$$

A neutralisation reaction can be shown as H^+ from an acid reacting with OH^- from an alkali to form water.

$$H^+(aq) + OH^-(aq) \rightarrow H_2O(l)$$

The problem with this definition of acids and bases is that it only applies to reactions that occur in aqueous solution and is not more widely applicable.

There is a more general theory of acids and bases that can be used in more situations:

- *An acid is a proton (hydrogen ion) donor.*
- *A base is a proton (hydrogen ion) acceptor.*

This is called the Brønsted–Lowry theory.

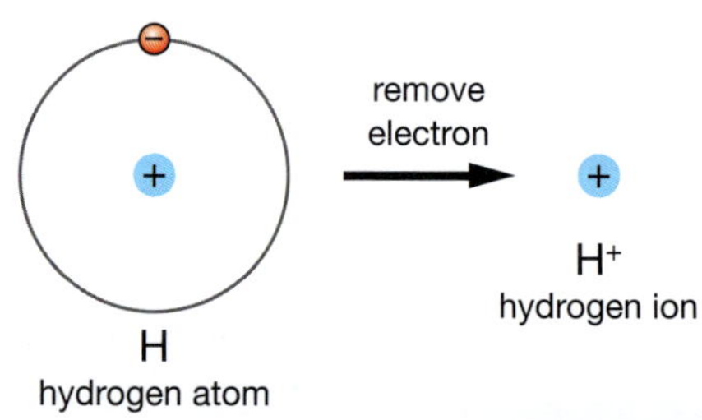

▲ Figure 13.9 A hydrogen ion (H^+) is a proton. If an electron is removed from a hydrogen atom, only a proton is left.

A better way of writing the reaction that occurs when hydrogen chloride dissolves in water is:

$$H_2O(l) + HCl(aq) \rightarrow H_3O^+(aq) + Cl^-(aq)$$

The HCl donates (gives) a proton (H^+) to an H_2O molecule. So, according to our definition, the HCl is an acid and H_2O is a base because it accepts the proton.

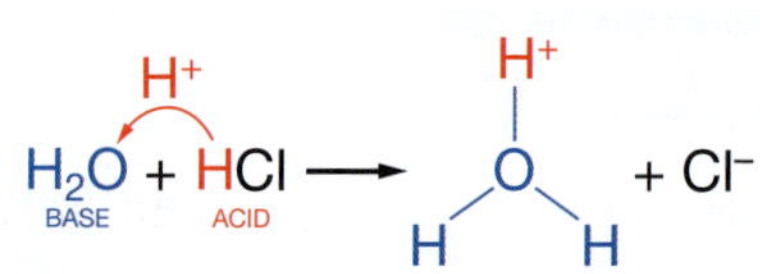

▲ Figure 13.10 HCl donates a proton and H_2O accepts it.

HINT

You do not have to remember the names of the theories.

EXTENSION WORK

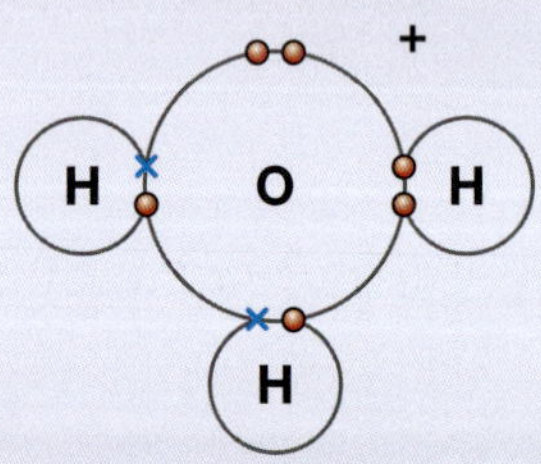

In the dot-and-cross diagram for the H_3O^+ ion you can see that the covalent bond that formed between the H_2O and the H^+ is unusual in that both the shared electrons come from the O. This is called a dative covalent bond or a co-ordinate covalent bond. Once it has been formed, it is exactly the same as a 'normal' covalent bond.

KEY POINT

You have already met the ammonium (NH_4^+) ion, which is obtained when H^+ is added to ammonia (NH_3). The hydroxonium ion is the equivalent ion for water. You do not have to remember the name *hydroxonium ion*.

KEY POINT

To understand the reaction between ammonia and hydrochloric acid in relation to the Arrhenius theory we have to realise that ammonia reacts with water to form OH^- ions:

$$NH_3(aq) + H_2O(l) \rightleftharpoons NH_4^+(aq) + OH^-(aq)$$

and that hydrochloric acid dissociates to form H^+ ions:

$$HCl(aq) \rightarrow H^+(aq) + Cl^-(aq)$$

and that the overall reaction involves H^+ ions reacting with OH^- ions to form water:

$$H^+(aq) + OH^-(aq) \rightarrow H_2O(l)$$

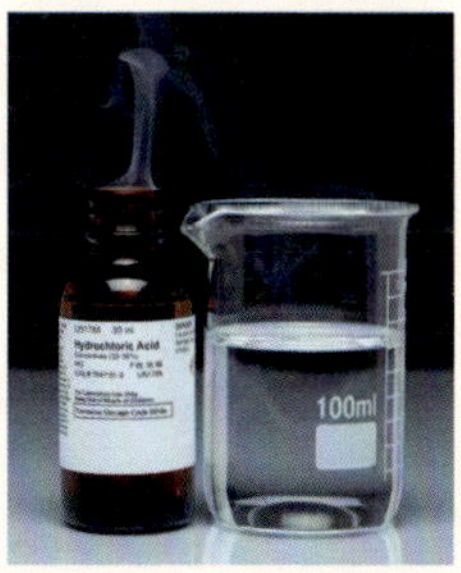

▲ Figure 13.12 Ammonia and hydrogen chloride gases also react to form ammonium chloride (the white smoke): $NH_3(g) + HCl(g) \rightleftharpoons NH_4^+Cl^-(s)$

The $H_3O^+(aq)$ ion is called the **hydroxonium ion**. This is the ion that we usually write simply as $H^+(aq)$. You can think of it as a hydrogen ion joined to a water molecule. Cl^- has a negative charge because the H^+ left an electron behind when it transferred to the H_2O.

THE REACTION BETWEEN NH_3 AND HCl

Dilute hydrochloric acid reacts with ammonia solution in a neutralisation reaction to form a salt, ammonium chloride:

$$NH_3(aq) + HCl(aq) \rightarrow NH_4Cl(aq)$$

Ammonium chloride is an ionic salt so we can show the ions that are present:

$$NH_3(aq) + HCl(aq) \rightarrow NH_4^+(aq) + Cl^-(aq)$$

We can see now that, in order to form ammonium chloride, the HCl must donate a proton (H^+) to the NH_3. The HCl is an acid because it donates a proton and the NH_3 is a base because it accepts the proton.

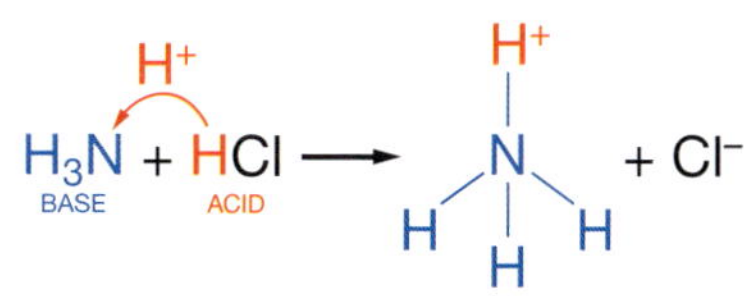

▲ Figure 13.11 HCl is an acid and donates a proton to NH_3 (a base).

MORE ACID-BASE REACTIONS

Acids in solution are acidic because they donate a proton (H^+) to water to form the hydroxonium ion. If we take a general acid (HA), this is what happens when it is put into water:

$$HA(aq) + H_2O(l) \rightarrow H_3O^+(aq) + A^-(aq)$$

HA donates a proton to H_2O, which acts as a base. For nitric acid this would be:

$$\underset{\text{acid}}{HNO_3(aq)} + \underset{\text{base}}{H_2O(l)} \rightarrow H_3O^+(aq) + NO_3^-(aq)$$

When bases, such as metal oxides (e.g. Na_2O), react with water they accept a proton from water, for example:

$$(Na^+)_2O^{2-}(s) + H_2O(l) \rightarrow 2Na^+(aq) + 2OH^-(aq)$$

The O^{2-} ion accepts a proton from the water. In this reaction the water acts as an acid because it donates a proton.

When sulfuric acid reacts with copper(II) oxide (CuO) we have:

$$Cu^{2+}O^{2-}(s) + H_2SO_4(aq) \rightarrow Cu^{2+}(aq) + SO_4^{2-}(aq) + H_2O(l)$$

H_2SO_4 is an acid, it donates protons to CuO, the base.

Ammonia is also a base:

$$\underset{\text{base}}{NH_3(aq)} + \underset{\text{acid}}{H_2O(l)} \rightleftharpoons NH_4^+(aq) + OH^-(aq)$$

The ammonia accepts a proton (H^+) from the water.

For reactions such as:

$$HCl(aq) + NaOH(aq) \rightarrow NaCl(aq) + H_2O(l)$$

HINT

Water can act as proton acceptor (base) or proton donor (acid) in reactions on this page. Do not get confused with what is happening here; remember, water is still neutral! We are simply understanding the reactions that occur in terms of proton transfer.

What actually happens is that the H_3O^+ ion formed when the acid reacts with water donates a proton to the base, OH^-.

$$\underset{\text{acid}}{H_3O^+(aq)} + \underset{\text{base}}{OH^-(aq)} \rightarrow 2H_2O(l)$$

But for International GCSE purposes, we almost always use the simplified version:

$$H^+(aq) + OH^-(aq) \rightarrow H_2O(l)$$

CHAPTER QUESTIONS

SKILLS CRITICAL THINKING 5th

1 State which of the following will react with dilute sulfuric acid:

a copper, copper(II) oxide, copper(II) hydroxide, copper(II) carbonate

SKILLS PROBLEM SOLVING 9th

b In the case of each of the substances which does react, write the equation (including state symbols) for the reaction. All of these substances are insoluble solids.

SKILLS CRITICAL THINKING 7th

2 Read this description of the chemistry of metal **A** and some of its compounds, and then answer the questions.

Metal **A** has no reaction with dilute hydrochloric acid or dilute sulfuric acid. It forms a black oxide, **B**, which reacts with hot dilute sulfuric acid to give a blue solution, **C**. Metal **A** also forms a green compound, **D**, which reacts with dilute nitric acid to give a colourless gas, **E**, and another blue solution, **F**. The colourless gas, **E**, turned limewater milky.

a State the names of **A**, **B**, **C**, **D**, **E** and **F**.

SKILLS PROBLEM SOLVING 9th

b Write equations for the reactions between:

i **B** and dilute sulfuric acid

ii **D** and dilute nitric acid.

SKILLS CRITICAL THINKING 6th

3 a Nickel, Ni, is a silvery metal just above hydrogen in the reactivity series. Nickel(II) compounds in solution are green.

i Describe what you would see if you warmed some nickel with dilute sulfuric acid in a test-tube.

ii State the name of any gas formed.

SKILLS PROBLEM SOLVING 9th

iii Write the equation for the reaction between nickel and dilute sulfuric acid.

b Nickel(II) carbonate is a green, insoluble powder. A spatula measure of nickel(II) carbonate is added to some dilute hydrochloric acid in a test-tube.

SKILLS CRITICAL THINKING 6th

i Describe what you would observe in this experiment.

SKILLS PROBLEM SOLVING 9th

ii Write an equation for the reaction that occurs.

SKILLS CRITICAL THINKING 6th

4 Organise the following compounds into two lists: those that are soluble in water and those that are insoluble.

sodium chloride, lead(II) sulfate, zinc nitrate, calcium carbonate, iron(III) sulfate, lead(II) chloride, potassium sulfate, copper(II) carbonate, silver chloride, aluminium nitrate, barium sulfate, ammonium chloride, magnesium nitrate, calcium sulfate, sodium phosphate, nickel(II) carbonate, chromium(III) hydroxide, potassium dichromate(VI)

SKILLS EXECUTIVE FUNCTION 6th

5 a Describe in detail the preparation of a pure, dry sample of copper(II) sulfate crystals, $CuSO_4{\cdot}5H_2O$, starting from copper(II) oxide.

SKILLS PROBLEM SOLVING 9th

b Write equations for i the reaction producing copper(II) sulfate solution and ii the crystallisation reaction.

SKILLS REASONING 7th

6 All of the following equations represent acid–base reactions. For each of the equations, state which substance is the acid and which the base.

a $CO_3^{2-}(s) + H_3O^+(aq) \rightarrow HCO_3^-(aq) + H_2O(l)$

b $MgO(s) + H_2SO_4(aq) \rightarrow MgSO_4(aq) + H_2O(l)$

c $HNO_3(aq) + NH_3(aq) \rightarrow NH_4^+(aq) + NO_3^-(aq)$

d $H_2SO_4(aq) + H_2O(l) \rightarrow HSO_4^-(aq) + H_3O^+(aq)$

e $NH_3(g) + HCl(g) \rightarrow NH_4Cl(s)$

f $CH_3COOH(aq) + NH_3(aq) \rightarrow CH_3COO^-\ (aq) + NH_4^+(aq)$

14 CHEMICAL TESTS

In this chapter we will look at how to identify substances using chemical tests.

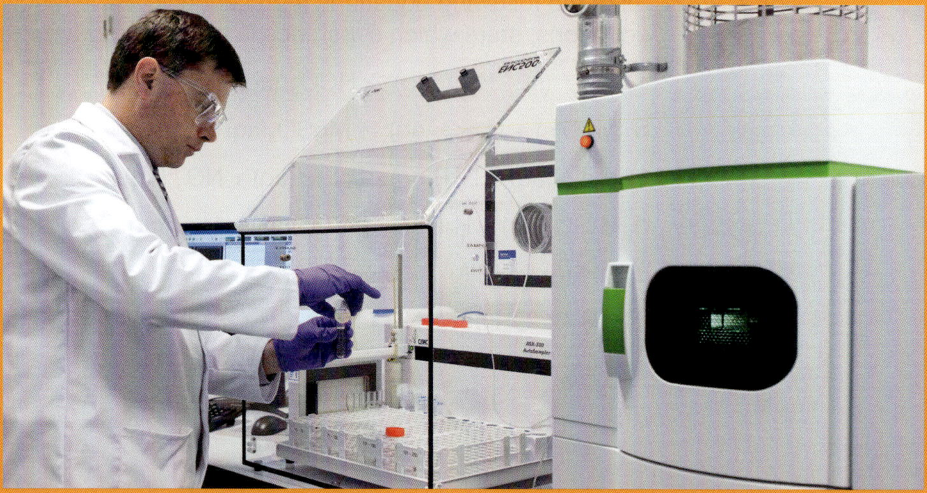

▲ Figure 14.1 Although the reactions we learn here are useful for identifying substances in the lab and we are also introduced to some interesting chemistry, analysis of substances is now routinely carried out using sophisticated machines.

LEARNING OBJECTIVES

- Describe tests for these gases:
  - hydrogen
  - oxygen
  - carbon dioxide
  - ammonia
  - chlorine
- Describe how to carry out a flame test
- Know the colours formed in flame tests for these cations:
  - Li^+ (red)
  - Na^+ (yellow)
  - K^+ (lilac)
  - Ca^{2+} (orange-red)
  - Cu^{2+} (blue-green)
- Describe tests for these cations:
  - NH_4^+ using sodium hydroxide solution and identifying the gas evolved
  - Cu^{2+}, Fe^{2+} and Fe^{3+} using sodium hydroxide solution
- Describe tests for these anions:
  - Cl^-, Br^- and I^- using acidified silver nitrate solution
  - SO_4^{2-} using acidified barium chloride solution
  - CO_3^{2-} using hydrochloric acid and identifying the gas evolved
- Describe a test for the presence of water using anhydrous copper(II) sulfate
- Describe a physical test to show whether or not a sample of water is pure

TESTING FOR GASES

HYDROGEN, H_2

THE TEST FOR HYDROGEN GAS

A lighted splint is held to the mouth of the tube. The hydrogen explodes with a squeaky pop.

The hydrogen combines explosively with oxygen in the air to make water.

$$2H_2(g) + O_2(g) \rightarrow 2H_2O(l)$$

OXYGEN, O_2

THE TEST FOR OXYGEN GAS

A glowing splint is put into the tube containing the gas. Oxygen relights a glowing splint.

CARBON DIOXIDE, CO_2

KEY POINT

If you keep bubbling the carbon dioxide through the limewater, the white precipitate will eventually disappear again. This is because the CO_2 reacts with the calcium carbonate to form calcium hydrogencarbonate, which is soluble in water:

$$CaCO_3(s) + H_2O(l) + CO_2(g) \rightarrow Ca(HCO_3)_2(aq)$$

THE TEST FOR CARBON DIOXIDE GAS

The carbon dioxide is bubbled through limewater. Carbon dioxide turns limewater milky/chalky/cloudy.

Limewater is calcium hydroxide solution. Carbon dioxide reacts with it to form a white **precipitate** of calcium carbonate.

$$Ca(OH)_2(aq) + CO_2(g) \rightarrow CaCO_3(s) + H_2O(l)$$

CHLORINE, Cl_2

THE TEST FOR CHLORINE GAS

A piece of damp litmus paper or universal indicator paper is put into the test-tube or held over its mouth. Chlorine is a green gas that bleaches (turns white) the damp litmus paper or universal indicator paper.

If blue litmus paper or universal indicator paper are used for this test, they go red first (the chlorine dissolves in the water to form an acidic solution) and then white.

Safety note: Wear eye protection. Avoid inhaling or 'sniffing' chlorine or ammonia, especially if you have a breathing problem such as asthma.

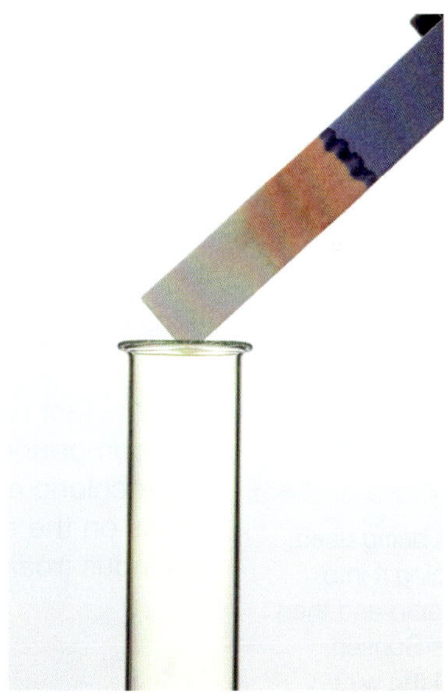

Figure 14.2 Chlorine bleaches damp litmus paper.

AMMONIA, NH_3

THE TEST FOR AMMONIA GAS

Hold a piece of damp universal indicator paper or red litmus paper at the mouth of the test-tube. Ammonia turns the universal indicator paper/litmus paper blue.

Ammonia is the only alkaline gas that you will meet at International GCSE.

TESTING FOR WATER

USING ANHYDROUS COPPER(II) SULFATE

Water turns white anhydrous copper(II) sulfate blue.

Anhydrous copper(II) sulfate lacks water of crystallisation and is white. Dropping water onto it replaces the water of crystallisation and turns it blue.

anhydrous copper sulfate	+ water	→	hydrated copper sulfate
$CuSO_4(s)$	$+ 5H_2O(l)$	→	$CuSO_4{\cdot}5H_2O(s)$
white			blue

If you aren't sure about water of crystallisation, see Chapter 13.

This test works for anything that contains water, so would work with sodium chloride solution or sulfuric acid. It does *not* show that the water is pure.

Safety note: Avid skin contact with the copper salts.

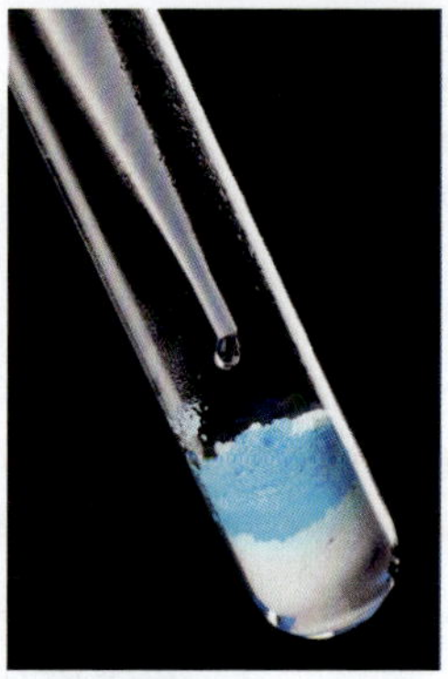

Figure 14.3 Testing for water with anhydrous copper(II) sulfate.

PHYSICAL TEST TO SHOW THAT WATER IS PURE

You can find out whether a sample of water is pure by measuring the freezing (melting) point or boiling point. Pure water freezes at exactly 0 °C and boils at exactly 100 °C at 1 atmosphere pressure. If the water is impure, it will usually freeze at a lower temperature and boil at a higher temperature.

TESTING FOR IONS

All salts contain at least one cation (positive ion) and anion (negative ion). In this section we will learn how to test for these anions and cations. We do the tests for these anions and cations separately.

FLAME TESTS

A flame test is used to show the presence of certain metal ions (cations) in a compound. A platinum or nichrome wire is dipped into concentrated hydrochloric acid and then into the salt you want to test, so that some salt sticks on the end. The wire and the salt are then held just within a non-luminous (roaring) Bunsen burner flame and the colour observed.

KEY POINT

If a new piece of wire is not being used, it is usually cleaned by dipping it into concentrated hydrochloric acid and then holding it in a non-luminous Bunsen flame. This is repeated until the wire doesn't give any colour to the flame.

HINT

The colour for sodium is described as yellow in the specification, but you will also see it described as orange. Both are usually acceptable.

KEY POINT

Lithium isn't the only ion to give a red flame colour. Strontium gives a very similar colour. The only way to be sure is to compare the flame colour next to the flame colour of a known compound of lithium or strontium.

Safety note: Wear eye protection and take great care with the concentrated acid. Do not get it on your skin and watch out for 'spitting' when heating it on the wire.

▲ Figure 14.4 Red shows lithium ions.

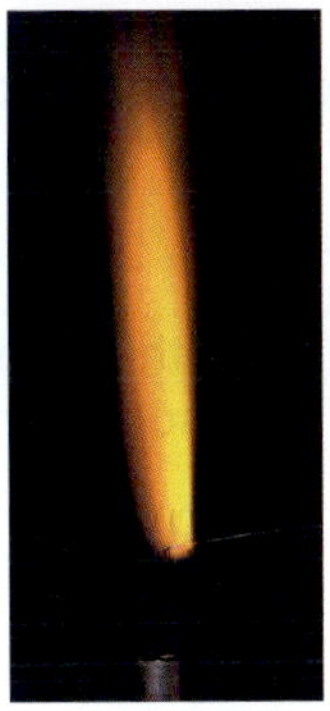

▲ Figure 14.5 Yellow shows the presence of sodium ions.

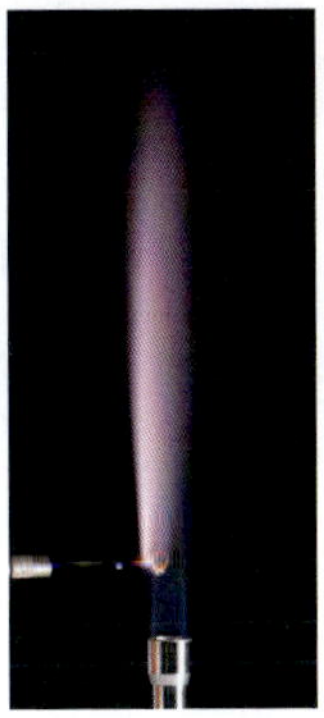

▲ Figure 14.6 Lilac shows potassium ions.

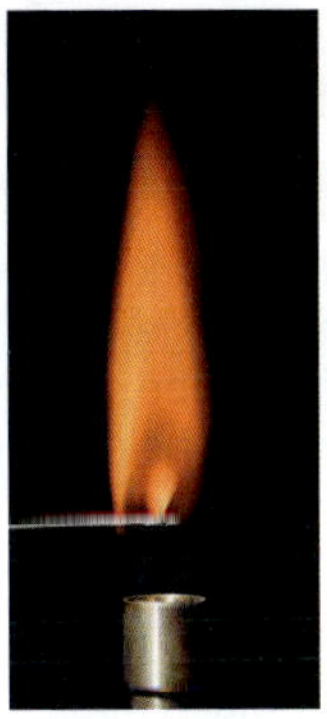

▲ Figure 14.7 Orange-red shows calcium ions.

▲ Figure 14.8 Blue-green shows the presence of copper(II) ions.

TESTING FOR CATIONS (POSITIVE IONS) USING SODIUM HYDROXIDE SOLUTION

Of the common hydroxides, only sodium, potassium and ammonium hydroxides dissolve in water to any extent. Most metal hydroxides are insoluble. That means that if you add sodium hydroxide solution to a solution containing the metal ions, you will get a precipitate of the metal hydroxide.

To carry out this test, you dissolve the salt in distilled (pure) water and put about 1 cm^3 in a test-tube. Add about the same volume of dilute sodium hydroxide solution. What you are looking for in most of these tests is the formation of a precipitate; the solution will go cloudy as a solid forms.

THE TEST FOR COPPER(II) IONS

HINT

Ionic equations, which just show the things that actually react, can be a useful way of showing what is happening in a precipitation reaction.

Formation of a blue precipitate shows the presence of copper(II) ions. The precipitate is copper(II) hydroxide.

$$Cu^{2+}(aq) + 2OH^-(aq) \rightarrow Cu(OH)_2(s)$$

Any copper(II) salt in solution will react with sodium hydroxide solution in this way. For example, with copper(II) sulfate solution, the full equation is:

$$CuSO_4(aq) + 2NaOH(aq) \rightarrow Cu(OH)_2(s) + Na_2SO_4(aq)$$

▲ Figure 14.9 The blue precipitate of copper(II) hydroxide.

THE TEST FOR IRON(III) IONS

Safety note: Wear eye protection for all these tests and avoid skin contact with the reactants and products.

Formation of an orange-brown precipitate shows the presence of iron(III) ions (Fe^{3+}). The precipitate is iron(III) hydroxide.

$$Fe^{3+}(aq) + 3OH^-(aq) \rightarrow Fe(OH)_3(s)$$

Any iron(III) compound in solution will give this precipitate. An example of a full equation might be:

$$FeCl_3(aq) + 3NaOH(aq) \rightarrow Fe(OH)_3(s) + 3NaCl(aq)$$

Notice how much more complicated the full equations for these reactions are. They also hide what is going on. Use ionic equations for **precipitation reactions** wherever possible.

▲ Figure 14.10 The orange-brown precipitate of iron(III) hydroxide.

THE TEST FOR IRON(II) IONS

KEY POINT

The green precipitate darkens on standing and turns orange-brown around the top of the tube. This is due to the iron(II) hydroxide being oxidised to iron(III) hydroxide by the air.

KEY POINT

You must carry out these three tests on a solution of the salt you are testing. If you tested the solid you would not be able to see whether a precipitate had been formed because there is already solid present.

Formation of a green precipitate shows the presence of iron(II) ions (Fe^{2+}). The precipitate is iron(II) hydroxide.

$$Fe^{2+}(aq) + 2OH^-(aq) \rightarrow Fe(OH)_2(s)$$

This could be the result of reacting, say, iron(II) sulfate solution with sodium hydroxide solution.

$$FeSO_4(aq) + 2NaOH(aq) \rightarrow Fe(OH)_2(s) + Na_2SO_4(aq)$$

Safety note: Wear eye protection for all these tests and avoid skin contact with the reactants and products.

Figure 14.11 The green precipitate of iron(II) hydroxide.

THE TEST FOR AMMONIUM IONS

KEY POINT

Recognising gases by smelling them has to be done with great care. In this case, there is usually so little ammonia gas present in the cold that it is safe to smell if you take the normal precautions. You shouldn't, however, make any attempt to smell the mixture when it is warm.
Safety note: Do not attempt to smell the ammonia gas if you have a breathing problem such as asthma.

This test shows the presence of an ammonium salt. Sodium hydroxide solution reacts with ammonium salts (either solid or in solution) to produce ammonia gas. In the cold, there is just enough ammonia gas produced for you to be able to smell it. If you warm it, you can test the gas coming off with a piece of damp red litmus paper or universal indicator paper. Ammonia is alkaline and turns the litmus paper/universal indicator blue. The ionic equation is:

$$NH_4^+(aq) + OH^-(aq) \rightarrow NH_3(g) + H_2O(l)$$

This test works on a sample of a solid or a solution as you are not looking for a precipitate.

A full equation for adding sodium hydroxide solution to solid ammonium chloride is:

$$NH_4Cl(s) + NaOH(aq) \rightarrow NaCl(aq) + NH_3(g) + H_2O(l)$$

Table 14.1 A summary of the reactions of positive ions with sodium hydroxide solution

Ion	Result of adding NaOH(aq)	Name of precipitate formed	Formula of precipitate
Cu^{2+}	blue precipitate	copper(II) hydroxide	$Cu(OH)_2$
Fe^{2+}	green precipitate	iron(II) hydroxide	$Fe(OH)_2$
Fe^{3+}	orange-brown precipitate	iron(III) hydroxide	$Fe(OH)_3$
NH_4^+	ammonia gas produced	no precipitate	

TESTING FOR CARBONATES (CO_3^{2-})

EXTENSION WORK

The ionic equation shows any carbonate reacting with any acid.

$CO_3^{2-}(s) + 2H^+(aq) \rightarrow CO_2(g) + H_2O(l)$

Add a little dilute hydrochloric acid to your sample of salt and look for fizzing/bubbles of gas. Fizzing indicates that a gas is given off. You can test the gas by bubbling it through limewater to show that it is carbon dioxide.

Most carbonates are insoluble in water and so you will usually be doing this test on a sample of a solid. Soluble carbonates are sodium carbonate, potassium carbonate and ammonium carbonate, and the test also works on solutions of these.

HINT

You can use any acid to do this test, but you have to be careful, especially with sulfuric acid, as some acid–carbonate combinations can produce an insoluble salt that coats the solid carbonate and stops the reaction. The test works well with dilute hydrochloric acid or dilute nitric acid.

Safety note: Wear eye protection for all these tests and avoid skin contact with the reactants and products.

For example, using zinc carbonate and dilute nitric acid:

$$ZnCO_3(s) + 2HNO_3(aq) \rightarrow Zn(NO_3)_2(aq) + CO_2(g) + H_2O(l)$$

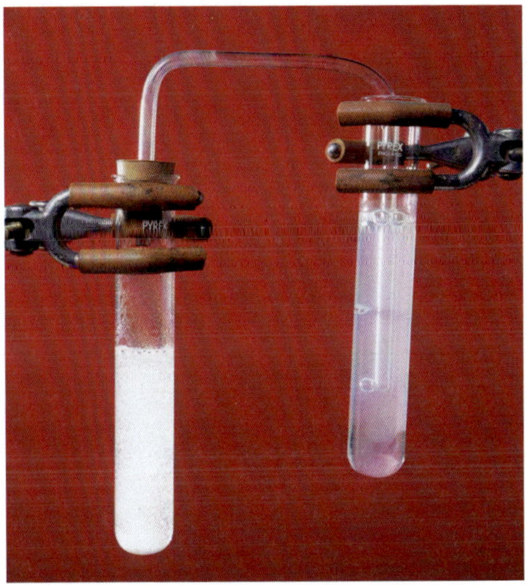

Figure 14.12 We can test to see if carbon dioxide is produced by bubbling the gas through limewater (in the tube on the right) and looking to see whether the limewater goes cloudy/milky (white precipitate of calcium carbonate formed).

TESTING FOR SULFATES (SO_4^{2-})

KEY POINT

You could also use nitric acid and barium nitrate solution in the same way.

Make a solution of your suspected sulfate in distilled (pure) water, add some *dilute hydrochloric acid* and then add some *barium chloride solution*. A sulfate will produce a white precipitate of barium sulfate.

$$Ba^{2+}(aq) + SO_4^{2-}(aq) \rightarrow BaSO_4(s)$$

You add acid to the solution to react with and remove other anions which might also produce white precipitates when you add the barium chloride solution. For example, if you didn't add acid, you would also obtain a white precipitate if there were carbonate ions present. This is because barium carbonate is also white and insoluble. The acid reacts with the carbonate ions and removes them. It is important to remember that the acid must be added *before* the barium chloride solution.

You must never acidify the solution with sulfuric acid because sulfuric acid contains sulfate ions. If you add those, you are bound to get a precipitate of barium sulfate because you have added sulfate ions.

TESTING FOR CHLORIDES (Cl^-), BROMIDES (Br^-) AND IODIDES (I^-)

Safety note: Wear eye protection for all these tests and avoid skin contact with the reactants and products.

KEY POINT

All of these precipitates tend to discolour to greys and pale purples on exposure to light.

Make a solution of your suspected chloride, bromide or iodide and add enough *dilute nitric acid* to make it acidic. Then add some *silver nitrate solution*.

A *white* precipitate (of silver chloride) shows the presence of chloride ions:

$$Ag^+(aq) + Cl^-(aq) \rightarrow AgCl(s)$$

A *cream* precipitate (of silver bromide) shows the presence of bromide ions:

$$Ag^+(aq) + Br^-(aq) \rightarrow AgBr(s)$$

A *yellow* precipitate (of silver iodide) shows the presence of iodide ions:

$$Ag^+(aq) + I^-(aq) \rightarrow AgI(s)$$

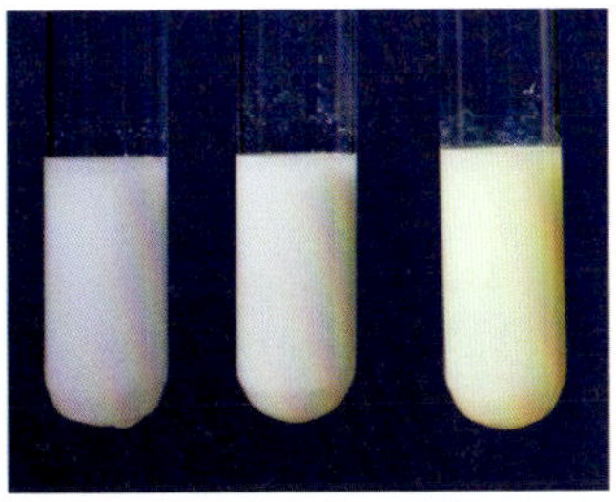

Figure 14.13 Precipitates of silver chloride, silver bromide and silver iodide

KEY POINT

The 1– ions formed by the halogens (Group 7) are collectively called *halide ions*. Chloride, bromide and iodide ions are all halide ions.

The acid is added to react with and remove other anions which might also produce precipitates with silver nitrate solution, for example carbonate and hydroxide ions. You must not use hydrochloric acid (or hydrobromic acid or hydroiodic acid) as you will be adding halide ions and you are certain to obtain a precipitate.

Table 14.2 A summary of the tests for negative ions (anions)

Ion	Test	Positive result	Product of reaction
CO_3^{2-}	add dilute hydrochloric acid then bubble any gas produced through limewater	fizzing, limewater goes cloudy (white precipitate)	CO_2 $CaCO_3$ (with limewater)
SO_4^{2-}	add dilute hydrochloric acid followed by barium chloride solution	white precipitate	$BaSO_4$
Cl^-	add dilute nitric acid followed by silver nitrate solution	white precipitate	AgCl
Br^-	add dilute nitric acid followed by silver nitrate solution	cream precipitate	AgBr
I^-	add dilute nitric acid followed by silver nitrate solution	yellow precipitate	AgI

CHAPTER QUESTIONS

SKILLS CRITICAL THINKING 5th

1 Name the gas being described in each of the following cases.

a A green gas that bleaches damp litmus paper.

b A gas that dissolves readily in water to produce a solution with a pH of about 11.

c A gas that produces a white precipitate with limewater.

d A gas that pops when a lighted splint is placed in it.

e A gas that relights a glowing splint.

SKILLS EXECUTIVE FUNCTION 6th

2 Describe in detail how you would carry out the following tests. In each case state whether you would carry out the test on the solid or a solution, and describe what you would expect to see happen.

a A flame test for lithium ions in lithium chloride.

b A test for ammonium ions in ammonium sulfate.

c A test for sulfate ions in ammonium sulfate.

d A test for carbonate ions in calcium carbonate.

e A test for iodide ions in potassium iodide.

3 **A** is an orange solid, which dissolves in water to give an orange solution. When sodium hydroxide solution is added to a solution of **A**, an orange-brown precipitate, **B**, is formed. Adding dilute nitric acid and silver nitrate solution to a solution of **A** gives a white precipitate, **C**.

SKILLS CRITICAL THINKING

a State the names of **A**, **B** and **C**.

SKILLS PROBLEM SOLVING 9th

b Write equations (full or ionic) for the reactions producing **B** and **C**.

SKILLS PROBLEM SOLVING, CRITICAL THINKING

6th

4 **D** is a green crystalline solid that dissolves in water to give a very pale green solution. Addition of sodium hydroxide solution to a solution of **D** produces a green precipitate, **E**, which turns orange-brown around the top after standing in air. Addition of dilute hydrochloric acid and barium chloride solution to a solution of **D** gives a white precipitate, **F**.

a State the names of **D**, **E** and **F**.

SKILLS PROBLEM SOLVING

9th

b Write equations (full or ionic) for the reactions producing **E** and **F**.

6th

5 **G** is a colourless crystalline solid which reacts with dilute nitric acid to give a colourless solution, **H**, and a colourless, odourless gas, **I**, which turns limewater milky. **G** has a lilac flame colour.

SKILLS CRITICAL THINKING

a State the names of **G**, **H** and **I**.

SKILLS PROBLEM SOLVING

9th

b Write an equation (full or ionic) for the reaction between **G** and dilute nitric acid.

6th

6 **J** is a colourless solid. When it is warmed with sodium hydroxide solution it produces a gas, **K**, which turns damp universal indicator paper blue. When nitric acid, followed by silver nitrate solution, is added to a solution of **J**, a cream precipitate of **L** is formed.

SKILLS CRITICAL THINKING

a State the names of **J**, **K** and **L**.

SKILLS PROBLEM SOLVING

9th

b Write an ionic equation for the formation of the cream precipitate.

SKILLS EXECUTVE FUNCTION

5th

7 A student has found that her sample of potassium nitrate is contaminated with small amounts of a green solid. She picks out a small piece of the green solid and finds that it is insoluble in water.

SKILLS CRITICAL THINKING

6th

a Describe how you would make a pure sample of potassium nitrate from the impure mixture.

b The student believes that the green solid could be copper(II) carbonate. Describe a series of tests that the student could use to confirm this.

5th

8 A student finds a bottle containing a colourless liquid in the laboratory.

a Describe a test to show that the bottle contains water.

4th

b Describe a test to show whether it is pure water.

SKILLS EXECUTIVE FUNCTION, REASONING

7th

c The student carried out the test in b and it showed that the water was not pure. He then carried out some more tests to try to identify the solution. The following results were obtained:

Test	Result
add sodium hydroxide solution	no visible reaction but the test-tube became warm
add dilute hydrochloric acid	no reaction
add dilute hydrochloric acid followed by barium chloride solution	no reaction
add nitric acid followed by silver nitrate solution	white precipitate

Explain what could be present in the bottle and how the student could confirm this.

UNIT QUESTIONS

You may need to refer to the Periodic Table on page 708.

SKILLS REASONING 8th

1 Lithium, sodium and potassium are three elements in Group 1 of the Periodic Table. All these elements are stored under oil so that they cannot react with air and water.

a Explain in terms of the structure of the atoms why these three elements are all placed in Group 1 of the Periodic Table. **(1)**

SKILLS CRITICAL THINKING 5th

b State the name of the product obtained when potassium reacts with air. **(1)**

c Only three of the statements about the reaction of lithium with water given below are true. Put a cross next to each of the correct statements. **(3)**

Statement	
The water turns blue	
The piece of lithium floats	
The lithium burns with a lilac flame	
Hydrogen gas is formed	
The lithium explodes	
The final solution is alkaline	
Lithium reacts more violently than sodium	

d Some data about the physical properties of lithium, sodium and potassium are shown in the table.

	Melting point / °C	Boiling point / °C	Density / g /cm^3
Li	181	1342	0.53
Na	98	883	0.97
K	63	760	0.86

Caesium is another element in Group 1 of the Periodic Table.

7th

i Which of the following are likely to be properties of caesium? Put crosses in two boxes. **(2)**

It forms a 1+ ion in compounds	
It has a melting point of 60 °C	
It is a non-metal	
It reacts with water and air	
It is an alkali	

SKILLS REASONING 8th

ii Explain why the data in the table cannot be used to predict whether caesium has a higher or lower density than potassium. **(2)**

(Total 9 marks)

SKILLS REASONING 6th

2 A student carried out some reactions between solutions of chlorine, bromine and iodine, and solutions of potassium halides. Some of their results are shown in the table:

	Potassium chloride solution	Potassium bromide solution	Potassium iodide solution
Chlorine solution		orange solution formed	
Bromine solution			
Iodine solution	no reaction	no reaction	

a Explain why the student did not carry out the experiments shaded in dark grey in the table. **(2)**

SKILLS INTERPRETATION

b Complete the table. **(3)**

SKILLS PROBLEM SOLVING 7th

c Write a word equation for the reaction between chlorine and potassium bromide. **(1)**

8th

d Complete and balance the ionic equation for the reaction between chlorine and potassium bromide solutions: **(3)**

$Cl_2(aq) + Br^-(aq) \rightarrow$

SKILLS REASONING 9th

e Explain in terms of electrons why the reaction between chlorine and potassium bromide solution is described as a redox reaction. **(3)**

f Chlorine can be prepared in the laboratory by the reaction between concentrated hydrochloric acid and potassium manganate(VII). The equation for the reaction is:

$2KMnO_4 + 16HCl \rightarrow 2KCl + 2MnCl_2 + 8H_2O + \ldots Cl_2$

SKILLS PROBLEM SOLVING 8th

i The equation is not balanced. Give the number that should be put in front of Cl_2 in order to balance it. **(1)**

SKILLS EXECUTIVE FUNCTION 5th

ii Describe a test for chlorine gas. **(2)**

Test:

Positive result:

iii When chlorine dissolves in water some chloride ions are formed. Describe a chemical test to show that a solution contains chloride ions. **(3)**

Test:

Positive result: **(Total 18 marks)**

SKILLS CRITICAL THINKING 5th

3 a State the name of the most common gas in the air. **(1)**

b A student carries out an experiment to measure the percentage of oxygen in the air. He used the following apparatus:

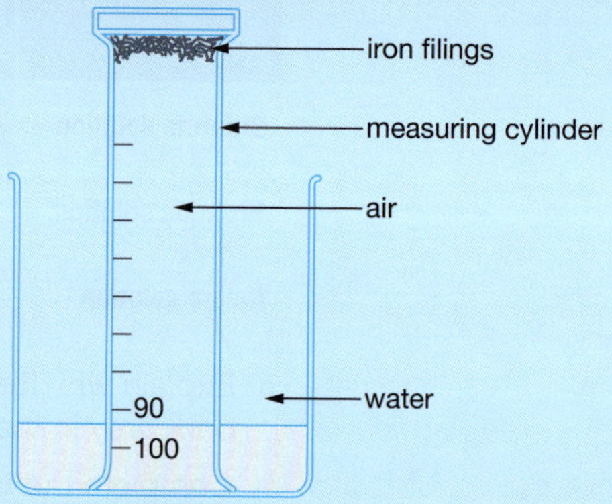

He carried out the following procedure:

- Put some damp iron filings at the bottom of a 100 cm^3 measuring cylinder.
- Invert the measuring cylinder in a beaker of water.
- Take the initial reading of the level of water in the measuring cylinder.
- Take a reading of the level of water in the measuring cylinder every day for 1 week.

The student's results were:

initial reading on measuring cylinder / cm^3	94
reading on measuring cylinder after 1 day / cm^3	85
reading on measuring cylinder after 2 days / cm^3	80
reading on measuring cylinder after 3 days / cm^3	77
reading on measuring cylinder after 4 days / cm^3	76
reading on measuring cylinder after 5 days / cm^3	75
reading on measuring cylinder after 6 days / cm^3	75
reading on measuring cylinder after 7 days / cm^3	75

SKILLS REASONING

i Explain why the water level rises. **(2)**

6th

ii Explain why the reading on the measuring cylinder eventually remains constant. **(1)**

SKILLS CRITICAL THINKING

iii Give the name of the iron compound that is formed in this experiment. **(1)**

SKILLS REASONING

iv The student trapped the gas in the tube and put a lighted splint into it. Explain why the splint goes out. **(2)**

SKILLS PROBLEM SOLVING

v Using the results in the table, calculate the percentage oxygen present in the air in the measuring cylinder after 1 day. **(4)**

SKILLS CRITICAL THINKING 7th

vi The student decided that 1 week is too long to wait for results so suggested using a more reactive metal such as calcium or lithium in this experiment. Explain one reason, other than that it might be too dangerous, why the experiment will not work with these metals. **(2)**

SKILLS EXECUTIVE FUNCTION 5th

vii Suggest one change that the student could make to the experiment so he does not have to wait so long for the results. **(1)**

c Sulfur reacts with oxygen. A teacher burns a piece of sulfur in a gas jar of oxygen.

SKILLS CRITICAL THINKING 5th

i State the colour of the flame. **(1)**

SKILLS PROBLEM SOLVING 9th

ii Write a balanced equation for the reaction that occurs. **(1)**

SKILLS REASONING 6th

iii A few drops of litmus solution are put into the gas jar at the end of the experiment. State and explain what colour will be seen. **(2)**

d Sodium reacts with oxygen to form sodium oxide.

SKILLS PROBLEM SOLVING 9th

i Write a chemical equation for this reaction. **(2)**

SKILLS CRITICAL THINKING 5th

ii When sodium oxide reacts with water an alkaline solution is formed. State the name of the ion responsible for making the solution alkaline. **(1)**

(Total 21 marks)

SKILLS DECISION MAKING 6th

4 This question is about copper(II) sulfate solution.

a Describe a procedure to make a solution of copper(II) sulfate starting from copper(II) oxide. **(3)**

5th

b Describe a chemical test that can be used to show that the solution contains sulfate ions. **(2)**

SKILLS CRITICAL THINKING

c A student added some sodium hydroxide solution to the copper(II) sulfate solution. State the name of the blue precipitate formed. **(1)**

d A student carried out an experiment to investigate displacement reactions of three different metals with copper(II) sulfate solution. She followed this method:

- Put some copper(II) sulfate solution into a polystyrene cup.
- Measure the initial temperature.
- Add some metal.
- Stir the solution.
- Record the maximum temperature.

SKILLS EXECUTIVE FUNCTION

i The student uses the same amount in moles of each metal in the experiments. State two other variables the student should keep the same in this experiment to allow her to be able to compare the different metals. **(2)**

SKILLS ANALYSIS 6th

ii The student recorded the following data.

Metal	Temperature change / °C
zinc	15
silver	0
nickel	7

Arrange the four metals, zinc, silver, copper and nickel, in order of reactivity, starting with the most reactive. **(1)**

SKILLS REASONING 7th

iii The student did not carry out the experiment with copper and copper(II) sulfate. Predict, giving a reason, what the temperature rise would be for this experiment. **(2)**

8th

iv The student carried out the experiment using 3.25 g of zinc (0.05 mol). She then used the same amount in moles of nickel and silver. Another student decided to use the same mass (3.25 g) of each metal. The results of the two students were very similar. Suggest reasons for this. **(3)**

SKILLS PROBLEM SOLVING 8th

v The ionic equation for the reaction between copper(II) sulfate solution and nickel is:

$$Ni(s) + Cu^{2+}(aq) \rightarrow Ni^{2+}(aq) + Cu(s)$$

Use the ionic equation to explain whether nickel is oxidised or reduced in this reaction. **(2)**

SKILLS EXECUTIVE FUNCTION 6th

e The student wants to make some anhydrous copper(II) sulfate. Describe how she could do this starting with copper(II) sulfate solution. **(2)**

f The student carried out a flame test on the anhydrous copper(II) sulfate.

5th

i Describe how to carry out a flame test. **(2)**

SKILLS CRITICAL THINKING

ii State the colour of the flame produced when the student carried out a flame test on copper(II) sulfate. **(1)**

(Total 21 marks)

SKILLS INTERPRETATION 8th

5 This question is about hydrogen chloride and hydrochloric acid.

a Hydrochloric acid is made when hydrogen chloride dissolves in water. Draw a dot-and-cross diagram for hydrogen chloride. **(2)**

SKILLS CRITICAL THINKING 7th

b When hydrogen chloride dissolves in water an acid–base reaction occurs. The equation for this reaction is:

$$HCl(aq) + H_2O(l) \rightarrow Cl^-(aq) + H_3O^+(aq)$$

Explain why this is classified as an acid–base reaction and identify the acid and the base. **(3)**

c A student wants to show that an unknown solution she has been given contains chloride ions. She puts a small amount of the solution in a test-tube and adds dilute nitric acid followed by silver nitrate solution.

5th

i Describe what would be seen if the solution contains chloride ions. **(1)**

7th

ii Explain why hydrochloric acid cannot be added instead of nitric acid. **(2)**

SKILLS PROBLEM SOLVING 9th

d Write an equation, including state symbols, for the reaction that occurs when hydrochloric acid is added to solid copper(II) carbonate. **(3)**

(Total 11 marks)

SKILLS CRITICAL THINKING 5th

6 This question is about chemical tests.

Samples of a very pale green solution, **X**, were tested as follows:

Test	Observation
A sample of **X** was acidified with dilute nitric acid and silver nitrate solution was added	A white precipitate (**A**) was formed
A small amount of sodium hydroxide solution was added to a sample of solution **X**	A dark green precipitate (**B**) was formed
Chlorine was bubbled through a sample of **X**	The pale green solution turned yellow (solution **C**)
A small amount of sodium hydroxide solution was added to solution **C**	An orange-brown precipitate (**D**) was formed

a Use the results from the first two tests to identify **X**. **(2)**

6th

b State the name and formula of **B**. **(2)**

c State the name and formula of **D**. **(2)**

7th

d Explain what type of reaction occurred when chlorine was bubbled through **X**. **(2)**

(Total 8 marks)

CHEMISTRY UNIT 3 PHYSICAL CHEMISTRY

In a world where the population has more than trebled in the last 100 years, fighting against hunger is an extremely important challenge. At the beginning of the 20th century scientists developed industrial processes to make artificial fertilisers that can be used to increase crop yields. In order to develop these processes, chemists and chemical engineers from around the world have had to understand the principles of energy changes, rates of reaction and reversibility. The world's resources are limited and it is vital that these processes are as efficient and environmentally friendly as possible. This is also the work of scientists.

15 ENERGETICS

Some chemical reactions produce heat. Others need to be heated constantly to make them occur at all. This chapter explores some examples of both kinds of reaction and examines how energy changes during reactions can be measured by experiments.

LEARNING OBJECTIVES

- Know that chemical reactions in which heat energy is given out are described as exothermic, and those in which heat energy is taken in are described as endothermic
- Describe simple calorimetry experiments for reactions such as combustion, displacement, dissolving and neutralisation
- Calculate the heat energy change from a measured temperature change using the expression $Q = mc\Delta T$
- Calculate the molar enthalpy change (ΔH) from the heat energy change, Q
- Practical: Investigate the temperature changes accompanying some of the following types of change:
  - salts dissolving in water
  - neutralisation reactions
  - displacement reactions
  - combustion reactions

EXOTHERMIC REACTIONS

Some chemical reactions give out energy in the form of heat. A reaction that *gives out heat to the surroundings* is said to be **exothermic**. If you are holding a test-tube in which an exothermic reaction is occurring, you will notice that the test-tube *gets warmer*.

An example of an exothermic reaction is adding water to calcium oxide. If you add water to solid calcium oxide, the heat produced is enough to boil the water and produce steam. Calcium hydroxide is produced.

$$CaO(s) + H_2O(l) \rightarrow Ca(OH)_2(s)$$

In an *exothermic* reaction, *the products of the reaction have less (chemical) energy than the reactants*. In the reaction, *chemical energy* (stored in the bonds of chemicals) *is converted to heat energy*, which is released to the surroundings. The temperature of the reaction mixture and its surroundings *goes up*.

DID YOU KNOW?
Calcium oxide is known as **quicklime**. Adding water to it is described as *slaking* it. The calcium hydroxide produced is known as **slaked lime**.

Safety note: It is less hazardous to use a lump of calcium oxide, rather than powered calcium oxide

▲ Figure 15.1 Calcium oxide reacting with water.

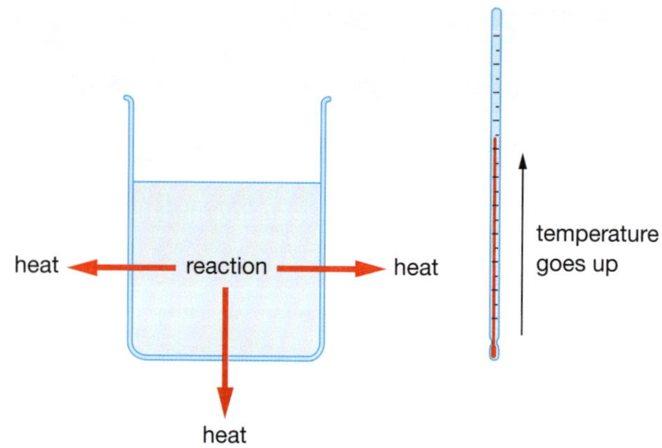

▲ Figure 15.2 In an exothermic reaction, chemical energy is converted to heat energy. Heat is released so the temperature goes up.

You will come across lots of exothermic reactions in this course. Some examples are given below.

COMBUSTION REACTIONS

▲ Figure 15.3 The burning of hydrogen is used in oxy-hydrogen cutting equipment underwater.

Any reaction that produces a flame is exothermic. Burning things produces heat energy.

For instance, hydrogen burns in oxygen, producing water and lots of heat:

$$2H_2(g) + O_2(g) \rightarrow 2H_2O(l)$$

Apart from burning, other exothermic changes include:

- the reactions of metals with acids
- neutralisation reactions
- displacement reactions.

THE REACTIONS OF METALS WITH ACIDS

REMINDER

This reaction is described in detail in Chapter 11 (pages 373–374).

When magnesium reacts with dilute sulfuric acid, for example, the mixture gets very warm:

$$Mg(s) + H_2SO_4(aq) \rightarrow MgSO_4(aq) + H_2(g)$$

NEUTRALISATION REACTIONS

REMINDER

You can read about this reaction in Chapter 12 (page 384). We will investigate how much heat energy is released in a typical neutralisation reaction later in this chapter (pages 423–425).

About the only interesting thing that you can observe happening when sodium hydroxide solution reacts with dilute hydrochloric acid is that the temperature rises:

$$NaOH(aq) + HCl(aq) \rightarrow NaCl(aq) + H_2O(l)$$

DISPLACEMENT REACTIONS

The thermite reaction between powdered aluminium and iron(III) oxide is a displacement (competition) reaction. This reaction releases a large amount of heat, which can be used in railway welding:

$$2Al(s) + Fe_2O_3(s) \rightarrow 2Fe(l) + Al_2O_3(s)$$

ENTHALPY CHANGE OF A REACTION

KEY POINT

ΔH is pronounced 'delta *H*'. The Greek letter Δ is used to mean 'change in'. ΔH means 'change in heat'. Note: it is not possible to measure how much enthalpy (*H*) something has – you can only measure the change in enthalpy (ΔH) when it reacts.

REMINDER

The mole is a unit for the amount of a substance. You can read more about it in Chapter 5.

KEY POINT

The units for ΔH can be written as kJ/mol or kJ mol^{-1}.

You can measure the amount of heat energy taken in or released in a chemical reaction. It is called the **enthalpy change** of the reaction and is given the symbol ΔH. The enthalpy change is *the amount of heat energy taken in or given out in a chemical reaction*. It is the difference between the energy of the products and the energy of the reactants.

ΔH is given a minus or a plus sign to show whether heat is being given out or absorbed by the reaction. You always look at it from the point of view of the reactants. For an exothermic reaction, ΔH is given a *negative* number because the reactants are *losing* energy as heat. That heat is transferred to the surroundings, which then get warmer. ΔH is measured in units of kJ/mol (kilojoules per mole).

In an equation, the amount of heat given out or taken in can be shown as, for example:

$$Mg(s) + H_2SO_4(aq) \rightarrow MgSO_4(aq) + H_2(g) \quad \Delta H = -466.9\,kJ/mol$$

The ΔH written next to an equation represents the enthalpy change of the reaction, i.e. 466.9 kJ of heat is given out when *one mole* of magnesium reacts in this way. You know heat has been given out because ΔH has a negative sign.

ENDOTHERMIC REACTIONS

A reaction that absorbs heat from the surroundings is said to be **endothermic**. If you hold a test-tube in which an endothermic reaction is occurring you will notice that it *gets colder*.

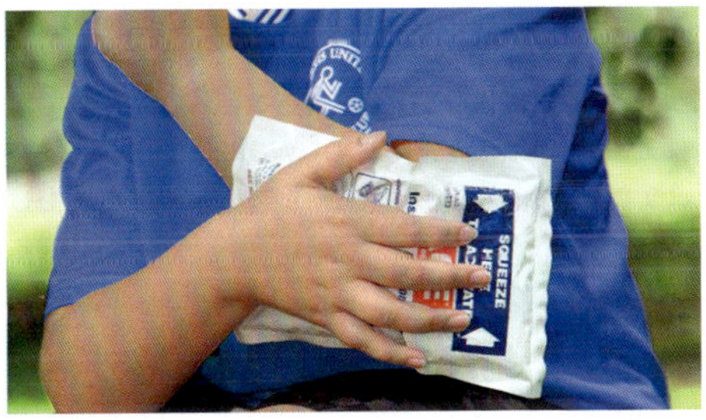

Figure 15.4 A boy using a cold pack to relieve pain in his elbow. Endothermic reactions occur in the chemical cold pack to absorb heat from the surroundings and reduce the temperature of his arm.

In an endothermic reaction, *the products have more (chemical) energy than the reactants*. In order to supply the extra energy that is needed to convert the reactants (lower energy) into the products (higher energy), heat energy needs to be absorbed from the surroundings. This *heat energy is converted to chemical energy* (energy stored in the bonds of chemicals). The temperature of the reaction mixture and the surroundings *goes down* because heat energy has been converted into a different form of energy.

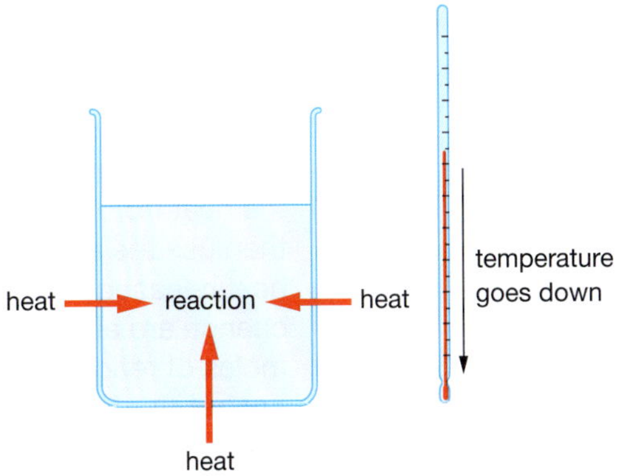

Figure 15.5 In an endothermic reaction, heat energy is converted to chemical energy. Heat is absorbed so the temperature goes down.

You have seen the *thermal decomposition* of metal carbonates before in Chapter 10. These are examples of endothermic reactions. You have to heat a carbonate constantly to make it decompose.

REMINDER

Not all reactions that have to be heated are endothermic reactions. Sometimes we just heat something to make it go faster.

For example, copper(II) carbonate (green) decomposes on heating to produce copper(II) oxide (black).

$$CuCO_3(s) \rightarrow CuO(s) + CO_2(g)$$

Similarly, zinc carbonate decomposes to form zinc oxide when heated.

$$ZnCO_3(s) \rightarrow ZnO(s) + CO_2(g)$$

MEASURING ENTHALPY CHANGES OF REACTIONS

Here we discuss how we can measure how much heat is taken in or given out by a chemical reaction, in other words the enthalpy change of a reaction.

SPECIFIC HEAT CAPACITY

KEY POINT

The unit for specific heat capacity is J/g/°C or J g^{-1} °C^{-1}.

When we heat something up, it gets hotter. The **specific heat capacity** tells us about *how much* energy has to be put in to increase the temperature of something. The specific heat capacity of a substance is defined as *the amount of heat needed to raise the temperature of 1 gram of a substance by 1 °C.*

For water, the value is 4.18 J/g/°C (joules per gram per degree Celsius). This means that 4.18 J of heat energy is needed if we want to increase the temperature of 1 g of water by 1 °C. If you want the temperature of 1 g of water to go up by 2 °C, then 4.18 × 2 = 8.36 J of heat energy must be supplied. If now you have 2 g of water, then 2 × 8.36 J of energy would be needed to raise the temperature by 2 °C.

KEY POINT

Again, we are using the delta (Δ) symbol to indicate a change, but this time a temperature change.
The concept of specific heat capacity also applies to the cooling of a substance. For example, to cool 1 g of water by 1 °C we need to take out 4.18 J of energy.

The amount of heat energy required is *directly proportional* to the mass (m) and the temperature change (ΔT) of the substance. The following equation can be used to calculate how much heat energy needs to be supplied to raise the temperature of mass m by ΔT °C:

heat energy change = mass × specific heat capacity × temperature change

$$Q = m \times c \times \Delta T$$

CALORIMETRY EXPERIMENTS FOR DETERMINING THE ENTHALPY CHANGES OF REACTIONS

It is fairly uncomplicated to measure the amount of heat absorbed or given out in several kinds of chemical reactions and physical changes. The technique used to do this is called **calorimetry** and it is based on the idea that if we use the heat from a reaction to heat another substance, such as water, we can then use the equation introduced above ($Q = mc\Delta T$) to calculate the amount of heat released. Here the mass, the specific heat capacity and the temperature change are all referring to *the substance heated*. If we know how many moles of reactants are used in the reaction, we can then work out the **molar enthalpy change**, ΔH, of the reaction in the unit kJ/mol.

The following activity illustrates how we can use calorimetry to determine the molar enthalpy change of combustion of an alcohol, i.e. how much heat energy is released when 1 mole of alcohol burns.

> **Safety note:** Wear eye protection. Do not carry a lit spirit burner and do not fill or re-fill one when there is a naked flame nearby.

KEY POINT

A *calorimeter* is simply something that we do a calorimetry experiment in; here it is a copper can, in other experiments it can be a polystyrene cup.

KEY POINT

You may see other versions of this experiment recommending a different temperature rise or suggesting that you heat the water for a fixed number of minutes. There's no ideal answer to this. The higher the temperature the water reaches, the greater the heat losses during the experiment. On the other hand, if you just increase the temperature of the water by a small amount, errors in reading the thermometer or in finding the mass change of the alcohol become too significant.

ACTIVITY 1

▼ PRACTICAL: MEASURING ENTHALPY CHANGES IN COMBUSTION REACTIONS

One of the most common calorimetry experiments at International GCSE is to measure the amount of heat given off when a number of small **alcohols** are burned. You could use methanol, ethanol, propan-1-ol and butan-1-ol.

The alcohols are burned in a small spirit burner, and the heat produced is used to heat some water in a copper can (the calorimeter).

The following procedure could be used:

- Measure 100 cm^3 of cold water using a measuring cylinder and transfer the water to a copper can.
- Take the initial temperature of the water.
- Weigh a spirit-burner containing ethanol with its lid *on*. The lid should be kept on when the **wick** is not lit to prevent the alcohol from evaporating.
- Arrange the apparatus as shown in Figure 15.6 so that the spirit-burner can be used to heat the water in the copper can. The apparatus is shielded as far as possible to prevent draughts.
- Light the wick to heat the water. Stop heating when you have a reasonable temperature rise of water (say, about 40.0 °C). The flame can be extinguished by putting the lid back on the wick.
- Stir the water thoroughly and measure the maximum temperature of the water.
- Weigh the spirit-burner again with its lid *on*.
- The experiment can be repeated with the same alcohol to check for reliability, and then carried out again with whatever other alcohols are available.

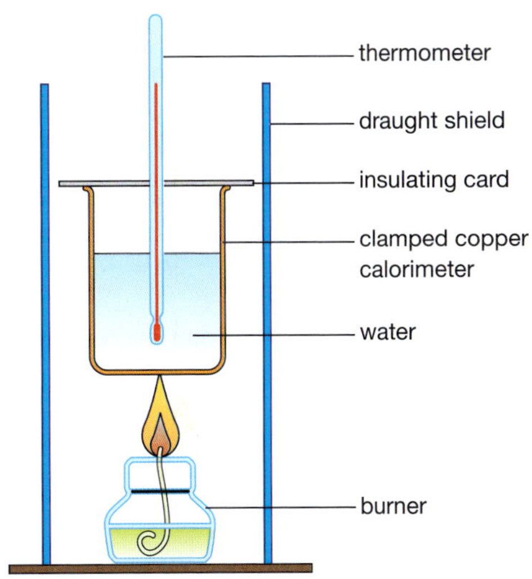

▲ Figure 15.6 A calorimetry experiment to measure the enthalpy change of combustion of alcohols.

SAMPLE DATA

volume of water / cm^3	100
mass of burner + ethanol before experiment / g	137.36
mass of burner + ethanol after experiment / g	136.58
original temperature of water / °C	21.5
final temperature of water / °C	62.8

Combustion is an exothermic reaction so the temperature of the water goes up. As ethanol is burned, the total mass of the burner and ethanol goes down.

Using the above data we can determine how much heat is released when one mole of an alcohol is burned, that is, the molar enthalpy change of combustion.

CALCULATIONS FOR ACTIVITY 1

We are going to use the equation $Q = mc\Delta T$ so we need to find out what each quantity is.

Temperature change of water = $\Delta T = 62.8 - 21.5 = 41.3\,°C$.

Mass of water being heated = m = 100 g, the density of water is approximately 1 g/cm^3 at room temperature, so 100 cm^3 of water has a mass of 100 g.

c is the specific heat capacity of the water (it is the water that is being heated): $c = 4.18$ J/g/°C

Heat gained by water = $Q = mc\Delta T = 100 \times 4.18 \times 41.3 = 17\,260$ J.

Divide Q by 1000 to give energy in kJ = 17.26 kJ.

KEY POINT

The enthalpy change when 1 mole of a substance is burned is called the *enthalpy change of combustion*.

This means 17.26 kJ of heat energy is released by the combustion of the ethanol in this experiment. To calculate the amount of heat produced when 1 mole of ethanol, CH_3CH_2OH, burns, you need to find out how many moles of ethanol are burned in your experiment.

Mass of ethanol burned = decrease in the mass of the burner
= 137.36 – 136.58 = 0.78 g

HINT

We have quoted the final answer to *3 significant figures*. In the exam, it is usually best to quote answers to 3 significant figures. When we are doing experiments we should actually base our answers on *the piece of data with the fewest significant figures*. When you are doing calculations carry more significant figures through on your calculator and then round the value at the end.

Ethanol has the formula C_2H_5OH. We can calculate the relative molecular mass of ethanol by adding up the relative atomic masses:
$(2 \times 12) + (5 \times 1) + 16 + 1 = 46$

Number of moles (n) of ethanol, CH_3CH_2OH, burned

$$n = \frac{\text{mass } (m)}{\text{relative molecular mass } (M_r)} = \frac{0.78}{46} = 0.01696\text{ mol}$$

Molar enthalpy change of combustion of ethanol (ΔH)

$$\Delta H = \frac{\text{heat energy change } (Q)}{\text{number of moles of ethanol burned } (n)}$$

$$= \frac{17.26}{0.01696} = 1020\text{ kJ/mol}$$

HINT

Always remember to put in the sign of the enthalpy change at this stage. You will be able to see whether the reaction is endothermic (ΔH +) or exothermic (ΔH –) from looking at the original temperature change: does it go up (exothermic) or down (endothermic)?

The amount of heat released in the **complete combustion** of 1 mole of ethanol is therefore:

$$CH_3CH_2OH + 3O_2 \rightarrow 2CO_2 + 3H_2O \qquad \Delta H = -1020\text{ kJ/mol}$$

The negative sign shows that heat is released and the combustion reaction is exothermic.

EVALUATION OF THE EXPERIMENTAL RESULTS

How accurate is the figure of −1020 kJ/mol for the enthalpy change of the combustion of ethanol? The accepted value found in data booklets for ethanol is −1370 kJ/mol, which means that 1370 kJ of heat should be given out when 1 mole of ethanol burns. You can see that the value we obtained is less exothermic than expected; our reaction seemed to give out less heat than expected.

There are many sources of error in this experiment, in particular *large amounts of heat loss*.

The warm water gives out heat to the air, heat is lost from the flame, which goes straight into the air rather than into the water, and heat is used to raise the temperature of the copper can and the thermometer.

Another major source of error is the *incomplete combustion* of alcohol. We will talk about incomplete combustion in more detail in Chapter 18. Incomplete combustion of an alcohol occurs when there is not enough oxygen present. Incomplete combustion releases less heat than complete combustion. We can see that the combustion in Activity 1 is incomplete because the flame of the wick is often yellow orange rather than blue, and **soot** (carbon) is produced at the bottom of the copper can. If the combustion is complete, the flame should be blue and carbon dioxide should be produced instead of carbon.

EXTENSION WORK

A bomb calorimeter can be used to obtain more accurate values of the enthalpy changes of combustion. The substance to be combusted is ignited electrically and burns in the presence of pure oxygen. The heat transferred to both water and the calorimeter itself is determined to give a more accurate value of the enthalpy change.

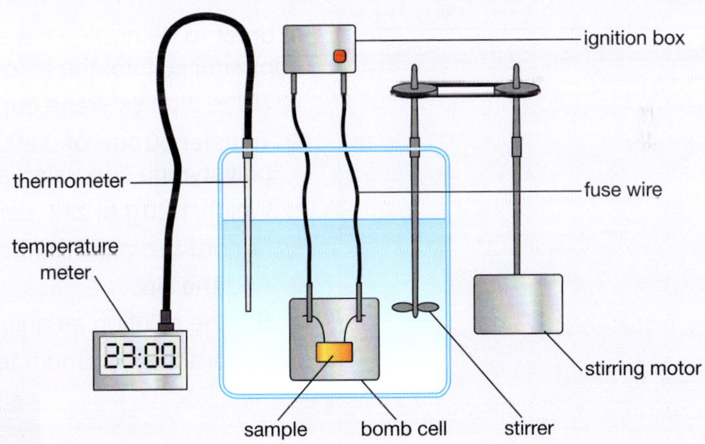

▲ Figure 15.7 Bomb calorimeter

That doesn't mean you can't use this experiment to make useful comparisons. If you repeat it with other alcohols, under conditions that are as similar as possible, you can find how the heat evolved (given out) changes as the alcohol gets bigger.

In Figure 15.8 we can see that the combustion reaction gets more exothermic as the alcohol chain becomes longer. In other words, longer alcohols give out more heat energy per mole when they burn than shorter ones.

The increase in the heat evolved as alcohol chain lengthens is regular. The difference between one alcohol and the next is always an extra CH_2, and so the number of extra bonds broken and made (see below) increases in a regular way. That means that the heat evolved will also increase in a regular way.

KEY POINT

You may sometimes see these plotted as smooth graphs, but that is technically wrong. A smooth curve should only be used for a continuous independent variable, one which can take any value. There is no such thing as an alcohol with 0.5 or 1.64 carbon atoms! The number of carbon atoms is a **non-continuous variable** because it can only take whole number values.

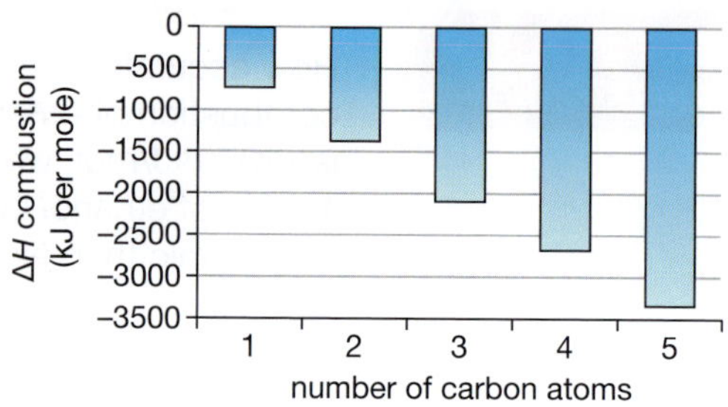

▲ Figure 15.8 Molar enthalpy change of the combustion of alcohols.

WORKING OUT ENTHALPY CHANGES FOR REACTIONS INVOLVING SOLUTIONS USING CALORIMETRY EXPERIMENTS

You can use very similar methods for measuring molar enthalpy changes in displacement reactions (e.g. zinc and copper(II) sulfate solution), dissolving (e.g. dissolving ammonium chloride in water to form a solution) and neutralisation reactions (e.g. between potassium hydroxide solution and dilute hydrochloric acid). These experiments also involve heating water, but this time the water is part of the solutions we are using. We will look at how to do this in the next few practicals.

Safety note: Avoid skin contact with the chemicals.

ACTIVITY 2

▼ PRACTICAL: MEASURING ENTHALPY CHANGES FOR DISPLACEMENT REACTIONS

In order to determine the enthalpy change of the reaction of zinc and copper(II) sulfate, the following procedure could be used:

- Place a polystyrene cup in a 250 cm^3 glass beaker.
- Transfer 50 cm^3 of 0.200 mol/dm^3 copper(II) sulfate solution into the polystyrene cup using a measuring cylinder.
- Weigh 1.20 g of zinc using a weighing boat on a balance.
- Record the initial temperature of the copper(II) sulfate solution.
- Add the zinc.
- Stir the solution as quickly as possible.
- Record the maximum temperature reached.

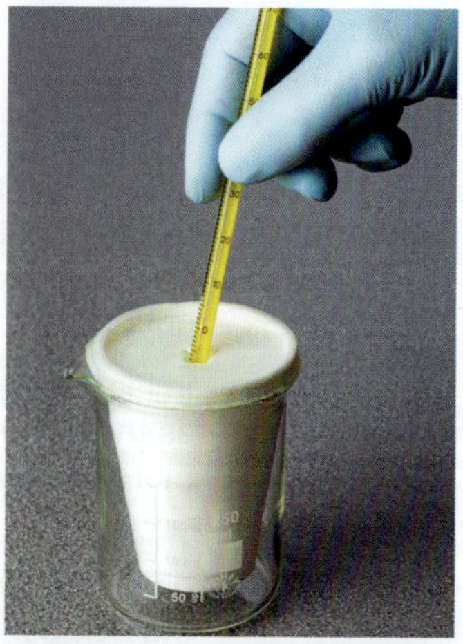

▲ 15.9 A calorimetry experiment to measure the enthalpy change of a displacement reaction.

SAMPLE DATA

initial temperature of copper(II) sulfate solution / °C	17.0
maximum temperature of the reaction mixture / °C	27.3

We can use this data to calculate the enthalpy change for this displacement reaction, when 1 mole of copper(II) sulfate reacts with zinc.

CALCULATIONS FOR ACTIVITY 2

Heat given out in this reaction: $Q = mc\Delta T = 50 \times 4.18 \times (27.3 - 17.0)$

$= 2152.7\,\text{J}$

$= 2.1527\,\text{kJ}$

Here we assume the following:

1. The density of the copper sulfate solution is the same as that of water, so 1 cm^3 of solution has a mass of 1 g.
2. The specific heat capacity of the mixture is the same as that of water. This is a fairly reasonable assumption because the reaction mixture is mostly water.

In this experiment we have used excess zinc. *Excess* means more than enough zinc is present to ensure all the copper(II) sulfate reacts. If you calculate the number of moles of copper(II) sulfate and the number of moles of zinc used in this procedure, you should spot that the number of moles of zinc used is more than that of copper(II) sulfate:

$$\text{number of moles } (n) \text{ of zinc added} = \frac{\text{mass } (m)}{\text{relative atomic mass } (A_r)} = \frac{1.20}{65} = 0.0185\,\text{mol}$$

$$\text{number of moles } (n) \text{ of copper(II) sulfate added} = \text{volume } (V) \times \text{concentration } (C) = 0.050 \times 0.200 = 0.0100\,\text{mol}$$

Now we need to calculate how much heat is released when 1 mole of copper sulfate reacts with excess zinc:

Molar enthalpy change of reaction (ΔH)

$$\Delta H = \frac{\text{heat energy change } (Q)}{\text{number of moles of copper sulfate reacted } (n)}$$

$$= \frac{2.1527}{0.0100} = 215\,\text{kJ/mol}$$

The amount of heat released in the displacement reaction when 1 mole of $CuSO_4$ reacts with excess Zn is therefore:

$$Zn(s) + CuSO_4(aq) \rightarrow ZnSO_4(aq) + Cu(s) \qquad \Delta H = -215\,\text{kJ/mol}$$

We have added the negative sign because we know that the temperature of the reaction mixture went up. The negative sign shows that this is an exothermic reaction; heat is released.

KEY POINT

1 mol of Zn reacts with 1 mol of $CuSO_4$, therefore 0.0100 mol of $CuSO_4$ reacts with 0.0100 mol of Zn. We added 0.0185 mol of Zn, so Zn is in excess.

REMINDER

Remember that we have to divide the volume by 1000 to convert it to dm^3 because the concentration is given in mol/dm^3.

EXTENSION WORK

You could repeat this experiment with metals of different reactivities. The more reactive a metal is, the more heat should be released in the displacement reaction. Make sure you keep everything else the same: the number of moles of the metals, the size of the solid particles, and the volume and concentration of the copper(II) sulfate solution. Do not use metals that are more reactive than magnesium, otherwise you are measuring the heat released when the metal reacts with water instead!

Safety note: Wear eye protection and avoid skin contact with the salts and their solutions.

ACTIVITY 3

▼ PRACTICAL: MEASURING ENTHALPY CHANGES WHEN SALTS DISSOLVE IN WATER

We can also use calorimetry experiments to work out the amount of heat given out/taken in when salts dissolve in water. The following procedure could be used:

- Place a polystyrene cup in a 250 cm^3 glass beaker.
- Transfer 100 cm^3 of water into the polystyrene cup using a measuring cylinder.
- Record the initial temperature of the water.
- Weigh 5.20 g of ammonium chloride using a weighing boat on a balance.
- Add the ammonium chloride to water and stir the solution vigorously until all the ammonium chloride has dissolved.
- Record the minimum temperature.

The set-up is very similar to the one used in Activity 2, see Figure 15.9.

SAMPLE DATA

initial temperature of water / °C	18.3
minimum temperature of salt solution / °C	15.1

Note: the temperature of the water decreases, so the reaction is endothermic and heat is absorbed from the surroundings for the dissolving process to occur.

We can use this data to calculate the molar enthalpy change for dissolving ammonium chloride.

CALCULATIONS FOR ACTIVITY 3

Heat absorbed: $Q = mc\Delta T = 100 \times 4.18 \times (18.3 - 15.1) = 1337.6\,J = 1.3376\,kJ$

Here we assume the following:

1. The specific heat capacity of the diluted solution of ammonium chloride is the same as that of water. This is quite a reasonable assumption because the mixture is mostly water.
2. The mass of the solution is 100 g. The mass of the ammonium chloride is relatively small and it is ignored in the calculation. There are other major sources of error in the experiment, for example heat absorbed from the surrounding air, which makes much more difference to the results.

Now we need to calculate how much heat is absorbed when 1 mole of ammonium chloride dissolves in excess water.

The relative formula mass of ammonium chloride (NH_4Cl) is $14 + 4 \times 1 + 35.5 = 53.5$.

Number of moles (n) of ammonium chloride dissolved

$$n = \frac{\text{mass } (m)}{\text{relative formula mass } (M_r)} = \frac{5.20}{53.5} = 0.0972\,\text{mol}$$

Molar enthalpy change of solution (ΔH)

$$\Delta H = \frac{\text{heat energy change } (Q)}{\text{number of moles of ammonium chloride dissolved } (n)}$$

$$= \frac{1.3376}{0.0972}$$

$$= 13.8\,\text{kJ/mol}$$

KEY POINT

Dissolving is a physical process rather than a chemical reaction. When some salts dissolve in water heat is given out (exothermic), but when others dissolve the process is endothermic.

The amount of heat absorbed when dissolving 1 mole of ammonium chloride in water is therefore:

$NH_4Cl(s) \rightarrow NH_4Cl(aq)$ $\Delta H = +13.8\,\text{kJ/mol}$

The positive sign shows that heat is absorbed and the dissolving of ammonium chloride in water is an endothermic process (the temperature goes down).

Safety note: Wear eye protection and avoid skin contact with the acid and alkali.

ACTIVITY 4

▼ PRACTICAL: MEASURING ENTHALPY CHANGES OF NEUTRALISATION BETWEEN AN ALKALI AND AN ACID

The reaction between an alkali and an acid is essentially between OH^- and H^+ ions to form water (see Chapter 12):

$OH^-(aq) + H^+(aq) \rightarrow H_2O(l)$

Let's look at the reaction between potassium hydroxide (an alkali) and hydrochloric acid. Suppose you know the concentration of the potassium hydroxide but are not so sure of the concentration of the dilute hydrochloric acid solution (the label has gone missing!). The following method could be used to find out the concentration of the acid and how much heat is released during the neutralisation reaction.

- Place a polystyrene cup in a 250 cm^3 glass beaker.
- Transfer 25 cm^3 of 2.00 mol/dm^3 potassium hydroxide into the polystyrene cup using a measuring cylinder.
- Record the initial temperature.
- Fill a burette with 50.00 cm^3 of dilute hydrochloric acid.
- Use the burette to add 5.00 cm^3 of dilute hydrochloric acid to the potassium hydroxide.
- Stir vigorously and record the maximum temperature reached.
- Continue adding further 5.00 cm^3 portions of dilute hydrochloric acid to the cup, stirring and recording the maximum temperature each time, until a total volume of 50.00 cm^3 has been added.

We can plot a graph of the temperature of the mixture versus the volume of acid added.

SAMPLE DATA

In this reaction the temperature increases at first but then decreases. The reaction between the acid and the alkali is exothermic. At the beginning the temperature goes up because the acid reacts with the alkali, giving out heat. But when all the alkali has been used up, we are just adding cold acid to our warm solution (there is no reaction because there is nothing for the acid to react with) and the temperature goes down.

Two lines of best fit can be drawn on our graph. The point where the lines cross represents complete neutralisation. From the graph, we can identify the maximum temperature reached during the experiment as 31.8 °C. At this point, 28.00 cm^3 of acid has been used.

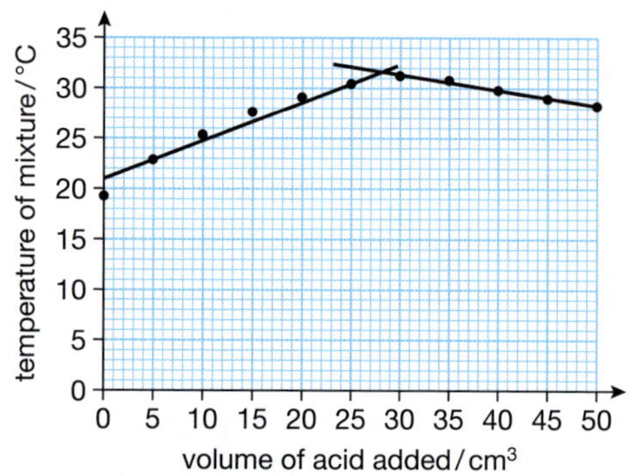

▲ Figure 15.10 Temperature change in the neutralisation reaction between KOH and HCl.

CALCULATIONS FOR ACTIVITY 4

To work out how much heat is released in the neutralisation reaction, we can use the same calculation as before.

The total volume of the solution at the neutralisation point is 25 + 28 = 53 cm^3.

Heat given out is shown by $Q = mc\Delta T = 53 \times 4.18 \times (31.8 - 19.3) = 2769.3$ J.

If we divide by 1000 we get 2.7693 kJ.

Here we assume the following:

1. The density of the reaction mixture is the same as that of water, so 1 cm^3 of solution has a mass of 1 g.
2. The specific heat capacity of the mixture is the same as that of water. This is a fairly reasonable assumption because the neutralised solution is mostly water.

Now we need to calculate how much heat is released when 1 mole of potassium hydroxide reacts with 1 mole of hydrochloric acid:

Number of moles of KOH (n) = concentration (C) × volume (V)

$$= 2.00 \times \frac{25}{1000} = 0.0500 \text{ mol}$$

The number of moles of HCl will be exactly the same because we have taken the temperature at the neutralisation point.

Molar enthalpy change of neutralisation (ΔH)

$$\Delta H = \frac{\text{heat energy change } (Q)}{\text{number of moles of KOH or HCl reacted } (n)}$$

$$= \frac{2.7693}{0.0500} = 55.4 \text{ kJ/mol}$$

The amount of heat released in the neutralisation reaction when 1 mole of KOH reacts with 1 mole of HCl is therefore:

$$KOH(aq) + HCl(aq) \rightarrow KCl(aq) + H_2O(l) \qquad \Delta H = -55.4 \text{ kJ/mol}$$

The negative sign shows that heat is released in this exothermic neutralisation reaction.

LOOKING AHEAD – ENTROPY

Many reactions we meet at International GSCE level are exothermic, for example combustion and neutralisation. Despite requiring a small amount of energy to get the reactions started (*activation energy*), these reactions release heat energy overall because the products are more stable than the reactants. This shows that enthalpy is certainly a driving force for a reaction to occur. However, endothermic processes do occur. How do they happen? Dissolving ammonium nitrate into water causes the temperature of the solution to decrease, but it dissolves anyway. This is possible because of a different factor called entropy. *Entropy is a measure of the number of ways for the energy in a system to be distributed*. It is greater in a more disordered system because the energy can be dispersed more flexibly. It follows that solids have lower entropy than liquids, which have lower entropy than gases, as shown in Figure 15.11.

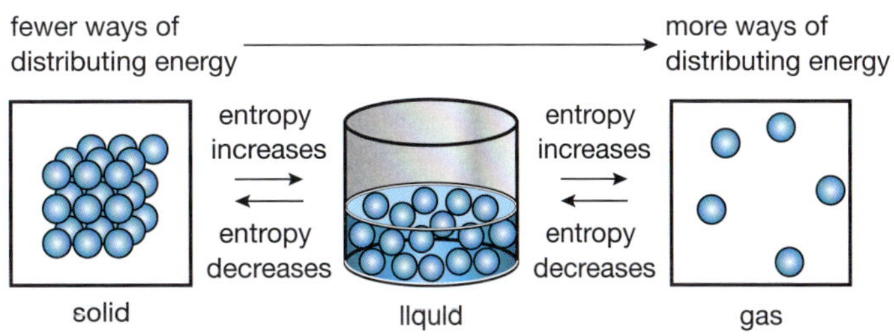

▲ Figure 15.11 Entropy is greater in a more disordered system.

If the entropy of a system increases during a reaction, it is more likely for that reaction to occur. When dissolving ammonium nitrate in water, although the process is endothermic, the NH_4^+ and NO_3^- ion particles in the giant ionic lattice become separated from each other. The ions have more freedom of movement in water and the entropy of the system increases, which outweighs the effect of enthalpy.

The reaction between baking soda and vinegar is another example of an endothermic reaction that occurs spontaneously. The reaction produces a gas which leads to an increase in the entropy of the system.

▲ Figure 15.12 The reaction between baking soda and vinegar is used to make papier mâché volcanos.

CHAPTER QUESTIONS

SKILLS CRITICAL THINKING, PROBLEM SOLVING

9th

1 Explain what is meant by an *exothermic reaction* and write balanced chemical equations for any two exothermic changes.

SKILLS REASONING

7th

2 Explain what is meant by an *endothermic reaction*.

SKILLS CRITICAL THINKING

9th

3 Identify each of the following changes as exothermic or endothermic. In some cases you will have to rely on your previous knowledge of chemistry. Several reactions are likely to be completely new to you.

a The reaction between sodium and water.

b Burning methane (major constituent of natural gas).

c The reaction between sodium carbonate and ethanoic acid. A thermometer placed in the reaction mixture shows a temperature drop.

d $S(s) + O_2(g) \rightarrow SO_2(g)$ $\Delta H = -297\,kJ/mol$

e $CuSO_4(s) \rightarrow CuO(s) + SO_3(g)$ $\Delta H = +220\,kJ/mol$

f If you dissolve solid sodium hydroxide in water, the solution becomes very hot.

SKILLS INTRAPERSONAL

11th

4 Self-heating cans are used to provide warm food in situations where it is inconvenient to use a more conventional form of heat. By doing an internet (or other) search, find out how self-heating cans work. Write a short explanation of your findings (not exceeding 200 words). You should include equation(s) for any reaction(s) involved, and a diagram or picture if it is useful.

SKILLS EXECUTIVE FUNCTION

4th

5 A student investigated the amount of heat given out when hexane, C_6H_{14}, burns using the apparatus in Figure 15.6. Hexane is a highly flammable liquid which is one of the components of petrol (gasoline).

In each case, the student calculated the amount of heat evolved per mole of hexane. Her first two experiments produced answers of –3200 and –3900 kJ/mol of heat evolved. She then decided to do a third experiment. Her results were as follows:

volume of water in copper calorimeter / cm^3	100
mass of burner + hexane before experiment / g	35.62
mass of burner + hexane after experiment / g	35.23
original temperature of water / °C	19.0
final temperature of water / °C	55.0

a Suggest a reason why the student decided to do a third experiment.

5th

b Apart from wearing eye protection, suggest two other safety precautions the student should take during the experiment.

SKILLS PROBLEM SOLVING

9th

c Use the results table to calculate the amount of heat in **kJ** evolved by the burning hexane during the experiment.

(Specific heat capacity of water = 4.18 J/g/°C; density of water = 1 g/cm^3.)

d Calculate the amount of heat energy released per gram of hexane.

SKILLS PROBLEM SOLVING

e Calculate the molar enthalpy change of combustion of hexane. (A_r: H = 1, C = 12)

SKILLS REASONING

f To calculate the average value of the heat evolved per mole when hexane burns, the student took an average of her results. She decided not to use the figure of −3900 in calculating the average because it was so different from the other two. Suggest two reasons why this reaction might have been more exothermic than the others.

g A data book gave a figure of −4194 kJ of heat evolved when 1 mole of hexane burns. Suggest two reasons why all the results in the student's experiment were less negative than this.

SKILLS PROBLEM SOLVING

6 When 5.15 g of lithium chloride (LiCl) is dissolved in 50 cm^3 of water the temperature of the solution goes from 17.0 °C to 33.5 °C.

a Calculate the heat energy released in this experiment. (Specific heat capacity of water = 4.18 J/g/°C; mass of 1 cm^3 of solution = 1 g.)

b Calculate the amount, in moles, of lithium chloride dissolved in the solution.

c Using your answers from a and b, calculate the enthalpy change when 1 mol of lithium chloride dissolves in water in kJ/mol.

SKILLS REASONING

d A data book gives a figure of −37.2 kJ/mol for heat released when 1 mole of lithium chloride is dissolved in water. Suggest two reasons why the value you calculated in c might be different from the value given in the data book.

16 RATES OF REACTION AND REVERSIBLE REACTIONS

Reactions can vary in speed between those that happen within fractions of a second – explosions, for example – and those that never happen at all. Gold can be exposed to the air for thousands of years and not react in any way.

This chapter looks at the factors controlling the speeds of chemical reactions. It also explores the idea of 'reversibility' in a reaction.

▲ Figure 16.1 Some reactions are very fast.

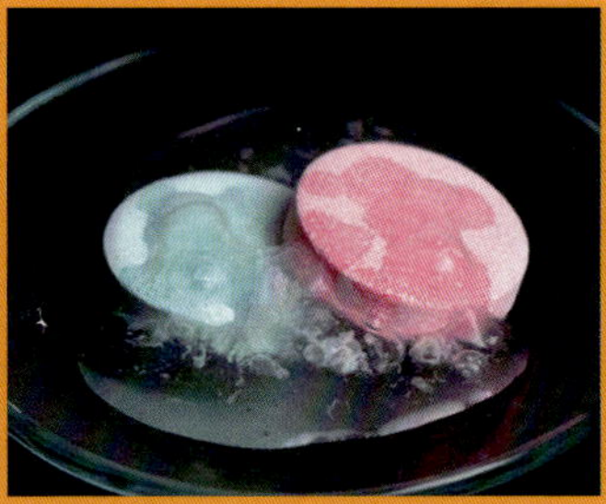

▲ Figure 16.2 Some reactions happen over several minutes.

▲ Figure 16.3 Rusting takes days or weeks.

▲ Figure 16.4 The weathering of limestone and the formation of stalagmites and stalactites takes a very long time.

LEARNING OBJECTIVES

- Describe experiments to investigate the effects of changes in the surface area of a solid, the concentration of a solution, the temperature and the use of a catalyst on the rate of a reaction
- Describe the effects of changes in the surface area of a solid, the concentration of a solution, the pressure of a gas, the temperature and the use of a catalyst on the rate of a reaction
- Explain the effects of changes in the surface area of a solid, the concentration of a solution, the pressure of a gas and the temperature on the rate of a reaction in terms of particle collision theory
- Know that a catalyst is a substance that increases the rate of a reaction, but is chemically unchanged at the end of the reaction
- Know that a catalyst works by providing an alternative pathway with lower activation energy
- Practical: Investigate the effect of changing the surface area of marble chips and of changing the concentration of hydrochloric acid on the rate of reaction between marble chips and dilute hydrochloric acid
- Practical: Investigate the effect of different solids on the catalytic decomposition of hydrogen peroxide solution
- Know that some reactions are reversible and that this is indicated by the symbol $\rightleftharpoons$ in equations
- Describe reversible reactions such as the **dehydration** of hydrated copper(II) sulfate and the effect of heat on ammonium chloride

EXPERIMENTS TO MEASURE THE RATE OF REACTION

The **rate** of a reaction is the speed at which the amount of reactants decreases or the amount of products increases. It is measured as *a change in the concentration (or amount) of reactants or products per unit time* (per second, per minute etc.).

$$\text{rate of reaction} = \frac{\text{change in concentration, volume or mass}}{\text{time}}$$

Safety note: Wear eye protection and avoid skin contact with the acid.

ACTIVITY 5

▼ PRACTICAL: AN INVESTIGATION OF THE RATE OF REACTION BETWEEN MARBLE CHIPS AND DILUTE HYDROCHLORIC ACID

Marble chips are made of calcium carbonate and react with hydrochloric acid to produce carbon dioxide gas. Calcium chloride solution is also formed.

$$CaCO_3(s) + 2HCl(aq) \rightarrow CaCl_2(aq) + H_2O(l) + CO_2(g)$$

Figure 16.5 shows some apparatus that can be used to measure how the mass of carbon dioxide produced changes with time. Part (a) is drawn as the apparatus would look before the reaction starts.

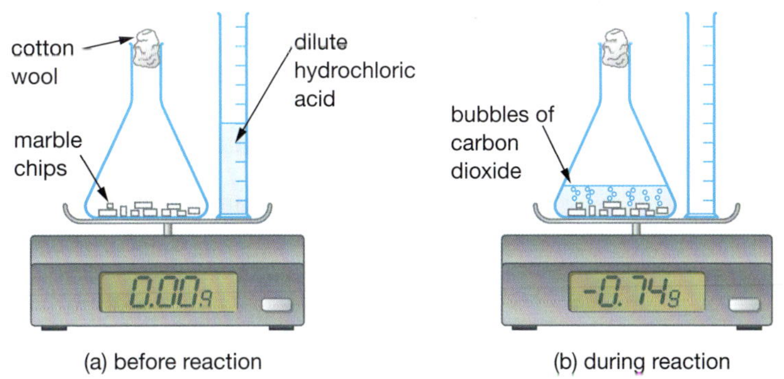

▲ Figure 16.5 Investigating the reaction between calcium carbonate and hydrochloric acid.

The following procedure could be used:

- Use a measuring cylinder to measure 25 cm^3 of 2.00 mol/dm^3 dilute hydrochloric acid.
- Add 5.00 g of large marble chips to a conical flask and place a piece of cotton wool at the opening of the flask. The cotton wool is there to allow the carbon dioxide to escape during the reaction, but to stop any acid spitting out. The marble is in *excess* – some of it will be left over when the acid is all used up.
- Place everything on a balance and reset it to zero.
- Add the acid to the marble chips and record the reading on the balance every 30 seconds.

Part (b) shows what happens during the reaction. The acid has been poured into the flask and everything has been replaced on the balance. Once the reaction starts, the balance shows a negative mass. The mass goes down because the carbon dioxide escapes through the cotton wool.

When we plot a graph of mass of carbon dioxide lost against time, we obtain something similar to the one in Figure 16.6.

The steeper the slope (gradient) of the line, the faster the reaction. We can see from Figure 16.6 that about 0.47 g of carbon dioxide is produced in the first minute. Only about 0.20 g of extra carbon dioxide is produced in the second minute, the reaction is slowing down.

HINT

You are unlikely to be asked to draw tangents and find rates like this in an exam.

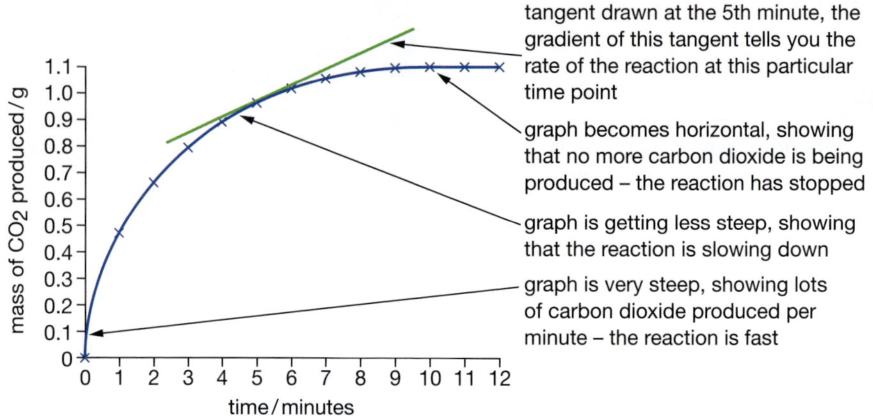

▲ Figure 16.6 The mass of carbon dioxide lost when calcium carbonate reacts with hydrochloric acid.

We can calculate the *average rate* of the reaction during any time interval by using

$$\text{rate} = \frac{\text{mass of CO}_2\text{ lost}}{\text{time}}$$

For example, the average rate of the reaction in the *first* minute

$$= \frac{0.47}{1} = 0.47\,\text{g/min}$$

The average rate of the reaction in the *second* minute

$$= \frac{0.20}{1} = 0.20\,\text{g/min}$$

The average rate of the reaction over the *first two* minutes

$$= \frac{0.67}{2} = 0.34\,\text{g/min}$$

We can see the reaction is fastest at the beginning. It then slows down, until it eventually stops because *all the hydrochloric acid has been used up*.

We can measure how fast the reaction is going *at any time point* by finding the slope (gradient) of the line at that point. This is the rate of the reaction *at that point* (rather than the average). This is done by drawing a **tangent** to the line at the time you are interested in and finding its slope (gradient). For example, at 5 minutes the carbon dioxide is being lost at the rate of about 0.05 g per minute (see Figure 16.6).

We can also follow the rate of this reaction by measuring the *volume* of carbon dioxide given off. The apparatus shown in Figure 16.7 can be used.

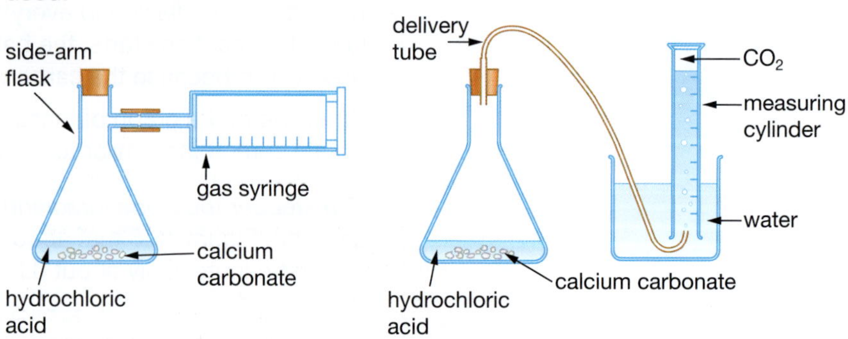

▲ Figure 16.7 Either method can be used to measure the volume of CO_2 given off.

REMINDER

Remember, the marble chips were in excess (there was more than enough to react with all the hydrochloric acid). There will still be unreacted marble chips in the flask at the end.

EXPLAINING WHAT'S HAPPENING

We can explain the shape of the curve by thinking about the particles present and how they interact. This is called the **collision theory**.

Reactions can happen only when particles collide. Not all collisions end up in a reaction. Many particles just bounce off each other. In order for a reaction to actually happen, *the particles have to collide with a minimum amount of energy*, called the **activation energy**. *The collisions with energy greater than or equal to the activation energy are usually called* **successful collisions**.

In the reaction between calcium carbonate and hydrochloric acid, particles in the acid have to collide with the particles at the surface of the marble chips. As the acid particles are getting used up, the collision rate decreases, and so the reaction slows down. The marble is in a large excess so that its shape doesn't change very much during the reaction.

KEY POINT

If you have studied Chapter 12, you may realise that the particles we are talking about in the acid are H^+ ions. A reaction occurs when the H^+ ions in the acid collide successfully with the CO_3^{2-} ions in the calcium carbonate. You should not talk about HCl molecules colliding with $CaCO_3$ molecules. If in doubt about what particles are actually colliding, it is probably safer to just use the word *particle*.

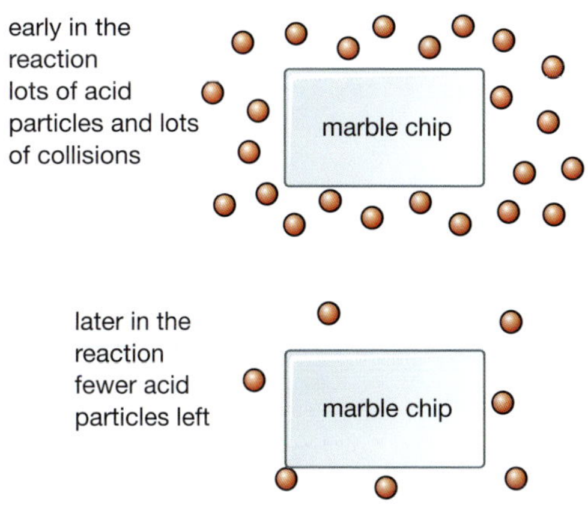

▲ Figure 16.8 As the reaction proceeds, the collision rate of acid particles with the marble chips decreases.

A DIFFERENT FORM OF GRAPH

At International GCSE you normally plot graphs showing the mass or volume of product *formed* during a reaction. It is possible, however, that you will see graphs showing the fall in the concentration of one of the *reactants* – in this case, the concentration of the dilute hydrochloric acid.

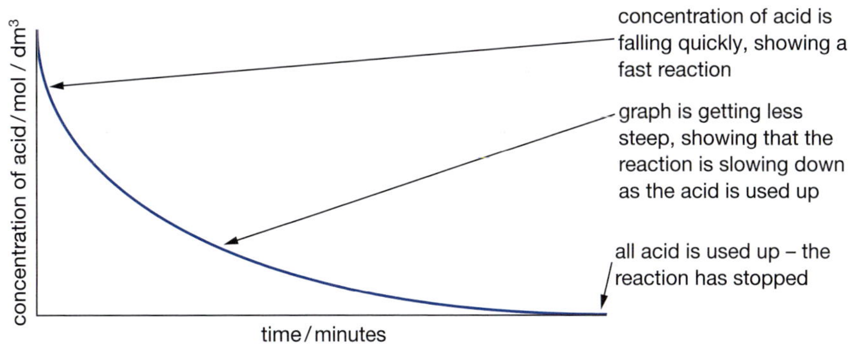

▲ Figure 16.9 The fall in concentration of hydrochloric acid over time

Where the graph is falling most quickly (is steepest), it shows that the reaction is fastest.

Eventually, the graph becomes horizontal because the reaction has stopped when all the acid has been consumed.

CHANGING THE SURFACE AREA OF THE REACTANTS

ACTIVITY 6

▼ PRACTICAL: INVESTIGATING THE EFFECT OF CHANGING THE SURFACE AREA OF MARBLE CHIPS ON THE RATE OF REACTION BETWEEN MARBLE CHIPS AND DILUTE HYDROCHLORIC ACID

Safety note: Wear eye protection and avoid skin contact with the acid.

We can repeat the experiment in Activity 5 using exactly the same quantities of everything, but using much smaller marble chips. The reaction with the smaller chips happens faster.

We can plot both sets of results (Activities 5 and 6) on the same graph (Figure 16.10). Notice that the same mass of carbon dioxide is produced because we are using the same quantities of everything in both experiments. However, the reaction with the smaller chips starts off much faster and finishes sooner.

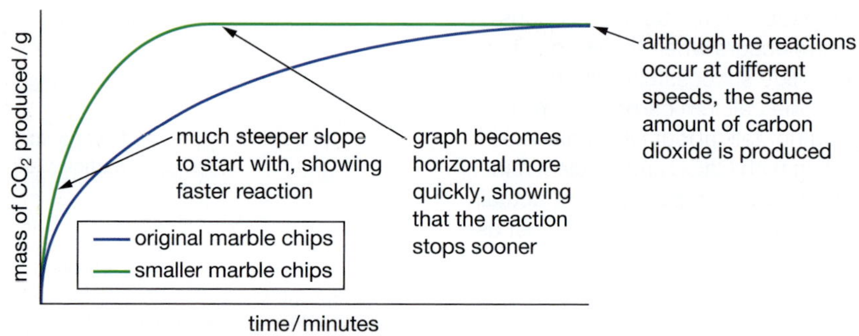

▲ Figure 16.10 The effect of using smaller marble chips

HINT

If we are going to investigate the effect of changing the size of the marble chips, it is important that everything else stays exactly the same to make this a valid (fair) test.

Reactions between solids and liquids (or solids and gases) are faster if the solids are present as a lot of small pieces rather than a few big ones. The more finely divided the solid, the faster the reaction. This is because the *surface area* in contact with the gas or liquid is *much greater* and there are more particles of the solid exposed on the surface. Only the particles on the surface are available for collisions. The *frequency of successful collisions increases* as the surface area of the solid increases.

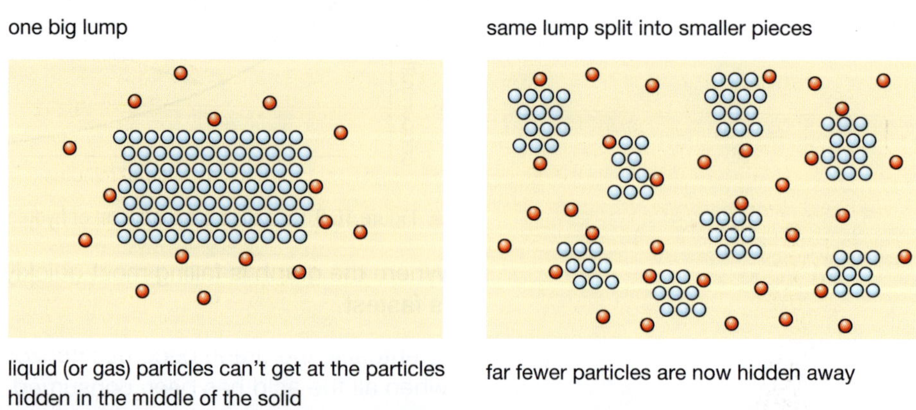

▲ Figure 16.11 The more divided the solid, the faster the reaction

▲ Figure 16.12 A catalytic converter has a honeycomb structure to give a very large surface area for the exhaust gases to flow through.

Large surface areas are frequently used to speed up reactions outside the lab. For example, a **catalytic converter** for a car uses expensive metals such as platinum, palladium and rhodium coated onto a honeycomb structure in a very thin layer to give the maximum possible surface area.

In the presence of these metals, harmful substances such as carbon monoxide and nitrogen oxides are converted into relatively harmless carbon dioxide and nitrogen. The large surface area means the reaction is very rapid. This is important because the gases in the exhaust system are in contact with the catalytic converter for only a very short time.

CHANGING THE CONCENTRATION OF THE REACTANTS

THE EFFECT OF CHANGING THE CONCENTRATION

We can repeat our original experiment with large marble chips and hydrochloric acid. Everything is kept the same except we use hydrochloric acid of half the concentration.

We find that reducing the concentration of the acid makes the reaction slower. We can see this on our graph because the graph (red line) is less steep than for our original experiment (blue line).

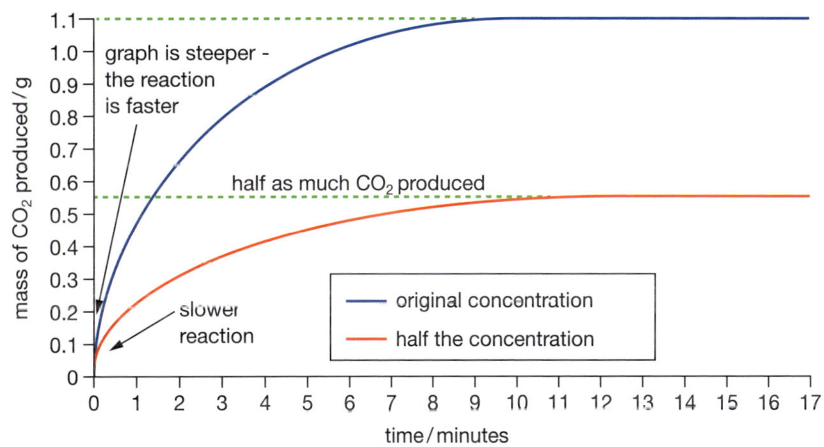

▲ Figure 16.13 The effect of changing the concentration of the acid

REMINDER

Remember, the marble chips were in excess, so this makes no difference.

In our original experiment we used 25 cm^3 of 2.00 mol/dm^3 hydrochloric acid. In this experiment we used 25 cm^3 of 1.00 mol/dm^3 hydrochloric acid. In the second experiment we have started with half the number of hydrochloric acid particles (half as many moles) and so we will produce half as much carbon dioxide.

KEY POINT

When explaining this, do not only say that there are more collisions. You must always include the idea of time. So, you should say things such as '*the particles collide more frequently or there are more collisions per second*'.

In general, if you increase the concentration of the reactants, the reaction becomes faster. *Increasing the concentration increases the number of acid particles within a fixed volume*, therefore the particles are closer together and collide more frequently. There are *more successful collisions* between the acid particles and the marble chips *every second*.

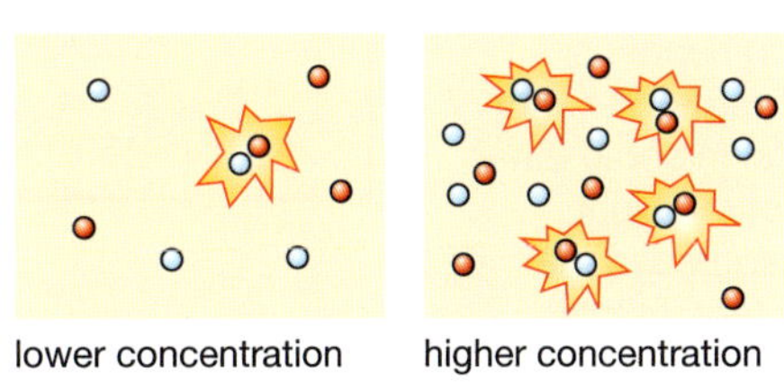

▲ Figure 16.14 At a higher concentration, more particles collide per second

Safety note: Wear eye protection and avoid skin contact with the acid.

KEY POINT

To calculate the concentration of hydrochloric acid you need to look at the proportions of acid and water. The equation to calculate the concentration of hydrochloric acid is:

$$\text{concentration (mol/dm}^3\text{)} = \frac{\text{volume of hydrochloric acid (cm}^3\text{)}}{\text{total volume of solution (25 cm}^3\text{)}} \times \text{original concentration (2.00 mol/dm}^3\text{)}$$

DID YOU KNOW?

The words *proportional* and *directly proportional* mean the same thing. If the graph we plotted was a straight line that did not go through the origin, this is not a proportional relationship. In that case we would describe the relationship as *linear.*

EXTENSION WORK

The relationship between the rate of a reaction and the concentration of the reactants is not always as uncomplicated as it seems. In some reactions, the rate of the reaction is proportional to the concentration of the reactants, as shown by the example in Figure 16.15. We say the reaction is first order with respect to a particular reactant.

If you go on to do chemistry at a higher level, you will come across reactions in which increasing the concentration of one of the reactants has no effect on how fast the reaction happens. These reactions are of zero order with respect to the reactants. In some other cases the rate of a reaction might be proportional to the square of the concentration of a reactant. In this case we say the reaction is of second order with respect to the reactant.

ACTIVITY 7

▼ PRACTICAL: INVESTIGATING THE EFFECT OF CHANGING THE CONCENTRATION OF THE ACID ON THE RATE OF REACTION BETWEEN MARBLE CHIPS AND DILUTE HYDROCHLORIC ACID

We can repeat our previous experiment in Activity 5 using the original large marble chips, but using hydrochloric acid of different concentrations. Everything else would be the same, that is, the mass of the marble chips (5.00 g) and the total volume of the acid (25 cm^3). We can dilute the acid by adding distilled water to the original 2.00 mol/dm^3 solution but making sure the total volume of water and acid remains at 25 cm^3.

For example, if 12.5 cm^3 of the original HCl is mixed with 12.5 cm^3 of distilled water, we get an acid solution of half of the original concentration (1.00 mol/dm^3). If only 5 cm^3 of the original HCl is mixed with 20 cm^3 of distilled water, the acid solution is now one-fifth (5 out of 25) of the original concentration (0.40 mol/dm^3).

In this experiment we are going to calculate the average rate during the first 30 seconds, so we record the mass of carbon dioxide lost in 30 seconds.

We can calculate the average rate of reaction within the first 30 seconds by dividing the mass loss by 30. For example, if we obtain a loss of 0.32 g:

$$\text{average rate} = \frac{0.32}{30} = 0.011 \text{ g/s}$$

To identify the effect of changing concentration on rate, we can plot the results for the different concentrations on a piece of graph paper with rate on the *y*-axis and concentration of acid on the *x*-axis (Figure 16.15). The line of best fit should go through the origin (0, 0). If there is no acid, there should be no rate. A straight line going through the origin shows that the rate of the reaction is *directly proportional* to the concentration of the hydrochloric acid. If the concentration doubles, the rate should double. If the concentration triples, the rate should triple.

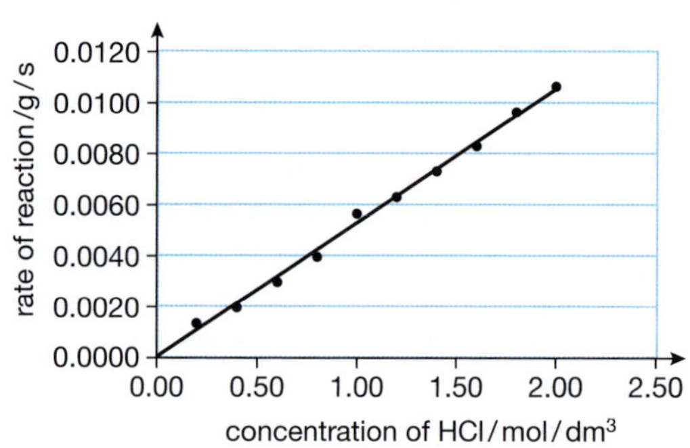

▲ Figure 16.15 The more concentrated the acid, the faster the reaction

CHANGING THE TEMPERATURE OF THE REACTION

We can do the original experiment again, but this time at a higher temperature. We keep everything else exactly the same as before.

Reactions get faster as the temperature is increased; the graph is *steeper* and *finishes sooner*. The same mass of gas is given off because we have used the same quantities of everything in the mixture.

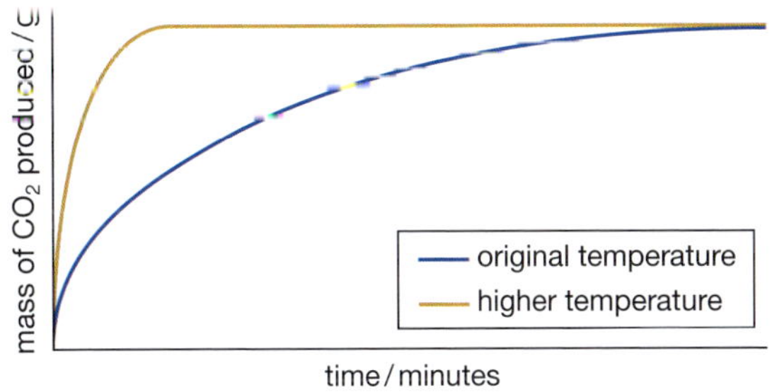

Figure 16.16 The effect of changing the temperature of the reaction

There are two factors that need to be considered when explaining why increasing temperature increases the rate of reaction:

- Increasing the temperature means that the particles are moving faster, and so collide more frequently. That will make the reaction go faster, but it only accounts for a small part of the increase in rate.
- We learned above that in order for a collision to cause a reaction (*a successful collision*), the particles have to collide with a minimum amount of energy, called the *activation energy*. A relatively small increase in temperature produces *a very large increase in the number of particles with energy greater than or equal to the activation energy*. This means that it is going to be much more probable that two particles which have sufficient energy to react collide with each other. So *the frequency of successful collisions increases*.

KEY POINT

As an approximation, a 10 °C increase in temperature approximately doubles the rate of a reaction. This works for quite a lot of reactions that we meet in the lab, as long as the temperature remains within a few tens of degrees of room temperature.

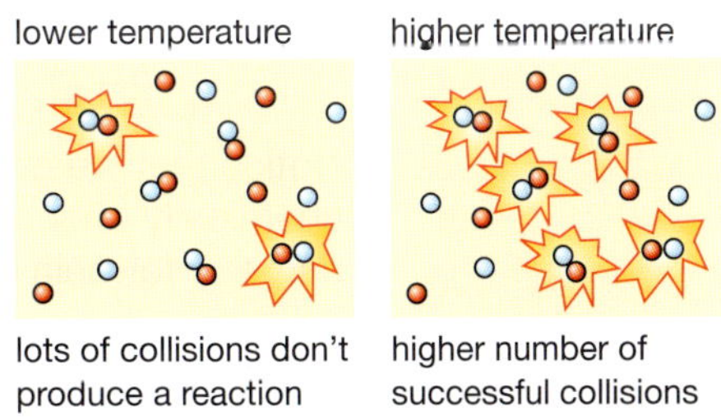

Figure 16.17 A small increase in temperature produces a large increase in the number of collisions with energy greater than the activation energy.

CHANGING THE PRESSURE ON THE REACTION

Changing the pressure of a reaction in which the reactants are only solids or liquids makes almost no difference to the rate of reaction. But increasing the pressure of a reaction where the reactants are *gases* does speed up the reaction.

If we have a fixed mass of a gas, we increase the pressure by squeezing it into a smaller volume.

This forces the particles *closer together*, so they *collide more frequently*. This is exactly the same as increasing the concentration of the gas.

KEY POINT

In solids and liquids, particles are packed closely together and there is hardly any space in between. Increasing the pressure would not change the volumes of the solids or liquids much, therefore there would hardly be any change in the number of particles in a certain volume.

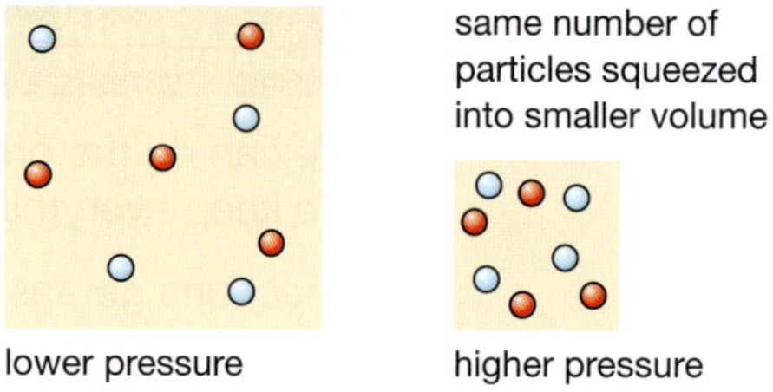

▲ Figure 16.18 Increased pressure means gas particles collide more frequently.

CATALYSTS

WHAT ARE CATALYSTS?

Catalysts are *substances that speed up chemical reactions*, but aren't used up in the process. They are still there, *chemically unchanged, at the end of the reaction*. Because they aren't consumed, small amounts of catalyst can be used to process lots and lots of reactant particles. Different reactions need different catalysts.

THE CATALYTIC DECOMPOSITION OF HYDROGEN PEROXIDE

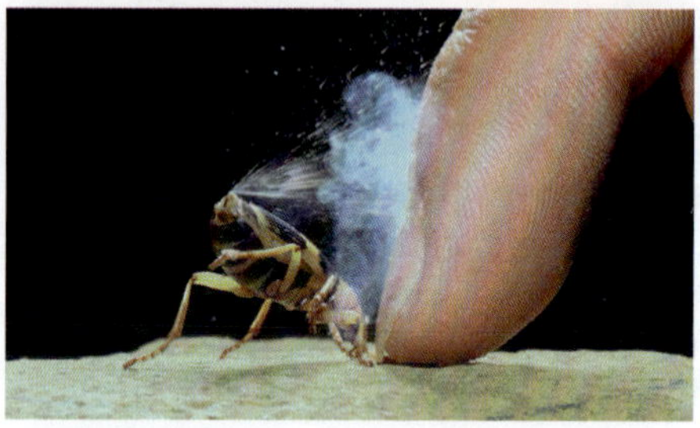

▲ Figure 16.19 Bombardier beetles use hydrogen peroxide as part of their defence mechanism.

Bombardier beetles defend themselves by spraying a hot, unpleasant liquid at their attackers. Part of the reaction involves splitting hydrogen peroxide into water and oxygen, using the enzyme catalase. **Enzymes** are *biological catalysts*. This reaction happens almost explosively, and produces a lot of heat. The same enzyme can be found in potatoes, or even liver tissues.

There are a lot of other things that also catalyse the decomposition of hydrogen peroxide. Some examples are manganese(IV) oxide (also called manganese dioxide), MnO_2, and lead(IV) oxide, PbO_2. Manganese(IV) oxide is what is normally used in the lab to speed up the decomposition of hydrogen peroxide.

The reaction happening with the hydrogen peroxide is:

hydrogen peroxide → water + oxygen

$$2H_2O_2(aq) \rightarrow 2H_2O(l) + O_2(g)$$

Notice that we don't write catalysts into the equation because they are chemically unchanged at the end of the reaction. If you like, you can write their name or formula over the top of the arrow.

SHOWING THAT A SUBSTANCE IS A CATALYST

▶ Figure 16.20 The beakers both contain hydrogen peroxide solution, the right-hand one has MnO_2 added to speed up oxygen production.

It isn't difficult to show that manganese(IV) oxide speeds up the decomposition of hydrogen peroxide to produce oxygen. Figure 16.20 shows two beakers, both of which contain hydrogen peroxide solution. Without the catalyst, there is only a trace of bubbles in the solution. With it, oxygen is given off quickly.

How can you show that the manganese(IV) oxide is chemically unchanged by the reaction? It still looks the same, but has any been used up? You can only find out by weighing it before you add it to the hydrogen peroxide solution and then reweighing it at the end.

You can separate the manganese(IV) oxide from the liquid by filtering it through a weighed filter paper, allowing the paper and residue to dry, and then reweighing to calculate the mass of the remaining manganese(IV) oxide. You should find that the mass hasn't changed.

Safety note: Wear eye protection and avoid skin contact with the solution.

HINT

The experiment in Figure 16.21 is very simple and easy to set up. However, using this setup has the disadvantage that some oxygen will escape at the beginning of the reaction when MnO_2 is added to H_2O_2 before the bung can be put back on the conical flask. Using a weighing bottle like the one in Figure 16.22 is a simple way of mixing the chemicals together without losing any oxygen before you can get the bung in. When you are ready to start the reaction, shake the flask so that the weighing bottle falls over and the manganese(IV) oxide comes into contact with the hydrogen peroxide. You need to keep shaking so that an even mixture is formed.

DID YOU KNOW?

'*vol*', meaning volume, is a measurement for concentration for hydrogen peroxide. 1 cm^3 of 2 vol hydrogen peroxide solution decomposes completely to give 2 cm^3 of oxygen.

ACTIVITY 8

▼ PRACTICAL: INVESTIGATE THE EFFECT OF DIFFERENT SOLIDS ON THE CATALYTIC DECOMPOSITION OF HYDROGEN PEROXIDE SOLUTION

Figure 16.21 shows apparatus that can be used to measure how the volume of oxygen produced changes with time.

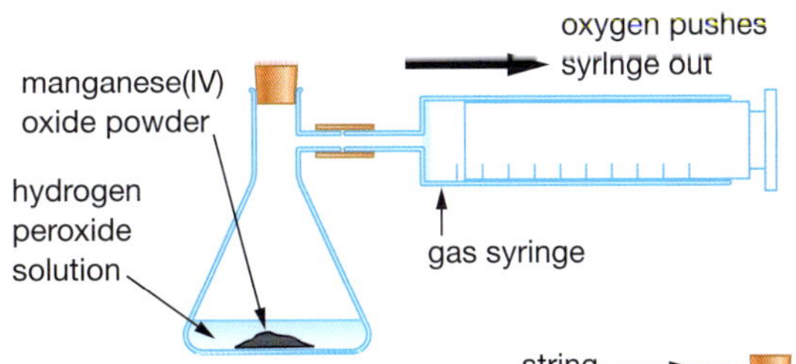

▲ Figure 16.21 Apparatus to measure the volume of oxygen evolved.

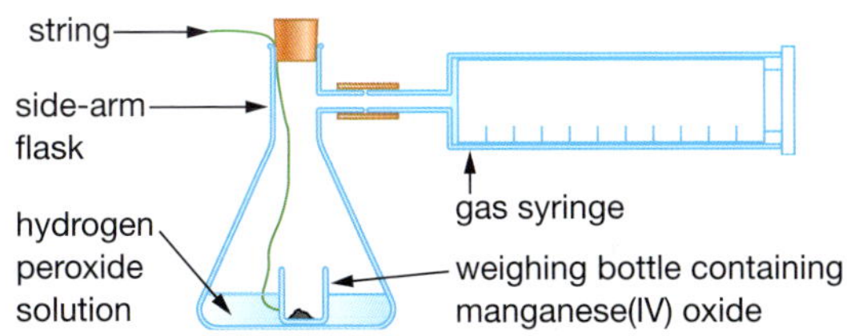

▲ Figure 16.22 Modified apparatus to avoid the loss of oxygen at the beginning of the experiment.

The following procedure could be used:

- Measure 100 cm^3 of 2 *vol* hydrogen peroxide and transfer to a 250 cm^3 conical flask.
- Weigh out 0.20 g of manganese(IV) oxide on a balance.
- Add the manganese(IV) oxide to the hydrogen peroxide and quickly replace the bung with the gas syringe already attached. Swirl the reaction mixture at a constant speed.
- Record the amount of oxygen produced every 20 seconds for 3 minutes and plot a graph of volume of oxygen versus time.
- Repeat the reaction with 0.20 g of lead(IV) oxide and copper(II) oxide but keep everything else the same.

The sample data below show manganese(IV) oxide is a very effective catalyst for the decomposition of hydrogen peroxide. In comparison, lead(IV) oxide is less effective as the rate of the reaction is much slower and copper(II) oxide does not act as a catalyst for this reaction at all.

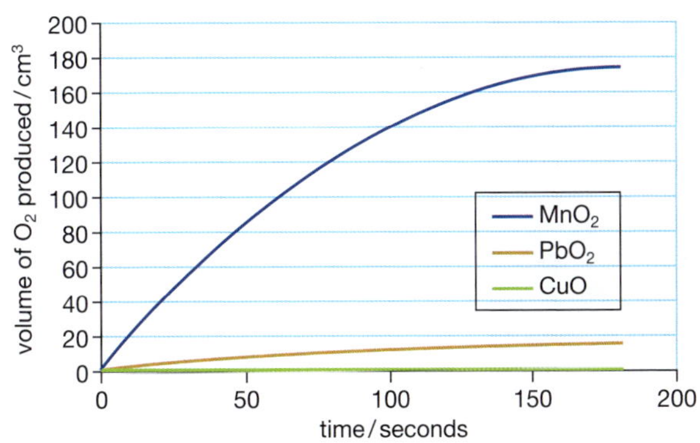

▲ Figure 16.23 The catalytic effect of different solids on the decomposition of H_2O_2.

HOW DOES A CATALYST WORK?

Not all collisions result in a reaction happening. Collisions have to involve at least a certain minimum amount of energy, called the *activation energy* (page 431).

If a reaction is slow, it means that very few collisions have this amount of energy; when most collisions happen, the particles simply bounce off each other.

Catalysts work by providing an alternative route for the reaction, involving a lower activation energy.

If the activation energy is lower, many more collisions are likely to be successful. The reaction happens faster because many more particles *have energy greater than or equal to the activation energy for the alternative route*. The energy of the particles has not changed but it has been made easier for them to react.

▲ Figure 16.24 Traffic passes easily through a road tunnel under a mountain.

You can illustrate this with a simple everyday example. Imagine you have a mountain between two valleys. Only a few very energetic people will climb over the mountain from one valley to the next. Now imagine building a road tunnel through the mountain. Lots of people will be able to travel easily from one valley to the next.

Be careful how you phrase the statement explaining how a catalyst works. You should say 'Catalysts provide an alternative route with a lower activation energy'.

They *do not* 'lower the activation energy' any more than building a tunnel lowers the mountain. The original route is still there, and if particles collide with enough energy they will still use it, just as very energetic people will still choose to climb over the top of the mountain.

CATALYSTS IN INDUSTRY

Catalysts are especially important in industrial reactions because they help substances to react quickly at lower temperatures and pressures than would otherwise be needed. This saves money.

REVERSIBILITY AND DYNAMIC EQUILIBRIA

TWO REVERSIBLE REACTIONS

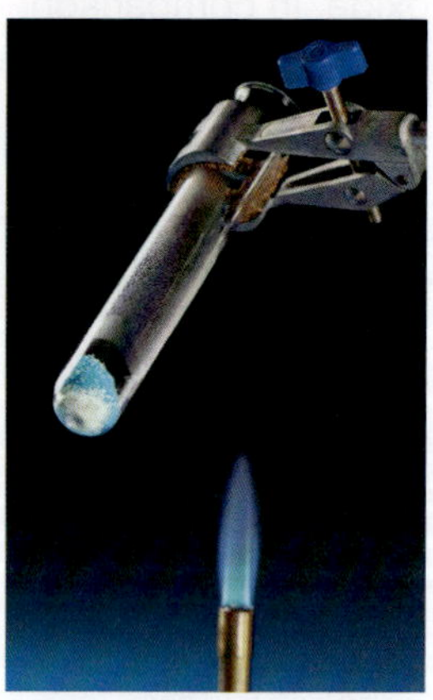

▲ Figure 16.25 Copper(II) sulfate crystals are split into anhydrous copper(II) sulfate and water on gentle heating.

DEHYDRATION OF COPPER(II) SULFATE CRYSTALS

If you heat blue copper(II) sulfate crystals gently, the blue crystals turn to a white powder and water is driven off. Heating causes the crystals to lose their *water of crystallisation* and white *anhydrous* copper(II) sulfate is formed. 'Anhydrous' simply means 'without water'.

$$\underset{\text{blue}}{CuSO_4{\cdot}5H_2O(s)} \rightarrow \underset{\text{white}}{CuSO_4(s)} + 5H_2O(l)$$

Heat is needed for this reaction to occur

If you add water to the white solid, it turns blue again; it also becomes very warm. See Figure 14.3 (page 400).

$$\underset{\text{white}}{CuSO_4(s)} + 5H_2O(l) \rightarrow \underset{\text{blue}}{CuSO_4{\cdot}5H_2O(s)}$$

Heat is released from this reaction

The original change has been exactly reversed. Even the heat that you put in originally has been given out again. This is called a **reversible** reaction and is indicated by a special arrow:

$$CuSO_4{\cdot}5H_2O(s) \rightleftharpoons CuSO_4(s) + 5H_2O(l)$$

KEY POINT

This reaction is an example of *thermal decomposition*.

KEY POINT

This is a reaction between an acid (HCl) and a base (NH_3) (see Chapter 13, page 394).

HINT

If you add water to the white solid, it turns blue again; it also becomes very warm. See Figure 14.3 (page 400).

HEATING AMMONIUM CHLORIDE

If you heat ammonium chloride, the white crystals disappear from the bottom of the tube and reappear further up. Heating ammonium chloride splits it into the colourless gases ammonia and hydrogen chloride.

$NH_4Cl(s) \rightarrow NH_3(g) + HCl(g)$ Heat is needed for this reaction to occur
white solid colourless gases

These gases recombine further up the tube, where it is cooler, to form a white solid:

$NH_3(g) + HCl(g) \rightarrow NH_4Cl(s)$ Heat is released from this reaction
colourless gases white solid

The reaction reverses when the conditions are changed from hot to cool.

Figure 16.26 Heating ammonium chloride

This can, again, be shown with the reversible arrow:

$$NH_3(g) + HCl(g) \rightleftharpoons NH_4Cl(s)$$

CHAPTER QUESTIONS

SKILLS CREATIVITY 5th

1 A student carried out an experiment to investigate the rate of a reaction between an excess of dolomite (magnesium carbonate) and 50 cm^3 of dilute hydrochloric acid. The dolomite was in small pieces. The reaction is:

$$MgCO_3(s) + 2HCl(aq) \rightarrow MgCl_2(aq) + H_2O(l) + CO_2(g)$$

He measured the volume of carbon dioxide given off at regular intervals, with the results shown in the table below.

Time / s	0	30	60	90	120	150	180	210	240	270	300	330	360
Volume / cm^3	0	27	45	59	70	78	85	90	94	97	99	100	100

a Draw a diagram of the apparatus you would use for this experiment and label it.

SKILLS INTERPRETATION

b Plot these results on a piece of graph paper, with time on the *x*-axis and volume of gas on the *y*-axis.

SKILLS ANALYSIS, REASONING 6th

c At what time is the gas being given off most quickly? Explain why the reaction is fastest at that time.

SKILLS PROBLEM SOLVING 5th

d Use your graph to find out how long it took to produce 50 cm^3 of gas.

6th

e Use your graph to calculate the average rate of this reaction in the first 80 seconds.

SKILLS REASONING

6th

f In each of the following questions, state and explain what would happen to the initial rate of the reaction and to the total volume of gas given off if various changes were made to the experiment.

i The mass of dolomite and the volume and concentration of acid were kept constant, but the dolomite was in one big lump instead of small pieces.

ii The mass of dolomite was unchanged and it was still in small pieces. 50 cm^3 of hydrochloric acid was used, which had half the original concentration.

iii The dolomite was unchanged again. This time 25 cm^3 of the original acid was used instead of 50 cm^3.

iv The acid was heated to 40 °C before the dolomite was added to it.

7th

2 The effect of concentration and temperature on the rate of a reaction can be explored using the reaction between magnesium ribbon and dilute sulfuric acid:

$$Mg(s) + H_2SO_4(aq) \rightarrow MgSO_4(aq) + H_2(g)$$

A student dropped a 2 cm length of magnesium ribbon into 25 cm^3 of dilute sulfuric acid (a large excess of acid) in a boiling tube. She stirred the contents of the tube continuously and timed how long it took for the magnesium to disappear.

a What would you expect to happen to the time taken for the reaction if the student repeated the experiment using the same length of magnesium with a mixture of 20 cm^3 of acid and 5 cm^3 of water? Explain your answer in relation to the collision theory.

b What would you expect to happen to the time taken for the reaction if she repeated the experiment using the original quantities of magnesium and acid, but first heated the acid to 50 °C? Explain your answer in relation to the collision theory.

c Give a reason why is it important to keep the reaction mixture stirred continuously.

3 Catalysts speed up reactions, but can be recovered chemically unchanged at the end of the reaction.

a Explain how a catalyst works to increase the rate of reactions.

SKILLS DECISION MAKING

b Describe how you would find out whether iron(III) oxide was a catalyst for the decomposition of hydrogen peroxide solution. Note: you need to show not only that it speeds the reaction up, but that it is chemically unchanged at the end.

SKILLS REASONING

6th

4 The thermal decomposition of ammonium chloride is a reversible reaction.

$$NH_4Cl(s) \rightleftharpoons NH_3(g) + HCl(g)$$

a Explain how the equation shows that the reaction is reversible.

SKILLS CRITICAL THINKING

b Give one observation associated with the **forward reaction**.

UNIT QUESTIONS

SKILLS ANALYSIS, PROBLEM SOLVING 3rd

1 A group of students wanted to investigate the energy changes when salts dissolve in water. The teacher suggested that they should measure the temperature changes that occur when the salts were dissolved.

This is the method they followed:

- Add 100 cm^3 of water to a beaker.
- Record the temperature of the water.
- Weigh 5.00 g of salt and add it to the water in the beaker.
- Stir the mixture with a glass rod vigorously until all the solid has dissolved.
- Record the maximum (or minimum) temperature of the solution.

a The diagram below shows the readings on the thermometer before and after the student dissolved a salt, potassium chloride, in water.

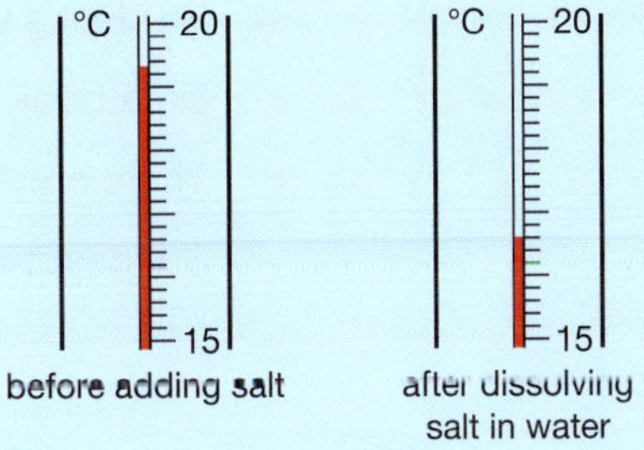

i Write down the thermometer readings and calculate the temperature change. **(3)**

Temperature before .... °C

Temperature after .... °C

Temperature change .... °C

SKILLS CRITICAL THINKING 8th

ii Which of the following statements is true about the dissolving of potassium chloride in water (choose one answer)? **(1)**

A The process is endothermic and ΔH is positive.

B The process is exothermic and ΔH is positive.

C The process is endothermic and ΔH is negative.

D The process is exothermic and ΔH is negative.

SKILLS PROBLEM SOLVING 8th

b Another student repeated the experiment with a different salt, calcium chloride, using the same method and recorded these results.

Volume of water = 100 cm^3

Starting temperature of water = 15.9 °C

Maximum temperature of solution = 23.2 °C

Mass of salt = 5.00 g

9th

i Calculate the heat energy released in this experiment. The specific heat capacity of the solution *c* = 4.2 J/g/°C and the mass of 1 cm^3 of mixture = 1 g. **(3)**

ii How many moles of calcium chloride dissolved in the solution? **(2)**

10th

iii Work out the molar enthalpy change, in kJ/mol, for dissolving calcium chloride in water. **(2)**

SKILLS REASONING 9th

c Another student dissolved magnesium chloride in water. She compared her result with a data book value.

Student's value = −105 kJ/mol

Data book value = −141 kJ/mol

There are no errors in the calculation of her result.

Suggest two reasons why the student's value differs from the data book value. **(2)**

(Total 13 marks)

SKILLS PROBLEM SOLVING

2 In an experiment to investigate the rate of decomposition of hydrogen peroxide solution in the presence of manganese(IV) oxide, a student mixed 10 cm^3 of hydrogen peroxide solution with 30 cm^3 of water and added 0.20 g of manganese(IV) oxide. She measured the volume of oxygen evolved at 60 s intervals. The results of her experiment are recorded in the table below.

Time / s	0	60	120	180	240	300
Volume / cm^3	0	30	48	57	60	60

a Write a balanced equation for the decomposition of hydrogen peroxide. **(2)**

SKILLS REASONING 6th

b Explain why the manganese(IV) oxide was added in a weighing bottle rather than directly into the hydrogen peroxide solution. **(1)**

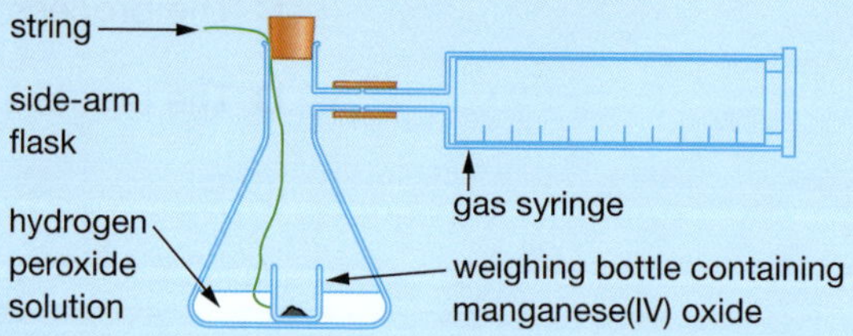

SKILLS INTERPRETATION 7th

c Plot a graph of her results and draw a line of best fit. Make sure that you label the axes. **(4)**

SKILLS ANALYSIS, PROBLEM SOLVING

d Use your graph to find out the following:

5th

i How long it took to produce 50 cm^3 of oxygen. **(1)**

ii The volume of gas produced after 100 seconds. **(1)**

6th

iii The average rate (with unit) in the first 150 seconds. **(2)**

SKILLS ANALYSIS, PROBLEM SOLVING 6th

e Explain why the graph becomes horizontal after 240 seconds. **(2)**

f Manganese(IV) oxide acts as a catalyst for this reaction.

SKILLS CRITICAL THINKING 7th

i A catalyst speeds up a chemical reaction by (choose one answer): **(1)**

A increasing the number of collisions between the reactant particles.

B providing an alternative reaction pathway with lower activation energy.

C increasing the energy of the reactant particles.

D changing the enthalpy of the reaction.

SKILLS DECISION MAKING 9th

ii Describe a method you could use to show that the manganese(IV) oxide is acting as a catalyst in this reaction. **(4)**

SKILLS INTERPRETATION 7th

g Suppose the experiment had been repeated using the same quantities of everything, but with the reaction flask immersed in ice.
Sketch the graph you would expect to get. Use the same grid as in **c**.
Label the new graph **G**. **(2)**

h On the same grid as in **c** and **g** sketch the graph you would expect to get if you repeated the experiment at the original temperature using 5 cm^3 of hydrogen peroxide solution, 35 cm^3 of water and 0.20 g of manganese(IV) oxide. Label this graph **H**. **(2)**

(Total 22 marks)

SKILLS EXECUTIVE FUNCTION 6th

3 A group of students investigated the effect of changing the concentration of dilute hydrochloric acid on the rate of its reaction with marble chips (calcium carbonate).

The equation for this reaction is

$$CaCO_3(s) + 2HCl(aq) \rightarrow CaCl_2(aq) + H_2O(l) + CO_2(g)$$

They used the following method:

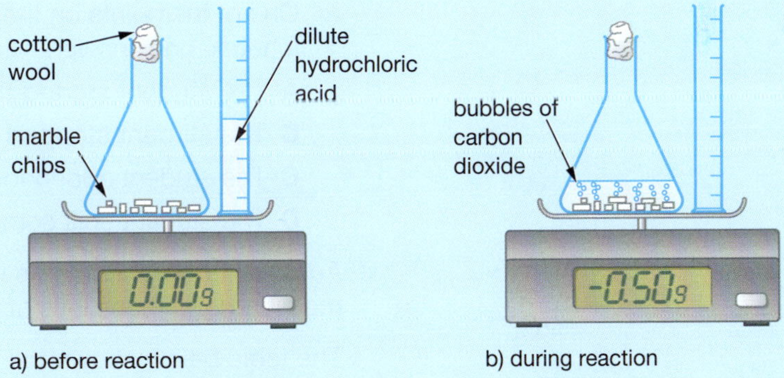

The students recorded the time taken for the mass of the flask and contents to decrease by 0.50 g.

The experiment was then repeated using different concentrations of hydrochloric acid.

a To ensure it was a valid (fair) test, the students kept the number of marble chips constant in each experiment. Suggest two other properties of the marble chips that should be kept the same in each experiment. **(2)**

SKILLS CRITICAL THINKING 5th

b What is the purpose of the cotton wool? **(1)**

c The teacher gave the students some hydrochloric acid that was labelled 100%. The table below shows the results.

Students	Mass of $CaCO_3$ / g	Volume of 2.00 mol / dm^3 HCl / cm^3	Volume of water / cm^3	Concentration of HCl / %	Time to lose 0.50 g / s
1	5.00	25	0	100	105
2	5.00	20	5	80	150
3	5.00	15		60	175
4	5.00	10	15	40	272
5	5.00	5	20	20	520

SKILLS PROBLEM SOLVING 6th

i The results of Student 3 are incomplete.
Calculate the volume of water the student should have used for the result to be comparable with the other four (choose one answer). **(1)**

A 5
B 10
C 15
D 20

SKILLS INTERPRETATION 7th

ii Plot a graph of the results on a separate piece of graph paper, with concentration of acid on the *x*-axis and time on the *y*-axis.
Draw a line of best fit. **(4)**

SKILLS ANALYSIS, PROBLEM SOLVING 5th

iii Use your graph in ii to find the time taken for the loss of 0.50 g of mass from the flask when the concentration of acid is 70%. **(1)**

SKILLS REASONING

iv One of the points on the graph is anomalous. Identify a reason for this (choose one answer). **(1)**

A The student started the stopwatch too late.
B The student stopped the stopwatch before mass loss reached 0.50 g.
C The student added too much water at the beginning of the experiment.
D The student spilt some water before adding it into the reaction mixture.

d Another group of students repeated the experiment, but this time they measured the mass loss after 1 minute.

The table below shows the results obtained by the students.

Mass of carbon dioxide given off / g	0.36	0.72	0.88	1.28	1.44	1.65
Concentration of acid / mol/dm^3	0.20	0.40	0.50	0.70	0.80	0.90

i Describe the relationship between the mass of carbon dioxide given off in 1 minute and the concentration of the acid. **(2)**

7th

ii Explain this relationship in terms of particles. **(3)**

(Total 15 marks)

SKILLS REASONING

7th

4 During the manufacture of nitric acid from ammonia, the ammonia is oxidised to nitrogen monoxide, NO, by oxygen in the air.

$$4NH_3(g) + 5O_2(g) \rightarrow 4NO(g) + 6H_2O(g)$$

The ammonia is mixed with air and passed through a stack of large circular gauzes made of platinum–rhodium alloy at red heat (about 900 °C). The platinum–rhodium gauzes act as a catalyst for the reaction.

a Gas particles have to collide before they can react. Use the collision theory to help you to answer the following questions.

i Because the gases are in contact with the catalyst for only a very short time, it is important that the reaction happens as quickly as possible. Explain why increasing the temperature to 900 °C makes the reaction very fast. **(3)**

ii Explain what will happen to the reaction rate if the pressure is increased. **(2)**

iii Explain why the platinum–rhodium alloy is used as gauzes rather than as pellets. **(2)**

b Platinum and rhodium are extremely expensive metals. Explain why the manufacturer can justify their initial cost. **(2)**

(Total 9 marks)

5 At temperatures above 150 °C, brown nitrogen dioxide gas dissociates (splits up reversibly) into colourless nitrogen monoxide and oxygen:

$$2NO_2(g) \rightleftharpoons 2NO(g) + O_2(g) \qquad \Delta H = +114 \text{ kJ/mol}$$

a Write down the meaning of the symbols $\rightleftharpoons$ and ΔH. **(2)**

b What does the positive sign of ΔH indicate about the reaction? **(1)**

c Give one observation associated with the backward reaction. **(1)**

(Total 4 marks)

CHEMISTRY UNIT 4 ORGANIC CHEMISTRY

Organic chemistry is the study of the compounds of carbon (there are some inorganic carbon compounds as well). There are more organic compounds than all the other compounds put together. These compounds include naturally occurring ones that are found in our bodies, for example proteins, DNA and fats. There are also artificially made compounds such as plastics, dyes and drugs. The artificial compounds are derived from chemicals obtained from crude oil. When all the crude oil has been used we will have to find new sources for more than just fuel for cars and making electricity. Organic chemists are involved in the synthesis of a huge variety of new compounds, including drugs and medicines used to treat diseases such as cancer, AIDS, influenza and asthma. The synthesis of these drugs can involve a large number of steps and requires the knowledge and understanding of a great number of organic chemistry reactions. It can take many years and millions of dollars to develop a new drug.

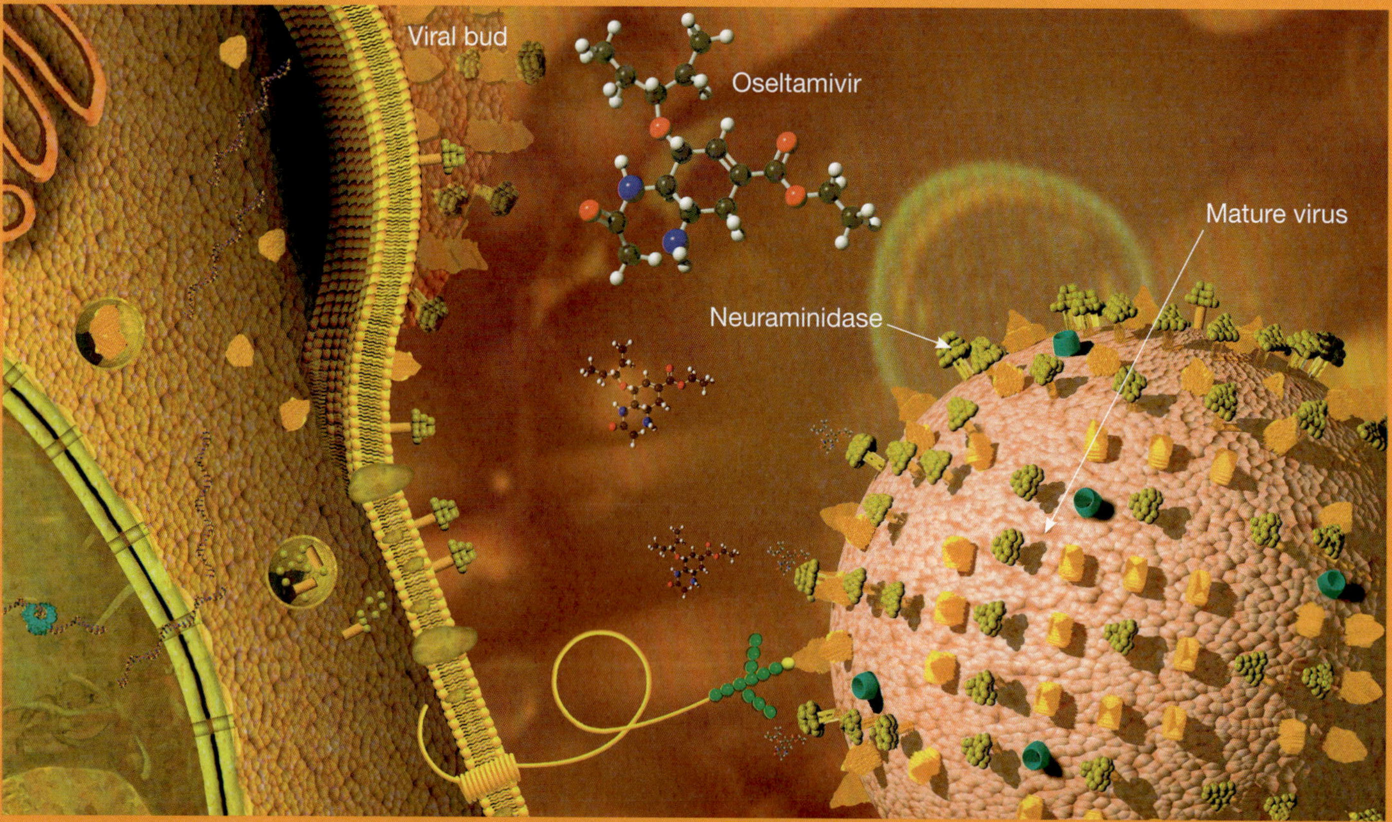

17 INTRODUCTION TO ORGANIC CHEMISTRY

There are millions of different organic compounds. They all contain carbon and hydrogen, and often other elements such as oxygen, nitrogen and chlorine. Carbon atoms can join together to form chains and rings, which is why there are so many carbon compounds. This chapter introduces you to some of the important ideas that you need to know before you can start to understand organic chemistry.

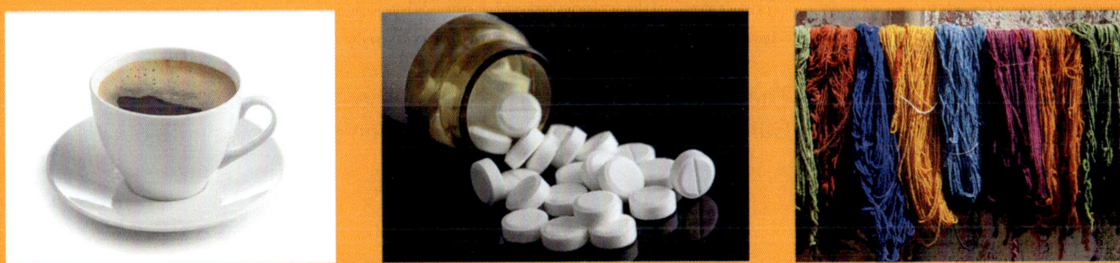

▲ Figure 17.1 What do caffeine, aspirin and dyes have in common? They are all organic compounds.

LEARNING OBJECTIVES

- Know that a hydrocarbon is a compound made up of hydrogen and carbon only
- Understand how to represent organic molecules using empirical formulae, molecular formulae, general formulae, structural formulae and displayed formulae
- Know what is meant by the terms homologous series, functional group and isomerism
- Understand how to name compounds (containing up to six carbon atoms) using the rules of International Union of Pure and Applied Chemistry (IUPAC) nomenclature
- Understand how to write the possible structural and displayed formulae of an organic molecule given its molecular formula
- Understand how to classify reactions of organic compounds as substitution, addition and combustion

In the next few chapters we will be looking at organic compounds. The term 'organic' was originally used because it was believed that organic compounds could only come from living things. Now it is used for any carbon compound except for the very simplest (carbon dioxide, carbon monoxide, the carbonates and the hydrogencarbonates).

Organic compounds can exist as chains, branched chains or rings of carbon atoms with hydrogens attached.

When you start doing organic chemistry, you are suddenly faced with a whole lot of new compounds with strange names and unfamiliar ways of drawing them. It can be quite scary!

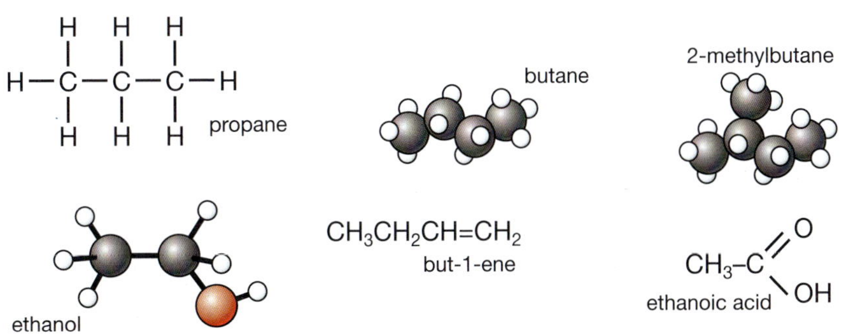

▲ Figure 17.2 Organic chemistry involves a lot of new compounds.

HINT

Your school may have models you can use. Otherwise, you can make your own out of modelling clay and matchsticks or small nails to use as bonds.

The secret at the beginning is to spend a lot of time exploring the subject – understanding names, drawing structures and making models.

HYDROCARBONS

The simplest organic compounds are **hydrocarbons**. *These are molecules that contain carbon and hydrogen only*.

HINT

The word *only* is important here. Virtually all organic compounds contain carbon and hydrogen but hydrocarbons contain *only* carbon and hydrogen.

The carbon atoms are joined together with single, double or triple bonds. Carbon atoms are joined to hydrogen atoms by single bonds.

KEY POINT

Organic compounds can be described as **saturated** (containing only single C–C bonds) or **unsaturated** (containing double or triple C–C bonds). This is discussed in Chapters 19 and 20.

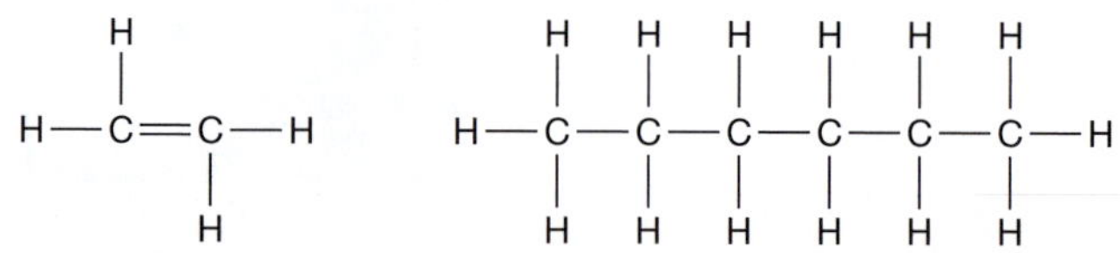

ethene hexane

▲ Figure 17.3 Examples of hydrocarbons

TYPES OF FORMULA FOR ORGANIC MOLECULES

EMPIRICAL FORMULAE

REMINDER

Empirical and molecular formula are introduced in Chapter 5.

An **empirical formula** tells you *the simplest whole number ratio of the atoms in a compound*. It can be calculated from experimental data. Without more information, it is not possible to identify the 'true' or 'molecular' formula. Sometimes the empirical formula is the same as the molecular formula. For example, the empirical formula of methane is CH_4, which is the same as its molecular formula. However, the empirical formula of ethane is CH_3 whereas its molecular formula is C_2H_6.

MOLECULAR FORMULAE

A **molecular formula** *counts the actual number of each type of atom present in a molecule*. For example, the molecular formula of butane is C_4H_{10} and the molecular formula of ethene is C_2H_4.

The molecular formula is a multiple of the empirical formula. For example, if a compound has empirical formula CH_2, the molecular formula could be C_2H_4, C_3H_6, C_4H_8, etc. The ratio of C:H must always be the same as in the empirical formula.

The molecular formula tells you nothing about the way the atoms are joined together. Both the compounds in Figure 17.4 have the same molecular formula.

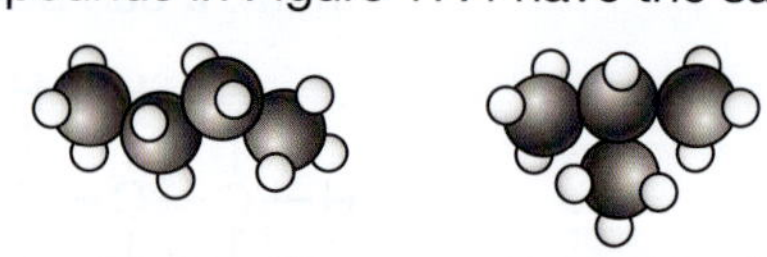

▲ Figure 17.4 These two compounds have the same molecular formula but different structures.

Molecular formulae are used very rarely in organic chemistry because they don't give any useful information about the bonding in the molecule. You might use them in equations for the combustion of simple hydrocarbons, where the structure of the molecule doesn't matter. For example:

$$2C_4H_{10}(g) + 13O_2(g) \rightarrow 8CO_2(g) + 10H_2O(l)$$

In almost all other cases, you use a structural or a displayed formula.

GENERAL FORMULAE

There are many different families of organic compounds, known as **homologous series**. Examples of homologous series are alkanes and alkenes. These homologous series will be discussed in more detail in later chapters.

A homologous series is a *series of compounds with similar chemical properties because they have the same functional group. Each member differs from the next by one* $-CH_2-$.

Members of a homologous series can be represented using a **general formula**. The first few members of the alkane series are shown in Table 17.1.

Table 17.1 The first few members of the alkane and alkene homologous series

Alkanes	Alkenes
CH_4	
C_2H_6	C_2H_4
C_3H_8	C_3H_6
C_4H_{10}	C_4H_8

In the case of alkanes, if there are n carbons in a molecule, there are always $2n + 2$ hydrogens. The general formula of alkanes is C_nH_{2n+2}. For methane, CH_4, there is 1 carbon atom in the molecule and $2 \times 1 + 2 = 4$ hydrogen atoms. For propane C_3H_8, there are 3 carbon atoms in the molecule and $2 \times 3 + 2 = 8$ hydrogen atoms. We can therefore work out that dodecane, which has 12 carbon atoms, will have 26 hydrogen atoms and the molecular formula $C_{12}H_{26}$.

Different homologous series usually have different general formulae. For example, the general formula for alkenes is C_nH_{2n}.

HINT

More features of a homologous series are discussed on page 469.

A **functional group** is *an atom or a group of atoms that determine the chemical properties of a compound*. All compounds in the same homologous series have the same functional group. For example, the functional group for alkenes is C=C.

HINT

A way of thinking about this is: the functional group is what makes the behaviour of a particular compound different from that of an alkane.

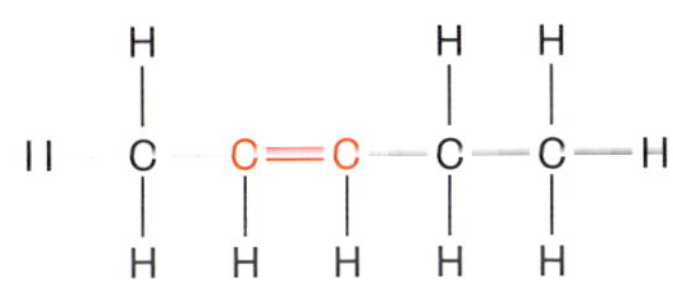

Figure 17.5 Alkenes contain the C=C functional group.

STRUCTURAL FORMULAE

A **structural formula** shows *how the atoms in a molecule are joined together*. There are two ways of representing structural formulae: they can be drawn as a **displayed formula** (full structural formula), or they can be written out in condensed form (*condensed structural formula*) by omitting all the carbon–carbon single bonds and carbon–hydrogen single bonds, for example $CH_3CH_2CH_3$. You need to be confident about using either way.

DISPLAYED FORMULAE

A displayed formula (sometimes called a full structural formula) shows *all* the bonds in the molecule as individual lines. You need to remember that each line represents *a pair of shared electrons in a covalent bond*.

Figure 17.6 shows a model of butane, together with its displayed formula. Notice that the way the displayed formula is drawn is different from the shape of the actual molecule. Displayed formulae are always drawn with the molecule straightened out and flattened. They do, however, show exactly how all the atoms are joined together.

REMINDER

It is important to remember when you draw structures that C always forms four bonds and H always forms one bond. Oxygen will form two bonds and a halogen (chlorine, bromine, etc.) atom one. If you are not sure about why these atoms form this number of bonds, you need to look back at Chapter 7.

Figure 17.6 Butane. The angles between neighbouring C–H bonds in butane are shown as 90° in the two-dimensional displayed formula. In reality they are about 109.5° in a tetrahedral arrangement in three dimensions, similar to the arrangement of C–C bonds in a diamond structure (see Chapter 7, page 334).

KEY POINT

If you are asked to draw the structure for a molecule in an International GCSE exam, always draw it as a displayed formula. You can't lose any marks by doing this, whereas you might if you use the simplified form. If, on the other hand, you are simply writing a structure in an equation, for example, you can use whichever version you prefer.

HINT

The best way to understand that these are all the same is to make some models. If you don't have access to molecular models, use blobs of modelling clay joined together with pieces of matchstick or small nails to represent the bonds. You will find that you can change the shape of the model by rotating around the bonds. That's what happens in real molecules.

KEY POINT

Structural formulae may be drawn in various ways. Sometimes no bonds are shown and other times some bonds are shown. The easiest way to think about it is like this: if all the bonds are shown, then it is a displayed formula but if not all of them are shown (but you can still see what the structure is), then it is a structural formula.

KEY POINT

In more advanced work the structural formula of propene would just be written as CH_3CHCH_2 but at International GCSE the C=C will normally be shown.

HOW TO DRAW A STRUCTURAL FORMULA

For anything other than the smallest molecules, drawing a fully displayed formula is very time-consuming. You can simplify the formula by writing, for example, CH_3 or CH_2 instead of showing all the carbon–hydrogen bonds.

The structural formula for butane can be shown as

$CH_3CH_2CH_2CH_3$ or $CH_3{-}CH_2{-}CH_2{-}CH_3$

These both show exactly how the atoms in the molecule are joined together. The corresponding molecular formula, C_4H_{10}, doesn't give you the same sort of useful information about the molecule.

All the structures in Figure 17.7 represent butane: even though they look different they are exactly the same molecule.

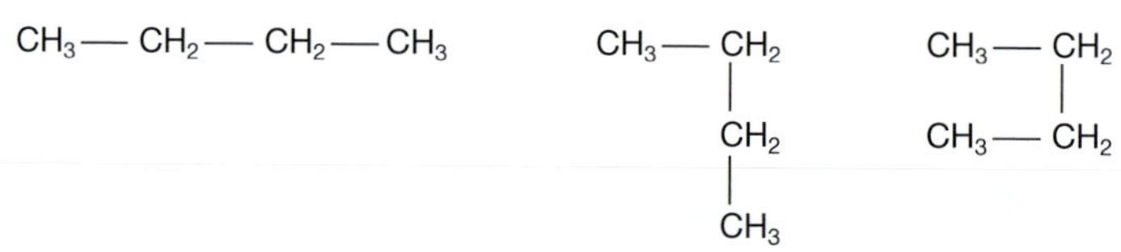

▲ Figure 17.7 All three structures represent butane. The convention is to write the structure with all the carbon atoms in a straight line.

Each structure shows four carbon atoms joined together in a chain, but the chain has simply twisted. This happens in real molecules as well: the atoms can rotate around single carbon–carbon bonds, as shown in Figure 17.8.

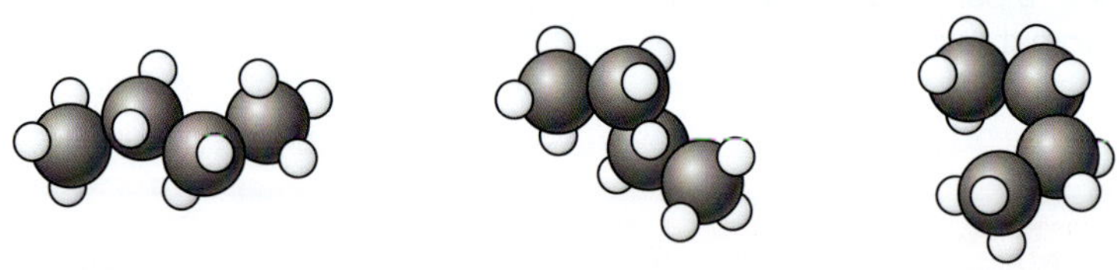

▲ Figure 17.8 These diagrams show the shape of a butane molecule better, but you would not draw these in an exam.

A molecule like propene, C_3H_6, has a carbon–carbon double bond. This is shown by drawing two lines between the carbon atoms to show *the two pairs of shared electrons*. You would normally write this in a simplified structural formula as $CH_3CH{=}CH_2$.

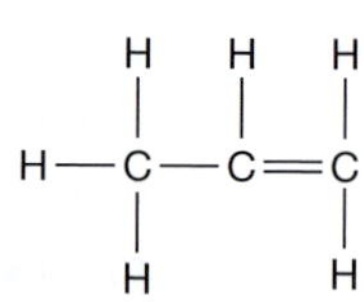

▲ Figure 17.9 The displayed formula for propene

NAMING ORGANIC COMPOUNDS

Names for organic compounds can appear quite complicated, but they are simply a code that describes the molecule. Each part of a name tells you something specific about the molecule. One part of a name tells you how many carbon atoms there are in the longest chain, another part tells you whether there are any carbon–carbon double bonds, and so on.

CODING THE CHAIN LENGTH

Look for the code letters in the name – these are given in Table 17.2.

Table 17.2 Coding the chain length

Code letters	Number of carbons in chain
meth	1
eth	2
prop	3
but	4
pent	5
hex	6

For example, **but**ane has a chain of four carbon atoms. **Prop**ane has a chain of three carbon atoms.

HINT

You have to learn these! The first four are the difficult ones because there isn't any pattern. However, a mnemonic can help, something like **M**onkeys **E**at **P**ink **B**ananas. Or you could think of one of your own that you can remember!
'**Pent**' means five (as in **pent**agon) and '**hex**' means six (as in **hex**agon).

CODING FOR THE TYPE OF COMPOUND

ALKANES

Alkanes are *a homologous series of similar hydrocarbons (compounds of carbon and hydrogen only) in which all the carbons are joined to each other with single covalent bonds*. Compounds like this are coded with the ending '**ane**'. For example, eth*ane* is a two-carbon chain (because of 'eth') with a carbon–carbon single bond, $CH_3{-}CH_3$.

HINT

In more complicated molecules, the presence of the code 'an' in the name again shows that the carbons are joined by single bonds. For example, you can tell that propan-1-ol contains three carbon atoms ('prop') joined together by carbon–carbon single bonds ('an'). The coding on the end gives you more information about the molecule. You will meet this later in the chapter.

ALKENES

Alkenes are *a homologous series of hydrocarbons which contain a carbon–carbon double bond*. This is shown in their name by the ending '**ene**'. For example, eth*ene* is a two-carbon chain containing a carbon–carbon double bond, $CH_2{=}CH_2$. With longer chains, the position of the double bond could vary in the chain. This is shown by numbering the chain and noting which carbon atom the double bond *starts* from.

Table 17.3 Indicating the position of the double bond in the name of alkenes

Formula	Name	Description
$CH_2{=}CHCH_2CH_3$	but-1-ene	a four-carbon chain with a double bond starting on the first carbon
$CH_3CH{=}CHCH_3$	but-2-ene	a four-carbon chain with a double bond starting on the second carbon

How do you know which end of the chain to number from? The rule is that *you number from the end which produces the smaller numbers in the name*.

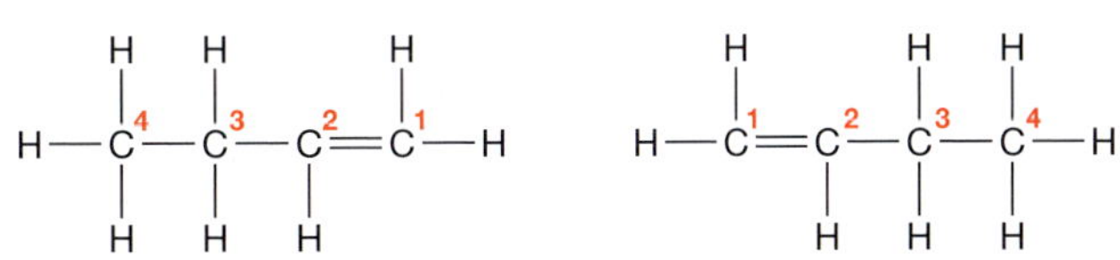

▲ Figure 17.10 Both structures represent but-1-ene.

HINT

Both parts of Figure 17.10 show the same molecule, but in one case it has been turned over so that what was originally on the left is now on the right, and vice versa. It would be silly to change the name every time the molecule moved! Both of the forms in Figure 17.10 are called but-1-ene.

CODING FOR BRANCHED CHAINS

Hydrocarbon chains can have side branches on them. You are only likely to come across two small side chains, shown in Table 17.4.

Table 17.4 Coding for branched chains

Side chain	Coded
CH_3–	methyl
CH_3CH_2–	ethyl

KEY POINT

Notice that the count of the number of carbons in the side chain is coded exactly as before: '**meth**' shows a *one*-carbon side chain, '**eth**' shows *two* carbons. The 'yl' shows that the group is attached to something else.

The name of a molecule is always based on the longest chain you can find in it. *The position of the side chain is shown by numbering the carbon atoms from the end of the longest chain which produces the smaller numbers in the name*, exactly as before with the carbon–carbon double bonds in alkenes.

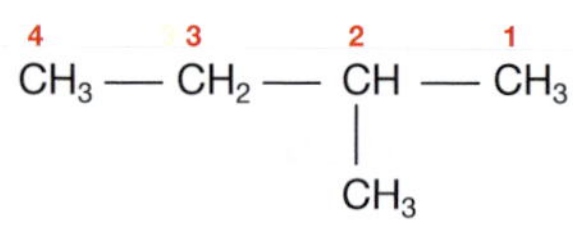

▲ Figure 17.11 Number from the end that produces the smaller number for the side chain branch.

The longest chain in the molecule in Figure 17.11 has four carbon atoms ('but') with no double bonds ('ane'). The name is based on butane. There is a methyl group branching from the number 2 carbon. (Remember to number from the end that produces the smaller number.) The compound is called 2-methylbutane.

Where there is more than one side chain, you describe the position of each of them.

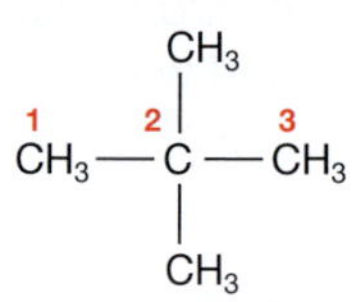

▲ Figure 17.12 Describe the position of each side chain.

The longest chain in the molecule in Figure 17.12 has three carbon atoms and no double bonds. Therefore the name is based on propane.

There are two methyl groups attached to the second carbon. The compound is 2,2-dimethylpropane. The '*di*' in the name shows the presence of the two methyl groups. '2,2' shows that they are both on the second carbon atom.

You can reverse this process and draw a structural formula from a name. All you have to do is decode the name.

For example, what is the structural formula for 2,3-dimethylbut-2-ene?

Start by looking for the code for the longest chain length. 'but' shows a four-carbon chain. 'ene' shows that it contains a carbon–carbon double bond starting on the second carbon atom ('-2-ene'). There are two methyl groups ('dimethyl') attached to the second and third carbon atoms in the chain ('2,3-'). All you have to do now is to fit all this together into a structure.

HINT

It is much more important to be able to decode names to give structures than the other way around. If you don't know what a teacher or an examiner is talking about, you are completely lost!

Start by drawing the structure without any hydrogen atoms on the main chain. It doesn't matter whether you draw the CH_3 groups pointing up or down. Then add enough hydrogens so that each carbon atom forms four bonds. Figure 17.13 shows how your thinking would work.

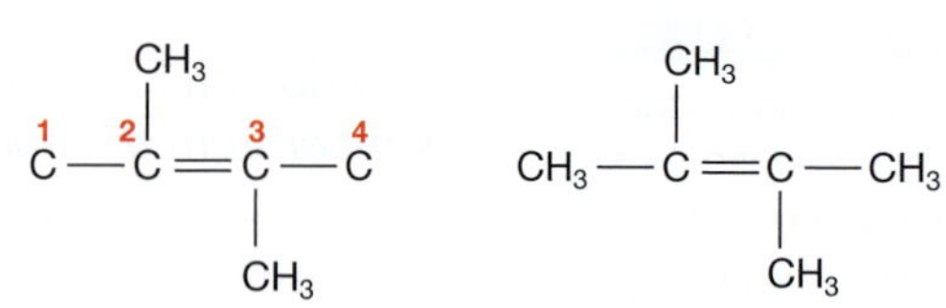

▲ Figure 17.13 First draw the carbon structure, then add hydrogens.

KEY POINT

Warning! Don't confuse the word isomer with isotope. *Isotopes* are different atoms of the same element with the same atomic number but different mass numbers.

STRUCTURAL ISOMERISM

***Structural isomers** are molecules with the same molecular formula, but different structural formulae.*

Examples will make this clear.

STRUCTURAL ISOMERISM IN THE ALKANES

ISOMERS OF C_5H_{12}

If you had some molecular models and picked out five carbon atoms and 12 hydrogen atoms, you would find it was possible to join them together in more than one way. The different molecules formed are known as isomers. All have the molecular formula C_5H_{12}, but different structures.

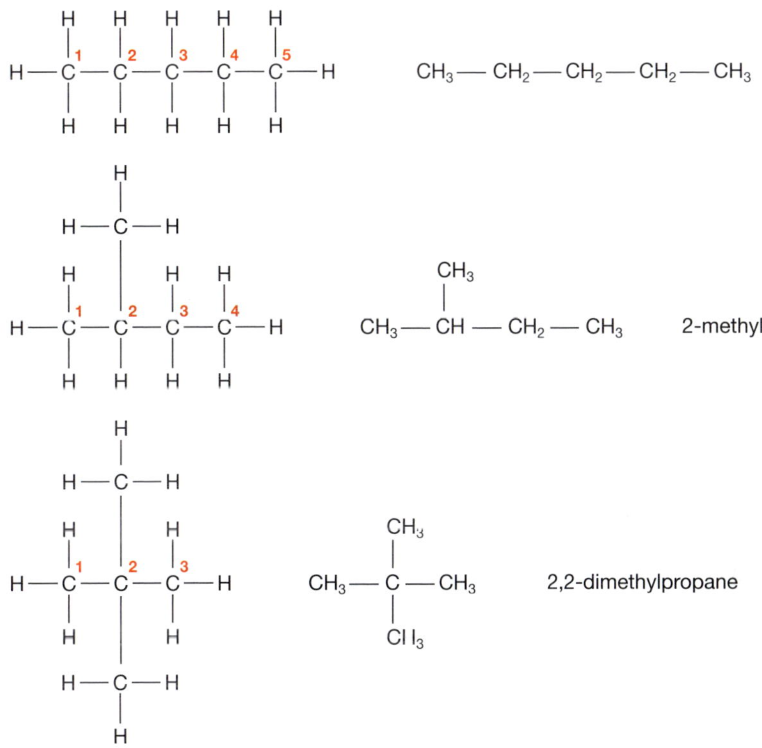

pentane

2-methylbutane

2,2-dimethylpropane

▲ Figure 17.14 There are three isomers for C_5H_{12}. These can be shown as either displayed formulae or structural formulae.

If you look carefully at the structures in Figure 17.14 you can see that you couldn't change one into the other simply by bending or twisting the molecule. You would have to break some bonds and reconnect the atoms. That's a simple way of telling that you have isomers.

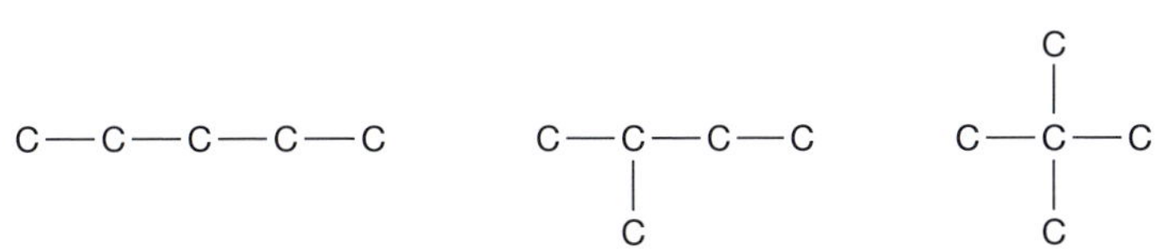

The **straight chain** isomer is called pentane. The *branched chain* isomer in the middle, which has a four-carbon chain ('butane') and a methyl group on the second carbon, is called 2-methylbutane. The final *branched chain* isomer, which has a three-carbon chain ('propane') and two methyl groups on the second carbon, is called 2,2-dimethylpropane. The prefix '*di*' indicates the presence of two identical branches in the molecule.

HINT

It is sometimes easier to see that the molecules are different by drawing only the C atoms joined together, without the hydrogens.

But you must show the hydrogen atoms in the exam!

REMINDER

A straight chain is an unbranched chain.

Students frequently think they can find another isomer as well. If you look closely at this 'fourth' isomer (Figure 17.15) you will see that it is just 2-methylbutane rotated in space.

To avoid this sort of problem, always draw your isomers so that *the longest carbon chain is drawn horizontally* (or draw them out again without the H atoms).

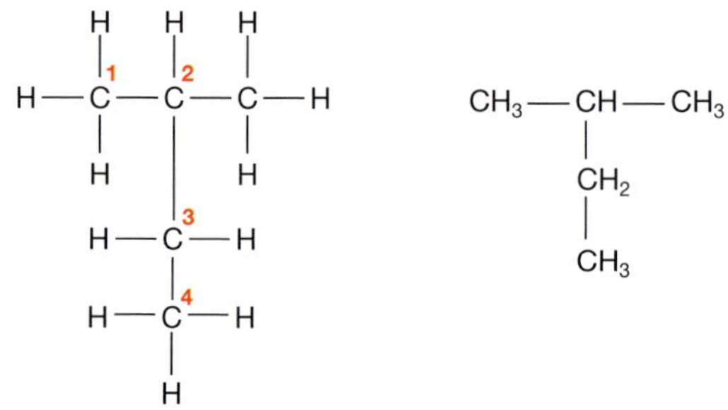

▲ Figure 17.15 There is no fourth isomer for C_5H_{12}.

LOOKING AHEAD

To be precise, the type of isomerism discussed here should be called **structural isomerism**: molecules have the same molecular formula but different structural formulae. The atoms in the different isomers are joined in a different order. There are also other forms of isomerism and one important type is called optical isomerism. Optical isomers have atoms joined in the same order (i.e. they have the same structural formula), but are arranged differently in three-dimensional space. These isomers are mirror images of each other but cannot be superimposed. A good analogy is to look at your left and right hands. They are exactly the opposite of each other but cannot lie on top of another and align perfectly (Figure 17.16).

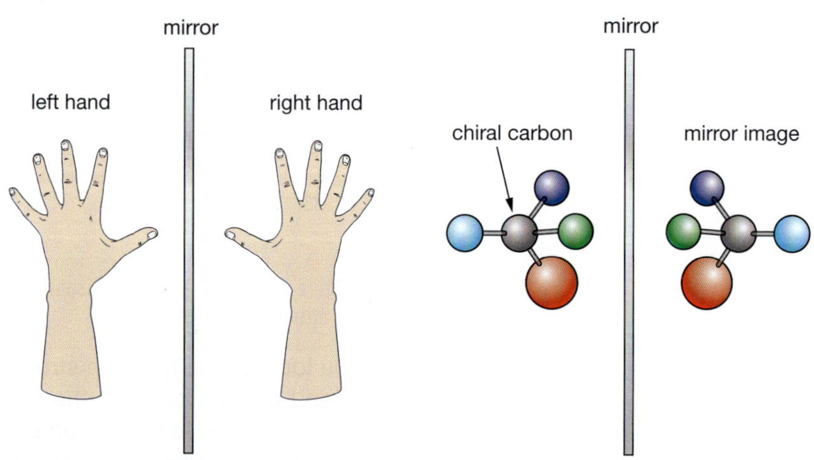

▲ Figure 17.16 Optical isomers are mirror images of each other and cannot be superimposed.

Optical isomerism occurs when a molecule has a *chiral centre*, that is to say it has a carbon atom that is connected to four different atoms or groups of atoms. These molecules have a tetrahedral shape around the chiral centre (molecular shape was mentioned in Chapter 7, pages 329–330). Figure 17.16 shows two molecules that are mirror images of each other. However, if you rotate one of the molecules 180° in space, it cannot be put on top of the other.

Optical isomers have identical chemical properties, except when they interact with something that is also chiral. For example, apart from glycine, all naturally occurring amino acids have optical isomers, which means that all the proteins in our body are chiral. This is why we can distinguish the two optical isomers in

EXTENSION WORK

The optical isomers are assigned a prefix (*R* or *S*) to show the configuration of atoms around the chiral centre.

Figure 17.17. One smells of spearmint and the other of caraway seed because the two molecules interact differently with the protein receptors in our noses.

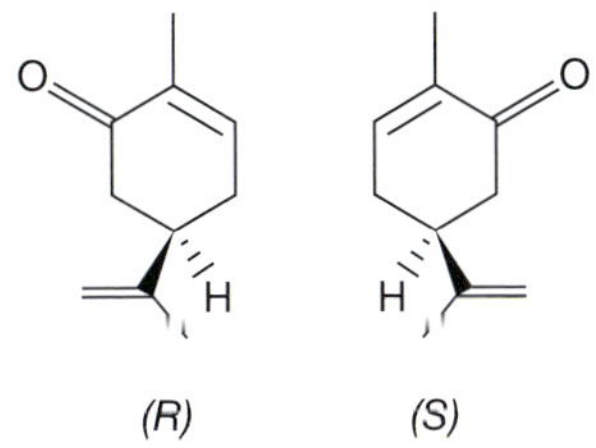

▲ Figure 17.17 Two optical isomers of carvone

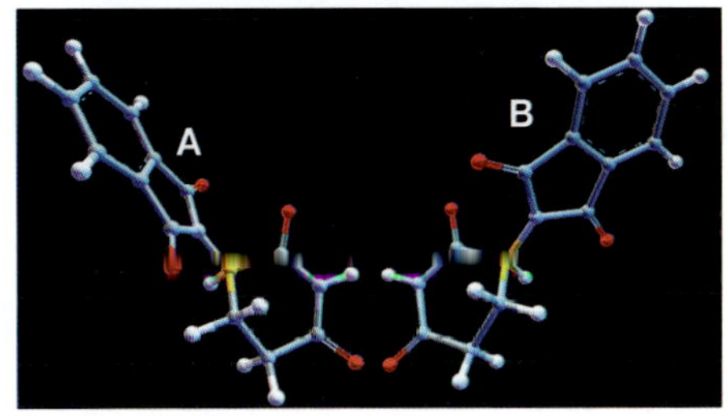

▲ Figure 17.18 Optical isomerism in drug molecules

An important application of optical isomerism is in the synthesis of pharmaceutical drugs. You might have heard of the thalidomide tragedy. Back in the 1960s in Germany, the molecule B shown in Figure 17.18 was found to have anti-nausea effects and was therefore used to treat morning sickness in pregnant woman. Unfortunately, molecule B was being manufactured together with its optical isomer A and little was known about the molecule A until many children born in that era were found to have deformed limbs. These days, many drug companies devote a great deal of money to separating optical isomers of new drugs just in case they have side effects.

STRUCTURAL ISOMERISM IN THE ALKENES

ETHENE AND PROPENE

Ethene, $CH_2{=}CH_2$, doesn't have any isomers. Propene, $CH_3CH{-}CH_2$, doesn't have a structural isomer that is still an alkene.

EXTENSION WORK

There is a structural isomer of C_3H_6 that doesn't have a carbon–carbon double bond. It has three carbon atoms joined in a ring. It is called cyclopropane, which indicates 'a ring of three carbons with only single bonds between them'.

ISOMERS OF C_4H_8

There are three structural isomers with the molecular formula C_4H_8 and containing a carbon–carbon double bond.

$\overset{4}{CH_3}-\overset{3}{CH_2}-\overset{2}{CH}=\overset{1}{CH_2}$

but-1-ene

$\overset{1}{CH_3}-\overset{2}{CH}=\overset{3}{CH}-\overset{4}{CH_3}$

but-2-ene

$\overset{3}{CH_3}-\overset{2}{C}(CH_3)=\overset{1}{CH_2}$

2-methylpropene

▲ Figure 17.19 Structural isomers with the molecular formula of C_4H_8.

HINT

If you aren't comfortable with the names, see pages 450–452 on organic names.

Notice the way that you can vary the position of the double bond as well as branching the chain.

SOME CHEMICAL REACTIONS OF ORGANIC COMPOUNDS

In this section we will look at how to classify the reactions of organic compounds. These reactions will be explained much more in the next few chapters.

COMBUSTION

All organic compounds that you will meet at International GCSE undergo combustion reactions. Combustion is just another way of saying *burning* and involves a reaction with oxygen.

Figure 17.20 The burning of a camping stove

Combustion of hydrocarbons in *excess oxygen* gives rise to *carbon dioxide* and *water*, together with the release of a large amount of heat energy. For example:

propane burning $C_3H_8(g) + 5O_2(g) \rightarrow 3CO_2(g) + 4H_2O(l)$

butene burning $C_4H_8(g) + 6O_2(g) \rightarrow 4CO_2(g) + 4H_2O(l)$

Propane is frequently used in camping stoves outdoors.

SUBSTITUTION

A **substitution** reaction occurs when an atom or group of atoms is *replaced* by a different atom or group of atoms. For example, the hydrogen atoms in an alkane can be replaced by halogen atoms. We will go into more detail on this reaction in Chapter 19.

ethane with bromine gas

$$CH_3CH_3(g) + Br_2(g) \rightarrow CH_3CH_2Br(g) + HBr(g)$$

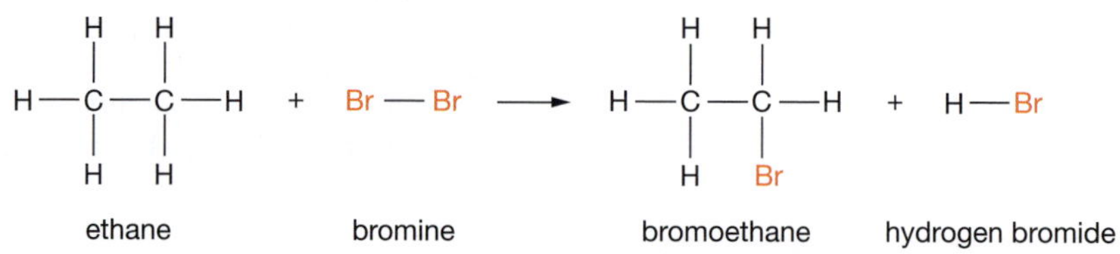

Figure 17.21 A substitution reaction between an alkane and a halogen

ADDITION

In an **addition** reaction something is added to a molecule without taking anything away. Alkenes undergo addition reactions. For example, ethene reacts with bromine:

ethene with Br_2

$$CH_2CH_2(g) + Br_2(l) \rightarrow CH_2BrCH_2Br(l)$$

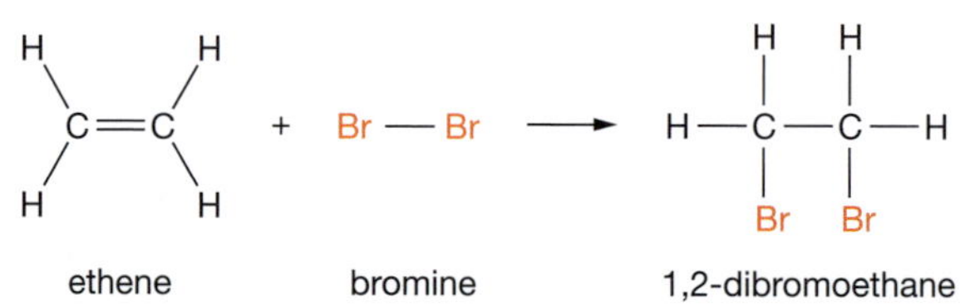

Figure 17.22 An addition reaction between an alkene and a halogen.

CHAPTER QUESTIONS

Note: the questions below deliberately include some examples which are slightly beyond the level which you would expect to meet in an International GCSE exam.

SKILLS CRITICAL THINKING

6th 7th

1 a Write down the names of the following hydrocarbons:

i CH_4

ii $CH_3CH_2CH_3$

iii $CH_3CH_2CH_2CH_2CH_2CH_3$

iv $CH_3CH{=}CH_2$

v $CH_2{=}CH_2$

vi $CH_2{=}CHCH_2CH_3$

SKILLS INTERPRETATION

b Draw structural and displayed formulae for:

i ethane
ii but-2-ene
iii hexane
iv 2-methylpropane
v methylpropene
vi pent-1-ene

SKILLS CRITICAL THINKING

2 a Explain the term *structural isomerism*.

SKILLS INTERPRETATION

b There are two structural isomers of C_4H_{10}. Draw their structures and name them.

c There are five structural isomers of C_6H_{14}. Draw their structures and name them.

SKILLS CRITICAL THINKING

d How many structural isomers containing a carbon–carbon double bond can you find with a molecular formula C_4H_8? Name the straight chain isomers.

SKILLS INTERPRETATION

e Draw two isomers of C_4H_8 that do not contain carbon–carbon double bonds.

3 Classify the following reactions as substitution, addition or combustion.

a
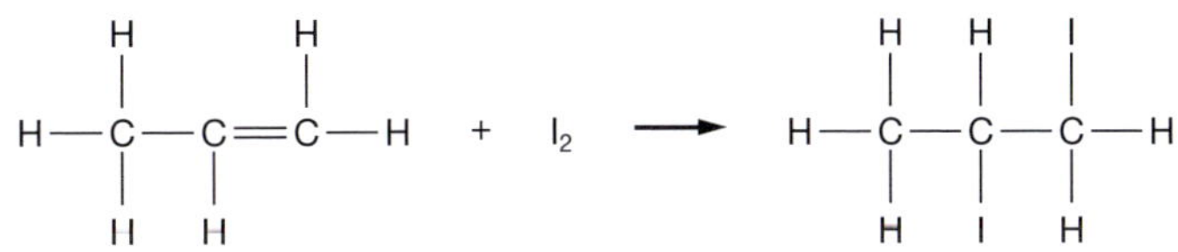

b $2C_8H_{18}(l) + 25O_2(g) \rightarrow 16CO_2(g) + 18H_2O(l)$

c $C_4H_8(g) + H_2(g) \rightarrow C_4H_{10}(g)$

d
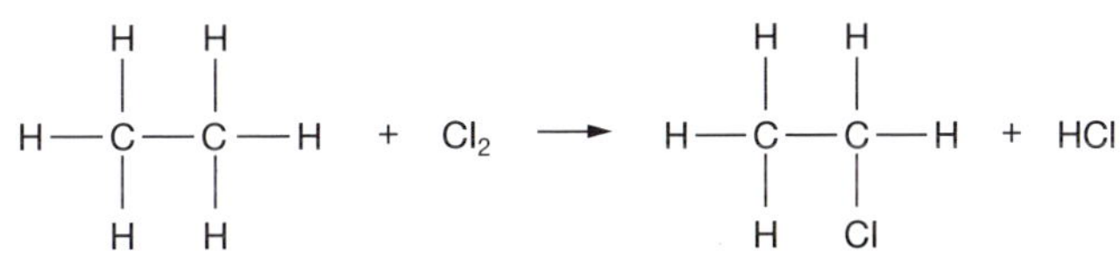

e $CH_3CH_2CH_2CH_3(g) + Br_2(g) \rightarrow CH_3CH_2CHBrCH_3(g) + HBr(g)$

SKILLS CRITICAL THINKING 6th

4 The table below shows the formulae of some organic compounds.

Compound	Formula
A	C_2H_6
B	$CH_3CH{=}CH_2$
C	$CH_3CH_2CH_2OH$
D	$CH_3CH_2CH_2CH_2CH_3$

a Select one compound from the table which is not a hydrocarbon. Explain your choice.

SKILLS INTERPRETATION 8th

b Draw a dot-and-cross diagram to show the bonding in compound **A**.

c Draw the full displayed formula of compound **B**. Include all bonds in your drawing.

SKILLS CRITICAL THINKING 6th

d Compounds **A** and **D** are from the same homologous series. State the general formula for this homologous series.

7th

e Other than having the same general formula, state *one* other characteristic of members of the same homologous series.

SKILLS PROBLEM SOLVING 9th

f Write a balanced chemical equation for the complete combustion of compound **D**.

18 CRUDE OIL

The oil industry is at the very heart of modern life. It provides fuels, plastics and the organic chemicals which go to make things as different as solvents, drugs, dyes and explosives. This chapter explores how an unappealing, sticky, black liquid is converted into useful things.

▲ Figure 18.1 The oil industry is BIG business!

LEARNING OBJECTIVES

- Know that crude oil is a mixture of hydrocarbons
- Describe how the industrial process of fractional distillation separates crude oil into fractions
- Know the names and uses of the main fractions obtained from crude oil: refinery gases, gasoline, kerosene, diesel, fuel oil and bitumen
- Know the trend in colour, boiling point and viscosity of the main fractions
- Know that a fuel is a substance that, when burned, releases heat energy
- Know the possible products of complete and incomplete combustion of hydrocarbons with oxygen in the air
- Know that in car engines the temperature reached is high enough to allow nitrogen and oxygen from air to react, forming oxides of nitrogen
- Explain how the combustion of some impurities in hydrocarbon fuels results in the formation of sulfur dioxide
- Understand how sulfur dioxide and oxides of nitrogen contribute to acid rain
- Describe how long-chain alkanes are converted to alkenes and shorter-chain alkanes by catalytic cracking (using silica or alumina as the catalyst and a temperature in the range of 600–700 °C)
- Explain why cracking is necessary in terms of the balance between supply and demand for different fractions
- Understand why carbon monoxide is poisonous, in terms of its effect on the capacity of blood to transport oxygen

WHAT IS CRUDE OIL?

THE ORIGIN OF CRUDE OIL

Millions of years ago, plants and animals living in the sea died and fell to the bottom. Layers of sediment formed on top of them. Their shells and skeletons formed limestone. The soft tissue was gradually changed by heat and high pressure into **crude oil**. Crude oil is a *finite,* ***non-renewable resource***. Once all the existing supplies have been used, they won't be replaced, or at least not for many millions of years.

▲ Figure 18.2 This sticky black liquid is essential to modern life.

CRUDE OIL CONTAINS HYDROCARBONS

Crude oil is a mixture of hydrocarbons, *compounds containing carbon and hydrogen only*. There are lots of different hydrocarbons of various sizes in crude oil, ranging from molecules with just a few carbon and hydrogen atoms to molecules containing over 100 atoms.

HOW THE PHYSICAL PROPERTIES OF HYDROCARBONS CHANGE WITH MOLECULE SIZE

As the number of carbon atoms in hydrocarbon molecules increases, the physical properties of the compounds change. Most of these changes are the result of increasing attractions between neighbouring molecules. *As the molecules become bigger, the intermolecular forces of attraction become stronger* and it becomes more difficult to pull one molecule away from its neighbours.

REMINDER

Intermolecular forces are explained in Chapter 7 (page 333).

As the molecules become bigger, the following changes occur.

- *Boiling point increases*: the larger the molecule, the higher the boiling point. This is because large molecules are attracted to each other more strongly than smaller ones. More energy is needed to break these stronger intermolecular forces of attraction to produce the widely separated molecules in the gas.
- *The liquids become less* **volatile**: the bigger the hydrocarbon, the more slowly it evaporates at room temperature. This is again because the bigger molecules are more strongly attracted to their neighbours and so don't turn into a gas so easily.
- *The liquids become more* **viscous** *and flow less easily*: liquids containing small hydrocarbon molecules are runny. Those containing large molecules flow less easily because of the stronger forces of attraction between their molecules.
- The liquids become darker in colour.
- Bigger hydrocarbons do not burn as easily as smaller ones. This limits the use of the bigger ones as fuels.

HINT

We usually count a substance as being volatile if it turns to a vapour easily at room temperature. That means it will evaporate quickly at that temperature.

SEPARATING CRUDE OIL

Crude oil itself has no uses and it has to be separated into *fractions* before it can be used. These fractions are all mixtures, but each one contains a narrow range of sizes of hydrocarbons with similar boiling points. We use **fractional distillation** to separate crude oil into fractions. This is carried out in an oil refinery.

FRACTIONAL DISTILLATION

Crude oil is heated until it boils and the vapours pass into a **fractionating column**, which is cooler at the top and hotter at the bottom. The vapours rise up the column. How far up the column a particular hydrocarbon moves depends on its boiling point.

KEY POINT

The boiling point is the same as the temperature at which a gas condenses to form a liquid; it could also be called the *condensation point*.

Suppose a hydrocarbon boils at 120 °C. At the bottom of the column, the temperature is much higher than 120 °C and so the hydrocarbon remains as a gas. As it travels up the column, the temperature of the column becomes lower. When the temperature falls to 120 °C, that hydrocarbon will turn into a liquid, it *condenses* and can be removed.

Smaller molecules have lower boiling points and get further up the column before they condense. Longer chain hydrocarbons have higher boiling points and condense lower down in the column. This way, the crude oil is split into various *fractions*.

HINT

You will find a lot of disagreement, from various sources, about exactly what fractions are produced in fractional distillation. Figure 18.3 matches the requirements of the Edexcel International GCSE specification, but this is a major simplification of what really goes on.

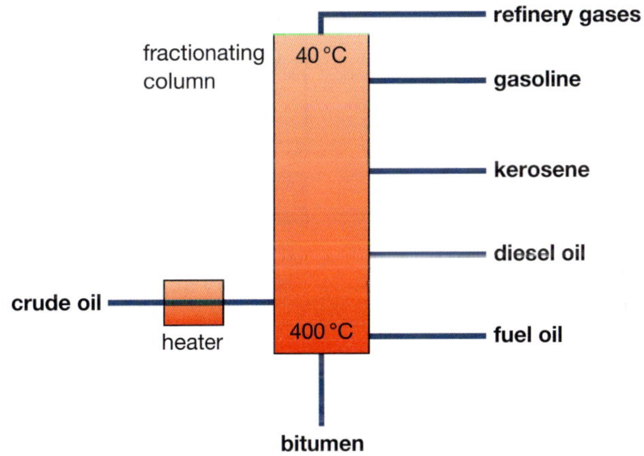

▲ Figure 18.3 Fractional distillation of crude oil

The hydrocarbons in the refinery gas fraction (see Figure 18.3) have very small masses and their boiling points are so low that the temperature of the column never falls low enough for them to condense to liquids. The temperature of the column isn't hot enough to boil some of the very large hydrocarbons found in the crude oil, and so they remain as a liquid. These are removed as a residue from the bottom of the column. Bitumen (see below), which is used in road making, is made from this.

USES OF THE FRACTIONS

AS FUELS

All hydrocarbons burn in air (oxygen) to form *carbon dioxide and water*, and release a lot of heat in the process. The various fractions can therefore be used as **fuels**.

A fuel is a substance which, when burned, releases heat energy.

HINT

Don't try to learn these equations as there are too many possible hydrocarbons you could be asked about. Provided you know (or are told) the formula of the fuel and remember the products of the combustion reaction, you can balance the equation yourself.

▲ Figure 18.4 As well as all the other poisonous or cancer-causing compounds, cigarette smoke contains carbon monoxide due to incomplete combustion.

For example, burning methane (the major constituent of natural gas):

$$CH_4(g) + 2O_2(g) \rightarrow CO_2(g) + 2H_2O(l)$$

or burning octane (one of the hydrocarbons present in gasoline, petrol):

$$2C_8H_{18}(l) + 25O_2(g) \rightarrow 16CO_2(g) + 18H_2O(l)$$

If there isn't enough air (or oxygen), you get **incomplete combustion**. This leads to the formation of *carbon (soot)* or *carbon monoxide* instead of carbon dioxide.

For example, if methane burns in a badly maintained gas appliance, there may not be enough oxygen available to produce carbon dioxide, and so you get toxic carbon monoxide instead:

$$2CH_4(g) + 3O_2(g) \rightarrow 2CO(g) + 4H_2O(l)$$

The formation of carbon monoxide from the incomplete combustion of hydrocarbons is very dangerous. Carbon monoxide is colourless and odourless, and is very poisonous. *Carbon monoxide is poisonous because it reduces the ability of the blood to carry oxygen around the body*. This will make you ill, or you may even die, because not enough oxygen gets to the cells in your body for respiration to provide energy.

DID YOU KNOW?

Carbon monoxide combines with *haemoglobin* (the molecule that carries oxygen in the red blood cells), preventing it from carrying the oxygen. It binds more strongly to the haemoglobin than oxygen does.

EXTENSION WORK

If you try to draw a dot-and-cross diagram for carbon monoxide, you will see that it is a very strange molecule because carbon does not form four bonds.

REFINERY GASES

Refinery gases are *a mixture of methane, ethane, propane and butane*, which can be separated into individual gases if required. These gases are commonly used as liquefied petroleum gas (LPG) for domestic heating and cooking.

GASOLINE (PETROL)

As with all the other fractions, petrol is a mixture of hydrocarbons with similar boiling points. It is used as a fuel in cars.

KEROSENE

Kerosene is used as a fuel for jet aircraft, as domestic heating oil and as 'paraffin' for small heaters and lamps.

▲ Figure 18.5 Kerosene is used as aviation fuel.

DIESEL

This is used as a fuel for buses, lorries, some cars, and some railway engines. Some is also converted to other more useful organic chemicals, including petrol, in a process called *cracking* (see page 464–466 for more details on cracking).

▲ Figure 18.6 A train powered by diesel

FUEL OIL

This is used as a fuel for ships and for industrial heating.

▲ Figure 18.7 Ships' boilers burn fuel oil.

BITUMEN

Bitumen is a thick, black material, which is melted and mixed with small pieces of rock to make the top surface of roads.

▲ Figure 18.8 Bitumen is used in road construction.

ENVIRONMENTAL PROBLEMS ASSOCIATED WITH THE BURNING OF FOSSIL FUELS FROM CRUDE OIL

KEY POINT

Fossil fuels include coal, gas and fuels derived from crude oil. These all come from things that were once alive.

There are major environmental problems associated with the burning of fossil fuels derived from crude oil. First of all, the carbon dioxide produced when hydrocarbons are burned is a greenhouse gas. Greenhouse gases *trap the heat radiated from the Earth's surface (originally from the Sun)* and many people believe that this could lead to climate change. For more discussion on the greenhouse effect, see Chapter 10.

ACID RAIN: SULFUR DIOXIDE AND OXIDES OF NITROGEN

KEY POINT

Several oxides of nitrogen are involved, including NO and NO_2. They are often given the general formula NO_x.

Rain is naturally slightly acidic (pH = ~5.6) because of dissolved carbon dioxide. Acid rain is rain with a pH lower than this (pH < 5.6) because of the presence of various pollutants. The pH of acid rain is often about 4.

Acid rain *is formed when water and oxygen in the atmosphere react with sulfur dioxide to produce sulfuric acid (H_2SO_4), or with various oxides of nitrogen, NO_x, to give nitric acid (HNO_3).* SO_2 and NO_x come mainly from power stations and factories burning fossil fuels, or from motor vehicles.

Fossil fuels contain a small amount of sulfur. When the fuel is burned, the sulfur reacts with oxygen, producing sulfur dioxide:

$$S(s) + O_2(g) \rightarrow SO_2(g)$$

Reactions in the atmosphere with oxygen and water can convert this to *sulfuric acid (H_2SO_4)*, a strong acid and an important component of acid rain:

$$2SO_2(g) + 2H_2O(l) + O_2(g) \rightarrow 2H_2SO_4(aq)$$

Note: when sulfur dioxide reacts with water, a weaker acid called *sulfurous acid (H_2SO_3)* is formed:

$$SO_2(g) + H_2O(l) \rightarrow H_2SO_3(aq)$$

▲ Figure 18.9 Use of very low-sulfur fuels limits the production of sulfur dioxide, but the spark in a petrol engine causes oxygen and nitrogen from the air to combine to make oxides of nitrogen, NO_x.

In petrol engines, **sparks** are used to ignite the petrol–air mixture to power the car. The temperature reached in the engine is high enough to allow nitrogen and oxygen in the air to combine to produce oxides of nitrogen. For example:

$$N_2(g) + O_2(g) \rightarrow 2NO(g)$$

These nitrogen oxides can be converted to *nitric acid (HNO_3)* in the atmosphere and therefore contribute to acid rain.

▲ Figure 18.10 Trees dying from the effects of acid rain.

Acid rain is a major problem, mainly because of its devastating effect on trees and on life in lakes. Acid rain kills trees and fish in lakes. In some lakes the water is so acidic that it won't support life at all. Limestone buildings and marble statues (both made of *calcium carbonate*) and some metals such as iron are also attacked by acid rain.

Reaction between limestone and sulfuric acid:

$$CaCO_3(s) + H_2SO_4(aq) \rightarrow CaSO_4(s) + H_2O(l) + CO_2(g)$$

The solution to acid rain involves removing sulfur from fuels (this is usually done for petrol used in cars), '**scrubbing**' the gases from power stations and factories to remove SO_2 and NO_x, and using catalytic converters in cars.

CRACKING

Although most of the fractions from the fractional distillation of crude oil are useful as fuels, some fractions are more useful and more profitable to sell than others.

The amounts of each fraction obtained will depend on the proportions of the various hydrocarbons in the original crude oil, not the amounts in which they are needed. The problem is:

- there are far too many long-chain hydrocarbons, which are not in such high demand and are not as profitable to sell
- there are not enough shorter-chain hydrocarbons that can be used as fuel for cars.

Far more petrol is needed than can be supplied by just separating crude oil into its fractions.

Cracking is a process in which *long-chain alkanes are converted to alkenes and shorter-chain alkanes*. The big hydrocarbon molecules in fuel oil, for example, can be broken down into the smaller ones needed for petrol. A very simple equation could be:

$$\underset{\text{alkane}}{C_{14}H_{30}} \rightarrow \underset{\text{alkane}}{C_{10}H_{22}} + \underset{\text{alkene}}{C_4H_8}$$

HOW CATALYTIC CRACKING WORKS

The fuel oil fraction is heated to give a gas and then passed over a catalyst of *silicon dioxide* (also called silica) and *aluminium oxide* (also called alumina) at about *600–700 °C*. Cracking can also be carried out at higher temperatures without a catalyst (*thermal cracking*).

Cracking is just an example of *thermal decomposition*: a big molecule splitting into smaller ones on heating. The majority of the hydrocarbons found in crude oil have single bonds between the carbon atoms. During the cracking process, C–C single bonds are broken and new C=C double bonds are formed.

The molecules are broken up in a fairly random way. One possibility is shown in Figure 18.11.

REMINDER

In Figure 18.11, the molecules have been drawn to show the various covalent bonds. They have also been 'straightened out' with bond angles of 90°.

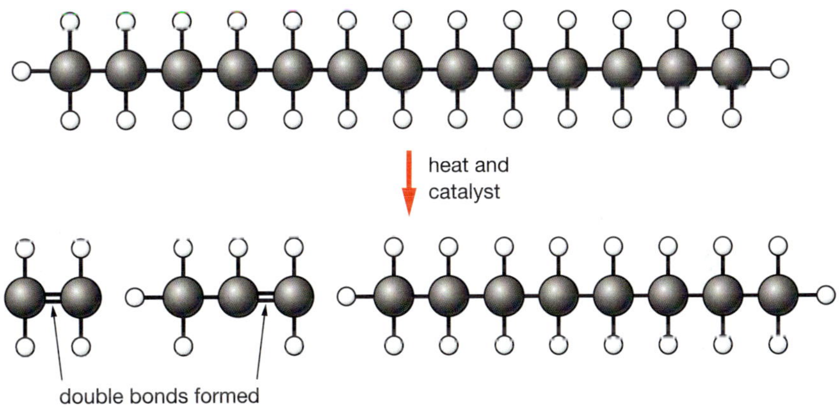

▲ Figure 18.11 How cracking works.

As an equation, this would read:

$$C_{13}H_{28}(l) \rightarrow C_2H_4(g) + C_3H_6(g) + C_8H_{18}(l)$$

HINT

Don't worry too much if you can't remember which are gases and which are liquids. State symbols are very commonly missed out in organic chemistry.

Cracking produces a mixture of alkanes and alkenes. In this case, two different alkenes are produced: ethene and propene. Octane, an alkane, is also formed. This particular cracking reaction has therefore produced two types of useful molecules for the chemical industry. Ethene and propene are both used to make important polymers. Both are also used in making other organic chemicals. The reaction also produces octane, which is a component of petrol (gasoline).

There are therefore two important reasons why oil companies carry out cracking:

- to produce more petrol
- to produce more alkenes that can be used for making polymers (plastics) (alkenes are more reactive than alkanes and also have other uses).

The molecule might have split quite differently. All sorts of reactions are happening in a catalytic cracker. Two other possibilities might be:

$$C_{13}H_{28}(l) \rightarrow 2C_2H_4(g) + C_9H_{20}(l)$$

$$C_{13}H_{28}(l) \rightarrow 2C_2H_4(g) + C_3H_6(g) + C_6H_{14}(l)$$

Some reactions might even produce a small percentage of free hydrogen. For example:

$$C_{13}H_{28}(l) \rightarrow 2C_2H_4(g) + C_3H_6(g) + C_6H_{12}(l) + H_2(g)$$

In this case, all the hydrocarbons formed will have double bonds. They are all alkenes.

There will also be very many other ways in which this particular molecule might have split up. Also, remember that the fraction being cracked contains a complex mixture of hydrocarbons, not just one. At the end of the cracking process you will have an equally complex mixture of smaller hydrocarbons, both alkanes and alkenes. This mixture will have to go through a lot of further processing (including further fractional distillation) to separate everything out into pure compounds.

HINT

It is essential that you don't try to learn these equations. In an exam, you could be given one of a wide range of possible hydrocarbons to start with. You need to understand what is happening, so that you can be adaptable.

EXTENSION WORK

In industry, catalytic cracking is done by passing hydrocarbons through a bed of zeolite (aluminosilicate) catalyst at about 500 °C and moderate pressures. Apart from breaking down large straight-chain molecules into smaller ones, isomerisation can occur during the process to produce branched-chain alkanes and alkanes with ring structures. The presence of these isomers in a fuel helps to increase the *octane number* of a fuel, which is a measure of the tendency of a fuel to not undergo auto-ignition in an engine. *Auto-ignition* is when fuel burns spontaneously out of control. It leads to wear in the engine and wastage of petrol. The higher the octane number, the lower the tendency for a fuel to undergo auto-ignition.

CHAPTER QUESTIONS

SKILLS CRITICAL THINKING

5th

1 Crude oil is a mixture of hydrocarbons.

a State which two elements are present in the compounds in crude oil.

7th

b Crude oil is separated into fractions by heating and passing the vapour into a fractionating column. Explain how the fractions separate in the column.

6th

c Two of the fractions are gasoline and diesel. State one use of each.

d Name two fractions formed in the fractional distillation of crude oil, other than gasoline and diesel.

e Describe the differences between gasoline and diesel. In your answer you should refer to the average size of the molecules in the two liquids, the colour of the two liquids and the viscosities of the two liquids.

7th

f One of the hydrocarbons found in the diesel fraction is $C_{18}H_{38}$. Suggest the formula of a hydrocarbon that could be found in the gasoline fraction.

SKILLS PROBLEM SOLVING

9th

g i Write a balanced chemical equation for the complete combustion of butane, C_4H_{10}.

SKILLS REASONING

6th

ii Incomplete combustion of hydrocarbons produces carbon monoxide. Explain why carbon monoxide is harmful to humans.

SKILLS REASONING 6th

2 Explain why:

a burning a fuel containing sulfur as an impurity causes acid rain

b petrol engines produce oxides of nitrogen

c the presence of too much sulfur dioxide, SO_2, in the atmosphere has a damaging effect on many buildings made of marble, a form of calcium carbonate, $CaCO_3$.

SKILLS CRITICAL THINKING

3 Cracking is a process that splits larger hydrocarbons into smaller ones.

a Give two reasons why an oil company might want to crack a hydrocarbon.

b Give the conditions under which cracking is carried out.

SKILLS PROBLEM SOLVING 9th

c A molecule of the hydrocarbon $C_{11}H_{24}$ was cracked to give two molecules of ethene, C_2H_4, and one other molecule. Write a balanced chemical equation for the reaction which took place. (You can omit the state symbols from your equation.)

d Write an equation for an alternative cracking reaction involving the same hydrocarbon, $C_{11}H_{24}$.

SKILLS CREATIVITY

4 Imagine a world in which fossil fuels such as coal, natural gas and oil had never formed. This would have effects other than the immediately obvious ones. For example, the iron and steel industry depends on coke made from coal, although in the past (on a much smaller scale) it used charcoal made from wood. Choose one aspect of the modern world and explain, in no more than 300 words, how it would be different in the absence of fossil fuels. You could choose from transport, use of materials, landscape, disease prevention, and power generation, for example, but you don't have to restrict yourself to this list.

Try not to be too simplistic about this, human beings are inventive! For example, it is possible to obtain organic chemicals from alcohol (from fermented sugar) and fuels from plant oils.

19 ALKANES

The hydrocarbons separated from the fractional distillation of crude oil are mainly alkanes. This is the simplest family of hydrocarbons, containing only carbon–carbon and carbon–hydrogen single bonds. Here we look into the structures and chemical reactions of these compounds in more detail. It is assumed that you have already read Chapter 17 (Introduction to Organic Chemistry).

LEARNING OBJECTIVES

- Know the general formula for alkanes
- Explain why alkanes are classified as saturated hydrocarbons
- Understand how to draw the structural and displayed formulae for alkanes with up to five carbon atoms in the molecule and to name the unbranched-chain isomers
- Describe the reactions of alkanes with halogens in the presence of ultraviolet radiation, limited to mono-substitution

▲ Figure 19.1 The small alkanes are gases and are burned as fuels.

The alkanes are the simplest family of hydrocarbons. Hydrocarbons are compounds that contain carbon and hydrogen only.

Many of the alkanes are used as fuels. Methane is the major component of natural gas. Ethane and propane are also present in small quantities in natural gas, and are important constituents of liquefied petroleum gases (LPG) from crude oil distillation (discussed in Chapter 18).

The first five members of the alkanes series are shown in Table 19.1.

Table 19.1 Some alkanes

Name	Molecular formula	Structural formula	Displayed formula
methane	CH_4	CH_4	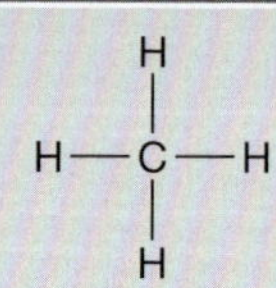
ethane	C_2H_6	CH_3CH_3	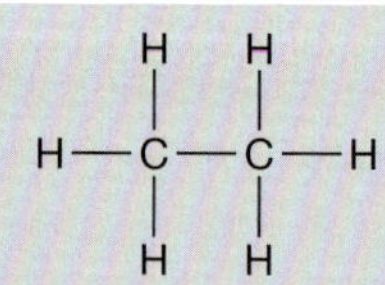
propane	C_3H_8	$CH_3CH_2CH_3$	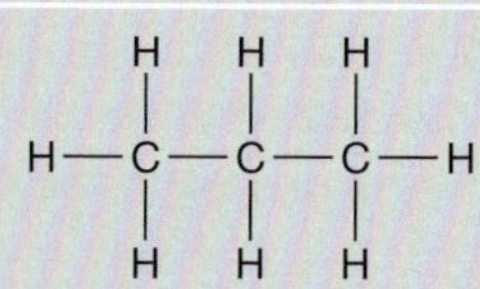
butane	C_4H_{10}	$CH_3CH_2CH_2CH_3$	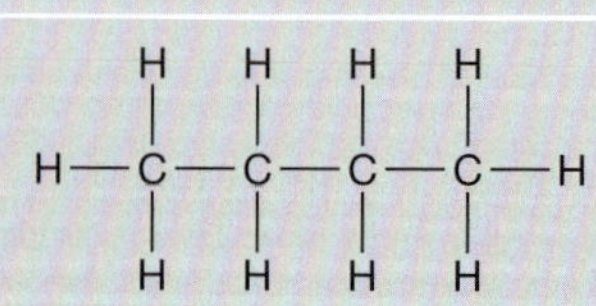
pentane	C_5H_{12}	$CH_3CH_2CH_2CH_2CH_3$	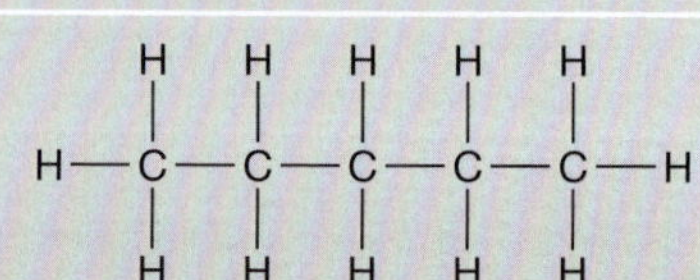

KEY POINT

The alkanes are described as *saturated* hydrocarbons because they contain only C–C single bonds and have no double (C=C) or triple (C≡C) bonds. A way of thinking about this is that the alkanes are saturated with hydrogen, in other words they have the maximum number of hydrogen atoms possible for that number of carbon atoms. But do not write this definition down in the exam!

ISOMERS OF ALKANES

Isomers are *compounds which have the same molecular formula but different structural formulae*. The alkanes shown in Table 19.1 can all be described as *straight-chain alkanes* or as having an unbranched chain. There are also isomers of butane and pentane that have branched chains. These are shown in Figure 19.2.

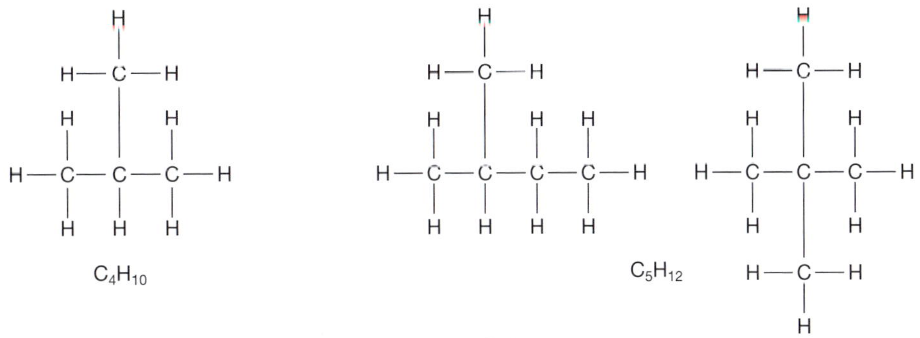

▲ Figure 19.2 Branched chain isomers of C_4H_{10} and C_5H_{12}.

HOMOLOGOUS SERIES

HINT

When asked about a homologous series in the exam, it is probably best to only write about the properties (the second and third bullet points). Sometimes you do not get separate marks for 'the same functional group' and 'similar chemical properties', and perhaps a better way of writing this is 'they have similar chemical properties because they have the same functional group'.

The alkanes form a homologous series. A homologous series is a series of compounds that:

- have the same functional group
- *have similar chemical properties*
- *show a trend (gradation) in physical properties*
- can be described by the same general formula
- differ from the next by a $-CH_2-$ unit.

The alkanes form the simplest homologous series. The alkanes do not really have a functional group as they just contain single C–C and C–H bonds, which are the basis of all other organic compounds.

MEMBERS OF A HOMOLOGOUS SERIES HAVE THE SAME GENERAL FORMULA

In the case of the alkanes, if there are *n* carbons, there are $2n + 2$ hydrogens.

The general formula for the alkanes is $\mathbf{C_nH_{2n+2}}$.

So, for example, if there are three carbons, there are $(2 \times 3) + 2 = 8$ hydrogens. The formula for propane is C_3H_8.

If you want the formula for an alkane with 15 carbons, you could work out that it is $C_{15}H_{32}$ and so on.

The reason that the alkanes and other homologous series can be described by a general formula is that each member differs from the next by a $-CH_2-$ unit.

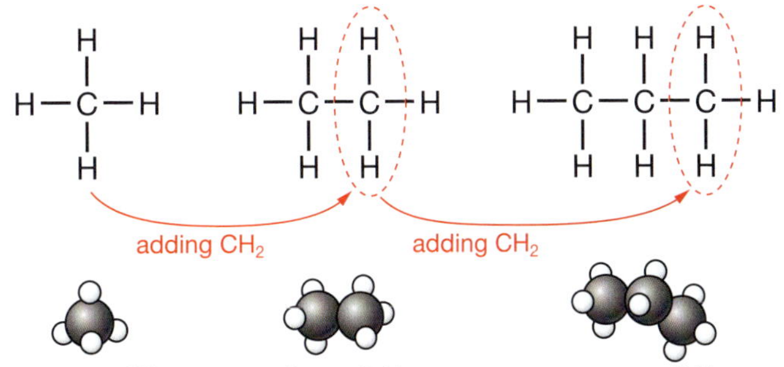

methane, CH_4 ethane, C_2H_6 propane, C_3H_8

▲ Figure 19.3 The three smallest alkanes. Each member differs from the next by a $-CH_2-$ unit.

MEMBERS OF A HOMOLOGOUS SERIES SHOW A TREND (GRADATION) IN PHYSICAL PROPERTIES

Figure 19.4 shows the boiling points of the first eight alkanes.

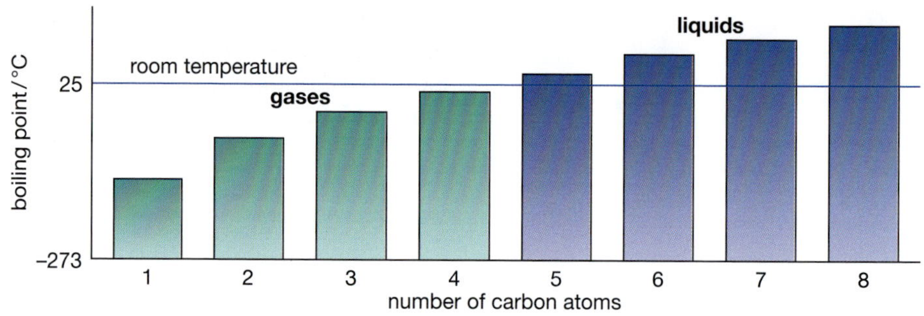

▲ Figure 19.4 Boiling points of the first eight alkanes

The first four alkanes are gases at room temperature (~25 °C). All the other alkanes you are likely to see at International GCSE are liquids. Solids start to appear at about $C_{18}H_{38}$.

The molecules of the members of a homologous series increase in size in a regular way and you can see that the *boiling points* also *increase* in a regular way.

As the molecules become bigger, the strength of the *intermolecular forces of attraction* between them *increases*. This means that *more energy* has to be put in to *break* the attractions between one molecule and its neighbours. One effect of this is that the boiling points increase in a regular way.

MEMBERS OF A HOMOLOGOUS SERIES HAVE SIMILAR CHEMICAL PROPERTIES

Chemical properties are dependent on the functional groups and bonding within the molecules. Because alkanes only contain carbon–carbon single bonds and carbon–hydrogen bonds, they are all going to behave in the same way. These are strong bonds, therefore alkanes are fairly unreactive organic compounds and are often thought of as being quite **inert**.

KEY POINT

The alkanes are not inert in the sense that they don't react with anything, like neon for example, but they are not very reactive for organic compounds and only really undergo two reactions.

TWO REACTIONS OF THE ALKANES

COMBUSTION

HINT

Don't try to learn these equations! Practise working them out for a wide range of different hydrocarbons. You will find guidance on how to work out the ethane equation in Chapter 5, page 293.

HINT

Remember, in combustion reactions it is highly unlikely that hydrogen, H_2, will be formed as a product because hydrogen is very flammable. You always obtain water, H_2O, even if there is insufficient oxygen.

All alkanes burn in air or oxygen. If there is enough oxygen, they burn *completely* to give *carbon dioxide* and *water*, for example:

$$CH_4(g) + 2O_2(g) \rightarrow CO_2(g) + 2H_2O(l)$$

$$2C_2H_6(g) + 7O_2(g) \rightarrow 4CO_2(g) + 6H_2O(l)$$

If there isn't enough oxygen, there is *incomplete* combustion of the hydrocarbon, and you obtain *carbon monoxide* or *carbon* (**soot**) instead of carbon dioxide, for example:

$$2C_2H_6(g) + 5O_2(g) \rightarrow 4CO(g) + 6H_2O(l)$$

or

$$2C_2H_6(g) + 3O_2(g) \rightarrow 4C(s) + 6H_2O(l)$$

SUBSTITUTION

Alkanes react with halogens in the presence of **ultraviolet radiation** (UV light), for example from sunlight. A hydrogen atom in the alkane is replaced by a halogen atom. This is known as a *substitution* reaction because *one atom has been replaced (or substituted) by a different one*.

EXTENSION WORK

UV light is required for substitution reactions to split halogen molecules into atoms. Energy is needed to break the covalent bonds between halogen atoms. The atoms formed are called *free radicals* due to the presence of unpaired electrons on them. These are very reactive species which then go on to react with the usually unreactive alkanes.

EXTENSION WORK

If bromine is in excess, this reaction can go on to substitute more of the hydrogens in the methane. What you obtain is a mixture of CH_3Br, CH_2Br_2, $CHBr_3$ and CBr_4, plus HBr of course. You will find out more about *multi-substitution* if you go on to do chemistry at a more advanced level.

A mixture of methane and bromine gas is orange because of the presence of the bromine. If it is exposed to sunlight, it loses its colour, and a mixture of bromomethane and hydrogen bromide gases is formed.

$$CH_4(g) + Br_2(g) \rightarrow CH_3Br(g) + HBr(g)$$

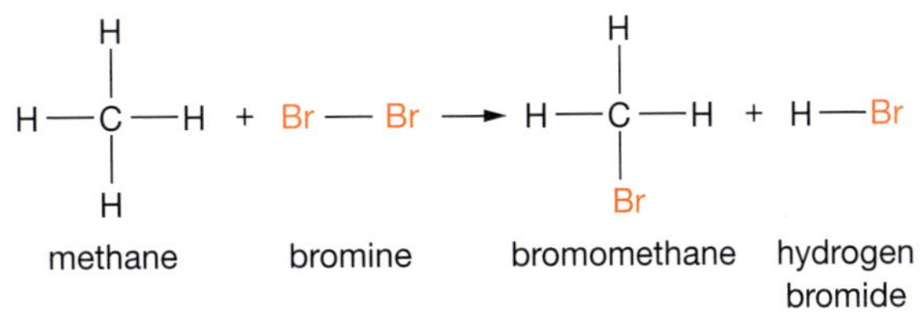

▲ Figure 19.5 A substitution reaction between methane and bromine.

An exactly similar reaction happens between ethane and chlorine exposed to UV light. In this case, you get a mixture of chloroethane and hydrogen chloride gases:

$$CH_3CH_3(g) + Cl_2(g) \rightarrow CH_3CH_2Cl(g) + HCl(g)$$

HINT

Notice the HCl(g) formed in this reaction is called hydrogen chloride rather than hydrochloric acid. To form an acid, hydrogen chloride gas must dissolve in water and dissociate to form H^+ ions (see Chapter 3).

Mono-substitution occurs when *only one hydrogen atom in the alkanes is replaced by a halogen atom*.

When propane reacts with bromine, it is possible to form two organic products even when only mono-substitution occurs. The two products are structural isomers of each other, they have the same molecular formula but different structural formulae.

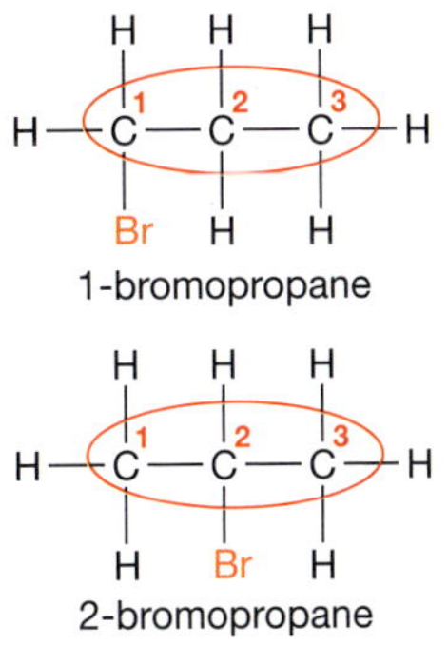

▲ Figure 19.6 Two isomers of bromopropane, formed from the mono-substitution of propane with bromine.

The products formed from substitution reactions of alkanes with halogens are called *halogenoalkanes*. They are named according to the format *x-haloalkane*, where *x* indicates the position of the halogen atom in the longest carbon chain. So, when bromine reacts with propane we get 1-bromopropane and 2-bromopropane.

CHAPTER QUESTIONS

SKILLS CRITICAL THINKING

1 a Alkanes are *saturated* hydrocarbons. Explain the term *saturated*.

b Undecane is an alkane with 11 carbon atoms.

i Write down the molecular formula for undecane.

SKILLS REASONING

ii What physical state (solid, liquid or gas) would you expect undecane to be in at room temperature (25 °C)?

SKILLS PROBLEM SOLVING

iii Write a balanced chemical equation for the complete combustion of undecane.

iv Write a balanced chemical equation for the incomplete combustion of undecane to produce carbon monoxide and explain why this reaction is harmful to humans.

SKILLS ANALYSIS

2 Write the molecular formulae of the following compounds.

a

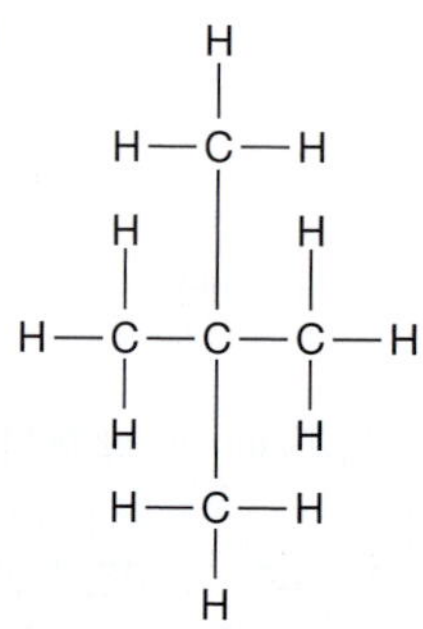

b

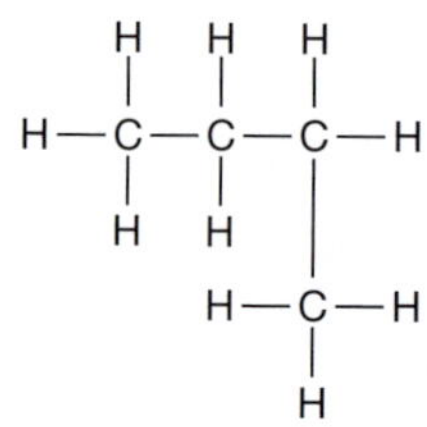

c

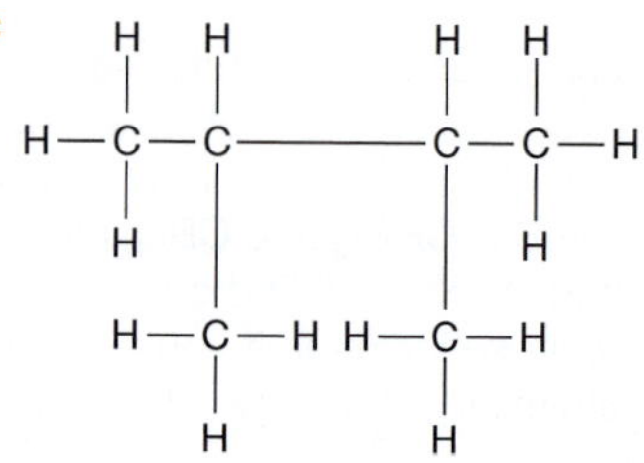

SKILLS INTERPRETATION

3 Draw two isomers of each of the following compounds.

a

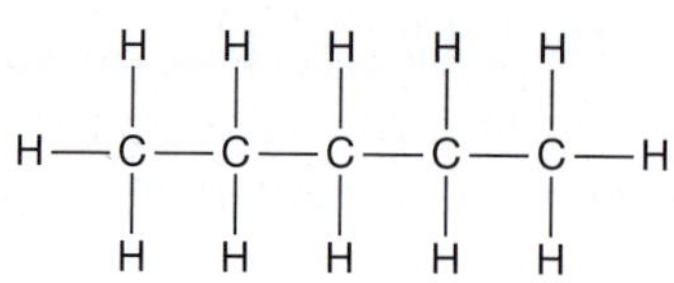

b

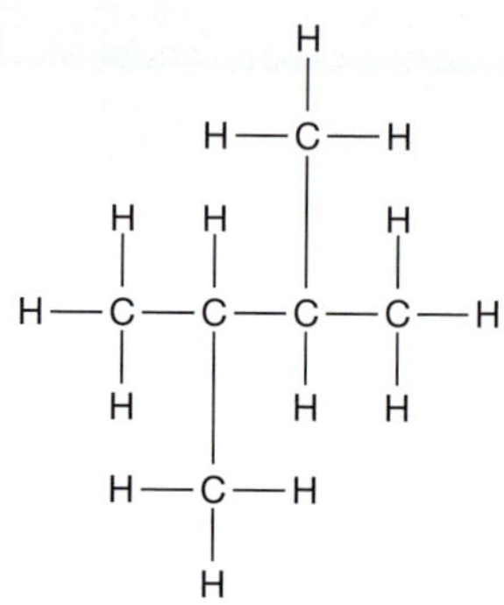

SKILLS CRITICAL THINKING

4 Ethane reacts with bromine under certain conditions.

a State the conditions needed for this reaction to occur.

b What is the type of reaction that occurs?

SKILLS PROBLEM SOLVING

c Write a balanced chemical equation for the reaction using displayed formulae and name the organic product produced.

SKILLS INTERPRETATION

5 Butane reacts with chlorine to form two organic compounds with the formula C_4H_9Cl.

a Write a balanced chemical equation for the formation of one of these compounds.

b Draw the structures and give the names of the two possible *organic* products of this reaction.

20 ALKENES

The alkenes are another family of hydrocarbons. They all contain a carbon–carbon double bond. Alkenes can be produced from alkanes by cracking and they are much more reactive than the alkanes.

▶ Figure 20.1 Sunflower oil is polyunsaturated and contains lots of C=C groups.

LEARNING OBJECTIVES

- Know that alkenes contain the functional group >C=C<
- Know the general formula for alkenes
- Explain why alkenes are classified as unsaturated hydrocarbons
- Describe the reactions of alkenes with bromine to produce dibromoalkanes
- Describe how bromine water can be used to distinguish between an alkane and an alkene
- Understand how to draw the structural and displayed formulae for alkenes with up to four carbon atoms in the molecule, and name the unbranched-chain isomers

The alkenes are a homologous series of hydrocarbons which contain a carbon–carbon double bond. The **C=C** bond is the functional group of the alkenes.

The first three members of the alkene series are shown in Table 20.1.

KEY POINT

It is not possible to have an alkene with one carbon atom because alkenes must contain a C=C group so you need a minimum of two carbon atoms.

Table 20.1 The first three alkenes

Name	Molecular formula	Empirical formula	Structural formula	Displayed formula
ethene	C_2H_4	CH_2	$CH_2{=}CH_2$	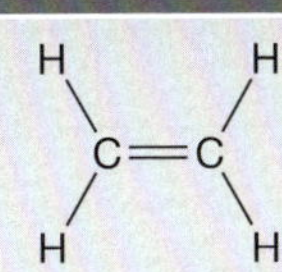
propene	C_3H_6	CH_2	$CH_2{=}CHCH_3$	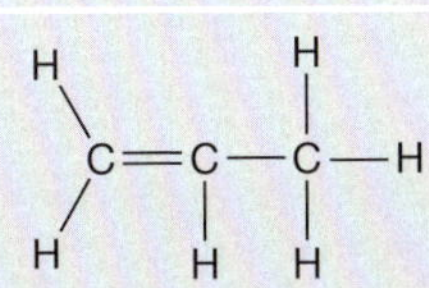
but-1-ene	C_4H_8	CH_2	$CH_2{=}CHCH_2CH_3$	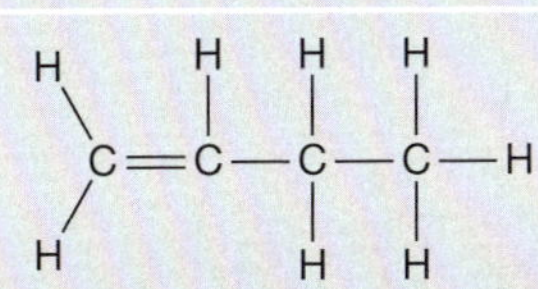

ISOMERS

There are two straight-chain isomers with the formula C_4H_8:

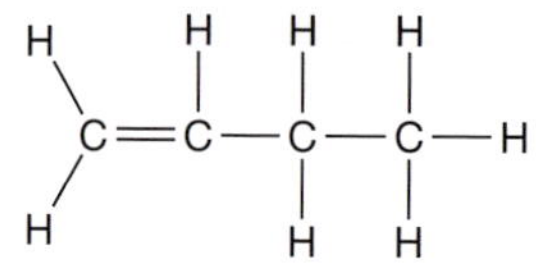

but-1-ene

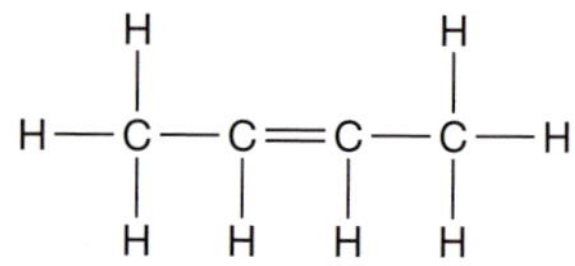

but-2-ene

and one branched-chain isomer:

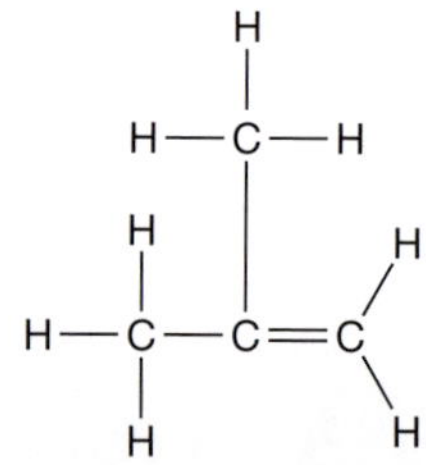

HINT

A way of thinking about this is that the alkenes are not saturated with H atoms, they do not have the maximum number of H atoms for that number of C atoms.

UNSATURATED HYDROCARBONS

Alkenes are ***unsaturated compounds*** because they contain a C=C bond. *A saturated compound contains single C–C bonds only whereas an unsaturated compound contains one or more double or triple C–C bonds*.

THE GENERAL FORMULA

Alkenes have the general formula $\mathbf{C_nH_{2n}}$. The number of hydrogen atoms is twice the number of carbon atoms. This means that all alkenes have the same empirical formula, CH_2.

The alkene with 11 carbon atoms will have 22 hydrogen atoms and the molecular formula $C_{11}H_{22}$.

PHYSICAL PROPERTIES

These are very similar to those of the alkanes. Remember that the small alkanes with up to four carbon atoms are gases at room temperature. The same is true for the alkenes. They are gases up to C_4H_8, and the next dozen or so are liquids. Again, the members of the homologous series *show a trend in physical properties*.

CHEMICAL REACTIONS OF THE ALKENES

COMBUSTION

In common with all hydrocarbons, alkenes burn in air or oxygen to give carbon dioxide and water, for example:

$$C_2H_4(g) + 3O_2(g) \rightarrow 2CO_2(g) + 2H_2O(l)$$

This isn't a reaction anybody would ever choose to do. Alkenes are much too useful to waste by burning them.

ADDITION

The C=C double bond is the functional group. The functional group determines the chemical properties of a compound. Alkenes have characteristic chemical properties which are different from those of alkanes. Alkenes are much more reactive than alkanes.

Alkenes undergo addition reactions. Part of the double bond breaks to become a single C–C bond and the electrons are used to join other atoms onto the two carbon atoms.

THE ADDITION OF BROMINE

Bromine adds to alkenes without any need for heat, light or a catalyst. The reaction is often carried out using bromine water (aqueous bromine solution) as, for example, in Figure 20.2, with ethene.

You know a reaction has happened because bromine water is *orange* but the product, called 1,2-dibromoethane, is a *colourless* liquid.

HINT

Decode the name and make sure you can see how it works. 'eth' shows a two carbon chain. 'ane' shows only carbon–carbon single bonds. The beginning of the name, '1,2-dibromo', shows two bromine atoms attached to the first and second carbon atoms.

You can write this as an equation in two ways: first, using displayed formulae and second, using structural formulae.

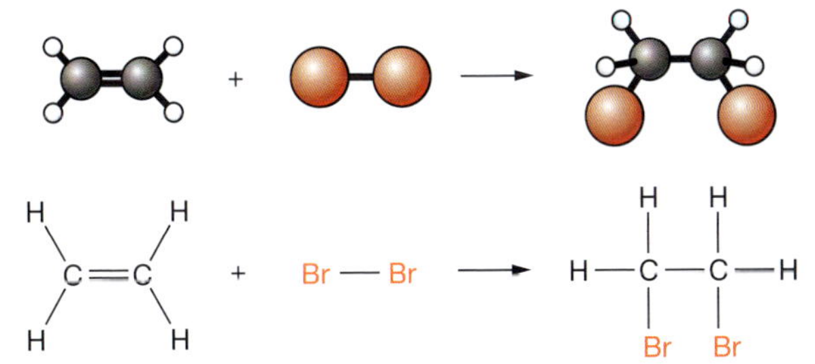

$CH_2{=}CH_2(g)$ + $Br_2(aq)$ → $CH_2BrCH_2Br(l)$.
ethene bromine 1,2-dibromoethane

▲ Figure 20.2 An addition reaction: an alkene plus bromine

HINT

Make sure you can see how these formulae relate to the full structures in the equation above.

THE TEST FOR UNSATURATED COMPOUNDS

HINT

You must be careful with the words you use here: the final mixture is *colourless* and not clear. Do not use the word clear. Clear means not cloudy, you can see through it. The bromine water is clear and any other solution can also be described as clear.

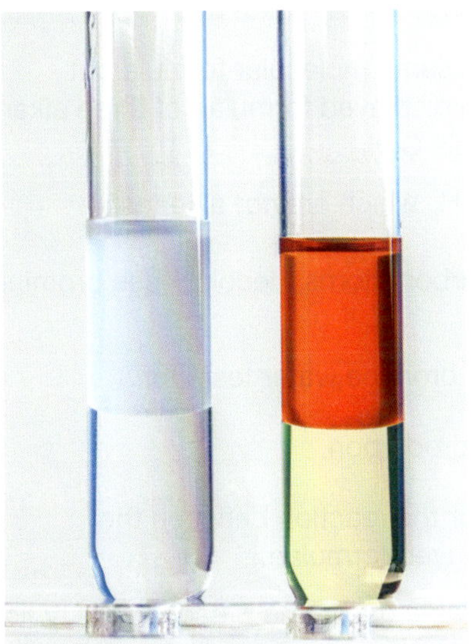

▲ Figure 20.3 The result of shaking a liquid alkene (left) or alkane (right) with bromine water.

Any compound with a carbon–carbon double bond will react with bromine in a similar way to ethene. This is used to *test for a carbon–carbon double bond*. If you shake an unknown organic compound with bromine water and the orange bromine water is *decolourised* (the colour changes from orange to colourless), the compound contains a carbon–carbon double bond. If your unknown compound is a gas, you can simply bubble it through bromine water with the same effect.

The left-hand tube in Figure 20.3 shows the effect of shaking a liquid alkene with bromine water. The organic layer (containing the alkene) is on top. You can see that the bromine water has been completely decolourised, showing the presence of the carbon–carbon double bond.

The right-hand tube in Figure 20.3 shows what happens if you use a liquid alkane, which doesn't have a carbon–carbon double bond. The colour of the bromine is still there. Alkanes do not decolourise bromine water because they do not contain a carbon–carbon double bond.

The addition reaction between bromine and propene is very similar to that of ethene. Part of the carbon–carbon double bond breaks and two bromine atoms add across the bond, as shown in Figure 20.4.

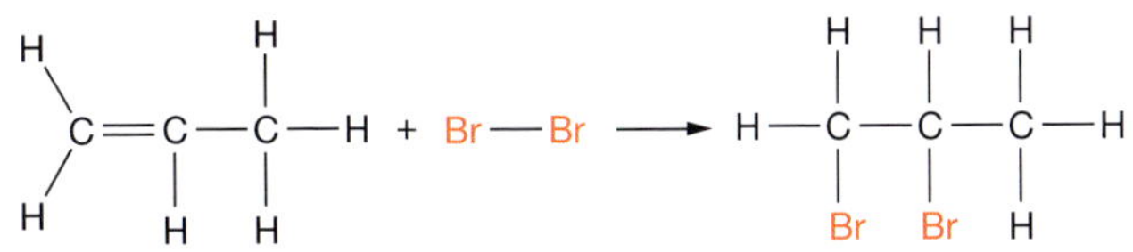

$CH_2{=}CHCH_3$ + Br_2 → $CH_2BrCHBrCH_3$
propene bromine 1,2-dibromopropane

▲ Figure 20.4 An addition reaction of propene with bromine

The product is called 1,2-dibromopropane. Its structure is based on propane and the prefix '1,2-dibromo' shows there are two bromine atoms, on the first and the second carbon atoms.

OTHER IMPORTANT ADDITION REACTIONS OF ALKENES

▲ Figure 20.5 Production of margarine

EXTENSION WORK

Hydrogenation

A **hydrogenation** reaction involves the *addition of hydrogen*. An alkene reacts with hydrogen to form an alkane, for example:

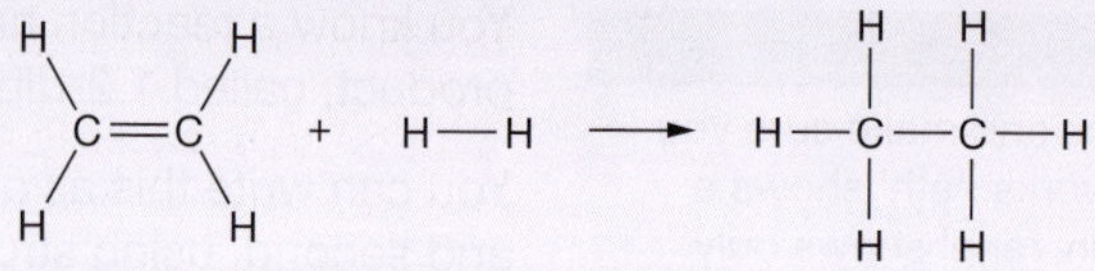

$$CH_2{=}CH_2 + H_2 \rightarrow CH_3CH_3$$

This reaction is used for the production of margarine, which is made by hydrogenation of polyunsaturated (i.e. many C=C bonds) plant oils.

CHAPTER QUESTIONS

SKILLS CRITICAL THINKING

1 The alkenes are a *homologous series* of *unsaturated* hydrocarbons.

a i State two characteristics of the members of a *homologous series*.

ii Explain the term *unsaturated*.

b Ethene is the simplest member of the alkenes. Bromine water can be used to distinguish alkenes from alkanes.

i Bromine water is added to ethene. State the starting colour of the bromine water and the finishing colour of the reaction mixture.

SKILLS PROBLEM SOLVING, INTERPRETATION

ii Complete the equation by drawing and naming the displayed formula of the product.

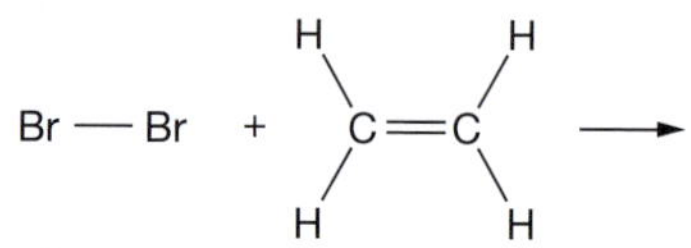

Name of the product:

SKILLS INTERPRETATION

c Isomers are compounds that have the same molecular formula but different displayed formulae. Draw the displayed formulae of three alkene isomers that have the molecular formula C_4H_8.

d Can you draw any other isomers of C_4H_8 which are *not* alkenes?

SKILLS CRITICAL THINKING

2 A gaseous hydrocarbon, **P**, with three carbon atoms, decolourises bromine water.

a Explain what the decolorisation of the bromine water tests for.

b Write the displayed formula for the hydrocarbon.

SKILLS PROBLEM SOLVING

c Write a balanced chemical equation for the reaction between the hydrocarbon and bromine, using displayed formulae.

d The reaction between ethane and bromine gas in the presence of UV light also causes the bromine to lose colour.

i Write a balanced chemical equation for this reaction.

SKILLS REASONING

7th

ii This reaction is described as a substitution reaction, whereas the reaction between **P** and bromine is an addition reaction. Using the equations you have already written, explain the difference between addition and substitution.

SKILLS CRITICAL THINKING

8th

3 Alkenes undergo addition reactions.

a Predict the structural formula of the compound formed when chlorine reacts with propene. Name the product formed.

b Ethene reacts with hydrogen. Give the name and structural formula of the product.

6th

4 Propene can be made by heating propane and sulfur.

a Name another method of making propene and state two conditions for making alkenes from alkanes.

SKILLS EXECUTIVE FUNCTION

b Describe a chemical test which can be used to distinguish between propane and propene.

Test:

Result with propane:

Result with propene:

SKILLS CRITICAL THINKING

8th

5 Give the structural formulae and names of the product when but-1-ene reacts with each of the following:

a steam

b hydrogen chloride (HCl)

c bromine.

21 SYNTHETIC POLYMERS

Polymers are everywhere, ranging from naturally occurring polymers, for example proteins (polypeptides) and sugar (polysaccharides), which you probably have met before, to synthetic polymers used for plastic bags and clothing. Polymers are large molecules consisting of many repeating units. This chapter looks at one way that polymers can be made: addition polymerisation for polymers such as poly(ethene) and PVC.

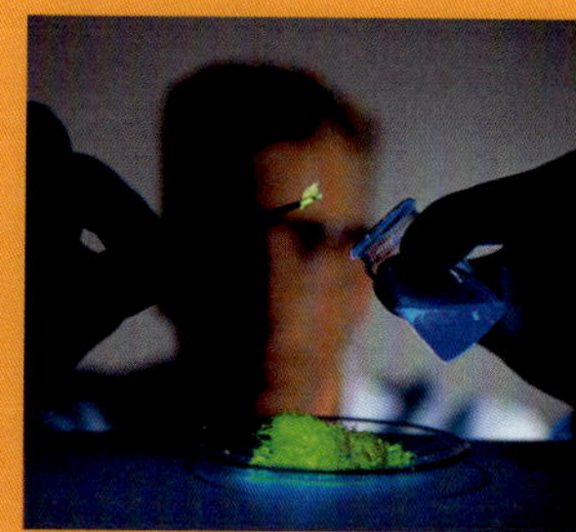

▲ Figure 21.1 Synthetic polymers are extremely useful for making a variety of products, from the coating for electrical wires to plastic bottles and intelligent label chips.

LEARNING OBJECTIVES

- Know that an addition polymer is formed by joining up many small molecules called monomers
- Understand how to draw the repeat unit of an addition polymer, including poly(ethene), poly(propene), poly(chloroethene) and poly(tetrafluoroethene)
- Understand how to deduce the structure of a monomer from the repeat unit of an addition polymer and vice versa
- Explain problems in the disposal of addition polymers, including:
  - their inertness and inability to biodegrade
  - the production of toxic gases when they are burned

ADDITION POLYMERISATION

THE POLYMERISATION OF ETHENE

Ethene is the smallest alkene and can be produced by cracking. It is the smallest hydrocarbon containing a carbon–carbon double bond. Figure 21.2 shows different ways of representing an ethene molecule.

C_2H_4 $CH_2{=}CH_2$

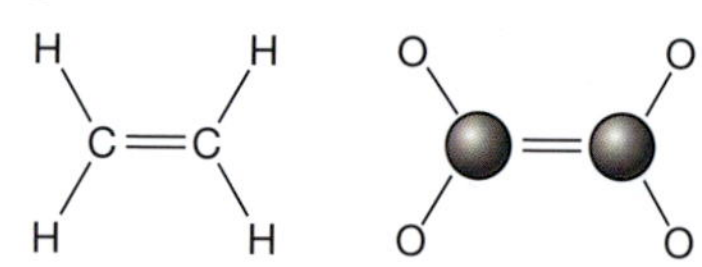

▲ Figure 21.2 Ethene

Under the right conditions, molecules containing carbon–carbon double bonds can join together to produce very long chains. Part of the double bond is broken to become a single bond, and the electrons in it are used to join to neighbouring molecules.

Polymerisation *is the joining up of lots of little molecules* (**monomers**) *to make one big molecule* (**polymer**). In the case of ethene, lots of ethene molecules join together to make *poly(ethene)*, which is more usually called *polythene*. *Molecules simply add onto each other without anything else being formed*. This is called **addition polymerisation**.

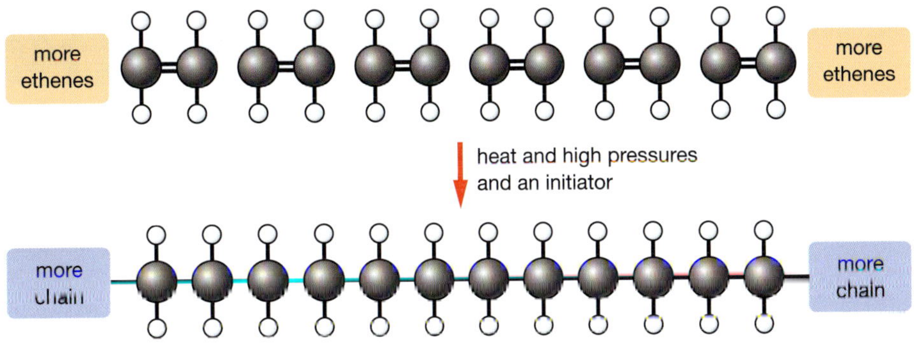

▲ Figure 21.3 The polymerisation of ethene

KEY POINT

An *initiator* is used to start the process. You mustn't call it a catalyst because it is consumed in the reaction.

EXTENSION WORK

People occasionally wonder what happens at the ends of the chains. They don't end tidily! Bits of the initiator are bonded on at either end. You don't need to worry about that for International GCSE.

The chain length can vary from about 4000 to 40 000 carbon atoms.

For normal purposes, the polymerisation reaction is written using displayed formulae.

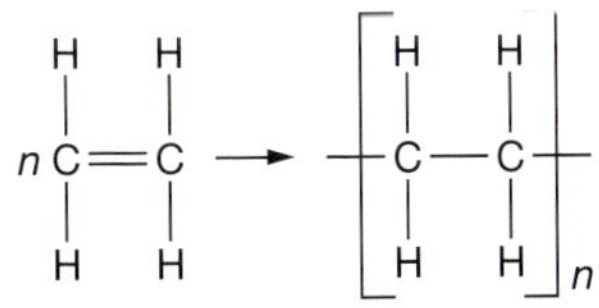

▲ Figure 21.4 Formation of poly(ethene)

KEY POINT

In this structure for poly(ethene) *n* represents a large but variable number. It simply means that the structure in the brackets (called the *repeat unit*) repeats itself many times in the molecule. When representing a polymer, the bonds on the two sides of the repeat unit should extend outside the square brackets to show that the carbon atoms are joined to the next ones in a chain, as shown in Figure 21.4.

HINT

Make sure you can distinguish between the different terms monomer, polymer and **repeat unit**. In the equation in Figure 21.4, the monomer is 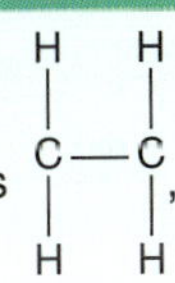, the polymer is 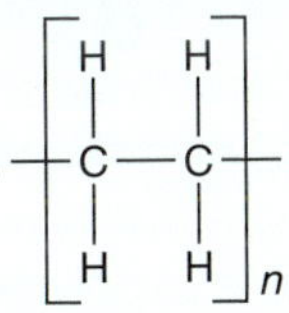 and the repeat unit is 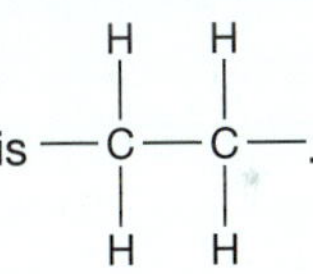.

USES FOR POLY(ETHENE)

KEY POINT

Although the polymer is called *poly(ethene)* it is actually an *alkane*. The polymer is saturated and will not decolourise bromine water.

Poly(ethene) comes in two types: low-density poly(ethene) (LDPE) and high-density poly(ethene) (HDPE). Low-density poly(ethene) is mainly used as a thin film to make polythene bags. It is very flexible and not very strong.

▲ Figure 21.5 Plastic bags made from poly(ethene)

High-density poly(ethene) is used where greater strength and rigidity are needed, for example to make plastic bottles such as milk bottles. If you can find a recycling symbol with the letters HDPE next to it, then the bottle is made of high-density poly(ethene). If it has some other letters there, then it is made of a different polymer.

HOW TO DEDUCE THE POLYMERISATION REACTION FOR ANY ALKENE

Figure 21.6 shows how to work out a polymerisation reaction starting from any alkene. The key thing is to always draw the alkene as shown with just the C=C in the middle.

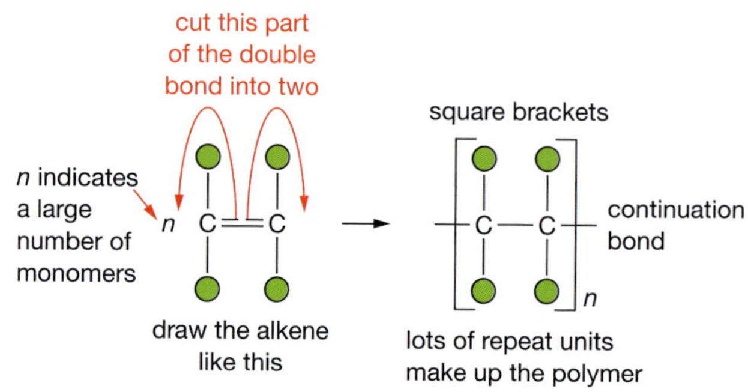

▲ Figure 21.6 How to work out a polymerisation reaction

THE POLYMERISATION OF PROPENE

Propene is another alkene, this time with three carbon atoms in each molecule. Its formula is normally written as $CH_3CH{=}CH_2$. Think of it as a modified ethene molecule, with a CH_3 group attached in place of one of the hydrogen atoms.

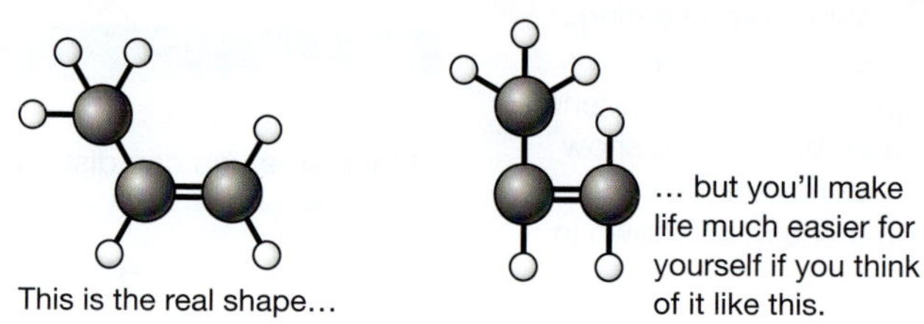

▲ Figure 21.7 Propene

When propene is polymerised you obtain *poly(propene).* This used to be called *polypropylene*.

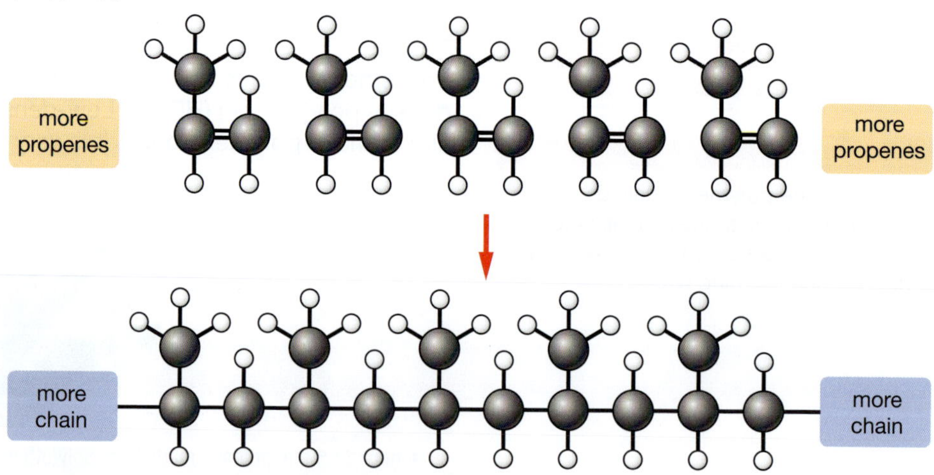

▲ Figure 21.8 The polymerisation of propene

Write this as:

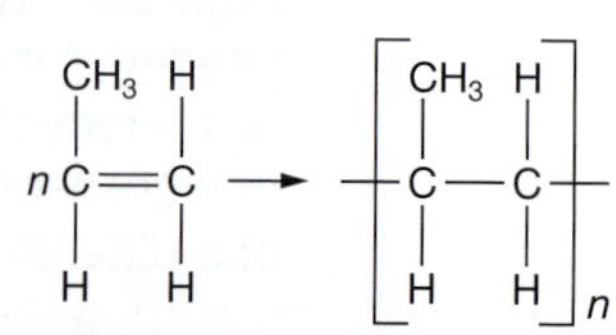

▲ Figure 21.9 Formation of poly(propene)

HINT

When you draw an addition polymerisation reaction never change anything except opening out the double bond and drawing the continuation bonds on each side.

USES OF POLY(PROPENE)

Poly(propene) is somewhat stronger than poly(ethene). It is used to make ropes and crates (among many other things). If an item has a recycling mark with PP inside it or near it, it is made of poly(propene).

▲ Figure 21.10 PP recycling symbol

▲ Figure 21.11 Poly(propene) is used to make crates . . .

▲ Figure 21.12 . . . and ropes.

THE POLYMERISATION OF CHLOROETHENE

Chloroethene is a molecule in which one of the hydrogen atoms in ethene is replaced by a chlorine. Its formula is CH_2=CHCl. In the past, it was called vinyl chloride. Polymerising chloroethene gives you *poly(chloroethene)*. This is usually known by its old name, polyvinylchloride or PVC.

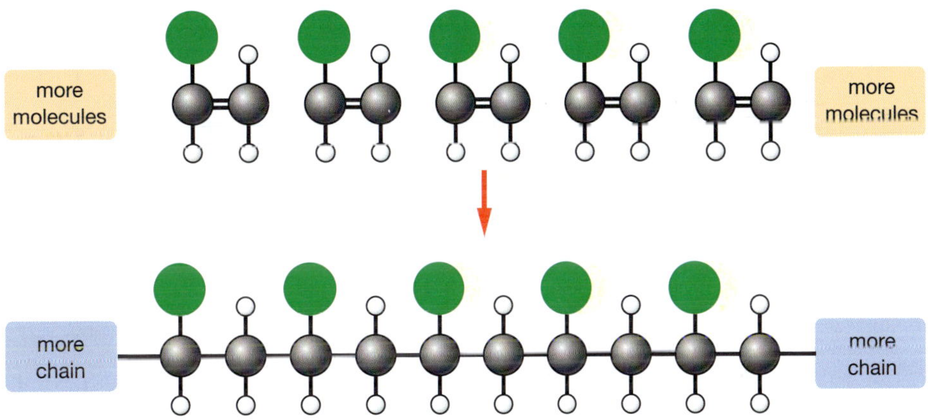

▲ Figure 21.13 The polymerisation of chloroethene

Write this as:

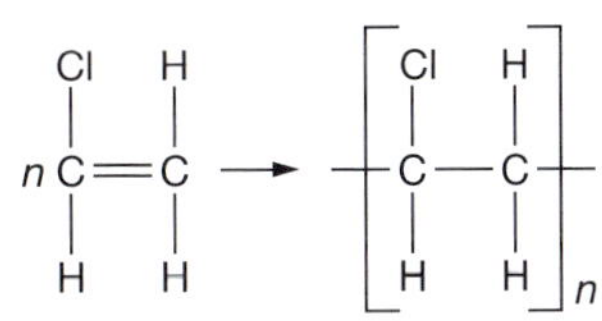

▲ Figure 21.14 Formation of poly(chloroethene)

HINT

When you draw this, it isn't important whether you put the chlorine atom on the left-hand carbon atom or the right-hand one.

USES OF POLY(CHLOROETHENE)

Poly(chloroethene), known as PVC, has a lot of uses. It is quite strong and rigid, and so can be used for water pipes or replacement windows. It can also be made flexible by adding *plasticisers*. This makes it useful for sheet floor coverings, and even clothing. These polymers don't conduct electricity, therefore PVC can be used for electrical insulation.

▲ Figure 21.15 PVC has a variety of uses.

THE POLYMERISATION OF TETRAFLUOROETHENE

Tetrafluoroethene is another molecule derived from ethene in which all four hydrogen atoms are replaced by fluorine. Its formula is $CF_2{=}CF_2$. Polymerising tetrafluoroethene gives you poly(tetrafluoroethene) or PTFE, more commonly known as Teflon®.

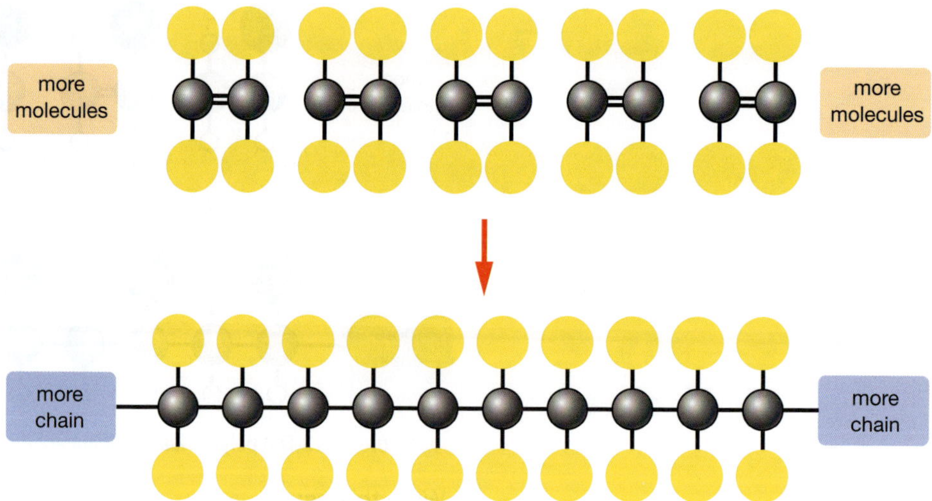

▲ Figure 21.16 The polymerisation of tetrafluoroethene

Write this as:

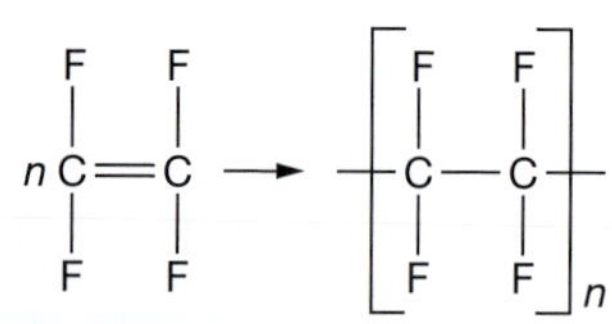

▲ Figure 21.17 Formation of poly(tetrafluoroethene)

KEY POINT

If you look at this reaction, you can see it is exactly the same as the polymerisation of ethene except that each H has been replaced by an F.

USES OF POLY(TETRAFLUOROETHENE)

Poly(tetrafluoroethene) is often used as a non-stick coating for pots and pans. It is very unreactive due to the strong carbon–fluorine bonds, and can be found lining containers for corrosive chemicals.

▲ Figure 21.18 PTFE is used for non-stick coatings.

WORKING OUT THE MONOMER FOR A GIVEN ADDITION POLYMER

In an exam you may find that you are given the structure of a polymer and asked to deduce what the repeat unit is or what monomer it was made from. Figure 21.19 shows you how to do this.

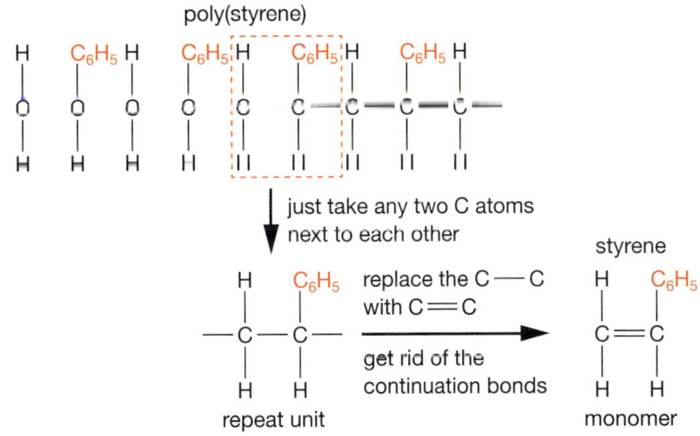

▲ Figure 21.19 How to work out the repeat unit and monomer for poly(styrene)

The C_6H_5 group is complicated, but we don't need to worry about that when we write the structure of the monomer; work from the structure you are given. First find the repeat unit, which can be done simply by taking any two adjacent carbon atoms in the main polymer chain. To derive the monomer, a double bond needs to be put back between the two middle carbon atoms of the repeat unit.

DISPOSAL OF ADDITION POLYMERS

Recycling of plastics is important, not just to save raw materials, but because it takes a very long time for addition polymers like poly(ethene) and poly(chloroethene) to break down in the environment. They contain strong covalent bonds, making them essentially *inert* at ordinary temperatures. They are **non-biodegradable**, meaning *they cannot be broken down by bacteria in the environment*.

One solution to the problem of their disposal is to *bury them in landfill sites*, which are basically just big holes in the ground, where they will remain unchanged for thousands of years.

▲ Figure 21.20 Plastics (and other rubbish) can be disposed of in landfill sites.

Some countries, including Denmark and Japan, *incinerate (burn) plastics* in order to tackle the problem of disposal. This releases a lot of heat energy, which can be used to generate electricity. However, there are problems associated with this. For example, carbon dioxide is produced, which contributes to **global warming**. Toxic gases are also released, including carbon monoxide and hydrogen chloride.

There are advantages and disadvantages for using either method to dispose of plastics.

Disposal method	Advantages	Disadvantages
Landfill	No greenhouse gases or toxic gases produced from plastics Cheap	Ugly, smelly and noisy; no one wants to live next to a landfill site Uses large areas of land The waste will be there for thousands of years
Incineration	Requires little space Can produce heat for local homes/offices and/or produce electricity	It is expensive to build and maintain the plant Produces greenhouse gases Releases toxic gases The ash produced must still be disposed of in landfill sites

CHAPTER QUESTIONS

SKILLS CRITICAL THINKING 6th

1 Ethene, C_2H_4, is an important molecule used in industry. It is an *unsaturated hydrocarbon*.

a Explain the terms *unsaturated* and *hydrocarbon*.

SKILLS PROBLEM SOLVING 9th

b Ethene burns easily and releases a large amount of heat during combustion. Write a balanced chemical equation for the complete combustion of ethene.

SKILLS REASONING 7th

c Explain why in industry ethene is considered too valuable to be used as a fuel.

SKILLS CRITICAL THINKING 6th

2 Propene, C_3H_6, can be polymerised to make poly(propene).

a Explain the term *polymerisation*.

SKILLS INTERPRETATION 7th

b Draw a displayed formula for propene.

8th

c Draw a diagram to represent the structure of a poly(propene) chain showing three repeat units.

SKILLS CRITICAL THINKING 6th

d The formation of poly(propene) is an example of *addition* polymerisation. Explain what is meant by the word *addition*.

SKILLS PROBLEM SOLVING 9th

e Styrene has the formula $C_6H_5CH{=}CH_2$. Write a balanced chemical equation to show what happens when styrene is polymerised to make polystyrene. Your equation should clearly show the structure of the polystyrene. (Show the C_6H_5 group as a whole.)

SKILLS INTERPRETATION 8th

f A small part of a Perspex molecule looks like this:

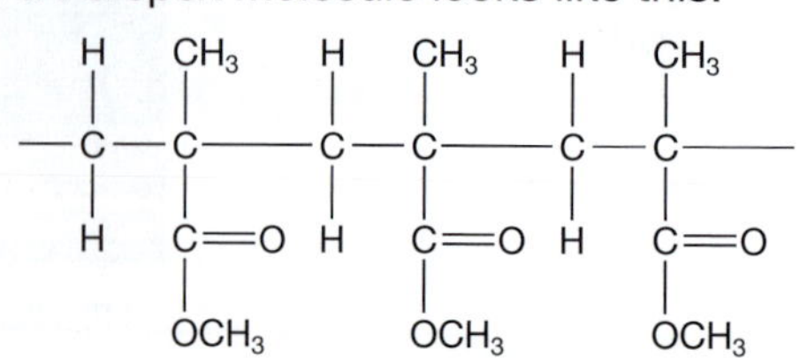

Draw the structure of the monomer from which Perspex is made.

SKILLS DECISION MAKING 7th

g Many addition polymers, for example those used for making plastic bags, are not biodegradable. Used plastic bags can be either buried underground in landfill sites or incinerated. State which method of disposal you think is better and give two reasons for your choice.

UNIT QUESTIONS

SKILLS ANALYSIS 6th

1 Crude oil is a complex mixture of hydrocarbons. The diagram shows the separation of crude oil into simpler mixtures called fractions.

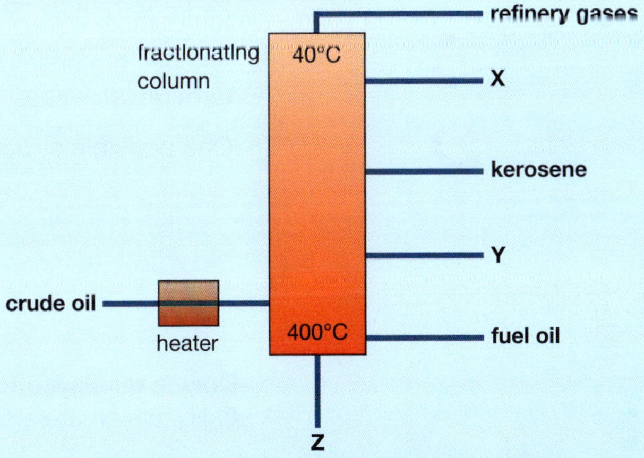

a What could X, Y and Z represent (choose one answer)? **(1)**

	X	Y	Z
A	gasoline	bitumen	diesel
B	diesel	gasoline	bitumen
C	bitumen	gasoline	diesel
D	gasoline	diesel	bitumen

SKILLS CRITICAL THINKING

b State a use for the refinery gas fraction. **(1)**

c Name the liquid that leaves the fractionating column at the lowest temperature. **(1)**

7th

d Describe how crude oil is separated into fractions in industry. **(4)**

e Write down and explain the relationship between the number of carbon atoms in a hydrocarbon and its boiling point. **(2)**

SKILLS PROBLEM SOLVING 9th

f One of the hydrocarbons, $C_{15}H_{32}$, called pentadecane, is present in the kerosene fraction. It could be used as a fuel in jet engines. Write an equation for the incomplete combustion of pentadecane to produce carbon monoxide. **(2)**

g The complete combustion of alkanes produces carbon dioxide, CO_2, which can dissolve in water to form a weakly acidic solution.

SKILLS INTERPRETATION 8th

i Draw a dot-and-cross diagram to show the bonding in CO_2. Show the outer electrons only. **(2)**

SKILLS REASONING 7th

ii Predict the most likely pH of a solution of CO_2 (choose one answer). **(1)**

A 1 **B** 5 **C** 7 **D** 9

SKILLS CRITICAL THINKING 6th

h $C_{15}H_{32}$ is a member of the alkane family. Long-chain alkanes are often cracked to form alkenes.

- **i** Write down two conditions used for cracking alkanes in industry. **(2)**
- **ii** Give two reasons why cracking is necessary in the oil industry. **(2)**
- 7th **iii** During cracking, one molecule of $C_{15}H_{32}$ is converted into one molecule of ethene, one molecule of another alkene C_4H_8 and one molecule of hydrocarbon **W**. State the molecular formula of **W**. **(1)**
- 6th **iv** Alkenes are unsaturated hydrocarbons. Write down what is meant by the term *unsaturated*. **(1)**

SKILLS INTERPRETATION 8th

- **v** One possible structure for C_4H_8 is

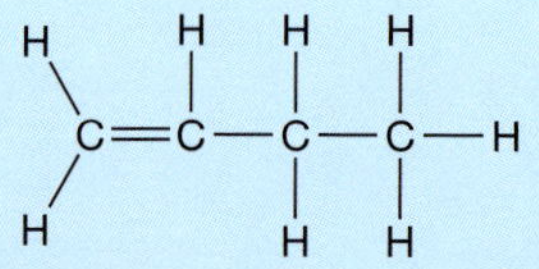

Draw a displayed formula for each of the other two isomers of C_4H_8, which are also alkenes. **(2)**

(Total 22 marks)

SKILLS ANALYSIS 6th

2 The table shows the formulae of some organic compounds.

A $CH_2{=}CHCl$	B $CH_3CH_2CH_3$	C $CH_2{=}CHCH_2CH_3$
D C_2H_6	E 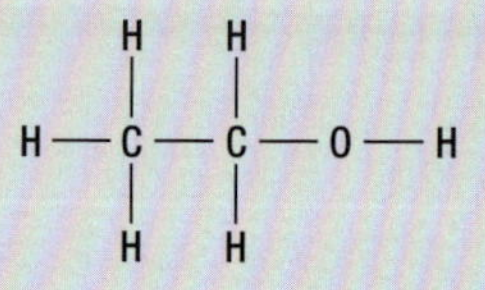	F 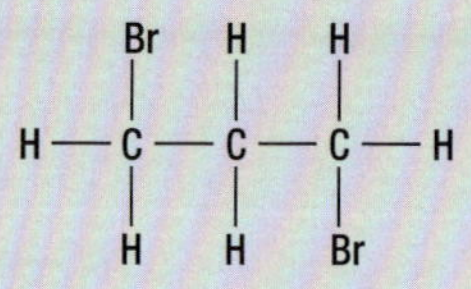

a Give one reason why compound **E** is *not* a hydrocarbon. **(1)**

b **i** State the name of compound **F**. **(1)**

SKILLS INTERPRETATION 8th

- **ii** Draw the displayed formula of an isomer of compound **F**. **(2)**

SKILLS PROBLEM SOLVING

c Compound **C** can undergo an addition reaction with bromine. Complete the equation below showing the structural formula of the product(s). **(1)**

$CH_2{=}CHCH_2CH_3 + Br_2 \rightarrow$

d Two of the compounds shown belong to the same homologous series.

SKILLS CRITICAL THINKING 6th

- **i** Give the letters of these two compounds. **(1)**
- **ii** Write down the general formula of this homologous series. **(1)**
- **iii** Write down *two* other characteristics of the compounds in a homologous series. **(2)**

e Compound **A** can undergo addition polymerisation.

- **i** Give the name of the addition polymer formed by compound **A**. **(1)**
- 7th **ii** Draw the repeat unit of the addition polymer of compound **A**. **(1)**

SKILLS REASONING

iii Explain the problems in the disposal of the addition polymer formed by compound **A**. **(2)**

iv Write down and explain the observations you would make if bromine water was added to the addition polymer of **A**. **(2)**

SKILLS CRITICAL THINKING

f Compound **B** undergoes a reaction with chlorine.

i Write down the condition required for this reaction to take place. **(1)**

ii Write down the type of reaction that occurs. **(1)**

SKILLS INTERPRETATION

iii Draw the displayed formulae for the two possible organic products from the reaction between compound **B** and chlorine. **(2)**

(Total 19 marks)

SKILLS PROBLEM SOLVING

3 Compound **X** contains 55% carbon, 9% hydrogen and 36% oxygen by mass.

a Calculate the empirical formula of **X**. **(3)**

b The relative molecular mass (M_r) of **X** is 88. Deduce the molecular formula of **X**. **(1)**

(Total 4 marks)

SKILLS EXECUTIVE FUNCTION

4 Below are two hydrocarbons with the molecular formula C_3H_6.

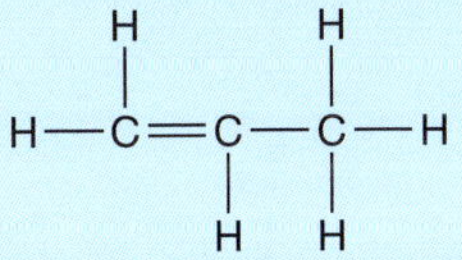

compound 1

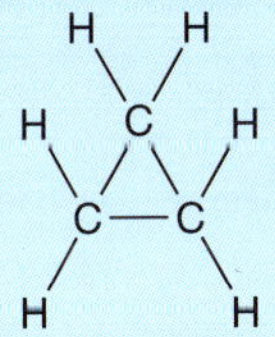

compound 2

a Describe a chemical test for distinguishing between the two hydrocarbons and give the results for this test. **(3)**

Test:

Result with compound 1:

Result with compound 2:

SKILLS CRITICAL THINKING

b Compound 3 is in the same homologous series as compound 1. Compound 3 can form an addition polymer. Draw the repeat unit of this polymer.

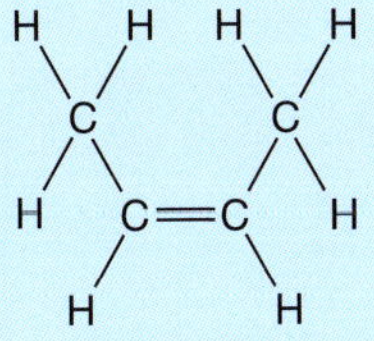

compound 3 **(2)**

c Name the addition polymer formed by compound 3. **(1)**

(Total 6 marks)

SKILLS INTERPRETATION

5 This question is about addition polymers.

a Poly(propene) is an addition polymer made from propene $CH_2=CHCH_3$. Draw a length of the poly(propene) chain showing two repeat units. **(2)**

b Another addition polymer, polyacrylamide, is used to make hydrogel in contact lenses, nappies and drug delivery systems. The structure of the polymer is shown in the diagram. Draw the structural formula of the monomer used to make polyacrylamide. **(1)**

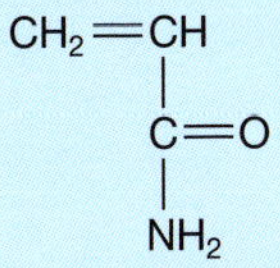

(Total 3 marks)

PHYSICS UNIT 1 FORCES AND MOTION

Forces make things move, like this Atlas V rocket carrying the Cygnus spacecraft up to the International Space Station. Forces hold the particles of matter together and keep us on the Earth. Forces can make things slow down. This is useful when we apply the brakes when driving a car! Forces can change the shape of things, sometimes temporarily and sometimes permanently. Forces make things rotate and change direction.

1 MOVEMENT AND POSITION

It is very useful to be able to make predictions about the way moving objects behave. In this chapter you will learn about some equations of motion that can be used to calculate the speed and acceleration of objects, and the distances they travel in a certain time.

▲ Figure 1.1 The world is full of speeding objects.

LEARNING OBJECTIVES

- Plot and explain distance–time graphs
- Know and use the relationship between average speed, distance moved and time taken:

  $$\text{average speed} = \frac{\text{distance moved}}{\text{time taken}}$$

- Practical: investigate the motion of everyday objects such as toy cars or tennis balls
- Know and use the relationship between acceleration, change in velocity and time taken:

  $$\text{acceleration} = \frac{\text{change in velocity}}{\text{time taken}} \qquad a = \frac{(v - u)}{t}$$

- Plot and explain velocity–time graphs
- Determine acceleration from the gradient of a velocity–time graph
- Determine the distance travelled from the area between a velocity–time graph and the time axis
- Use the relationship between final speed, initial speed, acceleration and distance moved:

  $(\text{final speed})^2 = (\text{initial speed})^2 + (2 \times \text{acceleration} \times \text{distance moved})$

  $$v^2 = u^2 + (2 \times a \times s)$$

KEY POINT

Sometimes average speed is shown by the symbols $v_{average}$ or $\overline{v}$ but in this book v will be used.

UNITS

In this section you will need to use kilogram (kg) as the unit of mass, metre (m) as the unit of length, and second (s) as the unit of time, You will find measurements of mass made in subdivisions of the kilogram, like grams (g) and milligrams (mg), measurements of length in multiples of the metre, like the kilometre (km), and subdivisions like the centimetre (cm) and millimetre (mm). You will also be familiar with other units for time: minutes, hours, days and years etc. You will need to take care to convert units in calculations to the base units of kg, m and s when you meet these subdivisions and multiples.

Other units come from these base units. In the first chapter you will meet the units for:

- speed and velocity: metre per second (m/s)
- acceleration: metre per second squared (m/s^2).

In later chapters you will meet the units for:

- force: newton (N)
- gravitational field strength: newton per kilogram (N/kg)

Speed is a term that is often used in everyday life. Action films often feature high-speed chases. Speed is a cause of fatal accidents on the road. Sprinters aim for greater speed in competition with other athletes. Rockets must reach a high enough speed to put communications satellites in **orbit** around the Earth. This chapter will explain how speed is defined and measured and how distance–time graphs are used to show the movement of an object as time passes. We shall then look at changing speed – **acceleration** and **deceleration**. We shall use velocity–time graphs to find the acceleration of an object. We shall also find how far an object has travelled using its velocity–time graph. You will find out about the difference between speed and velocity on page 492.

AVERAGE SPEED

KEY POINT

Sometimes you may see '*d*' used as the symbol for distance travelled, but in this book '*s*' will be used to be consistent with the symbol used in A level maths and physics.

A car travels 100 kilometres in 2 hours so the average speed of the car is 50 km/h. You can work this out by doing a simple calculation using the following definition of speed:

$$\text{average speed, } v = \frac{\text{distance moved, } s}{\text{time taken, } t}$$

$$v = \frac{s}{t}$$

The average speed of the car during the journey is the total distance travelled, divided by the time taken for the journey. If you look at the speedometer in a car you will see that the speed of the car changes from instant to instant as the accelerator or brake is used. The speedometer therefore shows the instantaneous speed of the car.

UNITS OF SPEED

Typically the distance moved is measured in metres and time taken in seconds, so the speed is in metres per second (m/s). Other units can be used for speed, such as kilometres per hour (km/h), or centimetres per second (cm/s). In physics the units we use are **metric**, but you can measure speed in miles per hour (mph). Many cars show speed in both mph and kilometres per hour (kph or km/h). Exam questions should be in metric units, so remember that m is the abbreviation for metres (and not miles).

REARRANGING THE SPEED EQUATION

If you are given information about speed and time taken, you will be expected to rearrange the speed equation to make the distance moved the subject:

$$\text{distance moved, } s = \text{average speed, } v \times \text{time, } t$$

and to make the time taken the subject if you are given the distance moved and speed:

$$\text{time taken, } t = \frac{\text{distance moved, } s}{\text{average speed, } v}$$

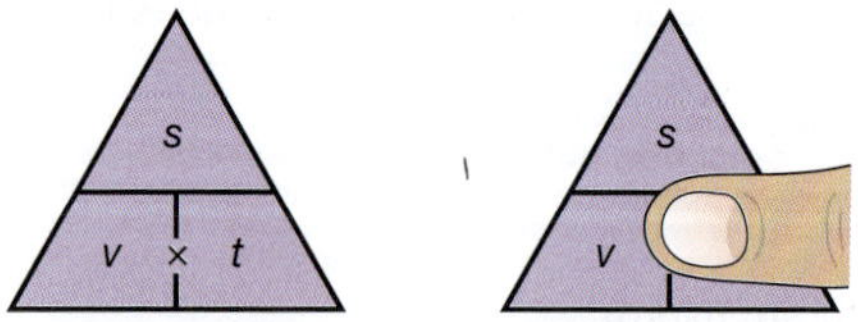

▲ Figure 1.2 You can use the triangle method for rearranging equations like $s = v \times t$.

REMINDER

To use the triangle method to rearrange an equation, cover up the part of the triangle that you want to find. For example, in Figure 1.2, if you want to work out how long (*t*) it takes to move a distance (*s*) at a given speed (*v*), covering *t* in Figure 1.2 leaves $\frac{s}{v}$, or distance divided by speed. If an examination question asks you to write out the equation for calculating speed, distance or time, always give the actual equation (such as $s = v \times t$). You may not get the mark if you just draw the triangle.

SPEED TRAP!

Figure 1.3 A stopwatch will measure the time taken for the vehicle to travel the distance.

Suppose you want to find the speed of cars driving down your road. You may have seen the police using a mobile speed camera to check that drivers are keeping to the speed limit. Speed guns use microprocessors (computers on a 'chip') to produce an instant reading of the speed of a moving vehicle, but you can conduct a very simple experiment to measure car speed.

Measure the distance between two points along a straight section of road with a tape measure or 'click' wheel. Use a stopwatch to measure the time taken for a car to travel the measured distance. Figure 1.4 shows you how to operate your 'speed trap'.

1 Measure 50 m from a start point along the side of the road.
2 Start a stopwatch when your partner signals that the car is passing the start point.
3 Stop the stopwatch when the car passes you at the finish point.

Figure 1.4 How to measure the speed of cars driving on the road

Safety note: No measurements should be taken on the public road or pavement but it is possible to do so within the school boundary within sight of the road.

KEY POINT

You can convert a speed in m/s into a speed in km/h.

If the car travels 12.8 metres in one second it will travel

12.8 × 60 metres in 60 seconds (that is, one minute) and

12.8 × 60 × 60 metres in 60 minutes (that is, 1 hour), which is

46 080 metres in an hour or 46.1 km/h (to one decimal place).

We have multiplied by 3600 (60 × 60) to convert from m/s to m/h, then divided by 1000 to convert from m/h to km/h (as there are 1000 m in 1 km).

Rule: to convert m/s to km/h simply multiply by 3.6.

Using the measurements made with your speed trap, you can work out the speed of the car. Use the equation:

$$\text{average speed, } v = \frac{\text{distance moved, } s}{\text{time taken, } t}$$

So if the time measured is 3.9 s, the speed of the car in this experiment is:

$$\text{average speed, } v = \frac{50\,\text{m}}{3.9\,\text{s}}$$
$$= 12.8\,\text{m/s}$$

DISTANCE–TIME GRAPHS

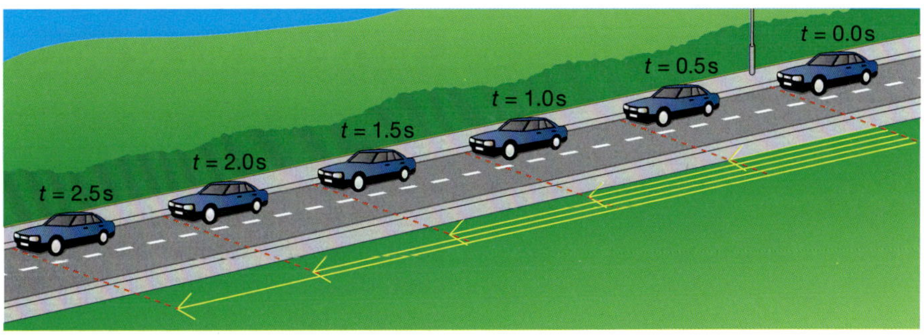

Figure 1.5 A car travelling at constant speed

Figure 1.5 shows a car travelling along a road. It shows the car at 0.5 second intervals. The distances that the car has travelled from the start position after each 0.5 s time interval are marked on the picture. The picture provides a record of how far the car has travelled as time has passed. The table below shows the data for this car. You will be expected to plot a graph of the distance travelled (**vertical** axis) against time (horizontal axis) as shown in Figure 1.6.

Time from start / s	0.0	0.5	1.0	1.5	2.0	2.5
Distance travelled from start / m	0.0	6.0	12.0	18.0	24.0	30.0

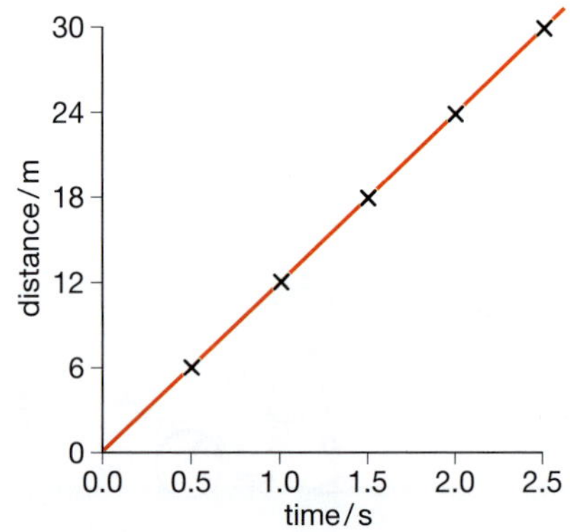

▲ Figure 1.6 Distance–time graph for the travelling car in Figure 1.5

The distance–time graph tells us about how the car is travelling in a much more convenient form than the series of drawings in Figure 1.5. We can see that the car is travelling equal distances in equal time intervals – it is moving at a steady or constant speed. This fact is shown immediately by the fact that the graph is a straight line. The slope or **gradient** of the line tells us the speed of the car – the steeper the line the greater the speed of the car. So in this example:

$$\text{speed} = \text{gradient} = \frac{\text{distance}}{\text{time}} = \frac{30\,\text{m}}{2.5\,\text{s}} = 12\,\text{m/s}$$

KEY POINT

A curved line on distance–time graphs means that the speed or velocity of the object is changing. To find the speed at a particular instant of time we would draw a tangent to the curve at that instant and find the gradient of the tangent.

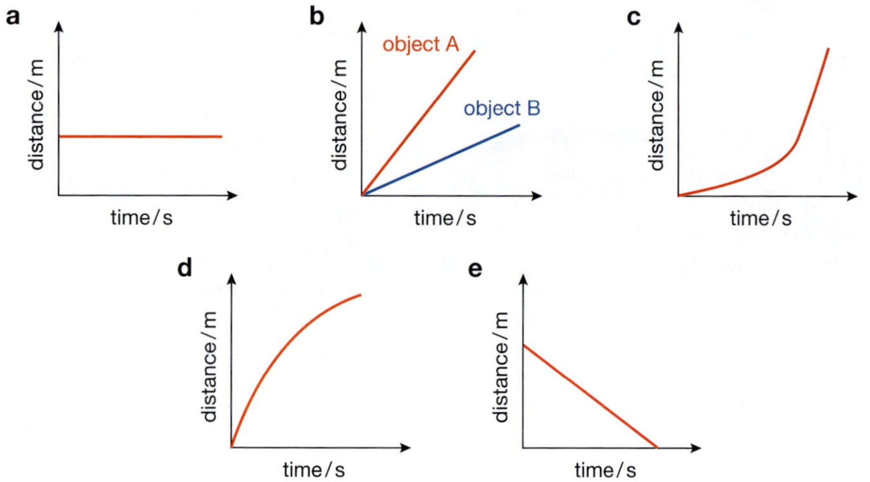

▲ Figure 1.7 Examples of distance–time graphs

In Figure 1.7a the distance is not changing with time – the line is horizontal. This means that the speed is zero. In Figure 1.7b the graph shows how two objects are moving. The red line is steeper than the blue line because object A is moving at a higher speed than object B. In Figure 1.7c the object is speeding up (**accelerating**) shown by the graph line getting steeper (gradient getting bigger). In Figure 1.7d the object is slowing down (decelerating).

THE DIFFERENCE BETWEEN SPEED AND VELOCITY

Some displacement–time graphs look like the one shown in Figure 1.7e. It is a straight line, showing that the object is moving with constant speed, but the line is sloping down to the right rather than up to the right. The gradient of such a line is negative because the distance that the object is from the starting point is now decreasing – the object is going back on its path towards the start. **Displacement** means 'distance travelled in a particular direction' from a specified point. So if the object was originally travelling in a northerly direction, the negative gradient of the graph means that it is now travelling south.

KEY POINT

A vector is a quantity that has both size and direction. Displacement is distance travelled in a particular direction. **Force** is another example of a vector that you will meet in Chapter 2. The size of a force and the direction in which it acts are both important.

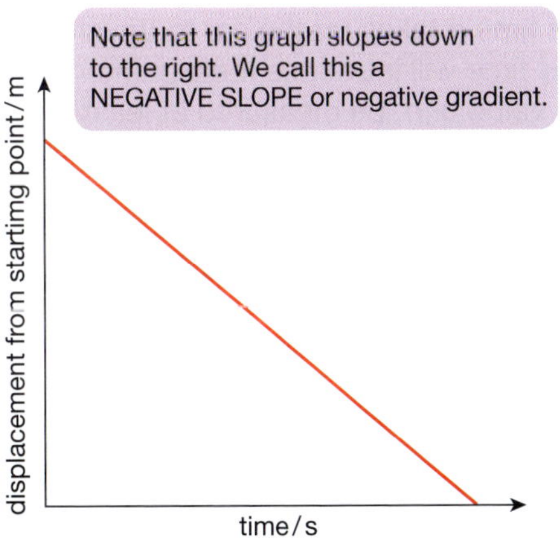

▲ Figure 1.8 In this graph displacement is decreasing with time.

KEY POINT

Always show your working when answering questions. You should show your working by putting the values given in the question into the equation.

Displacement is an example of a vector. Vector quantities have magnitude (size) and a specific direction.

Velocity is also a vector. Velocity is speed in a particular direction. If a car travels at 50 km/h around a bend, its speed is constant but its velocity will be changing for as long as the direction that the car is travelling in is changing.

$$\text{average velocity} = \frac{\text{increase in displacement}}{\text{time taken}}$$

EXAMPLE 1

The global positioning system (GPS) in Figure 1.9 shows two points on a journey. The second point is 3 km north-west of the first.

a A walker takes 45 minutes to travel from the first point to the second. Calculate the average velocity of the walker.

b Explain why the average speed of the walker must be greater than this.

a Write down what you know:

increase in displacement is 3 km north-west

time taken is 45 min (45 min = 0.75 h)

$$\text{average velocity} = \frac{\text{increase in displacement}}{\text{time taken}}$$

$$= 4 \text{ km/h north-west}$$

b The walker has to follow the roads, so the distance walked is greater than the straight-line distance between A and B (the displacement). The walker's average speed (calculated using distance) must be greater than his average velocity (calculated using displacement).

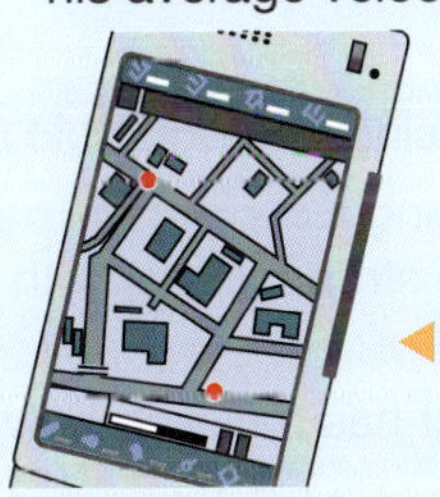

◀ Figure 1.9 The screen of a global positioning system (GPS). A GPS is an aid to navigation that uses orbiting satellites to locate its position on the Earth's surface.

ACTIVITY 1

▼ PRACTICAL: INVESTIGATE THE MOTION OF EVERYDAY OBJECTS SUCH AS TOY CARS OR TENNIS BALLS

You can use the following simple **apparatus** to investigate the motion of a toy car.

You could use this to measure the average speed, v of the car for different values of h.

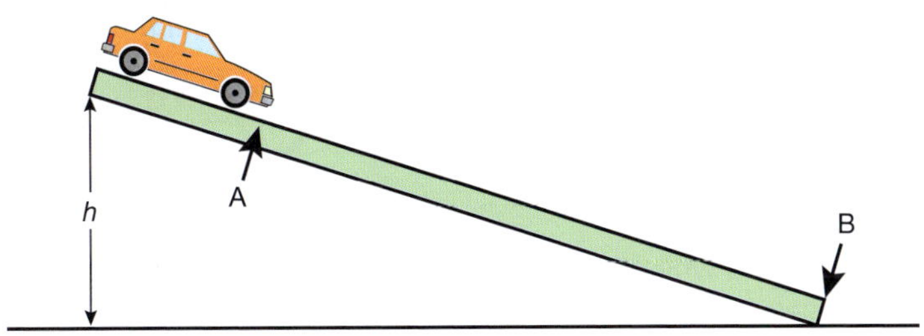

▲ Figure 1.10 Investigating how a toy car rolls down a slope

Safety note: Heavy wooden runways need to be stacked and moved carefully. They are best used at low level rather than being placed on benches or tables where they may fall off. If heavy trolleys are used as 'vehicles', a 'catch box' filled with bubble wrap or similar material should be placed at the end of the runway.

You need to measure the height, *h*, of the raised end of the wooden track. The track must be securely clamped at the height under test and *h* should be measured with a metre rule making sure that the rule is **perpendicular** to the bench surface. Make sure that you always measure to the same point or mark on the raised end of the track (a fiducial mark).

To find the average speed you will use the equation:

$$\text{average speed, } v = \frac{\text{distance moved, } s}{\text{time taken, } t}$$

so you will need to measure the distance AB with a metre rule and measure the time it takes for the car to travel this distance with a stop clock. When timing with a stop clock, human **reaction** time will introduce measurement errors. To make these smaller the time to travel distance AB should, for a given value of *h*, be measured at least three times and an average value found. Always start the car from the same point, A. If one value is quite different from the others it should be treated as anomalous (the result is not accurate) and ignored or repeated.

The results should be presented in a table like the one below.

You do not need to include these equations in your table headings but you may be asked to show how you did the calculations.

Distance / m	AB:

Height, h / m	Time, *t* / s			Average time, *t* / s $t = (t1 + t2 + t3) \div 3$	Average speed, *v* / m / s $v = AB \div t$
	*t*1	*t*2	*t*3		

In a question you may be given a complete set of results or you may be required to complete the table by doing the necessary calculations. You may be asked to plot a graph (see general notes above) and then draw a conclusion. The conclusion you draw must be explained with reference to the graph, for example, if the best fit line through the plotted points is a straight line and it passes through the origin (the 0, 0 point) you can conclude that there is a **proportional** relationship between the quantities you have plotted on the graph.

Some alternative methods

You could investigate the motion of moving objects using photographic methods either by:

- carrying out the experiment in a darkened room using a **stroboscope** to light up the object at regular known intervals (found from the **frequency** setting on the stroboscope) with the camera adjusted so that the shutter is open for the duration of the movement, or
- using a video camera and noting how far the object has travelled between each frame – the frame rate will allow you to calculate the time between each image.

In either case a clearly marked measuring scale should be visible.

Or you could use an electronically operated stop clock and electronic timing gates. This will let you measure the time that it takes for the moving object to travel over a measured distance. This has the advantage of removing timing errors produced by human reaction time.

You can also use timing gates to measure how the speed of the object changes as it moves.

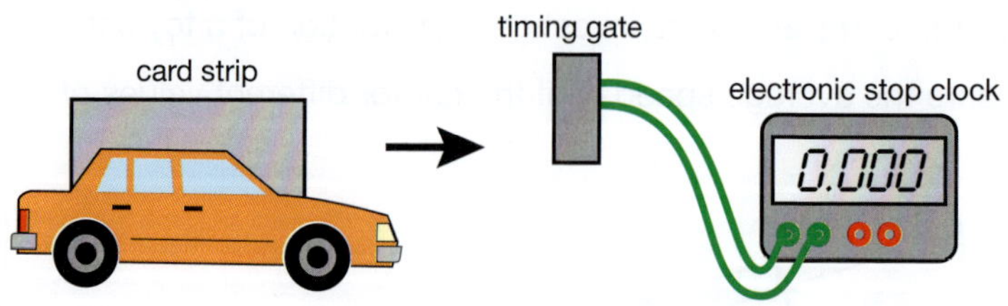

▲ Figure 1.11 Using a timing gate is a more accurate method for measuring time taken to travel a distance.

In this arrangement the stop clock will time while the card strip attached to the moving car passes through the timing gate. Measuring the length of the card strip and the time it takes for the card strip to pass through the timing gate allows you to calculate the average speed of the car as it passes through the timing gate.

ACCELERATION

Figure 1.12 shows some objects whose speed is changing. The plane must accelerate to reach take-off speed. In ice hockey, the puck (small disc that the player hits) decelerates only very slowly when it slides across the ice. When the egg hits the ground it is forced to decelerate (decrease its speed) very rapidly. Rapid deceleration can have destructive results.

▲ Figure 1.12 Acceleration …

… constant speed …

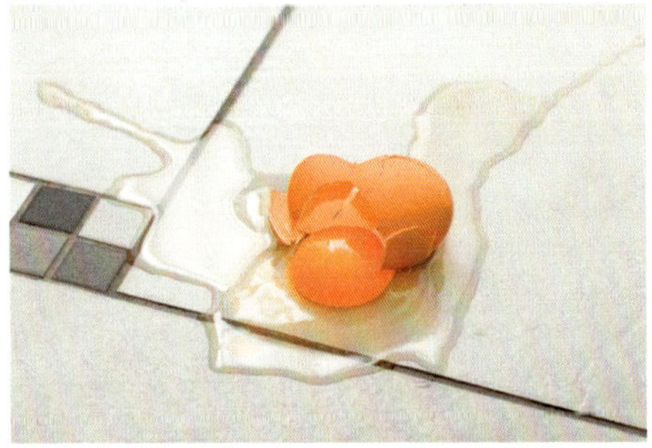

… and deceleration

Acceleration is the rate at which objects change their velocity. It is defined as follows:

$$\text{acceleration, } a = \frac{\text{change in velocity}}{\text{time taken, } t} \text{ or } \frac{\text{final velocity, } v - \text{initial velocity, } u}{\text{time taken, } t}$$

$$a = \frac{(v - u)}{t}$$

Why u? Simply because it comes before v!

Acceleration, like velocity, is a vector because the direction in which the acceleration occurs is important as well as the size of the acceleration.

UNITS OF ACCELERATION

Velocity is measured in m/s, so increase in velocity is also measured in m/s. Acceleration, the rate of increase in velocity with time, is therefore measured in m/s/s (read as 'metres per second per second'). We normally write this as m/s^2 (read as 'metres per second **squared**'). Other units may be used – for example, cm/s^2.

EXAMPLE 2

A car is travelling at 20 m/s. It accelerates steadily for 5 s, after which time it is travelling at 30 m/s. Calculate its acceleration.

Write down what you know:

initial or starting velocity, u = 20 m/s

final velocity, v = 30 m/s

time taken, t = 5 s

$$a = \frac{(v - u)}{t}$$

$$= \frac{30\,\text{m/s} - 20\,\text{m/s}}{5\,\text{s}}$$

$$= \frac{10\,\text{m/s}}{5\,\text{s}}$$

The car is accelerating at 2 m/s^2.

HINT

It is good practice to include units in equations – this will help you to supply the answer with the correct unit.

DECELERATION

Deceleration means slowing down. This means that a decelerating object will have a smaller final velocity than its starting velocity. If you use the equation for finding the acceleration of an object that is slowing down, the answer will have a negative sign. A negative acceleration simply means deceleration.

EXAMPLE 3

An object hits the ground travelling at 40 m/s. It is brought to rest in 0.02 s. What is its acceleration?

Write down what you know:

initial velocity, u = 40 m/s

final velocity, v = 0 m/s

time taken, t = 0.02 s

$$a = \frac{(v - u)}{t}$$

$$= \frac{0\,\text{m/s} - 40\,\text{m/s}}{0.02\,\text{s}}$$

$$= \frac{-40\,\text{m/s}}{0.02\,\text{s}}$$

$$= -2000\,\text{m/s}^2$$

In Example 3, we would say that the object is decelerating at 2000 m/s^2. This is a very large deceleration. Later, in Chapter 3, we shall discuss the consequences of such a rapid deceleration!

MEASURING ACCELERATION

EXTENSION WORK

Galileo was an Italian scientist who was born in 1564. He developed a telescope, which he used to study the movement of the planets and stars. He also carried out many experiments on motion (movement).

EXTENSION WORK

Though Galileo did not have a clock or watch (let alone an electronic timer), he used his pulse (the sound of his heart) and a type of water clock to achieve timings that were accurate enough for his experiments.

When a ball is rolled down a slope it is clear that its speed increases as it rolls – that is, it accelerates. Galileo was interested in how and why objects, like the ball rolling down a slope, speed up, and he created an interesting experiment to learn more about acceleration. A version of his experiment is shown in Figure 1.13.

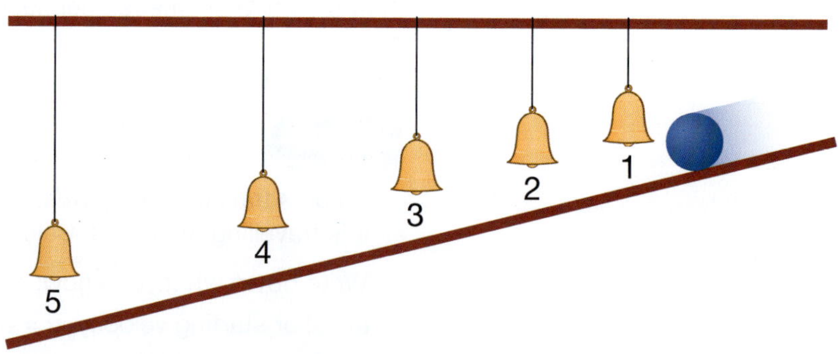

▲ Figure 1.13 Galileo's experiment. A ball rolling down a slope, hitting small bells as it rolls

Galileo wanted to discover how the distance travelled by a ball depends on the time it has been rolling. In this version of the experiment, a ball rolling down a slope strikes a series of small bells as it rolls. By adjusting the positions of the bells carefully it is possible to make the bells ring at equal intervals of time as the ball passes. Galileo noticed that the distances travelled in equal time intervals increased, showing that the ball was travelling faster as time passed. Galileo did not have an accurate way of measuring time (there were no digital stopwatches in seventeenth-century Italy!) but it was possible to judge equal time intervals accurately simply by listening.

Galileo also noticed that the distance travelled by the ball increased in a predictable way. He showed that the rate of increase of speed was steady or uniform. We call this uniform acceleration. Most acceleration is non-uniform – that is, it changes from instant to instant – but we shall only deal with uniformly accelerated objects in this chapter.

VELOCITY–TIME GRAPHS

The table below shows the distances between the bells in an experiment such as Galileo's.

Bell	1	2	3	4	5
Time / s	0.5	1.0	1.5	2.0	2.5
Distance of bell from start / cm	3	12	27	48	75

We can calculate the average speed of the ball between each bell by working out the distance travelled between each bell, and the time it took to travel this distance. For the first bell:

$$\text{velocity, } v = \frac{\text{distance moved, } s}{\text{time taken, } t}$$

$$= \frac{3\,\text{cm}}{0.5\,\text{s}} = 6\,\text{cm/s}$$

This is the average velocity over the 0.5 second time interval, so if we plot it on a graph we should plot it in the middle of the interval, at 0.25 seconds.

Repeating the above calculation for all the results gives us the following table of results. We can use these results to draw a graph showing how the velocity of the ball is changing with time. The graph, shown in Figure 1.14, is called a velocity–time graph.

Time / s	0.25	0.75	1.25	1.75	2.25
Velocity / cm/s	6	18	30	42	54

KEY POINT

The equations of motion we have learned work for uniform or constant acceleration only – therefore for objects with velocity–time graphs that are straight lines.

The graph in Figure 1.14 is a straight line. This tells us that the velocity of the rolling ball is increasing by equal amounts in equal time periods. We say that the acceleration is uniform in this case.

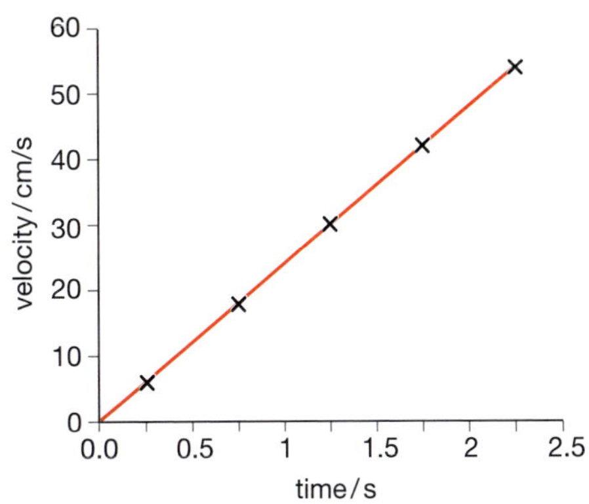

▲ Figure 1.14 Velocity–time graph for an experiment in which a ball is rolled down a slope. (Note that as we are plotting average velocity, the points are plotted in the middle of each successive 0.5 s time interval.)

A MODERN VERSION OF GALILEO'S EXPERIMENT

Safety note: A cylinder vacuum cleaner (or similar) used with the air-track should be placed on the floor as it may fall off a bench or stool. Also, beware of any trailing leads.

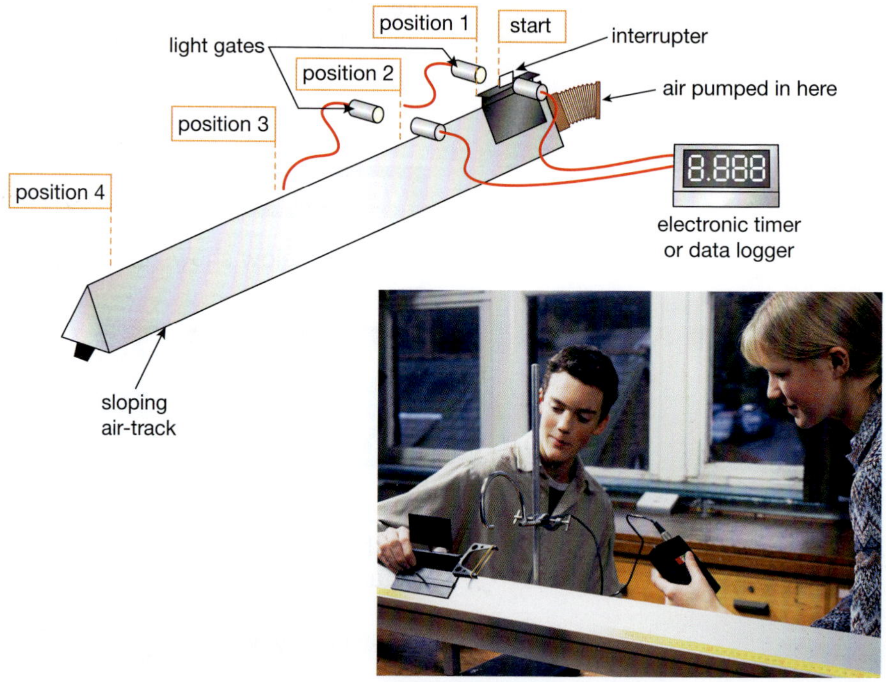

▲ Figure 1.15 Measuring acceleration

Today we can use data loggers to make accurate direct measurements that are collected and analysed by a computer. A spreadsheet program can be used to produce a velocity–time graph. Figure 1.15 shows a glider on a slightly sloping air-track. The air-track reduces **friction** because the glider rides on a cushion of air that is pushed continuously through holes along the air-track. As the glider accelerates down the sloping track the card stuck on it breaks a light beam, and the time that the glider takes to pass is measured electronically. If the length of the card is measured, and this is entered into the spreadsheet, the velocity of the glider can be calculated by the spreadsheet program using $v = \frac{s}{t}$.

Figure 1.16 shows velocity–time graphs for two experiments done using the air-track apparatus. In each experiment the track was given a different slope. The steeper the slope of the air-track the greater the glider's acceleration. This is clear from the graphs: the greater the acceleration the steeper the gradient of the graph.

The gradient of a velocity–time graph gives the acceleration.

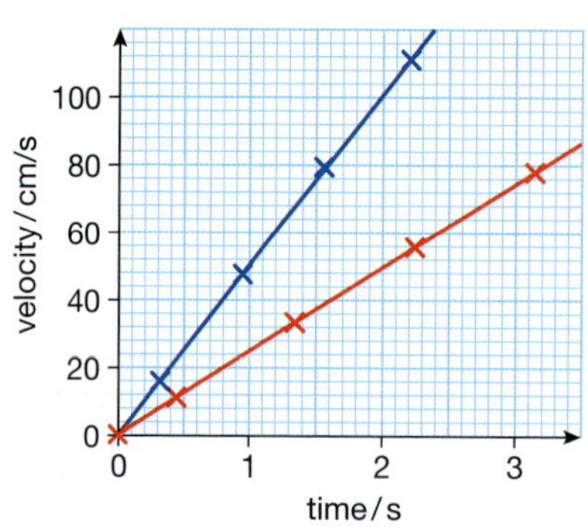

Air-track at 1.5°		Air-track at 3.0°	
Time / s	Av Vel. /cm/s	Time / s	Av Vel. /cm/s
0.00	0.0	0.00	0.0
0.45	11.1	0.32	15.9
1.35	33.3	0.95	47.6
2.25	55.6	1.56	79.4
3.15	77.8	2.21	111.1

▲ Figure 1.16 Results of two air-track experiments. (Note, once again, that because we are plotting average velocity in the velocity–time graphs, the points are plotted in the middle of each successive time interval – see page 497)

MORE ABOUT VELOCITY–TIME GRAPHS

GRADIENT

The results of the air-track experiments in Figure 1.16 show that the slope of the velocity–time graph depends on the acceleration of the glider. The slope or gradient of a velocity–time graph is found by dividing the increase in the velocity by the time taken for the increase, as shown in Figure 1.17. In this example an object is travelling at u m/s at the beginning and accelerates uniformly (at a constant rate) for t s. Its final velocity is v m/s. Increase in velocity divided by time is, you will recall, the definition of acceleration (see page 495), so we can measure the acceleration of an object by finding the slope of its velocity–time graph. The meaning of the slope or gradient of a velocity–time graph is summarised in Figure 1.17.

HINT

1. When finding the gradient of a graph, draw a big triangle.
2. Choose a convenient number of units for the length of the base of the triangle to make the division easier.

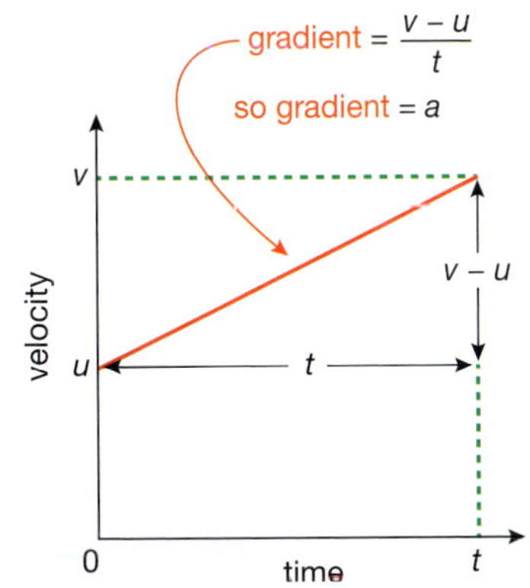

Figure 1.17 Finding the gradient of a velocity–time graph

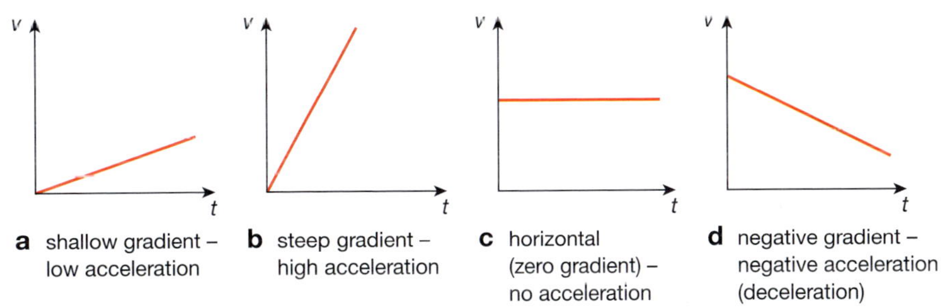

Figure 1.18 The gradient of a velocity–time graph gives you information about the motion of an object at a glance.

AREA UNDER A VELOCITY–TIME GRAPH GIVES DISTANCE TRAVELLED

Figure 1.19a shows a velocity–time graph for an object that travels with a constant velocity of 5 m/s for 10 s. A simple calculation shows that in this time the object has travelled 50 m. This is equal to the shaded (coloured) area under the graph. Figure 1.19b shows a velocity–time graph for an object that has accelerated at a constant rate. Its average velocity during this time is given by:

$$\text{average velocity} = \frac{\text{initial velocity} + \text{final velocity}}{2} \text{ or } \frac{u + v}{2}$$

In this example the average velocity is, therefore:

$$\text{average velocity} = \frac{0\,\text{m/s} + 10\,\text{m/s}}{2}$$

which works out to be 5 m/s. If the object travels, on average, 5 metres in each second it will have travelled 20 metres in 4 seconds. Notice that this, too, is equal to the shaded area under the graph (given by the area equation for a triangle: area = $\frac{1}{2}$ base × height).

HINT

Find the distance travelled for more complicated velocity–time graphs by dividing the area beneath the graph line into rectangles and triangles. Take care that units on the velocity and time axes use the same units for time, for example, m/s and s, or km/h and h.

The area under a velocity–time graph is equal to the distance travelled by (displacement of) the object in a particular time interval.

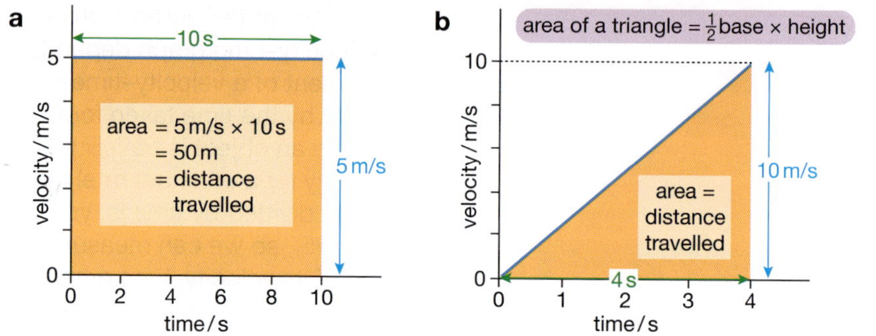

▲ Figure 1.19 a An object travelling at constant velocity; b An object accelerating at a constant rate

EQUATIONS OF UNIFORMLY ACCELERATED MOTION

You must remember the equation:

$$a = \frac{v - u}{t}$$

and be able to use it to calculate the acceleration of an object.

You may need to rearrange the equation to make another term the subject.

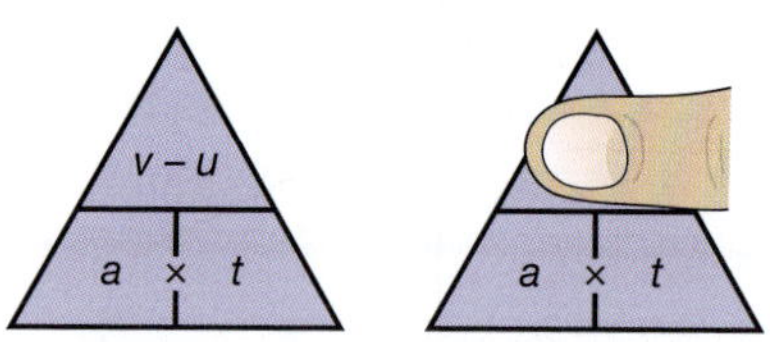

▲ Figure 1.20 Cover $v - u$ to find $v - u = a \times t$

EXAMPLE 4

A stone accelerates from rest uniformly at 10 m/s^2 when it is dropped down a deep well. It hits the water at the bottom of the well after 5 s. Calculate how fast it is travelling when it hits the water.

You will need to make v the subject of this equation:

$$a = \frac{v - u}{t}$$

You can use the triangle method to show that $v - u = a \times t$

then add u to both sides of the equation to give:

$$v = u + at$$

(In words this tells you that the final velocity is the initial velocity plus the increase in velocity after accelerating for t seconds.)

State the things you have been told:

initial velocity, u = 0 m/s (It was stationary (standing still) at the start.)

acceleration, a = 10 m/s^2

time, t, of the acceleration = 5 s

Substitute these into the equation: v = 0 m/s + (10 m/s^2 × 5 s)

Then calculate the result.

The stone hit the water travelling at 50 m/s (downwards).

You will also be required to use the following equation of uniformly accelerated motion:

(final speed)^2, v^2 = (initial speed)^2, u^2 + (2 × acceleration, a × distance moved, s)

$$v^2 = u^2 + 2as$$

EXAMPLE 5

A cylinder containing a vaccine is dropped from a helicopter hovering at a height of 200 m above the ground. The acceleration due to **gravity** is 10 m/s^2. Calculate the speed at which the cylinder will hit the ground.

You are given the acceleration, a = 10 m/s^2, and the distance, s = 200 m, through which the cylinder moves. The initial velocity, u, is not stated, but you assume it is 0 m/s as the helicopter is hovering (staying in one place in the air). Substitute these values in the given equation.

$$v^2 = u^2 + 2as$$

$$= 0\ \text{m/s}^2 + (2 \times 10\ \text{m/s}^2 \times 200\ \text{m})$$

$$= 4000\ \text{m}^2/\text{s}^2$$

$$\text{therefore } v = \sqrt{(4000\ \text{m}^2/\text{s}^2)}$$

$$= 63.25\ \text{m/s}$$

LOOKING AHEAD

The equations you have seen in this chapter are called the equations of uniformly accelerated motion. This means that they will give you correct answers when solving any problems that have objects moving with constant acceleration. In your exam you will only see problems where this is the case or very nearly so. Examples in which objects accelerate or decelerate (slow down) at a constant rate often have a constant acceleration due to the Earth's gravity (which we take as about 10 m/s^2).

In real life, problems may not be quite so simple! Objects only fall with constant acceleration if we ignore air resistance and the distance that they fall is quite small.

These equations of uniformly accelerated motion are often called the 'suvat' equations, because they show how the terms s (distance moved), u (velocity at the start), v (velocity at the finish), a (acceleration) and t (time) are related.

CHAPTER QUESTIONS

More questions on speed and acceleration can be found at the end of Unit 1 on page 526.

SKILLS PROBLEM SOLVING

7th

1 A sprinter runs 100 metres in 12.5 seconds. Calculate the speed in m/s.

8th

2 A jet can travel at 350 m/s. Calculate how far it will travel at this speed in:

a 30 seconds

b 5 minutes

c half an hour.

3 A snail crawls at a speed of 0.0004 m/s. How long will it take to climb a garden stick 1.6 m high?

SKILLS ANALYSIS

4 Look at the following distance–time graphs of moving objects.

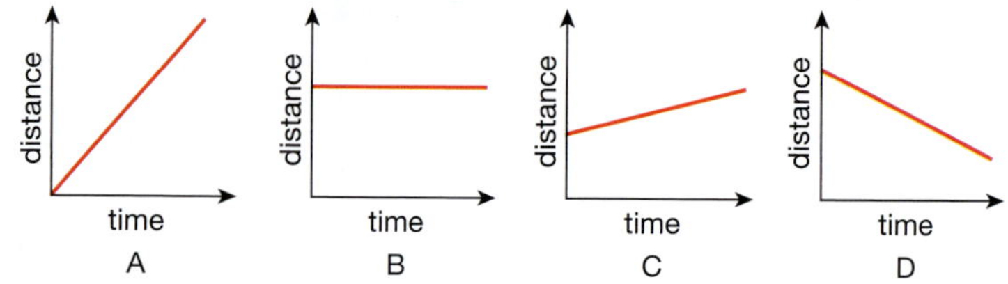

Identify in which graph the object is:

a moving backwards

b moving slowly

c moving quickly

d not moving at all.

SKILLS INTERPRETATION

5 Sketch a distance–time graph to show the motion of a person walking quickly, stopping for a moment, then continuing to walk slowly in the same direction.

6 Plot a distance–time graph using the data in the following table. Draw a line of best fit and use your graph to find the speed of the object concerned.

Distance / m	0.00	1.60	3.25	4.80	6.35	8.00	9.60
Time / s	0.00	0.05	0.10	0.15	0.20	0.25	0.30

SKILLS PROBLEM SOLVING

7 The diagram below shows a trail of oil drips made by a car as it travels along a road. The oil is dripping from the car at a steady rate of one drip every 2.5 seconds.

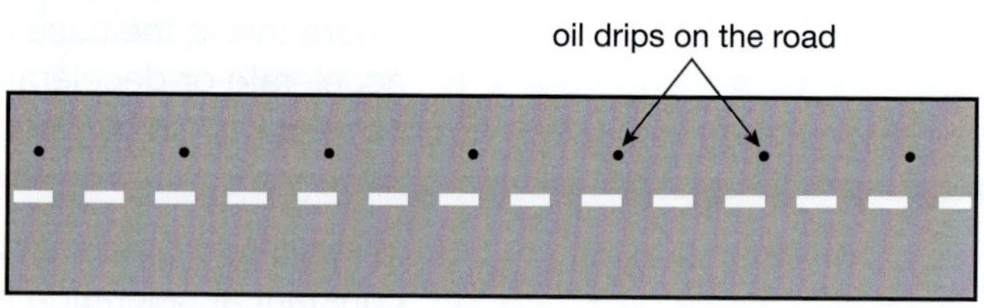

a Describe the way the car is moving.

b The distance between the first and the seventh drip is 135 metres. Determine the average speed of the car.

8 A car is travelling at 20 m/s. It accelerates uniformly at 3 m/s^2 for 5 s.

a Sketch a velocity–time graph for the car during the period that it is accelerating. Include numerical detail on the axes of your graph.

b Calculate the distance the car travels while it is accelerating.

SKILLS INTERPRETATION

9 Explain the difference between the following terms:

a average speed and instantaneous speed

b speed and velocity.

SKILLS PROBLEM SOLVING

10 A sports car accelerates uniformly from rest to 24 m/s in 6 s. Calculate the acceleration of the car.

SKILLS INTERPRETATION

11 Sketch velocity–time graphs for an object:

a moving with a constant velocity of 6 m/s

b accelerating uniformly from rest at 2 m/s^2 for 10 s

c decelerating to rest at 4 m/s^2 for 5 s.

Include numbers and units on the velocity and time axes in each case.

SKILLS PROBLEM SOLVING

12 A plane starting from rest accelerates at 3 m/s^2 for 25 s. Calculate the increase in velocity after:

a 1 s

b 5 s

c 25 s.

SKILLS ANALYSIS

13 Look at the following sketches of velocity–time graphs of moving objects.

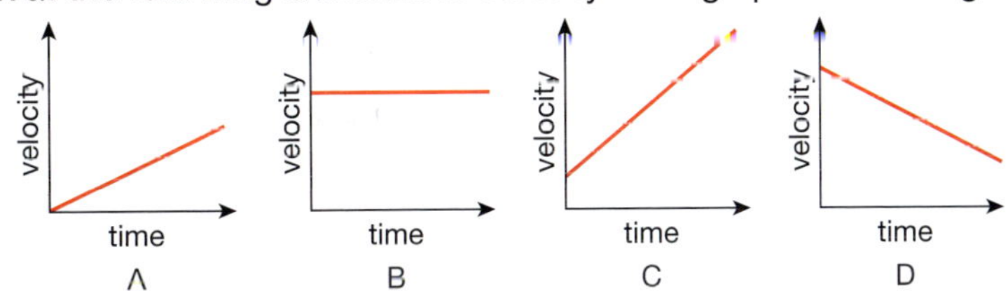

In which graph is the object:

a not accelerating

b accelerating from rest

c decelerating

d accelerating at the greatest rate?

SKILLS INTERPRETATION

14 Sketch a velocity–time graph to show how the velocity of a car travelling along a straight road changes if it accelerates uniformly from rest for 5 s, travels at a constant velocity for 10 s, then brakes hard to come to rest in 2 s.

15 **a** Plot a velocity–time graph using the data in the following table:

Velocity / m/s	0.0	2.5	5.0	7.5	10.0	10.0	10.0	10.0	10.0	10.0
Time / s	0.0	1.0	2.0	3.0	4.0	5.0	6.0	7.0	8.0	9.0

Draw a line of best fit and use your graph to find:

b the acceleration during the first 4 s

c the distance travelled in:

i the first 4 s of the motion shown

ii the last 5 s of the motion shown

d the average speed during the 9 seconds of motion shown.

SKILLS CRITICAL THINKING

16 The dripping car from Question 7 is still on the road! It is still dripping oil but now at a rate of one drop per second. The trail of drips is shown on the diagram below as the car travels from left to right.

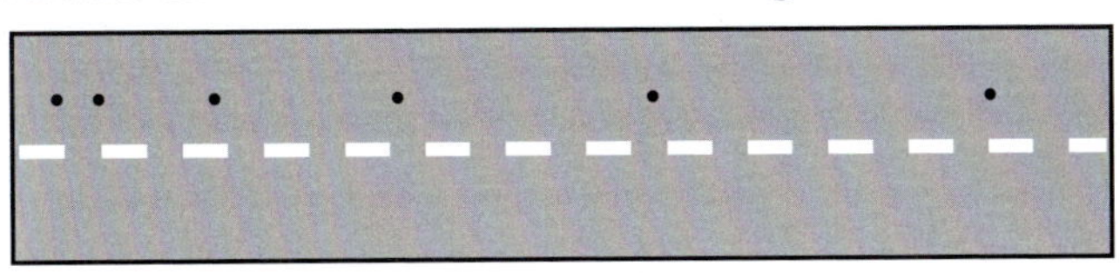

Describe the motion (the way the car is moving) using the information in this diagram.

SKILLS PROBLEM SOLVING

17 This question uses the equation $v^2 = u^2 + 2as$.

a Explain what each of the terms in this equation represents.

b A ball is thrown vertically upwards at 25 m/s. Gravity causes the ball to decelerate at 10 m/s^2. Calculate the maximum height the ball will reach.

2 FORCES AND SHAPE

Forces are acting on us, and on objects all around us, all the time. In this chapter you will learn about different kinds of forces, how they may change the speed and direction of objects and how they can affect the shape of objects.

▲ Figure 2.1 Forces include pulling, falling due to gravity and squashing

LEARNING OBJECTIVES

- Describe the effects of forces between bodies such as changes in speed, shape or direction
- Identify different types of force such as gravitational or electrostatic
- Understand how vector quantities differ from scalar quantities
- Understand that force is a vector quantity
- Calculate the resultant force of forces that act along a line
- Know that friction is a force that opposes motion
- Practical: investigate how extension varies with applied force for helical springs, metal wires and rubber bands
- Know that the initial linear region of a force–extension graph is associated with Hooke's law
- Describe elastic behaviour as the ability of a material to recover its original shape after the forces causing deformation have been removed

Forces are simply pushes and pulls of one thing on another. Sometimes we can see their effects quite clearly. In Figure 2.1, the tug is pulling the tanker; the bungee jumper is being pulled to Earth by the force of gravity, and then (hopefully before meeting the ground) being pulled back up by the stretched elastic rope; the force applied by the crusher permanently changes the shape of the cars. In this chapter we will discuss different types of forces and look at their effects on the way that objects move.

ALL SORTS OF FORCES

If you are to study forces, first you need to notice them! As we have already said, sometimes they are easy to see and their effect is obvious. Look at Figure 2.2 and try to identify any forces that you think are involved.

▲ Figure 2.2 What forces do you think are working here?

You will immediately see that the man is applying a force to the car – he is pushing it. But there are quite a few more forces in the picture. To make the task a little easier we will limit our search to just those forces acting on the car. We will also ignore forces that are very small and therefore have little effect.

The man is clearly struggling to make the car move. This is because there is a force acting on the car trying to stop it moving. This is the force of friction between the moving parts in the car engine, gears, wheel axles and so on. This unhelpful force opposes the motion that the man is trying to achieve. However, when the car engine is doing the work to make the car go, the friction between the tyres and the road surface is vital. On an icy road even powerful cars may not move forward because there is not enough friction between the tyres and the ice.

Another force that acts on the car is the pull of the Earth. We call this a gravitational force or simply **weight**. If the car were to be pushed over the edge of a cliff, the effect of the gravitational force would be very clear as the car fell towards the sea. This leads us to realise that yet another force is acting on the car in Figure 2.2 – the road must be stopping the car from being pulled into the Earth. This force, which acts in an upward direction (going up) on the car, is called the reaction force. (A more complete name is **normal** reaction force. Here the word 'normal' means acting at 90° to the road surface.) All four forces that act on the car are shown in Figure 2.3.

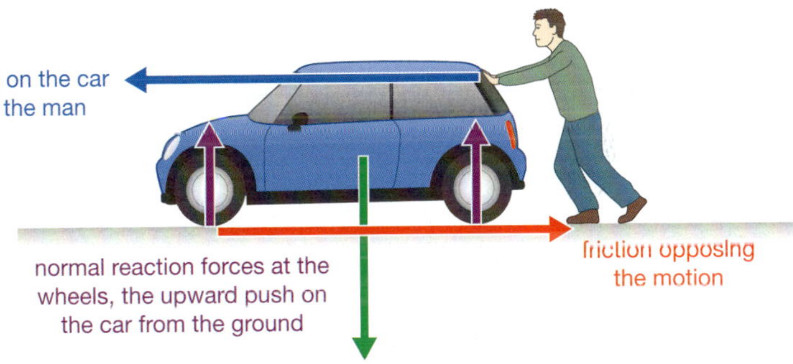

▲ Figure 2.3 There are four types of force at work.

You will have realised by now that it is not just the size of the force that is important – the direction in which the force is acting is important, too.

Force is another example of a vector.

KEY POINT

Like displacement, velocity and acceleration, force is a *vector quantity* because both its size and direction matter. Some quantities, such as temperature, have no direction connected with them. They are known as *scalar quantities*.

UNITS OF FORCE

The unit used to measure force is the newton (N), named after Sir Isaac Newton. Newton's study of forces is vital to our understanding of them today.

A force of one newton will make a **mass** of one kilogram accelerate at one metre per second squared.

This is explained more fully later (see Chapter 3). To give you an idea of the size of the newton, the force of gravity on a kilogram bag of sugar (its weight) is about 10 N; an average-sized apple weighs 1 N.

a

b

▲ Figure 2.4 More forces!

SOME OTHER EXAMPLES OF FORCES

It is not always easy to spot forces acting on objects. The compass needle in Figure 2.4a, which is a magnet, is affected by the magnetic force between it and the other magnet. Magnetic forces are used to make electric motors **rotate**, to hold fridge doors shut, and in many other situations.

If you comb your hair, you sometimes find that some of your hair sticks to the comb as shown in Figure 2.4b. This happens because of an electrostatic force between your hair and the comb. You can see a similar effect using a Van de Graaff **generator**.

A parachute causes the parachutist to descend more slowly because an upward force acts on the parachute called air resistance or drag. Air resistance is like friction – it tries to oppose movement of objects through the air. Designers of cars, high-speed trains and other fast-moving objects try to reduce the effects of this force. Objects moving through liquids also experience a drag force – fast-moving animals that live in water have streamlined (smooth and efficient) shapes to reduce this force.

Hot air balloons are carried upwards in spite of the pull of gravity on them because of a force called **upthrust**. This is the upward push of the surrounding air on the balloon. An upthrust force also acts on objects in liquids.

More types of force, such as electric and **nuclear** forces, are mentioned in other chapters of this book. The rest of this chapter will look at the effects of forces.

MORE THAN ONE FORCE

As we saw earlier, in most situations there will be more than just one force acting on an object. Look at the man trying to push the car, shown in Figure 2.5. The two forces act along the same line, but in opposite directions. This means that one is negative (because it acts in the opposite direction to the other) and, if they are equal in size, they add up to zero and the car will not move.

▲ Figure 2.5 The **resultant force** is zero because the two forces are balanced.

▲ Figure 2.6 The total pushing force is the **sum** of the two individual forces.

If the man gets someone to help him push the car, the forward force is bigger. Both of the forces pushing the car are acting in the same direction, so you can find the total forward force by adding the two forces together. If both people are pushing with a force of 300 N, then:

$$\text{total forward force} = 300\text{ N} + 300\text{ N} = 600\text{ N}$$

This means we can just add all the forces together to find the resultant force. As force is a vector quantity, we also need to think about the directions in which the forces are acting, and we do this by deciding which direction is the positive (+) direction. In this case, we can think of the force from the people as positive and the force from friction as negative. The + and – signs just show that the forces are acting in opposite directions.

So, if the force from friction is 300 N:

$$\textbf{unbalanced force} = 300\text{ N} + 300\text{ N} - 300\text{ N} = 300\text{ N}$$

BALANCED AND UNBALANCED FORCES

Figure 2.7 Balanced forces and unbalanced forces

Figure 2.7 shows two situations in which forces are acting on an object. In the tug of war contest the two teams are pulling on the rope in opposite directions. For much of the time the rope doesn't move because the two forces are balanced. This means that the forces are the same size but act in opposite directions along the line of the rope. There is no unbalanced force in one direction or the other. When the forces acting on something are balanced, the object does not change the way it is moving. In this case if the rope is stationary, it remains stationary. Eventually, one of the teams will become tired and its pull will be smaller than that of the other team. When the forces acting on the rope are unbalanced the rope will start to move in the direction of the greater force. There will be an unbalanced force in that direction. Unbalanced forces acting on an object cause it to change the way it is moving. The rope was stationary and the unbalanced forces acting on it caused it to accelerate.

The car in Figure 2.7 is designed to have an enormous acceleration from rest. As soon as it starts to move the forces that oppose motion – friction and drag – must be overcome. The **thrust** of the engine is, to start with, much greater than the friction and drag forces. This means that the forces acting on the car in the horizontal direction are unbalanced and the result is a change in the way that the car is moving – it accelerates! Once the friction forces balance the thrust the car no longer accelerates – it moves at a steady speed.

FRICTION

Friction is the force that causes moving objects to slow down and finally stop. The **kinetic energy** of the moving object is transferred to heat as work is done by the friction force. For the ice skater in Figure 2.8 the force of friction is very small so she is able to glide for long distances without having to do any work. It is also the force that allows a car's wheels to grip the road and make it accelerate – very quickly in the case of the racing cars in Figure 2.8.

Scientists have worked hard for many years to develop some materials that reduce friction and others that increase friction. Reducing friction means that machines work more efficiently (wasting less energy) and do not wear out so quickly. Increasing friction can help to make tyres that grip the road better and to make more effective brakes.

▲ Figure 2.8 The ice skater can glide because friction is low. The cars need friction to grip the road.

Friction occurs when solid objects rub against other solid objects and also when objects move through fluids (liquids and gases). Sprint cyclists and Olympic swimmers now wear special materials to reduce the effects of fluid friction so they can achieve faster times in their races. Sometimes fluid friction is very desirable – for example, when someone uses a parachute after jumping from a plane!

INVESTIGATING FRICTION

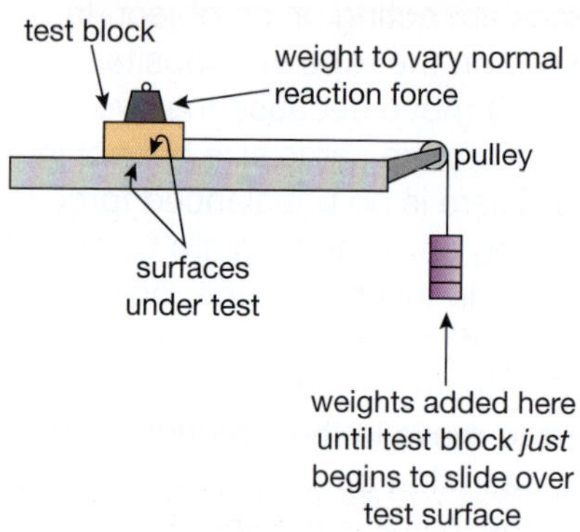

▲ Figure 2.9 This apparatus can be used to investigate friction.

Safety note: A 'catch box' filled with bubble wrap (or similar) under the suspended masses keeps hands and feet out of the 'drop zone'.

The simple apparatus shown in Figure 2.9 can be used to discover some basic facts about friction. The weight force on the line running over the pulley pulls the block horizontally along the track and friction acts on the block to oppose this force. The weight is increased until the block just starts to move; this happens when the pull of the weight force just overcomes the friction force. The friction force between the block and the track has maximum value.

The apparatus can be used to test different factors that may affect the size of the friction force, such as the surfaces in contact – the bottom of the block and the surface of the track. If the track surface is replaced with a rough surface, like a sheet of sandpaper, the force required to overcome friction will be greater.

It is important to remember friction when you are investigating forces and motion. Friction affects almost every form of motion on Earth. However it is possible to do experiments in the science laboratory in which the friction force on a moving object is reduced to a very low value. Such an object can be set in motion with a small push and it will continue to move at a constant speed even when the force is no longer acting on it. An experiment like this is shown in Figure 2.10.

You may also have seen scientists working in space demonstrating that objects keep moving in a straight line at constant speed, once set in motion. They do this in space because the objects are **weightless** and the force of air resistance acting on them is very small.

EXTENSION WORK

Objects in orbit, such as spacecraft, are described as 'weightless' because they do not appear to have weight. However the Earth's gravity is still acting on them, and on the spacecraft. You can think of a spacecraft in orbit as 'falling around the Earth'. As the objects inside the spacecraft are also falling around the Earth at the same rate, they do not seem to fall inside the spacecraft.

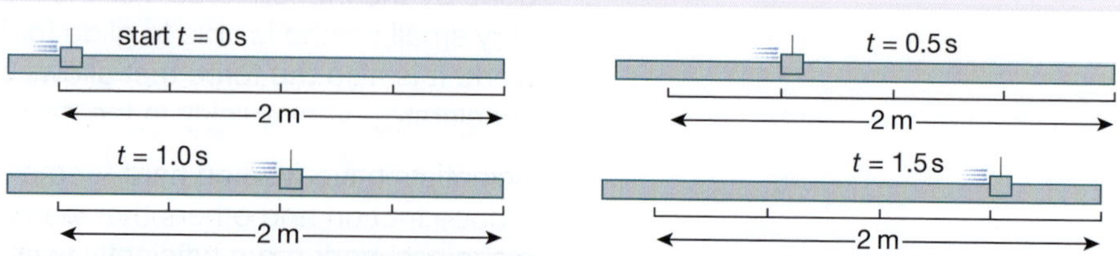

▲ Figure 2.10 A linear (straight line) air-track reduces friction dramatically. The glider moves equal distances in equal time intervals. Its velocity is constant.

▲ Figure 2.11 Forces can cause changes in shape.

CHANGING SHAPES

We have seen that forces can make things start to move, accelerate or decelerate. The examples in Figure 2.11 show another effect that forces can have – they can change the shape of an object.

Sometimes the change of shape is temporary, as in the suspension spring in the mountain bike (Figure 2.11a). Sometimes the shape of the object is permanently changed, like a crushed can or a car that has collided with another object. A temporary change of shape may provide a useful way of absorbing and storing energy, as in the spring in a clock (Figure 2.11b). A permanent change may mean the failure of a structure like a bridge to support a load. Next we will look at temporary changes in the lengths of springs and elastic bands.

TEMPORARY CHANGES OF SHAPE

If you apply a force to an elastic band, its shape changes – the band stretches and gets longer. All materials will stretch a little when you put them under tension (that is, pull them) or shorten when you compress or squash them. You can stretch a rubber band quite easily, but a huge force is needed to cause a noticeable extension in a piece of steel of the same length.

Some materials, like glass, do not change shape easily and are brittle, breaking rather than stretching noticeably. Elastic materials do not break easily and tend to return to their original shape when the forces acting on them are removed, like the spring in Figure 2.11b. Other materials, like putty and modelling clay, are not elastic but plastic, and they change shape when even quite small forces are applied to them.

We will look at elastic materials, like rubber, metal wires and metals formed into springs, in the next part of this chapter.

SPRINGS AND WIRES

Springs are coiled lengths of certain types of metal, which can be stretched or **compressed** by applying a force to them. They are used in many different situations. Sometimes they are used to absorb raised bumps in the road as suspension springs in a car or bicycle. In beds and chairs they are used to make sleeping and sitting more comfortable. They are also used in door locks to hold them closed and to make doors close automatically.

To choose the right spring for a particular use, we must understand some important features of springs. A simple experiment with springs shows us that:

> *Springs change length when a force acts on them and they return to their original length when the force is removed.*

This is true provided you do not stretch them too much. If springs are stretched beyond a certain point they do not spring back to their original length.

HOOKE'S LAW

Robert Hooke discovered another important property of springs. He used simple apparatus like that shown in Figure 2.12.

Hooke measured the increase in length (extension) produced by different load forces on springs. The graph he obtained by plotting force against extension was a straight line passing through the origin. This shows that the extension of the spring is proportional to the force. This relationship is known as Hooke's law.

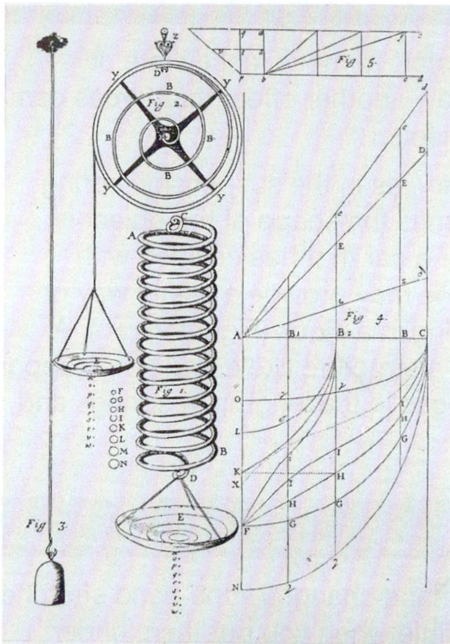

▲ Figure 2.12 Robert Hooke (1635–1703) was a contemporary of Sir Isaac Newton. This is a drawing of the apparatus Hooke used in his experimental work on the extension of a spring.

Safety note: Wear eye protection if heavy loads are being used and clamp stands securely to a bench or table. Keep hands and feet away from beneath the load. Do not use excessively large loads.

ACTIVITY 2

▼ PRACTICAL: INVESTIGATE HOW THE EXTENSION OF A SPRING CHANGES WITH LOAD

Figure 2.13a shows apparatus that may be used to investigate the relationship between the force applied to a spring and its extension.

The length of the unstretched spring is measured with a half-metre rule then the spring is loaded with different weights. The extension for each load is measured against a scale using a set square to improve measurement accuracy.

A table of results is recorded and a graph of load force against extension plotted as shown in Figure 2.13b. The extension measurements can be checked by unloading the weights one at a time and remeasuring the extension for each load.

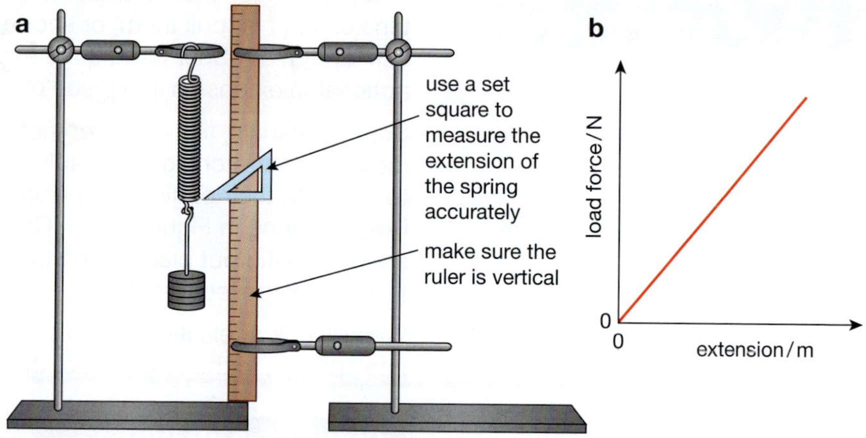

▲ Figure 2.13 **a** Apparatus for the investigation **b** Graph showing expected result

Here the result is a straight line graph passing through the origin of the axes. The spring obeys Hooke's law.

Hooke's law only applies if you do not stretch a spring too far. Figure 2.14 shows what happens if you stretch a spring too far. You can see that the line starts to curve at a point called the limit of proportionality. This is the point where the spring stops obeying Hooke's law and starts to stretch more for each increase in the load force. If the load is increased more, a point called the elastic limit is reached. Once you have stretched a spring beyond the elastic limit it will not return to its original length as you take the weights off the spring.

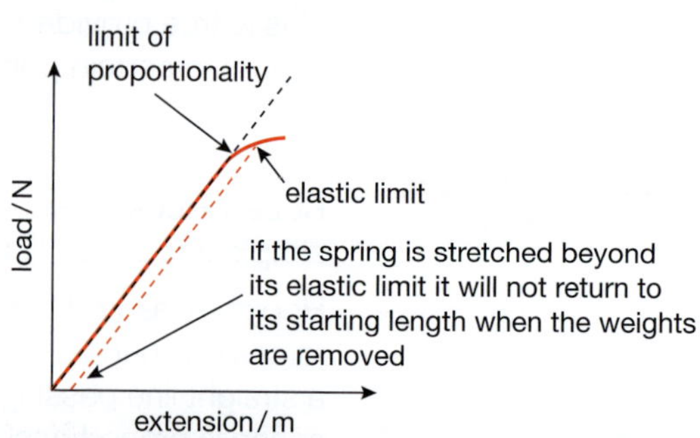

▲ Figure 2.14 Graph of load v extension showing spring going beyond elastic limit

Hooke's law also applies to wires. If you stretch a wire, you will find that the extension is proportional to the load up to a certain load then it may behave as the spring shown in Figure 2.14. Wires made of different metals will behave in different ways – some will obey Hooke's law until the wire breaks; other types of metal will stretch elastically and then plastically before breaking.

ELASTIC BANDS

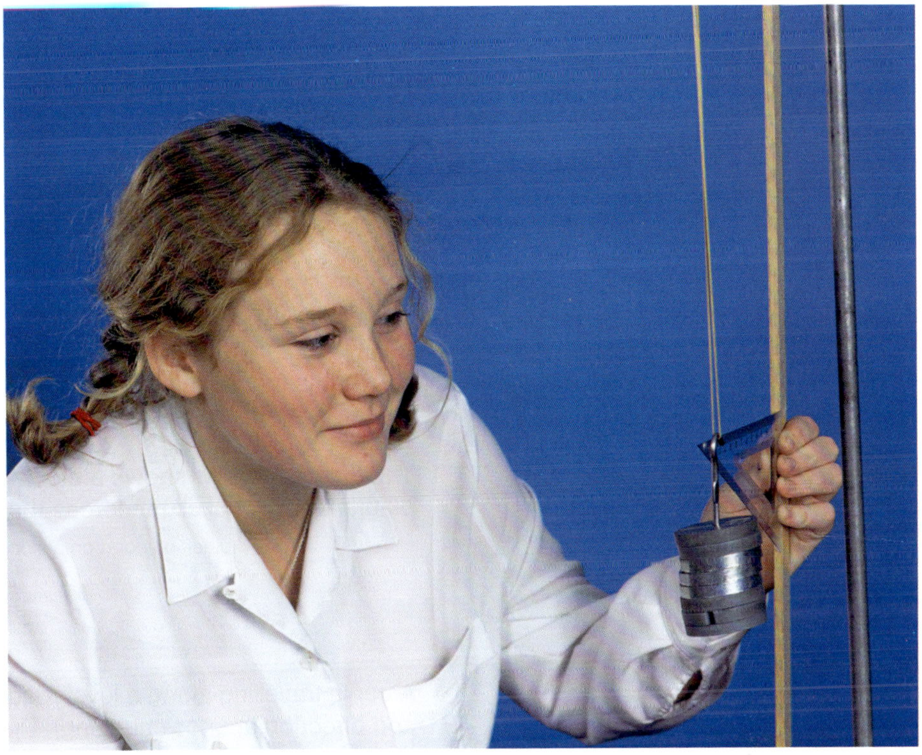

Figure 2.15 Stretching an elastic band

Safety note: Wear eye protection because if the elastic band breaks it can fly back with enough energy to cause serious eye damage.

Elastic bands are usually made of rubber. You can use the same apparatus shown in Figure 2.13a to investigate how an elastic band stretches under load. If you stretch an elastic band with increasing load forces, you get a graph like that shown in Figure 2.16. The graph is not a straight line, showing that elastic bands do not obey Hooke's law. You may also find that the extension produced by a given load force is different when you are increasing the load force to when you decrease the load force.

REMINDER

A wire that stretches elastically will return to its original length once the stretching force is removed. A wire that stretches plastically will not return to its original length once the stretching force is removed and may show signs of narrowing (necking).

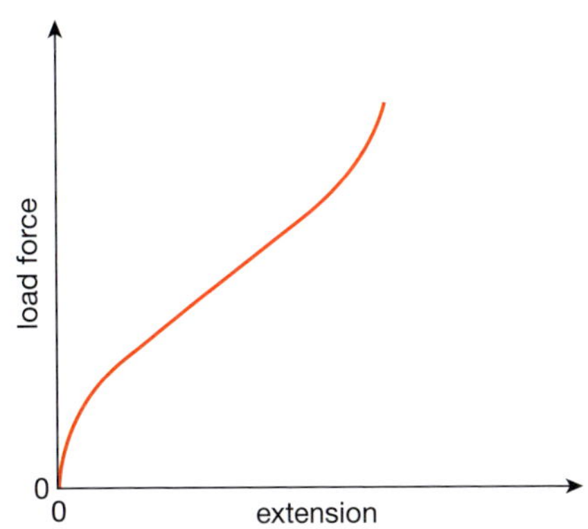

Figure 2.16 Rubber bands do not obey Hooke's law – the extension is not directly proportional to the force causing it.

CHAPTER QUESTIONS

More questions on forces can be found at the end of Unit 1 on page 526.

SKILLS CRITICAL THINKING

3rd

1 Name the force that:

a causes objects to fall towards the Earth

b makes a ball rolled across level ground eventually stop

c stops a car sinking into the road surface.

2 Name two types of force that oppose motion.

SKILLS PROBLEM SOLVING

3 The drawing shows two tug-of-war teams. Each person in the red team is pulling with a force of 250 N. Each person in the blue team is pulling with a force of 200 N.

5th

a What is the total force exerted by the blue team?

b What is the total force exerted by the red team?

6th

c What is the resultant (unbalanced) force on the rope?

d Which team will win?

SKILLS INTERPRETATION

4 The diagram below shows a block of wood on a sloping surface. Copy the diagram and label all the forces that act on the block of wood.

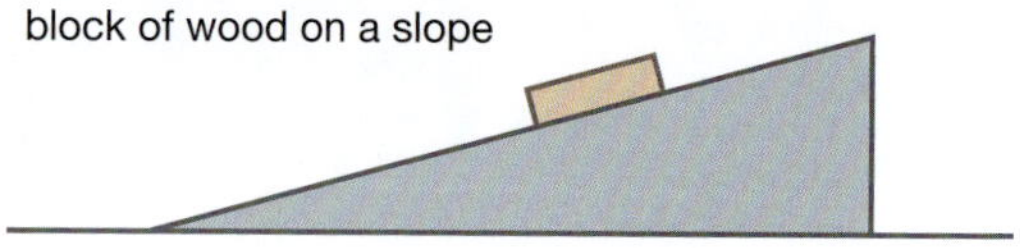

5 A car is travelling along a level road at constant velocity (that is, its speed and direction are not changing). Draw a labelled diagram to show the forces that act on the car.

SKILLS CRITICAL THINKING

4th

6 Describe two things that it would be impossible to do without friction.

SKILLS INTERPRETATION

5th

7 Copy the diagrams below and label the direction in which friction is acting on the objects.

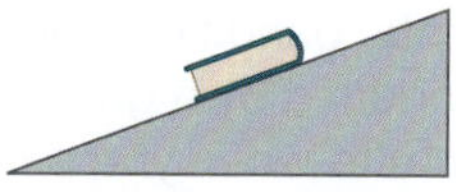

a a book on a sloping surface

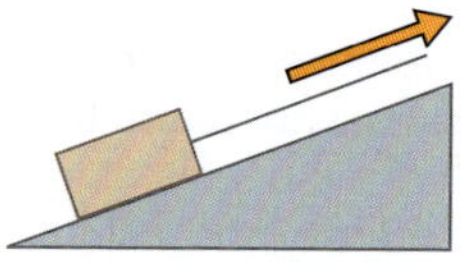

b a block of wood being pulled up a slope

6th

8 The drawing below shows a car pulling a caravan. They are travelling at constant velocity.

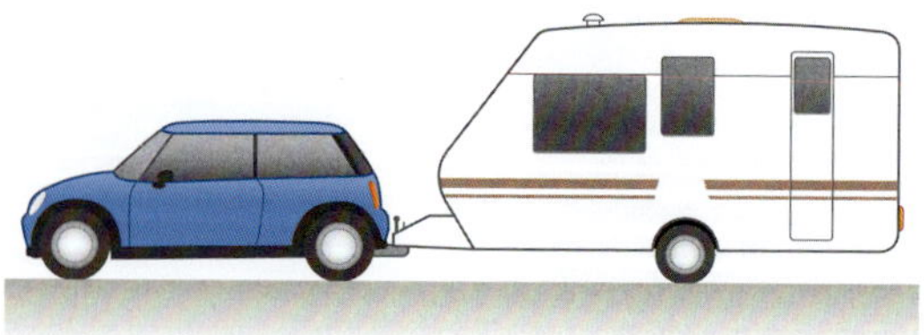

a Copy the drawing. Label the forces that are acting on the caravan with arrows showing the direction that they act in.

b Label the forces that act on the car.

SKILLS PROBLEM SOLVING

6th

9 The information in the following table was obtained from an experiment with a spring of original (unstretched) length 5 cm.

Load force on spring / newtons	Length of spring / cm	Extension of spring / cm
0	5.0	
2	5.8	
4	6.5	
6	7.4	
8	8.3	
10	9.7	
12	12.9	

5th

a Copy and complete the table by calculating the extensions produced by each load.

SKILLS INTERPRETATION

6th

b Use your table to plot a graph of force (*y*-axis) against extension (*x*-axis).

4th

c Mark on your graph the part that shows Hooke's law.

SKILLS REASONING

5th

d Sketch the shape of the graph you would expect if you carried out the same experiment using an elastic band instead of a spring.

3 FORCES AND MOVEMENT

The way an object moves depends upon its mass and the unbalanced force acting upon it. In this chapter you will find out how forces affect the way an object will move, particularly in the context of car safety.

a

b

▲ Figure 3.1 **a** This aircraft has only a short distance to travel before taking off and **b** a very short distance to land back on the aircraft carrier.

LEARNING OBJECTIVES

- Know and use the relationship between unbalanced force, mass and acceleration:

  force = mass × acceleration

  $F = m \times a$

- Know and use the relationship between weight, mass and gravitational field strength:

  weight = mass × gravitational field strength

  $W = m \times g$

- Know that the stopping distance of a vehicle is made up of the sum of the thinking distance and the braking distance
- Describe the factors affecting vehicle stopping distance, including speed, mass, road condition and reaction time
- Describe the forces acting on falling objects (and explain why falling objects reach a terminal velocity)

The aircraft in Figure 3.1 must accelerate to a very high speed in a very short time when taking off and decelerate quickly when landing back on the aircraft carrier. The unbalanced force on the plane causes the acceleration. The forces that act horizontally on the aircraft are the friction force between the wheels and the flight deck (where planes land on a ship), and air resistance, when the aircraft starts to move. At the start, the forward thrust of the aircraft engines is much greater than air resistance and friction, so there is a large unbalanced force to cause the acceleration. When the aircraft lands on the flight deck it must decelerate to stop in a short distance. Parachutes and drag wires are used to provide a large unbalanced force acting in the opposite direction to the aircraft's movement. An unbalanced force is sometimes referred to as a resultant force. In this chapter we look at how acceleration is related to the force acting on an object.

FORCE, MASS AND ACCELERATION

An object will not change its velocity (accelerate) unless there is an unbalanced force acting on it. For example, a car travelling along a motorway at a constant speed is being pushed along by a force from its engine, but this force is needed to balance the forces of friction and air resistance acting on the car. At a constant speed, the unbalanced force on the car is zero.

If there are unbalanced forces acting on an object, the object may accelerate or decelerate depending on the direction of the unbalanced force. The acceleration depends on the size of the unbalanced force and the mass of the object.

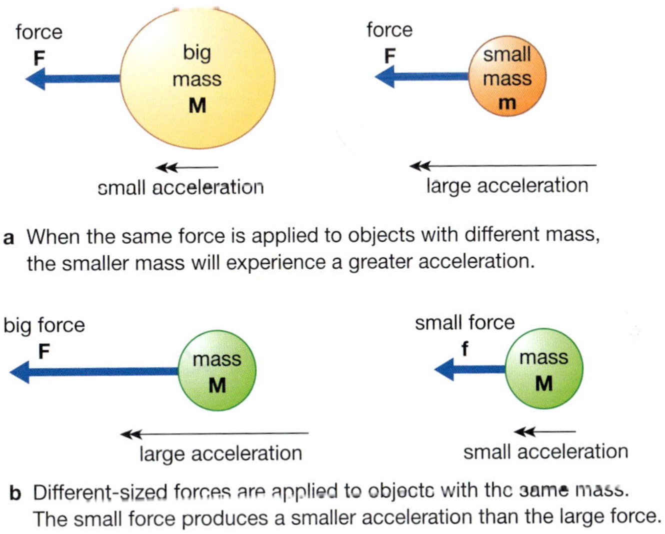

▲ Figure 3.2 The acceleration of an object is affected by both its mass and the force applied to it.

INVESTIGATING FORCE, MASS AND ACCELERATION

The experiment shown in Figure 3.3 shows how the relationship between force, mass and acceleration can be investigated. It uses a trolley on a slightly sloping ramp. The slope of the ramp is adjusted so that the trolley keeps moving down it if you push it gently. The slope is intended to overcome the friction in the trolley's wheels that could affect the results.

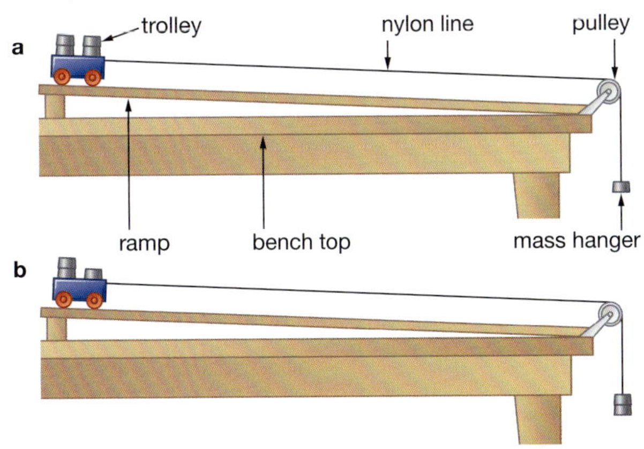

▲ Figure 3.3 You can use a trolley to find the acceleration caused by a particular force.

Safety note: Heavy wooden runways need to be stacked and moved carefully. They are best used at low level rather than being placed on benches or tables where they may fall off. If heavy trolleys are used as 'vehicles', a 'catch box' filled with bubble wrap or similar material should be placed at the end of the runway.

The force acting on the trolley is provided by the masses on the end of the nylon line. These masses accelerate as well as the trolley, so the force is increased by transferring one of the masses from the trolley to the mass hanger (Figure 3.3b). This increases the pulling force (explained later in this chapter) on the trolley, while keeping the total mass of the system the same.

The acceleration of the trolley can be measured by taking a series of pictures at equal time intervals using a digital video camera. Alternatively, a pair of **light gates** and a data logger can be used to find the speed of the trolley near the top of the ramp and near the end. The equation on page 495 can then be used to work out the acceleration.

EXTENSION WORK

The acceleration can be found using a digital video camera by measuring the distance travelled from the start for each image. Since the time between each image is known, a graph of displacement against time can be drawn. The gradient of the displacement–time graph gives the velocity at a particular instant, so data for a velocity–time graph can be obtained. The gradient of the velocity–time graph produced is the acceleration of the trolley.

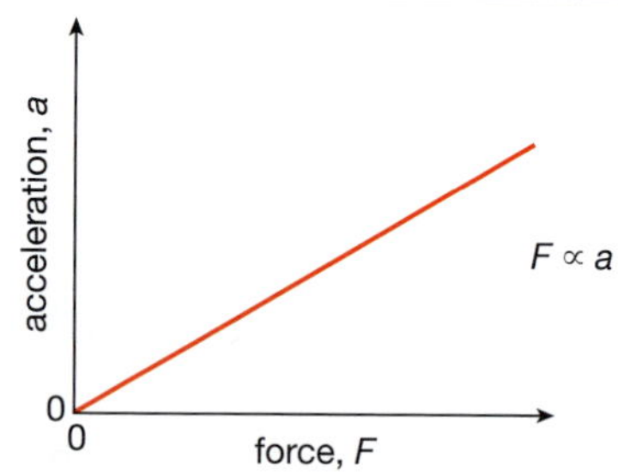

▲ Figure 3.4 Force is proportional to acceleration.

Figure 3.4 shows a graph of force against acceleration when the mass of the trolley and hanging masses is constant and the accelerating force is varied.

The graph is a straight line passing through the origin, which shows that:

force is proportional to acceleration

$$F \propto a$$

So doubling the force acting on an object doubles its acceleration.

In a second experiment, the accelerating force is kept constant and the mass of the trolley is varied.

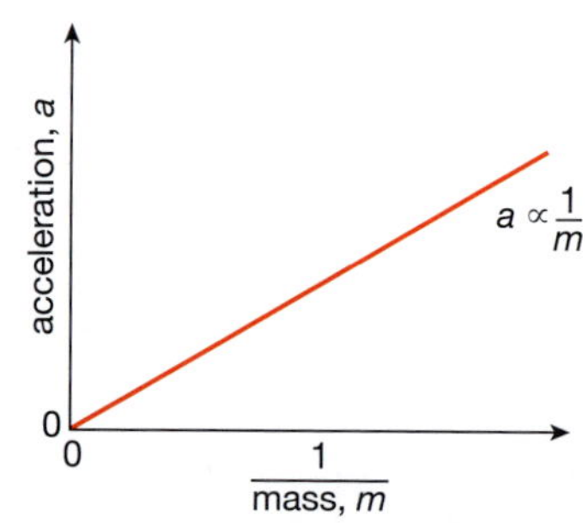

▲ Figure 3.5 Acceleration is inversely proportional to mass.

Figure 3.5 shows the acceleration of the trolley plotted against $\frac{1}{m}$. This is also a straight line passing through the origin, showing that:

acceleration is **inversely proportional** to mass

$$a \propto \frac{1}{m}$$

This means that for a given unbalanced force acting on an object, doubling the mass of the object will halve the acceleration.

Combining these results gives us:

force, F (N) = mass, m (kg) × acceleration, a (m/s^2)

$$F = m \times a$$

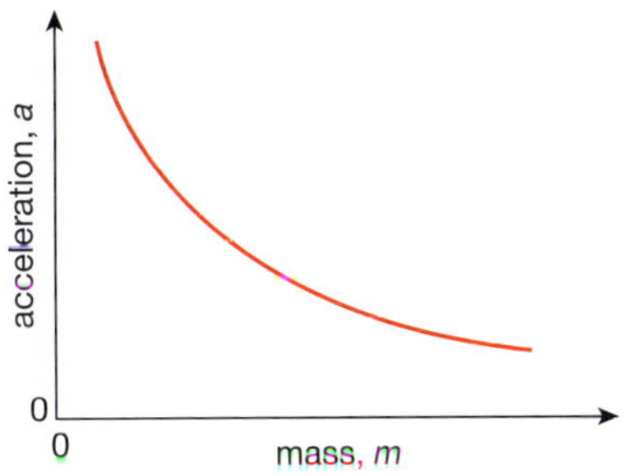

▲ Figure 3.6 The graph of a against m is a curve. Plotting a against $\frac{1}{m}$ (while keeping the force constant) gives a straight line. This makes it easier to spot the way that a is affected by m.

Force is measured in newtons (N), mass is measured in kilograms (kg), and acceleration is measured in metres per second squared (m/s^2). From this we see that:

One newton is the force needed to make a mass of one kilogram accelerate at one metre per second squared.

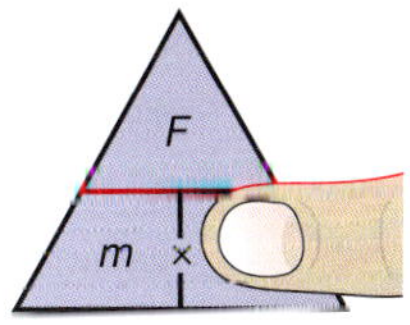

▲ Figure 3.7 The equation can be rearranged using the triangle method. If you need to find the acceleration that results when a known force acts on an object of known mass, cover up a; you can see that $a = \frac{F}{m}$.

HINT

If an examination question asks you to write out the equation for calculating force, mass or acceleration, always give the actual equation (such as $F = m \times a$). You may not get the mark if you just draw the triangle.

DECELERATION IN A COLLISION

REMINDER

v is the final velocity, u is the initial velocity and t is the time for the change in velocity to take place.

REMINDER

The minus sign in Example 1 for velocity change indicates that the velocity has decreased.

If you are designing a car for high acceleration, the equation $F = ma$ tells you that the car should have low mass and the engine must provide a high accelerating force. You must also consider the force needed to stop the car.

When a moving object is stopped, it decelerates.

A negative acceleration is a deceleration.

If a large deceleration is needed then the force causing the deceleration must be large, too. Usually a car is stopped by using the brakes in a controlled way so that the deceleration is not excessive (too much). In an accident the car may collide with another vehicle or obstacle, causing a very rapid deceleration.

EXAMPLE 1

A car travelling at 20 m/s collides with a stationary lorry and stops completely in just 0.02 s. Calculate the deceleration of the car.

$$\text{acceleration} = \frac{\text{change in velocity}}{\text{time taken}}$$ (see page 495)

$$a = \frac{v - u}{t}$$

$$= \frac{0\,\text{m/s} - 20\,\text{m/s}}{0.02\,\text{s}}$$

$$= \frac{-20\,\text{m/s}}{0.02\,\text{s}}$$

$$= -1000\,\text{m/s}^2$$

A person of mass 50 kg in the car experiences the same deceleration when she comes into contact with a hard surface in the car. This could be the dashboard or the windscreen. Calculate the force that the person experiences.

$$F = m \times a$$

$$= 50\,\text{kg} \times 1000\,\text{m/s}^2$$

$$= 50\,000\,\text{N}$$

FRICTION AND BRAKING

▲ Figure 3.8 Motorcycle disc brakes work using friction. Friction is necessary if we want things to stop.

The 'tread' of a tyre is the grooved pattern moulded into the rubber surface. It is designed to keep the rubber surface in contact with the road by throwing water away from the tyre surface.

Brakes on cars and bicycles work by increasing the friction between the **rotating** wheels and the body of the vehicle, as shown in Figure 3.8.

The friction force between the tyres and the road depends on the condition of the tyres and the surface of the road. It also depends on the weight of the vehicle. If the tyres have a good tread, are properly inflated (filled with air) and the road is dry, the friction force between the road and the tyres will be at its maximum.

Unfortunately, we do not always travel in ideal conditions. If the road is wet or the tyres are in bad condition the friction force will be smaller. If the brakes are applied too hard, the tyres will not grip the road surface and the car will skid (slide out of control). Once the car is skidding the driver no longer has control and it will take longer to stop. Skidding can be avoided by applying the brakes in the correct way, so that the wheels do not lock. Most modern cars are fitted with ABS (anti-lock braking system) to reduce the chance of a skid occurring. ABS is a computer-controlled system that senses when the car is about to skid and releases the brakes for a very short time.

SAFE STOPPING DISTANCE

The Highway Code used in the United Kingdom gives stopping distances for cars travelling at various speeds. The stopping distance is the sum of the thinking distance and the braking distance. The faster the car is travelling the greater the stopping distance will be.

THINKING DISTANCE

When a driver suddenly sees an object blocking the way ahead, it takes time for him or her to respond to the new situation before taking any action, such as braking. This time is called reaction time and will depend on the person driving the car. It will also depend on a number of other factors including whether the driver is tired or under the influence of alcohol or other drugs that slow reaction times. Poor visibility (for example, fog) may also make it difficult for a driver to identify a danger and so cause him or her to take longer to respond. Clearly, the longer the driver takes to react, the further the car will travel before braking even starts – that is, the longer the thinking distance will be. Equally clear is the fact that the higher the car's speed, the further the car will travel during this 'thinking time'. If the distance between two cars is not at least the thinking distance then, in the event of an emergency stop by the vehicle in front, a violent accident is inevitable.

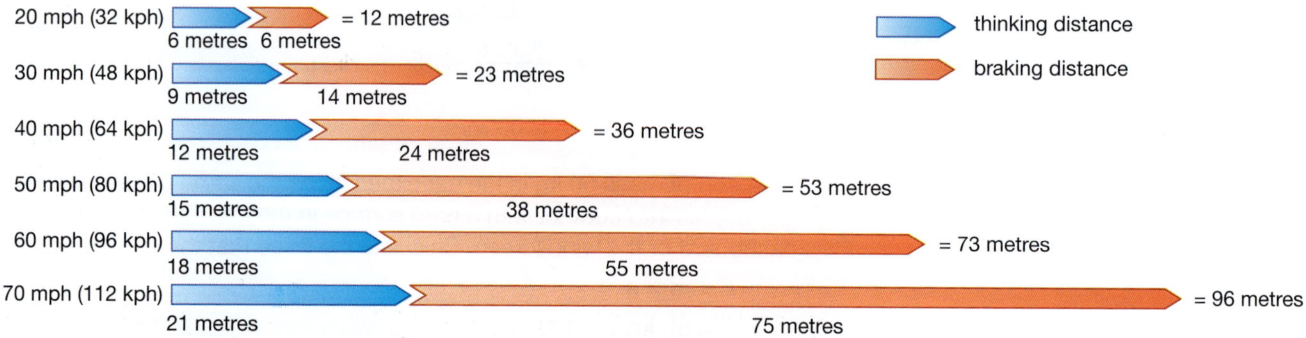

▲ Figure 3.9 The stopping distance is the distance the car covers from the moment the driver is aware of the need to stop to the point at which the vehicle comes to a complete stop.

BRAKING DISTANCE

With ABS (anti-lock braking system) braking, in an emergency you brake as hard as you can. This means that the braking force will be a maximum and we can work out the deceleration using the equation below.

$F = m \times a$, rearranged to give:

$a = \frac{F}{m}$ (shown in Figure 3.7)

It is worth pointing out here that vehicles with large masses, like lorries, will have smaller rates of deceleration for a given braking force – they will, therefore, travel further while braking.

Chapter 1 shows that the distance travelled by a moving object can be found from its velocity–time graph. The area under the graph gives the distance travelled. Look at the velocity–time graphs in Figures 3.10 and 3.11.

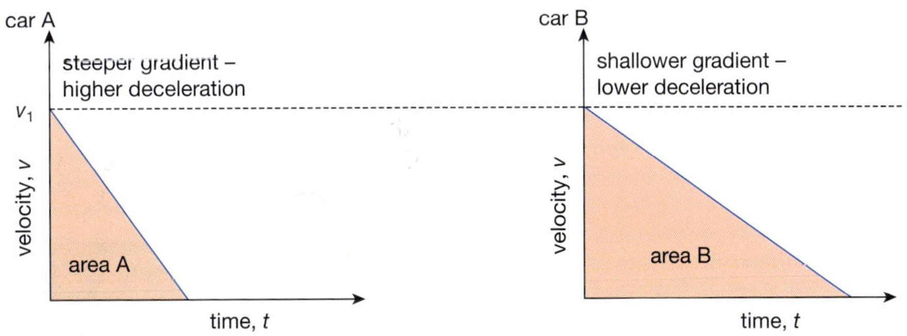

▲ Figure 3.10 Velocity–time graphs for two cars braking at different rates from the same speed, v_1, to rest.

Figure 3.10 shows two cars, A and B, braking from the same velocity. Car A is braking harder than car B and comes to rest in a shorter time. Car B travels further before stopping, as you can see from the larger area under the graph. Remember that the maximum rate of deceleration depends on how hard you can brake without skidding – in poor conditions the braking force will be lower.

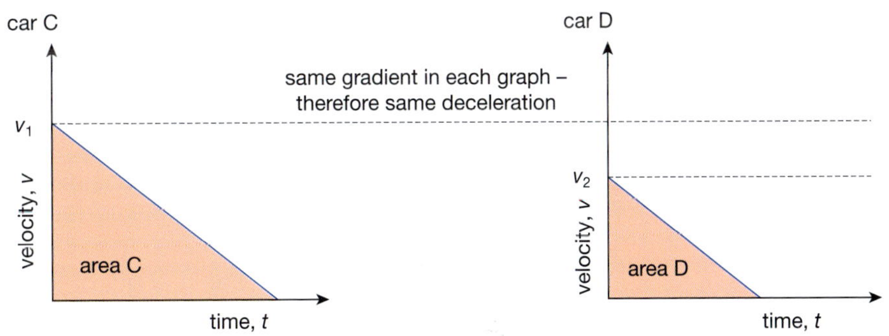

▲ Figure 3.11 Velocity–time graphs for two cars braking at the same rate to rest, from different speeds, v_1 and v_2.

Figure 3.11 shows two cars, C and D, braking at the same rate, as you can see from the gradients. Car C is braking from a higher velocity and so takes longer to stop. Again, the greater area under the graph for car C shows that it travels further while stopping than car D.

Vehicles cannot stop instantly! Remember also that the chart in Figure 3.9 shows stopping distances in ideal conditions. If the car tyres or brakes are in poor condition, or if the road surface is wet, icy or slippery, then the car will travel further before stopping.

WEIGHT

The weight of an object is the force that acts on it because of gravity. The weight of an object depends on its mass and the strength of gravity. The **gravitational field strength** (g) is the force that acts on each kilogram of mass. We can work out the weight of an object by using this equation:

weight, W (N) = mass, m (kg) × gravitational field strength, g (N/kg)

$$W = m \times g$$

You can use the triangle method to rearrange this equation.

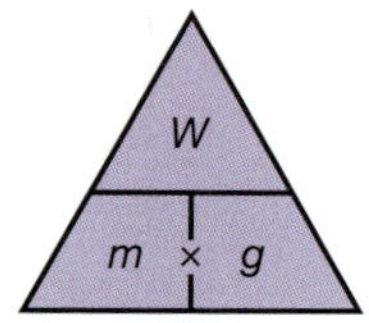

▲ Figure 3.12 Rearranging $W = m \times g$ using the triangle method

Near and on the Earth's surface the gravitational field strength is approximately 9.8 N/kg, but we often use 10 N/kg to make calculations easier. The gravitational field strength on the Moon is about 1.6 N/kg, so an object taken from the Earth to the Moon will have less weight even though it has the same mass.

▲ Figure 3.13 An astronaut jumping on the Moon enjoying the effect of low gravity

EXAMPLE 2

An astronaut in a space suit with a complete life support pack has a mass of 140 kg. How much will the astronaut weigh **a** on the Earth, and **b** on Mars where the gravitational field strength is about one third of that on Earth? (Take the strength of the Earth's gravitational field as 10 N/kg.)

The force of gravity or weight of an object is given by:

weight, W = mass, m × gravitational field strength, g

a weight on Earth = 140 kg × 10 N/kg

= 1400 N

b g on Mars = $\frac{10\text{ N/kg}}{3}$ = 3.34 N/kg

weight on Mars = 140 kg × 3.34 N/kg

= 468 N

AIR RESISTANCE AND TERMINAL VELOCITY

An object moving through air experiences a force that opposes its movement. This force is called air resistance or drag. The size of the drag force acting on an object depends on its shape and its speed. Cars are designed to have a low **drag coefficient**. The drag coefficient is a measure of how easily an object moves through the air. High-speed trains have an efficient streamlined shape so that air flows more smoothly around them. Streamlined, smooth surfaces produce less drag.

It is particularly important to make fast-moving objects streamlined because the drag force increases with the speed of the object. The fact that drag increases with speed affects the way that dropped objects accelerate, because the faster they move the greater the drag force opposing their motion becomes.

Objects falling through the air experience two significant forces: the weight force (that is, the pull of gravity on the object) and the opposing drag force.

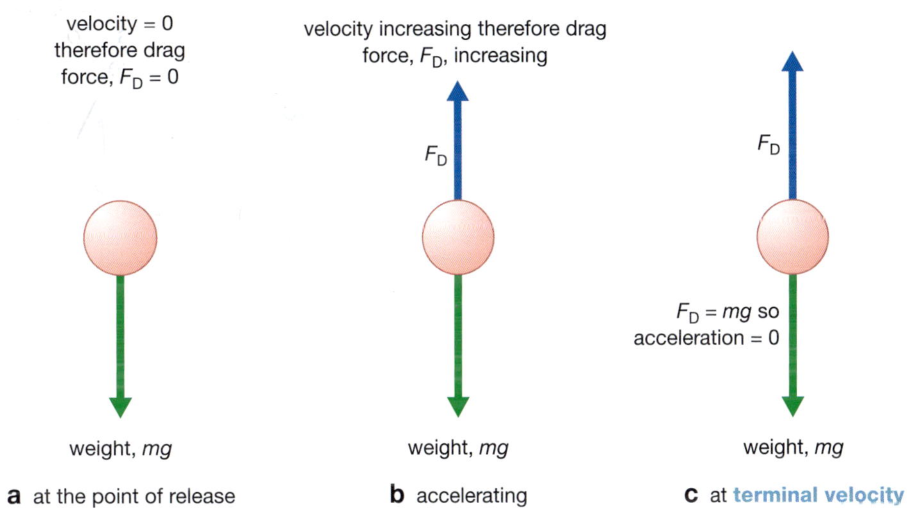

▲ Figure 3.14 How the forces acting on a object change as its velocity changes

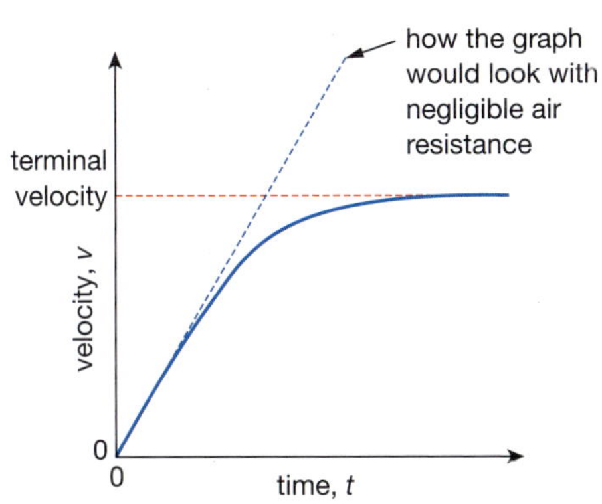

▲ Figure 3.15 The velocity–time graph for an object accelerating until it reaches terminal velocity

In Figure 3.14a the object has just been released and has a starting velocity of 0 m/s. This means that there is no drag. (Remember that the drag force acts on moving objects.) The resulting downward-acting force is just the weight force. This force makes the object accelerate towards the Earth.

Figure 3.14b shows the object now moving. Because it is moving it has a drag force, F_D, acting on it. The drag force acts upwards (up) against the movement. This means that the resulting downward force (acting down) on the object is $(mg - F_D)$. You can see that the drag force has made the resulting downward force smaller, so the acceleration is smaller. All the time that the object is accelerating it is getting faster. The faster the object moves the bigger the drag force is.

In Figure 3.14c the drag force has increased to the point where it exactly balances the weight force – since there is now no unbalanced force on the object its acceleration is also zero. The object has reached its terminal velocity and although it is still falling it will not get any faster. Figure 3.15 shows a velocity–time graph for an object falling through air and reaching terminal velocity.

PARACHUTES

▲ Figure 3.16 These skydivers have just left the aeroplane. They will accelerate until they reach terminal velocity.

When a skydiver jumps from a plane she will accelerate for a time and eventually reach terminal velocity. Typically this will be between 150 and 200 kph. When she opens her parachute this will cause a sudden increase in the drag force. At this velocity (around 200 kph) the drag force of the parachute is greater than the weight of the skydiver. This means that the unbalanced force acting on the parachutist acts upwards and, for a while, she will decelerate. As she slows down the size of the drag force decreases and, eventually, a new terminal velocity is reached. Obviously the new terminal velocity depends on the design of the parachute, but it must be slow enough to allow the parachutist to land safely. Figure 3.17 shows a velocity–time graph for a skydiver.

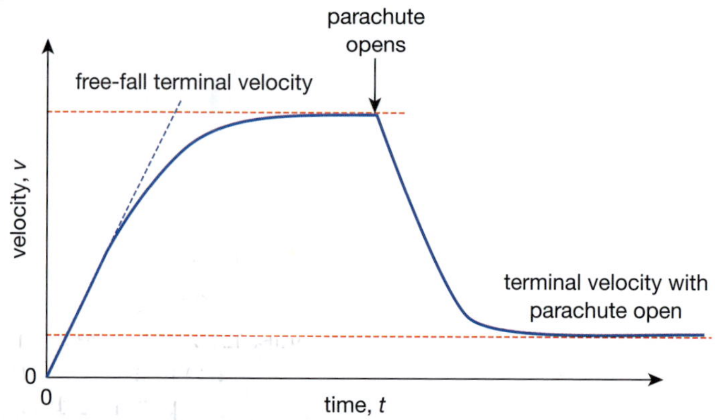

▲ Figure 3.17 Velocity–time graph for a free-fall parachutist reaching terminal velocity, then opening the parachute

MODELLING TERMINAL VELOCITY

Objects have to accelerate to quite high speeds in air to reach terminal velocity. This makes demonstrating the effect in a laboratory difficult. However, objects falling through liquids also experience a drag force that increases with speed. The sizes of drag forces in liquids are much higher than in gases. This means that objects falling through liquids have a much lower terminal velocity than objects falling through air, and can be used to model terminal velocity. You can use a tall measuring cylinder filled with water and drop small-**diameter** (1–2 mm) glass balls into it. Alternatively, use a much thicker liquid like oil and use small-diameter balls. As well as demonstrating terminal velocity this presents plenty of opportunities for investigations. You could measure the terminal velocity using a light gate and a data logger.

LOOKING AHEAD – WEIGHTLESSNESS

Figure 3.18 Scientists in the International Space Station experience weightlessness

Figure 3.19 Astronauts training for weightlessness in an aircraft

Figures 3.18 and 3.19 show astronauts in 'weightless' conditions in the International Space Station and training for weightlessness in an aircraft. In both cases the astronauts are still being pulled towards the Earth by gravity. They all experience the force we call weight, calculated using the equation *mg* that we met earlier in Chapter 3, yet they appear to float freely!

They are in a condition called free-fall. You may have noticed feeling very slightly 'lighter' when you are in a lift as it accelerates downwards. This effect is more noticeable if the lift accelerates at a greater rate. Further study of physics will explain all this.

Exploring the Solar System

Sir Isaac Newton worked out his laws of motion more than 300 years ago. Although Albert Einstein explained that these laws do not hold when objects are travelling at speeds close to the speed of light (3×10^8 m/s), Newton's laws give answers to calculations accurate enough for scientists to plan successful space missions like the Moon landing in 1969, the Phoenix lander to Mars in 2007 and the incredible achievement of landing the Philae lander (carried by the Rosetta spacecraft) on a **comet** in 2014.

CHAPTER QUESTIONS

More questions on force and acceleration can be found at the end of Unit 1 on page 526.

SKILLS CRITICAL THINKING 5th

1 Explain what is meant by an unbalanced force? Illustrate your answer with an example.

SKILLS REASONING 7th

2 Rockets burn fuel to give them the thrust needed to accelerate. As the fuel burns the mass of the rocket gets smaller. Assuming that the rocket motors provide a constant thrust force, explain what will happen to the acceleration of the rocket as it burns its fuel.

SKILLS PROBLEM SOLVING 9th

3 a Calculate the force required to make an object of mass 500 g accelerate at 4 m/s^2. (Take care with the units!)

b An object accelerates at 0.8 m/s^2 when a resultant force of 200 N acts upon it. Calculate the mass of the object.

c What acceleration is produced by a force of 250 N acting on a mass of 25 kg?

SKILLS CRITICAL THINKING 5th

4 Explain the meaning of the following terms used to describe stopping vehicles in an emergency:

a thinking distance

b braking distance

c overall stopping distance.

6th

5 What factors affect the braking distance of a vehicle?

SKILLS ANALYSIS

6 The diagram below shows the velocity–time graph for a car travelling from the moment that the driver sees an object blocking the road ahead.

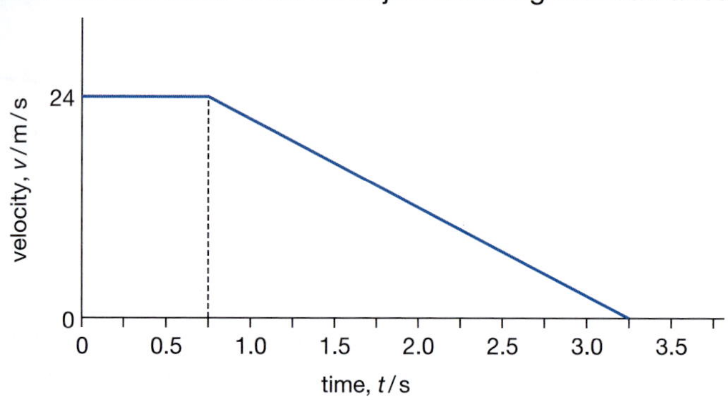

Use the graph to find out:

7th a how long the driver takes to react to seeing the obstacle (reaction time)

8th b how far the car travels in this reaction time

7th c how long it takes to bring the car to a halt once the driver starts braking

9th d the total distance the car travels before stopping.

SKILLS PROBLEM SOLVING 6th

7 Calculate the weight of an apple of mass 100 grams:

a on the Earth (g = 10 N/kg)

b on the Moon (g = 1.6 N/kg).

SKILLS CRITICAL THINKING 5th

8 What factors affect the drag force that acts on a high-speed train?

SKILLS DECISION MAKING 7th

9 Describe an experiment to demonstrate terminal velocity. Say what measurements you need to take in your experiment to show that a falling object has reached terminal speed.

SKILLS ANALYSIS 9th

10 Look at the velocity–time graph for a free-fall parachutist shown below.

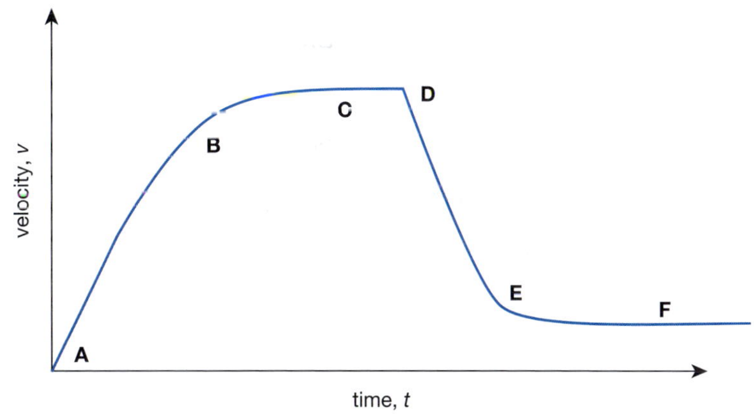

State and explain the direction and relative size of the unbalanced force acting on the parachutist at each of the points A–F labelled on the graph.

UNIT QUESTIONS

SKILLS CRITICAL THINKING 6th

1

a Which of the following quantities is not a vector quantity?

A force **B** area **C** displacement **D** velocity **(1)**

b Which of the following quantities is not a scalar quantity?

A speed **B** your age **C** volume **D** acceleration **(1)**

c Which of the following statements about the motion of an object on which unbalanced forces act is false?

A The object could continue moving at constant speed in a straight line.

B The object could accelerate.

C The object could slow down.

D The object could change the direction in which it is moving. **(1)**

d A ball is thrown vertically upwards in the air. Which of the following statements about the motion of the ball is false?

A The ball will be travelling as fast as it was when it gets back to the ground as it was when first thrown upwards.

B The ball will be stationary for an instant at the highest point in its flight.

C The direction of the force on the ball changes so the ball falls back to the ground.

D The direction of the acceleration is always downwards. **(1)**

(Total 4 marks)

SKILLS ANALYSIS

2

A tennis ball is dropped from a height of 3 m and bounces back to a height of 1 m after hitting the ground ($s = 0$).

a Which of the following distance–time graphs shows this motion correctly? **(1)**

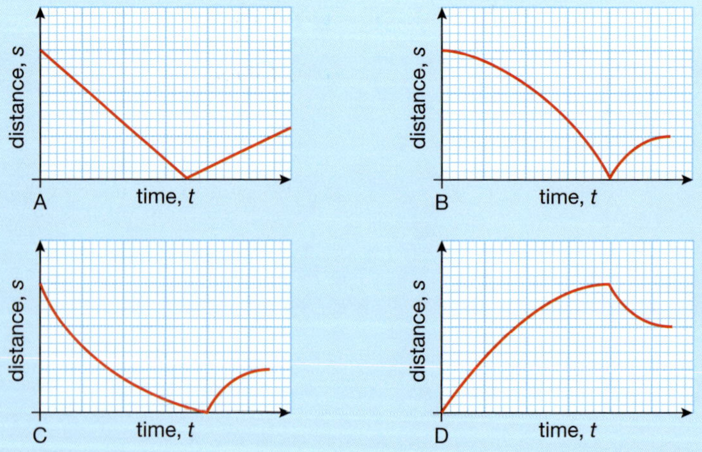

SKILLS CRITICAL THINKING 7th

b **i** Explain the difference between the terms distance and displacement. **(2)**

SKILLS PROBLEM SOLVING 8th

ii What is the displacement of the tennis ball at the end of the described motion? **(1)**

SKILLS PROBLEM SOLVING 9th

c **i** Use the equation $v^2 = u^2 + 2as$ to calculate the velocity of the tennis ball when it hits the ground. **(4)**

7th

ii What is the average speed of the tennis ball while it is falling to the ground? **(2)**

8th

iii Calculate how long it takes for the tennis ball to reach the ground. **(2)**

SKILLS CRITICAL THINKING 6th

d How can the distance travelled by the tennis ball be found from a velocity–time graph of its motion? **(1)**

SKILLS INTERPRETATION 8th

e Sketch a velocity–time graph for the tennis ball from the time that it is released to the time that it has rebounded to 1 m after the first bounce. Assume that the time that the ball is in contact with the ground is negligible (too short to show on your graph). Include as much numerical detail as you can without doing any further calculations. **(6)**

(Total 19 marks)

SKILLS CRITICAL THINKING

3 A student uses the following piece of apparatus to investigate how the extension of a length of wire varies with the force applied to it.

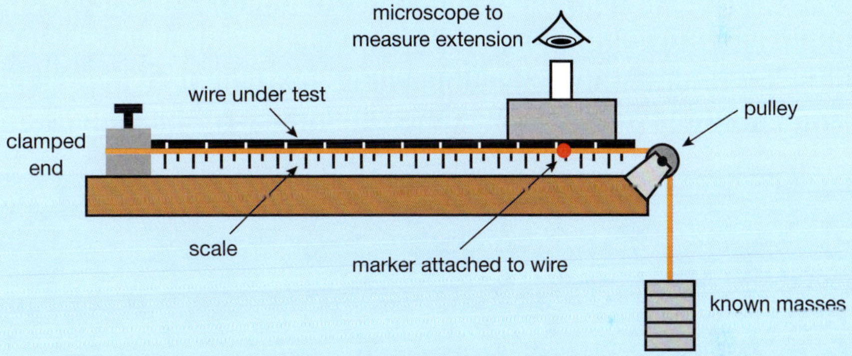

5th

a **i** Name the independent variable in this investigation. **(1)**

ii Name the dependent variable in this investigation. **(1)**

4th

iii Name one control variable in this investigation. **(1)**

5th

b How is the force being applied to the wire calculated? **(1)**

SKILLS DECISION MAKING

c Explain how the student should use the apparatus to determine if the wire obeys Hooke's law. **(5)**

SKILLS EXECUTIVE FUNCTION 6th

d The student also wants to know if the sample behaves elastically. Explain how the student can improve the investigation and discover whether or not the wire behaves elastically. **(3)**

(Total 12 marks)

PHYSICS UNIT 2 ELECTRICITY

It is sometimes really difficult to imagine how we could live without electricity. As we mmove around we use electricity from batteries and cells for our mobile phones, mp3 players and other mobile devices. In our homes and other buildings we use electricity from the mains for heating, lighting and providing the energy for household appliances such as televisions, radios, computers and their printers. Understanding what electricity is, where it comes from and how we can control it is important if we are to make maximum use of this important source of energy.

4 MAINS ELECTRICITY

The electricity that we use for heating, lighting and air conditioning in our homes is called mains electricity and is supplied to us by power stations.

In this chapter you will learn how mains electricity is brought to our homes and supplied to our appliances. You will also read about devices that protect us from electrical shocks.

▲ Figure 4.1 Most household appliances use mains electricity as their source of energy.

LEARNING OBJECTIVES

- Understand how the use of insulation, double insulation, earthing, fuses and circuit breakers protects the device or user in a range of domestic appliances
- Understand why a current in a resistor results in the electrical transfer of energy and an increase in temperature, and how this can be used in a variety of domestic contexts
- Know and use the relationship between power, current and voltage:

  power = current × voltage

  $P = I \times V$

  and apply the relationship to the selection of appropriate fuses
- Know the difference between mains electricity being alternating current (a.c.) and direct current (d.c.) being supplied by a cell or battery
- Use the relationship between energy transferred, current, voltage and time:

  energy transferred = current × voltage × time

  $E = I \times V \times t$

UNITS

In this unit, you will need to use ampere (A) as the unit of current, coulomb (C) as the unit of charge, joule (J) as the unit of energy, ohm (Ω) as the unit of resistance, second (s) as the unit of time, volt (V) as the unit of voltage and watt (W) as the unit of power.

When you turn on your computer, television and most other appliances in your home the electricity you use is almost certainly going to come from the mains supply. This electrical energy usually enters our homes through an underground cable. The cable is connected to an electricity meter, which measures the amount of electrical energy used. From here, the cable is connected to a consumer unit or a fuse box, which contains fuses or circuit breakers for the various **circuits** in your home. Fuses and circuit breakers are safety devices which shut off the electricity in a circuit if the current in them becomes too large (see page 531).

Most of the wires that leave the fuse box are connected to ring main circuits that are hidden in the walls or floors around each room. Individual pieces of electrical equipment are connected to these circuits using plugs.

▲ Figure 4.2 Circuit breakers in a consumer unit

Ring main circuits usually consist of three wires – the live wire, the neutral wire and the earth wire.

The live wire provides the path along which the electrical energy from the power station travels. The neutral wire completes the circuit.

The earth wire usually has no current in it. It is there to protect you if an appliance develops a fault (see page 531). It provides a path for current to escape without passing through the user.

EXTENSION WORK

Ring main circuits provide a way of allowing several appliances in different parts of the same room to be connected to the mains using the minimum amount of wiring. Imagine how much wire would be needed if there was just one mains socket in each room.

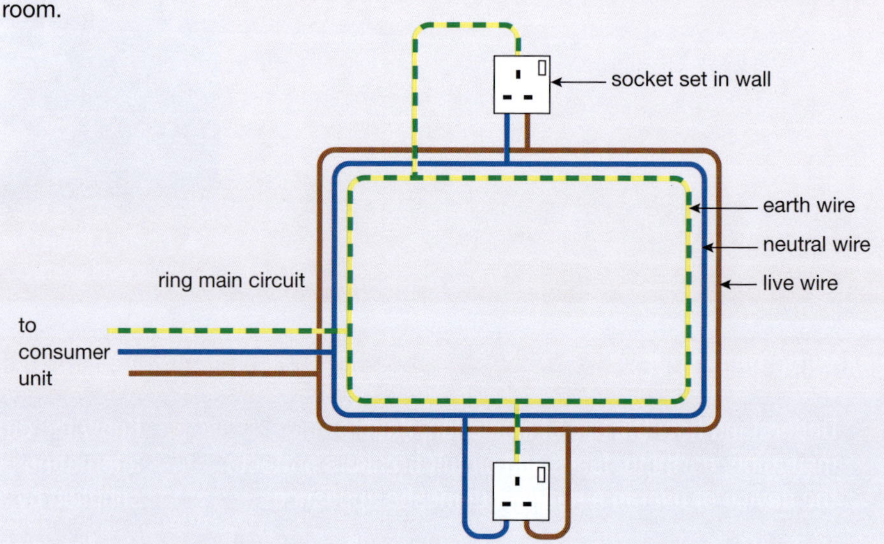

▲ Figure 4.3 Ring main circuits help to cut down on the amount of wiring needed in a house.

Plugs and sockets in different countries look different, but the principles (rules) of electrical wiring are similar.

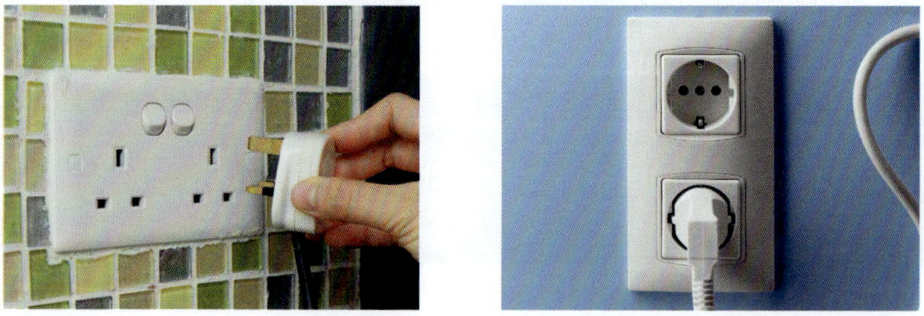

▲ Figure 4.4 Plug sockets in the UK and in Portugal

The mains electricity supplied to homes in the UK, China, India and many other countries is between 220 V and 240 V. This is a much higher **voltage** than the **cells** and batteries used in mobile electrical appliances. If you come into direct contact with mains electricity you could receive a severe electric shock, which might even be fatal. To prevent this the outer part of a plug, called the casing, is made from plastic, which is a good **insulator**.

Connections to the circuits are made via three brass pins, as the metal brass is an excellent **conductor** of electricity. Figure 4.5 shows the inside of a 3-pin plug used in the UK, but similar principles apply to all kinds of plug all over the world.

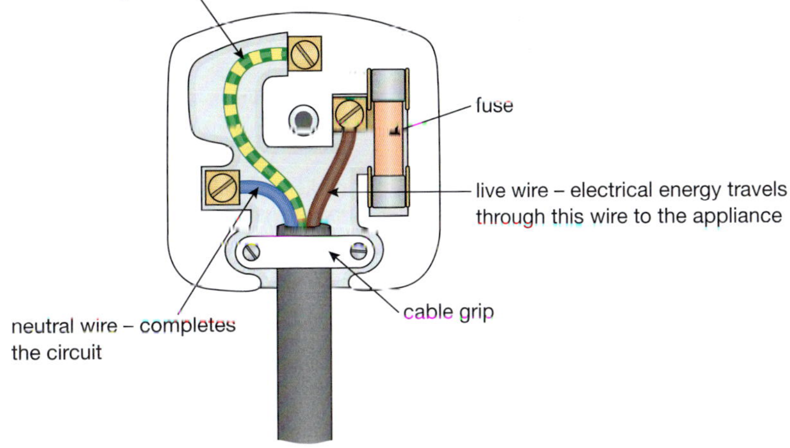

Figure 4.5 A labelled plug

SAFETY DEVICES

FUSES

Many plugs contain a fuse. The fuse is usually in the form of a cylinder or cartridge, which contains a thin piece of wire made from a metal that has a low melting point. If there is too large a current in the circuit the fuse wire becomes very hot and melts. The fuse 'blows'. The circuit is now incomplete so there is no current. This prevents you getting a shock and reduces the possibility of an electrical fire. Once the fault causing the increase in current has been corrected, the blown fuse must be replaced with a new one of the same size before the appliance can be used again.

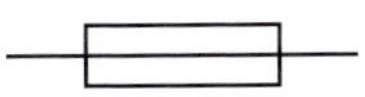

circuit symbol for a fuse

There are several sizes of fuses. The most common for domestic appliances in the UK are 3 A, 5 A and 13 A. The correct fuse for a circuit is the one that allows the correct current but blows if the current is a little larger. If the correct current in a circuit is 2 A then it should be protected with a 3 A fuse. If the correct current is 4 A then a 5 A fuse should be used. It is possible to calculate the correct size of fuse for an appliance but nowadays manufacturers provide appliances already fitted with the correct size of fuse.

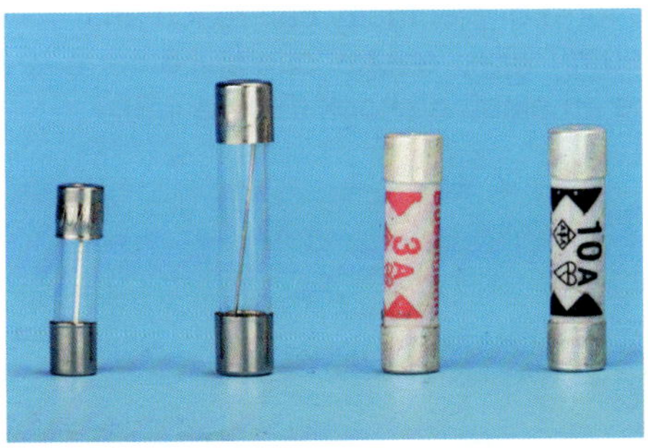

Figure 4.6 Fuses are important safety devices in electrical appliances.

Modern safety devices, such as those you might find in your consumer unit, are often in the form of trip switches or circuit breakers. If too large a current flows in a circuit a switch automatically opens making the circuit incomplete. Once the fault in the circuit has been corrected, the switch is reset, usually by pressing a reset button. There is no need for the switch or circuit breaker to be replaced, as there is when fuses are used. The consumer unit shown in Figure 4.2 uses circuit breakers.

EARTH WIRES AND DOUBLE INSULATION

Many appliances have a metal casing. This should be connected to the earth wire so that if the live wire becomes damaged or breaks and comes into contact with the casing the earth wire provides a low-resistance path for the current. This current is likely to be large enough to blow the fuse and turn the circuit off. Without the earth wire anyone touching the casing of the faulty appliance would receive a severe electric shock as the current passed through them to earth (Figure 4.7).

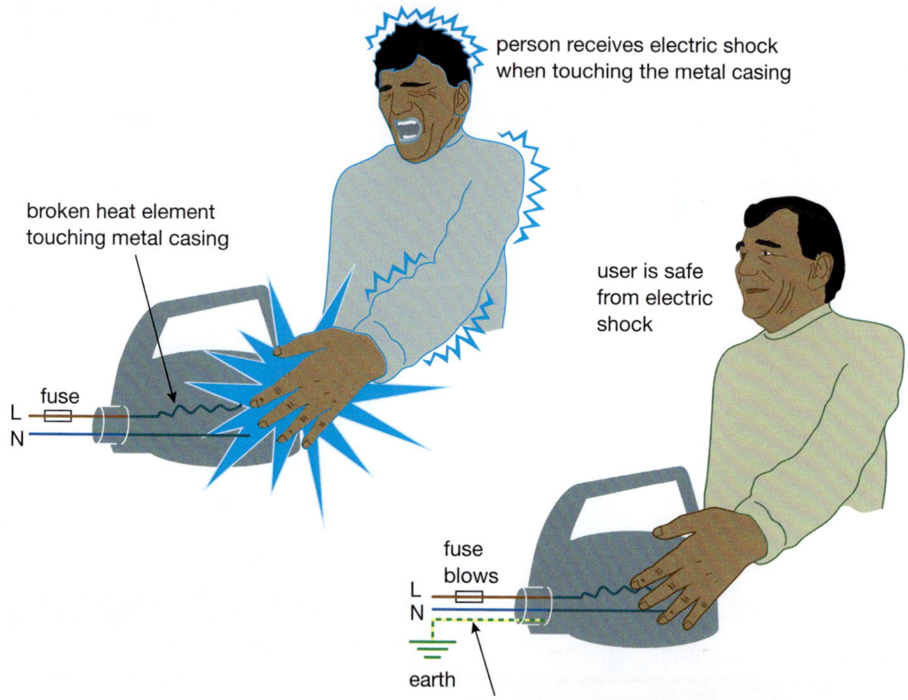

▲ Figure 4.7 The earth wire provides protection when electrical appliances develop a fault.

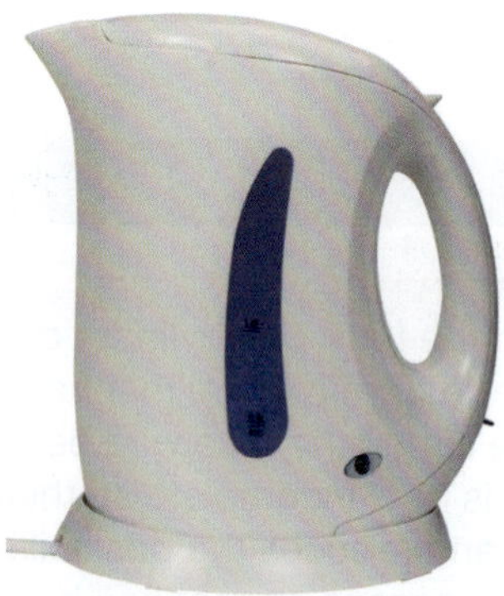

▲ Figure 4.8 This plastic kettle has double insulation which means that there is no need for an earth wire.

Some modern appliances now use casings made from an insulator such as plastic rather than from metal. If all the electrical parts of an appliance are insulated in this way, so that they cannot be touched by the user, the appliance is said to have double insulation. Appliances that have double insulation use a two-wire **flex**. There is no need for an earth wire.

SWITCHES

Switches in mains circuits should always be placed in the live wire so that when the switch is open no energy in the form of electricity can reach an appliance. If the switch is placed in the neutral wire, energy can still enter a faulty appliance, and could possibly cause an electric shock (Figure 4.9).

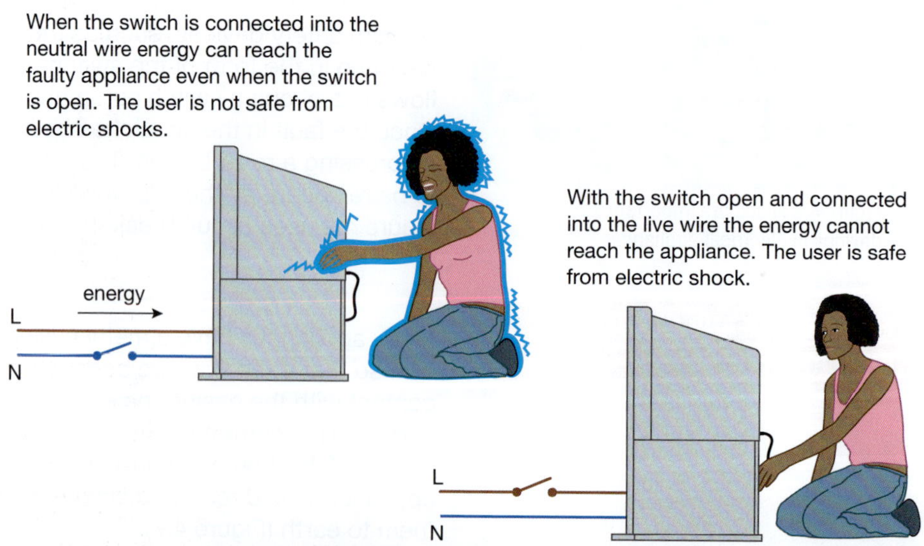

▲ Figure 4.9 The switch in a circuit should be in the live wire.

THE HEATING EFFECT OF CURRENT

Figure 4.10 The wires inside a toaster have a high resistance. They become very hot when a current passes through them.

The wiring in a house is designed to let current pass through it easily. As a result, the wires do not become warm when appliances are being used. We say that the wires have a low **resistance**. However, in some appliances, for example, kettles or toasters (Figure 4.10), we want wires (more usually called **heating elements**) to become warm. The wires of a heating element are designed to have a high resistance so that as the current passes through them energy is transferred and the element heats up. We use this heating effect of current in many different ways in our homes. You will learn more about resistance in Chapter 6.

Other common appliances that make use of the heating effect of electricity include kettles, dishwashers, electric cookers, washing machines, electric fires and hairdryers.

When current passes through the very thin wire (**filament**) of a traditional light bulb it becomes very hot and **glows** (shines) white. The bulb is transferring electrical energy to heat and light energy.

EXTENSION WORK

Incandescent bulbs like these are very inefficient. Often more than 90% of the energy transferred is lost to the surroundings as heat. As a result they are rapidly being replaced by modern halogen bulbs and LEDs, which give off much less heat and therefore waste less energy.

Figure 4.11 It is the heating effect of a current that is causing this bulb to glow.

ELECTRICAL POWER

Figure 4.12 shows a 50 W **halogen light bulb**. You can also buy 70 W light bulbs. Both bulbs transfer electrical energy to heat and light. The 70 W bulb will be brighter because it transfers 70 J of electrical energy every second. The dimmer 50 W halogen bulb shown transfers only 50 J of energy every second. A 70 W bulb has a higher power rating.

Figure 4.12 The dimmer 50 W bulb transfers less electrical energy to heat and light energy every second.

KEY POINT

You will learn more about voltage and current in Chapter 5.

Power is measured in joules per second or watts (W).

Devices that transfer lots of energy very quickly have their power rating expressed in kilowatts (kW).

1 kW = 1000 W

The power (P) of an appliance is related to the voltage (V) across it and the current (I) flowing through it.

The equation is:

power, P (watts) = current, I (amps) × voltage, V (volts)

$$P = I \times V$$

HINT

If an examination question asks for the equation for calculating power, voltage or current, always give the actual equation (such as $P = I \times V$). You may not be awarded a mark if you just draw the triangle.

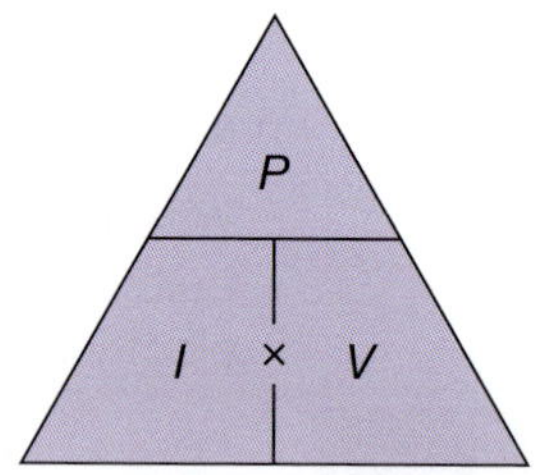

▲ Figure 4.13 You can use the triangle method for rearranging equations like $P = I \times V$.

EXAMPLE 1

A 230 V television takes a current of 3 A. Calculate the power of the television.

$$P = I \times V$$
$$= 3\text{ A} \times 230\text{ V}$$
$$= 690\text{ W}$$

EXAMPLE 2

Calculate the correct fuse that should be used for a 230 V, 1 kW electric hairdryer.

$$I = \frac{P}{V}$$
$$= \frac{1000\text{ W}}{230\text{ V}}$$
$$= 4.35\text{ A}$$

The correct fuse for this hairdryer is therefore a 5 A fuse.

CALCULATING THE TOTAL ENERGY TRANSFERRED BY AN APPLIANCE

The power of an appliance (P) tells you how much energy it transfers each second. This means that the total energy (E) transferred by an appliance is equal to its power multiplied by the length of time (in seconds) the appliance is being used.

energy, E (joules) = power, P (watts) × time, t (seconds)

$$E = P \times t$$

or since $P = I \times V$

$$E = I \times V \times t$$

EXAMPLE 3

Calculate the energy transferred by a 60 W bulb that is turned on for **a** 20 s, and **b** 5 min.

a $E = P \times t$

$= 60\text{ W} \times 20\text{ s}$

$= 1200\text{ J or } 1.2\text{ kJ}$

b $E = P \times t$

$= 60\text{ W} \times 5 \times 60\text{ s}$

$= 18\,000\text{ J or } 18\text{ kJ}$

ALTERNATING CURRENT AND DIRECT CURRENT

If we could see the current or voltage from the mains it would appear to be very strange. Its value increases and then decreases and then does the same again but in the opposite direction. If we could draw these changes as a graph they would look like a wave.

This happens because of the way in which the electricity is generated at the power station. A current or voltage that behaves like this is called an alternating current (a.c.) or **alternating voltage**. This is very different to the currents and voltages we get from batteries and cells.

Cells and batteries provide currents and voltages that are always in the same direction and have the same value. This is called direct current (d.c.) or direct voltage. If we drew this as a graph it would be a straight horizontal line.

Figure 4.14 shows how the voltage of an a.c. supply compares with the voltage of a d.c. supply.

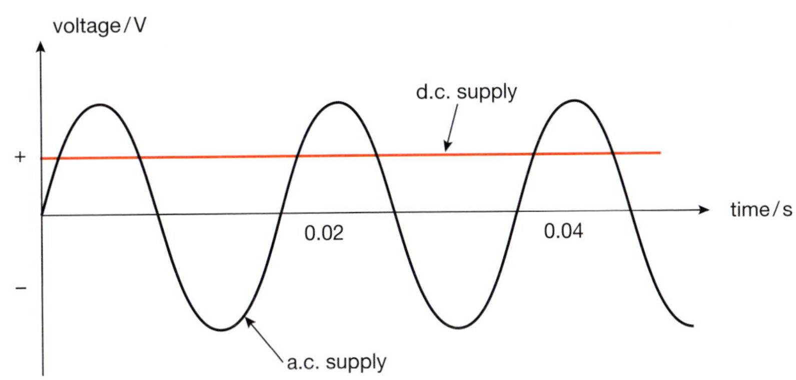

Figure 4.14 How the voltage of an a.c. supply compares with that of a d.c. supply

CHAPTER QUESTIONS

More questions on domestic electricity can be found at the end of Unit 2 on page 554.

SKILLS PROBLEM SOLVING

7th

1 a There is a current of 0.25 A in a bulb when a voltage of 12 V is applied across it. Calculate the power of the bulb.

8th

b Calculate the voltage that is being applied across a 10 W bulb with a current of 0.2 A.

c Calculate the current in a 60 W bulb if the voltage across it is 230 V.

7th

d How much energy is transferred if a 100 W bulb is left on for 5 hours?

SKILLS CRITICAL THINKING

2 An electric kettle is marked '230 V, 1.5 kW'.

a Explain what these numbers mean.

SKILLS PROBLEM SOLVING

6th

b Calculate the correct fuse that should be used.

SKILLS REASONING

c Explain why a 230 V, 100 W bulb glows more brightly than a 230 V, 60 W bulb when both are connected to the mains supply.

SKILLS CRITICAL THINKING

5th

3 a Give one advantage of using a circuit breaker rather than a wire or cartridge fuse.

b Why is the switch for an appliance always placed in the live wire?

c What is meant by the sentence 'The hairdryer has double insulation'?

SKILLS DECISION MAKING, CREATIVITY

6th

4 Think of a room in your house where there are lots of electrical appliances. Make a list of them. Now organise your list so that the appliances that you think have the highest power rating are at the top of your list and those with the lowest are at the bottom. How could you discover if your guesses are correct?

5 CURRENT AND VOLTAGE IN CIRCUITS

We rely on electricity in many areas of our lives. This chapter looks at what electric current is. You will learn what happens to electric current in different circuits, and what effect it has.

Look around the room you are in. If you are at home, you will probably be able to see a television, a radio or a computer. If you are in a science laboratory, you may be able to see a projector, a power supply or lights in the ceiling. These and many other everyday objects need electric currents if they are to work. But what are electric currents? How are they produced and what do they do in a circuit?

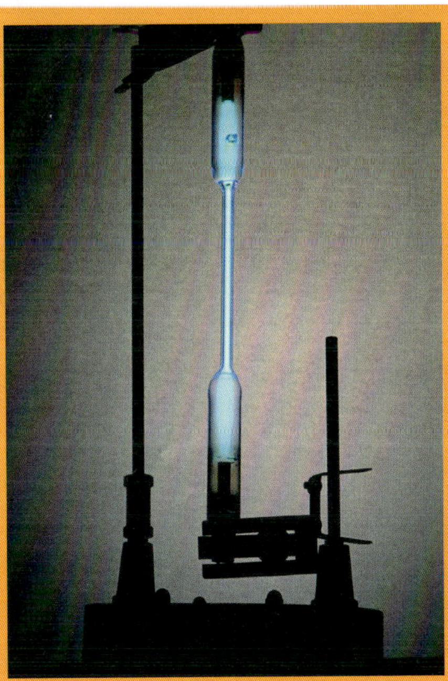

▲ Figure 5.1 The gas in this tube glows when there is a current.

LEARNING OBJECTIVES

- Explain why a series or parallel circuit is more appropriate for particular applications, including domestic lighting
- Know that electric current in solid metallic conductors is a flow of negatively charged electrons
- Know and use the relationship between voltage, current and resistance:

  voltage = current × resistance

  $V = I \times R$
- Know that current is the rate of flow of charge
- Know and use the relationship between charge, current and time:

  charge = current × time

  $Q = I \times t$
- Know that lamps and LEDs can be used to indicate the presence of a current in a circuit
- Know that the voltage across two components connected in parallel is the same
- Know that voltage is the energy transferred per unit charge passed
- Know and use the relationship between energy transferred, charge and voltage:

  energy transferred = charge × voltage

  $E = Q \times V$
- Know that the volt is a joule per coulomb
- Understand why current is conserved at a junction in a circuit

CONDUCTORS, INSULATORS AND ELECTRIC CURRENT

An electric current is a flow of charge. In metal wires the charges are carried by very small particles called electrons.

Electrons flow easily through all metals. We therefore describe metals as being good conductors of electricity. Electrons do not flow easily through plastics – they are poor conductors of electricity. A very poor conductor is known as an insulator and is often used in situations where we want to prevent the flow of charge – for example, in the casing of a plug.

In metals, some electrons are free to move between the **atoms**. Under normal circumstances this movement is random – that is, the number of electrons flowing in any one direction is roughly equal to the number flowing in the opposite direction. There is therefore no overall flow of charge.

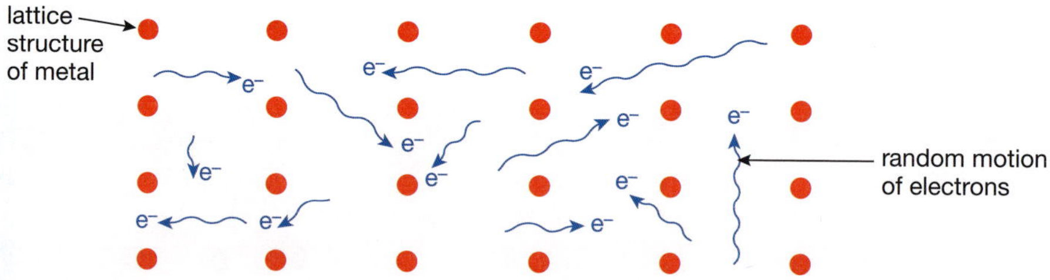

▲ Figure 5.2a With no voltage there is an equal flow of electrons in all directions.

If, however, a cell or battery is connected across the conductor, more of the electrons now flow in the direction away from the negative terminal and towards the positive terminal than in the opposite direction. We say 'there is now a net flow of charge'. This flow of charge is what we call an electric current.

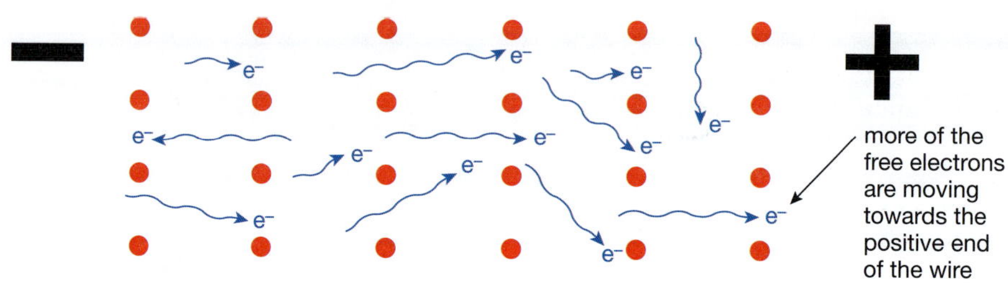

▲ Figure 5.2b When a voltage is applied more electrons will move towards the positive.

In insulators, all the electrons are held tightly in position and are unable to move from atom to atom. Charges are therefore unable to move through insulators.

EXTENSION WORK

When scientists first experimented with charges flowing through wires, they assumed that it was positive charges that were moving and that current travels from the positive to the negative. We now know that this is incorrect and that when an electric current passes through a wire it is the negative charges or electrons that move. Nevertheless when dealing with topics such as circuits and motors, it is still considered that electrons flow from positive to negative. This is conventional current.

MEASURING CURRENT

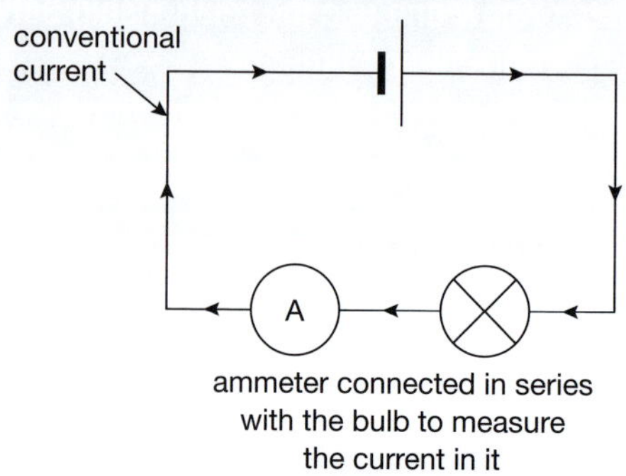

▲ Figure 5.3 An ammeter is used to measure current in a circuit. It has a very low resistance and so has almost no effect on the current.

We measure the size of the current in a circuit using an ammeter. The ammeter is connected in series (see page 542) with the part of the circuit we are interested in.

The size of an electric current indicates the rate at which the charge flows.

The charge carried by one electron is very small and would not be a very useful measure of charge in everyday life. It would be a little like asking how far away the Moon is from the Earth … and getting the answer in mm!

To avoid this problem we measure electric charge (Q) in much bigger units called coulombs (C). One coulomb of charge is equal to the charge carried by approximately six million, million, million (6×10^{18}) electrons.

We measure electric current (I) in amperes or amps (A). If there is a current of 1 A in a wire it means that 1 C of charge is passing along the wire each second.

1 C/s = 1 A

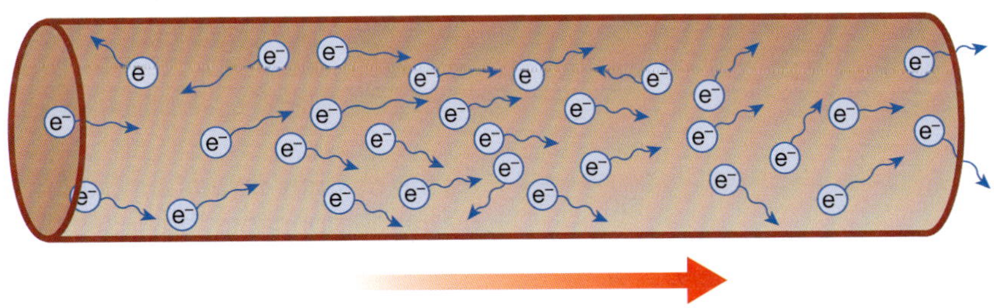

▲ Figure 5.4 One coulomb of charge flowing each second is one amp.

We can calculate the total charge that passes along a wire using the equation:

charge, Q (coulombs) = current, I (amps) × time, t (seconds)

$$Q = I \times t$$

HINT

If an examination question asks you to write out the equation for calculating charge, current or time, always give the actual equation such as $Q = I \times t$. You may not get the mark if you just draw the triangle.

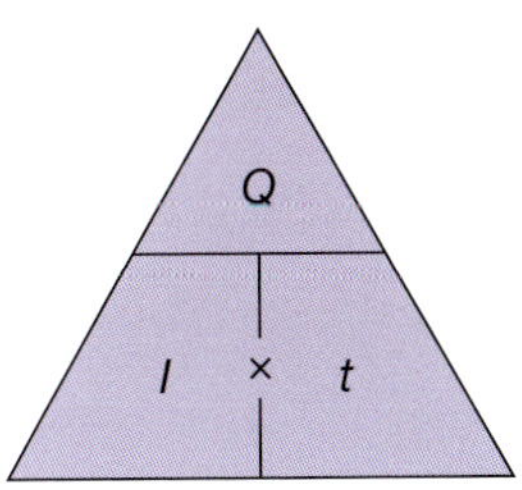

▲ Figure 5.5 You can use the triangle method for rearranging equations like this.

EXAMPLE 1

a Calculate the charge flowing through a wire in 5 s if the current is 3 A.

$Q = I \times t$

$= 3\ \text{A} \times 5\ \text{s}$

$= 15\ \text{C}$

b How many electrons flow through the wire in this time?

1 C of charge is carried by 6×10^{18} electrons

15 C of charge requires $15 \times 6 \times 10^{18}$ electrons $= 90 \times 10^{18}$ electrons

So 90 million, million, million electrons will flow along the wire in 5 s.

VOLTAGE

We often use cells or batteries to move charges around circuits. We can imagine them as being 'electron pumps'. They transfer energy to the charges. The amount of energy given to the charges by a cell or battery is measured in volts (V) and is usually indicated on the side of the battery or cell.

If we connect a 1.5 V cell into a circuit (Figure 5.6) and current flows, 1.5 J of energy is given to each coulomb of charge that passes through the cell.

If two 1.5 V cells are connected in series (Figure 5.7) so that they are pumping (pushing) in the same direction, each coulomb of charge will receive 3 J of energy.

The volt is a joule per coulomb.

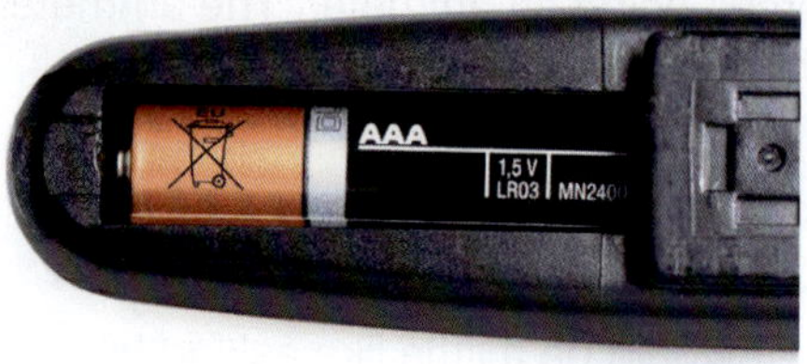

▲ Figure 5.6 When one coulomb of charge passes through this cell it gains 1.5 J of energy.

▲ Figure 5.7 When one coulomb of charge passes through both these cells in turn it gains 3 J of energy.

KEY POINT

When several cells are connected together it is called a battery.

KEY POINT

Cells and batteries provide current which moves in one direction. This is known as direct current (d.c.).

As the charges flow around a circuit the energy they carry is transferred by the components they pass through. For example, when current passes through a bulb, energy is transferred to the surroundings as heat and light. When a current passes through the speaker of a radio, most of the energy is transferred as sound.

In the external part of a circuit (outside the cell or battery) the voltage across each component tells us how much energy it is transferring. If the voltage across a component is 1 V this means that the component is transferring 1 J of energy each time 1 C of charge passes through it.

We can describe the relationship between the energy transferred, charge and voltage using the equation:

$$\text{energy transferred, } E \text{ (joules)} = \text{charge, } Q \text{ (coulombs)} \times \text{voltage, } V \text{ (volts)}$$

$$E = Q \times V$$

EXAMPLE 2

The voltage across a light bulb is 12 V. Calculate the electrical energy transferred when 50 C of charge passes through it.

$$E = Q \times V$$
$$= 50\text{ C} \times 12\text{ V}$$
$$= 600\text{ J}$$

Because $Q = I \times t$, we can also write this equation as $E = I \times t \times V$.

EXAMPLE 3

The voltage across a heater is 230 V. There is a current of 5 A through the heater for 5 mins. Calculate the total amount of energy transferred during this time.

$$E = I \times t \times V$$
$$= 5\text{ A} \times (5 \times 60)\text{ s} \times 230\text{ V}$$
$$= 345\,000\text{ J or } 345\text{ kJ}$$

MEASURING VOLTAGES

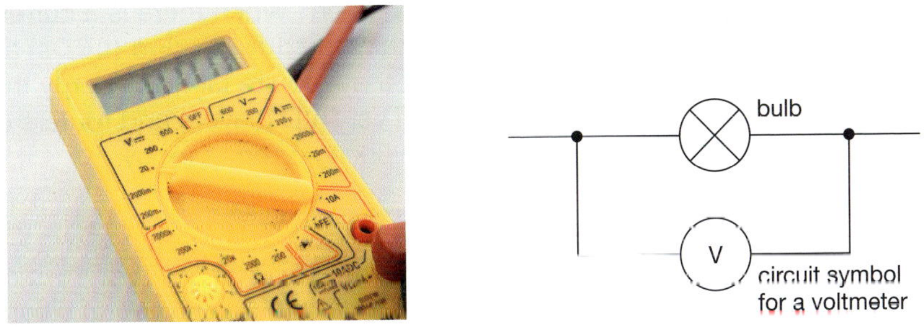

Figure 5.8 A voltmeter measures voltages across a component.

KEY POINT

A voltmeter has a very high resistance, so very little current flows through it.

We measure voltages using a voltmeter. This is connected across (in parallel with) the component we are investigating. A voltmeter connected across a cell or battery will measure the energy given to each coulomb of charge that passes through it. A voltmeter connected across a component will measure the electrical energy transferred when each coulomb of charge passes through it.

ELECTRICAL CIRCUITS

When the button on the torch shown in Figure 5.9 is pressed, the circuit is complete – that is, there are no gaps. Charges are able to flow around the circuit and the torch bulb glows. When the button is released the circuit becomes incomplete. Charges cease to flow and the bulb goes out.

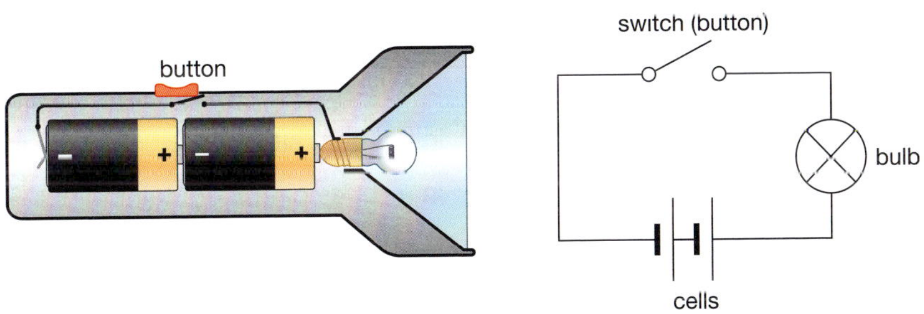

Figure 5.9 A torch contains a simple electrical circuit – a series circuit.

KEY POINT

Drawing diagrams of the actual components in a circuit is a very time-consuming and skilful task. It is much easier to use symbols for each of the components. Diagrams drawn in this way are called circuit diagrams. Figure 5.10 shows common circuit components and their symbols. You should know the common symbols but the less common ones will be given to you in the exam if you need them. Do not waste time memorising the less common ones.

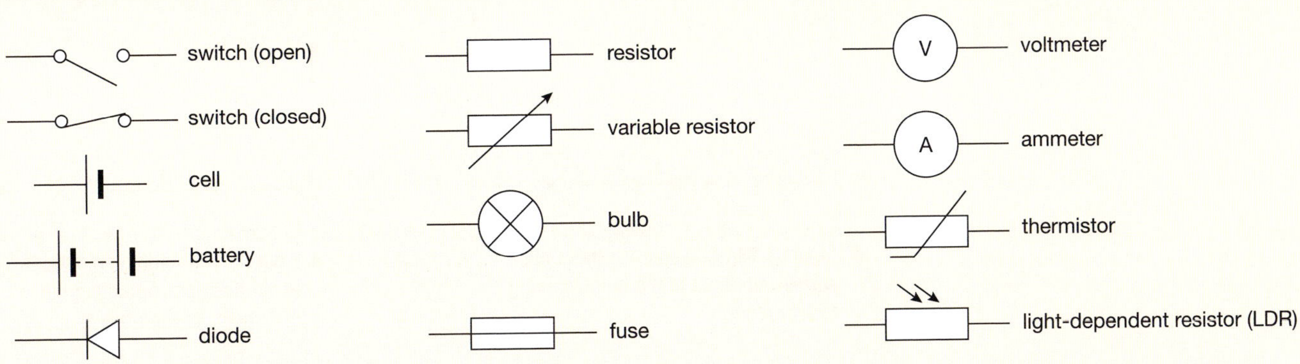

Figure 5.10 Circuit symbols

▲ Figure 5.11 Glowing LEDs indicate which circuits are working

IS IT ON?

We sometimes put a small bulb or lamp in a circuit to show us if a circuit is 'turned on'. When there is a current in the circuit the bulb glows or shines. **Light emitting diodes (LEDs)** also glow when there is a current in a circuit but they require far less energy than bulbs. This is why many appliances such as TVs, DVD players and routers use small LEDs to show when the appliance is working or on standby.

SERIES AND PARALLEL CIRCUITS

There are two main types of electrical circuit. There are those circuits where there are no branches or junctions and there is only one path the current can follow. These simple 'single loop' circuits are called series circuits.

Circuits that have branches or junctions and more than one path that the current can follow are called parallel circuits.

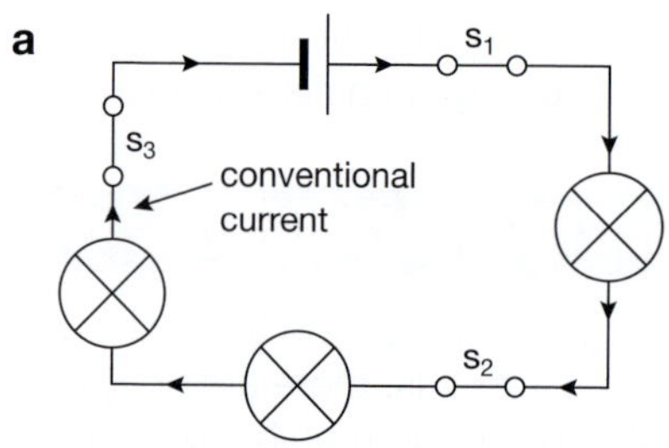

▲ Figure 5.12a A typical series circuit. Opening any one of these switches will turn all three bulbs off.

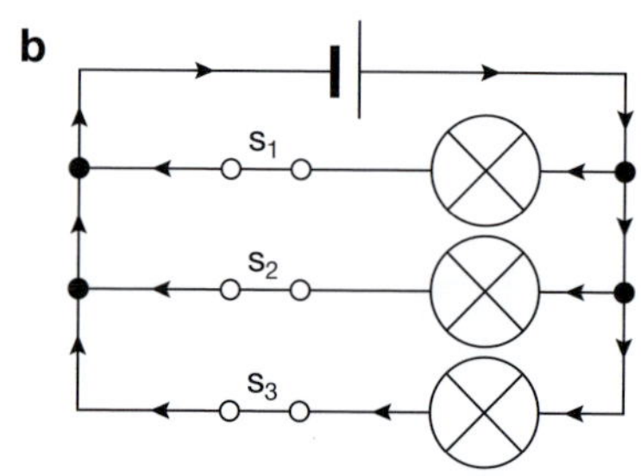

▲ Figure 5.12b A typical parallel circuit. Opening any one of these switches will turn off just the bulb in that part of the circuit.

Series circuits and parallel circuits behave differently. This makes them useful in different situations.

In a series circuit containing bulbs:

- One switch placed anywhere in the circuit can turn all the bulbs on and off.
- If any one of the bulbs breaks, it causes a gap in the circuit and all of the other bulbs will 'stop working'.
- The energy supplied by the cell is 'shared' between all the bulbs, so the more bulbs you add to a series circuit the less bright they all become.

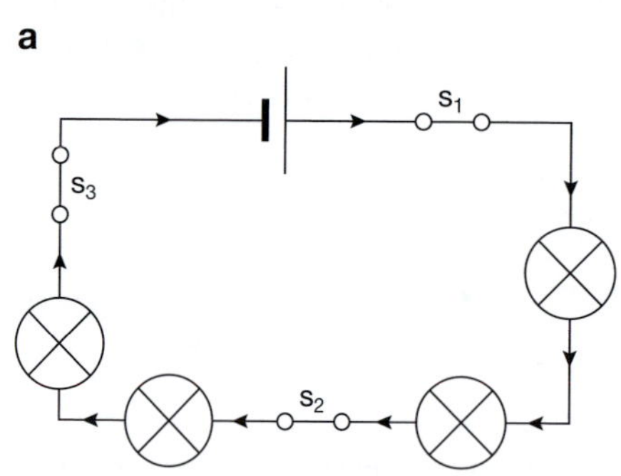

▲ Figure 5.13a Adding an extra bulb in series will result in the bulbs shining less brightly.

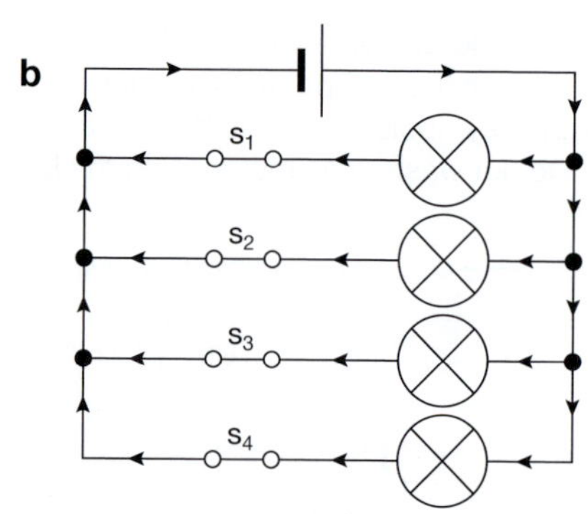

▲ Figure 5.13b Adding an extra bulb in parallel does not affect the brightness of the other bulbs.

In a parallel circuit containing bulbs:

- Switches can be placed in different parts of the circuit to switch each bulb on and off individually, or all together.
- If one bulb breaks, only the bulbs on the same branch of the circuit will be affected.
- Each branch of the circuit receives the same voltage, so if more bulbs are added to a circuit in parallel they all keep the same brightness.

▲ Figure 5.14 Decorative lights are usually wired in series.

Decorative lights are often wired in series. Each bulb only needs a low voltage, so even when the voltage from the mains supply is 'shared' out between them each bulb still gets enough energy to produce light. Unfortunately, if the filament in one of the bulbs breaks then all the other bulbs will go out.

The lights in your home are wired in parallel. We know this because lights can be switched on and off separately, and the brightness of each light does not change when other lights are on or off. Also, if a bulb breaks or is removed, you can still use the other lights.

CURRENT IN A SERIES CIRCUIT

In a series circuit the current is the same in all parts; current is not used up.

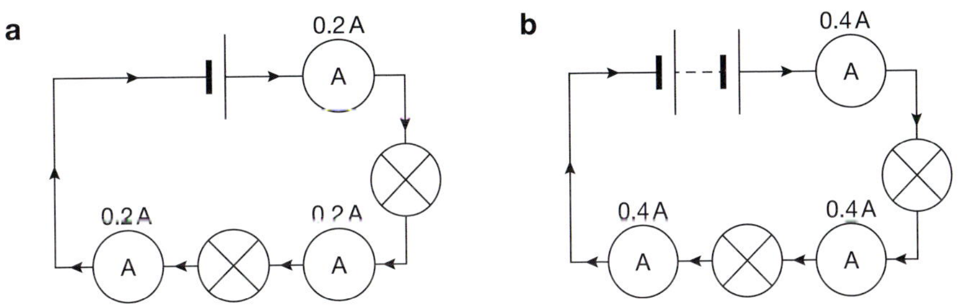

▲ Figure 5.15a In a series circuit the current does not vary.

▲ Figure 5.15b The addition of a second cell doubles the voltage applied to the circuit so the current will also double.

The size of the current in a series circuit depends on the voltage supplied to it, and the number and type of the other components in the circuit. If a second identical cell is added in series the voltage will double and so the current will also double.

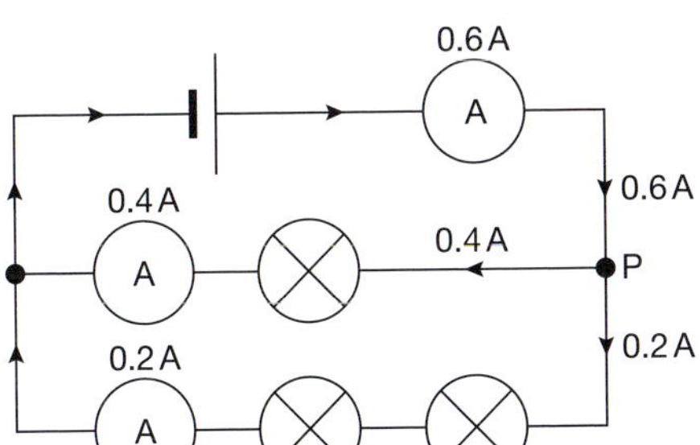

▲ Figure 5.16 There are different currents in the different parts of a parallel circuit.

CURRENT IN A PARALLEL CIRCUIT

In a parallel circuit the currents will not be the same in different parts of the circuit. The types of components in each of the different parts will affect the currents.

In a parallel circuit the number of electrons that flow into a junction each second must be equal to the number that leave each second. This means that the currents entering a junction must always be equal to those that leave. For example, in Figure 5.16 the current that enters junction P is 0.6 A. The current that leaves is 0.4 A + 0.2 A = 0.6 A.

CHAPTER QUESTIONS

More questions on electrical circuits can be found at the end of Unit 2 on page 554.

SKILLS CRITICAL THINKING

1 Current is a flow of charge.

5th a What are the charge carriers in metals?

6th b Explain why charges are able to flow through metals but not through a plastic.

SKILLS PROBLEM SOLVING

c If the current in a heater is 3 A, calculate the charge that flows through it in:

7th **i** 1 s

8th **ii** 10 min

iii 1 hour.

SKILLS CRITICAL THINKING

2 a Explain the differences between:

3rd **i** a complete circuit and an incomplete circuit

5th **ii** a series circuit and a parallel circuit.

SKILLS ANALYSIS

b Look carefully at the circuits shown below. Assuming that all switches are initially closed, decide which of the bulbs go out when each of the switches is opened in turn.

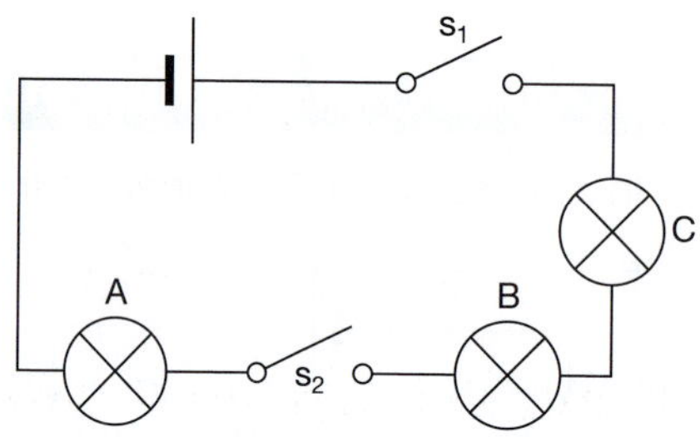

circuit A

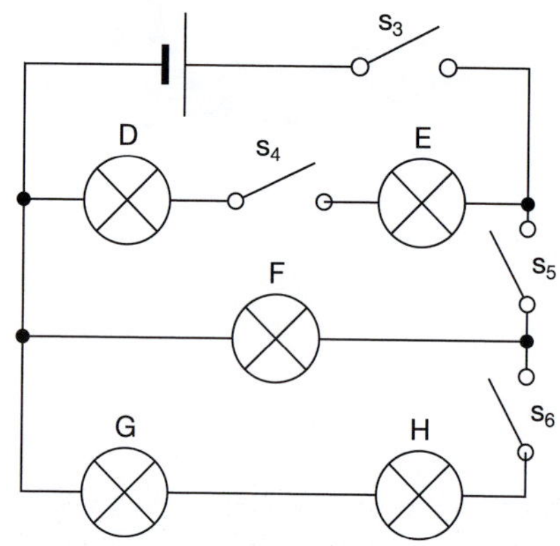

circuit B

c In circuit A, which bulb(s) glow the brightest when all the switches in the circuit are closed?

SKILLS CRITICAL THINKING

d Explain your answer to part **c**.

SKILLS INTERPRETATION

6th **3** The voltage between two points in a circuit is measured using a voltmeter.

a Draw a circuit diagram to show how a voltmeter should be connected to measure:

i the voltage across a bulb **ii** the voltage of a cell.

SKILLS CRITICAL THINKING

b Explain in your own words the phrase 'a cell has a voltage of 1.5 V'.

SKILLS REASONING

4th **4** The diagram below shows a circuit containing two 2-way switches.

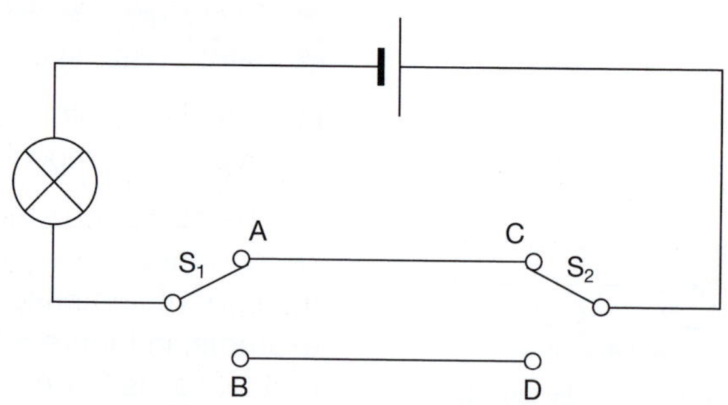

a Explain in your own words what happens when each of the switches is moved to a new position.

b Suggest one important application of this circuit in the home.

5th **5** Should the lights for the main street in a town be wired in series or in parallel? Explain your answer.

6 Why would it not be a good idea to connect all the different parts of an electric cooker (oven, grill, heating plates) in series?

6 ELECTRICAL RESISTANCE

In this chapter you will learn what resistance is and how it can be useful in electrical appliances. You will learn what factors affect resistance and how to work out the resistance of a component by measuring the current in it and the voltage across it (Ohm's law). You will also read about some special resistors, and their uses.

It is likely that almost every day of your life you will make some adjustments to at least one electrical appliance. You may turn up the volume of your radio or change the brightness of a light. In each of these examples your adjustments are changing the currents and the voltages in the circuits of your appliance. You are doing this by altering the resistance of the circuits. This chapter will help you understand the meaning and importance of resistance and how we make use of it.

▲ Figure 6.1 Turning this dial alters the resistance in the circuit which changes the volume of the sound.

LEARNING OBJECTIVES

- Understand how the current in a series circuit depends on the applied voltage and the number and nature of other components
- Describe how current varies with voltage in wires, resistors, metal filament lamps and diodes, and how to investigate this experimentally
- Describe the qualitative effect of changing resistance on the current in a circuit
- Describe the qualitative variation of resistance of light-dependent resistors (LDRs) with illumination and thermistors with temperature
- Calculate the currents, voltages and resistances of two resistive components connected in a series circuit

RESISTANCE

All components in a circuit offer some resistance to the flow of charge. Some (for example, connecting wires) allow charges to pass through very easily losing very little of their energy. We describe connecting wires as having very low resistance. The flow of charge through some components is not so easy and a large amount of energy may be used to move the charges through them. This energy is transferred, usually as heat. Components like these are said to have a high resistance.

REMINDER

We normally assume that connecting wires have zero resistance.

We measure the resistance (R) of a component by comparing the size of the current (I) in that component and the voltage (V) applied across its ends. Voltage, current and resistance are related as follows:

$$\text{voltage, } V \text{ (volts)} = \text{current, } I \text{ (amps)} \times \text{resistance, } R \text{ (ohms)}$$

$$V = I \times R$$

We measure resistance in units called ohms (Ω).

HINT

If an examination question asks you to write out the equation for calculating resistance, current or voltage, always give the actual equation such as $V = I \times R$. You may not get the mark if you just draw the triangle.

EXAMPLE 1

When a voltage of 12 V is applied across a doorbell there is a current of 0.1 A. Calculate the resistance of the doorbell.

$$V = I \times R$$

Rearrange the equation.

$$R = \frac{V}{I}$$

$$= \frac{12\text{ V}}{0.1\text{ A}}$$

$$= 120\ \Omega$$

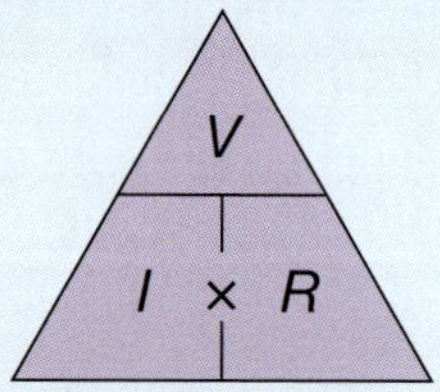

▲ Figure 6.2 You can use the triangle method for rearranging equations like $V = I \times R$.

If there are two or more resistors connected in series in a circuit, their total resistance is found by simply adding the individual resistances together. (This is not true for parallel circuits. You do not need to know how to do this.)

EXAMPLE 2

The circuit on the right contains a 12 V battery and two resistors connected in series.

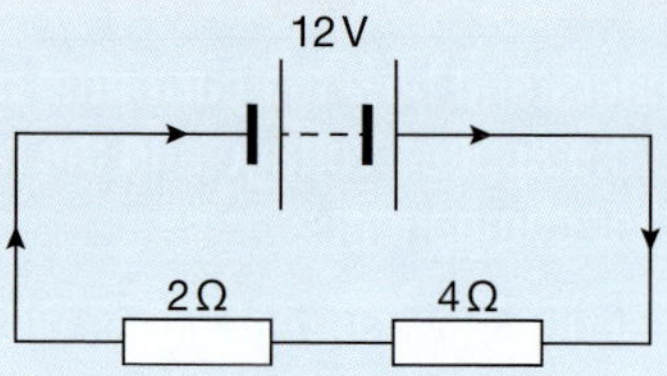

▲ Figure 6.3 Two resistor series circuit

Calculate

a the current in each of the resistors

b the voltage across each resistor.

a The total resistance the current must pass through is 2 Ω + 4 Ω = 6 Ω

The current in the circuit (I) is therefore:

$$I = \frac{V}{R}$$

$$= \frac{12\ V}{6\ \Omega}$$

$$= 2\text{ A}$$

The current in a series circuit is the same everywhere. So the current in both resistors is 2 A.

b Using $V = I \times R$

for the 2 Ω resistor: $V = 2\text{ A} \times 2\ \Omega = 4\text{ V}$

for the 4 Ω resistor: $V = 2\text{ A} \times 4\ \Omega = 8\text{ V}$

EXPERIMENT TO INVESTIGATE HOW CURRENT VARIES WITH VOLTAGE FOR DIFFERENT COMPONENTS

Safety note: The resistance wire in the circuit may get hot enough to burn skin if the current/voltage is increased too much.

1. Set up the circuit shown in Figure 6.4.
2. Turn the variable resistor to its maximum value.
3. Close the switch and take the readings from the ammeter and the voltmeter.
4. Alter the value of the variable resistor again and take a new pair of readings from the meters.
5. Repeat the whole process at least six times.
6. Place the results in a table (see the table below) and draw a graph of current (*I*) against voltage (V).

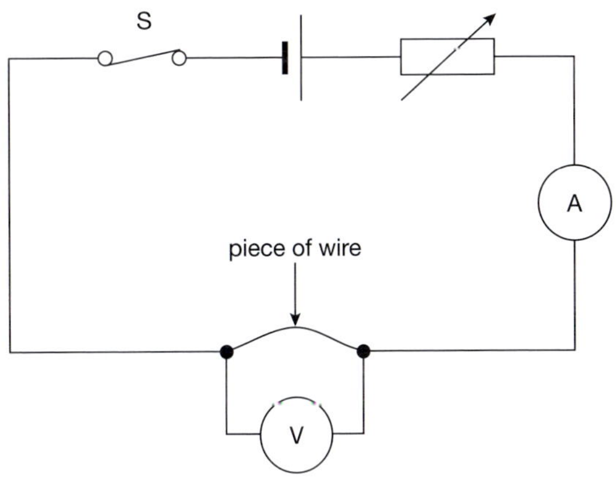

Figure 6.4 This circuit can be used to investigate the relationship between current and voltage.

Current / amps	Voltage / volts
0.0	0.0
0.1	0.4
0.2	0.8
0.3	1.2
0.4	1.6
0.5	2.0

Table 6.1 Typical results table

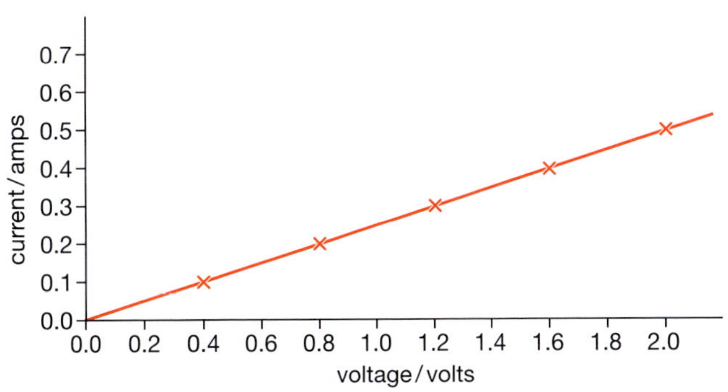

Figure 6.5 Graph of results

The graph in Figure 6.5 is a straight line graph passing through the origin. The slope of the graph tells us about the resistance of the wire. The steeper the slope the smaller the resistance of the wire.

If we repeat this experiment for other components, such as a resistor, a filament bulb and a diode, the shapes of the graphs we obtain are often very different to that shown in Figure 6.5. By looking very carefully at these shapes we can see how they behave.

CURRENT/VOLTAGE GRAPH FOR A WIRE OR A RESISTOR

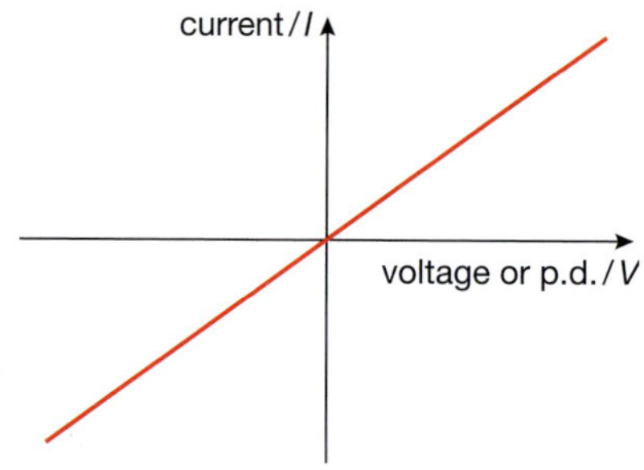

▲ Figure 6.6

The graph is a straight line. It has a constant slope. So the resistance of this component does not change.

CURRENT/VOLTAGE GRAPH FOR A FILAMENT BULB

HINT

The flatter the slope the higher the resistance.

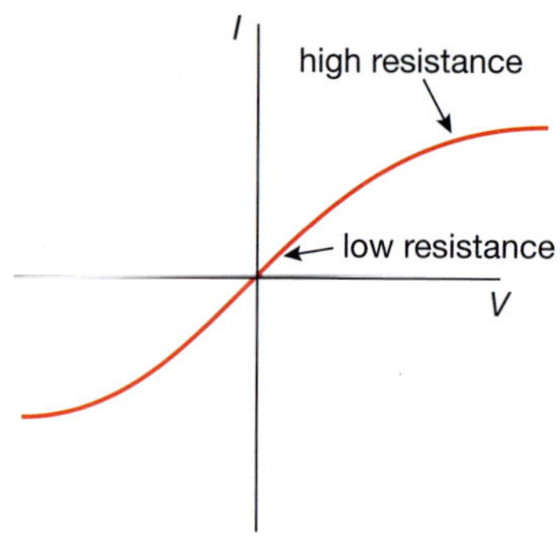

▲ Figure 6.7

This graph is not a straight line. The resistance of the bulb changes. At higher currents and voltages the slope of the graph shows us that the resistance of the filament bulb increases – that is, as the temperature of the filament increases the current decreases.

CURRENT/VOLTAGE GRAPH FOR A DIODE

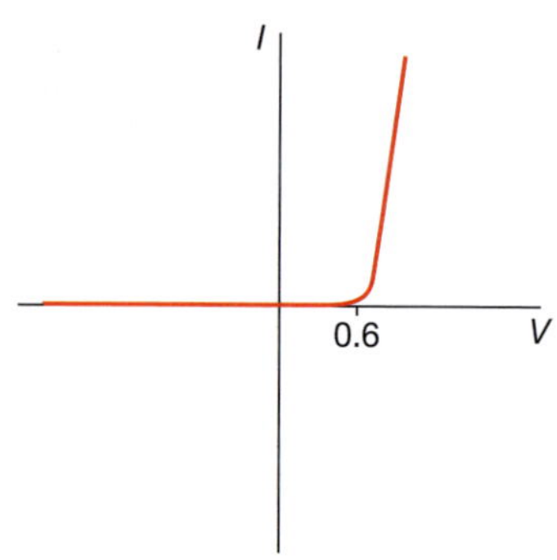

▲ Figure 6.8

This strangely shaped graph shows that diodes have a high resistance when the current is in one direction and a low resistance when it is in the opposite direction (see page 551).

USING RESISTANCE

FIXED RESISTORS

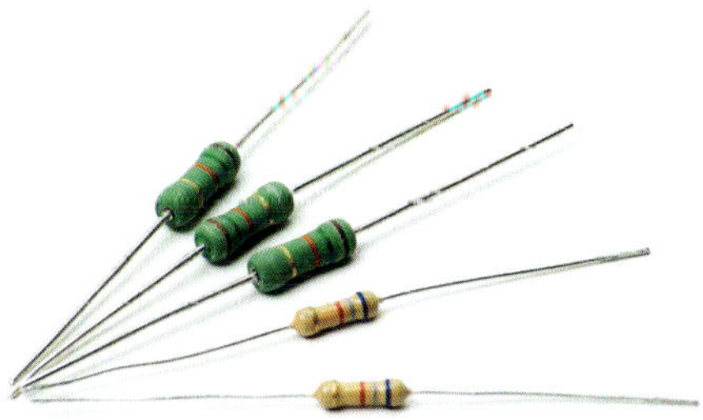

▲ Figure 6.9 A selection of resistors

In many circuits you will find components similar to those shown in Figure 6.9. They are called fixed resistors. They are included in circuits in order to control the sizes of currents and voltages. The resistor in the circuit in Figure 6.10 is included so that both the current in the bulb and the voltage applied across it are correct. Without the resistor the voltage across the bulb may cause too large a current and the bulb may 'blow' or break.

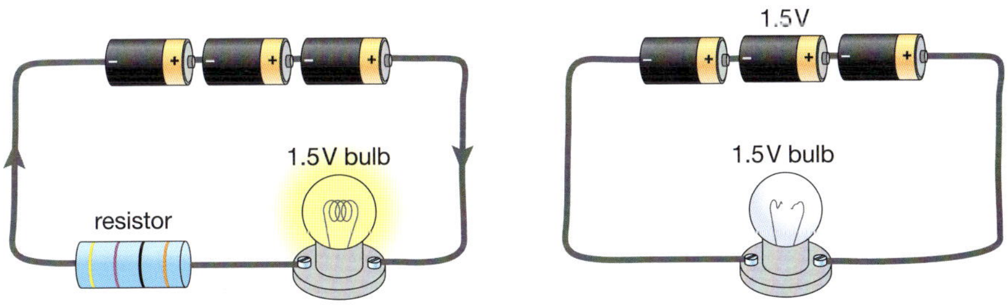

▲ Figure 6.10 The resistor in the first circuit limits the size of the current. Without the resistor the current in the second circuit is too high and the bulb breaks.

VARIABLE RESISTORS

Figure 6.11 shows examples of a different kind of resistor. They are called variable resistors as it is possible to alter their resistance. If you alter the volume of your radio using a knob you are using a variable resistor to do this.

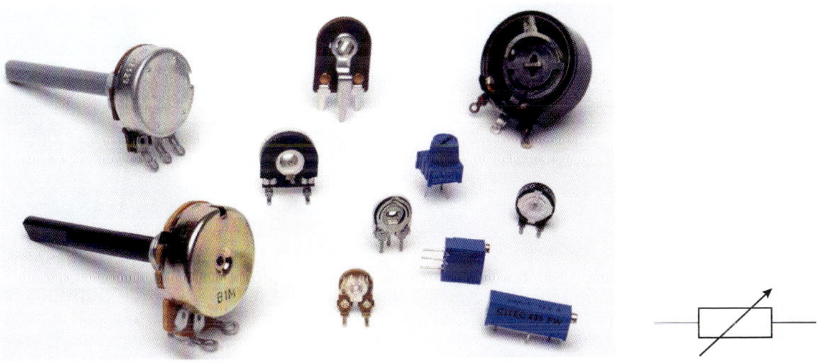

▲ Figure 6.11 Variable resistors and their symbol

In the circuit in Figure 6.12 a variable resistor is being used to control the size of the current in a bulb. If the resistance is decreased there will be a larger current and the bulb shines more brightly. If the resistance is increased the current will be smaller and the bulb will glow less brightly or not at all. The variable resistor is behaving in this circuit as a **dimmer switch**. In circuits containing electric motors, variable resistors can be used to control the speed of the motor.

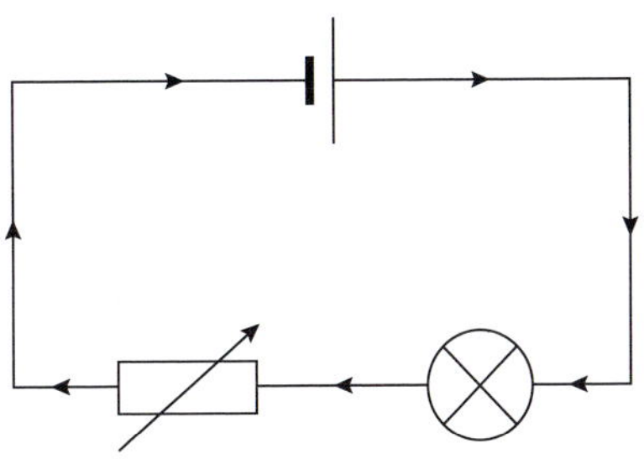

▲ Figure 6.12 Circuit with a variable resistor being used as a dimmer switch

SPECIAL RESISTORS

THERMISTORS

A **thermistor** is a resistor whose resistance changes quite a lot even with small changes in temperature.

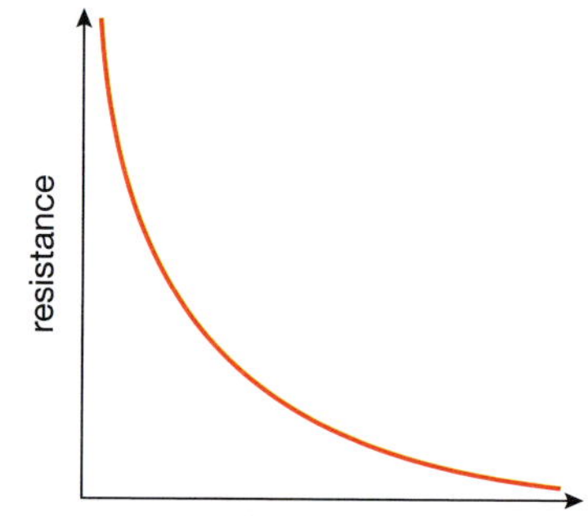

▲ Figure 6.13 A graph showing a thermistor's decreasing resistance with increasing temperature

KEY POINT

Some thermistors increase their resistance when the temperature increases. However, for your International GCSE Physics exam you only need to know about thermistors whose resistance decreases with increasing temperature.

Thermistors are used in temperature-sensitive circuits in devices such as fire alarms. They are also used in devices where it is important to make sure there is no change in temperature, for example, in freezers and computers.

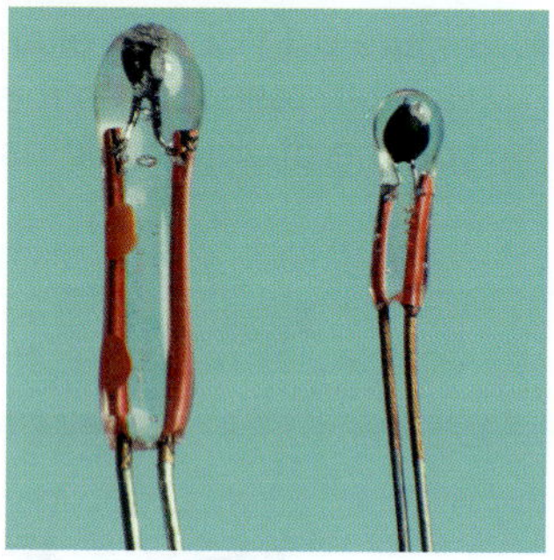

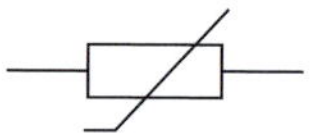

▲ Figure 6.14 Two examples of thermistors and their symbol – the resistance of a thermistor changes a lot as the temperature changes.

LIGHT-DEPENDENT RESISTORS (LDRs)

A light-dependent resistor (LDR) has a resistance that changes when light is shone on it. In the dark its resistance is high but when light is shone on it its resistance decreases.

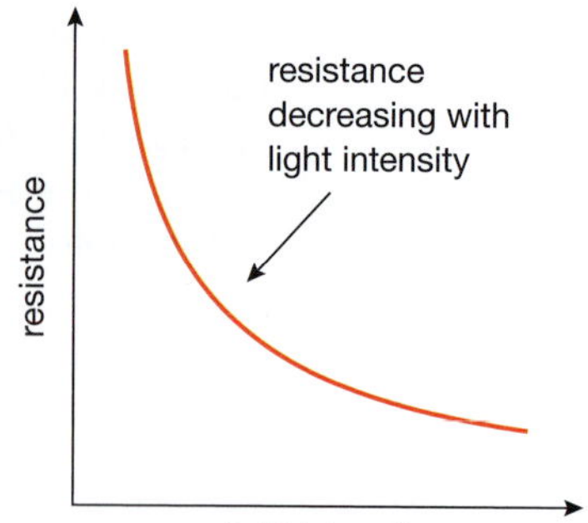

▲ Figure 6.15 A graph showing an LDR's decreasing resistance with increasing light intensity

▲ Figure 6.16 Light-dependent resistor

LDRs are often used in light-sensitive circuits in devices such as photographic-exposure equipment, automatic lighting controls and burglar alarms.

DIODES

Diodes are very special resistors that allow charges to flow through them easily but only in one direction.

When a diode is connected as shown in circuit A in Figure 6.17, the diode offers little resistance to the charges flowing through it. But if the diode is connected the opposite way round, the diode has a very high resistance and the rate at which the charges can flow through the diode is much less – that is, the current is very small. Diodes are often used in circuits where it is important that electrons flow only in one direction. For example, they are used in **rectifier circuits** that convert alternating current into direct current. Some diodes glow when charges flow through them. They are called light emitting diodes (LEDs).

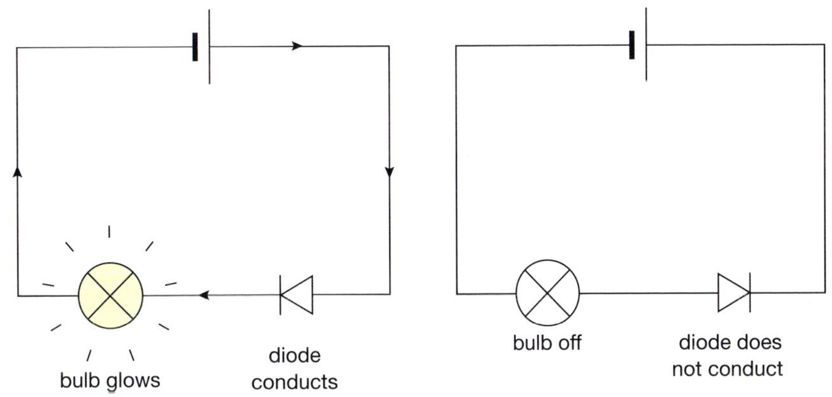

▲ Figure 6.17 Diodes will only let charges flow one way.

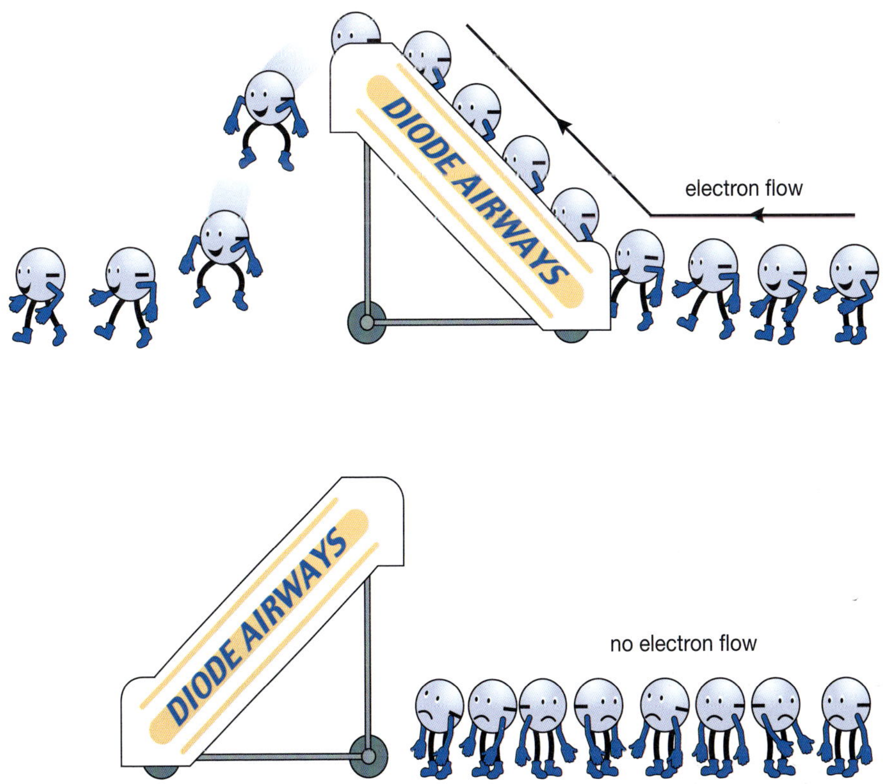

▲ Figure 6.18 Diodes are like aeroplane steps – from the ground, you can only climb them in one direction. In a diode the charge can only flow in one direction.

KEY POINT

You can imagine a diode as behaving like a set of aeroplane steps which the charges have to climb over. If the charges are moving towards the correct side of the steps they can 'flow through it'. If, however, they try to move the opposite way there are no steps for them to climb so the flow in this direction is almost zero.

LOOKING AHEAD – OHM'S LAW AND TEMPERATURE

The relationship between the voltage across a component and its current is described by Ohm's law, which states:

The current in a conductor is directly proportional to the potential difference across its ends, provided its temperature remains constant.

So the resistance of a wire can be found by measuring the voltage (V) across it and the current (I) in it when this voltage is applied to the wire and then calculating a value for the **ratio** $\frac{V}{I}$ (see page 545). But the law also states that the temperature of the wire must be constant. This is because if the temperature of the wire changes, its resistance also changes.

This happens because at higher temperatures the atoms in the wire **vibrate** more vigorously, making it more difficult for the electrons to flow.

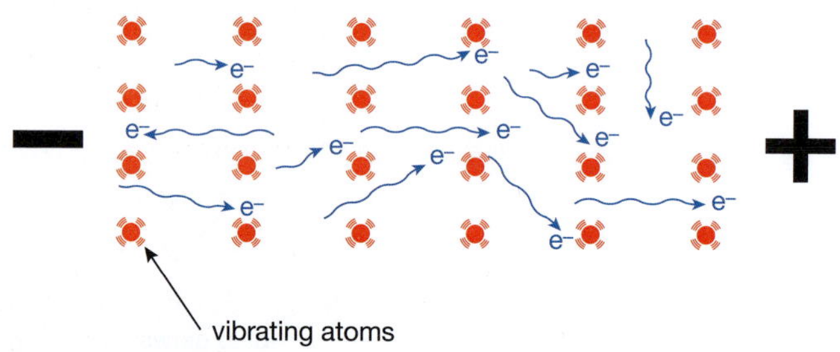

Figure 6.19 At higher temperatures the increased vibration of the atoms makes it more difficult for charges to flow.

If a wire or conductor is cooled the vibration of its atoms decreases and so its resistance decreases. At very low temperatures, close to absolute zero (–273 °C), these vibrations stop and the conductor offers no resistance to the flow of charge. This event is called superconductivity and could be extremely useful. For example, when electricity flows through a superconductor there is no loss of energy. This means that by using superconductivity we could transmit electrical energy from power stations without losses. Scientists around the world are now searching for materials that are superconductors at temperatures well above absolute zero.

Figure 6.20 Maglev trains use superconducting magnets to help them hover above the tracks.

CHAPTER QUESTIONS

More questions on electrical resistance can be found at the end of Unit 2 on page 554.

SKILLS CRITICAL THINKING 6th

1 a Describe how the current in a wire changes as the voltage across the wire increases.

SKILLS INTERPRETATION 7th

b Draw a diagram of the circuit you would use to confirm your answer to part a.

SKILLS DECISION MAKING 6th

c Describe how you would use the apparatus and what readings you would take.

SKILLS INTERPRETATION

d Draw an I–V graph for

i a piece of wire at room temperature

ii a filament bulb

iii a diode.

7th

Explain the main features of each of these graphs.

SKILLS PROBLEM SOLVING 8th

2 a There is a current of 5 A when a voltage of 20 V is applied across a resistor. Calculate the resistance of the resistor.

b Calculate the current when a voltage of 12 V is applied across a piece of wire of resistance 50 Ω.

7th

c Calculate the voltage that must be applied across a wire of resistance 10 Ω if the current is to be 3 A.

SKILLS INTERPRETATION 6th

3 a Describe how the resistance of

i a thermistor changes as its temperature changes

ii a light-dependent resistor changes as an increasingly bright light is shone on it.

7th

iii Draw graphs to illustrate these changes.

SKILLS CRITICAL THINKING

b Name one practical application for each of these resistors.

HINT

Remember when doing calculations like these to show all your working out and include units with your answer.

UNIT QUESTIONS

SKILLS CRITICAL THINKING 4th

1 **a** Which of the following is not used to protect us from the possibility of receiving an electric shock?

A double insulation

B live wire

C earth wire

D circuit breaker

(1)

6th

b Which of the following is true for a **negatively charged** object?

A It will attract another negatively charged object.

B It has too few electrons.

C It has too many neutrons.

D It has gained extra electrons.

(1)

4th

c Which of the following is true for all parallel circuits?

A Parts of the circuit can be turned off while other parts remain on.

B The current is the same in all parts of the circuit.

C There is only one path for the current to follow.

D There are no junctions or branches.

(1)

SKILLS PROBLEM SOLVING 7th

d When a voltage of 6 V is applied across a resistor there is a current of 0.1 A. The value of the resistor is

A 6 Ω

B 60 Ω

C 16.6 Ω

D 0.6 Ω

(1)

(Total 4 marks)

SKILLS CRITICAL THINKING 6th

2 Copy and complete the following passage about electricity, filling in the spaces.

An electric current is a flow of ______. A current of 1 amp is 1 ______ of charge flowing each second. The voltage is the ______ transferred per coulomb of charge.

The current in a component depends on the voltage and the ______; the higher the resistance, the ______ the current.

(Total 5 marks)

SKILLS ANALYSIS 6th

3 Asma set up the circuit shown below to investigate how the resistance of a bulb changes as the current in it changes.

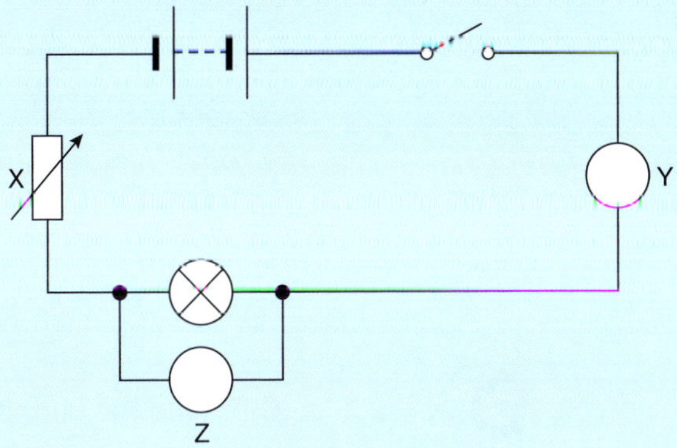

5th **a** What are the names of the instruments labelled Y and Z? **(2)**

b What is the name of the component labelled X? **(1)**

6th **c** What is the purpose of X in this circuit? **(1)**

Asma takes a series of readings. She measures the voltage across the bulb and the current in it. She then plots the graph shown below.

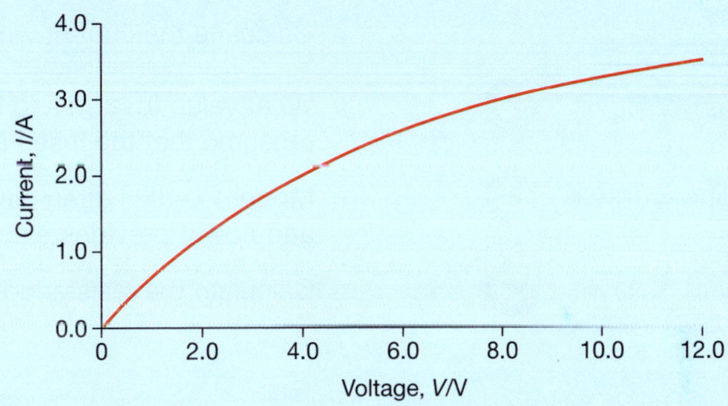

d What is the current in the bulb when a voltage of 6 V is applied across it? **(1)**

e What voltage is applied across the bulb when there is a current of 2 A? **(1)**

SKILLS PROBLEM SOLVING 7th **f** Calculate the resistance of the bulb when there is a current of 2 A. **(2)**

SKILLS REASONING 5th **g** What happens to the resistance of the bulb as the current increases? **(1)**

(Total 9 marks)

SKILLS PROBLEM SOLVING

4 A simple series circuit containing a 12 V battery and a 10 Ω resistor was constructed as shown below.

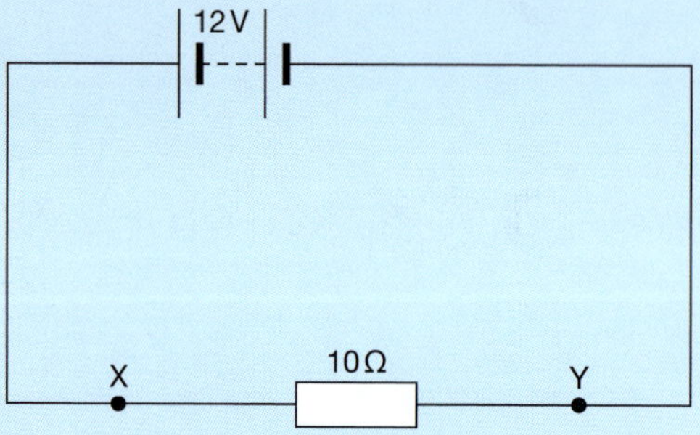

8th **a** Calculate the current between points X and Y. **(2)**

7th **b** Calculate the total charge that flows between X and Y in 5 s. **(2)**

c Calculate the energy transferred in the resistor in 1 minute. **(2)**

(Total 6 marks)

5 An electric kettle is rated at 2 kW when connected to a 230 V electrical supply.

a Calculate the current when the kettle is turned on. **(3)**

5th **b** What value fuse should be included in the circuit of the kettle? (Assume that the fuses available are 3 A, 5 A and 13 A.) **(1)**

SKILLS CRITICAL THINKING 6th **c** Modern kettles often have double insulation. Explain what this means and how it provides extra safety for the user. **(2)**

SKILLS PROBLEM SOLVING 8th **d** Calculate the resistance of the heating element of the kettle. **(3)**

(Total 9 marks)

SKILLS CRITICAL THINKING 6th **6** **a** Explain in detail how insulating materials can be charged by friction. **(4)**

SKILLS REASONING **b** When an aircraft lands it is important that it is earthed before it is refuelled.

7th **i** Explain why the aircraft should be earthed. **(3)**

6th **ii** Suggest one way in which the aircraft could be earthed. **(1)**

7th **c** Explain why electrostatic painting of objects, such as bicycle frames, makes good economic sense. **(3)**

SKILLS CRITICAL THINKING 6th **d** Describe briefly how an inkjet printer makes use of some of the properties of static electricity. **(3)**

(Total 14 marks)

5th 6th **7**

a Describe four uses of the heating effect of electricity in the home. **(4)**

b Explain why a double-insulated hairdryer does not need an earth wire in its cable. **(2)**

(Total 6 marks)

SKILLS PROBLEM SOLVING 7th **8**

Calculate

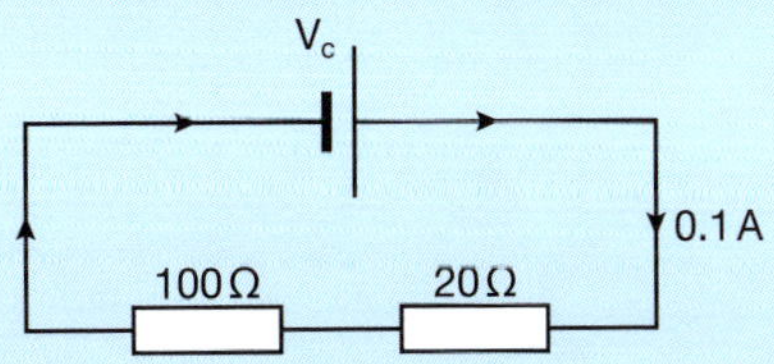

a the voltage across the 20 Ω resistor **(2)**

b the voltage across the 100 Ω resistor **(2)**

c the voltage of the cell (V_c). **(1)**

(Total 5 marks)

PHYSICS UNIT 3 WAVES

There are many different types of waves. They affect all of our lives. Sometimes they are useful and can be a tremendous benefit to the way we live. Sometimes they can be dangerous and pose a real risk to life. It is therefore very important that we understand the main features and properties of waves.

7 PROPERTIES OF WAVES

Talking to someone using a mobile phone is something most of us do several times a day. The technology that had to be developed for this to happen was based on a thorough understanding of the properties of waves.

In this chapter you will learn about different types of waves and their properties (characteristics).

▲ Figure 7.1 Using microwaves to communicate

LEARNING OBJECTIVES

- Explain the difference between longitudinal and transverse waves
- Know the definitions of amplitude, wavefront, frequency, wavelength and period of a wave
- Know that waves transfer energy and information without transferring matter
- Know and use the relationship between the speed, frequency and wavelength of a wave:

  wave speed = frequency × wavelength

  $v = f \times \lambda$
- Use the relationship between frequency and time period:

  $$\text{frequency} = \frac{1}{\text{time period}}$$

  $$f = \frac{1}{T}$$
- Use the above relationships in different contexts including sound waves and electromagnetic waves
- Explain that all waves can be reflected and refracted
- Explain why there is a change in the observed frequency and wavelength of a wave when its source is moving relative to an observer, and that this is known as the Doppler effect

UNITS

In this unit, you will need to use degrees (°) as the unit of angle, hertz (Hz) as the unit of frequency, metre (m) as the unit of length, metre per second (m/s) as the unit of speed and second (s) as the unit of time.

WHAT ARE WAVES?

Waves are a way of transferring energy from place to place. As we can see in Figure 7.1 we often use them to transfer information. All these transfers take place with no matter being transferred.

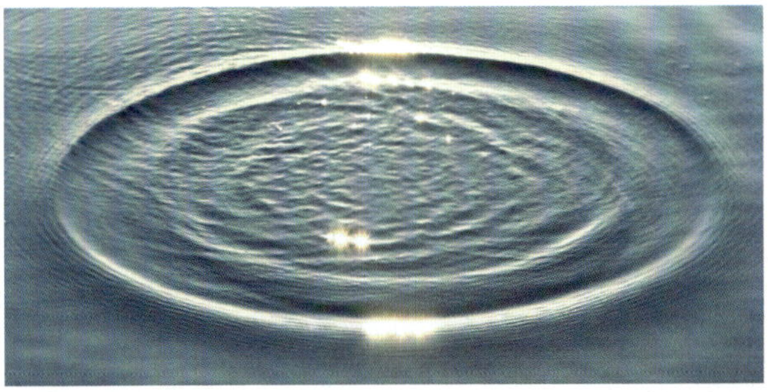

▲ Figure 7.2 Waves are produced if we drop a stone into a pond. The circular wavefronts spread out from the point of impact, carrying energy in all directions, but the water in the pond does not move from the centre to the edges.

WHAT ARE WAVEFRONTS?

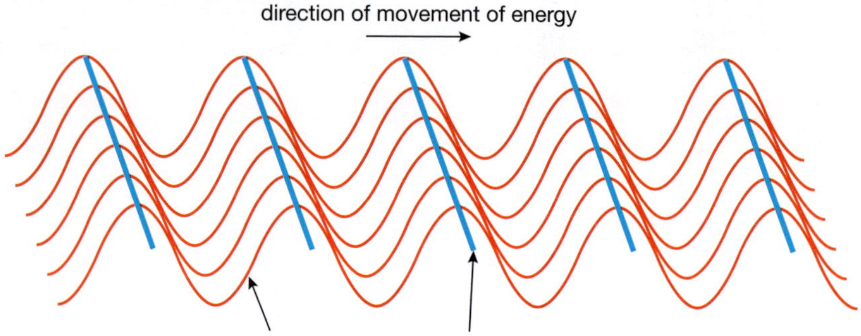

▲ Figure 7.3 Wavefronts are created by overlapping lots of different waves. A wavefront is a line where all the vibrations are in phase and the same distance from the source.

TRANSVERSE WAVES

Waves can be produced in ropes and springs. If you move one end of a spring from side to side you will see waves travelling through it. The energy carried by these waves moves along the spring from one end to the other, but if you look closely you can see that the coils of the spring are vibrating (shaking) across the direction in which the energy is moving. This is an example of a **transverse wave**.

A transverse wave is one that vibrates, or oscillates, at right angles to the direction in which the energy or wave is moving. Examples of transverse waves include light waves and waves travelling on the surface of water.

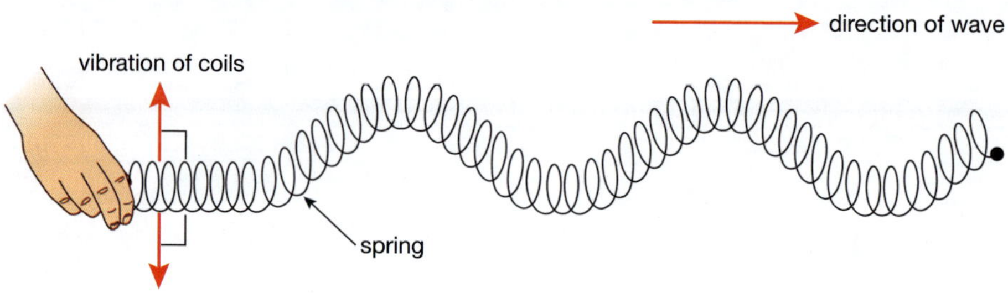

▲ Figure 7.4 A transverse wave vibrates at right angles to the direction in which the wave is moving.

LONGITUDINAL WAVES

If you push and pull the end of a spring in a direction parallel to its axis, you can again see energy travelling along it. This time however the coils of the spring are vibrating in directions that are along its length. This is an example of a **longitudinal wave**.

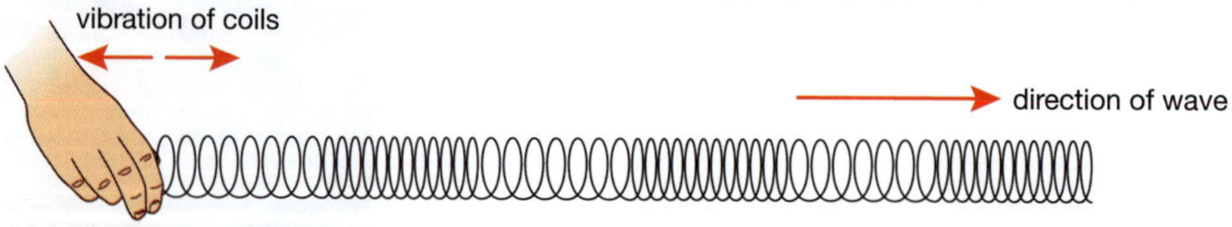

▲ Figure 7.5 A longitudinal wave vibrates along the direction in which the wave is travelling.

A longitudinal wave is one in which the vibrations, or oscillations, are along the direction in which the energy or wave is moving. Examples of longitudinal waves include sound waves.

DESCRIBING WAVES

When a wave moves through a substance, its particles will move from their equilibrium (resting position). The maximum movement of particles from their resting or equilibrium position is called its **amplitude** (A).

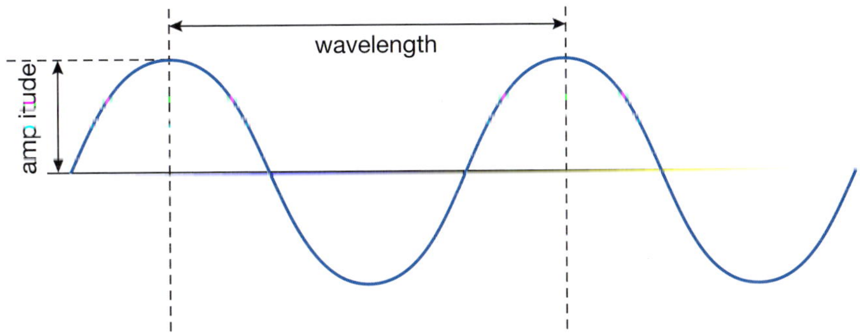

▲ Figure 7.6 A wave has amplitude and wavelength.

The distance between a particular point on a wave and the same point on the next wave (for example, from crest to crest) is called the **wavelength** (λ).

If the source that is creating a wave vibrates quickly it will produce a large number of waves each second. If it vibrates more slowly it will produce fewer waves each second. The number of waves produced each second by a source, or the number passing a particular point each second, is called the frequency of the wave (*f*). Frequency is measured in hertz (Hz). A wave source that produces five complete waves each second has a frequency of 5 Hz.

KEY POINT

λ is the Greek letter lambda and is the usual symbol for wavelength.

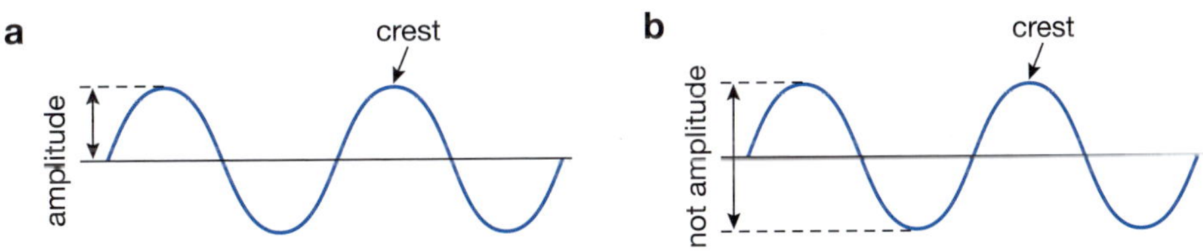

▲ Figure 7.7 The amplitude of a wave is as shown in **a**, and not as in **b**.

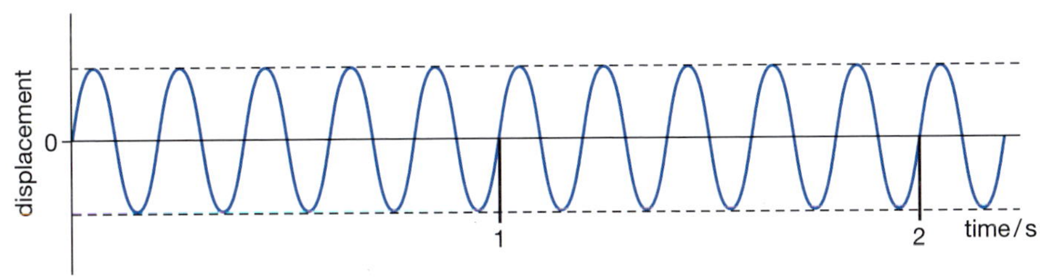

▲ Figure 7.8 This graph shows a wave with a frequency of 5 Hz.

The time it takes for a source to produce one wave is called the **time period** of the wave (*T*). It is related to the frequency (*f*) of a wave by the equation:

$$\text{frequency, } f\,(\text{Hz}) = \frac{1}{\text{time period, } T\,(\text{s})}$$

$$f = \frac{1}{T}$$

This equation can also be written as

$$T = \frac{1}{f}$$

EXAMPLE 1

Calculate the period of a wave with a frequency of 200 Hz.

$$T = \frac{1}{f}$$
$$= \frac{1}{200\text{ Hz}}$$
$$= 0.005 \text{ or } 5\text{ ms } (1000\text{ ms} = 1\text{ s})$$

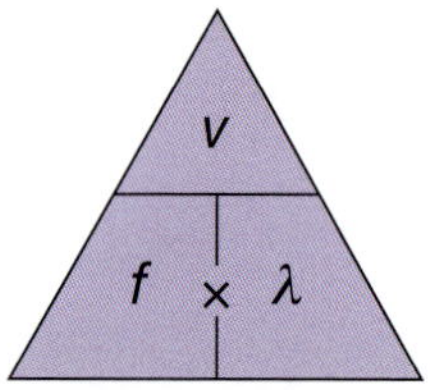

Figure 7.9 You can use the triangle method for rearranging equations like $v = f \times \lambda$.

HINT

If an examination question asks you to write out the equation for calculating wave speed, wavelength or frequency, always give the actual equation such as $v = f \times \lambda$. You may not be awarded a mark if you just draw the triangle.

THE WAVE EQUATION

There is a relationship between the wavelength (λ), the frequency (f) and the wave speed (v) that is true for all waves:

wave speed, v (m/s) = frequency, f (Hz) × wavelength, λ (m)

$$v = f \times \lambda$$

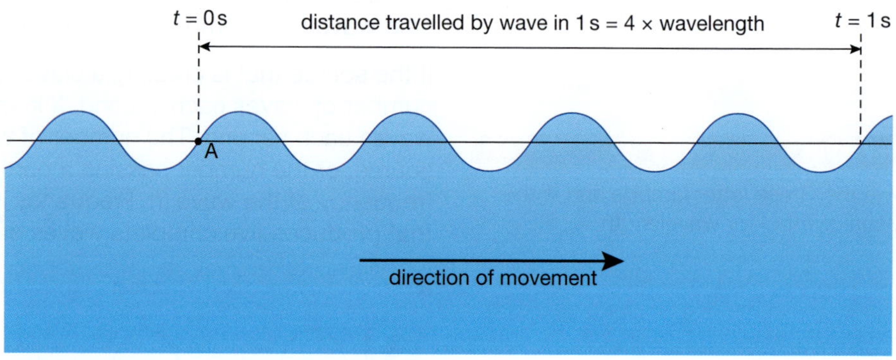

Figure 7.10 A wave with a frequency of 4 Hz

Imagine that you have created water waves with a frequency of 4 Hz. This means that four waves will pass a particular point each second. If the wavelength of the waves is 3 m, then the waves travel 12 m each second. The speed of the waves is therefore 12 m/s.

$$v = f \times \lambda$$
$$= 4\text{ Hz} \times 3\text{ m}$$
$$= 12\text{ m/s}$$

EXAMPLE 2

A **tuning fork** creates sound waves with a frequency of 170 Hz. If the speed of sound in air is 340 m/s, calculate the wavelength of the sound waves.

$$v = f \times \lambda$$

So $\lambda = \frac{v}{f}$

$$= \frac{340\text{ m/s}}{170\text{ Hz}}$$
$$= 2\text{ m}$$

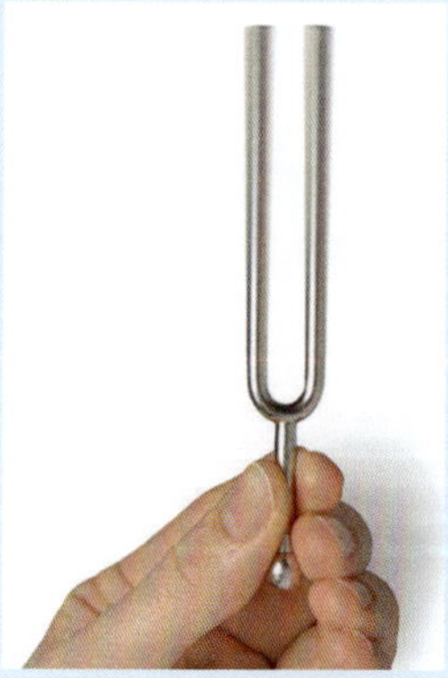

Figure 7.11 A tuning fork

THE RIPPLE TANK

We can study the behaviour of water waves using a ripple tank.

When the motor is turned on, the wooden bar vibrates creating a series of ripples or wavefronts on the surface of the water. A light placed above the tank creates patterns of the water waves on the floor. By observing the patterns we can see how the water waves are behaving.

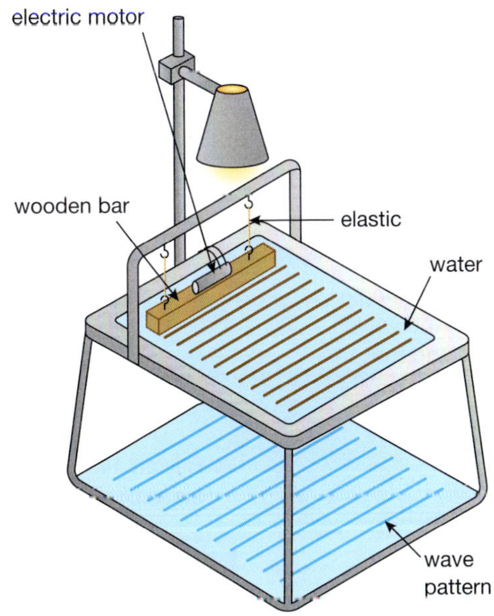

▲ Figure 7.12 The light shines through the water and we can see the patterns of the waves.

WAVELENGTH AND FREQUENCY

The motor can be adjusted to produce a small number of waves each second. The frequency of the waves is small and the pattern shows that the waves have a long wavelength.

At higher frequencies, the water waves have shorter wavelengths. The speed of the waves does not change.

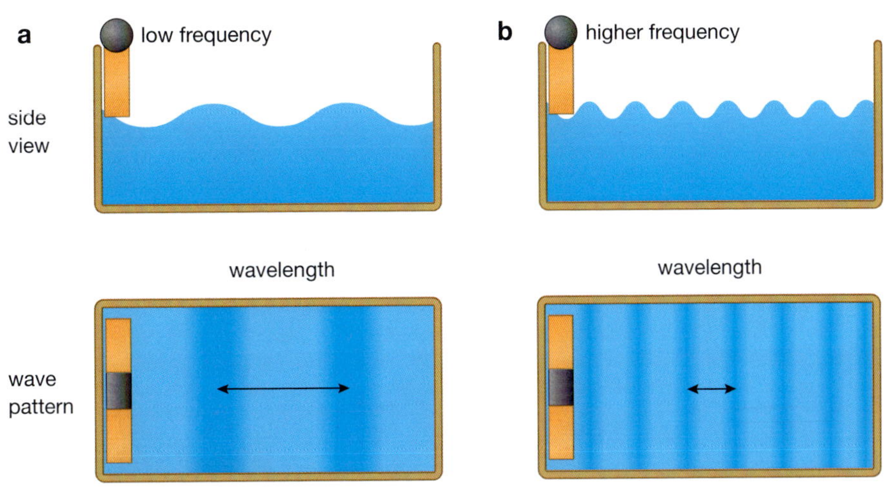

▲ Figure 7.13 When the frequency of the waves is low, the wavelength is long. When the frequency is higher, the wavelength is shorter.

REFLECTION

All waves can be reflected. If they hit a straight or flat barrier, the angle at which they leave the barrier surface is equal to the angle at which they meet the surface – that is, the waves are reflected from the barrier at the same angle as they strike it. This is described by the 'Law of Reflection' which states that:

The ***angle of incidence*** *is equal to the* ***angle of reflection****.*

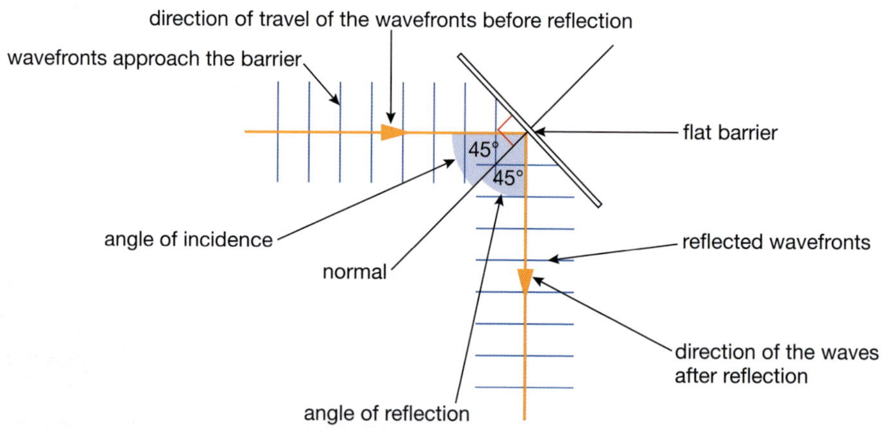

▲ Figure 7.14 Waves striking a flat barrier are reflected. The angle at which they strike the barrier is the same as the angle at which they are reflected.

KEY POINT

A normal is a line drawn at right angles to a surface.

The angle of incidence is the angle between the direction of the waves as they approach the barrier and the normal.

The angle of reflection is the angle between the direction of the waves after striking the barrier and the normal.

EXTENSION WORK

Although you will not be asked this in your exam, it is interesting to see how waves are reflected from curved surfaces.

When the waves strike a concave barrier, they are made to converge (come together).

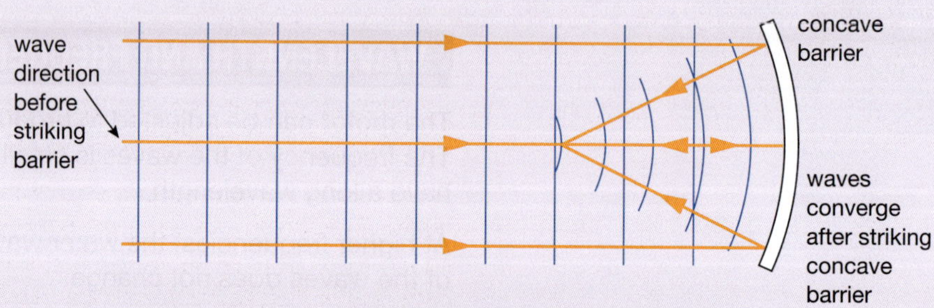

▲ Figure 7.15 Waves striking a concave barrier are reflected and converge.

▲ Figure 7.16 Radio telescopes have concave reflecting dishes so that the signals from space reflect and converge onto a detector that is placed in front of the dish.

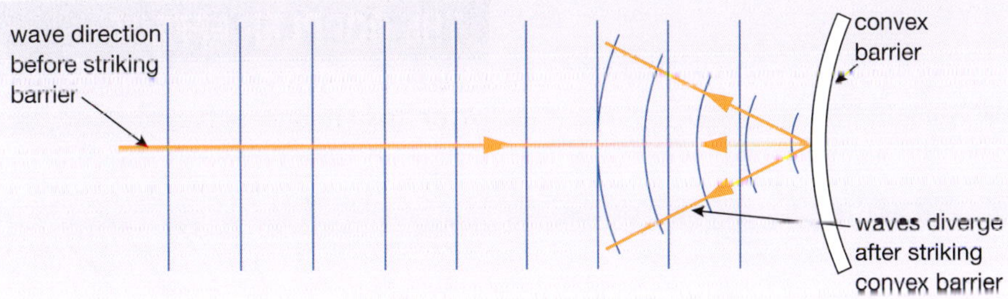

▲ Figure 7.17 Waves striking a convex barrier are reflected backwards and spread out.

When waves are reflected by a surface that is curved outwards (convex), they diverge (spread out).

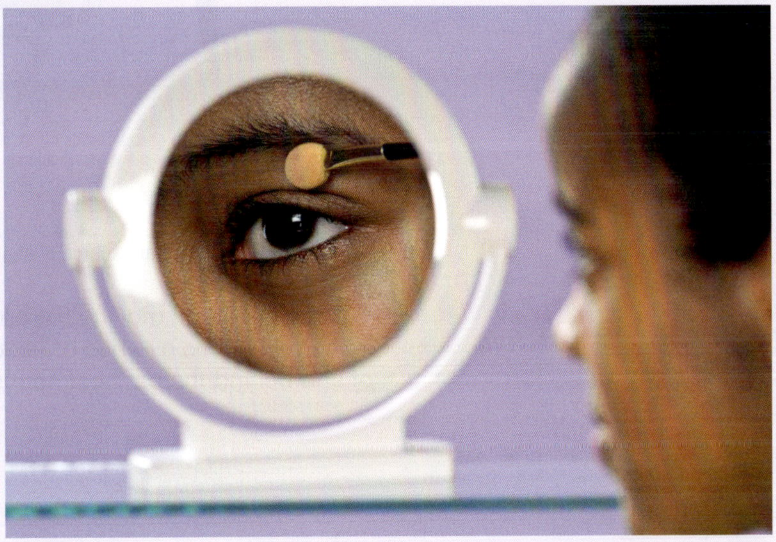

▲ Figure 7.18 The light waves reflected from this concave make-up mirror create a magnified image.

a

b

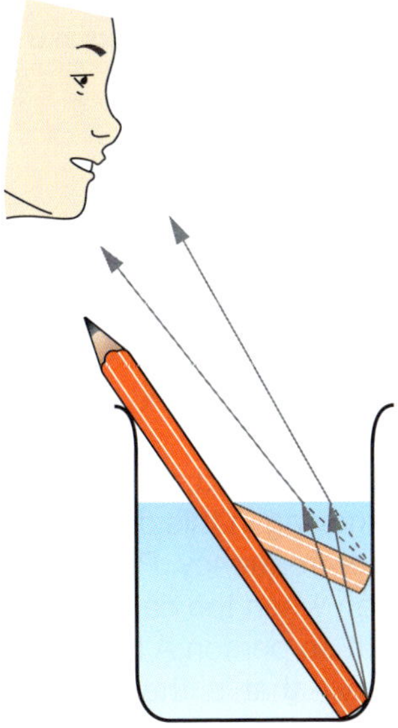

▲ Figure 7.19 **a** The pencil seems to bend at the air/water boundary. **b** Why the pencil appears to be bent. Rays of light are refracted at the water surface.

REFRACTION

The pencil in Figure 7.19 is straight but it seems to bend at the surface of the water. This happens because light waves in water travel more slowly than light waves in air. This change in speed as they leave the water causes the light waves to change direction. This change in direction is called refraction. All waves – light waves, sound waves, water waves – can be refracted.

EXTENSION WORK

Many optical instruments such as microscopes, telescopes and cameras use specially shaped pieces of glass or plastic (called lenses) to bend or refract light waves in a useful way.

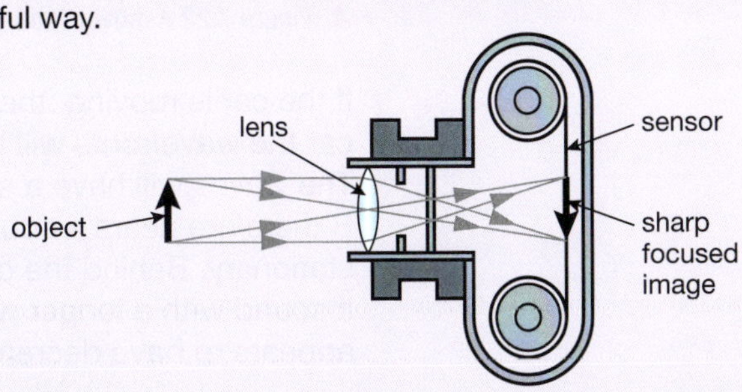

▲ Figure 7.20 In this camera, light waves are refracted by a glass lens to create a sharp image on the sensor or film. Refraction occurs because light travels more slowly in glass than in air.

THE DOPPLER EFFECT

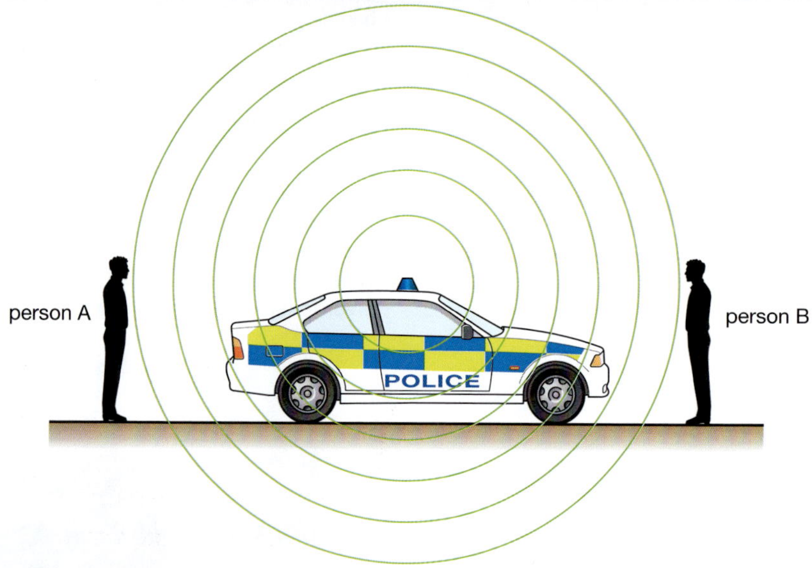

▲ Figure 7.21 A stationary source of sound

When a car is not moving the sound waves we receive from its engine or from its horn arrive as a series of equally (evenly) spaced wavefronts. People in front of and behind the car hear sound of the same frequency and wavelength.

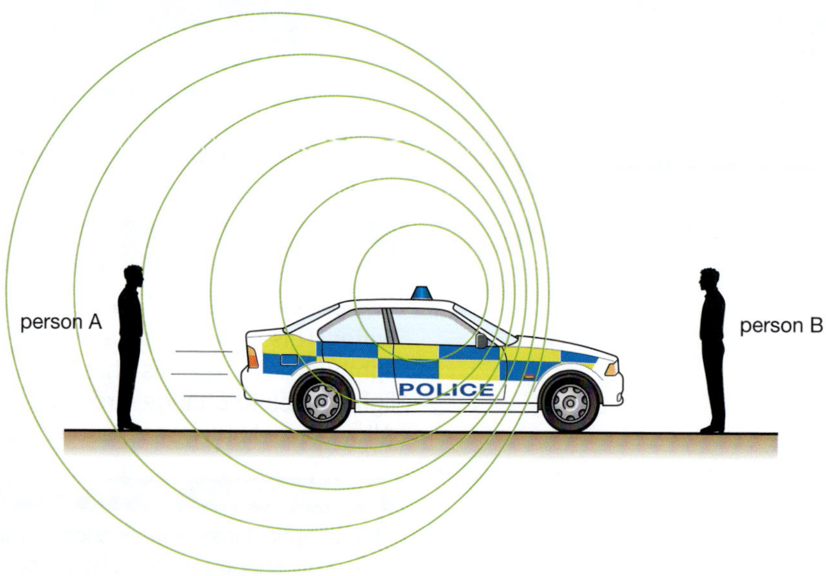

▲ Figure 7.22 A moving source of sound

If the car is moving, the wavefronts are no longer evenly spaced. Ahead of the car the wavefronts will be compressed as the car is moving in this direction. The waves will have a shorter wavelength and a higher frequency. Person B therefore hears a sound that has a higher **pitch** than when the car was stationary. Behind the car the waves are stretched out so person A hears a sound with a longer wavelength and lower frequency – that is, the pitch appears to have decreased.

These apparent changes in frequency, which occur when a source of waves is moving, is called the **Doppler effect** and is a property of all waves.

CHAPTER QUESTIONS

More questions on wave properties can be found at the end of Unit 3 on page 588.

SKILLS CRITICAL THINKING

1 a Explain the difference between a transverse wave and a longitudinal wave.

b Give one example of each.

SKILLS INTERPRETATION

c Draw a diagram of a transverse wave. On your diagram, mark the wavelength and amplitude of the wave.

SKILLS ANALYSIS, PROBLEM SOLVING

2 The diagram below shows the displacement of water as a wave travels through it.

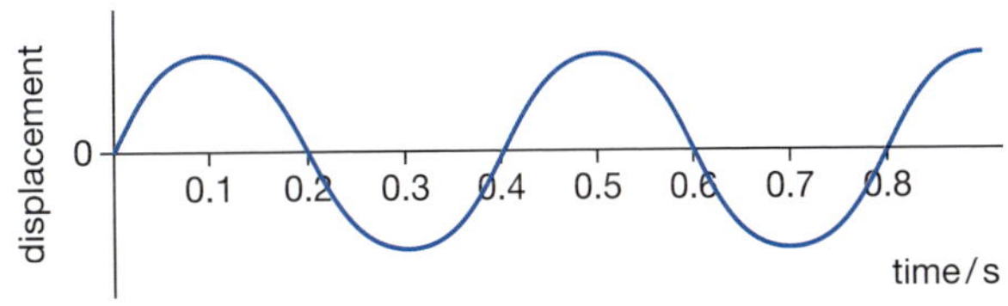

From the diagram calculate:

a the period of the wave

b the frequency of the wave.

SKILLS PROBLEM SOLVING

3 The speed of sound in water is approximately 1500 m/s.

a What is the frequency of a sound wave with a wavelength of 1.5 m?

b What is the period of this wave?

SKILLS CRITICAL THINKING

4 a Explain why the sound produced by the horn of an approaching car seems to have a higher frequency than one that is stationary.

SKILLS REASONING

b If the same car approached at a much higher speed how would this affect the frequency of the sound heard?

c Describe the frequency of the sound heard by the observer if the car is moving away at high speed.

5 Explain why this hunter should not aim at the fish he can see.

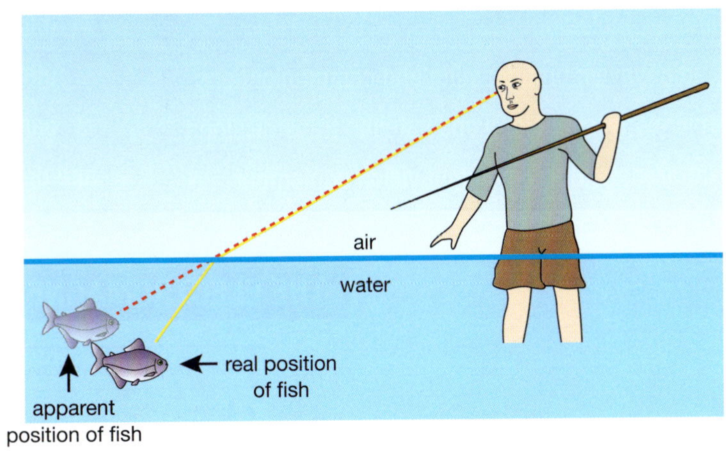

8 THE ELECTROMAGNETIC SPECTRUM

The electromagnetic spectrum is a family of waves, varying in wavelength and frequency. Although it is continuous, it is helpful to consider smaller groups of waves within the spectrum. These groups have distinct properties.
As we will see in this chapter, understanding the different properties allows us to use these waves in many situations including cooking and communication.

▶ Figure 8.1 When we shine white light through a prism it splits up forming a band of colours. This band is one small part of the electromagnetic spectrum.

LEARNING OBJECTIVES

- Know that light is part of a continuous electromagnetic spectrum that includes radio, microwave, infrared, visible, ultraviolet, x-ray and gamma ray radiations and that all these waves travel at the same speed in free space
- Know the order of the electromagnetic spectrum in terms of decreasing wavelength and increasing frequency, including the colours of the visible spectrum
- Explain some of the uses of electromagnetic radiations, including:
    - radio waves: broadcasting and communications
    - microwaves: cooking and satellite transmissions
    - infrared: heaters and night vision equipment
    - visible light: optical fibres and photography
    - ultraviolet: fluorescent lamps
    - x-rays: observing the internal structure of objects and materials, including for medical applications
    - gamma rays: sterilising food and medical equipment
- Explain the detrimental effects of excessive exposure of the human body to electromagnetic waves, including:
    - microwaves: internal heating of body tissue
    - infrared: skin burns
    - ultraviolet: damage to surface cells and blindness
    - gamma rays: cancer, mutation

  and describe simple protective measures against the risks

THE ELECTROMAGNETIC SPECTRUM

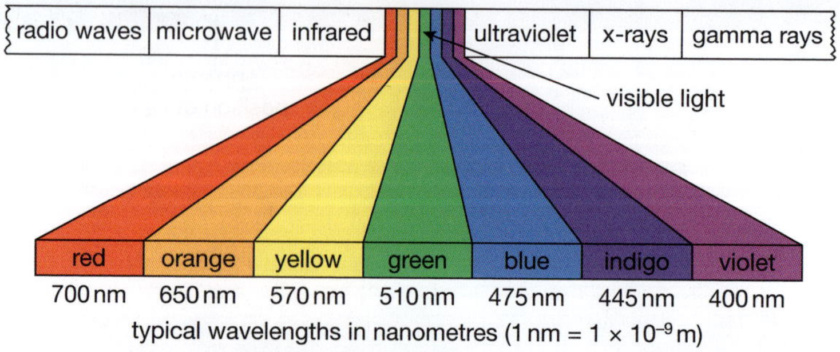

▲ Figure 8.2 The complete electromagnetic spectrum

The **electromagnetic spectrum** (EM spectrum) is a continuous spectrum of waves, which includes the visible spectrum. At one end of the spectrum the waves have a very long wavelength and low frequency, while at the other end the waves have a very short wavelength and high frequency. All the waves have the following properties:

1 They all transfer energy.
2 They are all transverse waves.
3 They all travel at 300 000 000 m/s, the speed of light in a **vacuum** (free space).
4 They can all be reflected and refracted.

Remember that the wave equations we met in the previous chapter can be applied to any member of the electromagnetic spectrum.

EXAMPLE 1

Yellow light has a wavelength of 5.7×10^{-7} m. What is the frequency and period of yellow light waves?

$$v = f \times \lambda$$

$$\text{So } f = \frac{v}{\lambda}$$

$$= \frac{3 \times 10^{8}\ \text{m/s}}{5.7 \times 10^{-7}\ \text{m}}$$

$$= 5.26 \times 10^{14}\ \text{Hz}$$

$$T = \frac{1}{f}$$

$$= \frac{1}{5.26 \times 10^{14}\ \text{Hz}}$$

$$= 1.9 \times 10^{-15}\ \text{s}$$

The table below shows the different groups of waves in order, and gives some of their uses.

	Typical frequency / Hz	Typical wavelength / m	Sources	Detectors	Uses
Radio waves	10^{5}–10^{10}	10^{3}–10^{-2}	radio transmitters, TV transmitters	radio and TV aerials	long-, medium- and short-wave radio, TV (UHF)
Microwaves	10^{10}–10^{11}	10^{-2}–10^{-3}	microwave transmitters and ovens	microwave receivers	mobile phone and satellite communication, cooking
Infrared (IR)	10^{11}–10^{14}	10^{-3}–10^{-6}	hot objects	skin, blackened thermometer, special photographic film	infrared cookers and heaters, TV and stereo remote controls, night vision
Visible light	10^{14}–10^{15}	10^{-6}–10^{-7}	luminous objects	the eye, photographic film, light-dependent resistors	seeing, communication (optical fibres), photography
Ultraviolet (UV)	10^{15}–10^{16}	10^{-7}–10^{-8}	UV lamps and the Sun	skin, photographic film and some fluorescent chemicals	fluorescent tubes and UV tanning lamps
X-rays	10^{16}–10^{18}	10^{-8}–10^{-10}	x-ray tubes	photographic film	x-radiography to observe the internal structure of objects, including human bodies
Gamma rays	10^{18}–10^{21}	10^{-10}–10^{-14}	radioactive materials	Geiger–Müller tube	sterilising equipment and food, radiotherapy

HINT

To remember the order of the waves in the electromagnetic spectrum try using 'Graham's Xylophone Uses Very Interesting Musical Rhythms'.

You do not need to remember the values of frequency and wavelength given in the table but you do need to know the order of the groups and which has the highest frequency or longest wavelengths. Most importantly, you need to realise that it is these differences in wavelength and frequency that give the groups their different properties – for example, gamma rays have the shortest wavelengths and highest frequencies, and carry the most energy.

RADIO WAVES

Radio waves have the longest wavelengths in the electromagnetic spectrum. They are used mainly for communication.

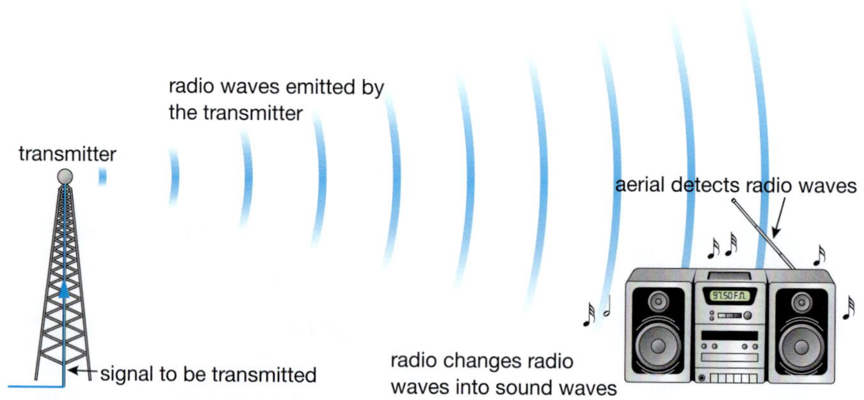

▲ Figure 8.3 Radio waves are emitted by a transmitter and detected by an aerial.

Radio waves are given out (**emitted**) by a transmitter. As they arrive at an aerial, they are detected and the information they carry can be received. Televisions and FM radios use radio waves with the shorter wavelengths to carry their signals.

MICROWAVES

Microwaves are used for communications, radar and cooking foods. Radar uses radio waves to find the position of things.

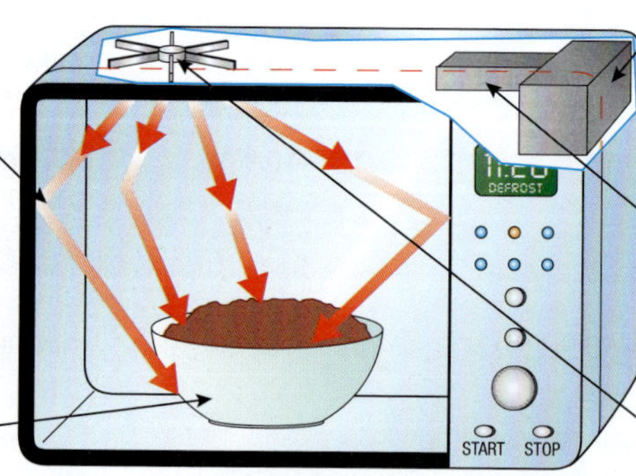

▲ Figure 8.4 Food cooks quickly in a microwave oven because water molecules in the food absorb the microwaves.

Food placed in a microwave oven cooks more quickly than in a normal oven. This is because water **molecules** in the food absorb the microwaves and become very hot. The food therefore cooks throughout rather than just from the outside.

Microwave ovens have metal screens that reflect microwaves and keep them inside the oven. This is necessary because if microwaves can cook food, they can also heat human body tissue! The microwaves used by mobile phones transmit much less energy than those used in a microwave oven, so they do not cook your brain when you use the phone.

Microwaves are used in communications. The waves pass easily through the Earth's atmosphere and so are used to carry signals to orbiting satellites. From here, the signals are passed on to their destination or to other orbiting satellites. Messages sent to and from mobile phones are also carried by microwaves. The fact that we are able to use mobile phones almost anywhere in the home and at work confirms that microwaves can pass through glass, brick and so on.

INFRARED

All objects, including your body, emit infrared (IR) radiation. The hotter an object is, the more energy it will emit as infrared. Energy is transferred by infrared radiation to bread in a toaster or food under a grill. Electric fires also transfer heat energy by infrared.

Special cameras designed to detect infrared waves can be used to create images even when there is no visible light. These cameras have many uses, including searching for people trapped in collapsed buildings, searching for criminals and checking for heat loss from buildings.

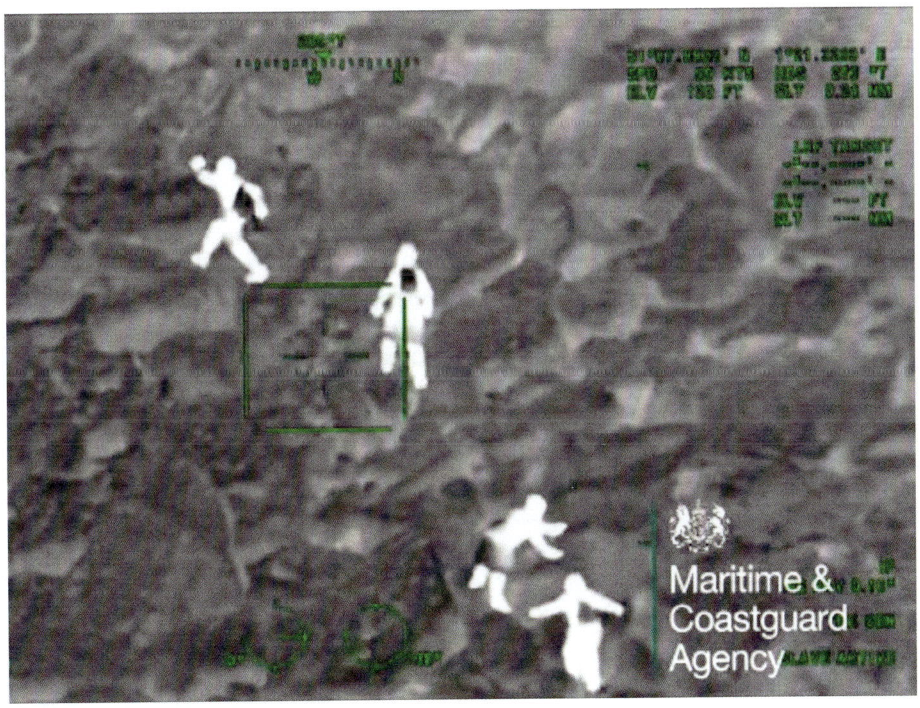

▲ Figure 8.5 It is not possible to see these people trapped at the bottom of a cliff using normal visible light. By using infrared detectors they can be found easily and rescued.

▲ Figure 8.6 Signals are carried from this remote control to a TV by infrared waves.

Infrared radiation is also used in remote controls for televisions, DVD players and stereo systems. It is very convenient for this purpose because the waves are not harmful. They have a low **penetrating power** and will therefore operate only over small distances, so they are unlikely to interfere with other signals or waves.

The human body can be harmed by too much infrared radiation, which can cause skin burns.

VISIBLE LIGHT

▲ Figure 8.7 Using visible light

> **EXTENSION WORK**
>
> When talking about light and colour, we often refer to the seven colours in the visible spectrum. These colours are red, orange, yellow, green, blue, indigo and violet; red light has the longest wavelength and lowest frequency. If you look back at Figure 8.1, you may only be able to make out six colours – most people have difficulty separating indigo and violet (two types of purple). Sir Isaac Newton (1642–1727) discovered that 'white' light can be split up into different colours. He believed that the number seven had magical significance, and so he decided there were seven colours in the spectrum!

This is the part of the electromagnetic spectrum that is visible to the human eye. We use it to see. Visible light from lasers is used to read compact discs and barcodes. It can also be sent along optical fibres, so it can be used for communication or for looking into hard-to-reach places such as inside the body of a patient (see page 583). Visible light can be detected by the sensors in digital cameras, and used to take still photographs or videos. Information stored on DVDs is also read using visible light.

ULTRAVIOLET LIGHT

▲ Figure 8.8 UV light can cause sunburn so we need to protect our skin.

Part of the light emitted by the Sun is ultraviolet (UV) light. UV radiation is harmful to human eyes and can damage the skin.

UV light causes the skin to tan, but overexposure (too much) will lead to sunburn and blistering. Ultraviolet radiation can also cause skin cancer and blindness. Protective goggles or glasses and skin creams can block the UV rays and will reduce the harmful effects of this radiation.

The **ozone layer** in the Earth's atmosphere absorbs large quantities of the Sun's UV radiation. In recent years there was real concern that the amount of ozone in the atmosphere was decreasing due to pollution, which would increase numbers of skin cancer. However, there is now evidence to show that the ozone layer is recovering.

Some chemicals glow (shine), or fluoresce, when under UV light. This property of UV light is used in security marker pens. The special ink is invisible in normal light but becomes visible in UV light.

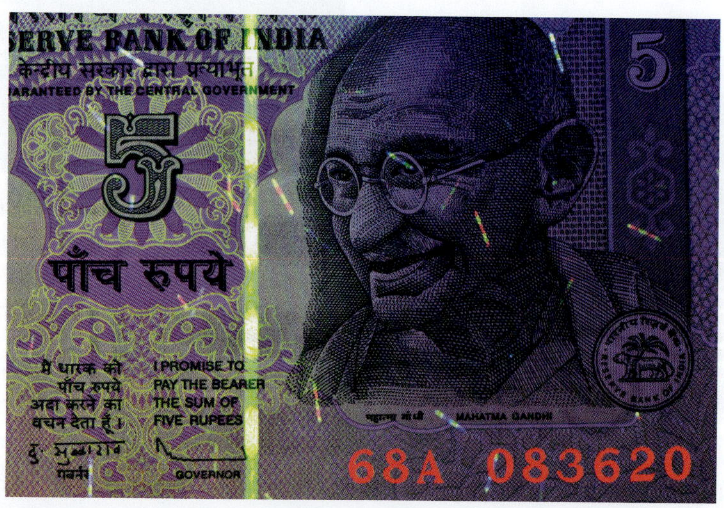

▲ Figure 8.9 This red code is only visible under UV light.

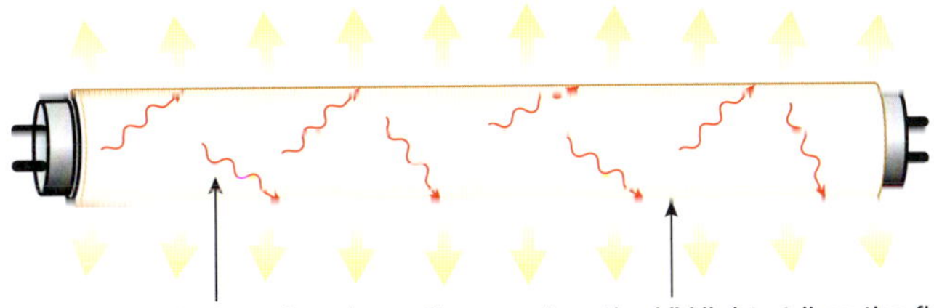

▲ Figure 8.10 Fluorescent tubes glow when UV light hits the fluorescent coating in the tube.

Fluorescent tubes glow (shine) because the UV light they produce strikes a special coating (covering) on the inside of the tube, which then emits visible light.

X-RAYS

X-rays pass easily through soft body tissue but cannot pass through bones. As a result, radiographs or x-ray pictures can be taken to check a patient's bones.

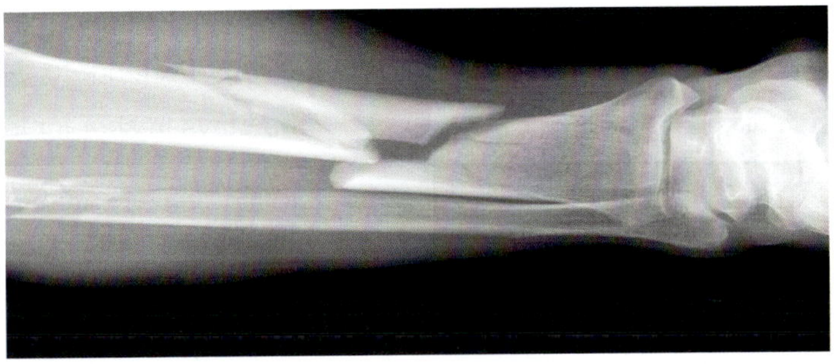

▲ Figure 8.11 X-ray of a broken leg

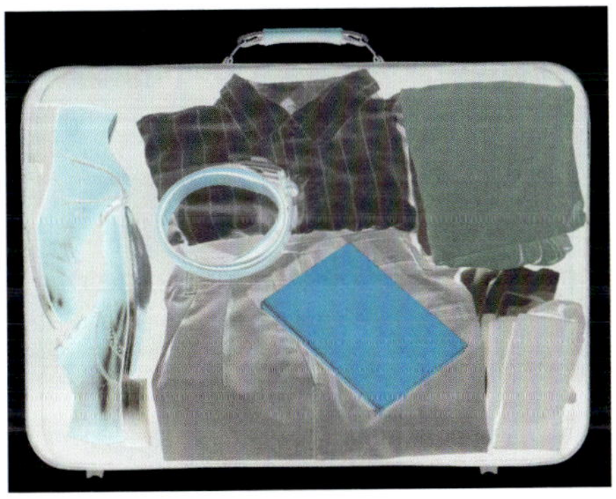

▲ Figure 8.12 X-rays were used to see what was in this suitcase.

Working with x-rays can cause cancer. Radiographers, who take x-rays, are at risk and have to stand behind lead screens or wear protective clothing.

X-rays are also used in industry to check the internal structures of objects – for example, to look for cracks and faults in buildings or machinery – and at airports as part of the security checking procedure.

GAMMA RAYS

Gamma rays, like x-rays, are highly penetrating rays and can cause damage to living cells. The damage can cause mutations (negative changes), which can lead to cancer. They are used to **sterilise** medical instruments, to kill microorganisms so that food will keep for longer and to treat cancer using radiotherapy. Gamma rays can both cause and cure cancer. Large doses of gamma rays targeted directly at the cancerous growth can be used to kill the cancer cells completely.

Like x-rays the use of lead screens, boxes and aprons can prevent the damage caused by gamma rays (overexposure).

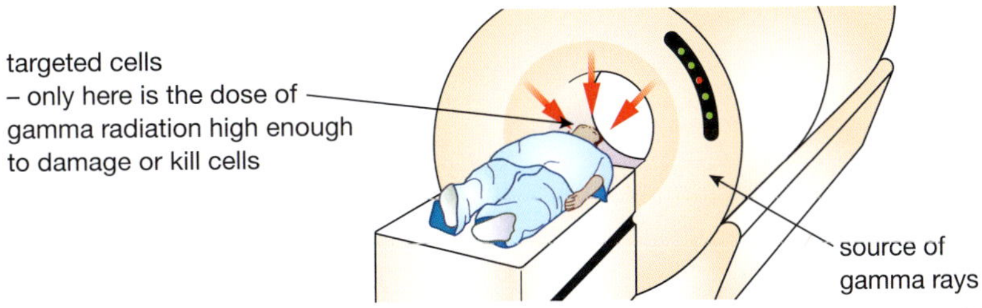

▲ Figure 8.13 The gamma rays are aimed carefully so that they cross at the exact location of the cancerous cells.

CHAPTER QUESTIONS

More questions on using waves can be found at the end of Unit 3 on page 588.

SKILLS CRITICAL THINKING 5th

1 a Name four wave properties that are common to all members of the electromagnetic spectrum.

b Name three types of wave that can be used for communicating.

c Name two types of wave that can be used for cooking.

d Name one type of wave that is used to treat cancer.

e Name one type of wave that might be used to 'see' people in the dark.

f Name one type of wave that is used for radar.

SKILLS REASONING 7th

2 Explain why:

a microwave ovens cook food much more quickly than normal ovens

b x-rays are used to check for broken bones

c it is important not to damage the ozone layer around the Earth

d food stays fresher for longer after it has been exposed to gamma radiation.

3 a Explain one way in which you could prevent overexposure (damage) by the following waves:

i x-rays

ii ultraviolet waves.

SKILLS CRITICAL THINKING

b Select one of the above waves and then describe one consequence of overexposure.

SKILLS INTERPRETATION 6th

4 Copy and complete the table below for four more different wave groups within the electromagnetic spectrum.

Type of radiation	Possible harm	Precautions
x-rays	cancer	lead screening

9 LIGHT AND SOUND WAVES

We see objects because they emit or reflect light. In this chapter you will learn how light behaves when it reflects from different surfaces, and what happens when light travels from one transparent material to another. Sound waves are longitudinal waves and not transverse waves like light. Nevertheless they can be reflected and refracted in just the same way. In this chapter you will learn about the nature and behaviour of sound waves, and how we make use of them in our everyday lives.

▲ Figure 9.1 In the Hall of Mirrors at the fairground the reflection of light can be very confusing!

LEARNING OBJECTIVES

- Know that light waves are transverse waves and that they can be reflected and refracted
- Use the law of reflection (the angle of incidence equals the angle of reflection)
- Draw ray diagrams to illustrate reflection and refraction
- Practical: investigate the refraction of light, using rectangular blocks, semi-circular blocks and triangular prisms
- Know and use the relationship between refractive index, angle of incidence and angle of refraction:

  $$n = \frac{\sin i}{\sin r}$$

- Practical: investigate the refractive index of glass, using a glass block
- Describe the role of total internal reflection in transmitting information along optical fibres and in prisms
- Explain the meaning of critical angle c
- Know and use the relationship between critical angle and refractive index:

  $$\sin c = \frac{1}{n}$$

- Know that sound waves are longitudinal waves that can be reflected and refracted

SEEING THE LIGHT

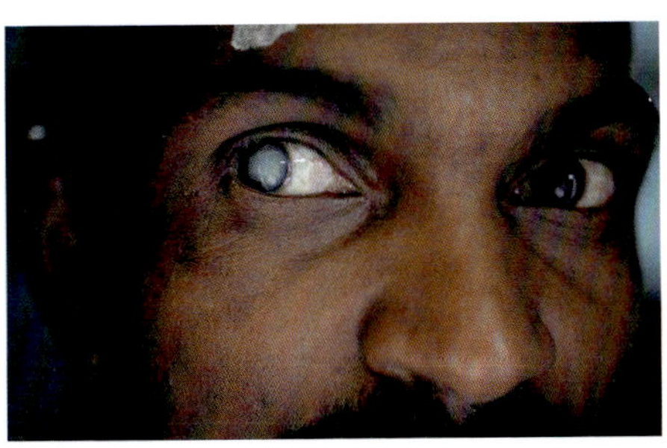

▲ Figure 9.2 Cataracts mean that light cannot enter the eye correctly.

The patient shown in Figure 9.2 has a cataract. The front of one of his eyes has become so cloudy that he is unable to see. Nowadays it is possible to remove this damaged part of the eye and replace it with a clear plastic that will allow light to enter the eye again.

There are many sources of light, including the Sun, the stars, fires, light bulbs and so on. Objects such as these that emit their own light are called luminous objects. When the emitted light enters our eyes we see the object. Most objects, however, are non-luminous. They do not emit light. We see these non-luminous objects because of the light they reflect.

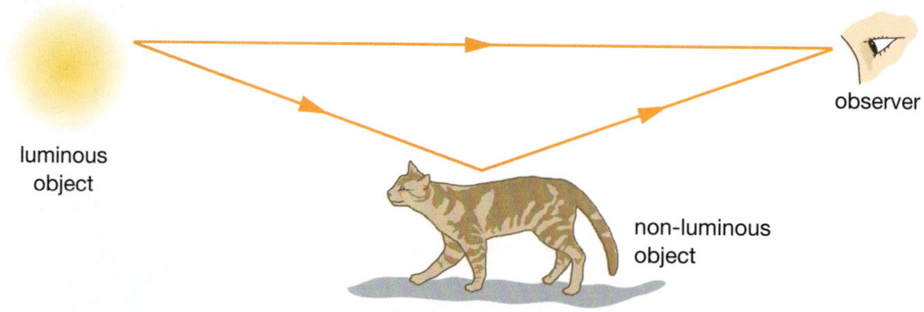

▲ Figure 9.3 Luminous objects, such as the Sun, give out light. Non-luminous objects only reflect light.

REFLECTION

When a ray of light strikes a plane (flat) mirror, it is reflected so that the angle of incidence (*i*) is equal to the angle of reflection (*r*).

KEY POINT

The angle of incidence is the angle between the incident ray and the normal.

The angle of reflection is the angle between the reflected ray and the normal.

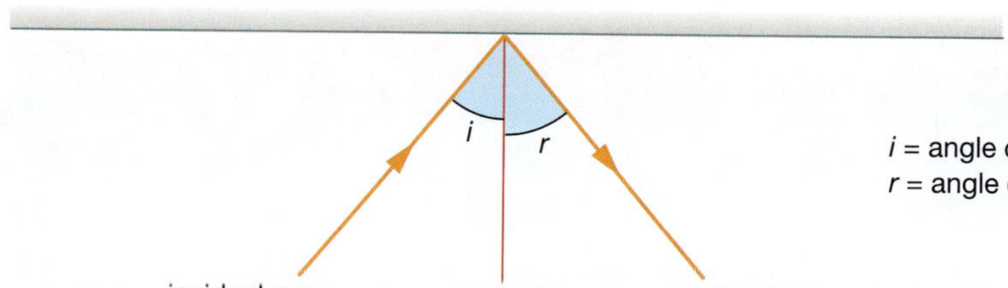

▲ Figure 9.4 Light is reflected from a plane mirror. The angle of incidence is equal to the angle of reflection. The normal is a line at right angles to the mirror.

Mirrors are often used to change the direction of a ray of light. One example of this is the simple periscope, which uses two mirrors to change the direction of rays of light.

Rays from the object strike the first mirror at an angle of 45° to the normal. The rays are reflected at 45° to the normal and so are turned through an angle of 90° by the mirror. At the second mirror the rays are again turned through 90°. Changing the direction of rays of light in this way allows an observer to use a periscope to see over or around objects.

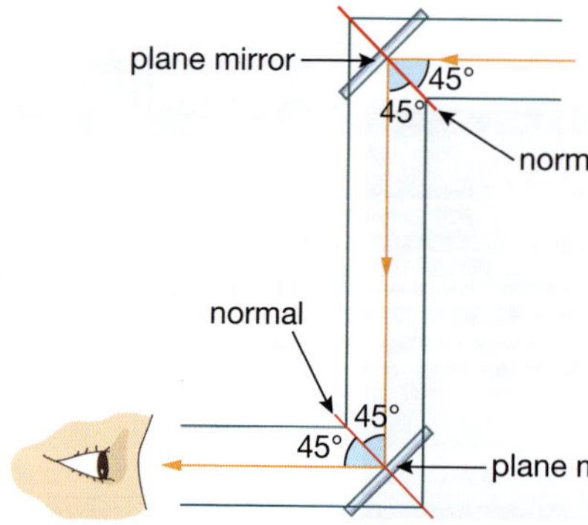

▲ Figure 9.5 A periscope is used to see over or around objects.

REFRACTION

▲ Figure 9.6 This rainbow is caused by refraction.

KEY POINT

A medium is a material, such as glass or water, through which light can travel. The plural of medium is media.

KEY POINT

Light does travel more slowly in air than in a vacuum but the difference is tiny.

Rays of light can travel through many different transparent media, including air, water and glass. Light can also travel through a vacuum. In a vacuum and in air, light travels at a speed of 300 000 000 m/s. In other media it travels more slowly. For example, the speed of light in glass is approximately 200 000 000 m/s. When a ray of light travels from air into glass or water it slows down as it crosses the border between the two media. This change in speed may cause the ray to change direction. This change in direction of a ray is called refraction.

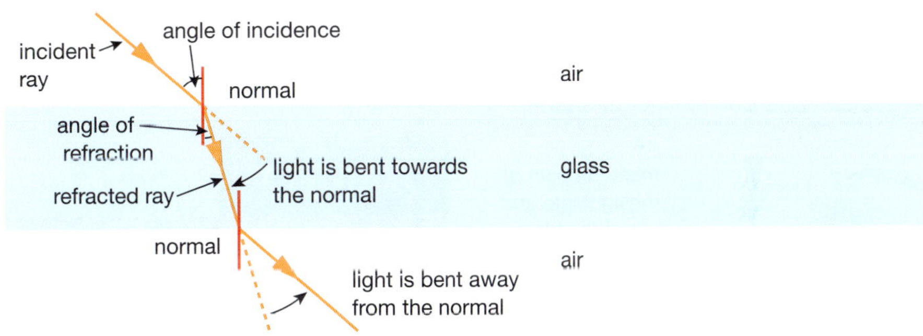

▲ Figure 9.7 This light ray is being refracted twice – once as it travels from air into glass and then as it travels from glass to air.

As a ray enters a glass block, it slows down and is refracted towards the normal. As the ray leaves the block it speeds up and is refracted away from the normal.

If the ray strikes the boundary between the two media at 90°, the ray continues without change of direction (Figure 9.8).

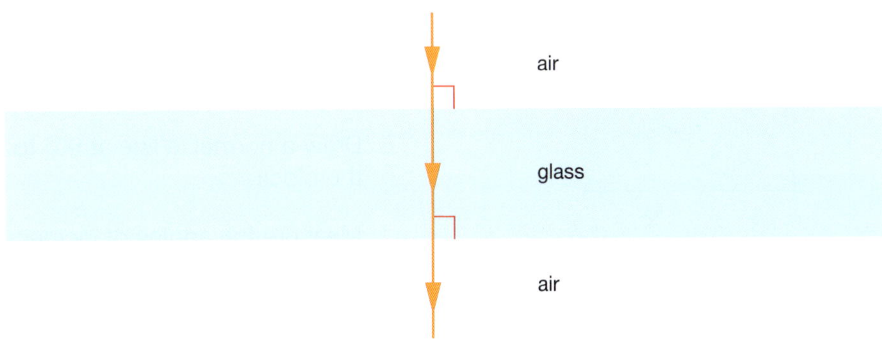

▲ Figure 9.8 If the light hits the boundary at 90° the ray does not bend.

REFRACTIVE INDEX

Different materials can bend rays of light by different amounts. We describe this by using a number called the **refractive index** (n). The refractive index of glass is about 1.5 and water is 1.3. This tells us that under similar circumstances glass will refract light more than water.

We can use the equation below to calculate the refractive index of a material:

$$n = \frac{\sin i}{\sin r}$$

where i is the angle of incidence and r is the **angle of refraction**.

EXAMPLE 1

In an experiment similar to the one shown in Figure 9.9, the angle of incidence was measured as 30° and the angle of refraction as 19°. Calculate the refractive index of the glass block.

$$n = \frac{\sin i}{\sin r}$$

$$= \frac{\sin 30}{\sin 19}$$

$$= \frac{0.5}{0.33}$$

$$= 1.52$$

Safety note: Ray box lamps get hot enough to burn skin and char paper. Glass blocks and prisms should be handled carefully and not knocked together – they can splinter or shatter.

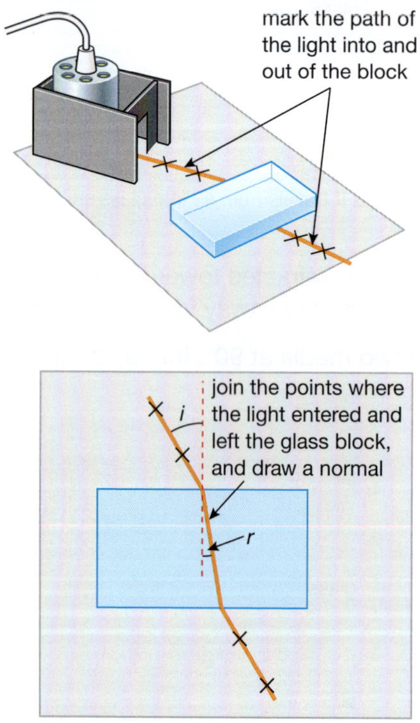

▲ Figure 9.9 How to investigate refraction using a rectangular glass block

ACTIVITY 1

▼ PRACTICAL: INVESTIGATE THE REFRACTIVE INDEX FOR GLASS

You can investigate the refractive index of glass using a ray box and a rectangular glass block.

1 Shine a ray of light onto one of the sides of the glass block, so that the ray emerges on the opposite side of the block. Mark the directions of both of these rays with crosses.

2 Draw around the glass block before removing it.

3 Using the crosses, draw in the direction of both rays.

4 Draw in the direction of the ray that travelled inside the glass block.

5 Draw a normal (a line at 90° to the glass surface) where the ray enters the block.

6 Measure the angles of incidence (i) and refraction (r) (see Figure 9.9).

7 Use the equation $n = \frac{\sin i}{\sin r}$ to find the refractive index of the glass block.

TOTAL INTERNAL REFLECTION

When a ray of light with a small angle of incidence passes from glass into air, most of the light is refracted away from the normal but if we look carefully we can see that there is a small amount that is reflected from the boundary. Total internal reflection only occurs when rays of light are travelling towards a boundary with a less optically dense medium (a medium with a lower refractive index).

KEY POINT

The symbol '*r*' is used for both the angle of reflection and the angle of refraction.

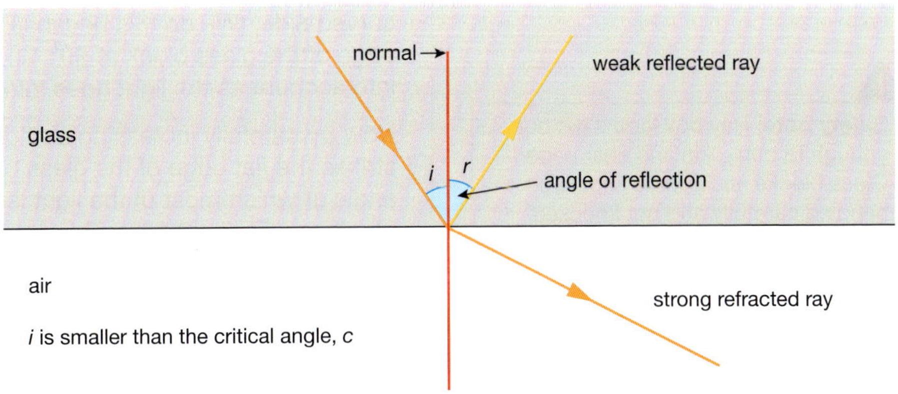

▲ Figure 9.10 A ray of light travelling from glass to air

But as the angle of incidence in the glass increases, the angle of refraction also increases until it reaches a special angle called the critical angle (*c*). The angle of refraction now is 90°.

The critical angle is the smallest possible angle of incidence at which light rays are totally internally reflected.

a

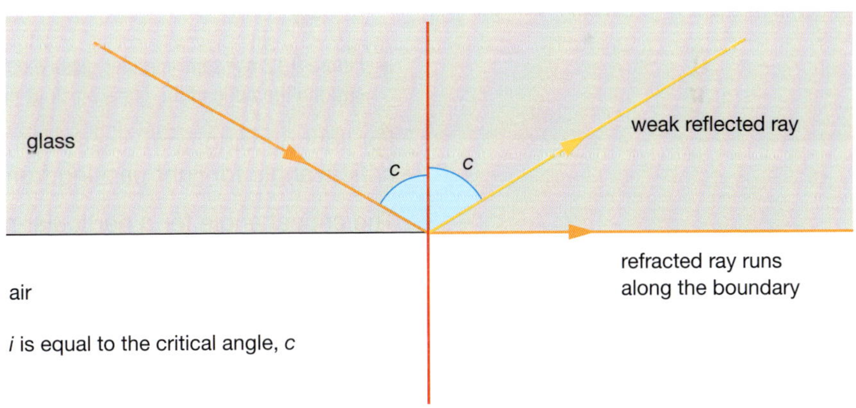

▲ Figure 9.11a Ray of light strikes glass/air boundary at the critical angle

b

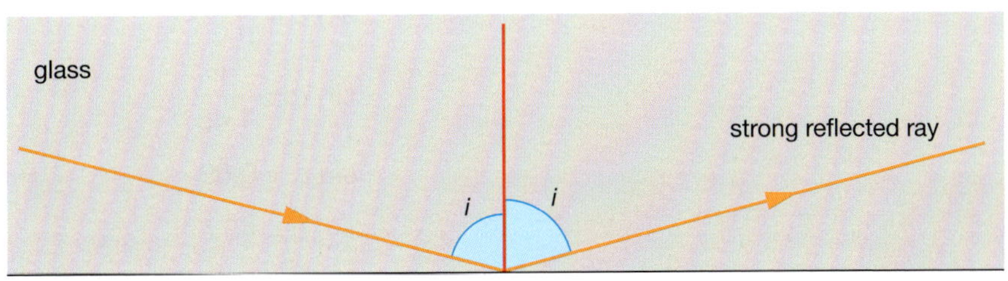

▲ Figure 9.11b When *i* is greater than *c* total internal reflection occurs.

When *i* is greater than the critical angle, all the light is reflected at the boundary. No light is refracted. The light is totally internally reflected.

Safety note: Ray box lamps get hot enough to burn skin and char paper. Glass blocks and prisms should be handled carefully and not knocked together – they can splinter or shatter.

ACTIVITY 2

▼ PRACTICAL: INVESTIGATE TOTAL INTERNAL REFLECTION

You can investigate total internal reflection in the laboratory using a semi-circular glass block and a ray box. As shown in Figure 9.12a, a ray of light is directed at the centre of the straight side of the block through the curved side. (We do this because the incident ray will then always hit the edge of the glass block at 90°, so there are no refraction effects to take into account as the light goes into the block.)

Now by carefully increasing and decreasing the angle at which the ray strikes the flat edge of the glass block, we can discover the smallest angle at which most of the light is refracted along the edge of the glass block (see Figure 9.12b). This angle is the critical angle.

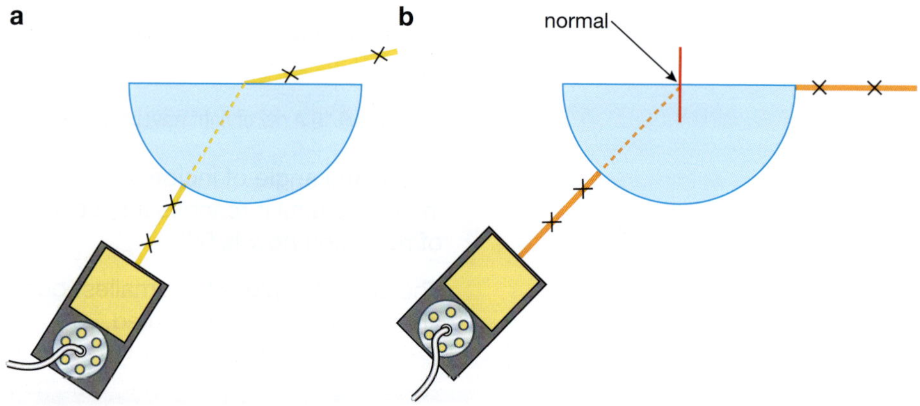

▲ Figure 9.12 **a** A semi-circular glass block used to demonstrate total internal reflection **b** Light striking the edge of the glass block at the critical angle

For light passing from glass to air, the critical angle is typically 42° and the critical angle for light passing from water to air is 49°.

The critical angle for a particular medium is related to its refractive index by this equation:

$$\sin c = \frac{1}{n}$$

EXAMPLE 2

The refractive index for a type of glass is 1.45. Calculate the critical angle.

$$\sin c = \frac{1}{n}$$

$$\sin c = \frac{1}{1.45}$$

$$\sin c = 0.69$$

$$c = 43.6°$$

We sometimes use **prisms** rather than mirrors to reflect light. The light is totally internally reflected by the prism.

Safety note: Ray box lamps get hot enough to burn skin and char paper. Glass blocks and prisms should be handled carefully and not knocked together – they can splinter or shatter.

ACTIVITY 3

▼ PRACTICAL: INVESTIGATE TOTAL INTERNAL REFLECTION IN PRISMS

If you shine a ray of light into a prism as shown in Figure 9.13 it will strike the far surface at an angle of 45°. The critical angle for glass is about 42° so the ray will be totally internally reflected. You will see therefore that the ray will be reflected through an angle of 90°.

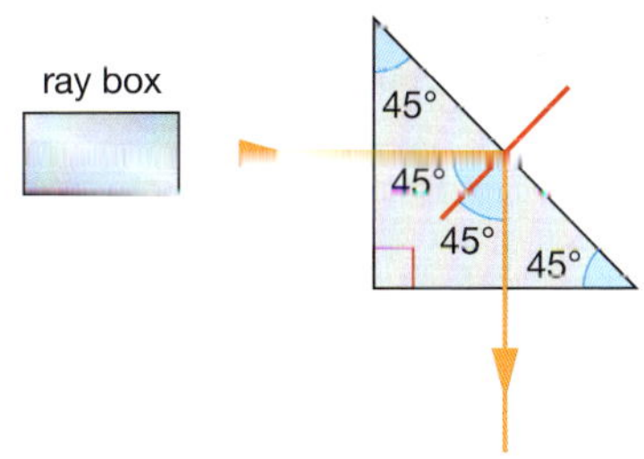

▲ Figure 9.13 Turning through 90° using total internal reflection

If you shine a ray into the prism as shown in Figure 9.14 the ray will be reflected through an angle of 180° – that is, it will go back in the direction from which it came.

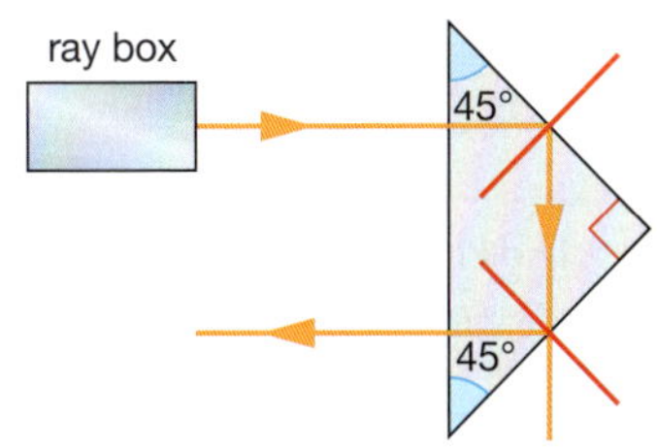

▲ Figure 9.14 Turning through 180° using total internal reflection

USING TOTAL INTERNAL REFLECTION

THE PRISMATIC PERISCOPE

The images produced by prisms are often brighter and clearer than those produced by mirrors. A periscope that uses prisms to reflect the light is called a prismatic periscope. Light passes through the surface AB of the first prism at 90° and so does not change direction (it is undeviated). It then strikes the surface AC of the prism at an angle of 45°. The critical angle for glass is 42° so the ray is totally internally reflected and is turned through 90°. When it leaves the first prism the light travels to a second prism. The second prism is positioned so that the ray is again totally internally reflected. The ray emerges parallel to the direction in which it was originally travelling.

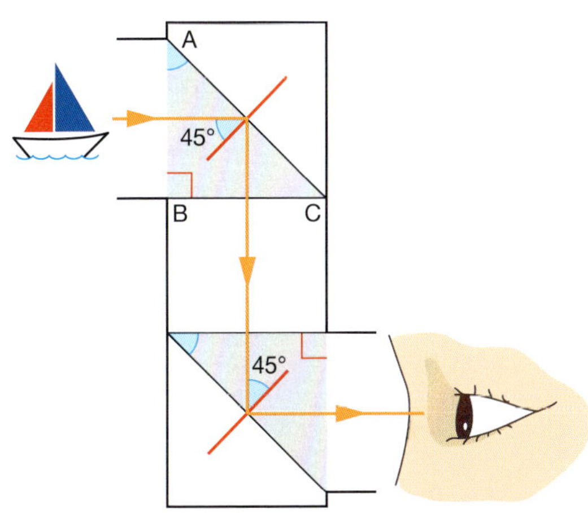

▲ Figure 9.15 Total internal reflection in a prismatic periscope

BICYCLE AND CAR REFLECTORS

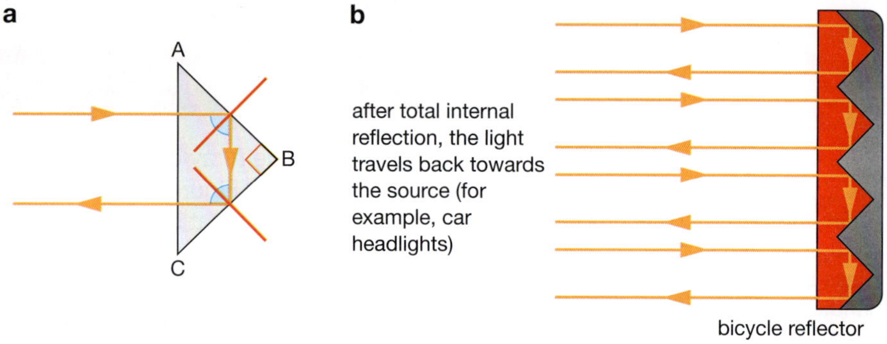

▲ Figure 9.16 Prisms can also be used as reflectors.

Light entering the prism in Figure 9.16 is totally internally reflected twice. It emerges from the prism travelling back in the direction from which it originally came. This arrangement is used in bicycle or car reflectors.

▲ Figure 9.17 Reflectors like these can save lives.

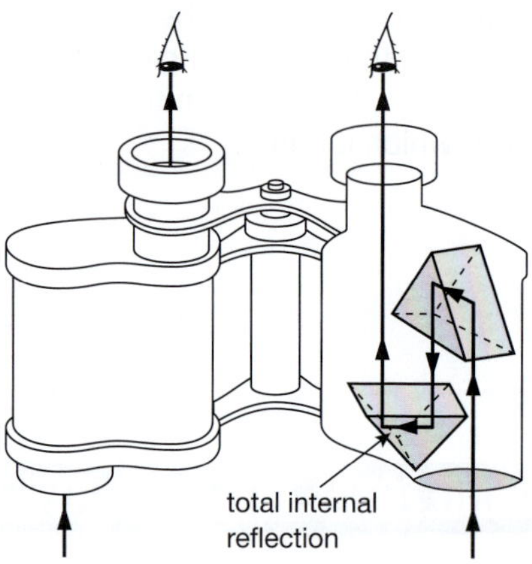

▲ Figure 9.18 Total internal reflection inside binoculars

▲ Figure 9.19 Prismatic binoculars

Binoculars also make use of total internal reflection within prisms.

Each side of a pair of binoculars contains two prisms to totally internally reflect the incoming light. Without the prisms, binoculars would have to be very long to obtain large **magnifications** and would look like a pair of telescopes.

OPTICAL FIBRES

One of the most important **applications** for total internal reflection is the optical fibre. This is a very thin piece of fibre composed of two different types of glass. The centre is made of a glass that has a high refractive index surrounded by a different type of glass that has a lower refractive index.

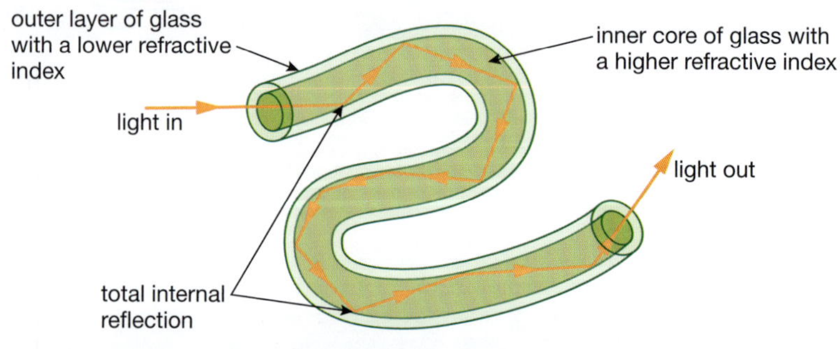

▲ Figure 9.20 In an optical fibre, light undergoes total internal reflection.

▲ Figure 9.21 Optical fibres

As the fibres are very narrow, light entering the inner **core** always strikes the boundary of the two glasses at an angle that is greater than the critical angle. No light escapes across this boundary. The fibre therefore acts as a 'light pipe' providing a path that the light follows even when the fibre is curved.

Large numbers of these fibres fixed together form a bundle. Bundles can carry sufficient light for images of objects to be seen through them. If the fibres are tapered (narrower at one end) it is also possible to produce a magnified image.

Figure 9.22 shows optical fibres in an endoscope. The endoscope is used by doctors to see the inside the body – for example, to examine the inside of the stomach. Endoscopes can also be used by engineers to see hard-to-reach parts of machinery.

Light travels down one bundle of fibres and shines on the object to be viewed. Light reflected by the object travels up a second bundle of fibres. An image of the object is created by the eyepiece.

THE ENDOSCOPE

By using optical fibres to see what they are doing, doctors can carry out operations through small holes made in the body, rather than through large cuts. This is called 'keyhole surgery'. This is less stressful for patients and usually leads to a more rapid recovery.

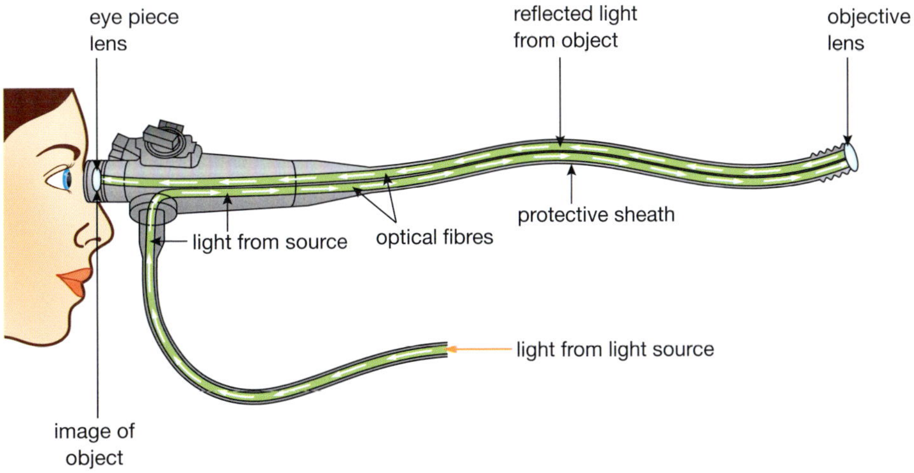

▲ Figure 9.22 Optical fibres are used in endoscopes to see inside the body.

OPTICAL FIBRES IN TELECOMMUNICATIONS

Modern telecommunications systems use optical fibres rather than copper wires to transmit messages as less energy is lost. Electrical signals from a telephone are converted into light energy produced by tiny lasers, which send pulses (small amounts) of light into the ends of optical fibres. A light-sensitive detector at the other end changes the pulses back into electrical signals, which then flow into a telephone receiver (ear piece).

SOUND WAVES

Figure 9.23 shows part of the sound system used by a band playing at a concert. This equipment must produce sounds that are loud enough to be heard by all the audience and the sound quality must be good enough for the music to be appreciated. We are going to look at how sounds are made and how they travel as waves.

▲ Figure 9.23 The sound produced by the speakers must be loud but also of good quality.

Sounds are produced by objects that are vibrating. We hear sounds when these vibrations, travelling as sound waves, reach our ears.

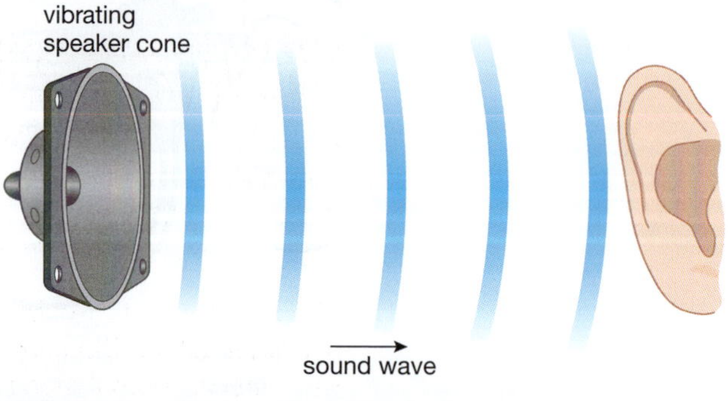

▲ Figure 9.24 The loudspeaker vibrates and produces sound waves.

EXTENSION WORK

You will not be tested on this more detailed description of how sounds from a loudspeaker are heard. As the speaker cone moves to the right, it pushes air molecules closer together, creating a **compression**. These particles then push against neighbouring particles so that the compression appears to be moving to the right. Behind the compression as the speaker cone moves to the left is a region where the particles are spread out. This region is called a rarefaction. After the cone has vibrated several times, it has created a series of compressions and rarefactions travelling away from it. This is a longitudinal sound wave (see page 560). When the waves enter the ear, they strike the eardrum and make it vibrate. These vibrations are changed into electrical signals, which are then detected by the brain.

REFLECTION

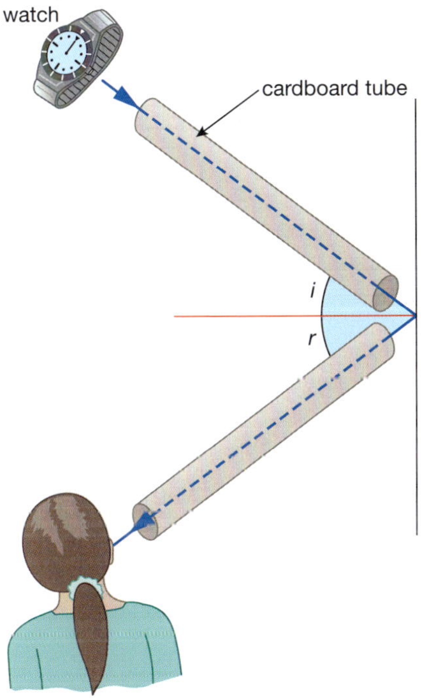

▲ Figure 9.25 Sound waves are reflected in the same way that light rays are reflected.

Sound waves behave in the same way as any other wave.

When a sound wave strikes a surface it may be reflected. Like light waves, sound waves are reflected from a surface so that the angle of incidence is equal to the angle of reflection (see Figure 9.25).

Ships often use echoes to discover the depth of the water beneath them. This is called echo sounding.

1 Sound waves are emitted from the ship and travel to the seabed (sea floor).
2 Some of these waves are reflected from the seabed back up to the ship.
3 Equipment on the ship detects these sound waves.
4 The time it takes the waves to make this journey is measured.
5 Knowing this time, the depth of the sea below the ship can be calculated.

The system of using echoes in this way is called **sonar** (Sound, Navigation And Ranging).

▲ Figure 9.26 Reflected sound can be used to tell ships about the depth of the sea beneath them.

REFRACTION OF SOUND

All waves can be refracted, even sound waves! For example, if some parts of a sound wave are travelling through warm air, they will travel more quickly than those parts travelling through cooler air. As a result the direction of the sound wave will change. It will be refracted.

Although it is not possible to see sound waves being refracted, we can sometimes hear their effect. Standing at the edge of a large pond or lake we can sometimes hear sounds from things on the other side of the water much more clearly than we would expect. This is due to refraction. Figure 9.27 explains how this happens.

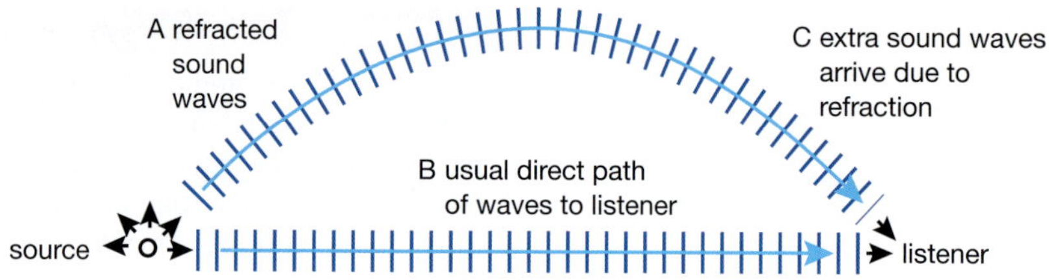

Figure 9.27 Why sometimes sounds travelling across water are louder than we expect

1 Most of the sound we hear travels to us in a straight line (Path B).

2 But some sound travels upwards (Path A).

3 If the temperature conditions are right, then as the sound waves travel through the air they are refracted and follow a curved path downwards (Path C).

4 We now receive two sets of sound waves.

5 So the sound we hear seems louder and clearer.

CHAPTER QUESTIONS

More questions on refraction can be found at the end of Unit 3 on page 588.

SKILLS INTERPRETATION, PROBLEM SOLVING (6th)

1 Draw a ray diagram to show how a ray of light can be turned through 100° using two plane mirrors. Mark on your diagram a value for the angle of incidence at each of the mirrors.

SKILLS INTERPRETATION

2 a Draw a diagram to show the path of a ray of light travelling from air into a rectangular glass block at an angle of about 45°.

b Show the path of the ray as it emerges from the block.

SKILLS CRITICAL THINKING

c Explain why the ray changes direction each time it crosses the air/glass boundary.

SKILLS INTERPRETATION

d Draw a second diagram showing a ray that travels through the block without its direction changing.

SKILLS PROBLEM SOLVING (7th)

3 In an experiment to measure the refractive index of a type of glass, the angle of refraction was found to be 31° when the angle of incidence was 55°.

a Calculate the refractive index of the glass.

b What would the angle of refraction be for a ray with an angle of incidence of 45°?

c Calculate the critical angle for the glass.

SKILLS INTERPRETATION (6th)

4 a Draw a diagram to show how a prism can create a rainbow of colours.

SKILLS CRITICAL THINKING

b Explain how these colours are produced by the prism.

SKILLS INTERPRETATION (7th)

5 Draw three ray diagrams to show what happens to a ray of light travelling in a glass block in the following situations. It hits a face of the block at an angle:

a less than the critical angle

b equal to the critical angle

c greater than the critical angle.

SKILLS CRITICAL THINKING

6th

6 a What is meant by 'total internal reflection of light' and under what conditions does it occur?

SKILLS INTERPRETATION

b Draw a diagram to show how total internal reflection takes place in a prismatic periscope.

SKILLS REASONING

c Give one advantage of using prisms in a periscope rather than plane mirrors.

SKILLS INTERPRETATION

7th

d Draw a second diagram to show how a prism could be used to turn a ray of light through 180°. Give one application of a prism used in this way.

SKILLS INTERPRETATION, CRITICAL THINKING

7 a Explain why a ray of light entering an optical fibre is unable to escape through the sides of the fibre. Include a ray diagram in your explanation.

SKILLS CRITICAL THINKING

b Explain how doctors use optical fibres to see inside the body.

6th

c Name one other use of optical fibres.

UNIT QUESTIONS

SKILLS CRITICAL THINKING 5th

1 a Which of the following does not move as a transverse wave?

A ultraviolet light
B sound wave
C surface water wave
D microwave

(1)

b Which of these effects describes the change in pitch we hear when a fast moving motorbike goes past?

A total internal reflection
B refraction
C reflection
D Doppler

(1)

6th

c Which of the following does not make use of total internal reflection?

A **oscilloscope**
B endoscope
C prismatic periscope
D optical fibres

(1)

(Total 3 marks)

SKILLS INTERPRETATION

2 The diagram below shows the cross-section of a water wave.

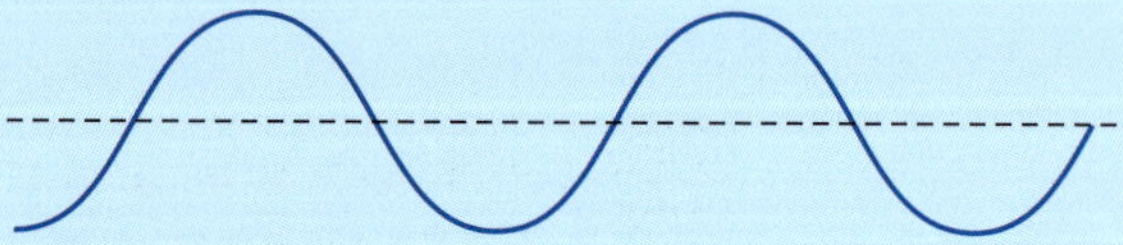

a Copy this diagram and mark on it:

5th

i the wavelength of the wave (λ) **(1)**

ii the amplitude of the wave (A). **(1)**

SKILLS PROBLEM SOLVING 8th

b i A water wave travelling at 20 m/s has a wavelength of 2.5 m. Calculate the frequency of the wave. **(3)**

ii Calculate the time period of the above wave. **(1)**

(Total 6 marks)

SKILLS ANALYSIS

3 The diagram below shows a ray of light travelling down an optical fibre.

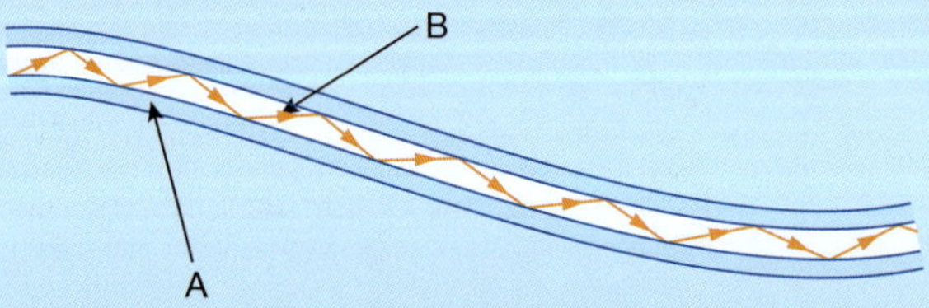

SKILLS ANALYSIS

a What is A? (1)

b What is B? (1)

c Why is light reflected from the boundary between A and B? (2)

SKILLS CRITICAL THINKING

d Describe one medical use for optical fibres. (1)

(Total 5 marks)

4 a i Explain the difference between a longitudinal wave and a transverse wave. (1)

ii Give one example of each type of wave. (2)

A girl stands 500 m from a tall building and bangs two pieces of wood together. At the same moment her friend starts a stopwatch. The sound waves created by the two pieces of wood hit the building and are reflected. When the two girls hear the echo they stop the stopwatch and note the time. The girls repeat the experiment four more times. The results are shown in the table below.

Experiment	Time (seconds)
1	2.95
2	3.00
3	2.90
4	3.20
5	2.95

SKILLS EXECUTIVE FUNCTION

b Why did the girls repeat the experiment five times? (1)

SKILLS PROBLEM SOLVING

c Calculate the speed of sound using the results. (6)

SKILLS EXECUTIVE FUNCTION

d One of the girls thought that their answer might be affected by wind. Was she correct? Explain your answer. (2)

(Total 12 marks)

SKILLS CRITICAL THINKING

5 The electromagnetic spectrum contains the following groups of waves: infrared, ultraviolet, x-rays, radio waves, microwaves, visible spectrum and gamma rays.

a Put these groups of waves in the order they appear in the electromagnetic spectrum starting with the group that has the longest wavelength. (2)

b Write down four properties that all of these waves have in common. (4)

c Write down one use for each group of waves. (7)

d Which three groups of waves could cause cancer? (3)

e Which three groups of waves can be used to communicate (3)

(Total 19 marks)

SKILLS PROBLEM SOLVING

6 a A ray of light hits the outside surface of a glass block with an angle of incidence of 38°. Its angle of refraction inside the block is 24°.

i Calculate the refractive index of the glass. (4)

ii Calculate the critical angle for this glass. (2)

b Calculate the refractive index for a piece of glass whose critical angle is 42°. (3)

(Total 9 marks)

PHYSICS UNIT 4 ENERGY RESOURCES AND ENERGY TRANSFER

Energy, energy resources and the transfer of energy! These are all vital to modern life.

The photo shows energy produced from a wind farm. We also obtain energy by burning fossil fuels like coal and oil, directly from the Sun in the form of heat, from hydroelectric power and nuclear power, and from many other resources.

We need to understand how to transfer energy from one store to another, to use it efficiently and to conserve resources that cannot be replaced. We also need to be aware of the advantages and disadvantages of different energy resources.

Physics is about energy!

10 ENERGY TRANSFERS

Whenever anything happens, energy is transferred from one store to another – indeed, without energy things simply can't happen! In this chapter, you will learn that energy can be transferred to many different stores, including sound, light, movement, thermal and potential energy. You will also find out that, although energy is never destroyed, in every energy transfer some energy is transferred to the surroundings, often as thermal energy.

▲ Figure 10.1 Energy is stored as sound, movement and light, for example.

LEARNING OBJECTIVES

- Describe energy transfers involving energy stores:
  - energy stores: chemical, kinetic, gravitational, elastic, thermal, magnetic, electrostatic, nuclear
  - energy transfers: mechanically, electrically, by heating, by radiation (light and sound)
- Use the principle of conservation of energy
- Know and use the relationship between efficiency, useful energy output and total energy output:

$$\text{efficiency} = \frac{\text{useful energy output}}{\text{total energy output}} \times 100\%$$

- Describe a variety of everyday and scientific devices and situations, explaining the transfer of the input energy in terms of the above relationship, including their representation by Sankey diagrams

UNITS

In this section you will need to use kilogram (kg) as the unit of mass, joule (J) as the unit of energy, metre (m) as the unit of length, metre per second (m/s) as the unit of speed and velocity, metre per second squared (m/s^2) as the unit of acceleration, newton (N) as the unit of force, second (s) as the unit of time and watt (W) as the unit of power. You have used all these units before.

For things to happen we need energy! Energy is used to produce sound. Energy is used to transport people and goods from place to place, whether it is by train, boat or plane or on the backs of animals or even by bicycles. Energy is needed to lift objects, make machinery work and run all the electrical and electronic equipment we have in our modern world. Energy is transferred by heating and as light radiation. The demand for energy increases every day because the world's population is increasing. People consume energy in the form of food and need energy for the basics of life, like warmth and light. As people become wealthier they demand much more than the basics, so the need for energy grows!

STORES OF ENERGY

Energy is found in many different stores:

- We get our energy from the food we eat. Food provides stored chemical energy that we can burn to transfer it to other types of energy.
- We use the energy from food to generate **thermal** energy (heat energy) to help to keep us warm.

EXTENSION WORK

Sound energy can be used to break up small stones that can form inside a person's body, without the need for an operation. Sound energy is also used in medicine to examine the inside of the body, as an alternative to x-rays.

- Our muscles transfer the chemical energy to movement energy (kinetic energy).
- Some of this movement energy is transferred to other stores by the radiation of sound.
- We need to transfer energy by heating to our homes, schools and workplaces. We also transfer energy in the form of light waves to illuminate our buildings, vehicles and roads.
- Most of the energy needed for these purposes is transferred electrically. The energy stores that are used in the production of electricity include chemical (burning gas, coal or oil) and nuclear.
- Some electrical energy is produced from the gravitational potential energy in water kept in reservoirs in mountainous areas. We can also use the energy in the hot core (centre) of the Earth. We see the evidence of this huge supply of heat in volcanoes and thermal springs.
- Energy from the thermal energy store underground is called geothermal energy.
- Energy can also be stored in springs as elastic potential energy. This type of stored energy is used in things like clocks and toys.

The main resource of energy for the Earth is our Sun. This provides us with heat, light and other stores of energy.

ENERGY TRANSFERS

For energy to be useful, we need to be able to transfer it from one store into whichever store we require. Unfortunately, when we try to do this there is usually some energy transferred to unwanted stores. We often refer to these energy transfers to unwanted stores as 'wasted' energy because it is not being used for a useful purpose.

Here are some examples of wasted energy:

- Energy can be transferred electrically to hot water in a tank (a thermal energy store) in a house to be used when needed. Although the tank may be well insulated, some energy will be transferred from the water in the hot water tank by heating other objects like the metal tank and then the surrounding air. These are unwanted energy stores.
- We provide our cars with an energy store, the tank of petrol (gas). We want energy from this store to be transferred to the kinetic energy of the moving car, and to gravitational energy if we are driving up a hill – both transfers are useful. Heating will also transfer thermal energy to the surroundings, sound will radiate energy to the surroundings and friction between moving parts and the air will cause mechanical work to be done making things get hot therefore transferring thermal energy to the surroundings. These are examples of chemical energy stored in the fuel being transferred to unwanted energy stores.

Unwanted energy transfers reduce efficiency. This problem is the same whether the system is a small one, like a car, or a large system, like the nationwide electricity generation and distribution industry. We need to be aware of where our energy is transferring to if we are to find ways of using it well.

SOME ENERGY TRANSFERS

We have many ways of transferring energy from one store to another.

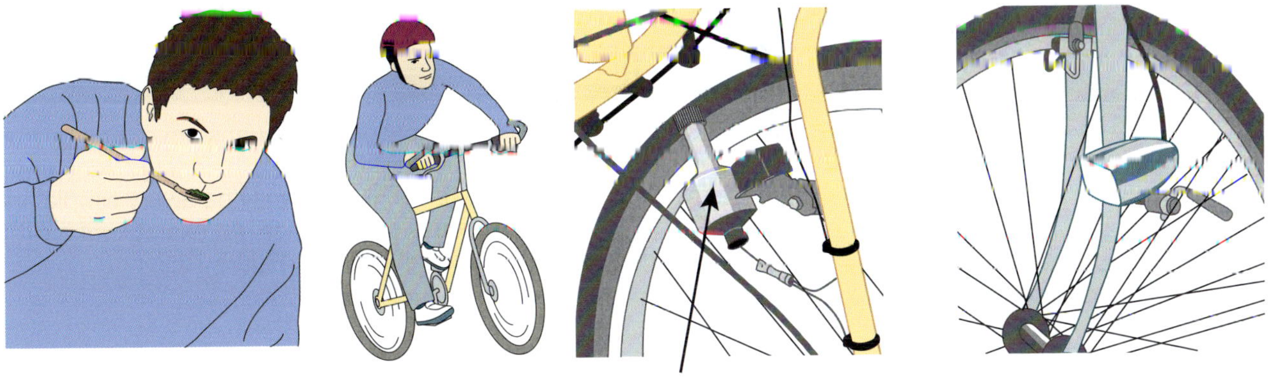

▲ Figure 10.2 Energy is transferred from one store to another, and to another, and so on.

In Figure 10.2, stored chemical energy in the food is needed to help our bodies make a range of other chemicals. Some of these – like carbohydrates – are used to produce heat to maintain our body temperature and energy for movement through muscle activity. Having eaten a meal, the cyclist in Figure 10.2 is transferring the chemical energy stored in his body to movement energy. The movement is initially in the cyclist's legs and is then transferred to the machine (the bicycle). The cyclist is transferring additional energy by heating the surroundings. Friction in various parts of the bicycle will also result in energy being transferred from movement to heat and sound.

The dynamo or generator fitted to the bicycle's wheel transfers some of the movement energy of the wheel to electrical energy. The lamp then transfers energy as light radiation and by heating. As electrons flow in the dynamo–lamp circuit, the conducting wires will be heated.

Examples of other energy transfers are given in the questions at the end of the chapter.

CONSERVATION OF ENERGY

The principle of conservation of energy is a very important rule. It states that:

Energy is not created or destroyed in any process.

(It is just transferred from one store to another.)

We often hear about the energy crisis: as our demand for more energy increases our reserves of energy in the form of fuels like oil and gas are rapidly being used up. The principle of conservation of energy makes it seem as if there is no real problem – that energy can never run out. We need to understand what the principle really means.

Physicists believe that the amount of energy in the Universe is constant – energy can be transferred from one store to another but there is never any more or any less of it. This means we cannot use energy up. However, if we consider our little piece of the Universe, the problem becomes more obvious. As we make energy do useful things – for example, move a car – some of it will be transferred to heat. Some of it will be transferred by heating. Some of the thermal energy stored will be radiated away into space. This means the energy is not available for us to use any more.

EXTENSION WORK

Even though the amount of energy in the Universe is constant, it is becoming more spread out and so less available for use. Some scientists think that all the energy in the Universe will eventually be transferred to heat and that everywhere in the Universe will end up at the same very low temperature. This possible 'end of the world' is sometimes referred to by the dramatic name of 'heat death'. If the Universe does end up this way, it is not expected to do so for some time yet, so carry on working for those exams!

This is just like a badly insulated house; if heat energy escapes, it is transferred away from the system we call our home, and is no longer available to keep us warm.

SANKEY DIAGRAMS

We use different ways to show how energy is transferred. Energy transfer diagrams show the energy input (contribution), the energy transfer process and the energy output (production). The system may be a very simple one with just one main energy transfer process taking place. An example of a simple system with its energy transfer diagram is shown in Figure 10.3.

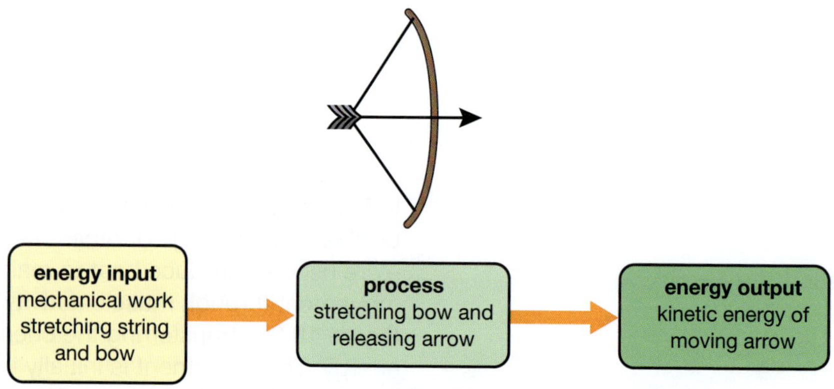

▲ Figure 10.3 Energy transfer diagram for an arrow being fired from a bow

Sankey diagrams are a simpler and clearer way of showing what happens to an energy input into a system. The energy flow is shown by arrows whose width is proportional to the amount of energy involved. Wide arrows show large energy flows, narrow arrows show small energy flows.

Figure 10.4 shows a Sankey diagram for a complex system – the energy flow for a car. Chemical energy in the form of petrol is the input to the car. The energy outputs from the car are:

- electrical energy (from the alternator) to drive lights, radio and so on, to charge the battery (transferred to chemical energy) and allow the car to switch on
- movement (kinetic) energy from the car engine
- wasted energy as electrical heating in wiring and lamp filaments, as frictional heating in various parts of the engine and alternator, and as noise.

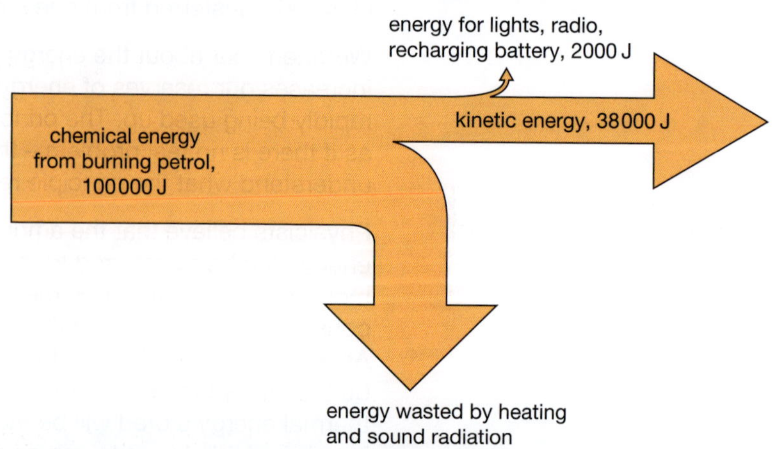

▲ Figure 10.4 Sankey diagram showing the energy flow in a typical car

Here the 100 000 J of chemical energy input might be shown by an arrow 20 mm wide, so the 60 000 J of energy wasted (60% of the input) would then be shown by an arrow that is 12 mm wide (60% of 20 mm). It is difficult to draw the 2% arrow for the energy output to scale; it is enough to show it as very small.

EFFICIENCY

Whenever we are considering energy transfers, we have to remember that a proportion of the energy input is wasted. Remember that wasted means transferred into stores other than the useful store required. We would like our energy transfer systems to be perfect with all the output energy being in the store that we want. For example, not all the output energy for an electric lamp is light (the useful energy output), some of the output energy is thermal energy (not useful when what we want is light).

Real systems always have an unwanted energy output so can never have 100% efficiency.

The efficiency of an energy conversion system is defined as:

$$\text{efficiency} = \frac{\text{useful energy output}}{\text{total energy output}} \times 100\%$$

HINT

If you calculate the efficiency of a system and get an answer bigger than 100% then you have put the numbers into the equation the wrong way round!

Efficiency does not have a unit because it is a ratio. Sometimes efficiency is shown as a **fraction** of the energy output that is in the wanted or useful store. In real energy transfers this fraction will always be less than 1 because some of the total output energy will be in an unwanted store.

EXAMPLE 1

A 60 W tungsten filament bulb uses 60 J of energy every second. It is 5% efficient. How much of the total energy output per second is useful light radiation?

$$\text{efficiency} = \frac{\text{useful energy output}}{\text{total energy output}} \times 100\%$$

$$5\% = \frac{\text{useful energy output}}{60\text{ J}} \times 100\%$$

$$\frac{5}{100} = \frac{\text{useful energy output}}{60\text{ J}}$$

So useful (light) energy from bulb $= \frac{5 \times 60\text{ J}}{100} = 3$ J each second.

CHAPTER QUESTIONS

More questions on the need for energy can be found at the end of Unit 4 on page 616.

SKILLS CREATIVITY 6th

1 Describe the main energy transfers taking place in the following situations:

a turning on a torch

b lighting a candle

c rubbing your hands to keep them warm

d bouncing on a trampoline.

SKILLS INTERPRETATION, PROBLEM SOLVING

7th

2 Copy and complete the following Sankey diagrams. Remember that the width of the arrows must be proportional to the amount of energy involved. This has been done for you in part a.

a for an electric lamp

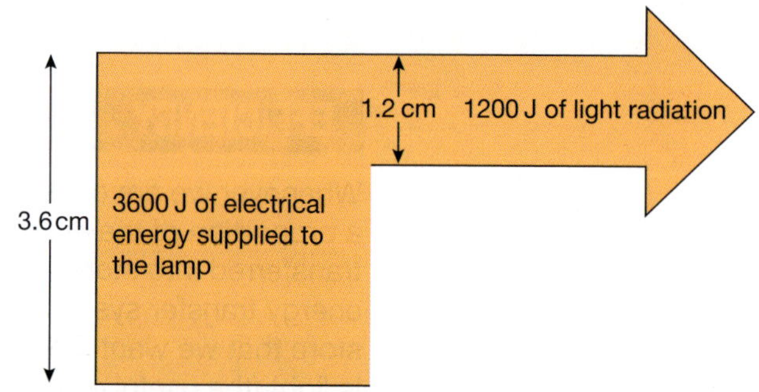

b In a typical wash in a washing machine 1.2 MJ is transferred to the kinetic energy of the rotating drum, 6 MJ of energy is transferred to heat the water and 0.8 MJ is wasted as heat transferred to the surroundings and sound.

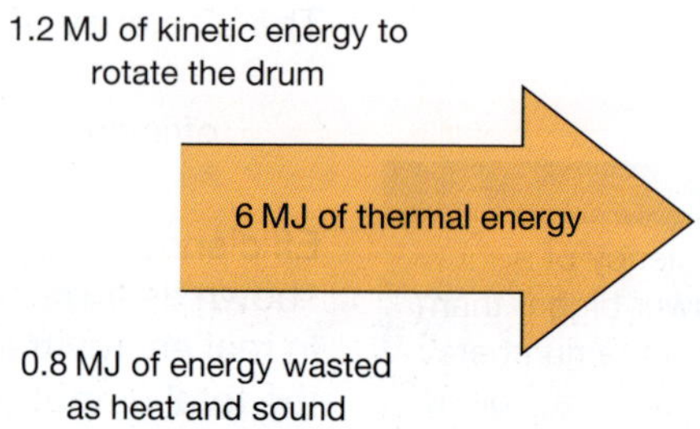

SKILLS INTERPRETATION

3 a Draw a Sankey diagram for the following situation. An electric kettle is used to heat some water. 350 kJ of energy are used to heat the water, 10 kJ raise the temperature of the kettle and 40 kJ escape to heat the surroundings.

SKILLS PROBLEM SOLVING

8th

b Calculate the efficiency of the kettle.

4 A ball is dropped. It hits the ground with 10 J of kinetic energy and bounces with 4 J of kinetic energy.

6th

a What happens to 6 J of the energy during the bounce?

SKILLS INTERPRETATION

7th

b Draw a Sankey diagram for the energy flow that takes place during the bounce.

11 THERMAL ENERGY

This chapter is about the ways in which thermal (heat) energy is transferred from a hotter place to a cooler place.

▲ Figure 11.1 The transfer of thermal energy from place to place can be useful – for example, rising warm air creates 'thermals' that can carry this glider up to great heights.

LEARNING OBJECTIVES

- Describe how thermal energy transfer may take place by conduction, convection and radiation
- Explain the role of convection in everyday **phenomena**
- Explain how emission and **absorption** of radiation are related to surface and temperature
- Practical: investigate thermal energy transfer by conduction, convection and radiation
- Explain ways of reducing unwanted energy transfer, such as insulation

Thermal or heat energy is energy that is stored in 'hot' matter. We shall see that 'hot' is a relative term. There is a temperature called absolute zero that is the lowest possible temperature. Any matter that is above this temperature has some thermal energy. The kinetic energy of the minute particles that make up all matter produces the effect we call heat.

Thermal energy is transferred from a place that is hotter (that is, at a higher temperature) to one that is colder (at a lower temperature). In this chapter, we will look at the different ways in which thermal energy is transferred between places that have different temperatures.

CONDUCTION

Thermal **conduction** is the transfer of thermal (heat) energy through a substance by the vibration of the atoms within the substance. The substance itself does not move.

If you have ever cooked kebabs on a barbecue with metal skewers, as shown in Figure 11.2, you will have discovered conduction! The metal over the burning charcoal becomes hot and the heat energy is transferred along the skewer by conduction. In metals, this takes place quite rapidly and soon the handle end is almost as hot as the end over the fire. Metals are good thermal conductors. If you use skewers with wooden handles you can hold the wooden

▲ Figure 11.2 Metal skewers allow heat to be transferred to parts that are away from the heat.

Safety note: The metal rods will quickly get hot enough to burn the skin and will remain hot long after the heat is removed.

EXTENSION WORK

'Free electrons' are electrons that are not connected with any particular atom in the structure of a substance. Metals usually have huge numbers of free electrons per unit volume. Copper, for example, has about 10^{29} free electrons in each cubic metre. As these free electrons carry electric charge as well as energy, it is no coincidence that good thermal conductors are usually good conductors of electricity too.

ends much more comfortably because wood does not conduct thermal energy very well. Wood is an example of a good thermal insulator.

The process of energy transfer by conduction is explained in terms of the behaviour of the tiny particles that make up all matter. In a hot part of a substance, like the part of the skewer over the hot charcoal, these particles have more kinetic energy. The more energetic particles transfer some of their kinetic energy store to particles near them mechanically. These therefore gain kinetic energy and then pass kinetic energy on to particles near to them. The energy transfer goes on throughout the substance. This process takes place in all materials.

In metals, the process takes place much more rapidly, because metals have free electrons that can move easily through the structure of the metal, making the transfer of energy happen faster.

ACTIVITY 1

▼ PRACTICAL: INVESTIGATE HOW WELL DIFFERENT METALS CONDUCT HEAT

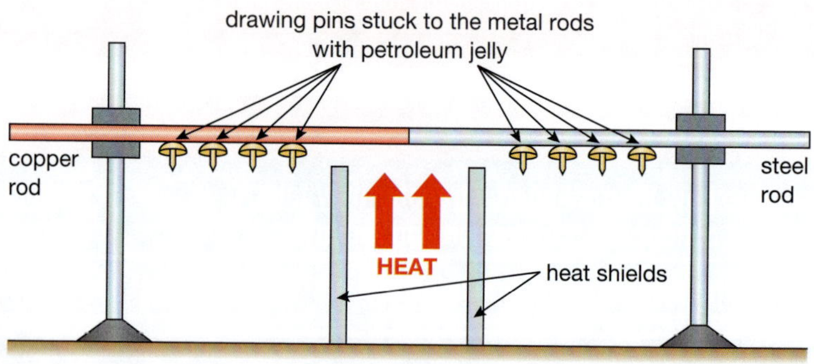

▲ Figure 11.3 Experiment to show thermal conduction in different metals

Figure 11.3 demonstrates how thermal energy is transferred along the metal rods from the heated ends towards the cooler ends away from the heat source. As the thermal energy passes along the rods the petroleum jelly holding the drawing pins in place melts and they drop off in sequence. This experiment also shows that copper conducts thermal energy better than steel because the drawing pins attached to the copper rod drop off sooner than those attached to the steel rod. The rods should be the same diameter and the drawing pins placed at the same distances from the heat source for this to be a fair test.

CONVECTION

Convection is the transfer of thermal energy through fluids (liquids and gases) by the upward movement of warmer, less dense regions of fluid.

You may have seen a demonstration of convection currents in water, like the one shown in Figure 11.4. The water is heated just under the purple crystal and the crystal colours the water as it **dissolves**, which lets you see the movement in the water. The heated water expands and becomes less dense than the colder surrounding water, so it floats up to the top of the glass beaker. Colder water sinks to take its place, and is then heated too. At the top, the warm water starts to cool, becomes more dense again and will begin to sink, so a circulating current is set up in the water. This is called a convection current.

Safety note: Avoid skin contact with the crystals and their solution.

ACTIVITY 2

▼ PRACTICAL: INVESTIGATE CONVECTION CURRENTS IN WATER

▲ Figure 11.4 Demonstration of convection currents, using a potassium manganate (VII) crystal in water

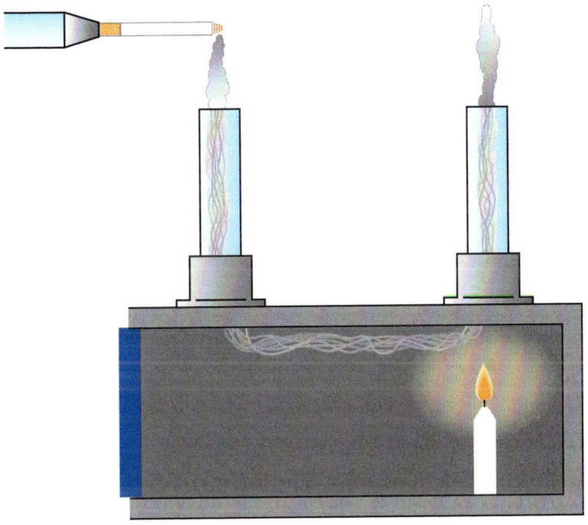

▲ Figure 11.5 Here, air warmed by the candle floats up the chimney on the right and colder air is drawn down the chimney on the left. Smoke from the burning candle shows up the circulation of the air.

EXTENSION WORK

Substances tend to expand when heated because the particles of which they are made have more kinetic energy. As they move around more, the average distance between the particles increases.

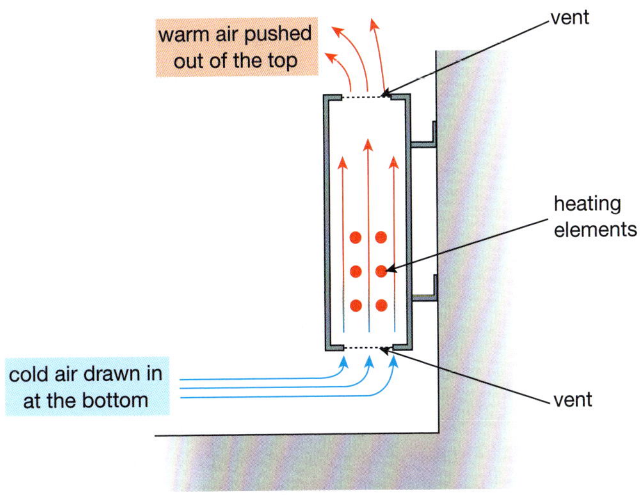

▲ Figure 11.6 A convector heater relies on the effects of convection.

Convection occurs in any fluid substance – that is, in things that can flow, such as liquids and gases. Convector heaters (Figure 11.6) heat air, which then floats out of the top of the heater to the top of the room. Cold air is drawn in at the bottom and this in turn is heated. In this way, thermal energy is eventually transferred to all parts of the room.

In many cooking ovens, the heating element is placed at the bottom of the oven. It heats the air near to it, and this air rises by convection. The top of the oven is generally warmer than the bottom, so you can cook foods at different temperatures. However many modern ovens are fan ovens, where hot air is blown into the oven and provides an even temperature throughout the oven.

▲ Figure 11.7 A diver wearing a wetsuit to keep warm in cold water

Air and water both allow thermal energy transfer to take place by convection as they are both fluids, but neither are good thermal conductors (they are insulators). This insulating property of both water and air is put to good use in situations where they are not able to circulate easily. For example, woollen clothing keeps you warm because air gets trapped in the fibres. The trapped air is heated by your body and forms a warm insulating layer that helps to stop you losing heat. In the same way, a wetsuit keeps a diver warm because a thin layer of water is trapped next to the diver's skin. (Figure 11.7)

Convection currents are responsible for many everyday events. One example is on-shore and off-shore breezes, also known as sea breezes and land breezes. These are explained in Figure 11.8.

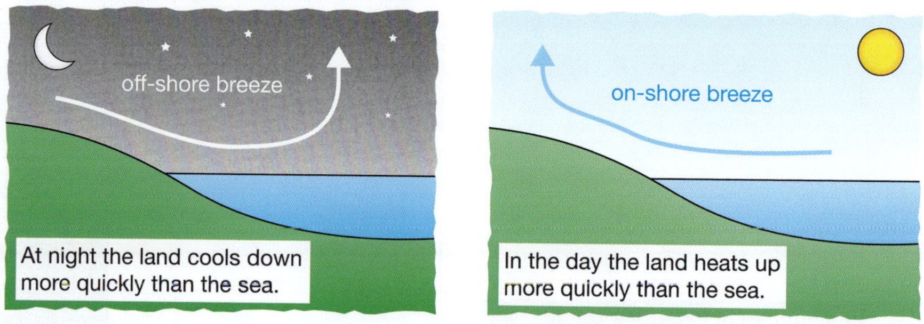

▲ Figure 11.8 At night the air over the warmer sea floats up causing cooler air to flow towards sea. During the day the situation is reversed. In Unit 5 you will learn that some things heat up and cool down more easily than others.

Another example is convection currents within the very tall 'thunder' clouds that are responsible for the build-up of charge at the cloud base resulting in lightning strikes.

RADIATION

Thermal radiation is the transfer of energy by infrared (IR) waves.

▲ Figure 11.9 Thermal energy is transferred from a heater by radiation.

REMINDER

Remember that we are talking about thermal energy transfer – this is thermal radiation not nuclear radiation!

EXTENSION WORK

The reflector in an electric fire is a special shape, called a **parabola**. You can see parabolic reflectors in torches and radio telescopes, for example.

When you turn on a bathroom heater, as shown in Figure 11.9, you will feel the effect almost instantly. Neither conduction nor convection can explain how heat is getting from the hot part to your hands. Conduction does not occur that rapidly, even in good thermal conductors, and air is a poor thermal conductor. Convection results in heated air floating upwards on colder, denser air.

There are two things you should notice about this example.

1 The heat that you feel so quickly is travelling from the heater in a straight line.

2 The design of the bathroom heater includes a specially shaped, very shiny reflector, similar to the reflector behind a fluorescent light or in a torch.

In this example, thermal energy is travelling in the form of waves, like visible light. Heat waves are called infrared (IR) waves or IR radiation. The army and the emergency services use special cameras, called thermal imaging cameras, that can detect objects giving out IR waves. These cameras show images of people because of the thermal energy radiation from their bodies, even when there is not enough visible light to actually see them. Thermal imaging is also an important tool in the diagnosis of certain illnesses. (Figure 11.10)

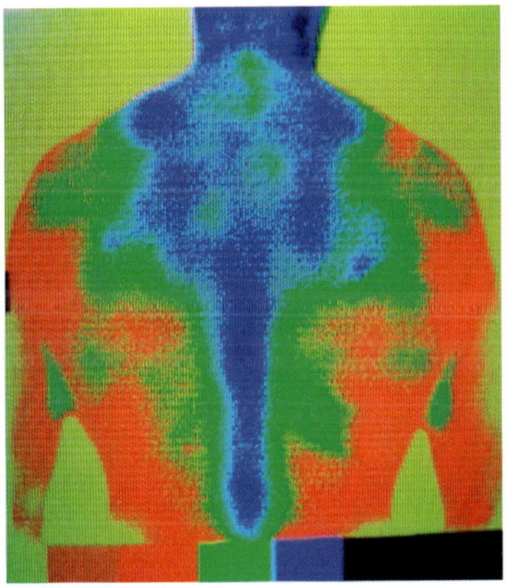

▲ Figure 11.10 This is a thermal image of a patient showing areas of different temperatures.

IR waves are part of the same family of waves as light, radio waves, ultraviolet and so on, called the electromagnetic (EM) spectrum (see page 568). IR waves, therefore, have the same properties as all the other waves in the EM spectrum. In particular, IR can travel through a vacuum and does so at the speed of light (3×10^8 m/s).

It is important that thermal energy can travel in this way, without the need for matter, otherwise we would not receive heat, as well as light, from the Sun.

IR waves can also be reflected and absorbed by different materials, just like visible light. Highly polished, shiny surfaces are good reflectors of thermal radiation. White surfaces also reflect a lot of IR. Matt (not shiny) black and dark surfaces are poor reflectors or, to put it more positively, are good absorbers of thermal radiation. Figure 11.12 shows how this can be useful in everyday life.

ACTIVITY 3

▼ PRACTICAL: INVESTIGATE HOW WELL DIFFERENT SURFACES RADIATE HEAT

This experiment shows that matt black surfaces radiate heat better than shiny white surfaces.

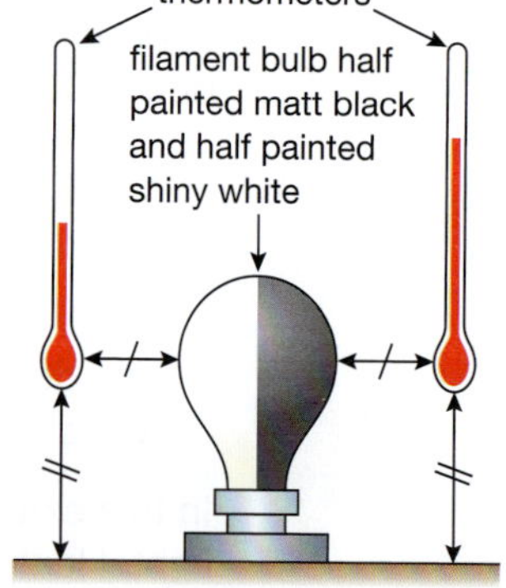

▲ Figure 11.11 Demonstrating that matt black surfaces radiate heat better than shiny white surfaces

Figure 11.11 shows the experiment. Put two identical (same type) thermometers on either side of a filament bulb that has been painted matt black on one side and shiny white on the other.

When you turn on the bulb you will notice that the temperature starts to rise more quickly on the thermometer facing the black side than on the other.

It is important that the thermometers are fixed at the same height and distance from the filament bulb.

Safety note: The bulb will quickly get hot enough to burn skin and ignite paper.

▲ Figure 11.12 Shiny and white surfaces reflect thermal radiation, while matt black surfaces, like in the solar heating panels, absorb it.

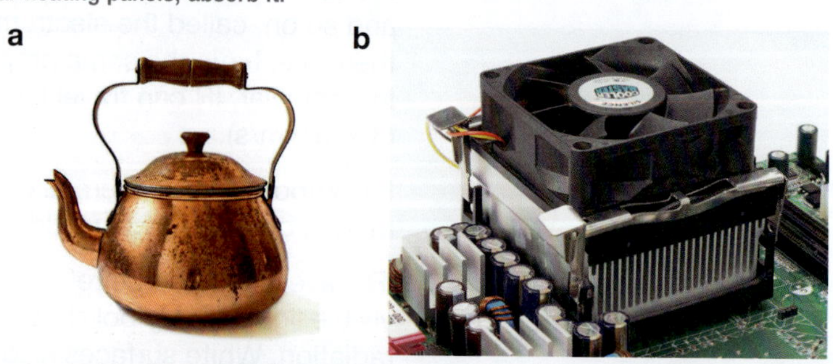

▲ Figure 11.13 **a** A shiny kettle stays warmer longer. **b** The heat sink needs to be matt black to lose heat to the surroundings quickly, and so stop the transistor overheating.

If a surface is a good reflector of IR then it is a poor radiator of IR. This means that a hot object with a shiny surface will emit thermal energy in the form of IR than another object at the same temperature with a matt black surface. The kettle in Figure 11.13a has a shiny surface to reduce the rate of thermal energy loss. Heat sinks are used in electronic equipment to stop parts getting too hot. A heat sink is shown in Figure 11.13b. The transistor is fixed to the black metal heat sink and thermal energy is transferred from the transistor to the heat sink by conduction. The matt black surface radiates thermal energy well and the shape of the heat sink helps convection air currents to transfer thermal energy away from the heat sink.

▲ Figure 11.14 A tungsten filament bulb

The amount and type of the energy radiated by a hot object does not only depend on its surface texture (how it feels to the touch) and colour – it also depends on how hot it is. Not only does the amount of energy radiated per second increase significantly with temperature but the nature of the EM waves also changes. At a low temperature most of the radiated energy is in the form of infrared waves (invisible to the human eye). As the temperature of a metal object increases it starts to radiate in the visible spectrum as well. Things that do not burn will start to glow a dull red. As the temperature rises further the colour changes through the visible spectrum, for example, the tungsten filament glows white hot when it reaches ~3000 °C.

ENERGY-EFFICIENT HOUSES

We pay for the energy we use in our homes, schools and places of work. Heating is the main use of energy in our homes and – since most domestic heating systems work by burning fuels like coal, oil and gas – it is the main producer of carbon dioxide. (Even if electric heaters are used, most electrical energy is produced by burning fuels in power stations.) Carbon dioxide is a greenhouse gas and contributes to global warming. It is, therefore, very important that houses are energy efficient.

Energy efficiency means using as much as possible of the energy we produce for the desired purpose. So when we turn on the central heating, we want to keep the insides of our homes warm and not allow the heat (thermal energy) to escape. If no heat can escape from a house then we will only need to heat it until it reaches the desired temperature.

The key to energy-efficient housing is insulation. Houses must be designed to reduce the rate at which energy is transferred between the inside and the outside.

EXTENSION WORK

The greenhouse effect

Infrared waves from the Sun can pass through ordinary greenhouse glass. The IR waves heat up the ground, which re-radiates the heat. However, the re-radiated heat is in the form of IR waves with much longer wavelengths. The longer wavelength IR waves cannot pass through glass, so they are trapped inside the greenhouse. Carbon dioxide in our atmosphere acts in the same way as the glass in a greenhouse. It traps the Sun's heat.

EXTENSION WORK

In cooler climates it is more appropriate to concentrate on keeping heat (thermal energy) in, rather than thinking about how to keep it out.

EXTENSION WORK

It is worth remembering that, in some countries, the problem is not keeping warm but keeping cool. Keeping cool also requires energy to run air-conditioning units, fans and other cooling devices. An energy-efficient house in a hot climate would stay cool by reducing the rate at which heat (thermal energy) entered the house.

HOW HEAT IS LOST

To insulate a house effectively we must look at all the ways in which thermal energy can escape. Conduction is the main way thermal energy is transferred between the inside of a building and the outside. Next we need to consider the places where conduction occurs: the walls, the windows (and doors) and the roof.

REMINDER

Energy lost here means energy transferred to unwanted energy stores. In the case of heating a house the wanted energy store will be the air in the rooms. An unwanted energy store in this example would be the outside environment.

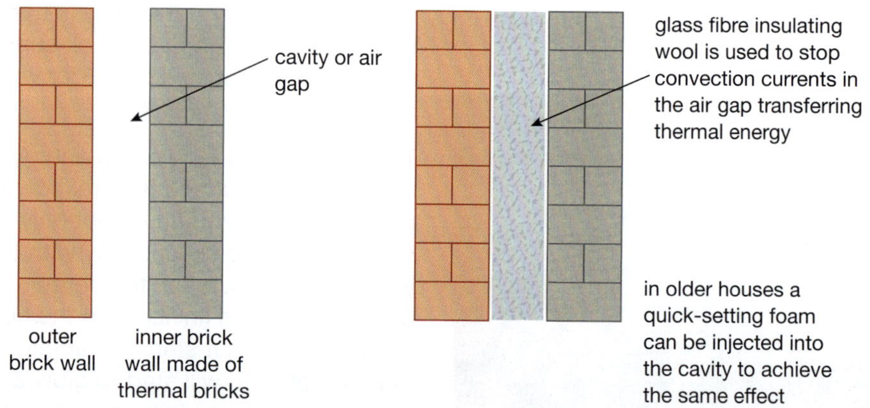

▲ Figure 11.15 Two-layered wall construction, with the gap filled with insulation panels, helps to reduce thermal energy loss by conduction, convection and even radiation.

Thermal energy loss by conduction through the walls can be reduced by using building materials that are good insulators. However, the materials used for building must also have other suitable properties like strength, durability and availability at a sensible price. For walls, bricks are a common building material.

Figure 11.15 shows the typical construction of a modern house in the UK built to follow the current energy efficiency regulations.

As you can see, the wall is made with layers of different materials. The outer layer is made with bricks – these have quite good insulating properties, are strong and will survive bad weather conditions. The inner layer is built with thermal bricks with very good insulation properties – they are also light, relatively cheap and quick to work with. The two layers of brick are separated by an excellent thermal insulator in the form of an air cavity or gap.

The walls also stop thermal energy being lost by convection. The cavity or gap between the two walls is wide enough for convection currents to circulate. This means thermal energy is circulated from the warmer surface of one wall to the colder surface of the other. To stop convection currents, the gap in modern houses is filled with insulating panels made of glass fibre matting. This is a lightweight, poor conductor that traps lots of air. The panels are usually surfaced with thin aluminium foil. This highly reflective surface reflects thermal energy in the form of infrared radiation.

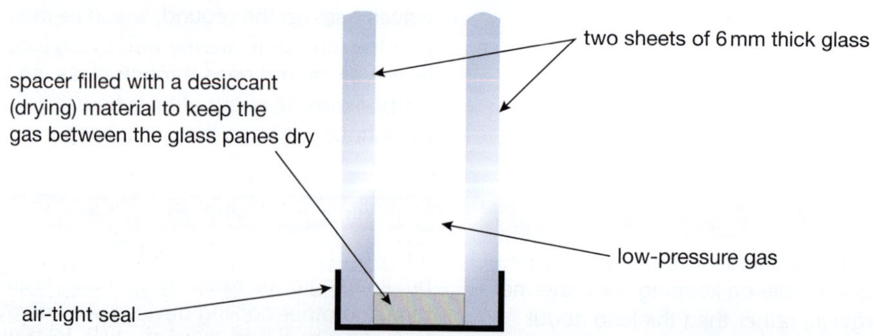

▲ Figure 11.16 Double glazing helps to stop thermal energy escaping from the home.

Figure 11.16 shows a cross-section of a typical double-glazed window, as used in modern houses. Glass is a poor thermal conductor but is used in thin layers. To improve the insulating properties, two layers of glass are used to trap a layer of air. The thickness of this layer is important. If it is too thin then the insulation effect is reduced, but if it is too thick then convection currents will be able to circulate and carry heat from the hotter surface to the colder one. In very cold countries triple glazing is used. Modern double glazing uses special glass to increase the greenhouse effect (thermal radiation from the Sun can get in but radiation from inside the house is mainly reflected back again).

Roof insulation in modern houses uses similar panels to those used in the wall cavities, trapping a thick layer of air. This takes advantage of the poor conducting property of air, while also preventing convection currents circulating. Again, reflective foil is used to reduce thermal energy loss by radiation. Figure 11.17 shows houses built before loft insulation was a compulsory building regulation. In some, the owners have installed loft insulation – you should be able to identify which!

▲ Figure 11.17 Loft insulation makes a big difference to heat loss through the roof.

There are other things that can be done to improve the energy efficiency of houses that do not relate directly to the mechanisms of thermal energy transfer discussed in this chapter. For example, thermostats and computer control systems for central heating can further reduce the heating needs of a house. They stop rooms being heated too much by switching off the heat when a certain temperature is reached. Another important energy-saving measure is the reduction or elimination of draughts (air currents) from poorly fitting doors and windows.

With your understanding of how thermal energy travels you can save your family money, keep warm and reduce global warming.

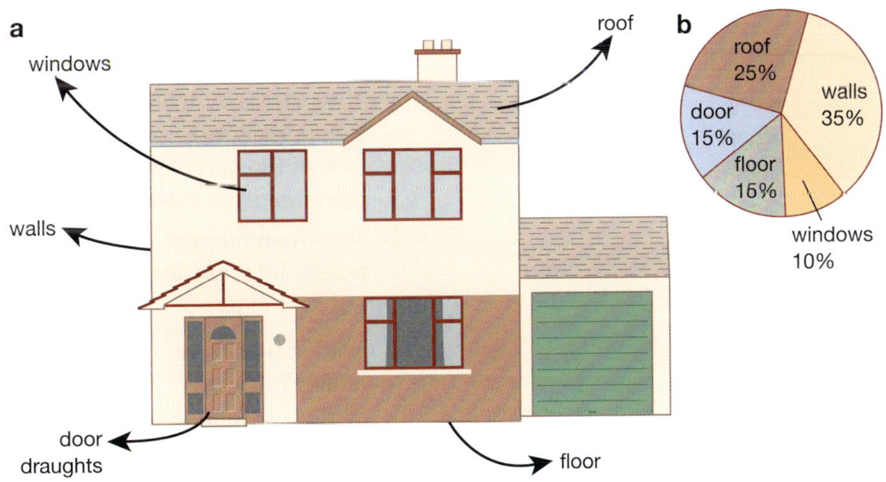

▲ Figure 11.18 **a** How thermal energy can be lost from the home; **b** Percentage of energy lost in different ways

INSULATING PEOPLE AND ANIMALS

Earlier in this chapter we saw a picture of a fire fighter in protective clothing designed to reduce the amount of heat getting to their bodies (Figure 11.12). Sometimes we have the opposite problem and want to keep warm. The obvious method of cutting down heat loss from the body is to wear clothes. Clothes that trap air around the body provide insulation because trapped air cannot circulate and is a very poor conductor. A large proportion of body heat (thermal energy) is lost from the head, so hats are the human equivalent of loft insulation.

Wind can cause rapid thermal energy loss from the body. It does this by forced convection – that is, making air circulate close to the body surface. It may also cause sweat to **evaporate** from the skin more quickly, causing rapid cooling. (The purpose of sweat is to help the body to lose thermal energy by evaporation, but, if it happens because of strong wind on a cold day, the effect can be life threatening.) These cooling effects of wind contribute to what is called the wind-chill factor. To reduce the wind-chill effect, a piece of wind-proof outer clothing should be worn.

When people do lose thermal energy at too great a rate they may become hypothermic, which means their body temperature starts to fall. If the heat loss is not significantly reduced the condition is potentially fatal. When people are rescued from mountains suffering from the effects of cold they are usually wrapped in thin, highly reflective blankets. The interior reflective surface reflects thermal energy back to their bodies while the outer reflective surface is a poor radiator of thermal energy. Marathon runners are often covered in these blankets at the end of the race to keep them warm when their energy reserves are low.

▲ Figure 11.19 Penguins stand close together for warmth.

Animals keep warm in different ways. You may have noticed birds fluffing up their feathers on cold days in winter. This increases the thickness of the trapped air layer around their bodies, so reducing thermal energy loss by conduction. Some birds, like penguins, will move close together for warmth (Figure 11.19). Other animals will curl into small balls. This cuts down thermal energy loss by making the surface area of their bodies exposed to the cold as small as possible.

CHAPTER QUESTIONS

More questions on thermal energy can be found at the end of Unit 4 on page 616.

SKILLS CREATIVITY, REASONING

7th

1 Explain the following observations, referring to the appropriate process of thermal energy transfer in each case.

  a Two cups of tea are poured at the same time. They are left for ten minutes. One of the cups has a metal teaspoon left in it. The tea in this cup is cooler than the tea in the other cup at the end of the ten-minute period.

  b Two fresh cups of tea are poured. (The others had gone cold!) A thin plastic lid is placed on top of one of the cups. The tea in this cup keeps hot for longer.

SKILLS REASONING

2 a Kettles heated on stoves used to be made of copper. Was this a good choice?

  b Copper kettles were usually kept highly polished (shiny). If it is not polished, copper turns matt and eventually blackens as it reacts with oxygen in the air. Apart from making the kettle look nice, what is a good physics reason for keeping a copper kettle polished?

8th

3 The diagrams below show a physics demonstration about thermal conduction.

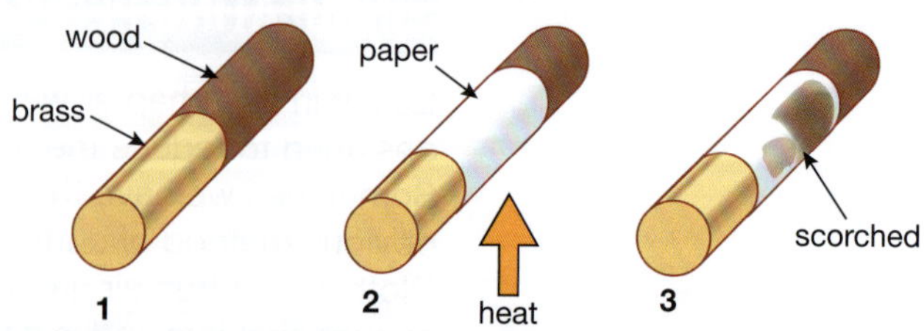

A cylinder is made from a piece of brass fitted to a piece of wood. A piece of paper is glued around the middle. The paper is then heated over a Bunsen burner flame. After a while one end of the paper is noticeably more burned than the other. Explain why this happens.

SKILLS CREATIVITY, REASONING

8th

4 There are two bench seats in a park, one made of metal, the other made of wood. The metal seat feels much colder to sit on than the wooden one. A student says that it is because the metal seat is at a lower temperature than the wooden one. Explain why this explanation is incorrect, and give a correct explanation of why the metal seat seems colder than the wooden one.

SKILLS REASONING

7th

5 a Why is the heating element (part) in an electric kettle positioned very close to the bottom of the kettle?

8th

b Where would you expect the cooling element to be placed in a freezer? Give a reason for your answer.

SKILLS CREATIVITY, REASONING

6 One model of a well-known brand of computer does not use a fan to keep the electronic circuits inside it cool, unlike other PCs. A student noticed that the ventilation (air) slots on most other PCs are positioned on the side, but the slots are on the top and bottom surfaces of this computer. The designer has applied physics to the problem of keeping the computer cool. Explain why the new computer does not need a fan.

7th

7 The diagram below shows how Roman mines used to be ventilated.

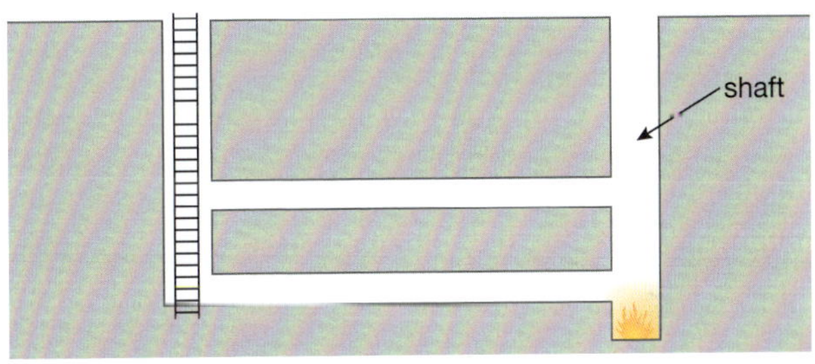

The mine system had a shaft with a fire lit at the bottom. Explain how this kept the air in the mine system fresh.

SKILLS EXECUTIVE FUNCTION

6th

8 a Describe an experiment to show that matt black surfaces absorb thermal radiation better than shiny metallic surfaces. Your description should include details of the apparatus; you may use a clearly labelled sketch diagram in your answer.

4th

b State what measurements you would take.

c Explain how you would make sure your investigation is fair.

5th

d How would your results show that the idea that a matt black surface absorbs thermal radiation better than a shiny metallic surface is correct?

12 WORK AND POWER

Work is calculated by multiplying the force applied by the distance through which the force moves – the bigger the force, or the longer the distance through which it moves, the more work is done. Work always involves an energy transfer. Power is the rate at which energy is transferred, and efficiency is a measure of how much of the input energy to a system is converted to useful output energy. In this chapter you will learn how to calculate the work done in a system and its power as energy is transferred.

▶ Figure 12.1 James Joule (1818–1889) was the son of a wealthy Manchester brewer. He was tutored by James Dalton and carried out scientific research in his own laboratory, built in the basement of his father's home.

LEARNING OBJECTIVES

- Know and use the relationship between work done, force and distance moved in the direction of the force:

  work done = force × distance moved

  $W = F \times d$

- Know that work done is equal to energy transferred
- Know and use the relationship between gravitational potential energy, mass, gravitational field strength and height:

  gravitational potential energy = mass × gravitational field strength × height

  $GPE = m \times g \times h$

- Know and use the relationship:

  kinetic energy = $\frac{1}{2}$ × mass × speed squared

  $KE = \frac{1}{2} \times m \times v^2$

- Understand how conservation of energy produces a link between gravitational potential energy, kinetic energy and work
- Describe power as the rate of transfer of energy or the rate of doing work
- Use the relationship between power, work done (energy transferred) and time taken:

  $\text{power} = \frac{\text{work done}}{\text{time taken}}$

  $P = \frac{W}{t}$

The unit of energy is named after James Joule. It was Joule who realised that heat was a store of energy. He showed that kinetic energy could be transferred to heat. At that time heat was measured in **calories**.

ENERGY AND WORK

Energy is the ability to do work.

This statement tells us what energy does rather than what energy is. We know that energy is found in a wide variety of different stores but we are really interested in what energy can do – the answer is that energy does work.

We need to define work in a way that is measurable. Some types of work are not easy to calculate the value of. Mechanical work, like lifting heavy objects, is easy to measure: if you lift a heavier object, you do more work; if you lift an object through a greater distance, again, you do more work. The definition of work in physics is:

work done, W (joules) = force, F (newtons) × distance moved, d (metres)

$$W = F \times d$$

If the force is measured in newtons and the distance through which the force is applied is measured in metres then the work done will be in joules.

Work done is equal to the amount of energy transferred.

1 J of work done is transferred when a force of 1 N is applied through a distance of 1 m in the direction of the force.

EXAMPLE 1

Figure 12.2 shows a weightlifter raising an object that weighs 500 N through a distance of 2 m. To calculate the work done we use:

$$W = F \times d$$
$$= 500\ \text{N} \times 2\ \text{m}$$
$$= 1000\ \text{J}$$

▲ Figure 12.2 Doing work by lifting a weight

This work done on the weight has increased its energy. This is explained in the section on gravitational potential energy (page 610).

EXAMPLE 2

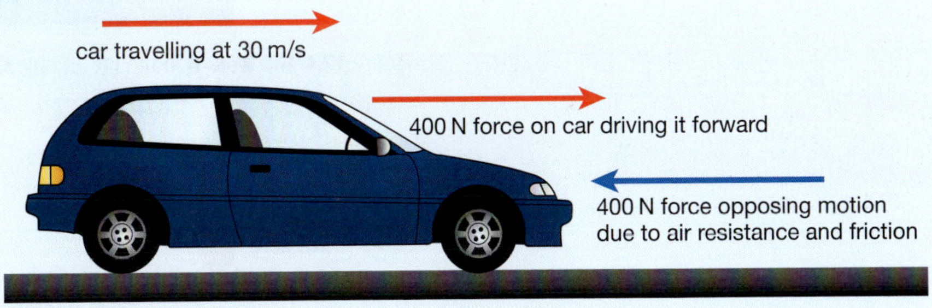

▲ Figure 12.3 A car travelling at a constant speed doing work

In the example shown in Figure 12.3 the force acting on the car is not accelerating it – instead, it is being used to balance the forces opposing its movement. The resultant force on the car is zero, so it keeps moving in a straight line at constant speed. To work out the work done on the car in one second we substitute the force required, 400 N, and the distance through which it acts in one second, 30 m, in the equation:

$$W = F \times d$$
$$= 400\ \text{N} \times 30\ \text{m}$$
$$= 12\,000\ \text{J or } 12\ \text{kJ}$$

GRAVITATIONAL POTENTIAL ENERGY (GPE)

The gravitational potential energy of an object that has been raised to a height, *h*, above the ground is given by:

gravitational potential energy, *GPE* (joules) = mass of object, *m* (kilograms) × gravitational field strength, *g* (newtons per kilogram) × height, *h* (metres)

$$GPE = m \times g \times h$$

The change in the GPE of an object will be an increase if we apply a force on it in the opposite direction to the pull of gravity – that is, if we lift it off the ground. When an object falls it loses GPE. To keep things simple, we usually assume that an object has no GPE before we do work on it.

In the weight-lifting example given on page 609, the weightlifter has used some chemical energy to do the work. We know that energy is conserved so what has happened to the chemical energy that the weightlifter used? Some has been transferred to heat in the weightlifter's body. The remainder has been transferred to the weight because he has increased its height in the gravitational field of the Earth. The energy that the weight has gained is called gravitational potential energy or GPE.

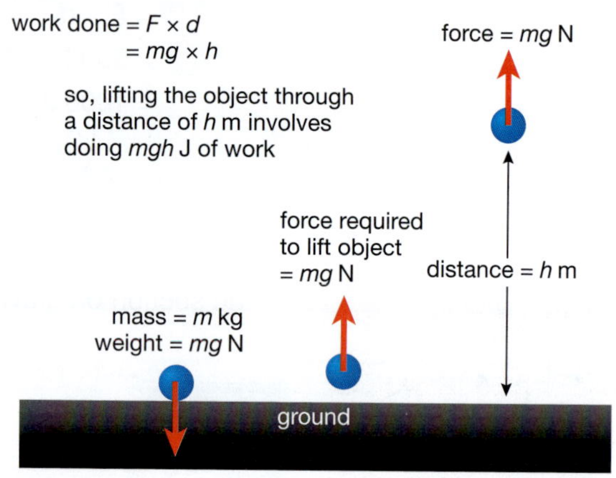

▲ Figure 12.4 The work done to lift an object is equal to the GPE the object has at its new height.

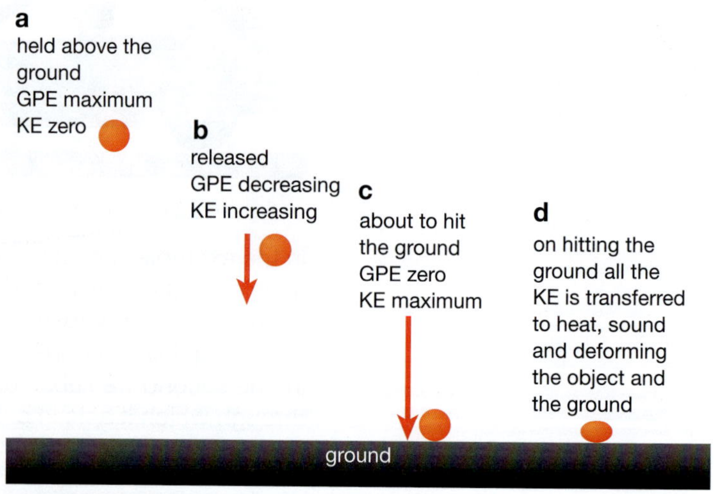

▲ Figure 12.5 When a raised object falls, its gravitational potential energy is transferred first to kinetic energy and then to heat and sound.

KEY POINT

Kinetic energy (KE) is the energy stored by moving objects.

In Figure 12.5, we can see the GPE stored by the weight is being transferred to other stores as the weight falls. The weight accelerates because of the force of gravity acting on it, so it gains kinetic energy. When it reaches the ground all the initial GPE is transferred to kinetic energy. When it hits the ground all the movement energy is then transferred to other stores, mainly heat and sound.

REMINDER

Gravitational field strength is the force acting per kilogram on a mass in a gravitational field. The gravitational field strength, g, on the surface of the Earth is approximately 10 N/kg. Since the weight of an object is mg, increase in GPE is a special version of the equation $W = F \times d$, with $F = mg$ and $d = h$.

KINETIC ENERGY, KE

The kinetic energy of a moving object is calculated using the equation:

kinetic energy, KE (joules) = mass, m (kilograms) × speed squared, v^2 (metres squared per seconds squared)

$$KE = \frac{1}{2}mv^2$$

EXTENSION WORK

In Chapter 1 we saw the equation of uniformly accelerated motion:

$$v^2 = u^2 + 2as$$

This equation allows us to work out the final velocity, v, of an object that has a uniform acceleration, a, and that has accelerated through a distance, s, starting with an initial velocity of u.

If we drop an object from rest its initial velocity, $u = 0$, its acceleration is g m/s^2 and the distance that it falls is usually represented by h, so the equation becomes

$$v^2 = 2gh$$

Multiplying both sides of the equation by m, the mass of the object, gives:

$$mv^2 = 2mgh \text{ which can be rearranged as } \tfrac{1}{2}mv^2 = mgh$$

showing that the gain in KE of the object is equal to its loss of GPE.

▲ Figure 12.6 Meteors burn up on entering our atmosphere – we see them as 'shooting stars'.

EXTENSION WORK

The meteorite that caused the Arizona crater is thought to have hit the Earth travelling at 11 000 m/s and to have had a mass of 109 kilograms. It hit the ground with an energy equivalent to a 15 megaton hydrogen bomb, 1000 times greater than the atomic bomb dropped on Hiroshima at the end of the Second World War.

We see that the amount of kinetic energy possessed by a moving object depends on its speed and its mass. As the Earth travels through space, orbiting the Sun, it runs the risk of colliding with chunks of matter that are drawn into the gravitational field of the Solar System. In fact, this is very common. If you have ever seen a shooting star – or, to give it its proper name, a meteor – you have seen the line of light produced as a small piece of space debris (waste) burns up on entering our atmosphere. This is an example of kinetic energy being transferred to heat and light by the friction produced between the air and the object passing through it.

▲ Figure 12.7 This crater was created when a meteorite collided with Earth in Arizona.

EXAMPLE 3

Calculate the kinetic energy carried by a meteorite of mass 500 kg (less than that of an average-sized car) hitting the Earth at a speed of 1000 m/s.

$$KE = \frac{1}{2}mv^2$$

$$= \frac{1}{2} \times 500 \text{ kg} \times (1000 \text{ m/s})^2$$

$$= 250\,000\,000 \text{ J (or 250 MJ)}$$

CALCULATIONS USING WORK, GPE AND KE

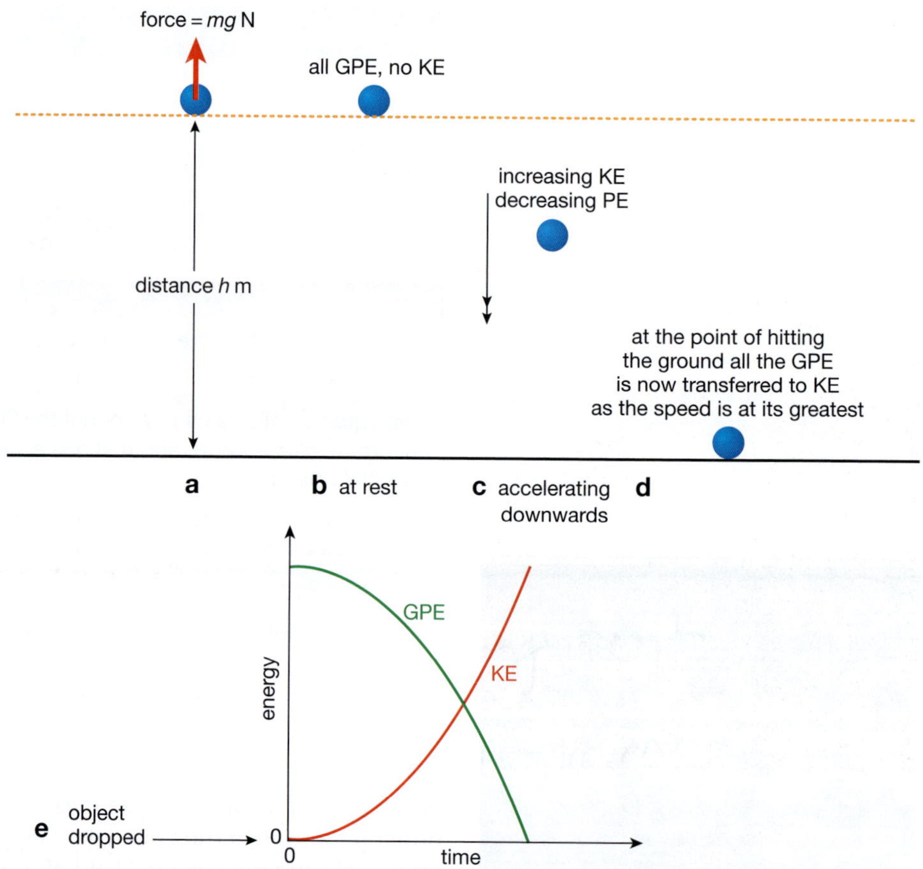

▲ Figure 12.8 GPE and KE of a falling object: **a** doing work to lift an object; **b** all GPE; **c** GPE transferring to KE during fall; **d** all KE at end of fall; **e** graph showing relationship between GPE and KE as the object falls

Work transfers energy to an object: $W = Fd$. An object of mass, m, weighs ($m \times g$) newtons so the force, F, needed to lift it is mg (Figure 12.8). If we raise the object through a distance h, the work done on the object is $mg \times h$. This is also the gain in GPE.

When the object is released, it falls – it loses GPE, but gains speed and so gains KE. At the end of the fall, all the initial GPE of the stationary (not moving) object has been transferred to the KE of the moving object. The graphs in Figure 12.8 show how the GPE of the object is changing into KE as it falls. The sum of the two graphs is always the same. Energy is conserved, so the loss of GPE is equal to the gain in KE.

work done lifting object = gain in GPE = gain in KE of the object just before hitting the ground

EXAMPLE 4

▲ Figure 12.9 A rollercoaster ride

In a rollercoaster ride the truck falls through a height of 17 m. Calculate the truck's speed at the bottom of this fall. (Take $g = 10$ N/kg)

If we assume that all the GPE of the truck at the top of the ride is transferred to KE at the bottom we can use the equation:

$$GPE = KE$$

$$mgh = \frac{1}{2}mv^2$$

The mass, m, of the truck appears on both sides of the equation, so it cancels out:

$$gh = \frac{1}{2}v^2$$

Substituting $h = 17$ m and $g = 10$ N/kg:

$$17\text{ m} \times 10\text{ N/kg} = \frac{1}{2}v^2$$

$$v^2 = 2 \times 17\text{ m} \times 10\text{ N/kg}$$

$$v = \sqrt{(2 \times 17\text{ m} \times 10\text{ N/kg})}$$

$$= 18.44\text{ m/s (about 66 kph)}$$

Some of the GPE the truck had at the start will be transferred to heat and sound, so the speed at the bottom of the fall will be a little slower than this.

▲ Figure 12.10 **a** James Watt (1736–1819) was a Scottish engineer who improved the performance of the steam engine and can be said to have started the Industrial Revolution – the beginning of the machine age. **b** A model of a steam engine that transfers the heat energy of steam to movement. Watt's engines were used to pump water out of mines.

POWER

Power is the rate of transfer of energy or the rate of doing work.

James Watt (Figure 12.10a) is remembered as the inventor of the steam engine and is said to have been inspired by watching the lid on a kettle being forced up by the pressure of the steam forming inside. Neither story is accurate, but what is true is that Watt, working in partnership with Matthew Boulton, developed improvements to the steam engine that made it a commercial product and completely changed industry and transport.

The SI unit of power is named in honour of James Watt. The watt (W) is the rate of transfer or conversion of energy of one joule per second (1 J/s).

$$\text{power, } P \text{ (watts)} = \frac{\text{work done, } W \text{ (joules)}}{\text{time taken, } t \text{ (seconds)}}$$

$$P = \frac{W}{t}$$

ACTIVITY 4

▼ PRACTICAL: INVESTIGATE YOUR POWER OUTPUT

You may have done a simple experiment involving running upstairs to measure your output power. You do work as you raise your GPE, and to find your power output in watts you divide the work done by the time taken. The experiment is shown in Figure 12.11. Notice that calculating the work you do against gravity using force × distance works just as well as using the equation for *GPE* (mass × gravitational field strength × height).

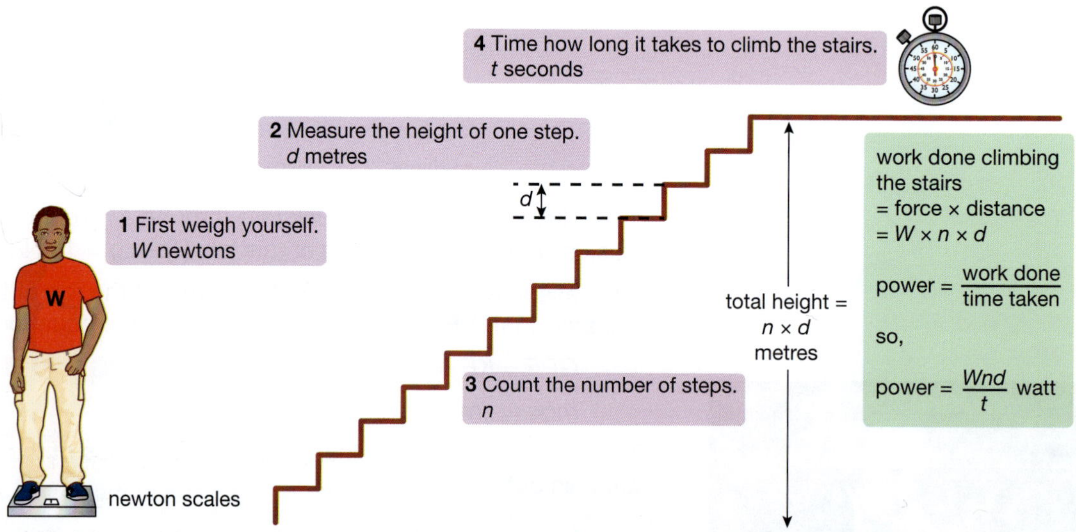

▶ Figure 12.11 An experiment to measure your output power

Safety note: Wear suitable footwear and only allow one person at a time on the staircase. Ensure the stairs are dry, in good condition and free of any obstacles.

A more convenient way of raising your GPE and getting to a higher floor in a building is to take a lift. The lift will transfer its energy input, usually electrical, to kinetic energy and then, if you are going up, to GPE. As usual, unwanted energy transfers are inevitable – sound and heat will be produced. If we know the weight of the lift and its contents and the height through which it moves, we can calculate the work done in the usual way. If we measure the time that the lift journey takes we can then calculate the power output of the lift motor. (Strictly this will be the useful power output – it will not take account of the wasted power due to unwanted energy transfers.)

EXAMPLE 5

If a lift and passengers have a combined weight of 4000 N and the lift moves upwards with an average speed of 3 m/s then what is the useful power output of the lift motor?

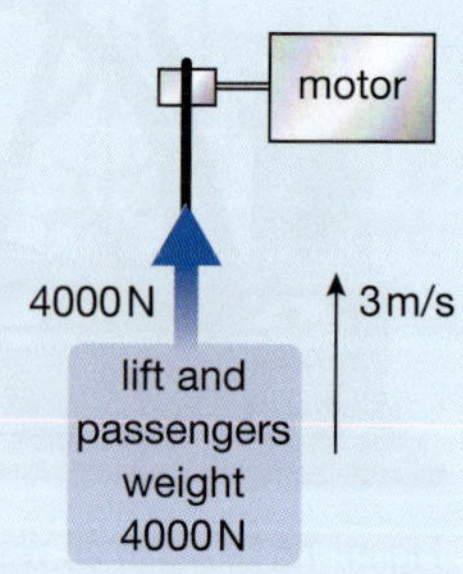

▲ Figure 16.12

To keep the lift moving upwards at a steady speed, the lift motor must provide an upward force to balance the weight of the lift. This is 4000 N.
In each second, this force is applied through a vertical distance of 3 m, so:

work done per second = 4000 N × 3 m/s

= 12 000 J/s

= 12 000 W

CHAPTER QUESTIONS

More questions on work, power and efficiency can be found at the end of Unit 4 on page 616.

In the questions below, where necessary, take the strength of the Earth's gravity to be 10 N/kg.

SKILLS CRITICAL THINKING

5th

1 James Joule showed that heat is a store of energy. He did this by showing that heat can be produced by using mechanical energy.

a Give an example of a process in which kinetic energy is transferred to heat.

b Describe how heat energy can be transferred to either kinetic energy or gravitational potential energy.

4th

2 a State the SI unit of work.

5th

b Define the unit of work.

SKILLS PROBLEM SOLVING

7th

c How much work is done in each of the following situations?

i A bag of six apples each weighing 1 N is lifted through 80 cm.

ii A rocket with a thrust of 100 kN travels to a height of 200 m.

iii A weightlifter raises a mass of 60 kg through a height of 2.8 m.

iv A lift of mass 200 kg lifts three people of mass 50 kg each through a distance of 45 m.

8th

3 Water from a **hydroelectric power** station reservoir is taken from a reservoir (artificial lake) at a height of 800 m above sea level to turbines (engines) in the power station itself. The power station is at sea level. The reservoir holds 200 million (2×10^8) litres of water. If a litre of water has a mass of 1 kg, how much gravitational potential energy is stored in the water in the reservoir?

SKILLS CRITICAL THINKING

4 a State how to calculate the kinetic energy stored by a moving object.

SKILLS PROBLEM SOLVING

b Work out the kinetic energy of the following:

i a man of mass 80 kg running at 9 m/s

ii an air rifle pellet of mass 0.2 g travelling at 50 m/s

iii a ball of mass 60 g travelling at 24 m/s.

9th

5 A catapult fires a stone of mass 0.04 kg vertically upwards. If the stone has an initial kinetic energy of 48 J, how high will it travel before it starts to fall back to the ground?

6 If a coin is dropped from a height of 80 m, how fast will it be travelling when it hits the ground? State any assumptions you may need to make.

SKILLS CRITICAL THINKING

5th

7 Define power and state its unit.

SKILLS PROBLEM SOLVING

8 A person with a mass of 40 kg runs upstairs in 12 s. The stairs have 20 steps and the height of each step is 20 cm.

6th

a How much does the person weigh, in newtons?

5th

b What is the total height that the person has climbed?

7th

c Calculate how much work is done in climbing the stairs.

d What is the power output of the person running up the stairs?

9 A drag car, of mass 500 kg, accelerates from rest to a speed of 144 km/h in 5 s.

6th

a What is its final speed in:

i m/h (metres per hour)

ii m/s?

8th

b What is the increase in KE of the drag car?

c What is the average power developed by the drag car's engine?

UNIT QUESTIONS

SKILLS PROBLEM SOLVING 6th

1 **a** A fluorescent lamp is 25% efficient. Choose the statement that correctly describes how the lamp performs.

A the lamp only works for a quarter of the time

B 25% of the energy transferred to the lamp is wasted

C the lamp does not work properly

D 25% of the energy supplied to the lamp is transferred to light **(1)**

SKILLS CRITICAL THINKING 5th

b A car uses energy stored in chemical form in petrol. When the engine is running this energy is transferred to other types of stored energy. Which of the following energy stores is useful?

A noise

B heat

C movement

D hot exhaust gases **(1)**

c Which of the following materials is a good thermal conductor?

A glass

B aluminium

C air

D water **(1)**

6th

d Which of the following statements about thermal radiation is false?

A It cannot travel through glass.

B It can travel through a vacuum.

C It travels at the speed of light.

D It is absorbed by black objects better than shiny ones. **(1)**

SKILLS PROBLEM SOLVING 7th

e Four students, A, B, C and D, measure their power output by running upstairs and timing how long it takes. Which of the four students has the greatest power output?

A mass of 50 kg, takes 20 s to gain a height of 10 m

B mass of 40 kg, takes 30 s to gain a height of 15 m

C mass of 45 kg, takes 10 s to gain a height of 5 m

D mass of 55 kg, takes 25 s to gain a height of 15 m **(1)**

(Total 5 marks)

SKILLS PROBLEM SOLVING 7th

2 An electric motor is used to raise a load that weighs 800 N through a distance of 30 m.

a How much work does it do in raising the load? **(3)**

b Calculate the power output of the motor if it takes 16 s to raise the load. **(2)**

c The motor is 75% efficient.

SKILLS CRITICAL THINKING 6th

i Explain what this means. **(2)**

SKILLS PROBLEM SOLVING 7th

ii Calculate the electrical power that must be supplied to the motor to raise this load in the time stated. Give your answer in kW. **(2)**

SKILLS INTERPRETATION

d Draw a labelled Sankey diagram to represent the energy transfers that take place as the motor raises the load. **(3)**

(Total 12 marks)

SKILLS ANALYSIS, REASONING

3 The diagram shows a toy rocket launcher that uses a spring in a tube.

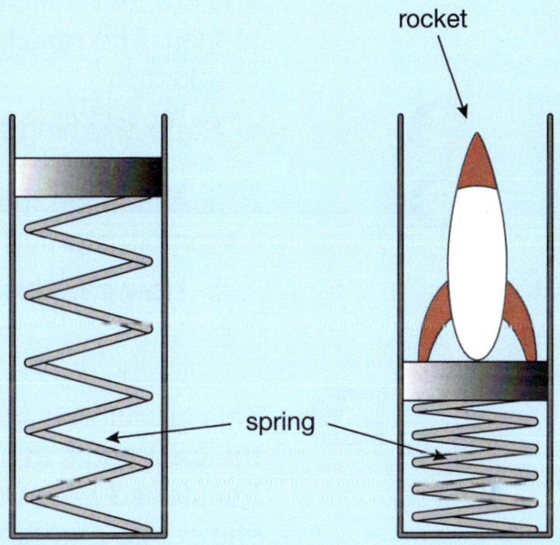

a Here are statements that describe the events leading to the launch of the toy rocket:

1 spring released

2 rocket leaves launcher

3 rocket gains kinetic energy

4 spring stores elastic potential energy

5 child does work squashing the spring

6 spring transfers stored energy to rocket

Choose from the following list the letter that describes the events in the order that they must happen. **(1)**

A 1 5 6 3 2 4 **B** 5 4 1 6 3 2 **C** 1 5 4 6 3 2 **D** 5 4 1 6 2 3

SKILLS CRITICAL THINKING

b Describe the energy transfers that take place after the rocket leaves the launcher, up to and including when it hits the ground. **(4)**

(Total 5 marks)

SKILLS EXECUTIVE FUNCTION

4 A student wants to show that water is a poor conductor of heat. The diagram below shows the investigation he sets up.

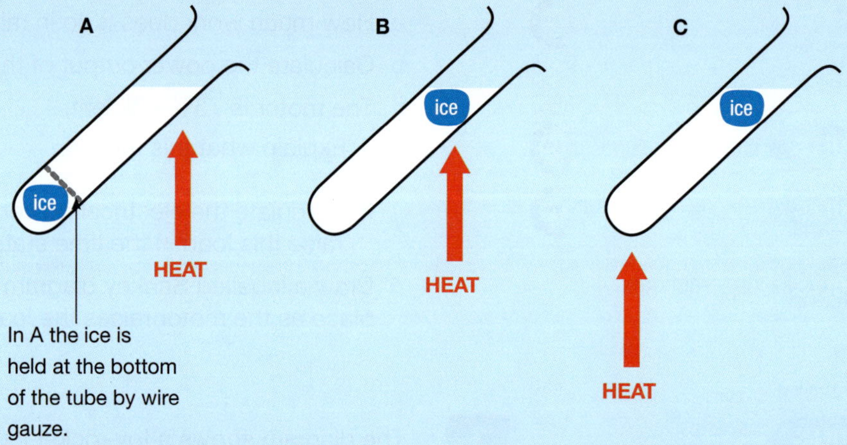

The student measures how long it takes for each piece of ice in the water to melt. The results will help him to show whether or not water is a poor conductor.

4th **a** State anything the student should do to make sure this is a fair test. **(3)**

SKILLS REASONING 7th **b i** Assuming that this is a fair test, in which order do you think the ice will melt, starting with the slowest? Give an explanation for your answer. **(4)**

SKILLS EXECUTIVE FUNCTION **ii** How can this investigation show that water is a poor conductor? **(3)**

(Total 10 marks)

5 This question is about PV **(photovoltaic) cells.** A student wanted find the best angle to set up a PV cell to get the maximum amount of energy transferred from the Sun's rays to electrical energy. Here is the apparatus she set up and the results she obtained.

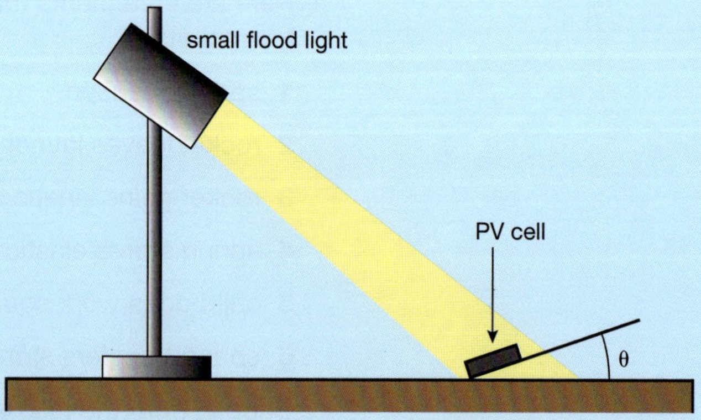

Angle θ / degrees	0	10	20	30	40	50	60	70	80	90
Current / mA	117	144	155	189	202	208	210	204	191	172

The PV cell was connected to a load and she measured the current, *I*, produced by the cell with the cell at different angles, θ, to the horizontal.

a State:

5th **i** the dependent variable **(1)**

ii the independent variable **(1)**

4th **iii** a control variable. **(1)**

SKILLS INTERPRETATION 7th

b On a graph grid, 18 cm by 22 cm, plot a graph of the current produced by the PV cell against the angle of the cell to the horizontal. **(5)**

SKILLS PROBLEM SOLVING 5th 6th

c Use the graph to find:

- **i** any anomalous result **(1)**
- **ii** the angle to get the maximum output from the PV cell in the set-up shown. **(1)**

SKILLS EXECUTIVE FUNCTION

d When installing PV panels it is important to have them pointing towards the Sun as you would expect. In the experimental set-up shown, the lamp is modelling conditions in the UK in early March at midday (when the Sun reaches its highest position in the sky).

- **i** How could the experiment be set up to model different positions of Sun? **(1)**

SKILLS INTERPRETATION 7th

- **ii** The experiment is repeated by another student at a time and place when the Sun is directly overhead at midday. Sketch a line on your graph to show how this student's results might appear. Label this line 'Sun overhead'. **(3)**

(Total 14 marks)

PHYSICS UNIT 5 SOLIDS, LIQUIDS AND GASES

Matter can exist in three basic forms: as a solid, a liquid or a gas. In this photo all three are present, though we can only see the solid iceberg and the liquid ocean. Fortunately the iceberg is surrounded by gas, the mixture of oxygen and nitrogen that makes up our atmosphere. Our atmosphere usually contains some water in gas form, which we cannot see. When gaseous water in the atmosphere condenses into tiny water droplets we can see these as clouds.

13 DENSITY AND PRESSURE

One way of characterising materials is by their density. This chapter looks at density and at how materials can affect things around them by exerting pressure.

▲ Figure 13.1 Some effects of density and pressure

LEARNING OBJECTIVES

- Know and use the relationship between density, mass and volume: density $= \frac{\text{mass}}{\text{volume}}$ $\rho = \frac{m}{V}$
- Practical: investigate density using direct measurements of mass and volume
- Know and use the relationship between pressure, force and area: pressure $= \frac{\text{force}}{\text{area}}$ $p = \frac{F}{A}$
- Understand how the pressure at a point in a gas or liquid at rest acts equally in all directions
- Know and use the relationship for pressure difference: pressure difference = height × density × gravitational field strength $p = h \times \rho \times g$

UNITS

In this section you need to use degree Celsius (°C) and Kelvin (K) as the units of temperature (these units both represent the same change in temperature but the Kelvin scale starts from absolute zero, as explained later), kilogram per cubic metre (kg/m^3) as the unit of density, cubic metre (m^3) as the unit of volume, pascal (Pa) as the unit of pressure and square metre (m^2) as the unit of area. It is important to remember 1 m^3 = 1 000 000 cm^3 (a cubic metre is 1 million cubic centimetres) and 1 m^2 = 10 000 cm^2 (a square metre is 10 thousand square centimetres).

KEY POINT

ρ is the Greek letter rho (pronounced 'row') and is the usual symbol for density. This is not to be confused with p which represents pressure.

The properties of a material affect how it behaves, and how it affects other materials around it. The balloon can fly because the gas inside it has a very low density. The skis spread the weight of the skier over the snow so she does not sink into it. The submersible is designed to explore the seabed – it has a very strong hull to withstand the high pressure from water deep in the oceans.

DENSITY

Solids, liquids and gases have different properties and characteristics. One such characteristic is density. Solids are often very dense – that is, they have a high mass for a certain volume. Liquids are often less dense than solids, and gases have very low densities.

The density (ρ) of a material can be calculated if you know the mass (m) of a certain volume (V) of the material, using this equation:

$$\text{density, } \rho = \frac{\text{mass, } m}{\text{volume, } V}$$

$$\rho = \frac{m}{V}$$

The units for density depend on the units used for mass and volume. If mass is measured in kilograms and volume in cubic metres, the units for density are kilograms per cubic metre (kg/m³). Density can also be measured in grams per cubic centimetre (g/cm³).

EXAMPLE 1

A piece of iron has a mass of 390 kg and a volume of 0.05 m³. What is its density?

$$\text{density} = \frac{\text{mass}}{\text{volume}}$$

$$= \frac{390\ \text{kg}}{0.05\ \text{m}^3}$$

$$= 7800\ \text{kg/m}^3$$

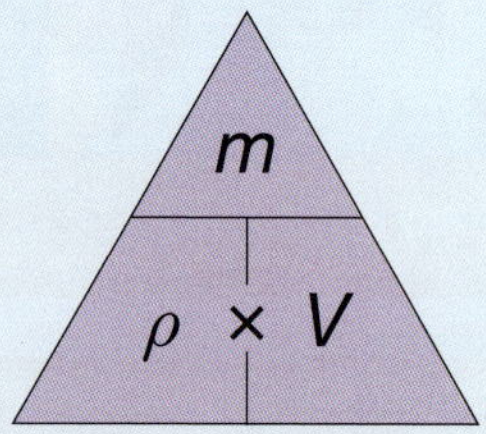

▲ Figure 13.2 The equation for density can be rearranged using the triangle method.

HINT

If an examination question asks you to write out the equation for calculating density, mass or volume, always give the actual equation in words or using standard symbols, such as $\rho = \frac{m}{V}$.

ACTIVITY 1

▼ PRACTICAL: INVESTIGATE THE DENSITY OF SOLIDS

The density of a substance can be determined by measuring the mass and volume of a sample of the material, and then calculating the density.

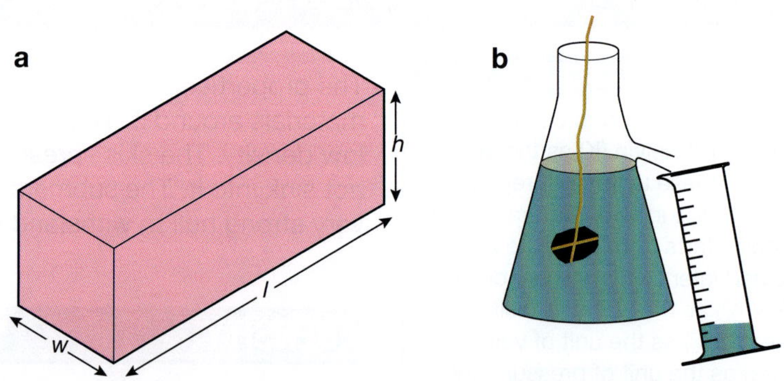

▲ Figure 13.3 **a** The volume of a regular solid can be calculated by multiplying its length (*l*), width (*w*) and height (*h*). **b** The volume of an irregular object can be determined using a displacement can and a measuring cylinder.

Use a half-metre rule to measure the length, width and height of a regular solid. When measuring the volume of the liquid that is displaced (pushed out) by an irregular solid make sure that the measuring cylinder is on a level (horizontal) surface and that you look at the scale straight on as shown (to avoid **parallax error**).

You then need to measure the mass of the solid. Use weighing scales for this.

EXAMPLE 2

The mass of 50 cm^3 of a liquid and a measuring cylinder is 146 g. The mass of the empty measuring cylinder is 100 g. What is the density of the liquid in kg/m^3?

$$\text{mass of 50 cm}^3\text{ of liquid} = 146\text{ g} - 100\text{ g} = 46\text{ g} = 0.046\text{ kg}$$

$$50\text{ cm}^3 = 0.000\,05\text{ m}^3$$

$$\rho = \frac{m}{V} = \frac{0.046\text{ kg}}{0.000\,05\text{ m}^3} = 920\text{ kg/m}^3$$

or

$$= \frac{46\text{ g}}{50\text{ cm}^3} = 0.92\text{ g/cm}^3 = 920\text{ kg/m}^3$$

HINT

Check the units when you are working out density – don't mix up g and m^3, for example. Also check which units the question asks for in your final answer.

1 kg = 1000 g

To convert kg to g, divide by 1000.

1 m^3 = 1 000 000 cm^3

To convert cm^3 to m^3, divide by 1 000 000 (or 10^6).

Alternatively, work out the density in g/cm^3, then multiply your answer by 1000.

PRESSURE UNDER A SOLID

You can push a drawing pin into a piece of wood quite easily, but you cannot make a hole in the wood with your thumb, no matter how hard you push! The small point of the drawing pin concentrates all your pushing force into a tiny area, so the pin goes into the wood easily. Similarly, it is easier to cut things with a sharp knife than a blunt one, because with a sharp knife all the force is concentrated into a much smaller area.

Pressure is defined as the force per unit area. Force is measured in newtons (N) and area is measured in square metres (m^2). The units for pressure are pascals (Pa), where 1 Pa is equivalent to 1 N/m^2.

Pressure (p), force (F) and area (A) are linked by the following equation:

$$\text{pressure, } p\text{ (pascals)} = \frac{\text{force, } F\text{ (newtons)}}{\text{area, } A\text{ (square metres)}}$$

$$p = \frac{F}{A}$$

REMINDER

When answering questions, start with the equation you need to use in words or recognised symbols.

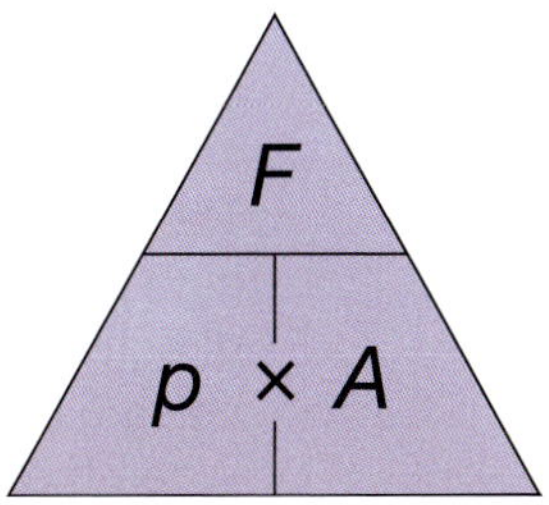

▲ Figure 13.4 The equation for pressure can be rearranged using the triangle method.

EXAMPLE 3

An elephant has a weight of 40 000 N, and her feet cover a total area of 0.1 m^2.

A woman weighs 600 N and the total area of her shoes in contact with the ground is 0.0015 m^2. Who exerts the greatest pressure on the ground?

Elephant:

$$p = \frac{F}{A}$$

$$= \frac{40\,000 \text{ N}}{0.1 \text{ m}^2}$$

$$= 400\,000 \text{ Pa (or 400 kPa)}$$

Woman:

$$p = \frac{F}{A}$$

$$= \frac{600 \text{ N}}{0.0015 \text{ m}^2}$$

$$= 400\,000 \text{ Pa (or 400 kPa)}$$

They both exert an equal pressure.

a b
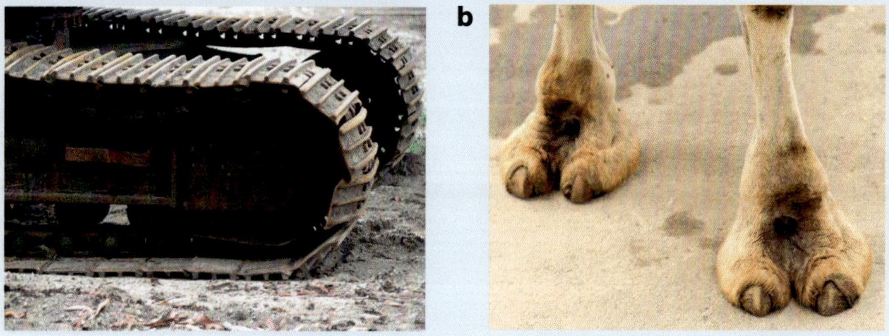

▲ Figure 13.5 **a** The caterpillar tracks on this vehicle spread its weight over a large area. **b** Camels have large feet so they are less likely to sink into loose sand.

Some machines, including cutting tools like scissors, bolt cutters and knives, need to exert a high pressure to work well. In other applications, a low pressure is important. Tractors and other vehicles designed to move over mud have large tyres that spread the vehicle's weight. The pressure under the tyres is relatively low, so the vehicle is less likely to sink into the mud. Caterpillar tracks used on bulldozers and other earth-moving equipment serve a similar purpose. (In Figure 13.5a the caterpillar tracks are very large.)

PRESSURE IN LIQUIDS AND GASES

The submersible shown in Figure 13.1 has a very strong hull to withstand the high pressure **exerted** on it by seawater. Pressure in liquids acts equally in all directions, as long as the liquid is not moving. You can easily demonstrate this using a can with holes punched around the bottom, as shown in Figure 13.6. When the can is filled with water, the water is forced out equally in all directions.

Gases also exert pressure on things around them. The pressure exerted by the atmosphere on your body is about 100 000 Pa (although the pressure varies slightly from day to day). However, the pressure inside our bodies is similar, so we do not notice the pressure of the air

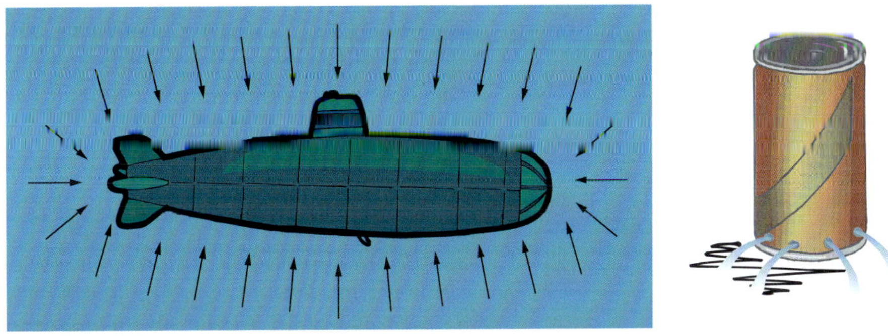

▲ Figure 13.6 Pressure in liquids acts equally in all directions. A can of water with holes can be used to demonstrate this.

One of the first demonstrations of the effects of air pressure was carried out by Otto van Guericke in 1654, in Magdeburg, Germany. Van Guericke had two large metal bowls made, put them together and then pumped the air out. The bowls could not be pulled apart, even when he attached two teams of horses to the bowls.

▲ Figure 13.7 Van Guericke's experiment at Magdeburg

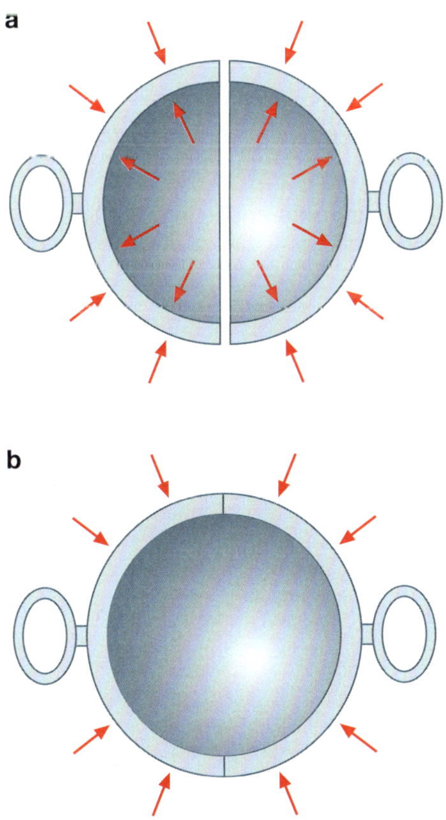

▲ Figure 13.8 **a** When the hemispheres are full of air, the forces are the same inside and outside. **b** When the air is taken out, there is only a force on the outside of the hemispheres.

You can do the same experiment in the laboratory, using much smaller bowls called Magdeburg **hemispheres**. When air is inside the spheres, the pressure is the same inside and outside. If the air is sucked out, pressure is only acting from the outside. The hemispheres cannot be pulled apart until air is let back into them.

EXAMPLE 4

A laboratory set of Magdeburg hemispheres has a surface area of 0.045 m^2. What is the total force on the outside of the hemispheres?

$$F = p \times A$$
$$= 100\,000 \text{ Pa} \times 0.045 \text{ m}^2$$
$$= 4500 \text{ N}$$

PRESSURE AND DEPTH

The experiment shown in Figure 13.9 demonstrates that the pressure in a liquid increases with depth. We can work out the pressure difference by thinking about a column of water, as shown in Figure 13.10.

▲ Figure 13.9 Pressure in a liquid increases with depth.

The force at the bottom of the column is equal to all the weight of water above it. The volume of this water (V) is found by multiplying the area of its base (A) by the height (h) of the column. We can work out the mass (m) of the water by multiplying the volume ($A \times h$) by the density (ρ).

mass of water, $m = (A \times h) \times \rho$

The force (F) on the bottom of the water column is equal to the weight of this volume of water, which is the mass, m ($A \times h \times \rho$), multiplied by the gravitational field strength (g) (see page 520).

$$F = (A \times h \times \rho) \times g$$

As we are concerned with the pressure on the base of the column, we divide the force by the area:

$$F = \frac{A \times h \times \rho \times g}{A}$$

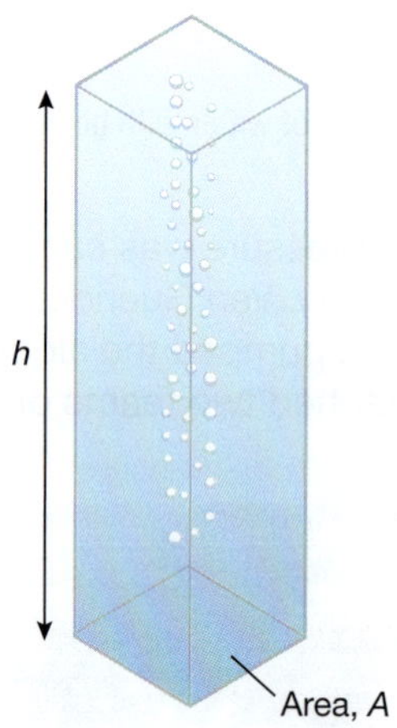

▲ Figure 13.10 We can work out the pressure difference between two points in a liquid by considering a column of the liquid.

The area of the column therefore does not matter, and we can calculate the pressure difference between two points in a liquid using the equation:

pressure difference, p (Pa) = height, h (m) × density, ρ (kg/m^3) × gravitational field strength, g (N/kg)

$$p = h \times \rho \times g$$

Be careful not to muddle the symbol for pressure, p, with the symbol for density, ρ.

This equation can be used for calculating pressure differences in other liquids or gases, as long as you know their densities.

KEY POINT

You need to learn this equation but you do not need to know the proof given here for the exam.

EXAMPLE 5

The first experiments on air pressure were carried out using a simple barometer. This was made by filling a long glass tube with mercury, and then inverting it into a bowl of mercury. The mercury falls until the weight of the column is supported by the pressure of the air on the mercury in the bowl.

If the column of mercury is 0.74 m high, what is the air pressure?

The density of mercury is 13 600 kg/m^3. Take the gravitational field strength as 10 N/kg.

$$p = h \times \rho \times g$$

$$= 0.74 \text{ m} \times 13\,600 \text{ kg/m}^3 \times 10 \text{ N/kg}$$

$$= 100\,640 \text{ Pa}$$

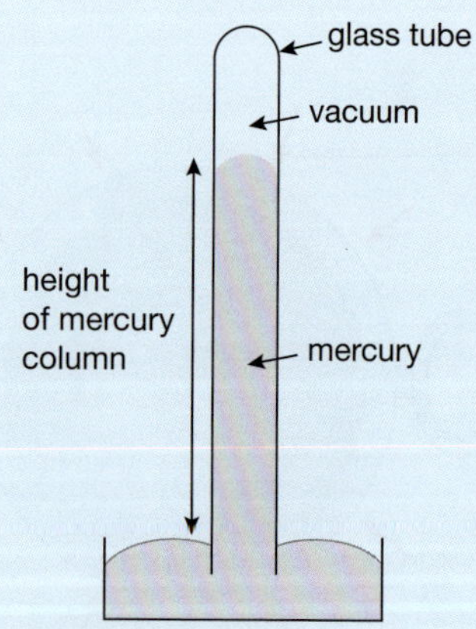

▲ Figure 13.11 A simple mercury barometer

EXTENSION WORK

The unit for pressure is named after Blaise Pascal (1623–1662). He was the first person to demonstrate that air pressure decreases with height. He persuaded his brother-in-law to take a mercury barometer up a mountain and measure the air pressure at different stages in the climb. He also arranged for someone at the base of the mountain to measure the air pressure at different times during the day. The measurements showed that the pressure of the air does decrease as you climb.

LOOKING AHEAD – WEATHER AND PRESSURE

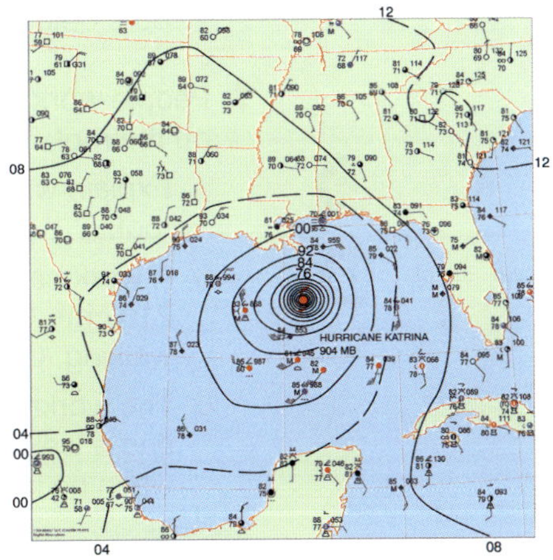

▲ Figure 13.12 Weather maps show isobars (lines of equal air pressure). The centre of hurricane Katrina is a very low pressure region surrounded by isobars that are very close together. The result of the pressure difference is very strong winds.

▲ Figure 13.13 Tornados regularly cause huge amounts of damage in many parts of the world.

Variations in atmospheric pressure are partly responsible for the weather systems around the world. Meteorologists produce maps showing how atmospheric pressure varies from place to place to help them make predictions about future weather systems. Regions of low pressure produce winds as air flows from surrounding areas of high pressure.

Sometimes the wind speeds cause violent weather systems with tornados and hurricanes causing extensive damage and loss of life. Physics provides important tools to enable meteorologists to make more accurate predictions about when and where these devastating events will occur.

CHAPTER QUESTIONS

More questions on density and pressure can be found at the end of Unit 5 on page 635.

SKILLS CREATIVITY, REASONING

1 A Greek scientist called Archimedes was asked to check the purity of the gold in a crown. He did this by comparing the density of the crown with the density of pure gold.

6th

a Describe how he could have measured the density of an irregular-shaped object such as a crown.

SKILLS PROBLEM SOLVING 8th

b Pure gold has a density of 19 000 kg/m^3. Suppose the crown had a volume of 0.0001 m^3. What mass should the crown be if it is made of pure gold?

2 People working on the roofs of buildings often lay a ladder or plank of wood on the roof. They walk on the ladder rather than the roof itself.

SKILLS REASONING 6th

a Explain why using a ladder or plank will help to prevent damage to the roof.

SKILLS PROBLEM SOLVING 7th

b A workman's weight is 850 N, and each of his boots has an area of 210 cm^2. Calculate the maximum pressure under his feet when he is walking. Give your answer in pascals.

c The workman lays a plank on the roof. The plank has an area of 0.3 m^2 and a weight of 70 N. What is the maximum pressure under the plank when he is walking on it?

HINT

Remember that all your weight is on one foot at some point while you are walking. To convert cm^2 to m^2, divide by 10 000 or 10^4.

3 A manometer can be used to find the pressure of a gas. The difference in the level of the liquid in each side of the tube indicates the difference in pressure on the water surface at A and the pressure of the gas on the water surface at B. (Assume atmospheric pressure is 100 kPa.)

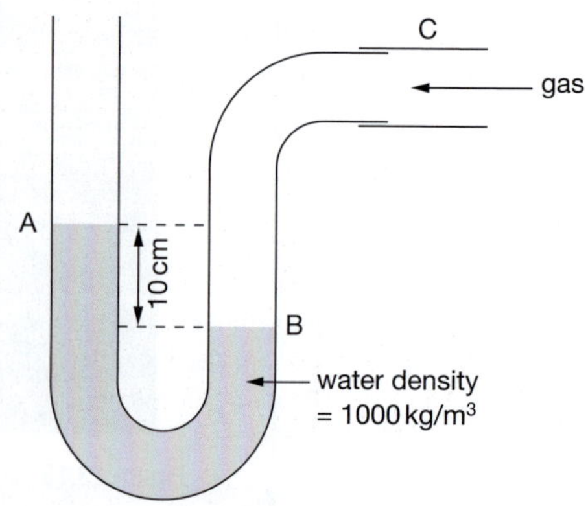

a What is the difference in pressure in Pa between A and B? Use g = 10 N/kg.

b What is the pressure of the gas in tube C?

SKILLS REASONING

c Describe what will happen when the gas is turned off and the pipe is removed from C.

14 SOLIDS, LIQUIDS AND GASES

All matter is made up of particles that are continuously moving. The arrangement and movement of the particles determine the properties of the material. In gases, scientists have discovered laws that describe the relationship between pressure, temperature and volume. In this chapter, you will learn what these laws are and how this relationship can be explained in terms of the behaviour of the particles.

▶ Figure 14.1 The botanist Robert Brown (1773–1858) made an observation while studying pollen grains under a microscope that has become known as Brownian motion in his honour. The observation led to the kinetic theory of matter that we use to explain the behaviour of solids, liquids and gases.

LEARNING OBJECTIVES

- Explain how molecules in a gas have random motion and that they exert a force and hence a pressure on the walls of a container
- Understand why there is an absolute zero of temperature which is –273 °C
- Describe the Kelvin scale of temperature and be able to convert between the Kelvin and Celsius scales
- Understand why an increase in temperature results in an increase in the average speed of gas molecules
- Know that the Kelvin temperature of a gas is proportional to the average kinetic energy of its molecules
- Explain, for a fixed amount of gas, the qualitative relationship between:
  - pressure and volume at constant temperature
  - pressure and Kelvin temperature at constant volume
- Use the relationship between the pressure and Kelvin temperature of a fixed mass of gas at constant volume: $$\frac{p_1}{T_1} = \frac{p_2}{T_2}$$
- Use the relationship between the pressure and volume of a fixed mass of gas at constant temperature: $$p_1V_1 = p_2V_2$$

THE GAS LAWS

We are now going to focus our attention on the properties of gases. We shall explain the different properties in terms of the movement of particles.

We have already said that gases are made up of molecules that are moving. We believe that the particles in gases are spread out and constantly moving in a random, haphazard way.

When the molecules hit the walls of a container they exert a force. The combined effect of the huge number of **collisions** results in the pressure that is exerted on the walls of the container.

SOLIDS, LIQUIDS AND GASES

BOYLE'S LAW

▲ Figure 14.2 Robert Boyle (1627–1691) was an Anglo-Irish chemist and philosopher. As well as discovering the law that bears his name, he worked with Robert Hooke at Oxford developing the air pump.

The scientist Robert Boyle (Figure 14.2) discovered something that you have probably noticed if you have ever used a bicycle pump: air is squashy! He noticed that you can squeeze air in a cylinder and that it springs back to its original volume when you release it. You can try this for yourself with a plastic syringe (Figure 14.3).

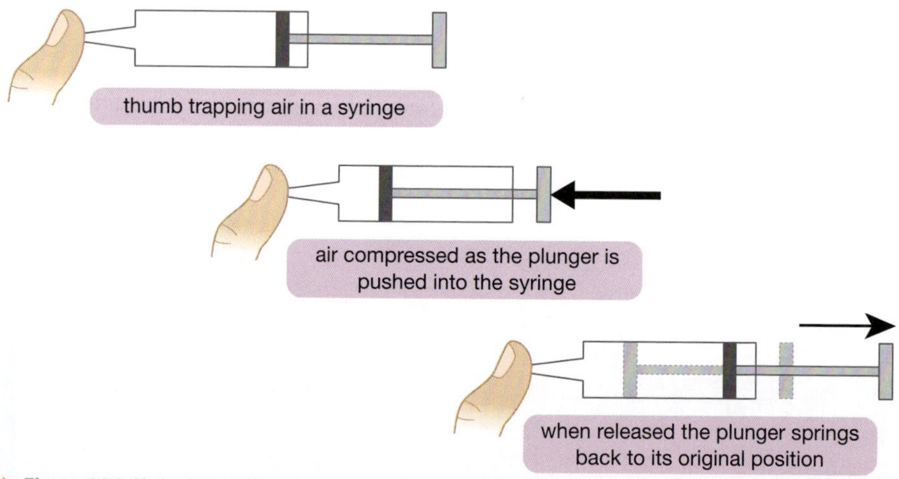

▲ Figure 14.3 Air is squashy!

Boyle devised an experiment to see how the volume occupied by a gas depends on the pressure exerted on it. Pressure is the force acting per unit area. This is measured in N/m^2. One N/m^2 is called a pascal (Pa). A version of Boyle's experiment is shown in Figure 14.4.

▲ Figure 14.4 A modern version of Boyle's experiment to see how the volume of a gas depends on the pressure exerted on it.

Boyle took care to make sure that the trapped gas he was studying stayed at the same temperature. He increased the pressure on the gas and made a note of the new volume. His results looked like the graph shown in Figure 14.5a.

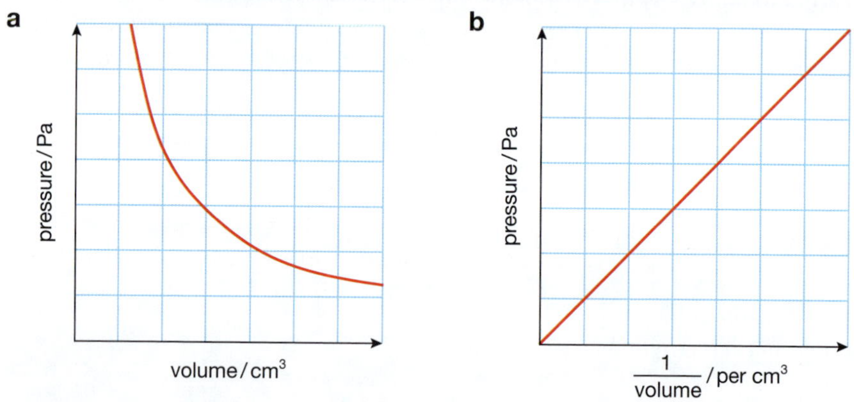

▲ Figure 14.5 **a** Graph to show how the pressure of a gas at constant temperature varies with the volume; **b** Graph of pressure against $\frac{1}{\text{volume}}$

> **!** **Safety note:** Eye protection is needed in case any tubing leaks or detaches, which will cause gas under high pressure to be ejected.

Boyle noticed that when he doubled the pressure, the volume of the gas halved. If we plot pressure (p), against $\frac{1}{\text{volume}}$ $\left(\frac{1}{V}\right)$, as in Figure 14.5b, we can see from the straight line passing through the origin that p is proportional to $\frac{1}{V}$. This discovery, called Boyle's law, is expressed in the equation:

$$p_1 V_1 = p_2 V_2$$

This means that if you take a fixed mass of gas that has a pressure p_1 and a volume V_1 and change either the pressure or the volume, the new pressure p_2 multiplied by the new volume V_2 will be the same as $p_1 \times V_1$, if the temperature of the gas remains the same.

EXAMPLE 1

Atmospheric pressure is 100 kPa (100 000 Pa). Some air in a sealed container has a volume of 2 m³ at atmospheric pressure. What would be the pressure of the air if you reduced its volume to 0.2 m³?

First write down what we know:

$$p_1 = 100 \text{ kPa}$$
$$V_1 = 2 \text{ m}^3$$
$$V_2 = 0.2 \text{ m}^3$$
$$p_1V_1 = p_2V_2$$
$$p_2 \times 0.2 \text{ m}^3 = 100 \text{ kPa} \times 2 \text{ m}^3$$
$$p_2 = \frac{100 \text{ kPa} \times 2 \text{ m}^3}{0.2 \text{ m}^3}$$
$$= 1000 \text{ kPa}$$

HINT

You can do all your working in kPa if you wish, rather than converting the pressure to pascals. You can also use cubic centimetres for volume if these units are given in the question. It does not matter which units you use, as long as you use the same ones throughout the question.

Gases can be compressed because the gas molecules are very spread out. When a gas is squashed into a smaller container it presses on the walls of the container with a greater pressure. This is explained in terms of particle theory as follows.

If the gas is kept at the same temperature, the average speed of the particles stays the same. (Remember that temperature is an indication of the kinetic energy of the particles.) If the same number of particles is squeezed into a smaller volume, they will hit the container walls more often. Each particle exerts a tiny force on the wall with which it collides. More collisions per second means a greater average force on the wall and, therefore, a greater pressure.

ABSOLUTE ZERO

Boyle took care to conduct his experiment at constant temperature. He was aware that temperature also had an effect on the pressure of a gas. Figure 14.6 shows an experiment to investigate how the pressure of a gas depends on its temperature.

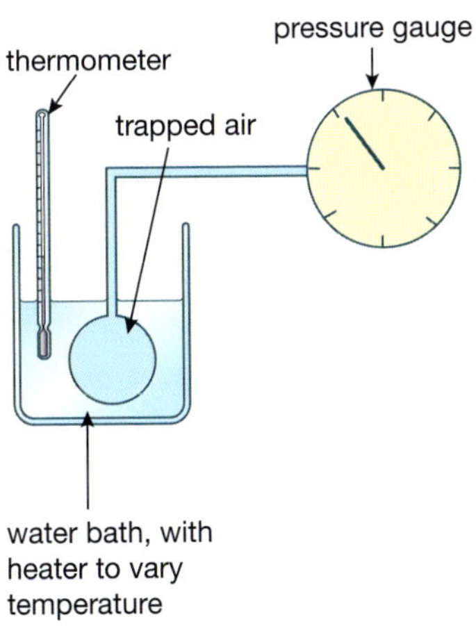

▲ Figure 14.6 Simple apparatus to measure the pressure of a fixed volume of gas at a range of temperatures

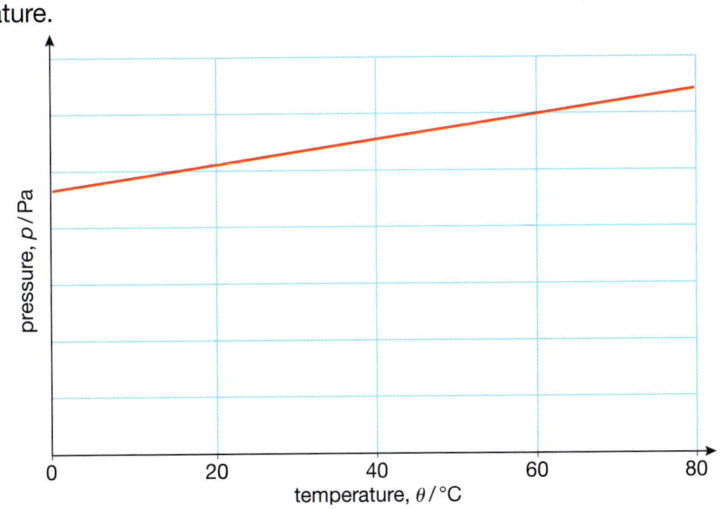

▲ Figure 14.7 Graph to show how the pressure of a fixed volume of gas varies with temperature

The gas is kept at constant volume, and its pressure is measured at a range of temperatures. The graph in Figure 14.7 shows typical results for this experiment.

The graph shows that the pressure of the gas increases as the temperature increases. We could also say that the gas pressure gets smaller as the gas is cooled.

What happens if we keep cooling the gas? The graph in Figure 14.8 shows this.

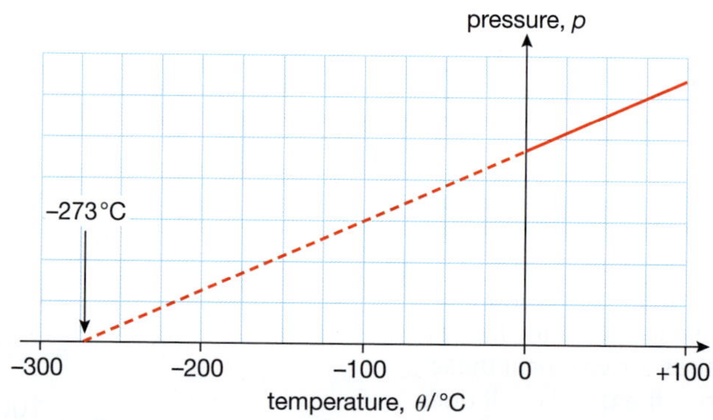

▲ Figure 14.8 At a temperature of −273 °C, the pressure of the gas would be zero. This temperature is known as 'absolute zero'.

As we cool the gas, the pressure keeps decreasing. The pressure of the gas cannot become less than zero. This suggests that there is a temperature below which it is not possible to cool the gas further. This temperature is called absolute zero. Experiments show that absolute zero is approximately −273 °C.

The Kelvin temperature scale starts from absolute zero. The Kelvin temperature of a gas is proportional to the average kinetic energy of its molecules.

To convert a temperature on the Celsius scale (in °C) to a Kelvin scale temperature (in K), add 273 to the Celsius scale temperature:

- temperature in K = temperature in °C + 273
- temperature in °C = temperature in K − 273

EXAMPLE 2

a At what temperature does water freeze, in Kelvin?

Water freezes at 0 °C. To convert 0 °C to Kelvin:

$T = (0\,°C + 273)\ K$

$= 273\ K$

b What is room temperature, in Kelvin?

Typical room temperature is 20 °C, so:

$T = (20\,°C + 273)\ K$

$= 293\ K$

c What temperature is 400 K on the Celsius scale?

$\theta = (400\ K - 273)\,°C$

$= 127\,°C$

If we redraw the graph of pressure against temperature using the absolute or Kelvin temperature scale, we get a graph that is a straight line passing through the origin, as shown in Figure 14.9. This shows that the pressure of the gas is proportional to its Kelvin temperature. For example, if you heat a gas from 200 K (–73 °C) to 400 K (127 °C), its pressure will double.

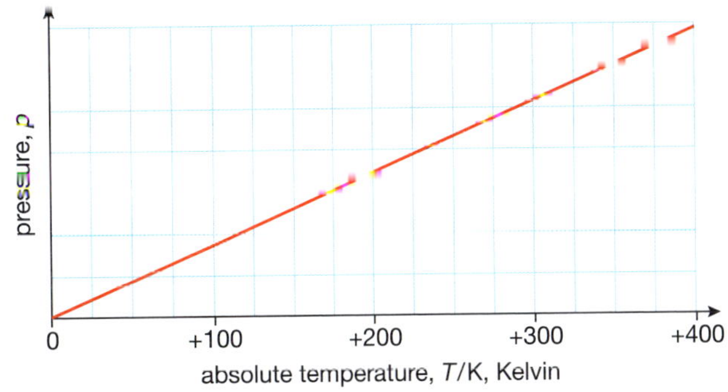

▲ Figure 14.9 Graph of pressure against absolute temperature for a fixed amount of gas at constant volume

For a fixed mass of gas at a constant volume:

$$\frac{p_1}{T_1} = \frac{p_2}{T_2}$$

NB T must be measured in Kelvin.

KEY POINT

We often use the symbol θ for temperature in °C. For temperature in K we always use the symbol T. Remember to convert Celsius temperatures to Kelvin when using gas law equations in which temperature change occurs.

EXAMPLE 3

You take an empty tin and put the lid on tightly. You heat it using a Bunsen burner until the temperature of the air inside is 50 °C. What is the pressure of the air inside the tin? The temperature of the room is 20 °C.

First write down what you know:

p_1 = 100 kPa (this is atmospheric pressure)

The starting temperature is 20 °C, but we must change this to Kelvin, so:

$$T_1 = 20 + 273\ \text{K} = 293\ \text{K}.$$

The end temperature, 50 °C, must also be converted so:

$$T_2 = 50 + 273\ \text{K} = 323\ \text{K}$$

$$\frac{p_1}{T_1} = \frac{p_2}{T_2}$$

$$p_2 = p_1 \times \frac{T_2}{T_1}$$

$$= 100\ \text{kPa} \times \frac{323\ \text{K}}{293\ \text{K}}$$

$$= 110\ \text{kPa}$$

EXTENSION WORK

Cooling things further becomes more and more difficult as they get closer to 0 K. Scientists have managed to cool gases down to within a few thousandths of a degree above absolute zero. At this temperature, even gases like helium and hydrogen can be liquefied. The gas laws do not apply once a gas is either cooled or compressed (forced into a small volume) to the point that they become liquid.

The relationship can be explained as follows.

The number of gas particles and the space, or volume, they occupy remain constant. When we heat the gas the particles continue to move randomly, but with a higher average speed. This means that their collisions with the walls of the container are harder and happen more often. This results in the average pressure exerted by the particles increasing.

When we cool a gas the kinetic energy of its particles decreases. The lower the temperature of a gas the less kinetic energy its particles have – they move more slowly. At absolute zero the particles have no thermal or movement energy, so they cannot exert a pressure.

SOLIDS, LIQUIDS AND GASES

CHAPTER QUESTIONS

More questions on solids, liquids and gases can be found at the end of Unit 5 on page 635.

SKILLS CRITICAL THINKING 6th

1 Explain how ideas about particles can account for the absolute zero of temperature.

SKILLS PROBLEM SOLVING 5th

2 a Convert the following Celsius temperatures to Kelvin temperatures.
   i 0 °C
   ii 100 °C
   iii 20 °C

   b Convert the following Kelvin temperatures to Celsius temperatures.
   i 250 K
   ii 269 K
   iii 305 K

SKILLS ANALYSIS 6th

3 State what happens in the situations shown in the diagram. Explain your answers using ideas about particles.

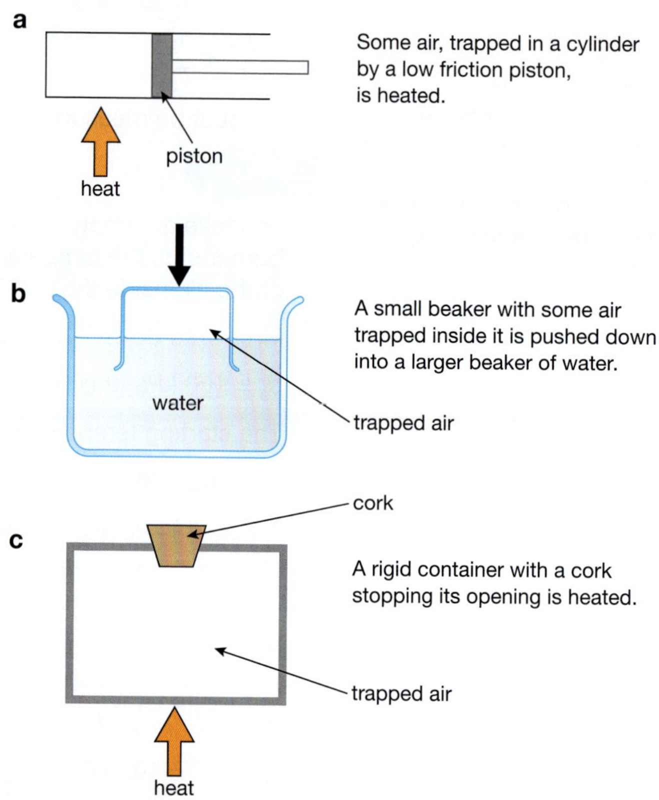

UNIT QUESTIONS

SKILLS PROBLEM SOLVING 7th

1

a A rectangular block of metal of density 8000 kg/m^3 measures 2 cm by 3 cm by 10 cm. What is the mass of the block?

A 48 g

B 0.48 kg

C 4.8 kg

D 48 kg **(1)**

b Which of the following will exert the greatest pressure when standing on the ground?

A an elephant: weight 50 000 N, area of one foot 0.2 m^2

B atmospheric pressure: 10^5 Pa

C ballerina: weight 450 N, on one point, area 0.0015 m^2

D man: weight 800 N, area of one foot 0.025 m^2 **(1)**

SKILLS CRITICAL THINKING 5th

c Which of the following descriptions most accurately describes a gas?

A very low density, easily compressed, cannot flow

B high density, cannot be compressed, definite shape

C very low density, easily compressed, expands to fill available space

D high density, difficult to compress, can flow **(1)**

d The specific heat capacity of a liquid is

A the amount of heat energy required to make 1 kilogram of the liquid boil

B the amount of heat energy required to raise the temperature of 1 kilogram of the liquid by 1 °F

C the amount of heat energy required to raise the temperature of 1 kilogram of the liquid by 1 °C

D the amount of heat energy required to raise the temperature of 1000 cm^3 of the liquid by 1 °C **(1)**

e Boyle's law states that

A if you double the pressure on a gas its volume doubles

B if you double the pressure on a gas its temperature halves

C if you double the pressure on a gas its volume doubles provided its temperature is constant

D if you double the pressure on a gas its volume halves provided its temperature is constant **(1)**

(Total 5 marks)

SKILLS INTERPRETATION 7th

2 Look at the diagram below showing a small gas bubble in a glass of fizzy drink, like cola.

a Copy the diagram and use eight arrows to shows how the pressure of the liquid acts on the gas bubble. **(2)**

SKILLS REASONING

b Describe what happens to the bubble as it floats up towards the top of the drink and explain the reason for your answer (assume that the amount of gas in the bubble does not change as the bubble rises up through the cola). **(3)**

(Total 5 marks)

SKILLS EXECUTIVE FUNCTION

3 The diagram shows part of the apparatus used by a student to find the density of a stone.

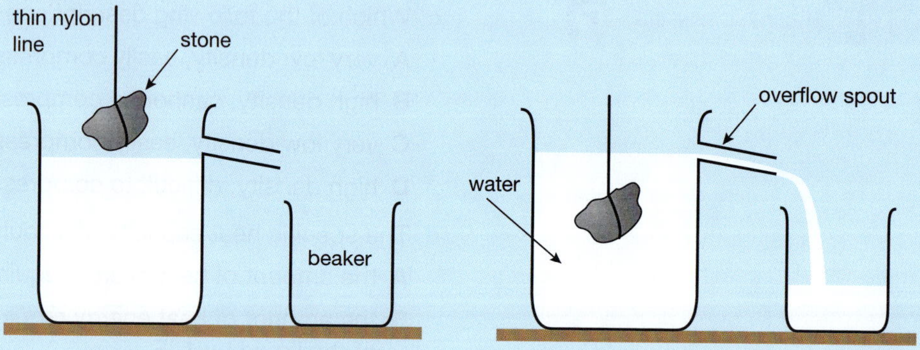

4th **a** **i** What is the student measuring? **(1)**

3rd **ii** What other piece of apparatus is required to complete the measurement? **(1)**

iii What precautions should the student take to ensure that the measurement is accurate? **(1)**

SKILLS CRITICAL THINKING 5th

b **i** State the equation that the student needs to calculate the density of the stone. **(1)**

SKILLS EXECUTIVE FUNCTION

ii What other measurement must be made? State the name of the apparatus needed to make this measurement. **(1)**

(Total 5 marks)

SKILLS PROBLEM SOLVING 7th

4 The diagram shows a simple mercury barometer made by filling a strong glass tube with mercury and turning it upside down (with the open end of the tube closed) in a dish of mercury and then opening the end below the level of mercury in the dish. Mercury runs out of the tube until the pressure of the mercury at X is equal to the pressure of the air acting on the surface of the mercury in the dish.

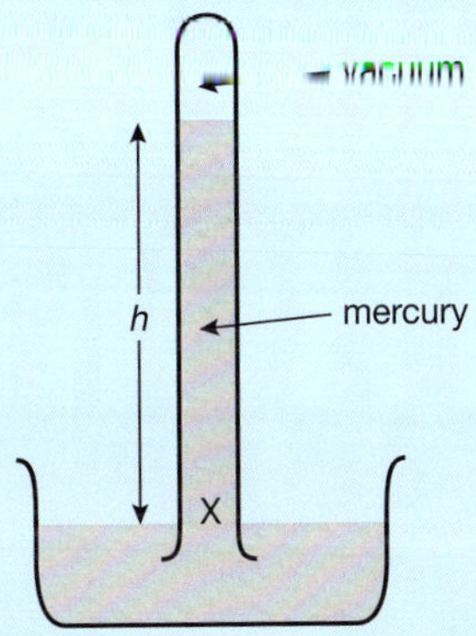

The height, h, of mercury in the tube is a measure of air (atmospheric) pressure. A typical value for h is 76 cm.

The density of mercury is 13 600 kg/m^3. Use this value to calculate the atmospheric pressure in Pa (pascals). **(3)**

(Total 3 marks)

PHYSICS UNIT 6 MAGNETISM AND ELECTROMAGNETISM

In Norse (Norwegian) mythology the spectacular light display we call the aurora borealis was seen as a bridge of fire that connected the Earth to the sky. Nowadays we know it is caused by charged particles, emitted by the Sun, interacting with the Earth's magnetic field and atmosphere. In this section we will be looking at magnetism and the crucial role it plays in our everyday lives.

15 MAGNETISM AND ELECTROMAGNETISM

There are two types of magnets that we use in our everyday lives. These are permanent magnets and electromagnets. A permanent magnet has a magnetic field around it all the time. The strength and direction of this field is not easy to change. An electromagnet when turned on also has a magnetic field around it but its strength and direction can be changed very easily. In this chapter you will learn about the factors affecting the magnetic field around an electromagnet and how electromagnets are used in several important devices.

▲ Figure 15.1 Electromagnets can be used to lift iron or steel objects.

The huge electromagnet in Figure 15.1 is being used in a scrapyard to pick up large objects that contain iron or steel. When the objects have been moved to their new position the electromagnet is turned off and the objects fall.

LEARNING OBJECTIVES

- Know that magnets repel and attract other magnets and attract magnetic substances
- Describe the properties of magnetically hard and soft materials
- Practical: investigate the magnetic field pattern for a permanent bar magnet and between two bar magnets
- Understand the term magnetic field line
- Know that magnetism is induced in some materials when they are placed in a magnetic field
- Describe how to use two permanent magnets to produce a uniform magnetic field pattern
- Know that an electric current in a conductor produces a magnetic field around it

UNITS

In this section you will need to use ampere (A) as the unit of current, volt (V) as the unit of voltage and watt (W) as the unit of power.

MAGNETISM AND MAGNETIC MATERIALS

Magnets are able to **attract** objects made from magnetic materials such as iron, steel, nickel and cobalt. Magnets cannot attract objects made from materials such as plastic, wood, paper or rubber. These are non-magnetic materials.

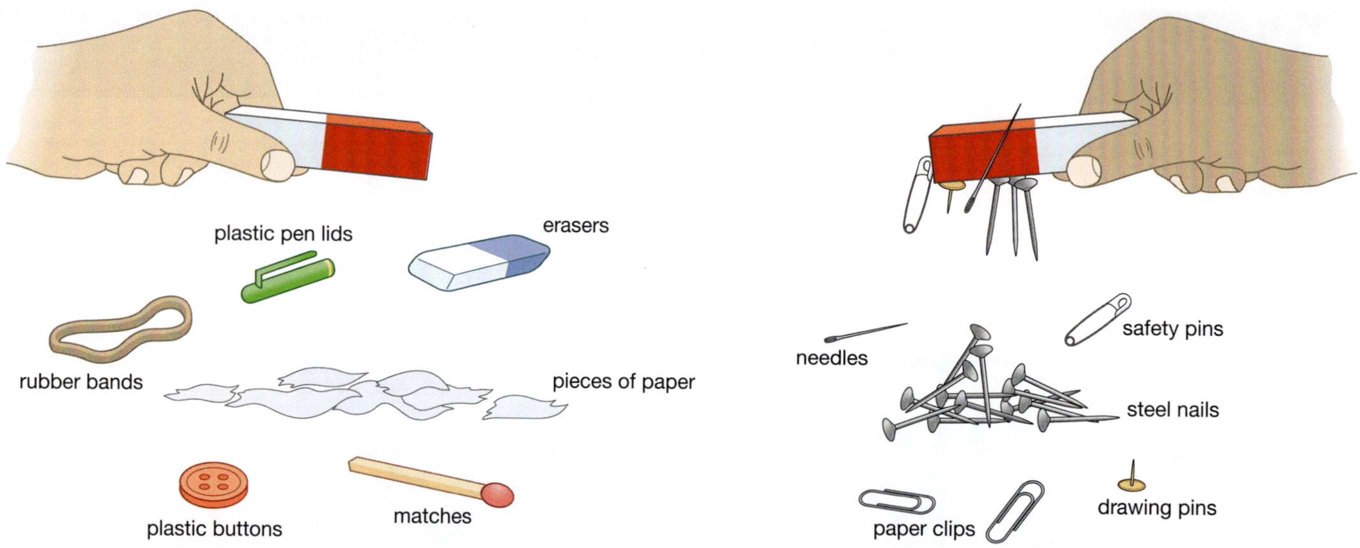

▲ Figure 15.2 Magnets attract some objects and not others.

MAGNETS

The strongest parts of a magnet are called its poles. Most magnets have two poles. These are called the north pole and the south pole.

If two similar poles are placed near to each other they **repel**. If two dissimilar (opposite) poles are placed near to each other they attract.

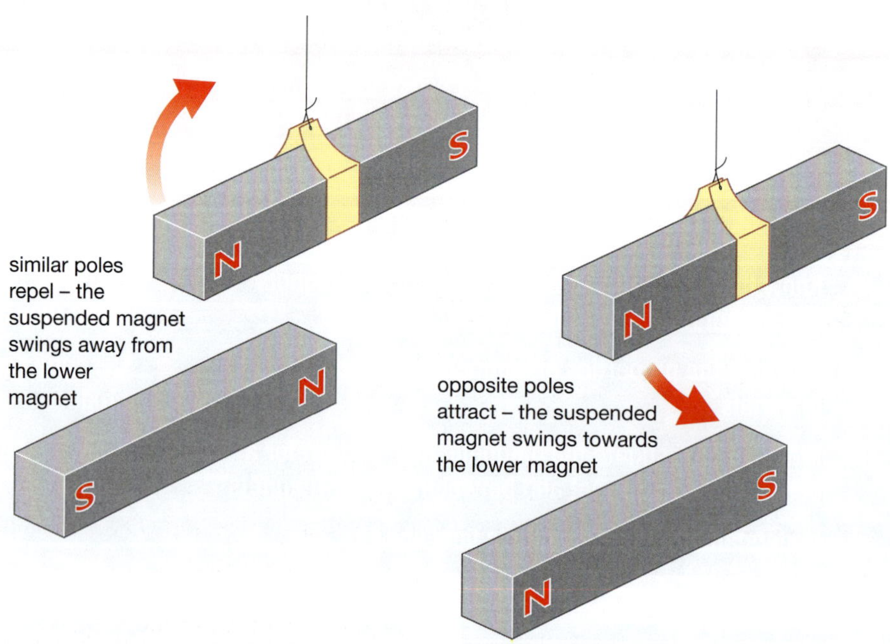

▲ Figure 15.3 Similar poles repel and opposite poles attract.

Permanent magnets like the bar magnets shown in Figure 15.3 are made from a magnetically hard material such as steel. A magnetically hard material keeps its magnetism once it has been magnetised. Iron is a magnetically soft material and is not suitable for a permanent magnet. Magnetically soft materials lose their magnetism easily and are therefore useful as temporary magnets.

EXTENSION WORK

Ancient travellers would construct a basic compass by placing a splinter (thin piece) of magnetised rock called lodestone onto a piece of wood floating in water. The splinter would turn to point in the direction of north–south. The end pointing towards the north was called the north pole.

 MAGNETISM AND ELECTROMAGNETISM

MAGNETIC FIELDS

Around every magnet there is a volume of space where we can detect magnetism. This volume of space is called a **magnetic field**. Normally a magnetic field cannot be seen but we can use iron filings or plotting compasses to show its shape and discover something about its strength and direction.

ACTIVITY 1

▼ PRACTICAL: INVESTIGATE THE MAGNETIC FIELD PATTERNS OF BAR MAGNETS

1 Place a bar magnet between two books and place a sheet of paper or thin card over it.

2 Sprinkle some iron filings on the paper above the magnet.

3 Tap the paper very gently.

4 The iron filings will move to show the magnetic field pattern.

OR

1 Place a bar magnet on a piece of paper.

2 Place a large number of small compasses on the paper near the magnet.

3 Look carefully at the pattern shown by the needles of the compasses.

Repeat the same experiment using two bar magnets, placing them about 5 cm apart.

Safety note: Avoid skin contact with iron filings, since they irritate the skin. Do not blow them off the paper, because they may get into the eyes, which is very painful.

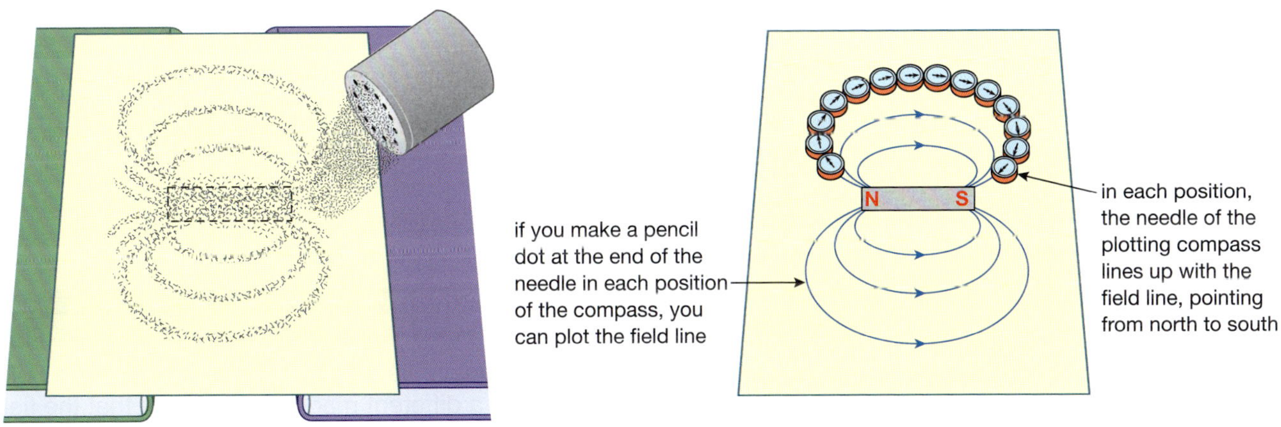

▲ Figure 15.4 We can see the shape of the magnetic field around a magnet by using iron filings or plotting compasses.

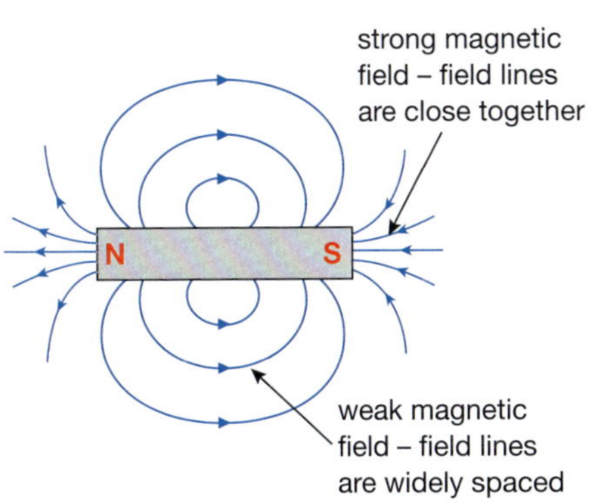

▲ Figure 15.5 The magnetic field around a bar magnet follows a pattern like this.

We draw magnetic fields like that in Figure 15.5 using magnetic field lines. Magnetic field lines don't really exist but they help us to visualise the main features of a magnetic field.

The magnetic field lines:

- show the shape of the magnetic field
- show the direction of the magnetic force – the field lines 'travel' from north to south
- show the strength of the magnetic field – the field lines are closest together where the magnetic field is strongest.

OVERLAPPING MAGNETIC FIELDS

If two magnets are placed near each other, their magnetic fields overlap and affect each other. We can investigate this using iron filings or plotting compasses. Figure 15.6 shows the different field patterns we would see.

EXTENSION WORK

Point X in Figure 15.6 is called a neutral point. It is a position where the effects of the two magnetic fields have cancelled each other out, meaning that there is no resultant magnetic field here. Can you find any other neutral points in these magnetic field patterns?

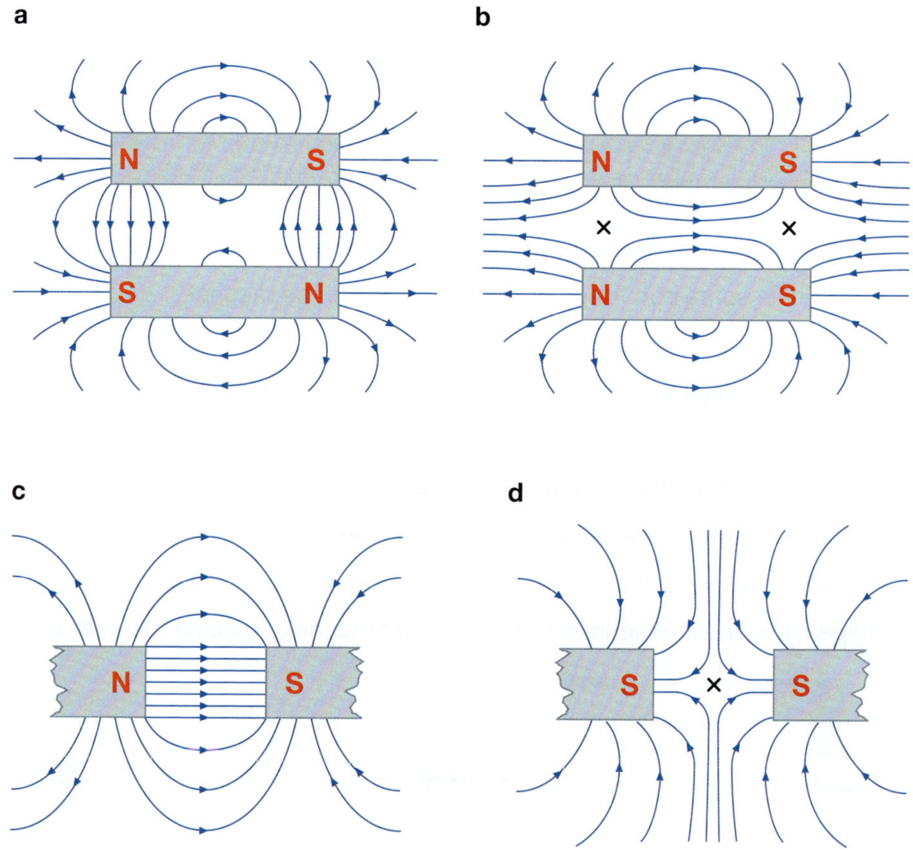

▲ Figure 15.6 Magnetic fields around pairs of magnets

CREATING A UNIFORM MAGNETIC FIELD

If we look very carefully at the magnetic field created between the north pole of one magnet and the south pole of a different magnet we will see that the field is shown as a series of straight field lines that are evenly spaced. A field like this is described as a uniform magnetic field – that is, its strength and direction is the same everywhere. Creating a uniform field like this is extremely useful as we will see later in this chapter and in the next chapter.

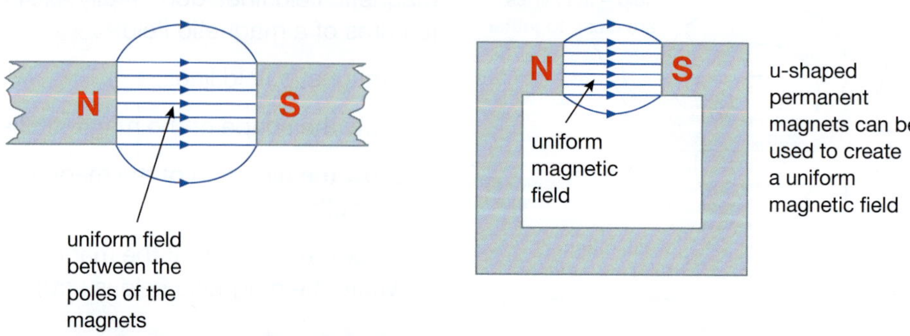

▲ Figure 15.7 Two examples of uniform magnetic fields

INDUCED MAGNETISM

If we place an object made from a magnetic material, for example, an iron nail, inside a magnetic field it becomes a magnet. We say that magnetism has been **induced** in the nail. Because iron is a magnetically soft material, its induced magnetism is temporary and disappears if the permanent magnet is removed. If the nail is made from a magnetically hard material such as steel it will retain some of its magnetism after the magnet is removed.

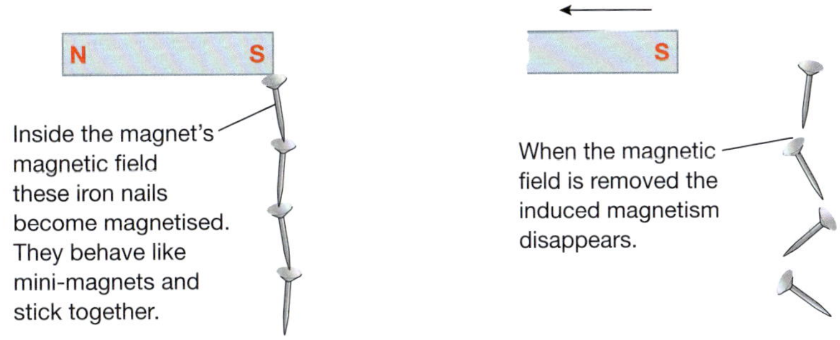

▲ Figure 15.8 Introducing magnetism in iron nails

EXTENSION WORK

It is not necessary to memorise how an electric bell or a circuit breaker works but understanding how they work might help reinforce some of the basic principles of magnets and electromagnets you will need in your exams.

The electric bell

When the bell push is pressed the circuit is complete and there is current in the circuit. As a result the soft iron core of the electromagnet becomes magnetised and attracts the piece of iron that is attached to the hammer (this is called the armature). When the armature is pulled down, the hammer strikes the bell. At the same time a gap is created at the contact screw. The circuit is now incomplete and the current stops. The electromagnet is now turned off so the springy metal strip pulls the armature up to its original position.
The circuit is again complete and the whole process begins again.

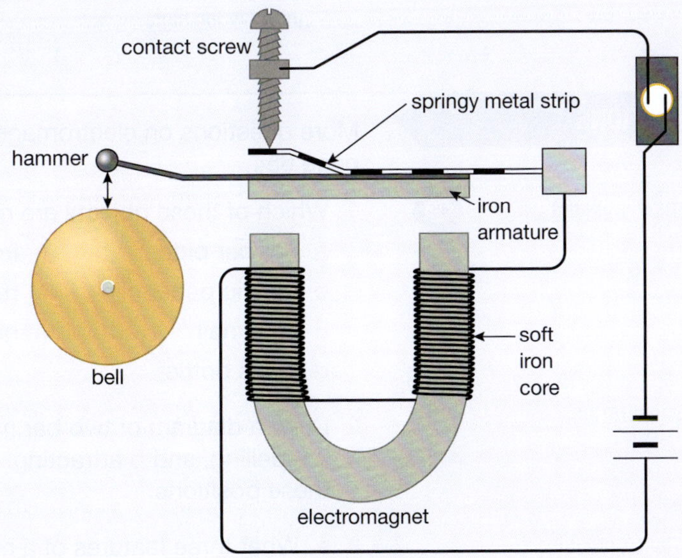

▲ Figure 15.9 An electric bell relies upon an electromagnet.

Circuit breaker

Circuit breakers also use electromagnets. The circuit breaker in Figure 15.10 uses electromagnetism to cut off the current if it becomes larger than a certain value. If the current is too high the electromagnet becomes strong enough to pull the iron catch out of position so that the contacts open and the circuit breaks. Once the problem in the circuit has been corrected the catch is repositioned by pressing the reset button.

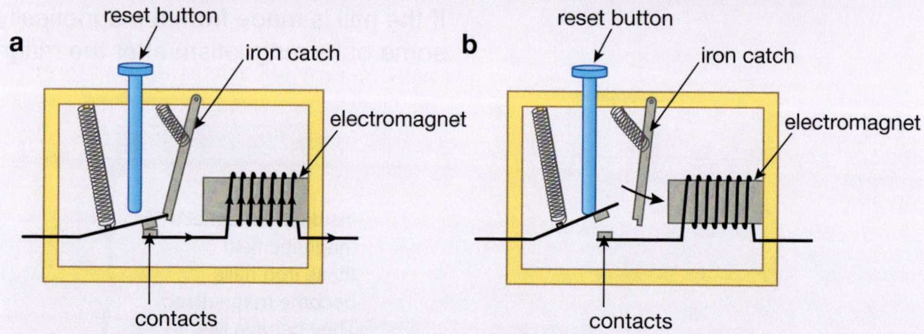

▲ Figure 15.10 **a** The circuit breaker allows a normal sized current. **b** When there is too large a current the circuit becomes incomplete.

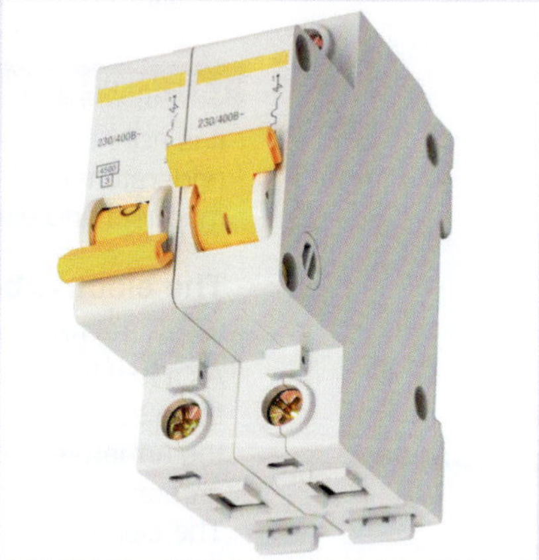

▲ Figure 15.11 These circuit breakers control the supply of electricity to different circuits in a building. The circuit breaker will 'trip' if there is something wrong with the circuit and the current is too high.

CHAPTER QUESTIONS

More questions on electromagnetism can be found at the end of Unit 6 on page 654.

SKILLS CRITICAL THINKING (4th)

1 Which of these objects are made from magnetic materials?

- a copper pipe
- b plastic paper clip
- c steel nail
- d glass bottle
- e iron bar
- f rubber tyre
- g nickel coins

SKILLS INTERPRETATION, REASONING

2 Draw a diagram of two bar magnets placed so that two of their poles are **a** repelling, and **b** attracting. Explain why you have drawn the magnets in these positions.

SKILLS CRITICAL THINKING

3 a What three features of a magnetic field do field lines show?

(3rd)

b What is a uniform magnetic field?

SKILLS INTERPRETATION (4th)

c Draw a diagram of a uniform field between two bar magnets.

SKILLS INTERPRETATION

SKILLS REASONING

7th

4 a Draw a diagram to show the shape of the magnetic field around a **solenoid**.

b How does your diagram show where the magnetic field is strong or weak?

c Explain what happens to the magnetic field if the direction of the current through the solenoid is reversed.

5 In 1819 a scientist named Hans Christian Oersted was using a cell to produce a current in a wire. Close to the wire there was a compass. When there was a current in the wire, Oersted noticed – much to his surprise – that the compass needle moved.

a Why did the compass needle move?

8th

b When there is a current in a horizontal wire, the needle of a compass placed beneath the wire comes to rest at right angles to the wire, pointing from left to right. In which direction will the compass needle point if it is held above the wire? Explain your answer.

c Would your answer to part b still be correct if the direction of the current in the wire was changed? Explain your answer.

7th

6 The diagram below shows a simple electromagnet.

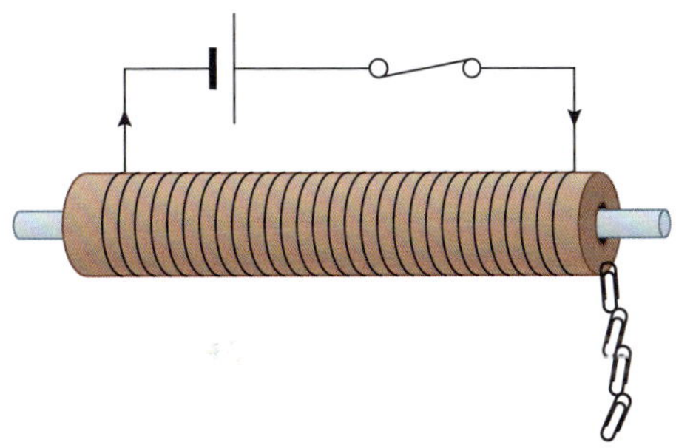

a Explain why the core (centre) of an electromagnet is made of soft iron and not steel.

b Suggest two ways in which the strength of this electromagnet could be increased.

16 ELECTRIC MOTORS AND ELECTROMAGNETIC INDUCTION

Trains in many cities use electric motors to transport millions of people to and from work each day. In the first part of this chapter, we are going to look at how an electric motor works. An electric motor creates motion from an electric current. Generators and alternators, on the other hand, transfer movement or kinetic energy into electrical energy by a process called electromagnetic induction. The second part of this chapter is going to look at this process.

▲ Figure 16.1 Electric train in Bangkok (the Skytrain)

LEARNING OBJECTIVES

- Understand why a force is exerted on a current-carrying wire in a magnetic field, and how this effect is applied in simple d.c. electric motors and loudspeakers
- Use the left-hand rule to predict the direction of the resulting force when a wire carries a current perpendicular to a magnetic field
- Describe how the force on a current-carrying conductor in a magnetic field changes with the magnitude and direction of the field and current
- Know that a voltage is induced in a conductor or a coil when it moves through a magnetic field or when a magnetic field changes through it and describe the factors that affect the size of the induced voltage
- Describe the generation of electricity by the rotation of a magnet within a coil of wire and of a coil of wire within a magnetic field, and describe the factors that affect the size of the induced voltage

MOVEMENT FROM ELECTRICITY

When a charged particle moves through a magnetic field it experiences a force, as long as its motion is not parallel to the field. We can demonstrate this effect by passing electrons (that is, an electric current) along a wire that is placed in a magnetic field as shown in Figure 16.2. When the switch is closed and electrons flow, the wire will try to move upwards.

OVERLAPPING MAGNETIC FIELDS

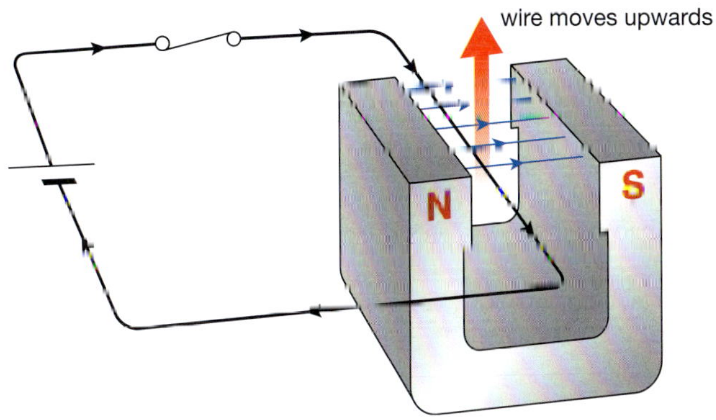

▲ Figure 16.2 The wire moves where there is a current in it.

We can explain this motion by looking at what happens when the switch is closed and the two magnetic fields overlap.

The two diagrams in Figure 16.3 show the shapes and directions of the magnetic fields **a** across the poles of the magnet, and **b** around the current-carrying wire before they overlap.

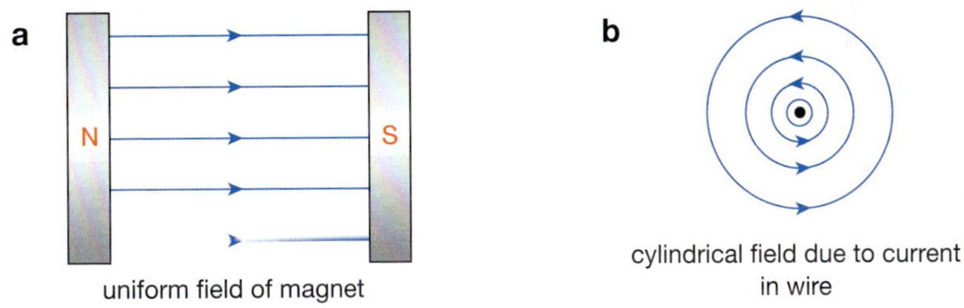

▲ Figure 16.3 **a** Magnet's uniform magnetic field **b** Magnetic field around a current carrying wire

If the wire is placed between the poles of the magnet, the two fields overlap.

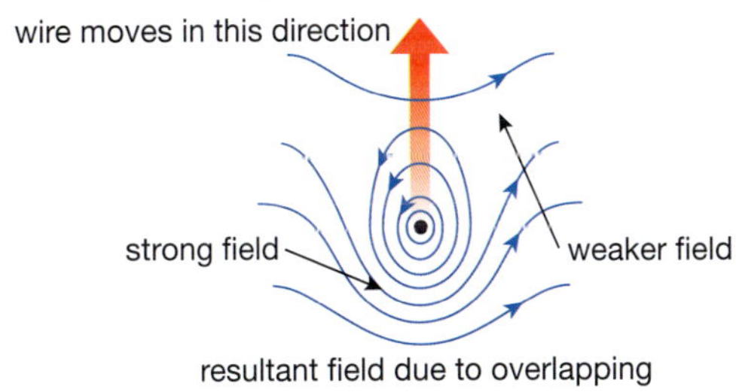

▲ Figure 16.4 The new magnetic field created by overlapping

In certain places, for example, below the wire, the fields are in the same direction and so reinforce each other. A strong magnetic field is produced here. In other places, for example, above the wire, the fields are in opposite directions. A weaker field is produced here. Because the fields are of different strengths the wire 'feels' a force, pushing it from the stronger part of the field to the weaker part – that is, in this case, upwards. The overlapping of the two magnetic fields has produced motion. This is called the motor effect.

A stronger force will be produced if the magnetic field is stronger or if the current is increased.

If we change the direction of the current or the magnet's field, a different overlapping pattern is created and we will see the wire move in the opposite direction.

KEY POINT

We can predict the direction of the force or movement of the wire using Fleming's left-hand rule.

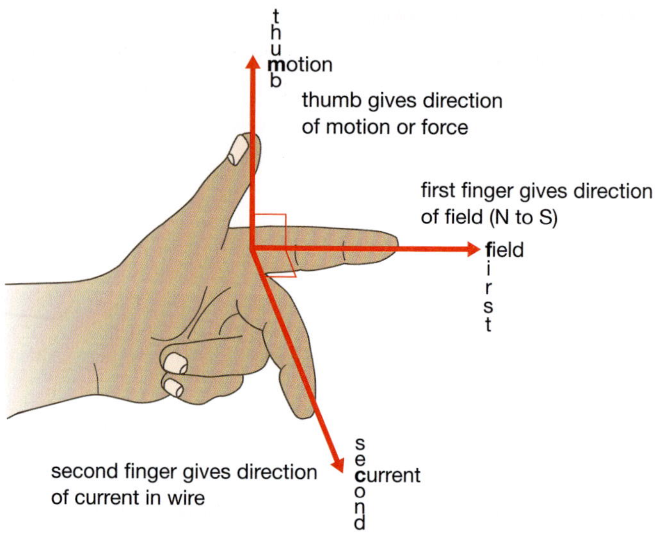

Figure 16.5 Fleming's left-hand rule helps you to work out the direction of the force.

THE MOVING-COIL LOUDSPEAKER

The moving-coil loudspeaker uses the motor effect to transfer energy to create sound.

- Electric currents from a source, such as a radio, pass through the coils of a speaker.
- These currents, which represent sounds, are always changing in size and direction, like vibrating sound waves.
- The fields of the coil and the permanent magnet are therefore creating magnetic field patterns which are also always changing in strength and direction.
- These fields in turn apply rapidly changing forces to the wires of the coil, which cause the speaker cone to vibrate.
- These vibrations create the sound waves we hear.

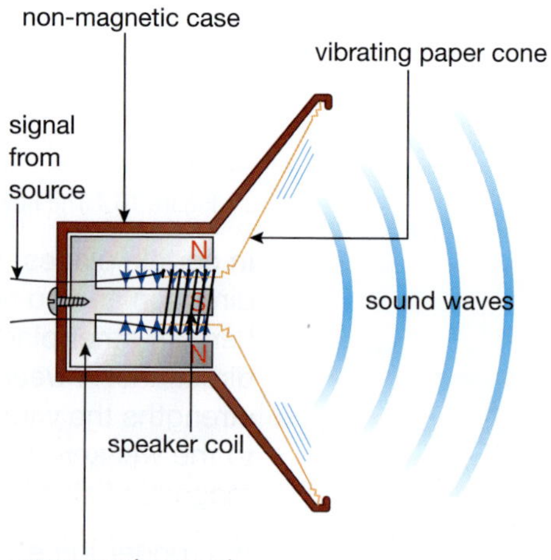

Figure 16.6 A loudspeaker transfers energy to create sound.

THE ELECTRIC MOTOR

The electric motor is one of the most important uses of the motor effect. Figure 16.7 shows the most important features of a simple d.c. electric motor.

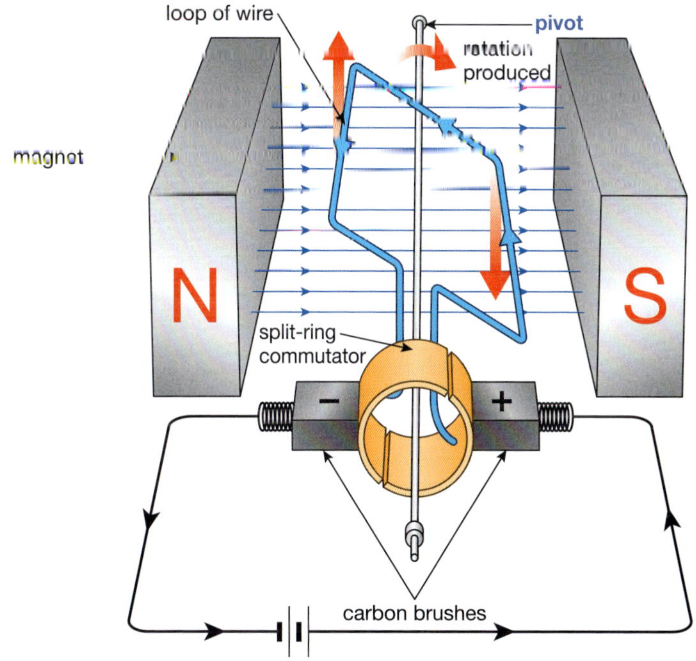

▲ Figure 16.7 A simple electric motor

When there is current in the loop of wire, one side of it will experience a force pushing it upwards. The other side will feel a force pushing it downwards, so the loop will begin to rotate (turn).

As the loop reaches the vertical position, its momentum takes it past the vertical. If the rotation is to continue the forces on the wires must now be reversed so that the wire at the top is now pushed down and the bottom one is pushed up.

This can be done easily by using a split ring to connect the loop of wire to the electrical supply. Now each time the loop of wire passes the vertical position, the connections change, the direction of the current changes, and the forces on the different sides of the loop change direction. The loop will rotate continuously.

To increase the rate at which the motor turns we can:

1 increase the number of turns or loops of wire, making a coil
2 increase the strength of the magnetic field
3 increase the current in the loop of wire.

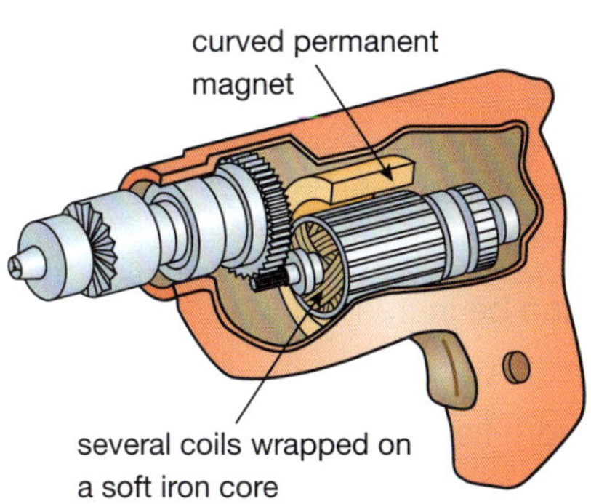

▲ Figure 16.8 A real electric motor

EXTENSION WORK

Although you will not be asked this in your exam it is interesting to know how commercial motors like the one used in this electric drill differ from the simple motor described in Figure 16.7.

- The permanent magnets are replaced with curved electromagnets capable of producing very strong magnetic fields.
- The single loop of wire is replaced with several coils of wire wrapped on the same axis. This makes the motor more powerful and allows it to run more smoothly.
- The coils are wrapped on a soft iron core that has been covered by a thin layer of plastic. This makes the motor more efficient and more powerful.

ELECTROMAGNETIC INDUCTION

Motors use electricity to produce movement. Generators and alternators are machines that use motion to produce electricity. They use a process called electromagnetic induction.

▲ Figure 16.9 Transportable generators are used to produce electricity for the lights and machinery used on roadworks.

The workers shown in Figure 16.9 need electricity for their machines and their lights. Instead of connecting into the mains supply, as we do at home, the workers have their own generator, which produces the electrical energy they need. In fact, the mains supply itself is produced by large generators in power stations. In this next section, you will discover how a generator produces electricity.

DEMONSTRATING ELECTROMAGNETIC INDUCTION

If we move a wire across a magnetic field at right angles, as shown in Figure 16.10, a voltage is induced or generated in the wire. If the wire is part of a complete circuit, there is a current. This event is called electromagnetic induction.

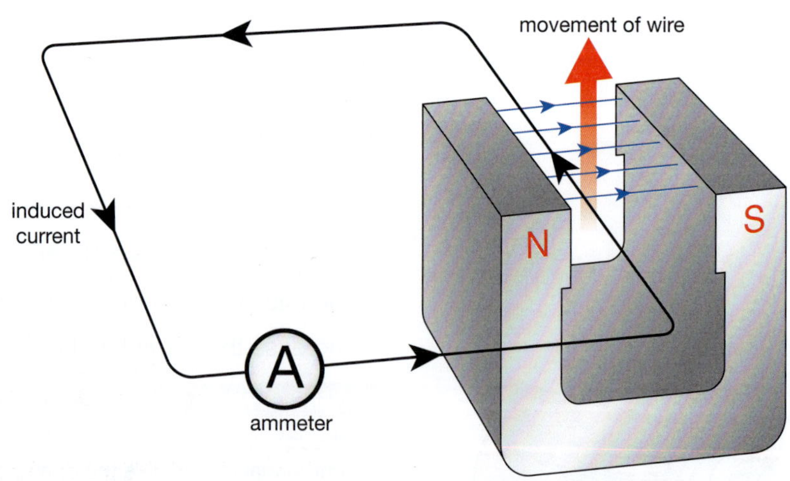

▲ Figure 16.10 When a wire moves across a magnetic field a voltage is generated in the wire.

The size of the induced voltage (and current) can be increased by:

1 moving the wire more quickly
2 using a stronger magnet so that there are more field lines 'cut'
3 wrapping the wire into a coil so that more pieces of wire move through the magnetic field.

We can also generate a voltage and current by pushing a magnet into a coil. In this situation and the previous one (Figure 16.10) we can see that it is the cutting action between the wires and the field lines that generates the voltage. If there is no cutting (that is, the wires and magnets are stationary) no voltage is generated.

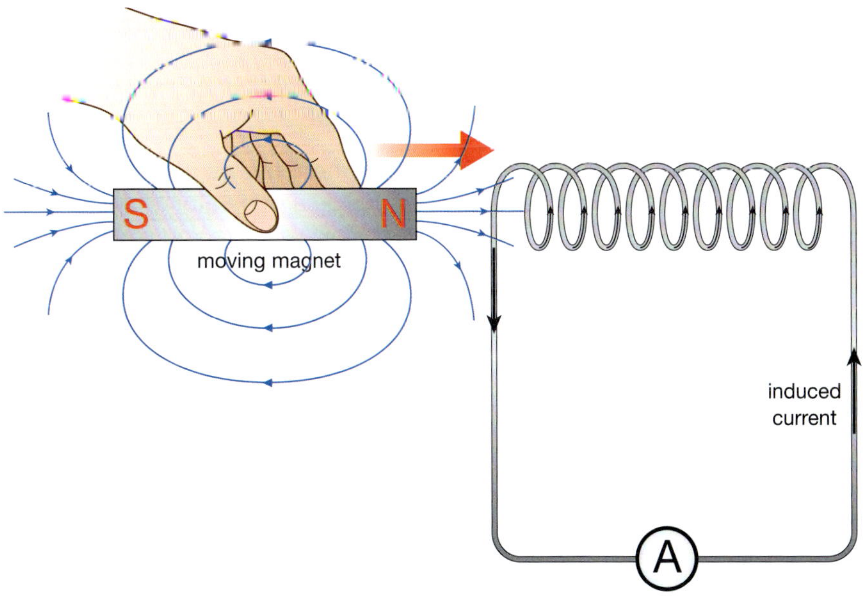

▲ Figure 16.11 A magnet moving in a coil will generate electricity.

This experiment also shows us that the size of the induced voltage (and current) can be increased by:

1 moving the magnet more quickly
2 using a stronger magnet
3 using a coil with more turns.

We can summarise all the discoveries from these experiments by saying:

- a voltage is induced when a conductor cuts through magnetic field lines
- a voltage is induced when magnetic field lines cut through a conductor
- the faster the lines are cut the larger the induced voltage.

EXTENSION WORK

It is interesting to note, but not necessary for your exam, that Michael Faraday was the first person to observe how the size of an induced voltage depends upon the rate at which the magnetic lines of flux (field lines) are being cut. He summarised his observations in Faraday's Law of Electromagnetic Induction. This states that:

> *The size of the induced voltage across the ends of a wire (coil) is directly proportional to the rate at which the magnetic lines of flux are being cut.*

GENERATORS

Figure 16.12 shows a small generator or dynamo used to generate electricity for a bicycle light.

As the cyclist pedals, the wheel rotates and makes a small magnet within the dynamo turn around. As this magnet turns, its magnetic field turns too. The field lines cut through the coil inducing a current in it. This current can be used to work the cyclist's lights.

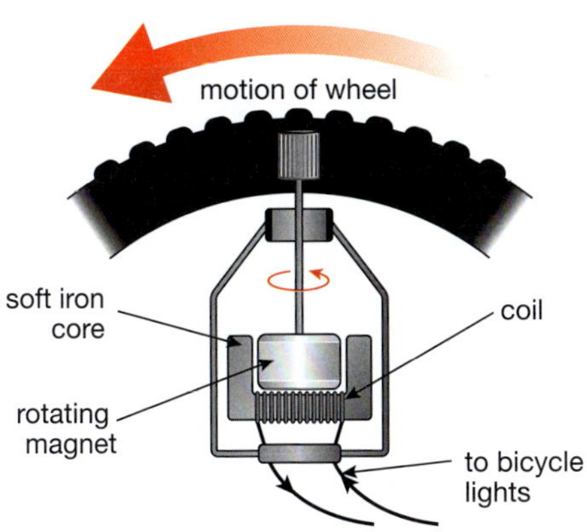

▲ Figure 16.12 A dynamo is a simple generator.

▲ Figure 16.13 This generator produces electricity on an industrial scale.

Figure 16.13 shows a much larger generator used in power stations to generate the mains electricity we use in our homes. In these generators the magnets are stationary and the coils rotate.

The size of the induced voltage is greater than in the bicycle dynamo because these generators **a** use much stronger magnets, **b** have many more turns of wire on the coil, and **c** spin the coil much faster.

LOOKING AHEAD

Higher Physics courses are likely to ask you what exactly is happening inside a generator and what is an alternator. The simple description given below will give you some idea of what is required.

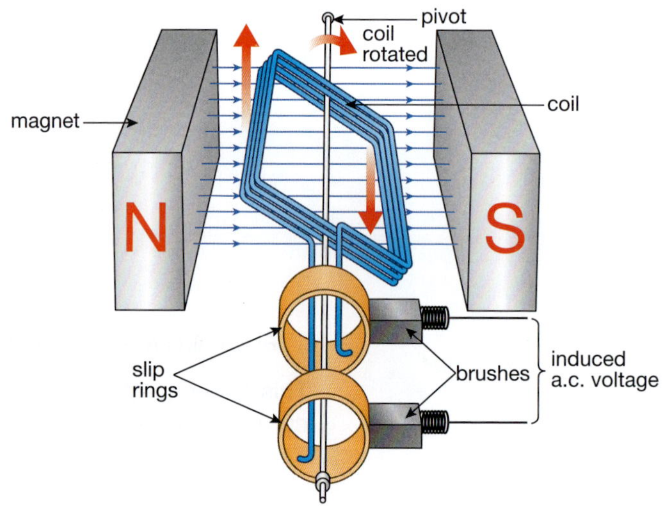

▲ Figure 16.14 The alternator produces alternating current.

As the coil rotates, its wires cut through magnetic field lines and a current is induced in them. If we watch just one side of the coil we see that the wire moves up through the field and then down for each turn of the coil. As a result the current is induced first in one direction and then in the opposite direction. This kind of current is called alternating current. A generator that produces alternating current is called an alternator.

The frequency of an alternating current is the number of complete cycles it makes each second. If an alternator coil rotates twice in a second, the frequency of the alternating current it produces is 2 Hz (2 cycles per second). The frequency of the UK mains supply is 50 Hz.

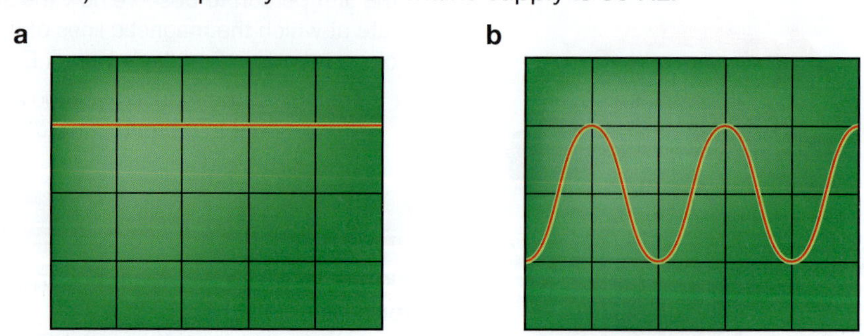

▲ Figure 16.15 **a** In a direct current (d.c) the charge flows in one direction. **b** Alternating currents (a.c.) keep changing direction.

CHAPTER QUESTIONS

More questions on electric motors and electromagnetic induction can be found at the end of Unit 6 on page 654.

SKILLS ANALYSIS, REASONING

7th

1 The diagram below shows a long wire placed between the poles of a magnet.

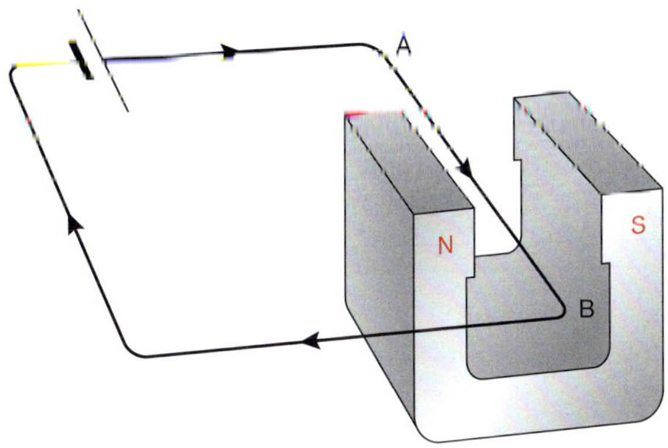

Describe what happens when:

a there is current in the wire from A to B
b the direction of the current is reversed – that is, from B to A
c with the current from B to A, the poles of the magnet are reversed
d there is a larger current in the wire.

SKILLS INTERPRETATION

2 a Draw a simple labelled diagram of a moving-coil loudspeaker.

SKILLS CRITICAL THINKING

b Explain how sound waves are made by the speaker when a signal is passed through its coil.

SKILLS REASONING

3 The diagram below shows a bar magnet being pushed into a long coil. A sensitive meter is connected across the coil.

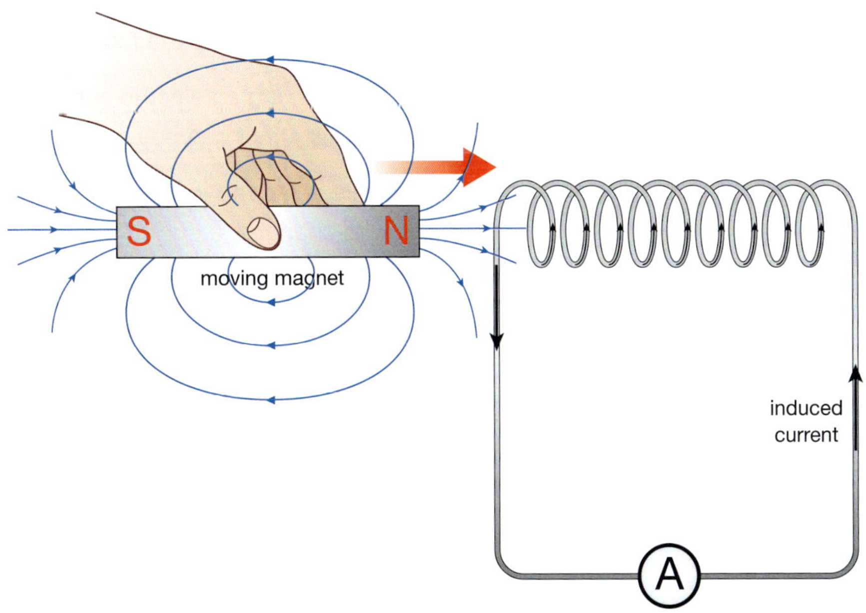

Describe what happens to the meter when:

a the magnet is pushed into the coil quickly
b the magnet is held stationary inside the coil
c the magnet is pulled out of the coil slowly
d the magnet is held stationary and the coil is moved towards it.

UNIT QUESTIONS

SKILLS CRITICAL THINKING 3rd

1

a Which of these objects is made from a magnetic material?

A a rubber band

B a piece of paper

C a steel nail

D a plastic ruler **(1)**

4th

b In which of these situations will you see attraction?

A The north poles of two magnets are placed close together.

B A wooden rod is placed close to a strong magnet.

C The south poles of two magnets are placed close together.

D The north pole of one magnet is placed close to the south pole of another magnet. **(1)**

c Which of these statements is true for a magnetically hard material?

A They are difficult to bend.

B They are used to make permanent magnets.

C They are electrical insulators.

D They are used in electromagnets. **(1)**

(Total 3 marks)

7th

2

Copy and complete the following passage, filling in the blanks.

A wire carrying an electric current experiences a ______ when it is in a ______ field. This effect can be used in ______ and electric ______.

If a wire is moved through a magnetic field, or the magnetic field near a ______ of wire changes, a current can be ______ in the wire. This effect is used in ______ and ______.

(Total 8 marks)

SKILLS REASONING

3

a Explain how a bicycle dynamo generates current. **(3)**

b Why does the dynamo produce no current when the cyclist has stopped? **(1)**

SKILLS CRITICAL THINKING 6th

c What is an alternator? **(1)**

SKILLS INTERPRETATION, CRITICAL THINKING

d Explain using diagrams the difference between a.c. and d.c. currents. **(3)**

SKILLS CRITICAL THINKING 5th

e Explain what is meant by this statement: 'The mains supply in the UK has a frequency of 50 Hz.' **(2)**

(Total 10 marks)

SKILLS CREATIVITY, REASONING

8th

4 A keen cyclist builds his own dynamo to generate electricity for his lights. Unfortunately, when he tries it out the lights are not bright enough. Suggest two changes he could make to his dynamo to generate more electricity. Is there a third solution to his problem?

(Total 3 marks)

SKILLS REASONING

7th

5 The diagram below shows the circuit for an electric bell.

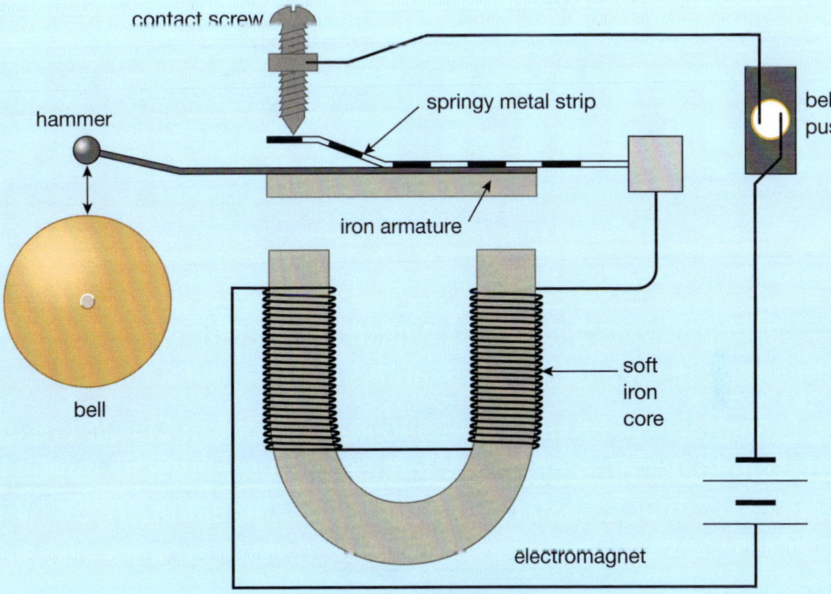

a Explain in your own words why the bell will not work if the electromagnet is replaced with a permanent magnet. **(2)**

b Explain why the core of the electromagnet used in an electric bell must not be made from steel. **(3)**

(Total 5 marks)

PHYSICS UNIT 7 RADIOACTIVITY AND PARTICLES

Henri Becquerel was a scientist whose pioneering work led to the discovery of radioactivity and set other scientists on a path of research that continues today.

Using radioactivity has enabled us to learn about the structure of matter, to develop new sources of energy and to understand a new force of nature: nuclear forces that bind matter together and control the processes that fuel stars and formed all the elements that we and the Universe are made of.

17 ATOMS AND RADIOACTIVITY

Atoms are made up of sub-atomic particles called neutrons, protons and electrons. It is the numbers of these particles that give each element its unique properties. In this chapter you will find out how atoms can break up and become transformed into different elements, and about the different types of radiation they give out.

LEARNING OBJECTIVES

- Describe the structure of an atom in terms of protons, neutrons and electrons and use symbols such as $^{14}_{6}C$ to describe particular nuclei
- Know the terms atomic (proton) number, mass (nucleon) number and isotope
- Know that alpha (α) particles, beta (β⁻) particles, and gamma (γ) rays are ionising radiations emitted from unstable nuclei in a random process
- Describe the nature of alpha (α) particles, beta (β⁻) particles, and gamma (γ) rays, and recall that they may be distinguished in terms of penetrating power and ability to ionise
- Investigate the penetration powers of different types of radiation using either radioactive sources or simulations
- Describe the effects on the atomic and mass numbers of a nucleus of the emission of each of the four main types of radiation (alpha, beta, gamma and neutron radiation)
- Understand how to balance nuclear equations in terms of mass and charge

UNITS

In this section you will need to use becquerel (Bq) as the unit of activity of a radioactive source, centimetre (cm) as the unit of length, and minute (min) and second (s) as the units of time.

ELECTRONS, PROTONS AND NEUTRONS

Atoms are made up of electrons, protons and neutrons. Figure 17.1 shows a simple model of how these particles are arranged.

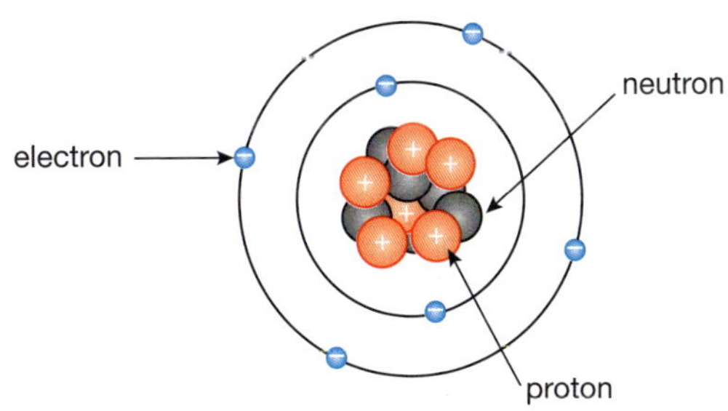

not to scale
The nucleus, made up of neutrons and protons, is about 10 000 times smaller than the atom itself.

▲ Figure 17.1 A simple model with protons and neutrons in the nucleus of the atom and electrons in orbits around the outside

The electron is a very small particle with very little mass. It has a negative electric charge. Electrons orbit the nucleus of the atom. The nucleus is very small compared to the size of the atom itself. The diameter of the nucleus is about 10 000 times smaller than the diameter of the atom. If the nucleus of an atom were enlarged to the size of a full stop on this page, the atom would have a diameter of around 2.5 metres.

The nucleus is made up of protons and neutrons. Protons and neutrons have almost exactly the same mass. Protons and neutrons are nearly 2000 times heavier than electrons. Protons carry positive electric charge but neutrons, as the name suggests, are electrically neutral or uncharged. The amount of charge on a proton is equal to that on an electron but opposite in sign.

EXTENSION WORK

The actual mass of an electron is 9.1×10^{-31} kg and its actual charge is -1.6×10^{-19} C. The table shows the approximate relative masses of the particles and the relative amount of charge they carry. The mass in atomic mass units is discussed below.

The properties of these three atomic particles are summarised in the table below. Protons and neutrons are also called nucleons because they are found in the nucleus of the atom.

Atomic particle	Relative mass of particle	Relative charge of particle
electron	1	−1
proton	2000	+1
neutron	2000	0

THE ATOM

The nucleus of an atom is surrounded by electrons. We sometimes think of electrons as orbiting the nucleus in a way similar to the planets orbiting the Sun. It is more accurate to think of the electrons as moving rapidly around the nucleus in a cloud or shell.

An atom is electrically neutral. This is because the number of positive charges carried by the protons in its nucleus is balanced by the number of negative charges on the electrons in the electron 'cloud' around the nucleus.

ATOMIC NUMBER, Z

The chemical behaviour and properties of a particular element depend upon how the atoms combine with other atoms. This is determined by the number of electrons in the atom. Although atoms may gain or lose electrons, sometimes quite easily, the number of protons in atoms of a particular element is always the same. The atomic number of an element tells us how many protons each of its atoms contains. For example, carbon has six protons in its nucleus – the atomic number of carbon is, therefore, 6. The symbol we use for atomic number is Z. Each element has its own unique atomic number. The atomic number is sometimes called the proton number.

ATOMIC MASS, A

The total number of protons and neutrons in the nucleus of an atom determines its atomic mass. The mass of the electrons that make up an atom is tiny and can usually be ignored. The mass of a proton is approximately 1.7×10^{-27} kg. To save writing this down we usually refer to the mass of an atom by its mass number or nucleon number. This number is the total number of protons and neutrons in the atom. The mass number of an element is given the symbol A.

ATOMIC NOTATION – THE RECIPE FOR AN ATOM

Each particular type of atom will have its own atomic number, which identifies the element, and a mass number that depends on the total number of nucleons, or particles, in the nucleus. Figure 17.2 shows the way we represent an atom of an element whose chemical symbol is X, showing the atomic number and the mass number.

So, using this notation, an atom of oxygen is represented by:

$$^{16}_{8}O$$

The chemical symbol for oxygen is O. The atomic number is 8 – this tells us that the nucleus contains eight protons. The mass number is 16, so there are 16 nucleons (protons and neutrons) in the nucleus. Since eight of these are protons, the remaining eight must be neutrons. The atom is electrically neutral overall, so the +8 charge of the nucleus is balanced by the eight orbiting electrons, each with charge −1.

KEY POINT

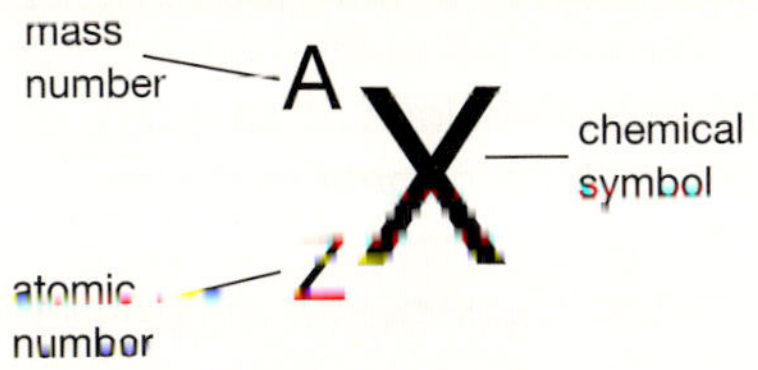

Figure 17.2 Atomic notation

mass number, A = number of neutrons + number of protons, Z = number of nucleons

so

number of neutrons = number of nucleons − number of protons = A − Z

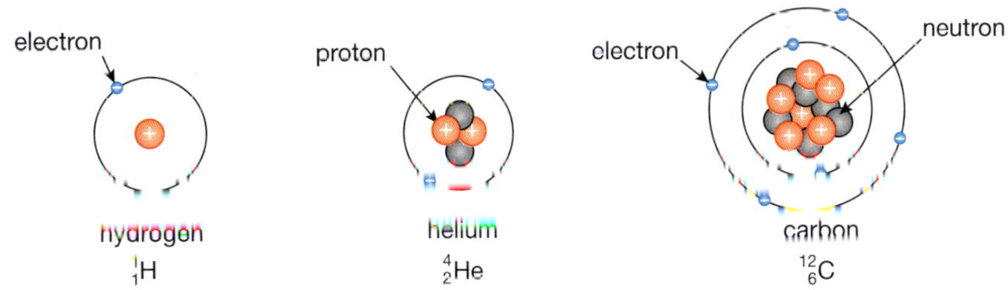

Figure 17.3 The hydrogen atom has one proton in its nucleus and no neutrons, so the mass number A = 1 + 0 = 1. As it has one proton, its atomic number, Z = 1. For helium, A = 4 (2 protons + 2 neutrons) and Z = 2 (2 protons). For carbon, A = 12 (6 protons + 6 neutrons) while Z = 6 (6 protons).

Figure 17.3 shows some examples of the use of this notation for hydrogen, helium and carbon, together with a simple indication of the structure of an atom of each of these **elements**. In each case the number of orbiting electrons is equal to the number of protons in the nucleus, so the atoms are electrically neutral.

ISOTOPES

The number of protons in an atom identifies the element. The chemical behaviour of an element depends on the number of electrons it has and, as we have seen, this always balances the number of protons in the nucleus. However, the number of neutrons in the nucleus can vary slightly. Atoms of an element with different numbers of neutrons are called isotopes of the element. The number of neutrons in a nucleus affects the mass of the atom. Different isotopes of an element will all have the same atomic number, Z, but different mass numbers, A. Figures 17.4 and 17.5 show some examples of isotopes.

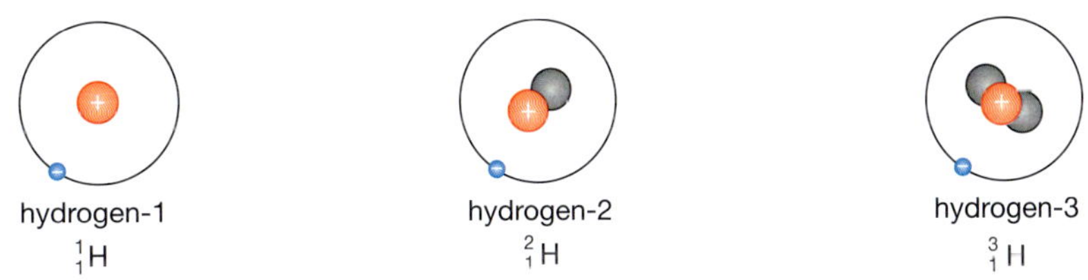

Figure 17.4 Isotopes of hydrogen – they all have the same atomic number, 1, and the same chemical symbol, H.

EXTENSION WORK

Hydrogen-2 is also called heavy hydrogen or deuterium. Hydrogen-3 is called tritium.

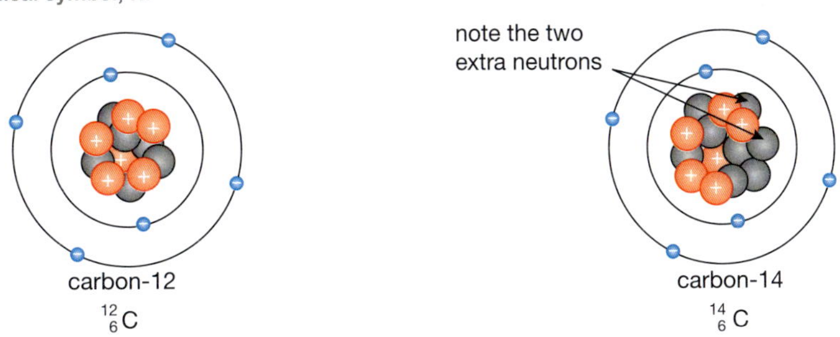

Figure 17.5 Two isotopes of carbon – they are referred to as carbon-12 and carbon-14 to distinguish between them.

THE STABILITY OF ISOTOPES

Isotopes of an element have different physical properties from other isotopes of the same element. One obvious difference is the mass. Another difference is the stability of the nucleus.

The protons are held in the nucleus by the nuclear force. This force is very strong and acts over a very small distance. It is strong enough to hold the nucleus together against the electric force repelling the protons away from each other. (Remember that protons carry positive charge and like charges repel.) The presence of neutrons in the nucleus affects the balance between these forces. Too many or too few neutrons will make the nucleus **unstable**. An unstable nucleus will eventually decay. When the nucleus of an atom decays it gives out energy and may also give out alpha or beta particles.

IONISING RADIATION

When unstable nuclei decay they give out ionising radiation. Ionising radiation causes atoms to gain or lose electric charge, forming ions. Unstable nuclei decay at random. This means that it is not possible to predict which unstable nucleus in a piece of **radioactive** material will decay, or when decay will happen. We shall see that we can make measurements that will enable us to predict the probability that a certain proportion of a radioactive material will decay in a given time.

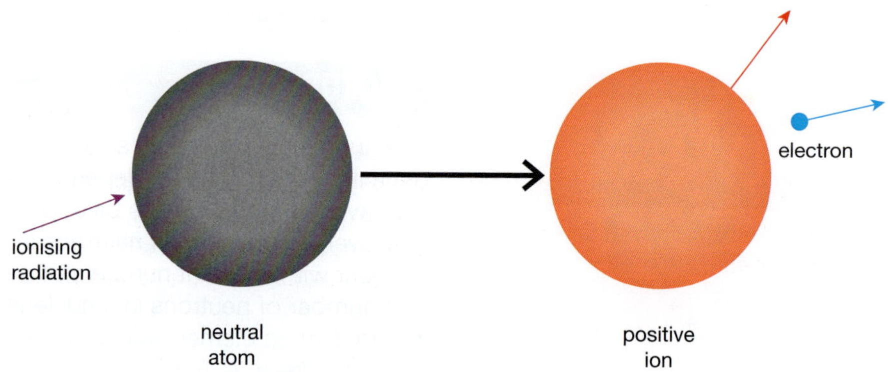

▲ Figure 17.6 When a neutral atom (or molecule) is hit by ionising radiation it loses an electron and becomes a positively charged ion.

There are three basic types of ionising radiation. They are: alpha (α), beta (β) and gamma (γ) radiation.

ALPHA (α) RADIATION

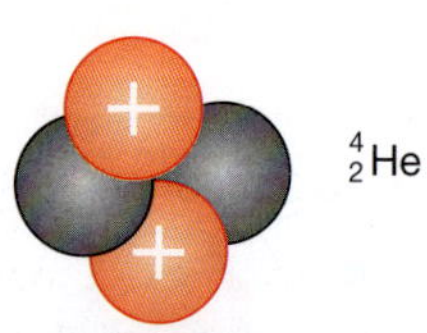

▲ Figure 17.7 An alpha particle (α particle)

EXTENSION WORK

Nucleons have roughly 2000 times the mass of an electron, and alpha particles are made up of four nucleons, so an alpha particle has 8000 times the mass of a beta particle.

Alpha radiation consists of fast-moving particles that are thrown out of unstable nuclei when they decay. These are called alpha particles. Alpha particles are helium nuclei – helium atoms without their orbiting electrons. Figure 17.7 shows an alpha particle and the notation that is used to denote it in equations.

Alpha particles have a relatively large mass. They are made up of four nucleons and so have a mass number of 4. They are also charged because of the two protons that they carry. The **relative charge** of an alpha particle is +2.

Alpha particles have a short range. The range of ionising radiation is the distance it can travel through matter. Alpha particles can only travel a few centimetres in air and cannot penetrate more than a few millimetres of paper. They have a limited range because they interact with atoms along their paths, causing ions to form. This means that they rapidly give up the energy that they had when they were ejected from the unstable nucleus.

BETA RADIATION (β^- AND β^+)

Beta minus particles (β^-) are very fast-moving electrons that are ejected by a decaying nucleus. The nucleus of an atom contains protons and neutrons, so where does the electron come from? The stability of a nucleus depends on the proportion of protons and neutrons it contains. The result of radioactive decay is to change the balance of protons and neutrons in the nucleus to make it

EXTENSION WORK

Antimatter will not be examined, but for all the particles that exist in ordinary matter there exists an antimatter particle. The positron is the antimatter equivalent of an electron. You will not be asked about neutrinos or antineutrinos either.

more stable. Beta minus decay involves a neutron in the nucleus splitting into a proton and an electron (an antineutrino is also emitted). The proton remains in the nucleus and the electron is ejected at high speed as a beta minus particle.

EXTENSION WORK

Sometimes a proton will decay into a neutron by emitting a beta plus particle (β^+). A beta plus particle is an antielectron, a particle with the same mass as an electron but with positive charge. The antielectron is called a positron.

Beta particles are very light – they have only 0.000 125 times the mass of an alpha particle. The relative charge of a β^- is −1 and the relative charge of a β^+ is +1.

Beta particles interact with matter in their paths less frequently than alpha particles. This is because they are smaller and carry less charge. This means that beta particles have a greater range than alpha particles. Beta particles can travel long distances through air, pass through paper easily and are only absorbed by denser materials like aluminium. A millimetre or two of aluminium foil will stop all but the most energetic beta particles.

GAMMA RAYS (γ)

Gamma rays are electromagnetic waves (see page 568) with very short wavelengths. As they are waves, they have no mass and no charge. They are weakly ionising and interact only occasionally with atoms in their paths. They are extremely penetrating and pass through all but the very densest materials with ease. It takes several centimetres thickness of lead, or a metre or so of concrete, to stop gamma radiation.

EXTENSION WORK

Gamma radiation is emitted in 'packets' of energy called photons.

NEUTRON RADIATION

Neutrons are emitted by radioactive material. They have roughly the same mass as a proton but have no electric charge. The symbol used for a neutron in radioactive decay equations is:

$${}^{1}_{0}n$$

If a neutron is emitted by a nucleus its mass number (A) goes down by 1 but the atomic number (Z) is unchanged. If a neutron is absorbed by a nucleus its mass number (A) goes up by 1 but the atomic number (Z) is unchanged.

EXTENSION WORK

As neutrons cause other atoms to emit radiation they must be screened. This is done using materials that have a lot of light atoms like hydrogen. Concrete and water are used to prevent neutrons escaping from nuclear reactors.

KEY POINT

As neutrons are not electrically charged they do not directly cause ionisation. They are absorbed by nuclei of other atoms and can cause them to become radioactive. The radioactive nuclei formed in this way will then decay emitting ionising radiation. Neutrons are the only type of radiation to cause other atoms to become radioactive. We shall see later (Chapter 20) that neutron radiation plays an important part in the process of fission used in nuclear reactors.

SUMMARY OF THE PROPERTIES OF IONISING RADIATION

We have said that ionising radiation causes uncharged atoms to lose electrons. An atom that has lost (or gained) electrons has an overall charge. It is called an ion. The three types of radioactive **emission** can all form ions.

As ionising radiation passes through matter, its energy is absorbed. This means that radiation can only penetrate matter up to a certain thickness. This depends on the type of radiation and the density of the material that it is passing through.

The ionising and penetrating powers of alpha, beta and gamma radiation are compared in the table on page 662. Note that the ranges given in the table are typical but they do depend on the energy of the radiation. For example, more energetic alpha particles will have a greater range than those with lower energy.

Radiation	Ionising power	Penetrating power	Example of range in air	Radiation stopped by
alpha, α	strong	weak	5–8 cm	paper
beta, β	medium	medium	500–1000 cm	thin aluminium
gamma, γ	weak	strong	virtually infinite	thick lead sheet

ACTIVITY 1

▼ PRACTICAL: INVESTIGATE THE PENETRATING POWERS OF DIFFERENT KINDS OF RADIATION

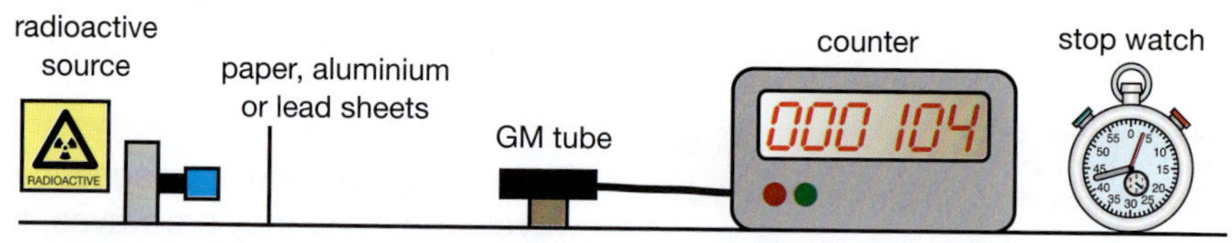

▲ Figure 17.8 Measuring the penetrating power of different types of radiation

Radioactive sources must be stored in lead-lined boxes and kept in a metal cupboard with a radiation warning label. The source must be handled with tongs away from the body. (See Chapter 19 page 683 for more details of safe practice with radioactive materials.)

Before the source is removed from its storage container, measure the background radiation count by connecting a Geiger–Müller (GM) tube to a counter. Write down the number of counts after 5 minutes. Repeat this three times and find the average background radiation count.

Take a source of alpha radiation and set it up at a measured distance (between 2 and 4 cm) from the GM tube.

Measure the counts detected in a 5 minute period. Repeat the count with a sheet of thick paper in front of the source. You should find that the counts have dropped to the background radiation count. This shows that alpha radiation does not pass through paper.

Now replace the alpha source with a beta source. After measuring the new count for 5 minutes place thin sheets of aluminium between the source and detector. When the thickness of the aluminium sheet is 1–2 mm thick you will find that the count has dropped to the background radiation level. This shows that beta radiation is blocked by just a few millimetres of aluminium.

Finally carry out the same steps using a gamma radiation source. Now you will find that gamma radiation is only blocked when a few centimetres of lead are placed between the source and the detector.

Safety note: All work with radioactive sources must be closely supervised by qualified science staff and no sources must be touched or pointed towards any part of the body. Source usage must be logged and they must be returned to their secure storage immediately after use. In the UK, students under 16 years are not permitted to handle sources; over 16, they are allowed to do this with close supervision.

KEY POINT

The Geiger–Müller (GM) tube is a detector of radiation. It is described in the next chapter.

As we said earlier, an unstable atom, or strictly speaking its nucleus, will decay by emitting radiation. If the decay process involves the nucleus ejecting either an alpha or a beta particle, the atomic number will change. This means that alpha or beta decay causes the original element to transform into a different element.

ALPHA (α) DECAY

Here is an example of alpha decay:

$^{222}_{88}Ra$	→	$^{218}_{86}Ra$	+	$^{4}_{2}He$	+	energy
radium atom	→	radon atom	+	α particle	+	energy

The radioactive isotope radium-222 decays to the element radon by the emission of an alpha particle. The alpha particle is sometimes represented by the Greek letter α. Radon is a radioactive gas that also decays by emitting an alpha particle. Note that the atomic number for radon, 86, is two less than the atomic number for radium.

This is a balanced equation:

- The total of the A numbers on each side of the equation is the same. (Remember that A is the total number of protons and neutrons.)
- The total of the Z numbers on each side of the equation is the same. (Remember that the Z number tells us the number of protons in the nucleus – the number of positively charged particles.)

The general form of the alpha decay equation is:

$$^{A}_{Z}Y \rightarrow {}^{A-4}_{Z-2}W + {}^{4}_{2}He + \text{energy}$$

↑ alpha particle, α

REMINDER

A is the mass number of the element and Z is the atomic number. The letters W and Y are not the symbols of any particular elements as this is the general equation.

In alpha decay, element Y is transformed into element W by the emission of an alpha particle. Element W is two places before element Y in the Periodic Table. The alpha particle, a helium nucleus, carries away four nucleons, which reduces the mass number (A) by four. Two of these nucleons are protons so the atomic number of the new element is two less than the original element, Z – 2. Notice that the mass number and the atomic number are conserved through this equation – that is, the total numbers of nucleons and protons on each side of the equation are the same.

KEY POINT

It is worth pointing out that the mass number refers to the number of nuclear particles, or nucleons, involved in the transformation – not the exact mass. Mass is not conserved in nuclear transformations, as some of it is transformed into energy.

EXAMPLE 1

Complete the following nuclear equation which shows the decay of uranium-238 to the element thorium by alpha decay (emitting an alpha particle).

$$^{238}_{92}U \rightarrow {}^{?}_{?}Th \rightarrow {}^{4}_{2}He$$

The atomic mass numbers (A) on both sides of the equation must add up to the same, so the atomic mass for thorium must be 234 (238 = 234 + 4).

The atomic numbers (Z) on both sides of the equation must add up to the same, so the atomic mass for thorium must be 90 (92 = 90 + 2). So the answer is:

$$^{238}_{92}U \rightarrow {}^{234}_{90}Th \rightarrow {}^{4}_{2}He$$

KEY POINT

A complete Periodic Table is shown in Appendix A on page 708. The numbers shown in the top left corner are the atomic numbers of the elements – the Z numbers in the nuclear equations. Remember that the Z numbers tell us the number of protons in the nucleus of an element. Some periodic tables show the atomic mass too but as elements have a number of different isotopes the mass numbers will be an average for the different isotopes.

Figure 17.9 shows the effect of alpha particle decay. Losing an alpha particle from the nucleus of a uranium atom turns it into thorium, two places back in the Periodic Table.

Ac	Th	Pa	U	Np
Actinium	Thorium	Protactinium	Uranium	Neptunium
89	90	91	92	93

▲ Figure 17.9 A part of the Periodic Table of elements

BETA (β^-) DECAY

Here is an example of beta minus decay:

$$^{14}_{6}C \rightarrow {}^{14}_{7}N + {}^{0}_{-1}e + \text{energy}$$

carbon-14 atom → nitrogen-14 atom + beta particle, β^- + energy (also an antineutrino)

The radioactive isotope of carbon, carbon-14, decays to form the stable isotope of the gas nitrogen, by emitting a beta particle. Remember that the beta minus particle is formed when a neutron splits to form a proton and an electron. Figure 17.10 shows the standard atomic notation for a beta particle (β^-).

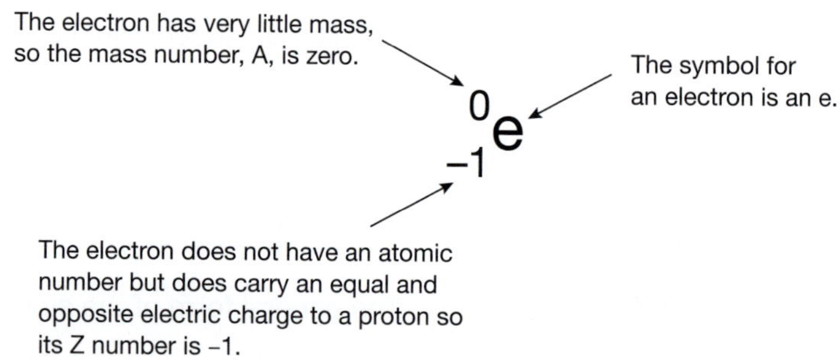

▲ Figure 17.10 A beta minus particle

The general form of the beta minus decay equation is:

$$^{A}_{Z}X \rightarrow {}^{A}_{Z+1}Y + {}^{0}_{-1}e + \text{energy}$$

↑ beta minus particle, β^-

In β^- decay, element X is transformed into element Y by the emission of a beta minus particle. Element Y is the next element in the Periodic Table after element X. The beta particle, an electron, has practically no mass so the mass number, A, is the same in X and Y. As the β^- particle has a charge of −1, the atomic number of the new element is increased to Z + 1. Again the mass number and the atomic number are conserved through this equation.

BETA (β^+) DECAY

EXTENSION WORK

You will not be asked about β^+ decay but the example here is included to show that the atomic mass numbers (A) and the atomic numbers (Z) on each side of the decay equation must balance. Here is an example of beta plus decay:

$$^{22}_{11}Na \rightarrow {}^{22}_{10}Ne + {}^{0}_{+1}e + \text{energy}$$

sodium-22 atom → neon-22 atom + beta particle, β^+ + energy (also a neutrino)

The radioactive isotope of sodium (Na), sodium-22, decays to form the stable isotope of the gas neon (Ne), by emitting a beta plus particle. Remember that the beta plus particle is formed when a proton splits to form a neutron and a positron. Figure 17.11 shows the standard atomic notation for a beta particle (β^+).

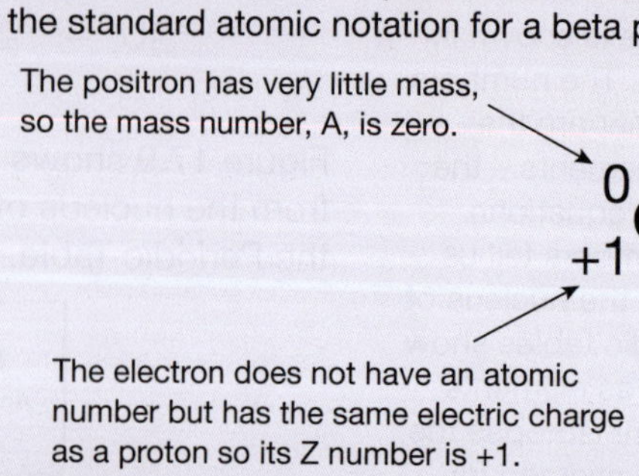

▲ Figure 17.11 A beta plus particle

The general form of the beta plus decay equation is:

$$^{A}_{Z}X \rightarrow {}^{A}_{Z-1}Y + {}^{0}_{+1}e + \text{energy}$$

beta plus particle, β^+

In β^+ decay, element X is transformed into element Y by the emission of a beta plus particle. Element Y is the element in the Periodic Table that comes before element X. The beta plus particle, a positron, has practically no mass so the mass number, A, is the same in X and Y. As this beta particle has a charge of +1, the atomic number of the new element is decreased to Z – 1.

EXAMPLE 2

An isotope of caesium $^{137}_{55}Cs$ decays by emitting an electron (β^-) and forms an atom of barium (Ba). Write a balanced nuclear equation for this decay.

$$^{137}_{55}Cs \rightarrow {}^{?}_{?}Ba + {}^{0}_{-1}e + \text{energy}$$

An electron has practically no mass so the mass number does not change. The emission of an electron happens when a neutron becomes a proton and an electron, so the atomic number increases by one. The barium isotope formed is therefore $^{137}_{56}Ba$ and the completed equation is:

$$^{137}_{55}Cs \rightarrow {}^{137}_{56}Ba + {}^{0}_{-1}e + \text{energy}$$

When an element decays by emitting an electron it changes to the element with the next higher atomic number. You can check this by looking at the Periodic Table on page 708.

REMINDER

You will not be asked questions involving positrons in the exam.

EXAMPLE 3

An isotope of magnesium $^{23}_{12}Mg$ decays by emitting a positron (β^+) and forms an atom of sodium (Na). Write a balanced nuclear equation for this decay.

$$^{23}_{12}Mg \rightarrow {}^{?}_{?}Na + {}^{0}_{+1}e$$

A positron has practically no mass so the mass number does not change. The emission of a positron happens when a proton in the nucleus becomes a neutron and a positron, so the atomic number decreases by one. The sodium isotope formed is therefore $^{23}_{11}Na$ and the completed equation is:

$$^{23}_{12}Cs \rightarrow {}^{23}_{11}Na + {}^{0}_{+1}e$$

When an element decays by emitting a positron it changes to the element with the next lower atomic number. You can check this by looking at the Periodic Table on page 708.

NEUTRON DECAY

Here is an example of neutron decay:

$$^{5}_{2}He \rightarrow {}^{4}_{2}He + {}^{1}_{0}n$$

helium-5 atom → helium-4 atom + neutron

As a neutron has no electric charge, the total positive charge is unchanged by the emission of a neutron – the Z number is 2 before and after the decay. The total number of particles (protons and neutrons) in the nucleus of the helium atom has decreased by 1 because of emission of the neutron.

EXAMPLE 4

An isotope of beryllium, $^{13}_{4}\text{Be}$, decays by emitting a neutron. Write a balanced nuclear equation for this transformation.

Write down what you know:

$$^{13}_{4}\text{Be} \rightarrow {}^{?}_{?}? + {}^{1}_{0}\text{n}$$

The emission of a neutron has no effect on the charge so the atomic number (Z) is unchanged at 4. Each element has its own atomic number so the element in this decay is unchanged – it is still an isotope of beryllium. The loss of a neutron from the beryllium nucleus means that the atomic mass decreases by one. The completed equation is:

$$^{13}_{4}\text{Be} \rightarrow {}^{12}_{4}\text{Be} + {}^{1}_{0}\text{n}$$

GAMMA (γ) DECAY

Gamma radiation is high-energy electromagnetic radiation (see page 568). After an unstable nucleus has emitted an alpha or beta particle it sometimes has surplus energy. It emits this energy as gamma radiation. Gamma rays are pure energy, so they do not have any mass or charge. When a nucleus emits a gamma ray there is no change to either the atomic number or the mass number of the nucleus.

LOOKING AHEAD

▲ Figure 17.12 Inside the Large Hadron Collider

Understanding the particles that make up all matter in the Universe, how they interact and the forces involved holding matter together remains a major area of research for physicists. This is an introduction to what has been called the 'particle zoo'. Large particle accelerators, like the Large Hadron Collider (LHC) on the Swiss/French border, have identified many new particles. Energy turned into matter! Research has recognised patterns in these particles and we now have a model that explains many complex nuclear processes – some of which have increased our understanding of how the Universe was formed.

We also understand how matter can be transformed into energy and the amazing amount of energy that results, revealed by Albert Einstein in his famous equation:

$$E = mc^2$$

CHAPTER QUESTIONS

More questions on the structure of the atom can be found at the end of Unit 7 on page 691.

SKILLS CRITICAL THINKING

7th

1 Copy and complete the table below. Identify the particles and complete the missing data.

Atomic particle	Relative mass of particle	Relative charge of particle
	1	−1
		+1
	2000	0

2 Identify the following atomic particles from their descriptions:

a an uncharged nucleon

b the particle with the least mass

c the particle with the same mass as a neutron

d the particle with the same amount of charge as an electron

e a particle that is negatively charged.

3 Explain the following terms used to describe the structure of an atom:

a atomic number

b mass number.

8th

4 Copy and complete the table below, describing the structures of the different atoms in terms of numbers of protons, neutrons and electrons.

	$^{3}_{2}He$	$^{13}_{6}C$	$^{23}_{11}N$
protons			
neutrons			
electrons			

5 Copy and complete the following sentences:

a An alpha particle consists of four ______. Two of these are ______ and two are ______. An alpha particle carries a charge of ______.

b A beta minus particle is a fast-moving ______ that is emitted from the nucleus. It is created when a ______ in the nucleus decays to form a ______ and the beta particle.

c A third type of ionising radiation has no mass. It is called ______ radiation. This type of radiation is a type of wave with a very ______ wavelength.

6th

d Gamma radiation is part of the ______ spectrum.

SKILLS PROBLEM SOLVING

6 The following nuclear equation showing beta plus decay:

$$^{1}_{1}p \rightarrow {}^{1}_{0}\square + {}^{\square}_{\square}e$$

a From the following list of particles:

A electron B neutron C proton D alpha particle

8th

i State which is the particle on the left of this balanced equation.

ii State which is the first of the terms on the right of this equation.

9th

b The second term on the right of this equation is a positron – the antiparticle of an electron. Copy and complete the above equation filling in the empty boxes shown.

SKILLS ANALYSIS, REASONING

11th

7 A certain radioactive source emits different types of radiation. The sample is tested using a Geiger counter. When a piece of card is placed between the source and the counter, there is a noticeable drop in the radiation. When a thin sheet of aluminium is added to the card between the source and the counter, the count rate is unchanged. A thick block of lead, however, causes the count to fall to the background level.

What type (or types) of ionising radiation is the source emitting? Explain your answer carefully.

HINT

Look at the table on page 662.

SKILLS PROBLEM SOLVING

9th

8 a The nuclear equation below shows the decay of thorium. Copy and complete the equation by providing the missing numbers.

$$^{234}_{90}\text{Th} \rightarrow {}^{\square}_{\square}\text{Pa} + {}^{0}_{-1}\text{e}$$

SKILLS CRITICAL THINKING

b What type of decay is taking place in this transformation?

SKILLS PROBLEM SOLVING

c The nuclear equation below shows the decay of polonium. Copy and complete the equation by providing the missing numbers and letters.

$$^{216}_{\square}\text{Po} \rightarrow {}^{\square}_{82}\text{Pb} + {}^{4}_{2}\square$$

SKILLS CRITICAL THINKING

d What type of decay is taking place in this transformation?

18 RADIATION AND HALF-LIFE

In this chapter you will learn about ways of detecting radiation, and where some of the radiation around us comes from. You will also learn why we use a value called half-life to describe the activity of radioactive isotopes.

LEARNING OBJECTIVES

- Know that photographic film or a Geiger–Müller detector can detect ionising radiation
- Explain the sources of background (ionising) radiation from Earth and space
- Know that the activity of a radioactive source decreases over time and is measured in becquerels
- Know the definition of the term half-life and understand that it is different for different radioactive isotopes
- Use the concept of the half-life to carry out simple calculations on activity, including graphical methods

DETECTING IONISING RADIATION

USING PHOTOGRAPHIC FILM

Wilhelm Röntgen (Figure 18.1a) discovered x-rays in 1895. Henri Becquerel (Figure 18.1b) believed that uranium emitted x-rays after being exposed to sunlight. To test this idea he placed some wrapped, unused photographic plates in a drawer with some samples of uranium **ore** on top of them. He found a strong image of the ore on the plates when he developed them. He later realised that this was due to a new type of ionising radiation. He had discovered radioactivity.

The unit of radioactivity is named after Becquerel. The becquerel (Bq) is a measure of how many unstable nuclei are disintegrating (breaking up) per second – one becquerel means a rate of one disintegration per second. The becquerel is a very small unit. More practical units are the kBq (an average of 1000 disintegrations per second) and the MBq (an average of 1 000 000 disintegrations per second).

Photographic film can still be used to detect radioactivity. Some scientists who work with radioactive materials wear a piece of photographic film in a badge. If the film becomes fogged (unclear) it shows that the scientist has been exposed to a certain amount of radiation. These badges are checked regularly to ensure that scientists are not exposed to too much ionising radiation.

a

b

▲ Figure 18.1 **a** Wilhelm Röntgen (1845–1923), **b** Henri Becquerel (1852–1908). Nobel prize winners in 1901 and 1903

THE GEIGER–MÜLLER (GM) TUBE

Figure 18.2 shows the basic construction of a Geiger–Müller (GM) tube. It is a glass tube with an electrically conducting surface on the inside. The tube has a thin window made of mica (a naturally occurring mineral that can be split into thin sheets). The tube contains a special mixture of gases at very low pressure. In the middle of the tube, electrically insulated from the conducting surface, there is an **electrode**. This electrode is connected, via a high-value resistor, to a high-voltage supply, typically 300–500 V.

When ionising radiation enters the tube it causes the low pressure gas inside to form ions. The ions allow a small amount of current to flow from the electrode to the conducting layer. This is detected by an electronic circuit.

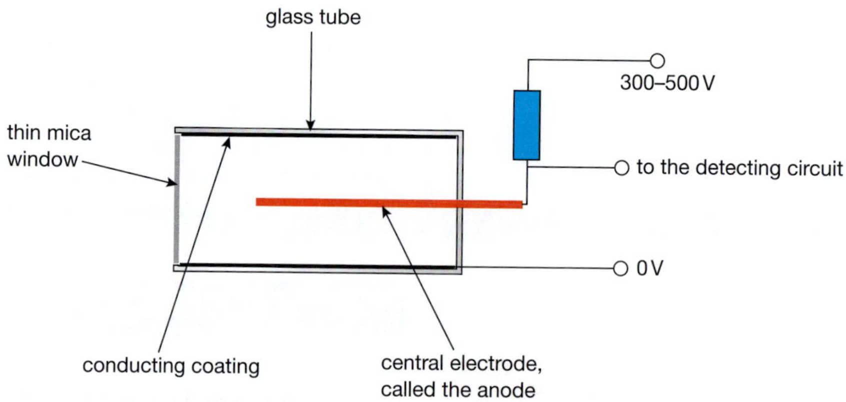

▲ Figure 18.2 A Geiger–Müller tube is used to measure the level of radiation.

The GM tube is usually linked up to a counting circuit. This keeps a count of how many ionising particles (or how much γ radiation) have entered the GM tube. Sometimes GM tubes are connected to rate meters. These measure the number of ionising events per second, and so give a measure of the radioactivity in becquerels. Rate meters usually have a loudspeaker output so the level of radioactivity is indicated by the rate of clicks produced.

BACKGROUND RADIATION

Background radiation is low-level ionising radiation that is produced all the time. This background radiation has a number of sources. Some of these are natural and some are artificial.

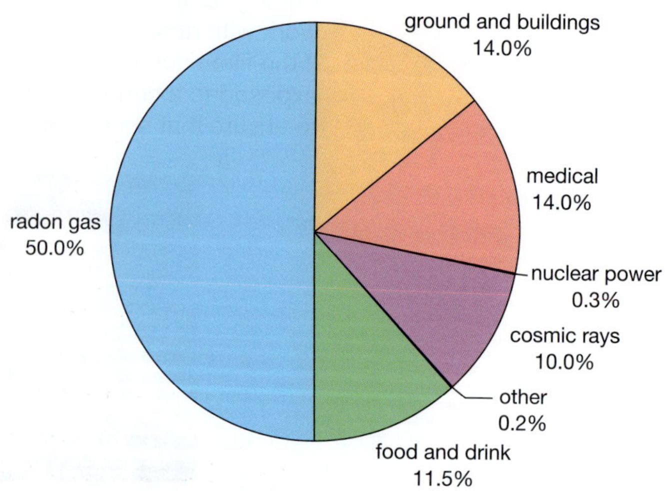

▲ Figure 18.3 Sources of background radiation in the UK. These are the average values – the true amounts and proportions vary from place to place.

NATURAL BACKGROUND RADIATION FROM THE EARTH

KEY POINT

When an atom of a radioactive element decays it gives out radiation and changes to an atom of another element. This may also be radioactive, and decay to form an atom of yet another element. The elements formed as a result of a radioactive element experiencing a series of decays are called decay products.

Some of the radiation we receive comes from rocks in the Earth's crust (hard outer layer). When the Earth was formed, around 4.5 billion years ago, it contained many radioactive isotopes. Some decayed very quickly but others are still producing radiation. Some of the decay products of these long lived radioactive materials are also radioactive, so there are radioactive isotopes with much shorter half-lives (see page 673) still present in the Earth's crust.

One form of uranium is a radioactive element that decays very slowly. Two of its decay products are gases. These are the radioactive gases radon and thoron. Radon-222 is a highly radioactive gas produced by the decay of radium-226. Thoron, or radium-220, is an isotope of radium formed by the decay of a radioactive isotope of thorium (thorium-232).

As these decay products are gases, they come out of radioactive rocks. They are dense gases so they build up in the basements of buildings. Some parts of the Earth's crust have higher amounts of radioactive material so the amount of background radiation produced in this way varies from place to place. In Cornwall in the UK, for example, where the granite rock contains traces of uranium, the risk of exposure to radiation from radon gas is greater than in some other parts of the UK.

NATURAL BACKGROUND RADIATION FROM SPACE

Violent nuclear reactions in stars and exploding stars called supernovae produce cosmic rays (very energetic particles) that continuously hit the Earth. Lower energy cosmic rays are given out by the Sun. Our atmosphere gives us fairly good protection from cosmic rays but some still reach the Earth's surface.

RADIATION IN LIVING THINGS

The atoms that make up our bodies were formed in the violent reactions that take place in stars that exploded (supernovae) billions of years ago. Some of these atoms are radioactive so we carry our own personal source of radiation around with us. Also, as we breathe we take in tiny amounts of the radioactive isotope of carbon, carbon-14. Because carbon-14 behaves chemically just like the stable isotope, carbon-12, we continuously renew the amount of the radioactive carbon in our bodies (see page 681).

Carbon-14 and other radioactive isotopes are eaten by humans (and animals which are in turn eaten by humans) because they are present in all living things.

ARTIFICIAL RADIATION

We use radioactive materials for many purposes. Generating electricity in nuclear power stations has been responsible for the leaking of radioactive material into the environment. The levels are usually small, but there have been a number of major incidents around the world, especially at Three Mile Island in the USA in 1979 and at Chernobyl in the Ukraine in 1986. The tsunami and earthquake that caused major damage and loss of life in Japan in 2011 also damaged the Fukoshima nuclear power station resulting in the release of radioactive materials into the air and the ocean as well as making a large area of land around the damaged power station unsafe for humans to live there.

Testing nuclear weapons in the atmosphere has also increased the amounts of radioactive isotopes on the Earth.

Radioactive **tracers** are used in industry and medicine. Radioactive materials are also used to treat certain forms of cancer. However, the majority of background radiation is natural – the amount produced from medical use in industry is very small indeed.

RADIOACTIVE DECAY

Radioactive decay is a random (unpredictable) process, just like throwing a coin. If we throw a coin we cannot say with certainty whether it will come down heads or tails. If we throw a thousand coins we cannot predict which will land heads and which will land tails. The same is true for radioactive nuclei. It is impossible to tell which nuclei will disintegrate (break down) at any particular time. However, if we threw a thousand coins we would be surprised if the number that landed as heads was not around 500. We know that a normal coin has an equal chance of landing as a head or a tail, so if we got 600 heads we would think it was unusual. If the proportion of heads were much greater than this we would be right to think that the coin was not fair.

▲ Figure 18.4 Throwing a coin

EXPERIMENTAL DEMONSTRATION OF NUCLEAR DECAY

We could, if we had the time, take 1000 coins and throw them. We could then remove all the coins that came down heads, note the number of coins remaining and then repeat the process. If we did this for, say, six trials we would begin to see the trend. A set of typical results is shown in the following table and in Figure 18.5.

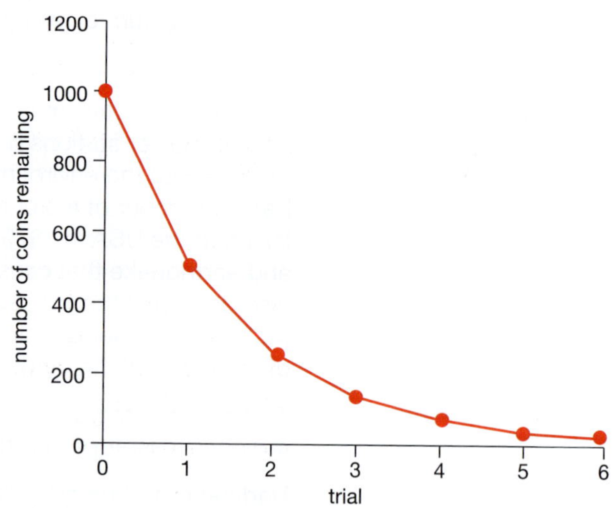

▲ Figure 18.5 Coin-throwing experiment. Each time the coins are thrown about 50% of them land as 'heads' and are removed from the pile. The graph decreases steeply at first but then does so more and more slowly.

Trial	Number of coins remaining
0	1000
1	610
2	261
3	140
4	72
5	33
6	19

EXTENSION WORK

The coin-throwing experiment is a model of radioactive decay. A good model will show the features of the real process. We must remember that models have limitations, however, and do not perfectly represent the actual process. One limitation of the experiment is that of scale. In just 1 g of uranium-235 there are millions of nuclei, and our model uses just 1000 coins. The model would be better if we used, say, 1 000 000 coins, but would take too long to perform. If we use a computer model to throw the coins we could deal with more realistic numbers.

Notice that the graph in Figure 18.5 falls steeply at first and more slowly after each throw. How quickly the graph falls depends on how many heads occur on each throw. But as the number of coins decreases, the number of coins that come up heads also gets smaller. This graph follows a rule: the smaller the quantity, the more slowly the quantity decreases. The quantity here is the number of coins still in the experiment. The name for this kind of decrease proportional to size is called exponential decay.

If we have a sample of a radioactive material, it will contain millions of atoms. The process of decay is random, so we don't know when an atom will decay but there will be a probability that a certain fraction of them will disintegrate in a particular time. This is the same as in the coin toss – there was a 50% probability that the coins would land heads each time we conducted a trial. Once an unstable nucleus has disintegrated, it is out of the game – it won't be around to disintegrate during the next period of time. If we plot a graph of number of disintegrations per second against time for a radioactive isotope we would, therefore, expect the rate of decay to fall as time passes because there are fewer nuclei to decay.

HALF-LIFE

Our coin-tossing model of radioactive decay shows a graph that approaches the horizontal axis more and more slowly as time passes. The model will produce a number of throws after which all the coins have been taken out of the game. The number is likely to vary from trial to trial because the model becomes less and less reliable as the number of coins becomes smaller. With real radioactive decay we use a measure of activity called the **half-life**. This is defined as follows.

The half-life of a radioactive sample is the average time taken for half the original mass of the sample to decay. If the amount of radioactive matter has halved then the activity of the decay halves – this activity is what is measured in finding the half-life of an isotope. The half-life is different for different radioactive isotopes.

Figure 18.6 shows what this means. After one half-life period, $t_{\frac{1}{2}}$, the amount of the original unstable element has halved. After a second period of time, $t_{\frac{1}{2}}$, the amount has halved again, and so on.

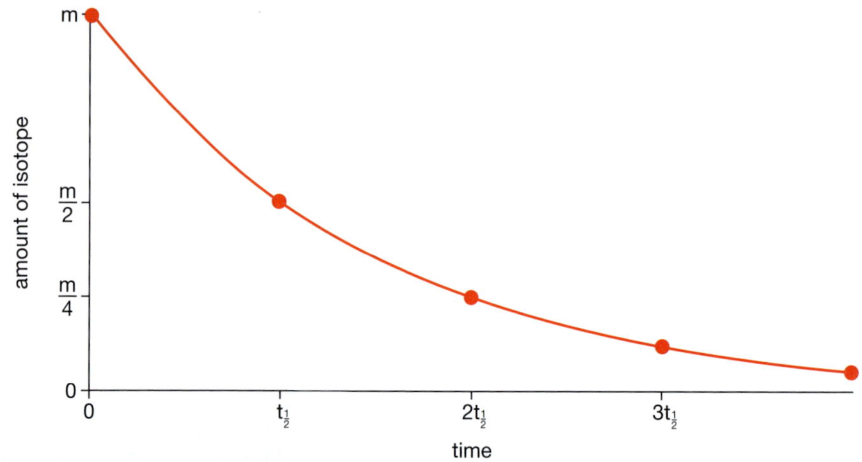

▲ Figure 18.6 Graph showing the half-life period for a radioactive isotope

MEASURING THE HALF-LIFE OF A RADIOACTIVE ISOTOPE

To measure the half-life of a radioactive material (**radioisotope**) we must measure the activity of the sample at regular times. This is done using a Geiger–Müller (GM) tube linked to a rate meter. Before taking measurements from the sample, we must measure the local background radiation. We must **subtract** the background radiation measurement from measurements taken from the sample so we know the radiation produced by the sample itself. We then measure the rate of decay of the sample at regular time intervals. The rate of decay is shown by the count rate on the rate meter. The results should be recorded in a table like the one shown below.

Average background radiation measured over 5 min = x Bq		
Time, *t* / min	Count rate / Bq	Corrected count rate, *C* / Bq
0	y_0	$y_0 - x$
5	y_5	$y_5 - x$

The rate of decay, *C*, corrected for background radiation, is proportional to the amount of radioactive isotope present. If we plot a graph of *C* against time, *t*, we can measure the half-life from the graph, as shown in Figure 18.7.

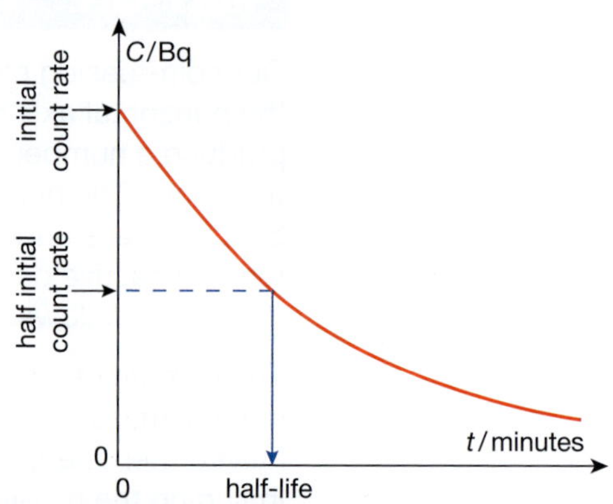

▲ Figure 18.7 You can find the half-life by reading from the graph the time taken for the count rate to halve.

As we have already mentioned, different isotopes can have very different half-lives. Some examples of different half-lives are shown in the table below.

Isotope	Half-life	Decay process
uranium-238	4.5 billion years	α particle emission
radium-226	1590 years	α particle emission, γ ray emission
radon-222	3.825 days	α particle emission

Isotopes with short half-lives are suited to medical use (see page 677). This is because the activity of a source will rapidly become very small as the isotope decays quickly.

Isotopes used for dating samples of organic material need to have very long half-lives. This is because the activity will become difficult to measure accurately if it drops below a certain level. In Chapter 19, we shall see that there are suitable isotopes for these different applications.

HALF-LIFE CALCULATIONS

Graphs of activity, in becquerels, against time can be used to find the half-life of an isotope, and this half-life information can be used to make predictions of the activity of the radioisotope at a later time.

EXAMPLE 1

The activity of a sample of a certain isotope is found to be 200 Bq.

If the isotope has a half-life of 20 minutes, what will the activity of the sample be after one hour?

After 20 minutes the activity will have halved to 100 Bq.

After 40 minutes (two half-lives) it will have halved again to 50 Bq. After 60 minutes it will have halved again, so the activity will be 25 Bq.

What is the level of activity of this sample after three hours?

Three hours = 9 × 20 minutes – that is, nine half-life periods. This means the activity will have halved nine times. The level of activity (and the amount of the radioisotope remaining) will be:

$$\frac{1}{2} \times \frac{1}{2} \times \frac{1}{2} \times \frac{1}{2} \times \frac{1}{2} \times \frac{1}{2} \times \frac{1}{2} \times \frac{1}{2} \times \frac{1}{2}$$

or $\frac{1}{2^9}$ of the original value, and so $\frac{1}{512}$ of the original activity or amount.

CHAPTER QUESTIONS

More questions on radioactive decay can be found at the end of Unit 7 on page 691.

SKILLS CRITICAL THINKING

9th

1 a Explain what is meant by background radiation.

b Explain the difference between natural background radiation and artificial background radiation.

8th

c Give three different sources of background radiation. Say whether your examples are natural or artificial sources.

SKILLS CRITICAL THINKING

2 a Explain simply the principle of the Geiger–Müller tube.

b The Geiger–Müller tube is often connected to a rate meter. Explain what this instrument measures.

c The rate meter is calibrated in kBq. How is this unit defined?

3 a Define what is meant by the half-life of a radioactive material.

b Radioactive decay is a random process. Explain what this means.

SKILLS PROBLEM SOLVING

4 The activity of a radioactive sample is measured. The activity, corrected for background radiation, is found to be 240 Bq. The activity is measured again after 1 hour 30 minutes and is now 30 Bq. What is the half-life of the sample?

5 In another model of radioactive decay, a student fills a burette with water, as shown in the diagram, and starts a timer at the instant the tap at the bottom is opened. She notes the height of the column of water at regular intervals. It takes 35 seconds to empty from 50 ml to 25 ml. Assuming that the arrangement provides a good model of radioactive decay:

a How long will it take for three quarters of the water in the burette to drain away?

b How much water should remain in the burette after 1¾ minutes?

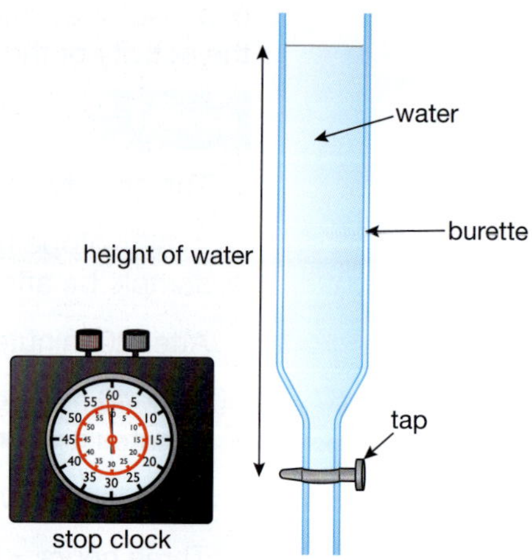

SKILLS EXECUTIVE FUNCTION

6 A student wants to measure the half-life of a radioactive isotope. He is told the isotope has a half-life of between 10 and 20 minutes. Illustrating your answers as appropriate, describe:

a the measurements that he should take

b how he should use the measurements to arrive at an estimate of the half-life for the isotope.

19 APPLICATIONS OF RADIOACTIVITY

Radioactivity has a wide variety of uses, including medicine, industry and power generation. In this chapter, you will read about these uses and also learn about the dangers associated with the use of radioactivity.

LEARNING OBJECTIVES

- Describe uses of radioactivity in industry and medicine
- Describe the difference between contamination and irradiation
- Be able to describe the dangers of ionising radiations including:
  - that radiation can cause mutations in living organisms
  - that radiation can damage cells and tissue
  - the problems arising from the disposal of radioactive waste and how the associated risks can be reduced

THE USE OF RADIOACTIVITY IN MEDICINE

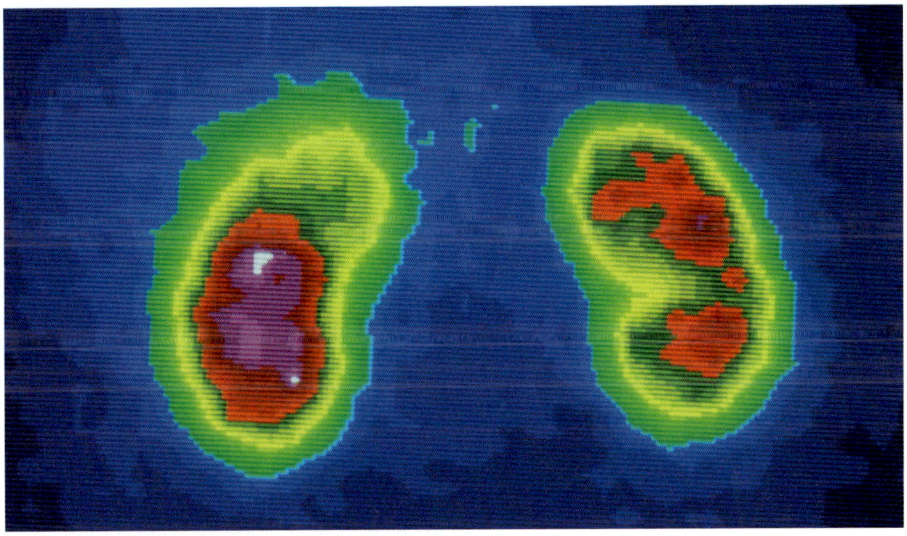

▲ Figure 19.1 This scan shows the kidneys in a patient's body.

USING TRACERS IN DIAGNOSIS

Radioactive isotopes are used as tracers to help doctors identify diseased organs (like the kidneys or the liver). A radioactive tracer is a chemical compound that emits gamma radiation. The tracer is taken orally (swallowed) by the patient or injected. Its journey around the body can then be traced (followed) using a gamma ray camera.

Different compounds are chosen for different diagnostic tasks. For example, the isotope iodine-123 is absorbed by the thyroid gland (a part of the body found in the neck that controls growth) in the same way as the stable form of iodine. The isotope decays and emits gamma radiation. A gamma ray camera can then be used to form a clear image of the thyroid gland.

The half-life of iodine-123 is about 13 hours. A short half-life is important as this means that the activity of the tracer decreases to a very low level in a few days.

EXTENSION WORK

The isotope used in medicine is what is called a metastable form of technetium-99 called technetium-99m.

Other isotopes are used to image specific parts of the body. Technetium-99 is the most widely used isotope in medical imaging. It is used to help identify medical problems that affect many parts of the body. Figure 19.1 shows a scan of a patient's kidneys. It shows clearly that one of the kidneys is not working properly.

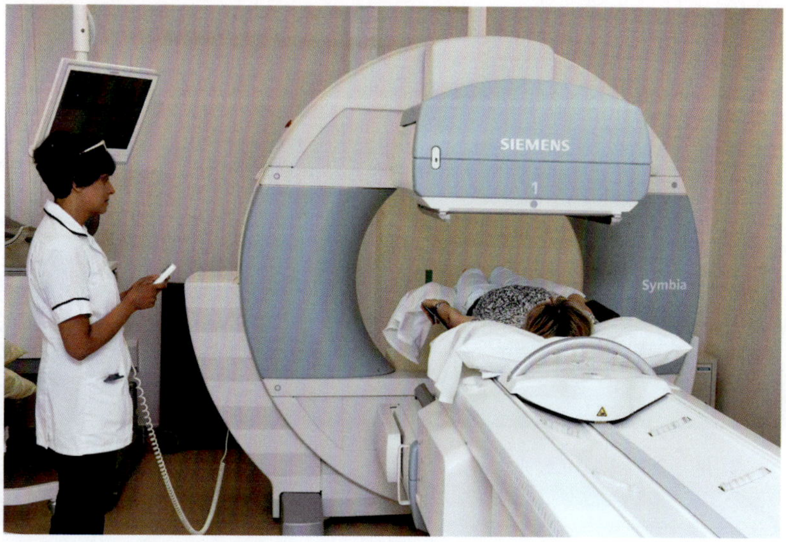

▲ Figure 19.2 Scanner used to provide 3D images of a patient's body

Imaging techniques enable doctors to produce three-dimensional (3D) computer images of parts of a patient's body. These are of great value in diagnosis. Figure 19.2 shows the kind of equipment used for three-dimensional imaging.

TREATMENT

Radiation from isotopes can have various effects on the cells that make up our bodies. Low doses of radiation may have no lasting effect. Higher doses may cause the cells to stop working properly as the radiation damages the DNA in the cells. This can lead to abnormal growth and cancer. Very high doses will kill living cells.

Cancer can be treated by surgery that involves cutting out cancerous cells. Another way of treating cancer is to kill the cancer cells inside the body. This can be done with chemicals containing radioactive isotopes. Unfortunately, the radiation kills healthy cells as well as diseased ones. To reduce the damage to healthy tissue, chemicals are used to target the location of the cancer in the body. They may emit either alpha or beta radiation. Both these types of radiation have a short range in the body, so they will affect only a small volume of tissue close to the target.

The radioisotope iodine-131 is used in the treatment of various diseases of the thyroid gland. It has a half-life of about eight days and decays by beta particle emission.

STERILISATION USING RADIATION

Gamma radiation can kill **bacteria** and viruses. It is therefore used to kill these microorganisms on surgical instruments and other medical equipment. The technique is called irradiation. The items to be **sterilised** are placed in secure bags to ensure that they cannot be re-contaminated before use. The gamma radiation will pass through the packaging and destroy bacteria without damaging the item.

KEY POINT

Irradiation will not destroy any poisons that bacteria may have already produced in the food before it is treated.

Irradiation does not destroy vitamins in the food like other means of killing bacteria, such as high-temperature treatment.

Some food products are treated in a similar way to make sure that they are free from any bacteria that will cause the food to rot or will cause food poisoning. The irradiation of food is an issue that causes concern among the public and is not a widely used procedure at the present time.

Irradiation such as the deliberate exposure of food products and surgical instruments to controlled amounts of radiation should not be confused with radioactive contamination. If radioactive waste is accidentally released either into the air or the sea it could result in fish, animals or agricultural crops being contaminated with radioactive material.

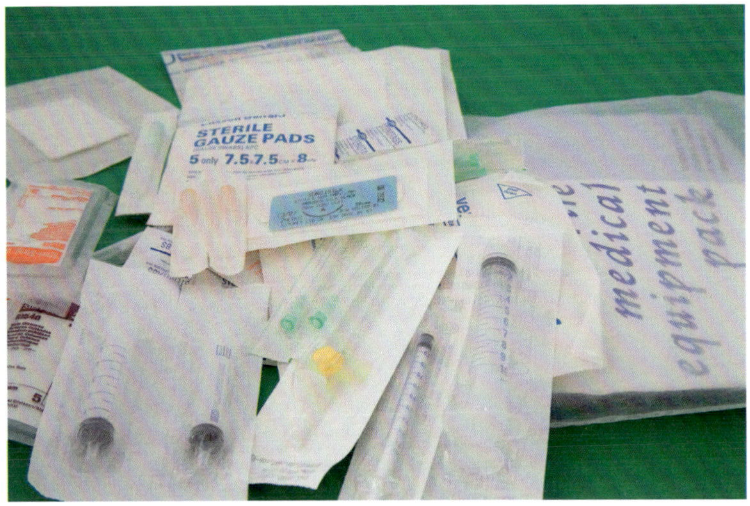

▲ Figure 19.3 Gamma radiation is used to sterilise medical equipment.

THE USE OF RADIOACTIVITY IN INDUSTRY

GAMMA RADIOGRAPHY

A gamma ray camera is like the x-ray cameras used to examine the contents of your luggage at airports. A source of gamma radiation is placed on one side of the object to be **scanned** and a gamma camera is placed on the other. Gamma rays pass through more objects than x-rays. They can be used to check for faults in casting (making things out of metal) or welding (joining metal objects together). Without the technique of gamma radiography, neither problem could be detected unless the welding or casting were cut through. An additional advantage of gamma radiography over the use of x-rays for this purpose is that gamma sources can be small and do not require a power source or large equipment.

GAUGING

In industrial processes, raw materials and fuel are stored in large tanks called hoppers. Figure 19.4 shows how radioactive isotopes are used to gauge, or measure, how much material there is in a storage container.

The coal absorbs a large amount of the radiation so the reading on the lower detector will be small. As the upper part of the hopper is empty the upper detector will have a high reading.

This method of gauging has several advantages over other methods. There is no contact with the material being gauged. Also, coal dust might cause false readings with an optical gauging system (one using light beams). Coal dust is much less dense than coal so the gamma ray system still works properly.

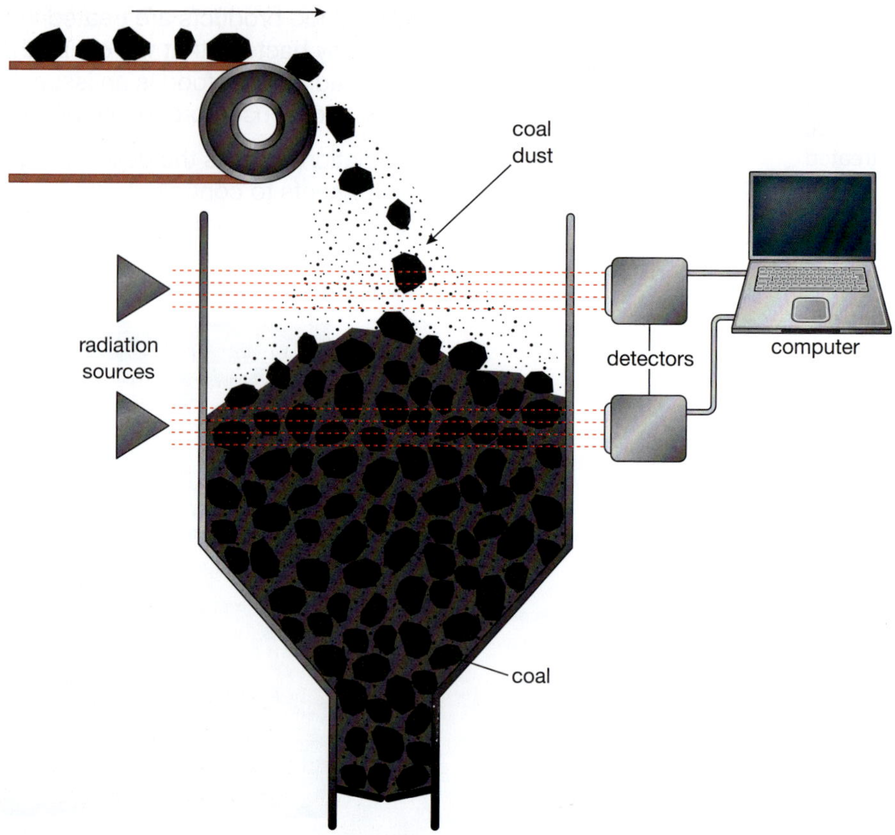

▲ Figure 19.4 The amount of coal in the hopper can be measured using gamma radiation.

Another example of gauging uses a similar process to monitor the thickness of plastic sheeting and film. The thicker the sheet, the greater the amount of radiation it absorbs and the amount passing through gets smaller. By measuring the amount of radiation that passes through the sheeting, its thickness can be closely controlled during manufacture.

TRACING AND MEASURING THE FLOW OF LIQUIDS AND GASES

Radioisotopes are used to check the flow of liquids in industrial processes. Very tiny amounts of radiation can easily be detected. Complex piping systems, like those used in in power stations, can be monitored for leaks. Radioactive tracers are even used to measure the rate of spread of sewage (human waste) (Figure 19.5)!

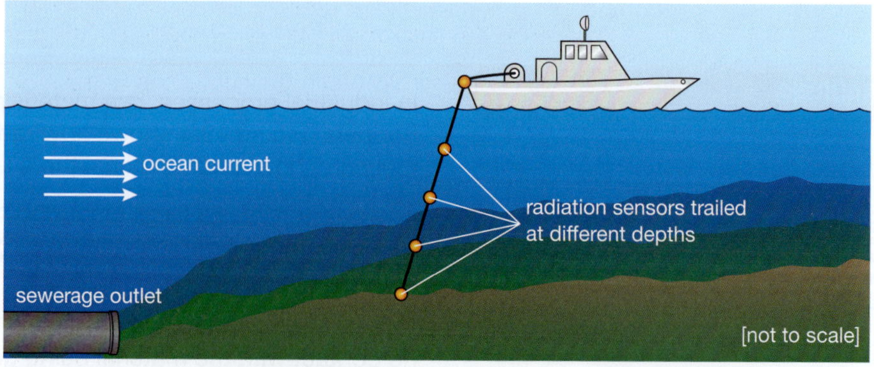

▲ Figure 19.5 Radioactive tracers released with the sewage allow its spread to be monitored to make sure the concentration does not reach harmful levels in any area.

RADIOACTIVE DATING

A variety of different methods involving radioisotopes are used to date minerals and organic matter. The most widely known method is radiocarbon dating. This is used to find the age of organic matter – for example, from trees and animals – that was once living. We shall also look at techniques that are used to find the age of inorganic material like rocks and minerals.

RADIOCARBON DATING

Radiocarbon dating measures the level of an isotope called carbon-14 (C-14). This is made in the atmosphere. Cosmic rays from space are continually raining down upon the Earth. These have a lot of energy. When they hit atoms of gas in the upper layers of the atmosphere, the nuclei of the atoms break apart. The parts fly off at high speed. If they hit other atoms they can cause nuclear transformations (changes) to take place. These transformations turn the elements in the air into different isotopes. One such collision involves a fast-moving neutron striking an atom of nitrogen. (Nitrogen forms nearly 80% of our atmosphere.) The nuclear equation for this process is:

$$^{14}_{7}N + ^{1}_{0}n \rightarrow ^{14}_{6}C + ^{1}_{1}p$$

Notice that, as in the other nuclear equations we have seen, the top numbers – which show the number of nucleons – add up to the same total on each side of the equation. This is because the mass number is conserved. The bottom numbers – which show the amount of charge on the particles – are also conserved.

You have seen the notation for neutrons and protons in Chapter 17. A reminder of neutron notation is shown in Figure 19.6, and of proton notation in Figure 19.7.

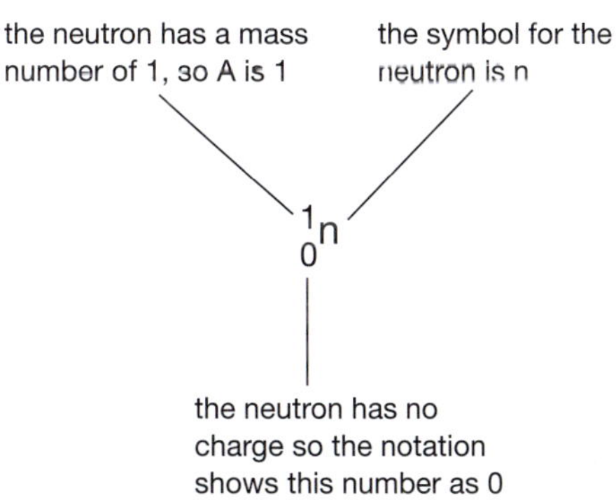

▲ Figure 19.6 The neutron

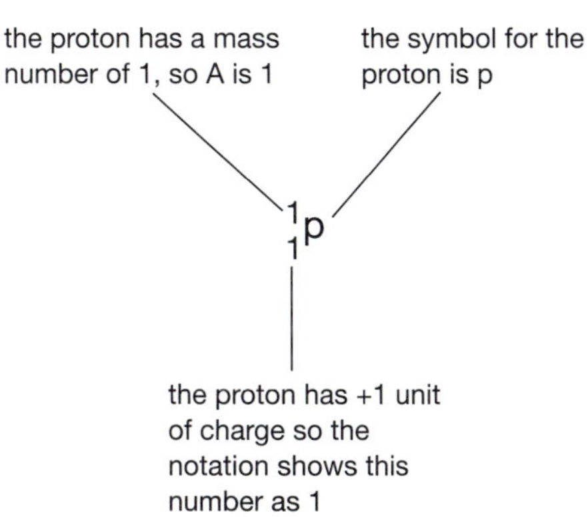

▲ Figure 19.7 The proton

The result of the collision of a neutron with a nitrogen atom is a nuclear transformation. The nitrogen atom is transformed into an atom of the radioactive isotope of carbon, carbon-14.

As we have already mentioned, isotopes of an element have the same chemical behaviour. This means that the carbon-14 atoms react with oxygen in our atmosphere to form carbon dioxide, just like the much more common and stable isotope, carbon-12. The carbon dioxide is then absorbed by plants in the process of **photosynthesis**. As a result, a proportion of the carbon that makes up any plant will be the radioactive form, carbon-14. Included in plant material, the radioactive isotope carbon-14 enters the food chain, which means that animals and humans will also have a proportion of carbon-14 in their bodies. These carbon-14 atoms will decay but, in living plants and animals, they are continuously replaced by new ones.

When an organism (living thing) dies, the replacement process stops. As time passes, the radioactive carbon decays and the proportion of radioactive carbon in the remains of the plant or animal, compared with the stable carbon isotope, decreases.

The half-life for the decay of carbon-14 is approximately 5600 years. This means that every 5600 years the proportion of carbon-14 in dead plant and animal material will halve. The amount of carbon-14 present in a sample of dead plant or animal material is found by measuring the activity of the sample. This is compared with the amount of carbon-14 that would have been present when the sample was part of a living organism. From this, it is possible to estimate when the source of the sample died.

EXAMPLE 1

120 g of living wood has a radioactive activity (corrected for background radiation) of 24 Bq. A 120 g sample of wood from an historical site is found to have an activity of 6 Bq. If the half-life of carbon-14 is 5600 years, estimate the age of the wood from the site.

$$6 \text{ Bq} = 24 \text{ Bq} \times \frac{1}{2} \times \frac{1}{2}$$

Since the activity of the sample has halved twice from that expected in living wood, two half-lives must have passed.

The age of the sample is therefore around 2 × 5600 years = 11 200 years.

There are limitations to the method of radiocarbon dating. It assumes the level of cosmic radiation reaching the Earth is constant, which is not necessarily accurate. Fortunately, the technique has been adjusted to take the variations of cosmic ray activity into account. This is done by testing samples of a known age, like material from the mummies (preserved corpses) of Egyptian Pharaohs and from very ancient living trees.

The radiocarbon method is not used to date samples older than 50 000–60 000 years because, after 10 half-lives, the amount of carbon-14 remaining in samples is too small to measure accurately.

EXTENSION WORK

Radiocarbon dating may be used as a context in questions about the half-life of radioactive isotopes. What follows on dating the age of rocks is included for interest only.

DATING THE AGE OF ROCKS

Inorganic, non-living matter does not absorb carbon-14, so different techniques must be used for finding out the age of rocks and minerals.

When a radioactive substance decays it transforms into a different isotope, sometimes of the same element, sometimes of a different element. The original radioisotope is called the parent nuclide (unstable nucleus) and the product is called the daughter nuclide. Many of the products of decay, the daughter isotopes, are also unstable and these too decay in turn. This means that as the parent isotope decays it breeds a whole family of elements in what is called a decay series. The end of the decay series is a stable isotope – one that does not decay further.

The table shows some radioactive parent isotopes with the stable daughters formed at the end of their particular decay series. The half-life quoted is the time for half the original number of parent nuclei to decay to the stable daughter element.

Radioactive parent isotope	Stable daughter element	Half-life / years
potassium-40	argon-40	1.25 billion
thorium-232	lead-208	14 billion
uranium-235	lead-207	704 billion
uranium-238	lead-206	4.47 billion
carbon-14	nitrogen-14	5568

For rocks containing such radioactive isotopes, the proportion of parent to stable daughter nuclide gives a measure of the age of the rock. Notice that the half-lives of most of the radioactive parent isotopes are extremely long, in some cases greater than the lifetime of the Earth.

The decay series of potassium-40 ends with argon gas. As potassium-40 decays in igneous rock, the argon produced remains trapped in the rock. Igneous rocks are formed when molten rock becomes solid. Igneous rocks are **non-porous**. The proportion of argon to potassium-40 again gives a measure of the age of the rock.

THE DANGERS TO HEALTH OF IONISING RADIATION

Ionising radiation can damage the molecules that make up the cells of living tissue. Cells suffer this kind of damage all the time for many different reasons. Fortunately, cells can repair or replace themselves given time so, usually, no permanent damage results. However, if cells suffer repeated damage because of ionising radiation, the cell may be killed. Alternatively the cell may start to behave in an unexpected way because it has been damaged. We call this effect cell mutation. Some types of cancer happen because damaged cells start to divide uncontrollably and no longer perform their correct function.

Different types of ionising radiation present different risks. Alpha particles have the greatest ionising effect, but they cannot pass through many materials. This means that an alpha source presents little risk, as alpha particles do not penetrate (pass through) the skin. The problem of alpha radiation is much greater if the source of alpha particles is taken into the body. Here the radiation will be very close to many different types of cells and they may be damaged if the exposure is prolonged. Alpha emitters can be breathed in or taken in through eating food. Radon gas is a decay product of radium and is an alpha emitter. It therefore presents a real risk to health. Smokers greatly increase their exposure to this kind of damage as they draw the radiation source right into their lungs (cigarette smoke contains radon).

Beta and gamma radiation do provide a serious health risk when outside the body. Both can penetrate skin and flesh (body) and can cause cell damage by ionisation. Gamma radiation, as we have mentioned earlier, is the most penetrating. The damage caused by gamma rays will depend on how much of their energy is absorbed by ionising atoms along their path. Beta and gamma emitters that are absorbed by the body present less risk than alpha emitters, because of their lower ionising power.

In all cases, the longer the period of exposure to radiation the greater the risk of serious cell damage. Workers in the nuclear industry wear badges to indicate their level of exposure. Some are pieces of photographic film that become increasingly 'foggy' (unclear) as the radiation exposure increases. Another type of badge uses a property called thermoluminescence. Thermoluminescence means that the exposed material will give out light when it is warmed. The radiation releases energy to make heat so the thermoluminescent badges give out more light when exposed to higher levels of radiation. Workers have their badges checked regularly and this gives a measure of their overall exposure to radiation.

SAFE HANDLING OF RADIOACTIVE MATERIALS

Samples of radioactive isotopes used in schools and colleges are very small. This is to limit the risk to users, particularly those who use them regularly – the teachers! Although the risk is small, certain precautions must be followed. The samples are stored in lead-lined containers to block even the most penetrating form of radiation, gamma rays. The containers are clearly labelled as a radiation hazard (danger) and must be stored in a locked metal cabinet. The samples are handled using tongs and are kept as far from the body as possible.

In the nuclear industry and research laboratories, much larger amounts of radioactive material are used. These have to be handled with great care. Very energetic sources will be handled remotely by operators who are protected by lead shields, concrete and thick glass viewing panels. As has been mentioned earlier, neutron radiation is absorbed by lighter elements and waste materials, like spent uranium fuel rods from nuclear reactors, are stored under water until the neutron radiation levels drop to a safe level.

▲ Figure 19.8 Radioactive samples are stored in lead-lined containers and are handled with tongs or protected fingers.

▲ Figure 19.9 Industrial sources of radioactivity must be handed with a lot of care.

The major problem with nuclear materials is long-term storage. Some materials have extremely long half-lives so they remain active for thousands and sometimes tens of thousands of years. Nuclear waste must be stored in sealed containers that must be capable of containing the radioactivity for enormously long periods of time.

CHAPTER QUESTIONS

More questions on applications of radioactivity can be found at the end of Unit 7 on page 691.

SKILLS REASONING 9th

1 The most widely used isotope in medicine is technetium-99m. It has a half-life of six hours and decays by the emission of low-energy gamma rays and beta particles.

a Explain why the characteristics of technetium-99m make it suitable for diagnostic use in medicine.

SKILLS CREATIVITY, REASONING

b Technetium-99m can be chemically attached to a wide variety of pharmaceutical products so that it can be targeted at particular tissues or organs. How can its progress through the body be measured and monitored?

SKILLS REASONING 10th

HINT
Look at Chapter 17.

2 Technetium-99m is produced from molybdenum-99 in a device called a technetium generator. Which decay process – α, β or γ – could cause molybdenum-99 to decay to technetium-99m? Explain your answer.

SKILLS CREATIVITY, REASONING 8th

3 A radioactive isotope of iodine is used in both the diagnosis and treatment of a condition of the thyroid gland. This gland naturally takes up ordinary iodine as part of its function. If a patient has an overactive thyroid it concentrates too much iodine in the gland and this has serious effects on the patient's health.

How might the radioisotope iodine-131 be used to:

a identify an overactive thyroid gland?

b treat the overactive thyroid?

(Iodine-131 has a half-life of eight days and is a high-energy beta emitter.)

SKILLS CRITICAL THINKING

8th

4 a Explain the difference between radioactive contamination and irradiation.

b Give an example of a use of irradiation.

SKILLS CREATIVITY, REASONING

12th

5 Paper is made in a variety of different 'weights', with different thicknesses. How could ionising radiation be used to check the thickness of paper during production? You should consider the following:

- the type of radiation to be used
- how it will be used to measure the paper thickness
- what checks should be made to ensure that the measurements are accurate
- safety procedures.

SKILLS CRITICAL THINKING

6 Radiocarbon dating is used to estimate the age of organic (once-living) materials. It uses a radioisotope of carbon, carbon-14 (C-14).

8th

a How is carbon-14 formed?

7th

b Why does all living matter contain a proportion of C-14?

8th

c What happens to the proportion of C-14 in an organism once it has died?

d What assumptions are made in the process of radiocarbon dating?

e Why is this method unsuitable for accurately dating material that is more than 50 000 years old?

SKILLS PROBLEM SOLVING

7 Most radioactive isotopes of elements have half-lives that are extremely short compared to the age of the Earth. The Earth is about 4.5 billion years old. Radium has a half-life of only about 1600 years.

10th

a How many half-lives of radium have there been since the Earth formed?

SKILLS ANALYSIS

Student A says all the radium formed when the Earth condensed out of the Sun's atmosphere, should have decayed away to an unmeasurably small amount by now.

Student B says that it depends on how much there was to start with.

Student C says that there is still a significant amount of radium on the Earth.

9th

b Which student or students are correct? Give reasons for your answer.

SKILLS REASONING

8 An isotope that decays by alpha emission is relatively safe when outside the body but very dangerous if absorbed by the body, either through breathing or eating.

a Explain why this is so.

10th

b Why is radon-220 a particularly dangerous isotope?

20 FISSION AND FUSION

Scientists have speculated about the nature of the atom for thousands of years, but it is only relatively recently that our current ideas were developed. In this chapter you will read about how our ideas about the structure of the atom have developed over the centuries and how we use nuclear energy to produce electricity.

LEARNING OBJECTIVES

- Know that nuclear reactions, including fission, fusion and radioactive decay, can be a source of energy
- Understand how a nucleus of U-235 can be split (the process of fission) by collision with a neutron, and that this process releases energy as kinetic energy of the fission products
- Know that the fission of U-235 produces two radioactive daughter nuclei and a small number of neutrons
- Describe how a chain reaction can be set up if the neutrons produced by one fission strike other U-235 nuclei
- Describe the role played by the control rods and moderator in the fission process
- Understand the role of shielding around a nuclear reactor
- Explain the difference between nuclear fusion and nuclear fission
- Describe nuclear fusion as the creation of larger nuclei resulting in a loss of mass from smaller nuclei, accompanied by a release of energy
- Know that fusion is the energy source for stars
- Explain why nuclear fusion does not happen at low temperatures and pressures, due to electrostatic repulsion of protons

NUCLEAR REACTIONS AS A SOURCE OF ENERGY

Nuclear reactions involve a change in the qualities of atoms. Heavy atoms may split into lighter atoms and other pieces in a process called **fission**. Lighter atoms may be forced to join together to make heavier atoms in a process called fusion. In either process, the mass of the starting atoms is greater than the mass of the products. This missing mass has been converted into energy.

Within the core of the Earth, radioactive isotopes of elements like uranium, thorium and potassium provide a large proportion of the heat within the Earth itself through radioactive decay.

In the Sun, hydrogen is converted into helium in a **fusion reaction** providing us with a continuous supply of energy in the form of heat and other electromagnetic radiation.

NUCLEAR FISSION

Uranium-235 is used as fuel in a nuclear reactor. It is used because its nuclei can be split by a neutron. The process of splitting an atom is called fission.

Uranium-235 is called a fissile material because it goes through the splitting process easily. The fission process is shown in Figure 20.1.

In the fission reaction, a slow-moving neutron is absorbed by a nucleus of uranium-235.

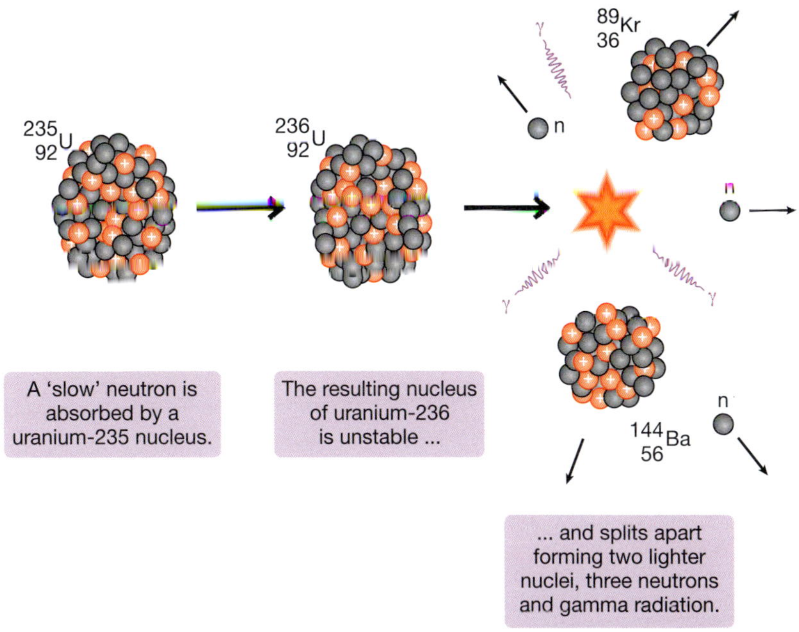

Figure 20.1 One example of fission of uranium-235

The resulting nucleus of uranium-236 is unstable and splits apart. The fragments of this decay are the two daughter nuclei of barium-144 and krypton-89. The decay also produces gamma radiation and three more neutrons. The equation for this decay is:

$$^{236}_{92}U \rightarrow ^{144}_{56}Ba + ^{89}_{36}Kr + 3\,^{1}_{0}n + \gamma \text{ radiation}$$

The fission reaction produces a huge amount of energy. This is because the mass of the products, the barium and krypton nuclei and the three neutrons, is slightly less than that of the original uranium-236 nuclei. This lost mass is converted to energy. Most of the energy is carried away as the kinetic energy of the two lighter nuclei. Some is emitted as gamma radiation. The three neutrons produced by the fission may hit other nuclei of uranium-235, so causing the process to repeat, as shown in Figure 20.2. If one neutron from each fission causes one nearby uranium-235 to split, then the fission reaction will keep going. If more than one neutron from each fission causes fission in surrounding nuclei, then the reaction gets faster and faster – a bit like an avalanche.

EXTENSION WORK

A 'slow' neutron is a low-energy neutron produced by a nuclear decay. Faster moving, more energetic neutrons do not cause fission.

This is called a chain reaction. Each fission results in more nuclei splitting apart. If the amount of uranium-235 is small, many of the neutrons released do not hit other uranium nuclei and the reaction does not get faster and faster. For a chain reaction to happen there must be a minimum amount of the uranium-235. This minimum amount is called the critical mass.

In an atomic bomb two pieces of fissile material (isotopes that can be triggered into splitting apart) that are smaller than the critical mass are forced together under high pressure to form a mass greater than the critical mass. The result is a chain reaction with the rapid and uncontrolled release of huge amounts of energy.

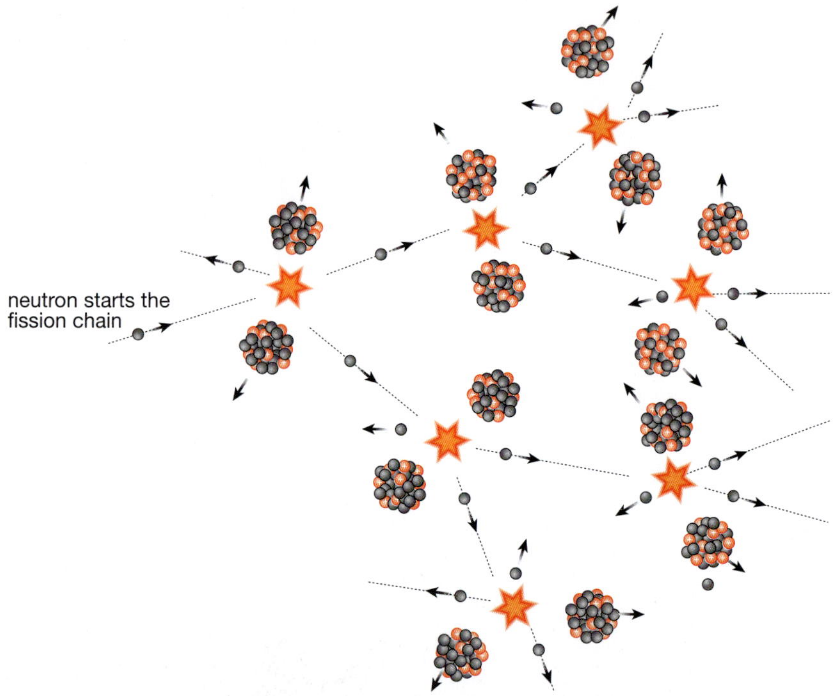

▲ Figure 20.2 A chain reaction in uranium-235

If this is allowed to take place in a nuclear reactor, the reactor core overheats, resulting in a nuclear explosion with the sudden release of enormous amounts of heat energy and radiation. In a nuclear reactor the process is controlled so that the heat energy is released over a longer period of time. The heat produced in the core or heart of the reactor is used to heat water. The steam produced then drives turbines (engines) to turn generators. The basic parts of a nuclear reactor are shown in Figure 20.3.

The reactor core contains fuel rods of enriched uranium. Enriched uranium is uranium-238 with a higher proportion of uranium-235 than is found in natural reserves of uranium. Graphite is used as a **moderator**. The job of

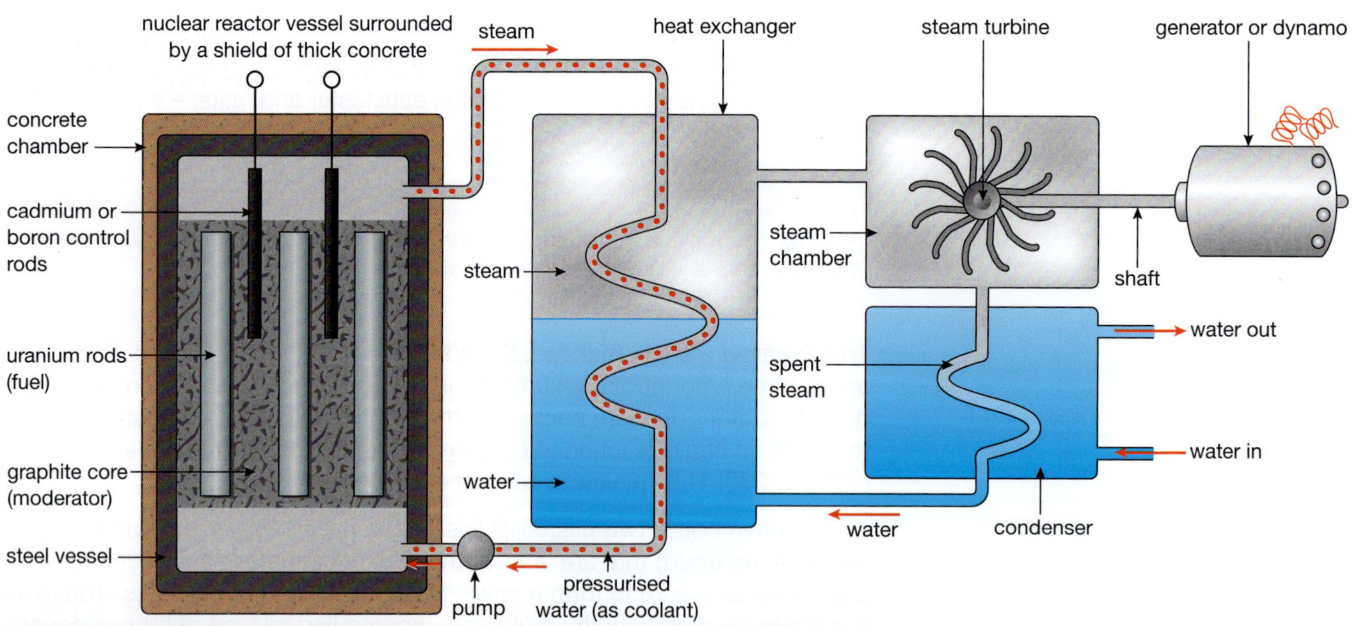

▲ Figure 20.3 A nuclear reactor controls a chain reaction so that heat energy is released slowly.

the moderator is to absorb some of the kinetic energy of the neutrons to slow them down. This is because slow neutrons are more easily absorbed by uranium-235. A neutron slowed in this way can start the fission process.

In the nuclear reactor there are also **control rods**, made of boron or cadmium. These absorb the neutrons and take them out of the fission process completely. When the control rods are fully inside the core, the chain reaction is almost completely stopped and the rate of production of heat is low. As the control rods are withdrawn, the rate of fission increases producing heat at a greater rate.

The reactor vessel is made of steel and surrounded by a concrete layer about 5 metres in thickness. This prevents any radiation escaping, even neutrons.

The nuclear process in a reactor produces a variety of different types of radioactive material. Some have relatively short half-lives and decay rapidly. These soon become safe to handle and do not present problems of long-term storage. Other materials have extremely long half-lives. These will continue to produce dangerous levels of ionising radiation for thousands of years. These waste products present a serious problem for long-term storage. They are usually sealed (closed) in containers which are then buried deep underground. The sites for underground storage have to be carefully selected. The rock must be water resistant and the geology of the site must be stable – storing waste in earthquake zones or areas of volcanic activity would not be sensible.

Some reactors are designed to produce plutonium. Plutonium is a very radioactive artificial element. Small amounts of plutonium represent a serious danger to health. Plutonium is another fissile material. If a large enough mass of plutonium is brought together a chain reaction will start. Plutonium can be used in the production of nuclear weapons.

Nuclear power stations do not produce carbon dioxide or acidic gases as fossil fuel power stations do. This means that nuclear power does not contribute to global warming or acid rain. Only small amounts of uranium are needed for a chain reaction and the supply of nuclear fuel will last many hundreds of years – unlike some **fossil fuels** that could run out in the next fifty years.

NUCLEAR FUSION

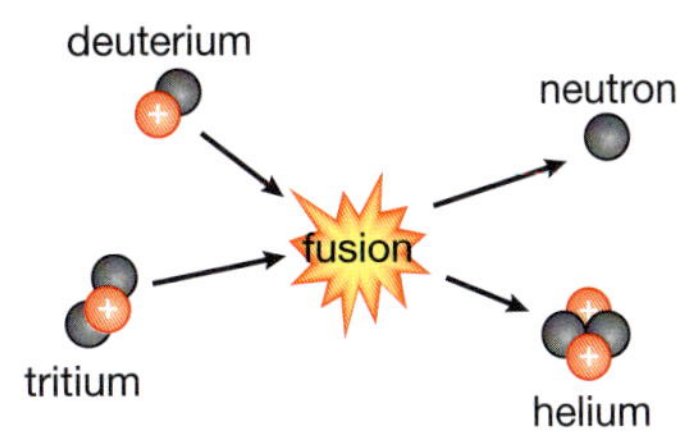

▲ Figure 20.4 Here a nucleus of deuterium collides with a nucleus of tritium. They undergo fusion to form the nucleus of helium, a neutron and a large amount of energy.

▲ Figure 20.5 The mass of the products of fusion is smaller than the two hydrogen nuclei.

Figure 20.4 shows a fusion process that is being used in projects to develop nuclear fusion reactors. Two isotopes of hydrogen, deuterium (H-2) and tritium (H-3), collide at very high speed. The result is the formation of a helium nucleus, a neutron and a large amount of energy. The fusion process is the energy source of our Sun and all stars.

This process uses materials that are more readily available than the uranium used in a conventional fission reactor and has the advantage of producing no radioactive waste. The problem is creating the very high temperatures needed to make the deuterium and tritium nuclei collide with enough energy to overcome the repulsive (pushing away) force between the positive electric charge in the nuclei of each isotope. The high temperature (100 million °C) liquid must be contained within a very strong magnetic field or 'magnetic bottle'. In order to increase the chance of fusion between the light nuclei in the hot liquid, the pressure within the liquid must be very high.

CHAPTER QUESTIONS

More questions on the structure of the atom can be found at the end of Unit 7 on page 691.

SKILLS CRITICAL THINKING

1 a (8th) Uranium-235 (U-235) is a fissile material. What does this mean?

b If there is a large enough mass of U-235, it may cause a chain reaction. (This is called the critical mass for the isotope.)

i (9th) Describe how a chain reaction may take place when a U-235 nucleus splits apart.

ii (10th) A chain reaction is unlikely to take place if there is only a small amount of U-235. Explain why this is so.

2 (7th) List two advantages and two disadvantages of nuclear fission as a way of producing energy.

SKILLS REASONING

3 In a nuclear fission reactor, fuel rods made up of a fissile material, like U-235, are lowered into tubes in a large block of graphite. In between the fuel rods are control rods made of boron which may be raised out of the reactor or lowered into it. The reactor container (vessel) is surrounded by steel and a very thick layer of concrete.

a (9th) Explain the purpose of the graphite around the fuel rods.

b (8th) Describe what effect the action of raising the control rods out of the reactor core has on the behaviour of the reactor.

c Explain how the workers in a nuclear power station are protected from the dangerous types of radiation produced by this nuclear reactor.

SKILLS CRITICAL THINKING

4 (9th) Describe the differences between nuclear fission and nuclear fusion.

5 Explain why creating energy in a nuclear reactor by fusion is so much more difficult than creating power by nuclear fission.

UNIT QUESTIONS

SKILLS PROBLEM SOLVING 7th

1 **a** Which of the following particles has the smallest mass?

A alpha

B neutron

C proton

D electron

(1)

SKILLS CRITICAL THINKING 8th

b When a radioactive isotope emits an alpha particle its

A atomic mass decreases and its atomic number decreases

B atomic mass increases and its atomic number decreases

C atomic mass decreases and its atomic number increases

D atomic mass is unchanged and its atomic number decreases

(1)

c The emission of which of the following particles from a radioisotope causes it to change into the next element in the Periodic Table?

A positron

B electron

C neutron

D alpha

(1)

SKILLS PROBLEM SOLVING 9th

d A radioactive isotope has an activity of 1000 Bq; after 5 hours its activity has fallen to 125 Bq. The half-life of this isotope is

A 1 hour

B 75 minutes

C 125 minutes

D 2.5 hours

(1)

SKILLS CRITICAL THINKING 8th

e Which of the following particles that may be emitted in radioactive decay is not ionising?

A alpha

B beta minus

C neutron

D beta plus

(1)

(Total 5 marks)

SKILLS PROBLEM SOLVING 9th

2 In the Sun and other stars the temperature and pressure make hydrogen nuclei fuse together to form heavier nuclei. This process produces a very large amount of energy, various types of radiation and helium. The steps of this fusion process are shown in the following nuclear equations.

Balance these equations by filling in the boxes:

a ${}^{1}_{1}H + {}^{1}_{1}H \rightarrow {}^{\square}_{1}H + {}^{0}_{\square}e$ **(2)**

b ${}^{2}_{1}H + {}^{1}_{1}H \rightarrow {}^{\square}_{\square}He$ **(2)**

c ${}^{\square}_{2}He + {}^{\square}_{2}He \rightarrow {}^{4}_{2}He + {}^{1}_{\square}\square + {}^{1}_{\square}\square$ **(3)**

(Total 7 marks)

8th

3 Here are descriptions of some nuclear particles:

Particle A has 0 mass and a charge +1.

Particle B has 1 mass and a charge 0.

Particle C has 1 mass and a charge +1.

Particle D has 0 mass and a charge −1.

Particle E has 4 mass and a charge +2.

a State which particle is an alpha. **(1)**

b State which particle is a beta minus. **(1)**

c State which particle is a positron. **(1)**

d State which particle is a proton. **(1)**

e State which particle is a neutron. **(1)**

(Total 5 marks)

SKILLS CRITICAL THINKING

4 Two types of nuclear reactor are used to produce energy. Fission reactors are already in use in nuclear power plants around the world. Fusion reactors are still at the experimental stage.

a Explain what is meant by:

i nuclear fission **(4)**

ii nuclear fusion **(4)**

b In a fission reactor the process of generating energy is a chain reaction using a suitable fissile fuel like uranium-235.

9th

i Explain what a chain reaction is, and **(4)**

ii how it be controlled or shut down completely. **(4)**

(Total 16 marks)

SKILLS CRITICAL THINKING 9th

SKILLS REASONING 8th

5

a Explain the conditions that are needed to cause nuclear fusion. **(3)**

b State two reasons why nuclear fusion reactors may be a better alternative to nuclear fission reactors. **(2)**

(Total 5 marks)

SKILLS CRITICAL THINKING 7th

SKILLS PROBLEM SOLVING 9th

6

a Explain what the letters A and Z tell us about the structure (make up) of the nucleus of any element X.

$^{A}_{Z}X$ **(2)**

b Here is a list of the type of radiation that may be emitted (given out) by an unstable nucleus:

A alpha **B** beta **C** gamma **D** neutron

i Which type affects A but not Z? **(1)**

ii Which type affects Z but not A? **(1)**

iii Which type affects both A and Z? **(1)**

iv Which type affects neither A nor Z? **(1)**

(Total 6 marks)

PHYSICS UNIT 8 ASTROPHYSICS

A supernova is an exploding star. The explosion occurs when the gravitational forces within a star are so great that its core collapses releasing huge amounts of energy. It is the largest explosion to take place in space. In this section we will see how important gravitational forces are in our Universe.

21 MOTION IN THE UNIVERSE

We live on a planet called Earth. It is one of many planets that, together with their moons, form our Solar System. Gravitational forces hold our Solar System together. These forces cause the planets, **asteroids** and comets to orbit the Sun, and moons and artificial satellites to orbit the planets. In this chapter we will look at the key role played by gravitational forces in controlling these movements.

▲ Figure 21.1 The force of gravity keeps these moons in orbit around Jupiter.

UNITS

In this section you will need to use kilogram (kg) as the unit of mass, metre (m) as the unit of length, metre/second (m/s) as the unit of speed, metre/second² (m/s²) as the unit of acceleration, newton (N) as the unit of force, second (s) as the unit of time and newton/kilogram (N/kg) as the unit of gravitational field strength.

LEARNING OBJECTIVES

- Explain that gravitational force causes moons to orbit planets; causes the planets and comets to orbit the Sun; causes artificial satellites to orbit the Earth
- Understand why gravitational field strength, *g*, varies and know that it is different on other planets and the Moon from that on the Earth
- Describe the differences in the orbits of comets, moons and planets
- Use the relationship between orbital speed, orbital radius and time period:

$$v = 2 \times \pi \times \frac{\text{orbital radius, } r}{\text{time period, } T}$$

THE SOLAR SYSTEM

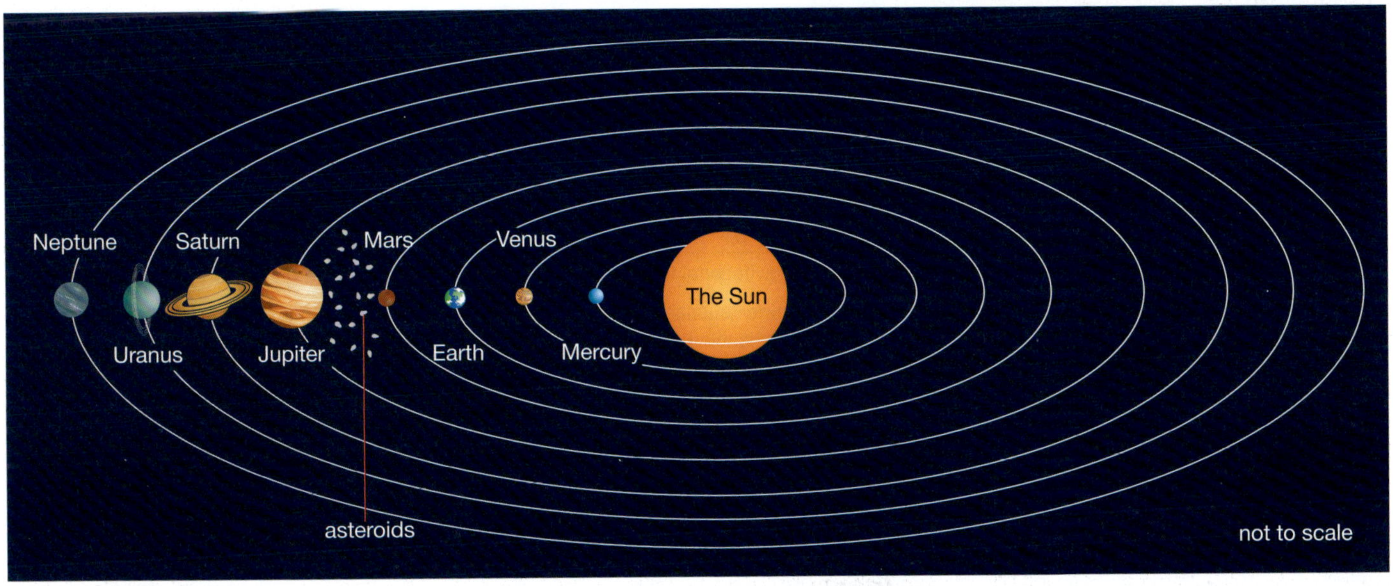

▲ Figure 21.2 The Earth is one of eight planets that orbit the Sun. The orbits of the planets are elliptical (an oval shape) with the Sun close to the centre.

WHY DO OBJECTS MOVE IN A CIRCLE?

Figure 21.3 shows a boy swinging a heavy ball around on a wire. To make this ball travel in a circle he needs to spin around and at the same time pull on the wire. Without this continuous pulling force the ball will not travel in a circle.

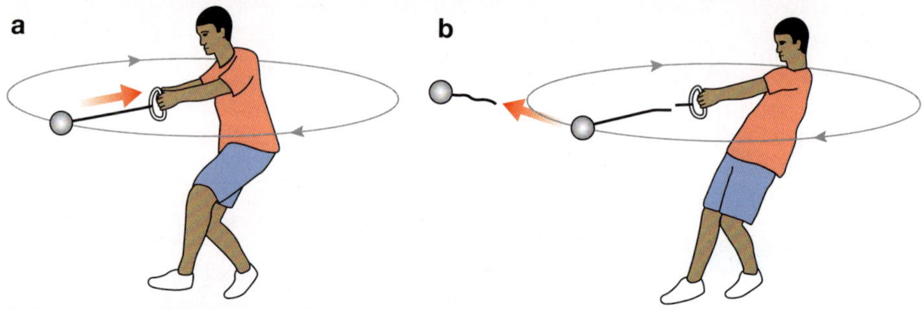

▲ Figure 21.3 **a** A 'pulling' force has to be applied to the ball to make it travel in a circle. **b** If the wire breaks or the boy releases the handle the ball flies away.

Planets and comets travel around the Sun. Moons and satellites travel around the planets. For this to happen there must be forces being applied to them. There is no string or wire to pull on as in the example above, so where do these forces come from? In 1687, Isaac Newton suggested his theory of gravity to explain these movements.

Newton suggested that between any two objects there is always a force of attraction. This attraction is due to the masses of the objects. He called this force gravitational force.

He suggested that the size of this force depends on the:

1 masses of the two objects
2 distance between the masses.

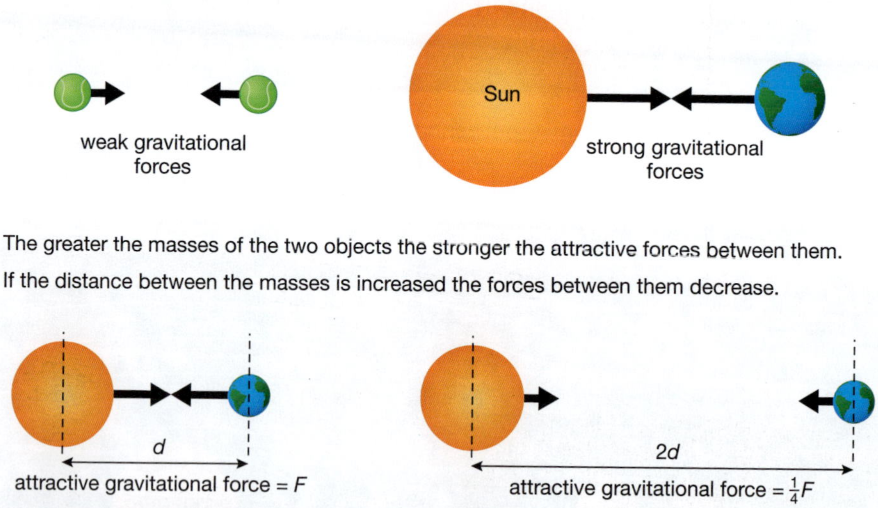

▲ Figure 21.4 Gravitational forces obey an inverse square law – that is, if the distance between the masses is doubled, the forces between them are **quartered**; if the distance between them is **trebled**, the forces become one ninth of what they were.

The gravitational attraction between two objects with small masses is tiny. Only when one or both of the objects has a very large mass – for example, a moon or a planet – is the force of attraction obvious.

Our Sun is massive. It contains over 99% of the mass of the Solar System. It is the gravitational attraction between this mass and each of the planets that holds the Solar System together and causes the planets to follow their curved paths.

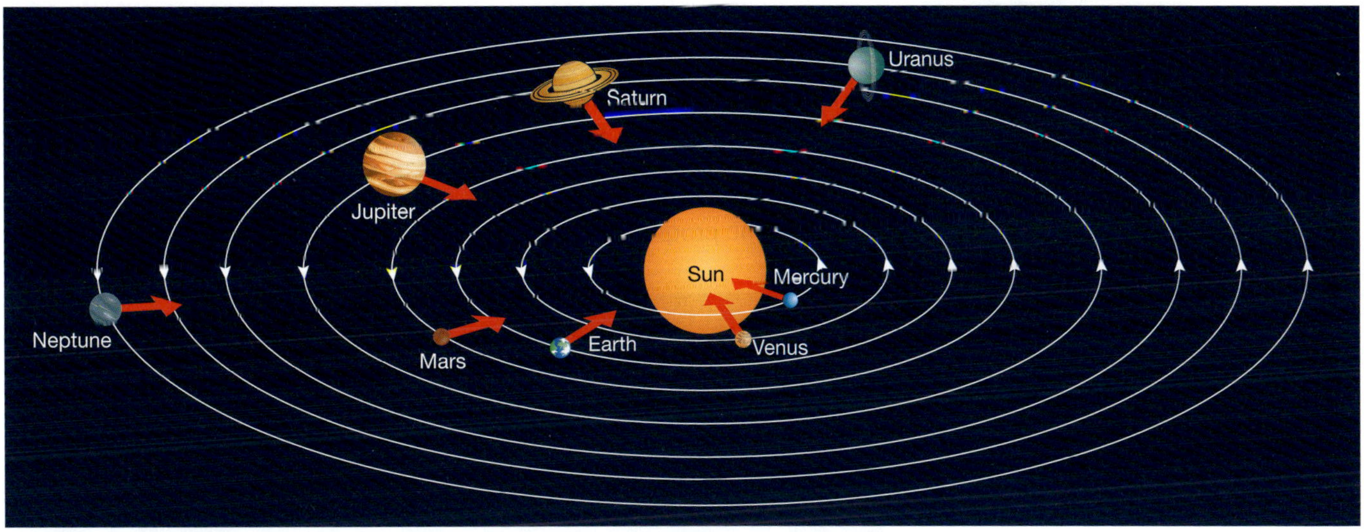

Figure 21.5 Gravitational forces make the planets follow nearly circular paths.

Those planets that are closest to the Sun feel the greatest attraction and so follow the most curved paths. Planets that are the furthest from the Sun feel the weakest pull and follow the least curved path.

EXTENSION WORK

The planet Neptune is a very long way from the Sun so the gravitational force between them is very small. This means that the orbit of Neptune is not very curved and it takes a very long time for it to complete one orbit.

Planet	Average distance from Sun compared with the Earth	Time for one orbit of the Sun in Earth years
Mercury	0.4	0.2
Venus	0.7	0.6
Earth	1.0	1.0
Mars	1.5	1.9
Jupiter	5.0	12
Saturn	9.5	30
Uranus	19	84
Neptune	30	165

Figure 21.6 Some of the many moons of Saturn.

SATELLITES AND MOONS

A satellite is an object that orbits a planet. There are two types of satellite: natural and artificial (human-made).

Natural satellites are called moons. The Earth has just one moon. It is the fifth largest moon in our Solar System, approximately 340 000 km from Earth, and takes just over 27 days to complete one orbit. Although we call our moon 'The Moon' it is not unique. Many planets have moons. Some have more than one, for example, Mars has two moons while Jupiter and Saturn have more than 60 each. All moons have circular orbits because of the gravitational forces between them and their planet.

▲ Figure 21.7 This satellite is held in orbit by the gravitational attraction between it and the Earth.

Since the late 1950s humans have been able to launch, and to put into orbit around the Earth, objects like the one seen in Figure 21.7. These are known as artificial satellites and are extremely useful. Some satellites are put into a very high orbit above the Earth and are used to help us communicate over large distances, for example, for international phone calls or video links, the internet and so on. Some satellites are put into a much lower orbit and are used to monitor in detail the Earth's surface, such as the temperature of the world's oceans or the progress of forest fires.

COMETS

Comets are large rock-like pieces of ice that orbit the Sun. They have very elliptical (elongated) orbits which at times take them very close to the Sun. At other times they travel close to the very edge of our Solar System.

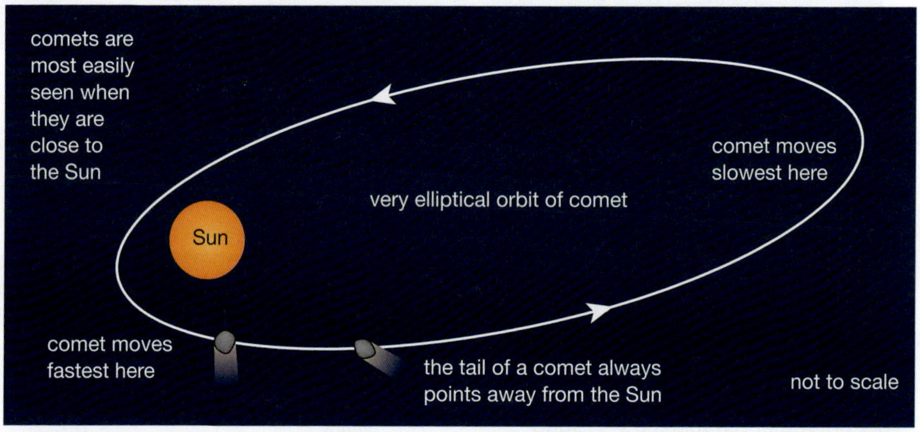

▲ Figure 21.8 The speed of a comet varies enormously. They travel at their fastest when they are very close to the Sun.

EXTENSION WORK

Although you will not be asked in your exam about the 'tails of comets' it is interesting to know that, close to the Sun, some of a comet's frozen gases evaporate to become gases again, forming a long tail that shines in the sunlight. These tails can be millions of kilometres in length. Perhaps the most famous of the comets is Halley's Comet, which visits our part of the Solar System every 76 years. It was last visible from Earth in 1986.

▲ Figure 21.9 Halley's comet could be last seen from Earth in 1986.

GRAVITATIONAL FIELD STRENGTH

The strength of gravity on a planet or moon is called its gravitational field strength, and given the symbol g. Different planets have different masses and different radii – both of these will affect their gravitational field strengths.

- The larger the mass of a planet the greater its gravitational field strength.
- The larger the radius of a planet the smaller the gravitational field strength at its surface.

The gravitational field strength on the Earth is approximately 10 N/kg while on the Moon it is approximately 1.6 N/kg.

Planet	Diameter compared with the Earth	Mass compared with the Earth	Gravitational field strength / N/kg
Mercury	0.4	0.06	4
Venus	0.9	0.38	9
Earth	1.0	1.0	10
Mars	0.5	0.10	4
Jupiter	11	320	23
Saturn	9	95	9
Uranus	4	15	9
Neptune	4	17.0	11

On the Moon, the gravitational field strength is only one sixth that of the Earth's. This means that on the Moon you would weigh six times less. If however you visited Jupiter you would weigh almost 2½ times more!

▲ Figure 21.10 The difference in one person's weight on the Moon and on Jupiter

ORBITAL SPEEDS OF PLANETS AND SATELLITES

The **orbital speeds** of satellites vary greatly depending on the tasks they are performing. For example, communication satellites are put in high orbits and travel at approximately 3 km/s, while those observing the whole surface of the Earth are put into low polar orbits with speeds of about 8 km/s.

We can calculate the speed of a satellite using the equation:

$$\text{speed, } v = \frac{\text{distance moved, } s}{\text{time taken, } t}$$

The distance moved is the circumference of the circular orbit, r:

distance moved = $2 \times \pi \times$ orbital radius, r

The time period, T, is the time for one complete orbit.

EXTENSION WORK

The orbital period of a communications satellite, and most weather satellites, is 24 hours, and it always remains above the same part of the Earth's surface. It is said to be 'geostationary'.

REMINDER

Remember to use the same units throughout your work. Distances here are likely to be given in kilometres and so must be converted into metres. In this example, you must multiply both 8.2 km and 6600 km by 1000. Times given in hours and minutes need to be converted into seconds.

So:

$$\text{orbital speed, } v = \frac{2 \times \pi \times \text{orbital radius, } r}{\text{time period, } T}$$

$$v = \frac{2 \times \pi \times r}{T}$$

The same equation can be used to calculate the speeds of the planets, where r is the average distance from the Sun.

EXAMPLE 1

Calculate the speed of a satellite that is orbiting 200 km above the Earth's surface and completes one orbit in 1 h 24 min. The radius of the Earth is 6400 km.

The radius of the orbit is measured from the centre of the Earth – that is, it is the radius of the Earth plus the height of the orbit above the Earth's surface.

radius of orbit, r = 200 km + 6400 km
= 6600 km
= 6 600 000 m

orbital period, T = (60 min + 24 min) × 60 seconds
= 5040 seconds

$$\text{orbital speed, } v = \frac{2 \times \pi \times r}{T}$$

$$= \frac{2 \times \pi \times 6\,600\,000\text{ m}}{5040\text{ s}}$$

$$= \frac{41\,500\,000\text{ m}}{5040\text{ s}}$$

$$= 8200\text{ m/s or } 8.2\text{ km/s}$$

CHAPTER QUESTIONS

More questions on motion in the Universe can be found at the end of Unit 8 on page 706.

SKILLS CRITICAL THINKING

1 a (3rd) What is the name of the force that keeps all the planets of the Solar System in orbit around the Sun?

b (4th) What two factors determine the size of this force on the surface of a planet.

c (6th) Describe one difference between the orbits of Mercury and Neptune. Give one reason for this difference.

d Describe how the speed of a comet changes as it orbits the Sun.

2 Describe the differences between the orbits of a moon, a planet and a comet.

SKILLS PROBLEM SOLVING

HINT

Convert the time period into hours.

3 A satellite is in an orbit 35 786 km above the surface of the Earth. The radius of the Earth is approximately 6400 km. The satellite is moving at 3.07 km/s.

a (10th) How long does the satellite take to orbit the Earth once?

SKILLS REASONING

b (7th) What do you notice about the time period of this satellite?

SKILLS PROBLEM SOLVING

4 (9th) If the Earth is approximately 150 million km from the Sun calculate the speed at which the following planets are moving around the Sun. The information you need is given in the table on page 697.

a Earth b Jupiter

22 STELLAR EVOLUTION

The Universe is mainly empty space within which are scattered large numbers of galaxies. Astronomers (scientists who study space and the Universe) believe that there are billions of galaxies in the Universe. The distances between galaxies are millions of times greater than the distances between stars within a galaxy. The distances between the stars in a galaxy are millions of times greater than the distances between planets and the Sun.

▲ Figure 22.1 Photograph of galaxies of the Universe taken by the Hubble space telescope

LEARNING OBJECTIVES

- Know that the Sun is a star at the centre of our Solar System
- Know that the Universe is a large collection of billions of galaxies; galaxies are a large collection of billions of stars; our Solar System is in the Milky Way galaxy
- Understand how stars can be classified according to their colour
- Know that a star's colour is related to its surface temperature
- Describe the evolution of stars of similar mass to the Sun through the following stages:
  - nebula
  - star (main sequence)
  - red giant
  - white dwarf
- Describe the evolution of stars with a mass larger than the Sun

THE MILKY WAY

Our nearest star is the Sun. It is approximately 150 million kilometres from the Earth. Its surface temperature is approximately 6000 °C and temperatures within its core are about 15 000 000 °C. Attractive gravitational forces between stars cause them to group together in enormous groups called galaxies. Galaxies consist of billions of stars. Our galaxy is a **spiral galaxy** called the Milky Way. We are approximately two-thirds of the way out from the centre of our galaxy along one of the arms of the spiral.

▲ Figure 22.2 Our galaxy, the Milky Way

▲ Figure 22.3 Our galaxy takes the shape of a spiral, like the one shown here.

CLASSIFYING STARS

▲ Figure 22.4 The colour of the light emitted by this piece of iron tells us how hot it is.

Even within our galaxy we can see a wide variety of stars (Figure 22.2).

Looking up into a clear night sky, especially if we use a telescope, we can see that stars are not all identical. They have different colours, different levels of brightness and appear to be different sizes. Scientists who study the stars in detail have created classes or star groups based upon these similarities and differences.

Why are some stars white, some red and others yellow? Surprisingly we can find the answer to this question in a traditional blacksmiths. To shape a piece of iron without it breaking the iron must be very hot. A skilled blacksmith will know when the temperature of the iron is high enough simply by taking it out of the furnace (very hot oven) and looking at its colour. If it is glowing white or bright orange it is very hot. If it is a dull red it is much cooler and not ready to be shaped.

In a similar way the colours of stars tell us about their temperatures. A very hot star emits more blue in its spectrum and therefore looks blue, a medium star like our Sun looks yellow and cooler stars appear red.

EXTENSION WORK

Scientists often subdivide these groups into 10 smaller groups by giving them a number between 0 and 9. Our Sun is classified as G2 – that is, it is two-tenths along from a G star towards a K star. (You will not be tested on this in your exam.)

Using the colours of stars and their surface temperatures, scientists have created seven different groups of stars. These groups are called O, B, A, F, G, K, M. O and B are the hottest stars and K and M the coolest.

Star classification	Surface temperature / K	Colour
O	more than 33 000	blue
B	33 000–10 000	blue-white
A	10 000–7500	white
F	7500–6000	yellow-white
G	6000–5200	yellow
K	5200–3700	orange
M	3700–2000	red

REMINDER

The brightness of a star depends on:
- the distance the star is from the Earth
- the luminosity of the star – that is, how much energy is transferred from the star each second.

THE BIRTH OF A STAR

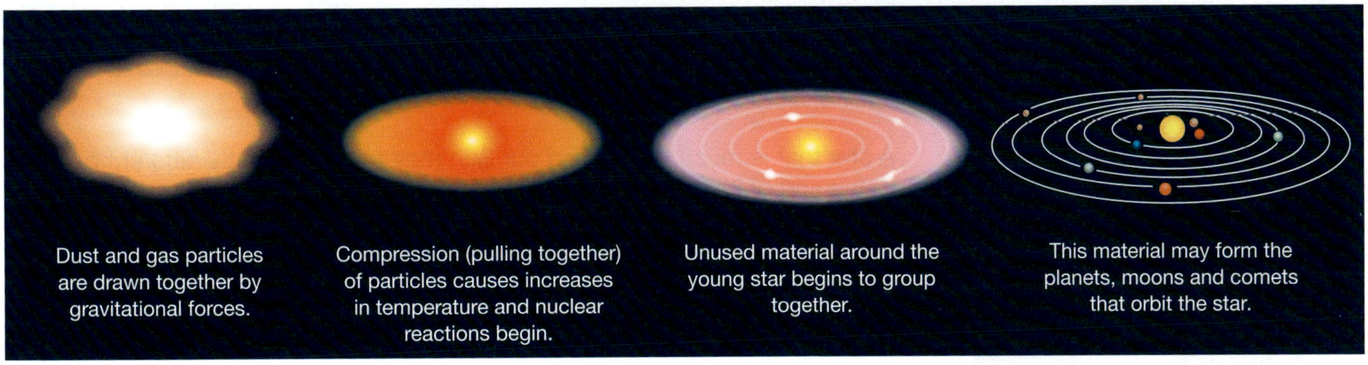

▲ Figure 22.5 Birth of a solar system

Stars like our Sun are formed from large clouds of dust and gas particles we call nebulae or stellar nebulae. These particles are drawn together over a very long period of time by gravitational forces. The particles are pulled together so tightly that there is a very large increase in temperature and pressure. As a result of this nuclear fusion reactions begin. Hydrogen nuclei join together to make larger nuclei and huge amounts of energy is transferred thermally and by radiation (light). This incredibly hot ball of gas is a very young star.

THE LIFE OF A STAR

The appearance of a star changes gradually with time. These changes follow a pattern.

When a star first forms, gravitational forces are pulling particles together. Then when nuclear reactions begin, the high temperatures create forces that try to push the particles apart – that is, make the gases expand. When these two forces are balanced, the star is said to be in its main stable period. A star in this main stable period is referred to as a main sequence star (you will learn why later). This period can last for many millions of years. At the moment our Sun is in this stable period.

Towards the end of this stable period, there are less hydrogen nuclei and eventually the hydrogen fusion reactions stop. Gravitational forces are now the largest forces and compress the star. As the star shrinks in size there is a large increase in temperature. So high that fusion reactions between helium nuclei begin. The energy released by these reactions causes the star to expand to many times its original size. As it expands it becomes a little cooler and more of its light energy is emitted in the red part of the spectrum. The star is changing into a red giant.

Sometime later when most of the helium nuclei have fused (joined) together, new nuclear reactions begin, but now the compressive or squashing forces are larger and the star begins to get smaller or contract. This contraction causes an increase in temperature so the star again changes colour. It now emits more blue and white light. It has changed into a white dwarf star. The matter from which white dwarf stars are made is millions of times more dense than any matter found on the Earth.

Finally as a white dwarf star cools it changes into a cold black dwarf star.

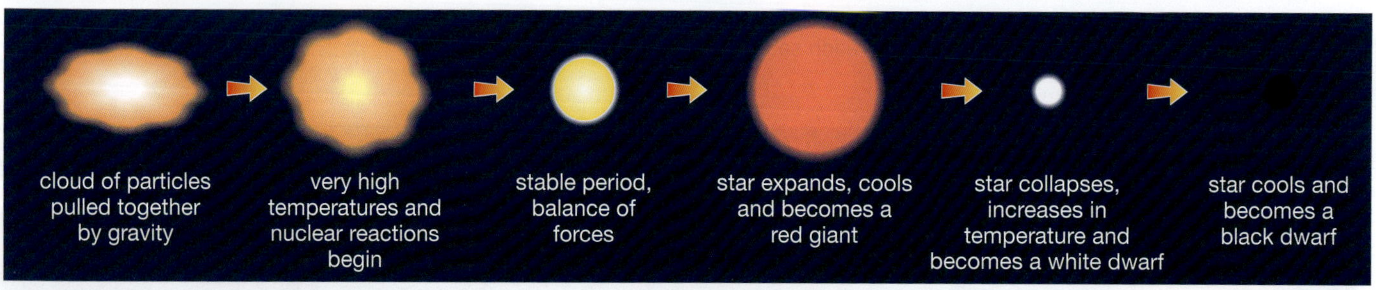

▲ Figure 22.6 The life-cycle of stars with a mass similar to that of our Sun

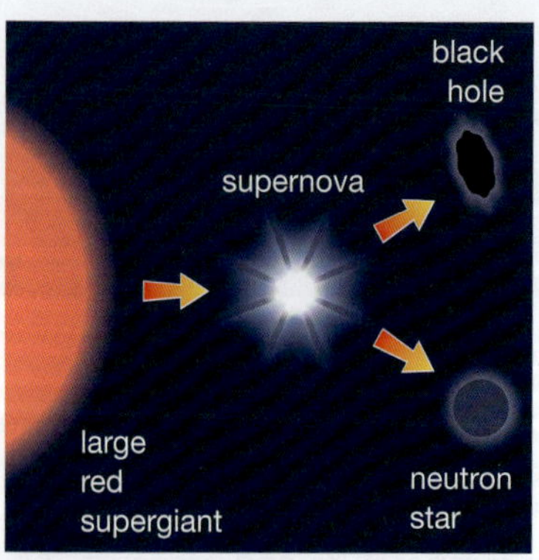

▲ Figure 22.7 The final stages for stars with masses much greater than our Sun

A star that is much larger than our Sun may follow a slightly different path at the end of its life. After the stable period it will expand into a large red supergiant. At the end of this period, as it contracts it becomes unstable. It explodes throwing dust and gas into space to form a new stellar nebula. This exploding star is called a supernova. Any matter remaining will form a very dense neutron star. If the neutron star has a mass that is approximately three times greater than that of our Sun or more, it collapses further to become a black hole.

EXTENSION WORK

The gravitational field of a black hole is so strong that even light is unable to escape from it. This is why they are called 'black holes'.
All the elements in the periodic table up to iron are formed in stars but elements heavier than these are only formed in supernova explosions.

CHAPTER QUESTIONS

More questions on stars and their life cycles can be found at the end of Unit 8 on page 706.

SKILLS CRITICAL THINKING

3rd

1 a What do we call a large group of stars?
  b Why do these groups form?
  c What is the name of the group where we live?
  d How many other groups of stars do we think exist in the Universe?

SKILLS ANALYSIS

4th

2 Using the table on page 703 answer the following questions.
  a Describe two properties of stars that belong in classes B and K.
  b To which group does a star belong if its surface temperature is 2500 K?
  c To which two groups might a star belong if it is emitting a lot of yellow light?
  d What range of surface temperatures might this star have?

SKILLS CRITICAL THINKING

6th

3 Explain the difference between the apparent and absolute brightness of a star.

4th

4 Describe the different stages of a life of a star that is much more massive than our Sun.

5 a What is a supernova?
  b Under what conditions does a supernova occur?

UNIT QUESTIONS

SKILLS CRITICAL THINKING 4th

1 **a** Which of the following statements is incorrect?

A Gravitational forces keep our Moon in orbit around the Earth.

B Comets and moons orbit planets.

C Planets orbit the Sun.

D Artificial satellites orbit a planet. **(1)**

SKILLS REASONING 3rd

b Which of the following sequences might be followed by a star that has a mass much larger than our Sun?

A main sequence, stellar nebula, red giant, white dwarf

B stellar nebula, main sequence, red supergiant, black hole

C stellar nebula, main sequence, white dwarf, black hole

D main sequence, red giant, neutron star, white dwarf **(1)**

SKILLS CRITICAL THINKING 5th

c Which are the most common reactions that take place in the core of a star that is in the main sequence?

A nuclear fission reactions between helium nuclei

B nuclear fission reactions between hydrogen nuclei

C nuclear fusion reactions between helium nuclei

D nuclear fusion reactions between hydrogen nuclei **(1)**

d Which of the following observations does not support the Big Bang theory?

A cosmic microwave background radiation

B blue-shift in the spectra of galaxies

C **red-shift** in the spectra of galaxies

D accelerating galaxies **(1)**

(Total 4 marks)

6th

2 Copy and complete the following passage about gravitational forces, filling in the spaces.

Gravitational forces cause planets and ______ to ______ the Sun. The planets ______ to the Sun, for example, ______ and ______, experience the ______ forces and so have the most ______ orbits. The planets ______ from the Sun, for example, ______ and ______, experience the ______ forces and so have the least ______ orbits. The shape of a planet's orbit is not quite ______. It is ______.

All objects that orbit a planet are called ______ but natural ones are called______.

(Total 16 marks)

SKILLS PROBLEM SOLVING, ANALYSIS 5th

3 A man has a mass of 80kg. On the Earth he weighs 800N. Using the table on page 699 calculate the weight of this man on the surface of:

a Venus **(3)**

b Mars **(3)**

c Neptune. **(3)**

(Total 9 marks)

SKILLS PROBLEM SOLVING 9th

4 Calculate the speed of a satellite that is orbiting 250 km above the Earth's surface and completes one orbit in 2 hr.

(Total 5 marks)

SKILLS ANALYSIS 4th

5 The table below contains information about some of the planets in our Solar System.

Planet	Surface gravity compared with the Earth	Distance from Sun compared with the Earth	Period / Earth years
Mercury	0.4	0.4	0.2
Venus	0.9	0.7	0.6
Mars	0.4	1.5	1.9
Jupiter	2.6	5.0	12
Saturn	1.1	9.5	30

a Name three planets that have a weaker gravitational pull on their surface than there is on Earth. **(1)**

b How long is a year on Saturn? **(1)**

HINT

circumference of a circle = $2\pi r$

SKILLS PROBLEM SOLVING 5th

c If the distance from the Earth to the Sun is 150 million kilometres, calculate the distance of Saturn from the Sun. **(2)**

9th

d Assuming that the orbital path for Saturn is circular, calculate its orbital speed in km/s. **(3)**

(Total 7 marks)

SKILLS INTERPRETATION 6th

6 **a** Draw a diagram to show the shape of the orbit of a comet around the Sun. **(2)**

SKILLS REASONING 7th

b Describe and explain how the speed of a comet changes as it travels around its orbit. **(4)**

(Total 6 marks)

APPENDIX A: PERIODIC TABLE

Period	1	2											3	4	5	6	7	0
1	1 H Hydrogen 1																	4 He Helium 2
2	7 Li Lithium 3	9 Be Beryllium 4											11 B Boron 5	12 C Carbon 6	14 N Nitrogen 7	16 O Oxygen 8	19 F Fluorine 9	20 Ne Neon 10
3	23 Na Sodium 11	24 Mg Magnesium 12											27 Al Aluminium 13	28 Si Silicon 14	31 P Phosphorus 15	32 S Sulfur 16	35.5 Cl Chlorine 17	40 Ar Argon 18
4	39 K Potassium 19	40 Ca Calcium 20	45 Sc Scandium 21	48 Ti Titanium 22	51 V Vanadium 23	52 Cr Chromium 24	55 Mn Manganese 25	56 Fe Iron 26	59 Co Cobalt 27	59 Ni Nickel 28	63.5 Cu Copper 29	65 Zn Zinc 30	70 Ga Gallium 31	73 Ge Germanium 32	75 As Arsenic 33	79 Se Selenium 34	80 Br Bromine 35	84 Kr Krypton 36
5	85 Rb Rubidium 37	88 Sr Strontium 38	89 Y Yttrium 39	91 Zr Zirconium 40	93 Nb Niobium 41	96 Mo Molybdenum 42	(98) Tc Technetium 43	101 Ru Ruthenium 44	103 Rh Rhodium 45	106 Pd Palladium 46	108 Ag Silver 47	112 Cd Cadmium 48	115 In Indium 49	119 Sn Tin 50	122 Sb Antimony 51	128 Te Tellurium 52	127 I Iodine 53	131 Xe Xenon 54
6	133 Cs Caesium 55	137 Ba Barium 56	■	178 Hf Hafnium 72	181 Ta Tantalum 73	184 W Tungsten 74	186 Re Rhenium 75	190 Os Osmium 76	192 Ir Iridium 77	195 Pt Platinum 78	197 Au Gold 79	201 Hg Mercury 80	204 Tl Thallium 81	207 Pb Lead 82	209 Bi Bismuth 83	(209) Po Polonium 84	(210) At Astatine 85	(222) Rn Radon 86
7	(223) Fr Francium 87	(226) Ra Radium 88	■■	(267) Rf Rutherfordium 104	(268) Db Dubnium 105	(269) Sg Seaborgium 106	(270) Bh Bohrium 107	(277) Hs Hassium 108	(278) Mt Meitnerium 109	(281) Ds Darmstadtium 110	(282) Rg Roentgenium 111	(285) Cn Copernicium 112	(286) Nh Nihonium 113	(289) Fl Flerovium 114	(290) Mc Moscovium 115	(293) Lv Livermorium 116	(294) Ts Tennessine 117	(294) Og Oganesson 118

■	139 La Lanthanum 57	140 Ce Cerium 58	141 Pr Praseodymium 59	144 Nd Neodymium 60	(145) Pm Promethium 61	150 Sm Samarium 62	152 Eu Europium 63	157 Gd Gadolinium 64	159 Tb Terbium 65	163 Dy Dysprosium 66	165 Ho Holmium 67	167 Er Erbium 68	169 Tm Thulium 69	173 Yb Ytterbium 70	175 Lu Lutetium 71
■■	(227) Ac Actinium 89	232 Th Thorium 90	231 Pa Protoactinium 91	238 U Uranium 92	(237) Np Neptunium 93	(244) Pu Plutonium 94	(243) Am Americium 95	(247) Cm Curium 96	(247) Bk Berkelium 97	(251) Cf Californium 98	(252) Es Einsteinium 99	(257) Fm Fermium 100	(258) Md Mendelevium 101	(259) No Nobelium 102	(266) Lr Lawrencium 103

Key: a / X / Name / b

a = relative atomic mass
X = atomic symbol
b = atomic number

(Masses in brackets are the mass numbers of the longest-lived isotope)

APPENDIX B: COMMAND WORDS

Command word	Definition
Add/Label	Requires the addition or labelling of a stimulus material given in the question, for example labelling a diagram or adding units to a table.
Calculate	Obtain a numerical answer, showing relevant working.
Comment on	Requires the synthesis of a number of variables from data/information to form a judgement.
Complete	Requires the completion of a table/ diagram.
Deduce	Draw/reach conclusion(s) from the information provided.
Describe	To give an account of something. Statements in the response need to be developed, as they are often linked but do not need to include a justification or reason.
Determine	The answer must have an element that is quantitative from the stimulus provided, or must show how the answer can be reached quantitatively. To gain maximum marks, there must be a quantitative element to the answer.
Design	Plan or invent a procedure from existing principles/ideas.
Discuss	Identify the issue/situation/problem/ argument that is being assessed within the question. Explore all aspects of an issue/situation/ problem/ argument. Investigate the issue/situation etc. by reasoning or argument.
Draw	Produce a diagram either using a ruler or freehand.
Estimate	Find an approximate value, number or quantity from a diagram/given data or through a calculation.
Evaluate	Review information (for example, data, methods) then bring it together to form a conclusion, drawing on evidence including strengths, weaknesses, alternative actions, relevant data or information. Come to a supported judgement of a subject's quality and relate it to its context.

Command word	Definition
Explain	An explanation requires a justification/ exemplification of a point. The answer must contain some element of reasoning/justification – this can include mathematical explanations.
Give/State/ Name	All of these command words are really synonyms. They generally all require recall of one or more pieces of information.
Give a reason/ reasons	When a statement has been made and the requirement is only to give the reason(s) why.
Identify	Usually requires some key information to be selected from a given stimulus/resource.
Justify	Give evidence to support (either the statement given in the question or an earlier answer).
Plot	Produce a graph by marking points accurately on a grid from data that is provided and then draw a line of best fit through these points. A suitable scale and appropriately labelled axes must be included if these are not provided in the question.
Predict	Give an expected result.
Show that	Verify the statement given in the question.
Sketch	Produce a freehand drawing. For a graph, this would need a line and labelled axes with important features indicated. The axes are not scaled.
State what is meant by	When the meaning of a term is expected but there are different ways for how these can be described.
Suggest	Use your knowledge to propose a solution to a problem in a novel context.
Verb proceeding a command word	
Analyse the data/ graph to explain	Examine the data/graph in detail to provide an explanation.
Multiple-choice questions	
What, Why	Direct command words used for multiple-choice questions.

INDEX

A

B

C

F

G